WORLD WAR II SEA WAR

VOLUME 4
GERMANY SENDS RUSSIA TO THE ALLIES

Day-to-Day Naval Actions from
June 1941 through November 1941

Donald A. Bertke
Don Kindell
Gordon Smith / Naval-History.net

Editor: Susan A. Bertke

BERTKE PUBLICATIONS
Dayton, Ohio, U.S.A.

World War II Sea War: Volume 4, Germany Sends Russia to the Allies.
Copyright 2012 by Donald A. Bertke, Don Kindell, and Gordon Smith. Printed in the United States of America. All rights reserved. No part of this book may be reproduced or transmitted in any form or by any means, electronic or mechanical, including photocopying, recording, computer bulletin board (BBS), Internet, or by any information storage and retrieval system without written permission from the author or publisher. Published by Bertke Publications, P.O. Box 291974, 1740 East Stroop Road, Dayton, OH 45429-9998. E-mail bertkepubs@email.com

First Edition.

Library of Congress Control Number: 2010900455

Bertke, Donald A.; Kindell, Don; and Smith, Gordon
World War II Sea War: Volume 4, Germany Sends Russia to the Allies / by Bertke, Donald A., et al.
Includes index.
ISBN 978-1-937470-03-6 (print)
ISBN 978-1-937470-04-3 (ebook)
1. Naval History 2. World War II 3. Subject. I. Title

Editor & Designer: Susan A. Bertke
Cover art © 2009, 2012 Susan Bertke

Acknowledgements

The authors have collected data from innumerable sources official and unofficial, published and unpublished. It is impossible to cite all the specific sources for all the naval activities as some involve dozens of articles. By presenting the data as actions, we have tried not to compromise anyone's previous work.

Books used to compile the data include many volumes. We would like to specifically mention the following:

History of United States Naval Operations in World War II by Samuel Eliot Morison, Little, Brown and Company, Boston.

Home Fleet Narrative, based upon dispatches of the Commander in Chief, Historical Section, Training and Staff Studies Division, Naval Staff, Admiralty.

Chronology of the War at Sea by Jurgen Rohwer, et al., Third Revised Edition, 2005, Naval Institute Press, Annapolis, Maryland

Web sites used to collect or verify information include, but are not limited to, the following:

www.naval-history.net (Gordon Smith) (The best site for information on the Royal Navy.)

www.ibiblio.org/hyperwar/ (A very good place to start when you want to learn about the war.)

www.uboat.net (An excellent source of information about the U-boats and the ships they sank.)

www.combinedfleet.com/kaigun.htm (*The* English language site for information on the Imperial Japanese Navy.)

www.warsailors.com (An excellent site for information about the Norwegian merchant ships during the war.)

www.wlb-stuttgart.de/seekrieg/chronik.htm (An expanded version of *Chronology of the War at Sea* by Jurgen Rohwer. Though in German, it is the best source for information on the German Navy during the war.)

Don Kindell would also like to acknowledge the work of those whose dedication preserved the records from the war: Commander Charles M. Stuart, RN Rtd, who passed away 21 January 1983; David Brindle, RN Rtd, who passed away 2 December 1988; Cdr William Edward May, RN Rtd, who passed away 26 April 1989; John Burgess, who passed away 16 September 1997; J. David Brown, who passed away 11 August 2001; George Ransome, who passed away 4 August 2004; and Lt Cdr Arnold Hague, RN Rtd, who passed away 14 February 2006.

Dedication

When Germany invaded Russia, most of the world held its breath.

Germany had conquered Poland in three weeks, Norway and Denmark in six weeks, and had taken Holland, Belgium and France in seven weeks, plus pushed the British Expeditionary Force out of the continent with heavy losses in materiel. Could Russia survive? Would her army fail on the battlefield as they had in Finland in 1939? These were the worries as the battle began.

In 1937, Russia had the largest and best trained army in the world. Then the German Secret Service made the best counter-intelligence coup ever seen. They managed to plant just enough information in Russian files to implicate the Russian Army leaders in a fictitious coup against Russian leader Josef Stalin. Stalin, supremely paranoid over his shaky position, immediately gutted the army leadership through ruthless executions and many imprisonments. He then installed "Political Officers" in most command levels in the army. Needless to say, that well trained Russian Army instantly became an incompetent, leaderless formation of scared officers and men.

It was this situation that led German leader Adolph Hitler to say, "All we have to do is kick in the door and the whole rotten structure will cave in on their heads!" In part, he was right; the Russian Army was in bad shape, but not all of the Russian leadership was incompetent or unable to influence the future of the army.

In Finland, Stalin saw the results of his great purge as the small Finnish Army easily repelled the massive Russian invasion and inflicted heavy casualties on the mostly leaderless Russian Army. The early failures alerted even Stalin as to the consequences of his own actions. When he finally relented, some of the officers were released from prisons and those remaining "politically reliable" officers were given the task of rebuilding the decimated officer corps.

In early 1940, some of the newly instituted changes bore fruit as the Russians finally used their strength to force Finland to quit. More importantly, the Russian leadership deeply analyzed the war to find out where the Russian Army had failed in Finland, while still not pointing the finger at Stalin. Part of the analysis showed where training and equipment needed improvement. One significant result was the adoption of the T-34 main battle tank, which had proven itself in the snowy battlefields in Finland and was much better than any of the German tanks the Russians had a chance to examine after the battle for Poland in 1939.

The other major change was the training and tactics developed by the Eastern Russian Army against Japan. Russian General Zhukov had used a coordinated combined arms approach, which literally destroyed the Japanese Army in Mongolia/Manchuria with heavy losses. So badly were the Japanese beaten, that their leadership all agreed that the only course for the expansion of the Japanese Empire was south against the old European colonies.

Based upon these and many other decisions, the Russian Army embarked upon a complete reorganization and retraining regimen. The army would be ready for a new contest in late 1942. Unfortunately, the Germans attacked in 1941.

What Germany had forgotten was that Russia had a very long history of invasions from just about every direction. They had beaten off the Mongols, the Huns, the Turks, the Poles, the Teutonic Knights, and the Swedes. The Russian people had developed many tried and true survival methods over the centuries.

When Sweden's Charles the XII invaded, he was lured deep into Russia with a series of small battles until his army was out of supplies, exhausted from the marching, and suffering from the brutal Russian summer. It was then that the Russians attacked and destroyed his army.

Napoleon failed to learn from this history lesson. He thought that all he needed was a larger army to conquer Russia. So he marched 600,000 men into Russia and occupied Moscow. He beat the Russian Army is several major clashes, but the Czar refused to surrender, abandoning Moscow and all its riches to the French. Napoleon wasted two months in Moscow as his men looted and burned most of the city, but his army, now down to only 200,000 men, began to experience the Russian winter at a time when the supply system for the French Army had become too long to feed the army.

Initially the French retreated in good order, but they carried the loot from Moscow, when they should have carried food. The Russian Army and people forced the French to retreat over the same land they had devastated when they marched into Russia. As a result, only about 50,000 men made it back to Paris.

So when German invaded, the Russian people and its army fought as best they could. Most of the best men were deep in Russia being retrained, so the frontline units were at a disadvantage, but fought nonetheless. In part, they fought because their Political Officers refused to let them retreat, even for tactical reasons. But mostly, they fought because Russia was their home, and the Germans were just another in a long line of invaders that they needed to destroy.

True, the Germans managed to capture millions of troops who gave up or who were surrounded and forced to stop fighting, but many men did not surrender, they just went to ground. Just like their ancestors, they hid out in the woods, the swamps and the steppes, waiting for the right time to strike back at the invader.

Luckily, the Germans, mostly through Adolph Hitler, kept the German Army from accomplishing its main mission of defeating the Russian Army. Hitler had convinced himself that the huge numbers of captured Russians meant that the army was destroyed. He could not have been more wrong.

While the Germans had dallied in western Russia, the Russian Army called up its millions of army reserves. Also, Russian spies in Japan confirmed that Stalin need not worry about the Japanese Army. They had learned their lesson in 1939 and were going after "easier" prey in the South Pacific.

So on a winner take all gamble, the Russians moved most of their well trained and battle hardened Eastern Army to the area just west of Moscow to create a Winter Surprise for the German Army.

Some of the German officers tried to warn Hitler that they needed to dig into winter quarters, but he would not hear of it. He wanted them to take Moscow and to end the war in 1941. They could quarter in Moscow after they took the city.

First came the mud, the like of which the German Army had never encountered. Whole vehicles were sucked under the viscous ooze. Then came the cold and the snow in an intensity never experienced in Germany. The cold froze motor vehicles where they stood in the mud. Motor oil froze solid. Troops had no winter gear and froze in their summer uniforms. Freezing and hungry, the German Army was ripe for the Russian counter-attack.

With a thunderous artillery barrage, the Russians attacked. Not only on the front lines, but everywhere throughout occupied Russian territory, small bands of Russian partisans attacked isolated German outposts, destroying rail tracks, supply dumps, bridges, and anything else that would aid the enemy. To the surprise of the world, the unbeatable German Army retreated. Thousands surrendered, many froze to death in the cold, and most of the German vehicles and heavy guns were left behind as the men tried to save themselves. When it was over, the German lines had been pushed hundreds of miles west and Moscow was saved.

What really saved the German Army from being totally annihilated was that the Russian Army ran out of supplies. Hitler's order to hold fast was only a factor after the Russians had stopped. It was only then that the German Army could reorganize and dig in, but the ugly truth had been exposed. The German Army was not going to beat the Russian Army, because the Russian people refused to be beaten. They defeated the Germans just like they had defeated the Mongols, the Turks and, more recently, the Swedes and the French.

The Russian people were like the willow that bends, but never breaks in the big storms. They scrambled to live until it was time to fight back. These skills they had learned and honed to a fine edge over the many centuries of invasion and war.

Some claim that the Russians were just lucky, but that ignores the history of the nation. The Russian people are survivors, and they have to be tough just to survive the extreme climate, terrain, and the vagaries of politics. Even many of the Germans in Russia admitted that it was impossible to defeat a dug-in Russian soldier. You could kill him, but you could not get him to give up once he had dug in.

So we dedicate this volume to the Russian people, for their bravery under adversity and their long tradition of resisting invaders. I pity the next fool who thinks he can defeat the Russians. Time has proven that they can take care of themselves, and they hate uninvited houseguests who stay too long.

Volume 4 Contents

Dedication	6
Overview	10
How to Use This Book	12
Equivalent Naval Officer Ranks	13
Abbreviations	14
JUNE 1941 DAY-TO-DAY OPERATIONS	15
JULY 1941 DAY-TO-DAY OPERATIONS	81
AUGUST 1941 DAY-TO-DAY OPERATIONS	141
SEPTEMBER 1941 DAY-TO-DAY OPERATIONS	207
OCTOBER 1941 DAY-TO-DAY OPERATIONS	273
NOVEMBER 1941 DAY-TO-DAY OPERATIONS	337
Volume 4 Index	410
Errata Form	451

Overview

In Volume 4, "Germany Sends Russia to the Allies," we see the consequences of the German invasion of Russia. The beginning of this titanic land struggle would eventually result in the defeat of the Axis powers. At sea, we see many little changes.

The German and Finnish Navies rushed to contain the Russian Baltic Fleet in the Gulf of Finland. A huge number of mines were laid, first across the mouth of the Gulf of Finland and then closer to Leningrad, as the Russian Baltic Sea Fleet retreated from its forward bases in Estonia, Latvia, and Lithuania. The German and Finnish naval forces also began operations against Russian bases in Finland and in the Russian-occupied Baltic States.

The German Northern Fleet rushed men and supplies east in an attempt retake the captured Finnish Petsamo region, rich in nickel ore, and to cut off the Russian port of Murmansk using a combined land and sea assault. The Russian troops quickly fought the Germans to a standstill while they successfully evacuated their civilian population to safer regions further east. In the end, a stalemate developed that would last for the next few years.

The Romanian Navy, supported by German aircraft, succeeded in forcing the Russian Black Sea Fleet to its bases in the Crimea. The Romanians set up defensive minefields and began to run supply convoys along the southern Ukrainian coast trying to keep pace with the rapid movement east by the German and Romanian Armies. The Romanians had to take on the Russian Fleet alone, as there were no German ships in the area. Both sides contested control, but German air superiority finally forced the Russians east.

The German U-boats and Italian submarines began full operation out of the new bases in western France. Even with the shortened route to the convoy lanes, the German submarine fleet was still too small to make much of an impact. The effectiveness of the British convoys made targets more scarce and attacking convoys more dangerous. The Axis submarines continued to sink ships, but there were only a dozen or so on station on any given day.

The British struggled to keep the Island of Malta as a base of operations against the German and Italian supply lines to North Africa. The constant air and sea attacks on the Axis supply lines kept the German and Italian troops on short rations while the British struggled to rebuild their army and free Tobruk from encirclement. Neither the Germans nor the Italians guessed that the British were reading most of their messages, which included departure times and cargo manifests.

While Italian aircraft managed to sink a number of British ships, the Italian Fleet was mostly harbour-bound as the shortage of oil made movements of the Italian heavy ships too expensive. They had to conserve their oil ration to support the convoys to Libya. The Royal Navy had convinced the Italians that they could not effectively engage the British on the open seas, so they avoided any further attacks on British warships.

The United States Navy (USN) took on a major role in escorting the North Atlantic convoys. Using the Danish invitation to occupy Iceland and Greenland to protect its neutrality as an excuse, the USN escorted convoys to and from Iceland, and the United States (US) invited any Allied merchant ship to share in its protection. The US was basically daring the Germans to attack and bring the United States into the war on the Allied side. In return, Hitler made it clear to the German U-boat commanders; they were to avoid sinking US ships at all cost.

The United States also threw down the gauntlet to the Japanese with their full oil and iron embargo. Japan had to quit their attacks and leave China or they would get no materials from the US. To the Japanese, it confirmed their decision to take what they needed from the poorly defended European colonies in the Pacific Ocean. They had no intention of ending their conquest of China, and the Japanese leadership was convinced that the United States was a paper tiger.

The Japanese quietly readied their forces in Japan, China, and French Indo-China for the now inevitable war with the United States and the European Allies. The Japanese leaders believed that both the US and European governments were too preoccupied with the war in Europe to stop Japan from greatly expanding the Japanese Empire at their expense. Those Pacific colonies had everything the Japanese needed, including a large pool of slave labour.

The Imperial Japanese Navy adopted a radical plan to destroy the US Pacific Fleet at Pearl Harbor, Hawaii. In strict secrecy, they worked out the details for an attack by carrier aircraft on the US Pacific Fleet and support facilities at Pearl Harbor, Oahu. The Japanese prepared 14-inch armour-piercing battleship shells and shallow diving aerial torpedoes to use against the US battleships. The Japanese hoped that, with their Pacific Fleet sunk and the base at Pearl Harbor destroyed, the US would rather negotiate a peace than fight, leaving Japan to its spoils. It was clear that no one in the Japanese government had researched United States history. Sinking the Pacific Fleet without warning was a sure way to unite all US citizens to a common purpose. Anger is a terrible emotion and, once unleashed, it is very hard to rein in.

The first British Arctic convoys took war materiel to Russia to support their struggling efforts against the German Army. It was the only real aid the Allies could send at this time, and most of the cargos came out of Britain's lend-lease allocations. The US eventually extended lend-lease terms to Russia, but both sides knew that Russia, and probably Britain as well, would never be able to repay the debt. Either way, these convoys would tie down the British Home Fleet for the duration of the war.

The United States began to slowly build up its defensive capabilities at all of its Pacific bases, especially in the Philippines. From information in broken Japanese diplomatic coded messages, the US was under no illusion that the Japanese would comply with the embargo terms. War was coming, but the US was woefully unprepared and trying to play catch up. The race to a full worldwide naval war was on.

How to Use This Book

Organization: Our goal is to provide the basic facts: who did what, where, and when. The authors organized the data chronologically by location. This approach gives the reader a better feel for the time it took to move between ports, to conduct searches, to refuel, to supply, and to perform other naval activities seldom provided in other historical documents. Once these elements are appreciated, a clearer picture can be drawn about the intricacies of naval warfare during World War II.

Geographical Organization: Each section begins in the Arctic and goes south to the Antarctic in longitudinal strips, beginning east of the Atlantic and encircling the Earth to the Pacific east coast. Within each geographic area and sub-area the data is presented day-by-day and, where possible, hour by hour. Days are only listed if an event took place in that area on that day. For more detail on the geographical areas, see Volume 1.

Ship Nationality: The original data base was focused on the activities of the Royal Navy of Great Britain, including Dominion and Indian Navy ships. Ships of other nationalities were later added to the record. For this reason, the reader should assume that all warships and convoys mentioned are British and Dominion unless otherwise identified.

Ship Losses: Ships lost are in **BOLD** type and include ships captured and renamed. Whenever possible in the loss of a warship or a merchant ship, the ship responsible for the rescue of crew survivors is shown. However, when no rescue ship is shown, this does not infer that there were no survivors, but merely that no information is available. Royal and Dominion Navy officers lost in action are in order of seniority by rank as listed in the Navy List but with regular Royal Navy first, then RNR, followed by RNVR. In this manner a Commander RNVR was technically junior to a Sub Lieutenant RN.

In the case of the positions of attacked and sunken ships, frequently you will find a discrepancy between the reported location radioed in haste by the attacked vessel and the location given by the attacking ship, aircraft, or submarine. This variation could be many miles. We have attempted to resolve this issue, as much as possible, by giving geographic location as well as latitude and longitude.

Time of Day: Times given in the text are Greenwich Mean Time or local time unless otherwise indicated.

Ship Tonnages: Merchant ship tonnages are British Registered Tons per Lloyds Register, abbreviated to grt.

Convoy Numbering: British east coast convoys between Southend and Methil and later only the Tyne were FN (north) and FS (south) convoys, respectively. On 20 February 1940, Commander-in-Chief Rosyth ordered that the hundreds be omitted in the numbering of future convoys. To avoid confusion, the convoys are shown by their actual number: i.e. FS.3 is listed as FS.203. The actual "centuries" for the period 1940-42 are as follows:

Convoy	FN sailed	FS sailed
101	23 Feb 40	20 Feb 40
201	21 Jun 40	21 Jun 40
301	6 Oct 40	5 Oct 40
401	5 Feb 41	31 Jan 41
501	3 Aug 41	28 May 41
601	10 Jan 42	21 Sep 41
701	6 May 42	16 Jan 42

Equivalent Naval Officer Ranks

Primary source—http://en.wikipedia.org/wiki/Ranks_and_insignia_of_NATO_Navies_Officers.
IJN information is from http://en.wikipedia.org/wiki/Naval_ranks_of_the_Japanese_Empire_during_World_War_II
and may not be exact equivalents to NATO designations.
The abbreviations come from a variety of sources, and some have been invented by the editor.

	OF-10	OF-9	OF-8	OF-7	OF-6	OF-5	OF-4	OF-3	OF-2	OF-1	OF(D)	Student Officer
FRANCE	Amiral de France	Amiral (Am)	Vice-amiral d'escadre (VAmE)	Vice-amiral (VAm)	Contre-amiral (CAm)	Capitaine de Vaisseau (CV)	Capitaine de frégate (CF)	Capitaine de corvette (CC)	Lieutenant de Vaisseau (LV)	Enseigne de Vaisseau de 1re classe (Ens/1) / Enseigne de Vaisseau de 2e classe (Ens/2)	Aspirant	
GERMANY		Admiral (Adm)	Vizeadmiral (VAdm)	Konteradmiral (KAdm)	Flottillenadmiral (FAdm)	Kapitän zur See (KptzS)	Fregattenkapitän (FKpt)	Korvettenkapitän (KKpt)	Stabskapitänleutnant / Kapitänleutnant (Kptlt)	Oberleutnant zur See (ObltzS) / Leutnant zur See (LtzS)	Oberfähnrich zur See (ObfzS) / Fähnrich zur See (FzS)	Seekadett
ITALY		Ammiraglio (only Chief of Defence Staff)	Ammiraglio di Squadra (AmS)	Ammiraglio de Divisione (AmDiv)	Contrammiraglio (CAm)	Capitano di vascello (CV)	Capitano di fregata (CF)	Capitano di corvette (CC)	Tenente di vascello (TV)	Sottotenente di vascello (S/TV) / Guardia marina (G)	Aspirante guardiamarina	
JAPAN		Kaigun Taishō (Adm)	Kaigun Chūjō (VAdm)	Kaigun Shōshō (RAdm)		Kaigun Daisa (Capt)	Kaigun Chūsa (Cdr)	Kaigun Shōsa (Lt Cdr)	Kaigun Daii (Lt)	Kaigun Chūi (S/Lt, Lt/JG) / Kaigun Shōi (Ens)	Kaigun Shōi (Warrant Officer)	Kaigun Shōi Kōhōsei (Midshipman)
NETHERLANDS	Admiraal (Adm)	Luitenant-Admiraal (Lt Adm)	Vice-Admiraal (VAdm)	Schout-bij-Nacht (SN)	Commandeur (Cdr)	Kapitein ter zee (KptZ)	Kapitein-luitenant ter zee (KptltZ)	Luitenant ter zee der 1ste klasse (LtZ/1)	Luitenant ter zee der 2de klasse oudste categorie (LtZ/2oc)	Luitenant ter zee der 2de klasse (LtZ/2) / Luitenant ter zee der 3de classe (LtZ/3)		
NORWAY		Admiral (Adm)	Viseadmiral (VAdm)	Kontreadmiral (KAdm)	Flaggkommandør (FKdr)	Kommandør (Kdr)	Kommandørkaptein (KdrKpt)	Orlogskaptein (OKpt)	Kapteinløytnant (Kptlt)	Løytnant (Lt) / Fenrik (F)		
POLAND		Admiral (Adm)	Admiral floty (AdmF)	Wiceadmiral (WAdm)	Kontradmiral (KAdm)	Komandor (Kdr)	Komandor porucznik (KdrPor)	Komandor podpodporucznik (KdrPod)	Kapitan marynarki (KptM)	Porucznik marynarki (PorM) / Podporucznik marynarki (PodM)		
ROMANIA	Maresal	Amiral (Am)	Viceamiral (VAm)	Contraamiral (CAm)	Contraamiral de flotila (CAmF)	Comandor (Cdr)	Capitan-comandor (CptCdr)	Locotenent-comandor (Lt Cdr)	Capitan (Capt)	Locotenent (Lt) / Aspirant		
USSR						Capt 1st Class	Capt 2nd Class	Capt 3rd Class				
UK	Admiral of the Fleet	Admiral (Adm)	Vice Admiral (VAdm)	Rear Admiral (RAdm)	Commodore (Cdre)	Captain (Capt)	Commander (Cdr)	Lieutenant-Commander (Lt Cdr)	Lieutenant (Lt)	Sub-lieutenant (Sub-Lt)	Midshipman	Officer Cadet
US	Fleet Admiral	Admiral (Adm)	Vice Admiral (VAdm)	Rear Admiral (UH) (RAdm)	Rear Admiral (LH) (RAdm)	Captain (Capt)	Commander (Cdr)	Lieutenant Commander (Lt Cdr)	Lieutenant (Lt)	Lieutenant, Junior Grade (Lt/JG) / Ensign (Ens)		Midshipman/ Officer Candidate

Abbreviations

(See previous page for abbreviations for naval officer ranks.)

SHIP & PLANE DESIGNATIONS (PREFIXES)

A. Submarine (Nor)	**I–** Submarine (Japan)	**S–** Submarine (USN)
ABEILLE. Tugboat (Fr)	**Ju** Junkers aircraft (Ger)	**S.** Motor torpedo boat (S-boat) (Ger)
AG– Naval auxiliary (USN)	**L–** Submarine (USSR)	**SCHIFF.** Armed merchant cruiser (Ger)
AO– Tanker (USN)	**L.** Submarine (UK)	**ShCh–** Submarine (USSR)
AP– Troop transport (USN)	**LCA.** Landing craft assault (UK)	**SM.** Tri-motor Savoia aircraft (Italy)
AV– Seaplane tender (USN)	**LCP(L).** Landing craft personnel (UK)	**SNA.** Steamer (Vichy France)
AVP– Seaplane tender (USN)	**LCM.** Landing craft mechanized (UK)	**SPERRBRECHER.** Minesweeper (Ger)
B. Submarine (Nor)	**M–** Submarine (USSR)	**SS–** Submarine (USN)
BB– Battleship (USN)	**M.** Minesweeper (Ger)	**T.** Torpedo boat (Ger or Yugo.)
C. Submarine chaser (France)	**MA/SB.** Motor antisubmarine boat (UK)	**U.** Submarine (U-boat) (Ger)
CA– Heavy cruiser (USN)	**MAC.** Motor attendant craft (UK)	**UJ.** Submarine chaser (Ger)
CAM Catapult Armed Merchant	**MAS.** Motor torpedo boat (Italy)	**V., Vs.** Auxiliary patrol vessel, trawler or drifter (Ger)
CH– Submarine chaser (Japan)	**MB.** Naval motorboat (UK)	
CH. Submarine chaser (Fr)	**Me** Messerschmitt aircraft (Ger)	**Vp.** Auxiliary patrol vessel (Ger)
CL– Light cruiser (USN)	**ML.** Motor launch (UK)	**W–** Minesweeper (Japan)
CR. Bi-plane fighter aircraft (Italy)	**MMS.** Motor minesweeper (UK)	**WPG–** Cutter (US Coast Guard)
CV– Aircraft Carrier (USN)	**MTB.** Motor torpedo boat (UK)	**X.** Lighter (auxiliary barge) (UK)
DD– Destroyer (USN)	**O.** Submarine (Neth)	**X.** Captured Italian submarine (UK)
Do Dornier aircraft (Ger)	**PB–** Patrol boat (Japan)	**YM–** Harbour patrol ship (USN)
Fw Focke-Wulf aircraft (Ger)	**PBY–** Consolidated PBY Catalina flying boat (USN)	**Z.** Destroyer or torpedo boat (Neth)
G. Torpedo boat (Neth)		**Z.** Destroyer (Ger)
G. Fiat fighter aircraft (Italy)	**PC.** Patrol sloop (UK)	**Z.** Cant seaplane (Italy)
H. Small submarine (Italy & UK)	**PR–** Patrol boat river (USN)	**ZH.** Destroyer (Ger)
He Heinkel aircraft (Ger)	**PT–** Patrol torpedo boat (USN)	

OTHER ABBREVIATIONS & ACRONYMS

(D.#)	Destroyer Division Commander	**Neth**	Netherlands
A.M.	*Ante Meridiem* (before noon)	**Nor**	Norway
A.S.I.S.	Armament Stores Issuing Ship (UK)	**OBV**	Ocean boarding vessel
AA	Antiaircraft	**RAAF**	Royal Australian Air Force
ABV	Armed boarding vessel	**RAF**	Royal Air Force (UK)
AMC	Armed merchant cruiser	**RAN**	Royal Australian Navy
BEF	British Expeditionary Force	**RCN**	Royal Canadian Navy
Belg	Belgium	**RFA**	Royal Fleet Auxiliary
CinC	Commander in Chief	**RIN**	Royal Indian Navy
CLAA	Light cruiser Antiaircraft (US, UK)	**RN**	Royal Navy
CO	Commanding Officer	**RNethN**	Royal Netherlands Navy
CS	Cruiser Squadron (UK)	**RNorN**	Royal Norwegian Navy
D/F	Direction Finding	**RNR**	Royal Navy Regular
DBS	Distressed British Seamen	**RNVR**	Royal Navy Reserve
DSO	Distinguished Service Order (UK)	**Rtd**	Retired
EMB	Explosive motorboat (Italy)	**SNO**	Senior Naval Officer
FAA	Fleet Air Arm (UK)	**SO**	Senior Officer
FFr	Free French	**SOE**	Special Operations Executive
Fin	Finland	**StG.#**	Dive Bomber Group (Ger)
Ger	Germany	**Swe**	Sweden
grt	Gross Registered Tons	**UK**	United Kingdom
HMS	His Majesty's Ship (UK)	**US**	United States of America
HQ	Headquarters	**USA**	United States Army
IJA	Imperial Japanese Army	**USCG**	United States Coast Guard
IJN	Imperial Japanese Navy	**USN**	United States Navy
JG.#	Fighter Group (Ger)	**USSR**	Union of Soviet Socialist Republics
KG.#	Bomber Group (Ger)	**VFr**	Vichy France
KGr.#	Tactical Reconnaissance Group (Ger)	**W/T**	Wireless Telegraphy
KGV.#	Air Transport Group (Ger)	**Yugo**	Yugoslavia
LG.#	Air Training Group (Ger)	**ZG.#**	Twin Engine Fighter Group (Ger)

JUNE 1941
DAY-TO-DAY OPERATIONS

SECTION CONTENTS

SUMMARY 17	BALTIC SEA..58
GENERAL 19	*Kattegat and Skagerrak* 58
NAVAL DEPLOYMENT—RUSSIA 22	*Southern Baltic Area*..........................58
NAVAL DEPLOYMENT—ROMANIA 22	*Gulf of Bothnia*...................................61
NAVAL DEPLOYMENT—HUNGARY 22	*Gulf of Finland*....................................61
NAVAL DEPLOYMENT—BULGARIA.....23	MEDITERRANEAN SEA & MIDDLE EAST 62
ARCTIC OCEAN 23	*East of Gibraltar* 62
Greenland Sea and Barents Sea........23	*Middle Mediterranean Sea*................64
White Sea 23	*Eastern Mediterranean Sea* 66
NORTH ATLANTIC OCEAN 24	*Black Sea*..72
Iceland and North of Britain..............24	*Red Sea* 73
Norwegian Sea 30	*Arabian Sea*...74
East of Canada....................................31	INDIAN OCEAN..74
East of United States..........................35	*East of South Africa* 74
Caribbean and Gulf of Mexico..........37	*South Indian Ocean* 74
Western Approaches 37	*Bay of Bengal* 74
Central Atlantic Crossing Zone........43	*Malaya* 75
UK East Coast.....................................47	PACIFIC OCEAN...75
North Sea 51	*South China Sea* 75
English Channel 51	*Dutch East Indies* 76
Bay of Biscay.......................................52	*East China Sea* 76
West of Gibraltar 52	*Sea of Japan*.......................................77
West of North Africa 56	*East of Australia*.................................77
SOUTH ATLANTIC OCEAN 57	*East of Japan*.......................................77
East of South America 57	*New Zealand* 79
West of South Africa 57	*West of United States* 79

SUMMARY

GERMANY

By opening the war with Russia, Germany added three new naval combat areas for the already over tasked German Navy. In the Baltic, the Germans relied on extensive minefields to contain the more powerful Russian Baltic Fleet in the Gulf of Finland. With the aid of Finland, the Gulf became an extremely hazardous place to transit.

In the Black Sea, Germany relied on its ally Romania and the German Air Force to contain the Russian Black Sea Fleet. Aerial mines were used extensively to damage the aggressive Russian ships without a major naval engagement.

In the Arctic, the Germans moved their already scarce destroyers to support the German troops fighting for Murmansk, Russia. The main effort to contain the Russian Arctic Fleet fell on the German Air Force.

Meanwhile in the North Atlantic, the German Navy finally fielded a sizable force of U-boats at sea. Aided by the Fw200 air reconnaissance, the convoy hunters continued to take a steady harvest of merchant shipping.

ITALY

The Italian Navy continued to support the convoy runs to Libya, but the cost continued to rise. British aircraft and submarines made the task more difficult and merchant-shipping losses steadily climbed. The lack of oil reserves prevented the Italian Fleet from openly attacking Malta, which stuck like an oversized fruit pit in the craw of the Italian convoy lanes.

The Italian submarines in the Atlantic continued to make a good showing. Their tally of kills continued to climb, but losses plus normal wear and tear on the submarines were slowly sapping their strength.

ROMANIA

The Romanian Navy took the brunt of the combat with the Russian Black Sea Fleet. They managed to hold the coastal areas with the help of the German air force and inflicted a number of losses on the Russian ships through their extensive minefields outside the important oil depot at Constanza, Romania.

HUNGARY

The Hungarians had only a small river patrol fleet, but they used it effectively to maintain barge traffic up and down the Danube.

JAPAN

The Japanese continued to steadily build up her fleet for the coming battle in the Pacific. New warships and fleet auxiliary ships were launched as fast as Japanese shipyards could run.

Japan also continued to isolate the Chinese by taking the major port cities along the southern Chinese coast. IJN patrol boats then blockaded the rest of the Chinese southern coast so that no western aid to get to the embattled Chinese forces inland.

FINLAND

As in the Russian War in 1940, the small Finnish Navy used minefields and submarines to inflict losses on the Russian Baltic Fleet. Unlike the Germans, Finland made a formal declaration of war and stressed that they were *not* part of the Axis Alliance, but were only acting to regain the territories taken by the Russians. The Finns were hedging their bets against a German loss in Russia.

VICHY FRENCH

The Vichy government found itself once again in combat with British and Free French troops in Syria. Since the Germans had staged an air group through Syrian territory, the Vichy government had supported the fight against the British and were therefore a legitimate target for British retaliation.

The stronger Vichy French Fleet in the Western Mediterranean did not sortie to defend Syria. Between the disarming of the fleet and the confiscation of nearly all of French oil, it is doubtful if the French navy could raise steam on any of its large warships.

BRITAIN

The Royal Navy was being stretched to the limit. Convoy losses continued to rise in the Atlantic, but luckily, captured German codes and maps enabled the British to destroy nearly all of the German supply ships supporting the U-boats at sea. The codes were also helping to sink U-boats being positioned to attack convoys. Even with this information, the merchant shipping losses were becoming alarming.

The Mediterranean Fleet was still recovering from a very bloody campaign in Greece and Crete when they were thrown into the Syrian attack. Luckily, they only encountered a few heavy air attacks from the Germans and were able to overpower the Vichy French forces in the Eastern Mediterranean.

The supply situation on Malta was becoming critical. The British had to resort to running critical supplies to the Island by using submarines as transports. Submarines can only carry a small fraction of cargo for even a small freighter, but the situation required the use of all means to salvage the situation.

UNITED STATES

The United States edged ever closer to war with Germany. Moving United States Marines to Iceland and establishing regular visits by American warships in the German declared war zone was tempting fates beyond control. Like a matador, the US Navy waved its red, white and blue cape in front of the U-boats, daring them to attack and draw the United States into the conflict.

RUSSIA

The Russian Navy was fully prepared for the German attack on Russia. In the Black Sea, the surface fleet quickly attacked the Romanian oil terminal at Constanza, only to lose several ships in the minefields. They deployed submarines in both offensive and defensive positions.

The Russian Baltic Fleet found itself too exposed in the forward bases in Latvia and Estonia. Consequently they suffered heavy losses in the offensive minefields laid by the Germans and the Finns along the coastal harbours.

The Russian Arctic Fleet quickly secured the northern areas before the Germans could intervene. They successfully evacuated most non-combatants to the east and set up strong defences in depth along the land and sea approaches to Murmansk.

CHINA

The Chinese continued to resist the Japanese attacks. Since the terrain was too mountainous for effective land combat, the Japanese relied on air attacks to force the Chinese government to the peace table.

Meanwhile small groups of Chinese partisans caused continuous trouble with small raids, destroying railroad bridges, cutting communication lines and destroying any small Japanese outpost too far away from quick support.

POLAND

Polish troops continued to support the British on all fronts. The Polish Navy escorted convoy ships while the Air Force flew combat missions over Britain and Germany. The Polish Army had over 20,000 men training in Palestine and learning English. They would soon be capable of supporting allied operations in the desert.

FREE FRENCH

The Free French embarked on their largest attack to date when they invaded Syria with British support. De Gaulle was convinced that the Vichy French forces in Syria would rally to his cause. He was mistaken as the Vichy troops launched a very determined counterattack.

Once again, General De Gaulle had not proven himself to be the strong French leader the Allies needed to retake France.

GERMANY SENDS RUSSIA TO THE ALLIES   JUNE 1941—19

GENERAL

DATE	COMMENTS
1 June	During the night, 110 German aircraft bombed Manchester.
1 June	British forces surrendered the island of Crete. About 18,000 Allied troops were taken off the beaches. The British and Dominion casualties were 1,742 killed, 1,737 wounded and 11,835 taken prisoner. For the Royal Navy the battle cost the Mediterranean Fleet: three cruisers and six destroyers sunk; one aircraft carrier, three battleships, six cruisers and nine destroyers damaged. Over 2,000 sailors were killed and almost 500 wounded. Crete proved to be a hollow victory; its significance in the overall war plan was minimal and it turned Hitler against conducting any future large-scale airborne actions, which could have helped his cause in other theatres. The cost to the Germans for Operation MERCURY was high. Of the 22,000 men committed for the operation approximately 6,000 were casualties. The mountain troops lost 20 officers and 305 other ranks, killed in action; the missing-most of them drowned when the Royal Navy sunk the boats transporting them, numbered 18 officers and 488 other ranks. Of the nearly 500 Ju52 transport aircraft involved, 271 were lost.
1 June	The British forces entered Baghdad, Iraq, ending the Iraqi bid for a pro-axis and free country.
1 to 30 June	During the month, German aircraft dropped six hundred aerial mines in British coastal waters. Over two hundred of the mines were put in the Thames and Humber estuaries.
2 June	Hitler and Mussolini met at the Brenner Pass on the German-Italian border to discuss the progress of the war.
2 June	In preparation for Operation BATTLEAXE, the British amassed 200 tanks verses 170 tanks for the Axis forces in Libya.
2 June	During the night, RAF Bomber Command dropped aerial mines in the Kaiser Wilhelm canal.
3 June	Using the German Naval Codes captured on **U.110** and weather observation ship **MUNCHEN**, the Home Fleet in connection with the German Operation RHEINBUNG, set out to destroy the U-boat re-supply network in the North Atlantic.
3 June	In Operation EXPORTER, the Royal Navy supported the invasion of Syria by British and Free French troops.
4 June	The British install a Pro-allied government in Iraq.
4 June	Luftwaffe bombers carry out a night raid on the port of Alexandria, Egypt.
4 June	Aircraft of German I/LG.1 group arrived at Maleme, Crete and became the main operational German air group on the island.
5 June	The United States landed 4000 Marines on Iceland to replace the British troops occupying the Island.
5 June	German Ju88 aircraft of I/LG.1 bombed Alexandria harbour during the night from their new base at Crete.
5 June	In Operation ROCKET, the Royal Navy flew forty-three Hurricane aircraft to Malta on 6 June.
6 June	Hitler issued a directive for the implementation of the Commissar Order, which called for the summary execution of all Russian political commissars attached to the Russian Army. Most German army and corps commanders tacitly disobeyed the order. They deem it contrary to German military custom and tradition.
6 June	The United States seized eighty foreign merchant ships in U.S. ports for use lend-lease convoys. Included were forty Danish, twenty-eight Italian, eleven French, two German, two Estonian, one Latvian and one Romanian ship. All German assets were frozen and the U.S. government requested that Germany close all American consulates and return the German personnel home.
8 June	In Operation ROCKET, British and Free French forces led by General Maitland, Wilson and Catroux, invaded Lebanon and Syria against stiff resistance by Vichy French troops.
10 June	During a reconnaissance flight over Deraa, the British air defence downed a well-known French pilot, Capitaine Emile Louis Roger Jacobi of 6 Squadron, 3rd Fighter Group.
10 June	In the afternoon the air crews of French 7 Squadron, 1st Fighter Group received orders to "drive off small units of the British Navy" that were firing uninterruptedly at the French-held coast; but it turned out that these "small units" were the whole of the British 15th Cruiser Squadron, and the French swiftly halted their operations.
10 June	The United States began preparing plans to invade the Azores in case Spain or German troops attempted to occupy neutral Portugal. These plans were dropped when the American Secret Service verified that there were no plans by Germany or Spain to invade Portugal.
10 June	In Operation CHRONOMETER, Indian troops were landed at Assab, Ethiopia.
11 June	A Japanese twin-engine military aircraft flew over Guam at very high altitude.
11 June	The RAF Bomber Command began a series of twenty consecutive raids against targets in the Ruhr, the Rhineland, as well as Hamburg and Bremen.
12 June	The German pocket battleship LÜTZOW (ex **DEUTSCHLAND**) was attacked and damaged by RAF aircraft off the southern coast of Norway.

12 June	RAF and Italian fighter aircraft engaged in fierce air battles over Malta.
12 June	All German ships were directed to depart from all Russian controlled ports and return immediately to Axis controlled ports.
13 June	The Luftwaffe carried out a raid on the British naval base at Chatham, but with little success.
13 June	During the night of 13/14 June, 110 RAF bombers attacked the German battleships and heavy cruisers at Brest, France.
14 June	A Japanese twin-engine military aircraft flew over Guam at very high altitude.
14 June	Croatia joined the Tripartite Pact with Germany, Italy and Japan.
14 June	Hitler and his top generals discussed matters concerning the upcoming campaign against Russia.
14 June	President Roosevelt ordered the freezing of all Axis assets and those of the occupied countries.
14 June	In Libya, the British Eighth Army began Operation BATTLEAXE to lift the siege of Tobruk, but the Axis Africa Corps counter attacked three days later and the British attack was abandoned.
14 June	In Operation TRACER, the Royal Navy launched forty-seven Hurricane aircraft to Malta.
15 June	While bombing Chunking, China, Japanese aircraft dropped bombs near the American river gunboat TUTUILA (PR-4). The men on board were convinced that the bombs were deliberately dropped on the American vessel.
15 June	In Libya, the British Eighth Army abandoned Gazala as Operation BATTLEAXE failed to reach the encircled troops at Tobruk.
15 June	The British begin using Naval Cipher 3 for Atlantic convoy control. The German B-Service began an intensive effort to break the code. From December 1942 through May 1943, the Germans could read 80% of the British message traffic.
15 June	In Operation SALVAGE, the Royal Navy continued to intercept German blockade-runners.
16 June	The U.S. State Department ordered the closing by July 10 of all German consular offices and tourist agencies in the United States.
16 June	German *Großadmiral* Karl Dönitz sent a message to all U-boats at sea identifying the secret rendezvous positions for re-supply. It is possible that the British already had the secret positions from the documents already captured on German ships.
18 June	Free French troops occupied Damascus, Syria.
18 June	Germany and Turkey sign a ten-year non-aggression pact.
19 June	Based on intercepted German propaganda messages about the evils of Communism and the plight of the Russian people under its evil boot, Russian Admiral N. G. Kuznetsov ordered the Russian Navy to implement Alert Status 2.
20 June	A Russian aerial formation, the 6th Fighter Corps, was set up in Moscow for the defence of the capital.
20 June	President Roosevelt, in a message to Congress, denounced the sinking of the American merchant ship **ROBIN MOOR** (4999grt) by U.69 (Kptlt Metzler) as 'an act of piracy'.
21 June	Hitler convinced Mussolini to allow General Rommel to invade Egypt and set aside the invasion of Malta, named Operation HERCULES. Mussolini accepted the proposal after heavy consideration. Malta was a strategic point for British convoys, which supplied the Commonwealth forces in Africa. The invasion of Malta would require the landing of three Italian parachute battalions and one German parachute division and bombardment by both Italian and German aircraft. After the capture of Malta, Rommel would then have a secure supply line to drive the Axis forces into Egypt.
21 June	General Auchinleck replaced General Wavell as C-in-C of the British Eighth Army in Libya.
21 June	At 2337, the Russian Fleet was ordered to Alert Status 1, authorizing deadly force against any ship violating Russian waters.
21 June	All German warships operating in the Eastern Baltic were directed to use a new code for the Russian operations. This code was used until November 1941.
22 June	Beginning of Operation BARBAROSSA, the German invasion of the Russian Union. At 3:15 a.m. CET, German, Rumanian and Finnish forces comprising 183 divisions (3,500,000 men), 3,350 tanks, 7,184 guns and 1,945 aircraft launch the biggest military operation in history on an 1,800-mile front from 'Finland to the Black Sea' (title of the German Army campaign song). Three army groups supported by powerful Panzer armies and Luftwaffe bomber fleets, Army Group South (von Rundstedt) with Panzer Group 1 (von Kleist), Army Group Middle (von Bock) with Panzer Group 2 (Guderian) and 3 (Hoth), and Army Group North (von Leeb) with Panzer Group 4 (Hoepner) went into action against 132 Russian divisions (2,500,000 men), 20,000 tanks and 7,700 aircraft. The overall objective of the campaign was to destroy the Russian forces in western Russia by fall and to occupy the European part of Russia up to the line from Archangel - Urals - Volga - Astrakhan. In the first few hours of the attack, the Luftwaffe destroyed 1,500 Russian aircraft on the ground at 60 airfields and another 300 aircraft in the air. The Russian Army forces along the border seemed unprepared for the assault and offered only limited resistance. At London, Winston Churchill announced Britain's support for Russia, thus making the Bolshevik state her much-needed ally.
22 June	Six Russian SB.2 and 3 DB.3 aircraft of the 63rd Aviation Brigade attacked Constanza and Sulina, Roma-

	nia.
22 June	The Russian Black Sea Fleet began laying defensive minefields off Sevastopol, Odessa, Kertsch, Novorossisk, Tuapse and Batumi.
22 June	The Russians begin to evacuate women and children from Murmansk, Russia to safe areas east.
22 June	German aircraft of II/KG.4 from the IV Air Corps laid 120 mines from Zilista to Sevastopol, and another 50 mines off Nikolaev, Russia.
23 June	The new independent country of Slovakia declared war on the Russia.
23 June	German Army Group South crossed the river Bug in southern Poland and captured the Russian city of Brest-Litovsk. (Authors note: some Russian soldiers continued to hold out in their defensive positions for another six weeks before they were taken by German assault.)
23 June	The Italian and German air forces bombed Tobruk, Libya.
23 June	Aircraft of the Russian Black Sea Fleet attacked Constanza and Sulina, Romania.
24 June	Hungary broke off diplomatic relations with Russia.
24 June	German Army Group North captured the cities of Kaunas and Vilna in Lithuania.
24 June	The United States extended Lend-Lease aid to Stalin.
24 June	Nine Russian DBS-3 aircraft of the 57th Attack Regiment (Col. Preobrashenski) attacked German troops at Memel, East Prussia.
25 June	German armoured forces of Panzer Group 1 (von Kleist) captured the cities of Lutsk and Dubno in eastern Poland (Russian territory).
25 June	Russian aircraft bombed several Finnish cities.
	In Operation EC, the Royal Navy departed Scapa Flow to capture a German weather ship operating near Jan Mayen Island in the Arctic.
26 June	Finland declared war on Russia. They called it the "Continuation War" as their goal was to recover the territory taken by the Russians in early 1940. Finland also informed the Russians that they were not part of the Axis invasion.
26 June	The Luftwaffe carried out air raids on Leningrad, Russia.
26 June	German Army Group North captured the city of Dünaburg, Latvia.
26 June	Hungarian Heinkel He70 aircraft were used for the first time by the I/LRG in co-operation with the Luftwaffe. They supported the attack of German and Hungarian troops into southern Russia.
27 June	Hungary declared war on Russia.
27 June	German forces encircle several Russian divisions near the Russian city of Minsk and captured the cities of Riga, Bobruisk and Przemysl.
27 June	During the night, RAF Bomber Command attacked Bremen, Cuxhaven, Emden and Wilhelmshaven.
27 June	In Operation VIGOROUS, the Royal Navy searched for German supply ships supporting German AMC's and U-boats in the area of the Canary Islands.
27 June	In Operation RAILWAY, the Royal Navy launched twenty-two Hurricane aircraft from a position south of the Balearic Islands to Malta led by Blenheim bomber aircraft flown from Gibraltar to Malta as navigation aids.
28 June	German troops of Army Group Middle captured the Russian city of Minsk.
29 June	Several divisions of the Russian West Front (Pavlov) were encircled near the Russian city of Bialystok.
29 June	On the Arctic front in northern Finland, the German XIX Mountain Corps (Dietl) launched Operation SILVER FOX, an offensive from Petsamo, Finland to capture the Russian port of Murmansk.
29 June	In Operation RAILWAY 2, the Royal Navy launched twenty-six Hurricane aircraft to Malta on 30 May.
30 June	Vichy France broke off diplomatic relations with Russia.
30 June	Pilots of Luftwaffe fighter wing JG.51 downed one hundred Russian bombers attacking German armoured forces east of Minsk; it's CO, Oberst (Colonel) Mölders, accounted for five of them.
30 June	German Army Group Centre (von Bock) captured the Russian city of Lvov (Lemberg).
30 June	The Russian 2nd and 40th Aviation Regiments and the 62nd Fighter Brigade made thirty-eight attacks with 285 Sorties.
30 June	RAF Bomber Command carried out a daylight attack with the new Halifax bombers on Kiel, Germany.
1 to 30 June	Atlantic Convoy statistics: convoys SC.33, SC.34, SC.35, HX.130, HX.131, HX.132, HX.134 and HX.135 plus outbound convoys OB.330 to OB.341 moved 512 ships across the Atlantic without a loss.

NAVAL DEPLOYMENT—RUSSIA

Russian Baltic Fleet
Under the command of Vice Admiral Tributs

Battleships MARAT and OKTYABRSKAYA REVOLUTSIYA
Heavy cruisers KIROV and MAKSIM GORKI
Destroyer leaders LENINGRAD and MINSK
Old destroyers YAKOV SVERDLOV, KALININ, KARL MARKS, LENIN, ARTEM, ENGLES and VOLODARSKI
Modern destroyers GNEVNY, GORDY, GROZYASHCHI, SMETLIVY, STEREGUSHCHI, STOROZHEVOI, SERDITY, STOIKI, SILNY, SUROVY, SLAVNY, and SMELY
Seven patrol boats (T-series), eleven large submarines, thirty-six medium submarines and twenty-three small submarines, six Minelayers, thirty-three minesweepers, one gunboat, forty-eight motor torpedo boats, and 656 airplanes.

Russian Northern Fleet
Under the command of Vice Admiral Golovko

Old destroyers KUYBYSHEV, URITSKI, and KARL LIBKNECHT
Modern destroyers GROZNY, GROMKI, SREMITELNY, SOKRUSHITELNY, and GREMYASHCHI
Seven patrol boats (three of them T-series), three large submarines, six medium submarines and six small submarines, two Minesweepers, fifteen patrol cutters, two torpedo boats and one auxiliary, plus 116 airplanes.

Russian Black Sea Fleet
Under the command of Vice Admiral Oktyabrsky

Battleship PARIZHSKAYA KOMMUNA
Modern cruisers VOROSHILOV and MOLOTOV
Old cruisers KRASNY KAVKAZ, KRASNY KRYM and CHERVONA UKRAINA
Training cruiser KOMINTERN
Destroyer leaders MOSKVA, KHARKOV and TASHKENT (newly constructed from an Italian design)
Old destroyers FRUNZE, DZERZHINSKI, NEZAMOZHNIK, SHAUMYAN, and ZHELEZNYAKOV
Modern destroyers BODRY, BYSTRY, BOIKI, BESPOSHCHADNY, BEZUPRECHNY, BDITELNY, SMYSHLENY, and SOOBRAZITELNY
Two patrol boats (T-series), forty-seven submarines, eighty-four torpedo boats, fifteen minesweepers, and 625 airplanes.

Russian Pacific Fleet
Under the command of Vice Admiral Yumashev

Two destroyer leaders, two old destroyers, five modern destroyers, eight patrol boats, eight minesweepers, thirteen large submarines, thirty-five medium submarines, and thirty-seven small submarines.

Russian Reserve Fleet

Five cruisers, two destroyer leaders, eighteen destroyers, five patrol boats, sixteen minesweepers, twelve large submarines, thirty-one medium submarines, and twenty-six small submarines.
Under Construction: three battleships, two battle cruisers, twenty-four destroyers, twelve patrol boats, eight minesweepers, eighteen medium submarines, and twenty-six small submarines.

NAVAL DEPLOYMENT—ROMANIA

Under the command of General Nicolae Sova at Constanza, Romania
Destroyers; MARASESTI, MARASTI, REGINA MARIA and REGELE FERDINAND.
Torpedo Boats; SBORUL, SMEUL and NALUCA
Minelayer ADMIRAL MURGESCU
Submarines; S.1, S.2 and DELFINUL
Gunboats: CAPITAN ROMANO MIHAIL, LOCOTENENT DIMITRIE CALINESCU, SUBLOCOTENENT CHICULESCU, CAPITAN DUMITRESCU, LOCOTENENT LEPRI REMUS and COMANDOR EUGEN STIHI.
River Gunboats; BISTRITSA, OTTUL, and SIRETUL.
Five Motor Torpedo Boats
River Monitors; ALEXANDRU LA ROVARI, MIHAIL KOGALRICEANU, ION C. BRATIANU, LASCAR CATARGIU, BASARABIA, ARDEAL and BUCOVINA.

NAVAL DEPLOYMENT—HUNGARY

Hungary had no ports on the Black Sea or the Adriatic. She did maintain a small river patrol flotilla for the Danube.

NAVAL DEPLOYMENT—BULGARIA

Under the command of General Russi Russev at Varna, Bulgaria

Motor torpedo boats; VARNA and RILA
Motor patrol boats; BELOMORETS, CHERNOMORETS, KAPITAN MINKOV and VZRIV
Coal burning patrol boats; STROGI and HRABRI
Motor launches; KATERINA GRUBO, LAPCHEV, FELVISHI, MAISTER IVAN, LILIYA, BALIK, KOMZIL, KALOSERKA, DOBROTITS and TILA
Auxiliary sail training vessels; TSAR ASSEN, KAMCHIYA, and SIMEON
Eight armed auxiliary sailing vessels
Five Siebel ferries
Two motor caiques
Yacht KAMCHIYA
Gunboat DOROSTOR
Thirty-eight F-boats.

ARCTIC OCEAN

Greenland Sea and Barents Sea
Long. W180, 00 – E180, 00   Lat. N90, 00 – N68, 00

17 JUNE 1941

	A German Me110 reconnaissance aircraft flew over the Russian port at Zapolyarny. Russian AA fired on the aircraft.

18 JUNE 1941

	Russian submarine M-176 arrived at Zyp Navolok to provide additional defensive force.

22 JUNE 1941

	The Russian Northern Fleet (VAdm A. G. Golovko) began combat operations. The Submarine Brigade (Capt 1st Class N. I. Vinogradov) sent D-3 to Nordkyn, SHCH-421 to Kirkenes, SHCH-401 to Vardø, and M-176 to Varangerfjord to attack German supply ships in Norwegian ports. Submarine SHCH-403 patrolled off Iokanga, and submarine SHCH-404 patrolled the entrance to the White Sea.
	Russian submarines M-175 and M-173 patrolled a defensive zone along the Russian Kola peninsula.

25 JUNE 1941

	Russian troopship MOSSOVET (2981grt) escorted by destroyers KUIBYSHEV and submarine chasers landed additional troops at Titovka. The convoy survived several German air attacks without damage.

27 JUNE 1941

	By the end of the month, one hundred fifty Russian merchant ships evacuated civilians from the Russian Kola Fjord area without a loss.

28 JUNE 1941

1850	In Operation EC, light cruiser NIGERIA with destroyers BEDOUIN, TARTAR, and JUPITER captured German weather ship **WBS.3/LAUENBURG** (344grt) off Jan Mayen Island in 73, 02N, 03, 13W. After a thorough search of the vessel, destroyer TARTAR sank the weather ship, and the force returned to Scapa Flow. The British recovered several code documents that allowed them to read ENIGMA traffic in German domestic waters until July.

30 JUNE 1941

	Russian destroyers KUIBYSHEV (Capt 2nd Class E. M. Simonov) and URITSKI with submarine chasers MO-121 and MO-123 landed parts of the Russian 14th Rifle Division at Petsamo, Finland, and provided gunfire support to the troops.
	German Ju87 aircraft of IV/LG.1 damaged submarine chaser MO-121 with bomb near misses off Petsamo.

White Sea
Long. E30, 00 – E60, 00   Lat. N68, 00 – N60, 00

22 JUNE 1941

	Russian destroyers GROZNY and SOKRUSHITELNY patrolled the entrance to the White Sea.

NORTH ATLANTIC OCEAN

Iceland and North of Britain
Long. W30, 00 – E03, 00   Lat. N68, 00 – N58, 30

1 JUNE 1941

	German aircraft sank steamer **PRINCE RUPERT CITY** (4749grt) north of Cape Wrath, Scotland, in 58, 46N, 04, 41W. Four crewmen were lost.
	British Deployment in the Area The Home Fleet at Scapa Flow included battleship KING GEORGE V, light cruisers MANCHESTER and GALATEA, and seven destroyers. Heavy cruiser SUFFOLK plus light cruisers KENYA and AURORA were at sea sweeping for German supply ships. Battleship NELSON, light cruisers NEPTUNE and SHEFFIELD, and fourteen destroyers would be available to the Home Fleet by 20 June.
	Light cruiser EDINBURGH departed Scapa Flow on Denmark Strait patrol.
	Light cruiser ARETHUSA departed the Denmark Strait patrol when relieved by light cruiser HERMIONE. She arrived in Iceland and then departed for a patrol in the Iceland-Faeroes passage.
	Destroyers COSSACK, ZULU, MAORI, and SIKH departed Scapa Flow for the Clyde to escort convoy WS.9A.
	U.204 sank Icelandic fishing trawler **HOLMSTEINN** (16grt) with gunfire north-northwest of Dyrafjord.
0300	Destroyer ELECTRA arrived at Scapa Flow from Rosyth, Scotland.
1400	Destroyer HAMBLEDON with sloops SUTLEJ and STORK arrived back at Scapa Flow after escort duty.
1500	Destroyers PUNJABI, ESKIMO, and ICARUS departed Scapa Flow for the Clyde to screen battleship RODNEY.
	Denmark Strait Patrol 1 to 4 June: light cruiser HERMIONE 4 to 10 June: light cruiser EDINBURGH 11 to 18 June: light cruiser MANCHESTER 13 to 16 June: light cruiser HERMIONE 17 to 24 June: heavy cruiser SUFFOLK 23 June to 1 July: light cruiser MANCHESTER.
	Iceland-Faeroes Passage Patrol 1 to 3 June: light cruiser MANCHESTER 3 to 10 June: light cruiser ARETHUSA 9 to 17 June: light cruiser KENYA 11 to 22 June: light cruiser NIGERIA 22 to 25 June: light cruiser AURORA 24 to 29 June: light cruiser ARETHUSA.

2 JUNE 1941

	Light cruiser BIRMINGHAM departed Scapa Flow for the Clyde to escort convoy WS.9A.
	A mine sank Finnish steamer **KASTEHOLM** (5417grt) in 63, 07N, 11, 18W. One crewman was lost and the rest of the crew were landed at Tórshavn.
2043 2221	U.108 (Kptlt Klaus Scholtz) heavily damaged catapult armed merchant (CAM) ship **MICHAEL E** (7628grt) (Master Murdo Macleod) after she was dispersed from convoy OB.327 southwest of Cape Clear in 48, 50N, 29W. Two crewmen and two gunners were lost. The CAM sank by the stern. Dutch steamer ALCINOUS (6189grt) rescued the master, forty-four crewmen, two gunners, and twelve RAF personnel, including two pilots and a fighter direction officer (FDO) the following day. Fighter pilot, A/Sub-Lt (A) M.A. Birrell, was among the survivors. The **MICHAEL E** had been the very first CAM ship, and the first successful aircraft launch occurred from this ship off Belfast, Ireland.
2230	Destroyer BEDOUIN arrived at Scapa Flow after escorting steamer BEN MY CHREE (2586grt) to Cape Wrath from Iceland.

3 JUNE 1941

	Light cruiser EDINBURGH arrived in Iceland to refuel.
	Using the German Naval Codes captured on **U.110** and weather observation ship **MUNCHEN**, the Home Fleet, in connection with German Operation RHEINBUNG, set out to destroy the U-boat re-supply network in the North Atlantic.

0200	Destroyers ELECTRA, IMPULSIVE, and ANTELOPE departed Scapa Flow for Londonderry, Northern Ireland, to refuel prior to joining the escort of arriving battleship NELSON.

4 JUNE 1941

	Light cruiser EDINBURGH departed Iceland to relieve light cruiser HERMIONE on Northern Patrol.
	Light cruiser NIGERIA arrived at Scapa Flow after refitting at Rosyth.
0615	Antiaircraft ship ALYNBANK departed Scapa Flow to join convoy WN.35 in Pentland Firth and escort it south-eastwardly. ALYNBANK transferred from convoy WN.35 to cover convoy EC.28 and remained in its company through the day.

5 JUNE 1941

	Antiaircraft ship ALYNBANK transferred from convoy EC.28 to convoy WN.36 west of the Orkneys.
	Light cruisers AURORA and KENYA arrived at Iceland after searching for German supply ships. AURORA continued on to Scapa Flow, arriving on the 7th.
	Light cruiser HERMIONE arrived at Iceland after her Denmark Strait patrol.
	AMC AURANIA arrived at Iceland after being withdrawn from Northern Patrol after a submarine was reported in her patrol area.
0001	Destroyer INTREPID departed Scapa Flow for Immingham to fit a new Targeting System Direction System (TSDS) and carry out repairs.

6 JUNE 1941

0900	Destroyer ANTHONY departed Scapa Flow and joined steamers AMSTERDAM (4220grt) and LADY OF MANN (3104grt) off the entrance to Aberdeen, Scotland.
2200	Steamer LADY OF MANN (3104grt) arrived at Long Hope, Orkneys, and destroyer ANTHONY and steamer AMSTERDAM (4220grt) arrived at Kirkwall.

7 JUNE 1941

0430	Destroyer ANTHONY departed Kirkwall with steamer AMSTERDAM (4220grt) for Lerwick, Scotland.
2000	Destroyer ACHATES arrived at Scapa Flow from Rosyth, Scotland.
2000	Home Fleet ships at Scapa Flow went to one hour's alert notice on a report of German heavy ship movements.
10000	Destroyer ANTHONY arrived at Lerwick with steamer AMSTERDAM (4220grt) from Kirkwall.

8 JUNE 1941

	Home Fleet ships returned to normal alert notice at Scapa Flow.
	Light cruiser KENYA departed Iceland to reinforce light cruiser EDINBURGH on Denmark Strait patrol. However, she was recalled to refuel and proceed to the Iceland-Faeroes passage patrol.
	A British mine sank trawler **HOPTON** (202grt) off Iceland in 62, 56N, 12, 30W. Eleven crewmen were lost. The master of trawler HONDO (229grt), who was in charge of **HOPTON**, was subsequently suspended for navigating in a prohibited area.
0030	Battleship NELSON arrived at Scapa Flow escorted by destroyers ELECTRA, IMPULSIVE, and ANTELOPE to rejoin the Home Fleet after duty in the South Atlantic.
0430	Destroyer ANTHONY departed Lerwick escorting steamer AMSTERDAM (4220grt) to Aberdeen.
0930	Steamer LADY OF MANN (3104grt) departed Scapa Flow and joined destroyer ANTHONY and steamer AMSTERDAM (4220grt) off Duncansby Head for the trip back to Aberdeen.
1930	Destroyers TARTAR, PUNJABI, and ESKIMO arrived at Scapa Flow after escorting battleship RODNEY.
2130	Destroyer ANTHONY returned to Scapa Flow.

9 JUNE 1941

	German Fw200 aircraft of I/KG.40 bombing sank steamer **DIANA** (942grt) northwest of the Faeroes Islands in 62, 04N, 13, 40W. One gunner was lost, and antisubmarine trawler CAPE PORTLAND rescued the survivors and took them to Tórshavn.
	Heavy cruiser SUFFOLK rejoined the Home Fleet at Scapa Flow after escorting inbound convoy HX.129 and searching for German supply ships.
	Light cruiser KENYA sailed from Iceland to patrol the Iceland Faeroes passage.
	Light cruiser MANCHESTER departed Scapa Flow for Iceland.
	Bombs from German Fw200 aircraft of I/KG.40 sank Finnish steamer **FENIX** (1894grt) northwest of the Faeroe Islands in 61, 56N, 12, 14W. One crewman was lost.
	Minelayers AGAMEMNON and MENESTHEUS with destroyers BRIGHTON, ST MARYS, IMPULSIVE, and ANTHONY departed Loch Alsh. Light cruiser NIGERIA departed Scapa Flow and joined the group at sea. They laid Minefield SN.64 in the Faeroes North Rona minefield.

	The minelayers arrived at Loch Alsh with destroyers BRIGHTON and ST MARYS on the 11th. Destroyers IMPULSIVE and ANTHONY parted company with the mining force off Cape Wrath and returned to Scapa Flow.
0100	Antiaircraft ship ALYNBANK arrived at Scapa Flow after detaching from convoy EC.29 off Cape Wrath.
0600	Destroyers IMPULSIVE and ANTHONY departed Scapa Flow for Loch Alsh to escort minelayers updating Minefield SN.64 (see 9 June).
1200	Destroyers INGLEFIELD, ICARUS, and ACHATES departed Scapa Flow for Reykjavik, Iceland.

10 JUNE 1941

	Light cruisers EDINBURGH and NIGERIA departed the Denmark Strait patrol to refuel at Hvalfjord. They were ordered by the Admiralty to prepare for a possible breakout of German heavy cruiser LÜTZOW into the North Atlantic in their area.
	Light cruiser ARETHUSA departed the Iceland-Faeroes passage patrol and arrived at Scapa Flow.
>1200	Destroyers INGLEFIELD, ICARUS, and ACHATES arrived at Reykjavik from Scapa Flow during the afternoon.
2315	Antiaircraft ship ALYNBANK departed Scapa Flow to join convoy WN.38 in Pentland Firth and escort it southeastwardly. During the afternoon of 11 June she transferred to convoy EC.31 south of Buchan Ness. Off Duncansby Head on the 12th, she shifted to convoy WN.39 and escorted it to Methil.

11 JUNE 1941

	Light cruiser NIGERIA arrived at Skaalefjord to refuel before proceeding on patrol.
	Light cruiser MANCHESTER arrived in Iceland escorted by destroyers INGLEFIELD and ICARUS and then sailed that day on a patrol with destroyers INGLEFIELD, ICARUS, and ACHATES. Destroyer ACTIVE departed Scapa Flow to join this force at sea.
	Heavy cruiser SUFFOLK departed Scapa Flow for Hvalfjord.
0430	The Home Fleet at Scapa Flow came to one hour's alert notice on the receipt of a report indicating that German heavy cruiser LÜTZOW was spotted in the Skagerrak approaching the North Sea.
1030	Destroyers IMPULSIVE and ANTHONY arrived at Scapa Flow after escorting the mining force to Cape Wrath.
2000	Polish destroyer KRAKOWIAK arrived at Scapa Flow to work up to combat efficiency.
2051	U.79 (Wolfgang Kaufmann) sank unescorted Norwegian steamer **HAVTOR** (1524grt) (Master Kjell Bugge) in 63, 35N, 28, 05W.
0033	U.79 began to shell the steamer to sink her more quickly after the crew abandoned the ship. Six crewmen were lost. The survivors, nine of them wounded, headed for Iceland in one lifeboat. Fishing vessel PILOT (grt) rescued the master and thirteen survivors the next day, five miles off Reykjanes.
2100	Destroyer HAMBLEDON departed Scapa Flow to escort steamers AMSTERDAM (4220grt) and LADY OF MANN (3104grt) from Aberdeen.

12 JUNE 1941

0127	Battleship KING GEORGE V, light cruisers AURORA and ARETHUSA plus destroyers BEDOUIN, PUNJABI, ESKIMO, and NESTOR departed Scapa Flow for a position in 64N, 28, 30W.
>0127	Light cruiser ARETHUSA intercepted Finnish steamer KRONOBORG (6537grt) and sent her to Kirkwall for cargo inspection.
>0127	Battleship NELSON and heavy cruiser DEVONSHIRE remained at Scapa Flow, but continued on one hour's alert notice. DEVONSHIRE had not yet worked up to combat efficiency after her extensive repairs and was only authorized by the Admiralty for combat in an extreme emergency.
1600	Destroyer HAMBLEDON arrived at Lerwick with steamer AMSTERDAM (4220grt). Steamer LADY OF MANN (3104grt) was detached en route to Scapa Flow when off Duncansby Head.
2330	Destroyers ELECTRA and ANTHONY departed Scapa Flow for the Clyde.

13 JUNE 1941

	Heavy cruiser SUFFOLK arrived at Hvalfjord from Scapa Flow.
0200	Light cruiser AURORA intercepted Finnish steamer ROLFSBORG (1831grt) while she was en route from Norfolk, Virginia, to Petsamo, Finland, in 61, 08N, 16W and ordered her to Kirkwall under armed guard.
0500	Destroyer HAMBLEDON departed Lerwick escorting steamer AMSTERDAM (4220grt), and they joined steamer LADY OF MANN (3104grt) off Duncansby Head. The two steamers were taken to Aberdeen.
0745	The battleship KING GEORGE V group departed their patrol area to return to Scapa Flow.
0900	Sloops BLACK SWAN and STORK departed Scapa Flow for Fair Isle Channel to search for a submarine reported by aircraft fifty miles southeast of Fair Isle. Two motor-launches and antisubmarine trawlers OPHELIA and CELIA later joined the sloops in the search. That evening, sloop STORK made a depth charge attack on a submarine contact fifteen miles 73° from Seal Skerry Light. Motor launch ML.218 also attacked a submarine contact.

	No further attacks were made and the ships returned to Scapa Flow on the 15th.
1500	Destroyer ANTELOPE departed Scapa Flow to join destroyers ELECTRA and ANTHONY at sea for a special convoy escort.
1915	Destroyer ACTIVE arrived in Iceland from Scapa Flow to join the light cruiser MANCHESTER force.
2200	Destroyer HAMBLEDON arrived back at Scapa Flow after her escort duty.

14 JUNE 1941

	CS.2 transferred his flag to light cruiser ARETHUSA at Scapa Flow.
1000	Indian sloop SUTLEJ departed Scapa Flow for the Clyde to join the Western Approaches Command after working up to combat efficiency.
1319	Battleship KING GEORGE V, light cruisers AURORA and ARETHUSA returned to Scapa Flow with destroyers BEDOUIN, PUNJABI, ESKIMO, and NESTOR from their patrol area.

15 JUNE 1941

0500	Sloops BLACK SWAN and STORK, antisubmarine trawlers OPHELIA and CELIA, and two motor launches returned to Scapa Flow after a submarine search near Seal Skerry Light.
1200	Antiaircraft ship ALYNBANK arrived in Scapa Flow after escort duty.

16 JUNE 1941

	Light cruiser EDINBURGH and destroyer INGLEFIELD departed Iceland.
	Minelayers AGAMEMNON and MENESTHEUS with destroyers BRIGHTON, CASTLETON, ST MARYS, and WELLS from Loch Alsh, plus light cruiser AURORA from Scapa Flow, laid Minefield SN.66 in the Iceland-Faeroes passage. Light cruisers NIGERIA and KENYA covered the mining group.
	Battleships KING GEORGE V and NELSON plus destroyers BEDOUIN, INTREPID, JUPITER, NESTOR, PUNJABI, and ESKIMO were brought to one hour's alert notice on the report of two unidentified ships departing the harbour at Brest, France. The alert notice was cancelled after it was found that these two ships were merchant vessels.
2230	Destroyer CHARLESTOWN arrived at Scapa Flow to work up to combat efficiency after her refit prior to rejoining the Minelaying Force at loch Alsh.
2359	Destroyer INTREPID arrived at Scapa Flow from the Humber with her newly installed TSDS equipment.

17 JUNE 1941

	Light cruiser KENYA arrived at Scapa Flow from the Iceland-Faeroes passage and covering the laying of Minefield SN.66.
	Light cruiser AURORA arrived at Scapa Flow after covering the laying of Minefield SN.66.
	Heavy cruiser SUFFOLK and destroyer ACTIVE departed Iceland for the Denmark Strait patrol.
	Light cruiser HERMIONE arrived at Iceland from her Denmark Strait patrol, refuelled, and then sailed for Scapa Flow.
1100	Destroyer LANCE departed Scapa Flow to join Western Approaches Command following her working up to combat efficiency.
1630	Destroyer WINCHESTER arrived at Scapa Flow to work up to combat efficiency following her repairs and prior to joining the NORE Command.

18 JUNE 1941

	Light cruiser HERMIONE arrived at Scapa Flow from Northern Patrol.
	Heavy cruiser CUMBERLAND arrived at Scapa Flow en route to her refit after duty in the South Atlantic and escorting convoy SL.76 north with light cruiser SHEFFIELD.
	Light cruiser EDINBURGH arrived at Scapa Flow from her Denmark Strait patrol.
	Light cruiser MANCHESTER and destroyer ACHATES arrived at Iceland from their Denmark Strait patrol.
0200	Destroyer ECHO arrived at Scapa Flow from Rosyth.
0200	Destroyer IMPULSIVE departed Scapa Flow for Immingham for a refit and the installation of TSDS equipment.
0630	Destroyer ECLIPSE arrived at Scapa Flow from Plymouth.
0630	Antiaircraft ship ALYNBANK departed Scapa Flow and escorted convoy WN.41 from Pentland Firth. In the afternoon, she transferred to escort convoy EC.34 until its arrival in Pentland Firth. She then returned to Scapa Flow.
1400	Destroyer BATH departed Scapa Flow for Liverpool after working up to combat efficiency.
2100	Destroyer INTREPID departed Scapa Flow for Iceland to join the antisubmarine force operating there.
2330	Antiaircraft ship ALYNBANK returned to Scapa Flow after escort duty.
2350	Destroyer WINDSOR arrived at Scapa Flow from Dundee to continue working up to combat efficiency.

19 JUNE 1941

	A/Vice Admiral A T. B. Curteis CB, Second in Command, Home Fleet, transferred his flag from light cruiser ARETHUSA to battleship PRINCE OF WALES at Scapa Flow. Rear Admiral E. N. Syfret CB, assumed command of 18th Cruiser Squadron on light cruiser KENYA.
0925	Destroyer ANTELOPE arrived at Hvalfjord from escort duty.
1240	Antiaircraft ship ALYNBANK departed Scapa Flow to join convoy WN.42 in the Pentland Firth and escorted the convoy to Methil.
2000	Destroyers ECLIPSE and ECHO departed Scapa Flow for Reykjavik to reinforce the antisubmarine screen for the cruisers on the Denmark Strait patrol. The destroyers arrived during the afternoon on the 21st.

20 JUNE 1941

	Polish destroyer KUJIWIAK arrived at Scapa Flow to work up to combat efficiency.
	RAdm E. N. Syfret CB transferred his flag to light cruiser EDINBURGH from the light cruiser KENYA.
	U.203 (Kptlt Mützelburg) sighted American battleship TEXAS (BB-35), escorted by destroyers TRIPPE (DD-403), RHIND (DD-404), and MAYRANT (DD-402) off Iceland. The U-boat followed the group for several hours without being detected. After reporting the contact, Kptlt Mützelburg received an order forbidding him to attack, even though the ships were within the German declared blockade zone.
	Light cruiser SHEFFIELD departed Scapa Flow to refit at Rosyth.
0300	Destroyer HAMBLEDON departed Scapa Flow to join steamers AMSTERDAM (4220grt) and LADY OF MANN (3104grt) off the entrance of Aberdeen.
1340	Destroyer INTREPID arrived at Reykjavik from Scapa Flow to join the antisubmarine force operating there.
2200	Destroyer ELECTRA arrived at Scapa Flow from escort duty and submarine hunting.
2200	Steamer LADY OF MANN (3104grt) was detached off Duncansby Head for Kirkwall. Destroyer HAMBLEDON later arrived at Lerwick with steamer AMSTERDAM (4220grt).

21 JUNE 1941

	Light cruiser HERMIONE was attached to the Western Approaches Command. She departed Scapa Flow for the Clyde to escort aircraft carrier FURIOUS to ferry aircraft to Gibraltar.
	Light cruiser AURORA departed Scapa Flow to relieve light cruiser NIGERIA on patrol west of the Iceland-Faeroes passage minefield.
	Destroyers ECLIPSE and ECHO arrived in Iceland. ECHO departed later in the day to join heavy cruiser SUFFOLK on a Denmark Strait patrol.
0100	Destroyer ANTHONY arrived at Scapa Flow from escort duty and submarine hunting.
0530	Sloop STORK departed Scapa Flow for Rosyth after working up to combat efficiency.
1015	Destroyer ELECTRA departed Scapa Flow for Sheerness for a refit.
1030	Destroyer HAMBLEDON departed Lerwick for Aberdeen with steamer AMSTERDAM (4220grt).
1115	Destroyer ANTHONY departed Scapa Flow for Rosyth to clean boilers.
1630	Steamer LADY OF MANN (3104grt) joined destroyer HAMBLEDON and steamer AMSTERDAM (4220grt) off Duncansby Head for escort to Aberdeen.

22 JUNE 1941

	German bombing sank naval trawler **BEECH** (540grt) (T/Lt A. P. Cocks RNVR) off Scrabster, Scotland. T/LT Cocks was lost.
	Antisubmarine trawler VISENDA attacked a U-boat with gunfire in 62, 24N, 14, 20W.
0932	Antiaircraft ship ALYNBANK arrived at Pentland Firth with convoy EC.35 and then continued on to Scapa Flow.
1700	Destroyer HEYTHROP arrived at Scapa Flow to work up to combat efficiency.

23 JUNE 1941

	Light cruiser NIGERIA arrived at Scapa Flow from her Iceland-Faeroes passage patrol.
	Light cruiser MANCHESTER and destroyer ECLIPSE departed Iceland to relieve heavy cruiser SUFFOLK on Denmark Strait patrol.
	Light cruisers KENYA and ARETHUSA departed Scapa Flow to cover the force laying Minefield SN.70B.
	Antisubmarine trawler VISENDA made seven depth charge attacks on a firm submarine contact in 61, 52N, 10, 44W. Antisubmarine trawlers NORTHERN SKY and NORTHERN REWARD joined VISENDA and continued the attack, but brought up no firm evidence of a kill.

24 JUNE 1941

	Heavy cruiser SUFFOLK and destroyer ECHO arrived at Iceland from their Denmark Strait patrol.
	Fast minelayer MANXMAN arrived at Scapa Flow to work up to combat efficiency.

2300		Antiaircraft ship ALYNBANK departed Scapa Flow to join convoy WN.44 in Pentland Firth.

25 JUNE 1941

	Minelayers AGAMEMNON and MENESTHEUS escorted by destroyers BRIGHTON, CASTLETON, and WELLS laid Minefield SN.70B in the Iceland-Faeroes passage. Light cruisers KENYA and ARETHUSA covered the mining group. Light cruiser AURORA relieved light cruiser ARETHUSA on the 25th. Light cruiser ARETHUSA went to the Iceland-Faeroes passage patrol area. Light cruiser KENYA and destroyer BRIGHTON collided on the 25th. The light cruiser proceeded to Scapa Flow, arriving on the 27th, and later to the Tyne for repairs. The destroyer was taken to Reydarfjord by light cruiser AURORA and destroyer WELLS. Destroyer ECLIPSE departed Reykjavik to provide additional antisubmarine support for the minelayers. Destroyer ECHO departed Hvalfjord to assist on the 25th and arrived on the 26th at Reydarfjord, where the damaged destroyer and cruiser AURORA had arrived. Destroyer ECLIPSE arrived at Loch Alsh on the 27th after assisting the escort. Light cruiser KENYA departed Scapa Flow for Rosyth on the 28th, arriving on the 29th. On the 28th, destroyer BRIGHTON departed for the Clyde in tow of tugs MARAUDER and THAMES escorted by light cruiser AURORA and destroyer ECHO. They were joined by destroyer LIGHTNING from Scapa Flow. The damaged destroyer was detached in the North Minches. Light cruiser AURORA and destroyers LIGHTING and ECHO arrived at Scapa Flow at 0200 on 1 July. Destroyer BRIGHTON arrived in the Clyde on 1 July. However, the destroyer's bow had broken away en route.
0100	Destroyers ACHATES, ACTIVE, ANTELOPE, INGLEFIELD, and INTREPID departed Iceland to join troop convoy TC.11 at sea. Destroyer ICARUS, detailed for the duty, was unable to proceed due to damaged propellers and was replaced by destroyer SHERWOOD.
1200	Antiaircraft ship ALYNBANK transferred to convoy EC.37 off Buchan Ness.
1300	Sloop BLACK SWAN departed Scapa Flow to provide additional protection for convoy EC.37. In North Channel, the sloop was detached and went to Belfast to join the Western Approaches Command following working up to combat efficiency at Scapa Flow.
2100	Light cruiser NIGERIA departed Scapa Flow with destroyers BEDOUIN, TARTAR, and JUPITER on Operation EC to locate German weather ship LAUENBURG (344grt). The ships proceeded to Skaalefjord to refuel. The ships departed on the 26th. On the 28th, weather ship LAUENBURG was captured off Jan Mayen Island in 73, 02N, 03,13W. After a thorough search of the vessel, destroyer TARTAR sank weather ship **LAUENBURG**. The ships arrived at Scapa Flow after the operation on the 30th.

26 JUNE 1941

	U.556, U.564 and U.201 again spotted convoy HX.133 south of Iceland.
	Indian sloop JUMNA departed Scapa Flow escorting tanker WAR BHARATA (5604grt) to the Faeroes, but returned to Scapa Flow after problems occurred with the tanker's machinery.
0500	Antiaircraft ship ALYNBANK transferred to convoy WN.45 and provided cover to Methil.
1030	Destroyer WINCHESTER departed Scapa Flow for the Clyde to form part of the escort for aircraft carrier VICTORIOUS for her transfer to Scapa Flow.
1830	Destroyer HAMBLEDON arrived at Scapa Flow from Chatham after the installation of Sound Acquisition (SA) equipment.

27 JUNE 1941

	Corvettes NASTURTIUM, CELANDINE, and GLADIOLUS sank **U.556** (Kptlt Wohlfarth) while she was attacking convoy HX.133 southwest of Iceland in 60, 18N, 29, 20W. The commanding officer, four other officers, and thirty-five crewmen were rescued, and an engineer officer and four ratings were missing.
	Aircraft reported a U-boat in 59, 41N, 07, 20W. Antisubmarine trawlers NORTHERN DUKE and NORTHERN FOAM searched the area unsuccessfully for two days.
	Aircraft reported a U-boat in 59, 20N, 04, 04W. A determined search by destroyers and motor launches found no submarine contacts in the area.
0400	Indian sloop JUMNA arrived back at Scapa Flow with tanker WAR BHARATA (5604grt) to repair problems with the tanker's machinery.
1030	Heavy cruiser CUMBERLAND departed Scapa Flow escorted by destroyers HAMBLEDON and WINDSOR to refit at Chatham.
1200	Destroyer ICARUS departed Reykjavik with damaged propellers to join convoy HX.133 at sea and then to proceed to Ardrossan for repair.
1400	Indian sloop JUMNA departed Scapa Flow escorting tanker WAR PINDARI (5559grt), which had taken the place of tanker WAR BHARATA (5604grt), to the Faeroes.
1930	Destroyers LIGHTNING, ESKIMO, NESTOR, and KRAKOWIAK departed Scapa Flow to search for a submarine reported by aircraft in 59, 20N, 04, 04W.

28 JUNE 1941

	U.651 maintained contact with convoy HX.133 south of Iceland. The convoy escorts forced U.201 to submerge and kept her from obtaining a firing position on the convoy.
0207	U.146 (ObltzS Ites) sank unescorted Finnish steamer **PLUTO** (3496grt) (Master Fritjof Ejder) about 100 miles north-northwest of the Butt of Lewis in 59, 39N, 08, 20W. (Heavy cruiser SUFFOLK had ordered her to Kirkwall for inspection eight days earlier.) She sank in thirty minutes with the loss of three crewmen. Armed boarding vessel NORTHERN DUKE rescued the master, twenty-five crewmen and ten Royal Marines and landed them at Kirkwall.
2200	Destroyers LIGHTNING, ESKIMO, NESTOR, and KRAKOWIAK returned to Scapa Flow after an unsuccessful submarine search.
2300	Indian sloop JUMNA departed the Faeroes escorting tanker WAR DIWAN (5551grt) and QUENTIN ROOSEVELT (grt) to Scapa Flow arriving at noon on the 30th.

29 JUNE 1941

	Destroyers MALCOLM and SCIMITAR, corvettes ARABIS and VIOLET, CAM ship MAPLIN, minesweepers NIGER and SPEEDWELL, and three antisubmarine trawlers joined beleaguered convoy HX.133 south of Iceland.
	U.201, U.562, U.564, U.561, U.559, U.557, U.553, U.202, U.111, U.108, U.98, U.96 and U.77 set up a patrol line in the North Atlantic.
	A German Fw200 aircraft of I/KG.40 spotted convoy HX.133, but no U-boats were close enough to attack.
	Heavy cruiser NORFOLK arrived at Scapa Flow after escorting convoy SL.77.
	Minelaying cruiser ADVENTURE arrived at Scapa Flow to work up to combat efficiency after repairs for her January mining damage.
	Battleship RAMILLIES arrived at Hvalfjord, Iceland. She was detached from convoy escort duties due to the increase in U-boat activity.
0030	U.651 (Peter Lohmeyer) sank steamer **GRAYBURN** (6342grt) (Master John William Sygrove) while attacking convoy HX.133 south of Iceland in 59, 30N, 18, 07W. Twenty-seven crewmen and eight gunners were lost. Corvette VIOLET (Lt F. C. Reynolds) rescued the master and sixteen survivors. Corvette ARABIS (Lt Cdr P. Stewart) rescued one survivor and landed him at Londonderry. Corvette VIOLET took the survivors to rescue ship ZAAFARAN (Capt Charles Kavanagh McGowan DSC). Antisubmarine trawler NORTHERN WAVE (Lt W. G. Pardoe-Matthews) took the survivors from ZAAFARAN and took them to Greenock.
0030	Destroyer ESKIMO departed Scapa Flow to join the aircraft carrier VICTORIOUS group and led them into Scapa Flow.
0031	**U.651** (Kptlt Lohmeyer) was sunk by destroyers MALCOLM (Cdr Howard-Johnston) and SCIMITAR, corvettes ARABIS and VIOLET, and minesweeper SPEEDWELL south of Iceland in 59, 52N, 18, 36W. The entire crew was rescued.
1130	Antiaircraft ship ALYNBANK arrived at Scapa Flow after escort duty.
1700	Destroyer LIGHTNING departed Scapa Flow to join the escort for damaged destroyer BRIGHTON en route to the Clyde in tow of tugs MAURADER and THAMES.
1800	Aircraft carrier VICTORIOUS arrived at Scapa Flow escorted by destroyers ESKIMO, ECLIPSE, and WINCHESTER.

30 JUNE 1941

	Heavy cruiser NORFOLK departed Scapa Flow for the Tyne.
	Heavy cruiser SUFFOLK departed Iceland to relieve light cruiser MANCHESTER on Denmark Strait patrol.
	Light cruiser ARETHUSA arrived at Scapa Flow after her Iceland-Faeroes passage patrol.
1200	Indian sloop JUMNA arrived at Scapa Flow from the Faeroes escorting tanker WAR DIWAN (5551grt) and QUENTIN ROOSEVELT (grt).
1630	Destroyers BEDOUIN and TARTAR arrived at Scapa Flow after Operation EC.
2200	Destroyer JUPITER arrived at Scapa Flow after Operation EC.

Norwegian Sea

Long. E03, 00 – E20, 00   Lat. N68, 00 – N58, 30

12 JUNE 1941

1230	German heavy cruiser LÜTZOW (KptzS Kreisch) passed the Skaw with German destroyer FRIEDRICH ECKHOLDT, HANS LODY, KARL GALSTER, Z.23 and Z.24 heading west.

13 JUNE 1941

0005	A Beaufort aircraft of RAF Coastal Command 42 Squadron damaged German heavy cruiser LÜTZOW (KptzS Kreisch) off Lindesnes, Norway.
0445	Destroyer FRIEDRICH ECKHOLDT took the heavy cruiser in tow while destroyers HANS LODY, KARL GALSTER, Z.23 and Z.24 screened the cruiser's withdrawal to the south. LÜTZOW was able to proceed under her own power an hour later. The German ships returned to Germany. British bombing damaged German destroyer Z.24 with a bomb near miss. LÜTZOW repaired at Kiel from 14 June to January 1942.

15 JUNE 1941

	A torpedo sank German steamer **FRANKENSTEIN** (3703grt) (ex **LÜBECK** (3703grt)) north of Florø, Norway.

20 JUNE 1941

	The German 6th Destroyer Flotilla with KARL GALSTER, HERMANN SCHOEMANN and FRIEDRICH ECKHOLDT departed from Norwegian ports and headed north to Kirkenes. Destroyers HANS LODY and RICHARD BEITZEN would follow later on 1 July. The flotilla arrived at Kirkenes on 11 July.

21 JUNE 1941

	A marine obstacle heavily damaged new German destroyer Z.25 south of Haugesund.

East of Canada Long. W70, 00 – W30, 00 Lat. N68, 00 – N43, 30

1 JUNE 1941

	American Coast Guard Cutters MODOC (CGC-39), COMANCHE (CGC-57) and RARITAN (CGC-72) arrived at Godthaab, Greenland with naval auxiliary BOWDOIN (IX-50) to set up a South Greenland Patrol group.
	Convoy HX.130 departed Halifax escorted by battleship RAMILLIES, corvettes PICTOU and RIMOUSKI, plus auxiliary patrol vessel RAYON D'OR. Convoy BHX.130 rendezvoused with convoy HX.130 on the 5th and the AMC ALAUNIA was detached. On the 4th, corvettes AGASSIZ, ALBERNI, and WETASKIWIN joined the convoy. Destroyers BURNHAM and CHURCHILL joined the convoy on 8 June and battleship RAMILLIES was detached on the 9th. AMC DERBYSHIRE joined the convoy on the 11th. Destroyers BURNHAM and CHURCHILL were detached from the convoy on 14 and 13 June, respectively. Corvettes AGASSIZ, ALBERNI, and WETASKIWIN plus AMC ALAUNIA were detached from the convoy on the 15th. Destroyers SARDONYX and WATCHMAN, corvettes HELIOTROPE, PETUNIA, VERBENA, and VIOLET, escort ships BANFF, CULVER, FISHGUARD, and HARTLAND, and catapult ship ARIGUANI joined the convoy on the 15th. Destroyer WATCHMAN and escort ship BANFF were detached from the convoy on the 18th. Destroyer SARDONYX and escort ships CULVER, FISHGUARD, and HARTLAND were detached from the convoy on the 19th. Antisubmarine trawlers NORTHERN GEM and NORTHERN PRIDE escorted the convoy in Home Waters before it arrived at Liverpool on the 20th.
	Convoy SC.33 departed Sidney CB escorted by AMC DERBYSHIRE, destroyer ST CROIX, and auxiliary patrol vessel RACCOON. ST CROIX was detached from the convoy on the 3rd and RACCOON was detached on the 4th, when corvettes AGASSIZ and WETASKIWIN joined the convoy. Destroyer BURNHAM and corvette ALBERNI joined the convoy on the 7th. Escort ship FISHGUARD joined the convoy on the 13th. BURNHAM was detached from the convoy on the 14th and AMC DERBYSHIRE was detached from the convoy the next day. On the 15th, destroyer BULLDOG, corvettes AUBRIETIA and CARNATION, escort ship BANFF, minesweepers BRITOMART and SALAMANDER, catapult ship ARIGUANI, and antisubmarine trawlers DANEMAN and ST APOLLO joined the convoy. Escort ships FISHGUARD and BANFF were detached from the convoy on the 18th. Destroyer BULLDOG was detached from the convoy on the 19th. The remainder of the escorts, less the two minesweepers, were detached from the convoy on the 20th. The convoy, escorted by minesweepers BRITOMART and SALAMANDER arrived at Liverpool on the 21st.

3 JUNE 1941

	Light cruisers AURORA and KENYA sank German tanker **BELCHEN** (6367grt) with gunfire in the Davis Strait between Greenland and Labrador near 59N, 47W, while she was supplying U.93 at sea. U.93 rescued some fifty

survivors.
(Other sources have only forty-nine survivors being rescued.)

5 JUNE 1941

Canadian corvettes BUCTOUCHE and SHERBROOKE were commissioned.

6 JUNE 1941

U.46 attacked a tanker south of Greenland. The U-boat heard a very heavy detonation, but did not observe a hit. The tanker then circled around and rammed the submerged submarine. The tanker remains unidentified.

Battle cruiser REPULSE arrived at Conception Bay after escorting convoy HX.129.

Convoy HX.131 departed Halifax escorted by AMC CHESHIRE with corvettes PICTOU and RIMOUSKI.
Convoy BHX.131 rendezvoused with convoy HX.131 on the 9th and AMC WOLFE was detached from the convoy. The convoy was joined on the 12th by corvette HONEYSUCKLE. All these escorts were detached on the 17th.
Joining on the 17th were destroyers BEAGLE, BOADICEA, and SALISBURY, catapult ship MAPLIN, corvettes GLADIOLUS, NIGELLA, ORCHIS, and POLYANTHUS, minesweepers SEAGULL and SHARPSHOOTER, and antisubmarine trawlers AYRSHIRE, LADY MADELEINE, and ST LOMAN.
Corvette GLADIOLUS was detached from the convoy on the 18th, destroyers BEAGLE and SALISBURY and corvette POLYANTHUS were detached from the convoy on the 19th, and destroyer BOADICEA and corvette NIGELLA were detached from the convoy on the 20th.
The remainder of the escort arrived with the convoy at Liverpool on the 23rd.

| 2024 | U.43 (Kptlt Lüth) sank Dutch steamer **YSELHAVEN** (4802grt) (Master M. P. de Waard) from dispersed convoy OB.328 east of Newfoundland in 49, 25N, 40, 54W. She sank in two minutes with the master and eight crewmen. The survivors made it to two lifeboats.
Finnish steamer HAMMARLAND (3875grt) rescued one lifeboat with first mate A. Boutkan and ten survivors on 15 June, after they survived a gale in the open boat.
Fifteen survivors in the other lifeboat were never found. |

7 JUNE 1941

Battle cruiser REPULSE departed Conception Bay for Halifax, Newfoundland.

9 JUNE 1941

Battle cruiser REPULSE arrived at Halifax from Conception Bay to escort Canadian troop convoy TC.11.

Canadian corvette SASKATOON was commissioned.

Canadian naval tugboat PATRICIA MCQUEEN was assigned to Gaspe.

Fleet oiler CLAM (7404grt) arrived at St John's, Newfoundland.

Leading Airman W. McCulloch of 31 Special Fleet Training Squadron (SFTS) at Kingston, Ontario, was killed when his Fairy Battle aircraft crashed near Gananoque, Ontario.

10 JUNE 1941

Convoy HX.132 departed Halifax, Nova Scotia, escorted by battleship REVENGE, destroyer ANNAPOLIS, and auxiliary patrol vessel REINDEER. The destroyer and the patrol vessel were detached later that day.
Convoy BHX.132 rendezvoused with convoy HX.132 on the 13th and AMC MALOJA was detached from the convoy.
Destroyers NIAGARA and SAGUENAY joined the convoy on the 14th.
Corvette COBALT joined the convoy on the 15th.
On the 16th, destroyers COLUMBIA, RAMSEY, RESTIGOUCHE, and RICHMOND and corvette CANDYTUFT joined the convoy.
Destroyers COLUMBIA and RESTIGOUCHE were detached from the convoy on the 18th.
Battleship REVENGE was detached from the convoy on the 20th.
Destroyers RICHMOND and SAGUENAY with corvette COBALT were detached from the convoy on the 23rd.
On the 23rd, destroyers BROKE and SALADIN, corvettes ABELIA, ANEMONE, and VERONICA, minesweeper HUSSAR, and antisubmarine trawlers ST ELSTAN, ST KENAN, and ST ZENO joined the convoy.
Corvette CANDYTUFT was detached from the convoy on the 24th.
The remainder of the escort arrived with the convoy at Liverpool on the 28th.

Convoy SC.34 departed Sidney, Cape Breton, escorted by AMC RANPURA plus auxiliary patrol boats RACCOON and REINDEER. The patrol vessels were detached in the harbour approaches on the 11th.
Destroyer RESTIGOUCHE joined the convoy on the 15th and was detached from the convoy on the 18th.
Destroyers COLUMBIA, NIAGARA, RAMSEY, RICHMOND, and SAGUENAY and corvettes CANDYTUFT and COBALT joined the convoy on the 16th.
Destroyers RAMSEY and RICHMOND were detached from the convoy on the 22nd.
The rest of the original escort, less destroyer NIAGARA, but including the AMC RANPURA, were detached from the convoy on the 23rd.
On the 23rd destroyer BROKE joined the convoy.

On the 24th, destroyers LINCOLN, SABRE, SHIKARI, and VENOMOUS, corvettes ALISMA and SUNFLOWER, minesweepers, GOSSAMER, HAZARD, and HEBE, and catapult ship PEGASUS joined the convoy.
Destroyers LINCOLN and NIAGARA and corvette ALISMA were detached from the convoy on the 27th.
Destroyers BROKE, SABRE, SHIKARI, and VENOMOUS and the minesweepers were detached from the convoy before it arrived in the Clyde on the 29th.

12 JUNE 1941

0251	U.48 (Kptlt Herbert Schultze) sank unescorted steamer **EMPIRE DEW** (7005grt) (Master John Edward Elsdon) north of the Azores in 51, 09N, 30, 16W. Two crewmen died and twenty-one were missing. Destroyer ST ALBANS rescued the master, sixteen crewmen and two gunners and landed them at Liverpool.

16 JUNE 1941

Convoy HX.133 departed Halifax, Nova Scotia, escorted by AMC WOLFE and destroyer ANNAPOLIS.
Destroyer ST CROIX joined the convoy on the 17th.
Destroyer ANNAPOLIS was detached from the convoy on the 20th.
Convoy BHX.133 rendezvoused with convoy HX.133 on the 20th and AMC LACONIA was detached from the convoy.
On the 20th, destroyer OTTAWA and corvettes CHAMBLY, COLLINGWOOD, ORILLIA, and VIOLET joined the convoy and destroyer ST CROIX was detached from the convoy.
Corvette POLYANTHUS joined the convoy on the 23rd.
Destroyers MALCOLM, RIPLEY, SCIMITAR, and WATCHMAN, sloop FLEETWOOD, corvettes ARABIS, CELANDINE, GLADIOLUS, and NASTURTIUM, and minesweepers NIGER and SPEEDWELL joined the convoy on the 27th.
AMC WOLFE and the OTTAWA escort group were detached from the convoy on the 27th. Sloop FLEETWOOD and corvette GLADIOLUS were detached from the convoy later on the 27th.
Destroyer RIPLEY and corvette NASTURTIUM were detached from the convoy on the 29th.
Destroyers MALCOLM, SCIMITAR, and WATCHMAN and corvette CELANDINE were detached from the convoy on the 30th.
In Home Waters, the convoy was escorted by destroyer ICARUS, catapult ship MAPLIN, and antisubmarine trawlers NORTHERN GEM, NORTHERN PRIDE, and NORTHERN WAVE.
The convoy arrived at Liverpool on 3 July.

20 JUNE 1941

Convoy HX.134 departed Halifax, Nova Scotia, escorted by battleship REVENGE, AMC MALOJA, corvettes DAUPHIN and NAPANEE, and auxiliary patrol vessel RAYON D'OR. The corvettes and the patrol vessel were detached later that day.
On the 23rd, convoy BHX.134 rendezvoused with convoy HX.134 and AMC ASCANIA was detached from convoy BHX.134.
On the 24th, sloops ABERDEEN and SANDWICH and corvettes HEPATICA, PRIMROSE, TRILLIUM, and WINDFLOWER joined the convoy.
This group, including the AMC, was detached from the convoy on 4 July.
Corvette BITTERSWEET joined the convoy on 3 July.
On 4 July, destroyers ROXBOROUGH, SALISBURY, and SHERWOOD, corvettes CARNATION, HOLLYHOCK, and NIGELLA, minesweepers BRITOMART and SALAMANDER, and antisubmarine trawler ST APOLLO joined the convoy.
Destroyer BULLDOG joined the convoy on 5 July.
Destroyer BULLDOG, sloop ABERDEEN and corvette AUBRIETIA were detached from the convoy on 8 July.
The remainder of the escorts arrived with the convoy at Liverpool on 9 July.

Convoy SC.35 departed Sidney, Cape Breton, escorted by AMC AUSONIA with auxiliary patrol boats RACCOON and REINDEER.
The patrol vessels were detached on the 24th.
On the 24th, sloop ABERDEEN plus corvettes TRILLIUM and WINDFLOWER joined the convoy.
The corvettes were detached from the convoy on 4 July.
On 4 July, destroyers BULLDOG and SALISBURY, corvettes AUBRIETIA, CARNATION, HOLLYHOCK, and NIGELLA, plus minesweepers BRITOMART and SALAMANDER joined the convoy.
Minesweepers SEAGULL and SHARPSHOOTER joined the convoy on 7 July.
Corvette PICOTEE joined the convoy on 8 July.
On 8 July, sloop ABERDEEN and the minesweepers were detached from the convoy.
The convoy arrived in the Clyde on 9 July.

21 JUNE 1941

Canadian troop convoy TC.11 departed Halifax, Nova Scotia, with troopships ANDES (25,689grt), BRITANNIC (26,943grt), INDRAPOERA (10,825grt), PASTEUR (29,253grt), STIRLING CASTLE (25,550grt), and WINDSOR

CASTLE (19,141grt).
   Battle cruiser REPULSE and battleship RAMILLIES, plus destroyers ASSINIBOINE, BUXTON, HAVELOCK, SKEENA, and ST LAURENT departed Halifax with the convoy.
   Battleship RAMILLIES was detached from the convoy on the 27th.
   Destroyer ASSINIBOINE was detached from the convoy on the 24th.
   Destroyer HAVELOCK was detached from the convoy on the 27th.
   Destroyers SKEENA and ST LAURENT were detached from the convoy on the 24th.
   REPULSE and destroyer BUXTON proceeded to Britain with the convoy.
   Destroyers ACHATES, ACTIVE, ANTELOPE, INGLEFIELD, SHERWOOD and INTREPID plus destroyers COSSACK and SIKH joined the convoy on the 28th.
   Dutch cruiser HEEMSKERK joined the convoy on the 26th.
   Destroyer SHERWOOD was detached from the convoy on the 28th.
   The rest arrived in the Clyde with the convoy on the 30th.

23 JUNE 1941

	U.203 (Kptlt Mützelburg) sighted convoy HX.133 east of Canada and radioed its position for a U-boat pack to form.

24 JUNE 1941

	U.371 (Kptlt Driver) sank Norwegian steamer **VIGRID** (4765grt) straggling convoy HX.133 in 55N, 41W. Nineteen crewmen, four passengers, and one gunner were missing. American destroyer CHARLES F. HUGHES (DD-428) rescued fourteen survivors on 7 July.
	The convoy H.133 escort drove U.71 underwater when she was spotted in front of the convoy. U.79 took over the attack coordination. U.111 experienced a problem and was forced to abandon the convoy pursuit. U.553, U.101, U.77 and U.558 pursued convoy OB.336 without any further success.
0331	U.203 (Kptlt Rolf Mützelburg) sank Norwegian steamer **SOLOY** (4402grt) (Master Arne H. Sørensen) while attacking convoy HX.133 in 54, 39N, 39, 43W. Steamer TRAVELLER (3963grt) rescued the entire crew of thirty-two and landed them at Liverpool on 3 July.
1200	U.203 sank steamer **KINROSS** (4956grt) (Master James Robson Reed) while attacking convoy OB.336 southeast of Cape Farewell at 55, 23N, 38, 49W.
1205	Corvette ORILLIA (Lt Cdr W. Edward S. Briggs) rescued the master and thirty-six crewmen and landed them at Reykjavik, Iceland.
2037	U.108 (Kptlt Klaus Scholtz) spotted unescorted Greek steamer ELLINICO (3059grt) and began a pursuit.
2106	U.651 (Kptlt Lohmeyer) sank steamer **BROCKLEY HILL** (5297grt) (Master James Howard Williams) as she was straggling behind convoy HX.133 southeast of Cape Farewell in 58, 30N, 38, 20W. Steamer SAUGOR (6303grt) rescued the master, thirty-seven crewmen and four gunners and landed them at Loch Ewe.

25 JUNE 1941

	U.77 (Kptlt Schonder) sank Greek steamer **ANNA BULGARIS** (4603grt) south of Greenland in 55N, 38W. The entire crew was lost.
0001	U.108 (Kptlt Klaus Scholtz) unsuccessfully attacked Greek steamer ELLINICO (3059grt) with two torpedoes.
0620	U.108 sank Greek steamer **ELLINICO** (3059grt) after she was dispersed from convoy OG.65 southwest of Iceland in 55N, 38W. The ship sank in three minutes.
1135	U.75 (Kptlt Helmuth Ringelmann) sank eastbound Dutch steamer **SCHIE** (1967grt) south of Greenland in 53, 02N, 42, 10W. The ship sank in four minutes, and there were no survivors from the crew of twenty-nine.
1614	U.108 torpedoed Greek steamer **NICOLAS PATERAS** (4362grt) after she was dispersed from convoy OB.336 in 55N, 38W.
1713	U.108 surfaced and began shelling the damaged steamer.
1755	U.108 finally sank the steamer after firing ninety-seven rounds from her deck gun, which was struggling in the heavy seas and strong winds to hit the steamer. The entire crew was lost.

26 JUNE 1941

	Convoy HX.135 departed Halifax, Nova Scotia, escorted by destroyer ST CROIX, sloop LONDONDERRY, corvettes BARRIE and MATAPEDIA, and auxiliary patrol vessel REINDEER. The corvettes and the patrol vessel were detached that day. The destroyer was detached from the convoy on the 29th. Convoy BHX.135 rendezvoused with convoy HX.135 on the 29th and AMC PRINCE DAVID was detached from the convoy. On 1 July, escort ships CULVER and HARTLAND joined the convoy. Escort ships BANFF and FISHGUARD joined the convoy on 4 July.

	Minesweeper HUSSAR and corvettes ABELIA and ANEMONE joined the convoy on 6 July. Destroyers BROKE, DOUGLAS, SALADIN, and SKATE, corvette VERONICA, and antisubmarine trawlers ST ELSTAN, ST KENAN, and ST ZENO joined the convoy. Destroyers SALADIN and SKATE were detached from the convoy on 10 July and the remainder of the escort was detached from the convoy on 11 July. The convoy arrived at Liverpool on 12 July.

27 JUNE 1941

0056	U.79 (Kaufmann) damaged Dutch tanker TIBIA (10,356grt) while attacking convoy HX.133 in 59, 55N, 30, 49W. The tanker was repaired in the Tyne.
0155	U.564 (ObltzS Reinhard Suhren) damaged Norwegian tanker KONGSGAARD (9467grt) (Master Leif Moen) while attacking convoy HX.133 in 60N, 30, 42W. Initially the crew abandoned the tanker, but the master, one mate and nine crewmen re-boarded the ship and put out the fire. The rest of the crew boarded the tanker and she arrived at Belfast Lough on 2 July.
0155	U.564 sank Dutch steamer **MAASDAM** (8810grt) (Master J. P. Boshoff) while attacking convoy HX.133 in 60N, 30, 35W. Two passengers were lost. The master, forty-seven crewmen, seventeen American Red Cross nurses and a group of American Marines (Maj Walter L. Jordan) reached the lifeboats before she sank. Norwegian tanker HAVPRINS (8066grt) rescued forty-four survivors and landed them at Barry. The USMC personnel were part of the advance detail for the Marine Detachment at the U.S. Embassy in London. All Americans survived the attack.
0155	U.564 sank steamer **MALAYA II** (8651grt) (Master W. Kragelund) while attacking convoy HX.133 east of Cape Farewell in 59, 56N, 30, 35W. The master, thirty-eight crewmen and four gunners were lost. Corvette COLLINGWOOD (Lt Cdr W. Woods) rescued six survivors and landed them at Reykjavik, Iceland.

28 JUNE 1941

	American destroyer MADISON (DD-425) was damaged when she ran aground at Argentia, Newfoundland.

29 JUNE 1941

1958	U.564 (ObltzS Reinhard Suhren) sank unescorted Icelandic steamer **HEKLA** (1215grt) south of Greenland in 58, 20N, 43W. Twelve crewmen were lost and seven spent ten days on a life raft. Corvette CANDYTUFT rescued the seven survivors. One man died that night after the rescue, but the remaining six were taken to St. John's, Newfoundland.

30 JUNE 1941

	Convoy HX.136 departed Halifax, Nova Scotia, escorted by AMCs ASCANIA and CALIFORNIA, corvettes ARROWHEAD, CAMELLIA, EYEBRIGHT, and MAYFLOWER, antisubmarine yacht PHILANTE, and antisubmarine trawler KOS XX. Convoy BHX.136 rendezvoused with convoy HX.136 on 3 July and AMC ASCANIA was detached from the convoy. On 4 July, destroyers BURNHAM and CHESTERFIELD, corvettes AGASSIZ and WETASKIWIN joined the convoy. Destroyer CHURCHILL joined the convoy on 6 July. On 13 July, the original escorts and those joining on 4 July (less trawler KOS XX) and 6 July were detached from the convoy. Destroyers KEPPEL, SABRE, and SHIKARI, corvettes DIANELLA and KINGCUP, minesweeper HEBE, and antisubmarine trawlers LADY ELSA and WELLARD joined the convoy. The convoy arrived at Liverpool on 18 July.

East of United States

Long. W85, 00 – W60,00 Lat. N43, 30 – N25, 00

1 JUNE 1941

	American Task Group TG.3 departed Bermuda with USN aircraft carrier RANGER (CV-4), heavy cruiser TUSCALOOSA (CA-37), plus destroyers MCDOUGAL (DD-358) and EBERLE (DD-430) on a neutrality patrol, which ended on 6 August when they arrived at Hampton Roads, Virginia.
	American Task Group TG.2.5 departed Bermuda with USN aircraft carrier YORKTOWN (CV-5), heavy cruiser VINCENNES (CA-44) plus destroyers SAMPSON (DD-394) and GWIN (DD-433) on a neutrality patrol to the Canary Islands, returning to Hampton Roads, Virginia, on 12 June.

2 JUNE 1941

	The first American escort aircraft carrier LONG ISLAND (AVG-1) was commissioned at Norfolk, Virginia.

4 JUNE 1941

	Convoy BHX.131 departed Bermuda escorted by AMC WOLFE.

8 JUNE 1941

Convoy BHX.132 departed Bermuda escorted by AMC MALOJA.

13 JUNE 1941

Battleship RODNEY arrived at Boston, Massachusetts, for a refit.

14 JUNE 1941

Convoy BHX.133 departed Bermuda escorted by AMC LACONIA.

17 JUNE 1941

USN light cruiser SAVANNAH (CL-42) arrived at Boston for repairs.

Petty Officer G. H. Fynn and Petty Officer S. G. Blatchford in a Walrus aircraft of 773 Squadron were lost when they failed to return to Bermuda after practice attacks at sea.

18 JUNE 1941

American authorities seized German steamer **PAULINE FRIEDRICH** (4645grt) at Boston, Massachusetts. She became the American ORMONDALE (4645grt).

American authorities seized Italian steamer **CLARA** (6131grt) at Savannah, Georgia. She became the Panamanian STONE STREET (6131grt).

USN light cruiser PHILADELPHIA (CL-41) arrived at Boston late in the day.

19 JUNE 1941

American light cruiser NASHVILLE (CL-43) arrived at Boston, Massachusetts, late in the day.

Convoy BHX.134 departed Bermuda escorted by AMC ASCANIA.

20 JUNE 1941

USN aircraft carrier WASP (CV-7) with VF-71, VS-72, and VMB-1, heavy cruiser TUSCALOOSA (CA-37), plus destroyers ANDERSON (DD-411) and ROWAN (DD-405) departed Hampton Roads, Virginia, as Task Force TF.2.6 on neutrality patrol. The patrol concluded on 4 July at Bermuda.

USN submarines O.6 (SS-167), O.9 (SS-170) and O.10 (SS-171) conducted deep diving tests off Portsmouth, New Hampshire. On one of the dives, **O.9** (SS-170) (LT H. J. Abbot) failed to surface. She was declared lost with all hands, which included Lt Howard J. Abbot, Ensign Marks P. Wangsness, and thirty-two enlisted men.

22 JUNE 1941

USN submarine TRITON (SS-201) held a memorial service over the last known position of lost submarine **O.9** (SS-170) off New Hampshire, USA.

24 JUNE 1941

Convoy BHX.135 departed Bermuda escorted by AMC PRINCE DAVID.

25 JUNE 1941

USN light cruisers PHILADELPHIA (CL-41) and SAVANNAH (CL-42) with destroyers LANG (DD-399) and WILSON (DD-408) departed Hampton Roads on a neutrality patrol that ended at Bermuda on 8 July.

28 JUNE 1941

Convoy BHX.136 departed Bermuda escorted by AMC ASCANIA.

29 JUNE 1941

American Task Force TF.2.8 departed Hampton Roads, Virginia, with USN aircraft carrier YORKTOWN (CV-5) with VF-42, VS-42, VMO-1, and half of VMS-1, heavy cruisers QUINCY (CA-39) and VINCENNES (CA-44), plus destroyers WAINWRIGHT (DD-419), HAMMANN (DD-412), MUSTIN (DD-413), and STACK (DD-406) on a neutrality patrol.

Aircraft carrier YORKTOWN (CV-5) was detached on 10 July with destroyers WAINWRIGHT (DD-419) and STACK (DD-406) and arrived back at Hampton Roads on 12 July.

Heavy cruisers QUINCY (CA-39) and VINCENNES (CA-44) with destroyers HAMMANN (DD-412) and MUSTIN (DD-413) continued on patrol and arrived at Bermuda on 15 July.

GERMANY SENDS RUSSIA TO THE ALLIES

Caribbean and Gulf of Mexico

Long. W100, 00 – W60, 00 Lat. N31, 00 – N05, 00

1 JUNE 1941

	Dutch sloop VAN KINSBERGEN captured Vichy French steamer **ARICA** (5390grt) in the Caribbean.

17 JUNE 1941

	AMC PRETORIA CASTLE captured Vichy French steamer **DESIRADE** (9645grt) east of the Antilles.

Western Approaches

Long. W30, 00 – W03, 00 Lat. N58, 30 – N49, 00

1 JUNE 1941

	Convoy WS.8X departed the Clyde with steamers PORT WYNDHAM (8580grt), DUCHESS OF BEDFORD (20,123grt), and WAIWERA (10,800grt) and AMC ESPERANCE BAY. Aircraft carrier VICTORIOUS and light cruiser NEPTUNE escorted the convoy from 31 May to 5 June. Heavy cruiser NORFOLK was with the convoy from 31 May to 11 June, when the convoy arrived at Freetown, Sierra Leone. Destroyers ASSINIBOINE and SAGUENAY escorted the convoy locally. Destroyers SHERWOOD, LEGION, PIORUN, WIVERN, WILD SWAN, VANSITTART, SAGUENAY, ST MARYS, and BRIGHTON escorted the convoy from 31 May to 3 June. All, but WIVERN, WILD SWAN, and VANSITTART, returning to England. AMC ESPERANCE BAY was detached from the convoy on 3 June. Destroyers WIVERN, WILD SWAN, and VANSITTART arrived at Gibraltar on 6 June. Destroyer VELOX and corvette ASTER joined the convoy on 9 June and escorted the convoy into Freetown on 11 June. The convoy departed Freetown escorted by light cruiser NEPTUNE. They arrived at Cape Town, South Africa, on 24 June. Convoy WS.8 X departed Cape Town on 28 June, escorted by light cruiser NEPTUNE. The convoy called at Kilindini on 6 July and departed the same day for Aden. The convoy arrived at Aden on 11 July, and the ships proceeded independently to Suez, arriving on 15 July.

2 JUNE 1941

	Destroyers COSSACK, ZULU, MAORI, and SIKH arrived in the Clyde from Scapa Flow to escort convoy WS.9A.
	U.147 (Kptlt Wetjen) damaged Belgian steamer MOKAMBO (4996grt) while attacking convoy OB.329 northwest of Ireland in 56, 38N, 10, 24W. MOKAMBO arrived in the Clyde on the 4th in tow. While escorting convoy OB.329, destroyer WANDERER and corvette PERIWINKLE sank **U.147** northwest of Ireland in 56, 38N, 10, 24W, after she torpedoed the Belgian steamer MOKAMBO (4996grt). The entire **U.147** crew of twenty-six was lost.
	Convoy OB.330 departed Liverpool escorted by corvette ALISMA and antisubmarine trawler NORTHERN DAWN. The convoy was joined on the 3rd by destroyers LINCOLN, SABRE, and VENOMOUS, corvettes ARROWHEAD, KINGCUP, and SUNFLOWER, CAM ship SPRINGBANK, and antisubmarine trawlers LADY ELSA and MAN O' WAR. The convoy was dispersed on the 7th.
	Dutch submarine O.14 was damaged in a collision and repaired at Grangemouth from 8 June to 9 July.
0730	Destroyers PUNJABI, ESKIMO, and ICARUS arrived at the Clyde and joined destroyer TARTAR, which was already there.

3 JUNE 1941

	Light cruiser BIRMINGHAM arrived in the Clyde from Scapa Flow to escort convoy WS.9A. Following this escort duty, she proceeded for duty in the South Atlantic.
	German bombing sank Belgian trawler **JOHN** (197grt) ninety miles south by east of Inglos Hofdi, northwest of St. Kilda, Hebrides. There were no casualties.
	Convoy WS.9A departed the Clyde with steamers SAMARIA (19,597grt), HIGHLAND BRIGADE (14,134grt), EASTERN PRINCE (10,926grt), AAGTEKERK (6811grt), CAPETOWN CASTLE (27,000grt), EMPRESS OF JAPAN (26,032grt), FRANCONIA (20,175grt), MOOLTAN (20,952grt), ORBITA (15,495grt), LLANGIBBY CASTLE (11,951grt), DURBAN CASTLE (17,388grt), EMPIRE CONDOR (7773grt), EMPIRE CURLEW (7101grt), EMPIRE EGRET (7248grt), and EMPIRE WIDGEON (6736grt). Antiaircraft cruiser CAIRO with destroyers RICHMOND, RAMSEY, COSSACK, MAORI, SIKH, ZULU, OTTAWA, RESTIGOUCHE, VANQUISHER, and WINCHELSEA were with the convoy form 3 to 7 June. AMC AUSONIA was with the convoy from 3 to 6 June. AMC DUNNOTTAR CASTLE and light cruiser BIRMINGHAM joined the convoy from 3 to 18 June.

	Destroyers VANSITTART and WILD SWAN joined the convoy on the 13th and escorted it to Freetown arriving on the 18th.
	Destroyers HIGHLANDER, VELOX, BOREAS, and BRILLIANT were with the convoy from 16 to 18 June when the convoy arrived at Freetown.
1300	Destroyers ELECTRA, IMPULSIVE, and ANTELOPE arrived at Londonderry, Northern Ireland, from Scapa Flow to refuel.
1900	Destroyers ELECTRA, IMPULSIVE, and ANTELOPE departed Londonderry to join battleship NELSON in 49N, 23W.
2200	Battleship RODNEY departed the Clyde escorted by destroyers TARTAR, PUNJABI, ESKIMO, and ICARUS for a refit in the U.S. Also sailing in company with the battleship was liner WINDSOR CASTLE (19,141grt).

4 JUNE 1941

	Destroyer ELECTRA damaged her ASDIC dome after hitting a whale at sea. Destroyer ICARUS was ordered to detach from the battleship RODNEY escort group and join the battleship NELSON escort group.
	Convoy OG.64 departed Liverpool escorted by antisubmarine trawlers CANNA, LADY SHIRLEY, LAERTES, and LORD IRWIN. Destroyers ROXBOROUGH, SALISBURY, and SKATE, sloop FOLKESTONE, ocean boarding vessel HILARY, plus corvettes ANEMONE, CLARKIA, and VERONICA joined the convoy on the 5th. HILARY was detached from the convoy that night. The destroyers and corvettes were detached on the 8th. On the 12th, corvettes COREOPSIS and FLEUR DE LYS and Dutch submarine O.21 joined the convoy. Corvettes COREOPSIS and FLEUR DE LYS were detached on the 13th. Destroyers AVON VALE, ERIDGE, and FARNDALE, arriving from the Irish Sea Force, and WRESTLER, which departed Gibraltar on the 13th, joined the convoy on the 17th. Antisubmarine trawler LADY SHIRLEY was detached from the convoy and arrived at Gibraltar on the 16th. The convoy arrived at Gibraltar on the 18th with sloop FOLKESTONE, the four destroyers, submarine O.21, mine disposal vessels SPRINGTIDE and SPRINGDALE, minesweeper CORBRAE and LORD IRWIN, antisubmarine trawler LAERTES, naval trawler CANNA, and whalers KOS VII, KOS X, KOS XI, and KOS XII.
2200	Destroyer MATABELE struck a submerged object after leaving Barrow for Scapa Flow.

5 JUNE 1941

	A German IX Air Corps aerial mine damaged steamer MYRMIDON (6278grt) in Crosby Channel. She returned to Liverpool for temporary repairs. Permanent repairs were accomplished later at New York City.
1700	Destroyer MATABELE returned to Barrow for repairs completing in August.

7 JUNE 1941

	A German IX Air Corps aerial mine sank **Examination vessel No.10** (281grt) off the entrance to Milford Haven.

8 JUNE 1941

	Convoy OB.331 departed Liverpool escorted by destroyers ASSINIBOINE and BULLDOG, corvettes ARROWHEAD, AUBRIETIA, CARNATION, HOLLYHOCK, and PRIMROSE, plus antisubmarine trawlers ANGLE, DANEMAN, and KING SOL. Minesweepers BRITOMART and SALAMANDER and catapult ship ARIGUANI joined the convoy on the 9th. ARIGUANI was detached from the convoy on the 11th, when sloops ABERDEEN and LONDONDERRY and corvette CAMELLIA joined the convoy. Destroyer BULLDOG, corvettes AUBRIETIA, CARNATION, and HOLLYHOCK, the minesweepers, and the antisubmarine trawlers were detached from the convoy on the 12th. Sloop LONDONDERRY and corvette ARROWHEAD were detached from the convoy on the 13th, while destroyer HARVESTER joined the convoy. The convoy was dispersed on the 18th.
	Convoy OB.332 departed Liverpool escorted by corvettes DIANTHUS, NASTURTIUM, and SPIKENARD and catapult ship MAPLIN. Destroyer CHESTERFIELD and corvettes HEPATICA, MAYFLOWER, TRILLIUM, and WINDFLOWER joined the convoy on the 9th. CHESTERFIELD was detached from the convoy on the 10th. On the 10th, destroyers HARVESTER and HAVELOCK, sloop SANDWICH, and antisubmarine yacht PHILANTE joined the convoy. HARVESTER was detached from the convoy on the 12th. On the 13th, sloop LONDONDERRY and corvettes ARROWHEAD, EYEBRIGHT, and SNOWBERRY joined the convoy. HAVELOCK was detached from the convoy on the 18th. Sloop SANDWICH with corvettes HEPATICA, SNOWBERRY, TRILLIUM, and WINDFLOWER were detached from the convoy on the 19th.

	The convoy arrived at Halifax, Nova Scotia, on the 23rd.

10 JUNE 1941

	Convoy OB.333 departed Liverpool escorted by destroyer WALKER plus corvettes GENTIAN, WALLFLOWER, and ZINNIA. Destroyers AVON VALE, ERIDGE, and FARNDALE joined the convoy on the 11th and were detached from the convoy on the 13th. WALKER and corvette WALLFLOWER were detached from the convoy on the 14th. The convoy was dispersed on the 21st.
1055	U.552 (Kptlt Topp) sank unescorted steamer **AINDERBY** (4860grt) (Master George Robert Cobb) about 130 miles west by north of Bloody Foreland in 55, 30N, 12, 10W. Eleven crewmen and one gunner were lost. Destroyer VETERAN (Cdr W. T. Couchman, OBE) rescued the master, twenty-seven crewmen and one gunner and landed them at Greenock, Scotland.

11 JUNE 1941

	German bombing heavily damaged steamer **BARON CARNEGIE** (3178grt) in St Georges Channel in 51, 55N, 05, 34W. Nine crewmen were killed and sixteen were missing. The steamer sank in tow of steamer SEINE (1358grt) in 52, 04N, 05, 01W.
	Convoy OB.334 departed Liverpool escorted by corvette POLYANTHUS and antisubmarine trawler AYRSHIRE. Destroyer BEAGLE and corvettes GLADIOLUS, NIGELLA, and ORCHIS, catapult ship MAPLIN, minesweepers SEAGULL and SHARPSHOOTER, and antisubmarine trawlers LADY MADELEINE and ST LOMAN joined the convoy the next day. BEAGLE, MAPLIN, corvettes GLADIOLUS and NIGELLA, and the minesweepers were detached from the convoy on the 17th. Destroyer BURNHAM and CHURCHILL, AMC AURANIA, and corvettes DIANTHUS and SPIKENARD joined the convoy on the 17th. Destroyer CHESTERFIELD was with the convoy on the 19th. AURANIA, BURNHAM, and corvettes DIANTHUS, ORCHIS, and SPIKENARD were detached from the convoy on the 20th. Battleship REVENGE joined on the 20th with AMC BULOLO and CALIFORNIA. The convoy arrived at Halifax on the 25th.
	Sub-Lt T. P. O'Donovan and Sub-Lt H. Morris were killed when their Fulmar aircraft of 800 Squadron collided with a Martlet aircraft of 881 Squadron off Lee. The Martlet's pilot, Lt J. A. Rooper was also killed.
	Submarine H.32 grounded in the Clyde and was repaired at Ardrossan.

12 JUNE 1941

	Light cruiser SHEFFIELD sank German tanker **FRIEDRICH BREME** (10,396grt) northwest of Cape Finisterre in 49, 48N, 24, 00W. SHEFFIELD rescued eighty-eight German survivors including twelve wounded. Two men later died of wounds.
	Ex-US Coast Guard cutter/escort ship SENNEN was damaged in a collision with harbour drifter ANIMATE (88grt) in the Clyde.
0326	U.371 (Heinrich Driver) damaged steamer **SILVERPALM** (6373grt) (Master Richard Long Pallett) with two torpedoes as she was sailing alone in 51N, 26W. He observed her sinking thirty-eight minutes later. The entire crew of sixty-eight were lost. Trawler CAVE found one lifeboat with eight bodies on 15 July. (Other sources credit U.101 (Kptlt Ernst Mengersen) with this attack on the 9th.)
0414	U.552 (Kptlt Topp) sank unescorted steamer **CHINESE PRINCE** (8593grt) (Master Wilma Finch) south of Rockall in 56, 12N, 14, 18W. Forty-five crewmen were lost. Corvettes ARBUTUS (Lt A. L. W. Warren) and PIMPERNEL (Lt F. H. Thornton) rescued the master, fifteen crewmen and three gunners and landed them at Londonderry, Northern Ireland.

13 JUNE 1941

	German bombing sank steamer **ST PATRICK** (1922grt) in St George's Channel in 52, 04N, 05, 25W. Seventeen crewmen, one gunner, and twelve passengers, including Surgeon Cdr A. R. Ewart MB, BCH, were lost.
	German bombing heavily damaged steamer **KINGSTOWN** (628grt) nine miles northwest of Bishops Light, Bristol Channel. The entire crew were rescued. She sank in the tow of a trawler six miles 287° from St Anne's Head.
	German bombing damaged Norwegian steamer BOKN (698grt) off St Ives, Cornwall. She returned to St Ives.
	P/T/A/Sub-Lt (A) M. Westerman RNVR was killed when his Hurricane aircraft of 759 Squadron crashed near Ilchester.
1630	Destroyers ELECTRA and ANTHONY arrived at the Clyde from Scapa Flow.

14 JUNE 1941

	Aircraft carrier ARGUS arrived in the Clyde with troopship NEA HELLAS (16,991grt) from Gibraltar.
	Destroyers COSSACK, MAORI, and SIKH escorted aircraft carriers FURIOUS and ARGUS, plus Greek troopship NEA HELLAS (16,991grt) to their berths in the Clyde.
	Destroyers ELECTRA, ANTHONY, and ANTELOPE departed the Clyde and topped off fuel at Londonderry, Northern Ireland, to escort a special outbound troop convoy LC.1 of AMCs CALIFORNIA and BULOLO for Halifax, Nova Scotia. BULOLO was then to go on to Baltimore, Maryland, for a refit. Steamer MENDOZA (5193grt) was destined for Montreal and steamer ULYSSES (14,652grt) was en route to the Far East. On the 17th the destroyers detached from the convoy, and steamer ULYSSES was detached for independent passage. Destroyers ELECTRA and ANTHONY proceeded to Scapa Flow, while destroyer ANTELOPE went to Iceland. Battleship REVENGE joined the convoy on the 19th and escorted the ships to Canada.
	Submarine THRASHER departed Holy Loch for Gibraltar.
	Convoy OG.65 departed Liverpool escorted by destroyer WESTCOTT, sloop DEPTFORD, and corvettes MARIGOLD and PERIWINKLE, and antisubmarine trawlers SYRINGA and HOLLY. Corvettes AURICULA, FREESIA, and HIBISCUS and antisubmarine trawler RUMBA joined the convoy on the 15th. Trawler RUMBA was detached from the convoy later on the 15th. Destroyer WESTCOTT with corvettes AURICULA, FREESIA, HIBISCUS, MARIGOLD, and PERIWINKLE were detached from the convoy on the 17th. Sloop DEPTFORD was detached from the convoy on the 18th. Submarine OLYMPUS joined the convoy on the 22nd with corvettes GERANIUM, JONQUIL, and SPIREA. The convoy arrived at Gibraltar on the 28th with sloop DEPTFORD, antisubmarine trawlers SYRINGA and HOLLY, whalers GOS II and GOS III, plus corvettes GERANIUM and JONQUIL and submarine OLYMPUS.
0346	U.751 (Kptlt Bigalk) sank steamer **ST LINDSAY** (5370grt) (Master Oliver John S. Hill) after she was dispersed from convoy OG.64 southwest of Iceland in 51N, 30W. The ship exploded and broke in two and sank in eighty seconds. The entire crew of forty-three was lost. Also lost in the steamer were P/T/Sub-Lt (A) P. G. Cliff RNVR, P/T/Sub-Lt (A) B. Burleston RNVR, and P/T/Sub-Lt (A) G. F. Robinson RNVR, en route to Fleet Air Arm base GOSHAWK for duty with 752 Squadron, T/LT (A) J. H. Crane RNVR, en route to Fleet Air Arm Base GOSHAWK for duty with 793 Squadron, and T/A/Lt Cdr C. J. Gordon-Canning RNVR, en route to duty in BENBOW.

15 JUNE 1941

1700	Destroyer ECLIPSE arrived at Greenock from Plymouth with engine problems.

16 JUNE 1941

	Convoy OB.335 departed Liverpool escorted by destroyers RIPLEY and SHERWOOD, sloop FLEETWOOD, and corvettes CELANDINE and NASTURTIUM. AMCs CHESHIRE and DERBYSHIRE joined the convoy on the 23rd. The escorts were detached on the 24th. The convoy arrived at Halifax, Nova Scotia, on 2 July.
	Convoy OB.336 departed Liverpool escorted by corvettes AGASSIZ and WETASKIWIN. Destroyers LINCOLN and SHIKARI joined the convoy on the 16th. On the 17th, destroyers SABRE and VENOMOUS, catapult ship PEGASUS, corvettes ALISMA and SUNFLOWER, and antisubmarine trawlers LADY ELSA, MAN O' WAR, and NORTHERN DAWN joined the convoy. Minesweepers GOSSAMER, HAZARD, and HEBE were with the convoy on the 18th. The convoy was dispersed on the 22nd.
	German bombing damaged steam trawler ATLANTIC (167grt) three miles southeast of Eddystone. The trawler returned to Plymouth later the same day.

17 JUNE 1941

	Submarine P.33 departed the Clyde for Gibraltar.
0315	U.43 (Kptlt Lüth) sank steamer **CATHRINE** (2727grt) (ex Estonian **ESTONIAN PEETER** (2727grt)) (Master Johannes Teng) while attacking convoy SL.76 at 250 miles southwest of Cape Clear in 49, 30N, 16W. The master and twenty-three crewmen were lost. Trawler BOREAS rescued three survivors on 19 August after thirty-three days at sea and landed them at Valentia, Co. Cork.
0900	Destroyer ECLIPSE departed Greenock for Scapa Flow.

18 JUNE 1941

0328	U.552 (Kptlt Topp) torpedoed unescorted steamer **NORFOLK** (10,948grt) (Master Frederick Lougheed) about 150 miles northwest of Malin Head in 57, 17N, 11, 14W.
0419	U.552 hit the steamer with a second torpedo.

0438	U.552 sank the steamer with a third torpedo. One crewman was lost. Destroyer SKATE (Lt F. Baker DSC) rescued the master sixty-three crewmen and six gunners and landed them at Londonderry.
0700	Destroyer LANCE arrived at Greenock from Scapa Flow to join the Western Approaches command following working up.

19 JUNE 1941

	En route to Scapa Flow, destroyers ELECTRA and ANTHONY were detailed to search for a submarine reported by aircraft in 56, 10N, 10, 58W.
1630	Destroyer BATH arrived at Liverpool from Scapa Flow after working up to combat efficiency.

20 JUNE 1941

	Convoy OB.337 departed Liverpool escorted by destroyers CHELSEA and VETERAN, CAM ship SPRINGBANK, plus corvettes ARBUTUS, BEGONIA, LARKSPUR, PIMPERNEL, and RHODODENDRON. Destroyers MANSFIELD and VERITY plus corvette JASMINE joined the convoy on the 21st. Destroyer VETERAN was detached from the convoy on the 21st. Destroyers MANSFIELD and VERITY were detached from the convoy on the 24th. The convoy was dispersed on the 28th.
0600	Destroyers ELECTRA and ANTHONY ended the submarine search in 56, 10N, 10, 58W and headed to Scapa Flow.
1730	Destroyer ANTHONY arrived at Loch Ewe to refuel and then continued on to Scapa Flow.

21 JUNE 1941

	Aircraft carrier VICTORIOUS arrived in the Clyde after ferrying aircraft to Malta.
	Convoy OB.338 departed Liverpool. On the 22nd, destroyers MALCOLM, SCIMITAR, and WATCHMAN, catapult ship MAPLIN, corvettes ARABIS and VIOLET, minesweepers NIGER and SPEEDWELL, and antisubmarine trawlers NORTHERN GEM, NORTHERN PRIDE, NORTHERN SPRAY, and NORTHERN WAVE joined the convoy outside Liverpool. This escort group was detached from the convoy on the 26th. On the 26th, destroyers NIAGARA and SAGUENAY, AMC RANPURA, plus corvettes PICTOU and RIMOUSKI joined the convoy. Destroyer NIAGARA was detached from the convoy on 2 July. The convoy was dispersed on 3 July.

22 JUNE 1941

	Light cruiser HERMIONE and aircraft carrier FURIOUS departed the Clyde for Gibraltar with destroyers LANCE and LEGION.
0329	U.141 (ObltzS Schuler) sank Swedish steamer **CALABRIA** (1277grt) after she was dispersed from convoy SL.76 about one hundred miles from Inishtrahull lightship off Ireland. Three crewmen were lost, while twenty-one survived.

24 JUNE 1941

	Convoy OG.66 departed Liverpool escorted by destroyers BATH and WALKER, sloop SCARBOROUGH, and ocean boarding vessel MALVERNIAN. On the 25th, destroyer VANOC and antisubmarine trawlers CORDELIA, FANDANGO, MORRIS DANCE, NORSE, and SARABANDE joined the convoy. Corvette HYDRANGEA joined the convoy on the 26th. The destroyers and the corvette were detached from the convoy on the 29th. The ocean boarding vessel was detached from the convoy on the 30th. On 3 July, destroyers FAULKNOR, FEARLESS, FORESTER, LANCE, and LEGION joined the convoy. On 4 July, corvette COREOPSIS and antisubmarine trawlers LADY HOGARTH and LADY SHIRLEY joined the convoy. Destroyers ERIDGE and FARNDALE joined the convoy on 6 July. Destroyers LEGION and LANCE were detached from the convoy on 3 July. Destroyer FAULKNOR was detached from the convoy on 5 July. Destroyers FEARLESS and FORESTER were detached from the convoy on 6 July. The convoy arrived at Gibraltar on 8 July with sloop SCARBOROUGH, antisubmarine trawlers FANDANGO, MORRIS DANCE, SARABANDE, CORDELIA, NORSE, and local escorts.

26 JUNE 1941

	Convoy OB.339 departed Liverpool escorted by destroyer BROADWATER, sloop LEITH, plus corvettes BITTERSWEET and FENNEL. On 2 July, destroyers RAMSEY and RICHMOND joined the convoy with corvettes COBALT and POLYANTHUS.

	RAMSEY was detached from the convoy on 3 July. AMC WOLFE joined the convoy on 6 July. On 9 July, destroyers BURWELL and RICHMOND plus sloop LEITH were detached from the convoy. On 10 July, destroyer BROADWATER and corvette COBALT were detached from the convoy. The convoy arrived at Halifax, Nova Scotia, on 12 July.

27 JUNE 1941

	Ships for convoy WS.9B departed Avonmouth on the 27th, Liverpool on the 28th, and the Clyde on the 29th. The three sections rendezvoused at sea on the 30th. The convoy included steamers TAMAROA (12,405grt), PULASKI (6345grt), ANSELM (5954grt) (which returned with defects), ORONSAY (20,043grt), ATHLONE CASTLE (25,564grt), MONARCH OF BERMUDA (22,424grt), CERAMIC (18,713grt), CLAN FORBES (7529grt), ARUNDEL CASTLE (19,118grt), MATAROA (12,390grt), PAMPAS (5415grt), RANGITATA (16,737grt), and ELISABETH BAKKE (5450grt). Destroyer WELLS escorted the convoy from 29 June to 1 July. Antiaircraft cruiser CAIRO plus destroyers ST FRANCIS, GARLAND, READING, PIORUN, VANQUISHER, WINCHELSEA, MAORI, and CASTLETON escorted the convoy from 29 June to 2 July. Light cruiser EDINBURGH and destroyer WOLVERINE escorted the convoy from 28 June to 3 July. AMC CATHAY was with the convoy from 29 June to 4 July. AMC CHITRAL was with the convoy from 29 June to 7 July. Light cruiser GALATEA and AMC MORETON BAY were with the convoy for the entire voyage to Freetown, Sierra Leone. Destroyers WIVERN, WILD SWAN, and BRILLIANT and corvette ASPHODEL joined the convoy on 10 July and escorted it to Freetown, and arrived on 13 July. On 16 July, the convoy departed Freetown escorted by destroyers BRILLIANT, VELOX, VANSITTART, and BOREAS from 16 to 18 July. Light cruiser GALATEA escorted the convoy through to Cape Town, South Africa. Steamers CERAMIC, CLAN FORBES, PAMPAS, ELISABETH BAKKE, PULASKI, and RANGITATA arrived at Cape Town on 27 July. Steamers ORONSAY, ATHLONE CASTLE, MONARCH OF BERMUDA, ARUNDEL CASTLE, TAMAROA, and MATAROA arrived at Durban on 30 July. Steamers CLAN FORBES, PULASKI, PAMPAS, and ELISABETH BAKKE departed Cape Town on 30 July escorted by AMC QUEEN OF BERMUDA. They rendezvoused with ORONSAY, ARUNDEL CASTLE, MONARCH OF BERMUDA, and ATHLONE CASTLE, which sailed from Durban on 3 August, escorted by light cruiser GALATEA, and arrived Aden on 14 August. The ships travelled independently to Suez from Aden.
	Convoy OB.340 departed Liverpool escorted by destroyers ASSINIBOINE and BULLDOG, corvettes AUBRIETIA, CARNATION, HOLLYHOCK, and NIGELLA, minesweepers BRITOMART and SALAMANDER, plus antisubmarine trawlers ANGLE, KING SOL, NOTTS COUNTY, and ST APOLLO. This escort group was detached from the convoy on 3 July when destroyer HAVELOCK, sloop FLEETWOOD, plus corvettes ALBERNI, CHAMBLY, COLLINGWOOD, and ORILLIA joined the convoy. The convoy was dispersed on 13 July.
	Submarine L.26 grounded on the west coast of Mull. The submarine was re-floated on the 28th and was repaired at Ardrossan, Scotland, from 8 July to 26 July. She was permanently repaired at Plymouth, England, from 19 September to 5 February 1942.

28 JUNE 1941

<2330	Aircraft carrier VICTORIOUS departed the Clyde for Scapa Flow escorted by destroyers CHARLESTOWN, ST MARYS and WINCHESTER.
2330	Destroyer ECLIPSE departed Loch Alsh to join the aircraft carrier VICTORIOUS escort.

30 JUNE 1941

	Convoy OB.341 departed Liverpool, England, escorted by destroyers ST ALBANS and WESTCOTT plus corvettes AURICULA, FREESIA, HIBISCUS, MARIGOLD, MYOSOTIS, and PERIWINKLE. Corvette PERIWINKLE was detached from the convoy on 4 July. The destroyers were detached from the convoy on 5 July with corvettes FREESIA and MYOSOTIS. The convoy was dispersed on 6 July.
0800	Canadian troop convoy TC.11 arrived in the Clyde.
0800	Battle cruiser REPULSE, Dutch light cruiser HEEMSKERK, plus destroyers COSSACK, SIKH, INGLEFIELD, ACHATES, ACTIVE, ANTELOPE, and INTREPID arrived in the Clyde after escorting troop convoy TC.11.
1630	Destroyer CROOME departed Greenock, Scotland, to work up to combat efficiency at Scapa Flow.

Central Atlantic Crossing Zone

Long. W60, 00 – W15, 00   Lat. 49, 00 – N05, 00

1 JUNE 1941

	U.43, U.46, U.66, U.93, U.111, and U.557 formed a new patrol line off Newfoundland until 22 June.
	German tanker BELCHEN (6367grt) supplied U.557 at sea during the night.
0022	U.105 (Kptlt Schewe) heavily damaged steamer **SCOTTISH MONARCH** (4719grt) (Master Graham Clegg Winchester) after she was dispersed from convoy OB.319 southwest of the Cape Verde Islands in 12, 58N, 27, 20W.
0036	U.105 hit the steamer with a second torpedo, which failed to explode.
0052	U.105 sank the steamer with a third torpedo near the bridge, and the ship sank by the bow. One crewman was lost. The forty-four survivors abandoned the ship after the first hit. Dutch steamer ALPHARD (5483grt) rescued the master and twenty-three survivors on the 8th and landed them at Freetown, Sierra Leone, on the 13th. Steamer CHRISTINE MARIE (3895grt) rescued chief officer M. Macleod and nineteen survivors on 11 June and landed at Freetown on 19 June.

2 JUNE 1941

>1200	U.75 (Kptlt Helmuth Ringelmann) spotted Dutch steamer **EIBERGEN** (4801grt) after she had dispersed from convoy OB.327. U.75 missed the steamer with a torpedo, but continued her pursuit. A short time later, U.75 missed the steamer with two torpedoes. (Action continues on 3 June.)

3 JUNE 1941

0101	U.48 (Kptlt Herbert Schultze) damaged tanker INVERSUIR (9456grt) (Master Robert Charles Loraine) after she was dispersed from convoy OB.327 north of the Azores in 48, 28N, 28, 20W. The crew abandoned the ship.
0111	U.48 hit the tanker with a second torpedo and then with fifty-one rounds of 88-mm deck gun shells.
0349	U.48 hit the tanker with a third torpedo and left her in sinking condition.
0345	U.75 (Kptlt Helmuth Ringelmann) heavily damaged Dutch steamer **EIBERGEN** (4801grt) (Master R. Hilbrandie) with her fourth torpedo after she was dispersed from convoy OB.327 about 600 miles north of the Azores in 48, 02N, 25, 06W. (See 2 June >1200.) U.75 sank the steamer with a fifth torpedo after the crew abandoned ship. Two crewmen and two gunners were lost. A destroyer rescued thirty-five survivors on the 7th and transferred them to antiaircraft ship CAIRO, which landed them at Gourock, Scotland.
2033	U.75 torpedoed the damaged tanker **INVERSUIR** (9456grt) (Master Robert Charles Loraine) north of the Azores in 48, 28N, 28, 20W.
2051	U.75 sank the tanker with a second torpedo. Norwegian steamer PARA (3986grt) rescued the master and twenty-three crewmen. Ocean boarding vessel CORINTHIAN (Cdr E. J. R. Pollitt) collected the survivors from PARA and took them to Greenock, Scotland, on the 21st. Destroyer WANDERER (Cdr A. F. St. G. Orpen) rescued nine crewmen and landed them at Holyhead, Wales. An unknown vessel rescued the remaining twelve crewmen, who were landed at Quebec, Canada.

4 JUNE 1941

	U.101 (Kptlt Ernst Mengersen) sank steamer **TRECARRELL** (5271grt), which was sailing alone in 47, 10N, 31W. Four crewmen were lost.
	Using information from captured German documents, ocean boarding vessel MARSDALE captured German tanker **GEDANIA** (8923grt) in the North Atlantic in 43, 38N, 28, 15W. She carried forty-eight torpedoes to replenish U-boats. Her crew attempted to scuttle the vessel, but she was captured and became the EMPIRE GARDEN (8923grt) for British use.
	AMC ESPERANCE BAY located German supply ship **GONZENHEIM** (4104grt) in the North Atlantic, but was not fast enough to intercept her. An aircraft from aircraft carrier VICTORIOUS sighted the **GONZENHEIM** in 43, 32N, 23, 56W. Battleship NELSON detached from convoy SL.75, intercepted the supply ship, and ordered light cruiser NEPTUNE to board the vessel. The crew scuttled **GONZENHEIM** when the NELSON was seen closing on the ship in 43, 29N, 24, 04W. Light cruiser NEPTUNE, which had been detached from convoy WS.8X, rescued sixty-three survivors and took them to Gibraltar.
	Heavy cruiser LONDON and destroyer BRILLIANT intercepted German tanker **ESSO HAMBURG** (9849grt) in 07, 35N, 31, 25W. After the crew scuttled the tanker, all eighty-seven officers and ratings were rescued. **ESSO HAMBURG** was on her way to join German tanker EGERLAND (9789grt).

5 JUNE 1941

	U.48 (Kptlt Herbert Schultze) sank tanker **WELLFIELD** (6054grt), which was sailing alone in the North Atlantic

	in 48, 34N, 31, 34W. Eight crewmen were lost. Norwegian steamer **HEINA** (4028grt) rescued sixteen survivors on 11 June.
	Heavy cruiser **LONDON** and destroyer **BRILLIANT** intercepted German tanker **EGERLAND** (9789grt) west of Freetown, Sierra Leone, in 07N, 31W. After the crew scuttled the ship, all ninety-four officers and ratings were rescued.
	Italian submarine **VELELLA** (TV Terra) sighted convoy OG.63 and called in Italian submarine **MARCONI** (TV Pollina) to conduct a coordinated attack the next night.

6 JUNE 1941

	U.48 (Kptlt Herbert Schultze) sank steamer **TREGARTHEN** (5201grt), which was sailing alone in the North Atlantic in 46, 17N, 36, 20W. The entire crew was lost.
	A Swordfish aircraft, flown by Sub-Lt (A) J.B. Murray of 824 Squadron, from aircraft carrier **EAGLE** sank German blockade runner **ELBE** (9179grt), which had left Darien, China, on 20 April, near the Azores in the North Atlantic in 23, 30N, 36, 09W. A search for survivors was unsuccessful. Ocean boarding vessel **HILARY** rescued nineteen survivors on 21 June.
	From 6 June to 13 June, U.38, U.103, U.106 and U.107 set up a patrol line in the middle Atlantic between the Canary Islands and Freetown, Sierra Leone.
0503	U.106 (Kptlt Oesten) sank steamer **SACRAMENTO VALLEY** (4573grt) (Master Harold L. Sharp) after she was dispersed from convoy OB.324 west of the Cape Verde Islands in 17, 10N, 30, 10W. Three crewmen were lost. Steamer **CAITHNESS** (4970grt) rescued the master and thirty-eight survivors the next day and landed them at Freetown on the 14th. Panamanian steamer **STANVAC CAPE TOWN** (grt) rescued seven survivors on 24 June and landed them at Aruba on 3 July.

7 JUNE 1941

	A German Fw200 aircraft of I/KG.40 spotted a convoy in the North Atlantic, but its reported position was two hundred sea miles away from the true position.
	In the morning, Italian submarine **BRIN** (CC Longanesi-Cattani) spotted outward-bound convoy OG.63 northeast of Madeira, but could not obtain a firing position.
	Italian submarine **MOCENIGO** failed to find convoy OG.63 after speeding to the location broadcast by submarine **BRIN**.

8 JUNE 1941

	Brazilian steamer **OSORIO** rescued eleven survivors from sunken American steamer **ROBIN MOOR** (4999grt) in the North Atlantic in 00, 16N, 37, 37W.
	U.108 (Kptlt Klaus Scholtz) sank Greek steamer **DIRPHYS** (4240grt) in 47, 44N, 39, 02W. Six crewmen were lost, while nineteen survived.
	Dutch steamer **ALPHARD** (5483grt) rescued twenty-four survivors from the sunken steamer **SCOTTISH MONARCH** (4719grt).
0001	U.46 (ObltzS Engelbert Endraß) hit steamer **PHIDIAS** (5623grt) (Master Ernest Holden Parks) with a dud torpedo after she was dispersed from convoy OB.330 north of the Azores in 48, 25N, 26, 12W.
0010	U.46 opened fire with her deck gun because she was out of torpedoes. **PHIDIAS** returned fire with her deck gun until she was set afire and the crew abandoned the ship.
0045	U.46 ceased fire after seventy-one rounds had turned the ship into a flaming wreck. The master and seven crewmen were lost. Steamer **EMBASSAGE** (4954grt) rescued forty-three survivors and landed them at Sydney, Newfoundland.
0006	U.108 sank steamer **BARON NAIRN** (3164grt) (Master John Kerr) after she was dispersed from convoy OB.328 west of Cape Race in 47, 35N, 39, 02W. One crewman was lost. Canadian corvette **CHAMBLY** (Cdr J. D. Prentice) rescued eighteen survivors and landed them at St. John's, Newfoundland. The master and twenty crewmen landed their lifeboat at Galway, Ireland, on the 27th.
0108	U.38 (Kptlt Heinrich Liebe) sank unescorted steamer **KINGSTON HILL** (7628grt) (Master William Edwin Niven) southwest of the Cape Verde Islands in 09, 35N, 29, 40W. The master and thirteen crewmen were lost. Destroyer **ACHATES** (Lt Cdr Viscount Jocelyn) rescued sixteen survivors and landed them at Greenock, Scotland. American tanker **ALABAMA** (7004grt) rescued twenty-six crewmen and six gunners and landed them at Cape Town, South Africa.
1234	U.103 (FKpt Viktor Schütze) sank steamer **ELMDENE** (4853grt) (Master Ernest Fear) after she was dispersed from convoy OB.324 two hundred miles west-southwest of Freetown, Sierra Leone, in 08, 16N, 16, 50W. Steamer **CARLTON** (5162grt) rescued the master and thirty-five crewmen in 08, 47N, 16, 37W, and landed them at Freetown.
1325	U.46 damaged tanker **ENSIS** (6207grt) in 48, 46N, 29, 14W. The tanker arrived at St John's, Newfoundland, on the 15th. The ship was repaired at Halifax, Nova Scotia.

1545	U.48 (Kptlt Herbert Schultze) sank Dutch tanker **PENDRECHT** (10,746grt) (Master A. Meinsma) after she was dispersed from convoy OB.329 about five hundred miles northwest of the Azores in 45, 18N, 36, 40W. The crew abandoned the ship in three lifeboats with twelve men in each after efforts to save her failed.
1617	U.48 sank the tanker with a third torpedo under the funnel. Steamer ALRESFORD (2472grt) rescued one lifeboat on the 10th and landed them at Sydney, Newfoundland. American liner EXCALIBUR (9359grt) rescued a second lifeboat on the 22nd and took them to New York City. PANDORA rescued the third lifeboat on 18 June.
night	German aircraft damaged trawler REMAGIO (174grt) near Bamburgh in 48, 46N, 29, 14W during the night of 8/9 June. The trawler was abandoned ashore one-quarter mile north of Bamburgh. She was re-floated on the 26th and brought to Holy Island.

9 JUNE 1941

	U.46 (ObltzS Engelbert Endraß) sank steamer **TREVARRACK** (5270grt), which had dispersed from convoy OB.330, north of the Azores in 48, 25N, 26, 12W. There were no survivors from the crew of forty-four. Other sources credit U.101 (Kptlt Ernst Mengersen) with sinking this ship.

10 JUNE 1941

	U.108 (Kptlt Klaus Scholtz) sank Norwegian steamer **CHRISTIAN KROHG** (1992grt) (Master Ingvart Hagen) after she was dispersed from convoy OB.328 in 45N, 36, 30W. The entire crew (seventeen Norwegians, three British, one Swedish, one Estonian and one Canadian) was lost. U.108 had tried an unsuccessful attack on this steamer the day before.
0248	U.204 (Kptlt Kell) heavily damaged unescorted Belgian steamer **MERCIER** (7886grt) in 48, 30N, 41, 30W.
0257	U.204 sank the steamer with a final torpedo. Seven crewmen were lost, while sixty-one survived.

11 JUNE 1941

	Steamer CHRISTINE MARIE (3895grt) rescued twenty survivors from the sunken steamer **SCOTTISH MONARCH** (4719grt) at sea.

12 JUNE 1941

	U.371 reported sinking a large steamer of the KENT or TONGARIO type. The ship was supposedly hit by two torpedoes and sank quickly. No identification or confirmation is available to support this claim.
	Italian submarine BRIN (CC Longanesi-Cattani) sighted convoy SL.75 east of the Azores and reported her position.
Early AM	U.553 (Kptlt Karl Thurmann) sank steamer **SUSAN MAERSK** (2355grt) in the North Atlantic. She sank in one minute with her entire crew lost.
1505	U.553 damaged Norwegian tanker **RANELLA** (5590grt) (Master Conrad Mørland) with one torpedo on her port side after she was dispersed from convoy OG.64 in 43, 39N, 28W.
1635	U.553 fired a second torpedo, but the tanker remained afloat after being hit behind the mast and she broke in two.
1706	U.553 surfaced and fired one hundred rounds from her deck gun until the tanker finally sank. The entire crew was rescued when their lifeboats reached Figueira da Foz, Azores Islands, after twelve days.

13 JUNE 1941

	U.77 (Kptlt Schonder) sank steamer **TRESILLIAN** (4743grt) in 44, 40N, 45, 30W. USCG cutter DUANE (WPG-33) rescued the entire crew of forty-six.
	Italian submarine BRIN (CC Longanesi-Cattani) sank steamer **DJURDJURA** (3460grt) while attacking convoy SL.75 west of Portugal in 38, 53N, 23, 11W. Thirty-three crewmen were lost and five were rescued.
	Italian submarine BRIN sank Greek steamer **EIRINI KYRIAKIDES** (3781grt) while attacking convoy SL.75 west of Portugal in 38, 53N, 23, 11W. The entire crew was lost. BRIN claimed sinking two more steamers, but no more were damaged.
	Italian submarines VENIERO and VELELLA plus U.204, U.43, U.73 and U.201 were ordered into a patrol line for convoy SL.75, but all failed to make contact.
1157	U.107 (Kptlt Hessler) sank unescorted Greek steamer **PANDIAS** (4981grt) west of Africa in 07, 49N, 23, 38W. Eleven crewmen were lost. U.107 surfaced and provided the twenty-three survivors with water, cigarettes and rum.

14 JUNE 1941

	Italian submarine MOROSINI sank steamer **RUPERT DE LARRINAGA** (5358grt) while attacking convoy OG.67 west of Portugal in 36N, 21W.
	Italian submarine MALASPINA sank Greek steamer **NIKOLKIS** (3575grt) while attacking convoy OG.67 west of Portugal in 36N, 21W.
	Italian submarine MOROSINI sank steamer **LADY SOMERS** (8194grt) west of Portugal in 37N, 21W.

	Italian submarine MALASPINA sank steamer **GUELMA** (4402grt) west of Portugal in 31N, 17W.

15 JUNE 1941

	German tanker **LOTHRINGEN** (10,746grt) surrendered when she was intercepted in Operation SALVAGE by light cruiser DUNEDIN and aircraft from aircraft carrier EAGLE of Force F west of Africa in 19, 49N, 38, 30W. She was renamed EMPIRE SALVAGE (10,746grt) for British use.
	Submarine THUNDERBOLT (Lt Cdr Crouch) unsuccessfully attacked U.557 with eight torpedoes during a storm in the North Atlantic in 42, 00N, 47, 00W.

20 JUNE 1941

	The German WEST GROUP formed in the middle Atlantic with U.71, U.96, U.203, U.79, U.651, U.371, U.108, U.553, U.556, U.562, U.201, U.751, U.75, U.558, U.557, U.77, U.101, U.111, U.43, U.559, U.202, and U.564. Only U.108, U.101, U.75, U.48, U.73, U.204, all previously operating south of Iceland and U.553, U.77, U.558 and U.751 found targets, mostly single steamers.

22 JUNE 1941

2236	U.77 (Kptlt Schonder) sank weather ship **ARAKAKA** (2379grt) (Master William Walker) east of St John's, Newfoundland, in 47N, 40W. The master, thirty-two crewmen, and twelve Admiralty personnel were lost.

24 JUNE 1941

	Italian submarine DA VINCI (CC Calda) began to patrol west of Gibraltar until 27 July.

25 JUNE 1941

	Italian submarine BARBARIGO sank steamer **MACON** (5135grt) in 32N, 26W.

26 JUNE 1941

	Italian submarine BARBARIGO sank tanker **HORN SHELL** (8272grt) in 33N, 23W.

27 JUNE 1941

0119	U.69 (Kptlt Jost Metzler) spotted convoy SL.78 while she was en route to refuel off Las Palmas from German tanker CHARLOTTE SCHLIEMANN (7747grt). U.69 fired two torpedoes at convoy SL.78 about two hundred miles southeast of the Azores and heard one detonation, but no hit can be confirmed from Allied sources.
0149	U.69 sank steamer **RIVER LUGAR** (5423grt) (Master William Frame) while attacking convoy SL.78 about two hundred miles southeast of the Azores in 24N, 21W. The master, thirty-five crewmen and two passengers were lost. Corvette BURDOCK (Lt H. J. Fellowes SANVR) rescued six survivors and landed them at Milford Haven.
0237	U.69 sank steamer **EMPIRE ABILITY** (7603grt) (ex-German **HANSA** (7603grt) (Master Herbert Flowerdew) during her third attack on convoy SL.78 in 23, 50N, 21, 10W. The ship caught fire and sank after twenty-one minutes with two crewmen missing. Steamer AMERIKA (10,218grt) rescued the master, sixty crewmen, two gunners, seventeen military personnel and twenty-seven passengers. Corvette BURDOCK (Lt H. J. Fellowes SANVR) collected the survivors and took them to Milford Haven.
2357	U.123 (Kptlt Reinhard Hardegen) sank steamer **P.L.M. 22** (5646grt) (ex-French) (Master Yves Le Bitter, MM and Chevalier du Mérite Maritime) while attacking convoy SL.78 west-southwest of the Canary Islands in 25, 43N, 22, 47W. Thirty-two crewmen were lost. Corvette ARMERIA (Lt Cdr H. M. Russell) rescued ten crewmen and two French gunners. (Other sources claim there were twenty-two survivors.) Corvette ASPHODEL (Lt Cdr K. W. Steward) collected the survivors and took them to Freetown, Sierra Leone, on 4 July.
2358	U.123 sank Dutch steamer **OBERON** (1996grt) (Master E. O. J. Jans) while attacking convoy SL.78 west-southwest of the Canary Islands in 25, 43N, 22, 47W. Six crewmen were killed. A corvette rescued twenty-eight survivors and landed them at Freetown.
2400	U.123 unsuccessfully attacked convoy SL.78 with her third torpedo.

28 JUNE 1941

1642	U.103 (FKpt Viktor Schütze) spotted unescorted Italian steamer ERNANI (6619grt) while she was en route from Las Palmas to Horta, Azores and began a pursuit.
2338	U.103 unsuccessfully attacked the steamer with one torpedo.

29 JUNE 1941

	U.95, U.97, U.98 and U.A were unable to reach convoy SL.78 in time to attack.

	U.66 (KKpt Richard Zapp) sank Greek steamer **GEORGE J. GOULANDRIS** (4345grt) while attacking stragglers from convoy SL.78 west of Africa in 29, 05N, 25, 10W. The entire crew of twenty-eight was rescued.
	A German Fw200 aircraft of I/KG.40 spotted a convoy (probably convoy OG.66) in the middle Atlantic, but reported her position off by seventy-six sea miles.
0051	U.103 (FKpt Viktor Schütze) accidentally sank Italian steamer **ERNANI** (6619grt), which had departed Tenerife to escape to Bordeaux, 450 miles west of Las Palmas in 27, 52N, 26, 17W. She sank by the stern in twenty-one minutes. While questioning the survivors, Schütze realized he had just sunk the Italian blockade-runner disguised as the Dutch steam merchant ENGGANO (5412grt).
1850	U.66 sank Greek steamer **KALYPSO VERGOTTI** (5686grt) while attacking stragglers from convoy SL.78 west of Africa in 29N, 25W. There were no survivors from the crew of thirty-six.
1930	U.66 spotted steamer SAINT ANSELM (5614grt) and began to pursue the zigzagging ship.
1936	U.123 (Kptlt Hardegen) sank steamer **RIO AZUL** (4088grt) (Master Thomas Vickers Sutherland) while attacking convoy SL.78 about two hundred miles southeast of the Azores in 29N, 25W. The ship broke in two and quickly sank. Two crewmen drowned, nine died on a raft or later on a rescue ship, and twenty-two crewmen were missing. In all, the master, thirty-one crewmen and one gunner were lost. AMC ESPERANCE BAY (Capt G. S. Holden) rescued six crewmen and three gunners and landed them at Scapa Flow.

30 JUNE 1941

	A German Fw200 aircraft spotted convoy OG.66 and reported its position. Only U.108 was in a position to intercept the convoy, but the convoy escorts forced her under before she could attack.
0110	U.66 (KKpt Richard Zapp) missed steamer SAINT ANSELM (5614grt) when the master spotted the torpedo and avoided it with quick ship movements.
0146	U.66 fired a second torpedo from 400 metres, but the ship again avoided being hit.
0328	U.66 fired a third torpedo from 1000 metres, which hit the ship but failed to explode.
0330	U.66 fired a fourth torpedo, which again failed to hit the ship.
0332	U.66 fired a fifth torpedo, but it also missed. All torpedo tubes were reloaded for another try.
0558	U.66 fired a sixth torpedo, which was another dud.
0559	The seventh torpedo finally sank steamer **SAINT ANSELM** (5614grt) (Master Thomas Ross) while she was straggling behind convoy SL.78 west of Madeira in 31N, 26W. Thirty-four crewmen were lost. Spanish steamer TOM (3056grt) rescued fifteen survivors and landed them at Buenos Aires. AMC MORETON BAY (Capt C. C. Bell) rescued the master and seventeen survivors and landed them at Freetown, Sierra Leone, on 13 July.

UK East Coast

Long. W04, 00 – E03, 00   Lat. N58, 30 – N51, 30

1 JUNE 1941

	German bombing damaged Norwegian steamer FERNBANK (4333grt) off Peterhead, Scotland. She arrived at Aberdeen later in the day and was taken to the Tyne for repairs.
	Minelayer TEVIOTBANK escorted by destroyer HOLDERNESS laid Minefield BS.63 off the east coast of England.

2 JUNE 1941

	He115 aircraft of 3S/KGR.506 reported sighting the aircraft carrier INDOMITABLE along the English east coast. Due to the structure of the German Naval Air Arm and the *Luftwaffe*, a single He111 aircraft modified to carry a torpedo was loaned to the reconnaissance group for an attack.
	German bombing damaged steamer THORPEBAY (2183grt) six miles off Coquet Lighthouse. She returned to the Tyne and arrived at Scapa Flow on the 17th in tow.
	During the night, the borrowed German He111 aircraft of 3S/KGR.506 torpedoed Fleet Tender C (7942grt) (ex-MARMARI (7942grt)) off the British east coast.
	Light cruiser NIGERIA was undocked at Rosyth, Scotland.
	Minelayer PLOVER escorted by patrol sloop GUILLEMOT laid Minefield BS.57 off the east coast of England. Minesweepers ELGIN, SUTTON, and ALBURY of the 4th Minesweeping Flotilla accompanied the mining group.
	German Ju88 aircraft of I/KGR.506 heavily damaged steamer **BEAUMANOIR** (2477grt) eight cables 180° from 19 Buoy, Robin Hood's Bay. She was taken in tow but then sank after a second air attack.
	German Ju88 aircraft of I/KGR.506 damaged trawler BEN SCREEL (195grt) in 55, 30N, 01, 30W. She returned to the Tyne.

3 JUNE 1941

	Light cruiser NIGERIA departed Rosyth, Scotland, for Scapa Flow.

	Fleet Tender C (decoy ship) **MARMARI** (7924grt) struck the sunken wreck of tanker **AHAMO** (8621grt) in 53, 22N, 00, 59E. She remained stuck in the wreckage, and attempts to remove the ship during the day were unsuccessful. During the night of 3/4 June, German S-boats of the 4th S-Boat Flotilla (KptLt Bätge) with S.22 (ObltzS Karcher) and S.24 (ObltzS v. Mirbach) sank the decoy ship in 53, 20N, 01, 05E, with one torpedo striking the **AHAMO**. Rescue tug SABINE picked up the crew and landed them at Grimsby.
	German bombing heavily damaged steamer **ROYAL FUSILIER** (2187grt) north of Blyth in 55, 22N, 01, 21W. The steamer sank four miles 200° from May Island. The entire crew was rescued.

4 JUNE 1941

	A mine sank Dutch minelayer **VAN MEERLANT** in the Thames Estuary. T/Sub-Lt N. Moore RNVR, T/Sub-Lt R. C. Palmer RNVR, and T/LT (E) R. R. G. Perrett RNR, were lost. T/LT R. H. Church RNR was wounded.
	A mine sank naval trawler **ASH** (505grt) (Lt A.G. Newell, NZRNVR) in the Thames Estuary. The mine wounded some of the ratings in the trawler.

5 JUNE 1941

	German aircraft attacked antiaircraft ship ALYNBANK and convoy WN.36 during the evening. A steamer was set afire, and a trawler was damaged. German bombing sank steamer **QUEENSBURY** (3911grt) in 56, 50N, 02, 07W. Ten crewmen and one gunner were lost.
	German bombing sank balloon barrage drifter **LAVINIA L.** (73grt) off Sheerness. One crewman was lost.
1700	Destroyer INTREPID arrived off the Humber from Scapa Flow to fit a new TSDS and to carry out repairs.

6 JUNE 1941

	The German 4th S-Boat Flotilla laid ten TMA mines off Cross Sand.
	German bombing sank Norwegian steamer **TAURUS** (4767grt) south of Aberdeen in 56, 47N, 02, 15W. The entire crew was rescued.
	German bombing damaged trawler EMULATOR (168grt) seven to eight miles east of Scarborough.
0900	Antiaircraft ship ALYNBANK arrived at Methil with convoy WN.36.

7 JUNE 1941

1100	Destroyer ACHATES departed Rosyth for Scapa Flow.
1100	Antiaircraft ship ALYNBANK departed Methil and escorted convoy EC.29 from May Island.

8 JUNE 1941

	German bombing sank naval drifter **COR JESU** (97grt) (ex-Belgian logger) off Alnmouth, Northumberland, in 55, 29N, 01, 27W. The entire crew was rescued.
1545	Destroyer ANTHONY arrived off Aberdeen, Scotland, with steamers AMSTERDAM (4220grt) and LADY OF MANN (3104grt). She then returned to Scapa Flow, arriving later that day.

10 JUNE 1941

	A German IX Air Corps aerial mine sank patrol sloop **PINTAIL** (580grt) (Lt J. L. E. McClintock) off the Humber while escorting convoy FN.477. McClintock, Lt J. Brunton RNR, T/Sub-Lt W. A. Johnson RNR, Gunner J. E. Lucie, Commissioned Engineer S. W. Paris, and forty-eight ratings were lost. Destroyer QUANTOCK and another ship rescued twenty-two survivors.
	German bombing damaged steamer CLEARPOOL (5404grt) off 18B Buoy, Scarborough. Two crewmen were lost. She arrived at Tees on the 11th and was repaired at Hartlepool.
	A German IX Air Corps aerial mine sank steamer **ROYAL SCOT** (1444grt) in the Humber.

11 JUNE 1941

	German bombing sank steamer **MOORWOOD** (2056grt) abeam 19 C Buoy, north of Whitby. The entire crew was rescued.
	German bombing damaged steamer WESTBURN (2842grt) three miles north of Skinningrove off Hartlepool. The steamer arrived at Hartlepool on the 11th in tow.
	During a night take off at Arbroath, Sub-Lt (A) S. H. Bunch was killed when his Sea Hurricane aircraft hit a Swordfish aircraft, flown by Sub-Lt R. P. Cross, who was not injured in the crash.

12 JUNE 1941

	A German IX Air Corps aerial mine sank minesweeper **SISAPON** off Harwich.
0400	Destroyer HAMBLEDON joined steamers AMSTERDAM (4220grt) and LADY OF MANN (3104grt) off Aber-

13 JUNE 1941

	Destroyer HAMBLEDON escorted steamer AMSTERDAM (4220grt) to Lerwick. HAMBLEDON then returned to Scapa Flow.
	German bombing sank gate vessel **KING HENRY** (162grt) at Lowestoft, Suffolk.
	German bombing damaged steamer DALEMOOR (5796grt) in 57, 04N, 01, 51W. Six crewmen were killed and two were missing. She was towed to Leith for repairs.
	German bombing damaged steamer EMPIRE CREEK (332grt) in 57, 16N, 01, 43W. The ship was disabled by bomb near misses. She later arrived at Aberdeen.
1200	Antiaircraft ship ALYNBANK arrived at Methil escorting convoy WN.39.

14 JUNE 1941

1200	Antiaircraft ship ALYNBANK departed Methil to provide escort for convoy EC.32. She returned to Scapa Flow after being detached from the convoy in Pentland Firth.

15 JUNE 1941

	A German IX Air Corps mine sank fishing vessel **AUDACIOUS** (7grt) in the Humber in 51, 28N, 00, 51E. One crewman was rescued.

17 JUNE 1941

	The German 4th S-Boat Flotilla (Kptlt Bätge) laid six TMB mines off Cromer, Norfolk.
	Minelayer PLOVER, escorted by patrol sloop GUILLEMOT, laid Minefield BS.58 off the east coast of England. Minesweepers ELGIN, SUTTON, and ALBURY of the 4th Minesweeping Flotilla covered the mining group.
	German bombing damaged steamer JIM (833grt) off the T.2 Buoy, in the Tyne. She returned to the Tyne the next day.
1500	Destroyer ECHO departed Rosyth for Scapa Flow.

18 JUNE 1941

	German aircraft attacked Polish destroyer KUJIWIAK while she was working up to combat efficiency off the British east coast. Machine gun fire from the aircraft set off the four-inch ready use ammunition locker. One man was killed and the destroyer called at Dundee to make repairs and land the dead crewman.
	A mine sank fishing vessel **DORIS II** (6grt) three cables southeast of Outer Bar Bell Buoy off Sheerness. The crew of two was missing.
1430	Destroyer WINDSOR departed Dundee, Scotland, on the completion of her repairs. She went to Scapa Flow to continue working up to combat efficiency.
1830	Destroyer IMPULSIVE arrived at Immingham from Scapa Flow for a refit and the installation of TSDS equipment.

19 JUNE 1941

	German bombing damaged destroyer VANESSA in the North Sea. She was then involved in a collision with antisubmarine trawler TURQUOISE (430grt). Destroyer VESPER towed her to Yarmouth, where she received temporary repairs at Great Yarmouth from 19 to 30 June. She was then towed to the Thames and was repairing at London to 15 April 1942.
	Minelayer PLOVER laid Minefield BS.59 off the east coast of England escorted by destroyer COTSWOLD. Minesweepers accompanied the mining group.
1900	Antiaircraft ship ALYNBANK arrived at Methil escorting convoy WN.42 from Pentland Firth.

20 JUNE 1941

	German bombing sank minesweeping trawler **RESMILO** (258grt) (Skipper R. D. Stephen RNR) at Peterhead, Scotland. There were no casualties.
	A German IX Air Corps aerial mine damaged steamer ILSE (2844grt) on the west side of Hartlepool Approach Channel, in 54, 41N, 01, 20W. One crewman was killed. The back of the ship was broken. The after-part of the ship was taken to Middlesbrough and a new forepart was added.
	German bombing sank Norwegian steamer **SCHIELAND** (2249grt) in convoy FS.520 in 53, 18N, 01, 01E. Destroyer MENDIP rescued nine survivors, one of whom later died of injuries.
	A German aerial torpedo damaged steamer CORMOUNT (2841grt) off Outer Dowsing Light Vessel. One gunner was killed.
1030	Destroyer HAMBLEDON arrived at the entrance of Aberdeen from Scapa Flow to escort steamers AMSTERDAM (4220grt) and LADY OF MANN (3104grt) to the Orkneys.

21 JUNE 1941

	A mine laid by the German 4th S-Boat Flotilla (Kptlt Bätge) sank steamer **GASFIRE** (2972grt) ten miles east of Southwold in 52, 19N, 01, 59E.
	A mine laid by the German 4th S-Boat Flotilla sank steamer **KENNETH HAWKSFIELD** (1546grt) in 52, 18N, 01, 59E. One crewman was lost.
	German bombing damaged steamer DORINE (3176grt) off Sheringham. She arrived at Hartlepool on the 23rd.
	German bombing damaged Norwegian steamer SKUM (1304grt) near No.57 Buoy. She was towed to Great Yarmouth and subsequently to London for repairs.
	Destroyer ARROW departed Chatham to rejoin the Home Fleet after repairs.
	A mine damaged destroyer PYTCHLEY while she was escorting convoy FN.483 two miles off Flamborough Head. There were no casualties. Destroyer VORTIGERN towed PYTCHLEY to the Tyne, where she was under repair until December 1942.
	Minesweeper PLOVER laid Minefield BS.60 off the east coast of England escorted by destroyer EGLINTON.
1130	Antiaircraft ship ALYNBANK departed Methil, Scotland, and escorted convoy EC.35 to Pentland Firth.
1930	Destroyer ANTHONY arrived at Rosyth from Scapa Flow to clean boilers.
2000	A mine heavily damaged destroyer ARROW off Flamborough Head.
2300	Destroyer HAMBLEDON arrived at Aberdeen from Scapa Flow with steamers AMSTERDAM (4220grt) and LADY OF MANN (3104grt). The destroyer then proceeded on to Chatham for the fitting of SA equipment prior to joining the NORE Command.

22 JUNE 1941

	Destroyer ARROW arrived at Middlesbrough for repairs completed on 20 November.
1330	Destroyer ELECTRA arrived at Sheerness from Scapa Flow for a refit.

23 JUNE 1941

	German bombing sank minesweeping trawler **NOGI** (299grt) (Skipper E. C. King DSC RNR) off Norfolk in 52, 57N, 01, 28E.
	A mine laid by the German 4th S-Boat Flotilla (Kptlt Bätge) sank steamer **HULL TRADER** (717grt) one mile 270° from No.57C Buoy, Cromer. Eleven crewmen were lost.
	German bombing sank steamer **TRELISSICK** (5265grt) 3½-miles 114° from Sheringham Buoy, Cromer. Two crewmen were lost.
	A mine damaged steamer CAMROUX II (324grt) one mile northeast of No.17 Buoy, Flamborough Head. The steamer was towed to Immingham for repairs.
	German bombing damaged steamer TOLWORTH (1351grt) north of Cromer in 53, 05N, 01, 25E. The steamer was dry-docked in the Tyne for repairs.

24 JUNE 1941

	German bombing damaged steamer LEVENWOOD (803grt) off Tees Bay. She arrived at Hartlepool in tow on the 25th.

25 JUNE 1941

	German bombing sank steamer **DASHWOOD** (2154grt) north of Dogger Bank in 52, 59N, 01, 52E. The entire crew was rescued.
	Minelayer TEVIOTBANK laid Minefield BS.65 off the east coast of England escorted by destroyer WALPOLE.
	German bombing damaged trawler ISLE OF WIGHT (176grt) off Scarborough.

26 JUNE 1941

	German bombing sank minesweeping trawler **TRANIO** (275grt) (T/LT A. L. G. Gillies RNR), in tow, near 57 Buoy (Smith's Knoll). There were no casualties on the trawler.
	Light cruiser EURYALUS was commissioned at Chatham.

27 JUNE 1941

	German bombing sank minesweeping trawler **FORCE** (324grt) (A/T/Skipper C. E. Smalley RNR) off Great Yarmouth.
	German bombing sank Dutch steamer **MONTFERLAND** (6790grt) off Dogger Bank in 52, 47N, 01, 50E. The entire crew was rescued.
	Destroyer FIREDRAKE departed Chatham after repairs to return to Gibraltar and duty with Force H.
1200	Antiaircraft ship ALYNBANK arrived at Methil with convoy WN.45.

28 JUNE 1941

	Heavy cruiser CUMBERLAND arrived at Sheerness for a refit.
	German bombing sank steamer **CASH HALL** (4972grt) off Dogger Bank.
	German bombing sank steamer **BARRHILL** (4972grt) in 52, 50N, 01, 46E. Five crewmen were lost.
1130	Antiaircraft ship ALYNBANK departed Methil and joined convoy EC.38 off May Island. She escorted the convoy to Pentland Firth and then continued on to Scapa Flow.

29 JUNE 1941

	German bombing sank steamer **CUSHENDALL** (626grt) south of Aberdeen, Scotland, in 56, 57N, 02, 03W. Two crewmen were killed.
	German bombing damaged steamer EMPIRE METEOR (7457grt) off Smith's Knoll in 53, 05N, 01, 30E. The steamer arrived in the Humber on the 30th in tow.
	Heavy cruiser CUMBERLAND began a refit at Chatham, which was completed on 11 October.
	Light cruiser KENYA began repairs for her collision damage and a refit in the Tyne.
	German bombing damaged steamer SILVERLAUREL (6142grt) in King George Dock, Hull.
	German bombing damaged tug EMPIRE LARCH (487grt) off Great Yarmouth. She arrived at Great Yarmouth on the 30th.
	A mine damaged Norwegian tanker LEIESTEN (6118grt) off B 3 Buoy, Barrow Deep. She arrived at Gravesend on the 30th in tow.

30 JUNE 1941

	A German IX Air Corps aerial mine damaged Norwegian tanker LEIESTEN (6118grt) in the Thames Estuary.
2200	Heavy cruiser NORFOLK arrived in the Tyne from Scapa Flow for a refit.

North Sea
Long. E03, 00 – E09, 00   Lat. N58, 30 – N51, 00

1 JUNE 1941

	The Germans set up the newly formed 4th S-Boat Flotilla (Kptlt Bätge) with the older S-boats S.19, S.20, S.22, S.24 and S.25 in Rotterdam, Holland. At the same time, the 1st, 2nd, and 3rd S-Boat Flotillas departed the North Sea for Swinemünde, Germany, in preparation for operations against Russia in the Baltic.

3 JUNE 1941

	German bombing damaged minesweeper FRANKLIN with two near misses in the North Sea. The minesweeper spent no time out of action due to the damage.
	In an attack on German shipping, a British Swordfish aircraft of 816 Squadron from Thorney Island was shot down. P/T/Sub-Lt (A) C. M. Richards RNVR, observer, and Leading Airman A. J. Atkin were killed. The pilot, T/A/Sub-Lt (A) E. K. Margetts RNVR, was taken prisoner.

6 JUNE 1941

	German steamer **CONSUL HINTZ** (1847grt) sank at Wilhelmshaven, Germany, after a collision with German steamer KAJE (1547grt).

20 JUNE 1941

	Minelayer TEVIOTBANK laid Minefield BS.64 escorted by destroyer MENDIP in the North Sea.

24 JUNE 1941

	The German 4th S-Boat Flotilla (Kptlt Bätge) departed Rotterdam, Holland, and set up a new base at Cherbourg, France. Their departure gave the ships along the British east coast a short respite from S-boat attacks.

25 JUNE 1941

	German bombing damaged destroyer LIDDESDALE in the North Sea, but she spent no time out of action.

English Channel
Long. W07, 00 – E01, 30   Lat. N51, 00 – N49, 00

2 JUNE 1941

	Ex-US Coast Guard cutter/escort ship HARTLAND was damaged in a collision with steamer WELSH COAST (646grt). The escort ship sustained minor damage, which was repaired at Falmouth during a scheduled refit from 8 June to 18 July.

3 JUNE 1941

	German bombing damaged steamer **DENNIS ROSE** (1600grt) five miles west by south of Start Point.

5 JUNE 1941

	German bombing sank coal hulk **HIMALAYA** (3540grt) at Portland.

9 JUNE 1941

	German bombing sank steamer **DAGMAR** (844grt) south of St. Alban's Head in 50, 35N, 01, 48W. Three crewmen were lost.

10 JUNE 1941

0700	Polish destroyer **KRAKOWIAK** departed Devonport for Scapa Flow to work up to combat efficiency.

13 JUNE 1941

	German bombing sank damaged Norwegian steamer **ALA** (933grt) while she was in the tow of tug **SECURITY** from Shoreham to Southampton in 50, 42N, 00, 52W. One crewman was lost.

14 JUNE 1941

1315	Destroyer **ECLIPSE** departed Plymouth for Scapa Flow on the completion of her refit.

20 JUNE 1941

	German bombing damaged tanker **INVERARDER** (5578grt) off the Isle of Wight. She was beached off Motherbank Buoy, Solent. She was later re-floated and taken to Southampton for repairs.

Bay of Biscay   Long. W15, 00 – E03, 00   Lat. N49, 00 – N40, 00

2 JUNE 1941

	German bombing damaged submarine P.32 while she was on passage to Gibraltar off Cape Finisterre, Spain. Considerable damage was done to the batteries.

3 JUNE 1941

	German heavy cruiser **PRINZ EUGEN** arrived at Brest, France.

7 JUNE 1941

	German heavy cruiser **PRINZ EUGEN** remained undamaged after an RAF bombing attack during the night at Brest, France.

22 JUNE 1941

	Ocean boarding vessel **MARSDALE** and a Catalina aircraft located German supply ship **ALSTERTOR** (3039grt) west of Portugal, but contact was lost.

23 JUNE 1941

	The crew scuttled German supply ship **ALSTERTOR** (3039grt) in 41, 12N, 13, 10W after destroyers FAULKNOR, FORESIGHT, FORESTER, FOXHOUND, and FURY of the 8th Destroyer Flotilla intercepted her two hundred miles southwest of Cape Finisterre, Spain. Survivors from the ship included seventy-eight British prisoners from sunken steamers **TRAFALGAR** (5542grt) and **RABAUL** (6809grt). The destroyers then proceeded to join aircraft carrier FURIOUS before she arrived at Gibraltar from the Clyde. Submarine P.33, which had also been searching for the German ship, was directed to continue her passage to Gibraltar.

27 JUNE 1941

	German blockade-runner **REGENSBURG** (8068grt) (Kpt Harder) arrived at Bordeaux, France, from Dairen, China.

West of Gibraltar   Long. W15, 00 – W05, 30   Lat. N40, 00 – N30, 00

1 JUNE 1941

	Italian submarine **MARCONI** (TV Pollina) sank Portuguese fishing trawler **EXPORTADOR I** (318grt) with gunfire 137 miles southwest of Cape St Vincent, in 35, 40N, 10, 30W. Two crewmen were killed and twenty were rescued.

	Italian submarine MARCONI sank fleet oiler **CAIRNDALE** (8447grt) west of Gibraltar in 35N, 09W.
	Submarine SEVERN departed Gibraltar for a patrol in the Middle Atlantic.

3 JUNE 1941

	Damaged submarine P.32 arrived at Gibraltar from Holy Loch.
	Corvette ASTER departed Gibraltar for Bathurst, Gambia.

4 JUNE 1941

	Convoy HG.64 departed Gibraltar escorted by sloop BIDEFORD, corvettes COREOPSIS and FLEUR DE LYS, Dutch submarine O.21, and antisubmarine trawler STELLA CARINA. Two motor launches departed Gibraltar with the convoy for local escort. Corvette WOODRUFF joined the convoy on the 5th and was detached the next day for Bathurst. STELLA CARINA was detached from the convoy on the 10th. Corvettes COREOPSIS and FLEUR DE LYS were detached from the convoy on the 12th to join convoy OG.64. On the 14th, ocean-boarding vessels LADY SOMERS and MALVERNIAN joined the convoy. Destroyers SKATE and WALKER plus corvettes HYDRANGEA and WALLFLOWER joined the convoy on the 15th. Convoy HG.64 arrived at Liverpool on the 19th.
	Aircraft carrier ARGUS and Greek troopship NEA HELLAS (16,991grt) departed Gibraltar for Britain escorted locally by destroyers FOXHOUND, FORESIGHT, and FURY. Corvettes GERANIUM and JONQUIL were to escort the ships during daylight on the 5th, but a forecast of bad weather, which would make the escorts inefficient, forced the ships to return to Gibraltar, arriving on the 5th.

6 JUNE 1941

	Italian submarine VENIERO missed steamer ARIOSTO (2176grt) with torpedoes while attacking convoy HG.64 west of Gibraltar in 34N, 11W. The Italian submarine reported attacking another steamer in this convoy, but there is no confirmation of this attack.
	Italian submarine MARCONI (TV Pollina) sank steamer **BARON LOVAT** (3395grt) while attacking convoy OG.63 in 35, 30N, 11, 30W. There were no casualties on the steamer.
	Italian submarine MARCONI sank Swedish steamer **TABERG** (1392grt) in 35, 36N, 11, 12W. Fifteen crewmen were lost. The Italian submarine also reported damaging an 8000grt tanker, but there is no confirmation for this attack.
	Italian submarines VELELLA and EMO (CC Roselli-Lorenzini) joined in the attack on convoy HG.64 or convoy OG.63. The two submarines claimed sinking two steamers each, but no confirmation was available.
	German Fw200 aircraft of I/KG.40 bombing sank steamer **GLEN HEAD** (2011grt) west of Gibraltar in 35, 40N, 10, 30W. Twenty-seven crewmen were lost.
	Destroyers WIVERN, WILD SWAN, and VANSITTART arrived at Gibraltar for refuelling after escort duty with convoy WS.8X.
	Aircraft carrier ARGUS and troopship NEA HELLAS (16,991grt) departed Gibraltar escorted by destroyers WIVERN, WILD SWAN, and VANSITTART to join inbound aircraft carrier VICTORIOUS and light cruiser NEPTUNE. The destroyers would return with VICTORIOUS and NEPTUNE to Gibraltar. ARGUS and NEA HELLAS continued on to the Clyde, arriving on the 14th.

7 JUNE 1941

	Battle cruiser RENOWN, aircraft carriers ARK ROYAL and FURIOUS plus light cruiser SHEFFIELD departed Gibraltar with destroyers FAULKNOR, FEARLESS, FOXHOUND, FORESTER, and FURY to join inbound aircraft carrier VICTORIOUS at sea.
	Submarine SEVERN arrived at Gibraltar after a patrol west of Gibraltar.

8 JUNE 1941

1100	Destroyers WIVERN, WILD SWAN, and VANSITTART joined aircraft carrier VICTORIOUS and light cruiser NEPTUNE at sea. Destroyer WRESTLER, after reinforcing the convoy OG.63 escort, also joined the VICTORIOUS escort.

9 JUNE 1941

	Aircraft carrier VICTORIOUS and light cruiser NEPTUNE escorted by destroyers WIVERN, WILD SWAN, and VANSITTART were joined at sea by Force H with battle cruiser RENOWN, aircraft carriers ARK ROYAL and FURIOUS, light cruiser SHEFFIELD, plus destroyers FAULKNOR, FEARLESS, FOXHOUND, FORESTER, and FURY. Light cruiser NEPTUNE was sent into Gibraltar to land German prisoners and captured documents from the German ship **GONZENHEIM** (4104grt). Destroyer WIVERN was sent into Gibraltar on the 9th, and destroyers WILD SWAN, VANSITTART, and

WRESTLER arrived on the 10th.
Aircraft carrier FURIOUS, transferred personnel and aircraft to aircraft carrier VICTORIOUS and then returned to Britain, accompanied by light cruiser SHEFFIELD and destroyer FURY.
Force H returned to Gibraltar with VICTORIOUS replacing FURIOUS.
FURY was later detached from SHEFFIELD at sea to rejoin Force H.
FURIOUS arrived in the Clyde on the 14th.
SHEFFIELD joined homebound convoy SL.76 on the 14th to return to Britain for a refit. She arrived at Scapa Flow on the 18th.

Light cruiser NEPTUNE departed Gibraltar for Freetown, Sierra Leone.

10 JUNE 1941

The crew scuttled Italian tanker **PAGAO** (6101grt) off Algeciras, Spain. She was later salvaged and became the Spanish ZARAGOZA (6101grt).

Antisubmarine trawlers ST MELANTE and RUNSWICK BAY departed Gibraltar for Bathurst, escorting salvage tug VALKYRIE, which was en route to the Eastern Mediterranean.

11 JUNE 1941

Force H, with aircraft carrier VICTORIOUS replacing aircraft carrier FURIOUS, returned to Gibraltar in time to support the new Malta supply mission.

14 JUNE 1941

Convoy HG.65 departed Gibraltar escorted by sloop WELLINGTON, submarine OLYMPUS, corvettes GERANIUM, JONQUIL, and SPIREA, and antisubmarine trawler LADY HOGARTH.
Destroyer FORTUNE departed Gibraltar on the 15th and joined the convoy for passage to Britain for a refit.
LADY HOGARTH was detached from the convoy on the 20th and the remainder of the escort, less sloop WELLINGTON, was detached from the convoy on the 22nd.
Destroyers CHELSEA, MANSFIELD, and VERITY, corvettes BEGONIA and JASMINE, and CAM ship SPRINGBANK joined the convoy on the 25th.
Destroyer VETERAN joined the convoy on the 26th.
Convoy HG.65 arrived at Liverpool on the 29th.

16 JUNE 1941

Force H departed Gibraltar with battle cruiser RENOWN, aircraft carriers ARK ROYAL and VICTORIOUS, plus destroyers FAULKNOR, FEARLESS, FOXHOUND, FORESIGHT, FORESTER, and HESPERUS for a position in 49N, 29, 30W.
Aircraft carrier VICTORIOUS and destroyer HESPERUS were detached from Force H at that position to return to Britain.

17 JUNE 1941

Ocean boarding vessel MARSDALE arrived at Gibraltar from her Western Patrol.

18 JUNE 1941

While returning to Gibraltar after escorting aircraft carrier VICTORIOUS, destroyers FAULKNOR (Capt de Salis), FEARLESS (Cdr Pugsley), FORESIGHT (Cdr Salter), FORESTER (Lt Cdr Tancock), and FOXHOUND (Cdr Peteo) sank **U.138** (ObltzS Gramitzky) seventy miles off Cape Trafalgar in 36, 04N, 07, 29W. FEARLESS picked up the entire crew of four officers and twenty-three ratings.
The destroyers arrived at Gibraltar later that day. The destroyers had used information gleaned from ENIGMA messages to approximate the position of **U.138**.

Destroyer WISHART departed Gibraltar to join troopship SCYTHIA (19,761grt) and destroyer DUNCAN, which were arriving from Freetown, and escort them into Gibraltar.

Ocean boarding vessel MARSDALE departed Gibraltar on a Western Patrol in company with Norwegian steamer SYDHAV (7587grt) and destroyer FURY as local escort.

19 JUNE 1941

German Fw200 aircraft of I/KG.40 bombing sank steamer **EMPIRE WARRIOR** (1306grt) after she broke away from convoy HG.64 two and three quarters miles off Guadiana Bar, Gulf of Cadiz, in 37, 06N, 07, 24W. A Portuguese destroyer rescued the entire crew.

German Fw200 aircraft of I/KG.40 bombing sank Swedish steamer **GUNDA** (1770grt) after she broke away from convoy HG.64 west of Portugal in 37, 36N, 09, 53W.
Steamer PETEREL took her in tow, but she later sank.
PETEREL and antisubmarine trawler IMPERIALIST rescued the entire crew.

Destroyer WRESTLER departed Gibraltar for Freetown, Sierra Leone, to join the South Atlantic Command.

20 JUNE 1941

	Submarine THRASHER arrived at Gibraltar from Holy Loch.
	U.123 (Kptlt Hardegen) sank Portuguese steamer **GANDA** (4333grt) west of Casablanca in 34, 10N, 11, 40W. Two crewmen and three passengers were lost, while sixty-one were rescued.
	Destroyers FAULKNOR, FEARLESS, FORESTER, and FOXHOUND departed Gibraltar to escort battle cruiser RENOWN and aircraft carrier ARK ROYAL into Gibraltar. Destroyer FURY was ordered to part company with ocean boarding vessel MARSDALE and join the escort group at sea.
	Deperming vessels SPRINGTIDE and SPRINGDALE departed Gibraltar with naval trawler CANNA for Freetown with destroyer AVON VALE as local escort. Norwegian tanker NORVINN (6322grt) sailed in company with the group and then proceeded independently to the west.

21 JUNE 1941

	Italian submarine TORELLI sank Norwegian tanker **IDA KNUDSEN** (8913grt) west of Gibraltar in 35N, 14W.
	Submarine OSIRIS arrived at Gibraltar from Holy Loch after refitting at Chatham from 25 January to 10 May.

22 JUNE 1941

	Force H returned to Gibraltar.
	In the afternoon, an RAF patrol aircraft spotted German supply ship ALSTERTOR (3039grt) west of Gibraltar returning from her supply mission to the Indian Ocean. Ocean boarding vessel MARSDALE and Force H destroyers FAULKNOR, FEARLESS, FORESTER, FOXHOUND and FURY were ordered to intercept the blockade-runner.
	Destroyers WISHART and DUNCAN arrived at Gibraltar with troopship SCYTHIA (19,761grt).
	Deperming ship CORBRAE departed Gibraltar with antisubmarine whalers KOS X and KOS XI for Freetown with local escort of destroyer ERIDGE.

24 JUNE 1941

	Convoy HG.66 departed Gibraltar escorted by destroyers FARNDALE and WISHART, sloop FOLKESTONE, corvette AZALEA, Dutch submarine O.21, antisubmarine trawler STELLA CARINA, and three motor-launches as additional local escort. STELLA CARINA was detached from the convoy later that day. WISHART was detached from the convoy on the 27th. FARNDALE was detached from the convoy on the 30th. Submarine O.21 was detached from the convoy on 1 July. On 4 July, destroyers GARLAND, MAORI, SARDONYX, and WESTCOTT joined the convoy. On 5 July, destroyer ST ALBANS plus corvettes FREESIA and MYOSOTIS joined the convoy. Sloop FOLKESTONE was detached from the convoy on 8 July and the convoy arrived at Liverpool on 9 July.

25 JUNE 1941

	Force H returned to Gibraltar after successfully intercepting German blockade-runner **ALSTERTOR** (3039grt).
	Aircraft carrier FURIOUS and light cruiser HERMIONE arrived at Gibraltar with destroyers LEGION and LANCE plus destroyers FAULKNOR, FEARLESS, FORESTER, FOXHOUND, and FURY, which joined on the 24th.

26 JUNE 1941

	Submarine P.33 arrived at Gibraltar from the Clyde.

27 JUNE 1941

	Destroyer WISHART sank Italian submarine **GLAUCO** (TV Baroni) west of Gibraltar in 35, 06N, 12, 41W. Seven officers and forty-four ratings were rescued. WISHART arrived at Gibraltar on the 28th.
	Submarine CLYDE departed Gibraltar heading westward for Operation VIGOROUS. Due to mistaken identity, she was attacked by destroyer AVON VALE in the Straits and sustained some damage. However, she was able to continue on her mission. She patrolled the area of the Canary Islands for a German supply ship, reportedly due to supply a German submarine on the 30th. However, nothing was found and the submarine returned to Gibraltar on 5 July.

28 JUNE 1941

	Submarine P.33 arrived at Gibraltar from the Clyde.
	Italian submarine DA VINCI (CC Calda) sank fleet tanker **AURIS** (8030grt) in 34, 27N, 11, 57W. Thirty-two crewmen were lost. Destroyer FARNDALE was detached from convoy HG.66 to assist and picked up twenty-seven survivors.
	Antisubmarine trawlers LORD IRWIN and LAERTES departed Gibraltar with whaler GOS VII for Freetown.

29 JUNE 1941

Destroyers WISHART and AVON VALE departed Gibraltar to join arriving AMC CILICIA escorting troopship CAMERONIA (16,297grt) from Freetown, Sierra Leone. The destroyers relieved the AMC and took the troopship to Gibraltar, arriving on 4 July.

Norwegian tanker SILDRA (7313grt) departed Gibraltar with the group and later detached to sail alone for the west.

30 JUNE 1941

Ocean boarding vessels MARSDALE and MALVERNIAN were ordered to sweep and locate an unidentified freighter sighted by aircraft on 25/26 June.

West of North Africa
Long. W15, 00 – E11, 00   Lat. N30, 00 – N00, 00

1 JUNE 1941

1409 — U.107 (Kptlt Hessler) sank steamer **ALFRED JONES** (5013grt) (Master Harold Harding), after she was dispersed from convoy OB.320, 140 miles west-southwest of Freetown, Sierra Leone, in 08N, 15W. Fourteen crewmen were lost. Corvette MARGUERITE (Lt Cdr A. N. Blundell) rescued the master, the commodore (Vice-Admiral G. T. C. P. Swabey CB DSO RN), six naval staff members, thirty-eight crewmen, four gunners and twelve passengers and landed them at Freetown.

4 JUNE 1941

A mine laid by U.69 (Kptlt Metzler) on 29 May sank dredger **ROBERT HUGHES** (2879grt) (Master D. Jones) at the entrance to Lagos harbour. Fourteen crewmen were lost, while seventeen survived.

8 JUNE 1941

Convoy SL.77 departed Freetown, Sierra Leone, escorted by AMC ARAWA to 2 July, corvettes GARDENIA and MARGUERITE to 13 June, and antisubmarine yacht SURPRISE from 8 to 13 June.
Corvette CYCLAMEN escorted the convoy on 10 and 11 June.
Heavy cruiser NORFOLK joined the convoy on the 15th and continued with the convoy to 27 June when she was detached to Scapa Flow.
On the 23rd, ocean-boarding vessels CAVINA and HILARY joined the convoy to 3 July.
On the 29th, destroyers BATH joined the convoy to 2 July, VANOC, and WALKER with corvettes HYDRANGEA and WALLFLOWER joined the convoy and arrived with it at Liverpool on 3 July.

0442 — U.107 (Kptlt Hessler) sank liner **ADDA** (7816grt) (Master John Tate Marshall) after she was dispersed from convoy OB.324 eighty-two miles west-southwest of Freetown in 08, 30N, 14, 39W. Seven crewmen, two passengers, and the Convoy Commodore, Captain W. H. Kelly CBE DSO, RD RNR, were lost.
Corvette CYCLAMEN (Lt H. N. Lawson) rescued the master, 141 crewmen, four gunners, five naval staff members and 264 passengers and landed them at Freetown on the 8th.

12 JUNE 1941

Heavy cruiser NORFOLK departed Freetown to escort convoy SL.77, which had departed Freetown on the 8th, to Britain. NORFOLK carried 181 German prisoners from the tankers **ESSO HAMBURG** (9849grt) and **EGERLAND** (9789grt).
She arrived at Scapa Flow on the 29th.

18 JUNE 1941

Convoy SL.78 departed Freetown, Sierra Leone, escorted by AMC ESPERANCE BAY to 27 June, sloop BRIDGEWATER to 21 June, and corvettes ARMERIA, ASPHODEL, ASTER, and BURDOCK to 28 June.
Heavy cruiser SHROPSHIRE was with the convoy on 26 to 27 June. She was ordered to detach from the convoy and take up a position one hundred miles west of the convoy.
After further U-boat attacks on the 27th, AMC ESPERANCE BAY also left the convoy.
Corvette FLEUR DE LYS departed Gibraltar on the 27th and was with the convoy on the 29th. The convoy was ordered dispersed on the 29th and the corvette returned to Gibraltar.
On 7 July, destroyers CHELSEA, MANSFIELD, and VERITY, catapult ship PEGASUS, corvettes ARBUTUS to 11 July, BEGONIA, CONVOLVULUS, JASMINE, LARKSPUR, PIMPERNEL, and RHODODENDRON escorted the convoy until it arrived at Liverpool on 12 July.

19 JUNE 1941

Captured Vichy French steamer **CRITON** (4564grt) joined convoy SL.78 at sea for passage to Belfast, Northern Ireland. However, the steamer experienced difficulties and fell out of the convoy to return to Freetown, Sierra Leone.
Vichy French auxiliary patrol vessel AIR FRANCE IV and armed trawler EDITH GERMAINE intercepted her on

20 JUNE 1941

Convoy WS.9A departed Freetown, Sierra Leone, with steamers BERGENSFJORD (11,015grt), ARONDA (4062grt), THYSVILLE (8351grt), and CHRISTIAAN HUYGENS (16,287grt). They were escorted by destroyers BOREAS, VELOX, WILD SWAN, and VANSITTART as local escort from 20 to 22 June and light cruiser BIRMINGHAM as ocean escort.

Steamers EASTERN PRINCE (10,926grt), CAPETOWN CASTLE (27,000grt), EMPRESS OF JAPAN (26,032grt), LLANGIBBY CASTLE (11,951grt), DURBAN CASTLE (17,388grt), and EMPIRE WIDGEON (6736grt) arrived at Cape Town on 1 July. The remaining ships continued towards Durban with light cruiser BIRMINGHAM.

Heavy cruiser HAWKINS relieved the light cruiser on 2 July. The convoy arrived at Durban on 4 July.

The Cape Town ships departed Cape Town on 5 July escorted by light cruiser BIRMINGHAM.

Durban ships ARONDA, AAGTEKERK, THYSVILLE, EMPIRE CONDOR, EMPIRE EGRET, and EMPIRE CURLEW departed on 8 July escorted by HAWKINS.

The two convoy sections rendezvoused on 9 July and light cruiser BIRMINGHAM was detached.

Steamers EMPRESS OF JAPAN, CAPETOWN CASTLE, and DURBAN CASTLE were detached from the convoy in 09, 10N, 51, 40E with AMC HECTOR as convoy WS.9 AX for Bombay, India. They arrived on 24 July.

Convoy WS.9 AX departed Bombay escorted by AMC ANTENOR and arrived at Colombo, Ceylon, on 30 July.

Steamers EMPRESS OF JAPAN and CAPETOWN CASTLE departed Colombo on 1 August escorted by light cruiser MAURITIUS. Light cruiser DURBAN relieved light cruiser MAURITIUS at sea and the convoy arrived at Singapore on 5 August.

The remaining ships arrived at Aden on 21 July and proceeded independently to Suez.

27 JUNE 1941

Convoy SL.79 departed Freetown, Sierra Leone, escorted by AMC DUNNOTTAR CASTLE to 10 July and by corvettes COLUMBINE, CROCUS, and CYCLAMEN to 5 July.

Ocean boarding vessel MARSDALE departed Gibraltar on 11 July and joined the convoy for passage to Britain.

On 14 July, the convoy joined with convoy HG.67 for the passage to Britain, and both arrived at Liverpool on 24 July.

SOUTH ATLANTIC OCEAN

East of South America
Long. W70, 00 – W30, 00   Lat. N05, 00 - S60, 00

24 JUNE 1941

Heavy cruiser LONDON intercepted German blockade-runner **BABITONGA** (4422grt) off the Brazilian coast. The crew scuttled the ship and were picked up by the cruiser.

West of South Africa
Long. W30, 00 – E25, 00   Lat. S00, 00 – S60, 00

17 JUNE 1941

German AMC SCHIFF.16/ATLANTIS sank steamer **TOTTENHAM** (4762grt) southwest of Ascension Island with the aid of her floatplane in 07, 38S, 19, 12W. Seventeen crewmen were landed at Trinidad on 2 July. Twenty-six crewmen became prisoners of war.

21 JUNE 1941

The crew scuttled German supply ship **BABITONGA** (4422grt) when she was intercepted by heavy cruiser LONDON near St Paul Rocks in 02, 05S, 27, 42W.

22 JUNE 1941

German AMC SCHIFF.16/ATLANTIS sank steamer **BALZAC** (5372grt) southwest of Ascension Island in 12S, 29W. Two crewmen were killed and one later died, while forty-five crewmen became prisoners of war.

24 JUNE 1941

Light cruiser NEPTUNE arrived at Simon's Town, South Africa.

Seaplane carrier ALBATROSS was docked for a refit at Simon's Town until 4 August.

BALTIC SEA

Kattegat and Skagerrak
Long. E09, 00 – E12, 00   Lat. N60, 00 – N53, 00

11 JUNE 1941

	German heavy cruiser LÜTZOW plus light cruisers EMDEN and LEIPZIG, departed the Baltic with destroyers HANS LODY, Z.23, Z.24, FRIEDRICH ECKHOLDT, and KARL GALSTER for Norway.

12 JUNE 1941

	German light cruisers EMDEN and LEIPZIG were detached from the heavy cruiser LÜTZOW group to enter Oslofjord, Norway. LÜTZOW passed out of the Skagerrak with the five destroyers.

14 JUNE 1941

>1200	Damaged German heavy cruiser LÜTZOW arrived at Kiel, Germany, and began repairs lasting until January 1942.

21 JUNE 1941

	RAF aircraft heavily damaged German troopship WESTERWALD (10,845grt) in the Skagerrak.

Southern Baltic Area
Long. E12, 00 – E22, 00   Lat. N60, 00 – N53, 00

12 JUNE 1941

	The German 2nd Minelaying Group (FKpt von Schönermark) with TANNENBERG, BRUMMER and HANSESTADT DANZIG plus the German 3rd Minelaying Group with COBRA, KAISER and KÖNIGIN LUISE assembled off Gotenhafen, Poland, to lay minefields along the entrance to the Gulf of Finland.

18 JUNE 1941

	The German 1st Minelaying Group (F.d.M, KptzS Bentlage) with PREUSSEN, GRILLE, SKAGERRAK and VERSAILLES with six small auxiliary minesweepers of the 6th Minesweeping Flotilla laid Minefield WARTBURG I between Memel and Öland. When completed, 1150 EMC and 1800 floating mines were laid in these fields.
	Russian light cruiser KIROV observed the Germans laying mines west of Libau, Latvia.

19 JUNE 1941

	The German 1st Minelaying Group and 6th Minesweeping Flotilla laid Minefield WARTBURG II between Memel and Öland.

20 JUNE 1941

	The German 1st Minelaying Group and 6th Minesweeping Flotilla laid Minefield WARTBURG III between Memel and Öland.

21 JUNE 1941

	The German 3rd Minelaying Group with COBRA, KAISER and KÖNIGIN LUISE escorted by six MTBs of the 1st S-Boat Flotilla and five boats of the 5th R-Boat Flotilla laid Minefield CORBETHA between Pakerort and Kallbada with 400 EMC and 700 floating mines. The Group observed Russian warships nearby while they were mining.
	While returning from laying Minefield CORBETHA, the German 3rd S-Boat Flotilla (Kptlt Kemnade) laid twelve TMB mines each off Libau and Ventspils, Latvia, named Minefield WEIMAR and Minefield ERFURT.
	While returning from laying Minefield CORBETHA, the German 5th S-Boat Flotilla (Kptlt Wisely) laid thirty TMB mines in the Irben Strait in Minefield EISENACH.

22 JUNE 1941

	The German 3rd S-Boat Flotilla laid twenty-four TMB mines off Ventspils, Latvia.
	U.140, U.142, U.144, U.145 and U.149 operated west of Memel, south of Gotland, west of Ventspils, west of Ösel-Dagö and off the entrance to the Gulf of Finland.
	U.48 arrived at Kiel, Germany, after her last patrol. In her twelve missions under the command of Kptlt Herbert Schultze (8 trips), KKpt Hans Rösing (2 trips) and Kptlt Heinrich Bleichrodt (2 trips) she managed to sink one sloop and fifty-four merchant ships for a total of 322,292grt and damaged another two ships for 11,024grt. She had the most success of any submarine of the war.
	The commander of the Russian Naval Base (Capt 1st Class M. S. Klevenski) at Libau, Latvia, coordinated its

Germany Sends Russia to the Allies

	defence with the Russian 67th Infantry Division (Major General Dedaev). There were fifteen submarines of the 1st Submarine Brigade (Capt 1st Class Egipko), one destroyer, six torpedo boats, twelve patrol boats, and one minesweeper in the harbour.
	Russian submarines KALEV, LEMBIT, M-77, M-78, S-7, S-8, and S-9 escorted transport ship ZHELEZNODOROZHNIK (2029grt), patrol boat MO-218 plus eight steamers from Libau to Ventspils, Latvia.
	During the night, Russian minesweeper T-204/FUGAS (Lt Gillerman) laid several minefields around Libau.
	Russian submarine S-4 was ordered to patrol off Memel. S-5 and S-6 patrolled off the Pomeranian coast. S-10 patrolled in Danzig Bay. S-7 and S-101 patrolled off Gotland. SHCH-305, SHCH-306, SHCH-309, SHCH-310, and SHCH-311 patrolled east of Gotland. SHCH-322, SHCH-323 and SHCH-324 patrolled along the Finnish coast. M-94, M-96, M-99, and M-102 patrolled off Utö, Finland. Submarines KALEV and LEMBIT were ordered to stop their mining operations and to begin offensive patrols against German ships.
	The Russian 1st Submarine Brigade (Capt 1st Class Egipko) laid a defensive minefield off Libau with submarines M-79, M-81, and M-83.
	Russian submarine L-3 (Capt 3rd Class Grishchenko) departed Libau to lay mines off Memel.
	German authorities seized the following Russian ships in German ports: Estonian steamer **HILDUR** (1856grt) at Stettin renamed RIMAGE (1856grt). Latvian steamer **AUSEKLIS** (1309grt) renamed CORTELSBURG (1309grt). Russian steamer **DNESTR** (3580grt) renamed PERNAU (3580grt). Russian steamer **ELTON** (1799grt) renamed INSTERBURG (1799grt). Russian steamer **KAGANOVITCH** (3663grt) renamed LIBAU (3663grt). Russian steamer **KHASAN** (3979grt) renamed PALATIA (3979grt). Russian steamer **MAGNITOGORSK** (3566grt) renamed TROSTBURG (3566grt). Latvian steamer **SPIDOLA** (2833grt) renamed RUDAU (2833grt). Russian steamer **TALLINN** (4479grt) renamed DITMAR KOEL (4479grt). Russian steamer **VOLGOLES** (3946grt) renamed CALMAR (3946grt). Russian steamer hopper **MAJA** was built at Hamburg for Russia, completing trials on the 19th.
0300	German S.59 (ObltzS Albert Müller) and S.60 (ObltzS Wuppermann) from the German 3rd S-Boat Flotilla sank Latvian steamer **GAISMA** (3077grt) off Ventspils in 57, 00N, 18, 48E.
0300	German S.31 (ObltzS Haag) from the German 3rd S-Boat Flotilla sank the Russian fishing steamer **SHUKA** (316grt) off Ventspils in 57, 00N, 18, 48E.
1822	A Russian patrol group (Capt 2nd Class I. G. Svyatov) departed Dvinsk, Russia, with cruiser MAKSIM GORKI plus destroyers GORDY, GNEVNY and STEREGUSHCHI to guard the Gulf of Finland entrance while the area was being mined.

23 JUNE 1941

	The German 3rd S-Boat Flotilla (KptIt Kemnade) laid eighteen TMB mines in the Irben Strait.
	Russian submarine S-3 (Lt Cdr Kostromichev) transferred the crew of Russian submarine S-1 aboard at Libau and departed for Ventspils.
	A mine from German Minefield APOLDA damaged Russian destroyer GORDY when struck by the destroyer's paravanes in the Irben Strait.
	A mine from German Minefield APOLDA heavily damaged Russian cruiser MAKSIM GORKI (Capt 2nd Class Petrov) in the Irben Strait. Her bow was blown off to frame 60. Russian destroyer STEREGUSHCHI detonated two mines using her paravanes and then towed the damaged cruiser to Worms, Germany. The cruiser was later towed to Tallinn, Estonia, for repairs.
0336 0645	German aircraft attacked Russian submarine M-78 off Uzava. U.144 (ObltzS v. Mittelstaedt) sank Russian submarine **M-78** (206grt) (Lt D. L. Shevchenko) with two torpedoes east of Ventspils, Latvia, in 57, 28N, 21, 17E. The entire crew of fifteen was lost. The commander of the Russian 4th Submarine-Division, Lt Cdr S. I. Matveev, was lost with the submarine. **M-78** was the first successful attack by a U-boat against a Russian submarine in the Baltic Sea.
0340	A mine from German Minefield APOLDA sank Russian destroyer **GNEVNY** (Capt 2nd Class Ustinov) in the Irben Strait.

24 JUNE 1941

	German S.35 (LtzS Weber) and S.60 (ObltzS Wuppermann) sank Russian submarine **S-3** (850grt) (Lt Cdr Kostromichev) off Stienort. The entire crew, along with the crew from Russian submarine S-1, was lost.
	The German 5th S-Boat Flotilla laid thirty-six TMB mines off Cape Tachkona, Estonia.
	German S.60 and S.27 encountered a Russian patrol group with twelve patrol boats and an auxiliary ship off Libau, Latvia. Neither side caused any damage in the short engagement.

	With the defence of Libau crumbling around him, the Russian commander ordered all vessels scuttled in the harbour. Submarines **S-1** (Capt 3rd Class Morskoi), **M-71** (Lt Cdr Kostylev), **M-80** (Lt Cdr Mochalov), **RONIS** (ex-Latvian) (Lt Cdr Madisson), and **SPIDOLA** (ex-Latvian) (Lt Boitsov) plus icebreaker **SILACH** (541grt) and auxiliary gunboat **TUNGUSKA** (947grt) were scuttled at Libau.
	Russian torpedo boat **TKA-27** went missing trying to break out of Libau harbour and was presumed sunk.
	The Russian 2nd Destroyer Flotilla laid mines in the Irben Strait with destroyers SERDITY, STOIKI and STOROZHEVOI. Cruiser KIROV (Rear Adm V. P. Drozd) supported the mining efforts with destroyers SILNY, STRASHNY, GROZYASHCHI and SMETLIVY and additional minelayers. Over the next two nights, over five hundred additional mines were laid in the Irben Strait.

25 JUNE 1941

	Russian small submarines M-102 and M-94 patrolled off the southern Finnish coast.
	Russian submarines SHCH-305 and SHCH-306 patrolled in the middle of the Baltic Sea.
	Russian submarine S-7 narrowly escaped an attack by the German 3rd S-Boat Flotilla in the Irben Strait.
	German minelayer BRUMMER escorted by the 5th S-Boat Flotilla and the 2nd S-Boat Flotilla laid Minefield D2 in the Moon Sound with 100 EMC and 50 floating mines.
	Russian submarine S-4 unsuccessfully attacked a German steamer or patrol boat in the Baltic.
	The German 1st S-Boat Flotilla captured Estonian steamer **ESTONIA** (1181grt) off Ventspils.

26 JUNE 1941

	While returning from covering the mining group west of the Irben Strait in the early morning, German S.34 (LtzS Lüders) or S.61 (ObltzS v. Gernet) of the 3rd S-Boat Flotilla sank Estonian steamer LIDAZA. S.54, S.60 and S.61 fired torpedoes into Ventspils harbour and obtained three hits on the Mole and one hit on another steamer.
	Russian minesweeper T-204/FUGAS (Lt Gillerman) laid several minefields off Libau, and then headed north. In all, she laid 207 mines off Libau.
	Russian minelayer MARTI (Capt 1st Class N. I. Meshcherski) laid additional mines in the entrance to the Gulf of Finland between Odensholm and Hangö.
	German minelayer BRUMMER escorted by the 2nd S-Boat Flotilla (S.43, S.106, S.42, S.105, S.44 and S.104) and the 5th S-Boat Flotilla (S.47, S.28, and S.46) laid mines between Minefield APOLDA and Minefield CORBETHA.
	U.149 sank Russian submarine M-101 or M-72 in 59, 20N, 21, 12E. Russian submarine M-72 was damaged and taken to Kronstadt, Kotlin Island. (It was unclear as to which submarine the German U-boat sank and which was lost to a mine.)
	Russian mines sank the German **S.43** and **S.106** of the 5th S-Boat Flotilla in the Moon Sound.

27 JUNE 1941

	Russian submarine L-3 (Capt 3rd Class Grishchenko) laid twenty mines off Memel.
	The crew of Russian submarine **M-83** (Lt Shalaev) scuttled the ship off Libau, Latvia. Other Russian submarines were re-routed to Ventspils.
	During the early morning hours, German S.59 (ObltzS Müller) and S.31 (LtzS Haag) sank Russian destroyer **STOROZHEVOI** (1686grt) (Capt 3rd Class Lomakin) in the Irben Strait in 57, 45N, 21, 30E.
	German S.59 and S.60 (ObltzS Wuppermann) sank Russian submarine **S-10** (850grt) in the Irben Strait.
	German S.35 (LtzS Weber) and S.60 sank Russian minesweeper **T-208/SHKIV** (441grt) in the Irben Strait.
	During the night, the Russians evacuated the naval base at Libau. MTBs TKA-37, TKA-57 and TKA-67 departed Libau for Ventspils, followed by TKA-17 (Lt Osipov with Cdr Capt Klevenski on board) and TKA-47.
	The German 3rd S-Boat Flotilla intercepted the fleeing Russians and, in a short engagement, S.35 captured Russian MTB **TKA-47** (16grt) off Backofen.
	German minelayer BRUMMER (KKpt Dr. Tobias) escorted by the 2nd S-Boat Flotilla with S.42, S.44, S.104, and S.105 plus the 5th S-Boat Flotilla with S.28, S.46, and S.47, laid Minefield D2 with one hundred EMC and fifty floating mines north of the Moon Sound.
	German motor minesweepers encountered the Russian minefields when they tried to enter the Irben Strait. A mine sank **R.205**, while other mines heavily damaged R.203 and auxiliary minesweeper M.201, with R.53, R.63 and R.202 damaged by mines in the Irben Strait.
0427	U.149 (Horst Höltring) sank Russian submarine **M-99** (206grt) (Ens B. M. Popov) with two torpedoes off Dago Island in 59, 20N, 21, 12E. There were no survivors from the crew of twenty.

28 JUNE 1941

	The crew scuttled Russian destroyer **LENIN** trapped at Libau, Latvia.

Gulf of Bothnia
Long. E16, 00 – E26, 00   Lat. N66, 00 – N60, 00

26 JUNE 1941

	Finnish submarines VESIHIISI and IKU-TURSO laid two new minefields—one with twenty mines south of Stenskär and one with eighteen mines south of Suur Tytärsaari.

Gulf of Finland
Long. E22, 00 – E30, 00   Lat. N61, 00 – N57, 00

13 JUNE 1941

	The Russian Navy began to transfer submarines from the Baltic Fleet to the White Sea using the White Sea Canal. K-23 departed on 13 June and arrived on 30 September. K-21 departed on 15 July and arrived on 24 October. S-101, S-102, L-20 and L-22 departed on 5 August and arrived on 8 September. K-22 departed on 22 August and arrived on 30 October. K-3 departed on 23 August and arrived on 8 November.

19 JUNE 1941

	Russian submarine S-7 departed Tallinn, Estonia, for the Irben Strait.

21 JUNE 1941

	Finnish submarines laid mines near Manni and Jussaro.
	The German 2nd Minelaying Group (FKpt. von Schönermark) with TANNENBERG, BRUMMER and HANSESTADT DANZIG escorted by four MTBs of the 2nd S-Boat Flotilla and five ships of the 5th R-Boat Flotilla laid Minefield APOLDA between Dago and the Fanofjord with five hundred EMC and seven hundred floating mines. Two Russian aircraft attacked the group, but did no damage and did not stop the mining.
	While returning from laying Minefield APOLDA, the German 2nd S-Boat Flotilla (KKpt Petersen) laid twelve TMB mines each in the Soelo Strait and the Moon Strait called Minefield COBURG and Minefield GOTHA.

22 JUNE 1941

	The German 2nd S-Boat Flotilla (KKpt Petersen) spotted and sank Estonian steamer **LIISA** (782grt) south of Hangö with gunfire.
	German S.44 (ObltzS Opdenhoff) from the 2nd S-Boat Flotilla sank Russian patrol boat **MO-238** off Hangö.
	German Ju88 aircraft of KGR.806 laid twenty-seven aerial mines in the harbour at Kronstadt.
	A German aerial mine sank Estonian steamer **RUHNO** (499grt) at Kronstadt.
	A German aerial mine sank Russian steamer **LUGA** (2329grt) at Kronstadt.
	Finnish submarines IKU-TURSO (Kptlt Pekkanen) and VETEHINEN (Kptlt Pakkala) laid twenty mines each east of Ekholm (Minefield F4) and Kunda Bay (Minefield F5).
1822	A Russian mining group (Rear Adm D. D. Vdovichenko) departed Tallinn, Estonia, with minelayers MARTI (Capt 1st Class Meshcherski) and URAL escorted by destroyer leaders MINSK and LENINGRAD plus destroyers KARL MARKS, ARTEM and VOLODARSKI to lay a minefield between Hangö and Osmussari. Destroyer SMELY, three BT-class minesweepers including T-204/FUGAS, and several submarine chasers (MO-class) covered the mining group. In all, the Russians laid 207 mines off Libau.

23 JUNE 1941

	Finnish submarine VETEHINEN (Kptlt Pakkala) laid twenty mines north of Ekholm, in Minefield F3.
	Six Russian submarines of the 2nd Submarine Brigade (Capt 2nd Class Orel) departed Tallinn, Estonia, to patrol in the Baltic. Submarines S-6 and S-10 headed for the Pomeranian coast and Danzig Bay. SHCH-309, SHCH-310 and SHCH-311 patrolled the entrance to the Gulf of Finland. M-90 patrolled off Helsinki, Finland.

24 JUNE 1941

	Finnish submarines IKU-TURSO (Kptlt Pekkanen) and VETEHINEN (Kptlt Pakkala) laid eighteen and twenty mines respectively east and southeast of Rodskar to increase Minefield F3, Minefield F4 and Minefield F5.
	U.140 unsuccessfully attacked a large Russian submarine in the Gulf of Finland.
	Russian submarine M-90 unsuccessfully attacked either a German steamer or a German patrol boat off Helsinki, Finland.

26 JUNE 1941

	Finnish minelayers RIILAHTI and RUOTSINSALMI laid Minefield KIPINOLA with two hundred mines.

27 JUNE 1941

	Finnish minelayers RIILAHTI and RUOTSINSALMI laid Minefield KULEMAJARVI with two hundred mines northeast of Kulemajarvi.
	Russian submarines S-5, S-8, S-101, and S-102 operated out of Riga, Latvia.
	Russian submarines SHCH-309, SHCH-310, SHCH-311, M-89, M-90, M-95, M-97, and M-98 operated out of Tallinn, Estonia.

28 JUNE 1941

	Finnish submarine VETEHINEN laid Minefield F6 between Suursaari and Tytärsaari islands.

29 JUNE 1941

	Finnish minelayers RIILAHTI and RUOTSINSALMI laid Minefield VALKJARVI with two hundred mines north of Cape Purikari.
	German bombers sank Estonian steamer **MARTA** (1414grt) in Saaremaa harbour on Ösel Island.

30 JUNE 1941

	Russian cruiser KIROV departed Riga, Latvia, escorted by destroyers GROZYASHCHI, SMETLIVY and STOIKI to pass through Moon Sound to Tallinn, Estonia.
	German mines damaged Russian submarines M-79 and M-77 when they departed Ventspils for Reval.

MEDITERRANEAN SEA & MIDDLE EAST

East of Gibraltar
Long. W05, 30 – E11, 00   Lat. N44, 30 – N35, 00

1 JUNE 1941

	Submarine CLYDE (Cdr Ingram) sank Italian steamer **SAN MARCO** (3076grt) five miles 90° from Cap Carbonara, southeast of Sardinia. The submarine made a second unsuccessful torpedo attack on another steamer on this date.

5 JUNE 1941

	In Operation ROCKET, battle cruiser RENOWN, aircraft carriers ARK ROYAL and FURIOUS, and six destroyers departed Gibraltar to launch forty-three Hurricane aircraft to Malta on 6 June. Group 1 included battle cruiser RENOWN, aircraft carrier FURIOUS, with destroyers FAULKNOR, FORESIGHT, FORESTER, and FOXHOUND. Group 2 included aircraft carrier ARK ROYAL, light cruiser SHEFFIELD, with destroyers FEARLESS and FURY. Force H safely returned to Gibraltar on the 7th after launching the aircraft to Malta.
	Italian submarines COLONNA and PROCIDA patrolled off Genoa, Italy, in case Force H was going to bombard the harbour again.
	Italian submarines BANDIERA, MANARA, and DIASPRO patrolled west of the Sicilian Strait in case Force H was escorting supply ships to Malta.

7 JUNE 1941

	Submarine REGENT departed Gibraltar for Malta.
	Dutch submarine O.24 departed Gibraltar to patrol in the Gulf of Genoa.

8 JUNE 1941

	Vichy French aircraft attacked Force H east of Gibraltar in retaliation for the British and Free French landings at Syria.

9 JUNE 1941

	An Italian mine sank Spanish steamer **SABINA** (2421grt) forty miles from Genoa. The entire crew was rescued.

13 JUNE 1941

	In Operation TRACER, Force H departed Gibraltar with battle cruiser RENOWN, aircraft carriers ARK ROYAL and VICTORIOUS, plus destroyers FAULKNOR, FEARLESS, FORESIGHT, FORESTER, FOXHOUND, HESPERUS, and WISHART to launch forty-seven Hurricane aircraft to Malta on the 14th. Force H arrived back at Gibraltar on the 15th.

14 JUNE 1941

	Force H launched forty-seven Hurricane aircraft led by four Hudson aircraft from Gibraltar, from a point south of the Balearic Islands for Malta. Forty-three aircraft made it to Malta.
	Italian submarines CORALLO and SANTAROSA patrolled south of Sardinia, but did not sight any Force H ships.
	Submarine SEVERN departed Gibraltar for a patrol in the Tyrrhenian Sea.

16 JUNE 1941

	Submarine CLYDE arrived at Gibraltar from her patrol in the western Mediterranean. She arrived with seven Italian prisoners from sunken Italian steamers **STURLA** (1195grt) and **GIOVANNI BOTTIGLIERE** (331grt).

17 JUNE 1941

	Dutch submarine O.24 unsuccessfully attacked a tanker off La Spezia.

22 JUNE 1941

	Dutch submarine O.23 claimed she sank a ship of 5371grt in the western Mediterranean. There was no confirmation for this claim.
	Submarine THRASHER departed Gibraltar with supplies for Malta.

23 JUNE 1941

	Dutch submarine O.24 arrived at Gibraltar from her patrol in the western Mediterranean.

25 JUNE 1941

	Submarine OSIRIS departed Gibraltar with seventy tons of petrol for Malta.
	Dutch submarine O.23 departed Gibraltar for a patrol in the Gulf of Genoa.

26 JUNE 1941

	Force H departed Gibraltar with battle cruiser RENOWN, aircraft carrier ARK ROYAL, light cruiser HERMIONE, plus destroyers FAULKNOR, FORESTER, FURY, FEARLESS, and FOXHOUND. Destroyers LANCE and LEGION were relieved by destroyers FEARLESS and FOXHOUND before the operation. On the 27th, aircraft carrier ARK ROYAL launched twenty-two Hurricane aircraft from a position south of the Balearic Islands to Malta led by Blenheim bomber aircraft from Gibraltar in Operation RAILWAY. Force H arrived back at Gibraltar on the 28th.

27 JUNE 1941

	Submarine OSIRIS unsuccessfully attacked a steamer in the Tyrrhenian Sea.

28 JUNE 1941

	Submarine P.33 departed Gibraltar for Malta.
	Submarine SEVERN (Lt Cdr Campbell) sank Italian steamer **UGO BASSI** (2900grt) five miles 24° from Capo Monte Santi in the Gulf of Orosei, Sardinia.
1800	For Operation RAILWAY 2, aircraft carrier FURIOUS and light cruiser HERMIONE, departed Gibraltar with destroyers FEARLESS, FOXHOUND, LANCE, and LEGION to conduct a feint movement to the west, as Force A. Destroyer LANCE was later transferred to the battle cruiser RENOWN group.

29 JUNE 1941

0130	Force B departed Gibraltar with battle cruiser RENOWN and aircraft carrier ARK ROYAL plus destroyers FAULKNOR, FURY, FORESTER, WISHART, and AVON VALE. Destroyers WISHART and AVON VALE were detached from Force B after providing local escort. Force A and Force B made up the Operation RAILWAY 2 and proceeded to Malta in company. ARK ROYAL launched twenty-six Hurricane aircraft to Malta on 30 June. Aircraft carrier FURIOUS launched eight Hurricane aircraft off to Malta. The operation suffered a mishap when one of the aircraft crashed into the bridge structure on FURIOUS and started a fire on the flight deck. Two officers and one rating were killed. One other officer and two ratings died of injuries on the 30th. Two officers and four ratings later died of wounds. Ten ratings were seriously injured. From FURIOUS, A/Sub-Lt (A) O. M. Wightman of 807 Squadron and A/Sub-Lt (A) J. G. Biddle, P/T/Sub-Lt (A) A. F. Hallett RNVR, and Sub-Lt (A) C. D. Livingstone of 816 Squadron and one rating were killed. Surgeon Lt D. A. Prothero, MRCS, LRCP, DA, and Sub-Lt (A) F. W. Follows of 816 Squadron died of wounds on 1 July. Four RAF officers and four ratings, one of which died of wounds, were injured. The mishap prevented the last six aircraft from being launched to Malta. The force returned to Gibraltar on 1 July.

30 JUNE 1941

	Dutch submarine O.23 (Lt Cdr v. Erkel) unsuccessfully attacked an Italian freighter in the Ligurian Sea.
	Dutch submarine O.23 sank Italian steamer **CAPACITAS** (5371grt) south of Livorno, seven miles off San Vincenzo, Italy, in 43, 06N, 10, 26E.

Middle Mediterranean Sea
Long. E11, 00 – E20, 00   Lat. N46, 00 – N30, 00

1 JUNE 1941

	An Italian return convoy departed Tripoli, Libya, with steamers ARSIA (736grt), COSTANZA (582grt) and tug COSTANTE NERI (100grt) escorted by gunboat GRAZIOLI LANTE for Trapani, Sicily.

2 JUNE 1941

	Submarine CLYDE made an unsuccessful torpedo attack on a small steamer off Terranova, in the Tyrrhenian Sea.

3 JUNE 1941

	An Italian supply convoy departed Naples, Italy, with troop transport AQUITANIA (4971grt), steamers NIRVO (5164grt), MONTELLO (6117grt), CAFFARO (6476grt), BEATRICE COSTA (6132grt) and tanker POZARICA (7599grt) escorted by Italian destroyers AVIERE, GENIERE, DARDO and CAMICIA NERA for Tripoli, Libya. Italian light cruisers DUCA DEGLI ABRUZZI and GARIBALDI with destroyers GRANATIERE, FUCILIERE, BERSAGLIERE, and ALPINO provided heavy cover for the convoy.
	An Italian return convoy departed Tripoli with the steamers ANDREA GRITTI (6338grt), SEBASTINO VENIER (6311grt), RIALTO (6099grt) and the German steamer ANKARA (4768grt) with escort by Italian destroyer VIVALDI and NOLI with torpedo boat CASTORE to Naples.
	The Italian 7th Cruiser Squadron of light cruisers EUGENIO DI SAVOIA, DUCA D'AOSTA, and ATTENDOLO plus the 4th Cruiser Squadron of light cruisers BANDE NERE and DI GUISSANO with destroyers PIGAFETTA, DA MOSTO, DA VERAZZANO, DA RECCO, USODIMARE, GIOBERTI, and SCIROCCO laid two minefields northeast of Tripoli.
	Submarine UNIQUE (Lt Collett) damaged Italian steamer **ARSIA** (736grt) off Lampedusa. **ARSIA** was salvaged, but declared a total loss.
	A mine sank Italian trawler **SANT ANTONIO** (736grt) north of Tripoli.

4 JUNE 1941

	An Italian supply convoy [see 3 June] was attacked twenty miles northeast of Kerkennah by British Martin Maryland aircraft. Steamers **BEATRICE COSTA** (6132grt) and **MONTELLO** (6117grt) were sunk.

5 JUNE 1941

	Submarine TRIUMPH sank small Italian gunboat **VALOROSO** (340grt) and Italian steamers **FRIEDA** (245grt) and **TRIO FRASSINETTI** (244grt) with gunfire off Buerat, Libya, in 31, 39N, 15, 39E. (Some sources credit submarine TAKU with sinking these ships, but she was not in the area at the time.)

8 JUNE 1941

	Submarine CLYDE (Cdr Ingram) unsuccessfully attacked an Italian destroyer off Naples.
	That evening, the CLYDE sank Italian steamer **STURLA** (1195grt) (ex **ASTRID** (1195grt)) with gunfire, five miles off Policastro in the Tyrrhenian Sea.

9 JUNE 1941

	Submarine URGE unsuccessfully attacked an Italian steamer northwest of Lampedusa, Pelagie Islands.
	An Italian supply convoy departed Tripoli with steamers SILVIO SCARONI (1367grt), CADAMOSTO (1010grt), and AOSTO (494grt) for Benghazi, Libya, escorted by Italian torpedo boats PALLADE and POLLUCE.

10 JUNE 1941

	An Italian supply convoy departed Naples with steamers AMSTERDAM (8673grt), GIULIA (5921grt), ERNESTO (7272grt), TEMBIEN (5584grt), COL DI LANA (5891grt) and the German steamer WACHTFELS (8467grt) escorted by Italian destroyer MALOCELLO plus torpedo boats PROCIONE, PEGASO, CLIO and ORSA for Tripoli.
	Submarine TAKU (Lt Nicolay) sank Italian steamer **SILVIO SCARONI** (1367grt) about 70 miles 283° from Benghazi in 32, 27N, 18, 42E. The Italian torpedo boats PALLADE and POLLUCE counterattacked TAKU with depth charges, while the Italian convoy arrived at Benghazi later in the day.

11 JUNE 1941

	Submarine RORQUAL arrived at Malta with supplies from Alexandria.
	Submarine TAKU (Lt Nicolay) sank German steamer **TILLY L. M. RUSS** (1600grt) in Benghazi Harbour. The steamer exploded and started fires aboard Italian sailing vessels **GIORGINA** (253grt), **NADIA** (247grt) and **CAROLINA** (227grt), which sank them in the harbour.
	A British Fulmar aircraft of 800X Squadron ditched off Delimara Point, Malta, while returning from a patrol over Sicily. Petty Officer A. W. Sabey and Lt J. S. Manning were rescued after dawn.

12 JUNE 1941

	Dutch submarine O.24 (Lt Cdr de Booy) sank Italian tanker **FIANONA** (6660grt) south of Vada, Italy, [in the Ligurian Sea in 43, 08N, 10, 30E.

13 JUNE 1941

	Dutch submarine O.24 (Lt Cdr de Booy) sank Italian auxiliary patrol trawler **V.121/CARLOFORTE** (143grt) with a demolition charge thirty-six miles 294° from Gorgara, Italy.
0220	Two Italian MTBs attacked antisubmarine trawler JADE seventeen miles 192° from Cape Passaro while she was searching for a downed Hurricane aircraft pilot. The trawler was able to drive off the two Italian craft without sustaining any damage, but Midshipman J. C. Creasy RNR, was killed by machine gun fire.

14 JUNE 1941

	Submarine CLYDE (Cdr Ingram) sank Italian patrol ship **V.125/GIOVANNI BOTTIGLIERE** (former **GUGLIELMO** (331grt)) twenty miles south of Cape Spartivento.
	Submarines URGE, UTMOST, UPRIGHT, URSULA, UNBEATEN and UPHOLDER sank no ships while on patrol from 1 June to 14 June.

16 JUNE 1941

	Submarine UNBEATEN unsuccessfully attacked a large, zigzagging liner south of the Messina Strait.

19 JUNE 1941

	An Italian supply convoy departed Naples for Tripoli with German steamer PREUSSEN (8230grt) plus Italian steamers MOTIA (2473grt), BAINSIZZA (7933grt), MADDALENA ODERO (5479grt) and NICOLO ODERO (6003grt) escorted by Italian destroyers FOLGORE, EURO, SAETTA and FULMINE. There were several British air attacks on the convoy, but it arrived intact on the 22nd.

20 JUNE 1941

	Italian steamer **BUCCARI** (4543grt) was lost in an explosion at Taranto. An investigation failed to identify the cause of the explosion, but a mine was highly suspected.
	Submarine SEVERN unsuccessfully attacked a steamer off Palermo.

21 JUNE 1941

	An Italian return convoy departed Tripoli with German steamers WACHTFELS (8467grt) and TEMBIEN (5584grt) plus Italian steamers AMSTERDAM (8673grt), GIULIA (5921grt), ERNESTO (7272grt) and COL DI LANA (5891grt) escorted by Italian destroyer MALOCELLO plus torpedo boats PROCIONE, PEGASO, CLIO, ORSA, and COSENZ for Trapani and Naples. Italian destroyers MAESTRALE, GRECALE and USODIMARE joined the group after attacks from Malta-based British aircraft.

22 JUNE 1941

	Submarine UNION (Lt Galloway) sank Italian steamer **PIETRO QUERINI** (1004grt) south of Pantelleria in 36, 11N, 12E.
	Allied Mediterranean submarines were reorganised as follows: 1st Submarine Flotilla based at Alexandria: TRUANT, TRIUMPH, TAKU, TETRARCH, TORBAY, REGENT, ROVER, OTUS, OSIRIS, RORQUAL, CACHALOT, PARTHIAN, PERSEUS, PANDORA, plus the Greek submarines KATSONIS, PAPANICOLIS, NEREUS, TRITON and GLAVKOS. 2nd Submarine Flotilla based at Gibraltar: CLYDE, SEVERN plus the Dutch submarines O.21, O.23, and O.24 with additional boats en route. 10th Submarine Flotilla based at Malta: URSULA, UTMOST, UPRIGHT, UNIQUE, UPHOLDER, UNBEATEN, URGE, UNION, P.32 and P.33.
	Submarine SEVERN unsuccessfully attacked an Italian submarine in 40, 44N, 14, 20E.

23 JUNE 1941

	Submarine UTMOST (Lt Cdr Cayley) dropped a sabotage group in the Gulf of Eufemia to damage the railroad

25 JUNE 1941

An Italian supply convoy departed Naples with troopships ESPERIA (11,398grt), MARCO POLO (12,272grt), OCEANIA (19,507grt), and NEPTUNIA (798grt) for Tripoli, but calling at Taranto on the 27th.
The convoy was escorted by destroyers AVIERE, GENIERE, GIOBERTI, and DA NOLI and was given cover by heavy cruisers TRIESTE and GORIZIA plus destroyers CORAZZIERE and CARABINIERE.
While attacking the Italian convoy, Sub-Lt (A) D. A. R. Holmes and Leading Airman J. R. Smith were lost when their Swordfish aircraft of the 830 Squadron hit the side of the ship being attacked.
Italian troopship ESPERIA received light damage from the air attacks.
Destroyer ASCARI arrived at Messina on the 29th. The convoy arrived at Tripoli on the 29th.

Italian destroyer ASCARI departed Messina to join the Italian convoy covering force.

Submarine URGE, already on patrol off Messina, plus submarines UNBEATEN and UPHOLDER at Malta, were ordered to intercept the Italian supply convoy.

26 JUNE 1941

Submarine SEVERN (Lt Cdr Campbell) sank Italian steamer **POLINNIA** (1292grt) southeast of Ischia Island in 40, 05N, 12, 08E.

Submarine UTMOST (Lt Cdr Cayley) sank Italian steamer **ENRICO COSTA** (4080grt) four miles from Cape Todaro in 38, 07N, 14, 37E.

27 JUNE 1941

Submarines UNBEATEN and UPHOLDER returned to Malta after failing to make contact with the Italian supply convoy.

28 JUNE 1941

The Italian 7th Cruiser Division (AmDiv Casardi) with light cruisers ATTENDOLO and DUCA D'AOSTA plus destroyers PIGAFETTA, PESSAGNO, DA MOSTO, DA VERAZZANO, and DA RECCO laid Minefield S.2 with 442 mines in the Sicilian Straits.

Submarine OSIRIS unsuccessfully attacked a steamer in the Tyrrhenian Sea.

Submarines UNIQUE, UPRIGHT, UNIQUE, and UPHOLDER departed Malta to intercept Vichy French warships expected to move east to support the fighting at Syria. All submarines except UPHOLDER arrived back at Malta without contact on 3 July. UPHOLDER arrived at Malta on 8 July.

29 JUNE 1941

	Submarine THRASHER arrived at Malta with supplies from Gibraltar.
0914	Submarine URGE unsuccessfully attacked an Italian heavy cruiser in 37, 55N, 15, 35E. Italian heavy cruiser BOLZANO was in the company of a second heavy cruiser and four destroyers. The submarine was heavily depth charged, but did not sustain any damage.
>0914	Submarine UTMOST unsuccessfully attacked the Italian heavy cruiser BOLZANO force later that day.

30 JUNE 1941

An Italian supply convoy departed Naples for Tripoli with steamers FRANCESCO BARBARO (6343grt), SEBASTINO VENIER (6311grt), ANDREA GRITTI (6338grt), RIALTO (6099grt), BARBARIGO (5293grt) and German steamer ANKARA (4768grt) escorted by Italian destroyers FRECCIA, STRALE, DARDO and TURBINE.

A mine sank sixty-year-old German steamer **JESUS ANTONIO** (988grt) off Imperia, Italy. She was one of the nine old ships purchased from Spain.

Eastern Mediterranean Sea
Long. E20, 00 – E38, 00   Lat. N43, 00 – N30, 00

1 JUNE 1941

MTB.215 arrived at Famagusta, Cypress, and MTB.68 arrived later in the day under tow.

Two German Ju88 aircraft of II/LG.1 sank antiaircraft cruiser **CALCUTTA** (4200grt) (Capt D. M. Lees) one hundred miles northwest of Alexandria in 31, 55N, 28, 05E.
Antiaircraft cruiser COVENTRY rescued 255 of the 372 man crew.

LCT.20 (372grt) and **LCT.6** (372grt) were lost in the Middle East.

Tugboat **IRENE VERNICOS** (250grt) was declared a constructive total loss.

Submarine TORBAY sank a caique carrying German troops and stores with gunfire in the Doro Channel.

Tanker PASS OF BALMAHA (758grt) departed Alexandria escorted by sloop AUCKLAND and trawler SOUTHERN MAID for Tobruk.

2 JUNE 1941

	Landing craft **LCT.16** (372grt) was declared lost at Crete.
	Naval whaler **KOS XXII** (353grt) (Lt H. D. Foxon RNR) was sunk while on passage from Crete to Alexandria.

3 JUNE 1941

	Submarine TORBAY sank a caique carrying oil drums with gunfire off Mitylene.
	Submarine PARTHIAN (Cdr Rimington) torpedoed Italian tanker **STROMBO** (5232grt) in Salamis Bay off Scaramanga in 39, 57N, 25, 38E. She was beached off the Dardanelles, a total loss.
	Troopship GLENGYLE (9919grt) departed Alexandria for Port Said escorted by two Greek destroyers to load equipment and landing craft for Operation EXPORTER, the invasion of Syria. Destroyers ILEX and HOTSPUR departed Alexandria for Famagusta, Cypress, to embark special service troops and transfer them to troopship GLENGYLE. The destroyers joined the troopship at Port Said on the 4th.
	Australian sloop PARRAMATTA arrived at Alexandria for duty with the Mediterranean Fleet, after duty in the Red Sea.
	A German air attack damaged antisubmarine trawler KLO (T/Skipper J. S. E. Ward RNR) while she was arriving at Mersa Matruh. Ward was killed. T/LT K. G. Pullman RNR died of wounds on 2 July.
	MTB.215 sank Turkish auxiliary schooner **IKI KARDESHLER** in 35, 56N, 32, 52E. The schooner was carrying petrol and was suspected of sailing under false orders.
2330	Tanker PASS OF BALMAHA (758grt) arrived at Tobruk from Alexandria escorted by New Zealand sloop AUCKLAND and trawler SOUTHERN MAID.

4 JUNE 1941

	During the night of 4/5 June, tanker PASS OF BALMAHA (758grt) departed Tobruk escorted by New Zealand sloop AUCKLAND for Alexandria after unloading.

5 JUNE 1941

	New Zealand light cruiser LEANDER arrived at Alexandria for duty with the 7th Cruiser Squadron.
	Submarine RORQUAL departed Alexandria with supplies for Malta.
	Antiaircraft cruiser COVENTRY departed Alexandria with destroyers ISIS and HERO to join troopship GLENGYLE (9919grt) at Port Said.
	Australian destroyers VOYAGER and VENDETTA departed Alexandria to deliver supplies to Tobruk during the night of 5/6 June. The destroyers unloaded and returned to Mersa Matruh.

6 JUNE 1941

	Landing ship GLENGYLE (9919grt) departed Port Said with destroyers ISIS and HOTSPUR for the attack on Syria.
	Submarine TORBAY damaged Vichy French tanker **ALBERTA** (3357grt) with artillery eight miles 75° from Cape Hellas. The tanker was boarded and further damage was done to the tanker. When Turkish tug TAXIARCHIS tried to tow the damaged tanker on the 9th, submarine TORBAY fired a torpedo, which missed. TORBAY finally sank tanker **ALBERTA** on the 10th.
	Destroyer HERO departed Port Said, Egypt for Haifa, Palestine to complete final arrangements with the Army for Operation EXPORTER.

7 JUNE 1941

	Force B departed Alexandria with light cruisers PHOEBE and AJAX plus destroyers KANDAHAR, KIMBERLEY, JACKAL, and JANUS to be off the Syrian coast at daylight on the 8th for Operation EXPORTER.
	Force C departed Port Said with troopship GLENGYLE (9919grt) escorted by antiaircraft cruiser COVENTRY plus destroyers ILEX, HOTSPUR, and ISIS to land troops at Syria on the 8th for Operation EXPORTER.

8 JUNE 1941

	Troopship GLENGYLE (9919grt) returned to Port Said with destroyers ILEX and HERO when the landing was cancelled due to heavy surf on the beach at Litani (Leontes) River. Orders were received to land the troops before dawn on the 9th. GLENGYLE departed Port Said with destroyers ILEX and HERO and the troops were landed as planned.
	Light cruisers PHOEBE and AJAX arrived off Syria with destroyers KANDAHAR, KIMBERLEY, JACKAL, and JANUS to support the Army landing at Syria.
	Destroyer KIMBERLEY engaged a French shore battery near Kahn Bridge, Syria and received shell damage.
	Two Fulmar aircraft of 803 Squadron from Dekheila were shot down. Lt J. M. Christian with Sub-Lt N. Cullen and Petty Officer J. A. Gardner with Leading Airman H. Pickering were lost.

	German Ju88 aircraft of I/LG.1 bombed Alexandria harbour from their new base on Crete. No damaged was recorded.
	Submarine PARTHIAN sank two schooners and a lighter in Mitylene Harbour with gunfire.
	Submarine TAKU (Lt Nicolay) landed a small sabotage group off Benghazi, Libya during the night of 8/9 June. They sank small Italian steamer **DRIN** (426grt) at Benghazi.
	Destroyer KELVIN and gunboat APHIS departed Alexandria for Port Said. APHIS for repairs at Port Said and KELVIN continued on to Bombay, India for repairs, arriving on the 19th.

9 JUNE 1941

	Light cruiser PHOEBE was attacked by Vichy French submarine CAIMAN off the Syrian coast, but was not damaged. At this point, Admiral King withdrew his cruisers to Haifa. Vichy French destroyers VALMY and GUÉPARD arrived from Beirut, Lebanon and bombarded the Australian troop positions in Syria. Destroyer JANUS, alone off Sidon, engaged the two Vichy French destroyers and was badly damaged by five shell hits. Destroyers HOTSPUR, ISIS, and JACKAL joined the battle and drove the Vichy French destroyers away from the landing area. Destroyers KIMBERLEY and KANDAHAR were bombarding the Khan Bridge and also joined destroyer JANUS off Sidon. JANUS was towed to Haifa by KIMBERLEY at a speed of 12 knots while ISIS, HOTSPUR, JACKAL pursued the Vichy French destroyers. JACKAL sustained slight damage from a shell hit. She had no time out of service. KANDAHAR covered the retirement of JANUS and recovered the pilots from a Vichy French fighter and a British Hurricane aircraft, which collided during the air attacks on JANUS. The Vichy French destroyers arrived back at Beirut. JANUS arrived at Haifa, Palestine on the 10th. She was towed from Haifa by netlayer PROTECTOR and escorted by sloop FLAMINGO on the 11th to Port Said, arriving on the 12th. PROTECTOR and FLAMINGO returned to Alexandria. JANUS was eventually taken to Simon's Town for repair through the end of 1941.
	Australian destroyer STUART departed Alexandria with destroyers JAGUAR, GRIFFIN, and DEFENDER to reinforce Force B off Syria.
	New Zealand light cruiser LEANDER departed Alexandria for Port Said to have her catapult removed and returned to Alexandria on the 10th.
	Troopship GLENEARN (8986grt) departed Alexandria towed by netlayer PROTECTOR and escorted by sloop FLAMINGO for Port Said. After arriving, PROTECTOR and FLAMINGO proceeded to Haifa to tow damaged destroyer JANUS back to Port Said.

10 JUNE 1941

	New Zealand light cruiser LEANDER and Australian destroyer STUART delivered supplies to the troops at Tyre, Syria.
	Submarine TORBAY unsuccessfully attacked an Italian six-ship convoy, including steamers UTILITAS (5342grt), ALBERTA (6131grt), and GIUSEPPINA GHIRARDI (3319grt), in the Dardanelle's. In a second attack, the submarine struck steamer UTILITAS with a torpedo which did not explode, but imbedded in her hull. In a third attack, submarine TORBAY sank Italian steamer **GIUSEPPINA GHIRARDI** (3319grt), which was straggling the convoy, fifteen miles off Cape Hellas.
	Submarine TORBAY sank Italian steamer **ALBERTA** (6131grt) in the Dardanelle's.
	The 15th Cruiser Squadron bombarded Vichy French shore positions in Lebanon.
	German Ju88 aircraft of I/LG.1 heavily damaged steamer DURENDA (7241grt) as she was approaching Port Said. Steamer RABY CASTLE (4996grt), travelling in company with DURENDA, was not damaged in the attack. The steamers were not escorted. DURENDA received temporary repairs at Port Said and permanent repairs at Bombay, India.
	Force B was in position off Syria with light cruisers PHOEBE and AJAX, antiaircraft cruiser COVENTRY, plus destroyers KANDAHAR, KIMBERLEY, JACKAL, ILEX, ISIS, HOTSPUR, and HERO. Destroyers STUART, JAGUAR, GRIFFIN, and DEFENDER acted as a separate antisubmarine force.

11 JUNE 1941

	Submarine TORBAY sank a caique carrying German troops and stores by ramming, fifteen miles south of Mitylene.
	Destroyer NUBIAN was sailed from Alexandria to Port Said escorted by New Zealand sloop AUCKLAND.
	Sub-Lt J. B. Musson RNVR was killed when his Buffalo aircraft of 805 Squadron flew into the ground at Dek-

	heila.

12 JUNE 1941

	Destroyer NUBIAN arrived at Port Said and was passed through the Suez Canal. New Zealand sloop AUCKLAND returned to Alexandria.
	A British torpedo aircraft damaged Vichy French tanker ADOUR (1105grt) off Syria. The tanker was able to proceed to Turkey where she was interned.
	Submarine TORBAY sank Italian schooner **GESUE E MARIA** (239grt) with gunfire off Skyros Island in 39, 10N, 25, 20E.
	New Zealand light cruiser LEANDER departed Alexandria with destroyers JERVIS and HASTY to relieve light cruiser AJAX plus destroyers STUART, KANDAHAR, JAGUAR, and HOTSPUR off Syria.
	Corvette HYACINTH arrived at Haifa, Palestine from Alexandria, Egypt.
	Submarine CACHALOT departed Alexandria with supplies for Malta.

13 JUNE 1941

	Minesweeper ABERDARE ran aground near Mersa Matruh, but was re-floated without serious damage to her hull.

14 JUNE 1941

	Destroyers JERVIS and GRIFFIN bombarded Sidon, Lebanon to ease the Vichy French opposition for the Australian troops ashore.
1620	Destroyer GRIFFIN sighted the two Vichy French destroyers off Beirut. When New Zealand light cruiser LEANDER closed to engage the destroyers, they retired into the harbour.

15 JUNE 1941

<1699	German and Vichy French bombers attacked light cruisers PHOEBE and the New Zealand LEANDER plus destroyers ILEX, HASTY, and ISIS off Syria. Destroyer JACKAL was struck by a bomb on the upper deck, which passed through the deck and into the sea. The bomb exploded in the sea causing superficial damage. The destroyer spent no time out of service.
1700	German Ju88 aircraft of II/LG.1 (Hptm. Kollewe) damaged destroyer ISIS with a bomb near miss off Sidon. The destroyer proceeded to Haifa, escorted by antiaircraft cruiser COVENTRY.
1900	Aircraft of the Vichy French 4th Naval Air Group heavily damaged destroyer ILEX off Sidon. She was taken to Haifa, towed part of the way by destroyer HASTY and finally under her own power at daylight on the 16th.

16 JUNE 1941

	Light cruiser NAIAD departed Alexandria with destroyers KINGSTON, HAVOCK, and JAGUAR to relieve light cruiser PHOEBE with destroyers GRIFFIN and DEFENDER off Syria.
0400	Six Swordfish aircraft of 815 Squadron sank Vichy French destroyer **CHEVALIER PAUL** near Latakia, fifty sea miles off Cypress in 35, 18N, 35, 18E as she attempted to carry supplies to Syria. One Swordfish was shot down and its crew of Lt M. G. W. Clifford and Sub-Lt P. Winter were taken prisoner. Vichy French destroyers VALMY and GUÉPARD rescued **CHEVALIER PAUL** survivors and also picked up the crew of the downed British aircraft. Six Vichy French sailors were lost and nine wounded.
>0401	Destroyers JERVIS and KIMBERLEY engaged Vichy French destroyers GUÉPARD and VALMY for a short time off the Syrian coast. Both Vichy French destroyers suffered some damage in the short gunfight.

17 JUNE 1941

	Vichy French destroyer leader VAUQUELIN reached Beirut, Lebanon with supplies, but was heavily damaged by British aircraft.
	Admiral King transferred his flag to light cruiser NAIAD from light cruiser PHOEBE off Syria. PHOEBE returned to Alexandria with destroyers GRIFFIN and DEFENDER arriving the next day.
	Minelayer ABDIEL departed Alexandria for Famagusta, Cypress with Fleet Air Arm torpedoes and a small quantity of stores.
	The flag of Rear Admiral Cruiser Squadron 7 was transferred from damaged light cruiser ORION to light cruiser AJAX at Alexandria.
	A Buffalo aircraft of 805 Squadron failed to return from a patrol over British ships northwest of Sidi Barrani. Lt K. L. Keith was taken prisoner, but died of wounds on the 26th.

18 JUNE 1941

	Vichy French destroyers VALMY and GUÉPARD briefly bombarded British troop positions in Syria.
	Australian sloop PARRAMATTA escorted tugboat ST ISSEY and antisubmarine whaler SOUTHERN SEA to

	Alexandria from Mersa Matruh.
	Troopship GLENROY (9809grt) arrived at Mersa Matruh, carrying five lighters, some stores, petrol, and military personnel, with netlayer PROTECTOR, which carried a full load of cased petrol. Both ships were unloaded during the day.

19 JUNE 1941

	Destroyers STUART, VENDETTA, WATERHEN, VOYAGER, VAMPIRE, DEFENDER, DECOY, and DAINTY with the sloops FLAMINGO, AUCKLAND, and PARRAMATTA continued to run supplies to Tobruk from Alexandria.

20 JUNE 1941

	Destroyers DECOY, HOTSPUR, and HAVOCK departed Alexandria for Haifa.
	Submarine PARTHIAN departed Alexandria to patrol off Syria to attack Vichy French warships.
	Submarine TETRARCH unsuccessfully attacked a steamer off Lemnos, Greece.
	Italian submarine ONDINA sank Turkish steamer REFAH (3805grt) forty miles south of Mersin, Turkey. Twenty-five crewmen and one hundred forty-two passengers were lost on the steamer.
1340	RAF aircraft sighted the Vichy French destroyer VAUQUELIN in 35, 56N, 29, 25E. However, the contact was lost and no attack was made.

21 JUNE 1941

	Destroyers HERO, KIMBERLEY, and JACKAL departed Haifa on relief for Alexandria.
	Minelayer LATONA arrived at Alexandria to join the Mediterranean Fleet. She had departed England on 16 May and travelled around Africa, via Cape Town to reach Alexandria.
	Corvette ERICA arrived at Alexandria to join the Mediterranean Fleet.
0840	Vichy French destroyer VAUQUELIN arrived at Beirut, Lebanon with supplies.
1400	Destroyer JACKAL intercepted Vichy French hospital ship CANADA (9684grt) in 34, 12N, 31, 05E. Force B supported the operation with light cruiser NAIAD plus destroyers DECOY, HOTSPUR, and HAVOCK. The hospital ship was taken to Haifa, escorted by destroyer JACKAL, for inspection and was released on the 22nd.

22 JUNE 1941

	British aircraft damaged Vichy French destroyer VAUQUELIN at Beirut, Lebanon.
	Tanker PASS OF BALMAHA (758grt) departed Alexandria escorted by sloops the New Zealand AUCKLAND and the Australian PARRAMATTA for Tobruk.
	Greek store ship ANTIKLIA (951grt) departed Alexandria for Tobruk, escorted by sloop FLAMINGO.

23 JUNE 1941

	Following temporary repairs at Alexandria, light cruiser ORION departed Alexandria for Port Said to have her catapult re-embarked. The cruiser departed Aden for Simon's Town on the 29th. At Simon's Town, her catapult was removed and installed on seaplane carrier ALBATROSS. The light cruiser went through the Panama Canal into the Pacific and departed Balboa, Canal Zone on 28 August. ORION arrived at Mare Island, San Francisco on 5 September and was under repair until 15 February 1942.
0148	Vichy French destroyer GUÉPARD was engaged by light cruisers NAIAD and the New Zealand LEANDER plus destroyers JAGUAR, KINGSTON, and NIZAM north of Beirut in 34, 05N, 35, 33E. British gunfire damaged GUÉPARD and one shell from the French destroyer struck LEANDER, but it did not explode. Destroyers JERVIS, HAVOCK, HOTSPUR, and DECOY were submarine hunting in the area and steamed to the battle area.
0315	German aircraft attacked Alexandria.
0510	German aircraft attacked Alexandria. Battleship WARSPITE was slightly damaged by a near miss of a heavy bomb. Two bulges were flooded.

24 JUNE 1941

	Thirty-one German Ju88 aircraft of LG.1 and four He111 aircraft of II/KG.26 attacked Alexandria harbour. The German bombing damaged battleship WARSPITE. The damage was too extensive to repair locally, so she steamed around Africa to the Panama Canal and was repaired in the Bremerton, Seattle shipyard.
	New Zealand light cruiser LEANDER shelled the Syrian coast north of Beirut with destroyers HASTY and JAGUAR at dawn.
	Minesweeper HARROW swept the Syrian coast off Sidon.
	Corvette PEONY departed Alexandria for Haifa.
	Corvette HYACINTH departed Alexandria for Famagusta.

>1200	Italian S.79 torpedo bombers attacked the Tobruk supply convoy east northeast of Tobruk. Hurricane fighter aircraft managed to fight off the attack and down two Italian aircraft. In the afternoon, twenty-four German Ju87 aircraft of II/STG.2 covered by Me109 fighter aircraft attacked and damaged tanker PASS OF BALMAHA (758grt) and her crew abandoned ship. (Other sources claim German Ju87 aircraft of I/STG.1 with Italian Ju87 aircraft of 239 Squadron were in the second attack.)
1530	German Ju87 aircraft of II/STG.2 sank New Zealand sloop **AUCKLAND** (1250grt) (Cdr M. S. Thomas DSO) off Tobruk in 32, 15N, 24,30E. LT (E) C. L. Meadley, thirty-two ratings and the NAAFI manager were killed. Three ratings died of wounds. Surgeon Lt C. J. Robarts and seven ratings were wounded. Australian sloop PARRAMATTA picked up the one hundred sixty-two survivors, including Cdr Thomas, Lt D. G. D. Hall-Wright, Lt A. P. Culmer, Lt J. F. House, Surgeon Lt C. J. Robarts, and T/A/Sub-Lt P. Whitehead RNVR and proceeded to Alexandria, arriving on the 25th. Australian destroyers VENDETTA and WATERHEN arrived to assist. They helped to pick up **AUCKLAND** survivors. Destroyer WATERHEN took the tanker PASS OF BALMAHA (758grt) in tow and proceeded to Tobruk, screened by destroyer VENDETTA. The tanker, with 750 tons of fuel, was unloaded on the 28th and escorted to Alexandria from Tobruk by sloop PARRAMATTA and antisubmarine whaler SOUTHERN MAID.
>1531	Due to heavy Axis air attacks on the tanker convoy, Greek store ship ANTIKLIA (951grt) and escort sloop FLAMINGO were ordered to remain at Mersa Matruh.

25 JUNE 1941

	New Zealand light cruiser LEANDER swept the area north of Beirut for shipping with destroyers DECOY, HAVOCK, and NIZAM during the night of 25/26 June.
	Destroyers HASTY and JAGUAR departed Haifa to return to Alexandria.
	Submarine RORQUAL departed Alexandria on a supply run to Malta.
1242	Submarine PARTHIAN (Cdr Rimington) sank Vichy French submarine **SOUFFLEUR** off Beirut, in 33, 49N, 35, 26E.
1530	Australian light cruiser PERTH and antiaircraft cruiser CARLISLE departed Alexandria to relieve cruisers LEANDER and COVENTRY off Syria. CARLISLE had been in the floating dock at Alexandria from 21 to 25 June. Light cruiser PERTH was only partially repaired from the Crete bombing damage. PERTH and CARLISLE relieved New Zealand light cruiser LEANDER and antiaircraft cruiser COVENTRY off Syria on the 26th. LEANDER and COVENTRY departed Haifa and joined the Mediterranean Fleet at sea. They returned to Alexandria on the 27th.

26 JUNE 1941

	At dawn, New Zealand light cruiser LEANDER bombarded the Damur area with destroyers DECOY, HAVOCK, and NIZAM.
	Battleships QUEEN ELIZABETH, WARSPITE, and VALIANT, light cruiser AJAX plus minelayer ABDIEL departed Alexandria with destroyers KANDAHAR, GRIFFIN, HERO, JAGUAR, DEFENDER, KIMBERLEY, and HASTY for gunnery and other exercises between Alexandria and Port Said. WARSPITE was detached that afternoon for Port Said, escorted by destroyers KANDAHAR, GRIFFIN, and KIMBERLEY. KIMBERLEY rejoined the Mediterranean Fleet. Light cruiser PHOEBE and minelayer LATONA joined the Mediterranean Fleet exercises later in the day.
2200	Battleship WARSPITE arrived at Port Said escorted by destroyers KANDAHAR, GRIFFIN, and KIMBERLEY. WARSPITE transited the Suez Canal and began the passage to the USA, via Colombo and Singapore. Destroyers KANDAHAR and GRIFFIN then proceeded to Haifa to patrol off Syria.

27 JUNE 1941

	Submarine TRIUMPH (Lt Cdr Become) sank Italian submarine **SALPA** off Mersa Matruh in 32, 05N, 26, 47E.
	Italian submarine JANTINA unsuccessfully attacked Australian sloop PARRAMATTA in 31, 34N, 27, 28E. The sloop counterattacked with depth charges and was joined by Australian destroyer STUART, but the submarine was not damaged.
	Light cruiser NAIAD bombarded Damur with destroyers KINGSTON, JERVIS, and HOTSPUR at dawn.
	Australian light cruiser PERTH carried out a T.S.D.S. sweep of Damur with destroyers KANDAHAR, GRIFFIN, HAVOCK, and JERVIS during the night of 27/28 June.

28 JUNE 1941

>1200	Australian light cruiser PERTH, antiaircraft cruiser CARLISLE bombarded Damur with destroyers JERVIS, DECOY, HAVOCK, HOTSPUR, and NIZAM during the afternoon.
1800	Destroyer ILEX was towed from Haifa by destroyer DECOY and escorted by antiaircraft cruiser CARLISLE plus destroyers HOTSPUR and NIZAM. On arrival at Port Said, NIZAM proceeded to Alexandria.

	CARLISLE returned to Haifa with destroyers HOTSPUR and DECOY. ILEX departed Port Said on 20 July after temporary repairs for Aden.

29 JUNE 1941

	Light cruiser NAIAD operated off Damur with two destroyers during the night of 29/30 June and carried out minor shore bombardments.
	Destroyer JERVIS was detached from operations off Syria to return to Alexandria.
	Greek steamers MIRANDA (279grt) and Greek ANTIKLIA (951grt) departed Mersa Matruh escorted by sloop FLAMINGO, trawler SOUTHERN ISLE, and gunboat CRICKET for Tobruk.
2005	Italian Ju87 aircraft of 239 Squadron heavily damaged Australian destroyer WATERHEN off Tobruk. As destroyer DEFENDER approached to tow the damaged destroyer, a submarine was sighted close ahead of the destroyer. Depth charge attacks forced Italian submarine TEMBIEN to leave, but no damage was done. DEFENDER tried to tow the damaged WATERHEN to port, but she sank early the next morning.

30 JUNE 1941

	Submarine TORBAY sank a caique with gunfire off Cape Malea.
	Greek cruiser GEORGIOS AVEROFF, destroyer PANTHER, torpedo boat SPHENDONI, submarine KATSONIS, and depot ship HIPHAISTOS departed Alexandria, escorted by Greek destroyers IERAX and AETOS, for the transit through the Suez Canal. These Greek ships were temporarily stationed at Suez.
	Destroyers DECOY and DEFENDER joined the group providing Tobruk with troop reinforcements and supplies.
0150	Damaged Australian destroyer **WATERHEN** (1100grt) capsized and sank while being towed in 32, 15N, 25, 20E. There were no casualties. Destroyer JACKAL departed Alexandria to assist the damaged destroyer, but when it was found she had been lost, she returned to Alexandria with destroyer DEFENDER.
1340	A large German bombing force of twenty-eight German and Italian dive-bombers attacked the convoy with Greek steamers MIRANDA (279grt) and Greek ANTIKLIA (951grt) escorted by sloop FLAMINGO, trawler SOUTHERN ISLE, and gunboat CRICKET for Tobruk. The German bombing damaged sloop FLAMINGO by a bomb near miss and heavily damaged gunboat CRICKET. She was towed back to Alexandria by sloop FLAMINGO and later by tugboat ST ISSEY. On 2 July, the gunboat arrived at Alexandria in the tow of tug ST ISSEY, escorted by FLAMINGO, and was judged to be a total loss.

Black Sea

Long. E27, 00 – E43, 00   Lat. N48, 00 – N41, 00

21 JUNE 1941

	The Romanian Navy (Rear Adm Bardescu) began deploying for war with Russia. The 1st Destroyer Flotilla (Kapitän Roman) included destroyers REGELE FERDINAND, REGINA MARIA, MARASESTI and MARASTI. The 2nd Section included Gunboats STIHI EUGEN, DUMITRESCU and GHIGULESCU. The 3rd Section included Torpedo boats NALUCA and SBORUL. The 4th Section included minelayers AMIRAL MURGESCU and DUROSTOR. The 5th Section included Submarine DELFINUL and MTBs VIJELIA, VISCOLUL and VIFORUL. The 6th Section included Auxiliary Cruisers, also used as mine layers, DACIA and REGELE CAROL I, plus the Danube-division with four river monitors and the Tulcea division with two river monitors.

22 JUNE 1941

	Russian cruisers KRASNY KAVKAZ and CHERVONA UKRAINA, destroyer Leader KHARKOV, destroyers BOIKI, BEZUPRECHNY, and BESPOSHCHADNY, minelayer OSTROVSKI and the training ship KOMINTERN laid mines off Sevastopol. When completed, the Sevastopol defence field included 3453 mines and 509 detection devices.
	Russian destroyer DZERZHINSKI laid mines off Batumi.
	Romanian Coastal Batteries at Reni in the Danube Estuary fired on Russian monitors ZHELEZNYAKOV, ZHEMCHUZHIN and ROSTOVTSEV.
	An II/KG.4 aerial mine sank Russian barge **DNEPR** off Sevastopol.
	An II/KG.4 aerial mine sank Russian **Floating Crane** off Sevastopol.
	An II/KG.4 aerial mine sank Russian tug **SP-12** off Sevastopol.
	An II/KG.4 aerial mine sank Russian destroyer **BYSTRY** off Sevastopol. She was later salvaged.
	The Russian 1st Submarine Brigade (Capt 1st Class P. I. Boltunov) sent submarines SHCH-205, SHCH-206, and SHCH-209 from Sevastopol to operate off Constanza, Mangalia and Varna.

23 JUNE 1941

	Russian destroyer SHAUMYAN and Minesweeper 27/T-413 laid seventy mines in the mouth of the Kilia river.
	Russian destroyer leader KHARKOV with destroyers SMYSHLENY and BESPOSHCHADNY plus torpedo boats ran a patrol to the mouth of the Danube near Fidonisi Island, but found no Axis ships there.

24 JUNE 1941

	The Russian Danube Flotilla (Rear Adm N. O. Abramov) with the Reni Group, monitors ROSTOVTSEV, ZHELEZNYAKOV and ZHEMCHUZHIN positioned themselves with four BKA-class armoured cutters to stop the Romanian monitors from advancing down the Danube through the Pruth estuary.
	From Ismailia, Russian monitors UDARNY and MARTYNOV plus twelve-BKA-class armoured cutters supported a limited landing by troops of the Russian 25th Rifle Division on the south bank of the Kilia river.

25 JUNE 1941

	A Russian bombardment group with destroyer leader KHARKOV (Capt 2nd Class M. F. Romanov) and MOSKVA departed Sevastopol covered by cruiser VOROSHILOV (Rear Adm T. A. Novikov) with destroyers SMYSHLENY and SOOBRAZITELNY to attack shipping and port facilities at Constanza, Romania.

26 JUNE 1941

	In the morning, Russian destroyer leaders KHARKOV and MOSKVA bombarded the oil tanks and harbour facilities at Constanza at the same time that aircraft of the Russian 63rd Naval Air Brigade attacked. Russian cruiser VOROSHILOV with destroyers SMYSHLENY and SOOBRAZITELNY covered the bombardment group. The burning oil tanks detonated an ammunition train at the port. The Romanian troops responded to the attack with 28-cm fire from the railway gun Tirpitz. Romanian destroyers REGINA MARIA and MARASTI were approaching the battle from the south. Russian submarine SHCH-206 (Lt Cdr Karakai), unaware of the bombardment mission, mistakenly torpedoed and sank Russian destroyer leader **MOSKVA** as the bombardment group retired, dodging Romanian shellfire. German bombing damaged destroyer leader KHARKOV with bomb near misses. While she was dead in the water, submarine SHCH-206 missed her with two torpedoes. SOOBRAZITELNY attacked the submarine with depth charges and sank Russian submarine **SHCH-206** off Constanza. Destroyers SMYSHLENY and SOOBRAZITELNY escorted destroyer leader KHARKOV from the area. Destroyer SOOBRAZITELNY set off a mine with her paravanes, which damaged cruiser VOROSHILOV off Constanza. Destroyers BESPOSHCHADNY and BODNY departed Sevastopol to join the cruiser and escort her back to port.
	Russian submarine SHCH-204 took up her patrol station in the southern Black Sea.
	Russian submarine SHCH-202 took up her patrol station off Novorossisk.
	Russian submarines A-4, M-33 and M-34 of the 2nd Submarine Brigade (Capt 1st Class M. G. Solovev) patrolled off Sevastopol. Submarines M-35, M-36, and M.31 relieved them at the end of the month. M-32 patrolled off the mouth of the Danube.

Red Sea
Long. E32, 00 – E43, 00   Lat. N30, 00 – N15, 00

2 JUNE 1941

	New Zealand light cruiser LEANDER arrived at Suez from Aden.

10 JUNE 1941

	In Operation CHRONOMETER, Indian troops were landed at Assab, Ethiopia from a transport covered by light cruiser DIDO, armed boarding vessel CHAKDINA, and Indian sloops CLIVE and INDUS. DIDO carried out a bombardment prior to the landing. On the 11th, DIDO departed Assab for Aden with sloops CLIVE and INDUS.

11 JUNE 1941

	Light cruiser DIDO departed Assab for Aden with Indian sloops CLIVE and INDUS.

26 JUNE 1941

	Troopship NIEUW AMSTERDAM (36,287grt) departed Suez with the King of Greece, members of the Royal Family, the Greek Prime Minister, other ministers and their families, British, Dutch, and Polish Ministers and families, 151 other passengers, five naval personnel, 1000 prisoners of war, and seventy-five escorts. Heavy cruiser CORNWALL joined the troopship on 3 July. They arrived at Durban, South Africa, on 7 July.

Arabian Sea
Long. E43, 00 – E77, 00   Lat. N31, 00 – N00, 00

1 JUNE 1941
	Light cruiser EMERALD departed Basra, Iraq, for Singapore.

11 JUNE 1941
	The crew scuttled Italian steamer **MONTE PIANA** (5890grt) when she was intercepted off Aden. She was later salvaged and became the EMPIRE BARON (5890grt).
	Convoy BA.3 departed Karachi, India (now Pakistan), escorted by AMC ANTENOR and arrived at Aden on the 20th.

INDIAN OCEAN

East of South Africa
Long. E25, 00 – E60, 00   Lat. S00, 00 – S60, 00

8 JUNE 1941
	Vichy French liner BOUGAINVILLE (7110grt) arrived at Diégo-Suarez.

27 JUNE 1941
	Light cruiser MAURITIUS arrived at Mombasa after escorting convoy CM.11 to Aden.
	Observer Sub-Lt (A) M. S. T. Broadwood of 700 Squadron, Petty Officer Airman H. D. Millington, Petty Officer Airman W. A. H. Peters, and Air Artificer 4/c T. G. Finan were killed in an air accident on heavy cruiser EXETER in Mozambique Channel, in 13, 38S, 42, 02E.

30 JUNE 1941
	Light cruiser DUNEDIN captured Vichy French steamer **VILLE DE TAMATAVE** (4993grt) east of St Paul.

South Indian Ocean
Long. E60, 00 – E95, 00   Lat. N00, 00 – S60, 00

6 JUNE 1941

	German AMC's SCHIFF.36/ORION and SCHIFF.45/KOMET experienced a shortage of targets in the Indian Ocean.
	    SCHIFF.36/ORION moved into the South Atlantic to supply SCHIFF.16/ATLANTIS with enough fuel to return to France and then took over her hunting zone.
	    SCHIFF.45/KOMET and SCHIFF.33/PINGUIN moved into the South Pacific towards Australia and New Zealand in hopes of finding better hunting.

Bay of Bengal
Long. E77, 00 – E95, 00   Lat. N22, 00 – N00, 00

20 JUNE 1941
	Light cruiser MAURITIUS relieved heavy cruiser SHROPSHIRE in the 4th Cruiser Squadron at Colombo, Ceylon.

24 JUNE 1941
	German AMC SCHIFF.41/KORMORAN, approached Madras, India, to lay mines, but encountered AMC CANTON. The German ship escaped undetected, but the mining was cancelled.

26 JUNE 1941
	German AMC SCHIFF.41/KORMORAN sank steamer **MAREEBA** (3472grt) in 08, 15N, 88, 06E. Twenty-six crewmen were lost and twenty-five were rescued and became prisoners of war.
	German AMC SCHIFF.41/KORMORAN sank Yugoslavian steamer **VELEBIT** (4153grt) in the Bay of Bengal. Six crewmen were rescued, of which two died. Twelve crewmen became prisoners of war. Seven crewmen were killed by the gunfire and seven crewmen were missing.

30 JUNE 1941
	Light cruiser ENTERPRISE departed Colombo, Ceylon, on a patrol.

Malaya

Long. E95, 00 – E105, 00   Lat. N17, 00 – N00, 00

3 JUNE 1941

Light cruiser DANAE departed Singapore.

9 JUNE 1941

Light cruiser DAUNTLESS completed her refit at Singapore.

14 JUNE 1941

A British mine damaged Swedish steamer NINGPO (6079grt) at Singapore when she picked up a floating mine in her screw. She was towed to Hong Kong for repairs.

15 JUNE 1941

Light cruiser DAUNTLESS departed Singapore for sea trials after her refit.

16 JUNE 1941

Light cruiser EMERALD collided with light cruiser DAUNTLESS near Malacca Light while she was arriving at Singapore from Basra, Iraq. Both ships were slightly damaged and repaired at Singapore.
DAUNTLESS had one rating killed.
EMERALD lost twelve ratings and one marine died of injuries. She was under repair until 2 August.

17 JUNE 1941

Light cruiser DAUNTLESS arrived at Singapore and was under repair until 13 August.

19 JUNE 1941

Steamer ELLENGA (5196grt) departed Singapore with forty-three personnel for Penang, Malaya.

21 JUNE 1941

Steamer ELLENGA (5196grt) arrived at Penang, Malaya, from Singapore and embarked eighty-three additional personnel. She then departed Penang escorted by light cruiser DURBAN to a position in 85E.

29 JUNE 1941

Light cruiser DANAE arrived at Penang, Malaya.
Light cruiser DAUNTLESS arrived at Singapore.

PACIFIC OCEAN

South China Sea

Long. E105, 00 – E120, 00   Lat. N27, 00 – N10, 00

1 JUNE 1941

IJN cargo ship MANKO MARU (4471grt) departed her position south of China for Sasebo, Kyushu.

10 JUNE 1941

Japanese cargo ship KENRYU MARU (4575grt) arrived at her support position south of China.
Japanese cargo ship KIMISHIMA MARU (5193grt) supported Japanese operations south of China.
Japanese cargo ship MYOKO MARU (5086grt) supported Japanese operations south of China.

11 JUNE 1941

Japanese cargo ship TATSUWA MARU (6335grt) departed her support position south of China for Takao, Formosa.

15 JUNE 1941

Japanese aircraft nearly missed American river patrol boat TUTUILA (PR-4) during an air attack at Chungking, China. The Japanese claimed the bombing was accidental and that the ship should not have been near the city, as it was a normal target for Japanese bombing. Observers at the scene claimed that the Japanese pilots deliberately targeted the American vessel during the air attack.

20 JUNE 1941

IJN oiler TOEN MARU (5232grt) departed Mako, Pescadores, to support operations in southern China.

25 JUNE 1941

Japanese cargo ship TATSUWA MARU (6335grt) supported Japanese operations south of China.

27 JUNE 1941

IJN oiler TOEN MARU (5232grt) arrived at Mako, Pescadores, after supporting operations in southern China.

29 JUNE 1941

Japanese cargo ship TOYO MARU (2470grt) departed her support position south of China.

Dutch East Indies
Long. E105, 00 – E120, 00   Lat. N10, 00 – S15, 00

1 JUNE 1941

Following rumours of a Japanese transport fleet escorted by warships in Chinese waters, Dutch ships were concentrated at the Gulf of Sukadana, Borneo.

4 JUNE 1941

Japanese liner ASAMA MARU (16,975grt) arrived at Batavia, Java, on her way to Kobe, Japan.

29 JUNE 1941

Japanese liner/AMC ASAMA MARU (16,975grt) departed Batavia, Java, with six hundred sixty-six German and Italian nationals detained in the Dutch East Indies since the invasion of the Netherlands by Axis forces. She was chartered by Germany for the mission.

30 JUNE 1941

Dutch light cruiser DE RUYTER, destroyers PIET HEIN and BANCKERT, submarines K-XVII and K-XVIII, supply ship JANSSENS and tanker TAN 8 were present at Gulf of Sukadana, Borneo.

East China Sea
Long. E120, 00 – E130, 00   Lat. N42, 00 – N20, 00

3 JUNE 1941

IJN river gunboat SAGA (785grt) departed Takao, Formosa, and arrived later that day at Guangdong, China.

6 JUNE 1941

IJN patrol boat SHURI MARU arrived at Ryojun, Korea, from a patrol of the North China coast.

7 JUNE 1941

IJN transport KOMAKI MARU (8525grt) arrived at Takao, Formosa.

9 JUNE 1941

IJN patrol boat SHURI MARU departed Ryojun, Korea, on a patrol of the North China coast.

10 JUNE 1941

IJN minesweepers W-13, W-17, W-19, W-15, W-18, W-16, and W-14 were assigned to the Japanese 2nd Base Force (Rear Admiral Hirose Sueto) of the Japanese Third Fleet (Vice Admiral Takahashi Ibo) at Takao, Formosa.

IJN river gunboat SUMIDA (350grt) arrived at Shanghai, China.

11 JUNE 1941

IJN river gunboat SUMIDA (350grt) entered the dry dock at Shanghai, China.

14 JUNE 1941

IJN patrol boat SHURI MARU arrived at Ryojun, Korea, from a patrol of the North China coast.

15 JUNE 1941

IJN oiler TOEN MARU (5232grt) arrived at Takao, Formosa.

18 JUNE 1941

IJN river gunboat SUMIDA (350grt) was undocked at Shanghai, China.

20 JUNE 1941

	German steamer ANNELIESE ESSBERGER (5173grt) departed Dairen, China, for Bordeaux, France.

30 JUNE 1941

	IJN river gunboat SUMIDA (350grt) departed Shanghai, China, and patrolled up the Yangtze River towards Hangkow, China.

Sea of Japan
Long. E128, 00 – E143, 00   Lat. N55, 00 – N33, 00

1 JUNE 1941

	IJN submarine chaser CH-39 was laid down at Harima Zosensho K. K.
	IJN oiler KORYU MARU (880grt) arrived at Sasebo, Kyushu.

2 JUNE 1941

	Japanese cargo ship NACHISAN MARU (4433grt) arrived at Korea.

10 JUNE 1941

	IJN minelayer ITSUKUSHIMA departed Sasebo, Kyushu, to operate off the South China coast.

21 JUNE 1941

	IJN aircraft carrier KAGA departed Sasebo, Kyushu.
	Japanese cargo ship NACHISAN MARU (4433grt) departed Korea for Sasebo, Kyushu.

East of Australia
Long. E140, 00 – E155, 00   Lat. S12, 00 – S40, 00

5 JUNE 1941

	Australian heavy cruiser AUSTRALIA and New Zealand light cruiser ACHILLES escorted convoy VK.2 with two ships from Sydney, Australia, to Wellington, New Zealand, where they arrived on the 9th.

East of Japan
Long. E130, 00 – E180, 00   Lat. N55, 00 – N30, 00

1 JUNE 1941

	IJN auxiliary CHIYODA began a modification to her stern to form a ramp to enable her to launch midget submarines at Kure, Japan.
	IJN minesweepers W-7, W-11, W-12, and W-8 were assigned to the Japanese Third Fleet (Vice Admiral Takahashi Ibo), 1st Base Force in Minesweeper Division 21 with W-8, W-9, W-10, W-11 and W-12.
	Japanese cargo ship AKITSU MARU (9186grt) was requisitioned at Aioi, Japan, by the IJA and was converted on the stocks into an assault landing ship. She was fitted with a flight deck above the hull, but had no hangar.
	Finnish cargo ship TORNATOR (4964grt) arrived at Yokohama, Japan.

2 JUNE 1941

	IJN seaplane tender KAMIKAWA MARU (6853grt) was designated as the flagship of the Japanese 12th Seaplane Tender Division. That same day, the flag was transferred temporarily to the aircraft transport FUJIKAWA MARU.

3 JUNE 1941

	IJN battleship KIRISHIMA departed Sukumo Bay, Japan, with battleships HIEI and HYUGA.
	Japanese steamer KAMIKAZE MARU (4916grt) was requisitioned by the IJN to become a torpedo recovery vessel.

4 JUNE 1941

	IJN battleship HIEI arrived at Yokkaichi, Japan.

5 JUNE 1941

	Japanese liner HIKAWA MARU (11,622grt) departed Yokohama, Japan, for Vancouver, Canada, carrying Jewish refugee passengers.
	IJN battleship KIRISHIMA arrived at Yokkaichi, Japan.

9 JUNE 1941

	IJN battleship KIRISHIMA departed Yokkaichi, Japan, and arrived at Ise Jinja (Ise Shrine), Japan.

13 JUNE 1941

	IJN oiler KOKUYO MARU (10,026grt) arrived at Tsurumi, Japan.
	IJN AMC SAIGON MARU (5350grt) departed Kobe, Japan, for Bangkok, Siam.

14 JUNE 1941

	Japanese liner/AMC ASAMA MARU (16,975grt) arrived at Kobe, Japan, after circling the globe gathering intelligence information and vital war supplies from Spain.

15 JUNE 1941

	IJN oiler KOKUYO MARU (10,026grt) was re-rated a converted transport (oil supply) and was fully manned by an IJN crew.
	IJN tanker KYOKUTO MARU (10,051grt) departed Tokuyama, Japan, for the South Seas area (probably Truk).
	IJN transport KOMAKI MARU (8525grt) departed Tateyama, Japan, for the South Seas area (probably Truk).

16 JUNE 1941

	Japanese cargo ship KUNISHIMA MARU (4083grt) arrived at Yokosuka, Japan.

18 JUNE 1941

	IJN battleship HIEI departed Yokkaichi, Japan, for Sukumo Bay, Japan.

19 JUNE 1941

	IJN battleship HIEI arrived at Sukumo Bay, Japan, from Yokkaichi, Japan.

21 JUNE 1941

	IJN battleship HYUGA arrived at Yokkaichi, Japan.
	IJN river gunboat FUSHIMI (374grt) entered the dry dock, probably at Fujinagata Zosensho.

22 JUNE 1941

	IJN battleship HIEI departed Sukumo Bay, Japan, for Ariake Bay, Japan.
	When the crew of Finnish cargo ship **TORNATOR** (4964grt) learned that Finland was at war with Russia and fighting with Germany, they realized that they could not reach Finland with their cargo of tobacco and fibre. The Japanese government chartered the vessel, and she was renamed the TORNATOR GO (4964grt).

23 JUNE 1941

	IJN battleship HIEI arrived at Ariake Bay, Japan, from Sukumo Bay, Japan.
	IJN battleship KIRISHIMA arrived at Ariake Bay, Japan, from Ise Jinja (Ise Shrine), Japan.

24 JUNE 1941

	IJN oiler HOYO MARU (8691grt) arrived at Yokkaichi, Japan.
	Japanese cargo ship KUNISHIMA MARU (4083grt) departed Yokosuka, Japan, for her assigned support position south of China.

25 JUNE 1941

	IJN oiler KOKUYO MARU (10,026grt) departed Kure, Japan, for the North American coast for another cargo of oil.
	IJN oiler TOEI MARU (10,023grt) arrived at Tokuyama, Japan.

27 JUNE 1941

	IJN battleships KIRISHIMA and HIEI departed Ariake Bay, Japan, for Yokosuka, Japan.
	IJN aircraft ferry FUJIKAWA MARU returned to Furue, Japan.

28 JUNE 1941

	IJN battleship HYUGA arrived at Ariake Bay, Japan, from Yokkaichi, Japan, and departed later the same day.
	IJN river gunboat FUSHIMI (374grt) was undocked, probably at Fujinagata Zosensho.

30 JUNE 1941

	IJN battleships KIRISHIMA and HIEI arrived at Yokosuka, Japan, from Ariake Bay, Japan.
	IJN battleships HYUGA and ISE arrived at Yokohama, Japan, from Ariake Bay, Japan.
	IJN oiler KYOEI MARU 3 (1189grt) was completed at Kyoei Tanker K.K., Kobe, Japan.

New Zealand   Long. E150, 00 – E180, 00   Lat. S25, 00 – S60, 00

10 JUNE 1941

	New Zealand light cruiser ACHILLES departed Wellington, New Zealand, escorting convoy AP.41. This convoy had previously sailed as convoy VK.12 to Wellington escorted by Australian heavy cruiser AUSTRALIA. ACHILLES escorted the convoy to a position 230 miles east of Chatham Island.

24 JUNE 1941

	New Zealand light cruiser ACHILLES departed Wellington, New Zealand, escorting troopship AQUITANIA (44,786grt) to Bass Strait, Australia. On the 30th, the ACHILLES joined troopships QUEEN MARY (81,235grt), and QUEEN ELIZABETH (83,673grt) to form troop convoy US.11A.

25 JUNE 1941

	German AMC ADJUTANT laid mines off Auckland, New Zealand.

27 JUNE 1941

	German AMC ADJUTANT laid mines off Wellington, New Zealand.

West of United States   Long. W130, 00 – W110, 00   Lat. N50, 00 – N30, 00

9 JUNE 1941

	The Canadian minesweepers CANSO and GRANBY were launched at Vancouver, BC.

JULY 1941
DAY-TO-DAY OPERATIONS

SECTION CONTENTS

SUMMARY	82
GENERAL	85
ARCTIC OCEAN	87
Greenland Sea and Barents Sea	*87*
White Sea	*90*
NORTH ATLANTIC OCEAN	90
Iceland and North of Britain	*90*
Norwegian Sea	*96*
East of Canada	*96*
East of United States	*98*
Caribbean and Gulf of Mexico	*99*
Western Approaches	*99*
Central Atlantic Crossing Zone	*104*
UK East Coast	*108*
North Sea	*110*
English Channel	*111*
Bay of Biscay	*112*
West of Gibraltar	*113*
West of North Africa	*116*
SOUTH ATLANTIC OCEAN	117
East of South America	*117*
West of South Africa	*117*
BALTIC SEA	118
Kattegat and Skagerrak	*118*
Southern Baltic Area	*118*
Gulf of Bothnia	*120*
Gulf of Finland	*120*
MEDITERRANEAN SEA & MIDDLE EAST	122
East of Gibraltar	*122*
Middle Mediterranean Sea	*124*
Eastern Mediterranean Sea	*128*
Black Sea	*134*
Red Sea	*134*
Arabian Sea	*135*
INDIAN OCEAN	135
East of South Africa	*135*
South Indian Ocean	*135*
Bay of Bengal	*135*
Malaya	*136*
PACIFIC OCEAN	136
South China Sea	*136*
South of Australia	*137*
East China Sea	*137*
Sea of Japan	*137*
East of Japan	*138*
Hawaii Area	*139*
South of Hawaii	*140*
West of United States	*140*

SUMMARY

GERMANY

The German Navy was hard pressed to support the German Army in their advance into Russia. With aid from Finland, the extensive minefields laid in the Gulf of Finland restricted Russian ship movements to coastal areas. The German Army slowly took the Baltic Naval bases one by one as they advanced towards Leningrad, Russia.

The German attack in the Arctic area was mostly hampered by the weather and the logistics. Everything that the Germans needed to advance towards Murmansk, Russia, had to sail around Norway and run the gauntlet of British aircraft and Allied submarines.

German operations in the Atlantic continued to achieve some success, but they were not expanding as the increase in the number of U-boats and heavy aerial reconnaissance should have permitted. The new bases in France helped, but the British eliminated most of the Atlantic supply boats after they broke the current German ENIGMA codes.

Axis operations in the Black Sea were confined to the coastal support provided by the Romanians. The strong presence of German air power negated the larger Russian Black Sea Fleet in the area.

Moving the German heavy ships to France did not result in any advantage for the Germans. The French ports were exposed to British bombers, and Allied submarines kept a vigilant watch while waiting to the heavy ships to enter regions where they could be attacked.

ITALY

The Italian Fleet continued to support the vital convoys to Libya, but the Italian and German merchant ships were being slowly whittled away by air and sea attack. While most of the convoy ships got through, they were under attack through most of the journey.

The Italians were marginally successful in keeping the British from supplying Malta. The combined German and Italian air forces made each attempt very costly.

The Italian heavy ships were still mostly bound to their ports due to the critical lack of oil reserves. With the Russian submarines patrolling the Romanian shores, the occasional tanker load that made it through the Dardanelles was a mere drop in the bucket.

ROMANIA

The Romanian Navy succeeded in maintaining naval support for German and Romanian troops advancing along the Russian coastline. The Axis defensive minefields kept the Russian heavy fleet units from interfering with either the naval support or the flow of oil from Constanza.

JAPAN

The United States oil embargo was the final straw for the Japanese. They either had to concede their war aims or fight. They chose to fight.

The Germans blessed the Japanese move into Vichy French Indochina and instructed the French to comply with all Japanese requests. The new airfields in southern Indochina put most of British Malaya and Burma within land based bomber reach. The new naval bases enabled the Japanese to begin stockpiling supplies for their projected advance through Malaya and the Dutch East Indies.

FINLAND

The Finnish Navy successfully deployed minefields across the Gulf of Finland. The Russian submarines could still move through them, but more and more of them just disappeared as they found each new minefield.

VICHY FRANCE

The Vichy French Navy tried to maintain supplies to Syria, but the German restrictions of Vichy ship movements and the confiscation of Vichy oil reserves gave the navy more than enough reasons to abandon any further offensive actions against the British and Free French forces.

The Vichy French put up a good show of resistance before abandoning Syria to the British and Free French forces. While some of the Vichy French were fighting hard to protect the integrity of French honour, most were unwilling to fight fellow Frenchmen who were trying to free more French territory from Axis control.

Still, it must have been very difficult for the Vichy French troops. Fighting fellow Frenchman had to be tough, but if they did not put up a good show of resistance, then the Germans or the Vichy government could take out their anger on their families back in France. War is a very ugly business!

BRITAIN

The British continued to spread their few assets over more and more areas of conflict. The aircraft carrier raid on the Kirkenes was very costly. British carrier aircraft were no match for the *Luftwaffe*.

Convoy escorts were finally beginning to reach an acceptable level in the North Atlantic. Using the decoded ENIGMA messages to find and destroy most of the German supply ships cut deeply into U-boat time on patrol and supplies to the German surface raiders.

The British forces in Gibraltar continued to ferry supplies and aircraft to Malta, but were encountering increasing levels of resistance from Italian air and naval units. Italian torpedo bombers were proving to be quite a challenging foe.

The Mediterranean Fleet continued to support the attack on Syria and the defence of Egypt. Supply runs to Tobruk and Malta were becoming more costly with time. German and Italian Ju87 attacks were very successful in sinking and damaging British warships.

UNITED STATES

The United States had taken off the gloves in dealing with the Axis powers. Establishing the oil and raw material embargo essentially pushed Japan into action against the United States possessions in the Pacific. Washington knew from reading the Japanese diplomatic messages that the Japanese could not continue fighting without the oil, and they also knew that the Japanese held Americans in enough contempt that they would attack. The fuse was lit.

Moving United States marines to Iceland also put the Germans into a dilemma. Not only was US war materiel going to Britain, but also US troops were relieving the British from occupation duties of a neutral country. US Atlantic Fleet aircraft were also now conducting air reconnaissance activities over large areas of the North Atlantic and reporting the position of German U-boats to the British.

Not only was the United States waving the red, white and blue in front of the German U-boats, but they had also dropped their pants and were mooning the Germans, daring them to do something about it.

RUSSIA

The Russian Navy was still fighting where it could. The Russian Northern Fleet was larger than the German forces in the area. Had it not been for the strong *Luftwaffe* presence, the Russians could have probably taken the Kirkenes.

The situation in the Baltic was problematic. The extensive German and Finnish minefields limited Russian Baltic Fleet movements. The strong *Luftwaffe* presence made daytime ship movements very costly. While some Russian submarines managed to operate in the Baltic, they were not having much success.

The Russian Black Sea Fleet was likewise constrained in the south. They had the advantage in strength over the Romanian Navy, but the *Luftwaffe* limited the Russians' ability to mount an effective attack against them.

While Stalin railed against Churchill about a British effort to tie down German soldiers, he overlooked one very important British contribution to the Eastern Front war. The loss of over three hundred German transport planes during the battle for Crete left the German airlift units greatly under strength.

The German rapid advance in France occurred in part because the *Luftwaffe* used the air transports to keep the combat aircraft flying from advanced airfields. In Russia, the *Luftwaffe* was mostly limited to ground supply. Time after time, the German armoured units outran their air support and were forced to stop while the forward airfields were set up and supplied by slow moving trucks.

The Russians did not realize it yet, but the British defence of Crete helped save a lot of Russian troops by slowing the German rate of advance. The Russian losses were bad enough, but if the *Luftwaffe* had been able to keep pace, it could have been a lot worse.

CHINA

The Chinese were very alarmed at the Japanese movements into Vichy French Indochina. The earlier Japanese movement into northern Indochina had significantly reduced the flow of foreign aid to China. The move south could only mean that the Japanese were preparing to cut the last British lifeline to China through Burma.

POLAND

The Polish Army in Exile continued to build its strength and to support the Allied effort. The new Polish destroyers were crewed with tough, experienced seamen. Small Polish units fought with the British and Free French in Syria. Polish aircraft flew missions over Britain and occupied Europe. Poland still fought.

FREE FRANCE

The Free French forces achieved a major victory in Syria. By outlasting the Vichy French forces, they obtained control of the Syrian oil resources and cut the last Axis link to the Middle East. They also obtained access to a fair amount of war materiel and new recruits to continue the fighting. France was also still fighting.

GENERAL

DATE	COMMENTS
1 July	In German Army Group Centre, the Second Panzer Group reached the Beresina River near Minsk, Russia. In Army Group North, the Fourth Panzer Group crossed the Dvina river and captured Riga, Latvia.
1 July	The British formed the 1st Burma Division with its headquarters at Toungoo, Burma.
1 July	In the Arctic, the German 136th Mountain Regiment managed to establish a bridgehead over the Titovka River on the Kola Peninsula, Russia.
1 July	During the month, the German IX Air Corps dropped two hundred aerial mines, mostly in the Thames Estuary.
1 July	In Operation SUBSTANCE, the Royal Navy escorted vital supply convoys to the eastern Mediterranean.
2 July	China ended diplomatic relations with Germany and Italy.
2 July	During the night, the RAF Bomber Command attacked Bremen and Cologne, Germany.
2 July	In German Army Group South, the German Eleventh Army with the Romanian Third and Fourth Armies crossed the Vinnitsa River to retake Moldavia and advanced on the Black Sea port of Odessa, Russia.
2 July	The Vichy French 4th Naval Air Group (Kptlt Hubert) attacked Haifa, Palestine.
2 July	During a high level meeting in Tokyo, the Japanese military agreed to continue the Empire expansion to the south and to defer any further efforts north into Russia. The military leaders also agreed to occupy Vichy French Indochina and to engage Britain and the United States in war if necessary.
3 July	For the first time since the beginning of the German attack on Russia, Stalin spoke to the Russian people over the radio. He demanded the utmost resistance 'in our patriotic war against German Fascism', he called for a policy of scorched earth if the Russian Army was forced to yield ground, the formation of 'people's partisan' groups behind enemy lines, as well as the summary execution of all cowards and shirkers.
3 July	The last Vichy French aerial reinforcements for Syria, twenty-one Dewoitine D.520 fighters of 3 Squadron, Second Fighter Group (GC II/3), landed at the German/Italian airbase at Rhodes after departing from Tunis on their way to Brindisi, Italy, and Athens, Greece.
4 July	German Army Group Centre captured Ostrov, south of Pskovsk, Russia.
4 July	The RAF Bomber Command attacked Bremen, Germany, during the day.
4 July	In Operation DN, the Royal Navy departed Scapa Flow to strike at German shipping near Stadlandet, Norway. German aircraft spotted the force during the night on 5/6 July, forcing the ships to return to Scapa Flow.
5 July	During the night, the RAF Bomber Command attacked Muenster and Bielefeld, Germany.
5 July	In the Ukraine, the German First Panzer Group advanced towards Zhitomir and Berdichev, Russia. In southern Poland, the German Sixth Army broke through the "Stalin Line" east of Lvov, Poland.
6 July	In Libya, German aircraft bombed Tobruk and Sidi Barrani.
6 July	The German Army Group North advanced to a line from Lake Peipus, through Reval to Parun, Estonia, north of the Gulf of Riga.
6 July	In the Arctic, the German 2nd and 3rd Mountain Divisions attacked over the Lisa River towards Murmansk, Russia.
7 July	Under the pretext of defending the Western Hemisphere against Nazi incursions, the United States 1st Marine Brigade was landed in Iceland to relieve the British garrison that had been there since the previous year.
8 July	Germany and Italy announced the dissolution of the state of Yugoslavia, with large portions of land being annexed by Italy. An independent state of Croatia, allied to the Axis and with its capital at Agram (Zagreb), was proclaimed.
8 July	German Army Group North captured Pskov with the Fourth Panzer Group and advanced toward Novgorod and Leningrad, Russia.
9 July	German Army Group Centre captured Vitebsk, Russia. To date, the Germans claimed to have destroyed 2500 Russian tanks and captured 300,000 Russian troops.
9 July	In Berlin, Hitler and his navy admirals discussed the new situation with United States troops and ships in Iceland. All agreed that the United States had positioned themselves for operations in the North Atlantic, but Hitler refused to authorize either an attack by U-boats on USN ships at Reykjavik or the use of AMC SCHIFF.45/KOMET to attack USN ships sailing from Los Angeles, California, to Manila, Philippines.
10 July	The Finnish Karelian Army began an offensive toward Lake Ladoga, northeast of Leningrad, Russia.
10 July	The German Army Group South repulsed a heavy Russian counter attack in the area of Korosten, west of Kiev, Ukraine, using the German First Panzer Group.
11 July	Stalin replaced three major Russian commanders appointing General Voroshilov to the northern, General Timoshenko to the central, and General Budjenny to the southern front.
11 July	The German First Panzer Group advanced to within ten miles of Kiev, Ukraine.
12 July	The German *Luftwaffe* made its first attack on Moscow, Russia, but created little damage, as the range was too extreme for the aircraft to carry a full bomb load.
12 July	The British and the Russians signed a Mutual Assistance Pact declaring that neither country would make a

	separate peace with the Axis Powers.
12 July	The last Vichy French troops in Syria surrendered to British and Free French forces.
12 July	British Admiral Vian flew by Catalina aircraft to Archangel, Russia. From there he took the train to Moscow to meet with the Russians about stationing British naval ships at Murmansk, Russia. The Russians only agreed to let the British send two submarines to operate out of Polyarny, Russia. Submarines TIGRIS and TRIDENT were selected for this operation.
13 July	The German Army Group North advanced from Pskov toward Luga, Russia, only seventy-five miles from Leningrad.
13 July	In the Arctic, the German 2nd Mountain Division expanded the Lisa River bridgehead in a reinforced attack.
13 July	In Operation SUBSTANCE, the Royal Navy supply convoy for Malta departed the Clyde.
14 July	In Syria, an armistice was signed at the city of Acre between the Vichy French and British/Free French forces.
14 July	Believing the campaign in the East would soon to be concluded in Germany's favour, Hitler ordered the German war industry to shift production away from guns and armoured vehicles to U-boats and airplanes.
15 July	In the outskirts of Leningrad, hundreds of thousands of Russian civilians, mostly women and teenagers, began constructing over three hundred miles of trenches and field fortifications.
15 July	The German Army Group Centre encircled 300,000 Russian troops in the Smolensk-Orsha pocket.
16 July	German bombers attacked Tobruk, Libya.
16 July	The German Army Group Centre began the destruction of the Russian Divisions encircled in the Uman pocket. Stalin's son, Lt Jacob Dugashvili, was taken prisoner near Vitebsk, Russia.
16 July	Finnish troops broke through Russian positions north of Lake Ladoga, Russia.
17 July	German and Italian aircraft bombed the port facilities at Malta.
17 July	The Romanian Fourth Army captured Kishinev, Russia, on the lower Dnestr River.
17 July	The German Army Group Centre crossed the Dnepr River near Mogilev, Russia.
18 July	Over 35,000 pro-Japanese Chinese soldiers attacked the Chinese New Fourth Army stronghold in Kiagnsu, China.
18 July	In Operation GUILLOTINE, the Royal Navy beginning moving troops and supplies from Port Said, Egypt, and Haifa, Palestine, to Famagusta, Cypress.
19 July	In a major change of operational plans, Hitler issued Directive 33 ordering the German Fourth Army and Second Panzer Group detached from Army Group Centre. He suspended attacks toward Moscow, Russia, and sent the German Fourth Army and Second Panzer Group to join the German Sixth Army and First Panzer Group of Army Group South with the objective of destroying the Russian Fifth, Sixth and Twelfth Armies west of the Dnepr-to-Dnestr line. The idea behind this directive was to begin exploiting the great agricultural and mineral riches of the Ukraine for the German war effort just as soon as the Russian forces in that region were defeated.
20 July	During the night, the RAF Bomber Command attacked Naples, Italy.
20 July	Stalin appointed himself as the People's Commissar for Defence.
21 July	The German Luftwaffe launched its first heavy bombing raid on Moscow, Russia, with 127 aircraft. Moscow would be bombed a further seventy-three times before the year's end.
21 July	The United States announced that Japanese ships could no longer use the Panama Canal.
22 July	The German Fourth Panzer Group reached Lake Ilmen, just outside of Leningrad, Russia.
22 July	Italian reconnaissance aircraft located part of the Royal Navy supply convoy for Operation SUBSTANCE, which had left Gibraltar the day before. The Italian Fleet stayed in port, expecting another aircraft ferry flight to Malta. Eight SM79 torpedo bombers and fifteen (SM79 and Cant Z1007) bombers took off from Sardinia to attack the convoy, but failed to find it.
23 July	German troops finally took the Russian fortress at Brest-Litovsk on the Polish border after a month-long siege.
24 July	The Japanese Army occupied southern French Indochina with the consent of the Vichy French Government. IJN Marines landed at Cam Ranh Bay to secure the port facilities before the army troops debarked.
24 July	In Operation EF, the Royal Navy departed Scapa Flow heading to the Arctic Ocean for air attacks on Kirkenes and Petsamo, Finland.
25 July	An Italian commando assault on Valletta harbour on the island of Malta was discovered and repulsed with fifteen Italians killed and the remaining eighteen captured.
25 July	German aircraft of KG.4 dropped forty aerial mines in the Moon Sound, off Estonia.
26 July	The Germans destroyed three Russian armies in the Mogilev, Russia, area.
26 July	US President Franklin D. Roosevelt ordered all Japanese assets in the United States frozen. He also ordered the suspension of all trade with Japan and established an oil embargo. He also authorized the activation of Western Hemisphere Defence Plan 4 (WPL-51), which integrated the United States Navy with British operations under a combined Chiefs of Staff. These actions by the president gave the Japanese the final impetus to authorize an attack on the United States Pacific Fleet at Pearl Harbor, Hawaiian Territory.
26 July	In Operation GIDEON, the Royal Navy bombarded Dieppe, France.
27 July	During the night, the German Luftwaffe bombed London.
27 July	The German Army Group North captured the Estonian capital Tallinn.

	The German Army Group Centre encircled Russian troops at Smolensk, Russia, after fierce fighting. The German Second Panzer Group turned away from Moscow to capture the Russian economic centres in the south of Russia.
28 July	The German Army Group Centre captured the Russian troops surrounded at Smolensk.
28 July	Finland ended diplomatic relations with Great Britain.
28 July	Japan froze all United States assets in Japan.
28 July	In Operation CHESS, the Royal Navy landed a commando team near Fécamp, France.
29 July	Under the Franco/Japanese "Common Defence" agreement signed in Vichy France by Deputy-Premier Admiral Darlan and Japanese Ambassador Kato, French Indochina was "integrated" into the "common defence" area and the Japanese were allowed to use Saigon as an advance base for operations in Southeast Asia. Subsequently, Japanese troops began to occupy southern Vichy French Indochina.
30 July	The United States announced that war materiel would be delivered to Russia under the Lend Lease Act.
30 July	In Operation EF, the Royal Navy launched an air strike of twenty Albacore torpedo bombers and nine Fulmar fighters on the German forces at Kirkenes, Norway.
31 July	In Operation FB, the Royal Navy attacked a German W/T station on Bear Island in the Arctic.
31 July	In Operation STYLE, the Royal Navy attacked Italian positions in Sardinia to divert attention from the supply convoy headed to Malta.

ARCTIC OCEAN

Greenland Sea and Barents Sea Long. W180, 00 – E180, 00   Lat. N90, 00 – N68, 00

1 JULY 1941

	Russian submarines SHCH-422, SHCH-402, and D-3 patrolled off northern Norway near Lopphavet.
	Russian submarine SHCH-401 patrolled off northern Norway near Kibergsneset.
	Russian submarine SHCH-403 patrolled off northern Norway off the Gorlo Strait.
	Small Russian submarines M-174, M-175, M-172, M-176 and M-171 patrolled off northern Norway near Varangerfjord and other German ports for a few days each.

4 JULY 1941

	Russian destroyers GROZA and SMERI provided fire support to Russian forces at Petsamo. The Russian 14th Infantry and the 52nd Rifle Division attacked the German bridgeheads over the Lisa river.

5 JULY 1941

	U.81 and U.652 began a patrol off the Russian Kola coast.

6 JULY 1941

	U.652 (ObltzS Fraatz) sank Russian **SKR-11/Patrol Boat 70** (ex-trawler RT-66 (1107grt) off Cape Teriberskiy, Russia.
	To support Russian troops defending the Lisa River, the Russian Arctic Fleet (Capt 1st Class Platonov) formed a support group with patrol boats GROZA, SKR-23/MUSSON, and TUMAN, minesweepers T-890 and T-891 plus submarine chasers MO-131, MO-132 and MO-133 to ferry troops from the Russian 14th and 52nd Divisions into the landing area.

9 JULY 1941

	German aircraft sank Russian minesweeper **T-890** off the Lisa River.

10 JULY 1941

	German destroyers HANS LODY, KARL GALSTER, HERMANN SCHOEMANN, FRIEDRICH ECKHOLDT, and RICHARD BEITZEN of the 6th Destroyer Flotilla arrived at Kirkenes, Norway.

12 JULY 1941

	U.81 unsuccessfully attacked Russian patrol boat SKR-29/BRILLIANT off Svyatoy.
	German destroyers HANS LODY, KARL GALSTER, HERMANN SCHOEMANN, FRIEDRICH ECKHOLDT, and RICHARD BEITZEN conducted a shipping sweep off the Kola coast. Destroyers LODY, GALSTER, and ECKHOLDT encountered a small Russian convoy near Cape Teriberskiy. They sank Russian patrol ship **SKR-22/PASSAT** (Lt Okunevich) and auxiliary patrol trawler **RT-67/MOLOTOV** (558grt) while auxiliary patrol trawler RT-32/KUMZHA was able to escape. The other two destroyers found no targets off Iokanga.

14 JULY 1941

	Russian submarine SHCH-402 unsuccessfully attacked German steamer HANAU (5892grt) off Porsangerfjord, Norway.
	German submarine chasers UJ.177 and UJ.178 attacked Russian submarine SHCH-401 off Vardø, Norway.
	A Russian naval force (Capt 1st Class Platonov) landed 1600 troops of the 235th Guards Regiment at Lisa Bay using three patrol boats, three minesweepers and ten submarine chasers. Russian destroyer KUIBYSHEV, patrol boat GROZA and four submarine chasers provided direct gunfire support to the troops. Russian destroyers GREMYASHCHI, GROMKI and STREMITELNY provided cover for the landing. In spite of the attack, the Germans held the bridgehead across the Lisa River.

16 JULY 1941

	A Russian naval group landed another battalion of troops in the Lisa River bay area with destroyer KUIBYSHEV, patrol boats GROZA, SMERCH and PRILIV plus four submarine chasers.

18 JULY 1941

	The German 6th Destroyer Flotilla sortied against Russian forces off the Kola coast, but could not find the Russian ships and was forced to return to Kirkenes, Norway, due to the threat of mines in the area.
	U.81 and U.652 were ordered to patrol the area off the Russian Kola coast until 6 August.

19 JULY 1941

	Russian aircraft attacked Russian submarine SHCH-421 off Polyarny. She sustained only light damage from the attack.

20 JULY 1941

	German Ju87 aircraft of 12/LG.1 (ObltzS J. Pfeiffer) sank Russian patrol boat **SKR-20/SHTIL** and destroyer **STREMITELNY** (Capt 2nd Class A. D. Vinogradov) at Ekaterinski Gavan in Kola Fjord, Russia.

21 JULY 1941

	RAF torpedo bombers of 42 Squadron sank German steamer **WANDSBEK** (2388grt) at Narvik, Norway.

22 JULY 1941

	German destroyers KARL GALSTER, HERMANN SCHOEMANN, FRIEDRICH ECKHOLDT, HANS LODY and RICHARD BEITZEN departed the Kirkenes to patrol off the Russian Kola coast. HANS LODY was forced to return due to mechanical defects. The remaining destroyers sank Russian survey ship **MERIDIAN** between Iokanga and Teriberski, Russia. The German destroyers fought off several Russian air attacks and arrived back at Kirkenes on the 24th.

24 JULY 1941

	U.652 missed Russian patrol boat SKR-23/MUSSON off Russian Kildin inlet.

28 JULY 1941

1530	Fleet oiler BLACK RANGER (3417grt) refuelled destroyers ICARUS and INGLEFIELD off the Russian Kola coast. She then refuelled the destroyers for Operation EF.

29 JULY 1941

	German destroyers KARL GALSTER, HERMANN SCHOEMANN, FRIEDRICH ECKHOLDT, and RICHARD BEITZEN conducted a shipping sweep towards the Russian Yugorsky and Kara Straits. However, the sweep was abandoned when the British carrier force was reported in the area.
0100	Fleet oiler BLACK RANGER (3417grt) completed refueling destroyers for Operation EF and minelayer ADVENTURE.

30 JULY 1941

0300	During the air strikes, minelayer ADVENTURE continued on to Russia escorted by destroyer ANTHONY. The minelayer was detached from the carrier group and proceeded to Archangel, Russia, alone until escorted by Russian destroyer SOKRUSHITELNY from Cape Gorodetski, with mines needed in Operation EF.
1346	In Operation EF, aircraft carrier VICTORIOUS launched an air strike of twenty Albacore torpedo bomber aircraft of 827 Squadron (Lt Cdr J. A. Stewart-Moore) and 828 Squadron (Lt Cdr D. E. Langmore) and nine Fulmar fighter aircraft of 809 Squadron (Lt Cdr V. C. Grenfell) on Kirkenes, Norway. Three additional Fulmar aircraft flew as fighter protection for the carrier. Minelayer BREMSE and other German ships were at Kirkenes. Some damage was done to piers and oil tanks, and steamer ROTTVER (grt) was damaged. German antiaircraft gunners and German fighter aircraft of 6/JG.5 downed six Albacores of 827 Squadron and

	five Albacores of 828 Squadron and two Fulmar fighters of 809 Squadron.
A/Leading Airman L. E. Barrow in a Fulmar of 809 Squadron was killed, and Sub-Lt (A) R. S. Miller, his pilot, was captured.
Pilot Lt M. G. McKendick, observer P/T/Midshipman (A) E. A. Mills RNVR, and A/Leading Airman F. Sharples in an Albacore of 827 Squadron were killed.
Pilot T/Lt (A) E. E. Hughes-Williams RNVR, observer Sub-Lt (A) J. J. R. Davies, and A/Leading Airman A. Fox and pilot T/Sub-Lt (A) D. R. McKay RNVR, observer T/Sub-Lt (A) J. G. Paton RNVR, and T/Leading Airman D. W. Corner in Albacores of 828 Squadron were killed.
Pilot Lt (A) T. E. Blacklock RNVR, and observer Lt (A) A. T. Easton, and pilot Lt (A) R. S. Miller from the Fulmars of 809 Squadron were captured.
Pilot Lt A. Turnbull RNVR, Observer Lt H. K. Serjeant, A/Leading Airman J. W. James of one Albacore of 827 Squadron were captured.
Pilot Lt H. F. Bond, Observer Lt H. H. Bracken, and A/Leading Airman E. Lancaster of another Albacore of 827 Squadron were captured.
Pilot Sub-Lt P. J. Greenslade RNVR, Observer Sub-Lt W. W. Parsons RNVR, A/Leading Airman H. Pickup of another Albacore of 827 Squadron were captured.
Pilot Sub-Lt (A) J. F. Olsen and Observer Sub-Lt (A) A. J. Bulford RNVR were captured and A/Leading Airman H. J. Wade was killed in another Albacore of 827 Squadron.
Pilot Lt (A) L. E. R. Bellairs and Observer T/Lt (A) D. M. Lubbock RNVR, of another Albacore of 828 Squadron were captured; their crewman A/Leading Airman C. F. Beer was killed.
An Albacore lost from 828 Squadron with Pilot Sub-Lt (A) C. V. Howard, Observer Sub-Lt (A) G. L. Turner RNVR, and T/Leading Airman D. E. Polmeer captured.
An Albacore lost from 828 Squadron with Pilot Lt (A) R. Ross-Taylor, Observer Sub-Lt (A) S. Clayton RNVR, T/A/Leading Airman L. W. Miles captured,
An Albacore lost from 827 Squadron with Pilot Sub-Lt (A) D. Myles RNVR, Observer Sub-Lt A. P. Keep, and A/Leading Airman H. C. Griffin captured.
In Albacores of 827 Squadron, one was damaged and able to return to aircraft carrier VICTORIOUS with its crew of Sub-Lt R. J. Grant-Sturgis, Sub-Lt W. A. Davies, and Naval Airman G. Dixon not wounded.
A damaged Albacore returned to the carrier with its crew of Lt J. C. Reed, Lt Cdr J. A. Stewart-Moore, and Petty Officer H. J. Lambert.
An Albacore with Sub-Lt R. B. Park and Sub-Lt O. G. W. Hutchinson, A/Leading Airman E. P. Fabien was downed and the crew were killed.
German AA flak damaged another Albacore, but its crew of Sub-Lt R. S. Meakin, Sub-Lt Scott, and Leading Airman F. Ward were not wounded.
An Albacore with Lt J. N. Ball, Lt B. J. Prendergast, and Petty Officer A. E. Sweet returned to the carrier, the only Albacore of the group undamaged.
A damaged Albacore returned to the carrier with Lt J. S. Bailey, Lt L. C. Williams, and TAG C. T. Roberts.
In 828 Squadron, a damaged Albacore with Lt R. L. Williamson, Lt F. Bedford, and Leading Airman F. A. J. Smith returned to the carrier.
An Albacore with Lt Cdr D. E. Langmore, Lt E. A. Greenwood, and A/Petty Officer Smith returned safely as did an Albacore damaged by flak with Sub-Lt R. D. Head, Lt G. M. Haynes, RAN, and Leading Airman J. Madeley.
The Fulmar aircraft with Lt Cdr V. C. Grenfell, Lt H. D. Mathews, Lt H. E. Yates RNR, T/Lt (A) D. A. Van Epps, Sub-Lt D. G. Carlisle, SARNVR, A/Sub-Lt P. R. J. Gilbert, T/Sub-Lt (A) J. B. Ganner RNVR, T/Lt K. J. Robertson, Lt J. Cooper, T/Sub-Lt (A) R. C. Wood RNVR, and T/A/Sub-Lt (A) A. E. R. Wilkinson returned to the carrier safely.
1346	Aircraft carrier FURIOUS launched an air strike of nine Swordfish aircraft of 812 Squadron (Lt Cdr W. E. Waters), nine Albacore torpedo bomber aircraft of 817 Squadron (Lt Cdr D. Sanderson), and six Fulmar fighter aircraft of 800 Squadron (Lt Cdr J. A. D. Wroughton DSC) on Petsamo, Finland.
Four Sea Hurricane aircraft of 880A Flight (Lt Cdr F. E. C. Judd) were flown off as protection for the aircraft carrier. Some damage was done to the piers by the torpedo bombers.
One Albacore torpedo plane of 817 Squadron with Lt (A) L. H. Lee RNVR, who was slightly wounded, Sub-Lt (A) G. Gorrie, and Leading Airman N. Train was shot down. The crew came ashore at Murmansk, Russia.
Two Fulmar fighter aircraft of 800 Squadron with Sub-Lt (A) F. J. G. Gallichan and Petty Officer Airman J. F. Black and P/T/Sub-Lt (A) E. S. Burke RNVR, Leading Airman J. Beardsley were shot down and their crews lost.
The following aircraft from 817 Squadron safely returned to FURIOUS: Lt L. E. D. Walthall, Lt Cdr W. E. Waters (Squadron CO), and Petty Officer (A) A. G. Brown; Sub-Lt P. McJ. Wilkinson, Sub-Lt (A) L. C. Plummer, and Leading Airman E. Kerridge; Sub-Lt (A) R. P. Cross RNVR, and Leading Airman E. A. Cowan; Lt R. S. Baker-Falkner, Sub-Lt (A) P. H. Phillips RNVR, and Petty Officer (A) D. V. Gill; Sub-Lt (A) F. L. Jones RNVR, Sub-Lt (A) K. Hyde RNVR, and Leading Airman A. F. Whitehouse; Sub-Lt (A) E. L. Heath and Leading Airman G. E. Cowsill; Lt (A) J. H. D. Maughan, Sub-Lt (A) G. F. Wild RNVR, and Leading Airman P. J. Nicholas; Lt C. J. K. Kindell, Sub-Lt L. A. Edwards, and Leading Airman J. Stewart, and Sub-Lt (A) J. D. Sinclair RNVR, Sub-Lt (A) K. A. Hovington RNVR, and Leading Airman S. W. Lock.
>1347	After recovering aircraft, the carrier strike force retired to the north after Operation EF.

31 JULY 1941

	Destroyer ANTHONY and minelayer ADVENTURE arrived at Murmansk, Russia.
	Force K arrived at Spitsbergen.

>Dawn	Aircraft carrier FURIOUS was sent back to Scapa Flow because of a fuel shortage. Five Albacore aircraft of 817 Squadron were transferred to aircraft carrier VICTORIOUS before her departure to make up some of her losses. During the aircraft transfer, a German reconnaissance aircraft appeared over the group and was soon shot down by the combat air patrol (CAP) over FURIOUS.
1400	In Operation FB, Force A joined the fleet oiler OLIGARCH (6897grt) group (trawlers SEALYHAM and WASTWATER) to refuel. Destroyer TARTAR was sent ahead to land a Norwegian officer (Lt Tamber) at the W/T station at Kap Linne, Spitsbergen. A Walrus aircraft flew Major A. S. T. Godfrey over Kap Linne and dropped leaflets to alert the local Norwegians not to use the radio transmitter until instructed further. The Walrus also did a reconnaissance of Isfjord.
1800	In Operation FB, light cruiser NIGERIA and destroyer TARTAR entered Advent Fjord, Spitsbergen. They found seven hundred Norwegians, but no German shipping. Light cruiser AURORA and destroyer PUNJABI proceeded to Gronfjord, where they found 1800 Russians. Destroyer GARLAND was engaged on antisubmarine patrol at the entrance to Isfjord. On 1 August, oiler OLIGARCH (6897grt) refuelled the ships at Spitsbergen. Destroyer GARLAND and Norwegian steamer DAGNY I (1392grt) joined the OLIGARCH group. Destroyer GARLAND, antisubmarine trawlers SEALYHAM and WASTWATER, and fleet oiler OLIGARCH proceeded out to sea. A shore party was landed at Bear Island on 2 August to demolish the W/T station and embarked the four Norwegian operators. The ships refuelled again on 3 August. Fleet oiler OLIGARCH was then sent with destroyer GARLAND and trawler SEALYHAM to Seidisfjord. Steamer DAGNY I was detached from the group on 3 August with whaler WASTWATER for escort to the Faeroes.

White Sea

Long. E30, 00 – E60, 00   Lat. N68, 00 – N60, 00

23 JULY 1941

	Russian destroyers GROZNY and SOKRUSHITELNY escorted minelayer KANIN as she laid a minefield across the White Sea entrance with 275 mines.

NORTH ATLANTIC OCEAN

Iceland and North of Britain

Long. W30, 00 – E03, 00   Lat. N68, 00 – N58, 30

1 JULY 1941

	Light cruiser MANCHESTER arrived at Hvalfjord from Denmark Strait patrol.
	Destroyer PUNJABI departed Scapa Flow for Scrabster to take part in the local War Weapons Week at Thurso, Scotland.
	Antiaircraft cruiser CURAÇOA arrived at Scapa Flow following her refitting at Rosyth and after she escorted convoy EC.39 from May Island to Pentland Firth.
1400	Destroyer CROOME arrived at Scapa Flow from Greenock to carry out working up to combat efficiency exercises.
1800	Indian sloop JUMNA departed Scapa Flow escorting convoy EC.39. She then joined the Western Approaches Command following her working up to combat efficiency.
2300	Destroyer PUNJABI arrived back at Scapa Flow from Scrabster.

2 JULY 1941

	Light cruiser MANCHESTER departed Hvalfjord for Scapa Flow, where she arrived the next day.
	Antiaircraft ship ALYNBANK departed Scapa Flow to join convoy EC.40 off Buchan Ness and provide escort to Pentland Firth.
	Steamer EMPIRE AUDACITY (5537grt) arrived at Scapa Flow escorted by sloop STORK. She departed the next day for Campbeltown, escorted by STORK, where she was converted into the auxiliary aircraft carrier AUDACITY.

3 JULY 1941

	Antiaircraft ship ALYNBANK transferred to convoy WN.48 in Pentland Firth and escorted the convoy to Methil.

4 JULY 1941

	USN Catalina PBY aircraft of VP-72 Squadron began reconnaissance flight operations from Reykjavik, Iceland, supported by USN seaplane tender GOLDSBOROUGH (AVD-5).
	Destroyer ESKIMO departed Scapa Flow for Sheerness and refitting at London.

0730	Destroyer ACTIVE arrived at Scapa Flow from Loch Ewe with defective machinery.
1000	Destroyers INGLEFIELD and ACHATES arrived at Scapa Flow from Greenock escorting battle cruiser REPULSE.

5 JULY 1941

	Heavy cruiser SHROPSHIRE arrived at Scapa Flow to join the Home Fleet from the East Indies carrying sixty prisoners of war.
	Antisubmarine trawler NORTHERN FOAM sighted a German U-boat on the surface in 62, 20N, 15, 37W. The U-boat escaped at high speed on the surface. Antisubmarine trawlers NORTHERN PRINCESS and NORTHERN SKY joined in the hunt, but no further contact was made with the U-boat in the area.
0630	For Operation DN, light cruiser NIGERIA, antiaircraft cruiser CURAÇOA, and destroyers BEDOUIN, PUNJABI, TARTAR, and ECLIPSE departed Scapa Flow to strike German shipping near Stadlandet, Norway, during the night. A German aircraft spotted the force during the night on 5/6 July, forcing the ships to return to Scapa Flow.
1700	Destroyer JUPITER departed Scapa Flow for Greenock to carry out minor repairs prior to joining Western Approaches Command. The destroyer was to have been in the escort for convoy WS.9C, but the repairs required longer than expected. Destroyer LIGHTNING replaced her in the convoy escort.
1900	Dutch destroyer ISAAC SWEERS arrived at Scapa Flow from Greenock to carry out working up to combat efficiency exercises.

7 JULY 1941

	USN Task Force TF.19 (RAdm David McC. Le Breton) arrived at Reykjavik, Iceland, from Argentia, Newfoundland, with the USMC 1st Marine Brigade. The cover force included USN battleships NEW YORK (BB-34) (Le Breton) and ARKANSAS (BB-33), light cruisers BROOKLYN (CL-40) and NASHVILLE (CL-43), with destroyers PLUNKETT (DD-431), NIBLACK (DD-424), BENSON (DD-421), GLEAVES (DD-423), MAYO (DD-422), CHARLES F. HUGHES (DD-428), LANSDALE (DD-426), HILARY P. JONES (DD-427), ELLIS (DD-154), BERNADOU (DD-153), UPSHUR (DD-144), LEA (DD-118), and BUCK (DD-420). The USN transport force included WILLIAM P. BIDDLE (AP-15), FULLER (AP-14), HEYWOOD (AP-12), ORIZABA (AP-24), ARCTURUS (AK-18), HAMUL (AK-30), SALAMONIE (AO-16), and tug CHEROKEE (ATF-66). Following disembarkation, the Task Force departed Iceland on the 12th and arrived at Argentia, Newfoundland, on the 19th.
	Submarine P.31 and the Free French submarine MINERVE patrolled in the Faeroes area.
	The Flag of the Rear Admiral Commanding 10th Cruiser Squadron was temporarily transferred to base ship DUNLUCE CASTLE at Scapa Flow.
	Destroyer HEYTHROP departed Scapa Flow for Loch Alsh.
	A Dominie aircraft of 782 Squadron crashed while ferrying passengers between Hatston and Donibristle. Petty Officer W. C. Jones, 1st Officer M. E. J. Dobson WRNS, Lt F. P. Tennyson of EXCELLENT, and passengers 2nd Lt J. L. Day RA, Mr. C. W. Young of Vickers Armstrong, and Mr. T. McCabe were all killed.
0800	Destroyers INTREPID and ANTELOPE were detached from convoy OB.341A escort and returned to Scapa Flow.

8 JULY 1941

	Light cruiser NIGERIA and later battle cruiser REPULSE departed Scapa Flow to cover the force that was laying Minefield SN.67A.
0900	Australian destroyer NESTOR departed Scapa Flow to join destroyer JUPITER at Greenock prior to proceeding to the Mediterranean.
0930	Destroyers INTREPID and ANTELOPE arrived at Scapa Flow after escorting convoy OB.341A.
1100	Antiaircraft ship ALYNBANK arrived at Scapa Flow after escorting convoy EC.41 from May Island to Pentland Firth.
1300	Light cruiser NIGERIA, antiaircraft cruiser CURAÇOA, plus destroyers BEDOUIN, PUNJABI, TARTAR, and ECLIPSE returned to Scapa Flow concluding the aborted Operation DN.
>1301	Antiaircraft cruiser CURAÇOA departed Scapa Flow to join convoy EC.42, south of Duncansby Head, and escort the convoy to Cape Wrath.
2300	Antiaircraft cruiser CURAÇOA transferred from convoy EC.42 to convoy WN.50 east of Cape Wrath and escorted it to Methil.

9 JULY 1941

	Minelayers AGAMEMNON, MENETHEUS, and PORT QUEBEC laid Minefield SN.67A of the Northern Barrage escorted by destroyers CASTLETON, WELLS, and HEYTHROP.
	Heavy cruiser SUFFOLK arrived at Hvalfjord, Iceland, after her Denmark Strait patrol. After refuelling, she departed for Scapa Flow, where she arrived on the 11th.
	Heavy cruiser DEVONSHIRE departed Scapa Flow for Hvalfjord. En route, she intercepted Panamanian

	steamer ST-CERGUE (4260grt) in 63, 28N, 07, 55W and sent her to Skopenfjord under armed guard. The cruiser arrived at Hvalfjord on the 10th and arrived back at Scapa Flow on the 15th.
	Light cruisers AURORA, ARETHUSA, and MANCHESTER departed Scapa Flow for the Clyde to escort convoy WS.9C.
2100	British aircraft reported a German U-boat in 60, 36N, 03, 20W. Polish destroyer KRAKOWIAK and destroyer ECHO departed Scapa Flow to search for the U-boat.

10 JULY 1941

	Light cruiser NIGERIA arrived back at Scapa Flow after covering the force laying Minefield SN.67A.
	The Flag of the Rear Admiral Commanding 10th Cruiser Squadron was transferred from base ship DUNLUCE CASTLE to light cruiser NIGERIA at Scapa Flow.
1200	Destroyer WINCHESTER departed Scapa Flow to replace Polish destroyer KRAKOWIAK, which was searching for a German U-boat reported in 60, 36N, 03, 20W.
1900	Minelayer MANXMAN departed Scapa Flow for Greenock, Scotland, after working up to combat efficiency.
2030	Destroyer HEYTHROP arrived at Scapa Flow from Loch Alsh after covering the force that was laying Minefield SN.67A.

11 JULY 1941

0030	Polish destroyer KRAKOWIAK arrived at Scapa Flow after being relieved by destroyer WINCHESTER.
0700	Destroyer ECLIPSE departed Scapa Flow providing escort for motor launches ML.122, ML.124, ML.125, ML.128, ML.208, ML.210, ML.213, and ML.233 of the 4th Motor Launch Flotilla proceeding to Skaalefjord and thence to Reykjavik, Iceland.
0830	Battleship NELSON departed Scapa Flow escorted by destroyers LIGHTNING, KRAKOWIAK, and KUJAWIAK for the Clyde.
0840	Destroyers ECHO and WINCHESTER arrived at Scapa Flow after an unsuccessful search for the German U-boat reported in 60, 36N, 03, 20W.
1800	Antiaircraft cruiser CURAÇOA arrived at Scapa Flow after escorting convoy EC.43 from May Island to Pentland Firth.
2300	Destroyer ECLIPSE arrived at Skaalefjord with motor launches ML.122, ML.124, ML.125, ML.128, ML.208, ML.210, ML.213, and ML.233 of the 4th Motor Launch Flotilla.

12 JULY 1941

	USN Task Force TF.19 departed Reykjavik, Iceland, for Argentia, Newfoundland.
	In a flying accident on aircraft carrier VICTORIOUS, T/Sub-Lt (A) J. B. Ganner RNVR and Leading Airman L. Powell in a Fulmar aircraft of 809 Squadron were killed.
0930	Antiaircraft ship ALYNBANK departed Scapa Flow to escort convoy WN.51 from the Pentland Firth to Tod Head, where she transferred to convoy EC.44. In the Pentland Firth, the ship was detached from convoy EC.44 and returned to Scapa Flow.
1000	Destroyer ICARUS returned to Scapa Flow after completing repairs at Ardrossan, Scotland.

13 JULY 1941

	Light cruiser AURORA arrived back at Scapa Flow from the Clyde.
	Destroyer ECLIPSE departed Skaalefjord for Reykjavik with motor launches ML.122, ML.124, ML.125, ML.128, ML.208, ML.210, ML.213, and ML.233 of the 4th Motor Launch Flotilla.
1130	Destroyer KUJAWIAK arrived at Scapa Flow from Greenock, Scotland.
1200	Antiaircraft ship POZARICA arrived at Scapa Flow from Chatham to carry out working up to combat efficiency exercises.
2100	Antiaircraft ship ALYNBANK returned to Scapa Flow after being detached from convoy EC.44 in the Pentland Firth.

14 JULY 1941

	Heavy cruiser BERWICK departed Scapa Flow for turbine repairs at Rosyth. En route, the cruiser experienced further engine defects.
	Cruiser minelayer ADVENTURE departed Scapa Flow for Loch Alsh, where she arrived that evening.
	A Swordfish aircraft of 821 Squadron crashed at Ballantrae, Scotland, en route from Detling-Prestwick to Hatston. T/A/Sub-Lt (A) S. F. J. Wood RNVR, Leading Airman F. B. Bavidige, and passenger Air Mechanic M. Robinson were killed.
0500	Destroyer TARTAR departed Scapa Flow to assist heavy cruiser BERWICK.
0600	Destroyer HEYTHROP departed Scapa Flow to assist heavy cruiser BERWICK. En route, HEYTHROP was recalled to Scapa Flow.
0900	Antiaircraft cruiser CURAÇOA departed Scapa Flow to carry out exercises in Pentland Firth and then joined

	convoy WN.52 off Duncansby Head.
2000	Destroyer WELLS arrived at Scapa Flow from Loch Alsh to carry out a short program of exercises.

15 JULY 1941

	Minelayer TEVIOTBANK laid Minefield SN.21A of the Northern Barrage escorted by destroyer CASTLETON and survey ship SCOTT.
0030	Destroyer HEYTHROP arrived back at Scapa Flow.
0900	Destroyer TARTAR returned to Scapa Flow after safely escorting heavy cruiser BERWICK to Rosyth.
1015	Destroyer ECLIPSE arrived at Reykjavik, Iceland, from Skaalefjord with motor launches ML.122, ML.124, ML.125, ML.128, ML.208, ML.210, ML.213, and ML.233 of the 4th Motor Launch Flotilla.
1800	Destroyer ECLIPSE departed Reykjavik for Scapa Flow.
1900	Antiaircraft cruiser CURAÇOA arrived at Scapa Flow after escorting convoy EC.45 to Pentland Firth.
2030	Antiaircraft cruiser CURAÇOA departed Scapa Flow to rejoin a portion of convoy EC.45, which had proceeded north of the Orkneys.

16 JULY 1941

1400	Destroyer WELLS departed Scapa Flow after her exercises to return to Loch Alsh.

17 JULY 1941

	Polish destroyer BURZA arrived at Scapa Flow escorting fleet oiler BLACK RANGER (3417grt). The destroyer later departed to return to the Western Approaches Command.
0500	Destroyer WINCHESTER departed Scapa Flow for Rosyth after working up to combat efficiency. En route, she joined convoy WN.53 as additional escort.
0500	Antiaircraft ship ALYNBANK departed Scapa Flow to provide antiaircraft protection for convoy WN.53 from Pentland Firth until south of Buchan Ness, where she transferred to convoy EC.46.
0530	Destroyer ECLIPSE arrived at Scapa Flow from Reykjavik, Iceland.
0630	Destroyer ORIBI arrived at Scapa Flow from Greenock to work up to combat efficiency.
1000	Destroyer HEYTHROP departed Scapa Flow escorting tankers WAR SUDRA (5627grt) and DAXHOUND (1128grt).
1700	Destroyer HEYTHROP escorting tankers WAR SUDRA (5627grt) and DAXHOUND (1128grt) joined trawler NORTHERN SKY with steamer LOCHGARRY (1627grt) in position 270 degrees at twenty-four miles from Noup Head. The group then proceeded to Skofenfjord in the Faeroes.
2000	Destroyer ESCAPADE arrived at Scapa Flow from the Tyne after completing her refit.

18 JULY 1941

	Battle cruiser REPULSE departed Scapa Flow escorted by destroyers ICARUS, ACTIVE, and ACHATES for Rosyth.
0700	Destroyer BEDOUIN departed Scapa Flow for a refit in the Humber.
1230	Destroyer ANTHONY arrived at Scapa Flow from Rosyth on the completion of her refit.
1630	Destroyer HEYTHROP arrived at Skofenfjord in the Faeroes with tankers WAR SUDRA (5627grt) and DAXHOUND (1128grt) plus trawler NORTHERN SKY with steamer LOCHGARRY (1627grt). HEYTHROP and WAR SUDRA and then proceeded on to Seidisfjord.
2000	Antiaircraft ship ALYNBANK transferred to convoy WN.54 off Cape Wrath.

19 JULY 1941

1930	Battleship PRINCE OF WALES arrived at Scapa Flow from Rosyth with destroyers ACTIVE, ACHATES, and ICARUS.

20 JULY 1941

	Antiaircraft ship ALYNBANK transferred to convoy EC.47 during the morning. On arrival in Pentland Firth, she was detached from the convoy and returned to Scapa Flow.
1600	Destroyer HEYTHROP arrived at Seidisfjord with tanker WAR SUDRA (5627grt).

21 JULY 1941

	Antiaircraft ship POZARICA departed Scapa Flow to join the Western Approaches Command after completing her fit.
	Minelaying cruiser ADVENTURE arrived at Scapa Flow, en route to Archangel, Russia.
0200	Antiaircraft ship ALYNBANK arrived at Scapa Flow after convoy escort duty.
0730	Destroyer HEYTHROP departed Seidisfjord for Skaalefjord.
1300	Antiaircraft ship PALOMARES arrived at Scapa Flow to begin working up to combat efficiency exercises.

1900	Aircraft carrier FURIOUS arrived at Scapa Flow from Greenock escorted by destroyers GARLAND, CASTLETON, and CHARLESTOWN after flying exercises in the Pentland Firth.

22 JULY 1941

	Minelayer TEVIOTBANK laid Minefield SN.21B in the Northern Barrage escorted by survey ship SCOTT.
0300	Destroyers ECLIPSE and ECHO departed Scapa Flow escorting tanker BLACK RANGER (3417grt) to Seidisfjord.
0630	Antiaircraft cruiser CURAÇOA departed Scapa Flow and joined convoy WN.55 in Pentland Firth.
0715	Destroyer CROOME departed Scapa Flow carrying Admiral Commanding 10th Cruiser Squadron and his staff to Rosyth.
0800	Destroyer HEYTHROP arrived at Skaalefjord from Seidisfjord.
1247	After receiving reports that German battle cruiser SCHARNHORST had departed Brest, battleship KING GEORGE V, heavy cruiser SHROPSHIRE, light cruisers NIGERIA and AURORA, and destroyers TARTAR, PUNJABI, ICARUS, INTREPID, ESCAPADE, and ACHATES were brought to one hour's alert notice.
1330	Destroyer HEYTHROP departed Skaalefjord with tankers DAXHOUND (1128grt) and WAR PINDARI (5559grt) plus antisubmarine trawler LORD AUSTIN to deliver the tankers to Kirkwall.
1616	Heavy cruisers DEVONSHIRE and SUFFOLK were brought to one hour's alert notice.
1720	Heavy cruisers DEVONSHIRE and SUFFOLK and light cruiser AURORA reverted to normal alert notice to allow urgent maintenance to be carried out.
1756	Aircraft carrier FURIOUS reverted to normal alert notice to allow urgent maintenance to be carried out.
1829	Aircraft carrier VICTORIOUS plus destroyers INGLEFIELD, ANTELOPE, ACTIVE, and ANTHONY were brought to one hour's alert notice.
2200	Antiaircraft cruiser CURAÇOA was detached from convoy WN.55 escort in Pentland Firth and joined convoy EC.48 and provided cover northward.

23 JULY 1941

	Heavy cruiser LONDON arrived at Scapa Flow from Gibraltar.
	Minelaying cruiser ADVENTURE departed Scapa Flow for Seidisfjord.
	Minesweepers NIGER, SALAMANDER, and HALCYON arrived at Scapa Flow en route to Iceland.
1226	The Home Fleet returned to normal alert notice when the German battle cruiser SCHARNHORST was located at La Pallice, France.
1520	Antiaircraft cruiser CURAÇOA arrived at Scapa Flow after escort duty.
2000	Destroyer HEYTHROP arrived at Scapa Flow after tankers DAXHOUND (1128grt) and WAR PINDARI (5559grt) were detached to Kirkwall escorted by antisubmarine trawler LORD AUSTIN.
2100	Polish destroyer KUJAWIAK departed Scapa Flow for Plymouth, England, on completion of working up to combat efficiency exercises.
2345	For Operation EF, heavy cruisers DEVONSHIRE (Flag Wake Walker) and SUFFOLK with aircraft carriers VICTORIOUS and FURIOUS, departed Scapa Flow with destroyers ESCAPADE, ACTIVE, ANTHONY, ACHATES, ANTELOPE, and INTREPID.

24 JULY 1941

	Destroyers ECLIPSE and ECHO arrived at Seidisfjord escorting tanker BLACK RANGER (3417grt) from Scapa Flow.
	Minelaying cruiser ADVENTURE arrived at Seidisfjord from Scapa Flow.
0800–2400	Antiaircraft ship ALYNBANK departed Scapa Flow and escorted convoy WN.56 from the Pentland Firth until she joined convoy EC.49 at approximately midnight.
1400	Fleet oiler OLIGARCH (6897grt) departed Scapa Flow for Seidisfjord escorted by destroyer GARLAND to support Force A.
2300	Light cruiser EURYALUS arrived at Scapa Flow from Rosyth escorted by destroyer CROOME.

25 JULY 1941

	For Operation EF, heavy cruisers DEVONSHIRE (Flag Wake Walker) and SUFFOLK, with aircraft carriers VICTORIOUS and FURIOUS, arrived at Seidisfjord from Scapa Flow with destroyers ESCAPADE, ACTIVE, ANTHONY, ACHATES, ANTELOPE, and INTREPID.
	Heavy cruiser SHROPSHIRE departed Scapa Flow for Hvalfjord and Denmark Strait patrol.
0300	Destroyer ACHATES struck a British mine of Minefield SN.69 in 64, 11N, 13, 00W and was badly damaged. (British sources claim the mine was from Minefield QZX.385.) She lost sixty-five ratings in the explosion and was towed into Seidisfjord by destroyer ANTHONY. Destroyer ACHATES was later towed by tugboat ASSURANCE and escorted by destroyer ANTELOPE to the Faeroes. Destroyer TARTAR escorted the towing group all the way to the Tyne. Destroyer ACHATES was under repair in the Tyne from 3 September to 13 March 1942.

1230	Destroyers INGLEFIELD and ICARUS departed Scapa Flow and relieved destroyer ECLIPSE and ECHO from their tanker escort. ECLIPSE and ECHO then joined the Operation EF Force to replace destroyers ACHATES and ANTELOPE.
1740	Admiral Vian hoisted his flag in light cruiser NIGERIA at Scapa Flow.
1800	Antiaircraft ship ALYNBANK arrived at Scapa Flow after she was detached from convoy EC.49 in Pentland Firth.

26 JULY 1941

	Submarine TIGRIS departed Scapa Flow for Murmansk, Russia. She would patrol northern Norway.
0900	Antiaircraft cruiser CURAÇOA departed Scapa Flow and escorted convoy WN.57 from Pentland Firth until transferring to convoy EC.50.
>1201	Minelayer ADVENTURE departed Seidisfjord with destroyer ANTHONY. ANTHONY returned the next day, while ADVENTURE continued on to Murmansk.
>1201	For Operation EF, Force F with heavy cruisers DEVONSHIRE (Flag Wake Walker) and SUFFOLK, aircraft carriers VICTORIOUS and FURIOUS, departed Seidisfjord for the Arctic with destroyers ESCAPADE, ACTIVE, ANTELOPE, and INTREPID.

27 JULY 1941

	Heavy cruiser SHROPSHIRE arrived at Hvalfjord, Iceland, from Scapa Flow before departing for a Denmark Strait patrol.
	Fleet oiler OLIGARCH (6897grt) arrived at Seidisfjord, Iceland, from Scapa Flow escorted by destroyer GARLAND to refuel Force A off Spitsbergen, Norway.
	Fleet oiler OLIGARCH (6897grt) escorted by destroyer GARLAND departed Seidisfjord later that day with trawlers SEALYHAM and WASTWATER to refuel Force A.
	AMC ESPERANCE BAY arrived at Scapa Flow on her way to London.
0600	Destroyers CROOME, HEYTHROP, and the Dutch ISAAC SWEERS departed Scapa Flow to escort inbound Canadian troop convoy TC.12.
1000	For Operation FB, light cruisers NIGERIA (Adm Vian) and AURORA departed Scapa Flow as Force A for Seidisfjord with destroyers TARTAR and PUNJABI.
	German bombing sank fishing trawler BEN STROME (198grt) fifteen miles southeast of Fuglo. All ten crewmen were lost.

28 JULY 1941

	Minesweepers HALCYON and SALAMANDER departed Scapa Flow for Seidisfjord, Norway, to provide antisubmarine protection.
	Heavy cruiser DORSETSHIRE arrived at Scapa Flow from the Tyne escorted by destroyers WINDSOR and WORCESTER.
	Heavy cruiser SHROPSHIRE departed Hvalfjord, Iceland, for patrol duties on a Denmark Strait patrol.
	German bombing sank fishing trawler **STRATHLOCHY** (212grt) 180 miles northwest of Rora Head, Orkneys.
1000	Antiaircraft ship ALYNBANK departed Scapa Flow and escorted convoy WN.58 from Pentland Firth. She transferred to convoy EC.51 during the next morning and escorted it back to Pentland Firth.

29 JULY 1941

0330	For Operation FB, Force A arrived at Seidisfjord, Iceland, from Scapa Flow with light cruisers NIGERIA (RAdm Vian) and AURORA plus destroyers TARTAR and PUNJABI to refuel from fleet oiler OLIGARCH (6897grt).
1330	Force A departed Seidisfjord for Spitsbergen, Norway.
1800	Antiaircraft ship ALYNBANK arrived at Scapa Flow after being detached from convoy EC.51 in Pentland Firth.

30 JULY 1941

	Minelayer PORT QUEBEC laid Minefield SN.21C in the Northern Barrage escorted by survey ship SCOTT.
1230	Antiaircraft cruiser CURAÇOA departed Scapa Flow and escorted convoy WN.59 from Pentland Firth to Methil.
2130	Battleship MALAYA and AMC ESPERANCE BAY departed Scapa Flow for Rosyth with destroyers CASTLETON, CHARLESTOWN, and CROOME. The AMC later continued on to London.

31 JULY 1941

	Minesweepers HALCYON and SALAMANDER arrived at Seidisfjord, Iceland, from Scapa Flow to provide antisubmarine protection.
	German bombing and gunfire damaged steam trawler ONWARD (209grt) twenty miles east of Nolsø, Faeroes.
2130	Destroyers CASTLETON, CHARLESTOWN and CROOME returned to Scapa Flow following escort duties.
2200	Heavy cruiser LONDON and Dutch destroyer ISAAC SWEERS, departed Scapa Flow for Greenock to escort convoy WS.10 after LONDON completed her working up to combat efficiency exercises.
2300	Destroyer ANTHONY departed Seidisfjord, Iceland, early in the morning and arrived at Scapa Flow after she

| | embarked part of the crew of damaged destroyer ACHATES. |

Norwegian Sea

Long. E03, 00 – E20, 00   Lat. N68, 00 – N58, 30

5 JULY 1941

| | A German Do18 aircraft spotted the Operation DN force with light cruiser NIGERIA, antiaircraft cruiser CURAÇOA, plus destroyers BEDOUIN, PUNJABI, TARTAR, and ECLIPSE when they were sixty-eight miles from Stadlandet, Norway. Having lost the element of surprise, the force aborted the shipping sweep and returned to Scapa Flow. |

8 JULY 1941

| | German fishing vessel **JAN HUBERT** (460grt) was sunk in a collision in southwest Norway. |

19 JULY 1941

| | RAF torpedo aircraft of 42 Squadron sank German patrol boat **NK.08/CANONIER** (ex Norwegian) west of Sirevaag, Norway. |

24 JULY 1941

| | RAF torpedo bombers of 42 Squadron sank Norwegian steamer **VESTKYST I** (370grt) off Skadberg, Norway. |

East of Canada

Long. W70, 00 – W30, 00   Lat. N68, 00 – N43, 30

1 JULY 1941

	USN Patrol Wing 7 began the first North Atlantic reconnaissance missions from Argentia, Newfoundland.
	USN Task Force TF.19 (RAdm McDougal Le Breton) with battleships ARKANSAS (BB-33) and NEW YORK (BB-34), light cruisers BROOKLYN (CL-40) and NASHVILLE (CL-43), plus destroyers PLUNKETT (DD-431), NIBLACK (DD-424), BENSON (DD-421), GLEAVES (DD-423), MAYO (DD-422), CHARLES F. HUGHES (DD-428), LANSDALE (DD-426) and HILARY P. JONES (DD-427) of DESRON 7 (Capt Kauffman), ELLIS (DD-154), BERNADOU (DD-153), UPSHUR (DD-144) and LEA (DD-118) of DESDIV 60 departed Argentia, Newfoundland, for Iceland.
	USCG cutters NORTHLAND (WPG-49) and NORTH STAR (WPG-59) set up a Northeast Greenland Patrol supported by naval auxiliary BEAR (AG-29) at Argentia, Newfoundland.
	Convoy SC.36 departed Sydney, Cape Breton, escorted by corvettes DAUPHIN and NAPANEE plus antisubmarine yacht PHILANTE. The corvettes were detached on the 4th. Destroyer CHESTERFIELD joined the convoy on the 3rd, corvettes AGASSIZ and WETASKIWIN joined on the 4th, and destroyer CHURCHILL joined on the 8th. On the 13th, the escort was detached when it was relieved by destroyers SABRE, SCIMITAR, and SHIKARI, sloop SANDWICH, corvettes ARABIS, DIANELLA, HELIOTROPE, KINGCUP, MALLOW, VERBENA, and VIOLET, minesweepers NIGER and SPEEDWELL, and antisubmarine trawlers NORTHERN GEM and NORTHERN SPRAY. The sloop, minesweepers, and trawlers were all detached on the 17th. The remainder of the escort, less corvette ARABIS, was detached on the 18th. The convoy arrived at Liverpool with corvette ARABIS on the 19th.

6 JULY 1941

| | USN troopships MUNARGO (AP-20) and CHATEAU THIERRY (AP-31) arrived at Tunugdliarfik Fjord, Greenland, with personnel and equipment to build an US Army Air Force support point. |
| | Convoy HX.137 departed Halifax, Nova Scotia, escorted by AMC CIRCASSIA plus corvettes DIANTHUS, SNOWBERRY, and SPIKENARD.
Corvettes BARRIE and MATAPEDIA joined the convoy on the 7th and were detached on the 8th.
On the 9th, destroyers READING and SALISBURY, AMC CHESHIRE, and corvette HONEYSUCKLE joined the convoy.
Convoy BHX.137 rendezvoused with HX.137 on the 10th. Corvette HONEYSUCKLE and AMC CHESHIRE were detached from the convoy on the 10th.
The remaining escorts were detached from the convoy when relieved by destroyers AMAZON, BULLDOG, BURZA, and GEORGETOWN, corvettes AUBRIETIA and NIGELLA, and antisubmarine trawlers DANEMAN and ST APOLLO.
Destroyer AMAZON was detached from the convoy later that same day and the rest of the escorts, less corvette AUBRIETIA, were detached on 21 August. Corvette AUBRIETIA arrived with the convoy at Liverpool on the 22nd. |

7 JULY 1941

| | Submarines TALISMAN and THUNDERBOLT were relieved from HX convoy escort duty and were ordered to cross the Atlantic and prepare for operations in the Mediterranean. |

GERMANY SENDS RUSSIA TO THE ALLIES

11 JULY 1941

Convoy HX.138 departed Halifax, Nova Scotia, escorted by destroyers ANNAPOLIS and ST CROIX plus AMC AURANIA.
Corvette RIMOUSKI joined the convoy on the 12th and sloop LEITH plus corvettes DAUPHIN and NAPANEE joined the convoy on the 13th.
RIMOUSKI, DAUPHIN and NAPANEE were detached from the convoy late in the day on the 13th.
AMC AURANIA was detached from the convoy on the 14th while destroyers ANNAPOLIS and ST CROIX were detached from the convoy on the 15th.
Destroyers BROADWATER and ST LAURENT joined the convoy on the 15th with corvette POLYANTHUS.
Destroyers BURWELL and RICHMOND joined the convoy on the 16th with corvette COBALT.
These escorts were detached from the convoy on the 23rd when relieved by destroyers BEAGLE, BOADICEA, and ROXBOROUGH, corvettes HEATHER, ORCHIS, and PICOTEE, and antisubmarine trawlers ARAB, LADY MADELEINE, and ST LOMAN.
The destroyers and corvette HEATHER were detached from the convoy on the 26th, and the convoy arrived at Liverpool on the 27th with the remainder of the escort.

12 JULY 1941

Convoy SC.37 departed Sydney, Cape Breton, escorted by corvettes BARRIE, CHICOUTIMI, and MATAPEDIA.
AMC AURANIA joined the convoy the next day and was detached on the 14th.
The three corvettes were detached from the convoy on the 15th. On the 15th, destroyers BURWELL and RICHMOND with corvettes COBALT and POLYANTHUS joined the convoy.
These escorts were detached from the convoy on the 23rd, when relieved by destroyers LEAMINGTON and SALADIN, corvettes ABELIA and ANEMONE, with antisubmarine trawlers ST ELSTAN and ST ZENO.
Destroyer DOUGLAS joined the convoy on the 24th.
Corvette ANEMONE was detached from the convoy on the 26th.
Destroyers DOUGLAS, LEAMINGTON, SALADIN, and SKATE, and trawler ST ZENO were detached from the convoy on the 27th.
Corvette ABELIA and trawler ST ELSTAN arrived with the convoy in the Clyde on the 28th.

16 JULY 1941

Convoy HX.139 departed Halifax, Nova Scotia, escorted by corvettes BITTERSWEET, FENNEL, and PICTOU, plus AMC RANPURA. Corvettes BITTERSWEET and FENNEL were detached later that day.
On the 17th, corvettes DAUPHIN and NAPANEE joined the convoy and were detached later the next day.
On the 18th, escort ships SENNEN and TOTLAND joined the convoy.
On the 19th, sloop FLEETWOOD joined the convoy.
On the 20th, corvette CHAMBLY joined the convoy.
Destroyers KEPPEL, LINCOLN, SHIKARI, and VENOMOUS and minesweeper HEBE joined the convoy, while AMC RANPURA and corvette CHAMBLY were detached from the convoy on the 26th.
Corvette PICTOU was detached from the convoy on the 28th.
Escort ships SENNEN and TOTLAND were detached from the convoy on the 29th.
Destroyers KEPPEL, LINCOLN, and SHIKARI were detached from the convoy on the 30th with sloop FLEETWOOD.
The convoy arrived at Liverpool on the 31st with destroyer VENOMOUS.

21 JULY 1941

Canadian troop convoy TC.12 departed Halifax, Nova Scotia, with troopships DUCHESS OF YORK (20,021grt), EMPRESS OF CANADA (21,517grt), ORION (23,371grt), STRATHMORE (23,428grt), and STRATHNAVER (22,283grt).
Destroyers ASSINIBOINE and BUXTON escorted the convoy from 21 to 23 July.
Destroyers HAVELOCK, HESPERUS, COLUMBIA, and RESTIGOUCHE escorted the convoy from 21 to 26 July. Battleship MALAYA escorted the convoy from 21 to 27 July.
Destroyers HARVESTER and RIPLEY escorted the convoy from 23 to 26 July.
Destroyer GURKHA, LANCE, LEGION, PIORUN, SALISBURY, VANQUISHER, and WINCHELSEA escorted the convoy from 26 to 29 July.
Destroyers CROOME, HEYTHROP, and ISAAC SWEERS joined the convoy on the 27th, from Scapa Flow. The destroyers escorted battleship MALAYA to Scapa Flow, where they arrived at noon on the 28th.
Antiaircraft cruiser CAIRO escorted the convoy from 27 to 29 July, when the convoy safely arrived at Liverpool.

22 JULY 1941

Convoy HX.140 departed Halifax, Nova Scotia, escorted by AMC ASCANIA with corvettes BITTERSWEET and FENNEL.
The convoy was joined on the 23rd by corvettes CHICOUTIMI and MATAPEDIA, which were detached later that day.
On the 24th, escorted ship WALNEY and corvette BUCTOUCHE joined the convoy.
Escort ship WALNEY was detached from the convoy the next day.

On the 25th, destroyers RAMSEY and COLUMBIA, corvettes CANDYTUFT, GLADIOLUS, MIMOSA, and NASTURTIUM, minesweeper SPEEDWELL, and antisubmarine trawlers NORTHERN SPRAY and NORTHERN WAVE joined the convoy.
 Corvette BUCTOUCHE was detached from the convoy on the 26th.
 NASTURTIUM was detached from the convoy on the 27th.
 Minesweeper SPEEDWELL was detached from the convoy on the 28th.
 Destroyer COLUMBIA was detached from the convoy on 1 August, as was AMC ASCANIA plus corvettes BITTERSWEET, CANDYTUFT, FENNEL, GLADIOLUS, and MIMOSA.
 Destroyers MALCOLM, SARDONYX, SCIMITAR, and WATCHMAN, corvettes AUBRIETIA, HEARTSEASE, NIGELLA, VERBENA, and VIOLET joined the convoy on 2 August.
 Destroyer AMAZON joined the convoy on 3 August.
 The destroyers were detached from the convoy on 5 August.
 The corvettes arrived with the convoy at Liverpool on 6 August.

Convoy SC.38 departed Sydney, Cape Breton, escorted by AMC CHITRAL with corvettes BARRIE, DAUPHIN, and NAPANEE.
 The corvettes were detached from the convoy on the 25th. Destroyer COLUMBIA plus corvettes GLADIOLUS, MIMOSA, and NASTURTIUM joined the convoy on the 25th.
 Corvette NASTURTIUM was detached from the convoy on the 27th.
 COLUMBIA was detached from the convoy on 1 August.
 AMC CHITRAL plus corvettes GLADIOLUS and MIMOSA were detached from the convoy on 2 August.
 Destroyer BURZA, corvettes AUBRIETIA, HEARTSEASE, and NIGELLA, and minesweeper BRITOMART joined the convoy on 2 August.
 Destroyers AMAZON and GEORGETOWN joined the convoy on 3 August.
 Destroyers AMAZON and GEORGETOWN were detached from the convoy on the 7th with corvette HEARTSEASE when antisubmarine trawlers DANEMAN and NOTTS COUNTY joined the convoy.
 Corvettes AUBRIETIA and NIGELLA were detached from the convoy on the 8th.
 The convoy arrived at Liverpool on 8 August escorted by the two trawlers.

27 JULY 1941

Convoy HX.141 departed Halifax, Nova Scotia, escorted by AMC MONTCLARE plus corvettes NANAIMO, ORILLIA, and TRAIL.
 Corvettes CHICOUTIMI and MATAPEDIA joined the convoy on the 28th.
 Corvettes CHICOUTIMI, NANAIMO, and TRAIL were detached from the convoy on the 30th.
 On the 30th, destroyer SKEENA joined the convoy with corvettes ALBERNI and PRIMROSE.
 The escort was detached from the convoy on 6 August when relieved by destroyers DOUGLAS, LEAMINGTON, and SKATE, corvette VERONICA, and minesweeper SPEEDY.
 VERONICA and SPEEDY were detached from the convoy on 8 August.
 DOUGLAS, LEAMINGTON and SKATE were detached from the convoy on 9 August.
 Antisubmarine trawlers ST ELSTAN and ST ZENO escorted the convoy in Home Waters until it arrived at Liverpool on 11 August.

East of United States   Long. W85, 00 – W60,00   Lat. N43, 30 – N25, 00

3 JULY 1941

USN battleship MISSISSIPPI (BB-41) began a Middle Atlantic patrol with destroyers O'BRIEN (DD-415), WALKE (DD-416), STACK (DD-406), STERETT (DD-407), and ROWAN (DD-405).

4 JULY 1941

Convoy BHX.137 departed Bermuda escorted by AMC CHESHIRE.

12 JULY 1941

USN Task Group TG.2.8 returned to Hampton Roads, Virginia, with aircraft carrier YORKTOWN (CV-5) with destroyers WAINWRIGHT (DD-420) and STACK (DD-406).

15 JULY 1941

USN heavy cruisers QUINCY (CA-39) and VINCENNES (CA-44) arrived at Bermuda with destroyers HAMMANN (DD-412) and MUSTIN (DD-413) following their Middle Atlantic patrol.
 USN Cruiser Division 7 (RAdm H. Kent Hewitt) with light cruisers PHILADELPHIA (CL-41), BROOKLYN (CL-40), SAVANNAH (CL-42), and NASHVILLE (CL-43) relieved heavy cruisers WICHITA (CA-45), QUINCY (CA-39), and VINCENNES (CA-44) from Central Atlantic Patrol.

16 JULY 1941

USN troopship WEST POINT (AP-23) departed New York City with German and Italian consular personnel and

	their families for transfer to Lisbon, Portugal.
	USN Task Group TG.2.7 departed Bermuda with light cruisers PHILADELPHIA (CL-41) and SAVANNAH (CL-42) plus destroyers MEREDITH (DD-434) and GWIN (DD-433) on a Middle Atlantic patrol.

19 JULY 1941

	The US Navy established Task Force TF.1 in the North Atlantic to protect US forces in Iceland and to support convoys from the United States to and from Iceland. 　The first convoy for TF.1 included aircraft carrier WASP (CV-7), with P-40 aircraft for Iceland, heavy cruisers QUINCY (CA-39) and VINCENNES (CA-44) with destroyers O'BRIEN (DD-415) and WALKE (DD-416). 　Other ships assigned to Task Force TF.1 included; 　DESRON 7 (Capt Kauffman) with BENSON (DD-421), NIBLACK (DD-424), HILARY P. JONES (DD-427), PLUNKETT (DD-431), MAYO (DD-422), MADISON (DD-425), GLEAVES (DD-423), CHARLES F. HUGHES (DD-428) and LANSDALE (DD-426). 　DESRON 11 with GRAYSON (DD-435), ROE (DD-418) and SAMPSON (DD-394). 　DESRON 30 (Capt Cohen) with DALLAS (DD-199), GREER (DD-145), TARBELL (DD-142), COLE (DD-155), BERNADOU (DD-153), LEA (DD-118), ELLIS (DD-154) and UPSHUR (DD-144). 　DESDIV 62 with MCCORMICK (DD-223), STURTEVANT (DD-240), REUBEN JAMES (DD-245) and BAINBRIDGE (DD-246).

25 JULY 1941

	USN Task Group TG.2.7 returned to Bermuda with light cruisers PHILADELPHIA (CL-41) and SAVANNAH (CL-42) plus destroyers MEREDITH (DD-434) and GWIN (DD-433) after a Middle Atlantic patrol.
	USN battleship NEW MEXICO (BB-40) departed Hampton Roads, Virginia, on a Middle Atlantic patrol with destroyers HUGHES (DD-410) and RUSSELL (DD-414).

27 JULY 1941

	USN Task Force TF.16 assembled at Norfolk, Virginia, with battleship MISSISSIPPI (BB-41), heavy cruisers QUINCY (CA-39) and WICHITA (CA-45), five destroyers, miscellaneous auxiliary SEMMES (AG-24), store ship MIZAR (AF-12), and cargo ship ALMAACK (AK-27). 　TF.16 joined aircraft carrier WASP (CV-7), which was carrying the air echelon of the 33rd Pursuit Squadron, heavy cruiser VINCENNES (CA-44), and destroyers WALKE (DD-416) and O'BRIEN (DD-415) at sea for transfer to Iceland.

30 JULY 1941

	USN Task Group TG.2.5 departed Hampton Roads, Virginia, with aircraft carrier YORKTOWN (CV-5) with VF-42, VS-41, and VT-5, light cruiser BROOKLYN (CL-40), plus destroyers ROE (DD-418), GRAYSON (DD-435), and EBERLE (DD-430) on a Middle Atlantic patrol ending at Bermuda on 10 August.

Caribbean and Gulf of Mexico
Long. W100, 00 – W60, 00   Lat. N31, 00 – N05, 00

1 JULY 1941

	Venezuelan authorities seized German steamer **DURAZZO** (1153grt) at Maracaibo, Venezuela. She was renamed PAMPERO (1153grt).

Western Approaches
Long. W30, 00 – W03, 00   Lat. N58, 30 – N49, 00

1 JULY 1941

	Landing craft **LCA.119** was lost in Home Waters to an unspecified cause.
	A mine sank fishing trawler **STRATHGAIRN** (211grt) about twenty miles southwest of Barra Head. Five of the crew were missing and six were landed at Stornoway.
	German bombing damaged steamers HIGHWOOD (1177grt) and JAMAICA PLANTER (4098grt) at Barry while in dry-dock. One crewman was killed on steamer HIGHWOOD.

2 JULY 1941

	Destroyers INTREPID, ACTIVE, and ANTELOPE departed Greenock for Loch Ewe to refuel, and then escort convoy OB.341A to the west until relieved by escort vessels from Iceland.
	Convoy OB.341A (there was no convoy OB.342) departed Liverpool, escorted by destroyers ANTELOPE and INTREPID with corvettes HEATHER and MIMOSA. The escort group, less corvette MIMOSA was detached on the 7th, when destroyer OTTAWA plus corvettes CANDYTUFT, GLADIOLUS, and NASTURTIUM joined the convoy. 　On the 8th, destroyer RIPLEY and AMC MALOJA joined the convoy. 　The escort group was detached from the convoy on the 15th and the convoy arrived at Halifax on the 18th.

0600	Destroyer ICARUS arrived at Ardrossan, Scotland, to begin repairs to her propellers, after arriving from Iceland in convoy HX.133.

3 JULY 1941

1400	Destroyers INGLEFIELD and ACHATES departed Greenock, Scotland, escorting battle cruiser REPULSE to Scapa Flow.
2200	Destroyer ACTIVE departed Loch Ewe for Scapa Flow with defective machinery. She had been withdrawn from convoy OB.341A escort duty.

4 JULY 1941

	A German IX Air Corps aerial mine sank steamer **LUNAN** (363grt) south of Cardiff, Wales, in 51, 26, 48N, 03, 10, 24W. Five of the six crewmen were lost. (Some sources claim German bombing sank her.)
	A German IX Air Corps aerial mine damaged motor vessel GOLDFINCH (454grt) ten miles 273° from St Bees Head, Solway Firth. She was towed to Whitehaven.
	Convoy OG.67 departed Liverpool escorted by destroyers CHELSEA and VERITY, sloop BIDEFORD, corvettes ARBUTUS, BEGONIA, CONVOLVULUS, JASMINE, LARKSPUR, and RHODODENDRON, plus ocean boarding vessel LADY SOMERS. LADY SOMERS was detached from the convoy that evening. On the 5th, catapult ship PEGASUS and corvette PIMPERNEL joined the convoy. On the 9th, destroyers CHELSEA and VERITY plus corvettes ARBUTUS, BEGONIA, CONVOLVULUS, JASMINE, and PIMPERNEL were detached from the convoy with PEGASUS. Corvette COREOPSIS, from Gibraltar, plus corvettes JONQUIL and SPIREA, from convoy HG.67, joined the convoy on the 14th. Corvette SPIREA was detached from the convoy on the 15th to assist OBV LADY SOMERS, which had been torpedoed. The convoy arrived at Gibraltar on the 20th escorted by sloop BIDEFORD, antisubmarine trawler ARCTIC RANGER, corvettes JONQUIL and COREOPSIS, Dutch submarine O.24, plus naval trawlers COPINSAY and ARRAN.
0100	Indian sloop JUMNA arrived at Greenock from Scapa Flow escorting depot ship GREENWICH.

5 JULY 1941

	A German He115 aircraft sank steamer **FOWEY ROSE** (470grt) with an aerial torpedo in the Bristol Channel in 51, 51N, 05, 28W. Eight crewmen were missing.
	German bombing damaged submarines TRAVELLER and TROOPER while they were being built at the Scott's yard at Greenock (Scotts Shipbuilding and Engineering Company).

6 JULY 1941

	Convoy OB.343 departed Liverpool escorted by destroyers SABRE, SHIKARI, and VENOMOUS, corvettes CLARKIA, DIANELLA, and KINGCUP, and antisubmarine trawlers LADY ELSA, MAN O' WAR, NORTHERN DAWN, and WELLARD. This escort group, except corvette CLARKIA, was detached from the convoy on the 12th, when destroyer HARVESTER, AMC AUSONIA, plus corvettes HEPATICA, PRIMROSE, TRILLIUM, TULIP, and WINDFLOWER joined the convoy. The convoy was dispersed on the 20th.
	P/T/A/Sub-Lt (A) T. Duncan RNVR, and Air Mechanic B. E. Randle were killed when their Fulmar aircraft of 759 Squadron crashed near Ilchester, England.
	German bombing sank steam trawler **WESTFIELD** (140grt) off St Govan's Head, near Lundy Island.

7 JULY 1941

	German bombing damaged Norwegian tanker FERNCOURT (9918grt) west of Pembroke in 51, 50N, 05, 29, 30W. Two gunners were lost. The tanker returned to Milford Haven and was docked at Swansea, England.
	Aircraft carrier ARGUS completed her refit at the Clyde. She was allocated for deck landing training duties.
	Convoy OB.344 departed Liverpool escorted by destroyers HESPERUS, SARDONYX, ST FRANCIS, and WATCHMAN, catapult ship ARIGUANI, plus escort ships SENNEN, TOTLAND, and WALNEY. Catapult ship ARIGUANI and destroyer SARDONYX were detached from the convoy on the 11th. The remainder of the escort was detached from the convoy on the 16th. Destroyers ASSINIBOINE and OTTAWA joined the convoy on the 15th and were detached on the 17th when the convoy was dispersed.
1800	Destroyer HEYTHROP arrived at Loch Alsh from Scapa Flow.

8 JULY 1941

	German bombing again damaged submarines TRAVELLER and TROOPER while they were being built at the Scott's yard at Greenock (Scott's Shipbuilding and Engineering Company).

9 JULY 1941

0400	Australian destroyer NESTOR arrived at Greenock to join destroyer JUPITER prior to proceeding to the Mediterranean.

10 JULY 1941

	Light cruisers AURORA, ARETHUSA, and MANCHESTER arrived at the Clyde from Scapa Flow to escort convoy WS.9C.
	German bombing by six He115 aircraft of KGR.406 sank Norwegian steamer **SVINT** (1174grt) seven miles northwest of Kellan Head, Trevose. One crewman was lost.
1130	Destroyer HEYTHROP was detached from the Minefield SN.67A force escort. After collecting mail at Loch Alsh she continued on to Scapa Flow.

11 JULY 1941

	Convoy OB.345 departed Liverpool escorted by destroyers ARROW, BULLDOG, and GEORGETOWN, corvettes AUBRIETIA and NIGELLA, and antisubmarine trawler ST APOLLO. This escort group was detached from the convoy on the 16th when AMC CALIFORNIA, destroyers CHESTERFIELD and CHURCHILL, and corvettes ARROWHEAD, CAMELLIA, and EYEBRIGHT joined the convoy. The second escort group was detached from the convoy on the 24th, and the convoy arrived at Halifax, Nova Scotia, on the 26th.
0500	Destroyer ICARUS, on completion of repairs, departed Ardrossan, Scotland, escorting tanker MONTENOL (2646grt) to Loch Alsh. She then proceeded to Scapa Flow.
0900	Minelayer MANXMAN arrived at Greenock from Scapa Flow. She replaced light cruiser AURORA for escorting convoy WS.9C. AURORA was ordered to return to Scapa Flow.

12 JULY 1941

	Steamer BLACKHEATH (4637grt) damaged corvette ARBUTUS in a collision in 55, 58N, 10, 38W. Corvette PIMPERNEL stood by ARBUTUS and escorted her to Liverpool, where she completed repairs on 19 August.
	Convoy OG.68 departed Liverpool escorted by destroyers BATH and WALKER, corvettes AZALEA, BLUEBELL, CAMPANULA, HYDRANGEA, WALLFLOWER, and ZINNIA. The convoy was joined on the 13th by ocean boarding vessels (OBV) CAVINA and HILARY. On the 14th, corvette AZALEA was detached from the convoy. On the 18th, the destroyers and OBVs were detached from the convoy. Destroyer WISHART and submarine CLYDE, from convoy HG.68, joined the convoy on the 22nd. On the 25th, the submarine was diverted to patrol in the vicinity of 40N, 15W. The convoy arrived at Gibraltar on the 26th with WISHART and the five corvettes.
1054	Battleship NELSON arrived at Greenock from Scapa Flow escorted by destroyers LIGHTNING, KRAKOWIAK, and KUJAWIAK. Destroyer LIGHTNING remained at Greenock to escort convoy WS.9C.
1430	Destroyer KUJAWIAK departed Greenock to return to Scapa Flow.
1500	Destroyer KRAKOWIAK, which had completed working up to combat efficiency, departed Greenock for Plymouth.

13 JULY 1941

	Convoy WS.9C formed at sea from ships sailing from Avonmouth, Liverpool, and the Clyde. Most of the ships in the convoy were part of the Operation SUBSTANCE convoy for Malta. The Clyde section, escorted by light cruisers ARETHUSA and the Dutch HEEMSKERK, departed on the 10th. The convoy consisted of battleship NELSON, light cruisers MANCHESTER, ARETHUSA, and HEEMSKERK, minelayer MANXMAN, and steamers DEUCALION (7516grt), AVILA STAR (14,443grt), LEINSTER (4302grt), PORT CHALMERS (8535grt), PASTEUR (29,253grt), MELBOURNE STAR (12,806grt), DURHAM (10,893grt), SYDNEY STAR (11,219grt), and CITY OF PRETORIA (8046grt). Destroyer WINCHELSEA escorted the convoy on the 12th. Sloop STORK escorted the Avonmouth convoy section and remained with the convoy until 13 July. Light cruiser HEEMSKERK escorted the convoy from 12 to 15 July with destroyers GURKHA, GARLAND, VANOC, and WANDERER. Battleship NELSON, light cruisers MANCHESTER and ARETHUSA, escorted the convoy from 12 to 17 July with destroyers COSSACK, MAORI, SIKH, NESTOR, and LIGHTNING. Troopship PASTEUR was detached from the convoy to Gibraltar on the 17th escorted by light cruiser MANCHESTER plus destroyers NESTOR and LIGHTNING. Troopship LEINSTER was detached from the convoy to Gibraltar escorted by destroyers COSSACK, SIKH, and MAORI. Minelayer MANXMAN escorted the convoy from 15 to 16 July. Steamer AVILA STAR was detached from the convoy to sail independently on the 16th. Destroyers FEARLESS, FOXHOUND, FURY, FORESIGHT, and FORESTER joined the convoy on the 18th from

	Gibraltar. Destroyer FIREDRAKE joined the convoy next day from Gibraltar. The destroyers remained with the convoy until its arrival on the 20th. Light cruiser EDINBURGH joined the convoy on the 20th and arrived with it at Gibraltar later in the day.

14 JULY 1941

	Minelayer ADVENTURE arrived at Loch Alsh from Scapa Flow in the evening.
	Convoy OB.346 departed Liverpool escorted by sloop WELLINGTON, corvettes CLOVER and VERVAIN, plus escort ships CULVER and LANDGUARD. On the 15th, destroyers ST ALBANS and WESTCOTT, catapult ship MAPLIN, plus corvettes AURICULA, HIBISCUS, MARIGOLD, and PERIWINKLE joined the convoy. Destroyers ST ALBANS and WESTCOTT were detached from the convoy on the 18th. Corvettes AURICULA and MARIGOLD were detached from the convoy on the 20th. Corvettes HIBISCUS and PERIWINKLE were detached from the convoy on the 21st. Corvettes CLOVER and VERVAIN were detached from the convoy on the 23rd. Catapult ship MAPLIN was detached from the convoy on the 28th. On the 31st, destroyer WRESTLER, sloop BRIDGEWATER, plus corvettes AMARANTHUS and BERGAMOT joined the convoy and all arrived at Freetown, Sierra Leone, on 1 August.

15 JULY 1941

	Steamer EMPIRE WAVE (7463grt) sank landing ship **PRINCE PHILIPPE** (2938grt) in a collision off the west coast of Scotland. T/Sub-Lt (E) F. G. Moncur RNR died of injuries sustained in the collision.
	U.558 sank Canadian steamer **VANCOUVER ISLAND** (9472grt) in the North Atlantic.
	German bombing sank steamer **FARFIELD** (468grt) five miles 250° from South Stack. One naval rating was saved, but the crew of eight was lost.

16 JULY 1941

	Convoy OB.347 departed Liverpool escorted by destroyers BEAGLE and BOADICEA, corvettes HEATHER, ORCHIS, and PICOTEE, minesweeper SHARPSHOOTER, plus antisubmarine trawlers ARAB, AYRSHIRE, LADY MADELEINE, and NORWICH CITY. Destroyers ROXBOROUGH and SALISBURY joined the convoy on the 18th. The initial escorts were detached from the convoy on the 22nd when destroyer BURNHAM with corvettes AGASSIZ, CELANDINE, MAYFLOWER, and Canadian WETASKIWIN joined the convoy. The convoy was dispersed on the 31st.
2130	Destroyer WELLS arrived at Loch Alsh from Scapa Flow after she completed working up to combat efficiency.

17 JULY 1941

	A German Fw200 aircraft of I/KG.40 spotted convoy OB.346 northwest of the North Channel and radioed its position. German aircraft spotted the convoy each of the next several days, but the British use of ULTRA intercepts enabled the convoy to avoid the waiting U-boats.
	Convoy OB.348 departed Liverpool escorted by destroyers DOUGLAS and SKATE, corvette ANEMONE, minesweeper LEDA, plus antisubmarine trawlers ST ELSTAN and ST ZENO. Destroyer LEAMINGTON and corvette ABELIA joined the convoy on the 22nd. The initial escorts were detached from the convoy on the 22nd, when destroyers READING and SAGUENAY plus corvettes DIANTHUS, HONEYSUCKLE, and SNOWBERRY joined the convoy. The new escorts were detached from the convoy off Halifax, Nova Scotia, on the 30th, and the convoy arrived at Halifax on the 31st.

18 JULY 1941

	A German Fw200 aircraft of I/KG.40 damaged steamer PILAR DE LARRINAGA (7046grt) in 54, 23N, 16, 53W. Four crewmen were killed. She was towed to Belfast Lough.

20 JULY 1941

	Convoy OG.69 departed Liverpool escorted by corvettes BEGONIA, JASMINE, LARKSPUR, PIMPERNEL, and RHODODENDRON plus antisubmarine trawler ST NECTAN. Corvettes ALISMA, DIANELLA, KINGCUP, and SUNFLOWER joined the convoy on the 21st. On the 26th, corvettes ALISMA, DIANELLA, and KINGCUP were detached from the convoy. On the 27th, corvette SUNFLOWER was detached from the convoy. Corvette BEGONIA was detached from the convoy on the 28th. Corvette RHODODENDRON was detached from the convoy on the 30th. Corvette FLEUR DE LYS joined the convoy on the 27th with antisubmarine trawlers LADY HOGARTH and LADY SHIRLEY. Destroyers FAULKNOR, FURY, and FORESTER departed Gibraltar on the 28th to escort this convoy, but they were recalled for Operation STYLE before they could join the convoy.

	Steamer ADJUTANT was detached from the convoy and arrived at Gibraltar on 1 August with corvettes JASMINE, PIMPERNEL, and LARKSPUR plus antisubmarine trawler ST NECTAN. The corvettes then departed Gibraltar and arrived with the convoy on 2 August.
0100	U.126 (Kptlt Bauer) spotted steamer CANADIAN STAR (8293grt) and began pursuit.
0242	U.126 missed CANADIAN STAR with two torpedoes, so she surfaced and attacked the ship with gunfire in 49, 15N, 21W. After shelling the ship for ten minutes, the armed guard fought back with great accuracy and forced the U-boat to dive. The damaged ship arrived at Curaçao on the 30th. (Some sources credit U.203 with this attack.)
0505	U.95 (Kptlt Schreiber) missed unescorted steamer PALMA (5419grt) with two torpedoes in 50, 14N, 17, 53W.
0528	U.95 surfaced and began shelling the zigzagging ship until the main gun experienced problems. Even after taking three shell hits, the steamer quickly outran the U-boat and escaped.

21 JULY 1941

	Convoy OB.349 departed Liverpool escorted by destroyers KEPPEL and SHIKARI, corvettes ALISMA, ALYSSE, DIANELLA, FREESIA, and SUNFLOWER, plus antisubmarine trawlers NORTHERN DAWN and WELLARD. Destroyer VENOMOUS joined the convoy on the 22nd. On the 26th, the initial escort group was detached from the convoy when destroyers BROADWATER and ST LAURENT, AMC CIRCASSIA, plus corvettes RIMOUSKI and SPIKENARD joined the convoy. The convoy was dispersed on 1 August. Convoy OB.349 was the last of the OB convoy series. Beginning on the 26th, the ON convoy series began with ON.1 departing Liverpool.

23 JULY 1941

	A German Fw200 aircraft spotted convoy OB.346 west of Ireland, but was driven off by a Hudson aircraft from RAF Coastal Command.

24 JULY 1941

	Convoy OS.1 departed Liverpool escorted by sloop FOLKESTONE plus corvettes AZALEA and PENSTEMON. The corvettes were detached on the 26th and 25 July, respectively. Destroyers BATH, VANOC, and WALKER joined the convoy on the 25th. The destroyers were detached from the convoy on the 28th, 26 July, and 3 August, respectively. Also joining the convoy on the 25th were antiaircraft ship ARIGUANI, which was detached from the convoy on the 28th, corvettes CARNATION, HELIOTROPE, LA MALOUINE, and MALLOW, which were detached from the convoy on the 28th, trawlers BALTA, KOS IX, and LORINDA, which were detached from the convoy on 3 August, plus boom defence vessels CONSBRO, LORD GAINSFORD, PANORAMA, and PHYLLISIA which were detached from the convoy on the 26th. Sloops LONDONDERRY and WESTON joined the convoy on the 26th and were detached from the convoy on 9 August. Destroyer CHELSEA joined the convoy on the 28th and was detached from the convoy on the 30th. Corvettes ANCHUSA, ASPHODEL, and CALENDULA joined the convoy on 9 August and arrived with the convoy at Freetown, Sierra Leone, on 10 August.

25 JULY 1941

	A German Fw200 aircraft of I/KG.40 reported the position of convoy SL.80 in the Western Approaches. No U-boats were near enough to attack.

26 JULY 1941

	Destroyers BROKE and VERITY collided near Londonderry, Northern Ireland, while escorting convoy SL.80. Destroyer BROKE sustained damage to her bow. Temporary repairs were done at Liverpool, and permanent repairs were done at the Hebburn on Tyne yard from 11 August to 12 September. Destroyer VERITY sustained extensive damage below the waterline. She was repaired at Belfast from 28 July to 21 September.
	Convoy ON.1 departed Liverpool escorted by sloop STORK. The sloop was detached from the convoy the next day when the convoy was joined by destroyers MALCOLM, SARDONYX, SCIMITAR, and WATCHMAN plus corvettes VERBENA and VIOLET, and antisubmarine trawlers NORTHERN PRIDE, NORTHERN SPRAY, and NORTHERN WAVE. Destroyers SARDONYX and SCIMITAR were detached from the convoy on the 30th and the remainder of the escort was detached from the convoy on the 31st, when relieved by destroyers BURWELL and RICHMOND with corvettes COBALT and POLYANTHUS. Destroyer BURWELL was detached from the convoy on 1 August. The remainder of the escort remained until the convoy was dispersed on 9 August.
	Leading Airman F. Andrew of 1 SFTS Netheravon was killed when his Hind aircraft crashed east of Shrewton. Leading Airman G. Ryalls was also lost in the crash.
0328	U.141 (ObltzS Schiller) damaged steamer ATLANTIC CITY (5133grt) while attacking convoy OS.1 north of Ire-

	land in 55, 42N, 09, 58W. The crew of forty-one initially abandoned the ship, but re-boarded when she remained afloat. She was later taken in tow and anchored off Buncrana, Ireland.
0328	U.141 (Philipp Schüler) sank steamer **BOTWEY** (5106grt) (Master Ebenezer Gordon) while attacking convoy OS.1 at 365 miles 270° from Bloody Foreland in 55, 42N, 09, 53W, sixty miles north of Tory Island. Rescue ship COPELAND (Master W. J. Hartley DSC) picked up the master, forty-eight crewmen and four gunners and landed them at Greenock, Scotland, on 28 July. U.141 reported torpedoing a third, unidentified, steamer, but only **BOTWEY** and ATLANTIC CITY were hit.
>0329	The 5th Escort Group led by destroyer WALKER (Cdr Macintyre) with destroyers VANOC, VOLUNTEER, SARDONYX, SCIMITAR, and Norwegian BATH plus corvettes BLUEBELL and HYDRANGEA dropped depth charges on U.141 for twenty hours after her attack on convoy OS.1.

27 JULY 1941

Convoy ON.2 departed Liverpool escorted by sloop BLACK SWAN and corvette CONVOLVULUS. Both escorts were detached from the convoy the next day.
On the 28th, destroyer BURZA, corvettes AUBRIETIA, NIGELLA, and SNOWDROP, minesweeper BRITOMART, and antisubmarine trawlers DANEMAN, NOTTS COUNTY, and ST APOLLO joined the convoy.
Destroyers AMAZON and GEORGETOWN joined the convoy on the 30th with corvette HEARTSEASE.
Destroyer GEORGETOWN and minesweeper BRITOMART were detached from the convoy on 1 August.
Destroyers AMAZON and BURZA, corvettes AUBRIETIA, HEARTSEASE, NIGELLA, and SNOWDROP, and antisubmarine trawlers DANEMAN and ST APOLLO were detached from the convoy on 2 August.
AMC RANPURA, destroyer BURWELL, plus corvettes CHAMBLY and PICTOU joined the convoy on 2 August.
The convoy was dispersed on 8 August.

30 JULY 1941

Convoy OG.70 departed Liverpool escorted by corvettes AURICULA, MARIGOLD, and SAMPHIRE.
On the 31st, catapult ship MAPLIN, sloop DEPTFORD, and corvette CONVOLVULUS joined the convoy.
Destroyers ST ALBANS, CAMPBELTOWN, and WANDERER were with the convoy during the day and were detached from the convoy that night.
Catapult ship MAPLIN was detached from the convoy on 1 August.
Corvettes COREOPSIS, JONQUIL, and SPIREA with antisubmarine trawler STELLA CARINA, from convoy HG.69, joined the convoy on 6 August.
Destroyers ENCOUNTER and NESTOR joined the convoy on 8 August from Gibraltar.
Destroyer FORESIGHT joined the convoy on 8 August from convoy HG.34F.
Destroyer ENCOUNTER, sloop DEPTFORD, plus corvettes AURICULA, CONVOLVULUS, JONQUIL, MARIGOLD, and SAMPHIRE were detached from the convoy on 10 August and arrived at Gibraltar on 13 August.
The convoy arrived at Gibraltar on 12 August with destroyers FORESIGHT and NESTOR plus corvettes COREOPSIS and SPIREA.

31 JULY 1941

Convoy ON.3 departed Liverpool escorted by corvette VERONICA and antisubmarine trawler ST ELSTAN.
Destroyers DOUGLAS, LEAMINGTON, and SKATE plus antisubmarine trawler ST ZENO joined the convoy on 1 August.
Corvettes MIMOSA and NASTURTIUM joined the convoy on 4 August.
The destroyers, corvette VERONICA, and the trawlers were all detached from the convoy on 5 August.
Destroyer COLUMBIA and corvette GLADIOLUS joined the convoy on 5 August.
AMC ASCANIA joined the convoy on 5 August and was detached from the convoy on 8 August.
Destroyer COLUMBIA plus corvettes GLADIOLUS, MIMOSA, and NASTURTIUM were detached from the convoy on 14 August when the convoy was dispersed.

Central Atlantic Crossing Zone
Long. W60, 00 – W15, 00   Lat. 49, 00 – N05, 00

1 JULY 1941

	U.108 (Kptlt Scholtz) sank steamer **TORONTO CITY** (2486grt), employed as a meteorological vessel, south of Greenland in 47, 03N, 30W. There were no survivors.
	U.201, U.562, U.564, U.561, U.559, U.557, U.553, U.202, U.111, U.108, U.98, U.96 and U.77 set up a new patrol line with slight success in the middle North Atlantic.
	A German Fw200 aircraft of I/KG.40 reported the location of convoy OG.66 in the North Atlantic. Only U.108 was able to intercept the convoy, while U.79, U.96, U.557 and U.77 failed to locate the convoy on its way south.
	A German Fw200 aircraft of I/KG.40 heavily damaged armed boarding vessel **MALVERNIAN** (3133grt) (Cdr J. W. B. Robertson RNR) in convoy OG.66 in the North Atlantic in 47, 37N, 19, 07W. The crew abandoned the vessel. T/Lt G. W. Jeffrey RNR, T/Lt (E) A. E. Magraw RNR, T/Lt J. R. Slimin RNR, A/Sub-Lt (E) K. J. Trineman RNVR,

and twenty ratings were lost. T/Sub-Lt P. Baddeley RNVR, and T/A/Sub-Lt A. England RNVR were wounded. Only fifty-seven from the crew of one hundred sixty-four survived.

Sloop SCARBOROUGH picked up a lifeboat of survivors, but could not locate the damaged vessel. She was finally sunk by German aircraft 11/7/1941 in position 47, 37N 19, 07W.

The captain and thirty-one others made it to Corunna in lifeboats on 21 July. Another twenty-one survivors arrived at Vigo in lifeboats on 22 July.

Finally, German minesweepers picked up the last boat; and P/T/Lt K. J. Dudgeon RNR, T/A/Sub-Lt (E) C. R. Keats RNVR, A/Major R. W. Madoc, RM, T/Lt T. G. Mitchell RNR, T/Paymaster Sub-Lt J. M. Moran RNR, T/Lt A. H. Rogers RNVR, T/A/Sub-Lt J. L. Wells RNVR, and others were made prisoners of war.

3 JULY 1941

	After ending attacks on convoy SL.78, U.66 and U.123 moved into the area off Freetown, Sierra Leone.
0436	U.69 (Kptlt Metzler) began a gun duel with steamer **ROBERT L. HOLT** (2918grt) (Master John Alexander Kendall) after she was dispersed from convoy OB.337 northwest of the Canary Islands in 24, 15N, 20, 00W.
0650	After U.69 expended 102 HE, thirty-four incendiary rounds from the deck gun, 220 rounds from the 20-mm gun, and 400 rounds of MG-34 fire, the steamer finally sank with the master, Vice Admiral N. A. Wodehouse, Commodore 2nd Class, forty-one crewmen, and six naval staff members. There were no survivors.

4 JULY 1941

	Ocean boarding vessel CAVINA intercepted German steamer **FRANKFURT** (5522grt) in 31, 34N, 37, 42W. The crew scuttled the ship and CAVINA rescued twenty-six survivors. Some twenty crewmen were missing.
0355	U.123 (Kptlt Hardegen) sank steamer **AUDITOR** (5444grt) (Master Edwin Bennett) after she was dispersed from convoy OB.337 about 600 miles northwest of the Cape Verde Islands in 25, 33N, 28, 23W. One crewman was lost. The master and fifty crewmen landed at St. Michael Island, Azores and twenty crewmen and four gunners landed at Taffalal Bay, San Antonio Island, Cape Verde Islands. Sloop GORLESTON (Cdr R. W. Keymer) took the survivors to Bathurst.

5 JULY 1941

0829	U.96 (Kptlt Lehmann-Willenbrock) attacked a group of ships composed of surveying ship CHALLENGER (Cdr W. C. Jenk OBE), AMC CHATHY (Master C. McC. Merewether) and troopship **ANSELM** (5954grt) (Master Andrew Elliott), carrying 1210 troops and RAF personnel for Takoradi, escorted by corvettes STARWORT, LAVENDER, and PETUNIA. These ships had departed the Clyde on 30 June for Freetown. Corvette PETUNIA had departed Londonderry on 30 June. The submarine sank steamer **ANSELM** with two torpedoes 300 miles north of the Azores in 44, 25N, 28, 35W. She went down in twenty-two minutes taking four crewmen and about two hundred fifty troops down from a crew of ninety-eight sailors and 1210 RAF and military personnel. CHALLENGER and corvette STARWORT (Lt Cdr N. W. Duck) rescued the master, ninety-three crewmen, three gunners, and 965 service personnel. All survivors were later transferred to AMC CATHAY, which landed them at Freetown, Sierra Leone.
>0830	Corvettes PETUNIA, LAVENDER and STARWORT damaged U.96 during an extensive depth charge attack with six salvoes north of the Azores. The U-boat had to abort her patrol and return to port for repairs.

6 JULY 1941

	Spanish steamer CORRIENTES (4565grt) re-supplied U.103 off Las Palmas and drew immediate protests from the British about Spain's neutrality.

7 JULY 1941

	Italian submarine TORELLI sighted another northbound convoy. Italian submarines DA VINCI, MOROSINI and BARACCA plus U.103 were arranged to intercept, but none found the convoy.
	Polish submarine SOKOL unsuccessfully attacked a large transport in 46, 41N, 20, 30W.
	Submarine CLYDE patrolled the area around the Cape Verde Islands.

9 JULY 1941

0155	U.98 (Kptlt Gysae) sank steamer **DESIGNER** (5945grt) (Master Donald Archibald McCallum) after she was dispersed from convoy OB.341 north-northwest of the Azores in 42, 59N, 31, 40W. The master and sixty-six crewmen were lost. Portuguese sailing ship SOUTA PRINCESCA (grt) rescued eleven survivors on the 10th in 42, 59N, 31, 40W, and landed them at Leixoes, Azores.
0528	U.98 (Robert Gysae) heavily damaged steamer **INVERNESS** (4897grt) (Master James Maxwell Henderson) after she was dispersed from convoy OB.341 north-northwest of the Azores in 42, 46N, 32, 45W.
0544	U.98 hit the ship with another torpedo and she broken in two and sank. Six crewmen were lost. The master, thirty-one crewmen and five gunners landed their lifeboats at Corvo Island, Azores.

14 JULY 1941

Italian submarine MOROSINI sank steamer **RUPERT DE LARRINAGA** (5358grt) after she was dispersed from convoy OG.67 in 36, 18N, 21, 11W.
Spanish tanker CAMPECHE (6382grt) rescued forty-four survivors.

Italian submarine MALASPINA sank Greek steamer **NIKOLKIS** (3576grt) after she was dispersed from convoy OG.67, 105 miles southwest of the Azores. Seventeen crewmen were lost.

15 JULY 1941

Italian submarine MOROSINI (Cdr Fraternale) sank ocean boarding vessel **LADY SOMERS** (Cdr G. L. Dunbar RD RNR) west of Gibraltar in 37, 12N, 20, 32W.
Corvette SPIREA of convoy OG.67 was ordered to her position to assist.
Spanish steamer CAMPECHE (6382grt) rescued the entire crew of one hundred thirty-eight.
Sloop BIDEFORD and antisubmarine trawlers LOCH OSKAIG and IMPERIALIST were ordered to intercept the steamer and remove the survivors due to the difficulty in obtaining the release of seamen from Spain. The Spanish ship landed the survivors at Lisbon and they arrived back at Gibraltar on the 18th in steamer PROCRIS (1033grt).

U.372, U.431, U.401, U.68, U.565, U.331, U.74, U.126, U.562, U.561, U.564, U.97, U.98, U.203 and U.95 set up a new patrol line in the North Atlantic.

17 JULY 1941

USN battleship TEXAS (BB-35) patrolled the middle Atlantic on a neutrality patrol with destroyers RHIND (DD-404) and MAYRANT (DD-402).

18 JULY 1941

After Spanish agents alerted the Germans that convoy HG.67 had sailed from Gibraltar, Italian submarines MALASPINA, MOROSINI, TORELLI, BAGNOLINI and BARBARIGO were positioned to intercept the convoy.
Using the ULTRA decoded messages; the Admiralty moved the convoy so she was able to avoid the submarine locations.

19 JULY 1941

1042	U.66 (Richard Zapp) sank steamer **HOLMSIDE** (3433grt) (Master Norman Caulfield) after she was dispersed from convoy OG.67 northeast of the Cape Verde Islands in 19N, 21, 30W. Twenty-one crewmen were missing. Portuguese steamer SETE CIDADES (grt) rescued the master, thirteen crewmen and two gunners and landed them at Lisbon on 1 August.

22 JULY 1941

Italian submarine BARBARIGO spotted convoy HG.67 and reported its position. U.93, U.94, U.124 and U.203 with Italian submarine BAGNOLINI (Cdr Chialamberto) failed to make contact with the convoy.

23 JULY 1941

Italian submarine BAGNOLINI (Cdr Chialamberto) made two attacks on convoy OG.68, claiming sinking one steamer and damaging another. No confirmation of damage was available.

U.93, U.94 and U.124 in a group with U.123 patrolled unsuccessfully west of Morocco.

24 JULY 1941

The German B-Service obtained the positions for convoy OG.69 and convoy SL.80.
U.431, U.565, U.401, U.74, U.95 and U.97 were set up to intercept convoy SL.80.
U.79, U.126, U.331, U.68, U.561, U.562, U.564 and U.203 set up to intercept convoy OG.69.

Italian submarine SQUALO claimed damaging a British tanker in 32, 20N, 24, 53E, but there are no confirmation records to support this claim.

25 JULY 1941

Italian submarine BARBARIGO (Cdr Murzi) sank steamer **MACON** (5135grt) west of North Africa in 32, 48N, 26, 12W. Twenty crewmen and one passenger were saved, twenty-five were missing, two crewmen died in the ship's lifeboat and one crewman were killed in the attack.

German Fw200 aircraft of I/KG.40 spotted convoy OG.69 twice west of Biscay.

26 JULY 1941

Italian submarine BARBARIGO (Cdr Murzi) sank tanker **HORN SHELL** (8272grt) west of North Africa in 33, 23N, 22, 18W. Seventeen crewmen were lost.
Portuguese trawler MARIA LEONOR (280grt) rescued the survivors. On 19 August, destroyer AVON VALE intercepted the MARIA LEONOR off Cape Juby and removed the survivors.

German Fw200 aircraft of I/KG.40 again spotted convoy OG.69 twice west of France. U.68 plus Italian subma-

27 JULY 1941

0021–0024	U.79 (Wolfgang Kaufmann) fired four torpedoes and claimed sinking two steamers and damaging two more while attacking convoy OG.69 at 800 miles southwest of Fastnet in 44, 55N, 17, 44W.
0021–0024	U.79 (Wolfgang Kaufmann) sank steamer **KELLWYN** (1459grt) (Master Alexander McLean) while attacking convoy OG.69 at 350 miles west-northwest of Cape Finisterre in 43N, 17W. The master, ten crewmen and three gunners were lost. Armed trawler ST NECTAN (Lt Cdr H. B. Phillips RNR) rescued nine survivors and landed them at Gibraltar on 1 August.
0254	U.203 (Kptlt Mützelburg) sank steamer **HAWKINGE** (2475grt) (Master Walter Aron Isaksson) while attacking convoy OG.69 at 800 miles southwest of Fastnet in 44, 55N, 17, 44W. Thirteen crewmen and two gunners were lost. Corvette SUNFLOWER (Lt Cdr J. T. Jones) rescued the master and five crewmen and landed them at Londonderry. Destroyer VANOC (Lt Cdr S. G. W. Deneys DSO) rescued seven crewmen and three gunners and landed them at Liverpool.
2351	U.126 (Kptlt Ernst Bauer) sank steamer **ERATO** (1335grt) (Master George D. Smail) (The convoy Commodore ship) while attacking convoy OG.69 at 200 miles west of Cape Finisterre in 43, 10N, 17, 30W. Eight crewmen and a gunner were lost. Corvette BEGONIA (Lt T. A. R. Muir) rescued the master, twenty-two crewmen and four gunners and landed them at Gibraltar.
2351	U.126 (Kptlt Ernst Bauer) sank Norwegian steamer **INGA I** (1304grt) (Master Lorentz Tvedt) while attacking convoy OG.69 at 200 miles west of Cape Finisterre in 43, 10N, 17, 30W. Three crewmen were missing. A convoy escort vessel rescued the master and fifteen crewmen.
2351	U.126 claimed sinking two more steamers during the attack.

28 JULY 1941

	Early in the morning, U.68 claimed she torpedoed a corvette.
	In the early morning, U.561 (ObltzS Bartels) sank steamer **WROTHAM** (1884grt) in convoy OG.69 northwest of Cape Finisterre in 43N, 17W. The entire crew was rescued. The U-boat also claimed sinking another steamer and damaging an AMC, but there are no supporting data.
	After a Spanish agent alerted the German Navy that convoy HG.68 had sailed from Gibraltar. U.79, U.126, U.66 plus Italian submarines CALVI, BAGNOLINI and BARBARIGO set up a patrol line.
0500	Destroyer HIGHLANDER rescued Norwegian steamer LIDVARD (4785grt) west of Africa in 12, 35N, 17, 52E. The steamer had escaped from Dakar during the night of 26/27 July. Vichy French auxiliary patrol vessel EDITH GERMAINE intercepted the steamer on the 27th. Destroyer BOREAS soon joined destroyer HIGHLANDER. Vichy French Light cruisers GLOIRE and GEORGES LEYGUES, submarine ACTÉON, and naval aircraft were at sea in an attempt to return the Norwegian steamer to Dakar. HIGHLANDER and BOREAS escorted LIDVARD to Freetown.
2127–2128	U.203 (Kptlt Mützelburg) sank steamer **LAPLAND** (1330grt) (Master James Stuart Brown) while attacking convoy OG.69 northwest of Cape Finisterre in 40, 36N, 15, 30W. Corvette RHODODENDRON (Sub-Lt R. H. Towersey) rescued the master, twenty-two crewmen and three gunners and landed them at Gibraltar on the 31st.
2127–2128	U.203 (Rolf Mützelburg) sank Swedish steamer **NORITA** (1516grt) in convoy OG.69 northwest of Cape Finisterre in 40, 10N, 15, 30W. Two crewmen were lost. Corvette RHODODENDRON (Sub-Lt R. H. Towersey), most likely rescued the eighteen survivors.

29 JULY 1941

	German AMC SCHIFF.36/ORION (FKpt. Weyher) sank steamer **CHAUCER** (5792grt) with ten torpedoes and gunfire west of Cape Verde Islands in 16, 46N, 38, 01W. Five torpedoes missed and the other five failed to detonate on impact, so the raider sank the ship using gunfire. The entire crew became prisoners of war.
	During the night, the escorts for convoy OG.69 forced U.331 under as she manoeuvred to reach firing range.
	Norwegian steamer LIDVARD (4785grt) arrived at Freetown escorted by destroyers HIGHLANDER and BOREAS

30 JULY 1941

0138	U.371 (Heinrich Driver) sank steamer **SHAHRISTAN** (6935grt) (Master Eric Henry Wilson) after she was dispersed from convoy OS.1 southeast of the Azores in 35,19N, 23, 53W. The master, thirty-eight crewmen and twenty-six passengers were lost. Panamanian steamer GLORIA (5896grt) rescuing nine survivors. Spanish tanker CAMPECHE (6382grt) rescuing thirty-three survivors. Corvette SUNFLOWER (Lt Cdr J. T. Jones) rescuing thirty-seven and landed them at Ponta Delgado, Azores.

	AMC DERBYSHIRE (Capt E. A. B. Stanley DSO MVO) rescuing six survivors and landed them at Gourock. (Some sources claim that all survivors were then transferred to ocean boarding vessel CORINTHIAN on 19 August.)
0246	U.371 (Heinrich Driver) heavily damaged Dutch steamer **SITOEBONDO** (7049grt) after she was dispersed from convoy OS.1 southeast of the Azores in 35,19N, 23, 53W. The seventy-one crewmen and six passengers abandoned the ship in three lifeboats.
0254	U.371 fired a second torpedo, but the steamer remained afloat.
0337	U.371 sank the steamer with a third torpedo.
	Seventeen crewmen and two passengers in the third lifeboat were never found.
	Spanish tanker CAMPECHE (6382grt) rescuing sixty-three survivors from two lifeboats the next day.
	Spanish tanker CAMPERO (6382grt) rescued two survivors from a raft after six days on the water.

31 JULY 1941

	Destroyer VANSITTART intercepted Vichy French steamer **OUED GROU** (792grt) in 13, 02N, 17, 20W. Destroyer HIGHLANDER was ordered to join VANSITTART. On 1 August, destroyer VELOX relieved HIGHLANDER and took the steamer into Freetown. HIGHLANDER proceeded to Bathurst to refuel en route to Gibraltar. On 3 August, VANSITTART was detached to proceed to Freetown. VELOX and the steamer arrived at Freetown on 4 August, despite an attempt by the crew to scuttle the ship.

UK East Coast

Long. W04, 00 – E03, 00   Lat. N58, 30 – N51, 30

1 JULY 1941

	A mine sank naval drifter **DEVON COUNTY** (86grt) (Skipper G. H. Barnard RNR) in the Thames Estuary in 51, 28, 51N, 00, 59, 14E. Three ratings were lost.
	German aircraft sank steamer **HOMEFIRE** (1262grt) north of Cromer in 53, 05, 30N, 01, 28E. Two crewmen were lost.

2 JULY 1941

	Minelayer PLOVER laid Minefield BS.66 off the east coast of England escorted by destroyer HAMBLEDON.
	Lt Cdr (A) F. D. G. Jennings, Commanding Officer of 768 Squadron, was killed when his Martlet aircraft dived into the sea after an engine failure at Abirlot, near Arbroath.

3 JULY 1941

	A German IX Air Corps aerial mine sank naval drifter **RECEPTIVE** (86grt) in the Thames Estuary in 51, 20, 50N, 00, 54, 35E. T/Lt R. H. A. Remington RNVR was lost.
	A German IX Air Corps aerial mine sank naval auxiliary ship **ROSME** (82grt) in the Thames Estuary in 51, 34, 12N, 01, 03E.

4 JULY 1941

	German bombing sank minesweeping trawler **AKRANES** (358grt) (T/Lt W. A. C. Harvey RNVR) off Bridlington Bay, Yorkshire. There were no casualties.
	Minelayer PLOVER laid Minefield BS.67, off the east coast of England escorted by destroyer HAMBLEDON.
	German bombing sank steamer **BALFRON** (362grt) 3½ miles 38° from Ravenscar, England. Four crewmen were missing.
1500	Antiaircraft ship ALYNBANK arrived at Methil with convoy WN.48 from Pentland Firth.

5 JULY 1941

	German bombing sank auxiliary minesweeper **SNAEFELL** (466grt) (A/T/Lt Cdr F. Brett RNR) off Sunderland in 54, 51N, 01, 27W. Brett was lost. T/Sub-Lt F. Greenwood RNVR and T/Lt A. R. D. Morgan RNVR were wounded.
1130	Antiaircraft ship ALYNBANK departed Methil to escort convoy EC.41 from May Island to Pentland Firth.

6 JULY 1941

	German bombing damaged Swedish steamer BIRGITTA (1363grt) northwest of Cromer in 53, 05N, 01, 19E. The steamer was towed to Great Yarmouth.
	German bombing damaged steamer NORTH DEVON (3658grt) off Sheringham in 53, 03N, 01, 38E. Five crewmen were killed. The steamer was towed to Immingham.

7 JULY 1941

	A German aerial mine sank naval drifter **LORD ST VINCENT** (115grt) (Skipper J. S. Alexander RNR) off North East Gunfleet Buoy in the Thames Estuary. One rating was killed and one rating died of wounds.

	A Fulmar aircraft of 804 Squadron was launched from catapult ship PEGASUS to intercept a German Fw200 bomber. The bomber was not located and the Fulmar proceeded towards Algergove in bad visibility. Sub-Lt T. R. V. Parke and Leading Airman E. F. Miller were killed when the aircraft crashed into Kerran Hill, near Southend, Kintyre.

8 JULY 1941

	Lt Cdr A. J. Tillard, Lt R. H. Furlong, and Lt Cdr W. Thompson were killed when their Walrus aircraft of 778 Squadron crashed off Arbroath.
1800	Destroyer ESKIMO arrived at Sheerness from Scapa Flow. Her refit was completed in September.

9 JULY 1941

	A mine sank steam vessel **BLUE MERMAID** (97grt) eight miles 185° from Clacton in 51, 39, 01N, 01, 08, 05E. Two crewmen were lost.

10 JULY 1941

	German bombing sank fishing trawler **ISABELLA FOWLIE** (196grt) seven miles east, northeast of Longstone, Scotland. Three crewmen were lost.
	Motorboat **CELANO** (14grt), being used as a tender to diving ship TEDWORTH, was sunk on a mine one cable 100° from Number 1 Channel Buoy. All six crewmen were lost.
0730	Antiaircraft cruiser CURAÇOA arrived at Methil with convoy WN.50.
1500	Antiaircraft cruiser CURAÇOA departed Methil to escort convoy EC.43 from May Island to Pentland Firth.

11 JULY 1941

	A German IX Air Corps aerial mine damaged motor vessel RIVER TRENT (246grt) west of Cromer in 53N, 01, 15E. She was towed to Great Yarmouth.

13 JULY 1941

	A German IX Air Corps aerial mine sank steamer **COLLINGDOC** (1780grt) four cables 200° from Southend Pier. Two crewmen were lost. She was re-floated on the 21st and towed to Gravesend, where she was converted to a hulk and towed to Rosyth.
	German bombing damaged steamer SCORTON (4813grt) two miles west of 57C Buoy, near Smiths Knoll. She arrived in tow at Immingham.

14 JULY 1941

	Minesweeper FRANKLIN was damaged in a collision with two merchant ships in the North Sea, and repaired at Aberdeen from 14 July to 23 August.

15 JULY 1941

	A collision sank Swedish steamer **IRIS** (1974grt) off the Scottish coast.
1100	Antiaircraft cruiser CURAÇOA arrived at Methil with convoy WN.52 from Duncansby Head.
>1101	Antiaircraft cruiser CURAÇOA departed Methil and joined convoy EC.45 off May Island. She was detached from the convoy in Pentland Firth and returned to Scapa Flow.

16 JULY 1941

	German bombing damaged steamer ELIZABETE (2039grt) halfway between 20C Buoy and T.2 Buoy, off the Tyne. She returned to the Tyne for repairs.
	P/T/Midshipman (A) R. L. Waddy RNVR was killed when his Swordfish aircraft of 767 Squadron crashed near Arbroath during exercises.

17 JULY 1941

	A collision sank drifter **FERTILE VALE** (91grt) off the River Tay.
	German bombing damaged steamer EMERALD QUEEN (481grt) northeast of Middlesbrough in 54, 39N, 00, 48W. She carried Admiralty Stores and ammunition and was towed to Hartlepool.
	Fishing steam trawler **BEN GLAMAIR** (198grt) was lost to an unknown cause near Dunstanburgh.
	Submarine UMPIRE (Lt Cdr M. R. G. Wingfield) departed Sheerness in convoy EC.47.

19 JULY 1941

	Antisubmarine trawler PETER HENDRIKS (266grt) escorting convoy FS.544 accidentally sank submarine **UMPIRE** (Lt Cdr M. R. G. Wingfield) in a collision off the Wash in 53, 09N, 01, 08E. Lt P. C. M. Banister DSC, Sub-Lt S. A. G. Godden, and fourteen ratings were lost. The crew of PETER HENDRIKS rescued Wingfield, T/Lt E. P. Young RNVR and fourteen ratings.

	Battleship PRINCE OF WALES departed Rosyth for Scapa Flow with destroyers ACTIVE, ACHATES, and ICARUS.
0630	Destroyer BEDOUIN arrived at the Humber from Scapa Flow for a refit.
0730	Battle cruiser REPULSE arrived at Rosyth from Scapa Flow escorted by destroyers ICARUS, ACTIVE, and ACHATES.

20 JULY 1941

	German bombing damaged steamer UMVUMA (4419grt) off Number 57 Buoy, in the Humber. The disabled vessel was able to proceed to Humber.
	Light cruiser EURYALUS arrived at Rosyth for a refit escorted by destroyer WORCESTER.

21 JULY 1941

	Destroyer ASHANTI was re-commissioned on the Tyne after extensive repairs.

22 JULY 1941

1500	Destroyer CROOME arrived at Rosyth from Scapa Flow to allow Admiral Commanding 10th Cruiser Squadron and his staff to embark in light cruiser KENYA.

23 JULY 1941

	A German IX Air Corps aerial mine sank steamer barge **OMFLEET** (130grt) in Alexandra Dock, Hull. There were no casualties.
	German IX Air Corps aerial mines damaged sailing vessels **ADAMANT** (80grt) and **SOAVITA** (80grt) at Alexandra Dock, Hull. Both vessels sank, but were later salvaged.

24 JULY 1941

0800	Light cruiser EURYALUS escorted by destroyer CROOME departed Rosyth for Scapa Flow.

27 JULY 1941

	Heavy cruiser DORSETSHIRE departed the Tyne for Scapa Flow, escorted by destroyers WINDSOR and WORCESTER.

29 JULY 1941

	German aircraft badly damaged steamer **ADAMS BECK** (2816grt) one mile 235° from 20C Buoy, Tyne. One crewman was missing, and the steamer sank the next day.
	Sub-Lt C. Wheatley, Midshipman L. E. W. Byam, and Leading Airman G. Curwen were lost when their Albacore aircraft of 832 Squadron crashed west of Kintyre.

31 JULY 1941

1130	Antiaircraft cruiser CURAÇOA arrived at Methil with convoy WN.59 from Pentland Firth.
1300	Battleship MALAYA and AMC ESPERANCE BAY arrived at Rosyth from Scapa Flow with destroyers CASTLETON, CHARLESTOWN, and CROOME. The AMC later continued on to London. The destroyers returned to Scapa Flow.
1600	Antiaircraft cruiser CURAÇOA departed Methil and joined convoy EC.52 off May Island. The convoy was escorted to Pentland Firth when the CURAÇOA was detached to Scapa Flow.

North Sea

Long. E03, 00 – E09, 00   Lat. N58, 30 – N51, 00

5 JULY 1941

	An RAF aerial mine sank Swedish steamer **STIG GORTHON** (2241grt) off Borkum, in the North Sea. The entire crew was rescued.
	Destroyer HOLDERNESS struck a mine in the North Sea. The damage required twenty-six days to repair.

7 JULY 1941

	RAF aircraft damaged Finnish steamer **DELAWARE** (2441grt) off the Hook of Holland.

14 JULY 1941

	German bombing sank Swedish steamer **ASPEN** (1305grt) forty-five miles from Rotterdam. Two crewmen were missing. (Other sources claim it was RAF bombers that sunk the ship.)

16 JULY 1941

	In a rare daylight attack, RAF bombers damaged seven steamers in Rotterdam, Holland.

19 JULY 1941

	RAF aircraft damaged German steamer HERMANN FRITZEN (3845grt) off the Dutch coast. She was towed into the Hook of Holland.

20 JULY 1941

	An RAF aerial mine damaged German steamer ASIA (7014grt) (ex Danish) off the Ems river mouth.

21 JULY 1941

	An RAF aerial mine sank German steamer **HANS CHRISTOPHERSON** (1599grt) off Terschelling.

23 JULY 1941

	German bombing damaged destroyer GARTH with a bomb near miss in the North Sea. The destroyer spent no time out of action.

27 JULY 1941

	An RAF aerial mine sank Danish steamer **KNUD VILLEMOES** (1582grt) north of Heligoland.

29 JULY 1941

	German steamer **BERNHARD** (1890grt) was lost in a collision with Swedish steamer FRODE (1535grt) near Norderney.

30 JULY 1941

	An RAF aerial mine sank German fishing vessel **PICKHUBEN** (238grt) off Esbjerg in the southern North Sea.
	RAF bombs damaged German steamer INGA ESSBERGER (grt) in the mouth of the Elbe river.

English Channel
Long. W07, 00 – E01, 30   Lat. N51, 00 – N49, 00

6 JULY 1941

	Fire destroyed motor gunboats **MGB.90** (33grt) and **MGB.92** (33grt) at Portland harbour. (Other sources place the fire occurring on 16 July.)

9 JULY 1941

	The German 4th S-Boat Flotilla (Kptlt Bätge) laid twenty-four TMA mines southeast and southwest of the Isle of Wight at 50, 33N 01, 26W.

10 JULY 1941

	An RAF attack on Cherbourg, France, damaged German tanker SCHLETTSTADT (8028grt).

16 JULY 1941

	A fire in Portland Harbour destroyed **MGB.90** and **MGB.92**. (Other sources place the fire occurring on 6 July.)

20 JULY 1941

	During the night, the German 4th S-Boat Flotilla (Kptlt Bätge) laid eighteen TMA mines southeast and southwest of the Isle of Wight.
	RAF aircraft damaged German tanker CARIBIA (12,049grt) in the English Channel. She was towed into Boulogne, France.

22 JULY 1941

	The German 4th S-Boat Flotilla (Kptlt Bätge) laid eighteen mines southeast of the Isle of Wight in 50, 25N, 01, 00W and southwest of the Isle of Wight in 50, 28N 02, 10W.

23 JULY 1941

	British MTBs sank German auxiliary patrol boat **Vp.1508/RAU III** (354grt) with a torpedo southwest of Boulogne.

25 JULY 1941

2100	Destroyers MENDIP, QUORN, and CATTISTOCK departed Portsmouth to bombard Dieppe in Operation

112 — JULY 1941

GIDEON. A brief bombardment was carried out early on the 26th, but the rest of the operation was cancelled due to bad weather.

27 JULY 1941

British MTBs unsuccessfully attacked German destroyer FRIEDRICH IHN while she was moving north to Calais.

28 JULY 1941

P/T/A/Sub-Lt (A) R. W. Langshaw RNVR was killed when his Hurricane aircraft of 759 Squadron crashed between Maiden Newton and Cerne Abbas.

0154 — In Operation CHESS, a patrol from an assault landing craft was landed near Fécamp. T/Lt (E) J. Templeton RNR, and one rating were killed. The landing craft was able to retire and joined with the covering force of motor launches ten miles southeast of Dover.

31 JULY 1941

French destroyer TRIOMPHANT departed Plymouth after her refit to join the Free French forces in the Pacific, via Panama. The destroyer arrived at St John's, Newfoundland, on 6 August, at Panama on 16 August, and at San Diego, California, on 25 August. She departed San Diego on 5 September, arriving at Honolulu, Hawaii, on 15 September, and at Papeete on 23 September. In the Pacific, the destroyer was used for escort duties between Australia and New Caledonia. She spent most of 1942 in Sydney, Australia, being overhauled.

Bay of Biscay

Long. W15, 00 – E03, 00   Lat. N49, 00 – N40, 00

1 JULY 1941

During the night, RAF bombers damaged German heavy cruiser PRINZ EUGEN at Brest. Sixty crewmen were lost when a bomb exploded in the ammunition bunker.

5 JULY 1941

Submarine TIGRIS (Cdr Bone) sank Italian submarine **MICHELE BIANCHI** (Cdr Tosoni-Pittoni) west of Bordeaux in 45N, 04W. There were no survivors.
(Some sources place this attack during the evening of 10/11 July.)

7 JULY 1941

Submarine SEALION (Cdr Bryant) sank Vichy French fishing trawlers **GUSTAV JEANNE** (39grt) and **GUSTAV EUGENE** (120grt) with gunfire off Ushant.

8 JULY 1941

Submarine SEALION (Cdr Bryant) sank Vichy French fishing trawler **CHRISTUS REGNAT** (28grt) with gunfire off Ushant.

9 JULY 1941

Submarine SEALION (Cdr Bryant) sank Vichy French fishing trawler **ST PIERRE D'ALCANTARA** (329grt) with gunfire off Ushant.

RAF aircraft accidentally attacked submarine TUNA (Lt Cdr Cavenagh-Mainwaring) while she was patrolling in the Bay of Biscay.

10 JULY 1941

Submarine TUNA (Lt Cdr Cavenagh-Mainwaring) unsuccessfully attacked a German U-boat (U.203 or U.124) in 46, 00N, 09, 40W.
(Some sources place this attack on 19 July.)

14 JULY 1941

Vichy French steamer ISAC (2385grt) departed Bordeaux, France, for Casablanca, Morocco, and then Dakar, Senegal.

17 JULY 1941

Submarine THRASHER (Lt Cdr Cowell) sank Vichy French fishing ship **VIRGO FIDELIS** (129grt) off San Sebastian with gunfire. She was beached, a total loss.

19 JULY 1941

Based upon ULTRA decoded messages, all Allied submarines were alerted to the possible arrival of German blockade-raiders arriving in the Gironde Estuary.

Germany Sends Russia to the Allies

Polish submarine SOKOL patrolled off the Gironde River estuary.

Submarine TUNA (Lt Cdr Cavenagh-Mainwaring) unsuccessfully attacked German tanker BENNO (8306grt) (former Norwegian **OLE JACOB** (8306grt)), escorted by minesweepers M.18, M.25, M.27, and M.30, sixty miles west of the Gironde. TUNA claimed hits on a steamer and a destroyer, but no ships were damaged. (According to German reports, the torpedoes detonated a mine. So the submarine thought it had hit the tanker, and the Germans did not know they were under torpedo attack, so they did not conduct any submarine sweeps.)

20 JULY 1941

German battle cruiser SCHARNHORST departed Brest escorted by destroyers ERICH STEINBRINCK, FRIEDRICH IHN, BRUNO HEINEMANN, Z.23 and Z.24 to conduct repair tests and to practice gun drills at sea.

23 JULY 1941

An RAF reconnaissance aircraft confirmed that German battle cruiser SCHARNHORST was at La Pallice, France.

24 JULY 1941

RAF Bomber Command sent 149 bombers against German battle cruisers GNEISENAU at Brest and SCHARNHORST at La Pallice during the night. Five bombs heavily damaged the SCHARNHORST, taking out nearly 200 Km of electrical wiring.
RAF bomb near misses also damaged German heavy cruiser PRINZ EUGEN at La Pallice.
RAF bomb near misses slightly damaged the GNEISENAU at Brest.
German AA and fighter defences downed ten Halifax bombers over La Pallice and accidentally downed a German Fw200 aircraft returning from a reconnaissance flight.

30 JULY 1941

Submarine SEAWOLF (Lt Cdr Raikes) unsuccessfully attacked U.562 off Lorient, France.

31 JULY 1941

German authorities requisitioned Italian trawler **SARDELLA** (329grt) at Arachon, France.

German steamer NATAL (3172grt) arrived at Gironde, France, after avoiding the British blockade.

West of Gibraltar
Long. W15, 00 – W05, 30   Lat. N40, 00 – N30, 00

1 JULY 1941

Destroyers FAULKNOR, FEARLESS, FORESTER, LANCE, and LEGION departed Gibraltar to join arriving convoy OG.66 and escort it to Gibraltar.

Light cruiser HERMIONE departed Gibraltar to patrol the area in 40N, 15W for enemy raider or supply ships.

Dutch submarine O.21, escorting convoy HG.66, was recalled to Gibraltar and ordered to establish a patrol in the vicinity of 43N, 11W to attack any enemy raiders making for Bay of Biscay ports.

2 JULY 1941

Antisubmarine whalers GOS II and KOS XII departed Gibraltar for Freetown, Sierra Leone, with minesweeping trawler HOLLY.

3 JULY 1941

Corvette COREOPSIS departed Gibraltar with antisubmarine trawlers LADY HOGARTH and LADY SHIRLEY to escort convoy OG.66. Upon joining the convoy, they relieved destroyers LANCE and LEGION, which proceeded to Gibraltar.

4 JULY 1941

Troopship CAMERONIA (16,287grt) arrived at Gibraltar from Freetown, Sierra Leone.
Aircraft carrier FURIOUS departed Gibraltar for the Clyde with troopships SCYTHIA (19,761grt) and CAMERONIA escorted by light cruiser HERMIONE plus destroyers LANCE, LEGION, WISHART, and FURY.
Light cruiser EDINBURGH relieved light cruiser HERMIONE after EDINBURGH was detached from convoy WS.9B on 3 July. Light cruiser HERMIONE proceeded to other patrol duties.
Destroyer FAULKNOR was detached from convoy OG.66 on the 5th to join aircraft carrier FURIOUS.
Destroyer WISHART was detached from the aircraft carrier FURIOUS escort on the 8th to refuel at Ponta Delgada and then return to Gibraltar.
On the 9th, aircraft carrier FURIOUS rendezvoused with battleship ROYAL SOVEREIGN at sea, and light cruiser EDINBURGH was detached from the aircraft carrier FURIOUS escort.
Light cruisers EDINBURGH and HERMIONE arrived back at Gibraltar on the 10th.
Destroyers FAULKNOR and FURY arrived back at Gibraltar on the 14th.

	Three German FW200 aircraft unsuccessfully bombed aircraft carrier FURIOUS in 36, 28N, 10, 51W on the 5th. The FURIOUS arrived in the Clyde on the 12th with battleship ROYAL SOVEREIGN, troopships SCYTHIA and CAMERONIA, carrying 188 prisoners of war, plus destroyers PIORUN, LANCE, and LEGION.
	Light cruiser HERMIONE arrived at Gibraltar from raider hunting.
	Antisubmarine whaler GOS III departed Gibraltar for Freetown.
	Destroyers LANCE and LEGION arrived at Gibraltar after escorting convoy OG.66.

5 JULY 1941

	Italian submarine TORELLI (Cdr de Giacomo) spotted a small convoy west of Gibraltar and called in Italian submarines DA VINCI, BARACCA, MALASPINA and MOROSINI for a coordinated attack. TORELLI made an unsuccessful attack on a destroyer.
	Submarine CLYDE returned to Gibraltar after Operation VIGOROUS.

6 JULY 1941

	Dutch submarine O.21 departed Gibraltar for a patrol off Cape Finisterre, Spain.
	A Catalina aircraft sighted a submarine on the surface in 37, 34N, 12, 22W. Destroyers FEARLESS and FORESTER were ordered to that position while escorting convoy OG.66, but they did not make any submarine contact.

7 JULY 1941

	Submarine SEVERN and Dutch submarine O.21 began escorting Gibraltar convoys.
	Destroyer AVON VALE arrived at Gibraltar towing in a Catalina aircraft, which has forced to land in the sea west of Gibraltar.
	Destroyer ERIDGE reported sighting a U-boat in 34, 46N, 09, 47W. A Catalina aircraft was ordered to assist. Destroyers ERIDGE and FARNDALE, which had departed from convoy OG.66, searched the area until the following day without result.

8 JULY 1941

	Convoy HG.67 departed Gibraltar escorted by sloop DEPTFORD, destroyers FOXHOUND and AVON VALE, corvettes JONQUIL, PETUNIA, and SPIREA, catapult ship MAPLIN, and Dutch submarine O.24. Captured Vichy French steamer **CAP CANTIN** (3317grt) was taken to Britain in this convoy. Destroyer FARNDALE and corvette COREOPSIS departed Gibraltar on the 9th and overtook the convoy. Destroyers AVON VALE and FARNDALE were detached from the convoy on the 12th. Early on the 13th, destroyer AVON VALE sighted a submarine on the surface in 35, 20N, 16, 35W near the convoy. AVON VALE and destroyer FARNDALE unsuccessfully searched for the submarine. On the 14th, the corvettes, less PETUNIA, and the Dutch O.24 were detached from convoy HG.67 to escort convoy OG.67 towards Gibraltar. On the 14th, convoy HG.67 merged with convoy SL.79 for better protection against U-boats and German aircraft. On the 19th, destroyers CAMPBELTOWN, ST ALBANS, and WANDERER joined the convoy. The combined convoy arrived at Liverpool on the 24th.
	Ocean boarding vessel MARSDALE arrived at Gibraltar from an Eastern Atlantic patrol.
	Dutch submarine O.21 arrived at Gibraltar from her patrol.

10 JULY 1941

	Light cruiser EDINBURGH, which had been with convoy WS.9B, arrived at Gibraltar with light cruiser HERMIONE. EDINBURGH was docked at Gibraltar the next day.

11 JULY 1941

	Antisubmarine trawlers FANDANGO, MORRIS DANCE, SARABANDE, SYRINGA, NORSE, and CORDELIA departed Gibraltar for Freetown, via Bathurst escorting steamer PINZON (1365grt).

12 JULY 1941

	Heavy cruiser LONDON arrived at Gibraltar from Freetown.

14 JULY 1941

	Sloop SCARBOROUGH and corvette GERANIUM departed Gibraltar for exercises in the Atlantic. SCARBOROUGH returned to Gibraltar to escort convoy HG.68 departing Gibraltar on the 18th, while GERANIUM arrived back at Gibraltar on the 18th, escorting Fleet oiler HORN SHELL (8272grt).
1746	Destroyers FEARLESS, FOXHOUND, FURY, FORESIGHT, and FORESTER departed Gibraltar to escort convoy WS.9C, arriving from Britain.

15 JULY 1941

	Destroyers FIREDRAKE, VIDETTE, VIMY, and BEVERLEY, arrived at Gibraltar with ML.126 of the 3rd Motor Launch Flotilla, and the 9th Motor Launch Flotilla with ML.169, ML.170, ML.172, ML.173, ML.174, ML.175, and ML.176.
	Destroyer FIREDRAKE departed Gibraltar later that day and joined the 8th Destroyer Flotilla, which was en route to convoy WS.9C at sea.

16 JULY 1941

	Destroyers AVON VALE, ERIDGE, and FARNDALE departed Gibraltar to join light cruiser MANCHESTER, troopship PASTEUR (29,253grt), plus destroyers LIGHTNING and NESTOR, arriving from Britain.

17 JULY 1941

	Submarine TALISMAN arrived at Gibraltar from Halifax, Nova Scotia.

18 JULY 1941

	Heavy cruiser LONDON departed Gibraltar to return to Scapa Flow.
	Destroyer VIDETTE departed Gibraltar to join tanker BRITISH HONOUR (6991grt) at sea and escort her to Gibraltar, arriving on the 21st.
	Corvette GERANIUM arrived at Gibraltar escorting Fleet oiler HORN SHELL (8272grt).
	Convoy HG.68 departed Gibraltar escorted by destroyers BEVERLEY and WISHART, sloop SCARBOROUGH, submarine CLYDE, plus antisubmarine trawlers LADY HOGARTH, LADY SHIRLEY, and LEYLAND. Captured Vichy French trawler **GROUIN DU COU** was en route to Britain in the convoy, but was forced to return to Gibraltar on the 22nd when she could not keep up. On the 24th, captured Vichy French trawler **L'ORAGE** returned to Gibraltar with boiler defects. Corvettes FLEUR DE LYS and GERANIUM departed Gibraltar on the 19th and joined the convoy at sea. Destroyer BEVERLEY was detached from the convoy on the 19th to capture Vichy French ship ISAC (2385grt). On the 22nd, submarine CLYDE, corvette FLEUR DE LYS, and destroyer WISHART were detached from the convoy. The CLYDE and WISHART joined convoy OG.68 heading towards Gibraltar. Corvettes CLOVER and VERVAIN joined the convoy on the 23rd. Trawlers LADY HOGARTH and LADY SHIRLEY were detached from the convoy on the 25th. On the 27th, corvettes ALISMA, DIANELLA, KINGCUP, and SUNFLOWER joined the convoy. Destroyers BATH, VANOC, and WALKER plus catapult ship ARIGUANI joined the convoy with corvettes CARNATION, HELIOTROPE, LA MALOUINE, and MALLOW. Corvettes CLOVER and VERVAIN were detached from the convoy on the 28th. On the 29th, corvettes CARNATION and LA MALOUINE were detached from the convoy. Corvette GERANIUM was detached from the convoy on the 31st to begin a refit in Britain. The convoy arrived at Liverpool on 2 August.

19 JULY 1941

	Free French troopship PASTEUR (29,253grt) arrived at Gibraltar escorted by destroyers LIGHTNING, NESTOR, AVON VALE, FARNDALE, and ERIDGE. She carried troops for transfer to Malta in Operation SUBSTANCE.
	Destroyer BEVERLEY intercepted Vichy French steamer **ISAC** (2385grt) west of Spain in 35, 12N, 09, 12W. BEVERLEY escorted the steamer towards Gibraltar until relieved by a tug that afternoon. The tug arrived at Gibraltar with the captured **ISAC** on the 21st.
0530	Minelayer MANXMAN arrived at Gibraltar after escorting convoy WS.9C. Her arrival in the harbour had been delayed by fog for one and a half hours.

20 JULY 1941

	Destroyer BEVERLEY arrived at Gibraltar.
0145	Light cruiser EDINBURGH and minelayer MANXMAN departed Gibraltar to join arriving convoy WS.9C with destroyers NESTOR, LIGHTNING, FARNDALE, AVON VALE, and ERIDGE.
0329	Light cruisers MANCHESTER and ARETHUSA arrived at Gibraltar with destroyers COSSACK, MAORI, and SIKH escorting troopship LEINSTER (4302grt).
>0329	Destroyers FEARLESS, FOXHOUND, FIREDRAKE, BEVERLEY, FURY, FORESIGHT, and FORESTER arrived at Gibraltar to refuel.

21 JULY 1941

	Italian submarine TORELLI (Cdr De Giacomo) sank Norwegian tanker **IDA KNUDSEN** (8913grt) in 34, 34N, 13, 14W. Five crewmen were missing. Portuguese trawler ALTAIR (341grt) rescued fourteen survivors and landed them at Las Palmas.

| | Submarine THUNDERBOLT arrived at Gibraltar from St John's, Newfoundland, for duty in the Mediterranean. |

22 JULY 1941

| | Antisubmarine trawler STELLA CARINA departed Gibraltar escorting tanker HORN SHELL (8272grt) to the west. The trawler would then join Panamanian tanker NORVINN (6322grt) at sea and escort her to Gibraltar. |
| | Trawler COPINSAY departed Gibraltar later in the day to join trawler STELLA CARINA. |

24 JULY 1941

| | USN troopship WEST POINT (AP-23) arrived at Lisbon, Portugal with German and Italian consular personnel and their families from the United States. |

26 JULY 1941

	Panamanian tanker NORVINN (6322grt) arrived at Gibraltar from Trinidad escorted by trawlers STELLA CARINA and COPINSAY.
	USN troopship WEST POINT (AP-23) departed Lisbon, Portugal with United States and Chinese consular personnel and their families from Europe for New York City, arriving on 1 August.
	U.109 entered Cadiz, Spain during the night and re-supplied from a tanker in the harbour and then began patrolling west of Gibraltar.

27 JULY 1941

| | U.371 spotted convoy OS.1 west of Portugal and maintained intermittent contact through the day. |
| | Ocean boarding vessel CORINTHIAN arrived at Gibraltar after a patrol west of Gibraltar. |

28 JULY 1941

| | Convoy HG.69 departed Gibraltar escorted by sloop BIDEFORD and antisubmarine trawler STELLA CARINA.
Destroyers BEVERLEY and DUNCAN, corvette COREOPSIS, JONQUIL, and SPIREA, and submarine SEVERN joined the convoy on the 29th.
Destroyer BEVERLEY refuelled at Ponta Delgada on 3 August and then rejoined the convoy.
Destroyer DUNCAN was detached from the convoy on 2 August and returned to Gibraltar.
On 5 August, submarine SEVERN and corvettes COREOPSIS, JONQUIL, and SPIREA were detached from the convoy. The corvettes joined convoy OG.70.
On 6 August, trawler STELLA CARINA was detached from convoy HG.69 to join convoy OG.70 while ocean boarding vessel HILARY joined convoy HG.69.
Destroyers LEGION and PIORUN joined the convoy on 7 August.
Destroyers CHELSEA and WOLVERINE plus corvettes GENTIAN, HIBISCUS, MYOSOTIS, and PERIWINKLE joined the convoy on 8 August.
Destroyers BEVERLEY, LEGION, and PIORUN were detached from the convoy on 9 August to Londonderry.
The convoy arrived at Liverpool on 11 August. |

29 JULY 1941

| | Supply ship BRECONSHIRE (9776grt) departed Gibraltar for Liverpool escorted by corvettes WALLFLOWER, ZINNIA, HYDRANGEA, CAMPANULA, and BLUEBELL. |
| | Submarine CLYDE arrived at Gibraltar from an Atlantic patrol. |

30 JULY 1941

| | Steamers SETTLER (6000grt) and CLAN MACNAUGHTON (6088grt) departed Gibraltar en route to Freetown, escorted by destroyers VIDETTE and VIMY plus trawlers ARRAN and COPINSAY. On the 31st, trawler ARRAN was forced to return to Gibraltar with defects.
Destroyer VIDETTE was detached from the steamers on 2 August and VIMY was detached from the steamers on 3 August to return to Gibraltar. Trawler COPINSAY continued with the steamers to Freetown. |
| | Steamers ARDEOLA (2069grt) and BRITISH HONOUR (6991grt) departed Gibraltar en route to Las Palmas and Trinidad respectively escorted by destroyers VIDETTE and VIMY and trawlers ARRAN and COPINSAY. |

31 JULY 1941

| | Ocean boarding vessel CORINTHIAN departed Gibraltar on Eastern Atlantic patrol. |

West of North Africa
Long. W15, 00 – E11, 00   Lat. N30, 00 – N00, 00

3 JULY 1941

| | Convoy SL.80 departed Freetown escorted by AMCs ESPERANCE BAY to 22 July and CANTON to 7 July.
Destroyer HIGHLANDER escorted the convoy to 8 July.
Corvettes AMARANTHUS and BERGAMOT escorted the convoy to 11 July. |

Antisubmarine yacht SURPRISE escorted the convoy to 9 July.
Antisubmarine trawler CANNA escorted the convoy to 11 July.
On the 23rd, destroyers BROKE and WOLVERINE joined the convoy to 29 July.
Destroyer VERITY joined the convoy on the 23rd, but was detached on 26 July after a collision with destroyer BROKE.
Corvettes HIBISCUS and PERIWINKLE joined the convoy to 29 July, when the convoy arrived at Liverpool.

15 JULY 1941

Convoy SL.81 departed Freetown escorted by AMCs CAPE SABLE to 8 August and MORETON BAY to 2 August, destroyer WRESTLER to 23 July, plus corvettes CLEMATIS, CYCLAMEN, MIGNONETTE, and WOODRUFF to 23 July.
On the 30th, corvettes CARNATION joined the convoy to 6 August, HELIOTROPE joined the convoy to 8 August, and MALLOW joined the convoy to 4 August.
On 3 August, destroyers CAMPBELTOWN, ST ALBANS, and WANDERER joined the convoy to 8 August, catapult ship MAPLIN joined the convoy to 7 August, plus corvettes BLUEBELL, CAMPANULA, HYDRANGEA joined the convoy to 5 August, LA MALOUINE joined the convoy to 6 August, WALLFLOWER joined the convoy to 8 August, and ZINNIA joined the convoy to 8 August.
On 3 August, a Hurricane aircraft from CAM MAPLIN shot down a German Fw200 aircraft in 50, 33N, 19, 40W. Pilot Lt R. W. H. Everett then bailed out and was picked up by a dingy from the catapult ship.
The convoy arrived at Liverpool on 8 August.

24 JULY 1941

Convoy SL.82 departed Freetown escorted by AMC DERBYSHIRE to 10 August, destroyer VANSITTART plus corvettes ARMERIA, ASTER, BURDOCK, and MARGUERITE to 31 July.
Corvette AMARANTHUS joined the convoy from 25 to 27 July.
On 10 August, destroyers VICEROY and WOOLSTON joined the convoy.
On 11 August, destroyers VANOC and WALKER joined the convoy.
The convoy arrived at Liverpool on 15 August.

27 JULY 1941

Corvette GARDENIA intercepted Vichy French auxiliary patrol vessel EDITH GERMAINE (130grt) in 12, 38N, 17, 55W.
Corvette AMARANTHUS was in company with GARDENIA. The EDITH GERMAINE was taken towards Freetown by the two corvettes, but when it was determined that the trawler was going to Dakar, she was allowed to continue.

SOUTH ATLANTIC OCEAN

East of South America
Long. W70, 00 – W30, 00   Lat. N05, 00 – S60, 00

20 JULY 1941

Steamer BANGALORE (6067grt) damaged steamer RICHMOND CASTLE (7798grt) in a collision in 01, 30N, 41, 54W.

21 JULY 1941

An escort ship sank steamer **BANGALORE** (6067grt) with gunfire in 00, 59N, 43W. She was damaged the previous day in a collision with steamer RICHMOND CASTLE (7798grt) and was unable to continue.

25 JULY 1941

Light cruiser NEWCASTLE intercepted German steamer **ERLANGEN** (6101grt) southeast of River Plate. The crew scuttled the ship to prevent her capture.

West of South Africa
Long. W30, 00 – E25, 00   Lat. S00, 00 – S60, 00

6 JULY 1941

German AMC SCHIFF.36/ORION began moving north to reach German controlled waters.

11 JULY 1941

AMC CANTON intercepted German steamer **HERMES** (7209grt) (formerly **KARNAK** (7209grt)) three hundred miles northwest of St Paul's Rock in S02, 27, 40W. The crew scuttled the steamer to prevent her capture.

22 JULY 1941

Light cruiser DUNEDIN captured Vichy French steamer **VILLE DE ROUEN** (5383grt) east of Natal in 19, 32S, 11, 12W.
She was taken to East London, South Africa, arriving on 4 August.

BALTIC SEA

Kattegat and Skagerrak Long. E09, 00 – E12, 00   Lat. N60, 00 – N53, 00

15 JULY 1941

An RAF aerial mine damaged auxiliary minesweeper M.509 in Kiel Bay.

20 JULY 1941

An RAF aerial mine damaged Norwegian steamer **BRYNJE** (3916grt) in the Great Belt.

23 JULY 1941

German fishing trawler **LENA REHDER** (262grt) was lost by stranding at Fage Bucht, Denmark.

31 JULY 1941

U.B (ex British **SEAL**) arrived at Kiel for test exercises.

Southern Baltic Area Long. E12, 00 – E22, 00   Lat. N60, 00 – N53, 00

1 JULY 1941

The German 5th and 31st Minesweeping Flotillas laid a minefield from Cape Tachkona to Libau.

2 JULY 1941

The German 5th and 31st Minesweeping Flotillas laid Minefield APOLDA off Libau.

A German mine sank Russian minesweeper **T-204/FUGAS** (ObltzS Gillerman) off Libau.

German minelayer BRUMMER laid a minefield east of the Minefield APOLDA off Libau.

3 JULY 1941

During the night, German minelayer BRUMMER covered by five S-boats of the 2nd S-Boat Flotilla and five motor minesweeping boats of the 5th R-Boat Flotilla, laid another minefield between Minefield APOLDA and Minefield CORBETHA off Libau.

Russian submarine S-7 began a patrol off Libau until the 21st.

Russian submarine S-9 began a patrol off Stolpmünde until the 21st.

4 JULY 1941

A Russian air attack damaged German mine destructor ships MDS.6 and MDS.11 of the 5th Minesweeper Flotilla off Libau.

5 JULY 1941

German minelayer BRUMMER and the 5th R-Boat Flotilla along with the 1st, 2nd, and 3rd S-Boat Flotillas laid 196 deep mines and 130 floating mines west of the Soelo Sound.

Russian submarine L-3 laid mines off Memel, East Prussia.

7 JULY 1941

A mine sank German fishing vessel **NEUENFELDE** (193grt) near Kolberg, Germany.

9 JULY 1941

Returning from Finland to Swinemünde, German minelayers **HANSESTADT DANZIG** (2461grt) (KKpt. Schroeder), **PREUSSEN** (2529grt) (KKpt. Barthel) and **TANNENBERG** (5504grt) (FKpt. von Schönermark) encountered a Swedish minefield just south of Oland and were all sunk in 56, 12N, 16, 17E.

Four Russian MO-class patrol boats attacked the first German convoy en route from Libau to Riga, Latvia, with six coastal motor ships and four logging ships. The Germans sustained no losses during the attack.

10 JULY 1941

A mine laid by Russian minesweeper **T-204/FUGAS** (Lt Gillerman) sank German submarine chaser **UJ.113/NORTHLAND** off Libau.

The German 1st S-Boat Flotilla with S.28, S.26, S.101, S.40, and S.39 sortied to attack a Russian force in the Gulf of Finland near Ekholm.
No contact was made with the Russian force, but they did sink the wreck of the Latvian steamer **RASMA** (3204grt).

A mine sank German auxiliary minesweeper **M.201** in the Irben Strait. She was later salvaged.

11 JULY 1941

German minesweepers SCHIFF.11/OSNABRUCK and M.23 were in transit from Riga, Latvia to Pernau, Latvia, via the Irben Strait when a mine heavily damaged **M.23**. She was beached and later salvaged.

The German 5th R-Boat Flotilla laid a minefield north of Juminda with ninety mines.

12 JULY 1941

The German 5th R-Boat Flotilla escorted a small convoy of motorised barges, lighters, artillery barges, attack boats and coastal steamers from Libau to Riga.

The German 2nd R-Boat Flotilla escorted a second convoy of motorised barges, lighters, artillery barges, attack boats and coastal steamers from Libau to Riga. As they reached Cape Domesnas, they encountered gunfire from the Russian coastal batteries on Svorbe.

13 JULY 1941

The German 5th R-Boat Flotilla laid ninety mines north of Juminda.

Russian MTBs (Lt Gumanenko) and aircraft sank a German attack boat, two large barges and twenty-three smaller barges off Riga.

Russian submarines S-11 (Lt Cdr Sereda) and S-8 patrolled off Poland.

Russian submarines SHCH-322, SHCH-323 and SHCH-406 patrolled an area between Stockholm and Bornholm until early August.

Russian submarine S-102 tried to attack a German convoy off Riga, but could not approach the ships due to the shallow water.

19 JULY 1941

Russian submarine S-11 (Lt Cdr Sereda) missed German minesweeper SCHIFF.11/OSNABRUCK off Poland.

Russian submarine L-3 (Capt 3rd Class Grishenko) laid a minefield off Brusterort.

20 JULY 1941

The German 5th R-Boat Flotilla laid ninety mines north of Juminda.

23 JULY 1941

A mine sank German auxiliary minesweeper **M.3131/NORDMARK** (462grt) in the Irben Straits.

25 JULY 1941

Russian MTBs and aircraft attacked the German 2nd R-Boat Flotilla in the Irben Strait.

Mines damaged German motor minesweepers R.53 and R.63 in the Irben Strait.

26 JULY 1941

Russian MTBs and aircraft attacked the German 2nd R-Boat Flotilla in the Irben Strait. The aircraft sank motor minesweeper **R.169**.

German torpedo boat T.3 claimed sinking a Russian destroyer in a surface action in the Baltic.
There were no confirming data for this claim.

Russian submarine K-3 began to lay a minefield off Bornholm, but technical problems forced her to abandon the mission.

27 JULY 1941

Russian bombing sank German steamer **ELBING III** (315grt) near Libau.

28 JULY 1941

A mine, laid by Russian minesweeper T-204/FUGAS, sank German patrol boat **V.309/MARTIN DONANDT** off Libau.

29 JULY 1941

A mine sank German trawler **LEONTES** (338grt) off Windau.

Gulf of Bothnia   Long. E16, 00 – E26, 00   Lat. N66, 00 – N60, 00

5 JULY 1941

A mine laid by Finnish submarine VESIHIISI on 23 June, damaged Latvian steamer **RASMA** (3204grt) north of Ekholm. The steamer was beached to avoid sinking, but was sunk by German S-boats S.26 and S.28 on the 10th.

9 JULY 1941

Finnish submarines IKU-TURSO (Lt Cdr Pekkanen) and VETEHINEN (Lt Cdr Pakkala) laid additional mines east of Ekholm.

11 JULY 1941

Finnish submarine IKU-TURSO (Lt Cdr Pekkanen) laid eighteen mines in Minefield F.15 east of Ekholm.

14 JULY 1941

The German 1st S-Boat Flotilla (Kptlt Birnbacher) with S.28, S.27, S.40, S.101, and S.26 unsuccessfully attacked a Russian convoy near Ekholm.

Gulf of Finland   Long. E22, 00 – E30, 00   Lat. N61, 00 – N57, 00

1 JULY 1941

German mines damaged Russian submarines M-79 and M-77 off Riga, Latvia.

A German mine in Minefield GOTHA, sank Russian submarine **M-81** (Lt Cdr Zubkov) off Riga.

2 JULY 1941

A mine heavily damaged Russian destroyer STRASHNY in Moon Sound. The rest of the Russian destroyer force (RAdm Drozd), destroyers SERDITY and SILNY laid mines in the Moon Sound covered by destroyers STOIKI, GROZYASHCHI and SMETLIVY.

3 JULY 1941

Finnish submarine VETEHINEN unsuccessfully attacked Russian steamer VIBORG (4100grt) with gunfire north of Stenskär.

4 JULY 1941

Finnish submarine VESIKKO (Lt Cdr Aittola) sank Russian steamer **VIBORG** (4100grt) south of Someri in 60, 08N, 27, 32E.

6 JULY 1941

A Russian destroyer force (Rear Adm Drozd) with SILNY, SERDITY, STRASHNY, STOIKI, GROZYASHCHI and SMETLIVY laid mines from the Irben Strait to the Moon Sound. A mine damaged SILNY in the Moon Sound.

Russian destroyer SERDITY chased German minesweepers M.31 and SCHIFF.11/OSNABRUCK out of the area. Both minesweepers dumped their mines overboard and reached Dunamunde after four separate Russian air attacks.

A Finnish mine from Minefield F.5 sank Latvian steamer **EVEROLANDA** (3379grt) in the Gulf of Finland.

A Finnish mine from Minefield F.5 damaged Russian minesweeper T-202/BUI in the Gulf of Finland.

8 JULY 1941

Russian destroyer SILNY attacked German motor minesweeper R.11 and minesweeper M.31 in the Irben Strait. In a brief encounter, destroyer SILNY was lightly damaged. The German ships were undamaged.

13 JULY 1941

A Russian naval group (RAdm Drozd) with destroyers ENGELS, GORDY, GROZJASHCHI, STOIKI, SILNY, STEREGUSHCHI and SERDITY plus torpedo boats TUCHA and SNEG unsuccessfully attacked German positions off the Duna River estuary.

15 JULY 1941

The German 3rd S-Boat Flotilla (Kptlt Kemnade) of S.54, S.47, S.58, and S.57 unsuccessfully attacked a Russian destroyer in the Bay of Riga. A torpedo from S.57 (ObltzS Erdmann) almost hit the destroyer.

16 JULY 1941

German SCHIFF.11/OSNABRUCK laid a new minefield off the Duna River estuary among the existing Russian minefields.

18 JULY 1941

The German 3rd S-Boat Flotilla (Kptlt Kemnade) sortied against Russian forces off Kübassare on Ösel Island. The encountered a small Russian convoy escorted by destroyers SERDITY and STEREGUSHCHI. After a short battle off Duna River estuary, the German force retired and the Russian convoy arrived without loss.

German Ju88 aircraft of KGR.806 damaged Russian destroyer **SERDITY** in Moon Sound during the night. Attempts to save the ship failed and the crew finally scuttled the wreck on 22 July.

20 JULY 1941

German aircraft damaged Russian submarine S-9 off the Soelo Sound.

U.140 missed Russian submarine S-9 with torpedoes off the Soelo Sound.

21 JULY 1941

Finnish minelayers laid Minefield F.16 with eighty-five deep mines and fifteen floating mines east of Minefield VALKJARVI.

Russian small submarines M-94 (Lt Dyakov) and M-98 patrolled the entrance to the Gulf of Finland.

22 JULY 1941

	The 3rd S-Boat Flotilla (Kptlt Kemnade) attacked a small Russian convoy off Arensburg, Osel. They sank a tugboat and S.29 sank Russian motor torpedo boat **TKA-71**.
0655	U.140 (Hans-Jürgen Hellriegel) sank Russian submarine **M-94** (206grt) (Lt Dyakov) at the entrance to the gulf of Finland in 58, 51N, 22, 02E. Eight crewmen were lost while three were rescued by Russian submarine M-98. (Some sources have this event occurring on 21 July and others on 31 July.)
0706	U.140 (Hans-Jürgen Hellriegel) unsuccessfully attacked Russian submarine M-98, which was travelling with Russian submarine **M-94** at the entrance to the gulf of Finland in 58, 51N, 22, 02E. M-98 later rescued three survivors from **M-94**.

26 JULY 1941

The German 3rd S-Boat Flotilla (Kptlt Kemnade) made an unsuccessful attack north of Riga.

27 JULY 1941

The German 3rd S-Boat Flotilla with S.54, S.55, S.57, and S.58 attacked Russian ships in the Gulf of Riga. S.54 (LtzS von Wagner), in company with S.55 sank Russian destroyer **SMIELY** (1690grt) in the Gulf of Riga. S.57 and S.58 unsuccessfully attacked two Russian minesweepers at Ösel.

28 JULY 1941

The German 3rd S-Boat Flotilla with S.54, S.55, S.57, and S.58 sank Latvian Ice Breaker **LASHPLESIS** (253grt) off Osel.

Russian submarine SHCH-307 sank **U.144** in the Gulf of Finland. The entire crew of twenty-eight were lost.

31 JULY 1941

Russian small submarines M-95 and M-96 patrolled the entrance to the gulf of Finland.

U.140 sank Russian submarine **M-94** (206grt) (Lt Dyakov) at the entrance to the gulf of Finland in 58, 51N, 22, 02E. (Some sources have this event occurring on 22 July.)

MEDITERRANEAN SEA & MIDDLE EAST

East of Gibraltar
Long. W05, 30 – E11, 00   Lat. N44, 30 – N35, 00

4 JULY 1941

	Italian submarines CORALLO and DIASPRO patrolled the area between Algeria and the Balearic Islands to guard against a sortie by the British Force H to send supplies to Malta.
	Submarine SEVERN arrived at Gibraltar from a patrol in the Tyrrhenian Sea.

5 JULY 1941

	Vichy French passenger/cargo ship LECONTE DE LISLE (9877grt) departed Marseilles, France, in a convoy bound to Dakar and Madagascar.

10 JULY 1941

	Dutch submarine O.23 arrived at Gibraltar after a patrol in the Gulf of Genoa. She was forced to depart the patrol area early on the 7th because of a fuel leak.
	Vichy French passenger/cargo ship VILLE DE VERDUN (7007grt) departed Marseilles, France, for Madagascar.

11 JULY 1941

	Aircraft carrier ARK ROYAL and light cruiser HERMIONE departed Gibraltar to exercise in the Mediterranean. A Swordfish aircraft ditched in the sea during the exercises and destroyer FEARLESS rescued the crew.

12 JULY 1941

	Battle cruiser RENOWN departed Gibraltar and joined aircraft carrier ARK ROYAL and light cruiser HERMIONE for exercises in the Mediterranean. The three ships arrived back at Gibraltar later that day.
	Submarine OTUS departed Gibraltar carrying stores for Malta.

16 JULY 1941

	Submarine OLYMPUS and Dutch submarine O.21 departed Gibraltar to patrol in the Tyrrhenian Sea to support Operation SUBSTANCE.

17 JULY 1941

	Italian submarines ALAGI and DIASPRO patrolled north of Cape Bougaroni in case Force H should sortie from Gibraltar for Malta.
	Dutch submarine O.23 (Lt Cdr van Erkel) torpedoed Italian tanker MADDALENA ODERO (5479grt) in the Tyrrhenian Sea.
	Submarine P.32 departed Gibraltar to patrol off Italy in support of Operation SUBSTANCE and then she was to proceed to Malta.

21 JULY 1941

	Italian battleships LITTORIO, VENETO, and DUILO at Taranto, heavy cruisers TRIESTE, BOLZANO, and GORIZIA at Messina, and light cruisers GARIBALDI, MONTECUCOLI, DI GUISSANO, and DA BARBIANO at Palermo were brought to alert notice, but the intention of the British forces was discovered too late for them to sortie for an attack.
0145	Operation SUBSTANCE (convoy GM.1) departed Gibraltar for Malta with steamers SYDNEY STAR (11,219grt), CITY OF PRETORIA (8046grt), PORT CHALMERS (8535grt), DEUCALION (7516grt), DURHAM (10,893grt), and MELBOURNE STAR (12,806grt), escorted by battleship NELSON, light cruiser EDINBURGH, minelayer MANXMAN, plus destroyers NESTOR, LIGHTNING, FARNDALE, AVON VALE, and ERIDGE.
0200	Light cruisers MANCHESTER and ARETHUSA plus troopship LEINSTER (4302grt) departed Gibraltar with destroyers COSSACK, SIKH, and MAORI. Troopship LEINSTER ran aground departing Gibraltar and was left behind.
0200	Fleet oiler BROWN RANGER (3417grt) departed Gibraltar escorted by destroyer BEVERLEY to be at sea to refuel destroyers during Operation SUBSTANCE. The two ships arrived back at Gibraltar on the 23rd. They sailed again on the 25th on the same mission, but were recalled later that day.
0300	To cover Operation SUBSTANCE, battle cruiser RENOWN, aircraft carrier ARK ROYAL plus light cruiser HERMIONE departed Gibraltar with destroyers FAULKNOR, FEARLESS, FIREDRAKE, FORESTER, FOXHOUND, FORESIGHT, FURY, and DUNCAN. Battleship NELSON and light cruisers ARETHUSA, EDINBURGH, and MANCHESTER were on temporary loan from the Home Fleet. Eight British and Dutch submarines were at sea to intercept the Italian Fleet should it attempt to intervene with the convoy headed to Malta.

	Submarines operating from Gibraltar included OLYMPUS, in the Tyrrhenian Sea, P.32 off Cagliari, and Dutch submarine O.21 in the Tyrrhenian Sea. Submarines operating from Malta included UNIQUE off the southern entrance to the Straits of Messina, UPHOLDER north of Marittimo, UPRIGHT off the southern approaches to the Straits of Messina, URGE off Palermo, and UTMOST north of Messina.

22 JULY 1941

	Italian submarines ALAGI and DIASPRO patrolled from Cape Bougaroni to the Balearic Islands. The Italian *Commando Supremo* decided that the British were only conducting another aircraft run to Malta.

23 JULY 1941

	Italian submarine DIASPRO attacked the Operation SUBSTANCE convoy and narrowly missed Australian destroyer NESTOR while she was escorting aircraft carrier ARK ROYAL near Bougie, Algeria, in 38, 10N, 05, 30E.
<0941	Italian reconnaissance aircraft spotted the Operation SUBSTANCE group north of Bône, Algeria. It was now too late to sortie the Italian Fleet, so torpedo bombers were ordered to attack.
<0941	Italian SM79 torpedo bombers of 280 and 283 Squadrons heavily damaged destroyer **FEARLESS** (1375grt) with an aerial torpedo north of Bone. **FEARLESS** was later scuttled by destroyer FORESTER in 37, 40N, 08, 20E. The destroyer had Lt R. A. Nares, RCNVR and seventeen ratings missing and twenty injured crewmen, of which nine died of wounds. Destroyer FIREDRAKE was also damaged by bombing and was towed for thirty seven hours back to Gibraltar by destroyer ERIDGE and escorted by destroyer AVON VALE, which was sent back to join the other destroyers after being relieved from escorting light cruiser MANCHESTER. Destroyer SIKH joined the FIREDRAKE group en route. FIREDRAKE arrived at Gibraltar, under her own power at the end, on the 27th, escorted by destroyers AVON VALE and ERIDGE. She was under repair for six months, including four months at the Boston Navy Yard from 23 September to 18 January 1942. Destroyer FOXHOUND was damaged by a bomb near miss but spent no time out of action.
0942	Italian SM79 torpedo bombers of 32 Stormo and 51 Stormo damaged light cruiser MANCHESTER, carrying 750 troops for Malta, with an aerial torpedo. Paymaster Cdr W. D. Stranack, A/Paymaster Sub-Lt C. D. Ballard, Paymaster Midshipman J. D. Pooley and twenty-three ratings were lost in the cruiser. P/T/Surgeon T. McG. Watt RNVR was wounded. The cruiser returned to Gibraltar escorted by destroyer AVON VALE making barely nine knots with three out of four engines inoperative. Before arriving at Gibraltar, destroyers VIDETTE and VIMY joined the screen. Destroyer WISHART later departed Gibraltar to relieve destroyer AVON VALE. (see <0942 above) Tug ST DAY departed Gibraltar to assist in towing the cruiser. The group arrived at Gibraltar shortly before midnight on the 25th. Motor launches ML.130, ML.126, ML.168, ML.121, and ML.129 departed Gibraltar to sweep ahead of the cruiser and provide additional escort. Later, tugs ROLLICKER and ST OMAR with ML.173, and ML.169 departed Gibraltar to join the cruiser. MANCHESTER, after temporary repairs at Gibraltar, sailed on 17 September for the Philadelphia Navy Yard where she was under repair from 23 September to 15 February 1942.
>0942	During the Italian bomber attack on Force H, British AA and Fulmar fighter aircraft from aircraft carrier ARK ROYAL downed two Italian bombers and five torpedo-bombers.

24 JULY 1941

	Axis aircraft damaged tanker HOEGH HOOD (9351grt) in convoy MG.1 but she was able to continue to Gibraltar.

25 JULY 1941

	P/T/Sub-Lt (A) K. G. Grant RNVR and his gunner Leading Airman H. McLeod in a Fulmar aircraft of 807 Squadron and Lt A. J. Kindersley and his gunner Petty Officer (A) F. A. Barnes in a Fulmar of 808 Squadron were lost when they were shot down 120 miles southwest of Sardinia. T/A/Sub-Lt (A) R. C. Cockburn RNVR and Petty Officer Airman W. E. Cuttriss of 808 Squadron were also shot down but were picked up by destroyer NESTOR.

26 JULY 1941

	Supply ship BRECONSHIRE (9776grt) and steamer TALABOT (6798grt) arrived at Gibraltar on the 26th escorted by destroyer ENCOUNTER. Destroyer FORESTER arrived later in the day with steamers AMERIKA (10,218grt) and THERMOPYLAE (6655grt).

27 JULY 1941

	Force H and the supporting cruisers arrived back at Gibraltar to conclude Operation SUBSTANCE.
	Steamers SETTLER (6000grt) and HOEGH HOOD (9351grt) arrived at Gibraltar.

28 JULY 1941

	Norwegian tanker SVENOR (7616grt) arrived at Gibraltar.
	Dutch submarine O.24 departed Gibraltar to patrol in the Gulf of Genoa and the Tyrrhenian Sea.

29 JULY 1941

	Italian bombing damaged submarine OLYMPUS (Lt Cdr Dymott) 3½ miles 107° Cavoli Light, Cavoli Light in the Tyrrhenian Sea. After emergency repairs to her heavily damaged batteries and plugging the many leaking fittings, the submarine was able to return to Gibraltar on 2 August.
	Submarine TALISMAN departed Gibraltar with stores for Malta.

30 JULY 1941

	Submarine OLYMPUS (Lt Cdr Dymott) made an unsuccessful attack on a steamer near Cape Camino in 40, 40N, 09, 50E.
	In Operation STYLE, battleship NELSON (Flag Vice Admiral Force H), battle cruiser RENOWN plus aircraft carrier ARK ROYAL departed Gibraltar with destroyers COSSACK, MAORI, NESTOR, FAULKNOR, FURY, FORESIGHT, FORESTER, FOXHOUND, ENCOUNTER, and ERIDGE to create a diversion. Force S departed Gibraltar with fleet oiler BROWN RANGER (3417grt) and destroyer AVON VALE. On the return to Gibraltar, destroyers AVON VALE and ERIDGE were exchanged.

31 JULY 1941

	In Operation STYLE, Force X departed Gibraltar with light cruisers HERMIONE and ARETHUSA plus minelayer MANXMAN with destroyers SIKH and LIGHTNING for Malta. They carried the troops and supplies that had been on troopship LEINSTER (4302grt) and light cruiser MANCHESTER, which had not reached Malta during Operation SUBSTANCE.
	In Operation STYLE, destroyers COSSACK and MAORI were detached from Force H to bombard the harbour of Alghero, Sardinia and fire star shells for a night raid by aircraft from aircraft carrier ARK ROYAL, on the night of 31st/1 August.
	Force H continued to provide cover for Force S as it continued towards Malta during the night.

Middle Mediterranean Sea
Long. E11, 00 – E20, 00   Lat. N46, 00 – N30, 00

2 JULY 1941

	During the month, Italian submarines ZOEA (2 trips), CORRIDONI (2 trips) and ATROPO (1 trip) delivered 268-tons of supplies to Axis forces at Bardia, Libya from Naples, Italy.
	During the night of 2/3 July, a British bombing raid on Tripoli, Libya damaged German steamer SPARTA (1724grt) and Italian steamer ERITREA (2517grt). Eight Swordfish aircraft of 830 Squadron laid mines at the entrance to Tripoli Harbour.
	Submarine URGE (Lt Cdr Tomkinson) unsuccessfully attacked an Italian AMC in 37, 48N, 15, 21E.

3 JULY 1941

	Submarine UPHOLDER (Lt Cdr Wanklyn) sank Italian steamer **LAURA COSULICH** (5870grt) east of Calabria, Italy, in 37, 55N, 15, 44E.
	Submarine OSIRIS arrived at Malta with seventy tons of bulk petrol.
	Submarine UTMOST arrived at Malta from her patrol.

4 JULY 1941

	Submarine URGE arrived at Malta from her patrol.

6 JULY 1941

	Submarine TRIUMPH (Lt Cdr Woods) sank Italian steamer **NINFEA** (607grt) and escorting gunboat **DE LUTTI** (266grt) in a long gun battle off Benghazi, Libya. In the encounter, TRIUMPH was hit by an Italian shore battery shell and was forced to return to Malta with damage to her forward torpedo tubes.
	Submarine P.33 arrived at Malta from Gibraltar.

7 JULY 1941

	Italian light cruisers ATTENDOLO and DUCA D'AOSTA of the 7th Cruiser Squadron with BANDE NERE and DI GUISSANO of the 4th Cruiser Squadron plus destroyers PIGAFETTA, PESSAGNO, DA RECCO, DA MOSTO, DA VERAZZANO, MAESTRALE, GRECALE, and SCIROCCO laid Minefield S.31 and Minefield S.32 in the Sicilian Channel. These minefields included 292 deep mines and 444 floating mines.

8 JULY 1941

	Submarine UPHOLDER arrived at Malta from her patrol.

9 JULY 1941

	During the night, RAF bombing damaged Italian destroyer DA MOSTO at Tripoli, Libya.

10 JULY 1941

2200	Submarine RORQUAL departed Malta on a patrol, but was forced to return with engine defects.

11 JULY 1941

	Submarines URSULA and P.33 departed Malta to intercept an Italian convoy west of Lampedusa.

12 JULY 1941

	Submarine URSULA returned to Malta with a defective generator.
	RAF bombing sank German steamer **SPARTA** (1724grt) at Tripoli, Libya. She was later salvaged in 1943.
	Submarine RORQUAL departed Malta for Alexandria with a new stem piece, forged at Malta, for damaged anti-aircraft ship COVENTRY.
	Submarine TRIUMPH arrived at Malta for repairs of damage incurred in her gunfire engagement off Benghazi.

13 JULY 1941

	Submarine TAKU (Lt Nicolay) sank Italian steamer **CALDEA** (2703grt) (ex **OGADEN** (2703grt)) while she was en route from Brindisi, Italy, to Benghazi, about ten miles 312° from Benghazi. Italian torpedo boat MONTANARI from Tripoli was escorting the steamer and conducted a submarine search but was unable to damage TAKU.
	RAF bombers sank Italian steamer **FRATELLI BERTOLLI** (429grt) in Tripoli harbour.

14 JULY 1941

	A German-Italian convoy departed Tripoli with steamers RIALTO (6099grt), ANDREA GRITTI (6338grt), SEBASTINO VENIER (6311grt), BARBARIGO (5293grt), and ANKARA (4768grt) for Naples escorted by Italian destroyers MALOCELLO, FUCILIERE, and ALPINO plus torpedo boats PROCIONE, PEGASO, and ORSA. The convoy arrived at Naples on the 16th.
	RAF bombing sank Italian fishing vessel **MARIA IMMACOLATA** (23grt) off Benghazi.
	Submarine OSIRIS (Lt Cdr Euman) damaged Italian steamer CAPO D'ORSO (5293grt) in 36, 27N, 11, 54E.
0100	Submarine UNION departed Malta to intercept an Italian convoy south of Pantellaria. Swordfish aircraft departed Malta on 14 and 15 July to attack this convoy, but no contact was made.

15 JULY 1941

	Submarine P.33 (Lt Whiteway-Wilkinson) sank steamer **BARBARIGO** (5293grt) eight miles south of Pantellaria in 36, 27N, 11, 54E. The submarine sustained hull damage from the heavy depth charge attack administered by Italian torpedo boats ORSA and PROCIONE.
	Submarine TAKU sank Italian patrol vessel **VINCENZO PADRE** (270grt) with gunfire east, SE of Ras Auegia. (Other sources indicate that two small auxiliary minesweepers were lost in addition to the two patrol boats.)
	Submarine UNBEATEN (Lt Woodward) sank Italian patrol vessel **NETTUNO** (500grt) with gunfire off Mara Zuag Roads. The submarine reported sinking a second patrol vessel.

16 JULY 1941

	Submarine CACHALOT arrived at Malta with supplies from Alexandria.
	Submarine P.33 arrived at Malta for battle damage repairs after she was depth charged on the 15th.
	Italian troopships MARCO POLO (12,272grt), NEPTUNIA (19,475grt), and OCEANIA (19,507grt) departed Taranto, Italy, for Tripoli escorted by destroyers GENIERE, GIOBERTI, LANCIERE, and ORIANI and torpedo boat CENTAURO. Italian heavy cruisers TRIESTE and BOLZANO plus destroyers ASCARI, CARABINIERE, and CORAZZIERE provided distant cover for the convoy. The convoy arrived at Tripoli on the 18th.
	Submarine UNBEATEN reported she damaged a large tanker twenty-three miles south, southwest of Messina, however there were no confirming evidence to support this claim.

17 JULY 1941

	A British aerial torpedo attack by three Swordfish aircraft of 830 Squadron from Malta damaged Italian tanker PANUCO (6212grt) at Tripoli. The tanker was unable to unload her cargo and departed Tripoli with her cargo still aboard on the 19th, escorted by Italian torpedo boats CENTAURO and MONTANARI. She arrived at Palermo, Sicily,

	on the 22nd.
	In preparation for Operation SUBSTANCE, submarine UTMOST (Lt Cdr Cayley) explored a new channel for submarines through the Sicilian Straits. Submarines UPHOLDER and URGE used this new route to reach their cover positions for the operation.
	An Italian convoy departed Tripoli with damaged German steamer MENES (5609grt) in tow of Italian tug CICLOPE and German tug MAX BERENDT escorted by Italian torpedo boat CIRCE.

18 JULY 1941

	Submarine UNBEATEN (Lt Woodward) unsuccessfully attacked Italian troopship OCEANIA (19,507grt) and barely missed her near Tripoli.

19 JULY 1941

	A mine damaged Italian tanker GADA (grt) off Brindisi, Italy. She was towed into port.
	Submarine UNBEATEN arrived at Malta from her patrol.
2200	Submarine UPHOLDER departed Malta for Operation SUBSTANCE.

20 JULY 1941

	Submarine OTUS arrived at Malta carrying stores from Gibraltar.
	Submarine **UNION** (Lt R. M. Galloway) attacked a small Italian convoy south southwest of Pantellaria and was sunk in return by torpedo boat CIRCE. Galloway, Lt D. L. Carr, Lt R. D. C. G. Simmons, Lt D. A. Tarrant RNR and twenty-eight ratings were lost.
	Submarine UTMOST (Lt Cdr Cayley) unsuccessfully attacked a steamer off Utica.
	Submarines UPRIGHT and UNIQUE departed Malta for Operation SUBSTANCE.

21 JULY 1941

	Italian motor tanker BRARENA (6996grt) (ex Norwegian) departed Palermo escorted by Italian destroyer FUCILIERE for Tripoli.
	A German-Italian convoy departed Naples, Italy, with steamers MADDALENA ODERO (5479grt), NICOLO ODERO (6003grt), CAFFARO (6476grt), and PREUSSEN (8230grt) for Tripoli escorted by Italian destroyers FOLGORE, EURO, SAETTA, and FULMINE. Italian destroyers ALPINO and FUCILIERE later joined the convoy at sea. Torpedo boat PALLADE joined the convoy on the 23rd from Tripoli.
	Submarine UTMOST (Lt Cdr Cayley) landed a commando group on the west tip of Italy to sabotage rail lines and delay train traffic.
	Submarine OLYMPUS unsuccessfully attacked a convoy of two steamers and one escort off Naples.

22 JULY 1941

	Swordfish aircraft of 830 Squadron sank German steamer **PREUSSEN** (8230grt) thirty miles southeast of Pantellaria. She exploded, leaving 190 crewmen dead. The other ships of the convoy reached Tripoli escorted by Italian destroyer ALPINO and torpedo boat PALLADE.
	British Blenheim bombers heavily damaged Italian motor tanker **BRARENA** (6996grt) (ex Norwegian) eighty miles south of Pantellaria. Italian destroyer FUCILIERE tried to tow the damaged tanker, but a second torpedo attack by the aircraft forced her to abandon the burning tanker. Italian Destroyer FOLGORE from another convoy assisted FUCILIERE in her attempts to save the tanker. (Other sources have Swordfish aircraft of 830 Squadron sinking the tanker.)
	Submarine URGE unsuccessfully attacked a small convoy off Palermo.

23 JULY 1941

	A mine sank German steamer **TIRPITZ** (7970grt) near Cape del Arma. (Other sources claim an aerial torpedo sank her.)
	Italian depth charges damaged submarine P.33 on patrol near Pantellaria, but she was able to continue patrol.
	Submarine OLYMPUS unsuccessfully attacked a troopship off Naples.
	Lt P. R. E. Woods was killed when his Martlet aircraft of 805 Squadron ditched in the sea one mile north of Ma'aten Bagush.
0500	Convoy MG.1 departed Malta with steamers SETTLER (6000grt), THERMOPYLAE (6655grt), AMERIKA (10,218grt), TALABOT (6798grt), HOEGH HOOD (9351grt), SVENOR (7616grt), and supply ship BRECONSHIRE (9776grt), in ballast, escorted by destroyer ENCOUNTER for Gibraltar. Steamer SVENOR hit the breakwater leaving harbour and had to be docked. She was able to depart the next day. Corvette GLOXINIA escorted the convoy during the first day and then returned to Malta. Destroyer FARNDALE had to remain at Malta with condenser problems.

24 JULY 1941

	Light cruisers EDINBURGH (Rear Adm Syfret) and ARETHUSA, minelayer MANXMAN, with destroyers COSSACK, MAORI, SIKH, NESTOR, and FARNDALE escorted the Operation SUBSTANCE convoy into Malta. The remainder of Force H returned to Gibraltar.
	Submarine UPRIGHT (Lt Wraith) unsuccessfully attacked Italian Floating Dock G022 off Cape dell'Armi. The submarine was then heavily depth charged by the escorts.
	Submarine UPHOLDER (Lt Cdr Wanklyn) damaged Italian steamer DANDOLO (4964grt), escorted by a destroyer, off the west coast of Sicily in 38, 08N, 12, 37E.
	Italian motor torpedo boats MAS.532 and MAS.533 attacked the Operation SUBSTANCE convoy off Pantellaria. The Italian boats escaped undamaged, despite claims by light cruisers EDINBURGH, destroyer COSSACK, and minelayer MANXMAN that they each sank an MAS boat. MAS.533 torpedoed steamer SYDNEY STAR (11,219grt) and she fell out of the convoy. Destroyer NESTOR and later light cruiser HERMIONE were detailed to protect the steamer and escort it to Malta, and without further incident they arrived later in the day. The SYDNEY STAR was dry-docked at Malta on 18 August. Destroyer NESTOR delivered 487 troops to Malta.

25 JULY 1941

	Italian fast sloop DIANA departed Augusta, Sicily, with eight explosive motorboats of the 10th MAS Flotilla aboard and one in tow, escorted by MAS.451 and MAS.452, each towing a two-man torpedo to Malta. British RADAR detected the group, but Major Tesei, the inventor of the Italian human guided torpedo (Maiali), blew up the harbour boom with his torpedo and two of the explosive motorboats. The explosion toppled the St Elmo bridge, blocking the harbour for the remaining six motorboats, which were soon destroyed by the shore batteries. British aircraft caught and sank **MAS.451** and **MAS.452** early the next morning as they tried to reach a safe port. Only DIANA returned safely to base.
	Submarine TETRARCH (Lt Cdr Greenway) sank Italian patrol vessel **B.247/MARIA IMMANCOLATA** off Gaidero Island. The submarine also reported an unsuccessful attack on a German ship.

27 JULY 1941

	The Italian 8th Cruiser Division with light cruisers MONTECUCOLI and GARIBALDI escorted by destroyers GRANATIERE, BERSAGLIERE, FUCILIERE and ALPINO put to sea to cover several convoys between Italy and Libya.
	An Africa Corps convoy departed Naples, Italy, with Italian steamers BAINSIZZA (7933grt), AMSTERDAM (8673grt), COL DI LANA (5891grt) and the German steamer SPEZIA (1825grt) escorted by Italian destroyers FRECCIA, DARDO, STRALE and TURBINE for Tripoli, Libya.
	A troop convoy departed Taranto, Italy, with troopships NEPTUNIA (19,475grt), OCEANIA (19,507grt) and MARCO POLO (12,272grt) escorted by Italian destroyers AVIERE, GENIERE, CAMICIA NERA, GIOBERTI and ORIANI to Tripoli.
	A return convoy departed Tripoli, Libya with steamers ERNESTO (7272grt), CASTELVERDE (6666grt), AQUITANIA (4971grt), NITA (6813grt), and NIRVA (5164grt) plus gunboat PALMAIOLO for Naples, Italy, escorted by destroyers FOLGORE, SAETTA, FUCILIERE, and ALPINO. Light cruisers GARIBALDI and MONTECUCOLI plus destroyers GRANATIERE and BERSAGLIERE provided cover for the convoy.

28 JULY 1941

	Submarine UTMOST (Lt Cdr Cayley) sank Italian steamer **FEDERICO C.** (1466grt) off western Calabria, Italy, in 39, 28N, 15, 52, 30E.
	Dutch submarine O.21 (Lt Cdr van Dulm) sank Italian steamer **MONTEPONI** (747grt) ten miles north of Cape Camino, Italy, in 39, 51N, 13, 46E.
	Submarine UPRIGHT arrived at Malta from her patrol.
	Submarine URGE arrived at Malta from her patrol.
1815	Italian destroyer FULMINE joined the Italian return convoy off Cape St Vito, Sicily.
1955	Submarine UPHOLDER torpedoed Italian light cruiser GARIBALDI off Marettimo, Sicily, in 38, 04N, 11, 57E.
2020	Italian destroyers FUCILIERE and ALPINO joined the damaged Italian light cruiser GARIBALDI off Marittimo.

29 JULY 1941

	A return convoy departed Tripoli, Libya with troopships NEPTUNIA (19,475grt), OCEANIA (19,507grt) and MARCO POLO (12,272grt) escorted by Italian destroyers AVIERE, GENIERE, CAMICIA NERA, GIOBERTI and ORIANI for Naples, Italy. Italian torpedo boat SIRTORI joined the return convoy and provided addition escort to Naples.
	A return convoy departed Tripoli with Italian steamers BAINSIZZA (7933grt), AMSTERDAM (8673grt), COL DI

	LANA (5891grt), and the German steamer SPEZIA (1825grt) for Naples escorted by Italian destroyers FRECCIA, DARDO, STRALE and TURBINE.
	A return convoy departed Tripoli with Italian steamers ERNESTO (7272grt), NITA (6813grt), CASTELVERDE (6666grt), NIRVA (5164grt) and AQUITANIA (4971grt) for Naples escorted by Italian destroyers FOLGORE, SAETTA, FULMINE and torpedo boat SIRTORI. Italian destroyers FUCILIERE and ALPINO provided local escort.
	Italian steamer FRANCESCO BARBARO (6343grt) departed Tripoli escorted by destroyer DA MOSTO for Naples as a separate convoy.
	An Italian supply convoy departed Naples for Tripoli with steamers ANDREA GRITTI (6338grt), RIALTO (6099grt), VETTOR PISANI (6339grt) and the German steamer ANKARA (4768grt) escorted by Italian destroyer MALOCELLO with torpedo boats PROCIONE, PEGASO, ORIONE and PARTENOPE. MALOCELLO downed an attacking RAF aircraft on the 31st.
0630	Italian destroyers FUCILIERE and ALPINO escorted the damaged Italian light cruiser GARIBALDI into Palermo, Sicily. She was under repair for four months to repair the damage.

30 JULY 1941

	Italian torpedo boat ACHILLE PAPA rammed and sank submarine **CACHALOT** (Lt Cdr H. R. B. Newton) north of Benghazi in 32, 49N, 20, 11E. Only one rating was lost. The remainder of the crew were rescued by the Italian torpedo boat. Newton, Sub-Lt C. E. S. Beale, Lt J. E. F. Dickson, T/Lt R. D. C. Hart RNVR, Lt (E) E. H. Player DSC, and sixty-two ratings were taken prisoner. Lt R. P. Lucey, on passage for submarine depot ship MEDWAY, T/Lt A. J. Piggot RNR, on passage for base ship ST ANGELO, and eighteen ratings, travelling as passengers for Alexandria, were also picked up and also made prisoners of war. Dickson later escaped captivity.
	Submarine UNIQUE (Lt Collett) landed a sabotage group at the western tip of Calabria, Italy, to destroy rail lines and trains.

31 JULY 1941

	Submarine REGENT (Lt Knox) sank Italian sailing ship **IGEA** (160grt) with gunfire seven miles northwest of Benghazi, Libya. (Other sources put the position as seven sea miles north of Carcura.)

Eastern Mediterranean Sea

Long. E20, 00 – E38, 00   Lat. N43, 00 – N30, 00

1 JULY 1941

	Vichy French destroyers GUÉPARD, VALMY, and VAUQUELIN departed Beirut, Lebanon to escort a troopship into Beirut.
	Light cruiser NAIAD departed Haifa, Palestine with destroyers KANDAHAR, DECOY, and HAVOCK for a night sweep off Syria.
	Corvette HYACINTH ran aground four miles south of Famagusta, Cyprus. She could not be readily re-floated and corvette ERICA was damaged in the attempt.
	MTB tender VULCAN sailed from Famagusta, Cypress with MTB.68 and MTB.215 to Haifa, Palestine.

2 JULY 1941

	Australian light cruiser PERTH and light cruiser NAIAD shelled Vichy French positions east of Damur with destroyers KANDAHAR, KINGSTON, HAVOCK, and GRIFFIN. PERTH was attacked in error by British aircraft, but was not damage.
	Destroyers JACKAL and HASTY departed Alexandria, Egypt for Haifa, Palestine.
	Vichy French aircraft of the 4th Naval Air Group (Lt Cdr Hubert †) attacked the British cruiser force off Damur, Syria. Several Vichy aircraft were lost, including the commander Hubert.
	Italian submarines MALACHITE, AMETISTA, SETTEMBRINI and DAGABUR patrolled off Cyrenaica and Egypt until the 17th.
	Submarine TORBAY sank Italian steamer **CITTA DI TRIPOLI** (2933grt) south of Athens, Greece in 37, 41, 50N, 24, 15, 50E.
	Destroyers JACKAL (D.7) and HASTY departed Alexandria for Haifa. On their arrival at Haifa, destroyers KANDAHAR and DECOY departed the port for Alexandria on the 3rd.
	Yugoslavian MTBs KAJMAKALAN and DURMITOR departed Alexandria for Haifa to operate under the orders of CS.15.
	Motor launch ML.1032 departed Alexandria for Famagusta.

3 JULY 1941

	Corvette PEONY departed Haifa, Palestine and tug ST ISSEY departed Alexandria, Egypt to re-float grounded corvette HYACINTH off Famagusta, Cypress.
	Light cruiser PHOEBE and Australian light cruiser PERTH swept for shipping off the Syrian coast with destroyers KINGSTON, HOTSPUR, and GRIFFIN.
	Italian submarine MALACHITE unsuccessfully attacked light cruiser PHOEBE in 32, 25N, 24, 40E.
	En route to Tobruk, Libya, Australian destroyer STUART sighted a submarine on the surface off Mersa Matruh, Egypt. Destroyer DEFENDER hunted for the submarine without success, while destroyers STUART and VENDETTA continued to Tobruk.
0100	Light cruisers AJAX (Rawlings) and PHOEBE departed Alexandria, Egypt with destroyers JACKAL and NIZAM and arrived off Syria later that day.

4 JULY 1941

	Axis bombers unsuccessfully attacked grounded corvette HYACINTH during the evening of 4 July off Famagusta, Cypress.
	Albacore aircraft of 822 Squadron sank Vichy French steamer **SAINT DIDIER** (2778grt) off the Anatolian coast near Beirut, Lebanon. Another Vichy French supply ship, the CHATEAU YQUEM (2536grt) returned to France after hearing of the sinking. The Vichy government determined that the British blockade of Syria was too effective to risk any additional ships.
	Light cruisers NAIAD and AJAX shelled Vichy French positions on the Syrian coast with destroyers JACKAL, NIZAM, KIMBERLEY, and HAVOCK.
	Submarine TORBAY (Lt Cdr Miers) sank two German caiques with troops and stores with gunfire in the Doro Channel.

5 JULY 1941

	Corvette PEONY successfully re-floated grounded corvette HYACINTH off Famagusta. Corvette PEONY and tug ST ISSEY returned to Alexandria, Egypt. Corvette HYACINTH proceeded to Alexandria via Haifa, Palestine, for repairs, completed on the 15th.
	Submarine TORBAY (Lt Cdr Miers) sank Italian submarine **JANTINA** south of Melos, Greece in 37, 309N, 25, 00E.
	An aerial mine laid by Ju88 aircraft of LG.1 sank steamer **BENCRUACHEN** (5920grt) 9.8 cables 297° from Mex High Light in Alexandria harbour. Three crewmen were lost. The mine explosion also sank motor yacht **WYREEMA** (31grt).
	Light cruisers AJAX and the Australian PERTH plus antiaircraft cruiser CARLISLE bombarded Vichy French positions at Damur, Syria with destroyers JACKAL, KINGSTON, NIZAM, GRIFFIN, HAVOCK, and HOTSPUR plus full air support.
	Light cruiser PERTH antiaircraft cruiser CARLISLE conducted a night shipping sweep along the Syrian coast with destroyers NIZAM and HAVOCK.

6 JULY 1941

	Light cruisers AJAX and the Australian PERTH plus antiaircraft cruiser CARLISLE bombarded Vichy French positions at Damur, Syria in support of army operations with destroyers JACKAL, KINGSTON, NIZAM, GRIFFIN, HAVOCK, and HOTSPUR (one of these destroyers were absent from the bombardment).
	Light cruisers NAIAD and PHOEBE conducted a night shipping sweep along the Syrian coast with destroyers KIMBERLEY and HASTY.

7 JULY 1941

	After a mine laying air raid on Haifa, Palestine, light cruisers NAIAD and PHOEBE remained at sea off the harbour with destroyers JACKAL, HOTSPUR, NIZAM, and HAVOCK. Antiaircraft ship CARLISLE had to be towed clear of a suspected mine dropped near her.
	During the night of 7/8 July, MTB.68 entered Beirut, Lebanon, harbour twice and dropped depth charges close to two merchant ships along the docking mole.

8 JULY 1941

	Submarine TORBAY (Lt Cdr Miers) sank German caiques **LXIV** and **LI** with gunfire east of Kithara, Greece.
	In the night of 8/9 July, twenty-five Ju88 aircraft of LG.1 from Crete attack Alexandria, Egypt and damaged the Greek steamer ANTIKLIA (951grt).

9 JULY 1941

	Vichy French destroyers GUÉPARD, VALMY, and VAUQUELIN departed Tripoli, Syria, for Salonika, Greece to pick up troops transported there by rail from France.

British aircraft located these destroyers before they were able to get within two hundred miles of Syria.

The Vichy French destroyers were ordered to retire to Toulon, putting an end to the naval phase of the Syria operations.

Vichy French sloop **ÉLAN**, auxiliary tanker **L'ADOUR** (4500grt), small tanker **CYRUS** (405grt), patrol vessels **DJEBEL SAMIN**, **JEAN MIC**, and **MASSALIA**, minesweepers **AVOCETTE** and **LE CID**, tugs **MARIUS**, **CHAMBRUM**, and **MARSEILLAISE**, and trawler **LA VAILLANTE** were interned at Iskanderun, Turkey.

Vichy French submarine CAIMAN proceeded to Bizerte, Tunisia from Syria.

On 18 September, the last of the interned ships had been moved, under Turkish escort, to Mersin and Erdek.

Submarine TORBAY (Lt Cdr Miers) sank German caiques **LVI** and **LV** and damaged **LXII** with gunfire and scuttling charges east of Kithera, Greece.

Submarine CACHALOT departed Alexandria on a supply run to Malta.

German bombing damaged destroyer **DECOY** and Australian destroyer **STUART** with bomb near misses, while they were leaving Tobruk Harbour. Both destroyers required repair on their return to Alexandria. Destroyer HERO replaced destroyer DECOY for the Tobruk supply operations.

Destroyer NAPIER departed Alexandria for Port Said to complete repairs on her turbines.

10 JULY 1941

Submarine TORBAY (Lt Cdr Miers) heavily damaged Italian tanker **STROMBO** (5232grt) with a torpedo attack off the Zea Canal, Greece, in 37, 30N, 24, 16E.

TORBAY was then damaged by depth charges dropped by the escorting torpedo boats CLIMENE and CALATAFIMI. The tanker was declared a total loss.

Light cruiser AJAX and Australian light cruiser PERTH were at sea off Syria with four destroyers on patrol during the night of 9/10 July in support of the Army operations ashore.

No contact was made with any Vichy French ships during the patrol.

Battleship VALIANT, light cruiser LEANDER, and destroyers were at sea from Alexandria, Egypt, exercising during the day.

11 JULY 1941

During the night of 10/11 July, light cruisers AJAX and PHOEBE with destroyers JACKAL, GRIFFIN, KINGSTON, HASTY, and KIMBERLEY searched the Syrian coast for Vichy French merchant ships reported by aircraft the previous day. There were no contacts and the ships arrived back at Haifa, Palestine, at daylight.

At midnight on 11/12 July, the Army ceased hostilities with Vichy French forces in Syria.

Tugboat ST ISSEY towed gunboat CRICKET from Alexandria, Egypt to Port Said, Egypt for docking, escorted by gunboat GNAT sailing on one engine.

0520 — German Ju88 aircraft of LG.1 from Crete heavily damaged destroyer **DEFENDER** (1,375t, 1932) and lightly damaged Australian destroyer **VENDETTA** after they had carried supplies to Tobruk, Libya in 31, 45N, 25, 51E. VENDETTA towed the damaged destroyer for a time before she sank seven miles north of Sidi Barrani. There was no loss of life and only five crewmen were wounded.

12 JULY 1941

About thirty German Ju88 aircraft of LG.1 from Crete sank Greek steamer **PATRAI** (1977grt) at Port Said, Egypt. She was raised and restored to service after the war.

About thirty German Ju88 aircraft of LG.1 from Crete damaged the Dutch steamer **ALPHARD** (5483grt) at Port Said. Four crewmen were lost.

About thirty German Ju88 aircraft of LG.1 from Crete damaged sloop **FLAMINGO** at Port Said.

After accepting the armistice, Vichy French submarines MORSE and CAIMAN departed Syria for Bizerte, Tunisia.

Submarines PARTHIAN, PERSEUS, REGENT, RORQUAL, CACHALOT, UPRIGHT, the Dutch O.23 and O.24, plus the Greek PAPANICOLIS, NEREUS and GLAVKOS sank no axis ships while on patrol since 1 July.

13 JULY 1941

Destroyer DECOY sighted a submarine off Bardia, Libya, while returning from a supply run to Tobruk, Libya. After an unsuccessful depth charge attack and due to the threat of axis air attack, the destroyer continued on to Alexandria, Egypt. Destroyer VOYAGER, in company with DECOY, was reduced to seventeen knots due to a mechanical defect and could not assist in the submarine hunt.

An RAF aerial mine sank tanker **PEGASUS** (3597grt) as she arrived at Beirut, Lebanon.

14 JULY 1941

Light cruiser AJAX remained on station along the Syrian coast with destroyers JACKAL, NIZAM, HASTY, and KINGSTON.

Antiaircraft ship CARLISLE remained at Beirut, Lebanon.

During the night of 14/15 July, destroyer HERO and Australian destroyer VENDETTA ran supplies to Tobruk, Libya. Destroyer VENDETTA was holed while alongside the dock, but she was able to return to Alexandria, Egypt

	after temporary repairs at Mersa Matruh, Egypt.
1800	Light cruisers NAIAD, PHOEBE and Australian light cruiser PERTH departed Haifa with destroyers GRIFFIN, HAVOCK, KIMBERLEY, and HOTSPUR to return to Alexandria.

15 JULY 1941

	Light cruisers NAIAD, PHOEBE and Australian light cruiser PERTH arrived at Alexandria, Egypt with destroyers GRIFFIN, HAVOCK, KIMBERLEY, and HOTSPUR from Haifa, Palestine.
	Axis dive-bombers attacked a small convoy escorted by sloop FLAMINGO with Lighter A.10 (Sub-Lt J. D. Thom RNVR) and Lighter A.11, en route to Tobruk in 32, 15N, 25, 26E. Lighter **A.10** was hit and was abandoned after attempts to take her in tow by A.11 failed. One rating was killed and three ratings were wounded in lighter **A.10**. T/A/Sub-Lt W. G. Jenkins RNVR was wounded in Lighter A.11.
	New Zealand light cruiser LEANDER departed Alexandria to reinforce the British forces at Haifa.

16 JULY 1941

	Italian submarine NEREIDE claimed damage on Greek submarine TRITON with a torpedo and gunfire in 37, 25N, 25, 52E.
	Antiaircraft cruiser CARLISLE arrived at Beirut, Lebanon carrying a base party, with minesweepers HARROW, MOY, and LYDIARD from Haifa, Palestine. Corvette SALVIA and ML.1032 arrived at Beirut from Famagusta, Cypress. Captain J. A. V. Morse was named Naval Officer in Charge of Syrian ports with his headquarters at Beirut.
	Corvette HYACINTH with LL equipped minesweeper FELLOWSHIP departed Alexandria, Egypt for Famagusta, Cypress.
	Destroyer KANDAHAR departed Alexandria for Port Said, Egypt to join the remainder of convoy LE.25. KANDAHAR departed Port Said with the two ships from convoy LE.25 on the 17th.
	Destroyer JAGUAR departed Alexandria with a petrol tanker from convoy LE.25 for Beirut.
	Destroyer JERVIS departed Alexandria for Haifa to operate with British forces there.

17 JULY 1941

	After destroyer JERVIS arrived at Haifa, Palestine, destroyers JACKAL, NIZAM, and HASTY departed Haifa for Alexandria, Egypt.
	Australian sloop PARRAMATTA departed Alexandria for escort duties at Port Said, Egypt.
	Minelayers ABDIEL and LATONA departed Alexandria for exercises.
1200	Antiaircraft cruiser COVENTRY departed Alexandria to join convoy LE.25 off Port Said and provide escort to Beirut. Light cruiser AJAX and two destroyers provided cover for the convoy. Convoy LE.25 arrived at Beirut, Lebanon later in the day. Cruiser COVENTRY relieved antiaircraft cruiser CARLISLE at Beirut and she sailed for Alexandria, arriving on the 19th.

18 JULY 1941

	Battleships VALIANT and QUEEN ELIZABETH plus light cruiser PHOEBE departed Alexandria, Egypt with destroyers JACKAL, NIZAM, HASTY, KIPLING, and HAVOCK for exercises.
	Australian light cruiser PERTH, after having been relieved by Australian light cruiser HOBART, departed Alexandria to return to Australia via Port Said, Egypt.
	In Operation GUILLOTINE, beginning on this date and continuing into August, troops and supplies were moved from Port Said and Haifa to Famagusta, Cypress in cruisers, minelayers ABDIEL and LATONA, plus destroyers. Australian steamer SALAMAUA (6676grt), carrying an antiaircraft battery and RAF 80 Squadron, departed Port Said for Famagusta escorted by sloop PARRAMATTA in convoy serial S.1. The ships arrived at Famagusta on the 21st.
	Destroyers HERO and HOTSPUR arrived back at Alexandria after delivering supplies to Tobruk, Libya.

19 JULY 1941

	Before departing the Mediterranean Fleet, Australian light cruiser PERTH had a quadruple pom-pom gun removed and a catapult, previously carried in light cruiser AJAX, mounted at Port Said, Egypt.
	Italian submarines UXUM, SQUALO and UARSCIEK patrolled off the Egyptian coast until the 31st.
	Battleships VALIANT and QUEEN ELIZABETH, light cruiser PHOEBE plus minelayer LATONA arrived at Alexandria, Egypt with destroyers JACKAL, NIZAM, HASTY, KIPLING, and HAVOCK after exercises at sea.
	Minelaying cruiser ABDIEL and destroyer DECOY departed Alexandria to carry supplies to Tobruk, Libya. The supplies were delivered and both ships arrived back at Alexandria on the 20th.

20 JULY 1941

	Submarine RORQUAL arrived at Alexandria, Egypt from Malta. Among the items brought to Alexandria was a

	new stem piece, forged at Malta, for damaged antiaircraft ship COVENTRY.
	Australian light cruiser PERTH passed through the Suez Canal to the Red Sea.
	Minelayer LATONA and Australian destroyer STUART departed Alexandria carrying supplies to Tobruk, Libya. At Tobruk, the cruiser was able to unload only fifty tons of her cargo due to a delay in arrival and difficulties in unloading. The ships arrived back at Alexandria on the 21st.
	Submarine TETRARCH unsuccessfully attacked a steamer in the Aegean Sea.
	In Operation GUILLOTINE, New Zealand light cruiser LEANDER and destroyer KINGSTON departed Haifa, Palestine, for Port Said, Egypt, where they arrived that day to embark troops and supplies in convoy serial S.2A. The supplies were unloaded at Famagusta, Cypress, during the night of 20/21 July. Destroyer JERVIS also disembarked troops from Haifa at Famagusta during the night of 20/21 July in convoy serial S.2B of Operation GUILLOTINE. LEANDER and destroyer KINGSTON arrived back at Haifa on the 21st.

21 JULY 1941

	Greek submarine GLAVKOS (Lt Cdr Zepos) sank Italian sailing vessel **SAN NICOLA** (21grt) four miles northwest of Rhodes with gunfire.
	Destroyer ILEX, after temporary repairs at Port Said, Egypt, passed through the Suez Canal for more repairs at Durban, South Africa.
	Corvette PEONY departed Port Said with Dutch steamer TRAJANUS (1712grt) in Operation GUILLOTINE. This movement, convoy series S.2C, arrived at Famagusta, Cypress, on the 23rd.
	Sloop FLAMINGO departed Alexandria, Egypt, for Port Said for an Operation GUILLOTINE escort of convoy serial S.3. The sloop departed Port Said on the 22nd escorting motor transport ship KEVINBANK for Famagusta, arriving on the 24th.
	Submarine PARTHIAN departed Alexandria for Malta and then on to Britain for a refit.
	Submarine TAKU sent a commando group into Benghazi harbour, Libya, where they attached explosive charges to one of the ships in harbour.

22 JULY 1941

	Light cruiser AJAX and New Zealand light cruiser LEANDER departed Haifa, Palestine with destroyers JERVIS, JAGUAR, KANDAHAR, and KINGSTON to rendezvous with the Mediterranean Fleet off Alexandria on the 23rd.
	Greek submarine GLAVKOS sank a caique with gunfire off Castellorizo, Italy.
	Yugoslavian torpedo boats DURMITOR and KAJMAKALAN departed Haifa to return to Alexandria, Egypt.
	Submarine TETRARCH shelled the harbour at Karlovassi, Greece, and claimed damage to a number of caiques.
	Axis bombing damaged destroyer HERO in Tobruk harbour, Libya during the night of 22/23 July. She received temporary repairs at Mersa Matruh, Egypt.
2100	In Operation SUBSTANCE, the Mediterranean Fleet sortied from Alexandria. Battleships QUEEN ELIZABETH and VALIANT, light cruisers NAIAD, PHOEBE, NEPTUNE, and HOBART, mine laying cruisers ABDIEL and LATONA, plus destroyers JACKAL, NIZAM, KIPLING, KIMBERLEY, GRIFFIN, HASTY, and HAVOCK operated to the west of Crete.

23 JULY 1941

	Aircraft carrier FORMIDABLE departed Alexandria, Egypt for repairs in the United States, escorted by minelayer LATONA plus destroyers JERVIS, KANDAHAR, and JAGUAR. She passed through the Suez Canal the next day into the Red Sea and arrived at Norfolk, Virginia on 26 August. Aircraft carrier FORMIDABLE was under repair until 12 December.
0600	Light cruiser AJAX and New Zealand light cruiser LEANDER with destroyers JERVIS, JAGUAR, KANDAHAR, and KINGSTON rendezvoused with the Mediterranean Fleet off Alexandria. Antiaircraft ship CARLISLE joined the Mediterranean Fleet at daylight. At dark, the Mediterranean Fleet turned backed eastward and light cruiser NEPTUNE and minelayer ABDIEL were detached from the Mediterranean Fleet to support convoy serial S.4 with destroyer KIMBERLEY for Operation GUILLOTINE. They departed Port Said, Egypt on the 24th. The troops were delivered on the 24th and the ships arrived back at Port Said on the 25th.

24 JULY 1941

	Submarines REGENT and PERSEUS created the impression by means of radio signals that the Mediterranean Fleet battleships were still at sea and that the Operation SUBSTANCE convoy was headed for Alexandria, Egypt.
	New Zealand light cruiser LEANDER and destroyer JAGUAR were detached from the Mediterranean Fleet for Port Said, Egypt where they arrived on the 25th.
	Australian sloop PARRAMATTA departed Port Said escorting motor transport ship GUJARAT (4148grt) to Famagusta, Cypress in Operation GUILLOTINE convoy serial S.5. The sloop arrived back at Port Said on the 28th.

	Australian destroyer VOYAGER departed Alexandria to return to Australia. The destroyer passed through the Suez Canal on the 25th into the Red Sea and arrived at Port Darwin, Australia, on 25 September.

25 JULY 1941

	The Main Body of the Mediterranean Fleet arrived back at Alexandria, Egypt.
	New Zealand light cruiser LEANDER and destroyer JAGUAR embarked troops for Famagusta, Cypress and departed Port Said, Egypt as convoy Serial S.6 with mine laying cruiser LATONA, arriving during the night of 25/26 July. LATONA was damaged in a collision with destroyer JAGUAR while berthing at Famagusta, but was able to depart with the destroyer on the 26th for Haifa, Palestine. LEANDER arrived at Alexandria, Egypt on the 26th.
	Rear Admiral, Mediterranean Aircraft Carriers, hoisted his flag in depot ship GREBE.
	A Swordfish aircraft of 815 Squadron was lost forty-four miles west of Cape Kormakiti, Cyprus, when the airframe and engine parted. Sub-Lt D. A. Wise and Sub-Lt A. H. Cann were killed.

26 JULY 1941

	Light cruiser NEPTUNE, minelayer ABDIEL, and destroyer KIMBERLEY departed Port Said, Egypt for Famagusta, Cypress on convoy serial S.7 of Operation GUILLOTINE. The troops were landed during the night of 26/27 July and the ships returned to Haifa, Palestine.
	New Zealand light cruiser LEANDER departed Alexandria, Egypt for Port Said and then to New Zealand after being relieved by light cruiser NEPTUNE. She departed Suez on the 31st on the long voyage to New Zealand.

27 JULY 1941

	Sloop FLAMINGO departed Port Said, Egypt with motor transport ship SALAMAUA (6676grt) for Famagusta, Cypress in convoy serial S.8 of Operation GUILLOTINE. The sloop arrived at Famagusta on the 28th and departed the same day.
	Submarine TETRARCH (Lt Cdr Greenway) sank Italian caique **NICITA** with gunfire five miles south of Kos, Greece.

28 JULY 1941

	Destroyer JERVIS departed Haifa, Palestine and joined light cruiser NEPTUNE, minelayers ABDIEL and LATONA, with destroyer JAGUAR to return to Alexandria, Egypt. Light cruiser HOBART with destroyers KANDAHAR and KIMBERLEY relieved the NEPTUNE group at Haifa. The NEPTUNE group arrived at Alexandria on the 29th.
	Corvette HYACINTH was detached from the escort for damaged destroyer ISIS off Port Said, Egypt. The corvette then escorted motor transport ship KEVINBANK to Famagusta, Cypress in convoy serial S.9 of Operation GUILLOTINE, arriving on the 30th. The corvette returned to Port Said on the 30th.
	Destroyer HOTSPUR and Australian destroyer VENDETTA departed Alexandria for Tobruk, Libya.

29 JULY 1941

	German Ju87 aircraft of I/STG.1 and Italian Ju87 aircraft of 239 Squadron sank **LCT.8** (372grt) and Lighter **A.8** (Sub-Lt R. M. Wright RNVR), but missed Lighter A.14 east of Bardia, Libya.
	Submarine THRASHER (Lt Cdr Cowell) arrived at Alexandria, Egypt with sixty-seven British and eleven Greek soldiers from Crete who had been in hiding since the island fell.
0900	Destroyer HOTSPUR and Australian destroyer VENDETTA loaded troops at Tobruk, Libya early in the morning and departed for Mersa Matruh, Egypt.

30 JULY 1941

	Destroyer HOTSPUR and Australian destroyer VENDETTA departed Mersa Matruh, Egypt for Alexandria, Egypt.
	Australian sloop PARRAMATTA departed Port Said, Egypt escorting motor transport ship GUJARAT (4148grt) to Famagusta, Cypress in convoy serial S.10 of Operation GUILLOTINE. The ships arrived at Famagusta on 1 August and sloop PARRAMATTA departed that day for Port Said, Egypt.
	Corvette DELPHINIUM departed Alexandria to relieve corvette PEONY, with defects, at Famagusta.
	MTB.104, which had been laid up with defects at Port Said, departed Port Said for Alexandria to be paid off.
2215	Destroyer HOTSPUR and Australian destroyer VENDETTA made a submarine contact while returning to Alexandria. Destroyer HOTSPUR attacked the contact and destroyer VENDETTA continued to Alexandria, arriving on the 31st.

31 JULY 1941

	A Sunderland Flying Boat attacked Italian submarine DELFINO off Mersa Matruh, Egypt.
	Submarines THRASHER, URSULA, UNIQUE, UNBEATEN, P.32 and the Greek TRITON scored no successes

during their patrols in the latter half of July.

Black Sea
Long. E27, 00 – E43, 00   Lat. N48, 00 – N41, 00

1 JULY 1941
Russian destroyer BYSTRY struck a German mine off Sevastopol and was beached to prevent her sinking.

6 JULY 1941
The Russian Black Sea Fleet patrolled off Romania with submarines D-5, SHCH-201, S-33, SHCH-210, SHCH-211, S-32 and S-34.
Smaller submarines M-62, M-33, M-34, M-32, M-36, M-31 and M-35 respectively took turns operating off Odessa, Ukraine, for one week each.

8 JULY 1941
The Russian Danube Reni Group broke through the Axis defences to reach Ismailia with three Monitors and four gunboats in the night of 8/9 July.
Russian gunboat **BKA-114** was sunk off Ismailia, Romania.

9 JULY 1941
The Russian 2nd Destroyer Division operated in the Fidonisi, Romania, area with destroyers TASHKENT, BODRY, BOIKI, BESPOSHCHADNY, and BEZUPRECHNY in the Black Sea on a shipping sweep, but did not make any contacts.
Romanian gunboat STIHI EUGEN, torpedo boat NALUCA and three MTBs sank Russian submarine **SC-206** near Mangalia, Romania, in 43, 51.5N, 28, 45E.

11 JULY 1941
Russian monitors ZHEMCHUZHIN, ROSTOVTSEV and MARTYNOV landed more Russian troops in the Danube Estuary in the Kilia channel, Romania. The defending Romanian forces sank Russian gunboats **BKA-111** and **BKA-134** with gunfire.

12 JULY 1941
German aerial mines dropped by II/KG.4 at Sevastopol heavily damaged Russian destroyer BDITELNY and slightly damaged destroyer leader KHARKOV.

14 JULY 1941
Russian steamer KRASNY KUBAN (3113grt) damaged Russian submarine M-52 in a collision off Sevastopol.
Russian submarines A-3, M-58, and S-31 had no success on their patrols along the Romanian coast.

18 JULY 1941
The Russian Donau Flotilla evacuated the Russian XIV Rifle Corps from the Kilia area through the Romanian positions at Periprava, Romania. At the mouth of the Danube, the monitors, armed cutters and patrol boats were joined by a force from Odessa, including cruiser KOMINTERN, gunboats KRASNAYA ARMENIYA and KRASNAYA GRUZIYA, ten torpedo cutters, six patrol cutters and the destroyers BODRY, KHARKOV and SHAUMYAN.

Red Sea
Long. E32, 00 – E43, 00   Lat. N30, 00 – N15, 00

12 JULY 1941
Australian light cruiser HOBART arrived at Suez, Egypt from Australia to join the Mediterranean Fleet. HOBART could not immediately be passed through the canal due to German aerial mines. HOBART and destroyer KIPLING, following her repairs at Suez, were able to proceed through the Suez Canal on the 16th.

14 JULY 1941
During the night, twenty-seven German Ju88 aircraft of LG.1 from Crete bombed the harbour at Suez, Egypt. At the same time, four German He111 aircraft dropped aerial mines in the Suez Canal.
Troopship **GEORGIC** (27,759grt) caught fire and drifted to the beach, fouling and slightly damaging landing ship GLENEARN (8986grt) en route. Twenty-six crewmen were killed. The troopship was salvaged in November and towed to Bombay, India for temporary repairs and then arrived in Britain on 1 March 1943 for full repairs.
An ammunition explosion damaged troopship GLENEARN anchored nearby.
Australian light cruiser HOBART was later able to pass a line to landing ship GLENEARN towing her free. Troopship GLENEARN departed Suez for Bombay on 1 August in the tow of steamer CITY OF KIMBERLEY (6169grt).

17 JULY 1941

Light cruiser NEPTUNE arrived at Suez, Egypt after her repairs. She passed through the Canal and arrived at Port Said, Egypt to disembark her catapult to make room for more antiaircraft weapons to be installed. NEPTUNE then proceeded to Alexandria, Egypt, arriving on the 19th.

21 JULY 1941

Australian light cruiser PERTH departed Suez, Egypt for Sydney, Australia where she was refitting and repairing defects from 11 August to 30 October.

Arabian Sea   Long. E43, 00 – E77, 00   Lat. N31, 00 – N00, 00

4 JULY 1941

Heavy cruiser EXETER arrived at Aden. She patrolled from Aden until the end of September 1941 when she was docked at Colombo, Ceylon.

23 JULY 1941

Troopship ERINPURA (5143grt) departed Madras, India for Penang, Malaya, escorted by light cruiser MAURITIUS to 10N, 92, 35E.
The light cruiser DANAE then relieved MAURITIUS and arrived with the troopship at Penang on the 27th.

24 JULY 1941

Destroyer ILEX arrived at Aden from Suez, Egypt. She remained there until 15 September when she departed for Durban, South Africa. Engine problems required further temporary repairs at Mombasa, Kenya and the destroyer did not arrive at Durban until November.

INDIAN OCEAN

East of South Africa   Long. E25, 00 – E60, 00   Lat. S00, 00 – S60, 00

4 JULY 1941

Dutch troopship SIBAJAK (12,226grt) departed Durban, South Africa with 800 personnel from convoy WS.8X. She was escorted to a position in 05, 20S, 50E, by light cruiser COLOMBO, where light cruiser MAURITIUS took over the escort.
MAURITIUS escorted the troopship to a position in 04, 25N, 86, 50E, where light cruiser DURBAN took over the escort. The troopship arrived at Singapore on the 19th.

9 JULY 1941

Heavy cruiser CORNWALL collided with the wharf at Durban, South Africa. The cruiser's stem was buckled.

South Indian Ocean   Long. E60, 00 – E95, 00   Lat. N00, 00 – S60, 00

6 JULY 1941

German AMC SCHIFF.16/ATLANTIS moved to patrol the area south of Australia in her search for merchant ships in the western Pacific Ocean.

Bay of Bengal   Long. E77, 00 – E95, 00   Lat. N22, 00 – N00, 00

6 JULY 1941

Troopship ELLENGA (5196grt) departed Madras, India for Penang, Malaya with personnel and lorries, escorted by Australian heavy cruiser CANBERRA to a position in 10N, 92E. Light cruiser DANAE relieved CANBERRA at sea and arrived with the troopship at Penang on the 10th.

27 JULY 1941

Light cruiser CERES damaged her port screw when it contacted the pier during docking at Trincomalee, Ceylon.

Malaya
Long. E95, 00 – E105, 00   Lat. N17, 00 – N00, 00

27 JULY 1941
IJN oiler HOYO MARU (8691grt) arrived at Pulau Sambu (near Singapore), Dutch East Indies.

29 JULY 1941
IJN oiler HOYO MARU (8691grt) departed Pulau Sambu (near Singapore), Dutch East Indies.

30 JULY 1941
IJN oiler SAN PEDRO MARU (7268grt) arrived at Pulau Sambu (near Singapore), Dutch East Indies.

PACIFIC OCEAN

South China Sea
Long. E105, 00 – E120, 00   Lat. N27, 00 – N10, 00

6 JULY 1941
IJN cargo ship TATSUWA MARU (6335grt) provided support for Japanese operations south of China.

7 JULY 1941
IJN cargo ship KENRYU MARU (4575grt) departed her support position south of China for Mako, Pescadores.

10 JULY 1941
IJN cargo ship MANKO MARU (4471grt) arrived at her support position to support Japanese operations south of China.

12 JULY 1941
Minesweepers PORTLAND and SEAFORD were laid down at Taikoo Shipbuilding and Engineering's Yard No.101 in Hong Kong.

IJN oiler HOYO MARU (8691grt) arrived at Sana, Hainan Island.

15 JULY 1941
IJN cargo ship MANKO MARU (4471grt) departed her support position south of China for Mako, Pescadores.

16 JULY 1941
IJN cargo ship NACHISAN MARU (4433grt) arrived at her support position south of China.

17 JULY 1941
IJN cargo ship KIMISHIMA MARU (5193grt) departed her support position south of China for Mako, Pescadores.

IJN cargo ship MYOKO MARU (5086grt) departed her support position south of China for Mako, Pescadores.

19 JULY 1941
IJN cargo ship MANKO MARU (4471grt) arrived at her support position south of China from Mako, Pescadores.

21 JULY 1941
IJN cargo ship NACHISAN MARU (4433grt) departed her support position south of China for Mako, Pescadores.

23 JULY 1941
IJN repair ship AKASHI (9000grt) arrived at Vichy French Indochina during the Japanese South Indochina (Cochinchina) Occupation Operation: Japanese and Vichy French authorities arrived at an "understanding" regarding the use of air facilities and harbours in southern Indochina. The Japanese allowed the Vichy French Colonial government to continue to administer the country. From the next day on, Japanese forces occupied southern Indochina. The AKASHI supported the occupation with IJN heavy cruiser ASHIGARA.

24 JULY 1941
IJN oiler HOYO MARU (8691grt) departed Sana, Hainan Island.

IJN cargo ship KIMISHIMA MARU (5193grt) supported Japanese operations south of China.

| | IJN cargo ship MYOKO MARU (5086grt) supported Japanese operations south of China. |

25 JULY 1941

| | IJN cargo ship NACHISAN MARU (4433grt) arrived at her support position south of China from Mako, Pescadores. |

29 JULY 1941

| | Vichy French liner CAP VARELLA (7677grt) was assigned to the Saigon-Shanghai-Manila route. |
| | Vichy French passenger/cargo ship ST PIERRE (10,086grt) was at Saigon, Vichy French Indochina. |

30 JULY 1941

| | Japanese aircraft bombed USN river patrol boat TUTUILA (PR-4) at Chungking, China. There were no personnel losses, but nearby motorboats were damaged. The Japanese referred to the matter as a tragic accident, but on the ground observers claimed that the Japanese pilots specifically targeted the ship. |
| | IJN cargo ship TATSUWA MARU (6335grt) departed her support position south of China for Yawata. |

South of Australia   Long. E125, 00 – E150, 00   Lat. S31, 00 – S60, 00

30 JULY 1941

| | Australian troop convoy US.1B departed Melbourne, Australia, with Dutch steamer JOHAN VAN OLDENBARNEVELDT (19,429grt), steamer KATOOMBA (9424grt), and Dutch steamers MARNIX VAN ST ALDEGONDE (19,355grt) and SIBAJAK (12,226grt). Steamer KATOOMBA only continued to Fremantle, Australia. Steamer SIBAJAK continued to Singapore. |

East China Sea   Long. E120, 00 – E130, 00   Lat. N42, 00 – N20, 00

1 JULY 1941

| | IJN patrol boat SHURI MARU (1857grt) arrived at Ryojun from a north China coastal patrol. |
| | IJN cargo ship TATSUWA MARU (6335grt) departed Takao, Formosa for her support position south of China. |

2 JULY 1941

| | IJN patrol boat SHURI MARU (1857grt) departed Ryojun for a north China coastal patrol. |

3 JULY 1941

| | IJN transport KOMAKI MARU (8525grt) arrived at Takao, Formosa. |

5 JULY 1941

| | IJN oiler SAN PEDRO MARU (7268grt) departed Keelung, Formosa. |

6 JULY 1941

| | IJN patrol boat SHURI MARU (1857grt) arrived at Ryojun from a north China coastal patrol. |

17 JULY 1941

| | IJN patrol boat SHURI MARU (1857grt) departed Ryojun for a north China coastal patrol. |

22 JULY 1941

| | Japanese passenger/cargo ship TEIZUI MARU (8428grt) (ex German steamer **MOSEL** (8428grt)) departed Ko Si Chang, China for Japan. |

Sea of Japan   Long. E128, 00 – E143, 00   Lat. N55, 00 – N33, 00

3 JULY 1941

| | IJN oiler KORYU MARU (880grt) departed Sasebo, Kyushu for the central China coast area. |

8 JULY 1941

| | IJN oiler ASHIZURI (7951grt) construction began at Mitsubishi Heavy Industries, Ltd. shipyard as an aviation gasoline tanker. |

15 JULY 1941

Russian defensive mines sank Russian submarines **M-49** (Lt Sibarinovski) and **M-63** (Lt Kapitsin) between Vladivostok and Petropavlovsk, Russia.

23 JULY 1941

IJN oiler KORYU MARU (880grt) returned to Sasebo, Kyushu from the central China coast area.

IJN cargo ship TOYO MARU (2470grt) operated in Korean waters.

25 JULY 1941

An unexplained cause sank Russian steamer **KAZAK POYAKOV** (1035grt) between Vladivostok, Russia and the La Perouse Strait.

26 JULY 1941

IJN oiler KORYU MARU (880grt) departed Sasebo, Kyushu for the central China coast area.

31 JULY 1941

IJN submarine chasers CH-17 and CH-18 were completed and registered in the IJN at the Sasebo Naval District.

East of Japan
Long. E130, 00 – E180, 00   Lat. N55, 00 – N30, 00

1 JULY 1941

Japanese tanker TOEI MARU (10,023grt) was re-rated a converted transport (oil supply) and was fully manned by IJN personnel. Captain Ishiguro was the Commanding Officer.

IJN aircraft carrier KAGA arrived at Yokosuka, Japan.

IJN patrol boat PB-34 was assigned to the Kure Naval District and attached to the Saeki Guard Unit of the Yokosuka Naval District.

IJN river gunboat FUSHIMI (374grt) completed her refit at Osaka, Japan.

3 JULY 1941

Japanese cargo ship MEITEN MARU (4474grt) arrived at Yokosuka, Japan.

4 JULY 1941

IJN tanker KYOKUTO MARU (10,051grt) arrived at Yokosuka, Japan.

5 JULY 1941

IJN oiler TOEI MARU (10,023grt) departed Tokuyama, Japan.

The flag of the Japanese 12th Seaplane Tender Division was transferred to IJN aircraft ferry FUJIKAWA MARU.

6 JULY 1941

Japanese steamer KIMIKAWA MARU (6863grt) was requisitioned by the IJN and began conversion into a seaplane tender at Kure Navy Yard.

IJN battleships HYUGA and ISE departed Yokohama, Japan.

8 JULY 1941

IJN aircraft carrier KAGA departed Yokosuka, Japan.

IJN battleships KIRISHIMA and HIEI departed Yokosuka, Japan.

9 JULY 1941

IJN vessel NAGOYA MARU (6072grt) completed her conversion into a submarine tender.

10 JULY 1941

Japanese liner TATSUTA MARU (16,975grt) departed Yokohama, Japan.

The IJN requisitioned Japanese cargo ship KAISHO MARU (4164grt).

11 JULY 1941

IJN aircraft carrier KAGA arrived at Ariake Bay, Kyushu with battleships KIRISHIMA, HIEI, ISE, and HYUGA.

14 JULY 1941

IJN transport KOMAKI MARU (8525grt) departed Furue, Japan for the central China coast.

16 JULY 1941

IJN battleships KIRISHIMA, HIEI, ISE, and HYUGA departed Ariake Bay, Kyushu.

17 JULY 1941

IJN battleships KIRISHIMA, HYUGA and HIEI arrived at Komatsujima, Kyushu from Ariake Bay, Kyushu.

18 JULY 1941

Japanese liner/AMC ASAMA MARU (16,975grt) departed Yokohama, Japan for San Francisco, California, carrying ninety-eight passengers, including forty-seven Japanese, born in the United States.

19 JULY 1941

IJN cargo ship LYONS MARU (7017grt) departed Yokosuka, Japan for the South Seas. Probably Truk.

The IJN requisitioned Japanese cargo ship NOJIMA MARU (7190grt).

20 JULY 1941

IJN battleship KIRISHIMA departed Komatsujima, Kyushu.

IJN battleship HIEI departed Komatsujima, Kyushu and arrived at Sukumo Bay, Kyushu later the same day.

21 JULY 1941

IJN submarine tender CHOGEI conducted a ceremony where Vice Admiral Shimizu Mitsumi assumed command of the Japanese Sixth Fleet. Vice Admiral Hirata was reassigned as CINC, Japanese Southern Expeditionary Fleet.

IJN battleship HYUGA departed Komatsujima, Kyushu.

22 JULY 1941

IJN battleships HYUGA and KIRISHIMA arrived at Sukumo Bay, Kyushu.

25 JULY 1941

IJN seaplane tender KAMIKAWA MARU (6853grt) was assigned to the Japanese Third Fleet, 2nd Base Unit.

The Japanese Fifth Fleet was reformed for the North Pacific under Vice Admiral Hosogaya Boshiro, after being disbanded in 1939.

IJN oiler TATEKAWA MARU (10,090grt) arrived at Shimotsu, Japan from San Pedro (Los Angeles), California.

26 JULY 1941

IJN oiler KOKUYO MARU (10,026grt) arrived at Amagasaki, Osaka, Japan.

The IJN requisitioned Japanese cargo ship SHINYO MARU (4163grt).

27 JULY 1941

IJN battleships HIEI and KIRISHIMA departed Sukumo Bay, Kyushu.

IJN battleship HYUGA departed Sukumo Bay, Kyushu and arrived at Beppu, Japan later the same day.

IJN cargo ship KUNISHIMA MARU (4083grt) arrived at Yokosuka, Japan, probably for maintenance and repairs.

28 JULY 1941

IJN battleships HIEI and KIRISHIMA arrived at Beppu, Japan from Sukumo Bay, Kyushu.

IJN liner TATSUTA MARU (16,975grt) set a new trans-Pacific crossing record.

29 JULY 1941

Japanese steamer KAMIKAZE MARU (4916grt) began her conversion into an IJN torpedo recovery vessel at Uraga Dock Co. Tokyo, Japan.

Hawaii Area

Long. W180, 00 – W140, 00   Lat. N30, 00 – N00, 00

31 JULY 1941

Japanese liner/AMC ASAMA MARU (16,975grt) arrived at Honolulu, Hawaiian Territory.

South of Hawaii
Long. W180, 00 – W140, 00   Lat. S00, 00 – S60, 00

1 JULY 1941

German AMC SCHIFF.45/KOMET captured Norwegian whaler **POL IX**/ADJUTANT and re-provisioned from German supply ship ANNELIESE ESSBERGER (5173grt) south of Tubuai Island. The AMC scuttled **ADJUTANT** before moving off east towards the Galapagos Islands.

West of United States
Long. W130, 00 – W110, 00   Lat. N50, 00 – N30, 00

7 JULY 1941

Japanese passenger/cargo ship HIE MARU (4943grt) arrived at Seattle, Washington.

19 JULY 1941

IJN oiler TOEI MARU (10,023grt) arrived at Los Angeles, California and probably loaded oil at San Pedro.

22 JULY 1941

IJN oiler TOEI MARU (10,023grt) departed Los Angeles, California to return to Japan.

28 JULY 1941

IJN oiler OTOWASAN MARU (9204grt) arrived at San Pedro, California to load oil, but two days prior to her arrival, the United States placed an embargo on oil exports to Japan to counter Japanese aggression in Asia. She returned to Japan in ballast.

AUGUST 1941
DAY-TO-DAY OPERATIONS

SECTION CONTENTS

SUMMARY 142	Gulf of Finland 180
GENERAL 144	MEDITERRANEAN SEA & MIDDLE EAST 183
ARCTIC OCEAN 145	
Greenland Sea and Barents Sea 145	East of Gibraltar 183
White Sea 148	Middle Mediterranean Sea 185
NORTH ATLANTIC OCEAN 148	Eastern Mediterranean Sea 189
	Black Sea 195
Iceland and North of Britain 148	Red Sea 196
Norwegian Sea 155	Arabian Sea 197
East of Canada 156	INDIAN OCEAN 198
East of United States 159	
Caribbean and Gulf of Mexico 161	East of South Africa 198
Western Approaches 161	Malaya 199
Central Atlantic Crossing Zone 167	PACIFIC OCEAN 199
UK East Coast 170	
North Sea 172	South China Sea 199
English Channel 173	Dutch East Indies 199
Bay of Biscay 173	East China Sea 200
West of Gibraltar 174	Sea of Japan 200
West of North Africa 177	East of Philippine Islands 201
SOUTH ATLANTIC OCEAN 178	New Guinea and Solomon Islands 201
	East of Australia 201
East of South America 178	East of Japan 201
West of South Africa 179	Gilbert – Marshall Islands 204
BALTIC SEA 179	New Zealand 204
	Hawaii Area 204
Kattegat and Skagerrak 179	West of United States 204
Southern Baltic Area 179	West of South America 205

SUMMARY

GERMANY

The German Arctic forces had limited success against the Russians. Targets were few, and the weather conditions quickly caused mechanical problems for the destroyers and other naval vessels. Moving U-boats to the north provided additional coverage, but took them away from better hunting grounds.

The German Baltic forces moved up the coast alongside the German army as they drove on Leningrad, Russia. Hitler's decision to surround the city and not attack it began a three-year ordeal for the Russians and Germans around the city.

The North Atlantic U-boats were still sinking ships, but not at a rate commensurate with their increased numbers. The Germans had not yet realized that their naval codes were compromised, allowing the convoys to avoid the German patrol lines.

The German surface raiders were finding it more difficult to find safe targets. Most ships now sailed in convoys or with air cover, making attack without discovery problematic. Since most of the raiders had been at sea for many months, they were in desperate need of a port to refit and make repairs.

ITALY

The Italian Fleet continued to maintain supply convoys to North Africa, but the price in ships lost steadily rose. The single fleet sortie against the British Force H resulted in heavy damage to a heavy cruiser and a waste of precious oil.

Meanwhile, the Italian Air Force continued to demonstrate its proficiency in hitting ships in the Mediterranean. Getting supplies in and out of Malta was getting steadily more expensive for the British. As was the cost to the Italians to move supplies closer to the Italian army around Tobruk, Libya.

ROMANIA

The Romanian Navy maintained support to the German and Romanian troops around Odessa, Ukraine, and southern Russia. They mostly engaged in moving troops and supplies plus laying extensive minefields to keep the larger Russian Black Sea Fleet at bay.

JAPAN

Japan continued to arm for war. Auxiliary merchant ships were upgraded as naval auxiliaries as fast as Japanese shipyards could work. Supplies flowed into the new Japanese bases in French Indochina. Japan was not going to agree to Western ultimatums and material embargoes without a fight.

FINLAND

The Finnish Navy rebuilt their minefields as they reclaimed coastal areas from Russian occupation. Other than taking back captured territory, the Finns did little to support the Germans. Finland was not going to waste Finnish blood for a new German Empire.

VICHY FRANCE

The Vichy French government continued to placidly follow their orders from Berlin. Meanwhile the French people were slowly organizing the beginning of an effective resistance movement throughout the country. The French people were slowly getting back into the war.

BRITAIN

The British decision to support Russia and provide aid severely stretched the already thinly spread Royal Navy. The Home Fleet operations in the Arctic made good press, but had little effect on the overall combat situation in Russia. Moreover, the cold miserable trips became a deadly ordeal for those ships unfortunate enough to be assigned duty in the arctic.

The British antisubmarine efforts were beginning to show an improvement in convoy escort and a reduction of merchant ship losses. Adding aerial escorts and Catapult Armed Merchantman (CAM) ships surprised the U-boats and the German long-range reconnaissance aircraft.

The Mediterranean Fleet was still recovering from the heavy losses incurred during the Crete evacuation. Moving supplies to forces trapped at Tobruk, Libya, and Malta became increasingly costly as the German and Italian aircraft became more proficient in sinking British ships. The use of submarines to carry supplies was entirely inadequate for the volume needed to sustain Malta

The surprise strike into Iran created a secure supply route to Russia, but it created a lot of Arab resentment.

The anti-British Iranians fought well, but were completely outclassed by the British forces, mostly from India, and quickly dispersed. The new Shah of Iran was more than willing to cooperate with the Allies as long as they continued to pay well.

British intelligence agents followed the Japanese operations with great interest. It was becoming quite clear that Malaya, Borneo, and probably Burma were at risk. Unfortunately, the British government had very few resources to send to the Pacific region.

UNITED STATES

The United States Navy continued to taunt the German U-boats in the North Atlantic by making bold patrols and convoy runs to Iceland. Using the new bases acquired under Lend-Lease, the Americans began establishing a comprehensive series of aerial reconnaissance zones all along the east coast from South America to Greenland.

In the Pacific, the Americans began to strengthen their far-flung bases against possible Japanese attack. The U.S. Army Air Force identified an alternative route to fly aircraft from Pearl Harbor to the Philippines without entering any Japanese-controlled air space. Unfortunately, the time needed to implement both the defences and new air routes was quickly ticking away.

RUSSIA

The Russian Northern Fleet managed to help contain the Germans attacking Murmansk, Russia, out of Finland. Russian and British submarines began attacking the long German supply route around Norway, forcing the Germans to allocate more ships to the far north for escort duty.

The Russian Baltic Fleet was having a much harder time. Though the fleet was much stronger than the German Navy in the Baltic, the German extensive use of mines and aircraft made a big difference. German land forces quickly overran most of the hastily established Russian naval bases in Estonia and Latvia. The Russian evacuation convoys took very heavy losses in ships and personnel, mostly civilians.

The Russian Black Sea Fleet was also having difficulty with German aircraft and extensive minefields. In spite of heavy losses, the Russian Navy continued to provide gunfire support to the hard-pressed Russian troops along the southern Russian coast.

The disappearance of several Russian ships in the Sea of Japan raised some concern with the Russian Pacific Fleet. It was entirely likely that some of the missing ships had accidentally stumbled upon the Japanese rehearsal areas for the coming attacks on Pearl Harbor and were sunk to maintain security.

CHINA

The Chinese continued to resist the Japanese wherever they could with whatever they had. Luckily, the preparations for the Japanese offensive to the south eased the pressure on the Chinese. Several of the best and most experienced Japanese infantry divisions were withdrawn from China. Their replacements were quite content to just occupy the areas already under Japanese control and live off the fat of the land.

POLAND

The Polish Brigade moved into Tobruk, Libya, was the first major Polish force deployed in combat since September 1939. The Polish troops were determined to support the British offensive and successfully break the German lines to relieve the city from siege.

FREE FRANCE

The Free French forces continued to consolidate their position in Syria and train forces to support the British in North Africa. The worsening conditions in Vichy France continued to provide volunteers and new agents working within France.

GENERAL

DATE	COMMENTS
1 August	In North Africa, fighting flared up around the perimeter of Tobruk, Libya, as German General Rommel tried to take the city.
1 August	A powerful Russian counter-offensive was launched at Gomel, Russia, south of Mogilev against German bridgeheads over the Dnieper River. Russian troops put up fierce resistance near Orsha and Vitebsk west of Smolensk. German Army Group Centre continued to destroy the Russian troops trapped in the Smolensk pocket.
1 August	The Japanese Foreign Office opened negotiations with Washington to resume passenger service between the two countries.
1 August	The Japanese Imperial Navy changed their operating code JN.25 from version B.6 to B.7. The new code was very difficult for the U.S. Navy to break.
1 August	In Operation STYLE, the Royal Navy fired fire star shells over Alghero, Sardinia, to support a night raid by carrier aircraft.
1 August	In Operation GUILLOTINE, the Royal Navy transferred men and material to Famagusta, Cypress.
2 August	The American government agreed to extend Lend-Lease materiel to the Russians.
2 August	During the night of 2/3 August, RAF Bomber Command attacked Hamburg and Kiel, Germany.
2 August	A determined German attack by the 136th Mountain Regiment broke through the Russian-reinforced 325th Rifle Regiment on the west bank of the Lisa River. The Russian Northern Fleet evacuated the remaining Russian troops the next day.
3 August	German Army Group Centre took 38,000 Russian prisoners after the battle at the Russian city of Roslavl.
3 August	The Royal Navy concluded Operation EF, the Royal Navy air strike on the German forces at Kirkenes, Norway, with all ships safely in British waters.
5 August	German Army Group Centre concluded the battle at Smolensk, Russia, and took 310,000 Russian prisoners.
5 August	Code breakers at Bletchley Park began decoding ENIGMA codes using the DOLPHIN cipher. They could now read messages to and from the German U-boats within thirty-six hours. Convoy HX.142 and convoy SC.39 were able to avoid the U-boats set up south of Iceland and arrived without a loss.
6 August	The American and British governments warned Japan not to invade Siam (Thailand). (Authors note: the warning was not needed as Siam had already signed agreements with Japan to support their invasion of Malaya and Burma.)
7 August	Joseph Stalin appointed himself Generalissimo of the Russian Army.
8 August	German Army Group Centre concluded the battle at Uman, Russia, taking 103,000 Russian prisoners.
9 August	Due to the increase in Allied escort for convoys, Hitler authorised the U-boats to sink any sized warship. Before this order, they were only allowed to attack warships of light cruiser size and above. Hitler did not allow the sinking of any American ship as long as they were clearly marked.
12 August	The United States Atlantic Fleet took over patrolling convoy routes in the North Atlantic and the tracking German U-boats for the Royal Navy in violation of the Neutrality Act.
12 August	The Russian Army made a counterattack against the German Army Group North at Staraja Russa south of Lake Ilmen.
12 August	United States President Franklin D. Roosevelt and British Prime Minister Winston Churchill signed the Atlantic Charter. In effect, the U.S. and Britain now conducted joint planning and combat operations against the Axis forces in the North Atlantic.
14 August	Hitler placed all German Navy and *Luftwaffe* units under the command of the German Army for the invasion of the Russian-held Baltic Islands.
16 August	German and Romanian forces of Army Group South captured Nikolaev, an important Russian naval base on the Black Sea.
16 August	The German LVI Panzer Corps of the 4th Panzer Group took Novgorod on the road to Leningrad, Russia.
17 August	German Army Group North captured Narva, Estonia.
17 August	In Operation RATION, the Royal Navy tried to intercept a Vichy French convoy that was rumoured to be carrying vital war contraband to France for Germany. The Operation was assigned the codename of KEDGREREE. The operation completed unsuccessfully on the 25th.
18 August	The German XX Mountain Army launched an offensive from Kairala, Finland, to capture the Russian port of Murmansk.
18 August	The German 1st Panzer Group established a bridgehead across the Dnepr River at Zaporoshe, Russia.
19 August	The Royal Navy began Operation TREACLE and ferried six thousand troops of the Polish Carpathian Brigade to Tobruk, Libya.
20 August	The German Eleventh Army captured Cherson, Ukraine, on the Black Sea, the gateway to the Crimea.

20 August	The German siege of Leningrad, Russia, began as German forces from the south joined with the Finnish forces from the north to encircle the city.
20 August	After weeks of negotiations between the German Navy and the *Luftwaffe*, aircraft dropped the new FAB-XI mine in British waters during the night of 20/21 August. The FAB-XI combined acoustic and magnetic triggers.
21 August	Hitler ordered the investment, but not the capture, of Leningrad, Russia, and then he transferred several German divisions from Army Group North and Army Group Centre to help Army Group South to capture the Crimea and the Donets river basin, an important industrial region vital to the Russian war effort.
21 August	In Operation GAUNTLET and Operation BENEDICT, the Royal Navy cleared German merchant shipping and land bases north of Norway along the Arctic convoy routes to Russia.
22 August	The German Navy reported to headquarters in Germany that the increase in convoy escorts and strong Allied air patrols caused the drop in Allied merchant ship losses, even though there were now three times the number of U-boats operating at sea than were available when the war began.
22 August	In Operation MINCEMEAT, the Royal Navy laid mines off the coast of Italy in the Gulf of Genoa.
23 August	Royal Navy ships departed Scapa Flow to operate in the northern waters around Archangel, Russia, and Murmansk, Russia, in Operation EGV.1 and Operation EGV.2.
24 August	In Operation CUTTING, the Royal Navy cut about sixty miles out of the Dakar-to-Pernambuco underwater communications cable.
24 August	The Royal Navy's Force H conducted ship movements in the western Mediterranean as a diversion for Operation MINCEMEAT.
25 August	British and Russian troops entered Iran to forestall any German incursions in the wake of the failed coup by anti-British elements in Iraq, which was supported by German special forces flown in from Greece. The occupation also saved the Abadan oilfields for Allied use and the important railways to Russia for the supply of war materiel to Russia. Operation COUNTENANCE was the overall operation supporting the British invasion of Iran. Operation RAPIER was the operation to capture Abadan and Khorramshahr, Iran, but was not used. Operation BISHOP was the capture of the port and shipping at Bandar Shahpur, Iran. Operation MARMALADE was aimed at the destruction of Iranian naval forces at Khorramshahr, Iran, at the junction of the Shatt Al-Arab and the Karun River. Operation CRACKLER was the capture of the island of Abadan, Iran, and its attendant oil refinery and facilities. Operation DEMON involved the landing of British Empire troops at Abadan, Iran.
25 August	The German 1st Panzer Group established a bridgehead across the Dnepr River at Dnepropetrovsk, Russia.
25 August	German Army Group South advanced from the Gomel, Russia, area toward Kiev in the Ukraine.
25 August	The German Naval High Command ordered that six medium class U-boats be sent to the Mediterranean. They were needed to stop the British from sending supplies to Malta and Tobruk, Libya.
26 August	German Army Group North surrounded and destroyed Russian forces in the area of Velikije Luki.
26 August	Retreating Russian troops destroyed the great dam on the Dnieper River, flooding the downsteam areas and denying the Germans its source of electrical power.
26 August	In Operation MOPUP, the Royal Navy and British Empire ground forces successfully cleared Iranian forces from the Khazalabad area between Khorramshahr and Abadan, Iran.
27 August	The Japanese government protested against the United States sending military materiel to Russia via Vladivostok, Russia, on the basis that it meant shipping war contraband through neutral Japanese waters.
29 August	Finnish troops captured the city of Vyborg from the Russians.
30 August	In Operation STRENGTH, the Royal Navy prepared for strong naval forces to cover Arctic convoys to and from Russia.
30 August	In Operation ILIAD, the Royal Navy searched the Bay of Biscay for German U-boats.

ARCTIC OCEAN

Greenland Sea and Barents Sea

Long. W180, 00 – E180, 00   Lat. N90, 00 – N68, 00

1 AUGUST 1941

	U.451, U.566 and U.652 patrolled off the entrance to the White Sea and along the Russian Kola coast until 20 August.
0001	Aircraft carrier FURIOUS group was detached from the aircraft carrier VICTORIOUS group about forty miles northeast of Bear Island to return to Scapa Flow.

2 AUGUST 1941

	A German aerial reconnaissance spotted and trailed Force K for about 130 miles. The attack on the Norwegian coast at Hammerfest, Norway, was cancelled when it was clear that surprise was not possible.

3 AUGUST 1941

	Force K (RAdm Vian) evacuated and destroyed the Norwegian weather station on Bear Island with light cruisers NIGERIA and AURORA covered by destroyers PUNJABI and TARTAR. They later refuelled from fleet oiler OLIGARCH (6897grt).

4 AUGUST 1941

	Aircraft carrier VICTORIOUS launched three Fulmar aircraft against Tromsø, Norway. One aircraft failed to return, and its crew became the guests of the Germans for the duration.
	Submarine TIGRIS arrived at Polyarny, Russia, to conduct patrols against German ships off northern Norway.
1300	Force K completed refuelling at sea. Fleet oiler OLIGARCH (6897grt), destroyer GARLAND, and trawler SEALYHAM departed the area to return to Seidisfjord.

5 AUGUST 1941

1600	Two German Dornier reconnaissance aircraft spotted Force A about two hundred miles from Norway. Since surprise was lost, the Force abandoned the planned attack and returned to Scapa Flow.

6 AUGUST 1941

	The German 6th Destroyer Flotilla and the 12th Antisubmarine Flotilla provided escorts to move the German 6th Mountain Division from Stettin, Germany, to Kirkenes, Norway. The German XIX Corps needed the troops for its attack on Murmansk, Russia.
	Russian submarines SHCH-421, M-175, SHCH-401, SHCH-402, M-174 and K-2 patrolled off the Norwegian polar coast until 30 August.
1900	U.652 (Kptlt Fraatz) sank Russian antisubmarine trawler **RT-70/KAPITAN VORONIN** (558grt) with one torpedo seven miles off Cape Teriberka, Russia. Forty-five crewmen were lost. Twelve survivors were rescued. The trawler was the first successful sinking for U.652. (Some sources refer to the ship as Dispatch Vessel **PS-70** (558grt).)

7 AUGUST 1941

	U.451 unsuccessfully attacked a Russian patrol boat off Cape Teriberka, Russia.

8 AUGUST 1941

	Russian destroyer KUJBYSHEV and two patrol boats escorted submarine TIGRIS to its new base at Polyarny, Russia.

9 AUGUST 1941

	German destroyers HANS LODY, FRIEDRICH ECKHOLDT, and RICHARD BEITZEN made a shipping sweep towards Kilden Island and the mouth of the Kola Inlet, and sank Russian patrol boat **SKR-12/TUMAN** (Lt Shestakov) after a heavy gun battle. On their return, Russian shore batteries and aircraft engaged the German destroyers. RICHARD BEITZEN was damaged by bomb near misses from Russian aircraft. The destroyers arrived back at their base on the 10th.

10 AUGUST 1941

	Submarine TRIDENT (Cdr Sladen) arrived at Polyarny, Russia, escorted by Russian destroyer URITSKI.
2112	U.451 (Eberhard Hoffmann) sank Russian patrol boat **SKR-27/ZHEMCHUG** (441grt) with one torpedo between Cape Svyatoy Nos and Cape Kanin Nos west of Kanin, Russia. The entire crew of sixty-one were lost.

11 AUGUST 1941

	Submarine TIGRIS departed Murmansk, Russia, on a patrol off the northern Norwegian coast.

13 AUGUST 1941

	Russian submarine M-173 conducted a reconnaissance of Petsamo Fjord, Finland.
	Russian submarine K-2 (Capt 3rd Class Utkin) unsuccessfully attacked German troopship HANSA (21,131grt) and steamer LÜBECK (3703grt) off Tanafjord, Norway.

16 AUGUST 1941

	The German Navy established an Arctic Ocean U-boat Command with U.451 and U.566 already on station plus U.571 and U.752 relieving the initial two boats U.81 and U.652.

	Submarine TRIDENT (Cdr Sladen) departed Polyarny, Russia, on a patrol off the Norwegian Arctic coast.

17 AUGUST 1941

	Submarine TIGRIS sank Norwegian coastal steamer **HAAKON JARL** (1482grt) off Svaerholt, Norway, in 70, 58N, 26, 48E.

19 AUGUST 1941

	Submarine TRIDENT (Cdr Sladen) damaged German steamer LEVANTE (4770grt) with gunfire off the Norwegian Arctic coast in 71, 01N, 24, 34E.

21 AUGUST 1941

	Submarine TRIDENT (Cdr Sladen) unsuccessfully attacked a Norwegian tanker and a German artillery training ship off the northern coast of Norway.

22 AUGUST 1941

	Submarine TRIDENT (Cdr Sladen) sank German troopship **OSTPREUSSEN** (3030grt) off Tromsø, Norway, in 70, 12N, 21, 05W.
	Russian submarine D-3 patrolled off Persfjord, Norway, but failed to penetrate the German defences.
	Russian submarine M-172 (Lt Cdr Fisanovich) unsuccessfully attacked German Hospital ship ALEXANDER VON HUMBOLDE at Petsamo Fjord, Finland.

23 AUGUST 1941

	U.571, U.752, U.451 and U.566 patrolled off the Russian Kola coast until 30 August.

24 AUGUST 1941

	Fleet Oiler OLIGARCH (6897grt) arrived near Spitsbergen, Norway, escorted by trawlers HAZEL and ELM.
	Force A arrived at a position sixty miles west of Isfjord, Spitsbergen.

25 AUGUST 1941

	Force K joined with Russian destroyers SOKRUSHITELNY and GROZNY for escort into Archangel, Russia.
	U.652 (ObltzS Fraatz) spotted two destroyers and a large ship off the Russian Kola coast, but could not reach an attack position.
	Fleet Oiler OLIGARCH (6897grt) entered Gronfjord, Spitsbergen, escorted by trawlers HAZEL and ELM.
1011	U.752 (ObltzS Schroeter) sank Russian minesweeping trawler **T-898/DVINA** (533grt) while she was on patrol about 80 miles east of Cape Chernyj northwest of Svyatoy, Russia, in 68, 41N, 38, 58E. Forty-one crewmen were lost. Only two survivors were rescued.

26 AUGUST 1941

	In Operation GAUNTLET, Force A demolished the Bergensburg coalfields.
	Light cruiser NIGERIA departed Spitsbergen, Norway, with destroyers ANTHONY, ANTELOPE, and ICARUS escorting troopship EMPRESS OF CANADA (21,517grt) to Archangel, Russia, with 1800 Russians taken from Spitsbergen.
	These ships returned to Spitsbergen on 1 September and joined light cruiser AURORA.
	Norwegian colliers **INGERTO** (3089grt), **NANDI** (1999grt), and **MUNIN** (1285grt) were taken as prizes by Norwegian Lt Tamber at Spitsbergen, Norway, and escorted by antisubmarine trawler SEALYHAM from there for Hvalfjord, Iceland, arriving on 1 September. Light cruiser AURORA covered the group until the morning of 27 August.
	This group was designated Convoy Drover with Lt Tamber as the Commodore.
0459	U.571 (Kptlt Mohlmann) damaged Russian steamer **MARIJA ULJANOVA** (3870grt) with two torpedoes north of Cape Teriberka, Russia, in 70, 08N, 36, 03E.
0502	U.571 hit the steamer with another torpedo, but she remained afloat and was beached at Teriberka, a total loss.
	U.571 was heavily depth charged and a screen of three destroyers prevented her from returning to sink the damaged steamer.

27 AUGUST 1941

	German destroyers RICHARD BEITZEN and HERMANN SCHOEMANN departed Kirkenes, Norway, to return to Germany for repairs. Their departure left the German 6th Destroyer Division at half strength after only six weeks on station off northern Norway.
	U.752 (ObltzS Schroeter) unsuccessfully attacked a Russian patrol boat off Svyatoy, Russia.

29 AUGUST 1941

	In Operation GAUNTLET, Russian destroyer GROZNY (Adm Dolini) joined troopship EMPRESS OF CANADA (21,517grt) off the Dvina light vessel. The 1800 Russians taken from Spitsbergen, Norway, were loaded into two Russian steamers. The troopship and her escort returned to Spitsbergen on 1 September and joined light cruiser AURORA. They carried two hundred Free French escaped prisoners of war who made it to Russia.

30 AUGUST 1941

	Submarine TRIDENT (Cdr Sladen) sank German steamers **DONAU II** (2931grt) and **BAHIA LAURA** (8561grt) off the Lofoten Islands, Norway, in 70, 27N, 21, 55E, from a convoy of German steamers DONAU II (2931grt) and BAHIA LAURA (8561grt), Vichy French CORNOUAILLE (3290grt), and Norwegian AUGUST BOLTEN (3665grt), escorted by destroyers HANS LODY and KARL GALSTER, submarine chaser UJ.178, and auxiliary submarine chasers Vp.6113 and Vp.6111, joined by UJ.176 and UJ.177 off Nordkyn, Norway. Over seven hundred German soldiers were lost, while KARL GALSTER rescued four hundred ninety, HANS LODY rescued thirty-eight, Vp.6111 rescued one hundred seventy-eight, Vp.6113 rescued three hundred sixty, Norwegian steamer MITTNATSOL rescued two hundred, and motor minesweeper R.153 rescued twenty-three survivors from the two steamers.
	Convoy DERVISH arrived at Spitsbergen, Norway, to refuel, escorted by antiaircraft ship POZARICA with minesweeping trawlers CELIA (545grt), HAMLET (545grt), and MACBETH (545grt), antisubmarine trawlers ST CATHAN (565grt) and LE TIGRE (516grt). The convoy included steamers LANCASTRIAN PRINCE (1914grt), NEW WESTMINSTER CITY (4747grt), ESNEH (1931grt), LLANSTEPHAN CASTLE (11,348grt), and TREHATA (4817grt), Dutch steamer ALCHIBA (4427grt), and oiler ALDERSDALE (8402grt) escorted by destroyers ELECTRA, ACTIVE, and IMPULSIVE, minesweepers HALCYON, HARRIER, and SALAMANDER, with minesweeping trawler OPHELIA. The convoy was covered by aircraft carrier VICTORIOUS, heavy cruisers DEVONSHIRE and SUFFOLK, and destroyers ECLIPSE, ESCAPADE, and INGLEFIELD from 24 to 30 August. The convoy arrived at Archangel, Russia, on the 31st.

31 AUGUST 1941

	Russian submarine SC-402 unsuccessfully attacked the German supply convoy in Kjoellefjord, Norway.
	Russian destroyers SOKRUSHITELNY, GROZNY, KUJBYSHEV, and URITSKI joined convoy DERVISH at sea and guided the ships to Archangel, Russia.

White Sea
Long. E30, 00 – E60, 00   Lat. N68, 00 – N60, 00

1 AUGUST 1941

	Minelayer ADVENTURE arrived at Archangel, Russia, with a cargo of parachute mines to be used to secure Russian northern ports.

4 AUGUST 1941

	Minelayer ADVENTURE departed Archangel, Russia, escorted by Russian destroyers SOKRUSHITELNY and GROZNY.

25 AUGUST 1941

	Russian submarines K-21, K-22, and K-23 arrived at Molotovsk, Russia, on the White Sea from the Baltic using the White Sea Canal.

NORTH ATLANTIC OCEAN

Iceland and North of Britain
Long. W30, 00 – E03, 00   Lat. N68, 00 – N58, 30

1 AUGUST 1941

	Heavy cruiser SHROPSHIRE arrived at Akreyri, Iceland, from her Denmark Strait patrol. Later that day, she departed for Hvalfjord, Iceland.
	Monitor EREBUS arrived at Scapa Flow escorted by destroyer QUORN.
	Submarine TRIDENT departed Scapa Flow for Murmansk, Russia.
0900	Destroyer LIVELY arrived at Scapa Flow from Greenock to work up to combat efficiency.
1400	Minesweeper HARRIER arrived at Scapa Flow to replace minesweeper NIGER, which had developed defects.

2 AUGUST 1941

	Heavy cruiser SHROPSHIRE arrived at Hvalfjord, Iceland, from Akreyri, Iceland.
0615	Antiaircraft cruiser CURAÇOA departed Scapa Flow to provide escort for convoy WN.60 from the Pentland Firth until joining convoy EC.53.
1300	Destroyer HEYTHROP departed Scapa Flow for Greenock upon the completion of her working up to combat efficiency exercises.
1630	Destroyer ORIBI departed Scapa Flow for Scrabster to convey Admiral Horton to Scapa Flow.
2030	Destroyer ORIBI arrived at Scapa Flow from Scrabster with Admiral Horton.
2300	Antiaircraft cruiser CURAÇOA joined with convoy EC.53 and provided escort to Pentland Firth.
2330	Minesweeper HARRIER departed Scapa Flow for Seidisfjord.

3 AUGUST 1941

	Heavy cruiser BERWICK arrived at Scapa Flow from Rosyth.
0300	Minesweeper NIGER departed Scapa Flow for Dundee to begin her refit.
0815	Destroyers HAVELOCK, HESPERUS, and HARVESTER arrived at Scapa Flow from Reykjavik, Iceland.
1000	Aircraft carrier FURIOUS and heavy cruiser SUFFOLK arrived at Seidisfjord, Iceland, with destroyers INTREPID, ECHO, and ECLIPSE upon completion of Operation EF. The ships went on to Scapa Flow after refuelling.
1200	Destroyer QUORN departed Scapa Flow after a short period of exercises for Rosyth.
1615	Destroyer ANTHONY departed Scapa Flow for Scrabster to embark special personnel and arrived back later that evening.
1800	Antiaircraft ship ALYNBANK departed Scapa Flow and escorted convoy WN.61 to southward.
2115	Antiaircraft cruiser CURAÇOA detached from convoy EC.53 at Pentland Firth and returned to Scapa Flow.

4 AUGUST 1941

	Antiaircraft ship ALYNBANK transferred to convoy EC.54 in the vicinity of Tod Head, and returned to Scapa Flow after escorting the convoy to the west of the Orkneys.
0720	Destroyers ORIBI and CROOME departed Scapa Flow for Scrabster to pickup personnel.
1130	Destroyers ORIBI and CROOME returned to Scapa Flow from Scrabster with personnel.
1730	Battleship PRINCE OF WALES departed Scapa Flow escorted by destroyers ORIBI, HAVELOCK, HARVESTER, and HESPERUS, but ORIBI returned to Scapa Flow that evening with defects.

5 AUGUST 1941

	Heavy cruiser DEVONSHIRE and aircraft carrier VICTORIOUS arrived at Seidisfjord, Iceland, with destroyers INGLEFIELD, ICARUS, and ESCAPADE. The ships departed the next day for Scapa Flow.
	Heavy cruiser SHROPSHIRE departed Hvalfjord, Iceland, to cover minelayer ADVENTURE as she returned from Archangel, Russia.
	Free French submarine MINERVE arrived at Scapa Flow from a patrol off the Faeroes.
0030	Destroyers HAVELOCK, HARVESTER, and HESPERUS were detached from battleship PRINCE OF WALES in heavy weather and proceeded independently to Reykjavik, Iceland.
0100	Minesweeper HARRIER arrived at Seidisfjord, Iceland, from Scapa Flow.
0830	Aircraft carrier FURIOUS arrived at Scapa Flow with destroyers ECHO and ECLIPSE from Seidisfjord.

6 AUGUST 1941

	Canadian destroyers RESTIGOUCHE and ASSINIBOINE plus destroyer RIPLEY, which came out from Iceland, joined battleship PRINCE OF WALES for her voyage across the North Atlantic.
	American aircraft carrier WASP (CV-7), battleship MISSISSIPPI (BB-41), heavy cruisers QUINCY (CA-39) and WICHITA (CA-45) and five destroyers arrived at Reykjavik, Iceland, with troopship AMERICAN LEGION (AP-35), stores ship MIZAR (AF-120) and cargo ship ALMAACK (AK-27) with U.S. Army troops. The group delivered the American 33rd Pursuit Squadron with P-40 aircraft and Catalina flying boats for patrol squadrons VP-73 and VP-74 operating out of Reykjavik.
0030	Antiaircraft ship ALYNBANK returned to Scapa Flow after being detached from convoy EC.54 west of the Orkneys.
1000	Destroyers CASTLETON, CHARLESTOWN, and ECHO departed Scapa Flow for Greenock to join destroyer INTREPID, which departed Loch Alsh for the Clyde, for escort duties with convoy WS.8C.
1000	Antiaircraft cruiser CURAÇOA departed Scapa Flow to join convoy EC.55 off Buchan Ness and escort it to Pentland Firth.
1830	Antiaircraft ship ALYNBANK departed Scapa Flow and escorted convoy WN.62 to May Island.

7 AUGUST 1941

	Heavy cruiser DEVONSHIRE and aircraft carrier VICTORIOUS arrived at Scapa Flow with destroyers INGLEFIELD, ICARUS, and ESCAPADE from Seidisfjord, Iceland.
	Minesweeper HARRIER departed Seidisfjord to investigate a submarine report and to conduct a minesweeping search in Vidfjord, Iceland.
	Captured Norwegian steamer DAGNY I (1392grt) arrived at Tórshavn from Spitsbergen, Norway, escorted by trawler WASTWATER.
0300	Antiaircraft ship ALYNBANK returned to Scapa Flow after being detached from convoy EC.56 in Pentland Firth.
0345	Antiaircraft cruiser CURAÇOA returned to Scapa Flow after her escort duty.
0600	Destroyers ANTELOPE and ACTIVE arrived at Seidisfjord on the completion of Operation EF. ACTIVE departed later in the day for Scapa Flow.
1630	Destroyer IMPULSIVE arrived at Scapa Flow from the Humber on the completion of her refit.
1815	Light cruisers NIGERIA and AURORA arrived at Scapa Flow with destroyers TARTAR and PUNJABI after aborting Operation FB.
2200	Destroyer ANTELOPE departed Seidisfjord escorting damaged destroyer ACHATES in the tow of tug ASSURANCE sailing for the Tyne.
2330	Heavy cruiser DEVONSHIRE and aircraft carrier VICTORIOUS arrived at Scapa Flow with destroyers INGLEFIELD, ICARUS, and ESCAPADE to complete Operation EF.

8 AUGUST 1941

	Polish destroyer GARLAND arrived at Hvalfjord, Iceland, with antisubmarine trawler SEALYHAM and fleet oiler OLIGARCH (6897grt), and then reverted to the Western Approaches Command after the escort duty.
0528	German bombing sank steam fishing trawler **OCEAN VICTOR** (202grt) (Master Marquis Silverstone Slater) southeast of Iceland. The entire crew of thirteen were lost. Other sources claim U.206 (ObltzS Herbert Opitz) sank the trawler on 9 August.
0528	German bombing damaged Minesweeper SELKIRK with a bomb near miss, but she did not spend any time out of action.
1200	Antiaircraft cruiser CURAÇOA departed Scapa Flow to escort convoy WN.63 from Pentland Firth southward. She continued on to Rosyth to clean boilers and carry out repairs.
1300	Destroyer PUCKERIDGE arrived at Scapa Flow from Rosyth to work up to combat efficiency.
1330	Destroyer ACTIVE arrived at Scapa Flow from Seidisfjord, Iceland.
1730	Destroyer CROOME departed Scapa Flow for Liverpool upon the completion of her working up exercises.
2000	Destroyer ACTIVE departed Scapa Flow for Rosyth for boiler cleaning.

9 AUGUST 1941

	U.206 (ObltzS Herbert Opitz) sank fishing trawler **OCEAN VICTOR** (202grt) southwest of Iceland. Other sources claim German aircraft sank the trawler on 9 August.
	Dutch submarine O.14 departed Scapa Flow for the Faeroes for an antisubmarine patrol.
	HM King George VI arrived at Scapa Flow for a visit.
1105	Norwegian steamer DAGNY I (1392grt) departed Tórshavn with whaler WASTWATER for Kirkwall.
1430	German bombers damaged Norwegian steamer DAGNY I (1392grt) near the Faeroes in 61, 40N, 06, 10W.
1700	Destroyer SOMALI arrived at Scapa Flow from Southampton.

10 AUGUST 1941

	Heavy cruiser SHROPSHIRE arrived back at Hvalfjord, Iceland, after her escort duty.
0600	Destroyer IMPULSIVE departed Scapa Flow and proceeded to Tórshavn to embark the sixty-one **DAGNY I** survivors.
0900	Damaged Norwegian steamer **DAGNY I** (1392grt) sank in tow of trawler LEICESTER CITY. Two passengers were lost. LEICESTER CITY rescued the survivors.
1800	Destroyer IMPULSIVE arrived at Tórshavn from Scapa Flow.
1930	Destroyer IMPULSIVE departed Tórshavn for Scrabster.
2130	Antiaircraft ship ALYNBANK departed Scapa Flow and escorted convoy WN.65 from Pentland Firth to Methil.
2200	Destroyer ANTELOPE arrived at the Faeroes with damaged destroyer ACHATES in the tow of tug ASSURANCE after having been hove to in bad weather.

11 AUGUST 1941

	Destroyer ELECTRA arrived at Scapa Flow from Sheerness after her refit.
	HM King George VI visited the destroyer depot ship TYNE during the forenoon and inspected representative contingents from the Home Fleet destroyers. He then visited destroyers ECLIPSE and CHARLESTOWN berthed

	alongside. The King inspected the Lyness Base facilities before departing.
	Minelayer PORT QUEBEC laid Minefield SN.22A in the Northern Barrage escorted by surveying ship SCOTT.
0600	Destroyer ECHO departed Scapa Flow for Sheerness for a refit.
0700	Destroyer IMPULSIVE arrived at Scrabster from Tórshavn and disembarked the **DAGNY I** survivors. She then departed Scrabster for Scapa Flow.
0840	Destroyer IMPULSIVE arrived back at Scapa Flow from Scrabster.
1230	Destroyer ANTELOPE arrived at Skaalefjord with damaged destroyer ACHATES in the tow of tug ASSURANCE. ANTELOPE then departed Skaalefjord and went on to Scapa Flow.
1230	HM King George VI departed Scapa Flow in destroyer INGLEFIELD for transport to Scrabster, escorted by destroyers TARTAR and PUNJABI.
1340	Destroyer ICARUS departed Scapa Flow for Scrabster to provide passage back to Scapa Flow for the Captain of the Fleet.
1530	Destroyers TARTAR, PUNJABI, and ESCAPADE departed Scapa Flow for Hvalfjord, Iceland.
2000	Destroyers INGLEFIELD, IMPULSIVE, and ECLIPSE departed Scapa Flow to join with the battle cruiser RENOWN in 55, 45N, 13W and escort her to Rosyth.
2200	Destroyer ANTELOPE arrived at Scapa Flow from Skaalefjord.

12 AUGUST 1941

	Light cruiser SHEFFIELD arrived at Scapa Flow in the evening from Rosyth after her refit to work up to combat efficiency.
	Minesweepers HARRIER, SALAMANDER, and HALCYON departed Seidisfjord, Iceland, for Reykjavik. HALCYON developed defects and put into Reydarfjord, Iceland, and then returned to Seidisfjord with SALAMANDER. HARRIER arrived at Reykjavik on the 13th.
0311	U.586 (Kptlt Preuss) sank corvette **PICOTEE** (900grt) (Lt R. A. Harrison RNR) while attacking convoy ONS.4 south of Iceland in 62, 00N, 16, 01W. She immediately broke in two and sank with her depth charges detonating as she went down. The entire crew with Harrison, T/Sub-Lt H. E. Brisland RNVR, A/Sub-Lt J. P. Roberts RNR, T/Lt T. H. Williams RNR, T/A/Sub-Lt J. A. Wymer RNVR, and sixty ratings was lost. U.586 also claimed hitting a steamer.
2030	Destroyer ANTHONY departed Scapa Flow escorting salvage tug LE LUTTEUR for Skaalefjord, where the tug was to effect repairs to damaged destroyer ACHATES to make her seaworthy for the passage to the Tyne.
2100	Destroyers TARTAR, PUNJABI, and ESCAPADE arrived at Hvalfjord, Iceland, from Scapa Flow.

13 AUGUST 1941

	A mine sank Faeroes fishing vessel **SJOBORG** (158grt) in 61, 31N, 05, 40W, while she was fishing in a prohibited area.
1000	Antiaircraft ship ALYNBANK arrived at Scapa Flow after escorting convoy EC.58 from May Island to Pentland Firth.

14 AUGUST 1941

	Destroyers TARTAR, PUNJABI, and ESCAPADE departed Hvalfjord, Iceland, to join with the battleship PRINCE OF WALES and escorted her to port.
0200	Destroyer ANTHONY arrived at Skaalefjord escorting salvage tug LE LUTTEUR to effect repairs to damaged destroyer ACHATES.
1145	Antiaircraft ship ALYNBANK departed Scapa Flow and escorted convoy WN.66 to the south. Off Buchan Ness that night, German aircraft attacked the convoy, but no damage was done. ALYNBANK transferred to convoy EC.59 shortly after midnight. On arrival in Pentland Firth, she left the convoy and returned to Scapa Flow.
1400	Destroyer FOXHOUND arrived at Scapa Flow for fuel while on passage from Force H to Sheerness.
1530	Destroyer LIGHTNING arrived at Scapa Flow from Greenock to rejoin the Home Fleet after operations in the Western Approaches Command and western Mediterranean.
2000	Destroyer ANTHONY departed Skaalefjord to return to Scapa Flow.

15 AUGUST 1941

	Heavy cruiser DORSETSHIRE departed Scapa Flow for the Clyde to escort convoy WS.10X. She arrived on the 16th.
	Convoy DERVISH arrived at Scapa Flow escorted by antiaircraft ship POZARICA with minesweeping trawlers CELIA (545grt), HAMLET (545grt), and MACBETH (545grt), antisubmarine trawlers ST CATHAN (565grt) and LE TIGRE (516grt) for Reykjavik, Iceland.
0700	Destroyer ANTHONY returned to Scapa Flow from Skaalefjord.

1400	Cancelled convoy WS.8C (Exercise LEAPFROG) with landing ships KARANJA (9891grt), ROYAL SCOTSMAN (3244grt), ULSTER MONARCH (3791grt), BACHAQUERO, MISOA, QUEEN EMMA, and PRINCE CHARLES, oilers DEWDALE and ENNERDALE, steamers NARKUNDA (16,632grt), WINCHESTER CASTLE (20,109grt), BATORY (14,287grt), ORMONDE (14,982grt), CLAN MACDONALD (9653grt), MACHARDA (7998grt), DUNEDIN STAR (11,168grt), and SILVERTEAK (6770grt) sailed for the Clyde escorted by destroyers DOUGLAS, LEAMINGTON, INTREPID, CHARLESTOWN, CASTLETON, GEORGETOWN, ANTELOPE, SALADIN, and antiaircraft ship POZARICA. The convoy arrived back in the Clyde on the 17th.
1700	Antiaircraft ship ALYNBANK returned to Scapa Flow following her escort duty.
1900	Battle cruiser REPULSE arrived at Scapa Flow escorted by destroyers IMPULSIVE, ECLIPSE, and ACTIVE.

16 AUGUST 1941

	Destroyer MATABELE arrived at Scapa Flow from Barrow.
0900	Battleship PRINCE OF WALES arrived at Hvalfjord, Iceland, escorted by TARTAR, PUNJABI, and ESCAPADE. Prime Minister Churchill went on to Reykjavik, Iceland, on Canadian destroyer ASSINIBOINE. Churchill addressed the crews of all ships at Hvalfjord on this date. Included were USN battleship NEW MEXICO (BB-40), battleship RAMILLIES, heavy cruisers SHROPSHIRE and USN QUINCY (CA-39), five destroyers, including the lend-lease CHURCHILL, five American destroyers and destroyer depot ship HECLA.
1430	Antiaircraft ship ALYNBANK departed Scapa Flow and escorted convoy WN.67 from the Pentland Firth to Methil.
1800	Convoy DERVISH departed Scapa Flow with destroyers ELECTRA, IMPULSIVE, and ACTIVE with light cruiser AURORA as additional escort until 18 August.
1845	Destroyer LIVELY departed Scapa Flow for Scrabster.
2045	Battleship PRINCE OF WALES departed Hvalfjord escorted by destroyers TARTAR, PUNJABI, and ESCAPADE.
2100	Destroyer LIVELY returned to Scapa Flow from Scrabster with the Senior Officer of Force A, Rear Admiral P. L. Vian DSO.

17 AUGUST 1941

	Destroyers ECLIPSE and ORIBI departed Scapa Flow to search for the submarine reported off Cape Wrath.
	Light cruiser ARETHUSA arrived at Scapa Flow from the Clyde.
0915	Antiaircraft ship PALOMARES departed Scapa Flow on completion of her working up to combat efficiency exercises. She joined join convoy EC.60 and proceeded to Belfast where she came under the Western Approaches Command.
1930	Destroyer LAMERTON arrived at Scapa Flow from Rosyth to carry out working up to combat efficiency exercises.
2359	Destroyers ECLIPSE and ORIBI joined the battleship PRINCE OF WALES with destroyers TARTAR, PUNJABI, and ESCAPADE at midnight.

18 AUGUST 1941

	Heavy cruiser LONDON arrived at Scapa Flow from convoy WS.10 escort and Bay of Biscay patrol.
	Destroyer ANTHONY departed Scapa Flow for Greenock to join destroyers INTREPID and ANTELOPE to provide escort for aircraft carrier ARGUS and troopship EMPRESS OF CANADA (21,517grt).
	Antisubmarine whaler WASTWATER departed Scapa Flow for Iceland escorting motor launches ML.1043 and ML.1045, via the Faeroes.
0900	Destroyer NEWARK arrived at Scapa Flow to carry out a short program of working up to combat efficiency exercises.

19 AUGUST 1941

	Heavy cruiser LONDON departed Scapa Flow for boiler cleaning in the Clyde.
	Destroyer INGLEFIELD arrived at Scapa Flow from Rosyth after her boiler cleaning.
1530	Force A departed Scapa Flow with light cruisers NIGERIA and AURORA plus destroyers TARTAR, ICARUS, and ECLIPSE to join the aircraft carrier ARGUS force.
1800	Antiaircraft cruiser CURAÇOA arrived at Scapa Flow after escorting convoy EC.61 to Pentland Firth.
2100	Force A and the aircraft carrier ARGUS force rendezvoused fifteen miles north of the Butt of Lewis. Aircraft carrier ARGUS proceeded to Scapa Flow with destroyers TARTAR, INTREPID, and ECLIPSE. The troopship EMPRESS OF CANADA (21,517grt) proceeded to Reykjavik, Iceland, with light cruisers NIGERIA and AURORA plus destroyers ICARUS, ANTELOPE, and ANTHONY. The troopship group was joined by destroyers TARTAR and ECLIPSE with fleet oiler OLIGARCH (6897grt) to become Force K to transfer 2000 people to Archangel, Russia, to handle the supply operations in Russia.

20 AUGUST 1941

	A mine sank Faeroes auxiliary trawler **SOLARRIS** (236grt) off Seidisfjord, Iceland. Four crewmen were rescued.
0900	Battleship PRINCE OF WALES arrived at Scapa Flow from Hvalfjord, Iceland, escorted by destroyers TARTAR, PUNJABI, ECLIPSE, ORIBI and ESCAPADE.
1000	Destroyer PUCKERIDGE departed Scapa Flow to convey the Commander in Chief, Home Fleet to Scapa Flow. On arrival, she returned to Scapa Flow, to carry out exercises in the Pentland Firth on passage.
2030	Aircraft carrier ARGUS arrived at Scapa Flow with destroyers TARTAR, INTREPID, and ECLIPSE.
2100	Battleship KING GEORGE V departed Scapa Flow for Rosyth, escorted by destroyers INGLEFIELD, LIGHTNING, and PUNJABI.
2200	Destroyer TARTAR departed Scapa Flow for Skaalefjord.

21 AUGUST 1941

	Convoy DERVISH (Capt Dowding) departed Hvalfjord, Iceland, with steamers LANCASTRIAN PRINCE (1914grt), NEW WESTMINSTER CITY (4747grt), ESNEH (1931grt), LLANSTEPHAN CASTLE (11,348grt), and TREHATA (4817grt), Dutch steamer ALCHIBA (4427grt), and oiler ALDERSDALE (8402grt) for Archangel, Russia. Destroyers ELECTRA, ACTIVE and IMPULSIVE, minesweepers HALCYON, HARRIER and SALAMANDER plus four antisubmarine trawlers escorted the convoy out to sea. Aircraft carrier VICTORIOUS (RAdm Wake-Walker) provided cover for the convoy with heavy cruisers DEVONSHIRE and SUFFOLK plus destroyers ECLIPSE, ESCAPADE and INGLEFIELD. The cover group joined the convoy west of Bear Island on the 26th and escorted the convoy to the White Sea on the 30th.
	Destroyers SOMALI and ORIBI departed Scapa Flow escorting aircraft carrier FURIOUS to Greenock.
	Heavy cruiser SHROPSHIRE departed Hvalfjord, Iceland, for Scapa Flow, via Akreyri and east of Iceland.
0600	Destroyer BADSWORTH arrived at Scapa Flow from Greenock to carry out working up to combat efficiency exercises.
0700	Antiaircraft cruiser CURAÇOA departed Scapa Flow and escorted convoy WN.70 from Pentland Firth to May Island. On this date, the antiaircraft ships operating with the WN and EC convoys came under the administration of Commander in Chief, Rosyth.
0730	The troopship EMPRESS OF CANADA (21,517grt) arrived at Reykjavik with light cruisers NIGERIA and AURORA plus destroyers ICARUS, ANTELOPE, and ANTHONY.
0800	Destroyer TARTAR arrived at Skaalefjord from Scapa Flow. TARTAR departed Skaalefjord escorting damaged destroyer ACHATES in tow of tugboat ASSURANCE and with salvage vessel LE LUTTEUR for the Tyne.
1500	Destroyers INGLEFIELD and LIGHTNING returned to Scapa Flow.
1730	Destroyer NEWARK departed Scapa Flow to rejoin the Minelaying Command at Loch Alsh.
2100	A U-boat was suspected of attempting to force a passage into Scapa Flow. A patrol was established through the night with destroyers LIGHTNING, MATABELE, INTREPID, and PUCKERIDGE, trawlers, and motor launches.
2200	Force K departed Hvalfjord, Iceland, with light cruisers NIGERIA and AURORA plus destroyers ANTHONY, ANTELOPE, and ICARUS escorting troopship EMPRESS OF CANADA (21,517grt) on Operation GAUNTLET and Operation BENEDICT. Fleet oiler OLIGARCH (6897grt) arrived at Spitsbergen, Norway, on the 24th, escorted by trawlers HAZEL and ELM. After demolishing the coalfields at Bergensburg, light cruiser NIGERIA departed Spitsbergen on the 26th with destroyers ANTHONY, ANTELOPE, and ICARUS escorting troopship EMPRESS OF CANADA to Archangel, Russia. On the 26th, Norwegian colliers INGERTO (3089grt), NANDI (1999grt), and MUNIN (1285grt) taken as prizes, escorted by antisubmarine trawler SEALYHAM, and until the morning of 27 August by light cruiser AURORA, which departed Spitsbergen for Hvalfjord, arriving on 1 September. This convoy was designated Convoy Drover. These ships returned to Spitsbergen on 1 September and joined light cruiser AURORA. Convoy DERVISH departed Liverpool on 12 August, escorted by antiaircraft ship POZARICA and minesweeping trawlers CELIA (545grt), HAMLET (545grt), and MACBETH (545grt), antisubmarine trawlers ST CATHAN (565grt) and LE TIGRE (516grt) for Reykjavik, Iceland. The convoy called at Scapa Flow on 15 August and departed at 1800/16th with destroyers ELECTRA, IMPULSIVE, and ACTIVE with light cruiser AURORA as additional escort until 18 August. The convoy departed Reykjavik, Iceland, on 21 August with steamers LANCASTRIAN PRINCE (1914grt), NEW WESTMINSTER CITY (4747grt), ESNEH (1931grt), LLANSTEPHAN CASTLE (11,348grt), and TREHATA (4817grt), Dutch steamer ALCHIBA (4427grt), and fleet oiler ALDERSDALE (8402grt) escorted by destroyers ELECTRA, ACTIVE, and IMPULSIVE, minesweepers HALCYON, HARRIER, and SALAMANDER, and minesweeping trawlers HAMLET, MACBETH, and OPHELIA. The convoy was covered by aircraft carrier VICTORIOUS, heavy cruisers DEVONSHIRE and SUFFOLK, and destroyers ECLIPSE, ESCAPADE, and INGLEFIELD from 24 to 30 August, when the ships called at Spitsbergen to refuel. The convoy arrived on the 31st at Archangel, Russia.

22 AUGUST 1941

	American destroyer CHARLES F. HUGHES (DD-428) was damaged in a collision with steamer CHUMLEIGH (5445grt) at Reykjavik, Iceland.
	Minelayer AGAMEMNON laid Minefield SN.22B in the Northern Barrage escorted by destroyer NEWARK.
0600	Destroyers LIVELY and LIGHTNING, which departed Scapa Flow to assist damaged Free French submarine RUBIS in the North Sea.

23 AUGUST 1941

	Heavy cruisers DEVONSHIRE (SO Force M) and SUFFOLK plus aircraft carrier VICTORIOUS departed Scapa Flow as Force M with destroyers INGLEFIELD, ECLIPSE, and ESCAPADE to operate in the northern waters around Archangel and Murmansk, Russia, in Operation EGV.1 and Operation EGV.2.
	An Albacore aircraft of 832 Squadron ditched in the sea off Cape Wrath. Destroyer INGLEFIELD rescued Sub-Lt H. Eyre, Sub-Lt D. J. R. Harvey, and Leading Airman T. E. J. St Vaughan.
	Minelayers SOUTHERN PRINCE, PORT QUEBEC, and ADVENTURE laid Minefield SN.70A east of Iceland escorted by destroyers CASTLETON, NEWARK, and CHARLESTOWN. The heavy cruiser DEVONSHIRE force provided cover for this mining as they proceeded on to their operations in the Arctic Ocean.
0700	Destroyer SOMALI returned to Scapa Flow from Greenock.
2347	U.143 (ObltzS Gelhaus) sank Norwegian steamer **INGER** (1418grt) (Master Jørgen G. Jørgensen) thirty miles northwest of Butt of Lewis, Scotland, in 58, 58N, 07, 50W. Nine crewmen were lost (Seven Norwegians and two British gunners).
	Trawler LADYLOVE rescued fourteen survivors from a lifeboat the next day and took them to Stornoway.

24 AUGUST 1941

	Heavy cruiser SHROPSHIRE arrived at Scapa Flow from Hvalfjord, Iceland.
	Light cruiser ARETHUSA departed Scapa Flow to refit in the Tyne.
1900	Destroyer VIVACIOUS arrived at Scapa Flow from Rosyth to carry out working up to combat efficiency exercises.
2100	Destroyers LIVELY and LIGHTNING returned to Scapa Flow after assisting damaged Free French submarine RUBIS in the North Sea.
2200	Destroyer SOMALI departed Scapa Flow for Loch Alsh to embark the First Lord of the Admiralty.

25 AUGUST 1941

	Catalina J aircraft (F/O Jewiss) of 209 Squadron and antisubmarine trawler VISENDA (Lt Walgate) sank **U.452** (Kptlt March) south of Iceland in 61, 30N, 15, 30W. The entire crew of forty-two were lost.
	Light cruiser KENYA arrived back at Scapa Flow from Rosyth after repairs. Her repair trial was not satisfactory, and speed was limited to a maximum of 28.5 knots.
	Minelayers SOUTHERN PRINCE, PORT QUEBEC, and ADVENTURE laid Minefield SN.70A in the Northern Barrage escorted by destroyers CASTLETON, NEWARK, and CHARLESTOWN.
0044	U.652 (ObltzS Fraatz) damaged auxiliary minelayer SOUTHERN PRINCE (10,917grt) returning from laying Minefield SN.70A west of the Faeroes in 62, 55N, 09, 55W. There were no casualties.
	U.652 tried to sink the damaged minelayer, but the torpedo missed.
0053	Destroyers LIGHTNING and LAMERTON arrived from Scapa Flow to assist the minelayer and escort her as far the Minches.
1200	Antiaircraft ship ULSTER QUEEN arrived at Scapa Flow from Belfast, Northern Ireland, to carry out working up to combat efficiency exercises.
1550	Destroyer SOMALI arrived at Stornoway from Loch Alsh with the First Lord of the Admiralty.
1630	Destroyer SOMALI departed Stornoway for Scapa Flow with the First Lord of the Admiralty.

26 AUGUST 1941

0600	Destroyer INTREPID departed Scapa Flow to join convoy ES.78 off May Island and act as additional escort to Sheerness.
0615	Destroyers LIGHTNING and LAMERTON departed Scapa Flow to assist torpedoed auxiliary minelayer SOUTHERN PRINCE west of the Faeroes. The minelayer was escorted as far the Minches. The destroyers arrived back at Scapa Flow on the 27th. The minelayer was repaired at Belfast, Northern Ireland.
0910	Cruiser minelayer WELSHMAN arrived at Scapa Flow from Rosyth. The cruiser then began working up to combat efficiency exercises.
0930	Destroyer SOMALI arrived at Scapa Flow from Stornoway. The First Lord of the Admiralty was transferred to battleship PRINCE OF WALES.

27 AUGUST 1941

	Heavy cruiser LONDON arrived at Scapa Flow after boiler cleaning at the Clyde.

	The German B-Service located convoy HX.145 south of Iceland and positioned U.570, U.38, U.82, U.202, U.652, U.501, U.569, U.84, U.567, U.553 and U.207 to intercept the convoy.
	RAF Hudson aircraft S of 269 Squadron (Sqn Ldr Thompson) damaged **U.570** (ObltzS Rahmlow) when it surfaced under the aircraft in heavy seas southwest of Iceland in 62, 15N, 18, 35W. The U-boat remained on the surface while the aircraft circled it to guide support ships to the position. A Catalina aircraft of 209 Squadron arrived in the evening to relieve the Hudson. Antisubmarine trawler NORTHERN CHIEF arrived during the evening of 27 August and took the entire crew of forty-four as prisoners. During the morning of 28 August, trawlers KINGSTON AGATE, WASTWATER, and WINDERMERE and destroyers BURWELL and NIAGARA arrived on the scene. Two trawlers towed **U.570** to Thorlakshavn, Iceland, and beached her to keep her from sinking. On 5 September, tug SALVONIA towed **U.570** off the beach and positioned her alongside depot ship HECLA at Hvalfjord, Iceland, on 6 September.
0100	Light cruiser EURYALUS and destroyer PUCKERIDGE departed Scapa Flow to join battleship MALAYA and destroyer PUNJABI off May Island and escort the battleship to Scapa Flow.
1435	U.202 (Kptlt Linder) sank antisubmarine trawler **LADYLOVE** (230grt) with one torpedo south of Iceland. She sank in fifteen seconds with her entire crew of fourteen.
1930	Destroyer LIVELY departed Scapa Flow for Greenock having completed her working up to combat efficiency exercises.
2000	Battleship MALAYA arrived at Scapa Flow escorted by light cruiser EURYALUS plus destroyers PUCKERIDGE and PUNJABI.

28 AUGUST 1941

	U.38, U.43, U.81, U.82, U.84, U.85, U.105, U.202, U.207, U.432, U.433, U.501, U.569 and U.652 set up a patrol line southwest of Iceland designated Wolfpack MARKGRAF.
1600	Destroyer PUCKERIDGE returned to Scapa Flow.
>1601	Destroyer PUCKERIDGE embarked the First Lord of the Admiralty and transported him from Scapa Flow to Scrabster.

29 AUGUST 1941

	Battle cruiser REPULSE and light cruiser SHEFFIELD departed Scapa Flow with destroyers LIGHTNING, BADSWORTH, and VIVACIOUS for the Clyde. The battle cruiser and light cruiser were required for escort duties with convoy WS.11.
1340	Destroyer LAFOREY (Capt R. M. J. Hutton, D.19) arrived at Scapa Flow to carry out working up to combat efficiency exercises.

30 AUGUST 1941

	After the report was received from U.S. Coast Guard cutter ALEXANDER HAMILTON (WPG-34), Task Group TG.1.1.2 with battleship NEW MEXICO (BB-40), heavy cruiser QUINCY (CA-39) plus destroyers SIMS (DD-409), CHARLES F. HUGHES (DD-428) and RUSSELL (DD-414) departed Hvalfjord, Iceland, to patrol the Denmark Strait in case the suspected German ship tried to reach Norway.
0800	Heavy cruiser SHROPSHIRE (SO Force L) and aircraft carrier ARGUS departed Scapa Flow with destroyers SOMALI, MATABELE, and PUNJABI for Seidisfjord, Iceland, in Operation STRENGTH. The ships arrived off Seidisfjord at 0500 on 1 September, but were unable to enter port due to thick fog. Destroyer PUNJABI was able to enter Seidisfjord at 1045 and sailed at 1300 to rejoin the Force.

31 AUGUST 1941

0730	Destroyers LIGHTNING, BADSWORTH, and VIVACIOUS returned to Scapa Flow from the Clyde.

Norwegian Sea

Long. E03, 00 – E20, 00   Lat. N68, 00 – N58, 30

10 AUGUST 1941

	A mine laid by a British submarine sank German auxiliary minesweeper **M.1102/H. A. W. MULLER** (460grt) off Lindesnes. Two Danish fishing ships also went missing in this area, probably mined.

12 AUGUST 1941

	German destroyer THEODOR RIEDEL arrived at Bergen, Norway, with a damaged screw caused by heavy seas.
	A German mine sank Norwegian coastal steamer **CITO** (124grt) in Sognefjord, Norway.

13 AUGUST 1941

	Free French submarine RUBIS claimed she sank a ship of 4360-grt west of Norway.

Free French submarines RUBIS and MINERVE patrolled the Norwegian west coast with Dutch submarine O.14 until 4 September.

East of Canada

Long. W70, 00 – W30, 00   Lat. N68, 00 – N43, 30

1 AUGUST 1941

Convoy HX.142 departed Halifax escorted by destroyer ANNAPOLIS, AMC AUSONIA, and corvettes COLLINGWOOD and ROSTHERN. Corvette ROSTHERN was detached from the convoy later that day.
Corvettes DAUPHIN and NAPANEE joined on the 2nd and were detached from the convoy later that day.
Destroyer ANNAPOLIS was detached from the convoy on the 3rd.
Destroyer CHESTERFIELD and corvettes HEPATICA, TRILLIUM, and WINDFLOWER joined the convoy on the 4th, destroyer CHURCHILL and corvettes ARROWHEAD and EYEBRIGHT joined the convoy on the 5th, and corvette CAMILLIA joined the convoy on the 6th.
Corvette COLLINGWOOD was detached from the convoy on the 5th and the remaining escorts were detached from the convoy on the 12th when relieved by destroyers BEAGLE, BOADICEA, KEPPEL, SABRE, SALISBURY, SHIKARI, and SKATE, corvettes HEATHER, ORCHIS, and SNOWDROP, minesweepers HAZARD, HEBE, and SEAGULL, and antisubmarine trawlers ARAB, AYRSHIRE, and NORWICH CITY.
Destroyers KEPPEL, SHIKARI, and SKATE, the minesweepers, and the trawlers were detached from the convoy on the 13th.
On the 14th, destroyer SALISBURY was detached from the convoy, on the 15th, destroyer SABRE and corvette ORCHIS were detached from the convoy, on the 16th, destroyer BEAGLE was detached from the convoy.
On the 17th, corvette ARABIS joined the convoy and on the 18th, the convoy arrived at Liverpool with destroyer BOADICEA and corvette ARABIS.

Convoy SC.39 departed Sydney, Cape Breton, escorted by AMC MALOJA plus corvettes BARRIE and CHICOUTIMI.
These three escorts were detached from the convoy on the 4th. On the 4th, destroyer CHESTERFIELD and corvettes BUCTOUCHE, HEPATICA, TRILLIUM, and WINDFLOWER joined the convoy.
Corvettes HEPATICA and TRILLIUM were detached from the convoy on the 8th and remainder of the escorts were detached from the convoy on the 12th, when relieved by destroyers KEPPEL, LINCOLN, and SHIKARI, corvettes ALISMA, DIANELLA, MATAPEDIA, and SUNFLOWER, minesweepers HAZARD and HEBE, and antisubmarine trawlers MAN O' WAR and NORTHERN DAWN. This escort group was detached from the convoy on the 17th.
Destroyers BOADICEA and SABRE joined the convoy on the 18th and the convoy arrived at Liverpool on the 19th.

2 AUGUST 1941

Dutch tanker MURENA (8252grt) sank Dutch steamer **ROZENBURG** (2068grt) in a collision off Halifax, Nova Scotia.

5 AUGUST 1941

Convoy HX.143 departed Halifax escorted by destroyers ANNAPOLIS and NIAGARA plus AMC WOLFE.
The destroyers were detached from the convoy that night.
Corvettes DAUPHIN and NAPANEE joined the convoy on the 6th and were detached from the convoy on the 7th.
Destroyer BURNHAM joined the convoy on the 8th with corvettes AGASSIZ, GALT, LEVIS, and MAYFLOWER.
The escorts were detached from the convoy on the 17th when relieved by destroyers MALCOLM, SARDONYX, SCIMITAR, and WATCHMAN, corvettes ARABIS, VERBENA, and VIOLET, plus antisubmarine trawlers NORTHERN GEM, NORTHERN PRIDE, and NORTHERN WAVE. The convoy arrived at Liverpool on the 20th.

7 AUGUST 1941

American heavy cruisers AUGUSTA (CA-31) and TUSCALOOSA (CA-37) arrived at Argentia, Newfoundland, from Massachusetts with President Franklin D. Roosevelt aboard escorted by five destroyers.

9 AUGUST 1941

Canadian destroyers RESTIGOUCHE and ASSINIBOINE with destroyer RIPLEY escorted battleship PRINCE OF WALES into Placentia Bay. In harbour at this time were American battleship ARKANSAS (BB-33), heavy cruisers AUGUSTA (CA-31) and TUSCALOOSA (CA-37), destroyers MCDOUGAL (DD-358), MADISON (DD-425), SAMPSON (DD-394), WINSLOW (DD-359), MOFFETT (DD-362), BELKNAP (AVD-8), RHIND (DD-404), and MAYRANT (DD-402), destroyer READING, and American oiler SALINAS (AO-19).
RESTIGOUCHE damaged her screws when she touched ground while refuelling. She was repaired at St John's and Halifax, completing on 9 October.
The Atlantic Charter was signed on the 10th.

10 AUGUST 1941

	American destroyer MCDOUGAL (DD-358) transferred President Roosevelt to battleship PRINCE OF WALES for Sunday services with Prime Minister Churchill.
	Convoy HX.144 departed Halifax escorted by destroyer ANNAPOLIS and AMC MALOJA. On the 11th, corvettes DAUPHIN and NAPANEE joined the convoy, and on the 13th the destroyers BURWELL and COLUMBIA plus corvettes DIANTHUS, HONEYSUCKLE, and SNOWBERRY joined the convoy. Corvettes DAUPHIN and NAPANEE were detached from the convoy on the 12th and destroyer ANNAPOLIS was detached from the convoy on the 13th. The remaining escorts were detached from the convoy on the 22nd when relieved by destroyers AMAZON, BELMONT, BULLDOG, GEORGETOWN, SKATE, WESTCOTT, WHITEHALL, and WITCH, corvettes AUBRIETIA and HEARTSEASE, minesweeper BRITOMART, plus antisubmarine trawlers ANGLE, CAPE WARWICK, DANEMAN, and NOTTS COUNTY. Destroyers SKATE, WESTCOTT, WHITEHALL, and WITCH, the minesweeper, and the trawlers were detached from the convoy later that day. Corvette NIGELLA joined the convoy on the 23rd. On the 24th, destroyers BURNHAM and CHURCHILL joined the convoy for the day only. Destroyers BELMONT and GEORGETOWN were detached from the convoy on the 27th, destroyers AMAZON and BULLDOG and corvette AUBRIETIA were detached from the convoy on the 28th, and corvettes HEARTSEASE and NIGELLA were detached from the convoy on the 29th. The convoy arrived at Liverpool on the 30th.
	Convoy SC.40 departed Sydney, Cape Breton, escorted by corvettes BARRIE, CHICOUTIMI, and MATAPEDIA. These escorts were detached from the convoy on the 13th, when relieved by destroyer NIAGARA and corvettes ALYSSE, CELANDINE, and COLLINGWOOD. AMC CHITRAL joined the convoy on the 19th. The escorts were detached from the convoy on the 22nd when relieved by destroyers DOUGLAS, LEAMINGTON, and VETERAN, corvettes ABELIA, ANEMONE, and VERONICA, plus minesweepers LEDA and SPEEDY. On the 28th, minesweepers GOSSAMER, HAZARD, and HEBE joined the convoy. The convoy arrived at Liverpool on the 29th.

12 AUGUST 1941

	American heavy cruisers AUGUSTA (CA-31) and TUSCALOOSA (CA-37) departed Argentia, Newfoundland, with destroyer MCDOUGAL (DD-358) to return President Roosevelt to the United States.
	Battleship PRINCE OF WALES departed Argentia, Newfoundland, with Canadian destroyers RESTIGOUCHE and ASSINIBOINE plus destroyer RIPLEY for Placentia Bay, Newfoundland.

14 AUGUST 1941

	Battleship PRINCE OF WALES departed Placentia Bay, Newfoundland, escorted by destroyers RIPLEY, ASSINIBOINE, SAGUENAY, and READING plus the American destroyers RHIND (DD-404) and MAYRANT (DD-402). RIPLEY and READING were detached from the group on the 16th.
	American heavy cruisers AUGUSTA (CA-31) and TUSCALOOSA (CA-37) with destroyer MCDOUGAL (DD-358) stopped off Cape Sable, Nova Scotia, for President Roosevelt to observe flight operations off escort carrier LONG ISLAND (AVG-1). F2A Buffalo and SOC Seagull aircraft of Scouting Squadron 201 (VS-201) demonstrated air operations of the first "jeep" aircraft carrier.
	American heavy cruisers AUGUSTA (CA-31) and TUSCALOOSA (CA-37) with destroyer MCDOUGAL (DD-358) arrived at Blue Hill Bay, Maine, to transfer President Roosevelt to the presidential yacht POTOMAC (AG-25).

15 AUGUST 1941

	American presidential yacht POTOMAC (AG-25) stopped off Deer Island, Maine, to allow President Roosevelt time for fishing.

16 AUGUST 1941

	American presidential yacht POTOMAC (AG-25) arrived at Rockland, Maine, to allow President Roosevelt to debark from the vessel for ground transfer back to Washington, DC.
	Convoy HX.145 departed Halifax escorted by destroyer BROADWATER, AMC CALIFORNIA, corvettes RIMOUSKI and SPIKENARD, plus antisubmarine whalers KOS IX and KOS VIII. The whalers were detached from the convoy that night. Corvettes ARVIDA and MATAPEDIA joined the convoy on the 17th for the day only. Corvette CHILLIWACK joined the convoy on the 20th. The escorts were detached from the convoy on the 25th when relieved by destroyers BEAGLE, BOADICEA, and SALISBURY, corvettes HEATHER and NARCISSUS, minesweeper SEAGULL, with antisubmarine trawlers ARAB, NORWICH CITY, and ST LOMAN. The minesweeper and the trawlers were detached from the convoy later that day.

158 — AUGUST 1941

On the 29th, destroyers SKATE and WITCH plus minesweepers HEBE and SPEEDWELL joined the convoy. Destroyer SALISBURY, corvettes HEATHER and NARCISSUS, and the minesweepers were detached from the convoy on the 30th and the convoy arrived at Liverpool on the 31st.

18 AUGUST 1941

0250 — U.38 (KKpt Schuch) sank unescorted Panamanian steamer **LONGTAKER** (1700grt) (ex Danish **SESSA** (1700grt)) (Master N. Nielsen) about 300 miles southwest Iceland in 61, 26N, 30, 50W.
She sank within one minute with only six crewmen getting off the ship alive, but three of them died at sea. American destroyer LANSDALE (DD-426) rescued the three survivors on 5 September. The rest of the crew of twenty-four was lost.

21 AUGUST 1941

Convoy HX.146 departed Halifax escorted by AMC WORCESTERSHIRE plus corvettes KENOGAMI, MOOSE JAW, and PRESCOTT.
Corvettes BARRIE and MATAPEDIA joined the convoy on the 22nd.
The corvettes were detached from the convoy on the 24th when relieved by destroyer BROADWAY with corvettes COBALT, POLYANTHUS, and TRAIL.
The entire escort, including the AMC was detached from the convoy on 2 September when relieved by destroyers KEPPEL, LINCOLN, NIAGARA, SABRE, SHIKARI, and VENOMOUS, corvettes ALISMA, ALYSSE, COLLINGWOOD, DIANELLA, and SUNFLOWER, with antisubmarine trawlers LADY ELSA and MAN O' WAR.
Destroyer NIAGARA with corvettes ALYSSE and COLLINGWOOD were detached from the convoy later that day.
Destroyers LINCOLN and SABRE, corvettes ALISMA, DIANELLA, and SUNFLOWER, and the trawlers were detached from the convoy on 5 September. The convoy arrived at Liverpool on 6 September.

23 AUGUST 1941

Canadian AMC PRINCE DAVID departed Halifax to search for a German auxiliary cruiser reported by radio intercepts and air reconnaissance south of Bermuda.

24 AUGUST 1941

Convoy SC.41 departed Sydney, Cape Breton, escorted by AMC RANPURA plus corvettes ARVIDA, CHICOUTIMI, and MATAPEDIA.
The corvettes were detached from the convoy on the 26th when relieved by destroyer ST CROIX with corvettes BUCTOUCHE, GALT, and PICTOU.
Destroyer RAMSEY joined the convoy on 2 September.
Corvettes ARABIS, MONKSHOOD, and PETUNIA with antisubmarine trawlers NORTHERN GEM, NORTHERN PRIDE, and NORTHERN WAVE joined the convoy on 5 September, destroyer SARDONYX joined the convoy on 6 September, plus destroyers MALCOLM and WATCHMAN joined the convoy on 11 September.
Destroyer ST CROIX was detached from the convoy on 5 September and destroyer RAMSEY with corvettes BUCTOUCHE and GALT were detached from the convoy on 6 September. The convoy arrived at Liverpool on 11 September.

26 AUGUST 1941

Canadian troop convoy TC.12B departed Halifax, Nova Scotia, with troopships DOMINION MONARCH (27,155grt), EMPRESS OF RUSSIA (16,810grt), and STRATHEDEN (23,722grt).
Destroyers ANNAPOLIS and RICHMOND escorted the convoy on 26 and 27 August.
On the 27th, destroyers ASSINIBOINE, HARVESTER, HAVELOCK, RIPLEY, SAGUENAY, and ST LAURENT joined the convoy and remained with it until its arrival on 1 September.

29 AUGUST 1941

Convoy HX.147 departed Halifax, Nova Scotia, escorted by AMC LACONIA plus corvettes GLADIOLUS, MIMOSA, and WETASKIWIN.
Destroyer COLUMBIA joined the convoy on 2 September.
On 8 September, the corvettes were detached from the convoy when relieved by destroyers AMAZON, BELMONT and BULLDOG, corvettes ACONIT (Free French), AUBRIETIA, HEARTSEASE, and NIGELLA, and antisubmarine trawlers DANEMAN, NORTHERN WAVE, and ST APOLLO.
Destroyer COLUMBIA was detached from the convoy on 8 September.
On 11 September, destroyers AMAZON, BELMONT, and BULLDOG and corvette ACONIT were detached from the convoy.
The convoy arrived at Liverpool on 12 September.

30 AUGUST 1941

Convoy SC.42 of sixty-five ships departed Sydney, Cape Breton, and was joined by five more ships from St John's, Newfoundland, on 2 September.

	The local escort of the convoy was Canadian destroyer SKEENA (Hibbard, SO) plus corvettes ALBERNI, KENOGAMI, and ORILLIA. Corvettes ARVIDA, BARRIE, and NAPANEE escorted the Sydney section of convoy SC.42. These corvettes were detached from the convoy on 2 September when corvettes ALBERNI, KENOGAMI, and ORILLIA joined the convoy. Corvette ORILLIA was detached from the convoy on 9 September. On 10 September, corvettes CHAMBLY, GLADIOLUS, MIMOSA, MOOSE JAW, and WETASKIWIN plus antisubmarine trawler BUTTERMERE joined the convoy. Destroyers DOUGLAS, LEAMINGTON, SALADIN, and VETERAN and antisubmarine trawler WINDERMERE joined the convoy on 11 September. Destroyers BELMONT, COLUMBIA, SKATE, SKEENA, and ST CROIX joined the convoy on 12 September. Corvettes ALBERNI, KENOGAMI, and MOOSE JAW were detached from the convoy on 13 September. American destroyers CHARLES F. HUGHES (DD-428), RUSSELL (DD-414), and SIMS (DD-409) escorted the convoy on 14 September and then were detached from the convoy later that day. Destroyer COLUMBIA, corvettes GLADIOLUS, MIMOSA, and WETASKIWIN, plus antisubmarine trawlers BUTTERMERE and WINDERMERE were detached from the convoy on 16 September. Destroyer SALISBURY and corvettes LOBELIA, NARCISSUS, and RENONCULE joined the convoy on 16 September. Destroyers SALADIN, SKEENA, and ST CROIX and corvette CHAMBLY were detached from the convoy on 17 September. Destroyers LEAMINGTON, SKATE, and VETERAN were detached from the convoy on 18 September and the convoy arrived Liverpool on 19 September.

East of United States

Long. W85, 00 – W60, 00   Lat. N43, 30 – N25, 00

1 AUGUST 1941

	American troopship WEST POINT (AP-23) arrived at New York City with the American and Chinese consular personnel and their families from Europe.
	American Task Group TG.2.5 departed Hampton Roads, Virginia, with aircraft carrier YORKTOWN (CV-5), light cruiser BROOKLYN (CL-40), plus destroyers ROE (DD-418), GRAYSON (DD-435) and EBERLE (DD-430) on a neutrality patrol that ended at Bermuda on the 10th.

2 AUGUST 1941

	American battleship NEW MEXICO (BB-40) returned to Hampton Roads, Virginia, with destroyers CHARLES F. HUGHES (DD-428) and RUSSELL (DD-414) from a neutrality patrol.

3 AUGUST 1941

	American presidential yacht POTOMAC (AG-25) and auxiliary CALYPSO (AG-35) departed New London, Connecticut, with President Roosevelt aboard.

4 AUGUST 1941

	The first American escort aircraft carrier LONG ISLAND (AVG-1) support landing exercises for the American 1st Marine Division at New River, North Carolina.
	American presidential yacht POTOMAC (AG-25) and auxiliary CALYPSO (AG-35) arrived off Massachusetts from New London, Connecticut, with President Roosevelt aboard. They rendezvoused with American heavy cruisers AUGUSTA (CA-31) and TUSCALOOSA (CA-37).

5 AUGUST 1941

	American heavy cruisers AUGUSTA (CA-31) and TUSCALOOSA (CA-37) with five destroyers departed Massachusetts for Newfoundland with President Roosevelt aboard.

7 AUGUST 1941

	American battleship ARKANSAS (BB-33) departed Hampton Roads, Virginia, with destroyers RHIND (DD-404) and MAYRANT (DD-402) on a neutrality patrol lasting until 15 August.

10 AUGUST 1941

	American Task Group TG.2.5 arrived at Bermuda with aircraft carrier YORKTOWN (CV-5), light cruiser BROOKLYN (CL-40), plus destroyers ROE (DD-418), GRAYSON (DD-435) and EBERLE (DD-430) after a neutrality patrol from Hampton Roads, Virginia.

12 AUGUST 1941

	American authorities seized Italian steamer **DINO** (5592grt) at Boston, Massachusetts. She became the Panamanian MERIDIAN (5592grt).

14 AUGUST 1941

American battleship NEW MEXICO (BB-40) departed Hampton Roads, Virginia, with destroyers CHARLES F. HUGHES (DD-428) and RUSSELL (DD-414) on a neutrality patrol until 23 August.

15 AUGUST 1941

American battleship ARKANSAS (BB-33) returned to Hampton Roads, Virginia, with destroyers RHIND (DD-404) and MAYRANT (DD-402) from a neutrality patrol.

American Task Group TG.2.5 departed Bermuda with aircraft carrier YORKTOWN (CV-5), light cruiser BROOKLYN (CL-40), plus destroyers ROE (DD-418), GRAYSON (DD-435) and EBERLE (DD-430) on a neutrality patrol.

16 AUGUST 1941

American battleship MISSISSIPPI (BB-41) returned to Hampton Roads, Virginia, with destroyers O'BRIEN (DD-415), WAKE (DD-416), STACK (DD-406), STERETT (DD-407) and ROWAN (DD-405) from a neutrality patrol.

22 AUGUST 1941

Battleship RODNEY departed Newport, Rhode Island, for Bermuda to work up to combat efficiency after repairs made in the American Naval Yard.

23 AUGUST 1941

American battleship NEW MEXICO (BB-40) returned to Hampton Roads, Virginia, with destroyers CHARLES F. HUGHES (DD-428) and RUSSELL (DD-414) from a neutrality patrol.

American authorities seized Italian steamer **LACONIA** (5932grt) at Norfolk, Virginia. She became the Panamanian ELWOOD (5932grt).

American authorities seized Italian steamer **ALBERTA** (6131grt) at New York City. She became the Panamanian BALLOT (6131grt).

American authorities seized Italian steamer **AUSSA** (5441grt) at New York City. She became the Panamanian AFRICANDER (5441grt).

American authorities seized Italian steamer **GUIDONIA** (5060grt) at Norfolk, Virginia. She became the Panamanian PLAUDIT (5060grt).

American authorities seized Italian steamer **PIETRO CAMPANELLA** (6140grt) at Norfolk, Virginia. She became the Panamanian EQUIPOISE (6140grt).

25 AUGUST 1941

American Task Group TG.2.6 departed Hampton Roads, Virginia, with aircraft carrier WASP (CV-7) and light cruiser SAVANNAH (CL-42) plus destroyers MEREDITH (DD-434) and GWIN (DD-433) on neutrality patrol ending on 10 September at Bermuda.

27 AUGUST 1941

American battleship MISSISSIPPI (BB-41) departed Hampton Roads, Virginia, with destroyers O'BRIEN (DD-415), WAKE (DD-416), STACK (DD-406), STERETT (DD-407) and ROWAN (DD-405) on a neutrality patrol until 11 September.

American Task Group TG.2.5 arrived at Bermuda with aircraft carrier YORKTOWN (CV-5), light cruiser BROOKLYN (CL-40), plus destroyers ROE (DD-418), GRAYSON (DD-435) and EBERLE (DD-430) after a neutrality patrol.

Battleship RODNEY departed Bermuda and followed American Task Force TG.2.6 with aircraft carrier WASP (CV-7), light cruiser SAVANNAH (CL-42) plus destroyers MONSSEN (DD-436), GWIN (DD-433), and MEREDITH (DD-434) towards the position where Canadian AMC PRINCE DAVID reported a German cruiser in the North Atlantic.

28 AUGUST 1941

American Task Group TG.2.7 departed Bermuda with escort aircraft carrier LONG ISLAND (AVG-1) with VGS-1, light cruiser NASHVILLE (CL-43), plus destroyers LIVERMORE (DD-429) and KEARNY (DD-432) on a neutrality patrol. The patrol concluded at Bermuda on 9 September.

30 AUGUST 1941

American Coast Guard cutter ALEXANDER HAMILTON (WPG-34) reported a HIPPER class cruiser between Bermuda and Newfoundland.

Caribbean and Gulf of Mexico

Long. W100, 00 – W60, 00   Lat. N31, 00 – N05, 00

14 AUGUST 1941

	American steamer NORLINDO (2686grt) sank American submarine chaser **PC-457** in a collision off San Juan, Puerto Rico.

23 AUGUST 1941

	American authorities seized Italian steamer **ADA O** (5234grt) at New Orleans, Louisiana. She became the Panamanian HERMIS (5234grt).

25 AUGUST 1941

	American authorities seized Italian tanker **COLORADO** (5039grt) at San Juan, Puerto Rico, and she became the Panamanian TYPHOON (5039grt).
	T/A/Sub-Lt (A) G. L. Stewart RNVR was killed when his Walrus aircraft of 749 Squadron crashed near Piarco, Trinidad. Two students, Leading Airman B. C. Hamilton, RNZNVR, and Leading Airman H. Hunt RNVR, were also killed.

28 AUGUST 1941

	American Task Force TF.3 departed Trinidad with light cruisers MEMPHIS (CL-13), MILWAUKEE (CL-5), and OMAHA (CL-4) plus destroyers SOMERS (DD-381), WARRINGTON (DD-383), DAVIS (DD-395) and JOUETT (DD-396) to patrol the channels to the Caribbean and the north coast of Brazil and Guinea.

31 AUGUST 1941

	Cuban authorities seized Italian steamer **RECCA** (5441grt) at Havana, Cuba, and she became the Cuban LIBERTAD (5441grt).

Western Approaches

Long. W30, 00 – W03, 00   Lat. N58, 30 – N49, 00

3 AUGUST 1941

	U.431, U.205, U.558, U.75, U.372, U.401, U.565 and U.559 converged on convoy SL.81 southwest of Ireland.
	CAM (Catapult Armed Merchantman) MAPLIN launched a Hurricane aircraft that shot down a German Fw200 of I/KG.40 over convoy SL.81. It was the first time that a fighter aircraft launched from a merchant ship at sea downed a German bomber. LT (A) R. W. H. Everett RNVR piloted the aircraft and after his success, safely landed in the sea near destroyer WANDERER and was rescued.
	Destroyers WANDERER and the Norwegian ST ALBANS with corvette HYDRANGEA sank **U.401** while escorting convoy SL.81 southwest of Ireland.
	Convoy WS.10 was formed at sea from ships departing Avonmouth on 30 July, Liverpool on 31 July, and the Clyde on the 2nd. The convoy included steamers PHEMIUS (7406grt), DIOMED (10,374grt), INDIAN PRINCE (6376grt), INDRAPOERA (10,825grt), ANDES (25,689grt), RANGITIKI (16,698grt), ORCADES (23,456grt), BRITANNIC (26,943grt), HIGHLAND MONARCH (14,139grt), MANCHESTER PORT (5469grt), STRATHALLAN (23,722grt), VOLENDAM (15,434grt), CAMERONIA (16,297grt), REINA DEL PACIFICO (17,702grt), NEA HELLAS (16,991grt), STIRLING CASTLE (25,550grt), WINDSOR CASTLE (19,141grt), WARWICK CASTLE (20,107grt), and NIGERSTROOM (4639grt). The convoy was escorted by AMC WORCESTERSHIRE and destroyers GURKHA, PIORUN, ISAAC SWEERS, BROADWAY, LANCE, and LEGION from 2 to 6 August. On the 6th, steamers WINDSOR CASTLE and WARWICK CASTLE collided. WARWICK CASTLE was detached from the convoy to Halifax escorted by AMC WORCESTERSHIRE. Antiaircraft cruiser CAIRO with destroyers WHITEHALL, WITCH, and WINCHELSEA escorted the convoy from 2 to 5 August. Heavy cruiser LONDON escorted the convoy from 2 to 10 August. On the 10th, light cruiser EDINBURGH, which departed Gibraltar on the 8th, relieved the heavy cruiser and escorted the convoy until 17 August when it arrived at Freetown. The heavy cruiser proceeded to 40N, 30W to attempt to intercept an armed enemy merchant ship reported by civilian aircraft. Destroyers WRESTLER and VELOX and corvette BERGAMOT escorted the convoy from 14 to 17 August and corvette CYCLAMEN escorted the convoy from 15 to 17 August. Destroyer JUPITER was involved in the escort of the convoy at some time prior to the arrival at Freetown. The convoy arrived at Freetown on the 17th. The convoy departed on the 21st, escorted by light cruiser EDINBURGH to 2 September when BRITANNIC, INDRAPOERA, REINA DEL PACIFICO, STIRLING CASTLE, STRATHALLAN, VOLENDAM, WINDSOR CASTLE, NIGERSTROOM, and PHEMIUS arrived at Cape Town, South Africa.
	Convoy OS.2 departed Liverpool.

	On the 4th, destroyers CHELSEA and WOLVERINE joined the convoy and were detached from the convoy on the 8th. Also joining on the 4th were sloop SANDWICH, which was detached from the convoy on the 19th, corvettes GENTIAN, HIBISCUS, and MYOSOTIS, which were detached from the convoy on the 8th, and antisubmarine yacht PHILANTE, which was detached from the convoy on the 19th. Free French sloop COMMANDANT DOMINE joined the convoy on the 4th and was detached from the convoy on the 18th. On the 7th, destroyers VICEROY and WOOLSTON joined the convoy and were detached from the convoy on 9 and 10 August, respectively. On the 19th, destroyer BRILLIANT with corvettes AMARANTHUS, ARMERIA, and WOODRUFF joined the convoy and provided escort all the way to Freetown, arriving on the 22nd.
0100	Destroyer HEYTHROP arrived at Greenock from Scapa Flow.
1115	Destroyer INTREPID became separated from the Operation EF group in bad weather and arrived at Loch Ewe to fuel. The destroyer later proceeded on to Greenock.

4 AUGUST 1941

	A German Fw200 aircraft sighted a convoy and sank steamer **TUNISIA** (4337grt) southwest of Ireland in 53, 53N, 18, 10W. Thirty-eight of a crew of forty-three were missing. The cargo included a valuable load of manganese ore. The aircraft also called in the location to U.558, U.431, U.559, U.75, U.83 and U.74, but none of them made contact with the convoy. U.71, U.77, U.96, U.751 and U.43 converged on convoy SL.81, but none could reach an attack position. U.565 sighted the convoy too late to call in other U-boats.

5 AUGUST 1941

	U.372 (Kptlt Heinz-Joachim Neumann), U.204 (Kptlt Walter Kell), U.75 (Kptlt Helmuth Ringelmann) and U.74 (Kptlt Eitel-Friedrich Kentrat) reached attack positions on convoy SL.81 by dark.
	A new German patrol line was set up southwest of Iceland with U.563, U.568, U.129, U.567, U.206, U.84, U.501, U.71, U.553, U.77, U.43, U.96, U.101, U.38, U.73, U.105, and U.751. later U.202, U.82, U.569 (from 11 August) and U.652 (from 23 August) joined the patrol.
0150	U.372 sank steamer **BELGRAVIAN** (3136grt) (Master Richard Sanderson Kearon OBE) while attacking convoy SL.81 west of Ireland in 53, 03N, 16, 54W. Three crewmen were lost. Corvette BLUEBELL (Lt Cdr Robert E. Sherwood RNR) rescued the master, forty crewmen and six gunners and landed them at Gourock.
0154	U.372 unsuccessfully attacked steamer VOLTURNO (3424grt) while attacking convoy SL.81 west of Ireland in 53, 03N, 16, 54W. U.204 made a similar claim for another large steamer, also unconfirmed.
0159	U.372 sank steamer **SWIFTPOOL** (5205grt) while attacking convoy SL.81 west of Ireland in 53, 03N, 16, 00W. Forty-two of forty-nine crewmen were lost.
0520	U.75 sank steamer **HARLINGEN** (5415grt) (Master Jack Willingham) while attacking convoy SL.81 west of Ireland in 53, 26N, 15, 40W. Three crewmen were lost. Corvette HYDRANGEA (Lt J. E. Woolfenden) rescued the master, thirty-four crewmen and four gunners and landed them at Gourock.
0520	U.75 badly damaged **CAPE RODNEY** (4512grt) (Master Peter Allan Wallace) while attacking convoy SL.81 west of Ireland in 53, 26N, 15, 40W. Corvette HYDRANGEA (Lt J. E. Woolfenden) rescued the master, thirty-one crewmen and four gunners and landed them at Gourock. Corvette ZINNIA (Lt Cdr C. G. Cuthberston) rescued three survivors and landed them at Londonderry. Dutch tugboat ZARTE ZEE took the **CAPE RODNEY** in tow for Rothesay Bay two days later in 52, 11N, 14, 42W, but she sank on the 9th in 52, 44N, 11, 41W.
0540–0542	U.74 made four attacks on convoy SL.81 and sank steamer **KUMASIAN** (4922grt) (Master William Edward Pelisser) west of Ireland in 53, 26N, 15, 40W, with the loss of one crewman. Corvette LA MALOUINE (Lt V. D. H. Bidwell RNR) rescued the master, forty-three crewmen, six gunners and nine passengers and landed them at Liverpool.

6 AUGUST 1941

	Convoy ON.4 departed Liverpool escorted by corvette SNOWDROP and minesweeper SEAGULL. The convoy was joined on the 7th by corvettes HEATHER, ORCHIS, and PICOTEE, plus antisubmarine trawlers ARAB, AYRSHIRE, and ST LOMAN. Destroyers BEAGLE, BOADICEA, ROXBOROUGH, and SALISBURY, plus antisubmarine trawlers LADY MADELEINE and NORWICH CITY joined the convoy on the 8th. These escorts were all detached from the convoy on the 12th. On the 11th, corvettes BITTERSWEET, CANDYTUFT, and FENNEL joined the convoy. On the 15th, corvettes ALBERNI, ORILLIA, and PRIMROSE joined the convoy. The corvettes escorted the convoy until it was dispersed on the 18th.
	Convoy ON.5 departed Liverpool escorted by antisubmarine trawlers MAN O' WAR and NORTHERN DAWN.

	On the 7th, destroyers KEPPEL, LINCOLN, and SHIKARI plus corvettes ALISMA, DIANELLA, and SUNFLOWER joined the convoy. Minesweepers HAZARD and HEBE joined the convoy on the 8th. These escorts were all detached from the convoy on the 11th. On the 11th, destroyer SKEENA, AMC MONTCLARE, plus corvettes ALBERNI, ORILLIA, and PRIMROSE joined the convoy until the convoy was dispersed on the 14th.

7 AUGUST 1941

0700	Destroyers CASTLETON, CHARLESTOWN, and ECHO arrived at Greenock from Scapa Flow to join destroyer INTREPID for escort duties with convoy WS.8C.

8 AUGUST 1941

0500	Convoy WS.8C (Exercise LEAPFROG) departed the Clyde with landing ships KARANJA (9891grt), ROYAL SCOTSMAN (3244grt), ULSTER MONARCH (3791grt), BACHAQUERO, MISOA, QUEEN EMMA, and PRINCE CHARLES, oilers DEWDALE and ENNERDALE, steamers NARKUNDA (16,632grt), WINCHESTER CASTLE (20,109grt), BATORY (14,287grt), ORMONDE (14,982grt), CLAN MACDONALD (9653grt), MACHARDA (7998grt), SUFFOLK (11,063grt), DUNEDIN STAR (11,168grt), SILVERTEAK (6770grt), and POTARO (5410grt), escorted by destroyers BULLDOG, INTREPID, ECHO, CHARLESTOWN, CASTLETON, WHITEHALL, WINCHELSEA, and WITCH. This convoy was the force for the intended seizure of the Azores Islands. The convoy entered Scapa Flow on the 10th. Steamers SUFFOLK (11,063grt) and POTARO (5410grt) were in a collision when entering Scapa Flow. Destroyers DOUGLAS, LEAMINGTON, GEORGETOWN, and SALADIN arrived at Scapa Flow on the 15th to escort the convoy. When the operation was cancelled, the ships, less SUFFOLK and POTARO, sailed for the Clyde on the 15th, escorted by destroyers DOUGLAS, LEAMINGTON, INTREPID, CHARLESTOWN, CASTLETON, GEORGETOWN, ANTELOPE, SALADIN, and antiaircraft ship POZARICA. The convoy arrived back in the Clyde on the 17th.
1700	Destroyer SOMALI arrived at Greenock from Southampton upon completion of her refit.
2200	Destroyer SOMALI departed Greenock for Scapa Flow.

9 AUGUST 1941

1500	Destroyer CROOME arrived at Liverpool from Scapa Flow.

10 AUGUST 1941

	U.75, U.559, U.204, and U.83 joined with the newly arrived U.106, U.201, U.564 and U.552 to patrol the area west of the North Channel.
	Light cruiser ARETHUSA arrived in the Clyde from Gibraltar.

11 AUGUST 1941

	Minelaying cruiser ADVENTURE arrived at Loch Alsh from Archangel, Russia.
	U.501 sighted the outbound convoy ONS.4 west of Ireland.
	Convoy ON.6 departed Liverpool escorted by corvette ARABIS and antisubmarine trawler NORTHERN SPRAY. Destroyers MALCOLM, SARDONYX, SCIMITAR, and WATCHMAN, corvettes VERBENA and VIOLET, plus antisubmarine trawlers NORTHERN PRIDE and NORTHERN WAVE joined the convoy on the 13th. Destroyers MALCOLM and WATCHMAN were detached from the convoy with corvette VERBENA on the 15th. Destroyer SCIMITAR with antisubmarine trawlers NORTHERN PRIDE and NORTHERN WAVE were detached from the convoy on the 16th. Corvettes ARABIS and VIOLET plus antisubmarine trawler NORTHERN SPRAY were detached from the convoy on the 17th. On the 17th, destroyers CHESTERFIELD and RIPLEY, AMC AUSONIA, plus corvettes HEPATICA, TRILLIUM, and WINDFLOWER joined the convoy until it was dispersed on the 24th.

12 AUGUST 1941

1700	Destroyers INGLEFIELD, IMPULSIVE, and ECLIPSE joined battle cruiser RENOWN in 55, 45N, 13W and escorted her to Rosyth for a refit.

13 AUGUST 1941

	Convoy OG.71 departed Liverpool escorted by destroyer BATH, sloop LEITH, and corvette ZINNIA. Corvettes BLUEBELL, CAMPANULA, CAMPION, HYDRANGEA, and WALLFLOWER joined the convoy on the 15th. BATH was detached from the convoy on the 18th and was sunk early the next day by U.204. Destroyers GURKHA and LANCE from convoy WS.10X joined the convoy on the 20th. Destroyer BOREAS joined the convoy on the 23rd.

	Destroyer WIVERN joined the convoy on the 20th to the 22nd. Destroyer VIDETTE joined the convoy on the 23rd. ZINNIA was sunk on the 23rd by U.564 in 40, 43N, 11, 39W. The convoy was dispersed on the 23rd to Lisbon. HYDRANGEA arrived at Gibraltar on the 22nd with nine survivors from BATH. Destroyers LANCE, GURKHA and corvettes WALLFLOWER, CAMPION, and CAMPANULA arrived at Gibraltar on the 24th. On the 25th, LANCE and corvette SPIREA departed Gibraltar to carry out an antisubmarine patrol off Cape St Vincent to cover steamers sailing independently from Lisbon to Gibraltar from the former convoy. Later in the day, destroyer WILD SWAN arrived at Gibraltar and departed again to join in the patrol off Cape St Vincent. WILD SWAN, VIDETTE, LEITH, BLUEBELL and SPIREA arrived at Gibraltar on the 27th.
	Convoy OS.3 departed Liverpool escorted by destroyer ST ALBANS which was detached from the convoy on the 18th and corvette CAMPION which was detached from the convoy on the 15th. On the 14th, destroyers CAMPBELTOWN and WANDERER joined the convoy and were detached from the convoy on the 17th and 29 August, respectively. AMC DUNNOTTAR CASTLE joined the convoy on the 14th and arrived with the convoy on 1 September. Escort vessel BANFF joined the convoy on the 14th and was detached from the convoy to Bathurst on the 29th. Ocean boarding vessel MARON joined the convoy on the 14th and was detached from the convoy on the 17th. On the 15th, sloop EGRET joined the convoy and was detached from the convoy on the 29th to Bathurst. On the 16th, escort vessel FISHGUARD joined the convoy and was detached from the convoy to Bathurst on the 29th. On the 29th, corvettes ASTER, BURDOCK, and STARWORT joined the convoy and arrived with the convoy at Freetown on 1 September.
2000	Destroyer LIGHTNING departed Greenock for Scapa Flow to rejoin the Home Fleet after operations in the Western Approaches Command and the western Mediterranean.

15 AUGUST 1941

	Convoy ON.7 departed Liverpool. The convoy was joined on the 16th by destroyers AMAZON, BULLDOG, BURZA, and GEORGETOWN, corvettes AUBRIETIA, HEARTSEASE, NIGELLA, minesweeper BRITOMART, plus antisubmarine trawlers ANGLE, CAPE WARWICK, DANEMAN, and NOTTS COUNTY. Destroyers AMAZON and BURZA were detached from the convoy on the 18th. The remainder of the escort was detached from the convoy on the 21st when destroyer CHURCHILL with corvettes ARROWHEAD, CAMELLIA, and EYEBRIGHT joined the convoy. CHURCHILL was detached from the convoy on the 23rd and the corvettes ARROWHEAD, CAMELLIA, and EYEBRIGHT were detached from the convoy on the 25th when the convoy was dispersed.

16 AUGUST 1941

	Heavy cruiser DORSETSHIRE arrived at the Clyde from Scapa Flow for escort duty with convoy WS.10X.
	Light cruiser ARETHUSA departed the Clyde for Scapa Flow.
	The two sections of Convoy WS.10X rendezvoused at sea. The convoy included troopships STRATHNAVER (22,283grt), PALMA (2715grt), STRATHMORE (23,428grt), BRISBANE STAR (11,076grt), ORION (23,371grt), and PORT JACKSON (9687grt). Light cruiser HEEMSKERK escorted the convoy with destroyers WHITEHALL and WITCH from 15 to 19 August. Destroyers GURKHA, LANCE, PIORUN, and ISAAC SWEERS escorted the convoy from 17 to 19 August. Heavy cruiser DORSETSHIRE escorted the convoy from 17 to 28 August, when the convoy arrived at Freetown. Destroyers BRILLIANT and WRESTLER with corvettes CROCUS and CLEMATIS escorted the convoy from 26 to 28 August. Destroyer VELOX escorted the convoy on 26 and 27 August. The convoy arrived at Freetown on the 28th and sailed on 1 September.
	Convoy ON.8 departed Liverpool escorted by corvettes ABELIA and ANEMONE. The convoy was joined on the 17th by corvette VERONICA plus antisubmarine trawlers ST ELSTAN and ST ZENO. On the 18th, destroyers DOUGLAS, LEAMINGTON, SALADIN, and VETERAN, minesweepers LEDA and SPEEDY, plus antisubmarine trawlers ST KENAN and VIZALMA joined the convoy. These escorts were all detached from the convoy on the 21st when relieved by destroyer BURNHAM, AMC WOLFE, and corvettes AGASSIZ, LEVIS, and MAYFLOWER. The convoy was dispersed on the 25th.

18 AUGUST 1941

	P/T/Midshipman (A) J. M. Down RNVR was killed when his Martlet aircraft of 802 Squadron crashed after an

19 AUGUST 1941

	engine failure on takeoff near Campbeltown.
	Leading Airman E. S. Ingle and Leading Airman G. R. Watson of 1 SFTS Netheravon were killed when their Hart aircraft crashed at Calverton, three miles east southeast of Bath.
	Convoy OG.72 departed Liverpool. On the 20th, destroyers CHELSEA, CROOME, HEYTHROP, and WOLVERINE, sloop ROCHESTER, corvettes CARNATION, HELIOTROPE, LA MALOUINE, and MALLOW, and catapult ship MAPLIN joined the convoy. Destroyer DUNCAN departed Londonderry on the 22nd and joined the convoy. Destroyers CHELSEA and WOLVERINE were detached from the convoy on the 23rd. Destroyers CROOME and HEYTHROP were detached from the convoy on the 27th and arrived at Gibraltar on the 30th. Destroyer LANCE joined the convoy from her patrol on the 26th and destroyer BOREAS departed Gibraltar on the 27th to join the convoy. Destroyer DUNCAN arrived at Gibraltar on the 31st. The convoy arrived at Gibraltar on 1 September with destroyers BOREAS and LANCE, sloop ROCHESTER, corvettes MALLOW, HELIOTROPE, CARNATION, and LA MALOUINE, and catapult ship MAPLIN.
0200	Destroyers ANTHONY, INTREPID and ANTELOPE departed Greenock escorting aircraft carrier ARGUS and troopship EMPRESS OF CANADA (21,517grt).
0208	U.559 (ObltzS Heidtmann) sank steamer **ALVA** (1584grt) (Master Cyril Spenser Palmer) while attacking convoy OG.71 at 600 miles west of Ushant in 48, 48N, 17, 46W. The U-boat also claimed sinking one more steamer and damaging another. One crewman was lost while steamer CLONLARA (1203grt) rescued the master, nine crewmen and four gunners, but they were lost when CLONLARA was sunk on the 22nd. Tugboat EMPIRE OAK rescued eleven crewmen, who also survived when she was sunk on the 22nd. Destroyer BOREAS rescued five survivors. Corvette CAMPANULA (Lt Cdr R. V. E. Case DSC) picked up the survivors on EMPIRE OAK and BOREAS to provide medical treatment. The **ALVA** survivors were later transferred to destroyer VELOX (Lt Cdr E. G. Ropner DSC) and taken to Gibraltar on the 25th.
0406	U.201 (ObltzS Adalbert Schnee) sank steamer **AGUILA** (3255grt) (Master Arthur Firth) while attacking convoy OG.71 west-southwest of Fastnet Rock in 49, 23N, 17, 56W. Fifty-eight crewmen, five gunners, Commodore (Vice Admiral P. E. Parker DSO Rtd), four of his staff, and eighty-nine passengers were lost. Among the passengers lost were Lt J. C. Graham, Surgeon Commander A. N. Forsyth, MB ChB, T/Sub-Lt (A) A. J. Ensor RNVR, T/A/Sub-Lt (A) R. A. Fawcett RNVR, P/T/Sub-Lt (A) W. P. Blewitt, P/T/Sub-Lt (A) M. Eden RNVR, and P/T/Midshipman (A) HM Bulpitt RNVR, en route to the aircraft carrier ARK ROYAL, A/Gunner (T) T. L. P. Melloy, en route to destroyer FORESIGHT, Surgeon Lt R. M. Calder, MB, ChB RNVR, en route to destroyer DUNCAN, T/A/Warrant Shipwright G. J. Lawson en route to submarine depot ship MAIDSTONE, Paymaster Lt Cdr D. G. Mackenzie RNR, T/Lt L. Beeching RNVR, T/Lt R. A. Crichton RNVR, T/Sub-Lt S. J. Golding RNVR, T/Sub-Lt G. M. Wright RNVR, T/Paymaster Sub-Lt R. W. Phillips RNVR, and T/Skipper A. V. Roberts RNR, en route to CORMORANT. Also lost were nine WREN officers and one nursing sister. Tugboat EMPIRE OAK (484grt) rescued six crewmen, but they were lost when U.564 (Suhren) sank the tug on 22 August. Corvette WALLFLOWER (Lt Cdr I. J. Tyson) rescued the master, six crewmen, one naval staffer and two passengers and landed them at Gibraltar. U.204 made two attacks on the 19th and reported sinking two steamers, but none were reported lost.
0406	U.201 sank steamer **CISCAR** (1809grt) (Master Edward Lenton Hughes) while attacking convoy OG.71 west-southwest of Fastnet Rock in 49, 10N, 17, 40W. Thirteen crewmen were lost Steamer PETEREL (1354grt) rescued the master, twenty-nine crewmen and five gunners and landed them at Lisbon, Portugal.

20 AUGUST 1941

	Heavy cruiser LONDON arrived in the Clyde from Scapa Flow for boiler cleaning.
	German bombing sank fishing trawler **JULIET** (173grt) thirty miles south of Old Head of Kinsale. The entire crew was rescued.
	Convoy ON.9 departed Liverpool escorted by destroyers BEAGLE, BOADICEA, SALISBURY, and WINCHELSEA, corvette NARCISSUS, minesweeper SEAGULL, plus antisubmarine trawlers AYRSHIRE and LADY MADELEINE. Corvette HEATHER joined the convoy on the 21st. Destroyers BOADICEA and WINCHELSEA and the trawlers were detached from the convoy on the 23rd. Destroyers BEAGLE and SALISBURY, corvettes HEATHER and NARCISSUS, and minesweeper SEAGULL were detached from the convoy when it was dispersed on the 25th.
0930	Destroyer BADSWORTH departed Greenock for Scapa Flow to carry out working up to combat efficiency exercises.

22 AUGUST 1941

	Due to a lack of convoy sightings, U.143, U.83, U.101, U.751, U.561, U.557, U.95 and U.141 set up a new patrol line west of the North Channel.
0245	Destroyers SOMALI and ORIBI arrived at Greenock from Scapa Flow escorting aircraft carrier FURIOUS. Destroyer ORIBI continued on to Glasgow for repairs. Destroyer SOMALI returned to Scapa Flow.

23 AUGUST 1941

Convoy OS.4 departed Liverpool escorted by destroyers CALDWELL, CASTLETON, VANOC, VOLUNTEER and WALKER. The destroyers were detached from the convoy on the 28th.
Also departing with the convoy was Free French sloop CHEVREUIL which was detached from the convoy on the 27th, special service vessel FIDELITY, which was detached from the convoy on 2 September, escort vessels GORLESTON and LULWORTH, which were detached from the convoy on 9 September, and Antiaircraft ship PALOMARES which as detached from the convoy on the 28th.
On the 31st, escort vessels SENNEN and TOTLAND joined the convoy and were detached from the convoy on 9 September. On 9 September, destroyer VANSITTART joined the convoy and escorted it into Freetown arriving on 11 September.

24 AUGUST 1941

Antisubmarine whaler **KOS XVI** (258grt) was sunk in a collision with destroyer WOLSEY in the Irish Sea. Damage to the destroyer was minor and did not remove her from service.
German bombing damaged sloop BLACK SWAN while she was escorting a convoy in the Irish Sea. The damage required three weeks to repair at Milford Haven.
A Catalina aircraft sighted and attacked a U-boat thirty miles southwest of the River Tagus. Destroyers BOREAS and WIVERN unsuccessfully searched the area.

25 AUGUST 1941

0800	Destroyer SOMALI arrived at Loch Alsh from Scapa Flow.
1400	After embarking the First Lord of the Admiralty, destroyer SOMALI sailed for Stornoway.

26 AUGUST 1941

	U.141 (ObltzS Schiller) spotted outbound convoy OS.4, but was forced to submerge by the aerial escort before she could reach an attack position.
	Heavy cruiser LONDON departed the Clyde after her boiler cleaning for Scapa Flow.

27 AUGUST 1941

	U.557 directed U.751 into an attack position on convoy OS.4 west of Ireland.
	Convoy ON.10 departed Liverpool. Destroyers KEPPEL, LINCOLN, SABRE, SHIKARI, and VENOMOUS, corvettes ALISMA and DIANELLA, plus antisubmarine trawlers LADY ELSA and MAN O' WAR joined the convoy on the 29th. On 1 September, corvettes DIANTHUS, HONEYSUCKLE, and SNOWBERRY joined the convoy. Destroyers KEPPEL, LINCOLN, SABRE, and SHIKARI were detached from the convoy on 1 September. On 2 September, destroyer NIAGARA plus corvettes ALYSSE, CELANDINE, and COLLINGWOOD joined the convoy. These escorts, less DIANTHUS, were detached from the convoy on 10 September. DIANTHUS was detached from the convoy when it was dispersed on 11 September.
	Leading Airman D. C. Stewart of 1 SFTS at Netheravon was killed when his Master aircraft crashed into the ground at Shrewton LG.
0125 to 0143	U.557 (Ottokar Arnold Paulshen) sank steamer **SAUGOR** (6303grt) (Master James Arthur Aitken Steel) while attacking convoy OS.4 in 53, 36N, 16, 40W. Fifty-two crewmen and seven gunners were lost. Rescue ship PERTH (Master Keith Williamson OBE) rescued the master and twenty-two survivors and landed them at Greenock the next day.
0125 to 0143	U.557 (Ottokar Arnold Paulshen) sank Norwegian steamer **SEGUNDO** (4414grt) (Master Karsten B. Wilhelmsen) while attacking convoy OS.4 in 53, 36N, 16, 40W. The master, five crewmen and the female secretary Gudrun Torgersen (the wife of the first mate) were lost. Escort vessel LULWORTH rescued twenty-seven survivors. Canadian T/Lt C. A. Keefer RCNVR, of escort vessel LULWORTH, drowned rescuing a passenger from Norwegian steamer **INGRIA** (4391grt). Both ships were in convoy OS.4. Keefer was awarded the Albert Medal.
0125 to 0143	U.557 (Ottokar Arnold Paulshen) sank steamer **TREMODA** (4736grt) attacking convoy OS.4 in 53, 36N, 16, 40W. Twenty-six crewmen and six gunners were lost.
0426	U.557 (ObltzS Paulshen) sank steamer **EMBASSAGE** (4954grt) (Master Edward Kiddie) while attacking convoy OS.4 in 54N, 13W. The master, thirty-two crewmen and six gunners were lost.

	Canadian destroyer ASSINIBOINE (Capt G. C. Jones) rescued three survivors on 31 August and landed them at Greenock.

28 AUGUST 1941

	U.557 directed U.71 and U.558 to attack positions on convoy OS.4 in the North Atlantic.
	German bombing damaged tanker DONOVANIA (8149grt) three miles 208° from St Ann's Head. The steamer proceeded to Milford Haven. One crewman was killed.
1230	Destroyer LIVELY arrived at Greenock from Scapa Flow after completing her working up to combat efficiency exercises.
1641	U.558 (Kptlt Krech) sank steamer **OTAIO** (10,298grt) (Master Gilbert Kinnell) while attacking convoy OS.4 about 330 miles west by north of Fastnet Rock in 52, 16N, 17, 50W. Four crewmen were lost and nine crewmen drowned in a small boat. Destroyer VANOC (Lt Cdr S. G. W. Deneys DSO) rescued the master, fifty-three crewmen and four gunners and landed them at Liverpool.

29 AUGUST 1941

	Destroyer ST MARYS was damaged in a collision with troopship ROYAL ULSTERMAN (3244grt) in convoy SD.10 off the west coast of Scotland. The destroyer proceeded to Greenock for temporary repairs, and then proceeded to Liverpool, arriving on 2 September. The destroyer was repaired at Liverpool, completing on 15 December.
	Convoy OG.73 departed Liverpool escorted by destroyers CAMPBELTOWN, ST ALBANS, WANDERER, and WESTCOTT, sloop FOWEY, corvettes GENTIAN, JASMINE, MYOSOTIS, PERIWINKLE, and STONECROP, CAM ship SPRINGBANK, and ocean boarding vessel HILARY. The ocean boarding vessel was detached from the convoy that night. Corvettes BEGONIA and LARKSPUR joined the convoy on the 30th. The destroyers were detached from the convoy on 2 September. On 2 September, corvette HIBISCUS joined the convoy. Corvette GENTIAN was detached from the convoy on 11 September. Destroyers DUNCAN and VIDETTE departed Gibraltar on 6 September joined the convoy on 8 September. Destroyers FARNDALE and WILD SWAN joined the escort on 8 September after refuelling at Ponta Delgada. Destroyer FURY also joined the convoy on 8 September. The convoy arrived at Gibraltar on 13 September.

30 AUGUST 1941

	U.143 spotted convoy ON.12 in the North Channel, but the escort forced her under and she lost contact.
	Convoy WS.11 departed Liverpool on the 30th and the Clyde on the 31st. The convoy included steamers KINA II (9823grt), BHUTAN (6104grt), BARRISTER (6200grt), GLAUCUS (7586grt), MOOLTAN (20,952grt), EMPRESS OF AUSTRALIA (19,665grt), NORTHUMBERLAND (11,558grt), ABOSSO (11,030grt), ORONTES (20,097grt), SCYTHIA (19,761grt), VICEROY OF INDIA (19,267grt), LARGS BAY (14,182grt), GUARDIAN, DUCHESS OF YORK (20,021grt), OTRANTO (20,032grt), CITY OF EDINBURGH (8036grt), GLENORCHY (10,000grt), CITY OF MANCHESTER (8917grt), and MANCHESTER PROGRESS (5620grt). The convoy was escorted by battle cruiser REPULSE, aircraft carrier FURIOUS, light cruiser SHEFFIELD, antiaircraft cruiser CAIRO, AMC DERBYSHIRE, destroyers COSSACK, ZULU, LEGION, LIVELY, ISAAC SWEERS, HIGHLANDER, PIORUN, GARLAND, and WINCHELSEA, sloop SUTLEJ, plus escort ships TOTLAND and SENNEN. Aircraft carrier FURIOUS suffered an engine room defect on the 31st and put into Bangor. She was able to sail at 0548 on 1 September, escorted by destroyer LIVELY, and rejoined the convoy.
	Convoy ON.11 departed Liverpool. The convoy was joined on 1 September by destroyers MALCOLM, SARDONYX, and WATCHMAN, corvettes ARABIS, MONKSHOOD, and PETUNIA, and antisubmarine trawlers NORTHERN GEM, NORTHERN PRIDE, NORTHERN SPRAY, NORTHERN WAVE, and WISTARIA. These escorts were detached from the convoy on 4 September when relieved by destroyer BURWELL, AMCs CALIFORNIA and MALOJA, plus corvettes CHILLIWACK, SPIKENARD, and TRAIL. These escorts were all detached from the convoy when it was dispersed on 11 September.
1000	Battle cruiser REPULSE, light cruiser SHEFFIELD, plus destroyers LIGHTNING, BADSWORTH, and VIVACIOUS arrived in the Clyde from Scapa Flow. The battle cruiser and light cruiser were required for escort duties with convoy WS.11. The destroyers were released to return to Scapa Flow.

Central Atlantic Crossing Zone   Long. W60, 00 – W15, 00   Lat. 49, 00 – N05, 00

2 AUGUST 1941

	U.204 (Kptlt Walter Kell) spotted convoy SL.81 and reported its position to the waiting U-boat attack group.

3 AUGUST 1941

	U.562, U.95, U.588, U.97, U.565, U.431, U.46, U.93, U.205 were allocated to the North Atlantic area, while U.A and U.124 covered the southern area of the North Atlantic until 28 August.

4 AUGUST 1941

	Ocean boarding vessel CAVINA intercepted German steamer **FRANKFURT** (5522grt) west of the Azores in 31, 34N, 37, 42W. The crew scuttled the steamer to avoid capture. CAVINA rescued twenty-six survivors, but a second boatload refused to be picked up and was subsequently lost at sea. CAVINA arrived at Gibraltar with the others on the 11th.
	Corvette VERVAIN broke down with boiler problems at 18, 50N, 20, 35W while on patrol duty. On the 5th, she was able to proceed on one boiler, but by mid-afternoon on the 8th, she could not steam at all with both boilers defective. Corvette CLOVER took her in tow for Freetown, arriving on the 9th.
2055	U.126 (Ernst Bauer) sank fishing trawler **ROBERT MAX** (172grt) with gunfire after she was stopped and the crew departed the ship in a lifeboat in 36, 47N, 21, 15W. The crew of seven landed at Ponta Delgada three days later. Sailing vessel JAMES AND STANLEY (grt) returned the crew to Grand Bank on 15 August.

6 AUGUST 1941

	The German B-service identified the position of convoy HG.68 and set up a patrol line with U.43, U.71, U.96, U.751, U.83, U.75, U.46, U.205, U.559, U.204 and U.372, which failed to make contact.
	U.331 patrolled between Gibraltar and the Azores. U.126, U.94, U.124, U.79, U.109, U.93 and U.371 assembled off Cadiz, Spain for operations against convoy HG.69, which Spanish agents reported as ready to sail. Italian submarines FINZI, MARCONI and VENIERO joined the group.

10 AUGUST 1941

	U.79 spotted convoy HG.69 and alerted U.93, U.94, U.109, U.124, U.126, U.331, and U.371 plus Italian submarines FINZI, MARCONI, and VENIERO to concentrate on the convoy.

12 AUGUST 1941

	After the hunt for convoy HG.69, U.331 and U.123 plus Italian submarine FINZI began their voyage back to port for rest and refits.
	U.129 sighted a convoy and alerted U.563, U.567 and U.206, but they could not find any ships to attack the next day.
	A German Fw200 aircraft of I/KG.40 spotted convoy HG.69 and reported its position.
	The Walrus aircraft from heavy cruiser LONDON bombed a submarine while on her Bay of Biscay patrol in 40, 24N, 29, 51W.

13 AUGUST 1941

	U.124 and Italian submarine VENIERO tried to reach an attack position on convoy HG.69, but failed. Italian submarines MARCONI and FINZI intermittently followed the convoy until forced under on the 14th.
	U.79, U.331 and U.109 were forced to return to port due to depth charge damage. U.93 was forced to return to France with bomb damage.

14 AUGUST 1941

	AMC CIRCASSIA captured Italian steamer **STELLA** (4272grt), which had departed Recife, west of Cape Verde Island at 24, 55N, 40, 23W. She was sent under prize crew to Bermuda, and became the EMPIRE PLANET (4272grt).
0955 1201 1515 1601	U.126 spotted Yugoslavian steamer **SUD** (2689grt) and began to set up a firing position. Italian submarine MARCONI (Cdr Pollina) missed the steamer with a torpedo and then heavily damaged **SUD** (2689grt) with twenty-five rounds of gunfire as she was straggling convoy HG.70 west of Portugal in 41N, 17, 41W. U.126 (KptLt Bauer) came later found the wreck and fired thirty-three rounds of gunfire at the ship, but she remained afloat. U.126 finally sank her with one torpedo. Portuguese steamer ALFERRAREDE (1452grt) later rescued the entire crew of thirty-three.

15 AUGUST 1941

	A patrol group with U.123, U.124, and U.126 plus Italian submarines MARCONI and FINZI found no targets.

16 AUGUST 1941

	A German Fw200 aircraft of I/KG.40 spotted convoy HG.69, but the continued tracking of the convoy became interrupted so that no further attacks could be made.

17 AUGUST 1941

	A German Fw200 aircraft of I/KG.40 spotted convoy OG.71 and reported its position.
	In the late evening, U.201 (ObltzS Adalbert Schnee) picked up convoy OG.71 in the North Atlantic and maintained intermittent track until the 19th.

18 AUGUST 1941

	A German Ju88 reconnaissance aircraft spotted convoy OG.71 in the North Atlantic and radioed its position.

19 AUGUST 1941

	A German Ju88 reconnaissance aircraft spotted convoy OG.71 in the North Atlantic and radioed its position.
	In the night, U.201 spotted convoy OG.71 and directed U.559 (ObltzS Heidtmann) and U.204 (Kptlt Walter Kell) into attack positions.
	U.106 spotted convoy OG.71 later in the evening, but was driven under by the convoy escorts before she could attack.
0205	U.204 sank Norwegian destroyer **BATH** (1060grt) (Lt Cdr C. F. T. Melsom RNorN) (Ex USN **HOPEWELL** (DD-181) while she was travelling behind convoy OG.71 about four hundred miles southwest of Ireland in 49N, 17W. The commander and eighty-eight crewmen were lost. Melsom, T/Sub-Lt J. R. A. Pennick RNVR, T/Surgeon Lt R. Taylor MB, ChB RNVR, and nine RN ratings were lost in the destroyer, including one who later died of wounds. Two more Norwegian officers and sixty-seven Norwegian ratings were lost in the destroyer. Corvette HYDRANGEA picked up thirty-nine and destroyer WANDERER four survivors from the destroyer. All but nine of the survivors in the corvette were transferred to the destroyer for medical attention; two died of wounds en route to Gibraltar.

20 AUGUST 1941

	Italian submarines MARCONI, FINZI and CAPPELLINI set up a patrol line to intercept convoy HG.71. They maintained their stations until the 24th without making any contact.
	Destroyers GURKHA and LEGION joined the escort for convoy OG.71 at sea.

21 AUGUST 1941

	Destroyer VIDETTE joined the convoy OG.71 escort from Gibraltar and was with the convoy until 23 August.
	In the afternoon, another German Fw200 aircraft spotted convoy OG.71 again, but U.201, U.108, U.564, U.106 and U.552 fail to make contact.

22 AUGUST 1941

	Destroyers BOREAS and WIVERN reinforced the convoy OG.71 escort from 22 to 23 August.

23 AUGUST 1941

	Italian submarine CALVI joined the patrol line for convoy HG.71, but also made no contacts.

27 AUGUST 1941

	Canadian AMC PRINCE DAVID reported sighting an unknown warship, possibly of the ADMIRAL HIPPER class, in the Middle Atlantic.

28 AUGUST 1941

	U.111, U.108 and U.125 patrolled the Middle Atlantic west of the Azores to the area around St Paul Rock until 24 September.
	Battleship REVENGE, heavy cruiser DIOMEDE with AMCs CIRCASSIA and ASCANIA formed a strike group to attack the reported German heavy cruiser (see 27 August) in the Middle Atlantic.
	American Task Group TG.2.5 with aircraft carrier YORKTOWN (CV-5), light cruiser BROOKLYN (CL-40), plus destroyers ROE (DD-418), EBERLE (DD-430) and GRAYSON (DD-435) began a search for the reported German heavy cruiser in the Middle Atlantic. YORKTOWN (CV-5) launched aircraft to search for the reported ship.

29 AUGUST 1941

	German air reconnaissance spotted convoy HG.71 southwest of Ireland, but could not make an attack or direct any U-boats to an intercept.

UK East Coast

Long. W04, 00 – E03, 00   Lat. N58, 30 – N51, 30

1 AUGUST 1941

	German bombing heavily damaged steamer **TRIDENT** (4317grt) four miles 208° from 20C Buoy, Tyne. The entire crew was rescued, but she sank the next day.

2 AUGUST 1941

	German bombing damaged steamer KOOLGA (1110grt) near 54.D Buoy, Smiths Knoll, in 52, 40, 03N, 02, 11E. She arrived in tow at Great Yarmouth on the 3rd.

3 AUGUST 1941

	Heavy cruiser BERWICK departed Rosyth for Scapa Flow and arrived later that day. Turbine problems had not yet been repaired and she was only capable of a maximum of 22.5 knots.
2100	Minesweeper NIGER arrived at Dundee from Scapa Flow for a refit, which was completed on 28 September. She returned to Dundee on 6 October for further refitting, which continued until 15 December.

4 AUGUST 1941

	Ex-American Coast Guard cutter/escort ship BANFF was damaged in a collision with a Thames lighter in the Thames Estuary. She had just departed Tilbury, and returned following the collision for more repairs, which were completed on the 8th.

6 AUGUST 1941

	Antisubmarine trawler **AGATE** (627grt) (Lt L. H. Cline RNVR) was lost when she ran aground off Cromer in heavy weather. Cline, T/Sub-Lt P. G. Beard RNVR, T/Sub-Lt A. G. Tree RNVR and the entire crew were lost.
1900	Destroyer IMPULSIVE departed the Humber for Scapa Flow after completing her refit.

7 AUGUST 1941

	A German aerial mine sank motor minesweeper **MMS.39** (226grt) in the Thames Estuary.
	German bombing damaged tanker GOLD SHELL (8208grt) north of Cromer in 55, 05N, 01, 32E. She was towed to Hull and then taken to Middlesbrough for repairs.
	T/Sub-Lt (A) J. R. Allen RNVR, Leading Airman A. A. Shields, and Mr. J. Goddard were killed when their Albacore aircraft of 820 Squadron crashed off Stokes Bay Pier.

9 AUGUST 1941

	German bombing damaged steamer GLENDALOUGH (868grt) north of Great Yarmouth in 52, 56N, 02, 02E. She was towed to Yarmouth Roads, and then to Hull.
	A battery and ammunition explosion damaged Norwegian submarine B.1 while she was under repair at Blyth.
0615	Destroyer ELECTRA, her refit completed, departed Sheerness as additional escort for convoy FN.503. German bombing sank steamer **CORDENE** (2345grt) while attacking the convoy off Cromer in 53, 00, 32N, 01, 48, 30E, but the entire crew was rescued. ELECTRA arrived at Scapa Flow on the 11th.
0700	Destroyer ACTIVE arrived at Rosyth from Scapa Flow for boiler cleaning.

10 AUGUST 1941

	Six RAF bombers damaged German patrol boat V.1506 off Ostend, Belgium.

11 AUGUST 1941

0600	Antiaircraft cruiser CURAÇOA arrived at Rosyth from Scapa Flow to clean boilers and carry out repairs.
2039	Antiaircraft ship ALYNBANK arrived at Methil with convoy WN.65 from Pentland Firth.

12 AUGUST 1941

	German bombing damaged steamer EAGLESCLIFFE HALL (1900grt) 1/2 mile south of S.2 Buoy, approximately two miles east of Sunderland. She was towed to Sunderland arriving on the 13th.
	Light cruiser SHEFFIELD departed Rosyth after her refit for Scapa Flow to work up to combat efficiency.
	A mine sank auxiliary vessel **EXPRESS** (16grt) one mile southwest of East Spaniard Buoy off Whitstable.
1130	Antiaircraft ship ALYNBANK departed Methil and escorted convoy EC.58 from May Island to Pentland Firth.

13 AUGUST 1941

1630	Destroyer ECHO arrived at Sheerness from Scapa Flow for a refit.

14 AUGUST 1941

	Free French submarine RUBIS departed Dundee to lay Minefield FD.33 off Jaederen.
0945	Destroyers INGLEFIELD, IMPULSIVE, and ECLIPSE arrived at Rosyth with battle cruiser RENOWN. RENOWN began a much-needed refit while INGLEFIELD began boiler cleaning.
1600	Destroyer MATABELE departed Barrow to carry out sea trials after her repairs and arrived at Scapa Flow on the 16th.

15 AUGUST 1941

0720	Battle cruiser REPULSE departed Rosyth escorted by destroyers IMPULSIVE, ECLIPSE, and ACTIVE for Scapa Flow.

16 AUGUST 1941

	German bombing damaged tugboat **NESS POINT** with a bomb near miss at Lowestoft. She sank, but was raised on the 23rd and repaired.
1800	Destroyer VIVACIOUS departed the Humber for Scapa Flow to work up to combat efficiency. En route, the destroyer developed engine defects and put into Rosyth for repairs.

17 AUGUST 1941

	German bombing damaged steamer KINDERSLEY (1999grt) three miles southeast by east of B.1 Buoy (Blyth). The steamer arrived at Blyth on the 18th.
	Light cruiser PENELOPE departed Rosyth for Scapa Flow to work up to combat efficiency after long repairs.
0500	Destroyer LAMERTON departed Rosyth for Scapa Flow to carry out working up to combat efficiency exercises.
1800	Antiaircraft cruiser CURAÇOA departed Rosyth after completing boiler cleaning and proceeded north to join with convoy WN.68 in Moray Firth. She escorted convoy WN.68 to May Island. Off May Island on the 18th, CURAÇOA transferred to convoy EC.61 and escorted it northward. The convoy was attacked off Aberdeen by German bombers, but no damage was done. In Pentland Firth on the 19th, the CURAÇOA parted company with convoy EC.61 and arrived at Scapa Flow.
1930	Antiaircraft ship ALYNBANK arrived at Methil with convoy WN.67 from Pentland Firth and continued on to Rosyth to clean boilers.

18 AUGUST 1941

	A mine damaged destroyer QUORN between Harwich and Chatham. The damage was repaired at Chatham and was completed on 13 September.

19 AUGUST 1941

	Destroyer INGLEFIELD departed Rosyth after boiler cleaning to return to Scapa Flow.
	A mine sank motor barge **GOLDEN GRAIN** (101grt) in 51, 35, 18N, 01, 03, 18E. The crew of three were all lost.

20 AUGUST 1941

	The German 4th S-Boat Flotilla (Kptlt Bätge) attacked a convoy off Cromer.
	S.48 (ObltzS v. Mirbach) sank Polish steamer **CZESTOCHOWA** (1971grt) off Cromer in 53, 11, 30N, 01, 06E. One crewman was lost.
	S.48 damaged steamer DALEWOOD (2774grt) off Cromer in 53, 11, 24N, 01, 05, 30E. Three crewmen and a naval gunner were lost. The steamer was towed to Humber badly damaged aft.

21 AUGUST 1941

0600	Battleship KING GEORGE V arrived off May Island escorted by destroyers INGLEFIELD, LIGHTNING, and PUNJABI. KING GEORGE V and destroyer PUNJABI continued to Rosyth, where PUNJABI began a boiler cleaning. Destroyers INGLEFIELD and LIGHTNING returned to Scapa Flow, arriving that mid afternoon.

24 AUGUST 1941

	Free French submarine RUBIS arrived at Dundee for repairs escorted by destroyer WOLFHOUND.
	A German FAB-XI aerial mine sank steamer **SKAGERAK** (1283grt) in the River Orwell, Harwich, in 51, 58, 08N, 01, 16, 06E. Seventeen crewmen and the pilot were killed. The steamer was believed to be the first ship sunk by the new German mine.
2300	Destroyer TARTAR arrived in the Tyne escorting damaged destroyer ACHATES in tow of tug ASSURANCE and with salvage vessel LE LUTTEUR from Skaalefjord.

25 AUGUST 1941

	Light cruiser KENYA departed Rosyth after repairs and returned to Scapa Flow.
2200	Cruiser minelayer WELSHMAN departed Rosyth to practice laying mines and then proceed to Scapa Flow.

26 AUGUST 1941

	Destroyer TARTAR departed the Tyne and joined convoy FS.577 as additional antiaircraft protection to the Humber.

27 AUGUST 1941

1222	Destroyer TARTAR arrived at Sheerness to disembark ammunition prior to going to London to begin her refit.

28 AUGUST 1941

1520	Destroyer INTREPID arrived at Sheerness to disembark ammunition. The destroyer then proceeded to London for her refit.
1600	Destroyer TARTAR arrived at London for her refit, which continued until 17 October.

29 AUGUST 1941

1400	Destroyer INTREPID arrived at London from Sheerness for her refit.

30 AUGUST 1941

	Heavy cruiser LONDON departed London for Akreyri and Hvalfjord, Iceland.
0530	Destroyer ASHANTI departed the Tyne to return to Scapa Flow after completing her long repairs, but a defect developed on passage and she arrived at Rosyth for repairs on 1 September.

31 AUGUST 1941

1945	Destroyer BEDOUIN departed the Humber to return to Scapa Flow upon the completion of her refit, and arrived at 1830 on 1 September.

North Sea
Long. E03, 00 – E09, 00   Lat. N58, 30 – N51, 00

8 AUGUST 1941

	A RAF aerial mine sank Danish steamer VENUS (2546grt) off the Schlei River delta.

9 AUGUST 1941

	A collision sank motor gunboat MGB.62 (28grt) in the North Sea.

10 AUGUST 1941

	German destroyer THEODOR RIEDEL departed Germany to join the 6th Destroyer Flotilla in northern Norway.

14 AUGUST 1941

	RAF Coastal Command aircraft sank German steamer LOTTE HALM (1198grt) off Borkum.

20 AUGUST 1941

	German trawler CHARLOTTE (200grt) became stranded and was lost in the North Sea.

21 AUGUST 1941

	Free French submarine RUBIS (Lt Cdr Rousselot) laid Minefield FD.33 off Egerö, Norway. Later in the day, a mine sank Finnish steamer HOGLAND (4360grt) northwest of EGERO in 58, 16N, 04, 48E. The German 11th Minesweeping Flotilla was ordered to clear the minefield.
1535	Free French submarine RUBIS attacked two steamers off Norway. In the attack, two torpedoes exploded shortly after leaving the torpedo tubes and damaged the submarine.

22 AUGUST 1941

	Early in the day, Free French submarine RUBIS was able to signal her situation (see 21 August) to the Fleet. Antiaircraft cruiser CURAÇOA, which was already at sea with convoy WN.70, destroyers LIVELY and LIGHTNING, destroyer WOLFHOUND, antisubmarine trawlers CLEVELLA and FILEY BAY, plus tug ABEILLE IV were sent to assist. Destroyers LIVELY and LIGHTNING returned to Scapa Flow on the 24th. En route, destroyer LIGHTNING rescued three Norwegians in a dinghy from Bergen, Norway.

23 AUGUST 1941

	RAF Coastal Command aerial mine damaged Finnish steamer WISA (3845grt) in the Ems estuary. She was towed into Emden for repairs.
	Minesweeper SPEEDWELL was damaged in a collision with steamer ST JULIEN (1952grt) in the North Sea. The damage to the minesweeper was minor.

25 AUGUST 1941

	The first ships of the German 12th Submarine Chaser Flotilla departed Wilhelmshaven for Norway.

26 AUGUST 1941

	RAF Coastal Command aircraft damaged German steamer CITY OF EMDEN (grt) northwest of the Hook of Holland.

English Channel

Long. W07, 00 – E01, 30   Lat. N51, 00 – N49, 00

7 AUGUST 1941

	Destroyer SOMALI departed Southampton for Greenock after completing her refit.

11 AUGUST 1941

	The German 4th S-Boat Flotilla (KptLt Bätge) attacked a convoy off Dungeness.
	S.49 (LtzS Günther) sank steamer **SIR RUSSELL** (1548grt) in heavy weather six cables 349° from No.10 Buoy in 50, 55N, 00, 58E. The entire crew was rescued.
	S.20 also claimed sinking a 4000-ton steamer, but there were no confirmation data.

20 AUGUST 1941

	Battleship DUKE OF YORK (Capt C. H. J. Harcourt, CBE) was completed.

21 AUGUST 1941

	German bombing damaged Free French drifter **GLORIA IN EXCELSIO DEO** off Southampton. The drifter sank, but was later raised and repaired.

22 AUGUST 1941

	German bombing sank netlayer **TONBRIDGE** (683grt) (T/A/Lt Cdr D. E. Brown RNR) three cables 108° from Scroby Elbow Buoy off Yarmouth. Brown and thirty-four ratings were lost.

28 AUGUST 1941

	Submarine PARTHIAN departed Portsmouth, England, for Portsmouth, New Hampshire, for a refit, which was completed on 30 January 1942.

30 AUGUST 1941

2000	Destroyers BERKELEY and ATHERSTONE departed Portsmouth to hunt for a U-boat in Operation ILIAD. After an unsuccessful search, the destroyers returned to Portsmouth.

Bay of Biscay

Long. W15, 00 – E03, 00   Lat. N49, 00 – N40, 00

9 AUGUST 1941

	After a commercial aircraft sighted a suspicious merchant ship in 46, 37N, 09, 22W, destroyer WISHART, which had been detached from convoy HG.34F on the 8th, was directed to investigate. Light cruiser HERMIONE departed Gibraltar on the 9th to attempt to locate merchant ship. On the 10th, heavy cruiser LONDON was detached from convoy WS.10 and also proceeded to this position. No contact was made by any of the searching warships on the suspicious merchant ship. On the 11th, HERMIONE was ordered to return to Gibraltar, arriving on the 13th.

22 AUGUST 1941

>1200	After several air reconnaissance reports, U.564 (ObltzS Suhren) spotted convoy OG.71 in the afternoon and directed U.201 into an attack position.
>1200	Eight German Ju88 aircraft of KGR.606 unsuccessfully attacked convoy OG.71. The convoy antiaircraft fire damaged the Ju88 of the Staffel leader (Hptm Heßling), who was killed when his aircraft crashed on landing at Bordeaux, France.
2331	U.564 (ObltzS Reinhard Suhren) made four attacks on convoy OG.71 and sank steamer **CLONLARA**

	(1203grt) (Master Joseph Reynolds) west of Aveiro, Portugal, in 40, 43N, 11, 39W. Six crewmen and all fourteen survivors from sunken steamer **ALVA** were lost. Corvette CAMPION (Lt Cdr A. Johnson) rescued the master and twelve crewmen and landed them at Gibraltar on 24 August.
2331	U.564 sank steam tug **EMPIRE OAK** (484grt) (Master Frederick Edward Christian) while attacking convoy OG.71 west of Aveiro, Portugal, in 40, 43N, 11, 39W. Eleven crewmen and three gunners were missing plus eight **ALVA** survivors and six **AGUILA** survivors were missing. Corvette CAMPANULA (Lt Cdr R. V. E. Case DSC) rescued the master, three crewmen and four gunners. Destroyer VELOX (Lt Cdr E. G. Ropner DSC) collected the survivors and rushed them to Gibraltar for medical treatment.

23 AUGUST 1941

	U.564 (ObltzS Reinhard Suhren) sank corvette **ZINNIA** (900grt) (Lt Cdr C. G. Cuthbertson DSO RNR) while attacking convoy OG.71 northwest of Lisbon in 40, 43N, 11, 39W. The corvette exploded and quickly sank. A/Sub-Lt M. T. Edwards RNVR, T/Sub-Lt J. Halliday RNVR, T/Sub-Lt J. B. Miller RNVR and forty-six ratings were lost. Corvette CAMPION (Lt Cdr A. Johnson) rescued the survivors.
	German AMC SCHIFF.36/ORION (FKpt Weyher) arrived at Bordeaux, France, escorted by U.75 and U.205, after raiding in the Atlantic, Pacific, and Indian Oceans for 510 days. She sank nine and a half ships for 57,744 tons and she shared seven kills with AMC SCHIFF.45/KOMET.
0214	U.201 (ObltzS Adalbert Schnee) sank tanker **ALDERGROVE** (1974grt) (Master Hugh William McLean) while attacking convoy OG.71 northwest of Lisbon in 40, 43N, 11, 39W. One naval rating was lost. Corvette CAMPANULA (Lt Cdr R. V. E. Case DSC) rescued the master, thirty-two crewmen and five gunners from lifeboats two hours later and landed them at Gibraltar the next day.
0214	U.201 sank steamer **STORK** (787grt) (Master Evan Atterbury Morris Williams) while attacking convoy OG.71 northwest of Lisbon in 40, 43N, 11, 30W. The master, sixteen crewmen and two gunners were lost. She was carrying canned gasoline and quickly went up in flames. Corvette CAMPION rescued one crewman and two gunners and landed them at Gibraltar on the 24th. Other sources claim that corvette WALLFLOWER (Lt Cdr I. J. Tyson) rescued the survivors.
0335	U.564 damaged Norwegian steamer **SPIND** (2129grt) (Master Johannes Berg Jonassen) after she was dispersed from convoy OG.71 at West of Portugal in 40, 43N, 11, 39W.
0648	U.552 (ObltzS Topp) unsuccessfully attacked damaged Norwegian steamer **SPIND** (2129grt) with two torpedoes in 40, 43N, 11, 39W.
0655 0715	U.552 fired twenty rounds of 88-mm shells and 200 rounds of 20-mm rounds before they were forced to dive when destroyer BOREAS arrived. **SPIND** managed to fire two shots from her gun before the twenty-five men aboard abandoned the ship. BOREAS attacked U.552 with depth charges, but caused no damage. BOREAS tried to extinguish the fire on the steamer after rescuing the crew and then finally scuttled the wreck with gunfire. The survivors were landed in Gibraltar on 25 August.

29 AUGUST 1941

	Italian blockade-runners HIMALAYA (6240grt) and AFRICANA (5869grt) arrived at the Gironde River, France, from Brazil.
	An RAF reconnaissance aircraft spotted the German battle cruisers SCHARNHORST and GNEISENAU with heavy cruiser PRINZ EUGEN at Brest, France, easing fears caused by the report of HIPPER Class cruiser at sea west of France.

30 AUGUST 1941

	German tanker BENNO (8306grt) (ex Norwegian **OLE JACOB** (8306grt)) departed Bordeaux, France, for Kobe, Japan.

West of Gibraltar
Long. W15, 00 – W05, 30   Lat. N40, 00 – N30, 00

1 AUGUST 1941

	Submarines SEVERN and CLYDE escorted convoys HG.69 and HG.70 until 21 August.

2 AUGUST 1941

	Tanker LAURELWOOD (7347grt) and Panamanian tanker NORVINN (6322grt) departed Gibraltar for Curaçao and Trinidad, respectively, escorted until dark on the 4th by destroyer WISHART and antisubmarine trawler LADY HOGARTH.

5 AUGUST 1941

	Minelaying cruiser MANXMAN and light cruiser ARETHUSA departed Gibraltar for Loch Alsh and the Clyde,

respectively. ARETHUSA arrived in the Clyde on the 10th.

6 AUGUST 1941

Destroyer HIGHLANDER arrived at Gibraltar from Freetown.

Convoy HG.34F departed Gibraltar with steamers THERMOPYLAE (6655grt) and TALABOT (6798grt) for New York plus LEINSTER (4302grt) and AMERIKA (10,218grt) for Liverpool, escorted by destroyers FORESIGHT, FOXHOUND, HIGHLANDER, and WISHART.
Destroyer WISHART was detached from the convoy on the 8th and proceeded to Southampton for a refit.
Destroyer FORESIGHT was detached from the convoy on the 8th to escort convoy OG.70 and return to Gibraltar.
Destroyer FOXHOUND was detached from the convoy on the 13th for her refit at Sheerness.
Destroyer HIGHLANDER arrived at Liverpool with LEINSTER and AMERIKA on the 14th.

7 AUGUST 1941

Submarine SEVERN unsuccessfully attacked a submarine west of Gibraltar in 34, 48N, 13, 04W. Some sources claim that SEVERN sank Italian submarine **BIANCHI**, but she had already been sunk by TIGRIS in July.

The 17th Motor Launch Flotilla of ML.242, ML.266, ML.256, ML.261, ML.263, ML.265, and ML.274 arrived at Gibraltar, escorted by antisubmarine whaler SOUTHERN GEM.

8 AUGUST 1941

ML.272 of the 17th Motor Launch Flotilla arrived at Gibraltar escorted by antisubmarine whaler SOUTHERN PRIDE.

Battle cruiser RENOWN and troopship PASTEUR (29,253grt) departed Gibraltar escorted by destroyers COSSACK, MAORI, SIKH and LIGHTNING to return to Britain.
PASTEUR carried fifteen officers and one hundred fifty-seven ratings from damaged light cruiser MANCHESTER to the Clyde.
U.93 spotted the group, but was unable to reach an attack position due to their high speed.

9 AUGUST 1941

Convoy HG.70 departed Gibraltar escorted by destroyers ERIDGE and AVON VALE, submarine CLYDE, corvettes BEGONIA, JASMINE, LARKSPUR, PIMPERNEL, and RHODODENDRON, plus antisubmarine trawlers LADY HOGARTH and LADY SHIRLEY. The trawlers were detached from the convoy that night.
Destroyer FAULKNOR joined the convoy on the 10th as Senior Office Escort. She was returning to England for turbine repairs at Portsmouth.
CLYDE was detached from the convoy and arrived at Gibraltar on the 11th. On the 11th, destroyers ENCOUNTER, NESTOR, sloop DEPTFORD, and corvette CONVOLVULUS joined the convoy. All but NESTOR were detached from the convoy that evening.
On the 12th, BOREAS and WILD SWAN joined the convoy. They had departed Gibraltar on the 11th with destroyers DUNCAN and FORESTER, later joined by destroyer FURY, for an antisubmarine sweep west. After the sweep, the two destroyers proceeded to join HG.70.
Sloop STORK joined the convoy on the 13th and was detached from the convoy that evening.
BOREAS and NESTOR were detached from the convoy on the 13th, AVON VALE and ERIDGE were detached from the convoy on the 14th, and WILD SWAN was detached from the convoy on the 15th. They all arrived at Gibraltar on the 16th.
Destroyer COSSACK joined the convoy on the 14th and was detached from the convoy that night.
Destroyer DUNCAN, which departed Gibraltar on the 13th, and sloop BLACK SWAN joined the convoy on the 15th. BLACK SWAN was detached from the convoy on the 21st.
DUNCAN arrived at Londonderry on the 20th; she departed on the 22nd to join convoy OG.72 for her return to Gibraltar. The convoy arrived at Liverpool on the 23rd.

Destroyer DUNCAN departed Gibraltar to join destroyers WIVERN, WILD SWAN, and BOREAS from Freetown. WIVERN had developed condenser problems and was in tow. The four destroyers arrived at Gibraltar on the 10th.

Submarine SEVERN sighted an Italian submarine in 35, 16N, 10, 09W, but the Italian submerged before SEVERN could attack.

| 2330 | Light cruiser HERMIONE departed Gibraltar to attempt to locate the unknown merchant ship sighted in the Bay of Biscay. |

10 AUGUST 1941

Corvettes FLEUR DE LYS and AZALEA departed Gibraltar to join arriving tanker CAPSA (8229grt) from Trinidad. Destroyer VIDETTE and antisubmarine trawler ST NECTAN departed Gibraltar to join arriving tanker BENEDICK (6978grt) from Curaçao. Both groups arrived at Gibraltar on the 17th.

Submarine SEVERN arrived at Gibraltar from her patrol in the Bay of Biscay.

11 AUGUST 1941

Submarine PARTHIAN departed Gibraltar for Portsmouth.

U.93 and U.94 made contact with convoy HG.69 west of Gibraltar, but were driven under by the escorts.

Italian submarine MARCONI (Lt Cdr Pollina) missed sloop DEPTFORD and corvette CONVOLVULUS with a torpedo attack west of Gibraltar in 37N, 10W. MARCONI claimed to have sunk sloop DEPTFORD, which had been detached from convoy OG.70 to join convoy HG.70 in 37, 16N, 09, 50W, but she was undamaged, and with corvette CONVOLVULUS carried out a search for the submarine.

A German Fw200 aircraft of I/KG.40 sank steamer **EMPIRE HURST** (2852grt), which had fallen astern of convoy HG.70, and was being escorted by antisubmarine trawler LADY HOGARTH in 36, 48N, 09, 50W. Twenty-six crewmen were killed. LADY HOGARTH rescued nine survivors.

Destroyers FORESTER, FURY, DUNCAN, BOREAS, and WILD SWAN departed Gibraltar on a shipping sweep. BOREAS and WILD SWAN were then ordered to join convoy HG.70, while FORESTER, FURY, and DUNCAN returned to Gibraltar late on the 11th.

16 AUGUST 1941

The 17th Motor Launch Flotilla of ML.242, ML.266, ML.256, ML.261, ML.263, ML.265, ML.272 and ML.274 departed Gibraltar escorted by antisubmarine whalers SOUTHERN PRIDE and SOUTHERN GEM plus antisubmarine trawler ARRAN for Bathurst.

Corvettes JONQUIL and COREOPSIS departed Gibraltar escorting ocean boarding vessel CAVINA. Once out of the local approaches, the corvettes joined arriving tanker CARDIUM (8236grt).

18 AUGUST 1941

Convoy HG.71 departed Gibraltar escorted by destroyer WILD SWAN, sloop DEPTFORD, corvettes AURICULA, CONVOLVULUS, MARIGOLD, and SAMPHIRE plus antisubmarine trawler ST NECTAN.
The trawler was detached from the convoy that night.
Destroyer WILD SWAN was detached from the convoy on the 23rd and destroyer VIMY, which departed Gibraltar on the 19th, relieved her in the convoy on that date.
Destroyer VIMY was detached from the convoy on the 25th and arrived at Gibraltar on the 28th.
Antiaircraft ship PALOMARES joined the convoy on the 29th.
Destroyers CALDWELL and CASTLETON joined the convoy on the 30th.
The convoy arrived at Liverpool on 1 September.

Destroyers AVON VALE and ERIDGE departed Gibraltar for Freetown, Sierra Leone, en route to the Mediterranean Fleet.

Submarine CLYDE departed Gibraltar for a patrol in the Atlantic.

20 AUGUST 1941

Destroyer VIDETTE departed Gibraltar to join the escort for convoy OG.71 at sea.

Submarine SEVERN departed Gibraltar for a patrol in the North Atlantic.

21 AUGUST 1941

Steamer ATLANTIC COAST (890grt) departed Gibraltar for Freetown, Sierra Leone, escorted by antisubmarine trawler STELLA CARINA until dark.

22 AUGUST 1941

Corvettes FLEUR DE LYS and AZALEA departed Gibraltar escorting tankers BENEDICK (6978grt) and CAPSA (8229grt) out to sea. The corvettes then joined arriving tanker CORDELIA (8190grt) and escorted her to Gibraltar, arriving on the 31st.

25 AUGUST 1941

Corvettes JONQUIL and COREOPSIS arrived at Gibraltar, escorting tanker CARDIUM (8236grt) from Curaçao, Lesser Antilles.

26 AUGUST 1941

Minelayer MANXMAN departed Gibraltar and arrived back in England on the 30th.

29 AUGUST 1941

Destroyers VIMY, VIDETTE, and WILD SWAN, corvettes CAMPANULA, WALLFLOWER, CAMPION, and HYDRANGEA departed Gibraltar with motor launches ML.170 and ML.172 to patrol in the Straits of Gibraltar to intercept any U-boats attempting passage into the Mediterranean from the North Atlantic.

31 AUGUST 1941

Australian destroyer NESTOR departed Gibraltar to refuel at Ponta Delgada prior to joining convoy WS.11.

	She then proceeded with the convoy to Freetown, Sierra Leone.
	Destroyer FORESIGHT, FURY, and FORESTER departed Gibraltar to carry out antisubmarine patrols in the Gibraltar Strait during the night.
	Destroyer DUNCAN arrived at Gibraltar after escorting convoy OG.72.
	Corvettes AZALEA and FLEUR DE LYS arrived at Gibraltar with tanker CORDELIA (8190grt), arriving from Curaçao.

West of North Africa
Long. W15, 00 – E11, 00   Lat. N30, 00 – N00, 00

1 AUGUST 1941

	The German B-service identified the location of Convoy SL.81 with eighteen ships escorted by destroyers WANDERER, CAMPBELTOWN, and the Norwegian ST ALBANS with corvettes LA MALOUINE, ZINNIA, CAMPANULA, BLUEBELL, WALLFLOWER, CARNATION, HELIOTROPE and HYDRANGEA. A new U-boat patrol line was established to engage the convoy.

3 AUGUST 1941

0800	Destroyers WIVERN, WILD SWAN, and BOREAS departed Freetown, Sierra Leone, and proceed to Bathurst to refuel en route to Gibraltar.

5 AUGUST 1941

	Convoy SL.83 departed Freetown, Sierra Leone, escorted by AMC CATHAY and AMC CITY OF DURBAN to 28 August, destroyer BRILLIANT to 11 August, sloop MILFORD to 9 August, plus corvettes ANCHUSA, ASPHODEL, and CALENDULA to 8 August and LAVENDER to 7 August. The corvettes joined convoy OS.1 and escorted it to Freetown. Sloop WELLINGTON escorted the convoy to 28 August and escort vessels CULVER escorted the convoy to 28 August and LANDGUARD escorted the convoy to 23 July after they joined the convoy on the 8th. On the 22nd, OBV CORINTHIAN joined the convoy and provided escort to 28 August. Destroyers CHELSEA and WOLVERINE joined the convoy on the 24th to 28 August. The convoy arrived at Liverpool on the 28th.

8 AUGUST 1941

	Destroyers VANSITTART and VELOX joined aircraft carrier EAGLE and light cruiser DUNEDIN at sea and escorted them to Freetown, Sierra Leone, arriving on the 10th.

12 AUGUST 1941

	Italian submarine TAZZOLI attacked and claimed to have damaged steamer SANGARA (5445grt) in 4N, 9W, but SANGARA was unharmed.

15 AUGUST 1941

	Convoy SL.84 departed Freetown escorted by destroyer BRILLIANT, corvettes AMARANTHUS, ARMERIA, MIGNONETTE, and WOODRUFF, plus antisubmarine trawlers SARABANDE and ST WISTAN to 19 August. On the 18th, sloops FOLKESTONE and LONDONDERRY joined the convoy to 8 September. Sloop WESTON joined the convoy on the 20th to 8 September. Destroyer ST ALBANS joined the convoy on 2 September to 8 September. CAM ship SPRINGBANK and destroyers CAMPBELTOWN, WANDERER, and WESTCOTT joined the convoy on 3 September to 8 September. The convoy arrived at Liverpool on 8 September.

19 AUGUST 1941

	Italian submarine TAZZOLI (CF Fecia di Cossato) sank Norwegian tanker **SILDRA** (7313grt) west of Africa in 05, 30N, 12, 50W. The entire crew was rescued.

23 AUGUST 1941

	AMC CIRCASSIA departed Freetown to search for a German auxiliary cruiser reported by radio intercepts and air reconnaissance in the Middle Atlantic, south of Bermuda.

24 AUGUST 1941

	In Operation CUTTING, steamer LADY DENISON-PENDER (1984grt) departed Freetown escorted by sloop MILFORD to lift and cut about sixty miles of the Dakar to Pernambuco communications cable. The ship arrived in position on the 28th and the operation required one week to complete.
	Convoy SL.85 departed Freetown escorted by destroyer VANSITTART to 28 August, sloop MILFORD to 28 August, plus corvettes ASTER, BURDOCK, STARWORT, and VERVAIN to 28 August. On the 28th, sloop SANDWICH, Free French sloop COMMANDANT DOMINE, and antisubmarine yacht

PHILANTE joined the convoy to 17 September.
On 2 September, corvette WALLFLOWER joined the convoy to 11 September.
On 11 September, destroyers BOREAS, CALDWELL, VANOC, VOLUNTEER, and WALKER plus corvettes BLUEBELL, CAMPANULA, CAMPION, CARNATION, HELIOTROPE, HYDRANGEA, LA MALOUINE, and MALLOW joined the convoy.
Sloop LEITH joined the convoy on 14 September. The convoy arrived at Liverpool on 17 September with ocean boarding vessel CAVINA and the escorts that joined on 11 and 14 September.

26 AUGUST 1941

Convoy ST.1 of four steamers departed Freetown and arrived at Takoradi on the 31st.

28 AUGUST 1941

Force F departed Freetown with aircraft carrier EAGLE, heavy cruiser DORSETSHIRE, light cruiser NEWCASTLE and tanker ECHODALE to cover troopship DURBAN CASTLE (17,388grt) and AMC QUEEN OF BERMUDA.

SOUTH ATLANTIC OCEAN

East of South America   Long. W70, 00 – W30, 00   Lat. N05, 00 - S60, 00

15 AUGUST 1941

After being intercepted by light cruiser DESPATCH and AMC PRETORIA CASTLE the crew of German steamer **NORDERNEY** (3667grt) scuttled the ship northeast of the Amazon estuary.

22 AUGUST 1941

Brazilian authorities captured Italian liner **CONTE GRANDE** (23,861grt) at Santos, Brazil. She became the American troopship MONTICELLO (AP-61) (23,861grt).

25 AUGUST 1941

Argentine authorities seized Italian steamer **CERVINO** (4363grt) at Buenos Aires. She became the Argentine RIO PRIMERO (4363grt).
Argentine authorities seized Italian steamer **DANTE** (4901grt) at Buenos Aires. She became the Argentine RIO SEGUNDO (4901grt).
Argentine authorities seized Italian steamer **INES CORRADO** (5159grt) at Bahia Blanca. She became the Argentine RIO DIAMANTE (5159grt).
Argentine authorities seized Italian steamer **MONTE SANTO** (5850grt) and she became the Argentine RIO COLORADO (5850grt).
Argentine authorities seized Italian steamer **MARISTELLA** (4862grt) and she became the Argentine RIO ATUELE (4862grt).
Argentine authorities seized Italian steamer **PELORUM** (5314grt) and she became the Argentine RIO CHICO (5314grt).
Argentine authorities seized Italian steamer **VITTORIO VENETO** (4595grt) at Bahia Blanca and she became the Argentine RIO GUALEGUAY (4595grt).
Argentine authorities seized Italian steamer **VOLUNTAS** (5597grt) at Nececheo and she became the Argentine RIO TEUCO (5597grt).
Argentine authorities seized Italian steamer **AMABILITAS** (5245grt) at Bahia Blanca and she became the Argentine RIO BERMEJO (5245grt).
Argentine authorities seized Italian steamer **CAPO ROSA** (4699grt) at Buenos Aires and she became the Argentine RIO DULCE (4699grt).
Argentine authorities seized Italian steamer **CASTELBIANCO** (4895grt) at San Lorenzo and she became the Argentine RIO CHUBUT (4900grt).
Argentine authorities seized Italian steamer **GIANFRANCO** (8081grt) at Buenos Aires and she became the Argentine RIO SALADO (8081grt).
Argentine authorities seized Italian steamer **TESEO** (4966grt) at Santa Fe and she became the Argentine RIO CORRIENTES (4966grt).
Argentine authorities seized Italian steamer **VALDARNO** (5696grt) at Buenos Aires and she became the Argentine RIO NEUQUÉN (5696grt).
Argentine authorities seized Italian steamer **FORTUNSTELLA** (4864grt) at Necocheo and she became the Argentine RIO TERCERO (4864grt).
Argentine authorities seized Italian steamer **PRINCIPESSA MARIA** (8918grt) at Buenos Aires and she be-

came the Argentine RIO DE LA PLATA (8918grt).

West of South Africa
Long. W30, 00 – E25, 00   Lat. S00, 00 – S60, 00

20 AUGUST 1941

Minesweeping trawler **LORINDA** (348grt) (Lt J. H. Seelye NZRNVR) was lost through engine trouble and a fire off Freetown in 06, 30S, 11, 37W, while en route to Port Harcourt, South Africa, in company with trawler BALTA. Corvette LAVENDER proceeded to the area to render assistance. Trawler BALTA rescued entire crew and took them to Freetown.

26 AUGUST 1941

Heavy cruiser HAWKINS arrived at Simon's Town, South Africa.

BALTIC SEA

Kattegat and Skagerrak
Long. E09, 00 – E12, 00   Lat. N60, 00 – N53, 00

8 AUGUST 1941

RAF bombing damaged Swedish steamer VENERSBORG (1065grt) in the Great Belt, and she was towed to a Danish port for repairs.

25 AUGUST 1941

German steamer **TROYBURG** (2288grt) became stranded and was lost at Faresund.

Southern Baltic Area
Long. E12, 00 – E22, 00   Lat. N60, 00 – N53, 00

3 AUGUST 1941

Russian submarines SHCH-318, SHCH-319 and SHCH-320 patrolled the Baltic along the Swedish coast until 18 August.

4 AUGUST 1941

German aircraft of KG.4 dropped sixteen LMB mines in the Irben Strait, south of Zerel, and sixteen LMB mines in the mouth of the river Triigi, near Kassarwik.

6 AUGUST 1941

Russian submarines S-4, S-5 and S-6 patrolled off the German coast and unsuccessfully attacked two convoys.

9 AUGUST 1941

A Russian mine sank German steamer **GERTRUD III** (210grt) near Ventspils, Latvia.

10 AUGUST 1941

Russian submarine S-4 (Lt Cdr Abrosimov) unsuccessfully attacked a large tanker off the Polish coast and returned to Tallinn, Estonia.

A mine sank Russian submarine **S-6** (Lt Cdr Kuligin) southeast of Oland.

11 AUGUST 1941

Russian submarine SHCH-301 (Lt Cdr Grashchev) joined the patrol group off the German coast.

13 AUGUST 1941

Estonian submarines KALEV (Lt Cdr Nyrov) and LEMBIT (Lt Cdr Poleshchuk) laid mines off Cape Ushava.

17 AUGUST 1941

Estonian submarines KALEV (Lt Cdr Nyrov) and LEMBIT (Lt Cdr Poleshchuk) laid mines off Bornholm.

23 AUGUST 1941

A German mine sank Finnish steamer **CISIL** (1847grt) off Kolberg, Germany.

Gulf of Finland

Long. E22, 00 – E30, 00　　Lat. N61, 00 – N57, 00

1 AUGUST 1941

	The German 2nd S-Boat Flotilla laid twenty-four TMB mines off Dago Island.
	Russian MTBs attacked the German 1st M-Boat Flotilla covered by two Russian destroyers off Cape Domesnas. During the short combat, Russian MTB **TKA-122** was sunk and the Germans departed without loss.
	During the night of 31 July / 1 August, aircraft of KG.4 dropped thirty-eight LMB mines in the mouth of the Triigi river.

2 AUGUST 1941

	The German 2nd S-Boat Flotilla laid thirty-six TMB mines off Cape Rista.
	During the night, aircraft of KG.4 dropped fifteen aerial mines east of the Moon Sound, twenty-two aerial mines north of the Moon Sound, and eighteen LMB mines west of Worms Island.
	A mine in the German Minefield COBURG sank Russian submarine **S-11** (Lt Cdr Sereda) off Soelo Sound in 58, 41, 03N, 22, 25E.
	Finnish submarine VESIHIISI (Lt Cdr Kijanen) laid Minefield F.17 with eighteen mines east of Odensholm.
	S.55 and S.58 unsuccessfully attacked Russian destroyer ARTEM in Riga Bay.

6 AUGUST 1941

	Russian destroyers SUROVY and STATNY bombarded the German coastal battery HAINASCH covering the Moon Sound.

8 AUGUST 1941

	Russian destroyers SUROVY and STATNY bombarded the German coastal battery MARKGRAF covering the Moon Sound.
	German Ju88 aircraft of KGR.806 sank Russian destroyer **KARL MARKS** in Loksa Bay at Tallinn, Estonia.
	German Minelayers COBRA (KKpt Dr. Brill), KÖNIGIN LUISE (Kptlt Wünning) and KAISER (KKpt Bohm) supported by the 5th R-Boat Flotilla (Kptlt Dobberstein) and the 1st S-Boat Flotilla (Kptlt Birnbacher) laid Minefield D.10 to Minefield D.30 in the Minefield Juminda with 673 EMC mines and 636 floating mines.
	Finnish Minelayers RIILAHTI (Lt Kivilinna) and RUOTSINSALMI (Lt Cdr Arho) laid Minefield F.18, Minefield F.19, Minefield F.20, Minefield F.21 and Minefield F.22 with 696 deep mines and 100 floating mines.

10 AUGUST 1941

	Russian submarine SC-307 (Lt Cdr Petrov) sank **U.144** (Kptlt v. Mittelstaedt) north of Dago Island in 59N, 23E.
	A Russian convoy departed Revel with troopship VYACHESLAV MOLOTOV (7484grt), carrying 3500 wounded soldiers, escorted by destroyer STEREGUSHCHI, BTSHCH-class minesweepers and several MO-class submarine chasers to Suursaari (Hogland Island) and Kronstadt, Kotlin Island,
	A mine sank Russian minesweeper **T-201/ZARYAD** and damaged troopship VYACHESLAV MOLOTOV (7484grt) off Suursaari.

11 AUGUST 1941

	During the night of 10/11 August, the German 2nd S-Boat Flotilla laid Minefield ALLIRAHU with twenty-four TMB mines in Riga Bay.
	During the night of 10/11 August, the German 5th M-Boat Flotilla laid Minefield PINNASS I, Minefield PINNASS II, Minefield PINNASS III, and Minefield PINNASS IV off Cape Domesnas with forty-seven EMC mines.

12 AUGUST 1941

	The German 1st S-Boat Flotilla (Kptlt Birnbacher) sank Russian motor minesweeper **R-101/RYBINCI** in the Gulf of Finland.

13 AUGUST 1941

	The German 1st S-Boat Flotilla (Kptlt Birnbacher) sank a Russian minesweeper in 59, 42N, 25, 25E.
	During the night of 12/13 August, the German 2nd S-Boat Flotilla laid Minefield MONA I with eighteen TMB mines in the south entrance to Moon Sound.
	During the night of 12/13 August, the German 5th M-Boat Flotilla laid Minefield PINNASS V and Minefield PINNASS VI with twenty-eight mines off Cape Domesnas.

14 AUGUST 1941

	German S-Boat laid mines sank Russian steamer **VODNIK** (125grt) and Lithuanian steamer **UTENA** (542grt)

GERMANY SENDS RUSSIA TO THE ALLIES

	in the Gulf of Finland.
	German bombing sank Russian steamer **SIBIR** (3767grt) at Reval, Estonia,. She carried 2500 wounded Russian troops and over 400 were lost. (Some sources have the **SIBIR** being lost on 19 August.)

15 AUGUST 1941

	A German S-Boat laid mine sank Russian minesweeper **T-202/BUJ** (441grt) off Suursaari (Hogland Island), Finland.
	A Russian mine sank German steamer **MEMELLAND** (542grt) south of Helsinki, Finland.

16 AUGUST 1941

	Mines from the German Minefield JUMINDA sank several ships of a Russian convoy led by ice breaker OKTYABR from Suursaari (Hogland Island) to Reval, Estonia.

17 AUGUST 1941

	S.58 sank Russian minesweeper **No.80** (ex **BP-21**, 140grt) in 58, 29N, 23, 31E.
	Four Russian TKA boats attacked German ships off Cape Domesnas. During the encounter, the German minesweeper **M.1707/LUNEBURG** came under fire from the Russian coastal artillery and was sunk when she strayed into a German minefield off Arensburg, Ösel Island.

18 AUGUST 1941

	A mine sank Russian destroyer **STATNY** in the Moon Sound off Ösel.
	German bombing sank Russian steamer **AXEL CARL** (2170grt) in Leningrad Harbour.

19 AUGUST 1941

	S.58 sank Russian minesweeper **T-51/PIRMUNAS** (210grt) off the south entrance to Moon Sound.

21 AUGUST 1941

	Russian aircraft unsuccessfully attacked the German 3rd Ferry Battalion moving troops in Riga Bay.
	Russian destroyers ARTEM and SUROVY also make an unsuccessful attack in Riga Bay.
	More Russian ships were lost in the German Minefield JUMINDA as they moved from Suursaari (Hogland Island), Finland, to Reval, Estonia.
	Russian submarine M-172 (Lt Cdr Fisanovich) with the Submarine Division commander Capt 2nd Class Kolyshkin on board entered the fjord into Liinakhamari, but unsuccessfully attacked German steamer MONSUN (6590grt) at the pier.

23 AUGUST 1941

	Russian cruiser KIROV, destroyer leaders LENINGRAD and MINSK with destroyer GORDY provided gunfire support to the Russian troops surrounded at Tallinn, Estonia (Reval).

24 AUGUST 1941

	A Russian convoy of nine ships led by ice breaker OKTYABR departed Reval, Estonia, for Suursaari (Hogland Island) and Kronstadt, Kotlin Island.
	A German mine sank Russian destroyer **ENGELS** off Cape Juminda.
	A German mine sank Russian minesweeper **T-209/KNECHT** off Cape Juminda.
	A German mine sank Russian minesweeper **T-213/KRAMBOL** off Cape Juminda.
	A German mine sank Russian minesweeper **T-212/SHTAG** off Cape Juminda.
	A German mine sank Russian steamer **LUNACHARSKI** (3618grt) off Cape Juminda.
	A German mine sank Russian steamer **DAUGAVA** (1430grt) off Cape Juminda.
	A German mine sank Russian tanker **ZHELEZNODOROZHNIK** (2029grt) off Cape Juminda.

25 AUGUST 1941

	The German 3rd S-Boat Flotilla laid thirty TMB mines at Cape Ristna (Dago).
	German minelayers BRUMMER and ROLAND laid Minefield RUSTO with 170 EMC mines north of Cape Ristna.

27 AUGUST 1941

	Four Russian TKA boats attacked a German motorboat convoy off Cape Domesnas, lightly damaging two of the German boats.
1118	The Russian Baltic Fleet began evacuating the X Rifle Corps and the remaining naval units from Tallinn, Estonia, to Kronstadt, Kotlin Island.
	The first convoy (Capt 2nd Class N. G. Bogdanov) departed Tallinn with destroyers SUROVY and SVIREPY,

	minesweepers MS-52/BUYOK, MS-56/BAROMETR, MS-57/IMANTA (ex Latvian), MS-71/KRAB, MS-72/DHZERZHINSKI, and MS-91/LYAPIDEVSKI, steamers VT-511/ALEV (1446grt) (ex Estonian), VT-524/KALPAKS (2190grt) (ex Latvian), VT-547/JARVAMAA (1363grt) (ex Estonian), VT-530/ELLA (1522grt) (ex Estonian), and VT-563/ATIS KRONVALDIS (1423grt) (ex Latvian), ice breaker KRISYJANIS VALDEMARS (2250grt) (ex Latvian), repair ship SERP I MOLOT, survey ship VOSTOK, training ship LENINGRADSOVIET (1270grt), submarines SHCH-307, SHCH-308, and M-97 escorted by destroyer SUROVY, patrol ships AMETIST (ex Estonian **SULEV**), BANYAN, and KASATKA, old minesweepers KTS-1201, KTS-1204, KTS-1205 and KTS-1206, submarine chasers MO-204 and MO-207, five patrol boats, rescue vessel SATURN and one tug.
1325	The second convoy (Capt 2nd Class N. V. Antonov) departed Tallinn with steamers VT-537/ERGONAUTIS (206grt) (ex Latvian), VT-505/IVAN PAPANIN (3974grt), VT-584/NAISSAAR (1839grt) (ex Estonian), VT-523/KAZAKHSTAN and VT-550/SIAULIA (1207grt) (ex Lithuanian), two netlayers, survey ship ASTRONOM, and one schooner escorted by destroyer leader MOSKVA, patrol boat CHAPAEV, old minesweepers KTS-1510, KTS-1511, KTS-1512, and KTS-1524, motor minesweepers TTS-43, TTS-44, TTS-47, TTS-84 and TTS-121, powered sailboat TIIR (ex Estonian) and submarine chaser MO-200.
1350	The third convoy (Capt 2nd Class Ya. F. Yanson) departed Tallinn with steamers VT-574/KUMARI (ex Estonian), VT-581/LAKE LUCERNE (2317grt) (ex Estonian), VT-518/LUGA (2329grt), VT-529/SKRUNDA (2414grt), VT-512/TOBOL (2758grt) and VT-543/VTORAYA PYATILETKA (3974grt), armed steamer HIIUSAAR (ex Estonian), rescue ship KOLYVAN and tanker TN-12 (1700grt), escorted by sloop AMGUN, patrol boats URAL and KOLYVAN, old minesweepers KTS-1101, KTS-1104, KTS-1105 and KTS-1107, minelayers MLR-33/OLONKA, MLR-35/SHUYA, MLR-58/OSETR and MLR-93, and submarine chasers MO-501 and MO-502. The Russians scuttled steamship **PK-233** (grt) before leaving the harbour.
	The Fourth convoy (Capt 3rd Class S. A. Gikhorovcev) departed Tallinn with nine small ships escorted by patrol boat RAZVECHIK, gunboat I-8, nine motor minesweepers, and two magnetic minesweepers.
1452	The Russian main force (Vice Adm. V. F. Tributs) departed Tallinn with light cruiser KIROV (FF), destroyer leader LENINGRAD, destroyers GORDY, SMETLIVY and YAKOV SVERDLOV, submarines S-4, S-5, SHCH-301, KALEV, and LEMBIT, ice breaker SUUR TOLL (ex Estonian), minesweepers T-204, T-205, T-206, T-207, and T-217, MTBs TKA-73, TKA-74, TKA-94, TKA-103, and TKA-113, plus submarine chasers MO-112, MO-131, MO-133, MO-142, and MO-202.
	The Russian convoy cover force (RAdm Ju. A. Panteleev) departed Tallinn with destroyer leader MINSK (F), destroyers SKORY and SAVNY, submarines SHCH-322, M-95, M-98, and M-102, minesweepers T-210, T-214, T-215, T-216, and T-218, submarine chasers MO-207, MO-212, MO-213, and MO-510, four MTBs and patrol boat NEPTUN.
	The second Russian convoy cover force (RAdm Ju. F. Rall) departed Tallinn with destroyer KALININ (F), ARTEM and VOLODARSKI, patrol boats SNEG, BURYA, and TSIKLON, two MTBs, five MO-IV class submarine chasers and minelayer VAINDLO. They departed Reval after laying extensive minefields and sinking the old minelayer **AMUR**, steamer **GAMMA** (696grt), tugboats **VIRRE** (80grt), **ALAR** (160grt) and **DIANA** as blockships in the channel.
	The Russians scuttled sailing ships **JUNO** (grt), **KODU** (grt), **LEIDUS** (grt), **MINNALAID** (grt), **DELPHIN** (109grt), and **KIHELKONNA** (120grt) plus small steamers **SALMI** (185grt) and **SATURN** (403grt) at Reval.

28 AUGUST 1941

	In the afternoon, Ju88 aircraft of II/KG.77 and KGR.806 attacked the Russian evacuation convoys off Reval, Estonia, and sank ice breaker **KRISYJANIS VALDEMARS** (2250grt), steamers **VT-529/SKRUNDA** (2414grt), **VT-581/LAKE LUCERNE** (2317grt), and **VT-563/ATIS KRONVALDIS** (1423grt) and damaged staff ship VIRONIA (2026grt).
	A mine sank staff ship **VIRONIA** (2026grt) when she tried to return to Reval.
	The Russian evacuation convoy tried to break through the German Minefield JUMINDA during the night of 28/29 August. Mines sank destroyers **YAKOV SVERDLOV**, **KALININ**, and **ARTEM**, patrol ships **SNEG**, **TSIKLON** and **JUPITER**, rescue ship **SATURN**, minesweepers **T-214**, and **T-216**, minelayers **TTS-56/BAROMETR**, **TTS-71/KRAB**, and **TTS-42/IZHORETS-17**, submarines **SHCH-301**, **S-5** and **S-6**, destroyer leader **MOSKVA**, gunboats **AMGUN** and **I-8**, netlayers **VYATKA** and **ONEGA**, MTB **TKA-103**, submarine chaser **MO-202**, steamers **VT-511/ALEV** (1446grt), **VT-512/TOBOL** (2758grt), **VT-547/JARVAMAA** (1363grt), **EVERITA** (3251grt), **VT-518/LUGA** (2329grt), **VT-512/KUMARI** (237grt), **BALKHASH** (2191grt), **JANA** (2917grt), **VT-584/NAISSAAR** (1839grt), **VT-537/ERGONAUTIS** (206grt), **VT-530/ELLA** (1522grt), **AUSMA** (1791grt), and **Tanker TN-12** (1700grt). Mines heavily damaged destroyer leader MINSK, destroyers GORDY and SLAVNY, minesweeper T-205 and other ships.
	Mines sank Russian destroyers **SKORY** and **VOLODARSKI** off Seiskaari.
	German bombing damaged Russian light cruiser KIROV off Tallinn, Estonia.
	The German 1st S-Boat Flotilla (Birnbach) departed Helsinki with S.26, S.27, S.39, S.40 and S.101 to attack the departing Russian convoys.

29 AUGUST 1941

	German Ju88 aircraft from II/KG.77 and KGR.806 again attacked the Russian convoys off Suursaari (Hogland Island). The aircraft sank Russian steamer **VT-543/VTORAYA PYATILETKA** (3974grt), steamer **VT-524/KALPAKS** (2190grt) and the training ship **LENINGRADSOVIET** (1270grt). Heavily damaged ships included steamer **VT-505/IVAN PAPANIN** (3974grt), steamer **VT-550/SIAULIA** (1207grt) and repair ship **SERP I MOLOT** (5920grt), which were all beached to prevent sinking at Suursaari. Only steamer VT-523/KAZAKHSTAN reached Kronstadt, Kotlin Island, after unloading 2300 of the 5000 troops she carried at Steinskar, but even she suffered extensive bomb damage.
	A special Russian cover/salvage group (Capt 2nd Class I. G. Svayatov) departed Suursaari with twelve old minesweepers, a division of patrol boats, six MTBs, eight submarine chasers, two tugs, four motorboats, two cutters and rescue ship METEOR. Over the next couple of days, this group rescued 12,160 Russian troops.
	Russian submarine **SHCH-322** covered the salvage group, but failed to return after the mission and was presumed lost.
	Finnish minelayers added twenty-four mines north of the Minefield JUMINDA.
	During the night of 29/30 August, the German 5th R-Boat Flotilla laid thirty-two mines between the old Finnish Minefield VALKJARVI and the German Minefield JUMINDA.
	German aircraft sank Russian transport **VT-581/LAKE LUCERNE** (2317grt) off Suursaari Island in 60, 01N, 27, 01E.
	German aircraft damaged Russian transport VT-550/SIAULIA (1207grt) off Rodskar. She was later towed to Hogland.
	German aircraft sank Russian transport **SIGULDA** off Lavansaari Island in 59, 55N, 27, 45E.
	German aircraft damaged Russian transport **VT-529/SKRUNDA** (2414grt) near Suursaari and sunk the next day after thirty-six attacks.
1507	German aircraft sank Russian transport **VT-520/EVALD** off Mohni Island.
1740	German aircraft sank Russian transport **VT-563/ATIS KRONVALDIS** (1423grt) off Lavansaari Island in 59, 55N, 27, 45E.
1740	German aircraft sank Russian transport **VT-546/AUSMA** (1791grt) off Lavansaari Island in 59, 55N, 27, 45E.
1740	A German mine sank Russian transport **VT-501/BALHASH** off Lavansaari Island in 59, 55N, 27, 45E.
1740	German aircraft sank Russian transport **VT-537/ERGONAUTIS** (206grt) off Lavansaari Island in 59, 55N, 27, 45E.

30 AUGUST 1941

	During the night of 30/31 August, the German 5th R-Boat Flotilla laid thirty-two mines between the old Finnish Minefield VALKJARVI and the German Minefield JUMINDA.
	The Russian Baltic Fleet began to provide gunfire support to the Russian troops along the Leningrad Front. The First Group (RAdm I. I. Gren) with destroyers STROGI, STROYNI and OPYTNY, gunboats ZEYA, SESTRORETSK and OKA operated in the Neva river to support the Russian Forty Second and Fifty Fifth Armies south of Leningrad. The Second Group (Capt 1st Class Vanifatév) with cruisers MAXIM GORKI and PETROPAVLOVSK, destroyer leader LENINGRAD, destroyers SVIREPY, GROZYASHCHI, SILNY, STOIKI, and STOROZHEVOI and minelayer MARTI supported Russian troops east of Leningrad. The Third Group with battleships OKTYABRSKAYA REVOLUTSIYA (RAdm M. S. Moskalenko) and MARAT (Capt 1st Class M. G. Ivanov), cruiser KIROV, destroyer leader MINSK, destroyers SUROVY, GORDY, SMETLIVY and SLAVNY, damaged destroyers STEREGUSHCHI and STRASHNY and gunboat VOLGA supported Russian troops defending Kronstadt, Kotlin Island,.
	Russian transport **VT-505/IVAN PAPANIN** (3974grt) ran aground at Suursaari (Hogland Island) and was destroyed by German bombers.

31 AUGUST 1941

	During the night of 31/1 August, the German 5th R-Boat Flotilla laid thirty-two mines between the old Finnish Minefield VALKJARVI and the German Minefield JUMINDA.

MEDITERRANEAN SEA & MIDDLE EAST

East of Gibraltar Long. W05, 30 – E11, 00   Lat. N44, 30 – N35, 00

1 AUGUST 1941

	During the night of 31st/1 August, Operation STYLE destroyers COSSACK and MAORI were detached from Force H to bombard the harbour of Alghero, Sardinia, and fire star shells for a night raid by aircraft from aircraft carrier ARK ROYAL.

During Operation STYLE, Force H aircraft carrier ARK ROYAL launched nine Swordfish aircraft to attack the Alghero airfield on Sardinia.

During Operation STYLE, a Swordfish aircraft of 810 Squadron crashed while landing on the aircraft carrier ARK ROYAL injuring the pilot, Lt (A) C. M. Jewell, who died of wounds and killing observer and the aircraft gunner Sub-Lt (A) L. A. Royall, and A/Lt D. G. Bowker, A/Lt (E) T. I. Gay, and two ratings of the deck party, Leading Airman H. F. Huxley and Stoker Hunt. The ARK ROYAL sustained light damage.

Force H (Vice Adm. Somerville) covered the Operation STYLE ships with battleship NELSON, battle cruiser RENOWN plus destroyers NESTOR, FAULKNOR, FURY, FORESIGHT, FORESTER, FOXHOUND and ENCOUNTER.

Submarine THUNDERBOLT departed Gibraltar with aviation spirits aboard for Malta.

2 AUGUST 1941

Also part of Operation STYLE, aircraft carrier ARK ROYAL launched Hurricane aircraft to Malta.

Dutch submarine O.23 departed Gibraltar for a patrol in the Tyrrhenian Sea.

Motor launches ML.130, ML.129, and ML.168 departed Gibraltar to conduct an antisubmarine search north of Alboran Island.

3 AUGUST 1941

Dutch submarine O.21 (Lt Cdr Van Dulm) unsuccessfully attacked a sailing vessel south of Sardinia. She did sink two smaller sailing ships with gunfire.

4 AUGUST 1941

Force H and the Malta reinforcement group of Operation STYLE returned to Gibraltar, and battle cruiser RENOWN was docked for repairs to her bulge plating. VAdm Somerville hoisted his flag on the battleship NELSON.

6 AUGUST 1941

Dutch submarine O.24 (Lt Cdr de Booy) sank Italian steamer **BOMBARDIERE** (613grt) six miles off Fregene in 41, 47N, 12, 06E.

Dutch submarine O.21 (Lt Cdr Van Dulm) arrived at Gibraltar from her patrol in the western Mediterranean.

9 AUGUST 1941

Submarine PARTHIAN arrived at Gibraltar from Malta.

12 AUGUST 1941

Dutch submarine O.24 unsuccessfully attacked an Italian steamer in the Ligurian Sea.

14 AUGUST 1941

Battleship NELSON, aircraft carrier ARK ROYAL, light cruiser HERMIONE and destroyers departed Gibraltar to the east for exercises.

On the 16th, NELSON, HERMIONE, and destroyer VIMY arrived back at Gibraltar, followed on the 17th, by ARK ROYAL with destroyers NESTOR, ENCOUNTER, FURY, FORESIGHT, and FORESTER.

15 AUGUST 1941

Dutch submarine O.24 arrived at Gibraltar after a patrol in the Gulf of Genoa and Tyrrhenian Sea.

16 AUGUST 1941

Battleship NELSON, light cruiser HERMIONE and destroyer VIMY arrived back at Gibraltar.

17 AUGUST 1941

Aircraft carrier ARK ROYAL returned to Gibraltar with destroyers NESTOR, ENCOUNTER, FURY, FORESIGHT, and FORESTER.

20 AUGUST 1941

Dutch submarine O.23 arrived at Gibraltar from a patrol in the western Mediterranean.

21 AUGUST 1941

Force H departed Gibraltar with battleship NELSON, aircraft carrier ARK ROYAL, light cruiser HERMIONE, and destroyers NESTOR, FORESTER, FURY, FORESIGHT, and ENCOUNTER for operations against Sardinia in Operation MINCEMEAT.

22 AUGUST 1941

In Operation MINCEMEAT, minelaying cruiser MANXMAN departed Gibraltar early in the morning disguised as a French LEOPARD-class destroyer for the passage to and from the Livorno area in the Gulf of Genoa, where she successfully laid mines.

23 AUGUST 1941

Italian aircraft damaged light cruiser MANCHESTER south of Sardinia.

Italian aircraft sank destroyer **FEARLESS** south of Sardinia.

24 AUGUST 1941

British air reconnaissance sighted the Italian battleship force west of Italy. After ARK ROYAL aircraft dropped incendiary bombs in the corkwood groves west and southeast of Tempio, Sardinia, she and Force H returned to Gibraltar. The Force H operations in Operation MINCEMEAT were a diversion for minelayer MANXMAN.

Minelayer MANXMAN laid seventy magnetic and seventy contact mines off Livorno, Italy.

Italian submarines SQUALO, BANDIERA, TRICHECO, TOPAZIO and ZAFFIRO set up a patrol line across the Sicilian straits with thirteen MAS boats to prevent another British convoy from reaching Malta from Gibraltar. Force H meanwhile was already east of the Balearic Islands.

Italian submarines ALAGI, SERPENTE, ARADAM and DIASPRO set up a patrol line southwest of Sardinia.

Ten Swordfish aircraft from aircraft carrier ARK ROYAL attacked the Tempio airport in northern Sardinia.

The Italian Fleet (AmS Angelo Iachino) waited in the entrance to the Sicilian straits for the British ships that never came.

25 AUGUST 1941

Minelayer MANXMAN returned to Gibraltar after laying mines off Livorno, Italy.

26 AUGUST 1941

Battleship NELSON, aircraft carrier ARK ROYAL, light cruiser HERMIONE, and the destroyers of Operation MINCEMEAT arrived back at Gibraltar.

27 AUGUST 1941

Dutch submarine O.21 departed Gibraltar for a patrol in the south Tyrrhenian Sea.

28 AUGUST 1941

Dutch submarine O.24 departed Gibraltar for a patrol in the Gulf of Genoa.

29 AUGUST 1941

Steamer DEUCALION (7516grt) and destroyer FARNDALE arrived at Gibraltar after sailing independently from Malta.

31 AUGUST 1941

Dutch submarine O.21 made an unsuccessful attack on an Italian submarine in the Tyrrhenian Sea.

Middle Mediterranean Sea

Long. E11, 00 – E20, 00   Lat. N46, 00 – N30, 00

1 AUGUST 1941

Italian submarines BANDIERA, MANARA, SETTIMO and ZAFFIRO patrolled off Malta, while SERPENTE, ALAGI and DIASPRO patrolled between Cape Bougaroni and Galita Island.

Submarines URGE, URSULA and UNBEATEN unsuccessfully patrolled off Sicily until 15 August.

2 AUGUST 1941

Light cruiser HERMIONE rammed and sank Italian submarine **TEMBIEN** off Tunis in 36, 21N, 12, 40E.

Destroyer FARNDALE, with her condenser problems repaired, departed Malta with the Operation STYLE ships. However, destroyer FARNDALE developed further problems at sea and had to return to Malta for additional repairs.

In Operation STYLE, light cruisers ARETHUSA and HERMIONE arrived at Malta with fast minelayer MANXMAN plus destroyers LIGHTNING and SIKH from Gibraltar. They unloaded 1750 men with 130 tons of supplies and then immediately departed to return to Gibraltar.

3 AUGUST 1941

British bombing sank Italian coastal steamer **ELISA** (216grt) off Benghazi, Libya.

Submarine UTMOST arrived at Malta from her patrol.

4 AUGUST 1941

An Italian supply convoy departed Naples, Italy, with steamers AQUITANIA (4971grt), NITA (6813grt), CASTELVERDE (6666grt), ERNESTO (7272grt), and NIRVO (5164grt) for Tripoli, Libya, escorted by destroyers AVIERE, GENIERE, CAMICIA NERA, GIOBERTI, ORIANI and torpedo boat CALLIOPE.
  Tanker POZARICA (7599grt) joined the convoy from Palermo, Sicily on the 5th.
  The convoy arrived at Tripoli on the 7th.

An Italian return convoy departed Tripoli with steamers AMSTERDAM (8673grt), BAINSIZZA (7933grt), MADDALENA ODERO (5479grt) and COL DI LANA (5891grt) escorted by destroyers FRECCIA, STRALE, TURBINE, and MALOCELLO plus torpedo boat PEGASO for Naples.
  British aircraft attacked the convoy on 5 August, but no damage was done.

Submarine UNIQUE arrived at Malta from her patrol.

6 AUGUST 1941

British aircraft of 830 Squadron from Malta sank Italian steamer **NITA** (6813grt) in a supply convoy twenty miles southwest of Lampedusa Island in 35, 15N, 12, 17E. Italian destroyer CAMICIA NERA and torpedo boat CALLIOPE assisted the survivors.

7 AUGUST 1941

Dutch submarine O.24 (LtZ/1 de Booy) sank Italian coastal steamer **MARGHERITA MADRE** (296grt) with gunfire fifteen miles off Anzio, Italy, in 41, 23N, 12, 38E.
  She had also made an unsuccessful attack on another steamer in the Ligurian Sea four hours earlier.

8 AUGUST 1941

Submarine THUNDERBOLT arrived at Malta from Gibraltar with aviation spirits (aviation gasoline).

10 AUGUST 1941

Submarine THUNDERBOLT departed Malta for Alexandria.

11 AUGUST 1941

Swordfish aircraft from 830 Squadron from Malta sank Italian hospital ship **CALIFORNIA** (13,060grt) at Syracuse, Sicily.

12 AUGUST 1941

Italian minelayers REGGIO and ASPROMONTE covered by destroyers ZENO, DA VERAZZANO, PIGAFETTA, DA MOSTO and PESSAGNO laid Minefield SN.41 in the Sicilian Strait.

Submarine TORBAY (Cdr Miers) attacked a convoy of steamers BOSFORO (3567grt) and ISEO, escorted by torpedo boat PARTENOPE, four miles west of Benghazi, Libya, without success.
  TORBAY suffered a very heavy depth charge attack from the torpedo boat.

Submarine RORQUAL arrived at Malta from Alexandria with petrol and stores.

Submarine P.33 departed Malta on a patrol.

13 AUGUST 1941

An Italian supply convoy departed Naples, Italy, with steamers ANDREA GRITTI (6338grt), RIALTO (6099grt), VETTOR PISANI (6339grt), FRANCESCO BARBARO (6343grt), and SEBASTINO VENIER (6311grt), escorted by destroyers VIVALDI, FOLGORE, STRALE, MALOCELLO, FULMINE and torpedo boat ORSA for Tripoli, Libya.
  On the 14th, during an air attack, one of the antiaircraft guns on VIVALDI exploded and she was forced to return to Italy.
  There were also submarine attacks reported during the air attack, but these claims were not confirmed.
  The convoy arrived at Tripoli on 15 August, undamaged by the British.

15 AUGUST 1941

British bombing sank Italian steamer **ADUA** (400grt) in the Gulf of Sirte, Libya, in 31, 31N, 15, 42E.

Submarine OSIRIS arrived at Malta from Alexandria to discharge petrol, stores, mail, and passengers.

16 AUGUST 1941

Italian minelayers REGGIO and ASPROMONTE covered by destroyers ZENO, DA VERAZZANO, PIGAFETTA, DA MOSTO and PESSAGNO laid Minefield SN.42 in the Sicilian Strait.

An Italian supply convoy departed Naples, Italy, for Tripoli, Libya, with steamers MADDALENA ODERO (5479grt), NICOLO ODERO (6003grt), CAFFARO (6476grt), MARIN SANUDO (5081grt), GIULIA (5921grt) and tanker MINATITLAN (7599grt) escorted by Italian destroyers FRECCIA, EURO and DARDO with torpedo boats

	PROCIONE, PEGASO and SIRTORI.
	Dutch submarine O.23 (LtZ/1 Van Erkel) unsuccessfully attacked a steamer in the Italian supply convoy southwest of Capri, Italy, in 39, 35N, 13, 18E.
	Submarine TORBAY (Cdr Miers) sank captured Greek sailing ship **EVANGELISTRA** (28grt) with gunfire near Benghazi, Libya.

17 AUGUST 1941

	RAF aircraft from Malta attacked the Italian supply convoy southeast of Malta twice during the day. In the first attack the RAF damaged Italian steamer **MADDALENA ODERO** (5479grt) with a torpedo. Torpedo boats PEGASO and SITORI towed the damaged steamer to Lampedusa Island. In the second RAF attack, a bomb set the cargo on fire, leaving the **MADDALENA ODERO** a total loss.

18 AUGUST 1941

	A mine damaged submarine **P.32** (540grt) (Lt D. A. B. Abdy) as she was attempting to attack an Italian convoy. The damage killed the eight crewmen in the submarine's forward section, and she was grounded on the bottom. Sub-Lt M. F. Millar, Lt R. L. S. Morris, Sub-Lt R. M. Smithard and twenty-seven ratings were lost. Only Abdy and one rating were able to successfully evacuate the submarine and were picked up by an Italian MAS boat.
	A mine or an Italian antisubmarine attack sank submarine **P.33** (540grt) (Lt R. D. Whiteway-Wilkinson DSC) north of Tripoli, Libya. Whiteway-Wilkinson, Lt R. H. Bygott, Lt R. L. Cunningham, Lt R. S. Frost RNR, and twenty-eight ratings were lost. (Some sources have her lost on 23 August.)
	Submarine TETRARCH (Lt Cdr Greenway) fired torpedoes into Benghazi Harbour, Libya, at Italian torpedo boat PERSEO. The torpedoes missed and exploded on the boom defence barrier.
	Submarines UNBEATEN and URGE departed Malta to intercept an Italian supply convoy north of Pantellaria Island.

19 AUGUST 1941

	Italian minelayers REGGIO and ASPROMONTE covered by destroyers ZENO, DA VERAZZANO, PIGAFETTA, DA MOSTO and PESSAGNO laid Minefield SN.43 in the Sicilian Strait.
	Submarine TETRARCH (Lt Cdr Greenway) unsuccessfully attacked Italian steamer CADAMOSTO (1010grt) escorted by torpedo boat CALLIOPE as they were arriving at Benghazi from Tripoli, Libya.
	An Italian convoy departed Naples, Italy, with troopships ESPERIA (11,398grt), MARCO POLO (12,272grt), NEPTUNIA (19,475grt), and OCEANIA (19,507grt) for Tripoli escorted by destroyers VIVALDI, DA RECCO, GIOBERTI, and ORIANI and torpedo boat DEZZA. After an unsuccessful attack by submarine UNBEATEN, Italian destroyers MAESTRALE, GRECALE, and SCIROCCO joined the convoy later the same day. The convoy arrived at Tripoli on the 20th.
	Submarine UNBEATEN (Lt Woodward) unsuccessfully attacked an Italian troop convoy north of Pantellaria Island and missed troopship ESPERIA (11,398grt).

20 AUGUST 1941

	Submarine UPHOLDER (Lt Cdr Wanklyn) sank Italian steamer **ENOTRIA** (852grt) six miles northwest of Cape St Vito, northwest Sicily.
	Submarine UNIQUE (Lt Hezlet) sank Italian troopship **ESPERIA** (11,398grt) with three torpedo hits eleven miles north of Tripoli, Libya, in 33, 03N, 13, 03E. Thirty-one troops were lost and 1139 men were rescued. The convoy arrived at Tripoli later that day.
	Submarine OTUS arrived at Malta from Alexandria, Egyp, with stores, including a submarine generator, twelve cases of U-class submarine spares, petrol, and eighteen passengers.
	Submarine URGE arrived at Malta from her patrol.

21 AUGUST 1941

	Steamer DURHAM (10,893grt) departed Malta independently for Gibraltar and was damaged by a mine west of Pantellaria Island. She arrived at Gibraltar on the 24th and was dry-docked for damage repair.
	Submarine TAKU arrived at Malta from Alexandria, Egypt, with stores.
	Submarine UNBEATEN arrived at Malta after her patrol.

22 AUGUST 1941

	An Italian convoy departed Palermo, Sicily, with Italian troopship LUSSIN (3958grt) with steamer ALCIONE (493grt) in tow and steamer ALBERTO FASSIO (2289grt) for Tripoli, Libya, escorted by torpedo boats CIGNO and PEGASO.
	Submarine UPHOLDER sank Italian troopship **LUSSIN** (3958grt) near Cape St Vito, Sicily.

23 AUGUST 1941

Italian minelayers REGGIO and ASPROMONTE covered by destroyers ZENO, DA VERAZZANO, PIGAFETTA, DA MOSTO and PESSAGNO laid Minefield SN.44 in the Sicilian Strait. In all, the minelayers laid 1125 mines and the destroyers laid another 3202 mines in the Sicilian Straits.

Italian battleships LITTORIO and VENETO departed Taranto with six destroyers, and heavy cruisers TRIESTE, TRENTO, BOLZANO, and GORIZIA departed Messina, Sicily, with four destroyers to guard against Force H operations. Five destroyers departed Trapani, Italy, and joined the Italian force at sea.
Light cruisers ABRUZZI, ATTENDOLO, and MONTECUCOLI of the 8th Cruiser Division departed Palermo with five destroyers and were stationed north of Tunisia.

Italian torpedo boat PARTENOPE sank submarine **P.33** (540grt) (Lt Whiteway-Wilkinson) as she was attacking a three-ship convoy off Pantellaria Island.
(Some sources claim she was lost on 18 August.)

Submarine TETRARCH (Lt Cdr Greenway) sank Italian steamer **FRATELLI GARRE** (413grt) twelve miles northwest of Sirte, Libya.

Submarine TETRARCH sank Italian steamer **FRANCESCO GARRE** (395grt) one mile from Sirte, Libya.

British Blenheim aircraft from Malta sank Italian steamer **CONSTANZA** (582grt) south of Lampedusa Island.

24 AUGUST 1941

Submarine UPHOLDER (Lt Cdr Wanklyn) reported sighting one Italian battleship, two heavy cruisers, and six destroyers in the Central Mediterranean between Sardinia and Sicily. She made an unsuccessful attack on light cruiser LUIGI DI SAVOIA in 38, 30N, 12, 00E.

The Italian 8th Cruiser Division with light cruisers DUCA DEGLI ABRUZZI, ATTENDOLO and MONTECUCOLI plus five destroyers departed Palermo, Sicily, to guard the Sicilian Straits.

RAF aircraft sank Italian auxiliary gunboat **GRAZIOLI LANTE** while attacking a small convoy between Tripoli and Benghazi, Libya.

25 AUGUST 1941

Submarine TAKU departed Malta for Gibraltar en route to Chatham, England, for a refit.

26 AUGUST 1941

While the Italian forces were returning to port, submarine TRIUMPH sighted Italian battleship LITTORIO, heavy cruisers BOLZANO and TRIESTE, and ten destroyers.
TRIUMPH torpedoed and badly damaged Italian heavy cruiser BOLZANO north of Messina, Sicily.

Steamer DEUCALION (7516grt) departed Malta and steamed independently to Gibraltar followed by destroyer FARNDALE. Both arrived at Gibraltar on the 29th. The steamer had sustained slight damage from a mine explosion.

Submarine URGE (Lt Cdr Tomkinson) spotted an Italian supply convoy with steamers ERNESTO (7272grt), AQUITANIA (4971grt), COL DI LANA (5891grt), and POZARICA (7599grt) escorted by Italian destroyers ORIANI and EURO with torpedo boats PROCIONE, ORSA, CLIO and PEGASO headed for Tripoli, Libya.

27 AUGUST 1941

Submarine URGE (Lt Cdr Tomkinson) unsuccessfully attacked Italian steamer POZARICA (7599grt) while attacking a supply convoy off Marittimo, Sicily.

Submarine URGE damaged Italian steamer AQUITANIA (4971grt) while attacking a supply convoy off Trapani, Italy, and was intensively attacked with depth charges from Italian torpedo boat CLIO. Torpedo boat ORSA took the damaged steamer to Trapani.

Submarine TRIUMPH (Cdr Woods) captured, and then sank a small fishing vessel off the Furiano River, Italy.

Submarine UPHOLDER arrived at Malta from her patrol.

28 AUGUST 1941

Submarine TRIUMPH (Cdr Woods) landed a commando group on the north coast of Sicily that succeed in destroying several water aqueducts and the main rail line into Palermo, Sicily.

Submarine UNBEATEN unsuccessfully attacked an Italian submarine north of Sicily.

Submarine UTMOST unsuccessfully attacked a steamer east of Calabria, Italy.

29 AUGUST 1941

An Italian troop convoy departed Naples, Italy, for Tripoli, Libya, with troopships NEPTUNIA (19,475grt), OCEANIA (19,507grt), and VICTORIA (13,098grt), escorted by destroyers AVIERE, DA NOLI, CAMICIA NERA, GIOBERTI, USODIMARE, and PESSAGNO.

Submarine URGE (Lt Tomkinson) made an unsuccessful attack on Italian troopship VICTORIA (13,098grt) off the island of Capri.

30 AUGUST 1941

	An Italian return convoy departed Tripoli for Naples with steamers MARIN SANUDO (5081grt), GIULIA (5921grt), CAFFARO (6476grt), NICOLO ODERO (6003grt), tanker MINATITLAN (7599grt) and minelayer ERITREA escorted by Italian destroyers ORIANI and EURO plus torpedo boats PEGASO, ORSA and CALLIOPE.
	Submarines UPHOLDER and URSULA departed Malta to intercept an Italian convoy east of Tripoli.

30 AUGUST 1941

	Submarine UNBEATEN (Lt Woodward) sank Italian auxiliary patrol boat **V.51/ALFA** (373grt) with gunfire off Augusta, Sicily.
	Swordfish aircraft of 830 Squadron from Malta sank Italian steamer **EGADI** (861grt) thirty miles northeast of Lampedusa Island.
	RAF Wellington aircraft sank Italian steamer **FIAMMETTA** (393grt) at Tripoli, Libya.
	RAF Wellington aircraft sank Italian steamer **GIUSEPPINA V.** (367grt) at Tripoli.
	RAF Wellington aircraft sank Italian steamer **NEPTUNUS** (395grt) at Tripoli.
	RAF Wellington aircraft sank Italian steamer **RIV** (6630grt) at Tripoli.
	RAF Wellington aircraft damaged Italian tanker POZARICA (7599grt) at Tripoli.
	Submarine TALISMAN damaged Italian auxiliary patrol boats SAN MICHELE and TENACEMENTE three miles north of Benghazi, Libya.

31 AUGUST 1941

	An Italian return convoy departed Tripoli, Libya, for Naples, Italy, with five steamers and a mine ship escorted by Italian destroyers ORIANI and EURO plus torpedo boats PEGASO, ORSA and COLLIOPE.
	An Italian convoy departed Tripoli with troopships NEPTUNIA (19,475grt), OCEANIA (19,507grt), VICTORIA (13,098grt), escorted by destroyers AVIERE, DA NOLI, CAMICIA NERA, GIOBERTI, USODIMARE, and PESSAGNO, for Taranto, Italy. Submarine UPHOLDER (Lt Cdr Wanklyn) made an unsuccessful attack on the convoy in the morning off the Tunisian coast. The convoy arrived at Taranto without loss on 2 September.
	Submarine UTMOST arrived at Malta from her patrol.

Eastern Mediterranean Sea

Long. E20, 00 – E38, 00   Lat. N43, 00 – N30, 00

1 AUGUST 1941

	Corvette HYACINTH departed Port Said, Egypt, with motor transport ship SALAMAUA (6676grt) in Operation GUILLOTINE convoy serial S.11 for Famagusta, Cypress. They arrived on the 3rd.
	Destroyers JERVIS, KINGSTON, JACKAL, and NIZAM departed Alexandria, Egypt, to sweep north of Bardia, Libya, for a reported submarine. Italian submarine DELFINO shot down a flying boat cooperating with the destroyers in the search. The destroyers made no contact and arrived back at Alexandria on the 2nd.
	Destroyers HERO and DECOY departed Alexandria on a supply run to Tobruk, Libya.

2 AUGUST 1941

	LL magnetic minesweeper SOIKA was recalled from Port Said, Egypt, to aid in minesweeping at Tobruk, Libya. Corvette SALVIA departed Beirut, Lebanon, to relieve her at Port Said. SOIKA proceeded to Alexandria, Egypt, and minesweeping whaler SOTRA departed Alexandria for Tobruk.
	Axis aircraft attacked Australian destroyer VENDETTA and destroyer HAVOCK while they were en route to Tobruk. The South African air support aircraft were able to repulse the attack and the destroyers were undamaged.

3 AUGUST 1941

	Greek submarine NEREUS claimed sinking a sailing ship and a troopship off Rhodes.
	German Me110 aircraft of ZG.26 attacked Mersa Matruh, Egypt, and damaged submarine chaser SOTRA during the night.
	Australian sloop PARRAMATTA arrived at Port Said, Egypt, from Famagusta, Cypress.
	Sloop FLAMINGO departed Port Said with motor transport ship KEVINBANK for Famagusta in Operation GUILLOTINE convoy serial S.12. They arrived on the 5th.
	Australian minesweeper BATHURST passed through the Suez Canal and proceeded to Alexandria, Egypt, for duty with the Mediterranean Fleet. BATHURST and LISMORE had been retained at Suez, Egypt, to assist with the large troopships of convoy US.11A.
	German bombing damaged tanker DESMOULEA (8120grt) at Suez off the west beacon, and she was towed to Bombay, India, for repairs.
Night	During the night of 3/4 August, four German He111 aircraft of II/KG.26 sank the Belgian motor ship ESCAUT (1087grt) 17.3 cables 232° from South Beacon Ships Head, Attika Bay, Suez. The Master and two crewmen were missing.

| Night | During the night of 3/4 August, four German He111 aircraft of II/KG.26 damaged Belgian tanker ALEXANDRE ANDRE (5322grt) off Zaafar, Egypt, with aerial torpedoes. The tanker was so heavily damaged that she was used only as an oil storage hulk for the remainder of the war. |

4 AUGUST 1941

Italian submarine DELFINO patrolled off Mersa Matruh, Egypt. She was attacked by a Sunderland flying boat, which she shot down, and then rescued the four crewmen and made them prisoners of war.

Light cruiser CARLISLE departed Alexandria, Egypt, for Suez, Egypt, to provide antiaircraft defence.

Light cruiser NEPTUNE and minelayer ABDIEL departed Alexandria with destroyers JACKAL and KIPLING for Port Said, Egypt, for one Operation GUILLOTINE convoy serial. The ships would then relieve light cruiser HOBART and destroyers at Haifa, Palestine.

Destroyers JAGUAR and NIZAM carried supplies from Alexandria to Tobruk, Libya.

German aircraft attacked minesweeping whaler SOTRA (A/Lt J. M. Davies RCNVR) off Mersa Matruh. T/Skipper W. T. Allen RNR was killed.

5 AUGUST 1941

Battleship QUEEN ELIZABETH and light cruiser NAIAD departed Alexandria, Egypt, with destroyer JERVIS, KINGSTON, HERO, and VENDETTA for exercises.
The QUEEN ELIZABETH and NAIAD arrived back at Alexandria, on the 6th with destroyers HERO and VENDETTA.
Destroyers JERVIS and KINGSTON were detached from the group for Mersa Matruh, Egypt, to intercept a reported enemy supply ship. No contact was made and they returned to Alexandria on the 7th.

Australian light cruiser HOBART arrived at Port Said, Egypt, with destroyers KANDAHAR, KIMBERLEY, and KIPLING from Haifa, Palestine. They sailed again later that day for Famagusta, Cypress, in Operation GUILLOTINE convoy serial S.14. They arrived at Famagusta on the 8th.

Light cruiser NEPTUNE, minelayer ABDIEL, with destroyers JACKAL and KIPLING arrived at Port Said from Alexandria. KIPLING departed that day in Operation GUILLOTINE convoy serial S.14.

Greek destroyer CONDOURIOTIS departed Alexandria carrying torpedoes for Fleet Air Arm Squadron 815 at Famagusta, and arrived back at Alexandria on the 7th.

Destroyers HERO and DECOY departed Alexandria and carried supplies to Tobruk, Libya.

6 AUGUST 1941

Australian sloop PARRAMATTA departed Port Said, Egypt, escorting motor ship GUJARAT (4148grt) to Famagusta, Cypress, in Operation GUILLOTINE convoy serial S.12. They arrived at Famagusta on the 7th.

Italian submarines ZOEA, CORRIDONI and ATROPO delivered 192-tons of supplies and fuel to Axis units at Bardia, Libya, between the 6th and 20th of August.
On one trip, ZOEA was attacked by aircraft and claimed downing a Bristol Blenheim bomber.

Destroyers HAVOCK and DECOY ran supplies to Tobruk, Libya, from Alexandria, Egypt. Destroyers NIZAM and JAGUAR also departed Alexandria later that day to carry additional supplies to Tobruk. These destroyers all arrived back at Alexandria on the 7th.

Netlayer PROTECTOR departed Alexandria for Suez, Egypt, with nets to be laid as anti-torpedo baffles.

7 AUGUST 1941

Light cruiser NEPTUNE, minelayer ABDIEL, and destroyer JACKAL departed Port Said, Egypt, for Famagusta, Cypress, in Operation GUILLOTINE convoy serial S.15. The troops were landed during the night of 7/8 August, after which the ships proceeded to Haifa, Palestine.

Destroyers KANDAHAR and KIMBERLEY departed Alexandria, Egypt, for Mersa Matruh, Egypt, but they were recalled at dusk.

German bombing sank tugboat **AMIRAL LACAZE** (332grt) at Famagusta, but she was later re-floated and repaired.

8 AUGUST 1941

Destroyers HERO and JAGUAR departed Alexandria, Egypt, for Mersa Matruh, Egypt, to intercept an enemy supply ship reported by aircraft. No contact was made, and the destroyers returned to Alexandria, arriving on the 9th.

Destroyers DECOY and HOTSPUR were at sea exercising with submarine OTUS.

Sloop FLAMINGO departed Port Said, Egypt, with motor transport ship SALAMAUA (6676grt) for Famagusta, Cypress, in Operation GUILLOTINE convoy serial S.16 of the. The sloop arrived at Famagusta on the 10th and sailed for Port Said, where she arrived on the 11th. Convoy serial S.17 was cancelled.

9 AUGUST 1941

Destroyers JERVIS and KINGSTON departed Alexandria, Egypt, for Mersa Matruh, Egypt, and returned to Al-

	exandria on the 10th.
	Destroyers DECOY and HAVOCK departed Alexandria with supplies for Tobruk, Libya.
	Destroyers KANDAHAR and VENDETTA departed Alexandria to rescue a bomber crew in the sea about 180 miles northwest of Alexandria, but were later recalled.

10 AUGUST 1941

	Destroyers KANDAHAR and KIMBERLEY departed Alexandria, Egypt, for Mersa Matruh, Egypt, to act as a strike force. Originally, their orders called for an attack on Bardia harbour, Libya, during the night of 10/11 August, but this order was later cancelled. They returned to Alexandria on the 11th.
	Destroyers DECOY and HAVOCK departed Alexandria with supplies for Tobruk, Libya, and arrived back at Alexandria on the 11th.
	Australian destroyer VENDETTA departed Alexandria for Haifa, Palestine, for mechanical repairs.

11 AUGUST 1941

	Destroyers JERVIS and KINGSTON departed Alexandria, Egypt, for Mersa Matruh, Egypt, to act as a striking force, and arrived back at Alexandria on the 13th.
	Australian sloop PARRAMATTA departed Port Said, Egypt, escorting motor transport ship KEVINBANK, for Famagusta, Cypress, in Operation GUILLOTINE convoy serial S.18. They arrived on 13 July.
1700	An Axis aerial torpedo heavily damaged netlayer PROTECTOR while she was on passage from Port Said to Alexandria in 31, 42N, 32, 04E. Destroyer HERO was sent from Alexandria to assist, and sloop FLAMINGO, corvette SALVIA, and trawlers were sent from Port Said. SALVIA was able to take her in tow to Port Said.

12 AUGUST 1941

	A German aerial mine laid by a Ju88 aircraft of LG.1 sank **Lighter A.14** (372grt) (Lt A. S. Mullens RNR) in Tobruk harbour, Libya. The lighter was also referred to as **LCT.14**.
	Minelayers ABDIEL and LATONA delivered 6000 fresh troops to Tobruk and evacuated 5000 battle weary Australian troops. The troop transfer lasted until the 18th. Australian heavy cruiser HOBART with Australian destroyers NAPIER and NIZAM supported the transfer convoys.
	Light cruiser NEPTUNE, minelayer ABDIEL and destroyer JACKAL departed Haifa, Palestine, for Port Said, Egypt, for an Operation GUILLOTINE supply mission.
	Destroyers KANDAHAR and KIMBERLEY departed Alexandria, Egypt, for Mersa Matruh, Egypt, to load supplies and then take them to Tobruk. They arrived back at Alexandria on the 13th.
0600	Corvette SALVIA arrived at Port Said towing damaged netlayer PROTECTOR. PROTECTOR received temporary repairs at Suez, Egypt, and on 25 November departed in tow of steamer EMPIRE KANGAROO (6219grt).

13 AUGUST 1941

	Schooner **KEPHALLINIA** (1267grt) foundered and sank off Alexandria, Egypt, while she was en route to Tobruk, Libya, with supplies. Destroyer HERO assisted her survivors.
	Light cruiser NEPTUNE, minelayer ABDIEL, and destroyer JACKAL departed Port Said, Egypt, with personnel for Famagusta, Cypress, in Operation GUILLOTINE convoy serial S.20. The troops were landed on the 14th, after which NEPTUNE proceeded to Alexandria, Egypt, with ABDIEL and JACKAL going to Port Said. Australian light cruiser HOBART departed Alexandria with destroyers DECOY and HAVOCK for Port Said to relieve NEPTUNE.
	Antiaircraft ship COVENTRY departed Beirut, Lebanon, to return to Alexandria, where she arrived on the 14th.
	Destroyers HASTY and JAGUAR departed Alexandria with supplies for Tobruk.

14 AUGUST 1941

	The German steamer BELLONA (1297grt) departed Bardia, Libya, alone due to the lack of any Italian escorts. German aircraft from Crete protected the vessel until she reached Suda Bay, Crete. From there, she safely reached Piraeus, Greece.
	Submarine TALISMAN fired torpedoes in error at submarine OTUS in 32, 41N, 27, 35E. At the time, TALISMAN was arriving at Alexandria, Egypt, while OTUS had just departed for Malta with stores. Neither submarine was damaged.
	Antiaircraft cruiser COVENTRY departed Alexandria with destroyers NIZAM and KINGSTON escorting troopship GLENROY (9809grt) to Port Said, Egypt. GLENROY passed through the Suez Canal on the 15th.
	Greek destroyer VASILISSA OLGA departed Alexandria for Famagusta, Cypress, and arrived on the 16th. She then departed that same day to return to Alexandria.

15 AUGUST 1941

	Submarine THRASHER unsuccessfully attacked German steamer ANKARA (4768grt) in the Mandri Channel, Greece, while she was escorted by Italian torpedo boat SIRIO.
	Australian light cruiser HOBART and minelayer ABDIEL departed Port Said, Egypt, with destroyers DECOY and HAVOCK for Famagusta, Cypress, with troops in Operation GUILLOTINE convoy serial S.21. Australian sloop PARRAMATTA was at Famagusta to provide antisubmarine protection. The HOBART group disembarked their troops at Famagusta during the night of 15/16 August. Minelayer ABDIEL departed for Alexandria, Egypt; the remainder of the group proceeded to Haifa, Palestine. Sloop PARRAMATTA departed Famagusta on the 16th for Port Said, where she arrived on the 17th.
	After departing Port Said on 13 August, corvette PEONY arrived at Famagusta with motor transport ship GUJARAT (4148grt) of convoy serial S.19 and then departed for Beirut, Lebanon.
	Destroyers HASTY and JAGUAR departed Alexandria, Egypt, with stores for Tobruk, Libya. The destroyers returned to Alexandria on the 16th.
	Destroyers KANDAHAR and KIMBERLEY landed stores at Tobruk during the night of 14/15 August and returned to Alexandria.

16 AUGUST 1941

	Sloop FLAMINGO departed Port Said, Egypt, escorting a motor transport ship SALAMAUA (6676grt) to Famagusta, Cypress, in Operation GUILLOTINE convoy serial S.22. The sloop arrived at Famagusta on the 18th and returned to Port Said.
	Destroyers KANDAHAR and KIMBERLEY carried supplies to Tobruk, Libya. The destroyers arrived back at Alexandria, Egypt, on the 17th.
	Yugoslav torpedo boats DURMITOR and KAJMAKALAN departed Alexandria to operate from Mersa Matruh, Egypt, against Axis shipping off Bardia, Libya.

17 AUGUST 1941

	Submarine REGENT was damaged at Alexandria when an air vessel of a torpedo exploded. There were no personnel casualties in the mishap.
Night	Destroyers KIPLING and NIZAM landed supplies at Tobruk, Libya, during the night of 17/18 August. The destroyers then returned to Alexandria, Egypt.

18 AUGUST 1941

	Submarine TORBAY (Lt Cdr Miers) entered Messara Bay, Crete, to pick up twenty-eight British and twelve Greek soldiers who had been hiding out since the island fell to the Germans. TORBAY picked up an additional ninety-two soldiers the following night and took them to Alexandria, Egypt.
	Destroyers JACKAL and KINGSTON departed Alexandria to carry supplies to Tobruk, Libya. The destroyers arrived back at Alexandria on the 19th.
	Australian minesweeper BATHURST arrived at Port Said, Egypt, from Alexandria to pass through the Suez Canal. The minesweeper joined the East Indies Fleet. Australian minesweeper LISMORE was also transferred to the East Indies Fleet, passing through the Canal on the 21st. In exchange, armed boarding vessels CHANTALA, which passed through the Canal on the 20th, and CHAKDINA, which arrived at Suez, Egypt, on the 29th, were attached to the Mediterranean Fleet. Armed boarding vessel CHAKDINA arrived at Alexandria on 2 September.
	Submarine THUNDERBOLT arrived at Alexandria from Malta.

19 AUGUST 1941

	Axis Ju87 aircraft sank whaler **THORBRYN** (305grt) (Lt Cdr J. F. Hall RNR), while she was towing two D lighters, off Tobruk, Libya, in 32N, 24, 09, 15E. T/Lt D. C. Wilson RNVR, T/Lt W. B. Chisholm RNVR, and six ratings were killed on the whaler. Hall, T/Sub-Lt (E) R. Firing RNVR, T/Lt (E) K. A. Larsen RNR, and sixteen ratings were taken prisoner. One D lighter, **LCT.12**, was sunk and the second drifted onto the enemy coast. Skipper P. D. Jackson RNR, was killed and T/Skipper J. J. Fortune RNR was taken prisoner.
	To begin Operation TREACLE, six thousand troops of the Polish Carpathian Brigade were ferried to Tobruk, covered by the cruisers of the 7th and 15th Cruiser Squadrons. On the first night, destroyers JERVIS, KIMBERLEY, and HASTY departed Alexandria, Egypt, for Tobruk in the first troop movement. The destroyers arrived back at Alexandria on the 20th.
	Antiaircraft cruiser COVENTRY departed Alexandria for the Suez Canal Area. The cruiser arrived at Suez, Egypt, on the 20th.
	Destroyer HOTSPUR departed Alexandria to relieve destroyer HAVOCK at Haifa, Palestine. Destroyer HAVOCK arrived back at Alexandria on the 20th.
	Australian sloop PARRAMATTA departed Port Said, Egypt, escorting motor transport ship KEVINBANK to

Famagusta, Cypress, in Operation GUILLOTINE convoy serial S.23. The sloop arrived on the 21st and then sailed for Port Said.

20 AUGUST 1941

Submarine THRASHER sank small Greek steamer **SAN STEFANO** with gunfire off Cape Malea, Greece.

Italian S.79 torpedo bombers (Capt Buscaglia) badly damaged tanker **TURBO** (4782grt) in 32, 08N, 31, 57E. Sloop FLAMINGO and trawlers from Port Said, Egypt, assisted the damaged tanker. The entire crew was rescued. The tanker arrived at Port Said on the 21st.
On 23 September, the tanker was moved to Suez. On 1 April 1942, the tanker departed Suez, Egypt, for Aden in the tow of steamer GLADYS MOLLER (5285grt). At 25, 16N, 35, 25E on 4 April, the tanker broke in half and sank.

Light cruisers AJAX and NEPTUNE departed Alexandria, Egypt, covering minelayer LATONA with destroyers KIPLING, NIZAM, and KINGSTON en route to Tobruk, Libya, in the second series of troop transfers for Operation TREACLE.

Destroyers HOTSPUR and DECOY departed Haifa, Palestine, for Beirut, Egypt.

21 AUGUST 1941

Destroyers KANDAHAR, GRIFFIN, and JACKAL departed Alexandria, Egypt, for Tobruk, Libya in the third Operation TREACLE transfer. The destroyers returned to Alexandria on the 22nd.

Destroyer NAPIER departed Port Said, Egypt, for Alexandria after turbine repairs to rejoin the Mediterranean Fleet. On her arrival at Alexandria on the 22nd, Captain D of the 7th Destroyer Flotilla re-embarked on his flagship.

A report that troopship DUNERA (11,162grt) was under attack by aircraft caused Australian minesweeper BATHURST to be diverted to search for her.
Antiaircraft cruiser COVENTRY departed Suez, Egypt, to protect shipping in anchorage F.
Sloop FLAMINGO departed Port Said, Egypt for Suez.
It was later discovered that the report was an inaccurate rebroadcast of the SOS of the tanker **TURBO** attack.

Gunboat GNAT departed Alexandria to relieve gunboat APHIS at Mersa Matruh, Egypt.

German bombing damaged Egyptian steamer EL FATH (311grt) at Famagusta, Cypress. Four crewmen were killed.

| 0630 | While returning from the Operation TREACLE troop transfer, German Ju88 aircraft of III/LG.1 damaged destroyer NIZAM with a bomb near miss north of Bardia, Libya. Destroyer KINGSTON towed NIZAM for a time until she could proceed under her own power. The light cruisers AJAX and NEPTUNE provided cover for the destroyer's return to Alexandria. |

22 AUGUST 1941

An explosion destroyed the wreck of Italian tanker **STROMBO** (5232grt) off Scaramanga, Italy.

Minelayer ABDIEL departed Alexandria, Egypt, with destroyers JERVIS, HASTY, and KIMBERLEY for Tobruk, Libya, in the fourth Operation TREACLE troop transfer.
Light cruisers PHOEBE, NAIAD, and GALATEA of the 15th Cruiser Squadron covered the ships carrying troops. The ships arrived back at Alexandria on the 23rd.

Australian destroyer STUART departed Alexandria with one engine inoperative to return to Australia, arriving on 16 September at Fremantle, Australia.
The 10th Destroyer Flotilla ceased to exist after her departure.
Australian destroyer VENDETTA was then attached to the 7th Destroyer Flotilla, and destroyer DECOY was attached to the 2nd Destroyer Flotilla.
STUART was sent on to Williamstown *(probably King William's Town)*, South Africa, for a refit.

German bombing damaged Greek steamer LESBOS (1009grt) at Tobruk, Libya.

23 AUGUST 1941

Destroyers NAPIER and JACKAL departed Alexandria, Egypt, to intercept any Italian supply ships attempting to enter Bardia, Libya. A merchant ship was sighted by submarine TALISMAN in 33, 30N, 24, 20E, however no further contact was made. The ship turned northward to avoid the British ships. The destroyers arrived back at Alexandria on the 24th.

There was no Operation TREACLE transfer on this day.

24 AUGUST 1941

Light cruisers AJAX and NEPTUNE departed Alexandria, Egypt, covering minelayer LATONA plus destroyers KIPLING, KINGSTON, and GRIFFIN in the fifth Operation TREACLE troop transfer to Tobruk, Libya. The ships arrived back at Alexandria on the 25th.

25 AUGUST 1941

Submarine RORQUAL (Lt Napier) laid mines off Cape Skinari, Greece, in the Aegean Sea.

	Light cruisers NAIAD, PHOEBE, and GALATEA departed Alexandria, Egypt, to cover minelayer ABDIEL with destroyers JACKAL, HASTY, and KANDAHAR on the sixth Operation TREACLE troop transfer to Tobruk, Libya. The light cruisers were unsuccessfully attacked at dusk on the 25th. All ships safely returned to Alexandria on the 26th.
	Yugoslav torpedo boats DURMITOR and KAJMAKALAN, completely out of service after two operations off Bardia, Libya, were ordered to depart Mersa Matruh, Egypt, and returned to Alexandria. The boats arrived on the 26th.

26 AUGUST 1941

	Light cruisers AJAX and NEPTUNE departed Alexandria, Egypt, escorting minelayer LATONA plus destroyers JERVIS (Rear Admiral Destroyers, Mediterranean Fleet embarked), GRIFFIN, and HAVOCK in the seventh Operation TREACLE troop transfer to Tobruk, Libya. The ships arrived back at Alexandria on the 27th.
	Antiaircraft ship CARLISLE arrived at Alexandria from Port Said, Egypt.
	Destroyers DECOY and HOTSPUR arrived at Alexandria from Haifa, Palestine.
	Submarine RORQUAL laid fifty mines off Skinari, Greece.
	Sub-Lt (A) G. B. Pudney was killed when his Hurricane aircraft of 806 Squadron was shot down ten miles north of Sidi Barrani, Libya.

27 AUGUST 1941

	German Ju87 aircraft sank whaler **SKUDD III** (245grt) (Lt R. C. Macmillan RCNVR) at Tobruk, Libya. T/Midshipman J. T. Bloxham RNR and two ratings were killed. T/Sub-Lt E. R. Swift RNVR died of wounds. Two ratings were missing and six ratings were wounded.
	Light cruisers NAIAD, GALATEA, and PHOEBE departed Alexandria, Egypt, covering minelayer ABDIEL plus destroyers KIPLING, KINGSTON, and HOTSPUR in the eighth Operation TREACLE troop transfer to Tobruk. ABDIEL and destroyers KIPLING, KINGSTON, and HOTSPUR returned to Alexandria from Tobruk, independently, arriving on the 28th.
	Australian sloop PARRAMATTA departed Port Said, Egypt, for Famagusta, Cypress, with motor transport ship SALAMAUA (6676grt) on the last Operation GUILLOTINE convoy serial 24. The ships, plus steamer RODI (3220grt), arrived at Famagusta on the 29th. The sloop then returned to Alexandria.
2145	Italian S.79 aircraft of 279 Squadron (Capt Masini) heavily damaged light cruiser PHOEBE with aerial torpedoes north of Sidi Barrani, Libya, in 32, 15N, 24, 53E. PHOEBE reported eight ratings killed. Destroyers JERVIS, KANDAHAR, KIMBERLEY, and HASTY departed Alexandria to escort the damaged ship. PHOEBE was able to proceed to Alexandria under her own power and after temporary repairs was sent to the United States for permanent repairs.

28 AUGUST 1941

	Submarine RORQUAL (Lt Napier) sank Italian steamer **CILICIA** (2747grt) with three torpedoes southwest of Navarino, Greece, in 36, 00N, 21, 30E. Italian torpedo boat ANTARES rammed the submarine and damaged her periscope and then covered the second steamer, ALFREDO ORIANI (3059grt), away from the attack area.
	Light cruisers AJAX and NEPTUNE departed Alexandria, Egypt, escorting minelayer LATONA with destroyers NAPIER, JACKAL, and DECOY in the ninth Operation TREACLE troop transfer to Tobruk, Libya. The ships arrived back at Alexandria on the 29th.

29 AUGUST 1941

	Destroyers GRIFFIN and HAVOCK departed Alexandria, Egypt, for Tobruk, Libya, in the tenth and final Operation TREACLE troop transfer to Tobruk. The destroyers arrived back at Alexandria on the 30th.
	Destroyers KINGSTON and HASTY departed Alexandria for Beirut, Lebanon.

31 AUGUST 1941

	Australian light cruiser HOBART departed Haifa, Palestine, for Alexandria, Egypt, where she arrived on 1 September.
	Sloop FLAMINGO departed Alexandria for Port Said, Egypt, for intended duty in the Red Sea.
	An Axis air raid on Alexandria late on the 31st and early on 1 September caused a number of casualties on shore, but no damage was done to ships or facilities. Cdr E. E. Addis Rtd of NILE and Sub-Lt J. Roper RNR of THORGRIM were killed and another officer wounded. There were also a number of rating casualties.

Black Sea

Long. E27, 00 – E43, 00   Lat. N48, 00 – N41, 00

1 AUGUST 1941

	Russian aircraft bombed the oil and harbour facilities at Constanza, Romania.
	Russian submarines SHCH-208, SHCH-209, M-33 and SHCH-211 patrolled the western Black Sea until 28 August.
	Russian submarines M-36, SHCH-215, M-34 and later M-35 and M-31, followed by M-62 took turns patrolling the northwest area of the Black Sea around Odessa, Ukraine.
	Russian submarine M-33 patrolled off Constanza.
	Russian submarines A-3, SHCH-212 and M-32 patrolled the middle and southern areas of the Black Sea.
	Russian submarines SHCH-201 and SHCH-202 patrolled the eastern areas of the Black Sea.

2 AUGUST 1941

	Russian submarine L-5 (Lt Cdr Zhdanov) laid fourteen mines off Mangalia, Romania.

8 AUGUST 1941

	The Russian Black Sea Fleet (RAdm G. V. Zhukov) established a Task Group under RAdm D. D. Vdovichenko to support the Russian Army along the coast northwest of Rayons. Included in this group was the cruiser KOMINTERN, destroyers SHAUMYAN and NEZAMOZHNIK, minelayer LUKOMSKI, gunboats KRASNAYA ABCHAZIYA, KRASNY ADZHARISTAN, KRASNAYA ARMENIYA and KRASNAYA GRUZIYA, the 2nd Torpedo Boat Brigade with three divisions of twelve, eighteen, and ten boats, and the 5th Minesweeping Division with seven auxiliary minesweepers based at Odessa and Ochakov, Ukraine.
	The Russian Danube Flotilla supported the withdrawal of Russian troops over the Bug River Delta until 12 August.

11 AUGUST 1941

	Russian submarine M-33 unsuccessfully attacked Romanian submarine DELFINUL off Constanza.
	Russian submarine SHCH-211 (Lt Cdr Devyatko) dropped two agents off Varna, Bulgaria.
	Russian submarine SHCH-301 (Lt Cdr Grashchev) unsuccessfully attacked two convoys off Landsort, Romania.

12 AUGUST 1941

	Romanian submarine DELFINUL began patrolling from Sevastopol to Odessa, Ukraine, to stop Russian supply convoys to the surrounded German garrison at Odessa.
	Romanian MTBs VISCOLUL, VIJELIA and VIFORUL patrolled the Russian coast from Sevastopol to Odessa to stop Russian supply convoys to the surrounded German garrison at Odessa.
	The Russian Danube Flotilla began evacuating Russian troops from the lower Dnepr River area. The evacuation continued until the 16th.
	Russian submarine L-4 (Lt Cdr Polyakov) laid twenty mines southeast of Mangalia, Romania.

13 AUGUST 1941

	Russian destroyers SHAUMYAN and NEZAMOZHNIK plus gunboat KRASNY ADZHARISTAN along with coastal defence batteries No.412 and No.726 supported a counterattack by the 1st Marine Rifle Regiment at Grigorevka, Ukraine.
	Russian destroyers SHAUMYAN, NEZAMOZHNIK, FRUNZE and DZERZHINSKI bombarded Romanian positions around Odessa and Ochakov, Ukraine, until 20 August.

14 AUGUST 1941

	The Russians evacuated the naval base at Nikolaev, Ukraine. All ships under construction, including battleship **SOVETSKAYA UKRANIA** (59,150grt), heavy cruiser **ORDZHONIKIDZE** (11,300grt), submarines **S-36**, **S-37** and **S-38** with two gunboats in the Marti South Yard and battle cruiser **SEVASTOPOL** (35,540grt), heavy cruiser **SVERDLOV** (11,300grt) plus destroyers **OTMENNY**, **OBUCHENNY**, **OTCHAYANNY** and **OBSHITELNY** in Kommunar 61 North Yard were destroyed to prevent capture. Ships undergoing a refit, heavy cruisers FRUNZE (11,300grt) and KUJBYSHEV (11,300grt), destroyer leaders KIEV and EREVAN, destroyers SVOBODNY, OGNEVOI and OZORNOI, submarines S-35, L-23, L-24, and L-25 with ice breaker MIKOYAN were towed away to other ports. Russian destroyers BODRY, BOIKI, BEZUPRECHNY, BESPOSHCHADNY, DZERZHINSKI, FRUNZE, NEZAMOZHNIK and SHAUMYAN covered the evacuation group.

15 AUGUST 1941

	Russian submarine L-5 laid a minefield off Sulina, Romania.
	Russian gunboats KRASNAYA ARMENIYA and KRASNAYA GRUZIYA provided Russian troops fire support at Grigorevka and Spridovka at Odessa, Ukraine.
	Russian submarine **S-39**, still under construction at Nikolaev, Ukraine, was scuttled to prevent her capture.
	Russian submarine SHCH-211 (Lt Cdr Devyatko) sank Romanian steamer **PELES** (5708grt) after SHCH-216 unsuccessfully attacked a convoy off Cape Emine, Romania.

16 AUGUST 1941

	Russian submarine L-5 (Lt Cdr Zhdanov) laid fourteen mines off Mangalia, Romania.

19 AUGUST 1941

	The Russian 2nd Destroyer Division with destroyer leader TASHKENT plus destroyers BEZUPRECHNY and BESPOSHCHADNY attacked German and Romanian supply ships near Meshchank, Mikhajiovka and Visarka near Odessa, Ukraine. The destroyers fired over 450 13-cm shells at the Axis ships.
	Russian submarine L-4 (Lt Cdr Polyakov) laid twenty mines off Cape Olinka, Romania.
	Russian submarine M-33 (Lt Surov) unsuccessfully attacked Romanian submarine DELFINUL off Constanza, Romania.

21 AUGUST 1941

	After German troops took Kherson, Ukraine, the Russian Black Sea Fleet decided to keep cruiser CHERVONA UKRAINA, KRASNY KRYM, KRASNY KAVKAZ, ice breaker MIKOYAN, destroyer leaders TASHKENT and KHARKOV with destroyers BODRY, BOIKI, BEZUPRECHNY, BESPOSHCHADNY, SPOSOBNY, SMYSHLENY and SOOBRAZITELNY on alert to support the Russian Army at Odessa, Ukraine.
Night	During the night of 21/22 August, Russian cruiser KRASNY KRYM, destroyers DZERZHINSKI and FRUNZE plus gunboat KRASNAYA ARMENIYA bombarded Romanian positions at Sverdlovka and Chebanka near Odessa, Ukraine.

24 AUGUST 1941

	Russian submarine L-4 (Lt Cdr Polyakov) laid twenty mines off Cape Olinka, Romania.
	Russian submarines S-32 and S-33 joined SHCH-212 and SHCH-216 along the Romanian coast while small submarines M-34 and M-36 patrolled off the Bulgarian coast.

28 AUGUST 1941

	Russian submarine L-5 (Lt Cdr Zhdanov) laid fourteen mines off Mangalia, Romania.

31 AUGUST 1941

	Russian submarine M-34 unsuccessfully attacked Italian tanker TAMPICO (4958grt) off Varna, Bulgaria.

Red Sea
Long. E32, 00 – E43, 00   Lat. N30, 00 – N15, 00

4 AUGUST 1941

	Light cruiser CALEDON departed Suez, Egypt, for Bombay, India, where she began a refit from 18 August to 13 October.

6 AUGUST 1941

	Antiaircraft ship CARLISLE arrived at Suez, Egypt, to give antiaircraft protection to ships in the anchorage.

11 AUGUST 1941

	A mine damaged American steamer IBERVILLE (5685grt) in the Red Sea.

15 AUGUST 1941

	Battleship BARHAM arrived at Suez, Egypt, after repairs of her Crete battle damages in Durban, South Africa. The battleship departed Port Said, Egypt, that evening escorted by antiaircraft ship COVENTRY with destroyers JACKAL, NIZAM, KIPLING, and KINGSTON. Troopship GLENGYLE (9919grt) sailed in company with the group. The ships arrived at Alexandria, Egypt, on the 16th.

19 AUGUST 1941

	Light cruiser GALATEA arrived at Suez, Egypt, to join the Mediterranean Fleet.

20 AUGUST 1941

Antiaircraft cruiser COVENTRY arrived at Suez, Egypt, and escorted troopships ÎLE DE FRANCE (43,450grt), NIEUW AMSTERDAM (36,287grt), and ORION (23,371grt) to Port Tewfik, Egypt.

21 AUGUST 1941

Greek light cruiser AVEROFF departed Port Sudan, Egypt, for Aden and Bombay, India, for boiler repairs.

26 AUGUST 1941

The 166th South African Minesweeping Group arrived at Suez, Egypt, with trawlers GRIBB, IMHOFF, SEKSERN, and TREERN. After passing through the Suez Canal, the trawlers were sent to Haifa, Palestine, to be equipped for duty in the Mediterranean.

31 AUGUST 1941

Antiaircraft ship CARLISLE arrived at Suez, Egypt.

Arabian Sea

Long. E43, 00 – E77, 00   Lat. N31, 00 – N00, 00

8 AUGUST 1941

Convoy BA.4 departed Bombay, India, escorted by AMC HECTOR, sloop CORNWALLIS, and auxiliary patrol ship DIPAVATI. The sloop and patrol vessel were detached from the convoy on the 9th. The convoy was dispersed on the 12th.

10 AUGUST 1941

Heavy cruiser EXETER arrived at Bombay, India, from Aden.

11 AUGUST 1941

Heavy cruiser EXETER departed Bombay, India, escorting convoy BP.12 with troopships KHEDIVE ISMAIL (7290grt), RAJULA (8478grt), TALMA (10,000grt), VARELA (4651grt), LANCASHIRE (9557grt), ROHNA (8602grt), SANTHIA (7754grt), and VARSOVA (4701grt) to Basra, Iraq. She returned to Bombay on the 17th.
There was no convoy BP.13.

24 AUGUST 1941

Light cruiser CERES was damaged in a collision with Norwegian tanker GYLFE (6129grt) off Bombay, India. The cruiser's stem was fractured, but she was able to depart Bombay later that day escorting convoy BM.8 to Trincomalee, Ceylon.

Convoy BM.8 departed Bombay with steamers EKMA (5101grt), NEVASA (9213grt), EGRA (5108grt), ETHIOPIA (5574grt), and EL MADINA (3962grt) escorted by light cruiser CERES to Trincomalee.
AMC ANTENOR escorted the convoy to 31 August, when light cruiser DAUNTLESS relieved her from the escort.
The convoy arrived at Port Swettenham on 2 September.

25 AUGUST 1941

Operation COUNTENANCE was the overall operation supporting the British invasion of Iran. There were three naval operations and two ground force operations in this plan.
Operation RAPIER was the original name for the capture of Abadan and Khorramshahr, but was not used.
In Operation BISHOP, the Royal Navy captured the port and shipping at Bandar Shahpur with AMC KANIMBLA (Capt Adams), gunboat COCKCHAFER, sloop LAWRENCE, corvette SNAPDRAGON, minesweeping trawlers ARTHUR CAVANAGH and LILAC, Anglo Iranian Oil Company salvage tugs ST ATHAN and DELAVAR, RAF Launch.20, and dhow DAIF.
Sloop LAWRENCE seized Iranian gunboats **CHAZBAAZ** (331grt) and **KARKAZ** (331grt).

German steamer **HOHENFELS** (7862grt) was captured by a boarding party from AMC KANIMBLA and renamed EMPIRE KEMAL (7862grt). The steamer left Bandar Shahpur under tow for Karachi, India, on 11 October.

German steamer **MARIENFELS** (7575grt) was captured by a boarding party from AMC KANIMBLA and was renamed EMPIRE RANI (7575grt). The steamer sailed for Karachi on 8 September.

German steamer **STURMFELS** (6288grt) was captured by corvette SNAPDRAGON and was renamed EMPIRE KUMARI (6288grt). The steamer sailed for Karachi on 5 September.

The crew of German steamer **WEISSENFELS** (7861grt) scuttled the ship at Bandar Shahpur to prevent her capture. The ship was beyond salvage.

German steamer **WILDENFELS** (6224grt) was captured by a boarding party from AMC KANIMBLA and was renamed EMPIRE RAJA (6224grt). The steamer departed on 2 September for Karachi, Sindh (Pakistan).

Australian sloop YARRA sank Iranian gunboat **BABR** (950grt) at Abadan, Iran.

	The crew of Italian tanker **BRONTE** (4769grt) set the ship on fire, but she was salvaged and renamed EMPIRE PERI (4769grt). On 4 September, tanker **BRONTE** left Basra, Iraq, in tow of sloop FALMOUTH for Karachi.
	The crew of Italian steamer **BARBARA** (3065grt) set the ship on fire, but sloop LAWRENCE put a fire-fighting unit aboard the steamer, assisted by antisubmarine trawler ARTHUR CAVANAGH and salvage tug DELAVAR. The steamer was renamed EMPIRE TAJ (3065grt) and departed Bandar Shahpur under of tow of corvette SNAPDRAGON on 3 September 1941 for Karachi. At Chahbar, Iran, on 9 September, Australian sloop YARRA took over the tow, and they arrived at Karachi on 13 September.
	The crew of Italian steamer **CABOTO** (5225grt) set the ship on fire to prevent her capture by sloop LAWRENCE, but the fire was extinguished by LAWRENCE, antisubmarine trawler ARTHUR CAVANAGH, and salvage tug DELAVAR. She was towed by sloop SHOREHAM to Karachi, departing on 1 September.
	Gunboat COCKCHAFER captured a floating dock at Bandar Shahpur, Iran.
	American steamers PUERTO RICO (6076grt) and ANNISTON CITY (5687grt) were at Bandar Shahpur during the operation.
	In Operation MARMALADE, the Royal Navy destroyed the Iranian naval forces at Khorramshahr at the junction of the Shatt Al-Arab and the Karun River. Sloops FALMOUTH and YARRA, Kenyan launch BALEEKA, and armed river tug SOURIYA operated at Khorramshahr. YARRA captured Iranian gunboats **CHAROGH** and **SIMORGH**, depot ship **IVY**, and tug **NEYROU**. The Iranian Naval Commander in Chief, RAdm Bayendor, was killed ashore while defending the base.
	In Operation CRACKLER, the Royal Navy captured the island of Abadan and its attendant oil refinery and facilities. Armed yacht SEABELLE, sloop SHOREHAM, Indian auxiliary minesweeper LILAVATI, armed river steamers IHSAN and ZENOBIA, five Eureka motorboats, two motor dhows, and one motor launch were deployed against Abadan. Sloop SHOREHAM sank Iranian gunboat **PALANG** (950grt) at Abadan. Operation DEMON involved the landing of troops at Abadan.
	Convoy BA.5 departed Bombay escorted by AMC HECTOR and auxiliary patrol vessels DIPAVATI and SONAVATI. The patrol vessels were detached from the convoy on the 26th. The convoy was dispersed on the 31st. There were no convoy BA.6 or convoy BA.7.

26 AUGUST 1941

	In Operation MOPUP, the Royal Navy successfully cleared Iranian forces from the Khazalabad area between Khorramshahr and Abadan.

27 AUGUST 1941

	Australian sloop YARRA captured Italian steamer **HILDA** (4901grt) at Banda Addas, Iran. The crew set the ship afire, but the fires were extinguished. The sloop towed her to Chahbar Bay before a salvage tug was required. The captured steamer departed Chahbar Bay for Karachi under tow of the tug SYDNEY THUBRON on 8 September. She became a Royal Navy repair ship.
	Heavy cruiser EXETER departed Aden escorting troopship MAURETANIA (35,677grt) and arrived at Durban, South Africa, on 2 September.

INDIAN OCEAN

East of South Africa
Long. E25, 00 – E60, 00   Lat. S00, 00 – S60, 00

17 AUGUST 1941

	Australian heavy cruiser AUSTRALIA and heavy cruiser HAWKINS were ordered to search for a Vichy French convoy which had departed Tamatave, Madagascar, on the 12th. The mission was named Operation RATION with the codename of KEDGREREE.

18 AUGUST 1941

2350	Australian heavy cruiser AUSTRALIA departed Durban, South Africa, to search for the Vichy French convoy in Operation RATION. The convoy consisted of Vichy French steamers VILLE D'ORAN (10,172grt), LINOIS (7473grt), DALNY (6672grt), LEPARI, and SAGITTAIRE (7706grt). Operation RATION ended on the 25th, without contact with the convoy.

19 AUGUST 1941

0800	Heavy cruiser HAWKINS departed Durban, South Africa, to search for the Vichy French convoy in Operation RATION.

25 AUGUST 1941

	Light cruiser EMERALD arrived at the Seychelles.

Malaya
Long. E95, 00 – E105, 00   Lat. N17, 00 – N00, 00

25 AUGUST 1941

	Light cruiser DANAE arrived at Singapore.

PACIFIC OCEAN

South China Sea
Long. E105, 00 – E120, 00   Lat. N27, 00 – N10, 00

1 AUGUST 1941

	IJN frigate SHIMUSHU was reassigned to the Japanese Southern Expeditionary Fleet (Vice Admiral Ozawa Jisaburo) and based at Camranh Bay, Vichy French Indochina.
	IJN oiler TOEN MARU (5232grt) departed Mako, Pescadores, to support operations in southern China.

6 AUGUST 1941

	IJN aircraft ferry FUJIKAWA MARU was based in the Amoy area, off the Chinese southern coast.
	IJN cargo ship MANKO MARU (4471grt) departed her support position south of China for Mako, Pescadores.

12 AUGUST 1941

	IJN cargo ship TATSUWA MARU (6335grt) provided support for Japanese operations south of China.

15 AUGUST 1941

	IJN cargo ship TOYO MARU (2470grt) arrived at her support position south of China.

16 AUGUST 1941

	IJN cargo ship KIMISHIMA MARU (5193grt) departed her support position south of China for Mako, Pescadores.

20 AUGUST 1941

	IJN cargo ship KIMISHIMA MARU (5193grt) arrived at her support position south of China from Mako, Pescadores.

21 AUGUST 1941

	IJN cargo ship NACHISAN MARU (4433grt) departed her support position south of China for Yawata, Japan.
	IJN cargo ship TOYO MARU (2470grt) departed her support position south of China.

26 AUGUST 1941

	IJN cargo ship TOYO MARU (2470grt) arrived at her support position south of China.

28 AUGUST 1941

	IJN cargo ship MANKO MARU (4471grt) arrived at her support position south of China.

29 AUGUST 1941

	IJN cargo ship KENRYU MARU (4575grt) departed her support position south of China for Osaka, Japan.

Dutch East Indies
Long. E105, 00 – E120, 00   Lat. N10, 00 – S15, 00

7 AUGUST 1941

	IJN oiler SAN DIEGO MARU (7269grt) arrived at Tarakan, Borneo.

East China Sea
Long. E120, 00 – E130, 00   Lat. N42, 00 – N20, 00

2 AUGUST 1941
	IJN patrol boat SHURI MARU (1857grt) arrived at Ryojun from a north China coastal patrol.

6 AUGUST 1941
	IJN patrol boat SHURI MARU (1857grt) departed Ryojun on a north China coastal patrol.

10 AUGUST 1941
	IJN oiler TOEN MARU (5232grt) arrived at Takao, Formosa.

19 AUGUST 1941
	IJN patrol boat SHURI MARU (1857grt) arrived at Ryojun from a north China coastal patrol.

22 AUGUST 1941
	IJN patrol boat SHURI MARU (1857grt) departed Ryojun on a north China coastal patrol.

Sea of Japan
Long. E128, 00 – E143, 00   Lat. N55, 00 – N33, 00

3 AUGUST 1941
	IJN transport KOMAKI MARU (8525grt) arrived at Sasebo, Kyushu.

6 AUGUST 1941
	Japanese cargo ship SANYO MARU (8360grt) was requisitioned by the IJN. She began conversion into a seaplane carrier/tender. Two 150-mm/45 cal single-mount guns, two Type 93 13-mm single-mount machine guns and a catapult were installed.

7 AUGUST 1941
	IJN cargo ship TOYO MARU (2470grt) departed Korean waters for Sasebo, Kyushu.

10 AUGUST 1941
	A mine sank Russian submarine **M-63** off Vladivostok, Russia. All hands were lost.

11 AUGUST 1941
	IJN transport KOMAKI MARU (8525grt) departed Sasebo, Kyushu, for the central China coast.
	IJN river gunboats ATAKA (725grt), SETA (340grt), FUSHIMI (374grt) and SUMIDA (350grt) were attached to the Japanese China Area Fleet of the Japanese First China Expeditionary Fleet (Vice Admiral, Prince, Komatsu Teruhisa).

14 AUGUST 1941
	IJN battleship KIRISHIMA arrived at Sasebo, Kyushu.

15 AUGUST 1941
	IJN seaplane tender SANYO MARU (8360grt) completed her conversion. She was re-rated as a converted seaplane tender and attached to the Sasebo Naval District. The SANYO MARU was issued the call sign JJLC. Her aircraft complement was six Type 0 Mitsubishi F1M2 "Pete" scout float biplanes and two Type O Aichi E13A1 "Jake" three-seat reconnaissance floatplanes with two Type 95 Nakajima E8N2 "Dave" two-seat reconnaissance float bi-planes in reserve. Her assigned aircraft code was "ZIII-xx."
	An unexplained cause sank Russian steamer **TUNGUS** (2607grt) between Vladivostok and the La Perouse Strait.

17 AUGUST 1941
	IJN oiler SAN PEDRO MARU (7268grt) arrived at Kudamatsu, Japan.

18 AUGUST 1941
	IJN auxiliary CHIYODA continued training crewmen for the midget submarines using CHIYODA as the target. During a subsequent conference, some crewmembers suggest using the new weapon to penetrate enemy naval bases to attack capital ships. They also suggested the use of "mother" submarines as midget submarine carriers to overcome the midget submarines' short-range problem. Soon thereafter, training of the second group was completed.

East of Philippine Islands
Long. E125, 00 – E140, 00   Lat. N20, 00 – N00, 00

5 AUGUST 1941

IJN oiler SAN PEDRO MARU (7268grt) departed Palau Sambu.

28 AUGUST 1941

IJN cargo ship SANTOS MARU (7266grt) arrived at Staring Bay, Kendari, in the Celebes, and assisted the salvaging of Japanese submarine I-5 from a reef, and then performed repairs on the submarine.

New Guinea and Solomon Islands
Long. E140, 00 – E180, 00   Lat. N00, 00 – S25, 00

13 AUGUST 1941

American heavy cruisers NORTHAMPTON (CA-26) and SALT LAKE CITY (CA-25) arrived at Port Moresby, New Guinea, from Brisbane, Australia, on a good will visit.

16 AUGUST 1941

American heavy cruisers NORTHAMPTON (CA-26) and SALT LAKE CITY (CA-25) arrived at Rabaul, New Britain, from Port Moresby, New Guinea, on a good will visit.

East of Australia
Long. E140, 00 – E155, 00   Lat. S12, 00 – S40, 00

1 AUGUST 1941

Japanese cargo ship ONOE MARU (6667grt) arrived at Sydney, Australia.

5 AUGUST 1941

American heavy cruisers NORTHAMPTON (CA-26) and SALT LAKE CITY (CA-25) arrived at Brisbane, Australia, on a good will visit.

East of Japan
Long. E130, 00 – E180, 00   Lat. N55, 00 – N30, 00

1 AUGUST 1941

IJN battleships KIRISHIMA, HYUGA and HIEI departed Beppu, Japan, and arrived at Saiki, Japan.

IJN seaplane tender KIMIKAWA MARU (6863grt) completed her conversion at Kure, Japan. She was assigned to the Sasebo Naval District. Her authorized aircraft allotment was six Type 0 Aichi E13A1 "Jake" three-seat reconnaissance floatplanes with two in reserve.

6 AUGUST 1941

IJN oiler TOEI MARU (10,023grt) arrived at Tokuyama, Japan.

The IJN requisitioned Japanese salvage vessel YAMABIKO MARU (6795grt).

The IJN requisitioned Japanese cargo ship KONGO MARU (8624grt). She was registered as an auxiliary light auxiliary cruiser.

7 AUGUST 1941

IJN oiler HOYO MARU (8691grt) arrived at Tokuyama, Japan.

8 AUGUST 1941

Japanese liner SHOKAKU (30,000grt) was commissioned at Yokosuka, Japan, and assigned as special duty ship. Captain Jojima Takatsugu was assigned as the Commanding Officer.

Japanese tanker NIPPON MARU (9975grt) began conversion into a naval auxiliary tanker at Kawasaki Heavy Industries shipyard, Kobe, Japan.

The IJN requisitioned Japanese oiler MANJU MARU (6515grt) when she arrived at Yokkaichi, Japan. She was chartered to support the Kure Naval district.

9 AUGUST 1941

The IJN requisitioned Japanese cargo ship KANTO MARU (8606grt). She began conversion into an armed auxiliary aircraft transport. 120-mm (4.7-inch) guns were installed at the bow and the stern. She was registered in the Kure Naval District.

	IJN oiler MANJU MARU (6515grt) departed Yokkaichi, Japan.

10 AUGUST 1941

	The IJN requisitioned Japanese liner KIKU MARU and converted her into a hospital ship.
	Japanese liner ASAMA MARU (16,975grt) returned to Yokohama, Japan.
	IJN oiler MANJU MARU (6515grt) arrived at Yokosuka, Japan, from Yokkaichi, Japan. She probably discharged fuel oil.

11 AUGUST 1941

	IJN battleship KIRISHIMA departed Saiki, Japan.
	IJN battleship MUTSU was attached to Battleship Division 1, Japanese Combined Fleet. She was stationed at Yokosuka, Japan, for crew rotations and repairs.
	IJN battleship NAGATO was attached to Battleship Division 1, Japanese Combined Fleet. She was stationed at Yokosuka, Japan, for crew rotations and repairs.

12 AUGUST 1941

	IJN aircraft carrier HOSHO became the flagship for Japanese Carrier Division 3.
	IJN battleship YAMATO departed Kure, Japan, for sea trials.
	The IJN requisitioned Japanese passenger cargo ship KEIYO MARU (6442grt). She began conversion into an armed auxiliary aircraft transport. 120-mm (4.7-inch) guns were installed at the bow and the stern.
	IJN oiler MANJU MARU (6515grt) departed Yokosuka, Japan, for Kawasaki and Kataoka Bay, Kuriles.

13 AUGUST 1941

	IJN submarine chaser CH-23 was launched.

15 AUGUST 1941

	IJN AMC HOKOKU MARU was fitted with one 1100-mm and one 900-mm searchlight and special heavy-duty booms for handling floatplanes. She carried one Type 94 Kawanishi E7K2 "Alf" floatplane and one spare plane. Equipment installation was completed. On the same day, the 24th Cruiser Squadron (Raider) (Rear Admiral Takeda Moriji) was formed and attached directly to the Japanese Combined Fleet. The HOKOKU MARU, AIKOKU MARU and the KIYOSUMI MARU were assigned to Cruiser Division 24.
	IJN salvage vessel YAMABIKO MARU (6795grt) was commissioned (registered) in the IJN and assigned to the Kure Naval District. She began conversion at the Fujinagata Zosensho shipyard in Osaka, Japan.
	The IJN requisitioned Japanese cargo ship BANGKOK MARU (5350grt) and she was registered as a specially installed cruiser in the Kure Naval District.
	IJN torpedo recovery vessel KAMIKAZE MARU (4916grt) was rated as a specially installed torpedo depot ship.
	The IJN requisitioned Japanese cargo ship HIDE MARU (5181grt) to be fitted as an ammunition ship.
	The IJN requisitioned Japanese oiler KUROSHIO MARU (10,383grt) at Tama, Japan.
	IJN cargo ship MEITEN MARU (4474grt) departed Yokosuka, Japan, for the South Seas area (probably Truk).

16 AUGUST 1941

	Japanese passenger cargo ship HEIAN MARU (11,614grt) returned to Yokohama, Japan, in ballast from Seattle, Washington. Her arrival marked the last voyage of a Japanese vessel to Seattle prior to the outbreak of the Pacific War.
	The IJN requisitioned Japanese cargo ship AWATA MARU (7397grt) and converted her into an auxiliary cruiser.
	The IJN requisitioned Japanese cargo ship ONOE MARU (6667grt).
	The IJN requisitioned Japanese cargo ship KOFUKU MARU (3209grt).

17 AUGUST 1941

	The IJN requisitioned Japanese cargo ship KENYO MARU (6486grt).
	The IJN requisitioned Japanese cargo ship SANUKI MARU (7158grt). She began conversion into a seaplane tender. Two 150-mm/45 cal single mount guns, two 80-mm single mount guns, two 13.2-mm single mount machine guns, and a catapult were installed.
	The IJN requisitioned Japanese liner KAMAKURA MARU (17,526grt) as a charter vessel and attached her to the Yokosuka Naval District.
	Japanese liner TATSUTA MARU (16,975grt) arrived at Yokohama, Japan.

18 AUGUST 1941

	The IJN requisitioned Japanese tanker SHINKOKU MARU (10,020grt), and she was registered as a converted merchant transport (oil supply) in the Kure Naval District.
	Japanese liner KAMAKURA MARU (17,526grt) departed Yokosuka, Japan.

20 AUGUST 1941

	The IJN requisitioned Japanese tanker TOHO MARU (9997grt) and registered her as a converted transport (oil supply) in the Yokosuka Naval District.
	IJN battleship HARUNA was assigned to the Japanese First Fleet (Vice Admiral Takasu Shiro) in Battleship Division 3 (Vice Admiral Mikawa Gunichi) at Hashirajima, Japan, with battleships KONGO, HIEI and KIRISHIMA.
	IJN submarine chasers CH-20 and CH-21 were completed and registered in the Kure Naval District.

21 AUGUST 1941

	IJN cargo ship SANTOS MARU (7266grt) departed Yokosuka, Japan.
	IJN battleships HIEI and HYUGA departed Saeki, Japan, and arrived at Hashirajima, Japan.
	The IJN requisitioned Japanese cargo ship SAIGON MARU (5350grt), and she was converted into an auxiliary cruiser.
	German steamer ODENWALD (5098grt) departed Yokohama, Japan, for Bordeaux, France.
	The IJN requisitioned Japanese cargo ship SENKO MARU (2618grt).
	IJN cargo ship TEISEN MARU (5019grt) (ex German **URSULA RICKMERS** (5019grt)) arrived at Tokyo, Japan, for her first voyage under charter. She carried coal and lumber from Kushiro, Hokkaido, to Nagoya, Japan.

22 AUGUST 1941

	Japanese oiler KUROSHIO MARU (10,383grt) began her conversion for the IJN at Tama Zosen shipyard.

23 AUGUST 1941

	IJN aircraft carrier SHOKAKU (30,000grt) departed Yokosuka, Japan, for a quick shakedown cruise to Ariake, Japan.
	Japanese cargo ship AWATA MARU (7397grt) arrived at Kobe, Japan, from Hankow, China. She began conversion into an auxiliary cruiser at Mitsubishi Heavy Industries' shipyard. She was fitted with four 140-mm single mount guns, a twin Type 96 25-mm AA guns, one quadruple-mount, one dual mount and four single mount Type 93 13.2-mm machine guns and three single mount 7.7-mm machine guns. Two 553-mm torpedo tubes were installed.
	Japanese cargo ship HIDE MARU (5181grt) arrived at Osaka Iron Works and began her conversion into an IJN ammunition ship.

24 AUGUST 1941

	IJN patrol boat PB-2 began reconstruction with Nos. 3 and Nos. 4, 4.7-inch/45 cal main guns. The second bank of torpedo tubes and her depth charge equipment were removed. Her stem was cut down to the waterline to form a ramp. She was fitted to carry and launch two 46-ft Daihatsu landing craft. Her interior spaces were modified to accommodate up to 250 troops.

25 AUGUST 1941

	Japanese tanker SHINKOKU MARU (10,020grt) began conversion into a naval auxiliary at Naniwa Dockyard, Osaka, Japan.
	IJN aircraft carrier SHOKAKU (30,000grt) arrived at Ariake, Japan, from Yokosuka, Japan. She became flagship of Japanese First Air Fleet after she completed working up to combat efficiency. She was assigned to Carrier Division 5.

26 AUGUST 1941

	The IJN requisitioned Japanese cargo ship ARATAMA MARU (6784grt) and she was assigned to Kure Naval District.

27 AUGUST 1941

	The IJN requisitioned Japanese cargo ship ONOE MARU (6667grt).

28 AUGUST 1941

	IJN submarine chaser CH-26 was launched.
	Japanese Army cargo ship GOSHU MARU (2211grt) arrived back at Yokosuka, Japan.
	IJN liner TATSUTA MARU (16,975grt) departed Kobe, Japan, with 349 Jewish war refugees.
	The IJN requisitioned Japanese cargo ship YAMASHIMO MARU (6776grt).

	The IJN requisitioned Japanese oiler KYOEI MARU No.2 (1192grt).
	IJN oiler MANJU MARU (6515grt) arrived at Odomari, Karafuto (Sakhalin Island).

29 AUGUST 1941

	The IJN requisitioned Japanese cargo ship HOKOKU MARU (10,439grt).
	Japanese tanker HOYO MARU (8691grt) began conversion into a naval auxiliary oiler.
	Japanese cargo ship BANGKOK MARU (5350grt) began conversion into an armed merchant cruiser at Ujina Zosen. Four 120-mm (4.7-inch) single mount guns, one 7.7-mm machinegun were fitted. Provisions were made for carrying and launching 500 mines.
	IJN oiler MANJU MARU (6515grt) departed Odomari, Karafuto (Sakhalin Island).

30 AUGUST 1941

	Japanese cargo ship HOKOKU MARU (10,439grt) began the installation of four 152-mm (6-inch) guns, two 76-mm/40 cal (3-inch) antiaircraft guns, type 93 type 13.2-mm MGs and two 533-mm torpedo tubes at the Mitsubishi Heavy Industries shipyard at Kobe, Japan.
	IJN battleship MUTSU arrived at Yokosuka, Japan.
	The IJN requisitioned Japanese cargo ship KOGYO MARU (6353grt) to be converted into an ammunition ship.
	IJN cargo ship KAIHEI MARU (4575grt) departed Tokyo, Japan.

31 AUGUST 1941

	Japanese passenger cargo ship AIKOKU MARU (10,437grt) was completed.
	IJN cargo ship LYONS MARU (7017grt) arrived at Yokosuka, Japan.
	IJN oiler MANJU MARU (6515grt) arrived at Nabilsky (Sakhalin Island).

Gilbert – Marshall Islands   Long. E150, 00 – E180, 00   Lat. N30, 00 – N00, 00

11 AUGUST 1941

	IJN coastal minelayer TOKIWA was assigned to the Japanese Fourth Fleet (VAdm Inouye Shigeyoshi) in Mine Division 19 (RAdm Shima) with transport MOGAMIGAWA MARU (7497grt), minelayer OKINOSHIMA and auxiliary minelayer TENYO MARU at Truk.

18 AUGUST 1941

	American cargo ship REGULUS (AK-14) arrived at Wake Island with the U.S. Marine Corps 1st Defence battalion.

28 AUGUST 1941

	IJN light cruiser TENRYU was based at Truk in the Japanese Fourth Fleet (Vice Admiral Inoue Shigeyoshi) in Cruiser Division 18 with light cruiser TATSUTA.

New Zealand   Long. E150, 00 – E180, 00   Lat. S25, 00 – S60, 00

29 AUGUST 1941

	New Zealand light cruiser ACHILLES departed Auckland, New Zealand, and joined steamer RIMUTAKA (16,576grt) off Cape Palliser. The steamer was escorted to 250 miles southeast of Chatham Island. On 2 September, the steamer was detached and the light cruiser joined another steamer, which was escorted to Wellington, New Zealand.

Hawaii Area   Long. W180, 00 – W140, 00   Lat. N30, 00 – N00, 00

1 AUGUST 1941

	Japanese liner ASAMA MARU (16,975grt) departed Honolulu, Hawaii, for San Francisco, California.

West of United States   Long. W130, 00 – W110, 00   Lat. N50, 00 – N30, 00

2 AUGUST 1941

	Japanese liner TATSUTA MARU (16,975grt) waited off San Francisco, California, unwilling to land until it was sure her cargo of $2,500,000 worth of raw silk would not be seized as a result of the U.S. embargo on Japanese

4 AUGUST 1941

Japanese liner ASAMA MARU (16,975grt) was recalled to Japan from a position 980 miles east of Honolulu, Hawaiian Territory.

Japanese liner TATSUTA MARU (16,975grt) departed San Francisco, California, with 320 kiloliters (84,489 gals.) of oil. She carried the last oil cargo exported to Japan from the United States.

14 AUGUST 1941

Japanese oiler ITSUKUSHIMA MARU (10,006grt) arrived at San Francisco, California.

West of South America
Long. W140, 00 – W70, 00   Lat. N05, 00 – S60, 00

14 AUGUST 1941

German AMC SCHIFF.45/KOMET (KAdm Eyssen) sank steamer **AUSTRALIND** (5020grt) off the Galapagos Islands in 04, 13S, 91, 03W. Two crewmen were killed and the rest became prisoners of war. One survivor later died on the raider.

17 AUGUST 1941

German AMC SCHIFF.45/KOMET (KAdm Eyssen) captured Dutch steamer **KOTA NOPAN** (7322grt) west of South America in 01, 22S, 89, 10W. The steamers cargo included 2800-tons of sago, 1500-tons of rubber, 1200-tons of tin and 1200-tons of manganese. After taking on fuel from the prise, the ship was sent to Vichy France and eventually arrived there on 14 November.

19 AUGUST 1941

German AMC SCHIFF.45/KOMET (KAdm Eyssen) sank steamer **DEVON** (9036grt) about two hundred miles southwest of the Galapagos Islands, in 05S, 91W. The entire crew was rescued and became prisoners of war.

SEPTEMBER 1941
DAY-TO-DAY OPERATIONS

SECTION CONTENTS

SUMMARY 208	MEDITERRANEAN SEA & MIDDLE EAST 249
GENERAL 210	*East of Gibraltar* *249*
ARCTIC OCEAN 212	*Middle Mediterranean Sea*..............................*252*
Greenland Sea and Barents Sea....................*212*	*Eastern Mediterranean Sea* *255*
White Sea *214*	*Black Sea*..*260*
NORTH ATLANTIC OCEAN 215	*Red Sea* *262*
Iceland and North of Britain..........................*215*	*Arabian Sea*..*263*
Norwegian Sea *221*	INDIAN OCEAN...263
East of Canada...*222*	*East of South Africa*......................................*263*
East of United States......................................*228*	*South Indian Ocean* *264*
Caribbean and Gulf of Mexico.......................*228*	*Bay of Bengal*...*264*
Western Approaches *228*	*Malaya*..*264*
Central Atlantic Crossing Zone.....................*233*	*West of Australia*..*264*
UK East Coast..*236*	PACIFIC OCEAN.......................................264
North Sea...*239*	*South China Sea* *264*
English Channel..*240*	*Dutch East Indies* *265*
Bay of Biscay..*240*	*South of Australia*..*265*
West of Gibraltar...*241*	*East China Sea* *265*
West of North Africa *244*	*Sea of Japan*...*266*
SOUTH ATLANTIC OCEAN 245	*East of Australia*..*266*
East of South America *245*	*East of Japan*..*266*
West of South Africa *245*	*Gilbert – Marshall Islands*.............................*270*
BALTIC SEA..246	*New Zealand* *271*
Kattegat and Skagerrak.................................*246*	*South of Hawaii*..*271*
Southern Baltic Area.....................................*246*	*West of South America*...................................*271*
Gulf of Finland..*247*	

SUMMARY

GERMANY

The German Navy began to feel the bite of British and Russian submarines against their arctic bound convoys. Heavy fog and rocky crags also took a toll of merchant shipping.

The German Navy put a full press on the Russian Baltic Fleet trying to eliminate it permanently. The combined land, air and sea attacks caused heavy Russian losses.

The new Wolfpack attacks showed great promise in the North Atlantic battle. Several allied convoys were heavily attacked with high losses. The rise in U-boat kills finally took some of the pressure off German *Großadmiral* Dönitz, who had promised he could strangle Britain if given enough U-boats.

The movement of German U-boats into the Mediterranean was begun in earnest. The first boat made it successfully through the Gibraltar Straits, but it was not yet ready to begin anti-shipping operations.

ITALY

The Italian Fleet sortie against the Operation SUBSTANCE convoy was one of the bravest acts of the war. An out-gunned Italian force entered into battle against a known larger British force without radar. Had the British found them, they would probably have been slaughtered. As it turned out, they managed to miss contact by a few hundred miles and returned safely to port with only a heavy use of oil to show for their valour.

Meanwhile, the Italian supply convoys continued to steadily lose precious cargo ships to the British Naval and Air Forces. If the September loss rate continued, the Italians would soon be unable to supply the Axis army in North Africa.

ROMANIA

The Romanians were slowly taking losses from the Russian Black Sea Fleet ships. Losses to Russian submarines and mines were beginning to have an effect on Romanians ability to support the Romanian and German Army movements into the Crimea.

JAPAN

The Japanese finally made the decision to enter into a war with the United States and the European Colonial Powers in the South Pacific. The Imperial Japanese Navy ran extensive war games to explore their options. Once they agreed upon a set of actions, they began the detailed planning to allocate ships and equipment to the various objectives.

The conversion of civilian ships to military support ships continued as fast as the Japanese shipyards could work. With the American embargo in place, many of the ships needed for the conversion were sitting idle and could be quickly put into the conversion queue.

FINLAND

In a high level meeting, the Finns made it very clear to the German high command that Finland would not participate in any military operations beyond their original 1939 border. The Finnish Navy continued to support mining operations and attacks on Russian bases still on Finnish territory, but that was the extent of their activities.

VICHY FRANCE

The Vichy Government continued to tacitly obey the directions from Berlin. The Pro-Nazi groups took on their orders with great enthusiasm, while most of the French people did the slow roll and only acted when they had too.

Meanwhile, the French people were getting very hungry on the short rations allocated to the civilian population. Many French men and women had to take jobs with the Vichy or German organizations to survive.

BRITAIN

The Royal Navy began the first of many long gruelling convoy runs to and from Russia. These Arctic convoys would tie up a large part of the Home Fleet for the next five years. It was a cold, miserable and hazardous duty, which was to take many lives before it was over.

The North Atlantic situation took a down turn as the new German Wolfpack tactics devastated a couple of convoys. While the overall loses were still manageable, the psychological impact was great as some convoys experienced 50% or greater losses.

The cost to supply Malta continued to rise. Italian aircraft caused considerable damage both to ships and port facilities. The extensive minefields in the Sicilian Straits were not discovered until a ship was lost in the area. While exploding mines with a ship identified the minefield, it was a very costly method of mine detection.

On the plus side, British air and sea forces were taking a steady harvest of Italian and German cargo ships supplying the Axis North African Army. With German General Rommel held impotent by the lack of fuel and supplies, the British poured new troops and equipment into Tobruk, Libya and along the Egyptian border for a renewed offensive into Libya to break the encirclement of Tobruk.

The British also began to strengthen their position at Singapore. Their intelligence agents throughout the area began to send firm information that the Japanese were building a force to attack through Malaya and into Burma and the Dutch East Indies. Neither the British nor the Dutch had much in the way of military forces in the area to stop them.

UNITED STATES

The United States basically ended its neutrality with the armed escort of British convoys to and from Europe. The attack on destroyer GREER (DD-145) was inevitable and she was lucky not to have been sunk. The shoot-on-sight order was borderline legal, as the Geneva Convention still called for the Germans to surface and identify themselves to neutral ships before attacking. So technically, the President was merely ordering his ships to treat any unidentified submarine as one committing an act of piracy until it proved its intentions were peaceful. These old laws enabled the President to broadly interpret the neutrality act.

Meanwhile, the United States sent small forces on their way to strengthened the long neglected defences in the Pacific. The United States intelligence agents also saw the signs of a pending Japanese attack and began to plan accordingly.

RUSSIA

The Russian Northern Fleet managed to take control over the Norwegian Arctic coast. Working in Cooperation with the British, the Russians put their submarines all along the German convoy routes and began to sink a few German ships. The Russian surface ships helped escort the Arctic convoys to and from Russian coastal waters.

The Russian Baltic Fleet was still fighting as hard as it could, but the accuracy of German dive-bombers was taking a heavy toll on the Russian capital ships. The extensive German and Finnish minefields sank a fair number of Russian submarines and smaller surface ships. The fleet was trapped at Leningrad and knew its fate was that of the city, so they supported the land war as best they could and formed Marine combat units to fight alongside the Russian Army.

The Russian Black Sea Fleet still had control, but they were taking heavy losses due to German aircraft and aerial mines. The Fleet took every opportunity to provide gunfire support to the Russian Army still fighting in the Crimea. The Russian submarine force patrolled off the Bulgarian and Romanian coasts and attacked any axis ship that came within range.

CHINA

The Chinese Army began to have limited success against the Japanese Army in China. As veteran Divisions were pulled out of China for the new offensives south, the Chinese were able to overpower the fresh, but un-blooded Japanese Divisions that replaced them. The Chinese showed that they could take the initiative when the Japanese underestimated their fighting ability.

POLAND

The newly formed Polish Brigade was successfully moved into Tobruk, to relieve the tired Australian units. Their orders were to hold Tobruk and advance out to meet the British Army once the offensive began. The Polish soldiers were more than ready to kill some Germans and Italians.

FREE FRENCH

The Free French forces were also providing units both to the British Eighth Army in Egypt, but also to the forces in Tobruk, Libya. Deep desert units provided the British with key intelligence information about German and Italian troop dispositions and their sorry supply state.

The Free French Navy provided convoy escorts and continued to train volunteers to take on more ships as they became available.

GENERAL

DATE	COMMENTS
1 September	In Shanghai, China, the U.S. Consul General, the Commander of the U.S. Navy's Yangtze Patrol, and the Commanding Officer of the 4th Marine Regiment, recommended that all U.S. naval forces in China, i.e., river gunboats and the U.S. Marines, be withdrawn.
1 September	The Royal Navy introduced a new naval code; but due to a mathematical error, the German B-Service quickly cracked the code and began to read the British dispatches.
1 September	OKW head Field Marschall Keitel visited Finnish Field Marshal Carl Gustaf Mannerheim to discuss joint operations on the Karelian peninsula and against the Russian-held Hanko area. Mannerheim make it clear that he opposed any actions beyond Finland's 1939 territorial borders, and he was not prepared to attack Hanko with Finnish troops. Such an operation would have to be done by the Germans alone.
1 September	During September, the *Luftwaffe* dropped 555 aerial mines in British waters.
3 September	Nationalist Chinese forces recaptured Fuchow, China, from the Japanese.
3 September	In Operation EGV.1 and Operation EVG.2, the Royal Navy evacuated all Norwegians from Spitsbergen and closed down the coalmines there.
4 September	A German U-boat attacked American destroyer GREER (DD-145) in the North Atlantic. The destroyer had trailed the U-boat and announced its position over the radio. When British aircraft dropped depth charges, the U-boat thought it was under attack by the American destroyer and retaliated.
4 September	In Operation EGV.1, the Royal Navy launched a carrier air attack on German ships off Tromsø, Norway.
5 September	The German Naval command decided to send six U-boats into the Mediterranean to intercept British ships taking supplies to Tobruk, Libya. A support base was set up at Salamis, near Athens, Greece, to support the U-boats.
6 September	The Japanese military leaders decided that they would go to war with the United States and its allies in Southeast Asia if the current negotiations did not succeed by 10 October.
6 September	German *Großadmiral Dönitz* ordered the MARKGRAF U-boat Group to spread out over a larger area southeast of Greenland.
7 September	The German Sixth Army broke through the Russian positions at Konotop in the Ukraine. The German Twentieth Army ended its offensive to capture the Russian port of Murmansk from Finland. The Russian forces were too strong for the Germans to advance, and many troops had already been moved south to support German Army Group South.
7 September	The RAF Bomber Command bombed Berlin, Germany, for the first time since the Battle of Britain. In the early war years, bombing Germany was the only means of striking directly at the enemy's homeland and war production. Plans for a major bombing offensive, known as the strategic air offensive, were ambitious, but limited by technical difficulties in the early stages.
7 September	In Operation STRENGTH, the Royal Navy delivered twenty-four Hurricane aircraft of the RAF 151 Fighter Wing to Vaenga Airfield, near Murmansk, Russia.
7 September	In Operation INDIGO III, American Task Force TF.15 departed Argentia, Newfoundland, for Iceland with an army brigade to replace the U.S. Marine Corps brigade delivered earlier.
8 September	German troops reached the Finnish Army at Schluesselburg to complete the encirclement of Leningrad, Russia.
8 September	British code breakers at Bletchley Park advised the Submarine Tracking Room of the new positions taken up by the German MARKGRAF U-boat group. Convoys ON.12S, HX.148 and SC.43 were moved far to the south to avoid their detection by the U-boats.
8 September	The Germans launched their amphibious invasion against the Estonian Islands from northern Kurland in Latvia. Operation BEOWULF I was a success, for within a very short period of time, all German objectives had been met. The operation was basically a repetition of the invasion plan the Germans used against the Estonian Islands in the First World War.
9 September	In Operation STATUS, the Royal Navy launched fourteen Hurricane aircraft to Malta.
10 September	The first use of German Wolf Pack tactics caused heavy losses for convoy SC.42 off Greenland.
10 September	The Imperial Japanese Navy began a series of war games to assess what strategies would work best for the Japanese in a war with the United States. After the analysis was completed and briefed to the Japanese Combined Fleet Commander Admiral Isoroku Yamamoto on the 13th, he concluded that the attack strategy recommended would work.
11 September	American President Franklin D. Roosevelt declared a shoot-on-sight order against all German and Italian shipping that threatened American ships. This order was his response to the U-boat torpedo attack on American destroyer GREER (DD-145) off Iceland.
11 September	The German U-boat command began using map coordinates based upon numbers and letters to identify a specific location. This new coordinate system was adopted to prevent the Allies from being able

	to locate the position of U-boats operating at sea from message interception.
12 September	German forces in the Kremenchug bridgehead across the Dnepr River in the Ukraine advanced north to aid in the encirclement of Kiev.
13 September	At 0400 hours, The main German attack against Muhu Island off Estonia began.
13 September	Hitler ordered that the transfer of six U-boats to the Mediterranean be expedited immediately.
13 September	During the night of 13/14 September, RAF Bomber Command attacked the German battleships in Brest Harbour, France.
13 September	In Operation STATUS, the Royal Navy launched nineteen Hurricane aircraft to Malta.
13 September	In Operation PROPELLER, a single steamer departed Gibraltar for Malta and safely arrived with supplies on the 19th.
14 September	In North Africa, British naval forces failed in their attempt to achieve a landing at Tobruk, Libya.
14 September	German Army Group Centre encircled two Russian armies at Kiev, Ukraine.
14 September	By the afternoon, German troops reached the village of Saastna on Muhu Island, Estonia. A short while later, the Germans had breached the Saaremaa-Muhu Island causeway and were pushing the Russian forces towards westwards.
15 September	The United States Atlantic Fleet began to escort convoys of British ships as far as Iceland. The Middle Ocean Meeting Point (MOMP) was set at 26W. The American Task Force TF.4 (RAdm Bristol), operating from Argentia, Newfoundland, and Hvalfjord, Iceland, would escort HX and ON convoys from Newfoundland and Iceland. The Canadian Newfoundland Escort Force (RAdm Murray) would escort the slower SC and ONS convoys to the MOMP, where British escort groups would hand over or take over escort. The German government protested that such escort violated American neutrality.
15 September	During the night of 15/16 September, RAF Bomber Command attacked Hamburg, Bremen, Cuxhaven, and Wilhelmshaven, Germany.
16 September	Riza Khan was forced to abdicate the Persian throne while British and Russian forces jointly occupied the country.
16 September	In Operation BEOWULF I, German troops expanded their attack to Dago Island off Estonia.
17 September	The United States government allocated a $100,000,000 loan to Russia for the purchase of war materiel.
17 September	In Operation SUPERCHARGE, the Royal Navy transferred 6300 British troops and 2100 tons of supplies to Tobruk, Libya, from 17 to 27 September.
18 September	German Army Group South captured Poltava, Ukraine.
18 September	The Japanese Naval Commander ordered the preparation for offensive actions in the Pacific.
19 September	German troops captured Kiev, Ukraine, after six weeks of heavy fighting. The German High Command claimed 650,000 Russian soldiers had been taken as prisoners of war, with 884 tanks and 3,718 guns captured. Russian civilian loses were estimated at half a million, Germany had lost 100,000 men so far on the Eastern Front.
19 September	During the night of 19/20 September, RAF Bomber Command attacked Stettin, Germany.
20 September	The 1st Yokosuka SNLF (Special Naval Landing Force) was formed, at Yokosuka Naval District, with a battalion of 520 paratroopers. This force became a part of the Sasebo Raiding Force.
20 September	In Operation ROMULUS, German AMCs were supplied in the Pacific Ocean off the Tuamotu Archipelago from a German steamer stationed in Japan.
21 September	German troops reached the town of Kuressaare on Saaremaa Island off Estonia.
21 September	The Allied Mid Ocean Meeting Place (MOMP) was moved from 26W to 22W longitude to shorten the British escort range.
24 September	German Army Group South attacked the land bridge at Perekop, Ukraine, to open the German advance into the Crimea.
24 September	In Operation GOEBEN, the German Navy began sending U-boats through the Gibraltar Straits into the Mediterranean. The last U-boat made the trip on 5 October.
25 September	Adolph Hitler ordered German Army Group North to lay siege to Leningrad, Russia, and starve the city into surrender. He also ordered that, after the city fell, it was to be levelled to the ground.
26 September	The Free French government in London under General de Gaulle signed an alliance with Russia.
26 September	One of the special German Brandenburg commando teams had to be withdrawn from Saaremaa Island after taking heavy casualties. The Russians had quickly found them after their arrival by gliders and kept them under heavy fire until they could be taken off the island.
26 September	In Operation HALBERD the Royal Navy supported a convoy taking supplies to Malta from Gibraltar.
27 September	In Operation CHOPPER, the Royal Navy landed a commando unit at St Vaast, near Cherbourg, France, during the night of 27/28 September.
27 September	In Operation EJ, the United States Atlantic Fleet and the Royal Navy held a conference in Iceland to conduct joint naval activities in the North Atlantic.
28 September	In a conference at Moscow, Josef Stalin, Ambassador Harriman (United States), and Lord Beaver-

	brook (United Kingdom) agreed that the United States would extend assistance to Russia through the Lend-Lease Act of March 1941.
29 September	German forces attacking into the Crimea failed to cross the land bridge.
29 September	The Germans downed a Russian courier aircraft carrying maps of the entire Russian defences on Saaremaa Island off Estonia.
29 September	During the night of 29/30 September, RAF Bomber Commander attacked Stettin and Hamburg, Germany.
30 September	During the night of 30 September/1 October, RAF Bomber Command attacked Stettin and Hamburg, Germany.
30 September	Armoured forces of German Army Group Centre captured Orel, Russia, to place German troops within one hundred miles of Moscow, Russia.

ARCTIC OCEAN

Greenland Sea and Barents Sea
Long. W180, 00 – E180, 00   Lat. N90, 00 – N68, 00

1 SEPTEMBER 1941

	Trawler HAZEL, Belgian trawler VAN OOST, and tanker OLIGARCH (6897grt) arrived at Sveagruva, Spitsbergen, Norway.
	Light cruiser NIGERIA plus destroyers ICARUS, ANTELOPE, and ANTHONY arrived at Gronfjord, Spitsbergen with troopship EMPRESS OF CANADA (21,517grt) from Archangel, Russia, to embark Norwegians from Spitsbergen, Norway.

2 SEPTEMBER 1941

	Light cruiser NIGERIA arrived at Isfjord, Spitsbergen, from Archangel, Russia, with destroyers ICARUS, ANTELOPE, and ANTHONY and troopship EMPRESS OF CANADA (21,517grt).
	Light cruiser AURORA departed Sveagruva, Spitsbergen, for Gronfjord, Spitsbergen.
	The aircraft carrier VICTORIOUS group departed Sardam Bay, Spitsbergen, to conduct an air attack on a German convoy north of Tromsø, Norway. Oiler ALDERSDALE (8402grt) refuelled the ships before they departed and awaited their return on the 5th with destroyer ESCAPADE.

3 SEPTEMBER 1941

	Trawler HAZEL, Belgian trawler VAN OOST, and tanker OLIGARCH (6897grt) departed Sveagruva, Spitsbergen, after Operation EGV.1 and Operation EVG.2 ended.
	The Spitsbergen community was embarked on the EMPRESS OF CANADA (21,517grt), and the town was then demolished. The cruisers, destroyers, and the troopship departed Spitsbergen for the Clyde. On the 4th, the cruisers were detached from the force.
	Russian submarines D-3, SHCH-402, M-173, K-1, SHCH-422, M-174 (two patrols), K-2, SHCH-401, M-171, M-172 and M-175 patrolled off the Norwegian Arctic coast until 26 September.
	Russian submarine K-1 (Capt 3rd Class M. P. Avgustinovich) operated off the Vestfjord, Norway, without success for twenty-eight days.
	Submarine TRIDENT unsuccessfully attacked U.566 while returning to Poljarnoe, Russia.
	Submarine TIGRIS (Cdr Bone) sank Norwegian steamer **RICHARD WITH** (905grt) off Breisund, Norway.
	Russian submarine SHCH-422 (Lt Cdr Malyshev) unsuccessfully attacked a target off Tanafjord, Norway.
	Trawler ELM departed Gronfjord, Spitsbergen, for Akureyri, Iceland, with four Norwegian prise ships.
0030	The aircraft carrier VICTORIOUS group launched aircraft to attack a German convoy off Tromsø, Norway. Due to the clear weather, the aircraft did not attack the convoy and returned to the VICTORIOUS as ordered.
0540	German air reconnaissance spotted Force M, and the rendezvous with Force L was altered to a position in 75, 25N, 06, 50E.

4 SEPTEMBER 1941

	Force M rendezvoused with Force L for Operation STRENGTH north of Hope Island in 75, 25N, 06, 50E.
	During the night, Force A detached troopship EMPRESS OF CANADA (21,517grt) with three destroyers for Scapa Flow, while the rest of the force searched for German shipping off Svaerholthavet, Norway.

5 SEPTEMBER 1941

	Russian submarine SHCH-422 (Lt Cdr Malyshev) unsuccessfully attacked a target off Tanafjord, Norway.
0730	Destroyers ELECTRA and ACTIVE arrived at Murmansk, Russia.
1800	Destroyers ELECTRA and ACTIVE departed Murmansk for Archangel, Russia.

7 SEPTEMBER 1941

	Minelayer ADVENTURE delivered a load of mines to the Russian Northern Fleet at Murmansk, Russia.
0130	In heavy weather, light cruisers NIGERIA and AURORA attacked a German convoy of steamers BARCELONA (3101grt) and TRAUTENFELS (6418grt), escorted by German gunnery ship BREMSE, in an inlet east of North Cape, Norway. German **BREMSE** was sunk in the action. Light cruiser NIGERIA was badly damaged by a Russian sunken wreck or mine during the engagement and could only make eight knots. The German steamers escaped in the fog carrying 1500 men of the German 6th Mountain Division aboard to Porsangerfjord, Norway.
1100	In Operation STRENGTH, aircraft carrier ARGUS with Force L of heavy cruiser SHROPSHIRE plus destroyers SOMALI, MATABELE, and PUNJABI and Force M of heavy cruisers DEVONSHIRE and SUFFOLK, aircraft carrier VICTORIOUS, plus destroyers INGLEFIELD, ECLIPSE, and ESCAPADE delivered twenty-four Hurricane aircraft of the RAF 151 Fighter Wing to Vaenga airfield, near Murmansk, Russia. The aircraft launched from a position south of Spitsbergen, Norway.

10 SEPTEMBER 1941

	Russian submarine K-2 (Capt 3rd Class Utkin with the commander of the 1st Submarine Division Capt 2nd Class Gadzhiev on board) laid the first Russian minefield off Vardø, Norway. The Germans later removed the mines after they discovered the field.
	In Operation STRENGTH, aircraft carrier ARGUS with heavy cruiser SHROPSHIRE plus destroyers MATABELE, PUNJABI and SOMALI launched twenty-four Hurricane aircraft of the 151 Fighter Wing to the Vaenga airfield outside of Murmansk, Russia. A further twenty-four Hurricane aircraft arrived by steamer at Archangel, Russia, and arrived at Vaenga airfield the next day.
	Minelayer ADVENTURE delivered more mines to Murmansk for Russian use.

11 SEPTEMBER 1941

	Russian destroyers GREMYASHCHI, GROMKI, GROZNY and SOKRUSHITELNY laid two minefields with British-supplied mines along the Russian Kola coast. The mining was completed by the 15th.
Night	During the night, Russian motor torpedo boats TKA-11 (Lt Cdr Svetlov) and TKA-12 (Lt Shabalin) attacked a German supply convoy off the Petsamo Fjord, Finland, escorted by German patrol boat NT.05/TOGO (ex Norwegian motor boat **OTRA**). No ships were lost in this first encounter by Russian MTBs operating against the German Navy in the Arctic.

12 SEPTEMBER 1941

	Russian submarine K-2 (Capt 3rd Class Utkin with the commander of the 1st Submarine Division, Capt 2nd Class Gadzhiev on board) damaged German steamer LOFOTEN (1517grt) with gunfire off Persfjord, Norway.
	Russian submarine SHCH-422 (Lt Cdr Malyshev) sank Norwegian steamer **OTTAR JARL** (1459grt) off Tanafjord, Norway.

13 SEPTEMBER 1941

	Submarine TIGRIS sank Norwegian steamer **RICHARD WITH** (905grt) off Breisund, Norway, in 70, 50N, 23, 57E.
	Russian submarine M-171 unsuccessfully attacked a ship off Liinahamari, Finland, in 69, 38N 031, 15E.

14 SEPTEMBER 1941

	Russian submarine M-173 (Lt Cdr Kunets) dropped off thirteen agents on the coast of the Norwegian Varanger Peninsula.
	Russian TKA-13 (Lt Polyakov) and TKA-15 (Lt Chapilin) damaged Norwegian steamer MIDNATSOL (978grt) on their way from Petsamo, Finland, to Kirkenes, Norway.

15 SEPTEMBER 1941

	Submarine TIGRIS unsuccessfully attacked German steamer BESSHEIM (1774grt) off Lopphavet, Norway.
	Russian TKA-14 (Lt Zhilyaev) torpedoed Norwegian steamer RANOY (286grt) off Petsamo, Finland.

16 SEPTEMBER 1941

	U.451 departed Kirkenes, Norway, and ran along the Norwegian coast, first to Bergen, Norway, and then finally to Kiel, Germany, on the 21st.

17 SEPTEMBER 1941

	Submarine TIGRIS unsuccessfully attacked German convoy R.152 one mile southwest of Loppa, Norway, in 70, 21N, 21, 30E.

21 SEPTEMBER 1941

	German motor minesweeper R.158 was damaged in a collision with German patrol boat NT.05/TOGO (ex Norwegian minelayer **OTRA**) off northern Norway.

23 SEPTEMBER 1941

	Submarine TRIDENT (Cdr Sladen) unsuccessfully attacked German troopship WESER (9179grt) off Rolvsöy, Norway.
	Russian submarine SHCH-401 began a four-week patrol off Svaerholt, Norway.
	Russian submarine D-3 (Lt Cdr Konstantinov with the commander of the 2nd Submarine Division Capt 2nd Class Kolyshkin on board) made unsuccessful attacks on German convoys off Tanafjord, Norway, on 26, 27 and 30 September.
	Small Russian submarines M-171, M-172, M-173, M-174, M-175, and M-176 took turns patrolling for six to eight days off Varangerfjord, Norway.

26 SEPTEMBER 1941

	Russian submarine M-174 (Lt Cdr N. E. Egorov) penetrated the German base at Petsamo fjord, Finland, but her torpedoes only damaged the pier.
	Submarine TIGRIS damaged German submarine chaser UJ.1201 (527grt) off Rolvsöy Fjord, Norway.

27 SEPTEMBER 1941

	Russian submarine D-3 unsuccessfully attacked German submarine chaser UJ.1201 (527grt) while attacking a convoy off Tanafjord, Norway.

28 SEPTEMBER 1941

	During the night of 28/29 September, submarine TRIDENT (Cdr Sladen) torpedoed and heavily damaged submarine chaser UJ.1201 (527grt) off Rolvsöy Fjord. She was towed to port and was eventually repaired at Rostock, Germany. She became operational again on 29 April 1944.

30 SEPTEMBER 1941

	Russian submarine M-176 tried to penetrate the German port in Bokfjord at Kirkenes, Norway, but got entangled in the antisubmarine nets and had to back out of the harbour.
	Submarine TRIDENT (Cdr Sladen) unsuccessfully attacked German hospital ship BIRKA (1000grt) at Rolvsöy, Norway, in 71, 03N, 24, 34E.

White Sea

Long. E30, 00 – E60, 00   Lat. N68, 00 – N60, 00

15 SEPTEMBER 1941

	Russian submarines K-21 and K-23 became operational in the Russian Northern Fleet.
	Russian submarines K-22, L-22, L-20, K-3, S-101 and S-102 were still in transit through the White Sea canal system and would become operational with the Russian Northern Fleet in January 1942.

25 SEPTEMBER 1941

	Russian submarines K-3, S-101 and S-102 reached Molotovsk, Russia, on the White Sea after passing through the White Sea canal system from the Baltic.
	Russian submarine L-20 was not yet combat ready, and L-22 was retained for Russian operations in the White Sea.

27 SEPTEMBER 1941

	Destroyers ACTIVE and ELECTRA with Russian destroyers GREMYASHCHI, GROMKI and SOKRUSHITELNY joined with heavy cruiser LONDON at sea and escorted her to Archangel, Russia.
1600	Heavy cruiser LONDON delivered Lord Beaverbrook, representing Britain, and Averell Harriman, representing the United States, to Archangel, Russia, for a meeting with Josef Stalin in Moscow, Russia.

28 SEPTEMBER 1941

1200	Convoy QP.1 departed Archangel, Russia, with Dutch steamer ALCHIBA (4427grt), tanker BLACK RANGER (3417grt), steamers ESNEH (1931grt), LLANSTEPHAN CASTLE (11,348grt), NEW WESTMINSTER CITY (4747grt), LANCASTRIAN PRINCE (1914grt), and TREHATA (4817grt), and Russian steamers SEVZAPLES (3947grt), SUKHONA (3124grt), ALMA ATA (3611grt), BUDENNI (2482grt), MOSSOVET (2981grt), RODINA (4441grt), and STARY BOLSHEVIK (2974grt). Minesweepers HALCYON, HARRIER, and SALAMANDER provided local escort from 28 to 30 September. Heavy cruiser LONDON escorted the convoy from 28 September to 2 October.

	Heavy cruiser SHROPSHIRE escorted the convoy from 2 to 10 October, relieving heavy cruiser LONDON in 74, 55N, 27, 30E.
	Destroyers ELECTRA escorted the convoy from 28 September to 9 October, ACTIVE from 28 September to 5 October, and ANTHONY from 4 to 9 October.
	Trawlers MACBETH and HAMLET of the 73rd Minesweeping Group escorted the convoy from 28 September to 9 October.
	Trawler OPHELIA escorted the convoy from 28 September to 5 October. Trawler OPHELIA developed defects while escorting tanker BLACK RANGER en route to convoy PQ.1, and was towed by destroyer ACTIVE to Akreyri, Iceland, arriving on 10 October.
	Russian steamers SUKHONA and MOSSOVET straggled from the convoy, but arrived at their destination ports safely.
	The convoy dispersed off the Orkneys on 10 October, and the steamers proceeding to their destinations in coastal convoy WN.91.
	Heavy cruiser SHROPSHIRE was detached on 10 October and arrived at Scapa Flow.
	Destroyer ANTHONY arrived at Scapa Flow on 11 October escorting oiler BLACK RANGER and steamer LLANSTEPHAN CASTLE.
	Destroyer ELECTRA arrived at Scapa Flow on 11 October.

NORTH ATLANTIC OCEAN

Iceland and North of Britain   Long. W30, 00 – E03, 00   Lat. N68, 00 – N58, 30

1 SEPTEMBER 1941

	U.652, U.105, U.432, U.38, U.84, U.501, U.43, U.202, U.82, U.207, U.569, U.433, U.85 and U.81 formed German U-boat group MARKGRAF southwest of Iceland.
	The United States Navy assumed the duty to patrol the Denmark Strait. The patrol group (RAdm Giffen) included battleships IDAHO (BB-42), MISSISSIPPI (BB-41), and NEW MEXICO (BB-40) (two of these battleships on patrol at a time), heavy cruisers WICHITA (CA-45) and TUSCALOOSA (CA-37), plus destroyers of Destroyer Squadron 2 (Capt Ainsworth) with MORRIS (DD-417) (Flag), ANDERSON (DD-411), HAMMANN (DD-412), RUSSELL (DD-414), SIMS (DD-409), WALKE (DD-416), CHARLES F. HUGHES (DD-428), O'BRIEN (DD-415), and MUSTIN (DD-413) and Destroyer Division 22 with GWIN (DD-433) (Flag), GRAYSON (DD-435), MEREDITH (DD-434), and MONSSEN (DD-436). The group operated out of Hvalfjord, Iceland.
	American battleship MISSISSIPPI (BB-41) was currently on the Denmark Strait patrol with destroyers O'BRIEN (DD-415), WALKE (DD-416), STACK (DD-406), STERETT (DD-407) and ROWAN (DD-405) until 11 September.
0500	Force L arrived off Seidisfjord, Iceland, with heavy cruiser SHROPSHIRE plus destroyers SOMALI, MATABELE, and PUNJABI, but could not enter the port due to the heavy fog. The heavy cruiser proceeded to rendezvous with Force M (heavy cruiser DEVONSHIRE group) with destroyers SOMALI and MATABELE in 74N, 08E.
1045	Destroyer PUNJABI entered Seidisfjord.
1300	Destroyer PUNJABI departed Seidisfjord to rejoin Force L in 74N, 08E.
1830	Destroyer BEDOUIN arrived at Scapa Flow after her refit to work up to combat efficiency.

2 SEPTEMBER 1941

	American battleship ARKANSAS (BB-33) began a patrol of the Denmark Strait with destroyers RHIND (DD-404) and MAYRANT (DD-402) until 11 September.
	Force M with aircraft carrier VICTORIOUS, heavy cruisers SUFFOLK and DEVONSHIRE, plus destroyers ECLIPSE, ESCAPADE, INGLEFIELD, ELECTRA, ACTIVE, and IMPULSIVE departed Sardam Bay after refuelling for a raid on a German convoy off Hammerfest on the 3rd. Senior Officer Force M transferred his flag from heavy cruiser DEVONSHIRE to aircraft carrier VICTORIOUS from 1 to 4 September, when he returned to the heavy cruiser.
	Heavy cruiser LONDON arrived at Hvalfjord, Iceland, from Scapa Flow, via Akreyri, Iceland.
	Light cruiser SHEFFIELD was detached from convoy WS.11 and steamed to Scapa Flow, arriving on the 4th.
	Light cruiser EURYALUS departed Scapa Flow for Rosyth to change a propeller.
	Antisubmarine trawler CAPE PALLISER (497grt) reported an enemy ship twenty miles 25° from 62N, 17W, while on Northern Patrol. At Scapa Flow, heavy cruiser BERWICK and light cruiser KENYA were brought to one hour's alert notice, and heavy cruiser LONDON was ordered to stand by alert notice at Hvalfjord, Iceland. These alerts were later cancelled when it was determined the ship was a motor vessel.

3 SEPTEMBER 1941

	Force K arrived at Scapa Flow with three Norwegian coal ships, an icebreaker, a tug, and two other small ships captured at Spitsbergen, Norway.

	Minelayer MANXMAN arrived at Scapa Flow from Loch Alsh.
1000	Minelayer MANXMAN escorted by light cruiser KENYA and destroyer LIGHTNING departed Scapa Flow to lay Minefield EH off Stadlandet, Norway, during the night of 3/4 September.

4 SEPTEMBER 1941

	Minelayer PORT QUEBEC escorted by destroyer NEWARK laid Minefield SN.23A.
1415	American destroyer GREER (DD-145) (Lt Cdr Frost) was cooperating with British Hudson aircraft "M" of 269 Squadron about 175 miles west-southwest of Iceland to locate a U-boat sighted from the air. Once the GREER (DD-145) located the U-boat, the aircraft dropped two depth charges on U.652 (ObltzS Fraatz), who assumed that the destroyer dropped them. The submarine fired a torpedo at destroyer GREER (DD-145), which missed. Destroyer WATCHMAN joined the GREER (DD-145) briefly and was then detached to other duties.
>1416	After the incident with American Task Unit TU.1.1.5 and convoy ONS.10, the Germans moved the MARKGRAF group 150 sea miles to the west to avoid any further incidents with American warships.
2100	Destroyers BEDOUIN and VIVACIOUS departed Scapa Flow to meet battleship KING GEORGE V at Oxcars Gate in the Firth of Forth and provide escort for her to Scapa Flow on the 5th.

5 SEPTEMBER 1941

	U.501 (KKpt Hugo Förster) sank Norwegian steamer **EINVIK** (2000grt) (Master Finn Wetteland) while she was straggling behind convoy SC.41 after she lost contact in heavy weather about 450 miles southwest of Iceland in 60, 38N, 31, 18W. The entire crew of twenty-three made it into two lifeboats and were rescued on the 12th.
	Light cruisers NIGERIA and AURORA refuelled from oiler OLIGARCH (6897grt) and departed Seidisfjord, Iceland, to operate against German shipping off Norway.
0015	Minelayer MANXMAN, light cruiser KENYA and destroyer LIGHTNING arrived back at Scapa Flow after laying Minefield EH. The MANXMAN departed Scapa Flow later on the 5th to return to Loch Alsh.
1230	Destroyer LAFOREY departed Scapa Flow to relieve destroyer VERDUN off Kinnaird Head.
1600	Monitor EREBUS escorted by motor launch ML.188 departed Scapa Flow for Lerwick to carry out special trials in the Shetlands.
1700	Destroyer LINCOLN arrived at Scapa Flow after escort duty in convoy ON.10 to refuel and carry out degaussing trials.
2012	Battleship KING GEORGE V arrived at Scapa Flow from Rosyth with destroyers BEDOUIN, VIVACIOUS, and LAFOREY.
Night	U.141 sank Icelandic fishing trawler JARLINN (190grt) during the night near Iceland in 61N, 12W.

6 SEPTEMBER 1941

	American destroyer LANSDALE (DD-426) rescued three survivors from the sunken Panamanian steamer **LONGTAKER** (1700grt).
	American Task Unit TU.1.1.7 turned convoy HX.147 over to Escort Group EG.20 with destroyer COLUMBIA plus corvettes WETASKIWIN, MIMOSA and GLADIOLUS.
0100	Light cruiser PENELOPE departed Scapa Flow to rendezvous with the Spitsbergen ships in 62N, 05W.
1330	Destroyer LINCOLN departed Scapa Flow to join convoy FS.588 and provide additional escort to the Thames.
1515	Destroyer ESKIMO arrived at Scapa Flow from Sheerness.
1530	Monitor EREBUS and motor launch ML.188 arrived at Lerwick from Scapa Flow to carry out special trials in the Shetlands for the next six days.
1800	Light cruiser PENELOPE rendezvoused with the Spitsbergen ships in 62N, 05W. Destroyers LIGHTNING and ICARUS escorted the troopship EMPRESS OF CANADA (21,517grt) to the Clyde. Destroyers ANTELOPE and ANTHONY were detached to Scapa Flow. Off Cape Wrath, light cruiser PENELOPE was detached and returned to Scapa Flow.
2200	Destroyer LIGHTNING departed Scapa Flow to rendezvous with the Spitsbergen force.
2330	U.141 (Philipp Schüler) sank fishing trawler **KING ERIK** (228grt) near Iceland in 61, 01N, 12W. The entire crew of fifteen was lost when the ship exploded and immediately sank.

7 SEPTEMBER 1941

	Light cruiser PENELOPE returned to Scapa Flow after escort duty.
	Light cruiser PENELOPE departed Scapa Flow for the Clyde to escort battleship DUKE OF YORK.
	Minelayer AGAMEMNON laid Minefield SN.61 escorted by destroyer CASTLETON. After the mining, CASTLETON departed Loch Alsh for Scapa Flow.
	German bombing damaged steam trawler NAIRANA (225grt) seven to eight miles off Myggenaes, Faeroes.
0230	Destroyers BEDOUIN and ESKIMO departed Scapa Flow for Seidisfjord, Iceland, and proceeded from that port to join with the cruisers NIGERIA and AURORA, which were returning from Norway.
1000	Destroyers ANTELOPE and ANTHONY arrived at Scapa Flow after escorting the Spitsbergen force (see 6 September) to the Clyde.

>1000	Destroyers ANTELOPE and ANTHONY departed Scapa Flow for Rosyth for boiler cleaning.
1545	Destroyer ASHANTI arrived at Scapa Flow to work up to combat efficiency after her long period of repairs.

8 SEPTEMBER 1941

0800	Destroyer VIVACIOUS departed Scapa Flow to join destroyers LIGHTNING and ICARUS at the Clyde to escort battleship DUKE OF YORK from the Clyde to Rosyth on the 9th.

9 SEPTEMBER 1941

	Battleship PRINCE OF WALES plus destroyers LAFOREY, PUCKERIDGE, ASHANTI, CASTLETON, LAMERTON, and BADSWORTH were brought to half hour's alert notice, and battleship KING GEORGE V was brought to one hour's alert notice, on a report that German heavy cruiser ADMIRAL SCHEER had departed Oslo, Norway. It was later found that the German heavy cruiser was returning to Swinemünde, Germany, after two unsuccessful bombing raids the ship had undergone while at Oslo on 5 and 8 September.
	Force M with heavy cruiser DEVONSHIRE, aircraft carrier VICTORIOUS, plus destroyers SOMALI, MATABELE, and PUNJABI refuelled at Bell Sound.
	Force L with aircraft carrier ARGUS, heavy cruiser SHROPSHIRE, and destroyers INGLEFIELD, IMPULSIVE, and ECLIPSE had been detached from Force M, accompanied for a time by heavy cruiser SUFFOLK, and was proceeding to Seidisfjord, Iceland.
0430	Heavy cruiser LONDON departed Hvalfjord, Iceland, with a salvage tug to assist damaged light cruiser NIGERIA.
0700	Destroyer CASTLETON arrived at Scapa Flow from Loch Alsh to dock and effect repairs to her antisubmarine fittings.
2000	Destroyers BEDOUIN and ESKIMO joined with the light cruisers NIGERIA and AURORA, which were returning from Norway.
2322	Heavy cruiser LONDON was recalled to Hvalfjord, Iceland, for operations against German heavy cruiser ADMIRAL SCHEER, which was currently reported to be at Oslo, Norway.

10 SEPTEMBER 1941

	Force M with heavy cruiser DEVONSHIRE, aircraft carrier VICTORIOUS, plus destroyers SOMALI, MATABELE, and PUNJABI departed Bell Sound for Operation EGV.2. Before sailing, the Commander of the Force transferred from heavy cruiser DEVONSHIRE to aircraft carrier VICTORIOUS.
	Heavy cruiser SUFFOLK rejoined Force M at sea to support Operation EGV.2.
	Minelaying cruiser MANXMAN departed Scapa Flow for Loch Alsh.
	Light cruiser SHEFFIELD departed Scapa Flow for the Clyde in her return to Gibraltar.
1300	Battleship PRINCE OF WALES departed Scapa Flow with destroyers LAMERTON, BADSWORTH, and PUCKERIDGE to exercise west of Hoy.
1330	Minelayer WELSHMAN departed Scapa Flow with destroyers LAFOREY and ASHANTI to relieve the HUNT-class destroyers in the battleship PRINCE OF WALES' screen. The battleship and screen would then proceed to Hvalfjord to prepare for operations against the German heavy cruiser ADMIRAL SCHEER, which was expected to attempt a break through into the North Atlantic. Heavy cruiser LONDON was ordered to patrol the western approaches to the Denmark Strait.
1430	Battleship PRINCE OF WALES was ordered to remain in her practice area.
1600	Destroyers LIGHTNING and ICARUS were released from the battleship DUKE OF YORK escort. Destroyer LIGHTNING returned to Scapa Flow. Destroyer ICARUS proceeded to the Humber to commence a refit at Immingham.
2000	Destroyers BEDOUIN and ESKIMO arrived at Scapa Flow with the light cruisers NIGERIA and AURORA.
2212	Battleship PRINCE OF WALES was ordered to Scapa Flow.

11 SEPTEMBER 1941

	Battleship PRINCE OF WALES returned to Scapa Flow with minelayer WELSHMAN plus destroyers LAFOREY and ASHANTI when the Home Fleet operation against the German heavy cruiser ADMIRAL SCHEER was cancelled.
	U.69, U.94, U.557, U.561, U.565, U.95 and U.98 formed U-boat group SEEWULF northwest of the Hebrides.
	Light cruiser KENYA departed Scapa Flow for repairs in the Clyde.
0530	Destroyer LIGHTNING arrived at Scapa Flow from Wick.
0800	Destroyer VIVACIOUS arrived at Scapa Flow from Rosyth after her escort duty.
1700	Damaged light cruiser NIGERIA departed Scapa Flow for the Tyne escorted by destroyers LAMERTON and BADSWORTH.
2025	All ships at Scapa Flow were ordered to revert to normal alert notice.
2051	Heavy cruiser LONDON was ordered to return to Hvalfjord.

12 SEPTEMBER 1941

	Heavy cruiser LONDON arrived back at Hvalfjord, Iceland.
	Destroyers ST CROIX from convoy SC.41 and COLUMBIA from convoy HX.147 joined the convoy SC.42 west of Iceland. Their arrival enabled Canadian destroyer SKEENA to steam to Hvalfjord, Iceland, with Canadian corvettes KENOGAMI and ALBERNI to refuel and unload rescued seamen.
	U.84 attacked and reported damaging a steamer in the convoy SC.42.
	U.S. Coast Guard cutters NORTHLAND (WPG-49) and NORTH STAR (WPG-59) captured Norwegian trawler **BUSKOE** in McKenzie Bay, Greenland. She was carrying German agents who were setting up a weather station.
	U.432, U.373 and U.433 maintained contact with convoy SC.42 in spite of heavy air and sea patrols around the convoy. Due to the heavy escort, they were unable to reach an attack position on the convoy to inflict further damage.
	Heavy cruiser BERWICK departed Scapa Flow to complete machinery repairs at Rosyth.
0500	Monitor EREBUS and motor launch ML.188 departed Lerwick to complete sea trials.
1700	Monitor EREBUS arrived at Scapa Flow after her sea trials.
1700	Destroyer PUCKERIDGE departed Scapa Flow for Portsmouth following her completion of working up to combat efficiency exercises.
<2000	Force L arrived Seidisfjord, Iceland, for refuel with aircraft carrier ARGUS, heavy cruiser SHROPSHIRE, plus destroyers INGLEFIELD, IMPULSIVE, and ECLIPSE.
2000	Force L departed Seidisfjord for Scapa Flow with aircraft carrier ARGUS, heavy cruiser SHROPSHIRE, plus destroyers INGLEFIELD, IMPULSIVE, and ECLIPSE.

13 SEPTEMBER 1941

	American destroyers SIMS (DD-409), CHARLES F. HUGHES (DD-428), and RUSSELL (DD-414) joined convoy SC.42 to allow the destroyers of the 2nd Escort Group, EG.2, to refuel.
	U.433, U.572, U.552, U.373 and U.575 failed to regain contact with convoy SC.42 due to a heavy fog that limited visibility.
	Canadian destroyer SKEENA departed Iceland with five steamers for British ports.
	German bombing sank steamer **BLOOMFIELD** (1417grt) east of the Faeroe Islands in 61, 50N, 06W. The entire crew was rescued.
	Light cruiser EURYALUS arrived at Scapa Flow from Rosyth.
1900	Aircraft carrier VICTORIOUS, heavy cruisers SUFFOLK and DEVONSHIRE, plus destroyers SOMALI, MATABELE, and PUNJABI arrived at Scapa Flow from operations off Norway.
2130	Destroyer ANTHONY arrived at Scapa Flow from Rosyth following boiler cleaning.

14 SEPTEMBER 1941

	Destroyer ESCAPADE, trawler HAZEL, Belgian trawler VAN OOST, and tanker OLIGARCH (6897grt) arrived at Reykjavik, Iceland, from Sveagruva, Spitsbergen, after Operation EGV.1 and Operation EGV.2.
	American destroyers TRUXTUN (DD-229), MACLEISH (DD-220) and SAMPSON (DD-394) dropped depth charges on submarine contacts detected near American Task Force TF.15.
	German reconnaissance aircraft spotted convoy SC.42, but only U.565 was able to get into an attack position. U.561 and U.95 were driven underwater by British aircraft.
	Canadian corvette CHAMBLY arrived at Hvalfjord, Iceland, to refuel.
	U.552 (ObltzS Topp) spotted convoy SC.42 for a short time before being forced under by the escorts.
	Heavy cruiser LONDON departed Hvalfjord, Iceland, for Scapa Flow.
	Light cruiser PENELOPE departed Scapa Flow for Akreyri, Iceland.
0730	Force L arrived at Scapa Flow from Seidisfjord, Iceland, with aircraft carrier ARGUS, heavy cruiser SHROPSHIRE, plus destroyers INGLEFIELD, IMPULSIVE, and ECLIPSE.
0900	Minelayer WELSHMAN departed Scapa Flow upon completion of gunnery and antisubmarine working up exercises. She proceeded to Loch Alsh.

15 SEPTEMBER 1941

	German reconnaissance aircraft spotted convoy SC.42, but no U-boats were in range to attack.
	American destroyers GLEAVES (DD-423), MADISON (DD-425), LANSDALE (DD-426) and CHARLES F. HUGHES (DD-428) followed convoy SC.44 to keep U-boats from catching up with the convoy on the surface.
	Heavy cruiser NORFOLK returned to Scapa Flow from the Tyne after a refit.
	Destroyer ESCAPADE arrived at Hvalfjord, Iceland, with tanker ALDERSDALE (8402grt) from the east.
0800	Battleship PRINCE OF WALES, light cruiser EURYALUS, plus destroyers CASTLETON and ESKIMO departed Scapa Flow for the Clyde for convoy WS.11X escort duties. Destroyer LAFOREY relieved destroyer CASTLETON soon after departure due to a defect. Destroyer CASTLETON returned to Scapa Flow.

1000	Destroyer CASTLETON departed Scapa Flow again and proceeded to Loch Alsh.
1730	Destroyer LIGHTNING departed Scapa Flow for the Clyde for repairs of her collision damage and to then join convoy WS.11X.

16 SEPTEMBER 1941

	Heavy cruiser LONDON arrived at Scapa Flow from Hvalfjord, Iceland.
	Light cruiser PENELOPE arrived at Akreyri, Iceland, from Scapa Flow.
	Heavy cruiser SUFFOLK departed Scapa Flow for the Clyde to boiler clean.
	An Albacore aircraft of 827 Squadron from aircraft carrier VICTORIOUS crashed landed in the sea thirteen miles off Brough Head, Orkneys. P/T/A/Sub-Lt (A) M. A. Lambert RNVR and P/T/A/Sub-Lt (A) J. H. C. Ashworth RNVR were drowned. The pilot Midshipman W. G. R. Beer was saved by the Walrus aircraft from heavy cruiser SHROPSHIRE and transferred to hospital ship AMARAPOORA (8173grt) at Scapa Flow.
	Minelayer PORT QUEBEC laid Minefield SN.23B escorted by destroyer NEWARK.
1630	Destroyers ASHANTI, BEDOUIN, MATABELE, PUNJABI, IMPULSIVE, ANTHONY, VIVACIOUS, LAMERTON, and BADSWORTH departed Scapa Flow to assist convoy SC.42. Destroyer ESKIMO, en route from the Clyde to Scapa Flow, joined this force off the Butt of Lewis. Convoy SC.42 was not joined as its position was uncertain, but the force was ordered to join convoy ON.16 in the same area. On the 17th, destroyers LAMERTON and BADSWORTH were ordered to join the escort of convoy ON.16 for twenty-four hours. The rest of the destroyers were detached from the convoy to return to Scapa Flow, except for destroyer VIVACIOUS, which had been detached to sink a floating mine while en route to Scapa Flow. Destroyers LAMERTON and BADSWORTH arrived at Scapa Flow on the 19th.
2100	Destroyer ESCAPADE departed Vestmannaeyjar, Iceland, escorting the 4th Motor Launch Flotilla to Stornoway. The motor launches were detached at the North Minch.
2311 2316	U.98 (Kptlt Gysae) sank steamer **JEDMOOR** (4392grt) (Master Robert Clifford Collins) while attacking convoy SC.42 northwest of St. Kilda in 59N, 10W. The master, twenty-five crewmen and five gunners were lost. Norwegian steamer KNOLL (1151grt) rescued three survivors. Steamer CAMPUS (3667grt) rescued two survivors.

17 SEPTEMBER 1941

0930	Aircraft carrier ARGUS and destroyer ECLIPSE departed Scapa Flow for the Clyde. Off Shianti Island, destroyer ECLIPSE was detached from the carrier and returned to Scapa Flow.

18 SEPTEMBER 1941

	German reconnaissance aircraft spotted convoy SC.42, but no U-boats were in range to attack.
0130	Destroyers ASHANTI, BEDOUIN, MATABELE, PUNJABI, IMPULSIVE, and ANTHONY returned to Scapa Flow after their escort duty.
0400	Destroyer VIVACIOUS returned to Scapa Flow after destroying a floating mine.
0600	Destroyer ECLIPSE returned to Scapa Flow following her escort duty.
0600	Destroyer ANTELOPE arrived at Scapa Flow up on the completion of boiler cleaning at Rosyth.
0800	Destroyer ECLIPSE departed Scapa Flow to carry out boiler cleaning at Rosyth.
1500	Destroyer INGLEFIELD departed Scapa Flow for the Humber to refit at Hull.
1500	Destroyer BEDOUIN departed Scapa Flow for Tórshavn with the Governor of the Faeroe Islands.
1800	Destroyer LANCASTER arrived at Scapa Flow from the Humber to carry out working up to combat efficiency exercises.
2030	Destroyers MATABELE and PUNJABI departed Scapa Flow to intercept a possible enemy minelayer off Saxavord, Faeroes. They proceeded to the intercept point west of the North Rona - Faeroes minefield.
2145	Destroyers ASHANTI, IMPULSIVE, and VIVACIOUS departed Scapa Flow to carry out a patrol between the Orkneys and Sule Skerry in support of destroyers MATABELE and PUNJABI.

19 SEPTEMBER 1941

0030	Destroyers ASHANTI, IMPULSIVE, and VIVACIOUS arrived back at Scapa Flow after their patrol.
0800	Destroyer BEDOUIN arrived at Tórshavn from Scapa Flow with the Governor of the Faeroe Islands.
0830	Destroyer ESCAPADE arrived at Scapa Flow from escorting motor launches to the North Minch from Iceland.
0918	Destroyers MATABELE and PUNJABI arrived back at Scapa Flow after an unsuccessful search off Saxavord, Faeroes.
0930	The 4th Motor Launch Flotilla arrived at Stornoway from Vestmannaeyjar, Iceland.
1800	Destroyer BEDOUIN departed Tórshavn to return to Scapa Flow.

20 SEPTEMBER 1941

	Destroyer BEDOUIN arrived at Scapa Flow from Tórshavn.

	A shore battery fired on American destroyer CHARLES F. HUGHES (DD-428) off Reykjavik, Iceland.
	Antiaircraft ship ULSTER QUEEN departed Scapa Flow for Belfast, Northern Ireland, after working up to combat efficiency.
0800	Monitor EREBUS departed Scapa Flow for Chatham after completing her working up to combat efficiency exercises.
1030	Destroyer VIVACIOUS departed Scapa Flow for Sheerness after completing her working up to combat efficiency exercises. The destroyer was ordered to overtake the monitor EREBUS and escort her to Sheerness.

21 SEPTEMBER 1941

0600	Norwegian destroyer DRAUG arrived at Scapa Flow from the Humber.

22 SEPTEMBER 1941

	Escort Group EG.3 with destroyers BULLDOG, AMAZON, RICHMOND and GEORGETOWN plus corvette HEARTSEASE, and the Free French ACONIT with four antisubmarine trawlers took over convoy SC.44 at the MOMP.
	Minelayer WELSHMAN laid Minefield SN.23C.
0715	Destroyer BADSWORTH departed Scapa Flow for Scrabster with the Captain of the Fleet.
1045	Destroyer BADSWORTH returned to Scapa Flow from Scrabster with the officers taking passage to Murmansk, Russia, in heavy cruiser LONDON. Heavy cruiser LONDON departed Scapa Flow later in the day to take the Anglo American supply mission to Archangel, Russia.
1730	Destroyers LAMERTON and BADSWORTH departed Scapa Flow after working up to combat efficiency to join the Western Approaches Command.
1900	Destroyer LANCASTER departed Scapa Flow after working up to combat efficiency to rejoin RAdm Minelaying at Loch Alsh.
1918	Destroyer BADSWORTH was ordered to proceed to Iceland and, after refuelling, to join convoy HX.150 at sea.

23 SEPTEMBER 1941

	Due to the impending actions of the German battleship TIRPITZ, an alert was sent to the American WHITE PATROL in the Denmark Strait with battleship NEW MEXICO (BB-40), heavy cruisers VINCENNES (CA-44) and QUINCY (CA-39) plus destroyers MOFFETT (DD-362), MCDOUGAL (DD-358), STACK (DD-406), CHARLES F. HUGHES (DD-428) and RUSSELL (DD-414).
	Light cruiser PENELOPE departed Hvalfjord, Iceland, and arrived back at Reykjavik, Iceland, on the 29th. The cruiser then proceeded to Hvalfjord.
1800	Battleship KING GEORGE V, aircraft carrier VICTORIOUS plus light cruiser AURORA departed Scapa Flow for Hvalfjord, Iceland, with destroyers SOMALI, MATABELE, BEDOUIN, ESKIMO, ASHANTI, and PUNJABI.

24 SEPTEMBER 1941

	Heavy cruiser SUFFOLK arrived at Scapa Flow from the Clyde.
	An engine room fire sank steamer **NIGARISTAN** (5993grt) southeast of Iceland. American destroyer EBERLE (DD-430) rescued the entire crew.
	American destroyers MADISON (DD-425), GLEAVES (DD-423), LANSDALE (DD-426), CHARLES F. HUGHES (DD-428), and SIMPSON (DD-221) under the command of Capt F. D. Kirtland assumed escort of convoy ON.18 at the MOMP. This was the first westbound convoy escorted by the United States Navy.
1700	Destroyer BADSWORTH arrived at Hvalfjord, Iceland, and, after refuelling, departed to join convoy HX.150 at sea.

25 SEPTEMBER 1941

	Norwegian MTB.56 arrived at Scapa Flow from Harwich.
	American Task Force TF.15 departed Hvalfjord, Iceland, for Argentia, Newfoundland, with battleship IDAHO (BB-42), heavy cruiser TUSCALOOSA (CA-37) plus nine destroyers and nine steamers and tankers.
	The Flag of RAdm, 1st Cruiser Squadron, was transferred from heavy cruiser DEVONSHIRE to heavy cruiser NORFOLK. The DEVONSHIRE then proceeded to the Clyde, where she arrived on the 27th, for duty escorting convoy WS.12.
1400	Battleship KING GEORGE V, aircraft carrier VICTORIOUS plus light cruiser AURORA arrived at Hvalfjord, Iceland, from Scapa Flow with destroyers SOMALI, MATABELE, BEDOUIN, ESKIMO, ASHANTI, and PUNJABI for Operation EJ.
1900	Sloop IBIS arrived at Scapa Flow from Rosyth to begin working up to combat efficiency.
2000	Heavy cruiser SUFFOLK departed Scapa Flow for Hvalfjord, Iceland, with destroyers IMPULSIVE, ANTHONY, and ANTELOPE to refuel prior to escorting convoy PQ.1 to Russia. The ships arrived at Hvalfjord on the 27th.

27 SEPTEMBER 1941

	German bombing sank Faeroes motor fishing vessel **FRAM** (92grt) at Vestmannhavn. There were no casualties.

28 SEPTEMBER 1941

	Minesweepers LEDA, BRITOMART, GOSSAMER, and HUSSAR arrived at Hvalfjord, Iceland, for escort duty in convoy PQ.1.
	Convoy ON.19A departed Reykjavik, Iceland, escorted by destroyer ST CROIX plus corvettes AGASSIZ, EYEBRIGHT, and PRESCOTT. The convoy was dispersed on 4 October.
1900	Heavy cruiser SHROPSHIRE departed Scapa Flow to escorted convoy QP.1 from 2 to 10 October, relieving heavy cruiser LONDON in 74, 55N, 27, 30E.
2100	Destroyer ESCAPADE departed Scapa Flow for Seidisfjord, Iceland, for refuelling.

29 SEPTEMBER 1941

	An Allied conference aboard battleship KING GEORGE V between Admiral Commanding, Home Fleet, Admiral Commanding, Western Approaches , Admiral Commanding, Iceland Command, Air Officer Commanding Iceland, U.S. RAdm R. C. Giffen (SO, U.S. Naval Forces in Iceland), and staffs concluded. Admiral Commanding, Western Approaches, who had arrived by air on the 26th, took passage back to Britain in destroyer ASHANTI.
1200	Destroyer OFFA arrived at Scapa Flow from the Clyde to begin working up to combat efficiency.
1845	Convoy PQ.1 departed Hvalfjord, Iceland, with steamers ATLANTIC (5414grt), BLAIRNEVIS (4155grt), ELNA II (3221grt), HARMONIC (4558grt), Panamanian NORTH KING (4934grt), Belgian VILLE D'ANVERS (7462grt), oiler BLACK RANGER (3417grt), Panamanian CAPIRA (5565grt), GEMSTONE (4986grt), LORCA (4875grt), and RIVER AFTON (5479grt) escorted by heavy cruiser SUFFOLK, destroyers ANTELOPE and IMPULSIVE, plus minesweepers BRITOMART, GOSSAMER, LEDA, and HUSSAR. Destroyer ANTHONY departed Hvalfjord with the convoy escorting oiler BLACK RANGER (3417grt). On 4 October, the destroyer and oiler joined returning convoy QP.1. Destroyer ANTELOPE was detached from the convoy on 2 October to Scapa Flow. Destroyer ESCAPADE departed Seidisfjord, Iceland, and joined the convoy on 2 October, escorting it to 11 October. Convoy PQ.1 arrived at Murmansk, Russia, on 11 October.

30 SEPTEMBER 1941

	U.S. Task Unit TU.4.1.5 with destroyers MAYO (DD-422), BROOME (DD-210), BABBITT (DD-128), LEARY (DD-158) and SCHENCK (DD-159) arrived with a convoy at the MOMP.
	Convoy ON.20 joined with U.S. Task Unit TU.4.1.3 for escort to the west.
0800	Destroyer ESCAPADE arrived at Seidisfjord, Iceland, for refuelling.
1900	Destroyer ECLIPSE arrived at Scapa Flow from Rosyth after completing boiler cleaning and minor repairs.

Norwegian Sea

Long. E03, 00 – E20, 00   Lat. N68, 00 – N58, 30

2 SEPTEMBER 1941

	An RAF aerial torpedo sank German steamer **OSLEBSHAUSEN** (4989grt) near Obrestad, Norway. (Other sources claim it was an aerial mine.)

3 SEPTEMBER 1941

	Swordfish aircraft from aircraft carrier VICTORIOUS sank Norwegian steamer **BAROEY** (424grt) off Vestfjord, Norway. Over thirty German soldiers and one hundred twenty Norwegians were lost.
	Aircraft carrier VICTORIOUS (RAdm Wake-Walker) launched air attacks on German ships off Tromsø, Norway, with heavy cruisers DEVONSHIRE and SUFFOLK in Operation EGV.1.
	Submarine TIGRIS patrolled the Norwegian coast between Tromsø and Hammerfest from 3 to 16 September.

5 SEPTEMBER 1941

	Dutch submarine O.14 unsuccessfully patrolled off Utsire, Norway, until 12 September. She reported moored mines in 60, 30N, 02, 26E while returning from her patrol area.

12 SEPTEMBER 1941

	Free French submarine MINERVE relieved Dutch submarine O.14 from the Norwegian coast patrol.
	RAF bombers sank Finnish steamer **TAURI** (2517grt) off Bergen, Norway.
	Heavy cruiser DEVONSHIRE (SO Force M), aircraft carrier VICTORIOUS, heavy cruiser SUFFOLK, with destroyers SOMALI, MATABELE, and PUNJABI carried out Operation EGV.2 when VICTORIOUS launched an aircraft attack against northern Norway with three striking forces.

The first force and second force searched for German shipping between Bodø and Jeldenfjord, Norway, while the third force attacked the power station and aluminium factory at Glomfjord, Norway.

The aircraft reported torpedoing a 2000-ton ship and attacked several small ships at Bodø, Norway, and damaged the power station in Glomfjord. They also dropped bombs on the German D/F station on the island of Røst, Norway.

An Albacore aircraft of 832 Squadron with a crew of Lt P. F. King, Lt T. L. Seccombe, and Leading Airman W. F. Lovell was damaged by flak and Lovell was slightly wounded.

14 SEPTEMBER 1941

Russian submarine M-172 unsuccessfully attacked a ship in Boknafjord, Norway.

16 SEPTEMBER 1941

Submarine TRIDENT replaced submarine TIGRIS from her patrol from Tromsø to Hammerfest, Norway.

17 SEPTEMBER 1941

RAF aircraft damaged small Norwegian tanker VARD (681grt) off Norway.

RAF aircraft attacked U.451 off Norway. One bomb detonated in the U-boats wake.

18 SEPTEMBER 1941

U.451 dodged three torpedoes off the Norwegian coast. No identification has been determined on who fired them.

21 SEPTEMBER 1941

Free French submarine MINERVE unsuccessfully attacked a steamer off Buefjord, Norway.

26 SEPTEMBER 1941

German steamer **GILLHAUSEN** (4339grt) became stranded south of Krakens, Norway, and later sank.

Free French submarine MINERVE reported three German U-boats, a submarine depot ship and a M-class minesweeper at Frosjoen, Norway. She was unable to reach an attack position.

East of Canada

Long. W70, 00 – W30, 00   Lat. N68, 00 – N43, 30

4 SEPTEMBER 1941

Convoy HX.148 departed Halifax escorted by AMC ALAUNIA plus corvettes LETHBRIDGE, SHEDIAC, and SHERBROOKE.

Destroyer RICHMOND with corvettes BITTERSWEET, CANDYTUFT, and FENNEL relieved the Halifax corvettes on 7 September.

Corvettes BITTERSWEET and CANDYTUFT were detached from the convoy on the 10th with destroyer RICHMOND and corvette FENNEL being detached from the convoy on the 11th.

On the 12th, destroyers MONTGOMERY, WHITEHALL, WINCHELSEA, and WITCH, corvettes ABELIA, ANEMONE, and VERONICA, plus antisubmarine trawler ST ZENO joined the convoy.

Destroyer BOADICEA joined the convoy on the 13th and destroyer WITCH was detached from the convoy.

Destroyers BEAGLE and SHIKARI joined the convoy on the 14th and destroyer MONTGOMERY was detached from the convoy.

On the 15th, destroyer BOADICEA, the AMC and corvette ANEMONE were detached from the convoy.

Destroyers BEAGLE and SABRE and corvettes ABELIA and VERONICA were detached before the convoy arrived at Liverpool on the 17th.

5 SEPTEMBER 1941

Convoy SC.43 departed Sydney, Cape Breton, escorted by AMC AUSONIA with corvettes ARVIDA, BARRIE, DAUPHIN, and HEPATICA.

The AMC was detached from the convoy on the 8th when destroyer READING and corvette PRESCOTT joined the convoy.

On the 16th, destroyer READING with corvettes HEPATICA and PRESCOTT were detached from the convoy, and destroyers KEPPEL, SABRE, and VENOMOUS joined the convoy.

Destroyers CAMPBELTOWN, ST ALBANS, and WESTCOTT joined the convoy on the 18th.

The convoy arrived at Liverpool on the 20th.

6 SEPTEMBER 1941

In Operation INDIGO III, American Task Force TF.15 departed Argentia, Newfoundland, with battleship IDAHO (BB-42), heavy cruisers TUSCALOOSA (CA-37) and VINCENNES (CA-44) plus destroyers WINSLOW (DD-359), ANDERSON (DD-411), MUSTIN (DD-413), O'BRIEN (DD-415), SAMPSON (DD-394), BENSON (DD-421),

	HILARY P. JONES (DD-427) and NIBLACK (DD-424) with a convoy with four troopships carrying an army brigade to Iceland to replace the U.S. Marine Corps brigade delivered earlier to Iceland. Also included in the convoy were three supply ships, fleet tanker CIMARRON (AO-22), repair ship DELTA (AR-9) plus destroyers BAINBRIDGE (DD-246), OVERTON (DD-239), REUBEN JAMES (DD-245), TRUXTUN (DD-229), MACLEISH (DD-220), WALKE (DD-416) and MORRIS (DD-417). The destroyers dropped depth charges on eight separate sonar contacts on the 11th and 12th, but all were false alarms. On the 14th, destroyer TRUXTUN (DD-229) detected a strong submarine contact. Destroyers TRUXTUN (DD-229), MACLEISH (DD-220) and SAMPSON (DD-394) kept the U-boat under with depth charges while the convoy continued on to arrive at Reykjavik and TF.15 at Hvalfjord, Iceland, on the 16th.
	Destroyers CHESTERFIELD and BURNHAM collided in St John's Harbour, Newfoundland. There was no serious damage to CHESTERFIELD and she departed St John's with convoys HX.149/SC 44 to Iceland. She arrived at Portsmouth on 6 October for a refit. Destroyer BURNHAM was sent to Boston, Massachusetts, for a refit and repairs. She arrived on the 17th and repairs were completed on 23 October. BURNHAM departed Boston on 1 November for Halifax, Nova Scotia.

8 SEPTEMBER 1941

	Convoy SC.42 (Commodore Mackenzie) with sixty-four ships escorted by escort group EG.24 (Lt Cdr Hibbard) with destroyer SKEENA plus corvettes ALBERNI, KENOGAMI and ORILLIA were directed to travel along the pack ice off Greenland to avoid the German MARKGRAF U-boat group patrolling south of Greenland.
	An American convoy departed Argentia, Newfoundland, for Reykjavik, Iceland. The convoy was escorted by battleships IDAHO (BB-42) and NEW MEXICO (BB-40), heavy cruiser VINCENNES (CA-44), with destroyers MORRIS (DD-417), SIMS (DD-409), CHARLES F. HUGHES (DD-428), HAMMANN (DD-412), MUSTIN (DD-413), and O'BRIEN (DD-415) of the 2nd Destroyer Squadron, NIBLACK (DD-424), HILARY P. JONES (DD-427), GLEAVES (DD-423), MADISON (DD-425), and LANSDALE (DD-426) of the 7th Destroyer Squadron, plus SIMPSON (DD-221), MACLEISH (DD-220), TRUXTUN (DD-229), OVERTON (DD-239), REUBEN JAMES (DD-245), and BAINBRIDGE (DD-246). The convoy and escort arrived on the 16th.

9 SEPTEMBER 1941

	Corvette CANDYTUFT, escorting convoy HX.148 with destroyer RICHMOND plus corvettes BITTERSWEET and FENNEL, was damaged when the ship's starboard boiler exploded in 51, 20N, 39, 08W. Lt D. M. Hall RNR and T/Sub-Lt H. F. T. Davies RNVR plus nine ratings were killed. The corvette was taken in tow by corvette BITTERSWEET and arrived at St John's on the 14th. She was later taken from St John's on 2 October for Halifax arriving on 6 October. Her damage was beyond the capacity of the Halifax repair facilities, so on 8 October the corvette was towed from Halifax for New York where she arrived on 11 October. The corvette was repaired from 11 October 1941 to February 1942 at the New York Navy Yard.
0655	U.81 (ObltzS Guggenberger) sank steamer **EMPIRE SPRINGBUCK** (5591grt) (ex American **SAN ANGELO** (5591grt)) (Master Walter O´Connell) with two torpedoes while she was straggling behind convoy SC.42 off Greenland in 61, 38N, 40, 40W. Her cargo of ammunition exploded, and the master and forty-one crewmen were all lost.
>1200	In the afternoon, U.85 (ObltzS Eberhard Greger) spotted convoy SC.42 off Cape Farewell, Greenland. Her initial attack failed, but she radioed the convoy position to other U-boats, which gathered during the night to attack the next day.
1359	U.85 (Robert Gysae) fired three torpedoes at convoy SC.42 in 61N, 40W. All missed, but their tracks were seen by steamer JEDMOOR (4392grt).

10 SEPTEMBER 1941

	Canadian corvettes CHAMBLY (Cdr Prentice) and MOOSE JAW sank **U.501** (KKpt Hugo Förster) as she was attacking convoy SC.42 southwest of Iceland in 62, 50N, 37, 50W. She was first driven underwater by a Catalina aircraft of RAF 209 Squadron operating from Iceland. The corvettes, on their way to support convoy SC.42, then dropped depth charges until the U-boat surfaced. Thirty-seven of the crew were rescued, but eleven were lost. One Canadian rating was lost after boarding the U-boat prior to her sinking, in an attempt to recover coding documents and material.
	U.85 (ObltzS Eberhard Greger) sank steamer **THISTLEGLEN** (4748grt) attacking convoy SC.42 off Cape Farewell, Greenland, in 61, 59N, 39, 46W. Three crewmen were missing. U.85 made two more attacks on the convoy and claimed sinking two steamers, but these were unconfirmed.
	Canadian destroyer SKEENA and Canadian corvette ALBERNI damaged U.85 with depth charges after the U-boat attacked convoy SC.42 off Greenland.
	Canadian corvette KENOGAMI forced U.569 to dive and then subjected her to depth charge attacks until convoy SC.42 cleared the area.
	Canadian corvette KENOGAMI attacked U.85 with depth charges off Greenland, while escorting convoy SC.42.
	Convoy HX.149 departed Halifax escorted by destroyers ANNAPOLIS and HAMILTON and AMC ASCANIA. Destroyer CHURCHILL joined the convoy on the 12th. Destroyers ANNAPOLIS and HAMILTON were relieved from the convoy on the 13th by corvettes

	ARROWHEAD, CAMELLIA, CELANDINE, and EYEBRIGHT.
	    Destroyers MALCOLM and WATCHMAN, corvettes ARABIS and PETUNIA, plus antisubmarine trawlers NORTHERN GEM, NORTHERN PRIDE, and NORTHERN SPRAY relieved destroyer CHURCHILL and the four corvettes from the convoy on the 20th.
	    Corvette MONKSHOOD joined the convoy on the 22nd.
	    The AMC and corvette PETUNIA were detached from the convoy on the 24th.
	    The convoy arrived at Liverpool on the 25th.

0230	U.432 (ObltzS Heinz-Otto Schultze) sank steamer **MUNERIC** (5229grt) (Master Frank Baker) while attacking convoy SC.42 off Cape Farewell, Greenland, in 61, 38N, 40, 40W. The master, fifty-five crewmen, five gunners and two stowaways were lost.
0452	U.652 (Georg-Werner Fraatz) damaged steamer TAHCHEE (6508grt) while attacking convoy SC.42 off Cape Farewell in 61, 15N, 41, 05W. TAHCHEE arrived at Iceland on the 15th in tow of Canadian corvette ORILLIA.

0452	U.652 damaged steamer BARON PENTLAND (3410grt) (Master Alexander Bleasby Campbell) while attacking convoy SC.42 off Cape Farewell in 61, 15N, 41, 05W.
	    Two crewmen were lost, while the master, thirty crewmen and eight gunners abandoned ship. Canadian corvette ORILLIA (Lt Cdr W. Edward S. Briggs) rescued the survivors and took them to Reykjavik, Iceland.
	    BARON PENTLAND remained afloat due to her cargo of timber and was later sunk by U.372 (Heinz-Joachim Neumann) on the 19th.

0707	U.432 sank Norwegian steamer **STARGARD** (1113grt) (Master Lars Larsen) while attacking convoy SC.42 off Cape Farewell in 61, 30N, 40, 30W. Two crewmen were lost. Norwegian steamer REGIN (1386grt) rescued ten survivors and took them to Reykjavik, Iceland. A corvette rescued the master and four men in a lifeboat about thirty minutes later and took them to Reykjavik, Iceland.
0709	U.432 sank Dutch steamer **WINTERSWIJK** (3205grt) while attacking convoy SC.42 off Cape Farewell in 61, 38N, 40, 40W. Twenty crewmen were missing.
0728 0729 0753	U.81 (ObltzS Guggenberger) fired two torpedoes at convoy SC.42 and observed one ship hit. U.81 fired two torpedoes at convoy SC.42 and heard two detonations, but the visibility prevented confirmation. U.81 fired a fifth torpedo that hit, but it was a dud. One of the torpedoes sank steamer **SALLY MAERSK** (3252grt) (ex Danish) (Master J. K. Lindberg) off Cape Farewell in 61, 40N, 40, 30W. Canadian corvette KENOGAMI (Lt P. J. B. Cook) rescued the master, twenty-eight crewmen and five gunners and landed them at Reykjavik, Iceland.

0957	U.82 (Siegfried Rollmann) sank CAM ship **EMPIRE HUDSON** (7465grt) (Master John Campbell Cooke) while attacking convoy SC.42 off Cape Farewell in 61, 28N, 39, 46W.
	    Four crewmen were lost. Steamer BARON RAMSAY (3650grt) and Norwegian steamer REGIN (1386grt) rescued the master, forty-seven crewmen, six gunners and nine RAF personnel and landed them at Loch Ewe.
	    (Other sources place the attack in 61, 28N, 40, 51W.)

11 SEPTEMBER 1941

	Canadian corvettes CHAMBLY and MOOSE JAW joined convoy SC.42 west of Iceland.
	Canadian corvette KENOGAMI dropped depth charges on U.569 west of Iceland.
	American destroyers MCDOUGAL (DD-358), MOFFETT (DD-362), MCCORMICK (DD-223) and TARBELL (DD-142) escorted three steamers from Argentia, Newfoundland, to Iceland. Before they arrived on 18 September, the destroyers made several depth charge attacks against possible U-boat detections.

	Convoy SC.44 departed Sydney, Cape Breton, escorted by AMC WOLFE plus corvettes LETHBRIDGE, NAPANEE, and SHEDIAC.
	    Corvette AGASSIZ joined the convoy on the 12th.
	    The escorts that departed with the convoy were detached on the 14th when relieved by destroyer CHESTERFIELD plus corvettes ALYSSE, HONEYSUCKLE, LEVIS, and MAYFLOWER.
	    Corvette LEVIS was lost on the 20th. Corvettes ARROWHEAD and EYEBRIGHT joined the convoy on the 20th.
	    Corvette HONEYSUCKLE was detached from the convoy on the 21st and destroyer CHESTERFIELD with corvettes AGASSIZ, ALYSSE, ARROWHEAD, EYEBRIGHT, and MAYFLOWER were detached from the convoy on the 22nd.
	    Destroyers AMAZON, BELMONT, BULLDOG, and GEORGETOWN with corvettes ACONIT and HEARTSEASE, and antisubmarine trawlers ANGLE, CAPE WARWICK, DANEMAN, NOTTS COUNTY, and ST APOLLO joined the convoy on the 22nd.
	    Destroyers AMAZON and BULLDOG with corvettes ACONIT and HEARTSEASE were detached from the convoy on the 27th. Destroyers BELMONT and GEORGETOWN and the trawlers were detached from the convoy on the 28th.
	    The convoy arrived at Liverpool on the 30th.

0151	U.82 (Siegfried Rollmann) sank tanker **BULYSSES** (7519grt) (Master Bartram Lamb) while attacking convoy SC.42 west of Iceland in 62, 40N, 38, 50W. One crewman was lost. Polish steamer WISLA (3106grt) rescued the master, fifty-three crewmen and six gunners and landed

	them at Liverpool.
0212	U.82 sank steamer **GYPSUM QUEEN** (3915grt) (Master Alban Jason Chapman) while attacking convoy SC.42 west of Iceland in 63, 05N, 37, 50W. She sank within a minute with nine crewmen and one gunner missing. Norwegian steamer VESTLAND (1934grt) rescued the master, twenty-two crewmen and three gunners and landed them at Belfast, Northern Ireland.
0245	U.207 (ObltzS Fritz Meyer) sank steamer **STONEPOOL** (4815grt) (Master Albert White) while attacking convoy SC.42 east of Cape Farewell, Greenland, in 63, 05N, 37, 50W. The master, thirty-three crewmen and eight gunners were lost. Canadian corvette KENOGAMI (Lt P. J. B. Cook) rescued six crewmen and one gunner and landed them at Loch Ewe.
0245	U.207 heavily damaged steamer **BERURY** (4924grt) (ex American **OLEN** (4924grt)) (Master Francis Joseph Morgan) while attacking convoy SC.42 east of Cape Farewell in 62, 40N, 38, 50W. One crewman was lost. Canadian corvettes KENOGAMI (Lt P. J. B. Cook) and MOOSE JAW (Lt L. D. Quick) rescued the master, thirty-six crewmen and four gunners and landed them at Loch Ewe. A convoy escort scuttled the wreck.
>0246	U.207 sank Canadian steamer **RANDA** (1558grt) while attacking convoy SC.42 east of Cape Farewell in 63N, 37W.
>0246	Destroyers LEAMINGTON (Lt Cdr Bowermann) and VETERAN (Cdr Eames) sank **U.207** (ObltzS Fritz Meyer) in the Denmark Strait in 63, 59N, 34, 48W with assistance from RAF aircraft from 209 and 269 Squadrons. The entire crew of forty-one was lost.
0406	U.432 (ObltzS Heinz-Otto Schultze) sank Swedish steamer **GARM** (1231grt) while attacking convoy SC.42 west of Iceland in 63, 02N, 37, 51W. Six crewmen were lost. Norwegian steamer BESTUM (2215grt) rescued fourteen survivors.
0408	U.433 (Hans Ey) damaged Norwegian steamer **BESTUM** (2215grt) while she stopped to rescue survivors from Swedish steamer **GARM** (1231grt) in convoy SC.42 west of Iceland in 63N, 37W. The SOE reported the hit on BESTUM, but it is believed that U.433 hit the Swedish ship. BESTUM arrived at Reykjavik, Iceland, three days later with twelve survivors from the Swedish ship. There were no reports of casualties on the BESTUM.
0705	U.82 (Siegfried Rollmann) sank steamer **EMPIRE CROSSBILL** (5463grt) (ex American **WEST ARMAGOSA**(5463grt)) (Master Eric Robinson Townend) while attacking convoy SC.42 west of Iceland in 63, 14N, 37, 12W. She immediately sank with the master, thirty-seven crewmen, ten gunners and one passenger.
0705	U.82 (Siegfried Rollmann) damaged Swedish steamer **SCANIA** (1980grt) while attacking convoy SC.42 west of Iceland in 63, 14N, 37, 12W. The entire crew of twenty-four was rescued.
<1159	Later in the morning, Canadian corvette WETASKIWIN, corvettes MIMOSA and GLADIOLUS, plus anti-submarine whaler BUTTERMERE joined convoy SC.42 west of Iceland.
>1200	In the afternoon, the 2nd Escort Group (EG.2) with destroyers DOUGLAS (SO), VETERAN, SALADIN, SKATE, and LEAMINGTON joined convoy SC.42.
1332 1347	U.202 sank the damaged and abandoned Swedish steamer **SCANIA** (1980grt) with two torpedoes as she was straggling behind the convoy in 63, 14N, 37, 12W.
1650	U.105 (Kptlt Schewe) sank unescorted Panamanian steamer **MONTANA** (1549grt) (ex Danish **PAULA** (1549grt)) about 400 miles northeast of Cape Farewell in 63, 40N, 35, 50W. Eighteen crewmen were lost. Seven survivors were rescued.

16 SEPTEMBER 1941

	Convoy HX.150 departed Halifax escorted by destroyer ANNAPOLIS plus corvettes ALGOMA and BRANDON. The destroyer was detached on the 17th. On the 17th in 46N, 55W, this convoy became the first trans Atlantic convoy to be assisted by the United States Navy when Captain M. L. Deyo relieved the Canadian escorts with his force of destroyers ERICSSON (DD-440), EBERLE (DD-430), UPSHUR (DD-144), ELLIS (DD-154), and DALLAS (DD-199). Corvettes ALGOMA and BRANDON were detached from the convoy on the 18th. On the 20th, destroyer EBERLE (DD-430) rescued the crew of steamer **NIGARISTAN** (5993grt), which had an engine room fire. Destroyers BLANKNEY, CHURCHILL, and WITCH with corvettes ARROWHEAD, CAMELLIA, CELANDINE, and HONEYSUCKLE relieved the American group on the 25th. Destroyer BADSWORTH joined the convoy on the 26th for the day only. Destroyer BLANKNEY was detached from the convoy on the 27th. The remaining destroyers plus corvettes CAMELLIA and CELANDINE were detached from the convoy on the 28th. Corvette ARROWHEAD was detached from the convoy on the 29th. The convoy arrived at Liverpool on the 30th with corvette HONEYSUCKLE.

18 SEPTEMBER 1941

	American Task Unit TU.4.1.1 with destroyers ERICSSON (DD-440), EBERLE (DD-430), ELLIS (DD-154), DALLAS (DD-199) and UPSHUR (DD-144) joined convoy HX.150 at sea.

	They joined destroyers CHURCHILL, CHESTERFIELD, and BROADWATER plus corvettes CAMELLIA, CELANDINE, ALYSSE (FF) and HONEYSUCKLE.
	U.74 (Kptlt Kentrat) spotted convoy SC.44 (Cdre Robinson, fifty-six ships) and called in U.373, U.94, U.552 and U.562.
	During the night, U.74, U.94, U.575, U.372, U.373, U.552, U.69, U.562 and U.572 set up attack positions and were designated as Wolfpack BRANDENBURG.
	Convoy SC.45 departed Sydney, Cape Breton, escorted by AMC RANPURA plus corvettes CHICOUTIMI, MATAPEDIA, and SHERBROOKE. Corvette SPIKENARD joined the convoy on the 19th. Corvettes BITTERSWEET, CHILLIWACK, COLLINGWOOD, DIANTHUS, PICTOU, and SNOWBERRY joined the convoy on the 21st and relieved the escort group-departing Sydney with the convoy. Destroyer ST LAURENT joined the convoy on the 22nd and was detached from the convoy on the 29th. The corvettes joining on the 21st were detached from the convoy on the 30th when relieved by destroyers BROADWATER, LEAMINGTON, SKATE, and VETERAN and corvettes ABELIA, ANEMONE, TRAIL, and VERONICA. The convoy arrived at Liverpool on 4 October.

19 SEPTEMBER 1941

	Submarine TRUANT departed St John's, Newfoundland, after refitting at Portsmouth, New Hampshire, for Gibraltar, but was delayed in arrival by engine defects.
0603	U.74 (Kptlt Kentrat) heavily damaged Canadian corvette LEVIS (925grt) (Lt C. W. Gilding RCNR) while attacking convoy SC.44 east of Cape Farewell, Greenland, in 60, 05N, 38, 48W. Seventeen Canadian and one British rating were lost.
0700	Canadian corvette MAYFLOWER (Lt Cdr G. Stephen) took the damaged LEVIS in tow.
0900	The tow parted.
1030	MAYFLOWER re-established the towline.
1910	**LEVIS** capsized to starboard and sank. Canadian corvettes MAYFLOWER and AGASSIZ rescued forty survivors. (Other sources claim MAYFLOWER rescued all ninety-one survivors.)
1433	U.372 (Kptlt Neumann) sank damaged abandoned steamer **BARON PENTLAND** (3410grt) (Master Alexander Bleasby Campbell) in 61, 15N, 41, 05W. *(See 10 September)*

20 SEPTEMBER 1941

	American destroyers WINSLOW (DD-359), OVERTON (DD-239), TRUXTUN (DD-229), BAINBRIDGE (DD-246) and REUBEN JAMES (DD-245) were detached from convoy SC.44. Free French corvette ALYSSE joined the convoy.
>0152	U.552 (Kptlt Erich Topp) sank tanker **T. J. WILLIAMS** (8212grt) while attacking convoy SC.44 south of Cape Farewell, Greenland, in 61, 34N, 35, 11W. Seventeen crewmen, including two gunners, were lost.
0113	U.74 (Kptlt Kentrat) sank CAM ship **EMPIRE BURTON** (6966grt) (Master John Mitchell) while attacking convoy SC.44 east of Cape Farewell in 61, 34N, 35, 05W. One crewman and one gunner were lost. Corvette HONEYSUCKLE (Lt Cdr G. W. Gregorie) rescued the master, forty-seven crewmen, four gunners and six RAF personnel and landed them at Reykjavik, Iceland.
0151	U.552 sank Panamanian steamer **PINK STAR** (4150grt) (ex Danish **LANDBY** (4150grt)) (Master John S. MacKenzie) while attacking convoy SC.44 south of Cape Farewell in 61, 36N, 37, 07W. Thirteen crewmen were lost. Twenty-two survived.
0327	U.552 heavily damaged Norwegian motor tanker **BARBRO** (6325grt) (Master Lauritz Knudsen) while attacking convoy SC.44 south of Cape Farewell in 61, 30N, 35, 00W. U.69 (Zahn) torpedoed the burning tanker, but the torpedo did not explode.
0430	The tanker sank after she had burned herself out. The entire crew of thirty-five was lost (twenty-two Norwegians, three Swedes, one Dane, five British and four Canadians).

21 SEPTEMBER 1941

	Canadian corvettes ARROWHEAD and EYEBRIGHT were detached from convoy SC.44 to provide other convoys with more escort support.
	Further attacks by U.74 and U.562 on convoy SC.44 were unsuccessful.

22 SEPTEMBER 1941

	U.94, U.372, U.562, U.431, U.564, U.575, U.69, U.373 and U.572 reformed Wolfpack BRANDENBURG southeast of Cape Farewell, Greenland.
	Convoy HX.151 departed Halifax escorted by destroyer ANNAPOLIS. ANNAPOLIS was detached from the convoy on the 24th when relieved by American destroyers DECATUR (DD-341), KEARNY (DD-432), LIVERMORE (DD-429), and PLUNKETT (DD-431). Destroyers BEAGLE, MONTGOMERY, ROXBOROUGH, and SALISBURY, corvettes HEATHER, LOBELIA,

	and NARCISSUS, with antisubmarine trawlers NORWICH CITY and ST LOMAN relieved the American destroyers on 1 October. Destroyers BEAGLE and SALISBURY were detached from the convoy on 4 October. Destroyer ROXBOROUGH and corvettes HEATHER, LOBELIA, and NARCISSUS were detached from the convoy on the 5th and destroyer MONTGOMERY was detached from the convoy on 6 October. The convoy arrived at Liverpool on 7 October.
0233	U.562 (Horst Hamm) sank steamer **ERNA III** (1590grt) (ex Danish **ERNA** (1590grt)) (Master Knud Christian Sorensen) with one torpedo while she was straggling behind convoy ON.16 northeast of Cape Farewell, Greenland, in 61, 45N, 35, 15W. She sank in fourteen minutes with her entire crew of twenty-three.

23 SEPTEMBER 1941

	Based upon an ULTRA intercept that the German battleship TIRPITZ was preparing to depart the Baltic and enter the North Atlantic, the American aircraft carrier YORKTOWN (CV-5), arrived at Argentia, Newfoundland, with light cruisers BROOKLYN (CL-40) and SAVANNAH (CL-42) to join the old battleships ARKANSAS (BB-33) and NEW YORK (BB-34).
	American battleship MISSISSIPPI (BB-41), aircraft carrier WASP (CV-7), plus heavy cruiser WICHITA (CA-45) departed Argentia, Newfoundland, for Hvalfjord, Iceland, with destroyers GWIN (DD-433), MEREDITH (DD-434), GRAYSON (DD-435) and MONSSEN (DD-436) plus repair ship VULCAN (AR-5).

24 SEPTEMBER 1941

	Convoy SC.46 departed Sydney, Cape Breton, escorted by corvettes LETHBRIDGE, NAPANEE, and SHEDIAC. Corvette GALT joined the convoy on the 25th. The original escort group was detached from the convoy on the 27th. Destroyers BROADWAY, BURWELL, and OTTAWA plus corvettes ALGOMA, BRANDON, BUCTOUCHE, and COBALT joined the convoy on the 27th. Destroyers CALDWELL, VANOC, VOLUNTEER, and WALKER joined the convoy on 4 October. The escort ships that joined on 27 September were detached from the convoy on 5 October. Destroyer VOLUNTEER was detached from the convoy on 9 October and the convoy arrived at Liverpool on 10 October.

26 SEPTEMBER 1941

	German Wolfpack BRANDENBURG was dispersed to allow some of the U-boats to return to port after their patrol time had been exceeded.
	Convoy HX.152 departed Halifax. Destroyer ANNAPOLIS joined the convoy on the 28th and was detached from the convoy on the 30th when relieved by American destroyers BABBITT (DD-128), BROOME (DD-210), LEARY (DD-158), MAYO (DD-422), and SCHENCK (DD-159). In heavy weather, all the American destroyers suffered varying degrees of storm damage. Destroyers KEPPEL, SABRE, SHIKARI, and VENOMOUS, corvettes DIANELLA and SUNFLOWER, and antisubmarine trawlers LADY ELSA, MAN O' WAR, and NORTHERN DAWN relieved the American group on 9 October. Destroyer SHIKARI was detached from the convoy on 9 October, the corvettes and the trawlers were detached from the convoy on 11 October, destroyer KEPPEL was detached from the convoy on 12 October, and destroyer SABRE was detached from the convoy on 13 October. The convoy arrived at Liverpool on 14 October.

29 SEPTEMBER 1941

	Convoy SC.47 departed Sydney, Cape Breton, escorted by corvettes CHICOUTIMI, MATAPEDIA, NAPANEE, and SHERBROOKE. Corvette CHAMBLY joined the convoy on 1 October and destroyers RAMSEY and RICHMOND with corvette ORILLIA joined the convoy on 4 October. Destroyers BROKE, MANSFIELD, and WOLVERINE, corvette EGLANTINE, and antisubmarine trawler KING SOL joined the convoy on 11 October. Destroyers RAMSEY and RICHMOND plus corvettes CHAMBLY, MATAPEDIA, ORILLIA, and SHERBROOKE were detached from the convoy on 12 October, destroyers BROKE, MANSFIELD, and WOLVERINE were detached from the convoy on 15 October, corvette EGLANTINE was detached from the convoy on 16 October, and antisubmarine trawler KING SOL was detached from the convoy on 17 October. The convoy arrived at Liverpool on 20 October.

East of United States
Long. W85, 00 – W60,00   Lat. N43, 30 – N25, 00

15 SEPTEMBER 1941

	Battleship RODNEY departed Bermuda after completing her refit in the United States to rendezvous with convoy WS.11 X during the morning of 21 September.

21 SEPTEMBER 1941

	The first of 2,751 Liberty Ships, the PATRICK HENRY (7191grt), Maritime Commission Hull 14, was launched at the Bethlehem-Fairfield Shipyards Inc. in Baltimore, Maryland.

23 SEPTEMBER 1941

	American battleship MASSACHUSETTS (BB-59) was launched at the Bethlehem Steel Co., Quincy, Massachusetts.

Caribbean and Gulf of Mexico
Long. W100, 00 – W60, 00   Lat. N31, 00 – N05, 00

1 SEPTEMBER 1941

	American Task Force TF.3 (RAdm Ingram) began regular Middle Atlantic patrols from Trinidad and Recife, Brazil to a point southwest of the Cape Verde Islands. The force was divided into four groups, each with a cruiser and a destroyer. TG.3.6 with MILWAUKEE (CL-5) and WARRINGTON (DD-383). TG.3.5 with OMAHA (CL-4) and SOMERS (DD-381). TG.3.7 with MEMPHIS (CL-13) and DAVIS (DD-395). TG.3.8 with CINCINNATI (CL-6) and JOUETT (DD-396).
	American TG.3.6 departed Trinidad with cruiser MILWAUKEE (CL-5) and destroyer WARRINGTON (DD-383) on a Middle Atlantic patrol lasting until 21 September.

23 SEPTEMBER 1941

	American TG.3.5 departed Trinidad with cruiser OMAHA (CL-4) and destroyer SOMERS (DD-381) on a Middle Atlantic patrol lasting until 11 October.

Western Approaches
Long. W30, 00 – W03, 00   Lat. N58, 30 – N49, 00

1 SEPTEMBER 1941

	U.77, U.568, U.553, U.206, U.567, U.563 and U.96 set up U-boat group KURFURST west of the North Channel.
	U.71, U.557, U.561, U.95, U.751, U.83, U.562 and U.558 set up U-boat group BOSEMULLER southwest of Ireland.
	Canadian convoy escort groups were reorganized as: EG.14 with destroyers ASSINIBOINE, HAVELOCK (RN) and ST LAURENT. EG.15 with destroyers BURWELL (RN) and SAGUENAY with corvettes DIANTHUS, HONEYSUCKLE and SNOWBERRY (all RN). EG.16 with destroyer BROADWATER (RN) plus corvettes CHILLIWACK, RIMOUSKI and SPIKENARD. EG.17 with destroyer BROADWAY plus corvettes POLYANTHUS, COBALT and TRAIL. EG.18 with destroyer CHURCHILL plus corvettes CARMELLA, ARROWHEAD and EYEBRIGHT. EG.19 with destroyer BURNHAM plus corvettes MAYFLOWER, AGASSIZ and LEVIS. EG.20 with destroyer COLUMBIA plus corvettes GLADIOLUS, MIMOSA and WETASKIWIN. EG.21 with destroyer ST CROIX plus corvettes CHAMBLY, PICTOU, BUCTOUCHE and GALT. EG.22 with destroyer RAMSEY plus corvettes CANDYTUFT, BITTERSWEET and FENNEL. EG.23 with destroyer CHESTERFIELD plus corvettes READING, HEPATICA and PRESCOTT. EG.24 with destroyer SKEENA plus corvettes ALBERNI, ORILLIA and KENOGAMI. EG.25 with destroyer NIAGARA plus corvettes ALYSSE, CELANDINE and COLLINGWOOD.
	Convoy ON.12 departed Liverpool, escorted by corvette HEARTSEASE plus antisubmarine trawlers ANGLE, CAPE WARWICK, and ST APOLLO. Antisubmarine trawler DANEMAN joined the convoy on the 2nd. On the 4th, destroyers AMAZON, AMBUSCADE, BELMONT, and BULLDOG, corvettes ACONIT, AUBRIETIA, and NIGELLA joined the convoy. Destroyer AMBUSCADE was detached from the convoy later that same day. The remaining escorts were detached from the convoy on the 7th. Destroyer BROADWAY plus corvettes COBALT and POLYANTHUS joined the convoy on the 7th and were detached from the convoy on the 10th. On the 10th, destroyer RAMSEY, AMC WORCESTERSHIRE, plus corvettes BUCTOUCHE and GALT joined and escorted the convoy until it was dispersed on the 14th.

2 SEPTEMBER 1941

	Free French destroyer LA CORDELIÈRE ran aground in Scottish waters and damaged her antisubmarine dome.
	P/T/Midshipman (A) J. F. Williams RNVR was killed when his Hurricane aircraft of 759/760 Squadron crashed near North Petherton.
	Convoy OS.5 departed Liverpool escorted by destroyers MANSFIELD and WOLVERINE, which were detached from the convoy on the 8th. Sloop ENCHANTRESS and escort vessel HARTLAND joined the convoy on the 3rd and were detached from the convoy on the 17th. Escort vessel WALNEY joined the convoy on the 6th and was detached from the convoy on the 17th. On the 17th, destroyer BRILLIANT, corvettes AMARANTHUS and ASPHODEL, and antisubmarine trawler SARABANDE joined the convoy. BRILLIANT, corvette AMARANTHUS, and SARABANDE were detached from the convoy on the 18th. Corvette ASPHODEL was detached on the 20th. The convoy arrived at Freetown on the 21st.

3 SEPTEMBER 1941

	Submarine PROTEUS departed Holy Loch for Gibraltar after completing her refit at Portsmouth.
2042	U.567 (Kptlt Fahr) sank steamer **FORT RICHEPANSE** (3485grt) (Master Charles Draper) while she was sailing alone at 450 miles southwest of Bloody Foreland in 52, 15N, 21, 10W. German bombing had slightly damaged the steamer seven hours before U.567 attacked. The master, thirty-five crewmen and five passengers were lost. Polish destroyers PIORUN picked up ten crewmen, five gunners and six passengers, and Polish destroyer GARLAND rescued one survivor. All survivors were landed at Greenock. (Other sources state that there were only twenty-two survivors.)

4 SEPTEMBER 1941

	German bombing sank steamer **ABBAS COMBE** (489grt) five miles north-northwest of Bardsey Island. Four crewmen were missing.
	German bombing damaged Dutch steamer TON S. (466grt) northwest of Bardsey Island in 52, 58N, 04, 55W. She arrived at Newport on the 6th for dry-docking.

5 SEPTEMBER 1941

	Convoy ON.13 departed Liverpool escorted by corvette VERONICA. Destroyers DOUGLAS, LEAMINGTON, SALADIN, SKATE, and VETERAN, corvettes ABELIA and ANEMONE, plus antisubmarine trawlers ST KENAN, ST ZENO, and VIZALMA joined the convoy on the 6th. Destroyer LEAMINGTON and trawler VIZALMA were detached from the convoy on the 8th while destroyers DOUGLAS, SALADIN, SKATE, and VETERAN were detached from the convoy on the 9th. The remaining escorts remained with the convoy until it was dispersed on the 11th.
2337	U.141 (Philipp Schüler) sank Icelandic trawler **ANDERS** (190grt) (Master Óskar Theódór Óskarsson) with one torpedo south of Iceland in 58, 24N, 11, 25W. She immediately sank with all eleven on board.

6 SEPTEMBER 1941

	Trawler **BRORA** (530grt) was lost by grounding in the Hebrides. She became a constructive total loss.
	German bombing heavily damaged steamer **EMPIRE GUNNER** (4492grt) (ex Italian **MOSCARDIN** (4492grt)) in St. Georges Channel in 52, 08N, 05, 18W. She sank early on the 7th in 52, 09N, 05, 16W with the entire crew rescued.
	Submarine TRUSTY departed Holy Loch for Gibraltar.

7 SEPTEMBER 1941

	Convoy ON.14 departed Liverpool. The convoy was joined at sea on the 8th by corvettes LOBELIA, NARCISSUS, and RENONCULE plus antisubmarine trawlers ARAB, AYRSHIRE, and LADY MADELEINE. Destroyers BEAGLE, BOADICEA, and SALISBURY with corvette HEATHER joined the convoy on the 9th. On the 11th, destroyer SALISBURY plus trawlers AYRSHIRE and LADY MADELEINE were detached from the convoy and on the 12th destroyers BEAGLE and BOADICEA were detached from the convoy. The remaining escorts were with the convoy until it was dispersed on the 14th.
2300	Destroyers LIGHTNING and ICARUS arrived in the Clyde escorting the troopship EMPRESS OF CANADA (21,517grt) with Norwegians evacuated from Spitsbergen.

8 SEPTEMBER 1941

	Light cruiser PENELOPE arrived at the Clyde from Scapa Flow to escort battleship DUKE OF YORK.
	Sloop ROSEMARY was damaged in a collision with Polish destroyer BURZA inside Milford Haven Harbour. The sloop was repaired at Milford Haven, completing on the 15th. The destroyer was repaired at Glasgow,

	completing on the 20th.
2100	Destroyer CASTLETON departed Loch Alsh for Scapa Flow.

9 SEPTEMBER 1941

| 0600 | Destroyer VIVACIOUS arrived in the Clyde and joined battleship DUKE OF YORK, light cruiser PENELOPE, plus destroyers LIGHTNING and ICARUS as they departed the Clyde for Rosyth to complete the DUKE OF YORK preparations for working up to combat efficiency. |

10 SEPTEMBER 1941

	Naval drifter **CHRISTINE ROSE** (T/Skipper R. W. Griffiths RNR) was lost when she grounded on Knap Rock, Argyll. Griffiths was lost.
	U.71, U.73, U.101, U.751, U.106, U.563, U.96, U.77, U.83, U.553, U.561 and U.569 formed a new patrol line west of Ireland until the 23rd.

11 SEPTEMBER 1941

	Light cruiser SHEFFIELD arrived at the Clyde from Scapa Flow to prepare for her return to Gibraltar.
	Convoy ON.15 departed Liverpool escorted by destroyers KEPPEL, SABRE, SHIKARI, and VENOMOUS, corvettes ALISMA, DIANELLA, and SUNFLOWER, plus antisubmarine trawlers LADY ELSA, MAN O' WAR, and NORTHERN DAWN. Destroyer VENOMOUS and corvette SUNFLOWER were detached from the convoy on the 13th, destroyer SABRE was detached from the convoy on the 14th, and destroyer KEPPEL was detached from the convoy on the 15th. The remainder of the escorts remained with the convoy until it was dispersed on the 16th.

12 SEPTEMBER 1941

	Light cruiser KENYA arrived in the Clyde from Scapa Flow to repair the damage from her collision with destroyer BRIGHTON on 25 June. The flag of CS.10 was transferred to light cruiser SHEFFIELD while KENYA was under repair.
	Convoy OG.74 departed Liverpool and the Clyde escorted by escort aircraft carrier AUDACITY, sloop DEPTFORD, plus corvettes PENSTEMON, MARIGOLD, and VETCH. Ocean boarding vessel CORINTHIAN and destroyer ROCKINGHAM joined the convoy on the 13th while corvettes ARBUTUS and RHODODENDRON joined the convoy on the 14th. The CORINTHIAN was detached from the convoy on the 18th. A Martlet aircraft, piloted by Sub-Lt (A) N. H. Patterson and Sub-Lt (A) G. R. P. Fletcher RNVR of 802 Squadron from aircraft carrier AUDACITY shot down the carrier's first German Fw200 aircraft on the 21st. Sloop DEPTFORD arrived at Gibraltar on the 25th. Corvette COWSLIP, which had steamed independently from Britain after failing to join up with the convoy at sea, also arrived at Gibraltar on the 25th. Aircraft carrier AUDACITY plus corvettes ARBUTUS and MARIGOLD arrived at Gibraltar on the 26th with survivors from the sunken ships, escorted by destroyer ROCKINGHAM, corvettes PENTSTEMON, VETCH, and RHODODENDRON plus antisubmarine trawler LAUREL.
	Convoy OS.6 departed Liverpool escorted by destroyer CAMPBELTOWN, which was detached from the convoy on the 15th. On the 13th, destroyers WESTCOTT and ST ALBANS plus sloops STORK and the New Zealand WELLINGTON joined the convoy. WESTCOTT and ST ALBANS were detached from the convoy on the 17th and STORK and WELLINGTON were detached from the convoy on the 29th. Indian sloop JUMNA joined the convoy on the 17th and was detached from the convoy on the 29th. On 1 October, corvettes CLOVER and CYCLAMEN joined and escorted the convoy into Freetown, arriving on 3 October. Destroyer BRILLIANT joined the convoy on 3 October outside Freetown.
2230	Light cruiser SHEFFIELD departed Greenock with three hundred service personnel for Gibraltar.

13 SEPTEMBER 1941

| | Convoy ON.16 departed Liverpool escorted by destroyers MALCOLM, SARDONYX, and WATCHMAN.
Antisubmarine trawlers NORTHERN GEM, NORTHERN PRIDE, and NORTHERN SPRAY joined the convoy on the 14th.
Corvettes ARABIS and PETUNIA joined the convoy on the 15th.
Destroyers BADSWORTH and LAMERTON were with the convoy on 17 and 18 September, and then they were detached from the convoy.
Destroyers MALCOLM, SARDONYX, and WATCHMAN were detached from the convoy on the 19th.
Destroyer COLUMBIA joined the convoy on the 19th.
Destroyer SKEENA plus corvettes ORILLIA, RIMOUSKI, and WETASKIWIN joined the convoy on the 20th when the corvettes ARABIS and PETUNIA and trawlers NORTHERN GEM, NORTHERN PRIDE, and NORTHERN SPRAY were detached from the convoy.
Destroyer COLUMBIA was detached from the convoy on the 24th and the convoy was dispersed on the 27th. |

15 SEPTEMBER 1941

	German Wolfpack BRANDENBURG patrolled southeast of Cape Farewell, Greenland.
	A German Fw200 aircraft bombing damaged Norwegian tanker VINGA (7321grt) in 58, 08N, 13, 17W. The tanker was towed to Rothesay Bay and later repaired at Glasgow.
	A German aerial mine sank tug **FLYING KITE** (260grt) off the Dalmuir Basin, Clyde. Five of the eight crewmen were lost.
	A German aerial mine damaged tug ATLANTIC COCK (182grt) near the Dalmuir Basin, Clyde. She was beached and re-floated on 11 October for docking.
	Destroyer BROCKLESBY and Dutch destroyer ISAAC SWEERS collided in the Irish Sea. There was minor damage to both ships, but both remained operational.
	Lt J. D. M. Briscoe and P/T/Sub-Lt (A) J. D. Pomfret RNVR were killed when their Hurricane aircrafts of 801 Squadron collided at Kingswill.
	German bombing sank steamer **DARU** (3854grt) in 51, 56, 30N, 05, 58W. There were no casualties.
0816	U.94 (ObltzS Otto Ites) sank steamer **NEWBURY** (5102grt) (Master Theodore Pryse OBE) while she was straggling behind convoy ON.14 southeast of Cape Farewell in 54, 39N, 28, 04W. The entire crew made it to the lifeboats; but the master, thirty-eight crewmen and six gunners were never seen again.
1800	Destroyer CASTLETON arrived at Loch Alsh from Scapa Flow.
2038	U.94 sank Greek steamer **PEGASUS** (5762grt) while she was straggling behind convoy ON.14 south of Greenland in 54, 40N, 29, 50W. Sixteen crewmen were lost. A Swedish steamer rescued the thirteen survivors.
2128	U.94 hit the abandoned steamer with another torpedo and she broke in two. Parts of the wreck remained afloat until they were shelled and sunk by an Allied warship in 54, 54N, 30, 32W.
2348	U.94 sank steamer **EMPIRE ELAND** (5613grt) (ex American **WEST KEDRON** (5613grt)) (Master Donald Cameron Sinclair) while she was straggling behind convoy ON.14 southeast of Cape Farewell in 54N, 28W. The entire crew of thirty-eight were lost, including the master, thirty-two crewmen and five gunners.

16 SEPTEMBER 1941

	Submarine P.34 departed Barrow (probably the Port of Barrow, *Barrow-in-Furness, England*) for Gibraltar.
1000	Battleship PRINCE OF WALES arrived at the Clyde with light cruiser EURYALUS plus destroyers LAFOREY, ESKIMO, and LIGHTNING to escort convoy WS.11X.
>1000	Destroyer ESKIMO departed the Clyde to return to Scapa Flow, but was diverted to join Captain (D) 6th Destroyer Flotilla in an antisubmarine sweep.
1230	Destroyer LIGHTNING arrived at the Clyde from Scapa Flow to escort convoy WS.11X.

17 SEPTEMBER 1941

	Heavy cruiser SUFFOLK arrived at the Clyde from Scapa Flow to boiler clean.
	Convoy WS.11X, which departed Liverpool on the 16th and the Clyde on the 17th, rendezvoused off Oversay on the 17th. The convoy included supply ship BRECONSHIRE (9776grt) plus steamers ULSTER MONARCH (3791grt), QUEEN EMMA, PRINCESS BEATRIX (4135grt), ROYAL SCOTSMAN (3244grt), LEINSTER (4302grt), STRATHEDEN (23,722grt), CLAN MACDONALD (9653grt), CLAN FERGUSON (7347grt), AJAX (7540grt), IMPERIAL STAR (10,733grt), CITY OF LINCOLN (8039grt), ROWALLAN CASTLE (7798grt), DUNEDIN STAR (11,168grt), and CITY OF CALCUTTA (8063grt). The convoy escort included battleship PRINCE OF WALES, light cruisers EURYALUS and KENYA, plus destroyers LAFOREY, LIGHTNING, and ORIBI, which departed the Clyde on the 16th, WHITEHALL, WITCH, BLANKNEY, PIORUN, GARLAND, and ISAAC SWEERS from Liverpool on the 17 September to Gibraltar. Destroyers HAVELOCK and HARVESTER escorted the convoy from 17 to 19 September when they were detached to escort troopship STRATHEDEN to Halifax. Destroyers FORESIGHT, FORESTER, FURY, and LEGION, escorting aircraft carrier FURIOUS, and ZULU, GURKHA, and LANCE departed Gibraltar on the 18th to join the convoy on the 19th in 42N, 22, 30W. Light cruiser SHEFFIELD departed Gibraltar on the 20th to join the convoy at sea. Destroyer LIVELY departed Gibraltar on the 20th to join the convoy, as did destroyers COSSACK, HEYTHROP, and FARNDALE on the 23rd. Troopships ULSTER MONARCH, QUEEN EMMA, PRINCESS BEATRIX, and ROYAL SCOTSMAN, and LEINSTER proceeded only to Gibraltar. The remainder of the convoy made up the Operation HALBERD convoy for Malta. During the night of 20/21 September, troopship PRINCESS BEATRIX and store ship AJAX were in a minor collision.
	Convoy ON.17 departed Liverpool escorted by destroyer BOREAS. On the 18th, destroyers BELMONT and BULLDOG, corvettes ACONIT and HEARTSEASE, plus antisubmarine trawlers ANGLE, CAPE WARWICK, DANEMAN, NOTTS COUNTY, and ST APOLLO joined the convoy. Destroyers AMAZON, GEORGETOWN, and ST CROIX joined the convoy on the 19th. They were detached from the convoy on the 21st when relieved by destroyer RICHMOND with corvettes FENNEL, GLADIOLUS, HEPATICA, and MIMOSA.

	RICHMOND was detached from the convoy on the 24th. The corvettes escorted the convoy until its dispersal on the 29th.

18 SEPTEMBER 1941

	Aircraft carrier ARGUS arrived unescorted at the Clyde from Scapa Flow.

19 SEPTEMBER 1941

	Convoy ON.18 departed Liverpool. Destroyers LEAMINGTON, SALADIN, SKATE, and VETERAN, corvettes ABELIA, ANEMONE, and VERONICA, and antisubmarine trawlers ST ELSTAN, ST KENAN, and VIZALMA escorted the convoy from 21 September. The Liverpool escorts were detached from the convoy on the 24th when relieved by American destroyers CHARLES F. HUGHES (DD-428), GLEAVES (DD-423), LANSDALE (DD-426), MADISON (DD-425), and SIMPSON (DD-221). The American destroyers escorted the convoy until it was dispersed on 2 October.

20 SEPTEMBER 1941

	A German aerial mine sank ferry **PORTSDOWN** (342grt) in St. Georges Channel in 50, 46, 07N, 06, 25W. Eight crewmen and fifteen passengers were lost.

21 SEPTEMBER 1941

	Convoy ON.19 departed Liverpool. Destroyers BEAGLE, MONTGOMERY, ROXBOROUGH, and SALISBURY, corvettes HEATHER, LOBELIA, and NARCISSUS, minesweepers BRITOMART, GOSSAMER, and LEDA, and antisubmarine trawler NORWICH CITY escorted the convoy from 22 September. Corvettes ALBERNI and KENOGAMI and minesweeper HUSSAR joined the convoy on the 23rd. BRITOMART, GOSSAMER, and LEDA were detached from the convoy on the 25th. Corvettes ALYSSE and MAYFLOWER joined the convoy on the 27th and corvettes ALBERNI and KENOGAMI escorted the convoy when rest of the escorts were detached. Corvette MAYFLOWER was detached from the convoy on 6 October. The convoy was dispersed on 7 October and the other three corvettes were detached.
1200	Antiaircraft ship ULSTER QUEEN arrived at Belfast, Northern Ireland from Scapa Flow to join the Western Approaches Command.

22 SEPTEMBER 1941

	Submarine THORN departed Holy Loch for Gibraltar.

23 SEPTEMBER 1941

	Heavy cruiser SUFFOLK departed the Clyde to return to Scapa Flow.
	Convoy OS.7 departed Liverpool. On the 24th, sloops FOLKESTONE and WESTON plus corvette AURICULA joined the convoy. The sloops were detached from the convoy on 12 October. AURICULA arrived with the convoy at Freetown on 14 October for duty in the South Atlantic Command. On the 26th, sloop LONDONDERRY and corvette VIOLET joined the convoy and were detached from the convoy on 12 October. On 10 October, destroyer BRILLIANT joined the convoy and, on 11 October, corvettes CLOVER and CYCLAMEN joined the convoy. All arrived with the convoy at Freetown on 14 October. Corvettes ANCHUSA, MIGNONETTE, and WOODRUFF joined the convoy on 14 October outside Freetown for local escort.
0630	Destroyer LANCASTER arrived at Loch Alsh from Scapa Flow to rejoin RAdm Minelaying.

24 SEPTEMBER 1941

	A German aerial mine damaged steamer DALTONHALL (7253grt) off Milford Haven in 51, 45, 06N, 05, 16, 30W. She arrived at Holyhead under her own power and later proceeded to Liverpool for full repairs.
1100	Destroyer LAMERTON arrived at Liverpool from Scapa Flow to join the Western Approaches Command.

25 SEPTEMBER 1941

	Convoy ON.20 departed Liverpool escorted by destroyers VANOC, VOLUNTEER, and WALKER and corvette HYDRANGEA. Destroyer CALDWELL joined the convoy on the 26th. American destroyers BENSON (DD-421), HILARY P. JONES (DD-427), NIBLACK (DD-424), REUBEN JAMES (DD-245), and WINSLOW (DD-359) relieved the escort on the 30th. Corvette ALGOMA joined the convoy on 3 October and was detached from the convoy the next day.

26 SEPTEMBER 1941

	Schooner **KANTARA** was lost—cause and location unknown.
	A German aerial mine damaged steamer ORIOLE (489grt) off South Bishops, Cardigan Bay. She was towed to Milford on the 27th.

27 SEPTEMBER 1941

	British air cover from Cornwall forced U.205 and U.203 underwater before they could attack convoy HG.73 southwest of Ireland. U.205 was damaged by bomb near misses.
	Convoy OG.75 departed Liverpool escorted by sloop ROCHESTER plus corvettes BLUEBELL, CAMPION, CARNATION, HELIOTROPE, and MALLOW. Minesweeping trawler BURKE and antiaircraft vessel ARIGUANI joined the convoy on the 28th. Corvette LA MALOUINE joined the convoy on 3 October. On 4 October, destroyer LAMERTON joined the convoy. Destroyers FORESIGHT, FORESTER, FURY, LEGION, and LIVELY departed Gibraltar on 7 October and joined the convoy on 8 October. Corvette FLEUR DE LYS departed Gibraltar on 8 October and joined the convoy. On 13 October, aircraft carrier ARK ROYAL, which was exercising east of Gibraltar, launched aircraft to provide the convoy with air cover. Destroyer VIDETTE joined the convoy and provided local escort into Gibraltar on 13 October.
0208 0211	U.201 (ObltzS Adalbert Schnee) sank CAM ship **SPRINGBANK** (5155grt) (Cap C. H. Godwin DSO) while attacking convoy HG.73 at 700 miles west of the Bishop Rock in 49, 10N, 20, 05W. T/A/Sub-Lt (E) J. Moir RNVR and thirty-one ratings were lost. Corvettes JASMINE (K 23) (Lt Cdr C. D. B. Coventry), which went alongside the burning ship to take off most of the survivors, HIBISCUS (Lt H. Roach) and PERIWINKLE (Lt Cdr P. G. MacIver) rescued two hundred one survivors. JASMINE later scuttled the **SPRINGBANK** with depth charges and gunfire. HIBISCUS landed survivors at Gibraltar. PERIWINKLE landed survivors at Milford Haven.
0208 0210	U.201 sank Norwegian steamer **SIREMALM** (2468grt) (Master Haakon Svendsen) while attacking convoy HG.73 at 700 miles west of the Bishop Rock in 49, 05N, 20, 10W. She sank immediately with her entire crew (twenty Norwegian, three Finnish, one Swede and three British).
2303	U.201 sank steamer **MARGARETA** (3103grt) (ex Finnish) (Master Holger Pihlgren) while attacking convoy HG.73 southwest of Cape Clear in 50, 15N, 17, 27W. There were no casualties. Corvette HIBISCUS (Lt Cdr H. Roach) rescued the master and thirty-three crewmen and landed them at Gibraltar.

28 SEPTEMBER 1941

	A German aerial mine heavily damaged fishing trawler **MURIELLE** (96grt) eight to nine miles southwest by south of Morecambe Bay Light Vessel. She sank in tow. There were no casualties.
	The Germans ended their attack on convoy HG.73, mostly due to the U-boats having used most of their torpedoes. In all, five U-boats sank ten steamers for 25,818grt lost.
	Convoy ON.21 departed Liverpool escorted by destroyer KEPPEL. On the 30th, destroyers SABRE and VENOMOUS, corvettes DIANELLA and SUNFLOWER, and antisubmarine trawlers LADY ELSA, MAN O' WAR, and NORTHERN DAWN joined the convoy. Destroyer SABRE was detached from the convoy on 2 October and destroyers KEPPEL and VENOMOUS were detached from the convoy on 5 October. The remaining escort ships were detached from the convoy on 6 October after destroyer ST LAURENT and corvettes BITTERSWEET, CHILLIWACK, COLLINGWOOD, SNOWBERRY, and TRAIL joined the convoy on 5 October. The convoy was dispersed on 14 October and the escorts were detached to other duties.
1400	Destroyer OFFA departed the Clyde to work up to combat efficiency at Scapa Flow.

30 SEPTEMBER 1941

1230	Destroyer DULVERTON departed the Clyde for Scapa Flow to work up to combat efficiency.

Central Atlantic Crossing Zone   Long. W60, 00 – W15, 00   Lat. 49, 00 – N05, 00

1 SEPTEMBER 1941

	U.111, U.108 and U.125 set up a patrol line around the area west of the Azores near St. Paul Rock in the North Atlantic.
	U.73 spotted convoy SL.84 during her return to France. She alerted the BOSEMULLER U-boat group, but

	they were unable to find the convoy in bad weather.
	A German Fw200 aircraft of I/KG.40 spotted convoy OG.73 and provided the KURFURST U-boat group with its position.

2 SEPTEMBER 1941

	U.557 tried to find convoy OG.73 in heavy fog. She did spot a corvette from the escort, but failed to locate the ships reported by aerial reconnaissance.

3 SEPTEMBER 1941

	U.98 spotted convoy OG.73 and reported its position.

5 SEPTEMBER 1941

	Italian submarine BARACCA sank Panamanian steamer **TRINIDAD** (434grt) west of France in 46, 06N, 17, 04W. Ten crewmen reached Oporto, Portugal, after twenty days in open boats. (Other sources have U.95 (Gerd Schreiber) sinking the steamer at that position.)

7 SEPTEMBER 1941

	A Sunderland aircraft of RAAF 10 Squadron sank Italian submarine **MALASPINA** west of Spain.

8 SEPTEMBER 1941

	Destroyer CROOME sank Italian submarine **MAGGIORE BARACCA** with gunfire and by ramming east of the Azores, in 40, 30N, 21, 15W, after forcing the submarine to the surface with depth charges. The captain, five officers, and twenty-eight ratings were picked up. The destroyer sustained damage to her stern. Destroyer CROOME arrived at Gibraltar on the 10th and was under repair from 12 September to 4 October.

10 SEPTEMBER 1941

	U.111 (Kptlt Kleinschmidt) sank unescorted Dutch steamer **MARKEN** (5719grt) (Master A. Kokké) north of Ceara in 01, 36N, 36, 55W. The entire crew of thirty-seven abandoned ship. The U-boat questioned the survivors in the lifeboats before giving them food. A Spanish steamer rescued them on the 21st.
	Italian submarines DA VINCI, MOROSINI, TORELLI and **MALASPINA** were ordered to patrol west of Gibraltar. At the time, the Italian command did not know that **MALASPINA** had already been lost.

20 SEPTEMBER 1941

	A Martlet aircraft from escort carrier AUDACITY and sloop DEPTFORD with corvette ARBUTUS forced U.201 (ObltzS Adalbert Schnee) to submerge before she could attack convoy OG.74.
	An aircraft from escort carrier AUDACITY downed a German Fw200 Condor aircraft that had been shadowing convoy OG.74 and reporting its position.
<2331	U.124 (Kptlt Johann Mohr) spotted convoy OG.74 southwest of Ireland and reported its position. The convoy included twenty-seven ships with OBV CORINTHIAN plus EG.36 (Lt Cdr White) with sloop DEPTFORD, corvettes ARBUTUS, PENTSTEMON, MARIGOLD, and PERIWINKLE. Convoy OG.74 also included the first escort carrier AUDACITY (ex German **HANNOVER**, Cdr Mackendrick) to provide air cover during the voyage.
2331	U.124 sank steamer **BALTALLINN** (1303grt) (Master Charles Walter Browne) while attacking convoy OG.74 north-northeast of the Azores in 48, 07N, 22, 07W. Seven crewmen were lost. Rescue ship WALMER CASTLE (906grt) (Master Gerald Lewis Clarke) rescued the master, twenty-two crewmen and five gunners. When the rescue ship was sunk the next day, sloop DEPTFORD (Lt Cdr H. R. White) rescued the master, twelve crewmen and four gunners and landed them at Gibraltar on the 28th.
2331	U.124 (Johann Mohr) sank steamer **EMPIRE MOAT** (2922grt) (Master James Fawcett Travis) while attacking convoy OG.74 north-northeast of the Azores in 48, 07N, 22, 07W. Rescue ship WALMER CASTLE (906grt) (Master Gerald Lewis Clarke) rescued the master, twenty-eight crewmen and three gunners. Unfortunately, five of the crew were lost when WALMER CASTLE was sunk.

21 SEPTEMBER 1941

	Italian submarine TORELLI made intermittent contact with convoy OG.74 during the night, but was heavily damaged by destroyer VIMY with depth charges.
	A German Fw200 aircraft of I/KG.40 heavily damaged rescue ship **WALMER CASTLE** (906grt) northeast of the Azores in 47, 16N, 22, 25W. She carried thirty-two survivors of steamer **EMPIRE MOAT** (five were lost), twenty-eight survivors from steamer **BALTALLINN** (ten crewmen and one gunner were lost), and twenty-three crewmen from steamer **CITY OF WATERFORD** (1071grt), which had been sunk in a collision with tug THAMES on the 19th. Ten crewmen and passengers were lost. Sloop DEPTFORD (Lt Cdr H. R. White) and corvette MARIGOLD (Lt W. S. Macdonald) rescued the survivors and landed them at Gibraltar on 28th. Sloop DEPTFORD then scuttled the wreck.

	After convoy OG.74 was dispersed, U.201 and U.124 set up a patrol line to intercept convoy HG.73.
	U.107 (KKpt Hessler) spotted convoy SL.87 and reported its position west of Portugal.
2250	U.201 (ObltzS Adalbert Schnee) sank steamer **RUNA** (1575grt) (Master Hugh McLarty) while attacking convoy OG.74 north-northeast of the Azores in 46, 20N, 22, 23W. Twelve crewmen and two gunners were lost. Sloop DEPTFORD (Lt H. P. White) rescued the master, seven crewmen and one gunner and landed them at Gibraltar.
2320	U.201 sank steamer **LISSA** (1511grt) (Master Donald MacQuarrie) while attacking convoy OG.74 north-northeast of the Azores in 47N, 22W. The master, twenty crewmen and five gunners were all lost.
2321	U.201 heavily damaged steamer **RHINELAND** (1381grt) (Master John Thorburn Gilroy) while attacking convoy OG.74 north-northeast of the Azores in 47N, 22W.
2341	U.201 sank the steamer with a final torpedo. The master, twenty-two crewmen and three gunners were lost.

22 SEPTEMBER 1941

	German U-boats spotted convoy SL.87 escorted by sloop BIDEFORD, cutter GORLESTON, corvette GARDENIA, and Free French sloop COMMANDANT DUBOC west of Africa.
0222 0224	U.68 (KKpt Merten) badly damaged steamer **SILVERBELLE** (5302grt) (Master Hilon Rowe) while attacking convoy SL.87 southwest of the Canary Islands in 25, 45N, 24W. Cutter GORLESTON took the damaged steamer in tow, but after a second attack on the convoy, the steamer was left and the cutter rejoined the convoy. Free French sloop COMMANDANT DUBOC took the damaged steamer in tow and took her towards Las Palmas.
0322	U.68 fired two torpedoes at the listing steamer, but both missed.
0415	U.68 fired two torpedoes at the listing steamer, but both missed. U.68 then departed, as she was out of torpedoes. Antisubmarine trawler LADY SHIRLEY and a tug was sent from Las Palmas relieved the sloop of the tow. **SILVERBELLE** was cut lose southwest of the Canary Islands on the 29th and sank in 26, 30N, 23, 14W. There were no casualties as COMMANDANT DUBOC removed the master, forty-seven crewmen, seven gunners and five passengers (among them two DBS) and landed them at Freetown.
2346	U.103 (Kptlt Winter) sank steamer **EDWARD BLYDEN** (5003grt) (Master William Exley) while attacking convoy SL.87 southwest of the Canary Islands in 27, 36N, 24, 29W. Sloop BIDEFORD (Lt Cdr W. J. Moore) rescued the master, forty-six crewmen, four gunners and twelve passengers and landed them at Londonderry, Northern Ireland, on the 5th.
2347	U.103 (Werner Winter) sank steamer **NICETO DE LARRINAGA** (5591grt) (Master Frederick Moulton Milnes) while attacking convoy SL.87 southwest of the Canary Islands in 27, 32N, 24, 26W. Two crewmen were lost. The master, forty-three crewmen, five gunners and four passengers (DBS) were rescued. Corvette GARDENIA (Lt Cdr H. Hill) rescued eleven and landed them at the Azores. Destroyer LULWORTH (Lt Cdr C. Gwinner) rescued forty-two survivors and landed them at Londonderry, Northern Ireland, on 4 Oct.

23 SEPTEMBER 1941

	Italian submarine DA VINCI reported the position of convoy HG.73 west of Gibraltar.

24 SEPTEMBER 1941

	A Fulmar aircraft from CAM ship SPRINGBANK (5155grt) downed a German Fw200 aircraft that spotted convoy HG.73 in the North Atlantic. Three U-boats were within interception range of the reported position.
0028	U.67 (Kptlt Müller-Stöckheim) sank steamer **ST CLAIR II** (3753grt) (ex French **SAINT CLAIR** (3753grt)) (Master Harry Readman) while attacking one group of convoy SL.87 west-northwest of the Canary Islands in 30, 25N, 23, 35W. Twelve crewmen and one gunner were lost. The master, twenty-six crewmen and four gunners were rescued. Sloop GORLESTON (Cdr R. W. Keymer) rescued twenty-six and landed them at Ponta Delgada, Azores. Destroyer LULWORTH (Lt Cdr C. Gwinner) rescued five survivors and landed them at Londonderry, Northern Ireland, on 4 Oct.
0631	U.107 (KKpt Hessler) sank steamer **DIXCOVE** (3790grt) (Master Richard Jones) while attacking one group of convoy SL.87 southwest of Madeira in 31, 13N, 23, 41W. Two crewmen were lost. Steamer ASHBY (4868grt) and Norwegian steamer FANA (1345grt) rescued the master, thirty-six crewmen, eight gunners and six passengers. Sloops GORLESTON (Cdr R. W. Keymer) and LULWORTH (Lt Cdr C. Gwinner) collected the survivors and took them to Londonderry, Northern Ireland, on 4 Oct.
0631	U.107 sank steamer **JOHN HOLT** (4975grt) (Master Cecil Gordon Hime) (Convoy Commodore Cdr A. MacRae DSC RNR) while attacking one group of convoy SL.87 southwest of Madeira in 31, 12N, 23, 32W. One gunner was lost. Sloop GORLESTON (Cdr R.W. Keymer) rescued the master, the commodore, five naval staff members, forty-five crewmen, seven gunners and nine passengers and landed them at Ponta Delgada, Azores.
0631	U.107 sank steamer **LAFIAN** (4876grt) (Master Evan Llewellyn Phillips) while attacking one group of convoy

	SL.87 southwest of Madeira in 31, 12N, 23, 32W. Sloop GORLESTON (Cdr R.W. Keymer) rescued the master, thirty-seven crewmen, five gunners and four passengers and landed them at Ponta Delgada, Azores.
>0631	After three nights of attacks, only four of the eleven ships remained from convoy SL.87. After completing the attack on convoy SL.87, U.103, U.107, U.66 and U.125 relocated to the area west of Freetown. Sierra Leone. U.108 patrolled on the line between Cape Verde and St. Paul, while U.68 patrolled between Ascension and St. Helena Islands.

25 SEPTEMBER 1941

0744	U.124 (Kptlt Mohr) sank steamer **EMPIRE STREAM** (2922grt) (Master Stanley Herbert Evans) while attacking convoy HG.73 north-northeast of the Azores in 46, 03N, 24, 40W. Four crewmen, two gunners, and two stowaways were lost. Corvette BEGONIA (Lt Cdr H. B. Phillips) rescued the master, twenty-four crewmen and two gunners and landed them at Milford Haven.

26 SEPTEMBER 1941

	Aircraft from CAM ship SPRINGBANK (5155grt) forced U.203, U.124 and U.205 underwater to stop them trailing and attacking convoy HG.73.
0031	U.203 (Kptlt Mützelburg) sank steamer **AVOCETA** (3442grt) (Master Harold Martin) (convoy commodore RAdm K. E. L. Creighton MVO RN) while attacking convoy HG.73 north of the Azores in 47, 57N, 24, 05W. Forty-three crewmen, four gunners, and seventy-six passengers were missing. Corvette PERIWINKLE (Lt Cdr P. G. MacIver) rescued the master, the convoy Commodore, five naval staff members, nineteen crewmen, two gunners and twelve passengers and landed them at Milford Haven. Steamer CERVANTES (1810grt) rescued three survivors. Surgeon Lt F. Bagot of battleship NELSON was lost. Sloop STARLING (Cdr Frederic John Walker) collected the three survivors on CERVANTES and took them to Liverpool.
0031 0634	U.203 heavily damaged steamer **CORTES** (1374grt) (Master Donald Ray McRae) while attacking convoy HG.73 north of the Azores in 47, 48N, 23, 45W. U.203 fired a final torpedo to sink the steamer. Steamer LAPWING (1348grt) rescued the master, thirty-five crewmen and six passengers. All but one of these survivors was lost when LAPWING was later sunk.
0031	U.203 sank Norwegian steamer **VARANBERG** (2842grt) while attacking convoy HG.73 north of the Azores in 47, 50N, 24, 50W. Twenty-one crewmen were missing.
0210	U.124 (Kptlt Mohr) sank steamer **LAPWING** (1348grt) (Master Thomas James Hyam) while attacking convoy HG.73 north of the Azores in 47, 40N, 23, 30W. The master twenty crewmen and five gunners were lost. Eight crewmen with nine **PETEREL** (1354grt) survivors landed their lifeboat at Slyne Bay, Co. Galway, Ireland, on 9 October.
0232	U.124 sank steamer **PETEREL** (1354grt) (Master John William Klemp) while attacking convoy HG.73 north of the Azores in 47, 40N, 23, 28W. She immediately sank with nineteen crewmen and three gunners lost. Eight crewmen from sunken steamer **LAPWING** (1348grt) rescued the master, seven crewmen and one passenger with their lifeboat. The lifeboat landed at Slyne Bay, Co. Galway, Ireland, on 9 October.
2335	U.124 sank steamer **CERVANTES** (1810grt) (Master Henry Austin Fraser) while attacking convoy HG.73 north of the Azores in 48, 37N, 20, 01W. Three crewmen, two gunners, and three passengers were lost. Sloop STARLING (Cdr Frederic John Walker) rescued the master, twenty-seven crewmen, three gunners and one DBS and landed them at Liverpool. The four passengers were DBS from sunken steamer **CISCAR** (1809grt).

27 SEPTEMBER 1941

	During the night of 27/28 September, U.79 and U.129 joined with captured steamer **KOTA PINANG** (7277grt) and escorted her north to the Bay of Biscay and France. British radio intercept learned about the passage and dispatched light cruisers SHEFFIELD and KENYA to intercept the captured steamer.
0330	During the night of 27/28 September, submarine CLYDE encountered U.111 (Kptlt Kleinschmidt) supplying U.67 and U.68 in Tarafal Bay, St Antao Island, Cape Verde Islands. CLYDE was missed by torpedoes from U.68 and was narrowly missed when the second submarine attempted to ram her. CLYDE was then damaged in a collision with U.67, but managed to escape and arrived at Gibraltar on 4 October.

UK East Coast

Long. W04, 00 – E03, 00   Lat. N58, 30 – N51, 30

1 SEPTEMBER 1941

	Destroyer ASHANTI was docked at Rosyth to correct a defect that developed during her passage to Scapa Flow.

2 SEPTEMBER 1941

1500	Destroyer ESKIMO departed London for Sheerness.
1845	Destroyer ESKIMO arrived at Sheerness from London. After completing her refit, the destroyer sailed to Chatham.

3 SEPTEMBER 1941

	Light cruiser EURYALUS arrived at Rosyth from Scapa Flow to change a propeller.

4 SEPTEMBER 1941

	Destroyer RIPLEY ran aground off Flamborough Head. She was towed off the same day and received temporary repairs at Grimsby until 25 September and permanent repairs at Middlesbrough to 15 March.

5 SEPTEMBER 1941

	Destroyer ESKIMO departed Sheerness for Scapa Flow.
0930	Battleship KING GEORGE V departed Rosyth for Scapa Flow with destroyers BEDOUIN, VIVACIOUS, and VERDUN. Destroyer LAFOREY relieved destroyer VERDUN off Kinnaird Head. VERDUN then returned to Rosyth.

6 SEPTEMBER 1941

	A German aerial mine sank minesweeping trawler **STRATHBORVE** (216grt) (T/Lt A. W. Johnston RNR) in the Humber. Johnston and three ratings were killed. T/Lt W. G. Lewis RNVR died of wounds and ten ratings were missing.
	German Do217 aircraft of KG.2 damaged steamer STANMOUNT (4468grt) off 54D Buoy off Great Yarmouth. The steamer arrived at Immingham the next day.

7 SEPTEMBER 1941

	German S-boats S.48, S.49, S.50, S.52, and S.107 of the 4th S-Boat Flotilla attacked a convoy off the Norfolk coast.
	S.50 (ObltzS Karcher) sank steamer **DUNCARRON** (478grt) three miles east of Sheringham in 53, 10N, 01, 23E. Six crewmen and three gunners were lost.
	S.52 (ObltzS Karl Müller) sank Norwegian steamer **EIKHAUG** (1436grt) off Norfolk in 53, 05, 52N, 01, 20, 50E. Fifteen crewmen were lost and four survivors were rescued.
	A German aerial mine sank fishing trawler **OPHIR II** (213grt) four miles northeast of Humber Light Vessel. Five crewmen were missing.
	German Do217 aircraft of KG.2 sank steamer **MARCREST** (4224grt) in the vicinity of 54D Buoy, two miles 90° from Yarmouth. The entire crew were rescued.
	German Do217 aircraft of KG.2 sank steamer **TRSAT** (1369grt) seven miles northeast by east of Kinnaird Head. Two crewmen and a gunner were lost.
	Destroyer ASHANTI departed Rosyth for Scapa Flow after repairing defects that developed on her earlier passage to Scapa Flow.

8 SEPTEMBER 1941

	A German aerial mine sank mine destructor ship **CORFIELD** (3000grt) (Lt Cdr W. J. Tucker RNVR) two miles south of the Humber Light Vessel. There were no casualties.
0930	Destroyers ANTELOPE and ANTHONY arrived at Rosyth from Scapa Flow for boiler cleaning.

10 SEPTEMBER 1941

	Destroyer LIGHTNING was in a collision with minesweeping trawler STRATHGELDIE (192grt) in 58, 12N, 02, 21W while en route to Scapa Flow after escorting battleship DUKE OF YORK. The destroyer was slightly damaged, while the trawler was badly damaged. Destroyer LIGHTNING escorted the trawler to Wick before continuing on to Scapa Flow.
<1900	Battleship DUKE OF YORK arrived at Rosyth with destroyer VIVACIOUS.
1900	Destroyer VIVACIOUS departed Rosyth to return to Scapa Flow.

11 SEPTEMBER 1941

	German bombing damaged steamer CORMEAD (2848grt) in 52, 33N, 02, 05E. She anchored at Great Yarmouth Roads on the 12th.
	German bombing damaged steamer trawler WAR GREY (246grt) off Sunderland.
1015	Destroyer ICARUS arrived at the Humber to begin a refit at Immingham.
1100	Destroyers HOLDERNESS and MEYNELL departed Sheerness to relieve destroyers LAMERTON and BADSWORTH off May Island and escort damaged light cruiser NIGERIA to the Tyne.

12 SEPTEMBER 1941

0600	Destroyers HOLDERNESS and MEYNELL relieved destroyers LAMERTON and BADSWORTH off May Island and escorted damaged light cruiser NIGERIA to the Tyne. LAMERTON and BADSWORTH returned to Scapa Flow. The NIGERIA was repaired at Newcastle, completing on 15 December.
0850	Destroyer BADSWORTH was ordered to search for a downed British aircraft off Kinnaird while returning to Scapa Flow after escorting damaged light cruiser NIGERIA. The search was not successful and the destroyer later arrived at Scapa Flow.
<2300	Heavy cruiser BERWICK arrived at Rosyth from Scapa Flow to complete machinery repairs.

13 SEPTEMBER 1941

	Light cruiser EURYALUS departed Rosyth for Scapa Flow.
	P/T/A/Sub-Lt (A) J. A. Dowling RNVR and Naval Airman W. Sands were killed when their Proctor aircraft of 755/756 Squadron crashed near Stratford on Avon.

15 SEPTEMBER 1941

	A German aerial mine heavily damaged steamer **BIRTLEY** (2873grt) off Cromer in 53, 06N, 01, 16, 30E. Three crewmen were lost. She sank the next day in 53, 03N, 01, 18E.
	A German aerial mine heavily damaged Belgian tanker PONTFIELD (8290grt) north of Harwich in 52, 03N, 01, 20, 30E. The tanker broke in two and the forepart sank. The aft part was towed to Salt End and later to the Tyne, where a new forepart was fitted.
	Heavy cruiser NORFOLK departed the Tyne to return to Scapa Flow after her refit. She was escorted part of the way by destroyers WINDSOR and WINCHESTER.

17 SEPTEMBER 1941

	German S-boats S.50, S.51, and S.52 of the 4th S-Boat Flotilla (Kptlt Bätge) attacked a coastal convoy off Cromer.
	German S-boat S.51 (ObltzS Meyer) heavily damaged steamer **TEDDINGTON** (4762grt) off Cromer in 54, 03N, 01, 35E. She was taken in tow, but went ashore on the 18th, two and three quarters miles east-southeast of Cromer Pier. The entire crew were rescued.
	German S-boat S.50 (ObltzS Karcher) torpedoed steamer **TETELA** (5389grt) off Cromer in 53, 04N, 01, 35E. She was taken in tow and beached at Haile Sand Flat. She was re-floated on the 18th and berthed at Hull for repairs.
	German aircraft attacked coastal convoy FS.605, escorted by destroyer MENDIP.
	Destroyer ANTELOPE departed Rosyth for Scapa Flow after completing her boiler cleaning.
1600	Destroyer LANCASTER departed the Humber for Scapa Flow after completing her refit.
Night	During the night, a German aerial mine sank steamer **BRADGLEN** (4741grt) two miles 230° from B.3 Buoy off Barrow Deep. Seven crewmen were missing and one crewman died in the hospital.

19 SEPTEMBER 1941

	German Do217 aircraft of KG.2 damaged steamer **PRESTATYN ROSE** (1151grt) three miles northeast of Sunk Buoy, Harwich in 51, 52, 25N, 01, 35, 45E. She arrived at Harwich in tow and was beached. She was re-floated on the 28th and taken to the Tyne on the 30th.
	A German aerial mine sank fishing vessel **GLEN ALVA** (6grt) off Jenkin Buoy, Southend. Both crewmen were lost.
1350	Destroyer INGLEFIELD arrived at the Humber from Scapa Flow to begin a refit at Hull.

20 SEPTEMBER 1941

	During the night 20/21, the German 4th S-Boat Flotilla (Kptlt Bätge) unsuccessfully patrolled along the English south coast.
	Trawler **MARCONI** (322grt) was lost in a collision off Harwich.
1130	Destroyer WINDSOR departed Harwich to join monitor EREBUS and destroyer VIVACIOUS off May Island and act as additional escort to Sheerness.
2000	Norwegian destroyer DRAUG departed the Humber for Scapa Flow.

21 SEPTEMBER 1941

	A German aerial mine sank tanker **VANCOUVER** (5729grt) about two miles 263° from Sunk Light Vessel in 51, 51N, 01, 31E.

22 SEPTEMBER 1941

	German Do217 aircraft of KG.2 sank Dutch steamer **VECHTSTROOM** (845grt) two miles east by north of 62 C

	Buoy. The entire crew was rescued.
1100	Norwegian MTB.56 departed Harwich for Scapa Flow, via the Tyne and Aberdeen.
1845	Monitor EREBUS and destroyer VIVACIOUS arrived at Sheerness from Scapa Flow.

23 SEPTEMBER 1941

	Dutch submarine O.23 arrived at Dundee from Gibraltar for a refit that completed 4 February 1942.

25 SEPTEMBER 1941

0500	Sloop IBIS departed Rosyth for Scapa Flow to work up to combat efficiency.

26 SEPTEMBER 1941

	German Do217 aircraft of KG.2 sank steamer **BRITISH PRINCE** (4979grt) south of the Humber in 53, 52N, 00, 25E. There were no casualties.

27 SEPTEMBER 1941

	During the night 27/28, the German 4th S-Boat Flotilla (KptIt Bätge) unsuccessfully patrolled along the English south coast.

28 SEPTEMBER 1941

	Destroyer SOUTHWOLD was damaged in a collision with patrol sloop SHEARWATER off Sheringham. Neither ship received more than minor damage. Destroyer SOUTHWOLD was repaired during refitting at Chatham from 10 October to 7 November. The sloop was repaired at Harwich from 4 to 8 October.

29 SEPTEMBER 1941

	During the night 29/30, the German 4th S-Boat Flotilla (KptIt Bätge) unsuccessfully patrolled along the English south coast.

30 SEPTEMBER 1941

	German bombing sank minesweeping trawler **EILEEN DUNCAN** (223grt) (T/Lt G. N. Ward RNVR) at the Bergen Wharf, River Tyne.
	German bombing sank minesweeping trawler **STAR OF DEVERON** (220grt) (T/Skipper G. F. Durrant RNR) at the Bergen Wharf, River Tyne. Durrant was killed in the attack.
	German bombing damaged submarine SUNFISH with bomb near misses, while she was refitting at Tyneside. Temporary repairs were completed at Tyneside from 3 October to 1 November. She was then taken to Portsmouth where full repairs were completed on 9 October 1943.
	German bombing damaged steamer CEDARWOOD (899grt) off Dover.
0700	Destroyer ECLIPSE departed Rosyth for Scapa Flow after completing her boiler cleaning and minor repairs.

North Sea

Long. E03, 00 – E09, 00   Lat. N58, 30 – N51, 00

2 SEPTEMBER 1941

	An RAF aerial mine sank German tug **PETER WESSELS** (135grt) off Juist.

3 SEPTEMBER 1941

	German aircraft damaged destroyer WOLFHOUND with a bomb near miss in the North Sea. The destroyer was under repair for nineteen months at Chatham.

10 SEPTEMBER 1941

	RAF aircraft sank German auxiliary minesweeper **M.1102/H. A. W. MULLER** (460grt) with an aerial torpedo off Norway in 58, 08N, 06, 38E.

12 SEPTEMBER 1941

	RAF aircraft damaged German steamer NARVIK (4281grt) (ex Swedish) off Ameland, Holland.

15 SEPTEMBER 1941

	RAF aircraft sank German steamer **JOHANN WESSELS** (4659grt) off Norderney. Some sources claim a mine sank her off Norway.
	RAF bombing sank Swedish steamer **YARRAWONGA** (4900grt) at Hamburg. She was salvaged and taken to Gothenburg for repairs.

20 SEPTEMBER 1941

An RAF aerial mine sank German steamer **METZ** (733grt) (ex **INDUS** (733grt)) off Vlaardingen, Holland.

21 SEPTEMBER 1941

Free French submarine RUBIS laid two groups of mines off Jaederen during the night. The next day she was severely damaged while attacking two steamers and could not dive. She reached Dundee on the 24th.

28 SEPTEMBER 1941

An RAF aerial mine sank Norwegian steamer **ASPE** north of Ameland, Holland.

English Channel
Long. W07, 00 – E01, 30   Lat. N51, 00 – N49, 00

1 SEPTEMBER 1941

RAF aircraft heavily damaged German patrol boat V.1512 off Barfleur, France.

9 SEPTEMBER 1941

Norwegian MTB.54 sank German steamer **TRIFELS** (6189grt) while attacking a small German convoy going from Calais to Boulogne escorted by German patrol boats V.202 and V.208. One of the patrol boats was damaged in a collision with MTB.54.

11 SEPTEMBER 1941

T/Sub-Lt M. S. Mills RCNVR was killed in motor gunboat MGB.67 in "action."

14 SEPTEMBER 1941

| 1400 | Destroyer PUCKERIDGE arrived at Portsmouth from Scapa Flow to join the 1st Destroyer Flotilla. |

18 SEPTEMBER 1941

Minelayer MANXMAN departed Plymouth and laid Minefield HF off Les Heaux, France.

20 SEPTEMBER 1941

An RAF aerial mine sank German tug **VULKAN** (395grt) northwest of Le Havre, France.

Minelayer MANXMAN departed Portsmouth and laid Minefield JT off Le Havre, France.

21 SEPTEMBER 1941

Minelayer MANXMAN departed Portsmouth and laid Minefield JU off Dieppe, France.

22 SEPTEMBER 1941

A German aerial mine sank motor launch **ML.144** (73grt) in the English Channel.

Naval specialty ship **VITA** was lost by a cause and a place unknown.

27 SEPTEMBER 1941

During the night of 27/28 September, landing ship PRINCE LEOPOLD accompanied by MGB.316, MGB.314 and MGB.312 landed a commando unit at St Vaast, near Cherbourg, France, in Operation CHOPPER. Destroyers FERNIE and VANITY provided cover. The force withdrew after obtaining the desired information.

30 SEPTEMBER 1941

| 0900 | Heavy cruiser KENT departed Devonport escorted by destroyer NORMAN after completing repairs and a refit. Both ships arrived at Scapa Flow on 1 October. |

Bay of Biscay
Long. W15, 00 – E03, 00   Lat. N49, 00 – N40, 00

6 SEPTEMBER 1941

German destroyers ERICH STEINBRINCK and BRUNO HEINEMANN departed Brest, France, to return to Germany for much needed refits and repairs.

A mine sank German auxiliary minesweeper **M.4030** off Brest.

9 SEPTEMBER 1941

German steamer **ERNA OLDENDORFF** (2095grt) was sunk in a collision with a tanker off Saint-Nazaire, France.

10 SEPTEMBER 1941

German steamer ANNELIESE ESSBERGER (5173grt) arrived safely at Bordeaux, France, from Japanese occupied China. She carried 3400 tons of vitally needed war materiel.

12 SEPTEMBER 1941

Submarines SEALION and SEAWOLF operated in the Bay of Biscay until 3 October without success.

15 SEPTEMBER 1941

RAF bombers sank auxiliary minesweeper **M.3823** off Le Havre, France.

21 SEPTEMBER 1941

German steamer RIO GRANDE (6062grt) departed Bordeaux, France, for Osaka, Japan.

Submarine P.34, en route to Gibraltar from Barrow, was ordered to conduct a diving patrol in the position in 42, 50N, 10, 40W and look for enemy submarines.

23 SEPTEMBER 1941

U.204 guided German steamer RIO GRANDE (6062grt) through the Bay of Biscay so that she could reach the open sea for her voyage to Japan. She arrived at Osaka, Japan, on 6 February.

West of Gibraltar
Long. W15, 00 – W05, 30   Lat. N40, 00 – N30, 00

2 SEPTEMBER 1941

Convoy HG.72 departed Gibraltar escorted by destroyers BOREAS, FARNDALE, VIDETTE, and WILD SWAN, sloop LEITH, CAM ship MAPLIN, plus corvettes CAMPION, CAMPANULA, BLUEBELL, WALLFLOWER, and HYDRANGEA.
  VIDETTE was detached from the convoy later in the day.
  BOREAS was detached from the convoy to refuel at Ponta Delgada, and then rejoined the convoy all the way to Londonderry.
  Destroyers CROOME and VIMY departed Gibraltar on the 4th to join the convoy.
  Destroyer CROOME then transferred to southbound convoy OG.73 from convoy HG.72.
  On the 7th, destroyers FARNDALE and WILD SWAN were detached from the convoy to refuel at Ponta Delgada and then joined south bound convoy OG.73.
  Sloop ROCHESTER plus corvettes CARNATION, LA MALOUINE, HELIOTROPE, and MALLOW departed Gibraltar on the 4th and joined the convoy on the 8th.
  Sloop DEPTFORD joined the convoy on the 10th, sloop SANDWICH, French sloop COMMANDANT DOMINE, and antisubmarine yacht PHILANTE joined the convoy on the 11th.
  Destroyers CALDWELL, VANOC, VOLUNTEER, and WALKER joined the convoy on the 12th.
  On the 14th, a Hurricane aircraft from MAPLIN drove off a German Fw200 bomber one hundred miles south of Ireland. Sub-Lt C. W. Walker bailed out of his aircraft and was picked up by sloop ROCHESTER.
  On the 15th, sloop DEPTFORD was detached from the convoy.
  The convoy arrived at Liverpool on the 17th.

3 SEPTEMBER 1941

Destroyer ENCOUNTER departed Gibraltar to join convoy WS.11F at sea. She refuelled at Ponta Delgada and then joined battle cruiser REPULSE, which was escorting convoy WS.11. The destroyer operated off East Africa for a time, before transferring to Alexandria and the Mediterranean Fleet.

Dutch submarine O.23 departed Gibraltar for Dundee for a refit.

4 SEPTEMBER 1941

Italian submarines CALVI, BARACCA, CAPPELLINI and DA VINCI set up a patrol line to intercept convoy HG.72, which was escorted by destroyers FAULKNOR, BOREAS, WILD SWAN, AVON VALE, ENCOUNTER and NESTOR.

Corvettes FLEUR DE LYS and AZALEA departed Gibraltar escorting tanker CORDELIA (8190grt) and steamer DEUCALION (7516grt) westwards. They joined tanker INVERLEE (9158grt) at and escorted her to Gibraltar.

Antisubmarine trawlers LADY SHIRLEY and LADY HOGARTH departed Gibraltar to join tanker NOREG (7605grt) for inbound escort to Gibraltar.

Submarine SEVERN arrived at Gibraltar from her eastern Atlantic patrol.

6 SEPTEMBER 1941

Submarine CLYDE departed Gibraltar on a patrol. She arrived back from the eastern Atlantic patrol on the 9th.

7 SEPTEMBER 1941

	Destroyer WIVERN departed Gibraltar for refitting in Britain.
1500	Aircraft carrier FURIOUS arrived at Gibraltar with destroyers COSSACK, LEGION, ZULU, and LIVELY from Britain. Twenty-six Hurricane aircraft were transferred from FURIOUS to aircraft carrier ARK ROYAL.

9 SEPTEMBER 1941

	Antisubmarine trawlers LADY SHIRLEY and LADY HOGARTH arrived at Funchal, Madeira, with LADY SHIRLEY under tow with condenser problems.

10 SEPTEMBER 1941

	Corvette JONQUIL arrived at Gibraltar with trawler LADY SHIRLEY.
	Submarine PROTEUS arrived at Gibraltar after refitting at Portsmouth from December 1940 to 17 August.

13 SEPTEMBER 1941

	Corvettes FLEUR DE LYS and AZALEA escorted tankers INVERLEE (9158grt) and BRITISH FREEDOM (6985grt) in to Gibraltar.
	Corvettes JONQUIL and SPIREA departed Gibraltar escorting tanker NOREG (7605grt) out to sea.
	Light cruiser MANCHESTER and destroyer FIREDRAKE departed Gibraltar for repairs received during the Operation SUBSTANCE. The ships proceeded for Philadelphia, Pennsylvania, and Boston, Massachusetts, respectively. Destroyer HEYTHROP provided the local escort to 25W.
	Submarine TRUSTY arrived at Gibraltar from Holy Loch.

15 SEPTEMBER 1941

	Polish submarine SOKOL arrived at Gibraltar from Dartmouth.

16 SEPTEMBER 1941

	Destroyer HIGHLANDER arrived at Gibraltar from Freetown via Bathurst, Gambia.
	Ocean boarding vessel MARON arrived at Gibraltar after her patrol.
	Antisubmarine trawlers LADY HOGARTH and ARCTIC RANGER departed Gibraltar escorting tanker INVERLEE (9158grt) westwards. They returned with tanker BENEDICK (6978grt), arriving on the 28th.

17 SEPTEMBER 1941

	Convoy HG.73 departed Gibraltar with destroyers DUNCAN, FARNDALE, and VIMY, sloop FOWEY, corvettes BEGONIA, GENTIAN, HIBISCUS, JASMINE, LARKSPUR, MYOSOTIS, PERIWINKLE, and STONECROP, and CAM ship SPRINGBANK (5155grt). Destroyer WILD SWAN departed Gibraltar on the 19th to join the convoy. Destroyers DUNCAN and FARNDALE were detached from the convoy on the 20th. Destroyers VIMY and WILD SWAN were detached from the convoy on the 22nd. The catapult ship **SPRINGBANK** was sunk on the 27th. Destroyer HIGHLANDER departed Gibraltar on the 20th and joined the convoy on the 22nd. She remained with the convoy until 26 September. Destroyer WOLVERINE joined the convoy on the 28th. The corvettes were detached from the convoy on the 30th. The convoy arrived at Liverpool on 1 October with destroyer WOLVERINE.
1500	Light cruiser SHEFFIELD arrived at Gibraltar from Greenock carrying three hundred service personnel.

18 SEPTEMBER 1941

	Italian submarines TORELLI, MOROSINI and DA VINCI patrolled west of Gibraltar. They were supposed to be joined by **MALASPINA**, but she had already been sunk on the 7th.
	Aircraft carrier FURIOUS departed Gibraltar for Bermuda escorted by destroyers FORESIGHT, FORESTER, FURY, and LEGION. Destroyer FURY arrived back at Gibraltar on the 22nd and sailed again on the 23rd to join convoy WS.11X.

19 SEPTEMBER 1941

	U.371 made brief contact with Italian submarines TORELLI and MOROSINI on her way to the Mediterranean through the Gibraltar Straits.

20 SEPTEMBER 1941

	Light cruiser SHEFFIELD departed Gibraltar to rendezvous with convoy WS.11X.

21 SEPTEMBER 1941

	Light cruiser EDINBURGH (CS.18) arrived at Gibraltar from Freetown for Operation HALBERD.
	Destroyer LIVELY departed Gibraltar to join convoy WS.11X.

22 SEPTEMBER 1941

	Submarine CLYDE departed Gibraltar for a patrol in the vicinity of the Canary Islands and then to proceed to Freetown. On the 25th, she was ordered to patrol in the Cape Verde Islands, as German U-boats were suspected of using Tarafa Bay to re-supply.
2300	Light cruisers KENYA and EURYALUS arrived at Gibraltar after being detached from convoy WS.11X on the 21st. The cruisers refuelled and departed on the 23rd before daylight to rejoin the convoy. The flag of CS.10 was transferred from light cruiser SHEFFIELD to light cruiser KENYA.

23 SEPTEMBER 1941

	Battleship PRINCE OF WALES arrived at Gibraltar with destroyers LAFOREY, LIGHTNING, and ORIBI from Greenock late in the day. The ships were refuelled and departed before daylight to rejoin convoy WS.11X.
	Destroyers COSSACK, HEYTHROP, and FARNDALE departed Gibraltar to join convoy WS.11X at sea.
<0600	Light cruisers KENYA and EURYALUS departed Gibraltar to rejoin convoy WS.11X.

24 SEPTEMBER 1941

	In Operation GOEBEN, U.371, U.559, U.97, U.331, U.75 and U.79 passed through the Gibraltar Straits into the Mediterranean, the last U-boat making the trip on 5 October.
	Corvettes SAMPHIRE and CONVOLVULUS arrived at Gibraltar escorting the 26th Motor Launch Flotilla of ML.209, ML.244, ML.251, ML.271, ML.277, ML.279, ML.281, and ML.289.
0800	Destroyers COSSACK, HEYTHROP, and FARNDALE joined convoy WS.11X west of Gibraltar.
0900	Battleship RODNEY arrived at Gibraltar with Dutch destroyer ISAAC SWEERS plus Polish destroyers PIORUN and GARLAND.
0900	Corvettes JONQUIL, SPIREA, and AZALEA departed Gibraltar to join the troopships of convoy WS.11X and bring them into Gibraltar.
1600	Destroyers FORESIGHT, FORESTER, GURKHA, and LANCE arrived at Gibraltar from convoy WS.11X.

25 SEPTEMBER 1941

	Australian destroyer NESTOR arrived at Gibraltar from Freetown, Sierra Leone.
	Ocean boarding vessel MARON departed Gibraltar for her eastern Atlantic patrol escorted by antisubmarine trawlers LADY SHIRLEY and ERIN. Trawler ERIN was to join arriving tanker LA CARRIERE (5685grt) and escort her to Gibraltar. Trawler LADY SHIRLEY was detached from the tanker escort on the 28th to relieve Free French sloop COMMANDANT DUBOC towing damaged steamer SILVERBELLE (5302grt) to Las Palmas.
0230	Corvettes JONQUIL, SPIREA, and AZALEA arrived at Gibraltar with the troopships from convoy WS.11X.

26 SEPTEMBER 1941

	Australian destroyer NESTOR departed Gibraltar for Devonport to make permanent repairs to her depth charge damage. Her repairs were completed on 5 December.
	Submarine P.34 arrived at Gibraltar from Barrow.

29 SEPTEMBER 1941

	Submarine ULTIMATUM arrived at Gibraltar from Barrow.
	The troopships from convoy WS.11X, less LEINSTER (4302grt), departed Gibraltar for Freetown escorted by destroyers VIMY and WILD SWAN. The troopships were turned over to corvettes WOODRUFF and MIGNONETTE on the 2nd. The destroyers, after spending 2 to 5 October at Bathurst, Gambia, were to join aircraft carrier EAGLE off Bathurst on 6 October. Aircraft carrier EAGLE and Free French sloop COMMANDANT DUBOC, escorted by light cruiser DUNEDIN, sloop BRIDGEWATER, and corvettes ARMERIA and ASTER, had departed Freetown 4 October. Destroyer VIMY was detached from the convoy. Destroyer WILD SWAN finally joined the aircraft carrier and sloop off Freetown. Destroyer CROOME departed Gibraltar on 5 October to join the EAGLE group and escorted them to Gibraltar, arriving at Gibraltar on 11 October.
	Submarines THORN and TRUANT arrived at Gibraltar.

30 SEPTEMBER 1941

	Corvette JONQUIL departed Gibraltar to join arriving tanker LA CARRIERE (5685grt), which had not been

joined by antisubmarine trawlers ERIN and LADY SHIRLEY. The tanker and corvette arrived at Gibraltar on 2 October.

West of North Africa

Long. W15, 00 – E11, 00   Lat. N30, 00 – N00, 00

1 SEPTEMBER 1941

Convoy WS.10X departed Freetown with troopships STRATHNAVER (22,283grt), PALMA (2715grt), STRATHMORE (23,428grt), BRISBANE STAR (11,076grt), ORION (23,371grt), and PORT JACKSON (9687grt).

Battleship REVENGE escorted the convoy from 1 to 11 September, when the convoy arrived at Cape Town, South Africa.

Corvette AMARANTHUS escorted the convoy on 1 and 2 September.

Corvettes WOODRUFF, MIGNONETTE, and ARMERIA escorted the convoy from 1 to 3 September.

Battleship REVENGE was in a collision with troopship ORION on 2 September and sustained slight damage to her bulges.

The convoy arrived at Cape Town, SA, on 11 September and sailed again on 14 September.

The convoy was escorted by battleship REVENGE until 23 September when light cruiser CERES took over the convoy.

Light cruiser CERES remained with the convoy until 27 September when the convoy arrived at Aden.

The troopships proceeded independently to Suez, Egypt.

2 SEPTEMBER 1941

Convoy ST.2 departed Freetown, Sierra Leone, escorted by corvettes ARMERIA and ASPHODEL.
The convoy arrived at Takoradi, Ghana, on the 7th.

4 SEPTEMBER 1941

Convoy SL.86 departed Freetown escorted by sloop EGRET to 24 September plus corvettes ASTER and BURDOCK to 7 September.

On the 7th, escort vessel BANFF joined the convoy to 24 September and on the 8th, escort vessel FISHGUARD joined the convoy to 24 September.

Ocean boarding vessel HILARY joined the convoy on the 18th to 25 September.

Destroyers BROKE, CHELSEA and MANSFIELD joined the convoy on the 22nd to 26 September.

Destroyer VANSITTART escorted the convoy on the 24th only and the convoy arrived at Liverpool on the 26th.

11 SEPTEMBER 1941

The premature explosion of a depth charge damaged Australian destroyer NESTOR off Bathurst, Gambia.

12 SEPTEMBER 1941

Australian destroyer NESTOR arrived at Freetown to repair damage from a close depth charge explosion. After temporary repairs at Freetown, the destroyer proceeded to Gibraltar.

13 SEPTEMBER 1941

Freetown based destroyers VELOX and WRESTLER joined convoy WS.11F with corvette STARWORT and escorted the ships to Freetown. Convoy WS.11F included MOOLTAN (20,952grt), EMPRESS OF AUSTRALIA (21,833grt), KINA II (9823grt), ORONTES (20,097grt), SCYTHIA (19,761grt), VICEROY OF INDIA (19,627grt), HMS LARGS BAY (14,182grt), HMS GUARDIAN, DUCHESS OF YORK (20,021grt), BHUTAN (6104grt), CITY OF EDINBURGH (8036grt), OTRANTO (20,032grt), and GLENORCHY (10,000grt) escorted by battle cruiser REPULSE with destroyers NESTOR and ENCOUNTER.

14 SEPTEMBER 1941

Convoy SL.87 departed Freetown escorted by destroyer BRILLIANT, corvettes AMARANTHUS and ASPHODEL, and antisubmarine trawler SARABANDE to 16 September.

Free French sloop COMMANDANT DUBOC joined the convoy on the 15th and continued with the convoy to 22 September.

Sloop BIDEFORD, corvette GARDENIA, with escort vessels GORLESTON and LULWORTH joined the convoy on the 16th and continued with the convoy to 6 October, when it arrived at Liverpool.

15 SEPTEMBER 1941

Convoy WS.11S arrived at Freetown with steamers GLAUCUS (7586grt), BARRISTER (6200grt), NORTHUMBERLAND (11,558grt), ABOSSO (11,030grt), oiler RAPIDOL (2648grt), and CITY OF MANCHESTER (8917grt) escorted by AMC DERBYSHIRE plus escort ships SENNEN and TOTLAND.

17 SEPTEMBER 1941

Light cruiser EDINBURGH (CS.18) arrived at Freetown from Simon's Town, South Africa, on her way to Gi-

18 SEPTEMBER 1941

Convoy WS.11 reassembled the Fast and Slow groups back into a single convoy and departed Freetown less ABOSSO (11,030grt), HMS GUARDIAN, and NORTHUMBERLAND (11,558grt), plus troopship NIEUW ZEELAND (11,069grt).
Destroyers WRESTLER and VELOX escorted the convoy from 18 to 20 September.
Battle cruiser REPULSE and AMC DERBYSHIRE escorted the convoy to the Cape Town, South Africa.

19 SEPTEMBER 1941

Convoy ST.3 departed Freetown escorted by corvettes BURDOCK and MARGUERITE.
Corvette CALENDULA joined the convoy on the 23rd.
The convoy arrived at Takoradi on the 24th.

23 SEPTEMBER 1941

Convoy ST.4 departed Freetown escorted by sloop BRIDGEWATER, corvettes ARMERIA and CALENDULA, and antisubmarine trawler COPINSAY. The convoy arrived at Takoradi, Ghana, on the 28th.

24 SEPTEMBER 1941

Convoy SL.88 departed Freetown escorted by destroyer VANSITTART to 27 September, sloop ENCHANTRESS to 8 October, corvettes ASTER, BURDOCK, and VERVAIN to 27 September, and antisubmarine trawlers FANDANGO and MORRIS DANCE to 27 September.
On the 27th, escort vessels HARTLAND and WALNEY joined the convoy to 8 October.
Destroyers VIMY and WILD SWAN escorted the convoy on 1 October only.
The convoy rendezvoused with convoy HG.74 on 8 October and both arrived at Liverpool on 18 October.

SOUTH ATLANTIC OCEAN

East of South America
Long. W70, 00 – W30, 00   Lat. N05, 00 - S60, 00

1 SEPTEMBER 1941

Uruguayan authorities seized Italian steamer **ADAMELLO** (5785grt) at Montevideo, Uruguay, and renamed her the MONTEVIDEO (5785grt).

Uruguayan authorities seized Italian steamer **FAUSTO** (5285grt) at Montevideo, and renamed her the MALSEDO (5285grt).

24 SEPTEMBER 1941

Brazilian authorities seized German steamer **MACERO** (3235grt) at Bahia, Brazil. She became the Brazilian SULOIDE (3235grt).

27 SEPTEMBER 1941

Brazilian authorities seized German steamer **BOLLWERK** (4173grt) at Bahia, Brazil. She became the Brazilian NORTELOIDE (4173grt).

29 SEPTEMBER 1941

Heavy cruiser HAWKINS arrived at Montevideo, Uruguay.

West of South Africa
Long. W30, 00 – E25, 00   Lat. S00, 00 – S60, 00

2 SEPTEMBER 1941

Part of convoy WS.10 arrived at Cape Town, South Africa, with BRITANNIC (26,943grt), INDRAPOERA (10,825grt), REINA DEL PACIFICO (17,702grt), STIRLING CASTLE (25,550grt), STRATHALLAN (23,722grt), VOLENDAM (15,434grt), WINDSOR CASTLE (19,141grt), NIGERSTROOM (4639grt), and PHEMIUS (7406grt).

6 SEPTEMBER 1941

Part of convoy WS.10 departed Cape Town, South Africa, with BRITANNIC (26,943grt), STIRLING CASTLE (25,550grt), WINDSOR CASTLE (19,141grt), VOLENDAM (15,434grt), INDRAPOERA (10,825grt), STRATHALLAN (23,722grt), NIGERSTROOM (4639grt), and PHEMIUS (7406grt) escorted by AMC CARNARVON CASTLE.

The ships not departing Cape Town with convoy WS.10 went forward to Aden in convoy CM.17.

11 SEPTEMBER 1941

	Light cruiser EDINBURGH (CS.18) departed Simon's Town, South Africa, for Gibraltar after escorting convoy WS.10 to Cape Town, SA.

20 SEPTEMBER 1941

	U.111 (Kptlt Kleinschmidt) sank unescorted steamer **CINGALESE PRINCE** (8474grt) (Master John Smith) east-southeast of St. Paul Rocks in 02S, 25, 30W. The master, forty-eight crewmen and eight gunners were lost. Sloop WESTON (Cdr J. G. Sutton) and sloop LONDONDERRY (Cdr J. S. Dalison) rescued one survivor each and landed them at Londonderry, Northern Ireland, on 3 November. Spanish steamer CASTILLO MONTJUICH (6581grt) rescued fifteen crewmen and three gunners on 1 October after twelve days at sea and landed them at St. Vincent, Cape Verde Islands.
	At St Helena, aircraft carrier EAGLE had a serious fire in her hangar deck. The salt water used to extinguish the fire seriously affected fourteen aircraft. The aircraft carrier sustained some structural damage. One rating died from injuries. On the 28th, the EAGLE departed St Helena for Freetown escorted by heavy cruiser DORSETSHIRE arriving 3 October. The EAGLE called at Gibraltar for emergency repairs and finally arrived back at Liverpool on 26 October. EAGLE began a refit lasting from 30 October to 9 January 1942.

26 SEPTEMBER 1941

2310	U.66 (KKpt Zapp) heavily damaged Panamanian tanker **I. C. WHITE** (7052grt) (ex American) (Master William Mello) while she was sailing alone in 10, 26S, 27, 30W. Three crewmen were missing.
0740	U.66 fired three more torpedoes to sink the tanker. American steamer DELNORTE (4982grt) (Master Hoehn) rescued one lifeboat on 3 October in 10, 16S, 23W. American steamer WEST NILUS (5565grt) (Master John Stern) rescued one lifeboat, also on 3 October.

30 SEPTEMBER 1941

	Steamers DUCHESS OF YORK (20,021grt), CITY OF MANCHESTER (8917grt), NIEUW ZEELAND (11,069grt), CITY OF EDINBURGH (8036grt), KINA II (9823grt), LARGS BAY (14,182grt), VICEROY OF INDIA (19,627grt), ORONTES (20,097grt), GLAUCUS (7586grt), BHUTAN (6104grt), and GLENORCHY (10,000grt) arrived at Cape Town, South Africa, escorted by AMC DERBYSHIRE.

BALTIC SEA

Kattegat and Skagerrak Long. E09, 00 – E12, 00   Lat. N60, 00 – N53, 00

4 SEPTEMBER 1941

	German heavy cruiser ADMIRAL SCHEER arrived at Oslo, Norway, escorted by three torpedo boats.

5 SEPTEMBER 1941

	RAF B-17 bombers of 2nd Group unsuccessfully tried to bomb the German heavy cruiser ADMIRAL SCHEER at Oslo, Norway.

8 SEPTEMBER 1941

	RAF B-17 bombers of 2nd Group unsuccessfully tried to bomb the German heavy cruiser ADMIRAL SCHEER at Oslo, Norway.

19 SEPTEMBER 1941

	An RAF aerial mine sank German fishing vessel **BUNTE KUH** (262grt) in the Kattegat north of Grenaa, Denmark.

Southern Baltic Area Long. E12, 00 – E22, 00   Lat. N60, 00 – N53, 00

10 SEPTEMBER 1941

	A mine sank German steamer **JULIUS HUGH STINNES 27** (2530grt) near Kolberg, Germany.
	A mine sank German steamer **MARIANN** (1991grt) (ex Dutch **HOLLAND** (1991grt)) off Kolberg.
	For Operation BEOWULF I, the Germans collected naval ships in the port-cities of Liepaja, Riga, Roja and Ventspils in Latvia. The ships included: Light cruisers: EMDEN, KÖLN and LEIPZIG

Germany Sends Russia to the Allies

Four heavy floating artillery barges
Two light floating artillery barges
Six coastal motor ships outfitted with special Sturmboot launching ramps
16 naval landing craft (Type AF.46; initially slated for Operation SEELOWE)
18 army landing craft
20 auxiliary naval craft (mostly converted civilian types)
The mother-ship H-27
Hospital ship PIETA
20 "Siebel" type landing craft.
Finnish naval forces consisted of the coastal battleships ILMARINEN and VAINAMOINEN and two ice breakers.

15 SEPTEMBER 1941

German motor ship **HANSEAT** (224grt) was lost in a stranding near Rugen, Germany.

16 SEPTEMBER 1941

In the Baltic, German light cruisers EMDEN and LEIPZIG bombarded the Sworbe Peninsula with torpedo boats T.7, T.8, and T.11 on 16/17 September.

17 SEPTEMBER 1941

In Stockholm Harbour, Swedish destroyers KLAS UGGLA, KLAS HORN, and GOTEBORG were seriously damaged in an explosion. Destroyer KLAS HORN was repaired from components of destroyers KLAS UGGLA and GOTEBORG. **GOTEBORG** was not repaired.

23 SEPTEMBER 1941

To prevent the Russian Baltic Fleet from escaping from Leningrad, Russia, the Germans set up two groups of heavy ships.
The Northern Group (VAdm Ciliax) included battleship TIRPITZ (KptzS Topp), heavy cruiser ADMIRAL SCHEER (KptzS Meendsen-Bohlken), light cruisers NÜRNBERG (KptzS v. Studnitz) and KÖLN (KptzS Hüffmeier), destroyers Z.25, Z.26 and Z.27, plus torpedo boats T.2, T.5, T.7, T.8 and T.11 with some S-boats in the Aaland Sea.
The Southern Group included light cruisers LEIPZIG (KptzS Stichling) and EMDEN (KptzS Mirow) with S-boats at Libau.
Both groups put to sea and returned on the 29th to Gotenhafen.

26 SEPTEMBER 1941

Mines sank German submarine tender **MOSEL** (796grt) and steamer **LEONTES** (338grt) off Ventspils.

Russian submarine SHCH-320 (Lt Cdr Vishnevski) sank German steamer **KAIJA** (244grt) (ex Latvian) off Danzig.

Gulf of Finland

Long. E22, 00 – E30, 00   Lat. N61, 00 – N57, 00

2 SEPTEMBER 1941

Finnish minelayer RIILAHTI dropped eighty-four new mines west of Minefield JUMINDA during the night.

German minelayer KAISER (Cdr Dr. Brill) dropped one hundred twenty new mines for Minefield JUMINDA during the night.

Finnish motor torpedo boat SYOKSY sank Russian steamer **MEERO** (1866grt) (ex Estonian) near the Koivisto Narrows.

7 SEPTEMBER 1941

Russian battleship MARAT and cruiser MAKSIM GORKI provided gunfire support to the Russian defenders by shelling the German Eighteenth Army positions south of Leningrad, Russia.

8 SEPTEMBER 1941

Russian gunboat KRASNOE ZNAMYA supported the Russian Eighth Army by providing gunfire support from Cape Shepelev.

Russian battleship OKTYABRSKAYA REVOLUTSIYA and cruiser KIROV bombarded German positions at Krasnoe Selo and Peterhof, Russia.

The German 5th R-Boat Flotilla laid forty-eight EMC mines north of Seiskari, Finland.

The German 1st S-Boat Flotilla laid forty mines north of Seiskaari.

A mine heavily damaged R.58 off Seiskaari and she was towed back to base.

Mines sank Russian submarines **L-2** and **KALEV** as they tried to carry supplies from Suursaari to Hangö, Finland.

11 SEPTEMBER 1941

During the night German 5th R-Boat Flotilla laid thirty-six EMC mines east of Suursaari, Finland.

During the night German 1st S-Boat Flotilla laid forty mines east of Suursaari, Finland.

12 SEPTEMBER 1941

To reduce German and Finnish mining operations in the Gulf of Finland, Russian submarine M-77 took up a patrol station off Someri, M-97 patrolled off Reval, M-98 and M-102 patrolled of Helsinki, and S-7 (Capt 3rd Class Lisin) patrolled off the Swedish coast until 18 September.

13 SEPTEMBER 1941

Operation BEOWULF I, the invasion of Ösel Island, began with a bombardment of Finnish monitors (KptzS Rahola) ILMARINEN (FKpt Göransson) and VAINAMOINEN (FKpt Koivisto) escorted by patrol boats (Kptlt Peuranheimo) VMV.1, VMV.14, VMV.15 and VMV.16 plus icebreakers JAAKARHU and TARMO.

German minelayer BRUMMER (KKpt Dr. Tobias) began the attack with five patrol boats of the 3rd VP-Boat Flotilla, two armoured tugboats, and eight assault boats.

German torpedo boats T.2, T.5, T.8 and T.11 attacked the west side of Ösel Island, escorted by the 2nd S-Boat Flotilla and 3rd S-Boat Flotilla plus nine assault boats.

From Riga, three groups totalling fifty German assault boats attacked the south coast of Ösel Island.

During the attack, a mine sank Finnish monitor **ILMARINEN** (FKpt. Göransson) with the loss of thirteen officers and two hundred fifty-eight men. The Finnish patrol boats rescued one hundred thirty-two survivors.

A Russian TKA boat sank German auxiliary patrol boat **VP.308/OSCAR NEYNABER** (314grt) off Porkkala, Finland.

14 SEPTEMBER 1941

Saboteurs sank German motor minesweepers **R.60**, **R.61** and **R.62** and damaged two tugboats at Helsinki, Finland.

Troops of the German 61st Infantry Division were landed on Moon Island, in Operation BEOWULF I.

15 SEPTEMBER 1941

The Russian Baltic Fleet ships bombarded the German coastal batteries at Peterhof, Russia.

16 SEPTEMBER 1941

Russian torpedo boat TKA-67 sank German auxiliary minesweeper **M.1707/LUNEBURG** (473grt) off Ösel Island.

German coastal batteries damaged Russian battleships MARAT and PETROPAVLOVSK with 15-cm shells in Kronstadt Bay, Russia.

17 SEPTEMBER 1941

A mine sank Russian submarine **P-1** (Lt Cdr Loginov) while she was carrying supplies from Suursaari to Hangö, Finland.

Russian submarine M-97 (Lt Cdr Mylnikov) unsuccessfully attacked a German convoy off Reval.

To prevent the Russian Baltic Fleet's escape to Sweden, German minelayers COBRA and KAISER laid additional mines off Cape Purikari (sixty-six EMC and one hundred floating mines) and west of Minefield JUMINDA (one hundred thirty-six EMC and two hundred floating mines).

18 SEPTEMBER 1941

German shore batteries heavily damaged Russian battleship PETROPAVLOVSK and lightly damaged destroyer MAKSIM GORKI in Kronstadt Bay, Russia.

20 SEPTEMBER 1941

Russian submarines SHCH-317, SHCH-319 and SHCH-320 departed Kronstadt, Kotlin Island, for operations in the Baltic. SHCH-317 (Lt Cdr Mochov) went to the aid of Russian troops on Ösel Island.

21 SEPTEMBER 1941

German minelayer KAISER laid eighty-six EMC and one hundred floating mines north of Minefield JUMINDA.

German Ju87 aircraft of the I/STG.2 and III/STG.2 (Oblt Dinort) attacked the Russian Baltic Fleet at Kronstadt, Russia.

One Ju87 (Oblt Rudel) landed a 1000-Kg bomb on Russian battleship **MARAT** and sank her next to the mole. The Russians were later able to get her 30.5-cm guns of turret C and D operating, and later turret B as well, so that she could still support the defence of Kronstadt.

Another Ju87 (Hptm Steen) damaged cruiser KIROV with his aircraft, which, damaged by the antiaircraft fire,

crashed next to the ship.
Six smaller bombs damaged the Russian battleship OKTYABRSKAYA REVOLUTSIYA.
Destroyer **STEREGUSHCHI** was sunk, but later raised.
Bombs damaged destroyers GORDY, GROZYASHCHI and SILNY, submarine tender SMOLNY and submarine SHCH-306.

22 SEPTEMBER 1941

German minelayer COBRA, escorted by motor minesweepers R.55 and R.57, laid one hundred twenty-six EMC and one hundred floating mines off Kallbadagrund, Finland.

Finnish MTB VINHA attacked shipping while MTB SYOKSY (ObBtsm Ovaskainen) sank Russian minesweeper **T-41/SERGEY KIROV** (400grt) in Suursaari harbour.

23 SEPTEMBER 1941

Russian TKA-12 sank German patrol boat **V.308/OSCAR NEYNABER** (314grt) at Porkkala, Finland. The other German patrol boats then sank **TKA-12** before she could escape.

German Ju87 aircraft of III/STG.2 damaged Russian cruiser MAKSIM GORKI while she was under repair at Leningrad, Russia.

German Ju87 aircraft of III/STG.2 further damaged Russian cruiser KIROV, destroyer GROZYASHCHI, and damaged submarines SHCH-302, SHCH-322 and SHCH-318 at Kronstadt, Russia.

German Ju87 aircraft of III/STG.2 sank Russian submarines **P-2** and **M-74** in the shipyard at Kronstadt.

German Ju87 aircraft of III/STG.2 sank Russian destroyer leader **MINSK** while she was under repair at Kronstadt. She was later raised.

German Ju87 aircraft of III/STG.2 sank Russian patrol boat **TAIFUN** at Kronstadt.

German Ju87 aircraft of III/STG.2 further damaged Russian battleships **MARAT** and OKTYABRSKAYA REVOLUTSIYA at Kronstadt.

During the night, a mine sank Russian submarine **SHCH-319** (Lt Cdr Agashin) off the Finnish coast.

Russian submarines S-4, SHCH-303, SHCH-309, SHCH-311, M-95, M-98 and LEMBIT were sent into the Gulf of Finland to intercept the German force spotted off Hangö, Finland.

Russian submarine L-3 remained off Suursaari, Finland.

24 SEPTEMBER 1941

During the night of 24/25 September, German minelayer KÖNIGIN LUISE laid eighty-six EMC mines off Kallbadagrund, Finland.

Russian minelayer MARTI laid a minefield across the entrance to Kronstadt Bay, Russia.

25 SEPTEMBER 1941

German light cruisers LEIPZIG (KptzS Stichling) and EMDEN (KptzS Mirow) with torpedo boats T.7, T.8 and T.11 bombarded Russian positions on the Sworbe peninsula.

Russian submarine SHCH-317 (Lt Cdr Mochov) with four TKA boats unsuccessfully attacked German light cruiser LEIPZIG off Halb Island.

A Russian mine sank German minelayer **KÖNIGIN LUISE** (2399grt) near Helsinki as she was returning from laying a minefield off Kallbadagrund.

29 SEPTEMBER 1941

Russian submarines S-4, SHCH-303, SHCH-311, M-95, M-98 and LEMBIT patrolled the western part of the Gulf of Finland, while L-3 patrolled of Suursaari Island.

MEDITERRANEAN SEA & MIDDLE EAST

East of Gibraltar
Long. W05, 30 – E11, 00   Lat. N44, 30 – N35, 00

3 SEPTEMBER 1941

Italian steamer **COMMANDANT BAFILE** (1790grt) was lost when she ran aground near Cape Comino, Sardinia. (Other sources claim that British aircraft sank her.)

5 SEPTEMBER 1941

Dutch submarine O.21 (Lt Cdr Van Dulm) sank Italian steamer **ISARCO** (5738grt) twenty-eight miles southeast of Ischia in 42, 48N, 09, 58E. The submarine picked up twenty-two survivors and arrived back at Gibraltar on the 12th. (Other sources place the sinking in 40, 12N, 13, 17E.)

6 SEPTEMBER 1941

	Dutch submarine O.24 (Lt Cdr de Booy) attacked Italian antiaircraft barque **A5/V63/CARLA** (347grt) off La Spezia, Italy, in 43, 45N, 09, 21E. The barque was heavily damaged by gunfire and was beached to prevent her sinking.

8 SEPTEMBER 1941

	Italian submarines ALAGI and SERPENTE unsuccessfully patrolled off the Algerian coast.
	Italian submarines AXUM, ADUA, ARADAM and SETTEMBRINI unsuccessfully patrolled off Cap Bon, Tunisia.
	In Operation STATUS, aircraft carrier ARK ROYAL and light cruiser HERMIONE departed Gibraltar with destroyers GURKHA, LIVELY, LANCE and FORESTER to launch fourteen Hurricane aircraft to Malta.

9 SEPTEMBER 1941

	In Operation STATUS, aircraft carrier ARK ROYAL launched her fourteen Hurricane aircraft to Malta.
	Dutch submarine O.24 (Lt Cdr de Booy) sank Italian steamer **ITALO BALBO** (5114grt) ten miles west of Elba off Cape Seere, Italy, in 42, 47N, 09, 57E.

10 SEPTEMBER 1941

0900	Force H returned to Gibraltar.
1900	In Operation STATUS, aircraft carrier FURIOUS departed Gibraltar with destroyers LEGION, FORESIGHT, and FORESTER.
2100	In Operation STATUS, aircraft carrier ARK ROYAL, battleship NELSON plus light cruiser HERMIONE departed Gibraltar with destroyers ZULU, GURKHA, LANCE, and LIVELY.

13 SEPTEMBER 1941

	In Operation STATUS, aircraft carriers ARK ROYAL launched twenty-six Hurricane aircraft and FURIOUS launched nineteen Hurricane aircraft to Malta. The force with battleship NELSON plus destroyers GURKHA, ZULU, LEGION, LIVELY, LANCE, FORESIGHT and FORESTER then returned to Gibraltar.
	Steamer EMPIRE GUILLEMOT (5641grt), which had arrived at Gibraltar in convoy OG.73, departed Gibraltar for Malta escorted through the day by corvettes GENTIAN and JASMINE in Operation PROPELLER. The steamer safely arrived on the 19th.

14 SEPTEMBER 1941

	Submarine PROTEUS departed Gibraltar with stores for Malta. When she did not send a message after her test dive, destroyer VIDETTE was dispatched to search for her. However, the submarine arrived back at Gibraltar on the 15th with radio problems. The submarine was able to proceed later on the 15th.

15 SEPTEMBER 1941

	U.79 successfully crossed through the Gibraltar Straits into the Mediterranean. She became the first U-boat to enter the sea since 1939.

16 SEPTEMBER 1941

	Lt (A) C. B. Lamb and T/A/Sub-Lt (A) J. E. Robertson RNVR were interned after they crashed landed their Swordfish aircraft of 830 Squadron near Sousse, Tunisia. Despite the crash, they had successfully delivered an agent to the area.
	Dutch submarine O.24 arrived at Gibraltar from her patrol in the Tyrrhenian Sea.

19 SEPTEMBER 1941

	Polish submarine SOKOL departed Gibraltar for a patrol in the Mediterranean and to support Operation HALBERD.

20 SEPTEMBER 1941

	Italian submarine SCIRE CF Borghese) entered Gibraltar Harbour during the night and released three two-men torpedo boats. They sank oil depot ship **FIONA SHELL** (2444grt) and oiler **DENBYDALE** (8145grt) and heavily damaged steamer DURHAM (10,893grt). One crewman was lost on **FIONA SHELL**. DURHAM was beached, re-floated and dry-docked to make temporary repairs. On the 3rd, DURHAM sailed in tow from Gibraltar for Falmouth.
	RAF aircraft sank Vichy French steamer **MONSELET** (3372grt) and Italian steamer **MARIGOLA** (5996grt) during an air attack on Sfax, Tunisia.
	Submarine TRUSTY departed Gibraltar for a patrol in the Mediterranean to support Operation HALBERD.

21 SEPTEMBER 1941

	Dutch submarine O.21 departed Gibraltar for a patrol in the Mediterranean to support Operation HALBERD.

23 SEPTEMBER 1941

	A mine sank Italian steamer **CARMELO NOLI** (109grt) south of Livorno, Italy.

24 SEPTEMBER 1941

1230	Light cruiser EDINBURGH departed Gibraltar to join the Operation HALBERD convoy.
1815	Battleship NELSON departed Gibraltar with Dutch destroyer ISAAC SWEERS plus Polish destroyers PIORUN and GARLAND in Operation HALBERD.
2000	Fleet oiler BROWN RANGER (3417grt) departed Gibraltar escorted by corvette FLEUR DE LYS as Force S to refuel destroyers in Operation HALBERD at sea.
2330	Battleship RODNEY, aircraft carrier ARK ROYAL plus light cruiser HERMIONE departed Gibraltar with destroyers DUNCAN, FORESIGHT, FORESTER, LIVELY, ZULU, GURKHA, LEGION, and LANCE for Operation HALBERD.

25 SEPTEMBER 1941

0130	Convoy GM.2 departed Gibraltar for Malta with steamers BRECONSHIRE (9776grt), CLAN MACDONALD (9653grt), CLAN FERGUSON (7347grt), AJAX (7540grt), IMPERIAL STAR (10,733grt), CITY OF LINCOLN (8039grt), ROWALLAN CASTLE (7798grt), DUNEDIN STAR (11,168grt) and CITY OF CALCUTTA (8063grt).
0130	Force A of battleships NELSON, RODNEY, and PRINCE OF WALES, aircraft carrier ARK ROYAL, with destroyers DUNCAN, LEGION, LIVELY, LANCE, GURKHA, GARLAND, PIORUN, and ISAAC SWEERS and Force X of light cruisers HERMIONE, KENYA, EDINBURGH, SHEFFIELD, and EURYALUS with destroyers LIGHTNING, LAFOREY, COSSACK, ZULU, ORIBI, FORESIGHT, FORESTER, FURY, HEYTHROP, and FARNDALE escorted convoy GM.2 for Operation HALBERD.

26 SEPTEMBER 1941

	Italian reconnaissance aircraft spotted the British Operation HALBERD forces south of the Balearic Islands.
	In the evening, Italian battleships LITTORIO (Adm Iachino) and VITTORIO VENETO departed Naples, Italy, with destroyers GRANATIERE, FUCILIERE, BERSAGLIERE, and GIOBERTI of the 13th Destroyer Division and DA RECCO, PESSAGNO, and FOLGORE of the 16th Destroyer Division. Italian heavy cruisers TRENTO, TRIESTE and GORIZIA departed Messina, Sicily, with destroyers CORAZZIERE, CARABINIERE, ASCARI, and LANCIERE of the 12th Destroyer Division. Italian light cruisers DUCA DEGLI ABRUZZI and ATTENDOLO departed Palermo, Sicily, with destroyers MAESTRALE, GRECALE, and SCIROCCO of the 10th Destroyer Division to intercept the British force southeast of Sardinia. The remainder of the Italian Fleet could not sail due to fuel shortages.
	Italian submarines DANDOLO, ADUA and TURCHESE patrolled north of Cape Ferrat.
	Italian submarines AXUM, SERPENTE, ARADAM and DIASPRO patrolled north of Cape Bougaroni.
	Italian submarines SQUALO, BANDIERA and DELFINO patrolled north of Cape Ferrat.
	Italian submarine NARVALO patrolled off Cap Bon, Tunisia.
	An Italian MAS group took up stations off Pantellaria Island.

27 SEPTEMBER 1941

	Italian torpedo bombers damaged battleship NELSON south of Sardinia. Her speed was reduced to eighteen knots as she took on over 3500 tons of seawater. Lt Cdr J. R. B. Longden, CBE, was wounded.
	Italian bombers damaged destroyer ZULU with bomb splinters from near misses.
	Battleships PRINCE OF WALES, NELSON, and RODNEY and six destroyers were detached to attack the Italian force. When the speed of battleship NELSON was reduced further to twelve knots, she was forced to drop out of the group so light cruisers EDINBURGH and SHEFFIELD replaced her. However, no contact was made with the Italian force.
	Italian aircraft heavily damaged troopship **IMPERIAL STAR** (10,733grt) off Cap Bon in 37, 31N, 10, 46E. Destroyers HEYTHROP and FARNDALE took off the survivors and destroyer ORIBI took the troopship in tow until it became necessary to scuttle the ship. There were no casualties.
	Battleship RODNEY shot down a Fulmar aircraft of 807 Squadron from aircraft carrier ARK ROYAL by mistake. Destroyer DUNCAN rescued Sub-Lt P. Guy and Leading Airman Jones. Battleship RODNEY also shot down a second Fulmar aircraft of 807 Squadron. Destroyer DUNCAN also rescued Lt G. C. M. Guthrie and Petty Officer A. T. Goodman.
	Fulmar aircraft from aircraft carrier ARK ROYAL downed five of the thirty Italian aircraft and antiaircraft fire from the ships downed a further seven. Two Fulmar aircraft were lost, both to "friendly" fire.
	The Italian Fleet (Admiral Iachino) passed through the area between Sardinia and the Skerki Bank without making contact with the British force.

	Dutch submarine O.21 (Lt Cdr van Dulm) made an unsuccessful attack on a steamer in 42N, 10E.
	Force X continued through the Sicilian Straits with the remaining steamers escorted by the five cruisers and nine destroyers.

28 SEPTEMBER 1941

	Lt M. W. Watson and A/Sub-Lt (A) P. W. N. Couch of the 808 Squadron of aircraft carrier ARK ROYAL were lost when their Fulmar aircraft was accidentally shot by gunfire from battleship PRINCE OF WALES.
	Battleship NELSON was detached from the group with five destroyers to return to Gibraltar at dark. Destroyers DUNCAN, PIORUN, and GARLAND escorted the NELSON back to Gibraltar. Destroyer ROCKINGHAM plus corvettes JONQUIL, FLEUR DE LYS, SAMPHIRE, and ARBUTUS departed Gibraltar on the 29th to join the escort. All ships arrived back at Gibraltar on the 30th.

29 SEPTEMBER 1941

	An unknown cause sank Italian steamer **ILVANIA** (487grt) at Port Torres, Sardinia.
	Steamer MELBOURNE STAR (12,806grt) arrived at Gibraltar from Malta.
0617	Italian submarine DIASPRO attacked destroyers in Force H off Algeria in 37, 32N, 06, 45E. Destroyer GURKHA damaged submarine DIASPRO during a depth charge attack.
1642	Italian submarine SERPENTE attacked destroyers in Force H off Algeria in 37, 22N, 06, 16E. Destroyers LEGION and LANCE damaged submarine SERPENTE during a depth charge attack.

30 SEPTEMBER 1941

	Steamers PORT CHALMERS (8535grt) and CITY OF PRETORIA (8046grt) arrived at Gibraltar from Malta.
0350	Italian submarine ADUA (Lt Cdr Riccardi) unsuccessfully attacked destroyers in Force H off Algeria. Destroyers GURKHA and LEGION sank **ADUA** east of Cartagena with depth charges.
1750	Battleship PRINCE OF WALES plus light cruiser KENYA and SHEFFIELD arrived at Gibraltar with destroyers LAFOREY, LIGHTNING, ORIBI, FORESIGHT, FORESTER, and FURY after completing Operation HALBERD.

Middle Mediterranean Sea
Long. E11, 00 – E20, 00   Lat. N46, 00 – N30, 00

1 SEPTEMBER 1941

	An Italian convoy departed Naples, Italy, with steamers ANDREA GRITTI (6338grt), RIALTO (6099grt), VETTOR PISANI (6339grt), FRANCESCO BARBARO (6343grt), and SEBASTINO VENIER (6311grt) escorted by destroyers DA RECCO, DARDO, FOLGORE, and STRALE. The convoy arrived at Tripoli, Libya, on the 4th.
	Submarines URSULA, UNIQUE, UPHOLDER, URGE, UTMOST, UPRIGHT and UNBEATEN formed the 10th Submarine Flotilla (Capt Simpson) at Malta.
	Submarine UPHOLDER arrived at Malta after her patrol.
	Submarine OTUS departed Malta for Alexandria, Egypt, with stores, mail, and fifteen passengers. Later in the day, she unsuccessfully attacked an Italian AMC in 35, 40N, 18, 07E.

2 SEPTEMBER 1941

	Submarine URSULA arrived at Malta from a patrol east of Tripoli, Libya.
	Submarine TRIUMPH arrived at Malta from patrol off the north coast of Sicily.

3 SEPTEMBER 1941

	Submarine OTUS attacked a southbound Italian convoy in 35, 40N, 18, 07E. The submarine reported two hits on a steamer.
0025	Nine British Swordfish of 830 Squadron from Malta sank Italian steamer **ANDREA GRITTI** (6338grt) south-southeast of Cape Spartivento, Italy, in 37, 33N, 16, 26E. Three hundred forty-seven crewmen and passengers were lost and there were only two survivors. In the same attack, the Swordfish damaged Italian steamer FRANCESCO BARBARO (6343grt). She was taken in tow by destroyer DARDO and escorted by destroyers ASCARI and LANCIERE to Messina, Sicily.

4 SEPTEMBER 1941

	An Italian supply convoy departed Tripoli, Libya, with steamers SIRENA (974grt), SPARVIERO (498grt), and IMPERIA (222grt) escorted by torpedo PALLADE and CENTAURO for Benghazi, Libya.
	Submarine UNBEATEN arrived at Malta from her patrol in the Straits of Messina.

5 SEPTEMBER 1941

	Torpedo boat PALLADE was detached from the Benghazi bound Italian supply convoy for other duty.

An Italian return convoy departed Tripoli, Libya, with steamers ERNESTO (7272grt), COL DI LANA (5891grt), and POZARICA (7599grt) for Naples, Italy, escorted by destroyers DA RECCO, FRECCIA, FOLGORE, and STRALE.
Torpedo boat CIRCE joined the escort on the 7th.
Dutch submarine O.21 (Lt Cdr Van Dulm) damaged steamer ERNESTO twenty miles north of Pantellaria Island on the 6th. ERNESTO arrived at Trapani, Italy, with destroyer STRALE and torpedo boat CIRCE on the 8th.
The rest of the convoy arrived at Naples later on the 8th.

Submarine OSIRIS departed Malta for Alexandria, Egypt, with stores and twelve passengers.

6 SEPTEMBER 1941

During the evening, Dutch submarine O.21 (Lt Cdr Van Dulm) damaged Italian steamer ERNESTO (7272grt) north of Pantellaria Island.

7 SEPTEMBER 1941

Submarine THUNDERBOLT (Lt Cdr Crouch) sank Italian steamer **SIRENA** (974grt) fifty miles west of Benghazi, Libya. The steamer was part of a small convoy covered by Italian torpedo boats CENTAURO and POLLUCE.

A supply convoy departed Naples, Italy, with German steamers LIVORNO (1829grt) and SPEZIA (1825grt) escorted by torpedo boat FABRIZI for Benghazi, Libya.
At Messina, torpedo boat FABRIZI was relieved by torpedo boats POLLUCE and CENTAURO.
The convoy arrived at Benghazi on the 11th.

8 SEPTEMBER 1941

Dutch submarine O.21 (Lt Cdr Van Dulm) unsuccessfully attacked a convoy in the Tyrrhenian Sea.

10 SEPTEMBER 1941

An Italian supply convoy departed Naples, Italy, with steamers TEMBIEN (5584grt), CAFFARO (6476grt), NIRVO (5164grt), BAINSIZZA (7933grt), NICOLO ODERO (6003grt) and GIULIA (5921grt) escorted by destroyers ORIANI and FULMINE plus torpedo boats PROCIONE, PEGASO, ORSA, CIRCE and PERSEO for Tripoli, Libya.

Submarine THUNDERBOLT (Lt Cdr Crouch) sank Italian steamer **SVAM I** (388grt) with gunfire in the Gulf of Sirte.

RAF bombing further damaged Italian heavy cruiser BOLZANO at Messina, Sicily. Twelve crewmen were killed and thirty were wounded. The bombers had flown from Malta.

11 SEPTEMBER 1941

Submarine THUNDERBOLT (Lt Cdr Crouch) sank German steamer **LIVORNO** (1829grt) off Bougie, Libya, in 31, 58N, 19, 23E. The Italian torpedo boats CENTAURO and POLLUCE could not find the submarine, which had sunk all three cargo ships of the convoy.

RAF Blenheim bombers sank Italian steamer **ALFREDO ORIANI** (3059grt) in 35, 05N, 20, 16E, after the steamer had departed Patrasso, Italy, escorted by torpedo boat CANTORE.

12 SEPTEMBER 1941

Swordfish aircraft of 830 Squadron from Malta sank Italian steamer **CAFFARO** (6476grt) northwest of Tripoli, Libya, in 34, 14N, 11, 54E. They also damaged Italian steamers TEMBIEN (5584grt) and NICOLO ODERO (6003grt).

Submarine UTMOST departed Malta to search for a crew of a downed RAF Blenheim aircraft. The crew was found and UTMOST returned to Malta with them on the 14th.

13 SEPTEMBER 1941

	Submarine THUNDERBOLT (Lt Cdr Crouch) unsuccessfully attacked Italian minesweeper ZIRONA off Benghazi, Libya.
	Submarine THRASHER unsuccessfully attacked a steamer in the Gulf of Sirte.
0600	Italian torpedo boat OERSEO joined an Italian supply convoy arriving from Naples, Italy, off Tripoli, Libya.

14 SEPTEMBER 1941

RAF bombers sank Italian steamer **NICOLO ODERO** (6003grt) off Tripoli, Libya. She had just arrived the previous day from Naples, Italy.

Submarine THUNDERBOLT (Lt Cdr Crouch) unsuccessfully attacked German steamer TINOS (2827grt), escorted by torpedo boat POLLUCE thirty miles northwest of Benghazi, Libya.

16 SEPTEMBER 1941

A North Africa supply convoy departed Taranto, Italy, with the troopships VULCANIA (24,469grt), OCEANIA

(19,507grt) and NEPTUNIA (19,475grt) escorted by Italian destroyers DA RECCO, DA NOLI, PESSAGNO, USODIMARE and GIOBERTI for Tripoli, Libya.

An unknown cause sank Italian submarine **SMERALDO** in the Aegean.

RAF aircraft attacked a small Italian convoy escorted by Italian torpedo boat CLIO.

RAF aircraft sank Italian tanker **FILUCCIO** (248grt) north of Zara.

Submarines URSULA, UNBEATEN, UPHOLDER, and UPRIGHT departed Malta to intercept a fast Italian convoy east of Tripoli, Libya.

Submarine TRIUMPH departed Malta for a special service mission and a patrol in the Adriatic.

17 SEPTEMBER 1941

Submarine URSULA unsuccessfully attacked Italian troopship VULCANIA (24,469grt) off Tripoli, Libya. British aerial reconnaissance spotted the convoy east of Calabria, Italy, and submarines UPRIGHT, UPHOLDER and UNBEATEN were set up northeast of Tripoli.

18 SEPTEMBER 1941

Submarine UPHOLDER (Lt Cdr Wanklyn) attacked an Italian convoy off Misurata, Sicily, and sank Italian troopship **NEPTUNIA** (19,475grt) and damaged troopship OCEANIA (19,507grt) sixty miles east-northeast of Tripoli, Libya, in 33, 02N, 14, 42E.

Submarine UPRIGHT was forced underwater by the Italian destroyers while submarine URSULA tried to set up a kill shot on damaged Italian troopship VULCANIA (24,469grt). Submarines THRASHER and UTMOST were too far away to reach the convoy.

Submarine UPHOLDER returned four hours later and sank the damaged Italian troopship **OCEANIA** (19,507grt). Italian troopship VULCANIA (24,469grt) escaped and continued on to Tripoli, Libya, escorted by Italian destroyer USODIMARE, while destroyers DA RECCO, DA NOLI, PESSAGNO and GIOBERTI searched for the submarine and rescued survivors.

Submarine TRIUMPH (Cdr Woods) torpedoed Italian steamer ARDOR (8960grt) Cape Cimiti, Italy, in the Adriatic. She was towed to Crotone, Italy.

Italian sailing ship **SAN FRANCISCO DI PAOLA** (50grt) was reported missing in the Tyrrhenian Sea.

19 SEPTEMBER 1941

RAF aircraft attacked an Italian supply convoy sailing from Naples, Italy, to Tripoli, Libya, with Italian steamers CATERINA (4786grt), COL DI LANA (5891grt), MARIN SANUDO (5081grt) and the tanker MINATITLAN (7599grt) escorted by destroyers FRECCIA, EURO, FOLGORE, DARDO and GIOBERTI. GIOBERTI escorted the damaged steamer COL DI LANA to Trapani, Italy.

20 SEPTEMBER 1941

Damaged Italian steamer COL DI LANA (5891grt) was escorted into Kuriat by Italian torpedo boat DEZZA.

Submarine TRIUMPH (Cdr Woods) landed a commando troop at Yugoslavia during the night.

22 SEPTEMBER 1941

During the night of 22/23 September, Italian destroyers CORAZZIERE, ASCARI, CARABINIERE, and LANCIERE of the 12th Destroyer Flotilla (KptzS Melodia) laid Minefield M.6 and Minefield M.6A southeast of Malta escorted by destroyers AVIERE and CAMICIA NERA.

Returning to Hal Far, Egypt, after searching for merchant ships between Kuriat and Pantellaria, T/Lt (A) L. F. E. Aldridge RNVR was killed and his gunner Leading Airman K. Pimlott died in hospital from injuries when their Swordfish aircraft of 830 Squadron crashed and exploded on landing.

Sub-Lt R. G. Drake was lost in a captured German He115 aircraft, flown by a Free French crew, that crashed shortly after takeoff from Malta. The two French crewmen were lost as well.

23 SEPTEMBER 1941

Submarine THRASHER (Lt Cdr Cowell) unsuccessfully attacked a group of three Italian destroyers southeast of Malta.

Submarine TRIUMPH (Cdr Woods) sank German steamer **LUVSEE** (2373grt) six miles northeast of Sebenico, Yugoslavia, in the Adriatic.

Submarine THRASHER made an unsuccessful attack on a steamer near Benghazi, Libya.

24 SEPTEMBER 1941

An Italian convoy with steamers CASTELVERDE (6666grt), PERLA (5741grt), and AMSTERDAM (8673grt) escorted by destroyers LAPINO, ORIANI, and FULMINE, and STRALE, reported a submarine attack off Pantellaria Island. No damage was done. There is no corresponding report from any British submarine to verify the attack.

Convoy MG.2 departed Malta for Gibraltar with empty steamers MELBOURNE STAR (12,806grt), PORT CHALMERS (8535grt) and CITY OF PRETORIA (8046grt).

	Submarine THRASHER (Lt Cdr Cowell) damaged Italian steamer **PROSPERO** (971grt) off Benghazi, Libya. She was sunk later the same day by British bombing at Benghazi.
	RAF aircraft heavily damaged German steamer **RUHR** (5954grt) during an attack on Palermo, Sicily.
	Submarine TRIUMPH (Cdr Woods) damaged Italian steamer **POSEIDONE** (6613grt) four miles off Ortona and damaged Italian steamer **SIDAMO** (2384grt) in Ortona Harbour, Italy.
	Submarine URGE (Lt Tomkinson) unsuccessfully attacked a small steamer off Libya.
	Submarines UTMOST, UPRIGHT, URGE, Polish SOKOL, TRUSTY and UPHOLDER took up positions north of Sicily to cover Operation HALBERD from the Italian Fleet. UTMOST patrolled the northern approach to Messina Straits. UPRIGHT patrolled the northeast approach to Messina Straits. URGE patrolled north of Palermo. UPHOLDER patrolled northward of Cape Marittimo to Cape St Vito. SOKOL patrolled north of Sicily. TRUSTY patrolled north of Sicily.
	Submarines UNBEATEN, URSULA and the Dutch O.21 took up positions off Cagliari and the Sicilian Straits to cover the passage of the Operation HALBERD convoys. UNBEATEN patrolled in the vicinity of Cape Spartivento and Cape del Armi, Italy. URSULA patrolled south of the Straits of Messina. O.21 patrolled off Cagliari.

25 SEPTEMBER 1941

	Submarine URGE (Lt Tomkinson) tried unsuccessfully to land a commando team on Sicily to blow up the main rail line.

26 SEPTEMBER 1941

	British bombing sank Italian fishing boat **CAPODOGLIO** (184grt) sixteen miles 346° from Marsa Dili, Libya.

27 SEPTEMBER 1941

	Submarine URGE (Lt Tomkinson) tried unsuccessfully to land a commando team on Sicily to blow up the main rail line.
	Submarine UPRIGHT (Lt Wraith) sank Italian torpedo boat **ALBATROS** off Messina, northeast of Sicily. U.371 rescued forty-two survivors.
1100	Steamers PORT CHALMERS (8535grt) and CITY OF PRETORIA (8046grt) departed Malta for Gibraltar.

28 SEPTEMBER 1941

	During the night of 27/28 September, light cruiser HERMIONE bombarded Pantellaria Island for five minutes. Steamers CITY OF CALCUTTA (8063grt) and ROWALLAN CASTLE (7798grt) in convoy MG.2 were damaged in a collision as they passed close to the Sicilian coast towards Gibraltar. An Italian submarine and three Italian torpedo bombers attacked the convoy during the night.
	The Italian MAS boats did not find either of the British Malta-Gibraltar convoys during the night in the Sicilian Straits.

29 SEPTEMBER 1941

	An RAF aerial mine sank Italian tanker **FLUVIOR** (389grt) at Tripoli, Libya.
1130	Steamers MELBOURNE STAR (12,806grt) departed Malta for Gibraltar.

Eastern Mediterranean Sea

Long. E20, 00 – E38, 00   Lat. N43, 00 – N30, 00

1 SEPTEMBER 1941

	The flag of Commander in Chief, Mediterranean Fleet, was transferred to the battleship QUEEN ELIZABETH. VAdm Commanding First Battle Squadron was transferred to battleship BARHAM.
	Motor torpedo boats MTB.68 and MTB.215 arrived at Alexandria, Egypt, from Haifa, Palestine. Both boats were out of action due to numerous serious defects.

2 SEPTEMBER 1941

	MTB depot ship trawler VULCAN arrived at Alexandria, Egypt.
	Heavy weather sank landing craft **LCP(L).59** (10grt) and **LCP(L).71** (10grt) while they were at anchor (presumably at Alexandria).

3 SEPTEMBER 1941

	Battleship VALIANT, light cruiser HOBART, and destroyers were at sea exercising from Alexandria, Egypt, dur-

ing the day.

Greek submarine PAPANICOLIS broke down while on passage from Alexandria to Port Said, Egypt, for docking. The submarine was towed back to Alexandria, arriving during the night of 3/4 September. It was determined the submarine would be out of action for at least two months.

Greek destroyer PANTHER departed Port Said to return to Alexandria after repairs at Suez, Egypt.

4 SEPTEMBER 1941

Australian destroyer VENDETTA arrived at Port Said, Egypt, for escort duties. She escorted steamer SALAMAUA (6676grt) from Port Said to Famagusta, Cypress, arriving on the 6th.
VENDETTA then proceeded to Haifa, Palestine.

Destroyers KINGSTON and HASTY departed Beirut, Lebanon, for Haifa.

An Italian convoy departed Piraeus, Greece, with Romanian steamer BALCIC (3495grt) and Italian tanker MAYA (3867grt) escorted by torpedo boat SIRIO for the Dardanelles.

5 SEPTEMBER 1941

Submarine PERSEUS (Lt Cdr Nicolay) damaged Italian tanker **MAYA** (3867grt) while attacking a convoy off the Dardanelles in 39, 43N, 25, 57E. Because the tanker could not be towed, she was beached. (Other sources state that Italian torpedo boat SIRIO scuttled the tanker.)

6 SEPTEMBER 1941

Italian submarine DAGABUR patrolled off the Egyptian coast between Tobruk, Libya, and Port Said, Egypt.

German aircraft damaged destroyer KANDAHAR with bomb near misses at Alexandria, Egypt. The destroyer had no time out of action.

German aircraft damaged depot ship WOOLWICH with bomb near misses at Alexandria.

German aircraft damaged hospital ship MAINE with bomb near misses. Surgeon Cdr R. W. Nesbitt, MB, FRCPI, and four ratings were killed. Fifteen ratings were wounded.

Destroyer GRIFFIN departed Alexandria to relieve destroyer KINGSTON at Haifa, Palestine. Destroyer KINGSTON arrived back at Alexandria on the 7th.

Australian sloop PARRAMATTA departed Alexandria to reinforce sloop FLAMINGO, which was operating in the Gulf of Suez. The sloop passed through the Suez Canal on the 7th.

| Night | Light cruiser NAIAD and destroyers HAVOCK and HOTSPUR were at sea during the night of 6/7 September to control Axis night fighters which might attack Alexandria or the Suez Canal area. |

7 SEPTEMBER 1941

Submarine TORBAY reported an Axis submarine in 32, 42N, 28, 55E.

Destroyers GRIFFIN and HASTY departed Haifa, Palestine; destroyer VENDETTA departed Port Said, Egypt; and destroyers HERO, HAVOCK, HOTSPUR, and KINGSTON departed Alexandria, Egypt, to carry out antisubmarine searches in the area. The search ended unsuccessfully. The destroyers returned to their respective ports of departure on the 10th.
(Authors' note: only Italian submarines were active in the area at this time.)

8 SEPTEMBER 1941

Destroyers KIPLING, JAGUAR, and DECOY departed Alexandria, Egypt, to carry supplies to Tobruk, Libya.
German bombing damaged destroyers DECOY and KIPLING with bomb near misses near Tobruk. Neither destroyer spent any time out of action.
German bombing damaged destroyer KIMBERLEY by bomb near misses while she was at sea covering the supply operation. She also spent no time out of action.
The destroyers arrived back at Alexandria on the 9th.

Light cruiser NAIAD with destroyers NAPIER and NIZAM were at sea off Alexandria controlling night fighters during the night of 8/9 September.

9 SEPTEMBER 1941

Battleship BARHAM, minelayers ABDIEL and LATONA, plus destroyers NAPIER and NIZAM were at sea from Alexandria, Egypt, for exercises. The light cruisers AJAX, NEPTUNE, and HOBART of the 7th Cruiser Squadron were also at sea exercising.

A Swordfish aircraft of 815 Squadron from Dekheila ditched offshore. Minelayer ABDIEL picked up the pilot, Sub-Lt D. W. Phillips and his crew after five and a half hours in the water.

Gunboat GNAT departed Mersa Matruh, Egypt, for Tobruk, Libya, but returned when her engines broke down. The gunboat later proceeded to Alexandria for repairs.

10 SEPTEMBER 1941

Submarine TORBAY (Lt Cdr Miers) damaged German steamer **NORBURG** (2392grt) with a torpedo in Candia

	Harbour at Crete. She sank but was later salvaged.
	Italian submarine TOPAZIO (Cdr Berengan) sank ferry **MUREFTE** (691grt) off the Syrian coast in 33, 12N, 34, 35E. One crewman was lost, and Egyptian steamer TALODI (1585grt) rescued the survivors.
	Destroyers KIPLING, JACKAL, HASTY, and HOTSPUR departed Alexandria, Egypt, and destroyers HERO and GRIFFIN departed Haifa, Palestine, to hunt for this submarine.
	Destroyers KIPLING and HASTY returned to Alexandria on the 13th. Destroyers HERO, GRIFFIN, JACKAL, and HOTSPUR arrived at Haifa on the 14th.
	German Ju87 aircraft damaged destroyers DECOY and KIMBERLEY during a night attack on Tobruk, Libya.
	Battleship QUEEN ELIZABETH, minelayers ABDIEL and LATONA, plus destroyers JACKAL and NIZAM were exercising off Alexandria, Egypt.
	Light cruiser NAIAD with destroyers JACKAL and HOTSPUR were at sea to direct night fighters over Alexandria, Egypt. Destroyer JACKAL rescued a party of two Army officers, three soldiers, and nine Greeks, who had escaped from Greece in a caique and were making for Alexandria.

11 SEPTEMBER 1941

	Submarine OTUS arrived at Alexandria, Egypt, from Malta.
	Destroyers NAPIER, KINGSTON, and HAVOCK departed Alexandria with supplies for Tobruk, Libya. On their return, Senior Naval Officer, Inshore Squadron, Captain A. L. Poland DSO DSC, took passage to Mersa Matruh, Egypt, in destroyer NAPIER. The destroyers returned to Alexandria on the 12th.

12 SEPTEMBER 1941

	Submarine OSIRIS arrived at Alexandria, Egypt, from Malta with stores and twelve passengers.
	Minelayers LATONA and ABDIEL began making supply runs from Alexandria to Tobruk, Libya. By the 22nd, they had delivered 6300 fresh troops plus 2100 tons of materiel to Tobruk and evacuated 6000 tired Australian troops to Alexandria.

13 SEPTEMBER 1941

	Corvette PEONY arrived at Alexandria, Egypt, from Beirut, Lebanon.

14 SEPTEMBER 1941

	Destroyers JACKAL and HOTSPUR departed Haifa, Palestine, for an antisubmarine sweep along the Syrian coast. The destroyers returned to Haifa on the 16th.
	Australian destroyer VENDETTA and corvette SALVIA arrived at Famagusta, Cypress, with steamer SALAMAUA (6676grt). VENDETTA remained with the steamer to escort it back to Haifa, Palestine. SALVIA proceeded to Beirut, Lebanon.

15 SEPTEMBER 1941

	Destroyers NAPIER, NIZAM, and HAVOCK departed Alexandria, Egypt, to carry supplies to Tobruk, Libya. Light cruisers AJAX, NEPTUNE, and HOBART with destroyers KINGSTON and KIMBERLEY departed Alexandria to cover the movement. All ships returned to Alexandria on the 16th.
	Light cruiser GALATEA departed Alexandria to operate in the Red Sea. The cruiser arrived at Suez, Egypt on the 16th.
	P/T/Sub-Lt (A) L. K. Harper RNVR, in a Martlet aircraft of 805 Squadron from Royal Navy air station GREBE, was killed when, while taking off at night, the aircraft went into a spin at the southwest side of Sidi Barrani North.

16 SEPTEMBER 1941

	Light cruiser NAIAD departed Alexandria, Egypt, to reinforce the Red Sea Escort Force. The cruiser arrived at Suez, Egypt, on the 17th.
	Destroyers HERO and GRIFFIN departed Haifa, Palestine, to conduct an antisubmarine sweep along the Port Said–to-Haifa shipping route. The destroyers returned to Haifa on the 17th.

17 SEPTEMBER 1941

	From 17 to 27 September, 6300 British troops and 2100 tons of supplies were moved to Tobruk, Libya, in Operation SUPERCHARGE. Light cruisers AJAX, NEPTUNE, and HOBART departed Alexandria, Egypt, for Beirut, Lebanon, to embark troops. Light cruisers AJAX and HOBART arrived at Beirut on the 18th. Light cruiser NEPTUNE was detached to spend the night of 18/19 September at Haifa, Palestine, rejoining at Beirut on the 19th. Minelayer ABDIEL plus destroyers JERVIS, JAGUAR, and HASTY departed Alexandria carrying supplies to Tobruk in convoy serial 1. The minelayer and destroyers arrived back at Alexandria on the 18th.
	Light cruiser GALATEA arrived at Port Said, Egypt.

18 SEPTEMBER 1941

In the Aegean from 18 to 30 September, submarine TORBAY made several attacks, including one on Italian supply ship CYCLOPS, but failed to sink or damage any ships.
Submarines OSIRIS and TALISMAN plus the Greek submarine TRITON also patrolled areas in the Aegean without success.

Minelayer LATONA departed Alexandria, Egypt, with destroyers NAPIER and NIZAM with supplies and some troops for Tobruk, Libya.
Destroyer HAVOCK sailed later to load supplies at Mersa Matruh, Egypt, and joined the ships en route in Operation SUPERCHARGE convoy serial 2.
While berthing alongside the wreck of Italian steamer **SERENITAS** (5171grt) at Tobruk, destroyer NIZAM was damaged forward when a crosswind blew the destroyer into the wreck.
The ships arrived back on the 19th.
Destroyer NIZAM was out of action for fourteen days to repair.

Australian destroyer VENDETTA and steamer FOUADIEH (1853grt) departed Port Said, Egypt, for Famagusta, Cypress.

19 SEPTEMBER 1941

In Operation SUPERCHARGE convoy serial 3, lighters A.2, A.9, and A.11 proceeded to Tobruk, Libya.
Convoy serial 4 was also conducted on this date with schooners KHEYR EL DINE and HILMI. However, these ships returned to Mersa Matruh, Egypt, and completed the operation on the 21st.

Light cruisers AJAX, NEPTUNE, and HOBART departed Haifa, Palestine, with 6000 troops for Tobruk, Libya.
Destroyers GRIFFIN and HOTSPUR from Haifa joined the cruisers off Beirut, Lebanon, and escorted them to Alexandria, Egypt, arriving on the 20th.

Submarine TORBAY unsuccessfully attacked a steamer off Gaidoro.

20 SEPTEMBER 1941

Minelayer ABDIEL departed Alexandria, Egypt, with destroyers JERVIS, KIMBERLEY, and HASTY with about 1000 troops, brought to Alexandria by the 7th Cruiser Squadron, and one hundred twenty tons of stores in Operation SUPERCHARGE convoy serial 5. The ships arrived back at Alexandria on the 21st.

Destroyers HERO and JACKAL departed Haifa, Palestine, for an antisubmarine sweep along the Haifa to Port Said to Alexandria shipping routes.

Destroyer HAVOCK grounded to the west of the Great Pass while waiting to enter harbour after an antisubmarine exercise. Both propellers were damaged beyond repair and both shafts and A bracket were distorted. Repairs in dry-dock required some fourteen days.

21 SEPTEMBER 1941

Italian submarine ASCIANGHI (TV di Derio) set the Palestinian steamer **ANTAR** (389grt) on fire with gunfire in 33, 57N, 35, 04E. The crew landed in lifeboats at Tyre, Lebanon. Whaler SOUTHERN ISLE went to the area and took the hulk in tow, but it sank on the 23rd before they could arrive in harbour.

Italian submarines MALACHITE and TRICHECO patrolled off the Cyrenaica coast.

Minelayer LATONA departed Alexandria, Egypt, with destroyers NAPIER, KINGSTON, and HOTSPUR on Operation SUPERCHARGE convoy serial 7. The ships arrived back at Alexandria on the 22nd.

Troopship GLENGYLE (9919grt) departed Alexandria for the Canal Area to relieve troopship GLENROY (9809grt) at the Combined Operations Training Centre at Kabret. Destroyers HERO and JACKAL joined troopship GLENGYLE off Alexandria and escorted her to Port Said, Egypt. Destroyers HERO and JACKAL arrived back at Alexandria on the 22nd.

Corvettes PEONY, HYACINTH, and ERICA departed Beirut, Lebanon, on an antisubmarine sweep.

At sunset, the flag of Cruiser Squadron 15 was hauled down from light cruiser NAIAD.
VAdm E. L. S. King CB, MVO was ordered to the appointment of Assistant Chief Naval Staff (Trade) in the Admiralty.
Captain W. H. A. Kelsey DSC assumed the duties of Senior Officer, 15th Cruiser Squadron, and Senior Officer, Suez Escort Force.

22 SEPTEMBER 1941

Minelayer ABDIEL departed Alexandria, Egypt, with destroyers KANDAHAR, JAGUAR, and GRIFFIN for Tobruk, Libya, in Operation SUPERCHARGE convoy serial 8.
Light cruisers AJAX, NEPTUNE, and HOBART departed Alexandria to cover the destroyers and rendezvous with minelayer ABDIEL at daylight on the 23rd. All ships involved arrived back at Alexandria on the 23rd.

23 SEPTEMBER 1941

Minelayer LATONA departed Alexandria, Egypt, with destroyers JERVIS, KIMBERLEY, and HASTY for Tobruk, Libya, in Operation SUPERCHARGE convoy serial 9. These ships arrived back at Alexandria on the 24th.

	Also sailing for Tobruk was petrol carrier PASS OF BALMAHA (758grt), Greek steamer SAMOS (1208grt), plus lighters A.2 and A.9, carrying tanks, escorted by antisubmarine whaler FALK and minesweeping trawler SOIKA (per Med Fleet WD -- SOTRA in Preliminary Narrative) in Serial 11. The convoy arrived on the 26th.
	Submarine TORBAY made an unsuccessful attack on a steamer off Suda Bay, Crete.

24 SEPTEMBER 1941

	Minelayer ABDIEL departed Alexandria, Egypt, with destroyers NAPIR, KINGSTON, and HOTSPUR for Tobruk, Libya, in Operation SUPERCHARGE convoy serial 10.
	Destroyers JAGUAR and GRIFFIN were at sea exercising off Alexandria and remained at sea for the night of 24/25 September.
	Submarine TETRARCH made an unsuccessful attack on a steamer in the Gulf of Athens.
	Greek submarine TRITON made an unsuccessful attack on Italian naval ship CYCLOPS off Suda Bay, Crete.

25 SEPTEMBER 1941

	Australian destroyer VENDETTA arrived at Alexandria, Egypt, from Haifa, Palestine.

26 SEPTEMBER 1941

	An Italian convoy departed Piraeus, Greece, for Candia, Crete, with steamers CITTA DI MARSALA (2480grt), CITTA DI BASTIA (2499grt), TRAPANI (1855grt), and SANTAGANTA (4299grt) escorted by Italian destroyer SELLA, torpedo boat LIBRA, and AMC BRIONI.
	Submarine TETRARCH (Lt Cdr Greenway) sank Italian steamer **CITTA DI BASTIA** (2499grt) while attacking a convoy off Piraeus, Greece in 36, 21N, 24, 23E. (Other sources claim the steamer was only (1499grt).)
	Minelaying cruiser LATONA departed Alexandria, Egypt, with destroyers JACKAL, KIMBERLEY, and HASTY for Tobruk, Libya, in Operation SUPERCHARGE convoy serial 12. The ships arrived back on the 26th.
	Antisubmarine whaler SOUTHERN SEA (344grt) attacked a submarine contact in 33, 29N, 34, 45E. Corvettes DELPHINIUM and ERICA joined the whaler, but the search was unsuccessful.
0900	The Mediterranean Fleet departed Alexandria, Egypt, with battleships QUEEN ELIZABETH, BARHAM, and VALIANT, light cruisers AJAX, NEPTUNE, and HOBART, plus destroyers JERVIS, JUPITER, KINGSTON, KIPLING, HERO, HOTSPUR, DECOY, and VENDETTA to act as a diversion for Operation HALBERD being carried out by Force H in the western Mediterranean.
1430	Destroyer NAPIER departed Alexandria after refuelling and joined the Mediterranean Fleet at sea.

27 SEPTEMBER 1941

	Submarine TETRARCH (Lt Cdr Greenway) made an unsuccessful attack on a steamer in Zea Channel.
	Later that day, TETRARCH sank Greek coastal steamer **PANAJOTIS KRAMOTTOS** (120grt) with gunfire southwest of Milos, Greece.
	Minelaying cruiser ABDIEL departed Alexandria, Egypt, with destroyers KANDAHAR, JAGUAR, and GRIFFIN for Tobruk, Libya, in Operation SUPERCHARGE convoy serial 13. The ships arrived back at Alexandria on the 28th, and Operation SUPERCHARGE came to an end.
	Also sailing on this date was Operation SUPERCHARGE convoy serial 14. Antisubmarine trawler WOLBOROUGH departed Alexandria with lighters A.7 and A.11 plus store ship MIRANDA. The convoy turned back to Alexandria on the 28th after bombing damaged lighter A.11. They sailed again from Alexandria on the 29th and arrived on 1 October.
	Store ship TIBERIO departed Alexandria, Egypt, on this date in Operation SUPERCHARGE convoy serial 15 and arrived at Mersa Matruh, Egypt. She sailed from Mersa Matruh on the 28th and was damaged by British bombing on the 30th. She finally arrived at Tobruk, Libya on 1 October.
	In Operation SUPERCHARGE; 6308 officers and men and 2100 tons of stores were carried to Tobruk, Libya, while 5444 officers and men, 544 wounded, and one prisoner of war were brought back to Alexandria, Egypt, from Tobruk.
1400	The Mediterranean Fleet returned to Alexandria.

28 SEPTEMBER 1941

	Corvette HYACINTH sank Italian submarine **FISALIA** (Cdr Acunto) off Jaffa, Palestine, in 32, 19N, 34, 17E.
	Submarine TETRARCH (Lt Cdr Greenway) damaged German steamer **YALOVA** (3750grt) twenty miles south of San Giorgio. The crew was able to beach the steamer to prevent her sinking, but she was finished off on 3 October by submarine TALISMAN.
	Destroyers NAPIER and JACKAL departed Alexandria, Egypt, to reinforce the Suez Escort Force. The destroyers passed through the Canal on the 29th.

29 SEPTEMBER 1941

	Light cruiser GALATEA departed Port Said, Egypt.

| | Australian destroyer VENDETTA departed Alexandria, Egypt, with two motor launches for Haifa, Palestine. |

Black Sea
Long. E27, 00 – E43, 00   Lat. N48, 00 – N41, 00

1 SEPTEMBER 1941

| | Russian cruisers CHERVONA UKRAINA and KOMINTERN with destroyers SOOBRAZITELNY, BESPOSHCHADNY, NEZAMOZHNIK, BOIKI and SHAUMYAN supported the Russian army units surrounded at Odessa, Ukraine. The ships bombarded Romanian positions at Dofinovka and Ilyichevka plus the Romanian coastal battery in Fontanka. The naval support continued until 5 September and caused considerable Romanian casualties. |

2 SEPTEMBER 1941

	Russian submarines S-31, S-32, S-33, S-34, SHCH-208, SHCH-213, and SHCH-214 operated off the southwest coast of Romania and Bulgaria until 14 September.
	Russian submarines SHCH-212 and SHCH-216 operated in the western part of the Black Sea.
	Small Russian submarines M-31, M-32, M-33, M-34, M-35, M-51, M-58, M-62 and M-111 operated off the Ukrainian southwest coast.

4 SEPTEMBER 1941

| | Russian submarine S-32 unsuccessfully attacked Hungarian steamer CORDELIA (1357grt) off the Bulgarian coast. |
| | Russian submarine S-33 unsuccessfully attacked Hungarian steamer SZEGED (grt) off the Bulgarian coast. |

5 SEPTEMBER 1941

| | Russian cruiser KOMINTERN bombarded the Romanian coastal battery at Fontanka. |

7 SEPTEMBER 1941

	Russian destroyer leader KHARKOV with destroyers BOIKI and SPOSOBNY bombard Romanian positions around Odessa, Ukraine, after delivering VAdm F. S. Oktyabrski to the city for discussions. Russian destroyer DZERZHINSKI joined the bombardment group. During the bombardment, German aircraft damaged destroyer SPOSOBNY with bomb near misses.
	Russian submarines M-34 and M-36 took up patrol positions off Constanza, Romania.
	Russian submarine S-34 unsuccessfully attacked Romanian gunboat DUMITRESCU off Constanza, Romania.
	Russian submarines SHCH-208 and SHCH-213 patrolled off Fidonisi with M-35 and then later with M-58 and M-62.
	Russian submarine L-4 (Capt 3rd Class Polyakov) laid a minefield off Varna, Bulgaria.

11 SEPTEMBER 1941

| | Russian cruiser KRASNY KAVKAZ bombarded Romanian positions around Odessa. |
| | Russian submarine M-111 relieved M-51 on patrol along the southwest Ukrainian coast. |

12 SEPTEMBER 1941

| | German aircraft damaged Russian cruiser KRASNY KAVKAZ off Odessa, Ukraine. She sustained minimal damage during the attacks. |

13 SEPTEMBER 1941

| | Russian submarine L-5 (Lt Cdr Zhdanov) laid mines off Kap Galata, Bulgaria. |

14 SEPTEMBER 1941

| | Russian submarine L-4 (Capt 3rd Class Polyakov) laid a minefield off Georgi, Bulgaria. |
| | Russian submarine L-5 (Lt Cdr Zhdanov) laid mines off Varna, Bulgaria. |

15 SEPTEMBER 1941

	Russian submarine L-4 (Capt 3rd Class Polyakov) laid a minefield off Varna, Bulgaria.
	Russian submarine L-5 (Lt Cdr Zhdanov) laid mines off Ochakov, Ukraine.
	A mine laid by Russian submarine L-4 sank Bulgarian steamer **CHIPKA** (2304grt) off Varna, Bulgaria. German motor minesweepers cleared the remaining mines out of the area.
	Russian submarines D-5, SHCH-209, SHCH-211 and S-31 patrolled along the Bulgarian coast until 29 September.
	Russian submarines M-34, M-35, M-36, M-51, M-58, M-59, M-60, M-62, M-111 and M-112 patrolled along the

	Romanian and southern Ukrainian coast until 29 September.

16 SEPTEMBER 1941

	The Russian Black Sea Fleet ran five convoys; each of two or three steamers to take the 157th Rifle Division from Novorossiysk, Russia, to Odessa escorted by cruisers CHERVONA UKRAINA, KRASNY KRYM and KOMINTERN, plus destroyers BODRY, BOIKI, BESPOSHCHADNY, BEZUPRECHNY, SPOSOBNY, SOOBRAZITELNY and FRUNZE.

17 SEPTEMBER 1941

	German aircraft damaged Russian troopships KRASNAYA ABCHAZIYA (grt), GRUZIYA (4857grt) and DNEPR (3071grt) south of Sevastopol. Russian cruiser CHERVONA UKRAINA with destroyers BOIKI, BEZUPRECHNY and NEZAMOZHNIK provided the troopships with cover.
	Russian cruiser VOROSHILOV and destroyer DZERZHINSKI bombarded German positions around Odessa, Ukraine.

18 SEPTEMBER 1941

	Russian submarine L-4 (Capt 3rd Class Polyakov) laid a minefield off Cape Galata, Bulgaria.

19 SEPTEMBER 1941

	Russian cruiser VOROSHILOV and destroyer DZERZHINSKI bombarded German positions around Odessa, Ukraine.
	A mine laid by Russian submarine L-4 sank Bulgarian steamer **RODINA** (4159grt) off Zarewo, near Varna, Bulgaria. (Other sources claim she hit an Axis mine.)
	German aircraft sank Russian monitor **UDARNY** off Tendra Island.
	Russian submarine M-111 (Lt Cdr Ioselliani) accidentally fired a torpedo at Russian minesweeper W-2 along the Ukrainian coast. Luckily it missed.

21 SEPTEMBER 1941

Night	During the night of 21/22 September, Russian cruisers KRASNY KAVKAZ and KRASNY KRYM each transported a battalion the 3rd Marine Regiment from Sevastopol to Odessa, Ukraine, and landed them behind the Romanian 13th and 15th Infantry Divisions at Grigorevka, Ukraine, as a diversion for the Russian 157th and 421st Rifle Divisions to attack the coastal batteries at Fontanka and Dofinovka. Russian destroyers BOIKI, BEZUPRECHNY and BESPOSHCHADNY escorted the cruisers. Destroyer FRUNZE preceded the landing force to coordinate with gunboat KRASNAYA ARMENIYA, departing Odessa with a tug, twenty-three cutters and ten barges to unload the troops on the beaches.
	Russian submarine D-5 unsuccessfully attacked Italian tanker TAMPICO (4958grt) north of Varna, Bulgaria. Later the same day, Russian submarine M-34 also unsuccessfully attacked the Italian tanker south of Constanza, Romania.
>1200	In the afternoon, Ju87 aircraft of STG.77 attacked the landing force and sank destroyer **FRUNZE** and gunboat **KRASNAYA ARMENIYA** plus tugboat **OP-8** off the Tendra peninsula.

22 SEPTEMBER 1941

	German Ju87 aircraft of STG.77 attacked Russian destroyers BOIKI, BEZUPRECHNY and BESPOSHCHADNY while they provided fire support to troops off Odessa, Ukraine. Bomb near misses damaged BEZUPRECHNY. Bomb hits heavily damaged BESPOSHCHADNY, and she was towed into Odessa by tug SP-14 covered by destroyer SOOBRAZITELNY.

24 SEPTEMBER 1941

	Mines laid by Russian submarine L-5 sank Romanian escort vessel **THERESIA WALLNER** plus tugboats **DROSSEL** and **BRUSTERORT** off Ochakov, Ukraine.

28 SEPTEMBER 1941

	Russian submarine M-34 unsuccessfully attacked Italian tanker TAMPICO (4958grt) off Varna, Bulgaria.

29 SEPTEMBER 1941

	Russian submarine L-5 (Lt Cdr Zhdanov) laid mines off Mangalia, Romania.
	Russian submarine SHCH-211 (Lt Cdr Devyatko) sank Italian tanker **SUPERGA** (6154grt) off Varna, Bulgaria, in 43, 00N, 27, 58E.
	A mine sank Russian submarine **SHCH-206** off Sulina, Romania.

30 SEPTEMBER 1941

A German aerial mine heavily damaged Russian destroyer SOVERSHENNY while she was conducting acceptance trials near Sevastopol, Ukraine.

Red Sea
Long. E32, 00 – E43, 00   Lat. N30, 00 – N15, 00

4 SEPTEMBER 1941

German Ju88 aircraft of I/LG.1 and II/LG.1 heavily damaged steamer HARPALYCUS (5629grt) off Ashrafi Reef, Gulf of Suez in the Red Sea. Steamers CITY OF AUCKLAND (8336grt), ROSS (4978grt), and KING EDGAR (4536grt) were also attacked, but were not damaged. HARPALYCUS arrived at Suez, Egypt, on the 5th.

5 SEPTEMBER 1941

South African antisubmarine trawler PROTEA arrived at Suez, Egypt, from South Africa to join the 22nd Anti Submarine Trawler Group.

7 SEPTEMBER 1941

During the night, German Ju88 aircraft of I/LG.1 and II/LG.1 sank American steamer **STEEL SEAFARER** (5718grt) about two hundred sea miles south of Suez, Egypt, in the Red Sea. Twenty-four survivors reached Shadwan Island by boat. These survivors were picked up by antiaircraft ship COVENTRY. A further twelve crewman reached Hurghada by boat. No crewmen were lost in the air attack.

8 SEPTEMBER 1941

Antiaircraft ship CARLISLE departed Suez, Egypt, to relieve antiaircraft ship COVENTRY at Anchorage F in the Red Sea in position 27, 49N, 33, 57E.

10 SEPTEMBER 1941

German Ju88 aircraft of I/LG.1 and II/LG.1 damaged Panamanian steamer HONDURAS (4524grt) off Suez in 28, 04N, 33, 29E. The steamer was able to arrive at Zafarana, Egypt, under her own power.

11 SEPTEMBER 1941

A German air attack damaged American steamer ARKANSAN (6997grt) at Port Suez, Egypt.

12 SEPTEMBER 1941

A mine sank tug **TAI KOO** (688grt) between Aden and Massawa, Eritrea, in 16, 45N, 40, 05E. Twenty-six crewmen were lost. Cdr J. R. Stenhouse DSO, OBE, DSC, RD RNR Rtd, on passage to SHEBA, was also lost. Thirty-seven crewmen were rescued.

15 SEPTEMBER 1941

Corvette PRIMULA arrived at Suez, Egypt, from Britain to join the 10th Corvette Group.

20 SEPTEMBER 1941

Steamer CLAN FORBES (7529grt) departed Suez, Egypt, with twenty-four officers and four hundred eight other ranks, and troopship GLENROY (9809grt) departed Suez with thirty-seven officers and five hundred forty-four other ranks for Port T, which was the Indian Ocean anchorage at Addu, Ethiopia. The ships were escorted from Aden by heavy cruiser CORNWALL and arrived on the 30th.

23 SEPTEMBER 1941

Destroyer JUPITER arrived at Suez, Egypt, to join the Mediterranean Fleet after having proceeded independently from Gibraltar. The destroyer was in need of docking for repair to serious leaks in her oil fuel tanks. The destroyer arrived at Alexandria, Egypt, on the 25th.

27 SEPTEMBER 1941

T/Sub-Lt (A) C. F. G. Carr-Gregg RNVR and Air Mechanic D. V. Blacklaws were killed when their Fulmar aircraft of RN Fulmar Flight Dekheila crashed off Hurguarda in the Red Sea during a practice attack on a warship.

29 SEPTEMBER 1941

Destroyers AVON VALE and ERIDGE arrived at Suez, Egypt, from Gibraltar, via Cape Town, South Africa. The destroyers were held at Suez for duty with Suez Escort Force until 5 October. At that time they proceeded to Alexandria, Egypt, and joined the 2nd Destroyer Flotilla in the Mediterranean Fleet.

Arabian Sea

Long. E43, 00 – E77, 00   Lat. N31, 00 – N00, 00

1 SEPTEMBER 1941

A fire destroyed naval auxiliary **TUNA** (662grt) at Aden. She was declared a constructive total loss.

17 SEPTEMBER 1941

Dutch steamer WESTERNLAND (16,231grt) departed Bombay, India, for Singapore with 2061 personnel. From Ceylon, light cruiser DAUNTLESS escorted the steamer.

20 SEPTEMBER 1941

Convoy WS.10 arrived at Bombay, India, escorted by light cruiser EMERALD.

23 SEPTEMBER 1941

Troopship STIRLING CASTLE (25,550grt) departed Bombay, India, for Singapore with 1650 personnel. Light cruiser EMERALD escorted the troopship to a position in 05, 26N, 80, 59E, then light cruiser GLASGOW escorted the troopship to a position in 06, 05N, 93E. Light cruiser DAUNTLESS escorted the troopship on to Singapore, arriving on the 29th.

26 SEPTEMBER 1941

Heavy cruiser EXETER departed Aden.

28 SEPTEMBER 1941

Convoy BP.16 departed Bombay, India, escorted by Greek cruiser GEORGIOS AVEROFF.
The cruiser was detached from the convoy en route and arrived back at Bombay on 4 October for boiler repairs.
The convoy arrived at Basra, Iraq, on 5 October.
Convoys BP.17 through BP.40 in April 1942 travelled without escort between Bombay and Basra.

INDIAN OCEAN

East of South Africa

Long. E25, 00 – E60, 00   Lat. S00, 00 – S60, 00

5 SEPTEMBER 1941

Heavy cruiser HAWKINS arrived at Durban, South Africa.

6 SEPTEMBER 1941

Part of convoy WS.10 arrived at Durban, South Africa, with troopships ORCADES (23,456grt), ANDES (25,689grt), CAMERONIA (16,297grt), HIGHLAND PATRIOT (14,172grt), NEA HELLAS (16,991grt), RANGITIKI (16,698grt), DIOMED (10,374grt), INDIAN PRINCE (6376grt), and MANCHESTER PORT (5469grt) escorted by heavy cruiser HAWKINS.

8 SEPTEMBER 1941

Troopship BRITANNIC (26,943grt) was detached from convoy WS.10 and arrived at Durban, South Africa, to embark passengers from troopship CAMERONIA (16,297grt).

9 SEPTEMBER 1941

Troopship BRITANNIC (26,943grt) and steamer ARONDA (4062grt) departed Durban, South Africa, and rejoined the part of convoy WS.10 escorted by heavy cruiser HAWKINS. After the rendezvous, AMC CARNARVON CASTLE was detached from convoy WS.10 with VOLENDAM (15,434grt), INDRAPOERA (10,825grt), PHEMIUS (7406grt), and NIGERSTROOM (4639grt) to Durban. Heavy cruiser HAWKINS then escorted the convoy until 15 September to a position in 03, 25S, 51, 12E, when light cruiser EMERALD took over the convoy escort.

15 SEPTEMBER 1941

Light cruiser EMERALD took the far east bound part of convoy WS.10 to Bombay, India, arriving on 20 September.

South Indian Ocean
Long. E60, 00 – E95, 00   Lat. N00, 00 – S60, 00

23 SEPTEMBER 1941

German AMC SCHIFF.41/KORMORAN (FKpt Detmers) sank Greek steamer **STAMATIOS G. EMBIRICOS** (3941grt) south of the Maldives in 01, 01S, 64, 30E. Five crewmen were lost, while five crewmen and the captain were picked up. Another twenty-four survivors in a boat lost touch in the dark and were rescued three days later by the German AMC. They became prisoners of war.

Bay of Bengal
Long. E77, 00 – E95, 00   Lat. N22, 00 – N00, 00

20 SEPTEMBER 1941

Steamer ELLENGA (5196grt) arrived at Madras, India, from Penang, Malaya.

Light cruiser EMERALD arrived at Colombo, Ceylon, from the Seychelles.

Malaya
Long. E95, 00 – E105, 00   Lat. N17, 00 – N00, 00

11 SEPTEMBER 1941

Steamer ELLENGA (5196grt) departed Singapore for Penang, Malaya.

13 SEPTEMBER 1941

Steamer ELLENGA (5196grt) departed Penang, Malaya, for Madras, India, escorted by light cruiser DAUNTLESS to a position in 10N, 84E.

25 SEPTEMBER 1941

Dutch steamer WESTERNLAND (16,231grt) arrived at Singapore from Bombay, India, with 2061 service personnel.

30 SEPTEMBER 1941

Light cruiser DAUNTLESS arrived at Singapore.

Light cruiser DANAE departed Singapore.

West of Australia
Long. E95, 00 – E125, 00   Lat. S15, 00 – S60, 00

12 SEPTEMBER 1941

Australian troop convoy US.12A departed Fremantle, Australia, with troopships QUEEN ELIZABETH (83,673grt) and QUEEN MARY (81,235grt).

28 SEPTEMBER 1941

Australian troop convoy US.12B departed Fremantle, Australia, with troopships AQUITANIA (44,786grt), JOHAN VAN OLDENBARNEVELDT (19,429grt), MARNIX VAN ST ALDEGONDE (19,355grt), and SIBAJAK (12,226grt).
Troopship SIBAJAK was later detached from the convoy to Singapore.

PACIFIC OCEAN

South China Sea
Long. E105, 00 – E120, 00   Lat. N27, 00 – N10, 00

7 SEPTEMBER 1941

IJN cargo ship KIMISHIMA MARU (5193grt) departed her support position south of China for Sasebo, Kyushu.

IJN cargo ship MYOKO MARU (5086grt) departed her support position south of China for Sasebo, Kyushu.

8 SEPTEMBER 1941

Vichy French light cruiser LAMOTTE-PICQUET departed Saigon, French Indochina, for Osaka, Japan, where she arrived on the 15th for urgent repairs.

10 SEPTEMBER 1941

IJN seaplane tender SANYO MARU (8360grt) was reassigned to the Japanese Third Fleet in the 12th Seaplane Tender Division with the seaplane tender KAMIKAWA MARU and moved to Cam Ranh Bay, French Indochina.

11 SEPTEMBER 1941

IJN cargo ship TATSUWA MARU (6335grt) departed French Indochina for Takao, Formosa.

18 SEPTEMBER 1941

IJN cargo ship TOYO MARU (2470grt) departed her support position south of China for Takao, Formosa.

22 SEPTEMBER 1941

IJN cargo ship NACHISAN MARU (4433grt) arrived at her support position south of China.

24 SEPTEMBER 1941

IJN cargo ship MANKO MARU (4471grt) departed her support position south of China for Takao, Formosa.

Dutch East Indies   Long. E105, 00 – E120, 00   Lat. N10, 00 – S15, 00

13 SEPTEMBER 1941

IJN oiler SAN DIEGO MARU (7269grt) departed Tarakan, Borneo.

28 SEPTEMBER 1941

A Dutch MLD (*Marine Luchtvaart Dienst,* the Dutch Naval Aviation Service) aircraft reported a suspect ship in the Ceram Sea. Two Dutch destroyers were sent to investigate, but did not find the intruder, "probably an IJN auxiliary". The destroyers were sent because Dutch patrol boat VALK, acting as the scouting vessel in the Eastern Archipelago, could not reach the position in time to intercept the ship.

South of Australia   Long. E125, 00 – E150, 00   Lat. S31, 00 – S60, 00

25 SEPTEMBER 1941

Australian light cruiser ADELAIDE departed Melbourne, Australia, escorting a steamer to southeast of Chatham Island. The light cruiser then proceeded to Wellington, New Zealand, arriving on the 30th.

East China Sea   Long. E120, 00 – E130, 00   Lat. N42, 00 – N20, 00

1 SEPTEMBER 1941

IJN cargo ship NACHISAN MARU (4433grt) departed Takao, Formosa, to support Japanese operations south of China.

3 SEPTEMBER 1941

IJN patrol boat SHURI MARU (1857grt) arrived at Ryojun from a north China coastal patrol.

10 SEPTEMBER 1941

IJN patrol boat SHURI MARU (1857grt) departed Ryojun on a north China coastal patrol.

15 SEPTEMBER 1941

Japanese liner TATSUTA MARU (16,975grt) arrived at Shanghai, China, in the evening.

20 SEPTEMBER 1941

IJN river gunboat TOBA (grt) was attached to the Japanese China Area Fleet (VAdm Koga Mineichi) Shanghai Base Force.

25 SEPTEMBER 1941

IJN seaplane tender SANUKI MARU was attached to the headquarters of the Japanese 2nd Base Unit, Japanese Third Fleet at Takao, Formosa.

Sea of Japan
Long. E128, 00 – E143, 00   Lat. N55, 00 – N33, 00

1 SEPTEMBER 1941

The Japanese Naval General Staff (NGS) liaison officer, Cdr Ariizumi Tatsunosuke, inspected naval auxiliary CHIYODA at Sasebo, Kyushu. Captain Harada informed him of the harbour-penetrating concept developed with the small two-men submarines and asked that Ariizumi forward the idea to the Japanese General Staff (NGS). Harada, Lt Iwasa Naoji and Lt/JG Matsuo Keiu compiled several studies about possible attacks on naval bases at Pearl Harbor, San Francisco, Hong-Kong, Singapore and Sydney, Australia.

The flag of Japanese Carrier Division 5, Japanese First Air Fleet was hoisted aboard aircraft carrier TAIYO at Sasebo, Kyushu.

2 SEPTEMBER 1941

IJN aircraft carrier TAIYO completed her conversion into an escort carrier at Sasebo.

5 SEPTEMBER 1941

IJN seaplane tender KIMIKAWA MARU arrived at Sasebo, Kyushu, and proceeded to Maizuru and Saeki, Japan, where she began working up to combat efficiency.

IJN oiler KUROSHIO MARU (10,383grt) was registered as an auxiliary oil transport in the Sasebo Naval District.

7 SEPTEMBER 1941

IJN aircraft ferry FUJIKAWA MARU arrived at Sasebo, Kyushu.

8 SEPTEMBER 1941

IJN oiler KORYU MARU (880grt) arrived at Sasebo, Kyushu.

10 SEPTEMBER 1941

IJN escort aircraft carrier TAIYO had the Flag of Japanese Carrier Division 5, Japanese First Air Fleet removed, and thereafter she was assigned to Japanese Carrier Division 4.

12 SEPTEMBER 1941

IJN oiler KORYU MARU (880grt) departed Sasebo, Kyushu, for the central China coast area.

13 SEPTEMBER 1941

IJN battleship KONGO arrived at Sasebo, Kyushu, and began to prepare for combat readiness.

20 SEPTEMBER 1941

IJN cargo ship SENKO MARU (2618grt) was registered as an auxiliary transport and attached to the Sasebo Naval District.

23 SEPTEMBER 1941

IJN oiler KORYU MARU (880grt) returned to Sasebo, Kyushu, from the central China coast area.

27 SEPTEMBER 1941

IJN oiler KORYU MARU (880grt) departed Sasebo, Kyushu, for the central China coast area.

East of Australia
Long. E140, 00 – E155, 00   Lat. S12, 00 – S40, 00

5 SEPTEMBER 1941

New Zealand light cruiser LEANDER departed Sydney, Australia with troopship AQUITANIA (44,786grt) for Wellington, New Zealand.

East of Japan
Long. E130, 00 – E180, 00   Lat. N55, 00 – N30, 00

1 SEPTEMBER 1941

The IJN requisitioned Japanese passenger/cargo ship AIKOKU MARU (10,437grt) for conversion into an armed merchant cruiser.

The IJN requisitioned Japanese tanker TOA MARU (10,052grt).

IJN converted minelayer TATSUMIYA MARU was attached to Japanese Minelaying Division 17.

	IJN battleship HYUGA was assigned to the Japanese First Fleet (VAdm Takasu Shiro) in Battleship Division 2 with battleships ISE (F), FUSO and YAMASHIRO. The HYUGA was home based at the Kure Naval Base for repairs and crew rotations.
	IJN battleship HIEI departed Hashirajima, Japan.
	IJN seaplane tender KIMIKAWA MARU (6863grt) was assigned to the Japanese Fifth Fleet in Cruiser Division 21 with the light cruisers TAMA and KISO. Her aircraft carried tail code "X-xx."
	IJN minelayer ITSUKUSHIMA was attached to Japanese Mine Division 17.
	IJN rescue ship SAWAKAZE was attached to the Tateyama air station to assist in flight training.
	Japanese liner KAMAKURA MARU (17,526grt) arrived at Yokosuka, Japan.
	IJN aircraft carrier SHOKAKU was assigned to Japanese Carrier Division 5, Japanese First Air Fleet, along with the KASUGA MARU (future light aircraft carrier TAIYO).
	IJN oiler TERUKAWA MARU (6433grt) departed Kobe, Japan, for Central and South America, Saigon, Indochina and Yokohama, Japan.

2 SEPTEMBER 1941

	The IJN requisitioned Japanese cargo ship KENYO MARU (6486grt).

3 SEPTEMBER 1941

	IJN auxiliary cruiser KONGO MARU (8624grt) began her modernization at Harima Zosen, Aioi, Japan, with 4.7-inch (120-mm) guns installed at the bow and the stern.
	Japanese cargo ship MITAKESAN MARU (4441grt) began her conversion at Uraga Shipyard, Uraga, Japan.

4 SEPTEMBER 1941

	IJN oiler TOEI MARU (10,023grt) began further conversion at Mitsubishi, Yokohama, Japan, probably to allow at-sea refuelling.
	IJN battleship HIEI arrived at Yokosuka, Japan.
	Japanese cargo ship ARATAMA MARU (6784grt) began conversion into a weapons/ammunition ship at Kawasaki Zosen, Kobe, Japan.
	Japanese liner KAMAKURA MARU (17,526grt) departed Yokosuka, Japan.
	IJN cargo ship KUNISHIMA MARU (4083grt) departed Yokosuka, Japan, for the South Seas area, probably Truk.

5 SEPTEMBER 1941

	IJN AMC AIKOKU MARU was registered as a warship and attached to the Kure Naval District. She began the installation of four single mount 152-mm guns, two 76-mm/40 cal antiaircraft guns, Type 93 13.2-mm MGs and two 533-mm torpedo tubes at Mitsui Engineering & Shipbuilding, Tamano, Japan.
	Japanese cargo ship KENYO MARU (6486grt) was registered as a converted merchant transport (oil supply) in the Yokosuka Naval District.
	IJN AMC AWATA MARU was registered in the IJN as a special auxiliary cruiser in the Kure Naval District.
	IJN seaplane tender SANUKI MARU completed her conversion and was registered in the IJN as a converted seaplane tender in the Maizuru Naval District. Her aircraft complement was six Type 95 Kawanishi E8N2 "Dave" two-seat float biplanes with two E8N2 aircraft in reserve. Her aircraft code was "IIB-xx" and her call sign was JGBN. She was assigned to the Japanese Third Fleet, 2nd Base Force.
	The IJN requisitioned Japanese cargo ship KAMOGAWA MARU (6441grt) and she began conversion to an armed auxiliary aircraft transport. 4.7-inch guns were installed at the bow and the stern.
	Japanese tanker AKEBONO MARU (10,182grt) completed several trips transporting heavy oil from Canada, Borneo, and Northern Sakhalin. Requisitioned by the IJN, she was registered in the Yokosuka Naval District as a converted merchant transport (oil supply).
	IJN AMC ASAKA MARU (7359grt) arrived at Japan and was approved for full conversion into an armed merchant cruiser.
	Japanese passenger/cargo ship KINRYU MARU (9310grt) began her conversion into an armed merchant cruiser at Kure, Japan.
	Japanese cargo ship ONOE MARU (6667grt) was rated a specially installed auxiliary transport in the Kure Naval District.
	IJN repair ship YAMASHIMO MARU departed Kure, Japan, for Otaru, Japan, and then she made calls at Nagoya, Kure, Nagasaki, Sasebo, Yokosuka, Osaka, Saitozaki, Hikari, Tama and Sakito.
	IJN ammunition ship KOGYO MARU (6353grt) was registered in the Kure Naval District as an auxiliary transport ship.
	IJN ammunition ship HIDE MARU (5181grt) was registered in the Maizuru Naval District as an auxiliary ammunition transport.
	IJN auxiliary cruiser KONGO MARU (8624grt) was attached to the Japanese Fourth Fleet (South Seas Force)

at Truk.

IJN cargo ship KOFUKU MARU (3209grt) was registered as an auxiliary transport and attached to the Maizuru Naval District.

IJN cargo ship NACHISAN MARU (4433grt) arrived at Yawata, Japan.

6 SEPTEMBER 1941

IJN AMC AWATA MARU was assigned to the IJN 22nd (Auxiliary Cruiser) Squadron (RAdm Horiuchi Shigenori) in the Japanese Fifth Fleet (VAdm Boshiro Hosogaya) with ASAKA MARU and AKAGI MARU.

IJN AMC ASAKA MARU was assigned to the IJN 22nd (Auxiliary Cruiser) Squadron (RAdm Horiuchi Shigenori) in the Japanese Fifth Fleet (VAdm Boshiro Hosogaya).

IJN aircraft carrier SHOKAKU departed Ariake, Japan, for Yokosuka, Japan.

7 SEPTEMBER 1941

The IJN requisitioned Japanese tanker NIPPON MARU (9975grt).

IJN transport KOMAKI MARU arrived at Tateyama, Japan.

Japanese cargo ship KOGYO MARU (6353grt) began her conversion into an ammunition ship at Kawasaki shipyard, Kobe, Japan.

8 SEPTEMBER 1941

IJN aircraft carrier SHOKAKU arrived at Yokosuka, Japan. The Commander of the Japanese First Air Fleet departed aboard the ship.

IJN minelayer ITSUKUSHIMA arrived at Yokosuka, Japan.

IJN AMC ASAKA MARU entered Osaka Tekkosho to begin full conversion into an armed merchant cruiser.

9 SEPTEMBER 1941

The IJN requisitioned Japanese tanker HISHI MARU No.2 (856grt) and she was registered at the Kure Naval District as a special transport ship (oiler).

The IJN requisitioned Japanese cargo ship TENYO MARU (6843grt) at Tokyo, Japan, and began conversion into an auxiliary minelayer.

Japanese passenger/cargo ship TEIKAI MARU (9492grt) (ex German **MOSEL** (9492grt)) was assigned the signal letters JWKQ for safe passage through Japanese controlled waters.

10 SEPTEMBER 1941

IJN aircraft carrier SHOKAKU became the flagship of Japanese Combined Fleet Carrier Division 5 and remained at Yokosuka for the rest of the month.

IJN battleship HIEI was assigned to the Japanese First Fleet (VAdm Takasu Shiro) at the Japanese Combined Fleet anchorage at Hashirajima, Japan, in Hiroshima Bay. Battleship Division 3 (VAdm Mikawa Gunichi) included battleships HARUNA, KONGO and KIRISHIMA.

IJN light cruiser NAGARA was assigned to the IJN Cruiser Division 16 in the Japanese Third Fleet (VAdm Takahashi Ibo) with ASHIGARA (F), light cruisers KUMA and NATORI plus Destroyer Squadron 5.

11 SEPTEMBER 1941

The IJN requisitioned Japanese cargo ship SAGARA MARU (7189grt) and she was converted into a seaplane tender.

The IJN requisitioned Japanese tanker SAN CLEMENTE MARU (7335grt).

The IJA requisitioned Japanese cargo ship TEIYO MARU (6081grt).

12 SEPTEMBER 1941

The IJN requisitioned Japanese passenger/cargo ship KIKU MARU and she was registered as a specially installed netlayer in the Yokosuka Naval District. She began conversion at the Yokosuka Navy Yard.

IJN oiler MANJU MARU (6515grt) departed Nabilsky, Sakhalin Island.

14 SEPTEMBER 1941

The IJN requisitioned Japanese cargo ship TATSUGAMI MARU (7064grt) to become an ammunition ship.

15 SEPTEMBER 1941

IJN battleship FUSO was assigned to the Japanese First Fleet (VAdm Takasu Shiro) in Battleship Division 2 with battleships ISE (F), YAMASHIRO and HYUGA.

Vichy French light cruiser LAMOTTE-PICQUET arrived at Osaka, Japan, from Saigon, French Indochina, for urgent repairs.

Japanese cargo ship TATSUGAMI MARU (7064grt) began her conversion into an IJN ammunition ship at the

	Mitsubishi Heavy Industries, Ltd. shipyard at Kobe, Japan.
	IJN auxiliary minelayer TENYO MARU (6843grt) arrived at Hirima shipyard.

16 SEPTEMBER 1941

	IJN oiler KYOEI MARU No.2 (1192grt) began her conversion into a fleet oiler.

17 SEPTEMBER 1941

	IJN minesweeper W-20 was launched and began equipping for operational use.
	IJN aircraft carrier HOSHO departed Hashirajima, Japan, and arrived at Kure, Japan, later the same day.

18 SEPTEMBER 1941

	Japanese tanker KOKUYO MARU (10,026grt) arrived at Kure Naval Yard and began conversion into a naval auxiliary.
	IJN battleship HYUGA was dry-docked at the Kure Navy Yard.
	IJN oiler MANJU MARU (6515grt) arrived at Tokuyama, Japan. She probably loaded fuel oil.

20 SEPTEMBER 1941

	IJN AMC HOKOKU MARU was registered in the Kure Naval District.
	Japanese tanker TOA MARU (10,052grt) was registered in the Kure Naval District. She arrived at Kure Naval Yard to begin conversion into a naval auxiliary.
	IJN aircraft carrier HOSHO was photographed alongside the starboard side of the battleship YAMATO while she was fitting out at Kure.
	The SAGARA MARU (7189grt) completed her conversion and was registered in the Yokosuka Naval District as a converted seaplane tender. Her aircraft complement was six Type 0 Mitsubishi F1M2 "Pete" two-seat float reconnaissance biplanes with two Type 95 Kawanishi E8N2 "Dave" two-seat float reconnaissance biplanes in reserve. Her aircraft code was "UVI-xx" and her call sign was JNPO.
	IJN oiler NIPPON MARU was registered in the IJN as a converted merchant transport (oil supply) in the Kure Naval District.
	IJN auxiliary ship MAMIYA (7,000grt) and light aircraft carrier HOSHO were anchored near a large fitting-out pontoon servicing battleship YAMATO during her later stage of construction. Heavy cruisers KAKO and KINUGASA were anchored nearby in the Kure Navy Yard.
	IJN submarine chaser CH-19 was completed and registered in the Kure Naval District.
	Japanese tanker SAN CLEMENTE MARU (7335grt) began conversion into a naval auxiliary that would allow her to perform at-sea refuelling at Osaka, Naniwa Dockyard.
	IJN AMC SAIGON MARU was registered as a special auxiliary cruiser in the Kure Naval District.
	IJN ammunition ship TATSUGAMI MARU (7064grt) was registered by the IJN as an auxiliary transport ship in the Maizuru Naval District.
	Japanese cargo ship TENYO MARU (6843grt) began her conversion into a large specially installed minelayer. She was registered in the Kure Naval District.
	Japanese oiler KUMAGAWA MARU (6641grt) began her conversion to a general transport. She was registered as an auxiliary transport (charter) in the Maizuru Naval District.
	IJN oiler KYOEI MARU No.2 (1192grt) was registered in the Kure Naval District as an auxiliary transport (oil supply).
	IJN cargo ship KAISHO MARU (4164grt) was registered as an auxiliary transport and attached to the Yokosuka Naval District.
	IJN cargo ship MITAKESAN MARU (4441grt) was registered as an auxiliary transport and attached to the Yokosuka Naval District.
	IJN cargo ship NOJIMA MARU (7190grt) was registered as an auxiliary transport and attached to the Kure Naval District.

21 SEPTEMBER 1941

	IJN Mine Sweeping Division 21 was assembled with minesweepers W-7, W-11, W-12, and W-8.
	IJN battleship MUTSU departed Yokosuka, Japan.
	German steamer BURGENLAND (7320grt) departed Kobe, Japan, for Bordeaux, France.
	IJN oiler MANJU MARU (6515grt) departed Tokuyama, Japan, with stops at Kanogawa, Japan, and later arrived at Kure, Japan.

22 SEPTEMBER 1941

	Japanese passenger/cargo ship HIE MARU (4943grt) departed Kobe, Japan, for India.
	IJN minelayer ITSUKUSHIMA arrived at Yokohama, Japan, and was dry-docked.

Japanese passenger/cargo ship TEIKAI MARU (9492grt) arrived at Kobe, Japan.

23 SEPTEMBER 1941

IJN battleship MUTSU arrived off Murozumi, Japan.

Japanese liner KAMAKURA MARU (17,526grt) arrived at Yokosuka, Japan.

IJN steamer SAIGON MARU began conversion at Harima Zosen into an armed merchant cruiser. Four 120-mm (4.7-inch) single mount guns, one 7.7-mm machine gun and provisions for carrying and launching 500 mines were fitted.

24 SEPTEMBER 1941

Japanese tanker TOHO MARU (9997grt) began her conversion into a IJN replenishment oiler at Mitsubishi Zosen, Yokohama, Japan.

IJN oiler SHINKOKU MARU completed her conversion into a IJN replenishment oiler.

IJN cargo ship MEITEN MARU (4474grt) arrived at Yokosuka, Japan.

25 SEPTEMBER 1941

IJN battleship ISE was assigned as the flagship of the Japanese First Fleet (VAdm Takasu Shiro) in Battleship Division 2 with battleships HYUGA, FUSO and YAMASHIRO.

IJN oiler SAN DIEGO MARU arrived at Yokohama, Japan.

IJN aircraft carrier ZUIKAKU was commissioned and assigned to Kure Naval Base, Japanese First Air Fleet. After the ceremony, she departed Kobe, Japan, for Kure, Japan.

26 SEPTEMBER 1941

IJN battleship HYUGA was undocked at the Kure Navy Yard.

Japanese cargo ship KENYO MARU (6486grt) completed her conversion into a naval auxiliary at Sanoyasu dockyard.

IJN aircraft carrier ZUIKAKU arrived at Kure, Japan, from Kobe, Japan.

27 SEPTEMBER 1941

Vichy French light cruiser LAMOTTE-PICQUET departed Osaka, Japan, for Saigon, French Indochina escorting Vichy French steamer KINDIA (1972grt). They arrived at Saigon on 9 October.

28 SEPTEMBER 1941

IJN light aircraft carrier HOSHO temporarily received the Flag of Japanese Carrier Division 3, which was transferred off the next day.

The IJN requisitioned Japanese cargo ship KIYOKAWA MARU (6862grt) and she began conversion into a seaplane carrier/tender at the Yokosuka Navy Yard.

29 SEPTEMBER 1941

Japanese liner KAMAKURA MARU (17,526grt) departed Yokosuka, Japan.

30 SEPTEMBER 1941

To verify the feasibility of penetrating an enemy harbour with midget submarines, Captain Harada conducted a series of night exercises off Shikoku Island. The midget submariners practiced attacking a defended harbour that, unknown to them, resembled Pearl Harbor and returning to the IJN auxiliary CHIYODA at night at Aki Nada, Inland Sea.

IJN torpedo depot ship KAMIKAZE MARU completed her conversion and was reassigned to the Japanese Second Fleet (VAdm Nobutake Kondo).

IJN cargo ship KAISHO MARU (4164grt) completed her conversion at the Yokohama Shipyard.

IJN cargo ship KENYO MARU (6486grt) completed her conversion.

IJN cargo ship KOFUKU MARU (3209grt) completed her conversion at the Osaka Shipyard.

IJN cargo ship MITAKESAN MARU (4441grt) completed her conversion.

Gilbert – Marshall Islands

Long. E150, 00 – E180, 00   Lat. N30, 00 – N00, 00

1 SEPTEMBER 1941

IJN cargo ship KAIHEI MARU (4575grt) delivered supplies to Truk.

5 SEPTEMBER 1941

IJN AMC KONGO MARU was attached to the Japanese Fourth Fleet (South Seas Force) at Truk.

New Zealand
Long. E150, 00 – E180, 00   Lat. S25, 00 – S60, 00

8 SEPTEMBER 1941

New Zealand light cruiser LEANDER arrived at Wellington, New Zealand, from Sydney, Australia, with troopship AQUITANIA (44,786grt).

15 SEPTEMBER 1941

New Zealand light cruiser ACHILLES departed Wellington, New Zealand, as the ocean escort for troopship AQUITANIA (44,786grt) for convoy US.12B. On the 18th, the light cruiser turned the troopship over to Australian light cruisers ADELAIDE and SYDNEY and returned to Auckland, New Zealand.

South of Hawaii
Long. W180, 00 – W140, 00   Lat. S00, 00 – S60, 00

11 SEPTEMBER 1941

German AMC SCHIFF.16/ATLANTIS (KptzS Rogge) captured Norwegian steamer **SILVAPLANA** (4793grt) east of the Kermadec Islands in 26, 16S, 164, 25W. Since the ship was carrying valuable war materiel, she was sent back to Germany as a prize.

20 SEPTEMBER 1941

German AMC SCHIFF.16/ATLANTIS (KptzS Rogge) re-supplied from German steamer MUNSTERLAND (6408grt) in Operation ROMULUS off the Tuamotu Archipelago. The MUNSTERLAND had departed Japan with war materiel to try to run through the British blockade.

West of South America
Long. W140, 00 – W70, 00   Lat. N05, 00 – S60, 00

27 SEPTEMBER 1941

German AMC SCHIFF.16/ATLANTIS (KptzS Rogge) and her prise **SILVAPLANA** (4793grt) ran through Cape Horn from the South Pacific into the South Atlantic.

OCTOBER 1941
DAY-TO-DAY OPERATIONS

SECTION CONTENTS

SUMMARY 274
GENERAL 277
ARCTIC OCEAN 278

    Greenland Sea and Barents Sea 278
    White Sea 280

NORTH ATLANTIC OCEAN 281

    Iceland and North of Britain 281
    Norwegian Sea 286
    East of Canada 287
    East of United States 291
    Caribbean and Gulf of Mexico 291
    Western Approaches 292
    Central Atlantic Crossing Zone 299
    UK East Coast 301
    North Sea 304
    English Channel 304
    Bay of Biscay 305
    West of Gibraltar 305
    West of North Africa 309

SOUTH ATLANTIC OCEAN 310

    East of South America 310
    West of South Africa 310

BALTIC SEA 310

    Kattegat and Skagerrak 310
    Southern Baltic Area 310

    Gulf of Finland 311

MEDITERRANEAN SEA & MIDDLE
EAST 312

    East of Gibraltar 312
    Middle Mediterranean Sea 314
    Eastern Mediterranean Sea 318
    Black Sea 323
    Red Sea 325
    Arabian Sea 326

INDIAN OCEAN 326

    East of South Africa 326
    Bay of Bengal 327

PACIFIC OCEAN 327

    South China Sea 327
    East China Sea 328
    West of Philippine Islands 329
    Sea of Japan 329
    New Guinea and Solomon Islands 330
    East of Australia 330
    East of Japan 330
    Bonin – Mariana Islands 335
    Gilbert – Marshall Islands 335
    New Zealand 336
    Hawaii Area 336
    South of Hawaii 336
    West of United States 336

SUMMARY

GERMANY

The German Navy's efforts in the Arctic were muted by the lack of ships and aircraft, along with an ever increasingly brutal winter environment. Hitler's orders to take Murmansk were just too unrealistic to be accomplished with the force allocated. The Russians were too many and the terrain and weather too rugged to accomplish any forward advance in the Arctic.

There was more success in the Baltic. Most of the Russian Baltic Fleet was bottled up next to Leningrad, trapped by ever increasing minefields and being attacked from land and air forces. The Germans managed to capture most of the Baltic Islands held by Russian forces. Except for an occasional Russian submarine, the Baltic was now a German-controlled sea.

The U-boat attacks in the North Atlantic demonstrated that the new Wolfpack tactics could be devastating when a convoy was found and continually tracked. The combination of massed U-boat attacks with air attacks sent an increasing number of ships to the bottom. The Allied cracking of the German ENIGMA code for Naval Operations was the only German impediment to achieving massive convoy losses.

The U-boats which were moved into the Mediterranean quickly made their presence felt by the British. The movement of men and materiel to Tobruk and Malta suddenly became much more expensive.

ITALY

The Italian Navy continued valiantly to supply the Axis forces in North Africa. The convoys from Italy to North Africa had to run a dangerous gauntlet of British aircraft, surface ships and submarines. Both sides fought hard to win control of the middle Mediterranean, but the Italians lacked RADAR and did not know that the British were reading their ENIGMA encoded messages.

The Italian submarines continued to sink British ships in the North Atlantic, but their number was slowly being whittled away. Allied convoys were now better-protected, which made attacking them much more dangerous than at any time in the past. Still the Italians pressed home their attack and won the respect of the British and the Germans.

ROMANIA

Though heavily outgunned, the Romanian naval units continued to support the German and Romanian Armies attacking in southern Russia. With the aid of German aircraft, they were slowly able to move the Russian Black Sea Fleet further east, while their extensive minefields secured their supply routes in the Black Sea.

JAPAN

While Japan continued the show of diplomacy, the Military Government was given full control by the Emperor to press an attack against the Western Allies if the Americans did not back off from the crippling oil and steel embargo. Japan was on a very tight clock: their oil reserves were dwindling fast, so they either had to act quickly or be forced into inactivity by the lack of oil.

The Imperial Japanese Navy thoroughly analysed the radical plan to attack the United States Pacific Fleet at Pearl Harbor. Their new aerial torpedo modifications proved that they could attack the United States Navy (USN) battleships in the very shallow water. The route chosen was seldom used commercially, so the element of surprise could be almost guaranteed. A quick victory was very likely and essential if Japan was to win the war.

Meanwhile, Admiral Isoroku Yamamoto continued to press for a peaceful solution. Having been to America, he knew that Japan could not win a long war. He also knew that if angered, the Americans would devastate Japan in the long run. Unfortunately, the Japanese generals ruled the government, and they believed that America would not fight if given a bloody nose at the opening phases of the war.

VICHY FRANCE

The Vichy Government found its power slowly eroding as the Germans made more demands on the French people. Most French merchant ships were allocated either to German convoys to Norway or to Italian convoys to North Africa.

Meanwhile, the French people continued to organize small resistance bands in both occupied and unoccupied France. With the help of British Special Operations Executive (SOE) operatives, they began to form independent networks that provided information on the German forces in France and assistance to downed airmen. The more living conditions worsened, the more French men and women began to actively oppose the Germans.

UNITED KINGDOM

The initiation of the Arctic convoys went smoothly. The mature convoy system, coupled with strong Home Fleet covering forces, enabled the British to begin sending small amounts of aid to Russia. While the aid was small, it enabled the Russian Arctic forces to continue to fight without drawing men or materiel from the vital defence of Moscow.

The new U-boat tactics caused a very heavy strain on British escorts. The Wolfpack approach overwhelmed the convoy escort group and allowed other U-boats to sink merchant ships almost unopposed. Even with the American escorts, once found, a convoy was in for a long period of attack as the U-boats swarmed the convoy like killer bees.

The British efforts against the Italian supply convoys steadily reduced the Italian merchant fleet. Conversely, the Italian attacks on British convoys to Malta were also becoming more costly as Italian air and sea forces coordinated with German air forces to attack even well defended merchant ships. The Italian torpedo bombers became very proficient and were much feared by the Royal Navy.

The British Mediterranean Fleet was slowly recovering from their heavy losses sustained during the Greek and Crete operations. Submarines were pressed into supply runs to Malta, because the Italian and German air attacks made surface convoys too vulnerable. The arrival of the German U-boats completely surprised the British and suddenly made the sea along the Egyptian coast very dangerous.

The British were also aware of the growing probability that the Japanese would attack Malaya and the Dutch East Indies. Unfortunately, the British had very few extra forces to send to these vital areas. Still, they did try to send a few brigades, a few aircraft, and a few warships in hope of bluffing the Japanese into aborting their attack.

UNITED STATES

The United States Atlantic Fleet was now very involved in the Battle for the Atlantic. American ships began to sail in convoys escorted by USN destroyers to bolster American forces in Iceland. The sinking of the USN destroyer REUBEN JAMES (DD-245) was inevitable. When you put ships in harm's way, they sometimes get hurt.

Meanwhile, the United States Pacific Fleet began to exercise and conduct manoeuvres to bring the fleet up to combat efficiency. Pacific Fleet submarines began long term patrols to evaluate procedures needed to sustain a submarine offensive should war breakout. Though mostly just going through the motions, United States armed forces were at least beginning to assess what was needed to conduct war in the vast Pacific Ocean.

RUSSIA

The Russian Northern Fleet cooperated with the Royal Navy to initiate the Arctic convoys. Russian destroyers and aircraft provided escorts while the merchant ships were in Russian-controlled waters. Russian submarines began patrolling the Norwegian coasts and began culling German supply ships supplying the German northern attack force.

The Russian Baltic Fleet, while mostly bottled up next to Leningrad, continued offensive operations with its submarine fleet into the Baltic shipping lanes. Unfortunately, the German and Finnish minefields sank a lot of Russian submarines going to or returning from patrols.

The Russian Black Sea Fleet continued to support the Russian Army in the defence of southern Russia and the Crimea. Unfortunately, the strong German air force sank a number of Russian surface ships. Still, the Russians successfully evacuated Odessa and began moving operations from Sevastopol to the east. While Sevastopol continued to hold out, it was impossible to sustain naval operations under German field guns.

Russian submarines continued to patrol the Romanian and Bulgarian coasts. They managed to pick off a few precious Axis tankers and merchants, but at the cost of a number of submarines that discovered the exact positions of Romanian minefields.

CHINA

With the Japanese mostly focussed on their attack into Southeast Asia, the Chinese were able to press Japanese forces away from Chinese-controlled areas. While Japan still controlled a large area of China, the Chinese continued to exact a payment in blood for every acre they occupied.

POLAND

Polish air, naval and ground forces were in action with British forces throughout the Mediterranean, Middle East and North Atlantic areas. The Polish Brigade replaced the gallant Australians holding Tobruk in preparation for the new British offensive against Rommel. Meanwhile, Polish destroyers escorted convoys and Polish submarines hunted German and Italian merchant ships.

FREE FRANCE

The Free French forces also moved into action alongside the British forces, primarily in Egypt and Libya. The Free French had built up a motorised brigade for the upcoming offensive.

The Free French navy provided escorts for convoys and submarines to patrol Norwegian ports. Free French aircraft supported the Royal Air Force (RAF) out of Britain and the Middle East.

GENERAL

DATE	COMMENTS
1 October	Nationalist Chinese forces repelled a Japanese offensive at Changla, China.
1 October	The Japanese General staff began a war game to evaluate their strategies for the upcoming attack into Southeast Asia at the Tokyo War Academy. The exercise was completed on the 5th.
1 October	A conference at Moscow between Britain, the U.S. and Russia concluded with promises of enormous amounts of aid to the Russian war effort, mostly from the United States.
1 October	Russian Naval Commissioner Vice Admiral G. I. Levchenko ordered his forces to prepare to evacuate Odessa.
1 October	During the night, RAF Bomber Command attacked Stettin and Hamburg, Germany.
1 October	Due to an ULTRA intercept message about the German U-boat patrol line southeast of Cape Farewell, Greenland, convoys SC.47, HX.152, ON.22 and ONS.23 were ordered south of the German patrol line.
1 October	The New Zealand Division of the Royal Navy became the Royal New Zealand Navy.
2 October	German Army Group South advanced against the Russian cities of Kursk and Kharkov. Adolph Hitler issued a special order to the troops proclaiming that "Today begins the last decisive battle of this year." German Army Group Centre began Operation TAIFUN, the final attack on Moscow.
2 October	The United States rejected the proposal submitted by Japanese Prime Minister Prince Konoye, bringing the two countries to a dead lock.
3 October	German Army Group Centre captured the Russian city of Orel, roughly one hundred miles from Moscow.
3 October	During the night of 3/4 October, RAF Bomber Command attacked Rotterdam, the Netherlands.
3 October	In Operation BAREFOOT, Norwegian MTBs attacked German shipping off Bergen during the night. Norwegian destroyers were standing off the port to provide the MTBs with cover, and they escorted the MTBs as they returned to Lerwick.
5 October	German Panzer Group 1 advanced in the southern Ukraine and reached the Sea of Azov.
5 October	A new key was added to the German U-boat ENIGMA machines. However, since they still used the old code for weather reports and ship-to-ship communications, Bletchley Park quickly broke the new code and continued to read German Naval messages through October and November, delayed by two to four days for deciphering.
6 October	German Army Group Centre captured the Russian city of Bryansk, close to the outskirts of Moscow.
7 October	Finland rejected a British demand for them to cease fighting the Russians.
7 October	German troops captured the Russian cities of Wyasma, Berjansk, and Mariupol.
7 October	The British rejected a proposed prisoner of war exchange with Germany between Newhaven and Dieppe due to the German demand for more German civilians to be exchanged for wounded British prisoners.
8 October	In a letter to Stalin, President Roosevelt promised U.S. military aid to Russia.
8 October	A shipping sweep in Vestfjord by Royal Navy destroyers in Operation EJ was cancelled due to the lack of available destroyers and poor weather.
9 October	President Roosevelt, in a message to Congress, urged the repeal of Section 6 of the Neutrality Act, which would allow the arming of U.S. merchant ships against "the modern pirates of the sea", the German U-boats.
9 October	Hitler announced that the war in the East, for all intents and purposes, had already been decided in favour of the *Reich*.
10 October	German Army Group South ended a battle with encircled Russian armies along the Sea of Azov and captured 100,000 Russian prisoners of war.
10 October	The Brazilian government allowed the United States to use its northern harbours (Pernambuco) to re-fuel and re-supply warships.
10 October	In Operation SIEGFRIED, the German 61st Infantry Division attacked Hiiumaa Island in the Baltic Sea.
11 October	Amid rumours that the Germans were about to capture Moscow, thousands of civilians fled the city.
11 October	During the night of 11/12 October, RAF Bomber Command attacked Emden, Germany.
12 October	German Army Group Centre captured the Russian city of Kaluga.
12 October	During the night of 12/13 October, RAF Bomber Command attacked Bremen, Germany.
12 October	In Operation WESTFALEN, the German Navy created a diversion off Cape Ristna for an attack by the German Army on Dagö (Hiiumaa Island).
12 October	In Operation EAST PRUSSIA, the German Navy created a diversion along the east coast of Dago, near the Russian coastal battery KERTEL to support the German Army attack.
12 October	In Operation CULTIVATE, the Royal Navy departed Alexandria for the first convoy serial to Tobruk, Libya, with reinforcements and supplies.
13 October	German Army Group Centre captured the Russian city of Kalinin, one hundred miles west of Moscow.

14 October	German Army Group Centre captured the Russian city of Rshev, one hundred miles west of Moscow. Other German units were within sixty miles of Moscow.
14 October	Hitler ordered the German Tenth Mountain Corps to attack and capture Murmansk, Russia, to cut the flow of Allied supplies to Russia.
15 October	The 2nd Yokosuka SNLF (Special Naval Landing Force) was formed at the Yokosuka port area with 746 men.
16 October	Following the evacuation of the Russian government and diplomatic corps from Moscow to Kuibyshev, panic began to spread among the civilian population, and thousands fled the city to places further east.
16 October	German and Romanian troops captured the Russian city of Odessa, on the Black Sea.
17 October	General Hideki Tojo became Prime Minister of Japan. The Emperor declared that, should negotiations with the United States not be resolved, General Tojo would have a free hand to conduct warfare in Southeast Asia against the United States and her allies.
18 October	German troops occupied the Russian city of Taganrog in the Crimea.
18 October	In Operation CALLBOY, the Royal Navy launched aircraft to Malta.
20 October	German Army Group Centre encircled Russian armies at Vjasma and Bryansk, leading to the capture of 673,000 Russian prisoners of war.
20 October	The Imperial Japanese Navy began making detailed plans to attack the U.S. naval base at Pearl Harbor, Hawaii, in case negotiations failed to resolve the issues between the two countries.
20 October	During the night of 20/21 October, RAF Bomber Command attacked Wilhelmshaven, Bremen and Emden.
21 October	The German Sixth Army captured the Russian city of Stalino in the industrial Donets Basin.
21 October	Operation SIEGFRIED came to an end with the Germans holding Hiiumaa Island and taking 3400 Russian prisoners.
23 October	During the night of 23/24 October, RAF Bomber Command attacked Kiel with sixty-four bombers (seventy-one bombers sortied) and all but one returned.
24 October	German Army Group Centre captured the Russian cities of Kharkov and Belgorod.
24 October	The Vichy French government allowed the Germans to move S-boats and motor barges through the canal system from the English Channel down the Rhone River into the Mediterranean Sea.
26 October	During the night of 26/27 October, RAF Bomber Command attacked Hamburg, Germany. Seventy-eight of the one hundred five bombers sortied dropped bombs on the target area. Five bombers failed to return.
27 October	The German Eleventh Army made a breakthrough at the Russian city of Perekop, opening the route to invade the Crimea.
28 October	President Roosevelt approved the appropriation by Congress of an additional $6 billion in Lend-Lease aid to Britain and Russia.
29 October	The German Crimean Army surrounded the Russians defending Sevastopol under the command of Vice Admiral F. S. Oktyabrski. The German Fifty-first Army pressed the attack to the Kertsch Peninsula, bypassing the Russian 7th Marine Infantry Brigade holding the west coast.
30 October	German troops began to occupy the Crimea and lay siege to the Russian city and Black Sea port of Sevastopol.
31 October	In the North Atlantic, the US destroyer REUBEN JAMES (DD-245) escorting convoy HX.156 was sunk by U.552 (Type VIIC, the "Red Devil" boat) (Kptlt Erich Topp) with the loss of one hundred of her crew. The destroyer was the first U.S. naval casualty in the hitherto undeclared war between Germany and the United States that existed after President Roosevelt authorized the use of USN vessels to escort Lend-Lease convoys bound for Britain.
31 October	During the night of 31 October/1 November, RAF Bomber Command attacked Hamburg and Bremen, Germany.

ARCTIC OCEAN

Greenland Sea and Barents Sea

Long. W180, 00 – E180, 00 Lat. N90, 00 – N68, 00

1 OCTOBER 1941

	Russian submarines SHCH-402, SHCH-422, M-171, M-175 and M-176 plus the TIGRIS patrolled off the Norwegian Arctic coast until the 25th.

2 OCTOBER 1941

	Russian submarine M-171 (Lt Cdr V. G. Starikov) unsuccessfully attacked two Norwegian steamers off Liinahamari in Petsamo Fjord. The torpedoes did damage the pier.
0500	Heavy cruiser SHROPSHIRE relieved heavy cruiser LONDON of convoy QP.1 escort duty in 74, 50N,

	56, 00E. LONDON returned to Archangel.
1700	Destroyer ESCAPADE relieved destroyer ANTELOPE of convoy PQ.1 escort duty in 70, 00N, 13, 00W. Destroyer ANTELOPE continued to Seidisfjord to refuel.

3 OCTOBER 1941

	Russian submarine M-176 unsuccessfully attacked a steamer off Varangerfjord.

5 OCTOBER 1941

	Russian TKA-12, TKA-14 and TKA-15 (Lt Cdr S. G. Korshunevich) patrolled between Kirkenes and Petsamo for German shipping.
	Heavy cruiser LONDON, carrying the British and American negotiating team, entered the Arctic Ocean escorted by Russian destroyer SOKRUSHITELNY from the White Sea to the Kanin Peninsula.
Night	During the night, TKA-12 (Lt A. O. Shabalin) sank Norwegian cutter BJORNUNGEN (163grt) off Ekkerøy, Norway.

7 OCTOBER 1941

	Destroyer ACTIVE, in the escort of convoy QP.1, took antisubmarine trawler OPHELIA in tow when she developed a defect to her boilers. The destroyer was ordered to take the trawler directly to Seidisfjord. Due to bad weather, the ships were diverted to Akureyri where they arrived on the 10th.

8 OCTOBER 1941

	Russian submarine M-175 unsuccessfully attacked a ship in Varangerfjord, Norway.

11 OCTOBER 1941

	Submarine TIGRIS unsuccessfully attacked a German eastbound convoy off North Cape.
0245	Convoy PQ.1 of steamers ATLANTIC (5414grt), BLAIRNEVIS (4155grt), ELNA II (3221grt), HARMONIC (4558grt), Panamanian NORTH KING (4934grt), Belgian VILLE D'ANVERS (7462grt), BLACK RANGER (3417grt), Panamanian CAPIRA (5565grt), GEMSTONE (4986grt), LORCA (4875grt), and RIVER AFTON (5479grt) arrived at Murmansk, Russia, from Hvalfjord, Iceland.

12 OCTOBER 1941

	Norwegian steamer VAAGEN (687grt) accidentally rammed German destroyer FRIEDRICH ECKHOLDT off Tromsø, causing heavy damage. Grand Admiral Raeder ordered the Norwegian captain arrested under the suspicion of sabotage. Meanwhile, destroyer KARL GALSTER escorted the damaged destroyer to Trondheim; where she spent twelve days in dry-dock for emergency repairs. She was later taken to Kiel, Germany, for a full refit and permanent repairs.
1240	Destroyer NORMAN arrived at Archangel from Seidisfjord with the Trade Mission Congress group.

14 OCTOBER 1941

	Submarine TIGRIS unsuccessfully attacked German steamers MINONA (grt) with Norwegian steamer HAVBRIS (1315grt) and TUGELA (5559grt) off North Cape in 71, 05N, 27, 10E.

17 OCTOBER 1941

	Russian submarine SHCH-402 (Lt Cdr N. G. Stolbov) sank Norwegian steamer **VESTERAALEN** (682grt) at Sørøysund.
2200	Destroyer NORMAN was recalled to Archangel, Russia.

18 OCTOBER 1941

1320	U.132 (Kptlt Vogelsang) damaged Russian steamer **ARGUN** (3487grt) (Master V. A. Greschner) while attacking a small convoy off Cape Gorodetski in 69, 30N, 33, 30E. (Other sources place the attack in 67, 41N, 41, 03E.)
1340	U.132 hit the steamer with a second torpedo and she began to sink north of Kackovski. When lost, **ARGUN** was under the command of the Russian pilot, Lt Cdr I. M. Ljubimov.
1400	U.132 missed the steamer with another torpedo and then departed the area. Russian auxiliary hydrographic vessel MGLA (Master I. E. Gorschkov) rescued the entire crew.
2017	U.132 (Kptlt Vogelsang) sank Russian steam trawler **RT-8/SELD** (608grt) while attacking a small convoy off Cape Gorodetski in 67, 41N, 41, 03E. There were no survivors. She was reported missing off the Gorlo Strait on the 26th.

19 OCTOBER 1941

	German steamer **ANDROMEDA** (658grt) became stranded and was sunk in Kongsfjord.
	Minesweepers HARRIER and BRITOMART arrived at Spitsbergen.

20 OCTOBER 1941

After a short stay at Polyarny, submarine TIGRIS departed to return to Holy Loch.

21 OCTOBER 1941

Russian submarines K-1 and K-23 laid mines off Kirkenes and North Cape, Norway.

Russian submarines M-176, SHCH-401, SHCH-404 and SHCH-421 departed Polyarny to patrol the Norwegian Arctic coast until 5 November.

22 OCTOBER 1941

Russian submarine SHCH-421 sank three fishing boats off Kirkenes.

29 OCTOBER 1941

Russian submarine K-1 (Capt. 3rd Class Avgustonovich) laid mines off Breisund, Norway.

Russian submarine K-23 (Capt. 3rd Class Potapov) laid mines off Kirkenes, Norway.

30 OCTOBER 1941

Submarine TRIDENT departed Murmansk on a patrol with orders to then return to the United Kingdom.

White Sea

Long. E30, 00 – E60, 00   Lat. N68, 00 – N60, 00

1 OCTOBER 1941

Convoy QP.1 departed Archangel, Russia, with Dutch steamer ALCHIBA (4427grt), tanker BLACK RANGER (3417grt), steamers ESNEH (1931grt), LLANSTEPHAN CASTLE (11,299grt), NEW WESTMINSTER CITY (4747grt), LANCASTRIAN PRINCE (1914grt), and TREHATA (4817grt), and Russian steamers SEVZAPLES (3947grt), SUKHONA (3124grt), ALMA ATA (3611grt), BUDENNI (2482grt), MOSSOVET (2981grt), RODINA (4441grt), and STARY BOLSHEVIK (2974grt).

Heavy cruiser LONDON escorted the convoy to 2 October.

Heavy cruiser SHROPSHIRE escorted the convoy from 2 to 10 October, relieving heavy cruiser LONDON in 74, 55N, 27, 30E.

Destroyers ELECTRA escorted the convoy 9 October, ACTIVE to 5 October, and ANTHONY from 4 to 9 October. Trawlers MACBETH and HAMLET of the 73rd Minesweeping Group escorted the convoy to 9 October.

Trawler OPHELIA escorted the convoy to 5 October.

Trawler OPHELIA, escorting tanker BLACK RANGER en route to convoy PQ.1, developed defects and was towed by destroyer ACTIVE to Akureyri, arriving on 10 October.

Russian steamers SUKHONA and MOSSOVET straggled from the convoy, but arrived safely.

The convoy dispersed off the Orkneys on 10 October, the steamers proceeding to their destinations in convoy WN.91.

Heavy cruiser SHROPSHIRE was detached on 10 October and arrived at Scapa Flow on 11 October.

Destroyer ANTHONY, escorting oiler BLACK RANGER and steamer LLANSTEPHAN CASTLE, arrived at Scapa Flow on 11 October.

Destroyer ELECTRA arrived at Scapa Flow on 11 October.

The Russian Northern Fleet reinforced its patrol boat group off the Kola Fjord using boats from the White Sea Fleet. Minesweepers HALCYON, HARRIER and SALAMANDER took over escort duties in the White Sea to compensate for the Russian ship movements.

Russian submarines L-20 and L-22 continued to work up to combat efficiency in the White Sea until the 25th.

3 OCTOBER 1941

1530 | Heavy cruiser LONDON returned to Archangel, Russia, after her escort of convoy QP.1.

4 OCTOBER 1941

Heavy cruiser LONDON departed Archangel for Scapa Flow.

14 OCTOBER 1941

Minesweepers HARRIER, HALCYON, SALAMANDER, and BRITOMART departed Archangel for Seidisfjord, Iceland.

15 OCTOBER 1941

Heavy cruiser SUFFOLK with destroyers IMPULSIVE, ESCAPADE, and NORMAN departed Archangel, Russia, late in the day to conduct a shipping sweep off the north coast of Finland, and then proceeded to Scapa Flow. The sweep was later cancelled and ships were ordered to return to Archangel.

GERMANY SENDS RUSSIA TO THE ALLIES

	Destroyer NORMAN was detached for the United Kingdom, via Seidisfjord, Iceland.

18 OCTOBER 1941

	U.132 (Kptlt Vogelsang) sank Russian trawler **RT-8/SELD** (608grt) off Cape Gorodetski in 67, 41N, 41, 03E.
	U.132 patrolled of the entrance to the White Sea from 14 September to 21 October.

19 OCTOBER 1941

1500	Destroyer NORMAN arrived back at Archangel.
1600	Heavy cruiser SUFFOLK departed Archangel with destroyers IMPULSIVE and ESCAPADE. En route to the United Kingdom, they carried out a shipping sweep off the north coast of Finland at Svaerholt Havet during the night of 21/22 October. No enemy ships were sighted.

20 OCTOBER 1941

	Russian patrol boat **SKR-11/RT-66/URAL** patrolled the entrance to the White Sea until the 24th. She went missing, probably on a mine, during that patrol.

23 OCTOBER 1941

	U.576 (Kptlt Heinicke) began a patrol of the mouth to the White Sea that lasted until the 31st.

27 OCTOBER 1941

	Destroyer NORMAN departed Archangel for Scapa Flow with the Trade Union Congress delegation and members of the Russian Labour Delegation.

30 OCTOBER 1941

1000	Convoy PQ.2 arrived at Archangel, Russia.

31 OCTOBER 1941

	U.576 (Kptlt Heinicke) completed an unsuccessful patrol across the mouth of the White Sea.

NORTH ATLANTIC OCEAN

Iceland and North of Britain
Long. W30, 00 – E03, 00   Lat. N68, 00 – N58, 30

1 OCTOBER 1941

	Norwegian destroyer DRAUG departed Scapa Flow towing Norwegian MTB.56 to Bergen, Norway, for Operation BAREFOOT.
0730	Destroyer DULVERTON arrived at Scapa Flow to begin working up to combat efficiency.
1830	Heavy cruiser KENT arrived at Scapa Flow escorted by destroyer NORMAN to work up to combat efficiency after repairs. Destroyer NORMAN arrived at Scapa Flow to begin working up to combat efficiency.
1845	Convoy PQ.1 departed Hvalfjord, Iceland, with steamers ATLANTIC (5414grt), BLAIRNEVIS (4155grt), ELNA II (3221grt), HARMONIC (4558grt), Panamanian NORTH KING (4934grt), Belgian VILLE D'ANVERS (7462grt), BLACK RANGER (3417grt), Panamanian CAPIRA (5565grt), GEMSTONE (4986grt), LORCA (4875grt), and RIVER AFTON (5479grt) escorted by heavy cruiser SUFFOLK, destroyers ANTELOPE and IMPULSIVE, and minesweepers BRITOMART, GOSSAMER, LEDA, and HUSSAR. Destroyer ANTHONY departed Hvalfjord with oiler BLACK RANGER and sailed with the convoy. On 4 October, the destroyer and oiler met returning convoy QP.1. Destroyer ANTELOPE was detached on 2 October to Scapa Flow. Destroyer ESCAPADE joined the convoy on 2 October and provided escort to 11 October. Convoy PQ.1 arrived at Murmansk, Russia, on 11 October.

3 OCTOBER 1941

1000	Destroyer ANTELOPE arrived at Seidisfjord, Iceland, to refuel after escorting convoy PQ.1.
1345	Destroyer ANTELOPE departed Seidisfjord for Scapa Flow.

4 OCTOBER 1941

	Norwegian destroyer DRAUG arrived at Lerwick, Shetlands, towing MTB.56 from Bergen, Norway, to conclude Operation BAREFOOT.
1300	Battleship KING GEORGE V departed Hvalfjord, Iceland, with destroyers ASHANTI, MATABELE, and SOMALI for Akureyri, Iceland.

	Aircraft carrier VICTORIOUS, light cruiser PENELOPE plus destroyers ASHANTI, PUNJABI, and MATABELE departed in company with the battleship group.
1700	Destroyer ANTELOPE arrived at Scapa Flow from Seidisfjord, Iceland.

5 OCTOBER 1941

	Battleship KING GEORGE V arrived at Akureyri, Iceland, with destroyers SOMALI, BEDOUIN, and ESKIMO from Hvalfjord, Iceland, and later departed that day for Seidisfjord, Iceland.
	Light cruiser AURORA departed Hvalfjord and proceeded to Seidisfjord, arriving the next day.
	Norwegian destroyer DRAUG and MTB.56 departed Lerwick, Shetlands, for Scapa Flow, where they arrived later that day.
0600	Minesweeper BRAMBLE arrived at Scapa Flow from Belfast, Northern Ireland, to await the sailing of convoy PQ.2.

6 OCTOBER 1941

	Battleship PRINCE OF WALES (flagship VAdm A. T. B. Curteis CB, Second in Command, Home Fleet) arrived at Scapa Flow from Gibraltar with destroyers LAFOREY, LIGHTNING, and ORIBI.
	Light cruiser PENELOPE arrived at Seidisfjord, Iceland, with destroyers PUNJABI, ASHANTI, and MATABELE to refuel. Aircraft carrier VICTORIOUS remained at sea.
	The Commander in Chief, Home Fleet, transferred to light cruiser AURORA for passage to Scapa Flow.
	Battleship KING GEORGE V, aircraft carrier VICTORIOUS plus light cruiser PENELOPE departed Seidisfjord with destroyers ASHANTI, BEDOUIN, ESKIMO, MATABELE, PUNJABI, and SOMALI for Operation EJ. Sub-Lt (A) P. G. F. Dumas and Leading Airman M. S. Eastment were lost in a practice flight in a Fulmar aircraft of 809 Squadron.
1600	Destroyer ANTELOPE departed Scapa Flow for Scrabster, Scotland, where she embarked a British trade delegation for transfer to Archangel, Russia.
1855	Destroyer ANTELOPE departed Scrabster for Seidisfjord, Iceland, to refuel en route. On the passage, the destroyer developed a defect to her main dynamo.
2200	Destroyer NORMAN departed Scapa Flow for Seidisfjord to replace destroyer ANTELOPE.

7 OCTOBER 1941

	U.502 (Kptlt v. Rosenstiel) damaged whaling ship SVEND FOYN (14,795grt) while she was straggling behind convoy HX.152 in 60, 37N, 21, 44W. The ship arrived at Iceland in tow on the 11th, assisted by corvette SUNFLOWER. She was later towed to Mersey, England, for repairs.
	Minelayer PORT QUEBEC laid Minefield SN.24A escorted by surveying ship SCOTT.
1000	Light cruiser AURORA arrived at Scapa Flow from Seidisfjord, Iceland, carrying the Commander in Chief, Home Fleet. The Commander in Chief transferred his flag to battleship PRINCE OF WALES.
1818	Destroyer HURWORTH anchored in Loch Eribol, Scotland, due to heavy fog and arrived at Scapa Flow after the fog cleared.
1930	Destroyer LIGHTNING departed Scapa Flow for Rosyth, Scotland, to carry out boiler cleaning and repairs.
2300	Destroyers ANTELOPE and NORMAN arrived at Seidisfjord, where the trade delegation was transferred to destroyer NORMAN.

8 OCTOBER 1941

	ANTELOPE departed Seidisfjord, Iceland, for Scapa Flow.
	USN destroyer DALLAS (DD-199) dropped depth charges on a submarine contact while escorting convoy ON.22.
	Heavy seas damaged USN fleet tanker SALINAS (AO-19), and destroyer BROOME (DD-210) escorted her to Iceland.
0700	Destroyers NORMAN departed Seidisfjord for Archangel, Russia, with the trade delegation (*see 6 Oct*) aboard.
0900	Destroyer ORIBI departed Scapa Flow carrying the Commander in Chief, Home Fleet to Scrabster.
0900	Norwegian destroyer DRAUG and motor torpedo boat MTB.56 departed Scapa Flow. The DRAUG proceeded to Grimsby and MTB.56 proceeded to Dover.
1430	Destroyer ORIBI returned to Scapa Flow from Scrabster.
2200	Destroyer ONSLOW arrived at Scapa Flow from Greenock, Scotland, to begin working up to combat efficiency.

9 OCTOBER 1941

0830	Heavy cruiser LONDON arrived at Scapa Flow from Archangel, Russia.
1000	The trade delegation (*see 6-8 Oct*) returning from Russia aboard heavy cruiser LONDON transferred to destroyer OFFA at Scapa Flow and was taken to Scrabster.

1330	Destroyer OFFA returned to Scapa Flow from Scrabster.
1530	ANTELOPE arrived at Scapa Flow from Seidisfjord.

10 OCTOBER 1941

	Light cruisers KENYA and SHEFFIELD departed Scapa Flow for the Clyde.
0700	Destroyer CHARLESTON arrived at Scapa Flow from Loch Alsh to carry out repairs to her oil tanks.
1000	Destroyer PUNJABI arrived independently at Scapa Flow after Operation EJ.
1000	The Operation EJ forces arrived back at Scapa Flow.
<1230	Destroyer ACTIVE arrived at Akureyri, Iceland, towing antisubmarine trawler OPHELIA.
1230	Destroyer ACTIVE departed Akureyri escorting tanker BLACK RANGER (3417grt) to Scapa Flow.
1900	Heavy cruiser SHROPSHIRE was detached from convoy QP.1 escort duty for Scapa Flow.

11 OCTOBER 1941

	Convoy HX.143 (forty-seven merchants and five escorts) and convoy SC.49 (thirty-one merchants) reached the MOWP line and were both routed north of the area where convoy SC.48 was attacked. According to ULTRA message intercepts, there were no U-boats on patrol in that area.
	Destroyer ORIBI departed Scapa Flow escorting steamer LLANSTEPHAN CASTLE (11,299grt) to the Clyde.
	German bombing damaged Norwegian motor vessel SILVA (127grt) at Klaksvig (Klaksvik), Faeroes.
0015	Heavy cruiser SHROPSHIRE arrived at Scapa Flow after convoy QP.1 escort duty.
>0015	Heavy cruiser SHROPSHIRE departed Scapa Flow for Sheerness, England, for a refit.
0900	Destroyer ANTHONY arrived at Scapa Flow escorting oiler BLACK RANGER (3417grt) and steamer LLANSTEPHAN CASTLE (11,299grt).
1039	Destroyer ELECTRA arrived at Scapa Flow after convoy QP.1 escort duty.
1900	Destroyer ELECTRA departed Scapa Flow for Rosyth for a boiler cleaning.

12 OCTOBER 1941

	German bombing damaged Faeroes auxiliary fishing vessel **FUGLOYGJIN** (81grt) at Klaksvig. The ship sank, but was later salvaged and returned to service.
	Light cruisers AURORA and PENELOPE departed Scapa Flow for Gibraltar.
0800	Destroyer ACTIVE arrived at Scapa Flow from Akureyri, Iceland, escorting tanker BLACK RANGER (3417grt).
1300	Sloop LOWESTOFT arrived at Scapa Flow from Harwich to work up to combat efficiency after her repairs.
1300	Destroyer ECLIPSE departed Scapa Flow to assist Russian steamer SUKHONA (3124grt), which had been in convoy QP.1 and made a distress signal seven miles north of the Orkneys. Antisubmarine trawler VASCAMA escorted the steamer to Kirkwall, and the destroyer returned to Scapa Flow. There was no apparent reason for the distress signal.
1600	Aircraft carrier VICTORIOUS departed Scapa Flow for the Clyde with destroyers BEDOUIN and ANTHONY. T/A/Sub-Lt (A) E. H. Archer RNVR, and Leading Airman W. M. James were killed when their Albacore aircraft of 817 crashed during night practice near Dunino while making a practice attack on aircraft carrier VICTORIOUS.

13 OCTOBER 1941

	During fire fighting exercises by men of the heavy cruiser NORFOLK on the hulk **INVERLANE** (9141grt), an explosion killed Lt W. J. Van De Kasteele, the cruiser's gunnery officer, and four ratings. The ship's executive officer Cdr A. C. Luce died of injuries on the 20th.
	Minelayer PORT QUEBEC laid Minefield SN.24B escorted by destroyer LANCASTER.

14 OCTOBER 1941

1000	Destroyer ACTIVE departed Scapa Flow for Hull, England, for a refit.
1730	Destroyer LIGHTNING arrived at Scapa Flow from Rosyth, Scotland, after boiler cleaning.

15 OCTOBER 1941

1300	Destroyer SOUTHWOLD arrived at Scapa Flow from Portsmouth, England, to begin working up to combat efficiency.
1745	Destroyer ICARUS arrived at Scapa Flow from the Humber after her refit.

16 OCTOBER 1941

0730	The Liverpool section of convoy PQ.2 arrived at Scapa Flow from Liverpool escorted by minesweepers SPEEDY and SEAGULL.
1230	Destroyers LAFOREY and LIGHTNING departed Scapa Flow to embark passengers and stores in the Clyde prior to transferring to Force H at Gibraltar.
1500	Battleship ROYAL SOVEREIGN arrived at Scapa Flow from the Clyde escorted by destroyers ORIBI and

17 OCTOBER 1941

	ANTHONY.
	Light cruiser EDINBURGH arrived at Scapa Flow from the Clyde.
	Damaged antisubmarine trawler OPHELIA departed Akureyri, Iceland, for Scapa Flow.
1630	Convoy PQ.2 departed Scapa Flow with steamers EMPIRE BAFFIN (6978grt), HARTLEBURY (5082grt), QUEEN CITY (4814grt), HARPALION (5486grt), ORIENT CITY (5095grt), and TEMPLE ARCH (5138grt), escorted by destroyers ICARUS and ECLIPSE plus minesweepers BRAMBLE, SEAGULL, and SPEEDY from 18 to 30 October. Heavy cruiser NORFOLK departed Scapa Flow early on the 18th and overtook the convoy and joined the escort. Destroyers ECLIPSE and ICARUS refuelled at Seidisfjord on the 20th and rejoined the convoy. On the 29th, minesweepers GOSSAMER, HUSSAR, and LEDA joined the convoy from Archangel and escorted it into the port on the 30th.

18 OCTOBER 1941

	USN repair ship VULCAN (AR-5) began temporary repairs on damaged USN destroyer KEARNY (DD-432) at Reykjavik, Iceland.
	Minesweepers FITZROY, ELGIN, ROSS, and LYDD arrived at Scapa Flow on passage to the Faeroes for a sweep for mines in the shipping channels.
1400	Destroyers ANTELOPE and ANTHONY departed Scapa Flow for the Clyde to escort destroyer depot ship FORTH from the Clyde to Rosyth.

19 OCTOBER 1941

	USN destroyer GLEAVES (DD-423) dropped depth charges on a submarine contact while escorting convoy HX.154 in 60, 00N, 23, 20W.
	Convoy ON.26 with thirty-two ships joined USN Task Unit TU.4.1.5 with destroyers MAYO (DD-422), SCHENCK (DD-159), LEARY (DD-158), BROOME (DD-210) and BABBITT (DD-128) at the MOMP, releasing escort group EG.4 with destroyers BEAGLE, SALISBURY and ROXBOROUGH, corvettes HEATHER, NARCISSUS and the Free French LOBELIA, attached destroyer SHERWOOD, plus antisubmarine trawlers LADY MADELEINE, NORWICH CITY and ARAB. Catalina aircraft of VP-73 Squadron also covered the convoy until they were north of the German Wolfpack REISSEWOLF identified by ULTRA intercepts.
	Dutch submarine O.14 and Free French submarine MINERVE departed the Faeroes to patrol off the Norwegian coast. Submarine O.14 arrived back at Scapa Flow after her patrol on the 29th.
<1615	Sloop IBIS departed Scapa Flow upon the completion of her working up exercises. She proceeded to Kirkwall for direction-finding calibration trials prior to going to Londonderry.
1615	Sloop IBIS arrived at Kirkwall from Scapa Flow.

20 OCTOBER 1941

	Heavy cruiser CUMBERLAND arrived at Scapa Flow from Chatham, England, after her refit.
<1029	In the early morning hours during a gale, heavy cruiser LONDON was dragged into the baffle, and heavy cruiser KENT was dragged into battleship MALAYA.
1030	Battleship MALAYA departed Scapa Flow escorted by destroyers BEDOUIN and PUNJABI for the Clyde. After the group joined with the escorts for aircraft carrier VICTORIOUS, destroyers LAFOREY and LIGHTNING, off Tiumpan Head, Scotland, destroyers BEDOUIN and PUNJABI returned to Scapa Flow.
1330	Destroyer SOUTHWOLD departed Scapa Flow to embark the Engineer in Chief at Scrabster and return to Scapa Flow.
1530	Aircraft carrier VICTORIOUS arrived at Scapa Flow from the Clyde unescorted due to the heavy weather.
1730	Destroyer CHIDDINGFOLD arrived at Scapa Flow from the Clyde, having been delayed by weather.
1730	Destroyer SOUTHWOLD returned to Scapa Flow from Scrabster.
1845	Destroyer CHARLESTON departed Scapa Flow for Loch Alsh upon the completion of her docking and repairs.

21 OCTOBER 1941

	Tug **HELEN BARBARA** was abandoned and lost in heavy weather.
	The British Submarine Tracking Room (STR) identified at least ten U-boats in a patrol line west of convoy ON.26, so it was ordered to the north.
	Heavy cruiser BERWICK arrived at Scapa Flow from Rosyth after completing engine repairs.
	Minesweepers FITZROY, ELGIN, LYDD, and ROSS of the 4th Minesweeping Squadron and minesweeping trawlers RONALDSAY, CAVA, and CAPE NYEMETSKI departed Scapa Flow for the Faeroes for a mine sweep. The ships arrived in the Faeroes on the 22nd and began the clearing the area of mines on the 23rd. On the 24th, minesweepers KELLETT and SELKIRK arrived in the Faeroes from Aberdeen, Scotland, to assist in the minesweeping work.

22 OCTOBER 1941

	USN Task Unit TU.4.1.5 joined convoy ONS.27 with sixty-two ships at the MOMP and the group moved further north of the route used by ON.26.
	Minelayer PORT QUEBEC laid Minefield SN.24C escorted by destroyer NEWARK.
	Minesweepers SALAMANDER and HALCYON arrived at Seidisfjord from Spitsbergen, Norway, to refuel.
0630	Destroyers ANTELOPE and ELECTRA returned to Scapa Flow.
0800	Sloop IBIS departed Kirkwall for Londonderry, Northern Ireland, after the completion of her D/F equipment calibration.

23 OCTOBER 1941

	An Albacore aircraft from aircraft carrier VICTORIOUS did not return from exercises near Rona off Scapa Flow. T/A/Sub-Lt (A) A. K. Hopkins RNVR, T/A/Sub-Lt (A) P. D. Sayer RNVR, and Leading Airman N. Weldon of the 832 Squadron were lost. In the same exercise, a Fulmar aircraft of 800 Squadron from aircraft carrier INDOMITABLE also failed to return. A/Sub-Lt (A) J. H. Miln and T/Sub-Lt (A) F. J. Stamper RNVR were lost.
0700	Battleship PRINCE OF WALES departed Scapa Flow for the Clyde with destroyers ELECTRA and EXPRESS.
0900	Minesweepers SALAMANDER and HALCYON departed Seidisfjord, Iceland, for Scapa Flow.
1800	Minesweepers HARRIER and BRITOMART arrived at Seidisfjord from Spitsbergen, Norway, to refuel and then departed again for Scapa Flow.

24 OCTOBER 1941

0930	Destroyer ANTELOPE departed Scapa Flow for Scrabster, Scotland, with the Engineer in Chief. After this transfer duty, the destroyer returned to Scapa Flow.

25 OCTOBER 1941

	Heavy cruiser SUFFOLK arrived at Seidisfjord, Iceland, from Spitsbergen, Norway, with destroyers IMPULSIVE and ESCAPADE to refuel.
	Convoy HX.155 joined with Escort Group EG.5 at the MOMP. The British STR, using ULTRA message intercepts, reported four U-boats off Strait of Belle Isle (Labrador Straits) and up to twenty U-boats patrolling the middle North Atlantic route, so the convoy was re-routed south.
	Convoy SC.50 with thirty-six ships departed Strait of Belle Isle escorted by USN Task Unit TU.4.1.3. Due to the large number of U-boats along her planned route, the convoy was ordered south away from the German patrol line.
	Convoy ON.28 joined with USN Task Unit TU.4.1.6 at the MOMP and proceeded southwards to avoid the U-boat patrol line to the west. TU.4.1.6 with destroyers SAMPSON (DD-394), LEA (DD-118), BERNADOU (DD-153), DUPONT (DD-152) and MACLEISH (DD-220) plus tanker SALINAS (AO-19) reached the MOMP from Iceland.
	Heavy cruiser LONDON departed Scapa Flow for the Tyne for a refit.
0900	Battleship ROYAL SOVEREIGN departed Scapa Flow for the Clyde escorted by destroyers ANTELOPE and DULVERTON after working up to combat efficiency.
1000	Minesweepers HARRIER and BRITOMART arrived at Scapa Flow from Seidisfjord.
1700	Destroyer INTREPID arrived at Scapa Flow from Sheerness, England.
1700	Destroyer MONTROSE arrived at Scapa Flow from Sheerness, via Methil, Scotland, to begin working up to combat efficiency.

26 OCTOBER 1941

0800	Heavy cruiser SUFFOLK departed Seidisfjord, Iceland, for Scapa Flow with destroyers IMPULSIVE and ESCAPADE.
1100	Minesweepers SALAMANDER and HALCYON arrived at Scapa Flow from Seidisfjord.

27 OCTOBER 1941

	U.74 (Kptlt Kentrat) spotted convoy ON.28 and radioed its position to the other German U-boats. USN destroyers DUPONT (DD-152) and SAMPSON (DD-394) dropped depth charges on a submarine contact while escorting convoy ON.28.
	Heavy seas damaged USN destroyer HILARY P. JONES (DD-427) while she was escorting convoy HX.156. The convoy was moved further south when radio intercepts indicated that the German Wolfpack had spotted convoy ON.28 north of them.
	Submarine SEALION arrived at Scapa Flow from Portsmouth, England.
1400	Destroyer ANTELOPE return to Scapa Flow from the Clyde.
1700	Heavy cruiser SUFFOLK arrived at Scapa Flow from Archangel, Russia, via Spitsbergen with destroyers IMPULSIVE and ESCAPADE.

28 OCTOBER 1941

	Convoy SC.50 joined with Escort Group EG.1 at the MOMP.
	U.568, U.77, U.73, U.751 and U.106 were all converging on convoy SC.50 for an attack. U.77 and U.74 were unable to reach an attack position on the convoy.
	Convoy ONS.29 with thirty-four ships joined with USN Task Unit TU.4.1.6 at the MOMP.
	German Wolfpack SCHLAGETOT with U.569, U.38, U.82, U.202, U.84, U.203, U.93 and U.85 formed a patrol line from Cape Farewell and Belle Isle Strait to intercept convoy ONS.29.
	Submarine SEALION departed Scapa Flow for Murmansk, Russia.
	Submarine P.35 departed Scapa Flow for Dundee, Scotland.
1200	Minesweepers HARRIER and BRITOMART departed Scapa Flow for Grimsby and Hartlepool, respectively, for refitting.

29 OCTOBER 1941

0800	Destroyers OFFA and ORIBI departed Scapa Flow for Loch Alsh, Scotland, under the orders of Rear Admiral Minelaying.
1700	Minesweepers SALAMANDER and HALCYON departed Scapa Flow for Aberdeen, Scotland, to carry out boiler cleaning and equipping for Arctic service.

30 OCTOBER 1941

0900	Destroyer ASHANTI departed Scapa Flow for Scrabster, Scotland, to embark a party of military officers taking passage in light cruiser KENYA to Archangel.
1200	Destroyer ONSLOW departed Scapa Flow and joined the Minefield SN.83A force in 58, 45N, 05, 42W.
1300	Destroyer ASHANTI arrived back at Scapa Flow from Scrabster.

31 OCTOBER 1941

	Submarine P.35 arrived at Scapa Flow from Dundee, Scotland.
	Minelayers MENETHEUS, PORT QUEBEC, and WELSHMAN laid Minefield SN.83A escorted by destroyers BRIGHTON, OFFA, ORIBI, and ONSLOW. Destroyers ONSLOW, OFFA, and ORIBI arrived back at Scapa Flow on 1 November. The minelayers arrived at Loch Alsh on 1 November escorted by destroyer BRIGHTON.
	Submarine SEAWOLF arrived at Scapa Flow from Portsmouth, England, and departed later that day for Murmansk, Russia.
0900	Light cruiser SHEFFIELD departed Scapa Flow to cover the force laying Minefield SN.83A.
0930	Destroyer ESCAPADE departed Scapa Flow for Scrabster to embark a Russian general for passage to Archangel in light cruiser KENYA.
1300	Destroyer ESCAPADE returned to Scapa Flow from Scrabster after dropping off a Russian general for passage to Archangel in light cruiser KENYA.
1400	Destroyer NORMAN arrived at Seidisfjord with the Trade Union Congress delegation and members of the Russian Labour Delegation to refuel, then departed on 1 November. The destroyer arrived at Scrabster on 2 November and reached Scapa Flow later that day.
2200	Light cruiser SHEFFIELD was detached from the mining group and returned to Scapa Flow on 1 November.
2300	Light cruiser KENYA departed Scapa Flow for Seidisfjord with destroyers BEDOUIN and INTREPID to refuel prior to escorting convoy PQ.3 to Archangel, Russia.

Norwegian Sea

Long. E03, 00 – E20, 00   Lat. N68, 00 – N58, 30

3 OCTOBER 1941

	In Operation BAREFOOT, Norwegian MTB.56 (S/Lt Danielsen) sank Norwegian tanker **BORGNY** (3015grt) off Bergen while she was en route to Trondheim escorted by German auxiliary minesweeper M.1101/FOCH & HUBERT and patrol boat V.5505/SEETEUFEL during the night. The MTB returned to Norwegian destroyer DRAUG, which was standing off the port, and they returned to Lerwick.

8 OCTOBER 1941

	Aircraft carrier VICTORIOUS launched aircraft to strike at Bodø escorted by battleship KING GEORGE V, light cruiser PENELOPE, and destroyers SOMALI, ESKIMO, ASHANTI, BEDOUIN, MATABELE, and PUNJABI. Two steamers were reported to be damaged in the air attack. The air attack damaged Norwegian steamer HAAKON ADALSTEIN (710grt). The only casualty was a slight wounding of one of the air gunners. Destroyer BEDOUIN lost two ratings overboard in heavy weather, but both were retrieved safely. A shipping sweep in Vestfjord by destroyers SOMALI and MATABELE in Operation EJ was cancelled due to

14 OCTOBER 1941

RAF bombing sank German auxiliary submarine chaser **UJ.1709/CARL KAMPF** (600grt) west of Lister, Norway.

18 OCTOBER 1941

Free French submarine MINERVE patrolled off Stavanger, Norway, until 4 November.

27 OCTOBER 1941

Russian submarine K-1 (Capt 3rd Class Avgustonovich) laid mines off Maakeröy Sound, Norway.

29 OCTOBER 1941

Free French submarine MINERVE unsuccessfully attacked a tanker off Stavanger.

RAF bombing sank German steamer **BARCELONA** (3101grt) near Aalesund, Norway.

East of Canada

Long. W70, 00 – W30, 00   Lat. N68, 00 – N43, 30

1 OCTOBER 1941

	U.94, U.372, U.562, U.431 and U.572, the last of the Wolfpack BRANDENBURG, were ordered into new patrol positions southeast of Cape Farewell, Greenland.
1810	U.94 (Otto Ites) spotted tanker SAN FLORENTINO (12,842grt) while she was straggling behind convoy ON.19 southeast of Cape Farewell.
2336	U.94 missed the tanker with the first torpedo.
2357	U.94 badly damaged tanker **SAN FLORENTINO** (12,842grt) (Master Robert William Davis) while she was straggling behind convoy ON.19 southeast of Cape Farewell in 52, 50N, 34, 40W. The tanker continued moving and fired shells at the U-boats direction.
0249	U.94 hit the tanker with a second torpedo in the bow and she radioed her position in 52, 42N, 34, 51W and dropped fog buoys, but continued to steam.
0426	U.94 hit the tanker with a third torpedo, but she still continued to steam.
0451	The tanker evaded the fourth torpedo fired by U.94.
0502	The tanker finally broke in two.
0552	U.94 sank the stern half with a torpedo that caused the boiler to explode. U.94 fired thirty-four rounds from her deck gun and then departed the area. The master, twenty-one crewmen and one gunner were lost. Canadian corvette MAYFLOWER (Lt Cdr George Stephen) rescued thirty-one crewmen and four gunners and landed them at St. John's, Newfoundland. USCG cutter CAMPBELL (WPG-32) scuttled the hulk. (Other sources have the Canadian corvette ALBERNI (Lt Cdr G. O. Baugh) scuttling the tanker on the 2nd.)

2 OCTOBER 1941

0652	U.562 (Horst Hamm) sank CAM ship **EMPIRE WAVE** (7463grt) (Master Clement Porter Maclay) while attacking convoy ON.19 about 500 miles east of Cape Farewell, Greenland, in 59, 08N, 32, 26W. The master, nineteen crewmen and nine RAF personnel were lost. In one of the ship's lifeboats one crewman died. T/Lt D. M. Bain RCNVR, en route to PRESIDENT III, was lost in the ship. Icelandic trawler SURPRISE rescued twenty-three crewmen, six gunners and two RAF personnel and landed them at St. Patrick's Fjord, Iceland. USN destroyer MEREDITH (DD-434) later took the survivors to Reykjavik, Iceland.
2345	U.431 (Kptlt Dommes) heavily damaged steamer **HATASU** (3198grt) (Master William Johnston Meek) while she was straggling behind convoy ON.19 about 600 miles east of Cape Race, Newfoundland.
0028 3 Oct	U.431 sank the wreck with one final torpedo. The master, thirty-three crewmen and six gunners were lost. USN destroyer CHARLES F. HUGHES (DD-428) rescued seven survivors after they spent seven days in a lifeboat and landed them at Reykjavik.

5 OCTOBER 1941

Convoy HX.153 departed Halifax, Nova Scotia, escorted by destroyer ANNAPOLIS.
ANNAPOLIS was relieved on the 7th by USN destroyers BERNADOU (DD-153), DUPONT (DD-152), LEA (DD-118), MACLEISH (DD-220), and SAMPSON (DD-394) with corvette GLADIOLUS. The corvette was detached the next day.
Destroyers MALCOLM, SARDONYX, and WATCHMAN, corvettes ARABIS, DAHLIA, MONKSHOOD, and SUNFLOWER, and antisubmarine trawlers NORTHERN PRIDE and NORTHERN WAVE relieved the USN escort

group on the 13th.

Corvette MONKSHOOD was detached from the convoy on the 16th, and the rest of the escorts were detached from the convoy on the 17th.

The convoy arrived at Liverpool on the 19th.

Convoy SC.48, departed Sydney, Cape Breton, escorted by corvettes BADDECK and SHEDIAC.

Corvette GLADIOLUS joined the convoy on the 8th, while corvettes CAMROSE, MIMOSA (FF), ROSTHERN, and WETASKIWIN joined the convoy on the 9th.

On the 16th, USN Task Unit TU.4.1.5 (Lt Cdr Davis) joined the convoy with destroyers PLUNKETT (DD-431), LIVERMORE (DD-429), KEARNY (DD-432), and DECATUR (DD-341) from convoy ON.24, destroyer GREER (DD-145) from other escort duties, plus destroyer BROADWATER and corvette ABELIA from Reykjavik.

Also on the 16th, destroyers HIGHLANDER and RICHMOND, corvettes PICTOU and VERONICA, plus antisubmarine trawler ST APOLLO joined the escort.

Corvette PICTOU was detached from the convoy later that day.

Corvette GLADIOLUS was lost on the 16th.

The initial escorts, less corvette ROSTHERN were detached from the convoy with the USN destroyers.

Corvette VERONICA was also detached from the convoy on the 17th.

On the 17th, destroyers AMAZON, BULLDOG, and GEORGETOWN, corvette HEARTSEASE, plus antisubmarine trawlers ANGLE and CAPE WARWICK joined the convoy.

On the 18th, destroyer BROADWATER was lost.

Destroyers HIGHLANDER and RICHMOND plus corvette ABELIA were detached from the convoy on the 20th, destroyers AMAZON, BULLDOG, and GEORGETOWN plus corvettes HEARTSEASE and ROSTHERN were detached from the convoy on the 21st, and the antisubmarine trawlers were detached from the convoy on the 22nd, before the convoy arrived at Liverpool.

9 OCTOBER 1941

USN destroyer UPSHUR (DD-144) dropped depth charges on a submarine contact while escorting convoy ON.22.

ULTRA message intercepts identified U.374, U.573, U.208 and U.109 in a patrol line southeast of Cape Farewell, Greenland.

Canadian troop convoy TC.14 departed Halifax, Nova Scotia, with troopships ANDES (25,689grt), AORANGI (17,491grt), CAPETOWN CASTLE (27,000grt), MONARCH OF BERMUDA (22,424grt), REINA DEL PACIFICO (17,702grt), and WARWICK CASTLE (20,107grt).

The convoy was escorted by destroyer ST FRANCIS from 9 to 12 October, destroyer RESTIGOUCHE from 9 to 15 October, destroyers HARVESTER and HAVELOCK from 9 to 17 October, destroyer SKEENA from 11 to 15 October, destroyer BUXTON from 11 to 17 October, destroyers HIGHLANDER and BROADWATER from 14 to 16 October, destroyer SHERWOOD from 14 to 17 October, antiaircraft cruiser CAIRO and destroyer BELMONT from 15 to 17 October. The convoy arrived at Liverpool on the 17th.

10 OCTOBER 1941

USN Task Group TG.17.4 with aircraft carrier YORKTOWN (CV-5), battleship NEW MEXICO (BB-40), heavy cruiser QUINCY (CA-39), light cruiser SAVANNAH (CL-42), and Destroyer Divisions 3 and 16 with RHIND (DD-404), HAMMANN (DD-412), ANDERSON (DD-411), SIMS (DD-409), MAYRANT (DD-402), ROWAN (DD-405), HUGHES (DD-410) and TRIPPE (DD-403) departed Argentia for Casco Bay.

Encountering heavy weather, YORKTOWN (CV-5), NEW MEXICO (BB-40), QUINCY (CA-39), SAVANNAH (CL-42), RHIND (DD-404), HAMMANN (DD-412), ANDERSON (DD-411), SIMS (DD-409), MAYRANT (DD-402), ROWAN (DD-405), HUGHES (DD-410), and TRIPPE (DD-403) arrived at Casco Bay on the Gulf of Maine on the 13th. All ships suffered varying degrees of weather damage.

Canadian destroyers RESTIGOUCHE, OTTAWA, and SKEENA with destroyers HAVELOCK, HARVESTER and BUXTON joined Canadian troop convoy TC.14 east of Newfoundland.

U.502, U.568 and U.553 joined the patrol line southeast of Cape Farewell, Greenland. Convoys ONS.23, ON.24, SC.48 and TC.14 were all moved south to avoid the waiting U-boats.

Convoy HX.154 departed Halifax, Nova Scotia, escorted by destroyer ANNAPOLIS and corvette AMHERST. The corvette was detached from the convoy the next day.

USN destroyers CHARLES F. HUGHES (DD-428), GLEAVES (DD-423), LANSDALE (DD-426), MADISON (DD-425), and SIMPSON (DD-221) joined the convoy on the 12th.

Destroyer ANNAPOLIS was detached from the convoy on the 13th.

On the 19th, destroyers DOUGLAS, SALADIN, SKATE, and VETERAN, corvettes ABELIA and VERONICA, plus antisubmarine trawlers ST ELSTAN and ST ZENO relieved the USN destroyers.

Destroyers DOUGLAS and SKATE were detached from the convoy on the 22nd with the corvettes.

The convoy arrived at Liverpool on the 23rd.

11 OCTOBER 1941

Convoy SC.49 departed Sydney, Cape Breton, escorted by corvette LETHBRIDGE.

On the 13th, corvettes AMHERST, EYEBRIGHT, MAYFLOWER, NANAIMO, and PRESCOTT joined the convoy. Destroyer ST FRANCIS and corvette KENOGAMI joined the convoy on the 14th.

Destroyer ST FRANCIS plus corvettes EYEBRIGHT and KENOGAMI were detached from the convoy on the 21st.

Corvettes AMHERST, LETHBRIDGE, MAYFLOWER, NANAIMO, and PRESCOTT were detached from the convoy on the 22nd when corvettes HEATHER, LOBELIA, and NARCISSUS joined the convoy.

On the 23rd, destroyers BEAGLE, ROXBOROUGH, SALISBURY, and SHERWOOD plus antisubmarine trawler NOTTS COUNTY joined the convoy.

Destroyer SALISBURY was detached from the convoy on the 24th.

The remainder of the escorts arrived with the convoy at Liverpool on the 27th.

12 OCTOBER 1941

ULTRA message intercepts identified that U.558, U.432, U.101, U.77, U.751 and U.73 were arriving from France to extend the German patrol line southeast of Cape Farewell, Greenland.

Convoys ONS.23, ON.24, SC.48 and TC.14 were diverted even further north to avoid detection by the German Wolfpack.

14 OCTOBER 1941

U.553 (Kptlt Thurmann) spotted convoy SC.48 (Commodore Elliot) after a heavy storm with forty-nine ships, eleven escorts including Canadian corvette WETASKIWIN, corvette GLADIOLUS, Free French corvette MIMOSA and Canadian corvette BADDECK.

U.432, U.502, U.558 and U.568 followed by U.73, U.77, U.101 and U.751 converged on the position of convoy SC.48.

16 OCTOBER 1941

Convoy HX.155 departed Halifax, Nova Scotia, escorted by corvettes DRUMHELLER and SUMMERSIDE.

USN destroyers BAINBRIDGE (DD-246), OVERTON (DD-239), ROE (DD-418), STURTEVANT (DD-240), and TRUXTUN (DD-229) relieved the corvettes on the 18th.

Destroyer VOLUNTEER and corvettes CAMPANULA, GENTIAN, HONEYSUCKLE, MYOSOTIS, PERIWINKLE, and SWEETBRIAR relieved the American group on the 25th.

All escorts but corvettes GENTIAN and PERIWINKLE were detached from the convoy on the 30th.

The convoy arrived at Liverpool on the 31st.

17 OCTOBER 1941

The USN escorts for convoy HX.154 made ASDIC contacts on possible U-boats.

USN destroyer CHARLES F. HUGHES (DD-428) dropped depth charges on a strong contact in 59, 58N, 23, 15W.

Convoy SC.50 departed Sydney, Cape Breton, escorted by corvette SOREL.

Corvette SOREL was detached from the convoy on the 19th when destroyer ST CROIX plus corvettes AGASSIZ, ALBERNI, ALYSSE, BITTERSWEET, COLLINGWOOD, and WINDFLOWER joined the convoy.

Corvette WINDFLOWER was detached from the convoy on the 20th.

Destroyer RESTIGOUCHE joined the convoy on the 25th.

Destroyer ST CROIX was detached from the convoy on the 26th, while corvettes AGASSIZ, ALBERNI, ALYSSE, BITTERSWEET, COLLINGWOOD were detached from the convoy on the 31st.

Destroyers KEPPEL, ROCKINGHAM, SABRE, and VENOMOUS, corvettes ALISMA and KINGCUP, plus antisubmarine trawler LADY ELSA joined the convoy on the 31st.

The convoy arrived at Liverpool on 4 November.

20 OCTOBER 1941

Wolfpack MORDBRENNER with U.573, U.374, U.208 and U.109 arrived to reconnoitre the area of Strait of Belle Isle off Newfoundland. However, the area was empty of ship traffic, as the Admiralty had alerted all ships to avoid the area based upon the ULTRA message intercepts of the group's pending arrival.

22 OCTOBER 1941

Convoy SC.49 departed the Strait of Belle Isle (Labrador Straits) with thirty-one ships covered by Escort Group EG.4 and were not bothered by any U-boats because the German patrol line had been pulled far to the east.

Convoy HX.155 departed Halifax, Nova Scotia, with fifty-nine ships escorted by USN Task Unit TU.4.1.7, which was relieved at the MOMP by Escort Group EG.5 on the 25th.

Convoy HX.156 departed Halifax escorted by destroyer ANNAPOLIS.

USN destroyers BENSON (DD-421), HILARY P. JONES (DD-427), NIBLACK (DD-424), REUBEN JAMES (DD-245), and TARBELL (DD-142) relieved her on the 24th.

Destroyer REUBEN JAMES (DD-245) was lost on the 31st.

Destroyers VERITY and WOLVERINE and corvettes CAMELLIA, LARKSPUR, and MONTBRETIA joined the convoy on the 31st.

The American group was detached from the convoy on 1 November when relieved by destroyers BROKE and

BUXTON, corvette BEGONIA and EGLANTINE, and antisubmarine trawler KING SOL.
The destroyers and corvettes BEGONIA and CAMELLIA were detached from the convoy on 4 November and the convoy arrived at Liverpool on 5 November.

23 OCTOBER 1941

Convoy SC.51 departed Sydney, Cape Breton, escorted by AMC WORCESTERSHIRE plus corvettes BATTLEFORD, DUNVEGAN, and SOREL.
The three corvettes were detached from the convoy on the 25th when corvettes ARROWHEAD, CHILLIWACK, POLYANTHUS, PRIMROSE, SNOWBERRY, and TRAIL joined the convoy.
Corvette POLYANTHUS was detached from the convoy on 2 November and the rest of the corvettes were detached from the convoy on 4 November.
Destroyers MALCOLM, SARDONYX, and WATCHMAN joined the convoy on 4 November with corvettes ARABIS, DAHLIA, and MONKSHOOD, plus antisubmarine trawlers NORTHERN GEM and NORTHERN SPRAY.
Corvettes ARABIS and MONKSHOOD were detached from the convoy on 7 November.
On 8 November, the AMC, destroyer SARDONYX, and corvette DAHLIA were detached from the convoy. The convoy arrived at Liverpool on 9 November.

25 OCTOBER 1941

USN destroyer HILARY P. JONES (DD-427) dropped depth charges on a submarine contact while escorting convoy HX.156 south of Greenland.

28 OCTOBER 1941

0719	U.106 (Hermann Rasch) sank steamer **KING MALCOLM** (5120grt) (Master James Wilson) as she was straggling behind convoy SC.50 southeast of St. John's in 47, 40N, 51, 15W. The master, thirty-three crewmen and four gunners were lost. There were no survivors. She was last seen on the 21st in 47, 40N, 51, 15W.
	USN Task Force TF.14 departed Halifax, Nova Scotia, with aircraft carrier YORKTOWN (CV-5), battleship NEW MEXICO (BB-40), light cruisers SAVANNAH (CL-42) and PHILADELPHIA (CL-41) plus destroyers MORRIS (DD-417), SIMS (DD-409), HUGHES (DD-410), HAMMANN (DD-412), ANDERSON (DD-411), MUSTIN (DD-413), RUSSELL (DD-414), O'BRIEN (DD-415) and WAKE (DD-416) escorting steamers EMPIRE PINTAIL (7773grt) (ex American **HOWELL LYKES** (7773grt)), EMPIRE EGRET (7248grt) (ex American **NIGHTINGALE** (7248grt)), EMPIRE FULMAR (7775grt) (ex American **HAWAIIAN SHIPPER** (7775grt)), EMPIRE WIDGEON (6736grt) (ex American **EXEMPLAR** (6736grt)), EMPIRE PEREGRINE (7842grt) (ex American **CHINA MAIL** (7842grt)), and EMPIRE ORIOLE (6551grt) (ex American **EXTANTIA** (6551grt)) to Britain. The steamers were part of a deal to provide ships to Britain from the United States.
On 2 November, Task Force TF.14 joined convoy CT.5 with troopships DUCHESS OF ATHOLL (20,119grt), SOBIESKI (11,030grt), ORCADES (23,456grt), WARWICK CASTLE (20,107grt), ANDES (25,689grt), DURBAN CASTLE (17,388grt), ORONSAY (20,043grt), and REINA DEL PACIFICO (17,702grt), escorted by antiaircraft cruiser CAIRO and destroyers NEWARK, CHARLESTON, CALDWELL, BEVERLEY, BADSWORTH, and CROOME.
The escorts traded convoys and Task Force TF.14 took convoy CT.5 towards Halifax.
The British escort took the convoy, designated TANGO, and proceeded to North Channel.
On 3 November, USN destroyers WAINWRIGHT (DD-420), MAYRANT (DD-402), TRIPPE (DD-403), RHIND (DD-404), ROWAN (DD-405), MCDOUGAL (DD-358), MOFFETT (DD-362), and WINSLOW (DD-359) relieved the Task Force TF.14 destroyer escort so they could refuel.
The convoy arrived at Halifax on 7 November and the troops carried in convoy CT.5 were transferred to American transports for convoy WS.12X.
	Convoy HX.157 departed Halifax escorted by destroyer ANNAPOLIS plus corvettes BUCTOUCHE and GALT. USN destroyers DALLAS (DD-199), EBERLE (DD-430), ELLIS (DD-154), ERICSSON (DD-440), and UPSHUR (DD-144) joined the convoy on the 30th.
On 3 November, the original escort was detached from the convoy.
Destroyer AMAZON joined the escort on 6 November.
The USN escort was detached from the convoy on 8 November when relieved by destroyers BELMONT and GEORGETOWN with corvettes HEARTSEASE, RENONCULE, and ROSELYS, plus antisubmarine trawlers ANGLE and CAPE WARWICK at the MOMP.
Destroyer DOUGLAS joined the convoy on 9 November.
Destroyers BELMONT and GEORGETOWN were detached from the convoy on 11 November, and destroyers AMAZON and DOUGLAS were detached from the convoy on 12 November.
The convoy arrived at Liverpool on 13 November.

29 OCTOBER 1941

USN destroyer HILARY P. JONES (DD-427) dropped depth charges on a submarine contact while escorting convoy HX.156 south of Greenland.

Convoy SC.52 departed Sydney, Cape Breton, escorted by corvettes BATTLEFORD, DUNVEGAN, and SOREL.
Destroyer BROADWAY with corvettes ACONIT, BUCTOUCHE, GALT, and WINDFLOWER joined the convoy

30 OCTOBER 1941

	USN destroyers DUPONT (DD-152), BERNADOU (DD-153), SAMPSON (DD-394) and MACLEISH (DD-220) dropped depth charges on submarine contacts while escorting convoy ON.28.
	USN fleet tugboat CHEROKEE (ATF-66) and USCG cutter CAMPBELL (WPG-32) joined convoy ON.28 at sea.
	U.568, U.751, U.77 and U.502 set up a patrol line off Newfoundland with U.571, U.577, U.133, U.567, U.552 and U.96. U.571, U.577, U.133, U.567, U.552 and U.96 for Wolfpack STOSSTRUPP and were ordered to attack shipping east of Newfoundland Bank.
0900	U.106 (Hermann Rasch) torpedoed American tanker SALINAS (AO-19) (8246grt) while attacking convoy ON.28 about seven hundred miles east of Newfoundland. USN destroyers DUPONT (DD-152) and LEA (DD-118) escorted the tanker to port.

31 OCTOBER 1941

	USN destroyers BABBITT (DD-128), BUCK (DD-420), DUPONT (DD-152), LEARY (DD-158) and SAMPSON (DD-394) dropped depth charges on submarine contacts while escorting convoy ON.28.
0903	U.374 (ObltzS v. Fischel) sank unescorted steamer **ROSE SCHIAFFINO** (3349grt) (ex French) (Master Thomas P. Evans) about 225 miles east of St. John's, Newfoundland, at 51N, 62W. The master, thirty-six crewmen and four gunners were lost.

East of United States
Long. W85, 00 – W60,00 Lat. N43, 30 – N25, 00

7 OCTOBER 1941

	Aircraft carrier FURIOUS arrived at Philadelphia, Pennsylvania, to begin a refit. She returned to Britain in April 1942.

25 OCTOBER 1941

	USN Task Force TF.14 departed Portland, Maine, with aircraft carrier YORKTOWN (CV-5) (with VF-42, VB-5, VS-5, and VT-5), battleship NEW MEXICO (BB-40), light cruisers SAVANNAH (CL-42) and PHILADELPHIA (CL-41) plus nine destroyers.

28 OCTOBER 1941

	Light cruiser CARADOC began a refit at the New York Navy Yard lasting until 26 February 1942.

Caribbean and Gulf of Mexico
Long. W100, 00 – W60, 00 Lat. N31, 00 – N05, 00

1 OCTOBER 1941

	The USN Task Force TF.3 conducted regular patrols between Trinidad and Recife, Brazil, to southwest of the Cape Verde Islands. Four patrol groups were formed, each with a cruiser and a destroyer. TG.3.5 included heavy cruiser OMAHA (CL-4) and destroyer SOMERS (DD-381), TG.3.6 included heavy cruiser MILWAUKEE (CL-5) and destroyer WARRINGTON (DD-383), TG.3.7 included heavy cruiser MEMPHIS (CL-13) and destroyer DAVIS (DD-395), and TG.3.8 included heavy cruiser CINCINNATI (CL-6) and destroyer JOUETT (DD-396).
	USN Task Group TG.3.7 departed Trinidad on a Middle Atlantic patrol with heavy cruiser MEMPHIS (CL-13) and destroyer DAVIS (DD-395), returning on the 19th.
	USN Task Group TG.3.5 was currently on patrol in the South Atlantic with heavy cruiser OMAHA (CL-4) and destroyer SOMERS (DD-381), returning to Trinidad on the 11th.

5 OCTOBER 1941

	Canadian steamer MONDOC (1926grt) was damaged when she struck Darien Rock off the east coast of Trinidad.

7 OCTOBER 1941

	USN Task Group TG.3.6 departed on a Middle Atlantic patrol with heavy cruiser MILWAUKEE (CL-5) and destroyer WARRINGTON (DD-383) returning on the 27th.

9 OCTOBER 1941

USN Task Group TG.3.8 departed Trinidad on a Middle Atlantic patrol with heavy cruiser CINCINNATI (CL-6) and destroyer JOUETT (DD-396) returning on the 27th.

11 OCTOBER 1941

USN Task Group TG.3.5 with heavy cruiser OMAHA (CL-4) and destroyer SOMERS (DD-381) returned to Trinidad from their Middle Atlantic patrol.

20 OCTOBER 1941

USN Task Group TG.3.5 departed Trinidad on a Middle Atlantic patrol with heavy cruiser OMAHA (CL-4) and destroyer SOMERS (DD-381) returning on 15 November.

Western Approaches
Long. W30, 00 – W03, 00   Lat. N58, 30 – N49, 00

1 OCTOBER 1941

German bombing damaged steamer SERENITY (557grt) with bomb near misses ten miles southeast by east of St Govan's Light in 51, 29N, 04, 45W.

Convoy WS.12 rendezvoused off Oversay and included steamers CLAN CAMPBELL (7255grt), EMPIRE TRUST (8143grt), HIGHLAND BRIGADE (14,134grt), SARPEDON (11,321grt), PERSEUS (10,286grt), ALMANZORA (15,551grt), EMPIRE PRIDE (9248grt), LEOPOLDVILLE (11,439grt), STRATHAIRD (22,281grt), EMPRESS OF RUSSIA (16,810grt), EMPRESS OF CANADA (21,517grt), NARKUNDA (16,632grt), CITY OF PARIS (10,902grt), ORMONDE (14,982grt), SAMARIA (19,597grt), FRANCONIA (20,175grt), MENDOZA (8199grt), DUCHESS OF RICHMOND (20,022grt), DOMINION MONARCH (27,155grt), HIGHLAND PRINCESS (14,133grt), PRINCE BAUDOUIN (3050grt), ROYAL ULSTERMAN (3244grt), CLAN LAMONT (7268grt), and PERTHSHIRE (10,496grt). Steamer HIGHLAND PRINCESS was detached from the convoy as convoy CT.4.

AMC CATHAY, minelayer AGAMEMNON, plus Canadian destroyers ASSINIBOINE and SAGUENAY escorted the convoy to 4 October.

Destroyer SIKH escorted the convoy to 5 October.

Destroyers BRADFORD, BADSWORTH, BRIGHTON, LANCASTER, and NEWARK escorted the convoy from 1 to 3 October.

Antiaircraft cruiser CAIRO and destroyers WHITEHALL, WITCH, and VERITY escorted the convoy from 1 to 4 October.

Destroyer BEVERLEY escorted the convoy on 2 and 3 October.

Destroyer BLANKNEY escorted the convoy from 1 to 7 October.

Aircraft carrier ARGUS escorted the convoy to 5 October, when she was detached to Gibraltar.

Heavy cruiser DEVONSHIRE escorted the convoy to 12 October, when she was detached to Freetown, Sierra Leone.

Heavy cruiser DORSETSHIRE escorted the convoy from 12 to 14 October.

Dutch destroyer ISAAC SWEERS departed Gibraltar on the 4th and escorted the convoy on the 7th.

Destroyer GURKHA departed Gibraltar on the 3rd and escorted the convoy on the 8th.

Destroyers WRESTLER, VELOX, VIMY, and VANSITTART plus corvettes AMARANTHUS and ARMERIA escorted the convoy from 11 to 14 October, when the convoy arrived at Freetown.

The convoy departed Freetown on the 19th, less steamer NARKUNDA (16,632grt), escorted by destroyers VELOX and WRESTLER plus corvettes MIGNONETTE, ANCHUSA, and CALENDULA from 19 to 22 October.

Heavy cruiser DEVONSHIRE escorted the convoy from 19 to 30 October.

Heavy cruiser DORSETSHIRE escorted the convoy from 19 October to 3 November.

AMC DERBYSHIRE escorted the convoy from 30 October to 3 November.

Steamers ULSTER MONARCH (3791grt) and ROYAL ULSTERMAN (3244grt) were detached from the convoy to Takoradi, Ghana, on the 21st.

Steamer PRINCE BAUDOUIN (3050grt) was detached from the convoy the same day to St Helena, arriving on the 24th. The steamer departed St Helena the same day and joined AMC DERBYSHIRE the same day. The steamer arrived at Cape Town, South Africa, with the convoy.

Steamers STRATHAIRD (22,281grt), EMPRESS OF CANADA (21,517grt), DOMINION MONARCH (27,155grt), EMPIRE PRIDE (9248grt), LEOPOLDVILLE (11,439grt), MENDOZA (8199grt), CLAN CAMPBELL (7255grt), EMPIRE TRUST (8143grt), PERTHSHIRE (10,496grt), and SARPEDON (11,321grt) arrived at Cape Town on the 29th.

T/Sub-Lt (A) J. W. T. Cooper RNZVR, and Leading Airman J. Stewart were killed when their Roc aircraft of 772 Squadron crashed near Crinan, Argyllshire.

2 OCTOBER 1941

U.575 (Kptlt Heydemann) sank Dutch steamer **TUVA** (4652grt) in 54,16N, 26, 36W. The submarine claimed sinking a second steamer. One crewman was lost.

USN destroyer WINSLOW (DD-359) from TU.4.1.3 was detached from convoy ON.20 to assist the crew of the

	torpedoed **TUVA**. She heavily depth charged the U-boat before assisting the crew.
	Two Fw200 aircraft of I/KG.40 spotted convoy OG.75 west of the North Channel with twenty-five steamers and nine escorts. Wolfpack BRESLAU was formed to attack the convoy.
	Convoy ON.22 departed Liverpool escorted by destroyers BROKE, MANSFIELD, and ST ALBANS, corvette EGLANTINE, plus antisubmarine trawlers COVENTRY CITY and KING SOL. Destroyer WOLVERINE joined the convoy on the 4th. USN destroyers DALLAS (DD-199), EBERLE (DD-430), ELLIS (DD-154), ERICSSON (DD-440), and UPSHUR (DD-144) relieved these escorts from the convoy on the 7th. The American escorts were detached from the convoy when the convoy was dispersed on the 15th.
	T/Sub-Lt (A) D. E. Smith RNVR was killed when his Walrus aircraft of 751 Squadron sank in River Tay.
	Submarine PORPOISE departed Troon, Scotland, for Gibraltar after her refit.

3 OCTOBER 1941

	A German Fw200 aircraft tracked convoy OG.75 as it moved south, but U.71, U.83, U.206, and U.563 failed to make contact.
	Aircraft carrier INDOMITABLE arrived in the Clyde to begin working up to combat efficiency.
	Convoy OS.8 departed Liverpool, England, escorted by sloop FLEETWOOD. The sloop was detached from the convoy off Freetown, Sierra Leone, on the 25th. On 4 October, sloops BLACK SWAN and SANDWICH plus naval trawler BURRA joined the convoy escort. Trawler BURRA was detached from the convoy on the 9th, sloop SANDWICH was detached from the convoy on the 20th, and sloop BLACK SWAN was detached from the convoy on the 25th. On the 5th, sloop SCARBOROUGH joined the convoy and was detached from the convoy on the 21st. Corvettes ARMERIA, ASTER, CYCLAMEN, and STARWORT joined the convoy on the 20th and escorted the convoy into Freetown, arriving on the 26th.

4 OCTOBER 1941

	A German Fw200 aircraft continued to track convoy OG.75 as it moved south.
	U.564 and U.204 were ordered to delay their return to France to rendezvous with blockade-runner RIO GRANDE (6062grt) and escort her into German controlled waters.
	Convoy ON.23 departed Liverpool. The convoy was joined on the 5th by destroyers MALCOLM, SARDONYX, and WATCHMAN, corvettes ARABIS, ARROWHEAD, CELANDINE, DAHLIA, MONKSHOOD, and PETUNIA, and antisubmarine trawlers LADY ELSA, NORTHERN GEM, NORTHERN PRIDE, and NORTHERN WAVE. Destroyer SARDONYX and the trawlers were detached from the convoy on the 9th. Destroyers BROADWAY and BURWELL plus corvettes BRANDON, BUCTOUCHE, COBALT, and GALT joined the convoy on the 10th. Corvette BRANDON was detached from the convoy later that day with destroyer MALCOLM and corvette PETUNIA. Destroyer WATCHMAN and corvette CELANDINE were detached from the convoy on the 11th. Corvettes ARROWHEAD and BUCTOUCHE were detached from the convoy on the 17th, while destroyers BROADWAY and BURWELL were detached from the convoy on the 18th. The convoy arrived at Halifax, Nova Scotia, on the 19th with corvettes COBALT and GALT.
0400	Minesweeper BRAMBLE departed Belfast, Northern Ireland, for Scapa Flow to await the sailing of convoy PQ.2.

5 OCTOBER 1941

	During the night, USN destroyer MAYO (DD-422) ordered Swedish motor ship KAAPAREN (3393grt) to turn off her lights while she was sailing with convoy HX.152 in the North Atlantic. After repeated requests went unanswered, the destroyer informed the ship that she would be fired upon if the lights were not turned off immediately. Shortly thereafter, the convoy returned to total darkness.

6 OCTOBER 1941

	Light cruisers KENYA and SHEFFIELD arrived in the Clyde from Gibraltar.

7 OCTOBER 1941

	USN escort Task Unit TU.4.1.1 joined convoy ON.22 at the MOMP and escorted the convoy to the west.
	USN Task Unit TU.4.1.6 delivered convoy HX.153 with fifty-nine ships to the MOMP exchange area.

8 OCTOBER 1941

	Convoy ON.24 departed Liverpool, England, escorted by destroyers AMAZON and BULLDOG, corvettes ACONIT, DIANTHUS, and HEARTSEASE, and antisubmarine trawler NOTTS COUNTY. Destroyer GEORGETOWN joined the convoy on the 10th. The destroyers, corvette HEARTSEASE, and the trawler were detached from the convoy on the 13th when

	USN destroyers DECATUR (DD-341), GREER (DD-145), KEARNY (DD-432), LIVERMORE (DD-429), and PLUNKETT (DD-431) joined the convoy.
	Destroyer KEARNY (DD-432) was detached from the convoy on the 14th.
	The remaining American destroyers plus corvettes ACONIT and DIANTHUS were detached from the convoy on the 15th when the convoy was dispersed.
0700	Destroyer ONSLOW departed Greenock, Scotland, for Scapa Flow to begin working up to combat efficiency.

9 OCTOBER 1941

| 1900 | Destroyer CHARLESTON departed Loch Alsh for Scapa Flow to carry out repairs to her oil tanks. |

10 OCTOBER 1941

| | Convoy ON.25 departed Liverpool escorted by destroyer DOUGLAS. Destroyers SALADIN, SKATE, and VETERAN, corvettes ABELIA, and VERONICA, plus antisubmarine trawlers ST ZENO and VIZALMA joined the convoy on the 11th. The trawlers were detached from the convoy on the 13th and the corvettes were detached from the convoy on the 15th. The destroyers were detached from the convoy on the 16th when relieved by corvettes ALGOMA, CHAMBLY, MATAPEDIA, NAPANEE, ORILLIA, and PICTOU. Corvette PICTOU was detached from the convoy later that day. On the 19th, destroyer OTTAWA joined the escort and the convoy was dispersed on the 24th. |

11 OCTOBER 1941

| | Light cruisers KENYA and SHEFFIELD arrived at the Clyde from Scapa Flow. |

12 OCTOBER 1941

| | U.563 again found convoy OG.75, but was forced under by aircraft covering the convoy. |
| | Minelayers MANXMAN and WELSHMAN departed Loch Alsh for Milford Haven, Wales. |

13 OCTOBER 1941

	Convoy ONS.25 moved much further south to join the American escort at the MOMP to avoid the new U-boat patrol line.
	Convoy OS.9 departed Liverpool escorted by Free French sloop COMMANDANT DOMINE, which was detached on the 24th. On the 14th, sloops EGRET, FOWEY, and LEITH joined the convoy. Sloops FOWEY, and LEITH were detached from the convoy on 1 November, and EGRET was detached from the convoy on 1 November. Also joining on the 14th were escort vessels BANFF and FISHGUARD, which were detached from the convoy on 1 and 2 November, respectively, plus corvettes HOLLYHOCK and STONECROP. Corvette HOLLYHOCK arrived with the convoy on 5 November and STONECROP was detached from the convoy on 1 November. Corvettes BURDOCK, CLOVER, and NIGELLA joined the convoy on the 31st and arrived with the convoy at Freetown, Sierra Leone, on 5 November.
	Minelayers MANXMAN and WELSHMAN arrived at Milford Haven, Wales, from Loch Alsh and embarked mines before heading to Plymouth.
0815	Destroyer ORIBI arrived at the Clyde from Scapa Flow escorting steamer LLANSTEPHAN CASTLE (11,299grt). The destroyer departed the Clyde later that day to return to Scapa Flow.
1030	The Liverpool section of convoy PQ.2 departed for Scapa Flow escorted by minesweepers SPEEDY and SEAGULL.

14 OCTOBER 1941

| | Convoy ON.26 departed Liverpool escorted by destroyers BEAGLE and SALISBURY, corvettes HEATHER and NARCISSUS, plus antisubmarine trawlers ARAB and LADY MADELEINE. The escorts were detached from the convoy on the 20th when relieved by USN destroyers BABBITT (DD-128), BADGER (DD-126), BROOME (DD-210), LEARY (DD-158), MAYO (DD-422), and SCHENCK (DD-159). The USN destroyers were detached from the convoy when the convoy dispersed on the 29th. |

15 OCTOBER 1941

	U.568, U.432, U.558 and U.502 converged on the position of convoy SC.48 while U.101, U.77, U.751 and U.73 set up another patrol line further east.
	U.558 (Günther Krech) sank Canadian steamer **VANCOUVER ISLAND** (9472grt) (ex German **WESER** (9472grt)) while attacking convoy SC.48 in 53, 37N, 25, 37W.
	USN Task Unit TU.4.1.4 was ordered to join with convoy SC.48 and provide additional escort against the converging U-boats.

	Convoy ON.24 was ordered to scatter after USN Task Unit TU.4.1.4 was sent to help convoy SC.48.
	Escort Group EG.3 with destroyer BULLDOG (Cdr Baker-Cresswell), AMAZON, RICHMOND, GEORGETOWN and BELMONT, corvette HEARTSEASE, antisubmarine trawlers ANGLE, ST APOLLO and CAPE WARWICK plus rescue ship ZAAFARAN were ordered to join convoy SC.48.
	Escort Group EG.2 with convoy ONS.25 was ordered to dispatch corvettes VERONICA and ABELIA to join convoy SC.48.
	Destroyers HIGHLANDER (Cdr Voucher) and BROADWATER were dispatched from Reykjavik, Iceland, to join convoy SC.48.
	Destroyer SHERWOOD plus three Canadian corvettes with convoy TC.14 were dispatched to join convoy SC.48.
	Canadian corvette PICTOU was detached from convoy ONS.21 to join the escort for convoy SC.48.
0815	U.553 (Kptlt Thurmann) sank steamer **SILVERCEDAR** (4354grt) (Master Thomas Keane) while attacking convoy SC.48 southeast of Cape Farewell, Greenland, in 53, 36N, 29, 57W. The master, eighteen crewmen, two gunners, and one passenger (DBS) were lost. Free French corvette MIMOSA rescued nineteen crewmen and seven gunners and landed them at Reykjavik, Iceland.
0817	U.553 missed a ship with another torpedo attack on convoy SC.48 southeast of Cape Farewell.
0823	U.553 sank Norwegian steamer **ILA** (1583grt) (Master Thore K. Johnsen) while attacking convoy SC.48 southeast of Cape Farewell in 53, 34N, 30, 10W. The ship exploded and sank immediately. Fourteen crewmen were lost. Free French corvette MIMOSA (Capt Roger Birot) rescued the master and six crewmen three hours later.
1200	Canadian destroyer COLUMBIA avoided a torpedo fired by U.553 and pursued the U-boat, dropping depth charges that forced the U-boat very deep.
1330	Battleship ROYAL SOVEREIGN with destroyers BEDOUIN and ANTHONY departed the Clyde for Scapa Flow.

16 OCTOBER 1941

	Corvette GLADIOLUS pursued U.568 using her ASDIC.
	U.573, U.374, U.208 and U.109 formed Wolfpack MORDBRENNER and continued across the North Atlantic to reconnoitre the area of Strait of Belle Isle (Labrador Straits) off Newfoundland instead of joining the attack on convoy SC.48.
	USN destroyer LIVERMORE (DD-429) depth charged U.553 after she was detected near convoy SC.48.
	USN destroyer KEARNY (DD-432) conducted antisubmarine sweeps astern of convoy SC.48 to prevent U-boats from running on the surface to reach new attack positions ahead of the convoy.
	USN destroyer CHARLES F. HUGHES (DD-428) rescued survivors from sunken steamer **HATASU** (3198grt).
	Light cruiser EDINBURGH departed the Clyde for Scapa Flow.
	Convoy ON.27 departed Liverpool. On the 17th, destroyers VANOC and VOLUNTEER plus corvettes CAMPANULA, GENTIAN, HIBISCUS, HONEYSUCKLE, MYOSOTIS, PERIWINKLE, and SWEETBRIAR joined the convoy escort. The destroyers were detached from the convoy on the 23rd when destroyers COLUMBIA and SKEENA with corvettes BRANDON, CAMROSE, MIMOSA, SHEDIAC, and WETASKIWIN joined the escort. The initial group of corvettes were detached from the convoy on the 24th. Corvette BRANDON was detached from the convoy on 1 November and the rest of the escort was detached from the convoy on 2 November when the convoy dispersed.
	German bombing damaged steamer EDENVALE (444grt) off Old Head of Kinsale.
0114	U.568 (Kptlt Preuß) sank steamer **EMPIRE HERON** (6023grt) (ex American **MOSELLA** (6023grt)) (Master James Dick Ross) while attacking convoy SC.48 in 56, 10N, 24, 30W. (Other sources place the attack in 54, 55N, 27, 15W.) The master, thirty-three crewmen and nine gunners were lost. Corvette GLADIOLUS rescued only one survivor, but this survivor was later lost with the corvette.
<1159	In the morning, U.568 and U.502 spotted convoy SC.48 for a short time and radioed its position to the Wolfpack.
1200	USN Task Unit TU.4.1.4 with destroyers PLUNKETT (DD-431), LIVERMORE (DD-429), KEARNY (DD-432), DECATUR (DD-341) and GREER (DD-145) joined with convoy SC.48.
>1201	U.553, U.568, U.558, U.502 and U.432 established contact with convoy SC.48.

17 OCTOBER 1941

	Destroyers HIGHLANDER, BULLDOG, AMAZON, GEORGETOWN, and RICHMOND plus corvettes PICTOU and VERONICA joined convoy SC.48 at sea.
	U.553 (Karl Thurmann) sank Panamanian steamer **BOLD VENTURE** (3222grt) (ex Danish **ALSSUND** (3222grt)) while attacking convoy SC.48 south of Iceland in 56, 10N, 24, 30W. Seventeen crewmen were missing.

	USN destroyer LIVERMORE (DD-429) immediately picked up the U-boat on ASDIC and began several depth charge attacks.
	U.553 unsuccessfully attacked USN destroyer PLUNKETT (DD-431) in 56, 10N, 24, 30W.
	From Iceland, air cover by USN Catalina aircraft squadrons VP-73 and VP-74 forced the U-boats under water.
	U.101, U.77, U.751 and U.73 converged on the position of convoy SC.48 to continue the battle the next day.
0128 0131 0149	U.558 (Günther Krech) fired torpedoes at 0128, 0131, and 0149 while attacking convoy SC.48 in the North Atlantic. During this action: U.558 sank corvette **GLADIOLUS** (965grt) (Lt Cdr H. M. C. Sanders DSC, DSC, RD RNR) while attacking convoy SC.48 in 57, 00N, 25, 00W. (It is possible that **U.432 (**ObltzS Schultze) sank the corvette when she fired torpedoes into the same general area.) Sanders, T/Lt S. H. Gifford RANVR, T/Lt J. G. Gifford-Hull RNVR, T/Lt J. C. Miller DSC RNVR, T/Sub-Lt R. B. Ross RNVR, and fifty-nine ratings were missing. There were no survivors. U.558 sank tanker **W. C. TEAGLE** (9552grt) while attacking convoy SC.48 in 57N, 25W. Thirty crewmen were lost. Destroyer BROADWATER rescued nine survivors, who were subsequently lost when the destroyer was sunk. U.558 heavily damaged Norwegian steamer **ERVIKEN** (6595grt) (Master Paul Heesch) while attacking convoy SC.48 in 56, 10N, 24, 30W. The master, eighteen Norwegians, five British and one Danish crewman were lost. She had stopped to rescue survivors from the other ships. Destroyer BROADWATER rescued two survivors, who were subsequently lost when the destroyer was sunk the next day.
0214	U.558 heavily damaged Norwegian steamer **RYM** (1369grt) (Master Conrad Rustad) while attacking convoy SC.48 in 57, 01N, 24, 20W. The master, the first engineer, a stoker and an able seaman remained aboard and tried to save the ship. The other seventeen crewmen abandoned the ship in the port side lifeboat. Corvette VERONICA (D. F. White RNR) arrived three hours later and rescued the entire crew of twenty-one. VERONICA scuttled the wreck and landed the crew at Londonderry on the 19th.
0342	U.432 (ObltzS Schultze) sank Greek steamer **EVROS** (5283grt) while attacking convoy SC.48 south of Iceland in 57N, 24, 30W. Thirty crewmen were lost, and only two survivors were rescued.
0400 0448	U.432 heavily damaged Norwegian tanker **BARFONN** (9739grt) (Master E. Ellingsen Vorberg) while attacking convoy SC.48 south of Iceland in 56, 58N, 25, 04W. U.432 sank the wreck with one last torpedo. Fourteen crewmen and one gunner were lost (eight Norwegian, two Canadians, two British, one Swede and one Dane). Corvette BADDECK rescued two, and corvette WETASKIWIN rescued twenty-four survivors. All survivors were taken to Reykjavik, Iceland.
0415	U.568 (Kptlt Preuß) damaged USN destroyer **KEARNY** (DD-432) (1630grt) (Lt Cdr Danis), which joined convoy SC.48 after escorting convoy ON.24, in 57N, 24W. Eleven enlisted men were killed and eight ratings were seriously wounded. Destroyer GREER (DD-145) assisted damaged destroyer KEARNY (DD-432). She was able to proceed to Hvalfjord under her own power at ten knots. After temporary repairs alongside USN repair ship VULCAN (AR-5) at Hvalfjord, she sailed on 25 December for Boston, Massachusetts, where full repairs were completed on 5 April 1942.
0900	Destroyers LAFOREY and LIGHTNING arrived at the Clyde from Scapa Flow to embark passengers and stores prior to transferring to Force H at Gibraltar.

18 OCTOBER 1941

	USN destroyers PLUNKETT (DD-431), LIVERMORE (DD-429) and DECATUR (DD-341) dropped depth charges on suspected U-boat contacts while escorting convoy SC.48 south of Greenland.
	Tug **ASSURANCE** (675grt) became grounded at Lough Foyle and was declared a total loss.
	During the night, U.101 (Kptlt Mengersen) sank destroyer **BROADWATER** (1190grt) (Lt Cdr W. M. L. Astwood) (ex USN **MASON** (DD-191)) south of Iceland while attacking convoy SC.48 in 57, 01N, 19, 08W. Lt J. S. Parker RNVR was killed. Parker was an American and was believed to be the first U.S. citizen killed in the Royal Navy. T/Lt R. J. Sampson RNVR and one rating died of wounds. Lt A. Knowles, T/A/Gunner (T) F. W. Turner, and thirty-nine ratings were missing.

19 OCTOBER 1941

	German bombing sank Norwegian steamer **RASK** (632grt) along the southeast coast of Ireland in 52, 08N, 06, 23W. Seven crewmen and one gunner were lost.
0900	Destroyers ANTELOPE and ANTHONY arrived at the Clyde from Scapa Flow to escort destroyer depot ship FORTH from the Clyde to Rosyth.
1330	Aircraft carrier VICTORIOUS with destroyers LAFOREY and LIGHTNING departed the Clyde for Scapa Flow. All three ships sustained weather damage during a gale.
1530	Destroyer CHIDDINGFOLD departed the Clyde to begin working up to combat efficiency at Scapa Flow.
1800	Destroyers ANTELOPE and ANTHONY departed the Clyde to escort destroyer depot ship FORTH to Rosyth.

20 OCTOBER 1941

	After ending the attack on convoy SC.48, U.568, U.502, U.432, U.77, U.751, U.73 and U.101 formed Wolfpack REISSEWOLF in the middle North Atlantic by the 22nd.
	A German aerial mine damaged steamer CORDELIA (8190grt) off Great Castle Head, Milford Haven, Wales. She arrived at Milford Haven later in the day.
	Convoy ON.28 departed Liverpool escorted by destroyers SABRE and WESTCOTT, corvettes ALISMA and KINGCUP, plus antisubmarine trawlers MAN O' WAR and WELLARD. The trawlers were detached from the convoy on the 23rd, and destroyer VENOMOUS relieved destroyer WESTCOTT. On the 25th, the escort group was detached from the convoy when relieved by USN destroyers BERNADOU (DD-153), DUPONT (DD-152), LEA (DD-118), MACLEISH (DD-220), and SAMPSON (DD-394). Destroyer LEA (DD-118) was detached from the convoy on the 30th. The USN escort group was further increased on the 31st by USCG cutter CAMPBELL (WPG-32) plus destroyers BABBITT (DD-128), BUCK (DD-420), LEARY (DD-158), LUDLOW (DD-438), and SCHENCK (DD-159). The Americans were detached from the convoy on 3 November when the convoy was dispersed.
1150	Off Tiumpan Head, Scotland, the destroyers hove to in the heavy weather, and aircraft carrier VICTORIOUS continued unescorted to Scapa Flow. The destroyers LAFOREY and LIGHTNING joined battleship MALAYA on its way back to the Clyde from Scapa Flow.
1500	Destroyer LAFOREY put into Stornoway to land a stretcher case, injured in the gale.
1700	Destroyer LAFOREY departed Stornoway to rejoin battleship MALAYA and destroyer LIGHTNING for the Clyde.

21 OCTOBER 1941

>1200	U.123 sighted convoy SL.89 west of Ireland and directed U.203 and U.82 to join her in an attack during the afternoon.
	U.123 (Kptlt Hardegen) damaged AMC **AURANIA** (A/Captain I. W. Whitehorn) as she travelled behind convoy SL.89 west of Ireland in 50, 45N, 18, 41W. Three ratings were lost. She arrived at Rothesay Bay on the 23rd. She was under repair for nineteen months and returned to service as base repair ship ARTIFEX.
>1800	In the evening, U.82 (Siegfried Rollmann) sank steamer **TREVERBYN** (5218grt) while attacking convoy SL.89 west of Ireland in 51N, 19W.
2203	U.82 (Siegfried Rollmann) sank steamer **SERBINO** (4099grt) (Master Lawrence Edwin Brooks) while attacking convoy SL.89 west of Ireland in 51, 10N, 19, 20W. Fourteen crewmen were lost. Corvette ASPHODEL (Lt Cdr K. W. Stewart) rescued the master and fifty crewmen and landed them at Gourock.

22 OCTOBER 1941

	U.569, U.123, U.38, U.82, U.202, U.84, U.203, U.93 and U.85, all fresh from French ports, formed Wolfpack SCHLAGETOT northwest of Wolfpack REISSEWOLF.
	A German reconnaissance aircraft spotted convoy SL.89 escorted by destroyer BEVERLEY, New Zealand sloop WELLINGTON, plus corvettes ASPHODEL and CLEMATIS. The escort successfully forced U.85, U.203 and U.202 to abort their attacks and dive to prevent being attacked.
	Convoy ON.28 departed Liverpool with forty ships and Escort Group EG.1, which was relieved by the USN Task Unit TU.4.1.6 from the convoy on the 25th. EG.1 then moved south and picked up convoy SC.50 with thirty-six ships on the 28th, relieving USN Task Unit TU.4.1.3 from the convoy at the MOMP.
	Battleship MALAYA departed the Clyde escorted by destroyer LIGHTNING for the Clyde to join Force H. Destroyer LAFOREY was delayed for docking to repair weather damage. Destroyers HAVELOCK and HARVESTER joined the battleship for escort from the Clyde.
	Convoy ON.29 departed Liverpool. The convoy was joined on the 23rd by destroyers BROKE, BUXTON, VERITY, and WOLVERINE, corvettes BEGONIA, CAMELLIA, EGLANTINE, LARKSPUR, MONTBRETIA and MOOSE JAW, naval trawlers BUTE, CELIA, HAMLET, and MACBETH, plus antisubmarine trawler KING SOL. Destroyer VERITY, corvette BEGONIA, and the naval trawlers were detached from the convoy on the 26th. USN destroyer WICKES (DD-441) with corvettes EYEBRIGHT, KENOGAMI, LETHBRIDGE, MAYFLOWER, NANAIMO, and PRESCOTT joined the convoy on the 28th. The remaining ships of the original escort were detached from the convoy on the 28th. Destroyer BROADWAY with corvettes ACONIT, COBALT, GALT, and WINDFLOWER joined the convoy on 4 November. All escorts were detached from the convoy on 5 November when the convoy was dispersed.

23 OCTOBER 1941

0630	Sloop IBIS arrived at Londonderry, Northern Ireland, from Kirkwall after working up.

24 OCTOBER 1941

0500	Battleship PRINCE OF WALES arrived at the Clyde with destroyers ELECTRA and EXPRESS from Scapa Flow. Vice Admiral Curteis transferred his flag to battle cruiser RENOWN, and Admiral Sir Tom S. V. Philips, KCB, raised his flag as Commander in Chief, Eastern Fleet.

1500	Force G with battleship PRINCE OF WALES plus destroyers HESPERUS, EXPRESS, and ELECTRA departed the Clyde for the Far East.
	    Destroyer LEGION, after refuelling in the Azores, joined the battleship screen on the 28th.
	    Destroyers EXPRESS and ELECTRA were detached to Ponta Delgada to refuel. On the destroyers' return to the screen on the 29th, destroyers LEGION and HESPERUS were detached.
	    Destroyer HESPERUS returned to the UK, and destroyer LEGION returned to Gibraltar.
	    On 5 November, the battleship group arrived at Freetown.
	    The battleship and destroyers EXPRESS and ELECTRA arrived at Simon's Town on 16 November and at Colombo on 28 November.
	    Battleship PRINCE OF WALES with destroyers EXPRESS and ELECTRA departed Colombo on 30 November and joined battle cruiser REPULSE and destroyers ENCOUNTER and JUPITER, which came out from Trincomalee. The ships arrived at Singapore on 2 December.

25 OCTOBER 1941

	Convoy OS.10 departed Liverpool.
	    On the 26th, sloop BIDEFORD, corvettes FREESIA and VERBENA, with escort vessels CULVER, LANDGUARD, and LULWORTH joined the convoy.
	    Corvette VERBENA was detached from the convoy on 4 November and the rest of the escort was detached from the convoy on 14 November to Bathurst.
	    On 1 November, destroyer STANLEY and escort vessel GORLESTON joined the convoy and were detached from the convoy on 14 November.
	    On 12 November, destroyer VANSITTART plus corvettes BURDOCK, MARGUERITE, and STARWORT joined the convoy and escorted it into Freetown, arriving on 18 November.

26 OCTOBER 1941

	Aircraft carriers EAGLE and ARGUS arrived at the Clyde from Gibraltar with destroyers FORESIGHT, FORESTER, and FURY.

	Convoy ON.30 departed Liverpool escorted corvettes ARABIS, DAHLIA and MONKSHOOD plus antisubmarine trawlers NORTHERN GEM and NORTHERN SPRAY.
	    Destroyers SARDONYX and WATCHMAN joined the convoy on the 29th.
	    These escorts were detached from the convoy on 2 November when USN destroyers CHARLES F. HUGHES (DD-428), GLEAVES (DD-423), LANSDALE (DD-426), MADISON (DD-425), and SIMPSON (DD-221) joined the convoy.
	    The USN destroyers were detached from the convoy on 9 November when the convoy dispersed.

1115	Battleship ROYAL SOVEREIGN arrived in the Clyde escorted by destroyers ANTELOPE and DULVERTON where ROYAL SOVEREIGN entered dock at Greenock prior to proceeding to the Mediterranean.
1800	Destroyer ANTELOPE departed the Clyde to return to Scapa Flow.

27 OCTOBER 1941

	Midshipman D. M. Jones and Naval Airman A. G. Davis were killed when their Proctor aircraft of 755/756 Squadron collided with an Oxford aircraft over Upper Heyford village.

28 OCTOBER 1941

	Convoy ON.31 departed Liverpool escorted by corvettes CELANDINE and HEARTSEASE plus antisubmarine trawlers ANGLE and ST APOLLO.
	    On the 20th, destroyers AMAZON and GEORGETOWN, corvettes RENONCULE, ROSELYS, and SUNFLOWER, naval trawler INCHKEITH, and antisubmarine trawler CAPE WARWICK joined the convoy.
	    Trawlers CAPE WARWICK and INCHKEITH were detached from the convoy on 2 November.
	    The remainder of the escort was detached from the convoy on 4 November when USN destroyers BAINBRIDGE (DD-246), OVERTON (DD-239), ROE (DD-418), STURTEVANT (DD-240), and TRUXTUN (DD-229) took over escort at the MOMP.
	    The USN destroyers were detached from the convoy on 15 November when the convoy was dispersed.

	Convoy OG.76 departed Liverpool on the 28th escorted by destroyer BRADFORD, sloop DEPTFORD, plus corvettes CONVOLVULUS, COWSLIP, MARIGOLD, PENTSTEMON, SAMPHIRE, and VETCH.
	    The convoy was joined on the 29th by escort aircraft carrier AUDACITY, which had departed the Clyde.
	    Corvette RHODODENDRON joined the convoy on the 31st and detached from the convoy on 9 November when destroyers VIDETTE and WISHART joined the escort from Gibraltar.
	    The convoy arrived at Gibraltar on 11 November.
	    The escort aircraft carrier was detached from the convoy on 11 November and arrived at Gibraltar for repairs lasting from 12 November to 13 December.

29 OCTOBER 1941

	USN destroyers LEA (DD-118), MACLEISH (DD-220), DUPONT (DD-152) and SAMPSON (DD-394) dropped depth charges on submarine contacts while escorting convoy ON.28.
1630	Destroyers OFFA and ORIBI arrived at Loch Alsh from Scapa Flow.

30 OCTOBER 1941

	Minelayers MENETHEUS, PORT QUEBEC, and WELSHMAN departed Loch Alsh to lay Minefield SN.83A escorted by destroyers BRIGHTON, OFFA, and ORIBI.
	T/Sub-Lt (A) P. Fahrenholtz RNVR, of 780 Squadron was killed when his Proctor aircraft collided with a Shark aircraft, piloted by A/Sub-Lt (A) J. E. Hampson RNVR, at Worthy Down.

31 OCTOBER 1941

	Escorts for convoy HX.156 forced U.552 under, while U.567 (Kptlt Endrass) tried to close with the convoy's position.
	While searching for convoy HX.156, U.96 (Kptlt Lehmann-Willenbrock) spotted convoy OS.10 and reported its position to U.568, U.502, U.77, U.751 and Italian submarine BARBARIGO. U.96 continued contact with the convoy, allowing U.572, U.201, U.98, U.373, U.103, U.107, and U.66 to converge on the convoy.
	A/T/Sub-Lt (A) P. Fahrenholtz RNVR was killed when his Proctor aircraft of 780 Squadron collided with a Shark aircraft at Worthy Down. A/A/Sub-Lt (A) J. E. Hampson RNVR of the Shark aircraft was not injured.
0834	U.552 (Kptlt Topp) sank USN destroyer **REUBEN JAMES (DD-245)** (1190grt) (Lt Cdr H. L. Edwards) while attacking convoy HX.156 west of Ireland in 51, 59N, 27, 05W. She broke in two and the forward section quickly sank, followed by the aft section five minutes later. Her unsecured depth charges exploded, killing many of the men in the water. USN destroyers BENSON (DD-421), HILARY P. JONES (DD-427) (ten), NIBLACK (DD-424) (thirty-six), and TARBELL (DD-142) (Cdr. Webb) (Flag) rescued forty-six enlisted men, including eight wounded. Edwards, Lt B. Ghetzler, Lt/JG D. G. Johnston, Lt/JG J. J. Daub, Lt/JG J. M. Belden, Ensign C. Spowers, Ensign H. V. Wade and eighty-eight enlisted men were missing. Two enlisted men were killed. One rescued crewman later died of wounds.
2247	U.96 (Heinrich Lehmann-Willenbrock) sank Dutch steamer **BENNEKOM** (5998grt) while attacking convoy OS.10 in 51, 20N, 23, 40W. Three gunners and five crewmen were lost. The forty-six survivors were later rescued. Escort ships LANDGUARD (SO 40th Escort Group), GORLESTON, CULVER, and LULWORTH, destroyer STANLEY, sloop BIDEFORD, plus corvettes VERBENA and FREESIA escorted convoy OS.10 at the time of the attack.

Central Atlantic Crossing Zone

Long. W60, 00 – W15, 00   Lat. 49, 00 – N05, 00

3 OCTOBER 1941

	A Walrus aircraft from light cruiser KENYA sighted German supply ship **KLARA** (7277grt) (ex-**KOTA PINANG** (7277grt)) and she was sunk north of the Azores in 42, 26N, 24, 30W. The presence of U.129 made stopping for survivors inadvisable. Four boatloads of survivors were left in the company of the submarine, which picked up one hundred nineteen survivors. The survivors were transferred to a Spanish tug on the 6th, after which U.129 continued on to her patrol area further south.
	U.204 (Kptlt Kell) patrolled west of Gibraltar.
	U.79 tried to enter the Mediterranean through the Gibraltar Straits.

4 OCTOBER 1941

	Antisubmarine trawler LADY SHIRLEY (Lt Cdr. Calloway) sank **U.111** southwest of Tenerife, 27, 10N, 20, 24N. Four crewmen on the trawler were wounded by machine gun fire from the submarine. The commanding officer and five ratings were killed in the submarine. Forty-five survivors were picked up; one died of wounds. Returning to Gibraltar, the trawler was joined by destroyer LANCE on the 8th. The destroyer escorted trawler LADY SHIRLEY into Gibraltar, arriving on the 9th. U.67 was returning to France with **U.111**, but was not involved in the action.

5 OCTOBER 1941

	U.67 attacked ocean boarding vessel MARON with her deck gun in 27, 59N, 18, 39W. The vessel returned fired on the submarine, which quickly submerged. Corvettes COREOPSIS and FLEUR DE LYS, which had escorted tanker BENEDICK (6978grt), were ordered to assist the boarding vessel. On the 6th, corvette COREOPSIS developed engine room defects and proceeded to Funchal. The ocean boarding vessel and corvette FLEUR DE LYS arrived at Gibraltar on the 8th. Corvette COREOPSIS arrived at Gibraltar on the 10th.

8 OCTOBER 1941

	A German Fw200 aircraft reported convoy OG.75 due west of Cape Finisterre, Spain. Convoy intercept positions were given to U.83 and U.71.

9 OCTOBER 1941

	Bad weather prevented German Fw200 aircraft from updating the position for convoy OG.75.

10 OCTOBER 1941

	A German Fw200 aircraft again located the position for convoy OG.75, but no U-boats were within intercept range.
0543	U.126 (Ernst Bauer) sank steamer **NAILSEA MANOR** (4926grt) (Master John Herbert Hewitt) as she was straggling behind convoy OS.7 in bad weather northeast of the Cape Verde Islands in 18, 45N, 21, 18W. Corvette VIOLET (Lt Cdr K. M. Nicholson) rescued the master, thirty-five crewmen, five gunners and one passenger. The survivors were put aboard the steamer CITY OF HONG KONG (9606grt) and they landed at Freetown, Sierra Leone, on the 14th. Also lost was **LCT.102** (450grt), which was carried as deck cargo on the steamer.

16 OCTOBER 1941

	U.103, U.107, U.66 and U.125 were ordered to delay their return to France to see if they could pick up any of the dispersed convoy OG.75 merchant ships, but none were encountered.
	U.564 (Kptlt Suhren) tried to attack convoy HG.75, but the escort's gunfire and depth charges drove her under.

17 OCTOBER 1941

	U.204 joined U.564 in pursuit of convoy HG.75.
	To intercept Allied convoys around Gibraltar, U.206, U.563 and U.564 set up a patrol line off Cape Trafalgar, and U.204, U.71 and U.83 set up a patrol line off Cape Spartel. Italian submarines ARCHIMEDE, FERRARIS and MARCONI also set up a patrol line further west.

19 OCTOBER 1941

	U.71 unsuccessfully attacked a destroyer west of Spain in 40, 06N, 19, 48W.

20 OCTOBER 1941

	Aircraft pursued and forced U.371 (Kptlt Driver) to dive and damaged her with aerial depth charges west of Portugal.
	U.84 (ObltzS Uphoff) spotted part of convoy SL.89 at sea and set up to attack it the next day.

22 OCTOBER 1941

1200	Escort Group EG.37 with sloop ROCHESTER, plus corvettes CAMPION, CARNATION, HELIOTROPE, LA MALOUINE (FFr), MALLOW and COMMANDANT DUBOC (FFr) joined convoy HG.75 to escort its seventeen ships.
>1201	Destroyers COSSACK, LEGION, LAMERTON, DUNCAN and VIDETTE joined convoy HG.75 as additional escort.

23 OCTOBER 1941

>0001	U.71 spotted convoy HG.75 shortly after midnight and made two unsuccessful attacks.
	During the day, U.206 and U.564 made unsuccessful attacks on convoy HG.75 due to the strong escort screen.

24 OCTOBER 1941

	Destroyers ZULU and SIKH detached from aircraft carriers EAGLE and ARGUS and joined battleship MALAYA and destroyer LIGHTNING in 48N, 17, 35W to escort them to Gibraltar.
	The Gibraltar section of convoy OS.9 was detached from the main convoy, escorted by sloops LEITH and FOWEY plus corvette STONECROP. Destroyer DUNCAN departed Gibraltar on the 24th and, after assisting destroyer COSSACK, refuelled at Ponta Delgada, Azores, on the 30th. She then sailed to join the convoy at sea. Destroyer WILD SWAN departed Gibraltar on the 25th to join the convoy. Destroyers GURKHA and Dutch ISAAC SWEERS departed Gibraltar on the 28th to join the convoy. Convoy OS.9G arrived at Gibraltar on 1 November.

25 OCTOBER 1941

	The air and sea escorts for convoy HG.75 forced U.71, U.83, U.206 and Italian submarine ARCHIMEDE to dive before they could attack the convoy.

	A RAF Catalina aircraft of 202 Squadron from Gibraltar damaged Italian submarine **FERRARIS** west of Gibraltar. Destroyer LAMERTON, supporting convoy HG.75, was sent to attack the submarine. The crew of the submarine scuttled the ship as the destroyer arrived. Forty-four survivors were picked up. A 3.9-inch shell from the destroyer exploded near the LAMERTON causing some damage. The destroyer spent no time out of action.

26 OCTOBER 1941

	U.563 unsuccessfully attacked corvette HELIOTROPE while attacking convoy HG.75.
	Corvette CAMPION was detached from the escort for convoy HG.75.
0354	U.83 (ObltzS Hans-Werner Kraus) damaged CAM ship **ARIGUANI** (6746grt) (Cdr R. A. Thorburn (ret)) while attacking convoy HG.75 in 37, 50N, 16, 10W. (Other sources claim U.84 torpedoed the ship.) Destroyer VIDETTE (Lt Cdr E. N. Walmsley) attempted to tow the ARIGUANI, but was unsuccessful. VIDETTE took eighteen badly wounded men to Gibraltar. In the tow of tug THAMES and escorted by corvettes JONQUIL, HELIOTROPE, and CAMPION (Lt Cdr A. Johnson), the ARIGUANI arrived at Gibraltar on 2 November.

27 OCTOBER 1941

	Destroyers LAMERTON and LEGION plus corvettes BLUEBELL, CARNATION, and HELIOTROPE were detached from the escort for convoy HG.75. Destroyers LAMERTON and LEGION proceeded to Ponta Delgada, Azores, to refuel. Destroyer LAMERTON then sailed to rejoin the convoy. Destroyer LEGION sailed to join battleship PRINCE OF WALES and escort her while destroyers ELECTRA and EXPRESS refuelled at Ponta Delgada.
	U.564 claimed sinking a steamer while attacking convoy HG.75. There was no confirming evidence.

28 OCTOBER 1941

	U.432 (ObltzS Schultze) sank steamer **ULEA** (1574grt) while attacking convoy HG.75 west of Portugal in 41, 17N, 21, 40W. Thirteen crewmen, three gunners, and three passengers were lost. Corvette BLUEBELL rescued nine survivors.
	Destroyer DUNCAN sank Italian submarine **MARCONI** (CC Piomarta) west of Portugal.

29 OCTOBER 1941

	Free French Sloop COMMANDANT DUBOC with corvettes LA MALOUINE and MALLOW detached from convoy HG.73 escort duty to return to Gibraltar.

30 OCTOBER 1941

	Sloop LONDONDERRY joined convoy HG.75 after being detached from convoy SL.90.

31 OCTOBER 1941

	Sloop ABERDEEN and destroyer HESPERUS joined convoy HG.75 from Britain.

UK East Coast

Long. W04, 00 – E03, 00   Lat. N58, 30 – N51, 30

2 OCTOBER 1941

	German bombing damaged steamer **SOUTHPORT** (572grt) when she was blown off the blocks in the Tyne Dock, South Shields.

3 OCTOBER 1941

	Destroyer MENDIP drove off a German S-boat attack while escorting convoy FS.615.

4 OCTOBER 1941

1250	Destroyer HURWORTH departed the Tyne for Scapa Flow to begin working up to combat efficiency. She called at Rosyth later in the day.
1612	Destroyer EXPRESS departed the Humber for Scapa Flow to begin working up to combat efficiency after long repairs.

5 OCTOBER 1941

1800	Destroyer HURWORTH departed Rosyth and spent the night at Methil.

6 OCTOBER 1941

0630	Destroyer HURWORTH departed Methil, but was delayed by thick fog and anchored in Loch Eribol during the night.

8 OCTOBER 1941

1430	Destroyer LIGHTNING arrived at Rosyth from Scapa Flow to carry out boiler cleaning and repairs.

10 OCTOBER 1941

	A German aerial mine sank Greek steamer **KYMA** (3959grt) off the Humber in 53, 53N, 00, 21E. The entire crew was rescued.
1200	Sloop LOWESTOFT departed Harwich for Scapa Flow to work up after repairs.

11 OCTOBER 1941

	ML.288 (73grt) was lost in heavy weather off Hartlepool, England.
	A German aerial mine damaged steamer ICEMAID (1964grt) off Orfordness near the Shipwash Light Vessel off Harwich. She arrived at Harwich in tow on the 12th.

12 OCTOBER 1941

	Heavy cruiser SHROPSHIRE arrived at Sheerness, England, escorted by destroyers QUORN and VIVACIOUS. She was refitting at Chatham from 17 October to 16 February 1942.
	The German 2nd S-Boat Flotilla with S.41, S.47, S.53, S.62, S.104, and S.105 attacked convoy FN.531 north of Cromer, England.
	German bombing heavily damaged steamer **GLYNN** (1134grt) east of Lowestoft about one and a half miles 223° from No.5 Buoy, in 52, 35N, 01, 56E. Two crewmen were lost. The Royal Navy scuttled the steamer, as she was deemed unsalvageable.
	New Zealand Sub-Lt L. E. Mitchell RNZN was killed when his Albacore aircraft of 778 Squadron from Arbroath crashed on takeoff.
1015	Destroyer ELECTRA arrived at Rosyth from Scapa Flow for boiler cleaning.

13 OCTOBER 1941

	In the early morning, S.53 sank Norwegian steamer **ROY** (1768grt) while attacking convoy FN.531 off Cromer in 52, 59, 36N, 01, 52E. Three crewmen were lost.
	In the early morning, S.105 (LtzS Howaldt) sank steamer **CHEVINGTON** (1537grt) while attacking convoy FN.531 off Cromer in 52, 59, 36N, 01, 52E. Seven crewmen and two gunners were lost.
	Destroyers WESTMINSTER, WOLSEY, and COTSWOLD from the convoy FN.531 escort were unable to damage to the German S-boats.

14 OCTOBER 1941

	A collision sank naval drifter **FORERUNNER** (92grt) (T/Skipper W. Harmon RNR) in the Thames Estuary. She became a constructive total loss.
0800	Destroyer LIGHTNING departed Rosyth for Scapa Flow upon the completion of her boiler cleaning.
1555	Destroyer ICARUS departed the Humber for Scapa Flow after her refit.

15 OCTOBER 1941

1310	Destroyer ACTIVE arrived at Hull, England, from Scapa Flow to begin her refit.

17 OCTOBER 1941

	A collision sank trawler **NUBIA** six miles off Tynemouth, England.
	A Swordfish aircraft of 767 Squadron crashed at Hallom Mill, Froickheim, Scotland. T/Sub-Lt (A) S. J. Carpenter RNVR died of injuries on the 20th.

18 OCTOBER 1941

	A German aerial mine sank steamer **EMPIRE GHYLL** (2011grt) in Barrow Deep, four to five cables from B 7 Buoy, in 51, 41N, 01, 19E. Five crewmen and two gunners were lost.
	A German aerial mine sank steamer **MAHSEER** (7911grt) in Barrow Deep, four to five cables from B 7 Buoy, in 51, 41N, 01, 19E. The entire crew were rescued.

19 OCTOBER 1941

	Heavy cruiser CUMBERLAND departed Chatham for Scapa Flow after refitting from 1 July to 11 October.

21 OCTOBER 1941

	Heavy cruiser BERWICK departed Rosyth for Scapa Flow after completing her engine repairs.
1500	Destroyers ANTELOPE and ANTHONY arrived off May Island with destroyer depot ship FORTH, which continued to Rosyth.

	Destroyer ANTHONY proceeded to Immingham for a refit.
	Destroyer ANTELOPE returned to Scapa Flow.
1600	Destroyer ELECTRA departed Rosyth for Scapa Flow and joined destroyer ANTELOPE at sea.
1730	Destroyer depot ship FORTH arrived at Rosyth.

22 OCTOBER 1941

	Minesweeping trawler **ALDER** (560grt) (T/Skipper G. E. Yates RNR) ran aground and was declared a total loss on the east coast of Scotland.
0650	Destroyer INTREPID departed London for Sheerness after her refit.
0700	Destroyer ANTHONY arrived at Immingham to begin her refit.

23 OCTOBER 1941

1230	Destroyer INTREPID departed Sheerness for Scapa Flow.

24 OCTOBER 1941

	A German aerial mine sank minesweeping trawler **EMILION** (201grt) (Sub-Lt J. W. S. Allison RNVR) in the vicinity of B.6 Buoy, Barrow Deep. There were no casualties.
	A German aerial mine sank minesweeping trawler **LUCIENNE JEANNE** (264grt) (Skipper S. E. George RNR) in the vicinity of B.6 Buoy, Barrow Deep.
0713	Destroyer MONTROSE departed Sheerness for Scapa Flow, via Methil, to begin working up to combat efficiency.

25 OCTOBER 1941

	Heavy cruiser LONDON arrived at the Tyne from Scapa Flow and began a refit lasting from 30 October to 25 January 1942.
1000	Destroyer MONTROSE arrived at Methil from Sheerness and, after landing trial parties, departed again for Scapa Flow.

27 OCTOBER 1941

	German bombing sank Dutch steamer **FRIESLAND** (2662grt) north of Cromer in 53, 04N, 01, 35E. Eleven crewmen and two gunners were lost.
	German bombing sank steamer **ANTIOPE** (4545grt) north of Cromer in 53, 10, 45N, 01, 06E. One crewman was lost.

29 OCTOBER 1941

	Naval trawler **FLOTTA** (530grt) (T/Sub-Lt A. Smith RNVR) ran aground off Buchan Ness. She foundered on 6 November.
1015	Destroyer TARTAR departed London for Sheerness after the completion of a long refit.
1415	Destroyer TARTAR arrived at Sheerness from London to embark ammunition and fuel and carry out a tilt test at Chatham before proceeding to Scapa Flow. She departed Sheerness on 1 November for Scapa Flow.
1935	Minesweeper HARRIER arrived in the Humber to begin her refit.

30 OCTOBER 1941

	Submarine P.35 departed Dundee for Scapa Flow.
0800	Minesweepers SALAMANDER and HALCYON arrived at Aberdeen from Scapa Flow to carry out boiler cleaning and equipping for Arctic service.
1300	Minesweeper BRITOMART arrived at Hartlepool, England, to begin her refit. She had to put into the Tyne to shelter from bad weather en route.

31 OCTOBER 1941

	German bombing sank tanker **BRITISH FORTUNE** (4696grt) one mile 265° from Aldeburgh Light Buoy, east of Felixstowe, England. Seven crewmen and a gunner were missing.
	German bombing sank Greek steamer **NICOLAOS PIANGOS** (4499grt) east of Felixstowe in 51, 58, 45N, 01, 37, 30E. Eight crewmen were lost.
0800	Destroyer MAORI departed London for Sheerness to embark ammunition and fuel after a long refit.
1300	Destroyer MAORI arrived at Sheerness from London to embark ammunition and fuel after a long refit.

North Sea

Long. E03, 00 – E09, 00   Lat. N58, 30 – N51, 00

3 OCTOBER 1941

	During the night, RAF Bomber Command attacked Rotterdam, Holland, and heavily damaged German patrol boats V.1106, V.1107, and V.1109 plus S.107, and lightly damaged S.51 and S.52.
	German bombing damaged destroyer VIVACIOUS in the North Sea. Her steering engine was damaged and she was repaired at Immingham, completing in November.

7 OCTOBER 1941

	A mine sank German trawler **PETER** (252grt) in the North Sea.

18 OCTOBER 1941

	British bombing damaged Swedish steamer **INGEREN** (6123grt) west of Borkum, Germany.

21 OCTOBER 1941

	RAF bombing sank Swedish steamer **HILDA** (1237grt) five miles west of IJmuiden, North Holland.

26 OCTOBER 1941

	German steamer **HERTA ENGELINE FRITZEN** (5100grt) became stranded near the Hook of Holland and later sank.

27 OCTOBER 1941

	RAF bombers sank Swedish steamer **GUNLOG** (1424grt) off Den Helder, Holland.

28 OCTOBER 1941

	Steamer **ROSLEA** (642grt) ran aground on the Belgian coast during a storm. The Germans captured her the next morning and her crew was taken prisoner. The ship was later salvaged for German use.

30 OCTOBER 1941

	RAF bombing sank Norwegian coastal steamer **SOLSKIN** (372grt) west of Egerö (Eigerøya).

English Channel

Long. W07, 00 – E01, 30   Lat. N51, 00 – N49, 00

1 OCTOBER 1941

	Eight RAF Hurricane aircraft attacked the German 3rd R-Boat Flotilla with R.38, R.33, R.35, R.36, R.165 and R.166 off Dieppe, France. R.38, R.33 and R.165 were slightly damaged, but R.35 and R.36 were heavily damaged with thirteen killed and eleven wounded.

3 OCTOBER 1941

	Light cruiser TRINIDAD was commissioned at Plymouth, England.

11 OCTOBER 1941

	German bombing sank the hulk of steamer **HAYTIAN** three and a half cables north of Castleton Pier, Isle of Portland, England.

13 OCTOBER 1941

1000	Destroyer SOUTHWOLD departed Portsmouth, England, for Scapa Flow to begin working up to combat efficiency.

15 OCTOBER 1941

	Submarine L.27 made an unsuccessful attack on a German steamer off Cherbourg, Normandy.

16 OCTOBER 1941

	T/A/Sub-Lt (A) A. C. Scott RNVR was killed when his Hurricane aircraft of 759 Squadron crashed at Yeovilton, Somerset, England.

21 OCTOBER 1941

	Minelayers MANXMAN and WELSHMAN departed Plymouth and laid Minefield HG off Lorient, France, during that night.

24 OCTOBER 1941

	Submarine P.36 passed the southwest tip of Cornwall on her sea trials.

25 OCTOBER 1941

	During the night of 25/26 October, minelaying cruiser WELSHMAN laid Minefield JXA off St Valery-en-Caux, and minelaying cruiser MANXMAN laid Minefield JXB off St Valery-sur-Somme in the English Channel.

26 OCTOBER 1941

	Light cruiser TRINIDAD departed Devonport for the Clyde, escorted by Polish destroyer KUJAWIAK. They arrived on the 27th, and the light cruiser began her sea trials.

Bay of Biscay
Long. W15, 00 – E03, 00   Lat. N49, 00 – N40, 00

5 OCTOBER 1941

	U.204 sank Panamanian steamer **C. JON** (744grt) while awaiting German blockade-runner RIO GRANDE (6062grt) in the Bay of Biscay in 48, 30N, 13, 00W. *(Also see 7 October.)* The entire crew became prisoners of war.

7 OCTOBER 1941

	A German Fw200 aircraft of I/KG.40 sank Panamanian steamer **JON** (744grt) (ex **GIBEL DRIS** (744grt)), which was sailing alone in the Bay of Biscay. (Author notes: It certainly looks like the same ship sunk by U.204 on the 5th.)

22 OCTOBER 1941

	German steamer PORTLAND (7132grt) departed Bordeaux, France, for Osaka, Japan. She carried supplies and parts for German AMC SCHIFF.41/KORMORAN.

23 OCTOBER 1941

	A mine sank German auxiliary minesweeper **M.6** south of Lorient, France.
	German destroyers Z.23 and Z.24 departed La Pallice, France, for Cherbourg, France, as they worked their way through the Dover Straits to the Wesermünde and then on to Norway.

West of Gibraltar
Long. W15, 00 – W05, 30   Lat. N40, 00 – N30, 00

1 OCTOBER 1941

	Flag Officer, Force H transferred his flag from battleship NELSON to battleship RODNEY.
	Corvettes COREOPSIS and FLEUR DE LYS departed Gibraltar escorting tanker BENEDICK (6978grt) until dark on the 4th.
0400	Light cruisers KENYA and SHEFFIELD departed Gibraltar to return to the Clyde and to search for a German supply ship reported off the coast of northern Spain.
0830	Battleship RODNEY, aircraft carrier ARK ROYAL plus light cruisers HERMIONE, EDINBURGH, and EURYALUS arrived at Gibraltar with destroyers FRANDALE, HEYTHROP, COSSACK, LEGION, LANCE, LIVELY, ZULU, Dutch ISAAC SWEERS, and GURKHA.
0900	Tug ST DAY arrived at Gibraltar.
2000	Battleship PRINCE OF WALES departed Gibraltar for Scapa Flow with destroyers LAFOREY, LIGHTNING, and ORIBI, escorted locally by destroyer LIVELY.
2345	Light cruiser EURYALUS departed Gibraltar for Freetown, Sierra Leone, with destroyers FARNDALE and HEYTHROP escorting steamers MELBOURNE STAR (12,806grt) and PORT CHALMERS (8535grt) for Buenos Aires, Argentina.

2 OCTOBER 1941

	Convoy HG.74 departed Gibraltar escorted by destroyers FORESIGHT and FORESTER, escort aircraft carrier AUDACITY, sloop DEPTFORD, plus corvettes ARBUTUS, CONVOLVULUS, COWSLIP, MARIGOLD, PENTSTEMON, RHODODENDRON, and VETCH. Destroyers FORESIGHT and FORESTER were detached from the convoy while destroyers DUNCAN and ROCKINGHAM departed Gibraltar on 4 October and joined the escort on the 6th. Sloop ENCHANTRESS, escort vessel HARTLAND, and corvette VERVAIN joined the escort on the 8th. Destroyer DUNCAN was detached from the convoy on the 9th. On the 8th, convoy SL.88 rendezvoused with the convoy. Destroyer BLANKNEY and ocean boarding vessel CORINTHIAN joined the convoy on the 9th and were detached from the convoy on the 11th.

	Destroyer ROCKINGHAM was detached from the convoy on the 12th and sloop ENCHANTRESS was detached from the convoy on the 17th. The convoy arrived at Liverpool on the 18th.
0130	Light cruiser EDINBURGH departed Gibraltar with destroyers COSSACK, ZULU, Polish PIORUN, and Polish GARLAND escorting steamers LEINSTER (4302grt) and CITY OF DURBAN (5850grt) to Britain. Light cruiser EDINBURGH arrived in the Clyde with Polish destroyer GARLAND, and Polish troopship SOBIESKI (11,030grt) on the 10th. Destroyers COSSACK and ZULU were detached en route and joined aircraft carrier ARGUS to escort her to Gibraltar.

8 OCTOBER 1941

	Submarine PORPOISE arrived at Gibraltar.
	Aircraft carrier ARGUS arrived at Gibraltar from the Clyde escorted by destroyers COSSACK, ZULU, and SIKH after being detached from convoy WS.12 escort duties.

9 OCTOBER 1941

	Escorts TOTLAND and SENNEN (ex-US Coast Guard cutters) arrived at Gibraltar from Freetown, Sierra Leone, escorting Norwegian tankers VANJA (6198grt) and SANDAR (7624grt).
	Corvettes AZALEA and SPIREA departed Gibraltar for Bathurst, the Gambia, escorting the 26th Motor Launch Flotilla. Tanker LA CARRIERE (5685grt) departed Gibraltar in company with the corvettes and proceeded independently to the West Indies. ML.244 later broke down at sea and returned alone to Gibraltar.
	Submarine PORPOISE arrived at Gibraltar from Troon, Scotland.

10 OCTOBER 1941

	U.83 (ObltzS Hans-Werner Kraus) sank a **floating crane** (500grt) with gunfire west of Gibraltar.
	Ocean boarding vessel MARON departed Gibraltar for a western patrol.

11 OCTOBER 1941

	Submarine P.31 arrived at Gibraltar from Dundee.
	Aircraft carrier EAGLE arrived at Gibraltar with destroyers CROOME and WILD SWAN plus Free French sloop COMMANDANT DUBOC.
	Antisubmarine trawlers LADY HOGARTH and STELLA CARINA departed Gibraltar escorting Norwegian tanker VANJA (6198grt) westwards. The trawlers then joined arriving tanker INVERLEE (9158grt) to escort her into Gibraltar.

12 OCTOBER 1941

1654	U.83 (ObltzS Hans-Werner Kraus) stopped Portuguese steamer **CORTE REAL** (2044grt) for inspection eighty miles west of Lisbon in 39, 40N, 11, 34W. When it was established that she was carrying contraband, the steamer was sunk. The entire crew of thirty-six were allowed to enter the lifeboats and were later rescued.

13 OCTOBER 1941

	A German Fw200 aircraft attacked antisubmarine trawler LOCH OSKAIG west of Portugal in 38, 15N, 09, 59W. Seven crewmen were wounded and considerable damage was done to the superstructure by the aircraft's cannon fire.

14 OCTOBER 1941

	U.206 (ObltzS Opitz) sank corvette **FLEUR DE LYS** (Lt A. Collins RNR) (925grt) (ex Fr **LA DIEPPOISE**) after she had detached from escort duty with convoy OG.75 west of Gibraltar, just as she was preparing to enter harbour in N36, 00N, 06, 30W. Collins and one rating were killed. Lt A. P. Godfrey RNR, T/Sub-Lt N. Higgs RNVR, T/Lt C. M. Nicholls RNVR, T/Lt J. G. Porter RNR, and sixty-four ratings were missing. Three survivors were picked up by a Spanish steamer and later transferred to corvette COREOPSIS.
	U.204 (Kptlt Kell) sank Portuguese sailing ship **AINGERU GUARDAKOA** (300grt) in the Bay of Cadiz off Cape Roche between Tangier, Morocco, and Lisbon, Portugal. The U-boat believed the vessel to be a British submarine chaser.
	Ex-US Coast Guard cutters/escorts SENNEN and TOTLAND departed Gibraltar to rendezvous with AMCs WOLFE, MALOJA, and RANPURA in 42N, 28W and escort them to Britain.
Night	During the night, U.564 entered neutral Cadiz harbour, refuelled and provisioned from German tanker THALIA (5875grt), and departed before daybreak.

15 OCTOBER 1941

	Destroyer CROOME departed Gibraltar to join the AMC group escort.

	Corvettes JONQUIL and COREOPSIS departed Gibraltar escorting Norwegian tanker SANDAR (7624grt) westwards and then joined arriving tanker VELMA (9720grt).
	Submarine SEVERN departed Gibraltar for Freetown, Sierra Leone.

16 OCTOBER 1941

	During the night, U.204 entered Cadiz harbour to refuel and supply from German tanker THALIA (5875grt).

17 OCTOBER 1941

	The departure of convoy HG.75 was delayed while two antisubmarine forces of destroyers LAMERTON, VIDETTE, and DUNCAN and of sloop ROCHESTER plus the 37th Escort Group of corvettes BLUEBELL, CAMPION, CARNATION, HELIOTROPE, MALLOW, and LA MALOUINE departed Gibraltar to sweep in the western approaches to the Gibraltar Strait.

18 OCTOBER 1941

2200	Light cruisers AURORA and PENELOPE arrived at Gibraltar from Scapa Flow.

19 OCTOBER 1941

0300	U.204 (Kptlt Walter Kell) sank unescorted motor tanker **INVERLEE** (9158grt) (Master Thomas Edward Alexander) thirty miles 240° from Cape Spartel, Spain. The master, twenty crewmen and one gunner were lost. Destroyer DUNCAN (Lt Cdr A. N. Rowell) plus trawlers LADY HOGARTH (Lt S. G. Barnes) and HAARLEM (Lt L. B. Merrick) rescued seventeen crewmen and four gunners and landed them at Gibraltar. Immediately after this sinking, the 37th Escort Group started a U-boat hunt off Cape Spartel and sank U-204 the same day.
>0301	Sloop ROCHESTER and corvette MALLOW sank **U.204** in the Straits of Gibraltar in 35, 48N, 06, 10W. The entire crew of forty-six was lost. Corvette BLUEBELL picked up debris from the submarine the next day.
0614	U.206 (Kptlt Opitz) sank unescorted steamer **BARON KELVIN** (3081grt) (Master William Lindsay Ewing) fourteen miles 100° from Tarifa Point, Spain, in 35, 51N, 06, 24W. Nineteen crewmen and seven gunners were lost. Spanish steamer UROLA (grt) rescued the master, twelve crewmen and two gunners and landed them at Gibraltar. Destroyer DUNCAN (Lt Cdr A. N. Rowell) rescued one survivor, and he was also landed at Gibraltar.

20 OCTOBER 1941

	Panamanian steamer **INDRA** (2032grt) was reported missing after this date. She had departed Bari, Italy, for Huelva, Spain, but did not arrive as scheduled. A ship's boat was washed ashore.
	Light cruiser HERMIONE departed Gibraltar to search for a tanker reported by aircraft in 44, 07N, 10, 07W. The cruiser arrived back at Gibraltar on the 25th without making contact with the tanker.
	Destroyer DUNCAN departed Gibraltar with antisubmarine trawlers ST NECTAN and ARCTIC RANGER to provide additional escort for tanker VELMA (9720grt) en route to Gibraltar, escorted by corvettes JONQUIL and COREOPSIS. The tanker arrived on the 22nd, escorted by the destroyer and the two corvettes.

21 OCTOBER 1941

	U.83 attacked aircraft carriers EAGLE and ARGUS west of Gibraltar.
<0915	Aircraft carriers EAGLE and ARGUS departed Gibraltar with destroyers FORESIGHT, FORESTER, and FURY for Britain. Destroyers VIDETTE and LAMERTON provided local escort.
0915	Destroyer VIDETTE detached from escorting aircraft carriers EAGLE and ARGUS to return to Gibraltar.
1140	Destroyer LAMERTON detached from escorting aircraft carriers EAGLE and ARGUS to return to Gibraltar.

22 OCTOBER 1941

	Convoy HG.75 departed Gibraltar escorted by sloop ROCHESTER (SO), catapult ship ARIGUANI, plus corvettes BLUEBELL, CAMPION, CARNATION, HELIOTROPE, LA MALOUINE, and MALLOW. Sloop COMMANDANT DUBOC joined the convoy on the 25th. Corvette CAMPION was detached from the convoy on the 26th and destroyers LAMERTON and LEGION plus corvettes BLUEBELL, CARNATION, and HELIOTROPE were detached from the convoy on the 27th. Destroyers LAMERTON and LEGION proceeded to Ponta Delgada to refuel. Destroyer LAMERTON then sailed to rejoin the convoy. Destroyer LEGION sailed to join battleship PRINCE OF WALES and escort her, while destroyers ELECTRA and EXPRESS refuelled at Ponta Delgada. Destroyers LAMERTON, COSSACK, LEGION, and VIDETTE reinforced the convoy escort at sea. Sloop COMMANDANT DUBOC with corvettes LA MALOUINE and MALLOW were detached from the convoy on the 29th. The convoy was joined on the 30th by sloop LONDONDERRY from convoy SL.90 and sloop ABERDEEN and destroyer HESPERUS on the 31st from Britain. The convoy arrived at Liverpool on 3 November.
	Destroyer GURKHA and Dutch destroyer ISAAC SWEERS arrived at Gibraltar from Freetown, Sierra Leone, after refuelling at Bathurst, Gambia.

24 OCTOBER 1941

0030	U.563 (ObltzS Bargsten) torpedoed destroyer **COSSACK** (Captain E. L. Berthon DSC) west of Gibraltar in 35, 36N, 10, 04W. 　One rating was killed and Berthon, Lt M. F. Isaac, Lt H. W. M. Rose, Lt W. G. Wheeler RAN, and 150 ratings were missing. Four ratings died of wounds. T/Paymaster Lt G. Craven RNVR, Lt H. T. Crispin, Lt A. Davies, Sub-Lt P. A. C. Day, Lt R. W. Hughes, and twenty-three ratings were wounded. 　Destroyer LEGION and sloop COMMANDANT DUBOC rescued sixty survivors. Corvette CARNATION was able to pass a towing line to **COSSACK** with destroyer LEGION standing by. 　Destroyer DUNCAN departed Gibraltar on the 24th with medical supplies and a surgeon. Destroyer DUNCAN was to then join convoy OS.9G. 　Tug THAMES and corvette JONQUIL departed Gibraltar on the 24th to assist the destroyer. 　**COSSACK** was towed by tug THAMES and escorted by corvettes JONQUIL and CARNATION, but she foundered on the 27th. Corvette JONQUIL took off the last of the crew on the destroyer. 　The tug THAMES had been diverted to assist damaged antiaircraft ship ARIGUANI, but tug ROLLICKER was already en route to assist.
0636	U.564 (ObltzS Reinhard Suhren) sank steamer **CARSBRECK** (3670grt) (Master John Dugald Muir) while attacking convoy HG.75 about 300 miles west of Gibraltar in 36, 20N, 10, 50W. The master, nineteen crewmen and four gunners were lost. Free French sloop COMMANDANT DUBOC rescued sixteen crewmen and two gunners. The survivors were transferred to damaged CAM ship ARIGUANI, which was sunk two days later. *(See 26 October.)*
0636	U.564 sank steamer **ARIOSTO** (2176grt) (Master Harold Hill) (convoy commodore F. L. J. Butler RNR RD) while attacking convoy HG.75 in 36, 20N, 10, 50W. Five crewmen and one gunner were lost. The master, the commodore, six naval staff members, thirty crewmen, three gunners, three passengers and one DBS were rescued. 　Swedish steamer PACIFIC (6034grt) rescued thirty-eight survivors and landed them at Barrow (Barrow-in-Furness), England. 　Destroyer LAMERTON (Lt Cdr H. C. Simms) rescued seven survivors and landed them at Gibraltar.
0636	U.564 sank steamer **ALHAMA** (1352grt) (Master Alexander Cameron) while attacking convoy HG.75 about 300 miles west of Gibraltar in 35, 42N, 10, 58W. 　Free French sloop COMMANDANT DUBOC rescued the master, twenty-five crewmen and seven gunners. They were later transferred to destroyer LAMERTON (Lt Cdr H. C. Simms). Later, destroyer HESPERUS (Lt Cdr A. A. Tait) landed eighteen survivors at Liverpool, England, and destroyer ROCHESTER (Cdr C. B. Allen) landed fifteen survivors at Londonderry, Northern Ireland.
1200	A German Fw200 aircraft of I/KG.40 spotted convoy HG.75 and reported its position.
>1800	U.71 spotted convoy HG.75 and reported its position and tried to set up for an attack.

25 OCTOBER 1941

	Corvette COREOPSIS departed Gibraltar with antisubmarine trawlers ST NECTAN and LADY SHIRLEY escorting tankers BRITISH FREEDOM (6985grt) and VELMA (9720grt) out to sea and then joined inbound tanker COWRIE (8197grt), which arrived at Gibraltar on 6 November.

27 OCTOBER 1941

	Battleship MALAYA arrived at Gibraltar escorted by destroyers LIGHTNING, ZULU and SIKH. On entering harbour, the battleship took a sheer and rammed steamers HOEGH HOOD (9351grt), which broke adrift, and CLAN MACDONALD (9653grt). The battleship sustained small holes in her forecastle and lost her sheet anchor. Damage to CLAN MACDONALD was minor, but HOEGH HOOD required six weeks repair.
	Light cruiser HERMIONE began repairs at Gibraltar lasting until 7 November.

28 OCTOBER 1941

	Submarine RORQUAL departed Gibraltar for Holy Loch, Scotland.
	Destroyer GURKHA and Dutch destroyer ISAAC SWEERS departed Gibraltar to join arriving convoy OS.9G.

29 OCTOBER 1941

	German bombing sank steamer **SARASTONE** (2473grt) off Huelva, Spain, in 37, 05, 10N, 06, 48, 30W. One crewman was lost.

30 OCTOBER 1941

	Destroyer WISHART arrived at Gibraltar after refitting in Britain.

West of North Africa

Long. W15, 00 – E11, 00   Lat. N30, 00 – N00, 00

5 OCTOBER 1941

Convoy SL.89 departed Freetown, Sierra Leone, escorted by destroyer BRILLIANT with corvettes ASPHODEL, CLEMATIS, CLOVER, COLUMBINE, and CYCLAMEN to 8 October.
On the 6th, destroyers VELOX and WRESTLER escorted the convoy for that day only.
New Zealand sloop WELLINGTON joined the convoy on the 8th to 25 October.
Sloop STORK joined the convoy on the 9th to 25 October.
Escort vessels SENNEN and TOTLAND escorted the convoy on the 21st only.
Destroyers BEVERLEY (to 24 October) and CROOME (for that day only) joined the convoy on the 22nd.
On the 23rd, Polish destroyers KRAKOWIAK and KUJAWIAK provided escort to 24 October, with VANQUISHER and WITCH continuing on to 25 October. The convoy arrived at Liverpool, England, on the 25th.

6 OCTOBER 1941

Convoy ST.5 departed Freetown, Sierra Leone, escorted by sloop MILFORD with corvettes BURDOCK, CROCUS, and MARGUERITE. The convoy arrived at Takoradi, Ghana, on the 11th.

15 OCTOBER 1941

Convoy SL.90 departed Freetown, Sierra Leone, escorted by destroyers BRILLIANT to 18 October, GURKHA and the Dutch ISAAC SWEERS to 17 October, and VANSITTART to 20 October, plus corvettes ARMERIA to 20 October, ASTER to 18 October, CLOVER to 18 October, CROCUS to 18 October, and CYCLAMEN to 18 October.
On the 18th, sloops FOLKESTONE joined the convoy and provided escort to 6 November, LONDONDERRY to 29 October, and WESTON to 6 November. The convoy arrived at Liverpool on 6 November.

17 OCTOBER 1941

Convoy ST.6 departed Freetown, Sierra Leone, escorted by sloop BRIDGEWATER plus corvettes AMARANTHUS, AURICULA, MARGUERITE, and WOODRUFF. The convoy arrived at Takoradi, Ghana, on the 22nd.

18 OCTOBER 1941

Corvettes AZALEA and SPIREA were directed to depart Bathurst, Gambia, to join RFA oiler DINGLEDALE (8145grt) and escort her to Gibraltar.
SPIREA arrived at Gibraltar on the 26th to refuel and then departed to rejoin the escort.
The three ships arrived at Gibraltar on the 29th.

19 OCTOBER 1941

1051	U.126 (Ernst Bauer) heavily damaged unescorted and unarmed neutral American steamer **LEHIGH** (4983grt) (Master Vincent Patrick Arkins) seventy-five miles west of Freetown, Sierra Leone, in 08, 26N, 14, 37W.
1310	The steamer sank stern first about 75 miles west of Freetown. The entire crew of forty-four was rescued. Destroyer VIMY rescued two lifeboats, and motor launches rescued the other two lifeboats.

20 OCTOBER 1941

0554	U.126 (Ernst Bauer) badly damaged tanker **BRITISH MARINER** (6996grt) (Master Henry Beattie) while attacking a small convoy west of Freetown in 07, 43N, 14, 20W. Three crewmen were lost, and she arrived at Freetown in tow of tugboat DONAU on the 22nd. Tugboat HUDSON rescued the forty-eight survivors and helped with the tow to Freetown.
The tanker was considered a constructive total loss and was used as an oil storage hulk at Freetown.

26 OCTOBER 1941

Convoy SL.91 departed Freetown escorted by destroyer WRESTLER to 31 October, sloop SANDWICH to 12 November and corvettes ANCHUSA to 12 November, BURDOCK to 31 October, CALENDULA to 12 November, CLOVER to 31 October, MIGNONETTE to 12 November, and NIGELLA to 31 October.
On the 28th, sloops BLACK SWAN, FLEETWOOD, and SCARBOROUGH joined the convoy to 12 November. Sloop FOWEY plus corvettes CAMPION, CARNATION, and HELIOTROPE joined the convoy on 8 November to 12 November.
Convoy SL.91 rendezvoused with convoy SL.91G on 8 November. After reforming, later on 8 November, the joined convoys SL.91 and SL.91G split into convoys SL.91GF and SL.91GS.
SL.91GF arrived at Liverpool on 18 November and SL.91GS on 19 November.

30 OCTOBER 1941

Convoy ST.7 departed Freetown escorted by destroyer VANSITTART plus corvettes ARMERIA and CYCLAMEN. The convoy arrived at Takoradi on 4 November.

SOUTH ATLANTIC OCEAN

East of South America
Long. W70, 00 – W30, 00   Lat. N05, 00 - S60, 00

4 OCTOBER 1941

	Argentine destroyer **CORRIENTES** sank in a collision with Argentine heavy cruiser ALMIRANTE BROWN during fleet manoeuvres off Tierra del Fuego.

West of South Africa
Long. W30, 00 – E25, 00   Lat. S00, 00 – S60, 00

3 OCTOBER 1941

	The Cape Town part of Convoy WS.11 departed without steamer GLAUCUS (7586grt), which departed the next day and overtook the convoy at sea, escorted by AMC DERBYSHIRE. These ships rendezvoused with the Durban portion of Convoy WS.11 on the 8th.

12 OCTOBER 1941

	U.126 arrived in the South Atlantic and took over control of operations there with U.68.
	U.68 (KKpt Merten) patrolled around Ascension Island until 18 October.

22 OCTOBER 1941

0142	U.68 (KKpt Merten) sank tanker **DARKDALE** (8145grt) (Master Thomas H. Card) while she was at anchor in Jamestown harbour, St Helena, in 15, 43S, 05, 43W. (Other sources place the attack in 15, 55S, 05, 43W.) Thirty-nine crewmen and two military personnel were lost. Harbour craft rescued the master and seven crewmen.

28 OCTOBER 1941

0343	U.68 (KKpt Merten) heavily damaged unescorted steamer **HAZELSIDE** (5297grt) (Master Charles Knight Evans) about 600 miles southeast of St. Helena into the area of the Walfisch bay in 23, 10S, 01, 36E.
0401	U.68 sank the steamer with a final torpedo. Two crewmen were lost. Steamer MALAYAN PRINCE (8593grt) rescued the master, thirty-seven crewmen and six gunners and took them to Cape Town.

BALTIC SEA

Kattegat and Skagerrak
Long. E09, 00 – E12, 00   Lat. N60, 00 – N53, 00

29 OCTOBER 1941

	A mine sank German steamer **PETER** (643grt) off Omösund, Denmark.

Southern Baltic Area
Long. E12, 00 – E22, 00   Lat. N60, 00 – N53, 00

1 OCTOBER 1941

	A mine laid by Russian minelayer MARTI, sank German submarine chaser **UJ.117/GUSTAV KRONER** twelve sea miles west of Hanko, Finland).
	German steamer ELIN (grt) sank Finnish minesweeper **HERTTA** (343grt) in a collision at Kalmarsund (Kalmar Strait).
	A mine sank a German **Floating Crane** during a salvage operation for the German submarine tender MOSEL off Ventspils, Latvia.
	A mine laid by Russian submarine L-3 (Capt. 3rd Class Grishenko) sank German captured steamer **KAIJA** (1876grt) (ex Latvian).

9 OCTOBER 1941

	German fishing vessel **GUNTHER** (252grt) was lost near Gotland, Sweden, to an unknown cause.

14 OCTOBER 1941

	A mine sank Russian submarine **S-8** (Lt Cdr Braun) off Suursaari (Hogland Island) in 56, 10, 07N, 16, 39, 08E.

17 OCTOBER 1941

	German steamer **PAULA FAULBAUM** (1922grt) became stranded near Stockholm, Sweden, and later sank.
	Salvaged Russian submarine **S-1** arrived at Gotenhafen (Gdynia), Poland, but the Germans could not agree on what would be done with her.

20 OCTOBER 1941

	Russian submarine L-3 laid mines off Danzig (Gdansk) Bay.
	Russian submarine LEMBIT (Lt Cdr Poleshchuk) laid mines off Koivisto (Primorsk), Russia. However, technical difficulties prevented the laying of the entire minefield.

23 OCTOBER 1941

	Russian submarine SHCH-323 (Lt Cdr Ivantsev) sank German steamer **BALTENLAND** (3724grt) off Västervik on the Swedish coast.

28 OCTOBER 1941

	A mine laid by Russian minesweeper **T-204/FUGAS** (Lt Gillerman) sank German auxiliary patrol vessel **Vp.309/MARTIN DONANDT** (367grt) south of Libau (Liepaya), Latvia.

31 OCTOBER 1941

	A mine laid by Russian minesweeper **T-204/FUGAS** (Lt Gillerman) sank German auxiliary minesweeper **M.1708/ALDEBARAN** off Libau (Liepaya), Latvia.

Gulf of Finland

Long. E22, 00 – E30, 00   Lat. N61, 00 – N57, 00

1 OCTOBER 1941

	Russian submarines L-3 and SHCH-309 patrolled off Suursaari (Hogland Island) until the 17th.
	Russian submarine SHCH-311 patrolled off Tytärsaari (Bolshoy Tyuters), Russia, until the 17th.
	Russian submarine SHCH-317 patrolled off Narva Bay until the 17th.
	Russian submarine M-98 patrolled off Narva Bay until the 9th.
	Russian submarine SHCH-320 (Lt Cdr I. M. Vishnevski) patrolled off Danzig (Gdansk) Bay, but only managed two unsuccessful attacks before departing on the 24th.
	A Finnish MTB damaged Russian submarine L-3 off Suursaari (Hogland Island) harbour.
	A mine sank German motor minesweeper **R.205** ten sea miles northwest of Cape Domesnas.

10 OCTOBER 1941

	Russian submarine M-95 patrolled Narva Bay until the 20th.
	Russian submarines SHCH-322 and SHCH-323 departed Kronstadt, Russia, to patrol in the Baltic.

11 OCTOBER 1941

	A mine or the collision with Russian patrol boat MO-310 sank Russian submarine **SHCH-322** (Capt 1st Class Ermilov) off the Finnish coast.
	Russian submarine S-8 (Lt Cdr Braun) departed Kronstadt, Russia, on a patrol.
	German bombing damaged Estonian steamers EESTIRAND (4444grt) and KAISSAAR (1893grt) carrying deportees from Tallinn to Leningrad off Wrangel Island.

12 OCTOBER 1941

	In Operation WESTFALEN, German light cruiser KÖLN (KptzS Hüffmeier), torpedo boats T.2, T.5, T.7 and T.8 plus seven minesweepers from the 1st and 4th M-Boat Flotillas created a diversion off Cape Ristna, Estonia, for an attack on Dagö (Hiiumaa), Estonia.
	In Operation EAST PRUSSIA, the German 2nd R-Boat Flotilla created a diversion along the east coast of Dagö, near the Russian coastal battery KERTEL. Both diversions tied down the Russian defenders while the Germans tested new landing boats along the south coast of Dagö supported by minesweepers of the German 5th M-Boat Flotilla.

13 OCTOBER 1941

	Russian submarine SHCH-323 (Lt Cdr Ivantsev) spotted German light cruiser KÖLN north of Dagö, but was forced under by the escorts before she could reach an attack position.

14 OCTOBER 1941

	German light cruiser KÖLN bombarded Russian positions at Cape Ristna, Estonia.

16 OCTOBER 1941

During the night, the Russians begin evacuating troops from Dagö Island to Odensholm (Osmussaar), Estonia, and Hanko, Finland. These evacuations continued until the 21st.

17 OCTOBER 1941

Russian submarines M-97 and KALEV began patrolling off Tallinn, Estonia.

19 OCTOBER 1941

Russian submarines S-4 and SHCH-304 departed their patrol areas to return to Suursaari (Hogland Island).

Russian submarines S-9 and S-7 departed for their patrol areas.
S-7 dropped two agents in Narva Bay, and then began a patrol off the port.
S-9 unsuccessfully patrolled in the Aaland Sea.

21 OCTOBER 1941

Russian submarine S-4 unsuccessfully attacked German steamer HOHENHORN (grt) off Tallinn, Estonia.

A mine sank Russian submarine **SHCH-324** west of Suursaari (Hogland Island).

A mine sank Russian submarine **L-2** west of Suursaari.

A mine sank Russian submarine **M-98** west of Suursaari.

23 OCTOBER 1941

A fast Russian convoy (Capt 3rd Class Likholetov) departed from Kronstadt, Russia, with three minesweepers and two submarine chasers with supplies for the Russian garrison at Hanko, Finland.

25 OCTOBER 1941

A mine sank Russian minesweeper **T-203/PATRON** between Hanko, Finland, and Kronstadt, Russia. The other ships of her group succeeded in delivering 499 troops and weapons to Oranienbaum, Russia.

During the night, Russian submarine M-97 (Lt Cdr Mylnikov) unsuccessfully attacked German steamer HOHENHORN (grt) off Nargon.

30 OCTOBER 1941

Russian submarine **KALEV** (Lt Cdr Nyrov) laid mines off Tallinn, Estonia. On her return journey to Kronstadt, she was lost to a mine in the German Minefield CORBETHA.

31 OCTOBER 1941

During the night, a Russian convoy (Vice Admiral V. P. Drozd) evacuated 4230 troops from Hanko, Finland, to Kronstadt, Russia.

MEDITERRANEAN SEA & MIDDLE EAST

East of Gibraltar   Long. W05, 30 – E11, 00   Lat. N44, 30 – N35, 00

1 OCTOBER 1941

Submarine THORN made an unsuccessful patrol east of Gibraltar until the 10th.

Submarine P.34 departed Gibraltar for Malta.

Dutch submarine O.24 departed Gibraltar for patrol in the Tyrrhenian Sea.

3 OCTOBER 1941

Dutch submarine O.21 (Lt Cdr van Dulm) sank Vichy French steamer **OUED YQUEM** (1369grt) off Cape Figari, Sardinia, in 40, 58N, 09, 59E.

4 OCTOBER 1941

Submarine THORN departed Gibraltar for Malta, arriving on the 10th.

8 OCTOBER 1941

Dutch submarine O.21 arrived at Gibraltar after a patrol in the Tyrrhenian Sea.

9 OCTOBER 1941

Submarine TRUANT departed Gibraltar for Malta.

11 OCTOBER 1941

	Submarine PORPOISE departed Gibraltar with supplies for Malta.

13 OCTOBER 1941

	Submarine P.31 departed Gibraltar for Malta.

14 OCTOBER 1941

	Force H (VAdm Somerville) departed Gibraltar with battleship RODNEY, aircraft carrier ARK ROYAL, and light cruiser HERMIONE plus seven destroyers to launch aircraft towards Malta.
	Force K (Capt Agnew) departed Gibraltar for Malta with light cruisers AURORA and PENELOPE plus destroyers LANCE and LIVELY.

16 OCTOBER 1941

	Force H departed Gibraltar with battleship RODNEY, aircraft carrier ARK ROYAL plus light cruiser HERMIONE with destroyers COSSACK, FORESTER, FORESIGHT, FURY, LEGION, SIKH, and ZULU for Operation CALLBOY.

17 OCTOBER 1941

	After receiving a report that Force H was in the Mediterranean, Italian submarine BANDIERA and ARADAM set up a patrol line between Galita and Cape Bougaroni.
	Italian submarines TURCHESE, SERPENTE, DIASPRO and ALAGI patrolled north of the Cap de Fer massif in Algeria.
	Italian submarines SQUALO and NARVALO patrolled off Cap Bon, Tunisia.
	Italian submarines DELFINO and SETTEMBRINI patrolled off Pantelleria.

18 OCTOBER 1941

	Force H reached a point 450 sea miles from Malta, where aircraft carrier ARK ROYAL launched eleven Albacore aircraft and two Swordfish torpedo bombers of 828 Squadron under Lt Cdr D. E. Langmore to Malta. One Swordfish aircraft was lost en route killing pilot T/Sub-Lt (A) D. M. Muller RNVR, and Observer T/Sub-Lt (A) A. S. Denby RNVR. Pilots T/Sub-Lt (A) T. G. Davison RNVR, and T/Sub-Lt (A) D. J. Dunyan RNVR, plus observer A/Sub-Lt (A) W. N. Jones RNVR, of 828 Squadron did not depart ARK ROYAL in Operation CALLBOY, but joined the Squadron at Hal Far, Malta, later.

19 OCTOBER 1941

	Force H arrived back at Gibraltar.
0515	Also in Operation CALLBOY, light cruisers AURORA and PENELOPE departed Gibraltar for Malta and joined destroyers LANCE and LIVELY forty miles off Europa Point. They arrived at Malta as Force K.

20 OCTOBER 1941

	Submarine PORPOISE departed Gibraltar for Alexandria, Egypt, with stores and personnel.

21 OCTOBER 1941

Night	Submarine RORQUAL (Lt Napier) laid mines off Sardinia during the night of 21/22 October. She laid ten mines southeast of Cavoli Island and forty mines southeast of Cape Ferrato, Sardinia.
	RAF bombers sank Italian steamer **ORSOLINA** (344grt) off Tunisia.
	Nine British aircraft sank Vichy French coastal steamer **DIVANA** (1530grt) off the Gulf of Hammamet, in Vichy French territorial waters. Nine crewmen were lost. After this incident, the Vichy French government ordered all French-flagged ships to shoot at all attacking aircraft.
	Dutch submarine O.24 arrived at Gibraltar from a patrol in the Tyrrhenian Sea.

22 OCTOBER 1941

	A mine laid by submarine RORQUAL sank Italian steamer **SALPI** (2710grt) off Cape Ferrato, Sardinia.
	Submarine URGE damaged Italian steamer MARIGOLA (5996grt) off the east coast of Tunisia in 35, 50N, 11, 06E.

23 OCTOBER 1941

	During the night, RAF aircraft further damaged Italian steamer MARIGOLA (5996grt) off the east coast of Tunisia.
	Unescorted merchant ships DUNEDIN STAR (11,168grt) and CITY OF LINCOLN (8039grt) were attacked

24 OCTOBER 1941

Italian sloop CORRISPONDENTE BETA sighted steamer **EMPIRE GUILLEMOT** (5641grt) off La Galita Island near Cap Bon, Tunisia. The sloop guided Italian S.79 torpedo bombers to the steamer, which was promptly sunk. Ten crewmen and one gunner were lost while twenty-eight crewmen and five gunners were taken prisoners.

Italian submarines AXUM, ALAGI, DIASPRO and SANTAROSA began a patrol off the Algerian and Tunisian coasts until 2 November.

26 OCTOBER 1941

Submarine RORQUAL arrived at Gibraltar from Malta.

27 OCTOBER 1941

A mine sank submarine **TETRARCH** (Lt Cdr G. H. Greenway) in the Sicilian Channel.
Greenway, Lt E. J. Cornish-Bowden, Lt K. W. M. Meyrick, Lt D. R. Stavert, Sub-Lt R. B. Houston, Lt (E) P. R. Phillips, Lt C. H. Walmsley RNR, Sub-Lt W. E. Evans RNR, and fifty-four men were lost.
Meyrick of submarine TALISMAN, Stavert of submarine UNIQUE, and Walmsley of submarine UPRIGHT were passengers for the voyage.

28 OCTOBER 1941

Submarine UTMOST torpedoed the already damaged Italian steamer MARIGOLA (5996grt) off Kuriat Island, Tunisia.

30 OCTOBER 1941

Submarine UTMOST (Lt Cdr Cayley) further damaged steamer **MARIGOLA** (5996grt) with gunfire 2.3 miles 165° from Kuriat Island. *(See 28 October.)* UTMOST returned and finally sank the steamer on 1 November.

Submarine OLYMPUS departed Gibraltar for patrol in the Gulf of Lyons (Lion).

Middle Mediterranean Sea
Long. E11, 00 – E20, 00   Lat. N46, 00 – N30, 00

1 OCTOBER 1941

An Italian supply convoy departed Naples escorted by Italian torpedo boats CALLIOPE and PEGASO.

Submarine THRASHER arrived at Malta from patrol in the Gulf of Sirte (Sidra).

Polish submarine SOKOL arrived at Malta from Gibraltar and her patrol supporting Operation HALBERD.

2 OCTOBER 1941

Submarine PERSEUS (Lt Nicolay) sank Italian steamer **CASTELLON** (2086grt) while attacking a convoy ten miles 311° from Benghazi escorted by Italian torpedo boats CALLIOPE and PEGASO from Naples in 32, 30N, 19, 09E.
PERSEUS unsuccessfully attacked Italian steamer SAVONA (2210grt), which was also in the convoy.

An Italian supply convoy departed Naples with Italian steamers VETTOR PISANI (6339grt), SEBASTINO VENIER (6311grt), FABIO FILZI (6835grt), and RIALTO (6099grt) with German steamers REICHENFELS (7744grt) and ANKARA (4768grt) escorted by Italian destroyers DA NOLI, USODIMARE, GIOBERTI, and EURO for Tripoli, Libya.

A mine sank Italian sailing ship **BARI** (120grt) off Tripoli.

Submarine UTMOST made an unsuccessful attack on a steamer in 37, 53N, 12, 05E.

Submarines TRUSTY and UPHOLDER arrived at Malta after a patrol off Cape Vito and Naples, Italy.

3 OCTOBER 1941

Submarine PERSEUS (Lt Nicolay) made an unsuccessful attack on a steamer off Benghazi, Libya.

Submarine UTMOST arrived at Malta after a patrol north of Messina, Sicily.

4 OCTOBER 1941

Submarine UPRIGHT arrived at Malta from patrol.

Submarine REGENT departed Malta on short notice to intercept an Italian convoy spotted east of Tripoli, Libya.

Polish submarine SOKOL departed Malta on short notice to search for a crew of a missing Blenheim aircraft. The search was unsuccessful and the submarine arrived back at Malta on the 6th. The aircrew was later rescued off Djerba, Tunisia.

5 OCTOBER 1941

Aircraft from 830 Squadron sank Italian tanker **RIALTO** (6099grt) eighty miles north-northeast of Misurata in 33, 30N, 15, 53E. Destroyer GIOBERTI rescued 145 survivors.

The tanker was from a convoy of Italian steamers VETTOR PISANI (6339grt), SEBASTINO VENIER (6311grt), FABIO FILZI (6835grt), and RIALTO with German steamers REICHENFELS (7744grt) and ANKARA (4768grt) escorted by destroyers DA NOLI, USODIMARE, GIOBERTI, and EURO, which had departed Naples for Tripoli with torpedo boats CALLIOPE and PARTENOPE from Tripoli.

6 OCTOBER 1941

Submarine URSULA arrived at Malta from a patrol south of Messina.

7 OCTOBER 1941

On a patrol over Sicily, a Fulmar aircraft of 800X Squadron made a forced landing off Syracuse. Petty Officer A. Jopling and Lt J. S. Manning were rescued and became prisoners of war.

8 OCTOBER 1941

Late evening	An Italian convoy departed Naples late in the evening with steamers GIULIA (5921grt), CASAREGIS (6485grt), NIRVO (5164grt), BAINSIZZA (7933grt), ZENA (5219grt), and tanker PROSERPINA (4869grt) (ex-French **BEAUCE** (4869grt)) escorted by Italian destroyers GRANATIERE (Capt. Capponi), BERSAGLIERE, FUCILIERE and ALPINO. Torpedo boat CASCINO joined from Trapani, Sicily. Steamer BAINSIZZA returned to Trapani with defects.

Royal Navy forces on Malta were alerted through ULTRA message intercepts about convoy GUILIA and sent out air reconnaissance to sight the convoy prior to attacking it. (It was standard procedure to use aerial reconnaissance prior to attacking any ULTRA-identified target so as to maintain the secret.)

Aircraft from 830 Squadron sank Italian steamer **PAOLO Z. PODESTA** (863grt) southwest of Favignana, Sicily.

Submarine PERSEUS arrived at Malta from a patrol off Benghazi, Libya.

Submarine P.34 arrived at Malta from Gibraltar.

Submarine THORN unsuccessfully attacked a steamer and a destroyer in the Tyrrhenian Sea.

9 OCTOBER 1941

Submarines UNIQUE, UPHOLDER and the Polish SOKOL departed Malta on short notice to intercept an Italian supply convoy between Pantelleria and Lampedusa Island, Sicily.
UPHOLDER returned to Malta that same day with generator problems.

10 OCTOBER 1941

Italian submarines SAINT BON, CAGNI and ATROPO begin supply runs from Taranto, Italy, to Bardia, Libya. By the 26th, they had delivered 354 tons of supplies and fuel.

11 OCTOBER 1941

Aircraft from 830 Squadron, from Malta, attacked the Italian convoy of steamers GIULIA (5921grt), CASAREGIS (6485grt), NIRVO (5164grt), ZENA (5219grt), and tanker PROSERPINA (4869grt) (ex-French **BEAUCE** (4869grt)) with aerial torpedoes south of Pantelleria.
One aerial torpedo sank Italian steamer **ZENA** (5219grt) south of Lampedusa, Sicily, in 34, 52N, 12, 22E.
Another aerial torpedo sank Italian steamer **CASAREGIS** (6485grt) south of Lampedusa in 34, 10N, 12, 38E.

12 OCTOBER 1941

An Italian convoy departed Trapani, Sicily, with Italian steamers BAINSIZZA (7933grt) and NIRVO (5164grt) and German tug MAX BERENDT escorted by Italian destroyers DA RECCO and SEBENICO plus torpedo boat CASCINO.

Italian light cruisers DUCA D'AOSTA, EUGENIO DI SAVOIA, and MONTECUCOLI plus destroyers VIVALDI, MALOCELLO, PIGAFETTA, DE VERAZZANO, AVIERE, and CAMICIA NERA were scheduled to lay Minefield B off Benghazi, Libya, during the night of 12/13 October. However, the mine laying was cancelled when it was reported that the British Mediterranean Fleet was at sea.

Submarine RORQUAL arrived at Malta after laying mines in the Aegean.

Polish submarine SOKOL arrived at Malta after a patrol off Lampedusa, Sicily.

13 OCTOBER 1941

Dutch submarine O.24 (LtZ/1 de Booy) made an unsuccessful attack on a steamer in the southern Tyrrhenian Sea. (Other sources claim he attacked an Italian tanker.)

RAF bombing sank Italian coastal steamer **ROSA** (246grt) at Tripoli, Libya.

	RAF bombing sank Italian torpedo boat **PLEIADI** off Tripoli. She was hit by several bombs and became a total loss.
	Submarine THORN departed Malta on patrol and then to proceed to Alexandria, Egypt.

14 OCTOBER 1941

	Aircraft of 830 Squadron made a torpedo attack on the Trapani, Italy, to Tripoli, Libya, convoy and damaged steamer **BAINSIZZA** (7933grt) in 34, 15N, 12, 12E. She was taken in tow by the German tug MAX BERENDT, sailing with the convoy, and later by Italian tug CICLOPE, escorted by torpedo boat POLLUCE, both of which had come out from Tripoli. The steamer sank the next day.
	Submarines TALISMAN and TORBAY landed a commando force that attacked the headquarters of German General Rommel in Libya. He was not there during the attack.
	Submarine UNIQUE unsuccessfully attacked a steamer in 40, 26N, 14, 20E.
	Submarines UNBEATEN, URGE, and UPRIGHT departed Malta on short notice for an operation off Cape Passero, Sicily. The submarines arrived back at Malta on the 16th, having sighted nothing but a hospital ship during the operation.

15 OCTOBER 1941

	Italian destroyers DA NOLI, ZENO and PESSAGNO began supply runs from Augusta, Sicily, to Benghazi, Libya, through the 21st. In two trips they carried 1670 troops to Benghazi and evacuated 222 wounded soldiers.

16 OCTOBER 1941

	Submarine TRUANT arrived at Malta from Gibraltar.
	An Italian convoy departed Naples for Tripoli with steamers MARIN SANUDO (5081grt), PROBITAS (5084grt), BEPPE (4859grt), PAOLINA (4994grt), and CATERINA (4786grt), escorted by destroyers FOLGORE, FULMINE, USODIMARE, GIOBERTI, DA RECCO, and SEBENICO. Torpedo boat CIGNO escorted the convoy until Trapani, Sicily. Torpedo boat CALLIOPE also escorted the convoy. Steamer AMBA ARADAM (405grt) joined the convoy from Trapani. Torpedo boat CASCINO joined the convoy from Tripoli.
1000	As part of Operation CALLBOY, steamers CLAN MACDONALD (9653grt) and EMPIRE GUILLEMOT (5641grt) departed Malta, independently, for Gibraltar. EMPIRE GUILLEMOT soon returned with engine problems, but was able to sail on the 22nd with a second group of steamers.

17 OCTOBER 1941

	Submarine PORPOISE arrived at Malta from Gibraltar with stores.
	Submarines URSULA, P.34, and RORQUAL departed Malta for patrols off Kuriat Island, Tunisia. Submarine RORQUAL was forced to return to Malta later with defects.

18 OCTOBER 1941

	Submarine URSULA (Lt Hezlet) damaged Italian steamer BEPPE (4859grt) near Lampedusa, Sicily, using information from an ULTRA message intercept. The steamer was taken in tow by German tug MAX BERENDT and arrived at Tripoli on the 21st escorted by Italian destroyer DA RECCO and torpedo boat CALLIOPE.
Evening	In the evening, British bombing heavily damaged Italian steamer **CATERINA** (4786grt) and she sank sixty-two miles 350° from Tripoli on the 19th. The rest of the convoy arrived at Tripoli on the 19th.
	Submarines UPHOLDER, UPRIGHT and UNBEATEN patrolled unsuccessfully off the Tunisian coast.
	Submarine THORN patrolled unsuccessfully off the Tunisian coast until 30 October.
	Submarine TRUANT departed Malta for a patrol in the Adriatic.
	Submarine RORQUAL departed Malta to lay mines off the south coast of Sardinia. After the mining on 21 and 22 October, the submarine arrived at Gibraltar on the 26th.

19 OCTOBER 1941

	Submarines THORN, TRUSTY and TRUANT were sent to the location of an Italian convoy running from Taranto to Benghazi identified from an ULTRA message intercept. The submarines made no contacts.
	Submarine TRUSTY departed Malta on a patrol off Argostoli, Ionian Islands.
	Submarine URSULA returned to Malta after a patrol.

20 OCTOBER 1941

	Submarine P.31 arrived at Malta from Gibraltar.
	RAF bombers sank Italian steamer **NEREO** (214grt) off Tripoli, Libya.

21 OCTOBER 1941

	A submarine attacked Italian destroyers DA NOLI, ZENO, and PESSAGNO fifteen miles north of Benghazi, Libya, after they departed Benghazi for Augusta, Sicily.
	Submarine UNIQUE arrived at Malta from a patrol.
0915	As part of Operation CALLBOY, Force K (Capt Agnew) arrived at Malta with light cruisers AURORA and PENELOPE plus destroyers LANCE and LIVELY from Gibraltar.

22 OCTOBER 1941

	Several small Italian convoys between Brindisi and Benghazi were recalled due to an *Alarme Navale* and were ordered into the nearest port until the 24th.
	A mine sank Italian steamer **MARIA POMPEI** (1407grt) at Cattaro (Kotor), Montenegro.
1000	As part of Operation CALLBOY, steamers CITY OF LINCOLN (8039grt), DUNEDIN STAR (11,168grt), and EMPIRE GUILLEMOT (5641grt) departed Malta to make an unescorted passage to Gibraltar.

23 OCTOBER 1941

	Italian escort ship ARBOREA led a convoy of Greek steamer VIRGINIA S. (3885grt) plus Romanian tanker BALCIC (3495grt) and Bulgarian steamer BALKAN (3838grt) from Patrasso to Brindisi, Italy.
	Submarine TRUANT (Lt Cdr Haggard) sank Greek steamer **VIRGINIA S.** (3885grt) while attacking a small convoy in the Ionian Sea in 39, 48N, 19, 06E. The submarine also claimed damage to the escort, which was not hit.
	Submarine TRUANT damaged Italian steamer **PADENNA** (1589grt) with a torpedo and gunfire off Bari, Italy. Though the ship burnt out, the wreck was later towed away.
	RAF bombing sank Italian steamer **ACHILLE** (2415grt) west of Sicily in 38, 26, 11, 24E.

24 OCTOBER 1941

	Submarine TETRARCH arrived at Malta from Alexandria with stores and kerosene.
	Steamer CLAN FERGUSON (7347grt) departed Malta to proceed independently to Gibraltar. The steamer was attacked by aircraft shortly after leaving Malta and was recalled.

25 OCTOBER 1941

	Submarine TRUSTY made an unsuccessful attack on Italian steamer MARIA POMPEI (1407grt) off Cattaro in 38, 24N, 20, 13E.
	Force K departed Malta with light cruisers AURORA and PENELOPE plus destroyers LANCE and LIVELY to intercept an Italian return convoy from Benghazi with Italian steamer CAPO ORSO (3149grt), German steamer TINOS (2827grt), escorted by destroyer STRALE. No contact was made and Force K returned to Malta on the 26th. The convoy arrived at Brindisi on the 28th.
	Submarine THUNDERBOLT arrived at Malta from a patrol.
0900	Steamer CLAN FERGUSON (7347grt) returned to Malta as ordered.

26 OCTOBER 1941

	Based upon an ULTRA message intercept, submarines UPRIGHT, URGE and UNBEATEN were ordered to intercept an Italian destroyer convoy. Unfortunately, the submarines were set up too far south and missed the convoy.
	Submarine TRUANT (Lt Cdr Haggard) landed commandos off Ancona, Italy, to damage the rail line running along the Italian east coast.

27 OCTOBER 1941

	Submarine UNBEATEN unsuccessfully attacked a German submarine off Augusta, Sicily.

28 OCTOBER 1941

	Submarine THRASHER (Lt Mackenzie) sank Italian coastal steamer **ESPERIA** (384grt) with gunfire northeast of Benghazi, Libya.
	Polish submarine SOKOL unsuccessfully attacked Italian steamer CITTA DI PALERMO (5413grt) off Naples in 40, 42N, 13, 47E.
	Seven Albacore aircraft of 828 Squadron attacked Comiso airfield on Sicily. Midshipman P. A. Brown RNVR, and Sub-Lt F. A. J. Smith RNVR were killed when their Albacore failed to return to Hal Far, Malta, after the attack.
	Submarine URGE arrived at Malta after a patrol off Kuriat Island, Tunisia.
	Submarine URSULA arrived at Malta after a patrol off Calabria, Italy.

29 OCTOBER 1941

	An Italian supply convoy departed Brindisi, Italy, with steamer CAPO ARMA (3195grt) escorted by torpedo boat PEGASO to Benghazi, Libya.

30 OCTOBER 1941

	During the night, submarine TRUANT (Lt Cdr. Haggard) sank Italian tanker **METEOR** (1685grt) two sea miles off Point Penna, south of Ortona, Italy.

Eastern Mediterranean Sea

Long. E20, 00 – E38, 00   Lat. N43, 00 – N30, 00

1 OCTOBER 1941

	Submarine TALISMAN (Lt Cdr Willmott) unsuccessfully attacked an Italian convoy of steamers LAURETTA (grt) and ARKADIA (grt), escorted by torpedo boat LIBRA, off the Zea Channel in the Cyclades.
	Submarines PROTEUS and REGENT unsuccessfully patrolled off Zante (Zakynthos) in the Ionian Islands and Khoms, Libya, respectively, until the 10th.
	Submarine RORQUAL departed Alexandria, Egypt, for Malta to return to Britain. The submarine arrived at Malta on the 12th and Gibraltar on the 27th, laying two minefields en route.
	Minesweeping whaler SOTRA was damaged below the water line by gunfire at Tobruk. One rating was wounded.

2 OCTOBER 1941

	The Mediterranean Fleet was at sea from Alexandria for exercises. The Fleet returned to Alexandria on the 3rd.
	Antisubmarine trawler KLO reported being attacked by a submarine off Alexandria. Destroyers KANDAHAR and JAGUAR searched the area, but were unable to make contact.
	Antisubmarine trawler LYDIARD attacked a submarine contact off Haifa, Palestine. Destroyer VENDETTA and corvette HYACINTH joined the trawler in the hunt, without success. The destroyer and the corvette returned to port on the 3rd.
	An accidental explosion sank A.S.I.S. **CHURRUCA** (1847grt) at Alexandria. The cargo and the ship were later salvaged.
1900	Minesweeping whaler SOTRA departed Tobruk with lighter A.9 and minesweeping whaler SOIKA.

3 OCTOBER 1941

	Submarine TALISMAN (Lt Cdr Willmott) sank damaged German steamer **YALOVA** (3750grt) south of Piraeus, Greece, near Giorgio Island.
	Corvette PEONY proceeded to Akrotiri Bay, Cyprus, to act as a Q ship against Axis submarines.
	A supply convoy with Italian tanker TORCELLO (3336grt) and Vichy French steamer THEOPHILE GAUTIER (8194grt) departed Salonika, Greece, for Piraeus escorted by torpedo boats MONZAMBANO, CALATAFIMI, and ALDEBARAN.

4 OCTOBER 1941

	Submarine TALISMAN (Lt Cdr Willmott) sank Vichy French steamer **THEOPHILE GAUTIER** (8194grt) in the Doro Channel off Euboea Island, Greece, in 37, 45N, 24, 35E.
	U.559, U.331, U.75, U.97, U.79 and U.371 began patrolling off Egypt from Alexandria to Tobruk.
	U.559 (Kptlt Heidtmann) unsuccessfully attacked a steamer off the Egyptian coast during the night.
	German bombing sank antisubmarine whaler **WHIPPET** (ex Norwegian **KOS XXI** (353grt)) (Lt A. R. J. Tilston RNR) while she was towing a D-lighter off the coast of Egypt. She was in company with minesweeping whaler SVANA (286grt). Four survivors reached Tobruk in SVANA. The remainder of the crew returned in the D-lighter to Mersa Matruh. T/Sub-Lt (E) A. Hodgson RNVR was the only fatality.
	Allied aircraft reported a submarine north of Bardia in 33, 00N, 25, 30E steering towards Alexandria.
	Minesweeper ABERDARE departed Alexandria with twelve torpedoes for the Fleet Air Arm at Cyprus. After delivering the torpedoes, the minesweeper relieved minesweeper BAGSHOT at Beirut, Lebanon.

5 OCTOBER 1941

	Destroyers KIPLING, GRIFFIN, JUPITER, and HOTSPUR departed Alexandria and were ordered to search the area north of Bardia for the submarine reported there *(see 4 October)*.
	Axis aircraft attacked U.559 while she was operating northeast of Tobruk. Three bombs missed her and no damage was done in this "friendly aircraft" engagement.

7 OCTOBER 1941

	A convoy with German steamers SALZBURG (1756grt) and TRAPANI (1855grt), escorted by Italian destroyer SELLA and torpedo boat CASTELFIDARDO, departed Suda Bay, Crete, for Piraeus, Greece.
	Submarine TALISMAN (Lt Cdr Willmott) unsuccessfully attacked the convoy north of Crete in 35, 45N, 24, 08E.

8 OCTOBER 1941

	Submarine RORQUAL (Lt Napier) laid fifty mines in the Gulf of Athens in 37, 22N, 23, 52E.
	Battleship QUEEN ELIZABETH was at sea exercising with her escort destroyers from Alexandria.
	Antiaircraft cruiser COVENTRY departed Alexandria for Port Said. COVENTRY and Greek destroyer VASILISSA OLGA passed through the Suez Canal on the 9th en route to India. The cruiser provided antiaircraft support for troopships NEA HELLAS (16,991grt) and INDRAPOERA (10,825grt). After calling at Aden to fuel on the 11th, the cruiser then sailed and rejoined the ships at sea. Steamers NEA HELLAS and INDRAPOERA joined steamers VOLENDAM (15,434grt) and DUNERA (11,162grt) at Aden and departed on the 13th as convoy SW.10, escorted by AMC CARTHAGE. COVENTRY departed Aden on the 13th and escorted a Norwegian tanker back to Aden, arriving on the 14th. COVENTRY departed Aden on the 15th with Greek destroyer VASILISSA OLGA. COVENTRY proceeded to Bombay, India, for a refit, which included the installation of a new bow, replacing her temporary bow installed from her December 1940 torpedoing. COVENTRY and Greek destroyer VASILISSA OLGA both arrived at Bombay on the 20th. VASILISSA OLGA departed Bombay on the 23rd for Calcutta, India, for the installation of ASDIC equipment.
	Corvette PEONY attacked a submarine contact in 34, 08N, 35, 21E. Destroyer VENDETTA, corvettes DELPHINIUM, SALVIA, and HYACINTH, plus two antisubmarine aircraft joined in the search, but no further contact was made. The corvettes were recalled to Beirut, Lebanon, on the 10th.

10 OCTOBER 1941

	U.559 (Kptlt Heidtmann) unsuccessfully attacked a convoy off Tobruk, Libya, during the night.
	Submarine THUNDERBOLT (Lt Cdr Crouch) sank Italian sailing ship **CITTA DI SIMI** (25grt) with gunfire twelve miles from Cape Sidero, Crete, in 35, 31N, 26, 25E.
	Destroyers HERO, NIZAM, and KIPLING departed Alexandria to join the Mediterranean Fleet at sea.
0402	Lighters A.2 (AKA LCT.2) (Sub-Lt E. L. Clark RNVR), A.7 (AKA LCT.7) (Sub-Lt A. C. Bromley RNVR), and A.18 (AKA LCT.18) (Sub-Lt L. D. Peters RNVR), en route to Tobruk from Mersa Matruh, encountered U.331 (ObltzS Freiherr Hans-Diedrich v. Tiesenhausen) near Ashaila Rocks off Sidi Barrani.
0417	U.331 fired three torpedoes at the three landing craft, which all missed. (Authors note: The draft of the LCT would make it very difficult for a torpedo hit.)
0439	U.331 slightly damaged A.18 with gunfire in 31, 10N, 26, 42E. Sub-Lt G. S. Sinclair RNR, the group navigator in A.18, was wounded.
0520	The lighters damaged the U-boat with their AA (pom-pom) guns, wounding two German sailors in the forward gun crew (one later died of wounds) and damaging the conning tower.
	Damaged lighter A.18 (LCT.18) returned to Mersa Matruh, while the other two lighters continued on to Tobruk.
<1759	Battleships BARHAM and VALIANT plus light cruisers AJAX and HOBART departed Alexandria with destroyers JERVIS, JAGUAR, JUPITER, KANDAHAR, GRIFFIN, HASTY, HOTSPUR, DECOY, AVON VALE, and ERIDGE to sweep westward.
1800	Destroyers KANDAHAR, GRIFFIN, JUPITER, DECOY, AVON VALE, and ERIDGE were detached from the Mediterranean Fleet to conduct a U-boat sweep towards Bardia.
>1801	Battleships BARHAM and VALIANT plus light cruisers AJAX and HOBART turned back eastwards towards Alexandria with destroyers JERVIS, JAGUAR, JUPITER, KANDAHAR, GRIFFIN, HASTY, HOTSPUR, DECOY, AVON VALE, and ERIDGE.

11 OCTOBER 1941

	Australian destroyer VENDETTA departed Haifa, Palestine, for Alexandria with a small convoy.
0730	Destroyer JERVIS attacked a submarine contact in 31, 14N, 29, 14E. She remained in the area searching for the contact for three hours before continuing after the fleet to Alexandria.
1130	The Mediterranean Fleet returned to Alexandria.
1430	Destroyers KANDAHAR, GRIFFIN, JUPITER, DECOY, AVON VALE, and ERIDGE returned to Alexandria after an unsuccessful U-boat search.

12 OCTOBER 1941

0005	U.75 (Kptlt Ringelmann) began a gun battle with lighters **A.2** (372grt) (AKA **LCT.2**) (Sub-Lt E. L. Clark DSC, DSM RNVR) and **A.7** (372grt) (AKA **LCT.7**) (Sub-Lt A. C. Bromley RNVR), which had departed Tobruk, Libya, earlier that day, in 32, 08N, 24, 56E.

0234	**A.2** (372grt) sank from shell damage.
0700	**A.7** (372grt) sank from shell damage.
	Clark, Bromley, Skipper J. C. Norton RNR, of lighter **A.2**, T/Skipper J. R. Peel RNR, of **A.7**, twenty-six ratings, an officer in the Royal Engineers, four Australian soldiers, and two Italian prisoners of war were lost.
	Only one crewman survived; A/Petty Officer W. A. Henley, DSM, from **A.7** was rescued the next day and taken prisoner by the submarine. He was taken to Piraeus and later to Germany.
<1759	Battleships QUEEN ELIZABETH and VALIANT plus light cruisers AJAX, HOBART, and GALATEA departed Alexandria with destroyers JERVIS, JAGUAR, GRIFFIN, JUPITER, KANDAHAR, HASTY, HOTSPUR, DECOY, AVON VALE, and ERIDGE and proceeded westward.
1800	Light cruisers AJAX, HOBART, and GALATEA with destroyers JERVIS, JAGUAR, and JUPITER were detached from the Mediterranean Fleet to reach a position in 33, 00N, 24, 30E at midnight and then rejoin the Fleet at daylight.
<1949	Operation CULTIVATE began when minelaying cruiser ABDIEL departed Alexandria, Egypt, with destroyers HERO, KIPLING, and NIZAM for the first convoy serial to Tobruk with reinforcements and supplies.
1950	Minelaying cruiser ABDIEL with destroyers HERO, KIPLING, and NIZAM saw oil and heard cries from survivors of the sunken lighters **A.2** and **A.7** while approaching Tobruk, but they were unable to stop and search for survivors because they were already behind schedule on their supply mission.

13 OCTOBER 1941

	At daylight, the Mediterranean Fleet set course for Alexandria.
	MTB.68 and MTB.215 were ordered to patrol off Bardia to intercept a reported submarine.
1315	The Mediterranean Fleet turned westward when a report indicated that three Italian cruisers and six destroyers were at sea. No further contact was made with these Italian ships.
1800	Light cruisers AJAX, HOBART, and GALATEA with three destroyers were again detached from the Mediterranean Fleet for a night patrol and then rejoined at daylight on the 14th.

14 OCTOBER 1941

	Antisubmarine whaler SOIKA and tug C.307 departed Alexandria, Egypt, on Operation CULTIVATE convoy serial 1A. The tug returned to Mersa Matruh.
0800	Corvettes DELPHINIUM, SALVIA, PEONY, and ERICA rendezvoused off Capa Gata with antisubmarine whaler PROTEA and carried out an antisubmarine search of the area.
1530	The Mediterranean Fleet arrived back at Alexandria.

15 OCTOBER 1941

	Italian submarines DAGABUR, TOPAZIO and ZAFFIRO patrolled off the Gulf of Mersin until 23 October.
	Italian submarine ZYPERN patrolled west of Haifa until the 23rd.
	Italian submarine UARSCIEK patrolled off Cyrenaica until the 23rd.
	Polish submarine SOKOL (Lt Cdr Karnicki) made two unsuccessful attacks on steamers in the Gulf of Athens.
	Submarine THUNDERBOLT (Lt Cdr Crouch) made an unsuccessful attack on a tanker in the Aegean.

16 OCTOBER 1941

0055	U.97 (Udo Heilmann) spotted a small convoy escorted by an armed trawler about fifty miles west of Alexandria, Egypt.
0217	U.97 attacked the convoy with three torpedoes, but all missed.
0325	U.97 sank Greek steamer **SAMOS** (1208grt) while attacking Operation CULTIVATE convoy serial 4 escorted by antisubmarine whaler KOS XIX about 50 miles west of Alexandria in 31, 14N, 28, 50E. Twenty-four crewmen, three gunners, and four British personnel were lost. Three survivors were rescued.
0400	U.97 sank tanker **PASS OF BALMAHA** (758grt) (Master Stanley Kirby Hardy) while attacking Operation CULTIVATE convoy serial 4 escorted by antisubmarine whaler KOS XIX in 31, 14N, 28, 50E. The tanker exploded with a cloud of smoke and flames towering 300 metres high. The master, fifteen crewmen and two gunners were all lost.
	The sunken ships were to have joined gunboat GNAT and A-lighters A.13, A.17, and A.18 off Mersa Matruh before proceeding to Tobruk.
	Destroyers HASTY, AVON VALE, ERIDGE, and DECOY departed Alexandria, joined later by destroyer HERO and HOTSPUR, to search for the submarine.
	Destroyers HASTY and ERIDGE were detached during the night of 17/18 October to sweep ahead of gunboat GNAT and the A-lighters.
	MTB.68 and MTB.215 joined gunboat GNAT. After an unsuccessful search, the destroyers returned to Alexandria on the 18th. The gunboat and the A-lighters arrived at Tobruk, Libya, on the 19th.

17 OCTOBER 1941

	Minelaying cruiser LATONA departed Alexandria, Egypt, with destroyers NIZAM, JACKAL, and HAVOCK on

	the second Operation CULTIVATE convoy series to Tobruk. The ships returned to Alexandria on the 18th.
	Armed boarding vessel CHANTALA departed Alexandria to carry cargo to Syria.

18 OCTOBER 1941

	Minelaying cruiser ABDIEL departed Alexandria, Egypt, with destroyers KANDAHAR, GRIFFIN, and JAGUAR on Operation CULTIVATE convoy serial 3.
	Destroyers JERVIS and JUPITER departed Alexandria escorting landing ship GLENROY (9809grt) from Port Said to Alexandria. The destroyers and landing ship arrived at Alexandria on the 19th.
	Submarine THUNDERBOLT made an unsuccessful attack on a steamer in the Aegean.
2144	U.559 (Kptlt Heidtmann) unsuccessfully attacked a destroyer escorting three lighters in 32, 40N, 24, 34E.
2354	U.79 (Kptlt Kaufmann) damaged LCT.18 (372grt) while attacking Tug No.307, LCT.13, LCT.17 and LCT.18 off Tobruk in 32, 10N, 24, 18E.

19 OCTOBER 1941

	Destroyers HOTSPUR, HASTY, HAVOCK, and DECOY departed Alexandria, Egypt, to bombard the Axis military rest camp at Marsa Lucch during the night of 19/20 October. Late on the 19th, destroyer HAVOCK ran aground in 32, 02N, 24, 53E. The destroyer's propellers and shaft were damaged. The other destroyers escorted her back to Alexandria and the bombardment was cancelled. The destroyers arrived back at Alexandria during the night of 20/21 October.
	Sloop FLAMINGO departed Alexandria, Egypt, to escort steamer MANCHESTER PORT (5469grt) from Port Said to Alexandria.
	Antisubmarine whaler KOS XIX reported a submarine contact off Alexandria while escorting tanker TONELINE (811grt) to Tobruk, Libya, in Operation CULTIVATE convoy serial 4A. ML.1023 had departed Alexandria with the two ships, but had to return with defects. Destroyer ENCOUNTER and two antisubmarine trawlers joined the convoy to search for the submarine, without success. The tanker and its escort safely arrived at Tobruk on the 21st.
0330	Returning from Tobruk, destroyer KANDAHAR attacked a submarine contact off Bardia, Libya.
1200	Minelaying cruiser ABDIEL arrived back at Alexandria.
>1201	Destroyers KANDAHAR, GRIFFIN, and JAGUAR arrived back at Alexandria after their submarine search.

20 OCTOBER 1941

	Italian torpedo boat ALTAIR with AMC BARLETTA plus torpedo boats LUPO and MONZAMBANO were escorting a convoy including steamers CITTA DI AGRIGENTO (2480grt), CITTA DI MARSALA (2480grt), TAGLIAMENTO (5448grt), and SALZBURG (1756grt). **ALTAIR** struck a mine in the Gulf of Athens in 35, 45N, 23, 52E and later sank in tow. Torpedo boat LUPO rescued the survivors. Torpedo boat **ALDEBARAN** also struck a mine while going to assist **ALTAIR** and was sunk. Both mines were part of a minefield laid by submarine RORQUAL on the 8th.
	Minelaying cruiser LATONA departed Alexandria with destroyers KINGSTON, NIZAM, and ENCOUNTER on Operation CULTIVATE convoy serial 5. The ships arrived back at Alexandria, Egypt, on the 21st.
	Australian destroyer VENDETTA departed Alexandria for Singapore and passed through the Suez Canal on the 21st. The destroyer was refitting at Singapore in December. She departed Singapore on 2 February in the tow of destroyer STRONGHOLD.
Night	Light cruisers AJAX, HOBART, and GALATEA departed Alexandria with destroyers GRIFFIN and JAGUAR and bombarded an Axis gun battery near Tobruk during the night of 20/21 October.

21 OCTOBER 1941

	Depth charges damaged U.371 off Tobruk, Libya.
	Destroyers JERVIS, JUPITER, and KANDAHAR departed Alexandria, Egypt, to bombard the enemy gun battery near Tobruk. The battery was bombarded during the night of 21/22 October.
	Minelaying cruiser ABDIEL departed Alexandria with destroyers NAPIER, HASTY, and DECOY on Operation CULTIVATE convoy serial 6. The ships returned to Alexandria on the 22nd.
	Antisubmarine trawler WOLBOROUGH and steamer GEBIL KEBIR (grt) departed Alexandria with motor launch ML.1061 on Operation CULTIVATE convoy serial 8. The steamer was damaged by German bombing off Tobruk and was towed into harbour by the trawler. Two motor launches intended as escorts for damaged steamer GEBIL KEBIR were attacked by German bombers at dusk on the 22nd, sustaining only superficial damage. Both motor launches arrived at Tobruk.
0445	U.79 (Wolfgang Kaufmann) damaged gunboat **GNAT** (625grt) with a torpedo thirty miles northeast of Bardia, Libya, in 32, 08N, 25, 22E. The gunboat's bow was blown away to the 6-inch gun position. There were no casualties. Destroyers GRIFFIN and JAGUAR were detached by the 7th Cruiser Squadron plus destroyers KINGSTON and NIZAM were detached from minelaying cruiser LATONA to assist.

However, all ships were ordered to turn eastward to avoid threat of air attack during daylight hours. Destroyers GRIFFIN and JAGUAR were to remain in the vicinity of Mersa Matruh and were joined by destroyers ERIDGE and AVON VALE. These destroyers contacted the gunboat before sunset.

Destroyer GRIFFIN towed the damaged gunboat escorted by destroyer JAGUAR plus antisubmarine whalers SOUTHERN MAID and KLO.

Off Mersa Matruh, the tow was turned over to tug ST MONACE.

Destroyers JAGUAR, AVON VALE, and ERIDGE returned to Alexandria arriving on the 22nd.

Destroyer GRIFFIN joined destroyer JERVIS to conduct an antisubmarine sweep ahead of whaler KOS XIX and tanker TONELINE (811grt), which had departed Tobruk at dark on the 22nd.

The gunboat arrived at Alexandria on the 23rd. Later, an attempt was made to weld the bow of sunken gunboat **CRICKET** to the remaining stern section of gunboat **GNAT**, but this effort was unsuccessful. The gunboat was then declared a total loss.

22 OCTOBER 1941

Minelaying cruiser LATONA departed Alexandria, Egypt, with destroyers KINGSTON, ENCOUNTER, and HOTSPUR on Operation CULTIVATE convoy serial 7.

The LL sweep equipment of minesweeping whaler SOIKA was cut in an air raid at Tobruk, Libya. The cable fouled the propeller on HOTSPUR, but she was able to return to Alexandria at reduced speed, with no permanent damage being done. The group returned to Alexandria on the 23rd.

Corvette PEONY departed Haifa, Palestine, with armed boarding vessel CHANTALA and steamer BRITISH COLONEL (6999grt) for Alexandria.

Corvette ERICA escorted cable ship BULLFINCH from Alexandria to Port Said. The corvette then departed Port Said and escorted mine carrier GURNA to Haifa, Palestine.

1052	Aircraft reported U.75 in 32, 07N, 29, 44E so destroyers JUPITER and KANDAHAR were detached to hunt for the U-boat. Another report was received some five hours later. Destroyer JUPITER, short of fuel, was sent into Alexandria. Destroyer DECOY departed Alexandria to join destroyer KANDAHAR in the U-boat hunt. Also, sloop FLAMINGO, which had departed Alexandria earlier for Port Said, was diverted to the U-boat hunt. Destroyers KANDAHAR and DECOY arrived at Alexandria on the 23rd. Sloop FLAMINGO was detached from the U-boat hunting group to continue her voyage to Port Said and to return to the Suez Escort Force.

23 OCTOBER 1941

Submarine TRIUMPH (Lt Cdr. Woods) sank Greek caique **PANGIOTIS** (120grt) and damaged caique **AGHIA PARASKEVA** (120grt) with gunfire in the Gulf of Petali. German sources claim both were sunk.

U.97 unsuccessfully attacked a steamer in the eastern Mediterranean.

Light cruisers AJAX, NEPTUNE, and HOBART departed Alexandria with destroyers NAPIER, NIZAM, JUPITER, HASTY, ERIDGE, and AVON VALE to bombard enemy positions at Bardia.

Destroyers NAPIER, NIZAM, JUPITER, and HASTY were detached from the cruisers and conducted a separate bombardment of Sollum, Egypt. The light cruisers bombarded Bardia escorted by destroyers ERIDGE and AVON VALE.

All ships returned to Alexandria on the 24th.

Antiaircraft ship CARLISLE departed Alexandria to return to the Red Sea for duty in the Suez Escort Force. The ship arrived at Suez on the 25th.

24 OCTOBER 1941

Minelaying cruiser ABDIEL departed Alexandria with destroyers KANDAHAR, KINGSTON, and GRIFFIN on Operation CULTIVATE convoy serial nine. The ships arrived back at Alexandria on the 25th.

Submarine TRIUMPH unsuccessfully attacked Spanish steamer ISORA (316grt) in the Aegean.

25 OCTOBER 1941

Minelaying cruiser LATONA departed Alexandria, Egypt, with destroyer HERO, HOTSPUR, and ENCOUNTER on the last Operation CULTIVATE convoy, serial 10.

Late in the day, German Ju87 aircraft of I/STG.1 sank minelaying cruiser **LATONA** (2650grt) (Captain S. L. Bateson) off Bardia in 32, 15N, 24, 14E.

Commissioned Gunner (T) G. F. W. Bruce, Midshipman R. Kennedy, T/Lt (E) E. W. Pillinger, Cdr (E) T. G. B. Winch, sixteen ratings, and seven soldiers were lost.

Destroyer HERO was damaged by a bomb near miss while standing by **LATONA** and her speed was reduced to ten knots. The destroyer was later able to increase speed to twenty knots.

Destroyers ENCOUNTER and HERO took the **LATONA** survivors to Alexandria.

Operation CULTIVATE transported 7138 fresh troops to Tobruk, Libya, with 7234 tired troops and 727 wounded brought back to Alexandria, Egypt on the return trips.

Minelaying cruiser ABDIEL delivered troops and supplies to Tobruk.

	U.75 (Kptlt Ringelmann) unsuccessfully attacked a destroyer off the northern Egyptian coast.
	Submarine TRIUMPH (Lt Cdr. Woods) sank Italian steamer **MONROSA** (6703grt) off Hydra, in the Aegean in 37, 41N, 23, 53E while attacking a convoy with steamers MONROSA and SANTAGANTA (4299grt) escorted by Italian destroyer SELLA and torpedo boat SIRIO en route from Piraeus, Greece, to Candia, Crete. The Italian depth charge attack damaged the submarine.
	Light cruisers AJAX, NEPTUNE, and the Australian HOBART departed Alexandria with destroyers JERVIS, JAGUAR, JUPITER, KIMBERLEY, HASTY, NAPIER, and NIZAM on a bombardment operation. However, due to the loss of minelaying cruiser **LATONA**, the bombardment was cancelled. Destroyers JERVIS, JAGUAR, KIMBERLEY, and JUPITER were detached from the cruisers to assist **LATONA** and escorted damaged destroyer HERO to Alexandria. The light cruisers bombarded Bardia prior to returning to Alexandria with destroyers NAPIER, NIZAM, and HASTY.

26 OCTOBER 1941

1400	Damaged destroyer HERO arrived at Alexandria and was under repair for four weeks.
Night	MTB.68 and MTB.215 laid mines in Bardia Harbour during the night of 26\27 October. The boats returned to Mersa Matruh after the mining.

31 OCTOBER 1941

	Destroyers ERIDGE and AVON VALE departed Alexandria escorting ocean boarding vessel CHANTALA to Port Said. From there they passed through the canal to join the Suez Escort Force.

Black Sea

Long. E27, 00 – E43, 00   Lat. N48, 00 – N41, 00

1 OCTOBER 1941

	Russian submarines SHCH-201, M-32, M-52, and M-58 followed by SHCH-202, SHCH-203, M-60 and M-59 took turns patrolling the south-eastern Ukrainian coast.
	Russian submarine M-33 and M-34 took turns patrolling off Constanza, Romania.
	Russian submarines S-33, SHCH-215 and SHCH-210 patrolled off the Bulgarian coast.

3 OCTOBER 1941

	Over the next three days, the Russian 157th Rifle Division was evacuated from Odessa to Sevastopol. The men were transported in steamers ARMENIYA (4727grt), KOTOVSKI (grt), BOLSHEVIK (1412grt), ZHAN ZHORES (grt), VOLGA (3113grt), and BELOSTOK (grt) plus tankers SERGO (7956grt) and MOSKVA (6086grt). The evacuation was covered by Russian cruisers KRASNY KRYM, CHERVONA UKRAINA and KRASNY KAVKAZ plus destroyers BODRY, BOIKI, NEZAMOZHNIK, SHAUMYAN and DZERZHINSKI.

4 OCTOBER 1941

	The Odessa evacuation continued with Russian steamers URALETS (grt) and EQURTSA (grt) with tugboat SP-14. Russian cruisers KRASNY KRYM, CHERVONA UKRAINA and KRASNY KAVKAZ plus destroyers BODRY, BOIKI, NEZAMOZHNIK, SHAUMYAN and DZERZHINSKI provided cover.

5 OCTOBER 1941

	Russian steamers ABKHAZIYA (4727grt), KALININ (4156grt) and DNEPR (3071grt) continued to evacuate troops from Odessa to Sevastopol escorted by patrol boats SKR-113/BUG and SKR-114/DNESTR, gunboat KRASNY ADZHARISTAN, with minesweepers T-38/RAIKOMVOD, T-39/DOROTEYA, and T-41/KHENKIN. Russian cruisers KRASNY KRYM, CHERVONA UKRAINA and KRASNY KAVKAZ with destroyers BODRY, BOIKI, NEZAMOZHNIK, SHAUMYAN and DZERZHINSKI provided cover.
	Russian submarine L-4 (Lt Cdr Polyakov) laid mines off Mangalia, Romania, and unsuccessfully attacked Romanian destroyer REGINA MARIA.

7 OCTOBER 1941

	Romanian minelayers DACIA, REGELE CAROL I, and AMIRAL MURGESCU (KKpt Niculescu, German Adviser KKpt v. Davidson) escorted by Romanian torpedo boats SBORUL, NALUCA, and SMEUL with cutters GHIGULESCU and DUMITRESCU plus occasional escort by Bulgarian torpedo boats SMELI, DERZKY, and KHABRI began to lay four full minefields and one partial minefield along the Bulgarian coast, completing on the 16th.

8 OCTOBER 1941

	Russian steamers CHEKHOV (grt) and KALININ (4156grt) with tanker MOSKVA (6086grt) evacuated heavy equipment, weapons, auxiliary services, party organizations and labour forces from Odessa to Sevastopol escorted by minelayer SYZRAN and minesweeper T-32/ZEMLJAK.

	Russian cruiser KOMINTERN, destroyer SHAUMYAN and three patrol boats covered the operation.
	Incomplete Russian cruiser FRUNZE was towed to Mariupol from Nikolaev to prevent her capture. While there, German air attacks damaged the FRUNZE, and she was towed out of the harbour before the Germans occupied the city on the Sea of Azov.

9 OCTOBER 1941

	Russian steamers ARMENIYA (4727grt) and tanker SERGO (7956grt) continued to evacuate troops from Odessa to Sevastopol covered by cruiser KOMINTERN, destroyer SHAUMYAN and three patrol boats.

10 OCTOBER 1941

	A mine laid by Russian submarine L-4 sank Romanian minelayer **REGELE CAROL I** (2369grt) off Varna, just after she had been loaded with 150 mines for the minefields off Bulgaria.

13 OCTOBER 1941

	The Russian Black Sea Fleet military council approved the evacuation of the Odessa defence area.

14 OCTOBER 1941

	Russian steamers UKRAINA (4727grt), GRUZIYA (4857grt), ABKHAZIYA (4727grt), ARMENIYA (4727grt), KOTOVSKI (grt), ZHAN ZHORES (grt), VOSTOK (grt), KALININ (4156grt), BOLSHEVIK (1412grt), KURSK (5801grt), and CHAPAEV (2638grt) plus minelayer LUKOMSKI and SYZRAN, plus survey ships CHERNOMORETS and TSENIT arrived at Odessa to begin the evacuation.
	Russian cruiser KRASNY KAVKAZ and CHERVONA UKRAINA, destroyers SMYSHLENY, BODRY, NEZAMOZHNIK and SHAUMYAN, patrol boats SKR-102/PETRAS, SKR-113/BUG and SKR-114/DNESTR, fast minesweepers T-404/SHCHIT, T-405/VZRYVATEL, T-406/ISKATEL and T-408/YAKOR, auxiliary minesweeper T-39/DOROTEYA plus numerous small patrol boats, tugs and harbour craft supported and covered the evacuation force.
	German aircraft damaged Russian steamer GRUZIYA (4857grt) with several bombs at Odessa. The evacuation force also faced artillery fire as the Russian army pulled back to the coast.
	Russian minesweeper T-405/VZRYVATEL laid mines in Odessa harbour as the Russian evacuation fleet departed.

15 OCTOBER 1941

	During the evening the Russian troops quickly withdrew to their embarkation positions around Odessa harbour for evacuation.

16 OCTOBER 1941

0300	During the night, 35,000 men of the Russian 421st and 95th Rifle Divisions and the remnants of the 2nd Cavalry Division were loaded aboard transports at Odessa.
0300	During the troop embarkation, Russian destroyers SMYSHLENY and BODRY laid thirty-two mines off the fortress at Ilyichevka, which were later removed by the Romanian Danube Flotilla.
0600	The Russian rear guard was embarked on the cruisers and destroyers in Odessa harbour. Patrol boat SKR-107/KUBAN took on 1200 men from the rear guard and demolition parties.
0900	The evacuation force departed Odessa while minesweeper T-405/VZRYVATEL laid magnetic mines in the harbour. It was not until the afternoon that the German and Romanian forces realised that the Russians had departed and ordered aircraft to attack the convoy.
>1200	German aircraft sank Russian steamer **BOLSHEVIK** (1412grt) and damaged other ships, including steamer GRUZIYA (4857grt), between Odessa and Sevastopol.

18 OCTOBER 1941

	Russian submarines S-34, SHCH-207, SHCH-212 and SHCH-216 patrolled off the mouth of the Dnepr River.
	Russian submarine SHCH-210 unsuccessfully attacked Vichy French tanker LE PROGRÈS (grt) off St Ivan in the mouth of the Dnepr River.
	A mine heavily damaged Russian submarine SHCH-212 (Lt Cdr Burnashev) off the mouth of the Dnepr River. The crew was able to bring the damaged vessel back to port after a very perilous voyage.

20 OCTOBER 1941

	Russian submarine SHCH-216 unsuccessfully attacked Romanian steamer SZEGED (grt) off the Dnepr River mouth.
	Russian submarines D-5, M-33, M-35, M-36, M-58, and M-62 unsuccessfully patrolled off the Romanian coast.

21 OCTOBER 1941

	Romanian minesweeper THERESE WALLNER (KKpt Petzel) arrived at Odessa, Ukraine, with three motor

minesweepers and three auxiliary minesweepers of the Donau Flotilla. They cleared thirty-two mines and cleared a shipping lane from the mouth of the Chilia River to the mouth of the Dnepr River. Axis ships could now access Odessa and Ilyitschevka, south of Odessa.

A mine sank Russian submarine **M-58** (Lt Cdr Eliseev) off the Romanian coast.

22 OCTOBER 1941

Russian submarines SHCH-207, M-59, M-60, L-6, D-4, M-34, S-31, M-112, A-3, SHCH-214 and SHCH-213 took turns patrolling the western Black Sea until the 31st.

23 OCTOBER 1941

The Romanian Danube Flotilla cleared mines off Otschakov, Ukraine.

24 OCTOBER 1941

Mines laid by Russian destroyers SMYSHLENY and BODRY, sank Romanian tugboat **DROSSEL** (175grt) west of Otschakov in 46, 35N, 32, 34E.

The minesweepers of the Romanian Danube Flotilla expanded their sweep to Kherson.

Russian submarine L-4 (Lt Cdr Polyakov) laid additional mines off Mangalia.

25 OCTOBER 1941

A Russian destroyer laid mine sank Romanian minesweeper **THERESE WALLNER** (101grt) off Kherson in 46, 35N, 32, 34E.

A Russian destroyer laid mine sank Romanian tugboat **BRUSTERORT** (101grt) off Kherson in 46, 35N, 32, 34E.

A Russian destroyer laid mine sank Romanian motorised barge **SF.16** off Kherson in 46, 35N, 32, 34E.

The Romanian Danube Flotilla began sweeping the lower Dnepr River area for mines.

26 OCTOBER 1941

Russian submarine M-35 (Lt Greshilov) sank Romanian motorised barges **SF.25** and **SF.36** off Odessa.

A mine sank Russian submarine **M-58** near the mouth of the Dnepr River.

27 OCTOBER 1941

Russian submarine M-35 (Lt Greshilov) unsuccessfully attacked Romanian submarine chaser SHIP.19/LOLA off Sulina.

28 OCTOBER 1941

A mine sank Russian submarine **M-59** off Sulina.

29 OCTOBER 1941

During the night, Russian cruiser KRASNY KAVKAZ evacuated the 8th Marine Infantry Brigade from Novorossisk to Sevastopol. At Sevastopol, the 16th, 17th, 18th and 19th Marine Infantry Battalions were formed from ships crews to support the defence of the city.

30 OCTOBER 1941

A mine sank Russian submarine **M-34** off Constanza, Romania.

Russian battleship PARIZHSKAYA KOMMUNA, cruiser MOLOTOV, destroyer leader TASHKENT with destroyer SOOBRAZITELNY departed Sevastopol for ports in the Caucus.

Russian cruisers CHERVONA UKRAINA (Capt 1st Class V. A. Andreev) and KRASNY KRYM with destroyers BODRY, NEZAMOZHNIK and SHAUMYAN continued to provide naval gunfire for the defence of Sevastopol.

31 OCTOBER 1941

Russian cruiser KRASNY KAVKAZ and destroyers ZHELEZNYAKOV and DZERZHINSKI provided gunfire support for the defence of Sevastopol.

Russian destroyers BDITELNY and BOIKI provided gunfire support for the defence of Sevastopol where German Ju87 aircraft of STG.77 damaged BOIKI with the loss of fifty crewmen off Nikolaev.

Red Sea

Long. E32, 00 – E43, 00   Lat. N30, 00 – N15, 00

4 OCTOBER 1941

Antiaircraft ship COVENTRY was withdrawn from the Suez Escort Force and passed through the Suez Canal for Alexandria. This trip was in preparation for her to leave the area for repairs at Bombay, India.

5 OCTOBER 1941

A German aerial mine sank tanker **TYNEFIELD** (5856grt) at the south end of the Suez Canal. Four crewmen were lost.

6 OCTOBER 1941

German He111 aircraft sank steamer **THISTLEGORM** (4898grt), which was carrying munitions, at Anchorage F, inner channel Strait of Jubal, near the south entrance to the Suez Canal. Four crewmen and five gunners were lost on the steamer.

German He111 aircraft damaged Norwegian tanker NORFOLD (6370grt) at Ras Gharib.

German He111 aircraft attacked steamer SCALARIA (5683grt), but she was not damaged

German He111 aircraft damaged Australian steamer SALAMAUA (6676grt) in the same attack.

Antiaircraft cruiser NAIAD plus destroyers AVON VALE and ERIDGE passed through the Suez Canal en route to Alexandria to operate with the Mediterranean Fleet.

7 OCTOBER 1941

Sloops SHOREHAM and FALMOUTH arrived at Suez from the East Indies to join the Suez Escort Force.

German bombing damaged Egyptian lighthouse tender **AIDA** at Zafarana, in the Gulf of Suez. The tender was beached to avoid sinking. There were no casualties.

8 OCTOBER 1941

German bombing sank steamer **ROSALIE MOLLER** (3963grt) at Anchorage H, Suez Canal. Two crewmen were missing, and Australian sloop PARRAMATTA rescued the survivors.

9 OCTOBER 1941

Light cruiser GALATEA departed Anchorage H (Towila) for Suez with the survivors from the **ROSALIE MOLLER** (3963grt). After landing the survivors, the light cruiser passed through the Suez Canal on the 10th for Alexandria.

Sloop FLAMINGO passed through the Suez Canal to return to Alexandria to rejoin the Mediterranean Fleet.

13 OCTOBER 1941

Destroyers NAPIER and JACKAL passed through the Suez Canal northbound to return to the Mediterranean Fleet after being relieved in the Suez Escort Force by sloops FALMOUTH and SHOREHAM.

15 OCTOBER 1941

Antiaircraft ship CARLISLE passed through the Suez Canal northbound to rejoin the Mediterranean Fleet.

Destroyer ENCOUNTER arrived in the Canal area to rejoin the Mediterranean Fleet.

30 OCTOBER 1941

Corvette SNAPDRAGON arrived at Suez from Britain to join the Mediterranean Fleet. The corvette arrived at Alexandria on the 31st.

Arabian Sea
Long. E43, 00 – E77, 00   Lat. N31, 00 – N00, 00

18 OCTOBER 1941

Heavy cruiser EXETER arrived at Bombay, India.

22 OCTOBER 1941

Heavy cruiser EXETER departed Bombay for Colombo, Ceylon.

INDIAN OCEAN

East of South Africa
Long. E25, 00 – E60, 00   Lat. S00, 00 – S60, 00

3 OCTOBER 1941

Part of convoy WS.11 arrived at Durban, South Africa, with MOOLTAN (20,952grt), EMPRESS OF AUSTRALIA (19,665grt), SCYTHIA (19,761grt), OTRANTO (20,032grt), BARRISTER (6200grt), and MANCHESTER PROGRESS (5620grt).

7 OCTOBER 1941

Convoy WS.11 departed Durban, South Africa, with troopships MOOLTAN (20,952grt), EMPRESS OF AUSTRALIA (19,665grt), SCYTHIA (19,761grt), OTRANTO (20,032grt), BARRISTER (6200grt), and MANCHESTER PROGRESS (5620grt) plus steamers DILWARA (11,080grt), CITY OF CANTERBURY (8331grt), PULASKI (6345grt), EASTERN PRINCE (10,926grt), LLANDAFF CASTLE (10,786grt), NIEUW HOLLAND (11,066grt), and JOHAN DE WITT (10,474grt).

On 8 October, the convoy, less EMPRESS OF AUSTRALIA and SCYTHIA, rendezvoused with the Cape Town ships. Upon rendezvous, AMC DERBYSHIRE returned to Cape Town.

Battle cruiser REPULSE escorted the convoy to 13 October, when she was relieved by light cruiser CERES.

On 17 October, GLENORCHY (10,000grt), CITY OF EDINBURGH (8036grt), BARRISTER, ORONTES (20,097grt), NIEUW ZEELAND (11,069grt), VICEROY OF INDIA (19,627grt), LARGS BAY (14,182grt), JOHAN DE WITT, OTRANTO, DUCHESS OF YORK (20,021grt), KINA II (9823grt), and GLAUCUS (7586grt) were detached from convoy WS.11 as convoy WS.11 X escorted by light cruiser GLASGOW.

On 19 October, steamers GLENORCHY and CITY OF EDINBURGH were detached from the convoy to sail independently for Basra, Iraq. The rest of the convoy arrived at Bombay, India, on 22 October.

The convoy departed Bombay on 27 October with steamers GLAUCUS, KINA II, JOHAN DE WITT, ELLENGA (5196grt), ORION (23,371grt), NIEUW ZEELAND, and LARGS BAY (14,182grt), escorted by AMC HECTOR.

The convoy arrived at Colombo, Ceylon, on 30 October, except for steamer KINA II, which was detached from the convoy on 29 October. On 31 October, the convoy, plus RANGITIKI (16,698grt), departed Colombo, escorted by light cruiser MAURITIUS and arrived at Singapore on 6 November.

Bay of Bengal
Long. E77, 00 – E95, 00   Lat. N22, 00 – N00, 00

22 OCTOBER 1941

Australian heavy cruiser AUSTRALIA departed Colombo, Ceylon, after embarking mines from a lighter in the harbour. She proceeded to Mauritius, where she re-fuelled.

She arrived at the Kerguelen Islands on 1 November and, after searching the various islands by landing party and aircraft, laid eighteen mines in Gazelle Basin, Long Island Sound, Island Harbour, and Tucker Strait.

She searched the Crozet Islands on 6 and 7 November.

Heavy cruiser AUSTRALIA finally arrived at Durban, South Africa, on 11 November.

PACIFIC OCEAN

South China Sea
Long. E105, 00 – E120, 00   Lat. N27, 00 – N10, 00

1 OCTOBER 1941

IJN torpedo depot ship KAMIKAZE MARU arrived at Mako, Pescadores Islands.

IJN transport MIKAGE MARU No.3 (3111grt) completed her conversion at Mako, Pescadores.

3 OCTOBER 1941

IJN oiler HOKUAN MARU (3712grt) departed her support position south of China for Takao, Formosa.

6 OCTOBER 1941

IJN naval auxiliary TATSUWA MARU (6335grt) arrived at her support station south of China.

9 OCTOBER 1941

Vichy French light cruiser LAMOTTE-PICQUET departed Saigon, French Indochina, for Osaka, Japan, where she obtained urgent repairs.

10 OCTOBER 1941

USN river patrol boat MINDANAO (PR-8) arrived at Hong Kong.

IJN passenger/cargo ship NACHISAN MARU (4441grt) departed her support position south of China for Sasebo, Kyushu.

12 OCTOBER 1941

IJN naval auxiliary TATSUWA MARU (6335grt) departed her support station south of China for Mako, Pescadores.

14 OCTOBER 1941

IJN cargo ship TOYO MARU (2470grt) arrived at her support station south of China.

16 OCTOBER 1941

IJN oiler TOEN MARU departed Mako, Pescadores, to support operations in southern China.

19 OCTOBER 1941

IJN river gunboat SAGA (785grt) arrived at Mako, Pescadores, and departed later the same day.

20 OCTOBER 1941

IJN naval auxiliary TATSUWA MARU (6335grt) arrived at her support station south of China.

31 OCTOBER 1941

IJN minelayer HATSUTAKA was assigned to the Japanese Southwest Area Fleet, First Southern Expeditionary Fleet, Ninth Base Force based at Camranh Bay, French Indochina.

East China Sea   Long. E120, 00 – E130, 00   Lat. N42, 00 – N20, 00

1 OCTOBER 1941

IJN cargo ship LYONS MARU (7017grt) was attached to the Japanese 11th Air Fleet (Vice Admiral Tsukahara Nishizo).

A fire damaged Vichy French liner D'ARTAGNAN (15,105grt) at Shanghai.

IJN passenger/cargo ship TATSUWA MARU (6335grt) departed Sakito, Formosa, for Takao, Formosa. She departed Takao later the same day.

IJN cargo ship TOYO MARU (2470grt) departed Takao, Formosa.

6 OCTOBER 1941

IJN ammunition ship KOTOKU MARU (6702grt) arrived at Takao, Formosa.

7 OCTOBER 1941

IJN patrol boat SHURI MARU arrived at Ryojun and departed again later that day to resume her north China coast patrol.

8 OCTOBER 1941

IJA antiaircraft vessel SAKURA MARU (9246grt) arrived at Humen, China, from Moji, Japan.

14 OCTOBER 1941

IJN patrol boat SHURI MARU arrived at Ryojun from a north China coast patrol.

15 OCTOBER 1941

IJA antiaircraft vessel SAKURA MARU (9246grt) departed Humen, China, for Moji, Japan.

17 OCTOBER 1941

IJN patrol boat SHURI MARU departed Ryojun on a north China coast patrol.

18 OCTOBER 1941

IJN cargo ship LYONS MARU (7017grt) departed Takao, Formosa, for the south China area.

21 OCTOBER 1941

German steamer SPREEWALD (5083grt) departed Dairen, China, for Bordeaux, France.

IJA antiaircraft vessel SAKURA MARU (9246grt) arrived at Canton, China, from Moji, Japan.

26 OCTOBER 1941

IJN aircraft carrier TAIYO arrived at Takao, Formosa, from Sasebo, Kyushu.

28 OCTOBER 1941

IJN cargo ship LYONS MARU (7017grt) returned to Takao, Formosa.

30 OCTOBER 1941

IJN river gunboat FUSHIMI (374grt) was attached to the Japanese First China Fleet, Nanking Base Force.

IJN river gunboat TOBA (grt) arrived at Shanghai and was assigned to the Shanghai Base Force (Vice Admiral Makita Kakusaburo) as its flagship.

West of Philippine Islands
Long. E120, 00 – E125, 00   Lat. N20, 00 – N00, 00

16 OCTOBER 1941

USN destroyers PEARY (DD-225) and PILLSBURY (DD-227) were damaged when they collided at Manila, Philippine Islands.

Sea of Japan
Long. E128, 00 – E143, 00   Lat. N55, 00 – N33, 00

3 OCTOBER 1941

IJN battleship KONGO docked at Sasebo, Kyushu. Degaussing coils were added to her hull.

4 OCTOBER 1941

IJN coastal minelayer ITSUKUSHIMA arrived at Tachibana Bay, Kyushu.

IJN battleship KIRISHIMA departed Sasebo, Kyushu.

5 OCTOBER 1941

IJN destroyer MINEKAZE departed Chinkai, Korea, and conducted an antisubmarine patrol in the waters between Korea and Japan.

7 OCTOBER 1941

IJN battleship HIEI arrived at Sasebo, Kyushu, from Murozumi, Japan.

IJN oiler KORYU MARU (880grt) arrived at Sasebo, Kyushu.

10 OCTOBER 1941

IJN oiler KORYU MARU (880grt) departed Sasebo, Kyushu, for the central China coast area.

11 OCTOBER 1941

IJN transport KINAI MARU (5047grt) completed her conversion at Sasebo, Kyushu.

14 OCTOBER 1941

IJN battleship KONGO departed Sasebo, Kyushu, for training off Saiki, Japan.

German steamer ELSA ESSBERGER (6103grt) departed Sasebo for El Ferrol, Spain.

15 OCTOBER 1941

IJN oiler MOJI MARU was registered as a specially installed transport ship (oil supply) in the Sasebo Naval District.

IJN oiler TOEN MARU was registered in the Sasebo Naval District as a specially installed transport ship (oil supply).

IJN oiler KORYU MARU (880grt) was registered as an auxiliary transport ship (oil supply) in the Sasebo Naval District.

IJN passenger/cargo ship SHINYO MARU (4163grt) was registered as an auxiliary transport and attached to the Sasebo Naval District.

IJN cargo ship TOYO MARU (2470grt) was registered as an auxiliary transport and attached to the Sasebo Naval District.

IJN auxiliary gunboat SHINKYO MARU (2670grt) was attached to the 3rd Naval District, Sasebo Guard Force in the Sasebo Local Defence Squadron (RAdm Tashiro Sohei), which included auxiliary patrol boat SHINKO MARU No.5.

IJN auxiliary transport YAMAGIRI MARU (6438grt) completed her conversion and was attached to the Sasebo Naval District as an auxiliary transport, (Ko) category.

The IJN requisitioned oiler HOKUAN MARU (3712grt) and attached her to the Sasebo Naval District.

18 OCTOBER 1941

IJN cargo ship MANKO MARU (4471grt) departed Sasebo, Kyushu, for her support position south of China.

21 OCTOBER 1941

IJN oiler HOKUAN MARU (3712grt) departed Sasebo Naval Base for Korea.

23 OCTOBER 1941

IJN oiler KORYU MARU (880grt) arrived at Sasebo, Kyushu.

24 OCTOBER 1941

IJN aircraft carrier TAIYO departed Sasebo, Kyushu, for Takao, Formosa.

25 OCTOBER 1941

IJN transport KOMAKI MARU (8525grt) departed Sasebo, Kyushu, for the south China coast.

IJN oiler KORYU MARU (880grt) departed Sasebo, Kyushu, for the central China coast area.

26 OCTOBER 1941

IJN oiler HOKUAN MARU (3712grt) arrived at Korea.

28 OCTOBER 1941

IJN aircraft carrier SHOKAKU arrived at Sasebo, Kyushu.

29 OCTOBER 1941

IJN aircraft carrier SHOKAKU departed Sasebo, Kyushu, for Oita Bay, Japan, with a stop at Ariake Bay, Japan.

IJN auxiliary gunboat SEIKYO MARU (2606grt) departed Yushin, Chosen's east coast (now Sokcho, South Korea).

30 OCTOBER 1941

IJN oiler HOKUAN MARU (3712grt) departed Korea for Sasebo, Kyushu.

31 OCTOBER 1941

IJN submarine I-10 was completed and registered in the Sasebo Naval District.

New Guinea and Solomon Islands Long. E140, 00 – E180, 00   Lat. N00, 00 – S25, 00

4 OCTOBER 1941

New Zealand light cruiser ACHILLES departed Suva, Fiji Islands, to search for German merchant raiders with Australian light cruiser ADELAIDE and AMC MONOWAI.
Light cruiser ADELAIDE was detached from the group on the 6th for escort duties.
Light cruiser ACHILLES and AMC MONOWAI returned to Auckland, New Zealand, on the 10th.

17 OCTOBER 1941

Free French destroyer TRIOMPHANT departed Suva, Fiji Islands, for Bora Bora.

East of Australia Long. E140, 00 – E155, 00   Lat. S12, 00 – S40, 00

14 OCTOBER 1941

New Zealand light cruiser ACHILLES relieved Australian light cruiser ADELAIDE from the escort of a liner to New Zealand.
ADELAIDE returned to Sydney, Australia.
ACHILLES and the liner arrived at Auckland, New Zealand, on the 16th.

East of Japan Long. E130, 00 – E180, 00   Lat. N55, 00 – N30, 00

1 OCTOBER 1941

IJN seaplane tender NOTORO was assigned to Patrol Squadron 2. The tail code of her aircraft was "Z1-xx".

IJN submarine chaser CH-17 was reassigned to Submarine Chaser Division 21.

IJN battleship HIEI departed Hiroshima, Japan.

IJN seaplane tender SAGARA MARU was attached to the Japanese Southern Expeditionary Fleet (VAdm Ozawa Jisaburo).

IJN liner/transport ASAMA MARU entered the dry dock at Mitsubishi Heavy Industries, Ltd. Shipyard in Kure, Japan.

IJN oiler KIRISHIMA MARU was requisitioned and registered as an auxiliary transport. She was assigned di-

	rectly to the Japanese Combined Fleet Supply and Support Unit.
	German tanker BENNO (8306grt) (ex Norwegian **OLE JACOB** (8306grt)) arrived at Kobe, Japan, from Bordeaux, France.
2000	IJN ammunition ship KASHINO departed Kure, Japan, carrying the first of nine Type 94 457-mm (18.1-inch) main guns and a turret for Battleship No.2 (later named MUSASHI). KASHINO arrived at Mitsubishi's Nagasaki shipyard. The turret and the gun were hoisted aboard the battleship's deck by a 350-ton capacity derrick. Once aboard, the turret and gun were covered with canvas to maintain secrecy. Later, KASHINO transported ordnance and general goods from Kure to Nagasaki at regular intervals.
	IJN passenger/cargo ship KAISHO MARU (4164grt) was assigned to the Yokosuka Naval District as an auxiliary transport.
	IJN cargo ship KENYO MARU (6486grt) was assigned to the Yokosuka Naval District as an auxiliary transport.
	IJN passenger/cargo ship MITAKESAN MARU (4141grt) was assigned to the Yokosuka Naval District as an auxiliary transport. She was scheduled to support the Japanese Mandate Islands.

2 OCTOBER 1941

	IJN coastal minelayer ITSUKUSHIMA departed Yokosuka, Japan.
	IJN battleship HIEI arrived at Murozumi, Japan, from Hiroshima, Japan.
	Japanese cargo ship MEITEN MARU (4474grt) began conversion at the Yokosuka Naval Yard into a military auxiliary transport.
	IJN transport HOKKAI MARU (5105grt) began her conversion into an auxiliary transport at Yokohama, Japan.

3 OCTOBER 1941

	Japanese passenger cargo ship HEIAN MARU (11,614grt) was requisitioned by the IJN. She was converted into a submarine tender.
	IJN battleship HYUGA departed Kure, Japan, and arrived later the same day at the Murozumi Bight, Japan.
	IJN passenger/cargo ship YAMAGIRI MARU (6438grt) began her conversion into an auxiliary transport at Yokohama, Japan.

4 OCTOBER 1941

	IJN aircraft ferry GOSHU MARU departed Muroran, Japan, for the South Seas, probably calling at Truk and Kwajalein.
	IJN battleship KIRISHIMA arrived at Murozeki, Japan.
	IJN seaplane tender KIYOKAWA MARU completed her conversion and was registered (commissioned) in the Yokosuka Naval District. She had six Type 95 Kawanishi E8N "Dave" two-seat reconnaissance floatplanes with two in reserve and three Type 94 Kawanishi E7K2 "Alf" two-seat reconnaissance floatplanes with one in reserve. Her aircraft code was "R-xx" and her call sign was JNZL.
	IJN aircraft carrier SHOKAKU departed Yokosuka, Japan, for Oita Bay, Japan.
	IJN transport TATSUHO MARU (6334grt) completed her conversion.
	IJA antiaircraft vessel SAKURA MARU (9246grt) departed Moji, Japan, for Humen, China.

5 OCTOBER 1941

	Japanese cargo ship ONOE MARU (6667grt) began conversion into an ammunition ship at Mitsubishi Heavy Industries Shipyard, Kobe, Japan.

6 OCTOBER 1941

	IJN oiler TOEI MARU (10,023grt) was reassigned to the Yokosuka Naval District.
	IJN battleship HIEI departed Murozumi, Japan, for Sasebo, Kyushu.
	IJN aircraft carrier SHOKAKU arrived at Oita Bay, Japan, from Yokosuka, Japan.
	IJN transport MITAKESAN MARU (4441grt) departed Moji, Japan.
	IJN transport SHOHEI MARU (7255grt) completed her conversion at Kure, Japan.

7 OCTOBER 1941

	IJN submarine chaser CH-25 was launched.
	IJN aircraft carrier ZUIKAKU departed Kure, Japan, for Oita Bay, Japan.
	IJN cargo ship NARUTO MARU (7149grt) departed Yokohama, Japan, on NYK's American route with calls at Manzanillo and Tocopilla, Mexico.
	IJN transport CUBA MARU (5950grt) completed her conversion at Yokosuka, Japan.

8 OCTOBER 1941

IJN aircraft carrier ZUIKAKU arrived at Oita Bay, Japan, and joined her new sister-carrier SHOKAKU for the first time. They spent the remainder of the month moving around in the Kure, Oita, and Saeki, Japan, area.

IJN transport HEITO MARU (4468grt) completed her conversion at Yokohama, Japan.

9 OCTOBER 1941

War games were conducted aboard IJN battleship NAGATO to explore various attack options for the coming war.

German tanker BENNO (8306grt) (ex Norwegian **OLE JACOB** (8306grt)) departed Kobe, Japan, for Bordeaux, France.

10 OCTOBER 1941

IJN battleship HYUGA departed Kure, Japan.

Japanese oiler TONAN MARU NO. 2 (19,262grt) was requisitioned by the IJN and registered in the Kure Naval District.

IJN transport HOKUROKU MARU (5046grt) completed her conversion at Tokyo, Japan.

11 OCTOBER 1941

IJN oiler HOYO MARU completed her conversion and was rated as a converted transport (oil supply). She was attached to the Japanese Fourth Fleet based at Truk.

12 OCTOBER 1941

IJN oiler TOEI MARU (10,023grt) completed her conversion to a fleet oiler.

IJN submarine chaser CH-22 was completed and registered in the Yokosuka Naval District.

Japanese cargo ship BANGKOK MARU (5350grt) completed her conversion into IJN AMC BANGKOK MARU.

The American and Japanese Press announced the schedules for three NYK liners to renew service. TATSUTA MARU (16,975grt) would depart Yokohama, Japan, for San Francisco, California, via Honolulu, Hawaiian Territory, on 15 October. NITTA MARU would depart Yokohama for Seattle, Washington, on 20 October. TAIYO MARU (14,457grt) would depart Yokohama for Honolulu on 22 October 1941.

IJN aircraft carrier SHOKAKU arrived at Saeki Bay, Japan, from Oita Bay, Japan.

IJN transport TOKAI MARU (5038grt) was registered by the IJN.

14 OCTOBER 1941

IJN oiler SHIRETOKO MARU (6500grt) was reassigned to the Japanese Fourth Fleet.

IJN oiler SATA (6500grt) rescued the survivors of Lt Cdr Hirokawa Takashi's submarine **I-61**, which sank after colliding with converted gunboat KISO MARU on 10 October off Iki Island in 33, 40N, 129, 40E. (Some sources claim that the entire crew of seventy were lost.)
The submarine was salvaged in 1942 and broken up at Sasebo, Japan.

IJN AMC KONGO MARU (8624grt) completed her conversion at Aioi, Japan.

IJN AMC SAIGON MARU (5350grt) completed her conversion.

Japanese liner TATSUTA MARU (16,975grt) was requisitioned by the IJN as a charter vessel and attached to the Yokosuka Naval District.

IJN aircraft carrier SHOKAKU arrived at Sukumo Bay, Japan, from Saeki Bay, Japan.

IJN oiler KYOEI MARU No.2 (1192grt) completed her conversion into a fleet oiler at Kure, Japan.

IJN transport CHOKO MARU No.2 GO (3515grt) completed her conversion.

IJN transport SHOAN MARU (5624grt) completed her conversion.

15 OCTOBER 1941

Japanese passenger cargo ship AIKOKU MARU (10,437grt) was equipped with one 1100-mm and one 900-mm searchlight and special heavy-duty booms for handling floatplanes. She was equipped to carry one Type 94 Kawanishi E7K2 "Alf" floatplane and one spare E7K2. When her conversion was completed, the 24th Squadron (Raider) was officially established under RAdm Takeda Moriji and attached directly to the Japanese Combined Fleet. The AIKOKU MARU, HOKOKU MARU and KIYOSUMI MARU were assigned to the Japanese Cruiser Division 24.

IJN submarine tender CHOGEI was assigned directly to the Japanese Combined Fleet as flagship of Submarine Squadron 6 (RAdm Kono Chimaki) and Submarine Division 9 with (I-123, I-124) and Submarine Division 13 with (I-121, I-122).

Japanese passenger/cargo ship HEIAN MARU (11,614grt) was registered as a prospective submarine tender in the Yokosuka Naval District. She began conversion at Mitsubishi Heavy Industries' shipyard at Kobe. Six 6-inch (152-mm) 1941 Type single mount guns, one 3.5 m range finder, two Type 93 dual 13-mm machine guns and one 1100-mm diameter and one 900-mm diameter search light were fitted. A degaussing cable (anti-magnetic mine

	device) was also installed.
	HIJMS submarine I-25 was completed by Mitsubishi at Kobe, commissioned in the IJN and based in the Yokosuka Naval District. She was assigned to Submarine Squadron 1 in Submarine Division 4 in the Japanese Sixth Fleet (Submarines).
	IJN oiler KOKUYO MARU (10,026grt) was re-rated back into a converted merchant transport (oil supply).
	IJN oiler TOEI MARU (10,023grt) was re-rated a converted merchant transport (oil supply) and manned mostly by civilian merchant marine personnel.
	IJN salvage vessel YAMABIKO MARU (6795grt) completed her conversion to an auxiliary specially installed construction warship. She was assigned to the Japanese Third Fleet (VAdm Takahashi Ibo), Southern Force, based at Takao, Formosa.
	IJN AMC AWATA MARU was assigned to the Japanese Fifth Fleet in the Northern Patrol.
	IJN oiler HOYO MARU (8691grt) was re-rated back to a converted merchant transport (oil supply).
	IJN hospital ship KIKU MARU completed her conversion and was assigned to the Ominato Guard Unit.
	IJN AMC SAIGON MARU began to conduct patrols in the Kii and Bungo Straits. She also laid mines and escorted convoys.
	IJN liner TATSUTA MARU (16,975grt) departed Yokohama, Japan, with an entirely new crew, on a repatriation voyage for American and Japanese nationals wishing to return to their homelands. The ship maintained radio silence during the entire voyage.
	Vichy French light cruiser LAMOTTE-PICQUET arrived at Osaka, Japan, from Saigon, French Indo-China, for urgent repairs.
	IJN oiler HISHI MARU (856grt) was registered in the Kure Naval District as an auxiliary transport (oil supply) and attached to the Yokosuka Naval Base.
	IJN naval auxiliary KAIHEI MARU (4575grt) arrived at Yokosuka, Japan. She was registered in the Yokosuka Naval District.
	IJN cargo ship KUNISHIMA MARU (4083grt) completed her conversion and was registered in the Yokosuka Naval District.
	IJN cargo ship NANIWA MARU (4857grt) was registered in the Yokosuka Naval District.
	IJN cargo ship TOYO MARU No.2 (2480grt) was registered as an auxiliary transport and assigned to the Yokosuka Naval District.
	IJN auxiliary gunboat SEIKYO MARU (2606grt) was detached from the 1st Gunboat Division and attached to the Chinkai Guard District.

16 OCTOBER 1941

	IJN oiler GOYO MARU was requisitioned by the IJN as a general transport registered in the Maizuru Naval District and assigned directly to the Japanese Combined Fleet.
	IJN submarine tender ARATAMA MARU completed her conversion.
	IJN AMC ASAKA MARU completed her conversion.
	IJN aircraft carrier ZUIKAKU departed Oita Bay, Japan, for Saeki Bay, Japan.

17 OCTOBER 1941

	IJN battleship KIRISHIMA departed Murozeki, Japan, and arrived at Saiki, Japan, later the same day.
	IJN AMC ASAKA MARU departed Osaka, Japan.
	IJN oiler KUROSHIO MARU (10,383grt) completed her conversion into a fleet oiler at Tama, Japan, and was later attached to the Japanese Combined Fleet.
	IJA antiaircraft vessel SAKURA MARU (9246grt) arrived at Moji, Japan.

18 OCTOBER 1941

	IJN AMC AWATA MARU departed Kure, Japan.
	IJN AMC ASAKA MARU arrived at Yokohama from Osaka, Japan.
	IJN ammunition ship HIDE MARU (5181grt) arrived at Kure Navy Yard and completed her conversion. She was assigned directly to HQ, Japanese Combined Fleet.
	IJA antiaircraft vessel SAKURA MARU (9246grt) departed Moji, Japan, for Canton, China.

19 OCTOBER 1941

	Japanese cargo ship ONOE MARU (6667grt) completed her conversion into an ammunition ship.

20 OCTOBER 1941

	Japanese liner HIKAWA MARU (11,622grt) departed Yokohama, Japan, for Seattle, Washington, USA.
	IJN AMC AWATA MARU departed Yokosuka to patrol the Kuriles.
	Japanese passenger/cargo ship KINRYU MARU (9310grt) completed her conversion into a troopship.

	IJN battleship HYUGA departed Saeki, Japan.
	IJN aircraft carrier SHOKAKU arrived at Terajima Strait, Japan.
	IJN aircraft carrier ZUIKAKU departed Saeki, Japan, for Sukumo Bay, Japan.
	IJN transport TOKAI MARU (5038grt) arrived at Kobe, Japan.

21 OCTOBER 1941

	IJN oiler KOKUYO MARU (10,026grt) completed her conversion into a fleet oiler.
	IJN battleship HIEI departed Murozumi, Japan.
	IJN auxiliary aircraft transport KEIYO MARU completed her conversion and was registered with the IJN.
	Early in the morning, IJN submarines I-66 and I-7 collided during manoeuvres in Saeki Bay, but the damage was minor to both vessels.
	IJN oiler HISHI MARU No.2 completed her conversion into a fleet oiler.
	IJN transport TOKAI MARU (5038grt) departed Kobe, Japan, for Yokohama, Japan. She would later reach Shibaura, Tokyo.

22 OCTOBER 1941

	IJN coastal minesweeper TSUGARU was completed and commissioned in the IJN.
	IJN battleship HIEI arrived at Saeki, Japan.
	IJN submarine I-22 departed Saeki, Japan, for Kure, Japan, where she is converted to carry a top-secret 46-ton two-man Type "A" midget submarine. I-22 was the first submarine to undergo such conversion.
	IJN transport CHOKO MARU No.2 GO (3515grt) departed Kure, Japan for Osaka, Japan and then to Tokyo, Japan.
	IJN transport OKITSU MARU (6666grt) completed her conversion at Kure, Japan.
	Japanese passenger/cargo ship TAIYO MARU (14,503grt) departed Yokohama, Japan, for Hawaii. She carried the last foreigners who remained in Japan. Among other passengers were three IJN officers disguised as crewmen, Cdr Maejima Toshihide, Cdr Suzuki Suguru and midget submarine pilot Lt Matsuo Keiu. The TAIYO MARU took the North Pacific route that would be followed by the IJN's Kido Butai (carrier striking force) in the Pearl Harbor, Hawaii, Operation.

23 OCTOBER 1941

	The Flag of the Japanese Combined Fleet Carrier Division 1 was shifted from aircraft carrier KAGA to aircraft carrier AKAGI.
	IJN ammunition ship TATSUGAMI MARU (7064grt) completed her conversion and was attached to the Japanese 11th Naval Air Fleet.
	IJN cargo ship MEITEN MARU (4474grt) departed Yokosuka, Japan, for her support position off Nanyang, China.

24 OCTOBER 1941

	IJN submarine chaser CH-17 was designated as the flagship of Submarine Chaser Division 21.
	IJN aircraft carrier ZUIKAKU departed Sukumo Bay, Japan, for Saeki, Japan, arriving later the same day.

26 OCTOBER 1941

	IJN battleship HYUGA was dry-docked at the Kure Navy Yard.
	IJN oiler KUMAGAWA MARU (6641grt) completed her conversion and was assigned to the Japanese Combined Fleet, Japanese Third Fleet in the Second Base Force as an auxiliary charter ship. She was later reassigned to the First Base Force.

27 OCTOBER 1941

	The Chief of Staff of the Japanese 1st Air Fleet (Rear Admiral Kusaka Ryunosuke) arranged for IJN oilers TOHO MARU (9997grt) and SHINKOKU MARU (10,020grt) to join the 1st Air Fleet by about 10 November. In the meantime, the two oilers were equipped for re-fuelling at sea. The equipment included special fenders and lines.
	Vichy French light cruiser LAMOTTE-PICQUET departed Osaka, Japan, for Saigon, French Indo-China, escorting Vichy French steamer KINDIA (1972grt).

28 OCTOBER 1941

	IJN oiler SAN CLEMENTE MARU completed her conversion into a fleet oiler.
	IJN AMC KONGO MARU (8624grt) departed Aioi, Japan, for Truk.
	Japanese passenger/cargo ship KINRYU MARU (9310grt) departed Aioi, Japan.
	IJN naval auxiliary KAIHEI MARU (4575grt) departed Yokosuka, Japan, for Kwajalein Atoll in the Marshall Islands.

29 OCTOBER 1941

	Japanese liner KAMAKURA MARU (17,526grt) arrived at Yokosuka, Japan.

30 OCTOBER 1941

	The Chief of Staff of the Japanese 1st Air Fleet (RAdm Kusaka Ryunosuke) signalled IJN tankers KYOKUTO MARU (10,051grt) and SHINKOKU MARU (10,020grt) that when the installation of gear for re-fuelling at sea and preparations for action were completed, they were to depart Sasebo and Kure, respectively, on 13 November and proceed to Kagoshima Bay, conducting exercises with aircraft carriers en route. Kusaka further requested their COs load fuel oil for refuelling at sea before their departure.
	IJN submarine I-22 became the flagship for the Commander, Submarine Division 3 (Captain Sasaki Hankyu).

31 OCTOBER 1941

	IJN AMC AIKOKU MARU departed Tamano, Japan, and arrived at Kure, Japan, the same day.
	IJN seaplane tender SAGARA MARU arrived at the Mitsubishi shipyard at Yokohama, Japan, for the installation of equipment.
	Japanese cargo ship KUNIKAWA MARU (6863grt) was requisitioned by the IJN and began conversion into a seaplane tender.
	IJN oiler IRO (6500grt) was assigned to the Japanese Fourth Fleet.
	Japanese tanker NICHIEI MARU (10,020grt) was requisitioned by the IJN and registered in the Kure Naval District.
	IJN aircraft carrier SHOKAKU arrived at Oita Bay, Japan, from Sasebo, Kyushu.
	IJN auxiliary minelayer TENYO MARU (6843grt) completed her conversion and was assigned to the Japanese Fourth Fleet (VAdm Inouye Shigeyoshi) in Mine Division 19 (RAdm Shima Kiyohide) with minelayer OKINOSHIMA and auxiliary minelayer TOKIWA.
	The IJN requisitioned transport EIKO MARU (3535grt) at Kure, Japan, and she entered the Naval Arsenal to start her conversion into her military role.

Bonin – Mariana Islands   Long. E130, 00 – E150, 00   Lat. N30, 00 – N00, 00

31 OCTOBER 1941

	IJN seaplane tender KIMIKAWA MARU (6863grt) began a patrol off Chichi-jima.

Gilbert – Marshall Islands   Long. E150, 00 – E180, 00   Lat. N30, 00 – N00, 00

1 OCTOBER 1941

	IJN hydrographic survey ship KATSURIKI (1540grt) was based at Kwajalein, Marshall Islands. During the month, USN code breakers tracked her movements from Kwajalein to Tarawa Atoll, Gilbert Islands. The code breakers determined KATSURIKI was performing oceanic surveys and soundings in the vicinity of Tarawa preparatory to a Japanese invasion. (In fact, the Japanese invaded Tarawa in December 1941.)
	IJN naval auxiliary KAIHEI MARU (4575grt) operated in the Japanese Mandate Islands.

15 OCTOBER 1941

	IJN auxiliary gunboat NIKKAI MARU (2562grt) was attached to Japanese Combined Fleet, Japanese Fourth Fleet, 4th Base Force in the 5th Gunboat Division (Captain Kamiyama T), also consisting of auxiliary gunboats KEIJO MARU and SEIKAI MARU, based at Truk, Carolines.

16 OCTOBER 1941

	IJN auxiliary gunboat NIKKAI MARU (2562grt) engaged in gunfire drills off Truk.

19 OCTOBER 1941

	IJN transport SHOKA MARU (4467grt) departed Truk.

25 OCTOBER 1941

	IJN light cruiser YUBARI arrived at Truk.

26 OCTOBER 1941

	USN submarines NARWHAL (SS-168) and DOLPHIN (SS-169) arrived at Wake Island on a training patrol from Pearl Harbor.

30 OCTOBER 1941

	IJN hydrographic survey ship KATSURIKI (1540grt) was assigned to the Japanese Fourth Fleet Survey and Patrol Division with survey vessel (ex submarine tender) KOMAHASHI and transport KOSHU.

New Zealand
Long. E150, 00 – E180, 00   Lat. S25, 00 – S60, 00

20 OCTOBER 1941

	New Zealand light cruiser ACHILLES departed Auckland, New Zealand, to escort an American liner to the equator. The light cruiser ended the escort on the 27th and steamed for Suva, Fiji, arriving on the 31st.

Hawaii Area
Long. W180, 00 – W140, 00   Lat. N30, 00 – N00, 00

22 OCTOBER 1941

	USN battleships OKLAHOMA (BB-37) and ARIZONA (BB-39) were damaged in a collision in the Hawaiian Operating Area.

23 OCTOBER 1941

1000	IJN liner TATSUTA MARU (16,975grt) arrived at Honolulu, Hawaii, and disembarked American nationals.

24 OCTOBER 1941

	IJN liner TATSUTA MARU (16,975grt) departed Honolulu, Hawaii, for San Francisco, California.

South of Hawaii
Long. W180, 00 – W140, 00   Lat. S00, 00 – S60, 00

21 OCTOBER 1941

	Free French destroyer TRIOMPHANT arrived at Bora Bora from Suva, Fiji Island, and was damaged in a very minor collision in the harbour. She then sailed from Bora Bora to Papeete, Tahiti.

22 OCTOBER 1941

	Free French destroyer TRIOMPHANT arrived at Papeete, Tahiti, from Bora Bora.

West of United States
Long. W130, 00 – W110, 00   Lat. N50, 00 – N30, 00

30 OCTOBER 1941

	IJN liner TATSUTA MARU (16,975grt) arrived at San Francisco, California, and disembarked Americans and other repatriates, including Consul General Leon Siguenza of El Salvador, Cdr P. D. Perkins of the Japanese Foreign Office, and other foreign nationals. That same day, she embarked Japanese nationals and departed.

NOVEMBER 1941
DAY-TO-DAY OPERATIONS

SECTION CONTENTS

SUMMARY 338	MEDITERRANEAN SEA & MIDDLE EAST 377
GENERAL 341	*East of Gibraltar 377*
ARCTIC OCEAN 343	*Middle Mediterranean Sea 378*
Greenland Sea and Barents Sea 343	*Eastern Mediterranean Sea 383*
White Sea 345	*Black Sea 389*
NORTH ATLANTIC OCEAN 346	*Red Sea 391*
Iceland and North of Britain 346	*Arabian Sea 391*
Norwegian Sea 352	INDIAN OCEAN 392
East of Canada 352	*East of South Africa 392*
East of United States 356	*Bay of Bengal 393*
Caribbean and Gulf of Mexico 356	*Malaya 393*
Western Approaches 357	*West of Australia 393*
Central Atlantic Crossing Zone 362	PACIFIC OCEAN 394
UK East Coast 363	*South China Sea 394*
North Sea 366	*Dutch East Indies 395*
English Channel 367	*East China Sea 395*
Bay of Biscay 368	*West of Philippine Islands 397*
West of Gibraltar 369	*Sea of Japan 397*
West of North Africa 371	*East of Philippine Islands 399*
SOUTH ATLANTIC OCEAN 372	*New Guinea and Solomon Islands 399*
East of South America 372	*East of Australia 399*
West of South Africa 372	*East of Japan 400*
BALTIC SEA 373	*Bonin – Mariana Islands 407*
Kattegat and Skagerrak 373	*Gilbert – Marshall Islands 407*
Southern Baltic Area 373	*New Zealand 408*
Gulf of Finland 374	*Alaska 409*
	Hawaii Area 409
	West of United States 409

SUMMARY

Several critical decisions were made during November 1941 that literally changed the outcome of the war.

For Germany, when Hitler refused to let his generals establish winter quarters and a defensible Russian winter defence line, he needlessly sacrificed the main strength of the German Army. The losses in men and equipment, not to mention the German loss in confidence, from the coming Russian December attack were never to be replaced, and Germany would cease to control the war outcome on the European continent.

For Japan, the decision to attack the United States and European colonial powers committed Japan to a war she could never win, against a foe she fully underestimated. The Neo-Samurai spirit running rampant among the Imperial Japanese Army officer corps doomed the nation to near obliteration. Japan could only win if the war ended quickly; she did not have the resources to survive a protracted fight. The lack of progress in China should have alerted the Japanese to the problems they faced, but they were already counting their victories.

For the United States, President Roosevelt knew that he had pushed the Japanese into an attack position. When he refused to rescind the oil boycott, the Japanese had to act. The Japanese oil reserves were at a critical point; they either had to attack or bow to American dictates. Based upon decoded Japanese diplomatic messages, the Commander of the Joint Chiefs of Staff issued a "war warning" to all US forces in the Pacific. Unfortunately, the United States underestimated the Japanese fighting ability as much as the Japanese underestimated the United States. This mutual ignorance doomed both nations to many years of bitter fighting.

GERMANY

In the Arctic, the German naval forces had all but ceased operations for the winter. Other than maintaining critical supply convoys, the conditions were too extreme to enable the Germans to disrupt the Russian convoys at this time.

In the North Atlantic, winter sea conditions also made effective operations impossible, and German U-boats had to move south. The Middle Atlantic offered calmer waters and better flying conditions for the Fw200 aircraft. The bad sea conditions in the Atlantic also made it possible for Germany to send U-boats into the Mediterranean, where their presence quickly cut into the Royal Navy's capital ships.

In the South Atlantic, German U-boats found slim pickings. The Allied convoy system had been extended along the western coast of Africa, so only the ships crossing back and forth to South America were at risk.

The Germans and Finns had all but sealed the Russian Baltic Fleet into the eastern Baltic with extensive minefields and air patrols. The Germans once again turned the Baltic into their own private lake.

ITALY

The battle for the Mediterranean was slowly eroding the Italian Fleet away. Italy's fuel shortage prevented the deployment of the heavier ships, but without radar, they were at a heavy disadvantage anyway. It took brave men to continually take to the sea against an enemy with so many advantages.

Meanwhile, the Italian Air Force continued to be a very deadly opponent for the British. The Italian S.79 torpedo bombers were greatly feared by the Royal Navy. Their skill and daring somewhat made up for the gap in surface ships for the Italian Navy.

ROMANIA

The Romanian Navy continued to support the German advance into the Crimea. While still no match for the Russian surface ships, they continued to clear mines and provide supplies in the Black Sea at a time when Russian roads were sticky glue.

JAPAN

The Japanese crossed their "Rubicon," in their case, the North Pacific. Japan came out to fight, fully confident that they could defeat the weaker European colonial powers and the United States.

Though they still had the ability to call things off if the Americans came to reason, there was little belief in Tokyo that events would not run their course. General Tojo knew Japan had to strike fast and win quickly or be totally destroyed. He did not believe that the United States would fight a prolonged war. He should have read up on American history! The United States always took up a good fight and Japan was giving them the excuse many had waited for. Plus, things did not end well for Julius Caesar either.

VICHY FRANCE

The Vichy government was still trying to hold France and her colonies together. German oversight in France was continually tightening the noose around the French people. Freedom and food quickly became a luxury.

UNITED KINGDOM

The Arctic convoys began rather successfully, as the Germans had few vessels to use against them. While still dangerous, just from a weather standpoint, the initial shipments of aid got through to the Russians. While insignificant to the current battles, the supplies demonstrated to Stalin that the Allies were at least trying to help.

The North Atlantic convoys also got a reprieve as the winter weather forced the U-boats south. The losses were still high if a Wolfpack managed to strike a convoy, but the decoded ULTRA messages and a sufficient supply of convoy escorts made the task more manageable.

The Mediterranean Fleet suffered two major losses with the sinking of the ARK ROYAL and the BARHAM. These losses overshadowed the success of the Royal Navy surface units against Italian supply convoys to North Africa. The Royal Navy continued to hold up its end to make Operation CRUSADER a success.

In the Pacific, the modest reinforcements sent to Malaya had no effect on the Japanese plans for the area. The additional troops and ships were not matched by a drastic increase in modern aircraft for the RAF. As events unfolded, the lack of air power played a major role in the British naval losses sustained in the region.

UNITED STATES

The United States thought it was prepared for war in the Pacific, but it is very difficult to move a peace time military into a wartime military. The Joint Chiefs of Staff, armed with the decoded PURPLE messages, had a much better picture of Japanese movements than did the American commanders in the field. The lack of this critical information at the local level would play a major role in the events of December.

The United States Navy's Atlantic Fleet, for all intents and purposes, was already at war. By anyone's definition, escorting convoys and attacking submarine contacts was far above the normal peacetime operations of any navy. All that was missing was the formalization that Germany and the United States were at war. Men were dying regardless of the technical details.

The American Volunteer Group (Flying Tigers) were training at an RAF base in Burma. Their arrival was the result of a long effort by the United States, Britain and China to provide air power for the defence of China. Their presence in Burma was about to become a major surprise for the Japanese.

RUSSIA

The Russian Northern Fleet made good progress in suppressing the Germany naval activities in the Arctic. They provided escorts and merchant ships to help bring the promised aid from Britain to Murmansk and Archangel.

The Russian Baltic Fleet continued to fight against the combined German and Finnish navies. The extensive minefields effectively bottled up the Russian heavy ships near Leningrad and made the passage of smaller ships and submarines very costly through the Gulf of Finland. Hitler's decision not to take Leningrad saved both the city and the Russian Fleet.

The Russian Black Sea Fleet continued to fight the losing battle in the Crimea. Sevastopol was holding out on sheer guts and the determination of the Russian people. Luckily, the Russian admirals had enough sense to move as many ships and as much materiel as possible to the Caucuses so that they could continue to fight after the city fell. Their largest opponent continued to be the German *Luftwaffe*, which continued to attack the ships helping in the defence of the area.

CHINA

The Chinese continued to maintain pressure on the Japanese occupation forces, but were very relieved when many of the best Japanese units were taken out of the line. The Chinese had been close to collapse after the last summer offensive and used the new quiet period to rebuild their forces. They were also looking forward to the arrival of the American Volunteer Group (The Flying Tigers) to help take control of the sky above China.

POLAND

In Libya, the Polish Brigade played a solid role in Operation CRUSADER. Having replaced many of the Australians in Tobruk, they manned the defensive line against continuing Axis attacks while the British tried to defeat Rommel on the Libyan border.

FREE FRANCE

The Free French forces also supported the British offensive in North Africa. The newly equipped Free French Brigade fought with the forces attacking Rommel in Libya.

Meanwhile, the Free French Navy continued to pick up more French colonies to the Free French cause. The capture of Reunion Island took one more area away from the Vichy government.

GENERAL

DATE	COMMENTS
1 November	The German Eleventh Army captured the Russian city of Simferopol in the Crimea.
1 November	The German government issued a statement denying the charges made by American President Franklin D. Roosevelt that the USN destroyers GREER and KEARNY were attacked by German U-boats without any provocation, stating that the exact opposite was true in that the U-boats fired torpedoes only after they were tracked and depth-charged for hours by these USN warships.
1 November	Ships departed San Francisco, California, with fifty-two crated A-24 aircraft for the 27th Light Bombing Group of the American Far East Asian Air Force in the Philippine Islands.
2 November	A furious battle began between the Yugoslavian "Chetniks" led by Mihailowitsj and the Yugoslavian Communist partisans led by Tito.
2 November	In Operation GLENCOE, the Royal Navy carried troops to Famagusta, Cypress, to relieve the troops garrisoned there.
2 November	In Operation BELLRINGER, the Royal Navy intercepted a Vichy French convoy south of the Cape of Good Hope, which carried 900 tons of graphite and 30,000 tons of rice.
3 November	German Panzer Group 2 captured the Russian city of Kursk.
4 November	Finnish forces captured the Russian Baltic naval base of Hangö, that Finland had been compelled to lease to the Russians in 1940.
4 November	The German Eleventh Army captured the Russian city of Feodosia in the Crimea.
7 November	Speaking in Red Square at Moscow, with the spearheads of the German Army less than a hundred miles from the capital, Josef Stalin predicted that the Fascist German invaders were facing disaster.
7 November	During the night of 7/8 November, the greatest combined British air-operation to date began with 387 bombers sent to different targets at the other side of the North Sea, including Berlin (1700 km). Whitley, Wellington, Stirling, and Halifax bombers took part in the raid.
8 November	The German Army Group North advanced across the Volchov River and captured the Russian city of Tichvin, outside Leningrad.
9 November	During the night of 9/10 November, RAF Bomber Command attacked Hamburg, Cuxhaven and Emden.
11 November	In Operation PERPETUAL, the Royal Navy departed Gibraltar to launch aircraft to Malta.
12 November	The German Panzer units achieved a numerical superiority, in respect of tank strength, over the Allies in North Africa. After a day of heavy fighting around Sidi Rezegh, the British 4th, 7th and 22nd Armoured Brigades were badly mauled. New Zealand troops joined the Allies in the area, as part of XIII Corps.
13 November	President Roosevelt announced the arming of American merchant vessels carrying Lend-Lease cargo to Britain. With the consent of Congress, the American Neutrality Act was modified to allow the ships to enter the war zone and defend themselves if attacked.
13 November	In Operation APPROACH, the Royal Navy carried stores to Tobruk, Libya.
14 November	American and Japanese representatives began talks in Washington, D.C., to try to ease tensions between the two countries.
14 November	In Operation ASTROLOGER, single merchant ships tried to run supplies to Malta.
15 November	German Army Group Centre began the second phase in the attack on Moscow, using Panzer Group 2, Panzer Group 3, and Panzer Group 4, supported by the Second, Fourth and Ninth Armies.
16 November	The American V Bomber Command and V Interceptor Command were created in the Philippine Islands.
16 November	In Operation CHIEFTAIN, a convoy departed Gibraltar as a diversion for Operation CRUSADER in the eastern Mediterranean.
17 November	The German Eleventh Army captured the Russian port of Kerch in the Crimea.
17 November	The British Army begin Operation CRUSADER with 756 tanks plus reserves against 249 German and 150 Italian tanks.
18 November	Operation CRUSADER began in Libya where the British 8th Army (General Cunningham) tried to break through the Axis ring around Tobruk and to defeat the German and Italian forces in Libya. The Royal Navy transferred ammunition and supplies to the British forces along the Egyptian and Libyan coast.
18 November	In response to deteriorating political conditions in China, Admiral Thomas C. Hart, CINC, United States Asiatic Fleet, ordered Rear Admiral William A. Glassford, CO of the Yangtze River Patrol, to return to Manila with five of his larger gunboats.
18 November	In Operation Z, the Imperial Japanese Navy began collecting the supply ships, primarily oilers, needed for the carrier strike on Pearl Harbor, Hawaiian Territory.
20 November	German Army Group South reached the Russian city of Rostov on the Don River.
20 November	The Japanese Kawaguchi Brigade was activated in Tokyo, Japan, and placed under the direct com-

	mand of the Japanese Southern Army. Major-General Kiyotake Kawaguchi was in command of the Brigade, which was comprised mainly of units stationed at Canton in southern China.
21 November	German Panzer Group 1 captured the Russian city of Rostov on the Don river.
21 November	The Allied garrison at Tobruk, Libya, began an eastward attack to join with the attacking British 8th Army.
21 November	At Bletchley Park, England, decoded ULTRA messages indicated that the Germans were sending the long range U-boats west of Gibraltar, and new U-boats were being transferred from Germany to French ports. With no U-boats allocated to the North Atlantic convoy routes, the Admiralty informed all HX, SC and ON convoys to use the shortest routes across the Atlantic.
21 November	In Operation LANDMARK, the Royal Navy sailed from Malta with a convoy in order to draw out the Italian Fleet into combat.
22 November	In North Africa, a large tank battle raged near Sidi Rezegh in Libya. At the end of this confusing battle, British units withdrew away from Tobruk. Separately the German 15th Panzer Division mauled the British 4th Armoured Brigade, leaving the Germans with the initiative.
23 November	New Zealand forces attacked and captured the HQ of the German *Afrika Korps* and much of Rommel's communications equipment. Due to heavy British losses, General Cunningham lost confidence and became depressed. Noting the change in communications with Cunningham, General Auchinleck, the overall commander, went to the forward command post. In the end, he had to take command and move the British Army to safety further east.
23 November	In North Africa, fierce battles took place southeast of Sidi Rezegh. In the afternoon, German Panzer Divisions were joined by the Italian ARIETE Armoured Division in making a sharp charge against the British Armour Brigade and both South African brigades.
23 November	The German offensive against Moscow continued with a fifty-mile front northwest of the city. The Germans captured the Russian city of Klin; German forces were now within thirty-five miles of the Russian capital.
24 November	In North Africa, Rommel, believing the opposing British Armour Brigade destroyed, ignored the New Zealand forces in the area and advanced along the Trig-el-Abd to the Egyptian border. During Rommels advance, he lost touch with his senior commanders, causing confusion at the Axis headquarters. His advance cut through the British rear areas, causing the British support troops to panick and they began an unordered retreat. Though the attack was successful, the German troops took losses they could not afford and the bulk of the British Army escaped before they could be captured.
24 November	Due to heavy Russian counterattacks, the Russian city of Rostov was evacuated of German units to prevent being cut off. Field Marshal von Rundstedt made this move in the face of express orders from Hitler to stand fast.
24 November	In Operation AR, the Royal Navy and Russian Northern Fleet attacked German shipping between Nordkyn and Vardø, Norway.
24 November	In Operation SUNSTAR, the Royal Navy supported a commando raid on the coast of Normandy. The landing force covered the beach while samples were taken of the beach material. The allies needed to know if the beaches would support the movement of armoured vehicles.After the information was gained, the ships returned to Portsmouth.
25 November	President Roosevelt instructed his Secretary of State to hand the Japanese Ambassador a ten point note, outlining the actions Japan needed to take to get the United States to remove the oil embargo. The United States knew that the contents would be unacceptable to Japan. Roosevelt had concluded that war between the two countries was unavoidable.
25 November	The United States Navy introduced a compulsory convoy system for all merchant ships in the Pacific Ocean.
27 November	Some German armed patrols penetrated the western suburbs of Moscow and got a good look at the Kremlin.
27 November	The German Army Group Centre continued its attack on Moscow in extremely difficult wintry conditions. The German Ninth Army reached the Volga Canal sixty miles northwest of the city.
27 November	The Russian Army re-captured the city of Rostov.
27 November	Based upon classified messages decoded by American intelligence agents, the Commander of the Joint Chiefs of Staff issued a "War Warning" to all forces in the Pacific. Japanese ship concentrations were identified between Formosa, Hainan Island and Vichy French Indo-China. Other Japanese forces were identified near Palau. It appeared that Japanese forces were preparing to strike in Southeast Asia. While the United States could read messages using the Japanese "PURPLE" diplomatic code, they did not successfully crack the JN.25 code used by the Imperial Japanese Navy until after the war.
27 November	The Royal Navy began evacuating RAF personnel from Murmansk, Russia. They had arrived there as part of Operation STRENGTH, but the weather made conditions too difficult for them to stay.
28 November	Overextended and short of supplies, German Panzer Group 1 evacuated Rostov-on-Don and withdrew to the Mius River thirty miles to the west.
29 November	Depleted by continuous savage fighting and extreme weather conditions in below-zero temperatures,

	German forces of Army Group Centre suspended all offensive operations in positions less than fifty miles from Moscow.
29 November	In Operation GI, IJN ships departed Truk with the Japanese Gilbert Islands Invasion Force.
30 November	Units of the 16th Indian Infantry Brigade began arriving at Rangoon, Burma, from Calcutta, India, and were placed under direct command of Burma Army HQ.

ARCTIC OCEAN

Greenland Sea and Barents Sea
Long. W180, 00 – E180, 00   Lat. N90, 00 – N68, 00

2 NOVEMBER 1941

	The Russian Northern Fleet sent submarines SHCH-401, M-171, M-172, M-173 and M-175 to patrol off the Norwegian Arctic coast until 15 November.
	Russian submarine SHCH-421 (Lt Cdr N. A. Lunin) unsuccessfully attacked a German convoy off Lopphavet, Norway.
	Russian submarine K-22 had an unsuccessful patrol off Vestfjord, Norway.

3 NOVEMBER 1941

	Submarine TRIDENT sank German submarine chaser **UJ.1213** (ex whaler **RAU IV** (354grt)) off Honningsvåg, Norway in 70, 58N, 26, 58E. TRIDENT missed German steamer ALTKIRCH (4713grt) in the same attack.
	Russian submarine K-1 unsuccessfully attacked a German convoy off Lopphavet, Norway.

5 NOVEMBER 1941

	A mine laid by Russian submarine K-23 damaged German auxiliary minesweeper M.22 off Kirkenes, Norway.

6 NOVEMBER 1941

	Submarine SEALION arrived at Murmansk, Russia, from Scapa Flow.

7 NOVEMBER 1941

	Russian submarine K-1 unsuccessfully attacked a German convoy off Lopphavet, Norway.
	Submarine TRIDENT made an unsuccessful attack on German minesweeper MRS.3 (ex steamer **BALI** (1428grt)) in 71, 06N, 26, 57E.

8 NOVEMBER 1941

	Russian submarine M-175 unsuccessfully attacked a German convoy off Lopphavet, Norway.
	A mine laid by Russian submarine K-1 sank German steamer **FLOTTBEK** (1930grt) in Maakeröy Sund, Norway.

9 NOVEMBER 1941

	Russian submarine SHCH-421 (Lt Cdr N. A. Lunin) unsuccessfully attacked a German convoy off Lopphavet.
	Russian submarine K-21 (Capt 3rd Class Zhukov) unsuccessfully attacked a German convoy off Lopphavet.

10 NOVEMBER 1941

	Russian submarine SHCH-421 (Lt Cdr N. A. Lunin) unsuccessfully attacked a German convoy off Lopphavet.
	Russian submarine K-21 (Capt 3rd Class Zhukov) laid mines in the Sørøysund, Norway.
	Submarine SEAWOLF arrived at Murmansk from Scapa Flow.

11 NOVEMBER 1941

	Russian submarine K-21 (Capt 3rd Class Zhukov) laid mines off Hammer Fest, Norway.

12 NOVEMBER 1941

	Russian submarine K-21 (Capt 3rd Class Zhukov) unsuccessfully attacked a German convoy off Lopphavet, Norway. Her torpedoes narrowly missed German patrol boat V.6109.
	Russian MO-IV class submarine chasers laid thirty-four mines off Petsamo, Finland.
	Submarine SEALION departed Murmansk for a patrol off Svaerholt Havet, Norway.

15 NOVEMBER 1941

	Russian submarine M-171 unsuccessfully attacked a German convoy off Lopphavet, Norway.
	Submarine TRIDENT departed Poljarnoe, Russia, for Blyth, England.

16 NOVEMBER 1941

	Russian submarine K-23 (Capt 3rd Class Potapov) departed Murmansk, Russia, for operations off the Norwegian Arctic coast.
	Minesweepers GOSSAMER, HUSSAR, and SPEEDY arrived at Murmansk from Archangel, Russia.

18 NOVEMBER 1941

	Submarine SEALION (Lt Cdr Colvin) sank Norwegian tanker **VESCO** (331grt) with gunfire in Svaerholt Havet, Norway, in 70, 57N, 26, 50E.

19 NOVEMBER 1941

	Russian submarine K-23 (Capt 3rd Class Potapov) laid mines off Bergsfjord, Norway.

20 NOVEMBER 1941

	Russian submarine K-23 (Capt 3rd Class Potapov) laid mines off Kvaenangenfjord, Norway.

21 NOVEMBER 1941

	A mine laid by Russian submarine K-21 sank Norwegian steamer **BESSHEIM** (1774grt) off Soroysund, Norway.
	Russian submarine K-3 (Capt 3rd Class Malofeev with the commander of the 1st Submarine Division, Capt 2nd Class Gadzhiev on board) departed Murmansk, Russia, on a mining mission.
1100	Convoy PQ.3 arrived at Murmansk with light cruiser KENYA. The convoy continued to Archangel with local escort only, arriving on the 22nd.

22 NOVEMBER 1941

	Destroyers BEDOUIN and INTREPID arrived at Murmansk, Russia, with minesweeper BRAMBLE.
	Submarine SEAWOLF (Lt Raikes) unsuccessfully attacked a steamer three and a half miles off Syltefjord, Norway.

23 NOVEMBER 1941

	Russian submarine K-3 (Capt 3rd Class Malofeev) laid mines at Reinøya sound and Magerøya sound, Norway.

24 NOVEMBER 1941

	Minesweepers SEAGULL and SPEEDY arrived at Murmansk from Archangel.
	Submarine SEAWOLF (Lt Raikes) unsuccessfully attacked a convoy of steamers ASUNCION (4626grt), the Norwegian GRAZIELLA (2137grt), and WENDINGEN (grt) in Syltefjord, Norway in 70, 30N, 30, 30E.
	Russian MO-IV-class submarine chasers laid twenty mines off Kirkenes, Norway.
	Light cruiser KENYA, destroyers BEDOUIN and INTREPID, plus Russian destroyers GREMYAHCHI and GROMKI departed Murmansk to sweep for German shipping between Nordkyn and Vardø, Norway, in Operation AR. The ships arrived at back Murmansk later on the 25th.

25 NOVEMBER 1941

0731	In Operation AR, light cruiser KENYA, destroyers BEDOUIN and INTREPID, plus Russian destroyers GREMYAHCHI and GROMKI shelled Vardø, Norway, and then arrived at back Murmansk later in the day.

26 NOVEMBER 1941

	Russian submarine K-3 (Capt 3rd Class Malofeyev) sank Norwegian fishing ship **START** (grt) with gunfire off Lopphavet, Norway. Shell fragments wounded seven crewmen.
	Russian submarine D-3 (Lt Cdr Bibeyev) laid two minefields off Porsangerfjord, Norway.

27 NOVEMBER 1941

1500	Destroyers BEDOUIN and INTREPID departed Murmansk carrying officers and other ranks of RAF 151 Wing from Operation STRENGTH. They joined convoy QP.3 and provided escort from the 28th to 2 December.

28 NOVEMBER 1941

	Light cruiser KENYA departed Murmansk carrying two hundred personnel from RAF 151 Wing, which had arrived in Operation STRENGTH. The cruiser joined convoy QP.3A with six more ships for Seidisfjord at daylight on the 29th and escorted the convoy to 3 December. Two steamers returned to Murmansk with weather damage.
1030	Heavy cruiser BERWICK arrived at Murmansk with destroyers OFFA and ONSLOW plus trawlers BUTE and STELLA CAPELLA after escorting convoy PQ.4. German bombers unsuccessfully attacked the group as they entered the harbour.

30 NOVEMBER 1941

0900	Light cruiser SHEFFIELD joined convoy PQ.5 in 70, 20N, 05, 00W from Seidisfjord. The light cruiser continued with the convoy to 7 December, when she was detached to Murmansk.
1600	Heavy cruiser BERWICK, carrying RAF personnel of 151 Wing brought to Russia in Operation STRENGTH, departed Murmansk with destroyers ONSLOW and OFFA for Scapa Flow. The force was carrying out a search for enemy shipping between Tanafjord and North Cape, Norway, on 1 December. That mission was later cancelled, and the force proceeded to Scapa Flow.

White Sea
Long. E30, 00 – E60, 00   Lat. N68, 00 – N60, 00

1 NOVEMBER 1941

	A Russian aircraft unsuccessfully attacked U.576 (Kptlt Heinicke) off the White Sea entrance.

2 NOVEMBER 1941

2214	Heavy cruiser NORFOLK departed Archangel, Russia, to escort convoy QP.2.
2214	Destroyers ECLIPSE and ICARUS departed Archangel to escort convoy QP.2.

3 NOVEMBER 1941

	Convoy QP.2 departed Archangel, Russia, with steamers ATLANTIC (5414grt), Panamanian CAPIRA (5565grt), GEMSTONE (4986grt), Russian IJORA (2815grt), Panamanian NORTH KING (4934grt), BLAIRNEVIS (4155grt), Russian CHEYNYSHEVSKI (3588grt), HARMONIC (4558grt), LORCA (4875grt), RIVER AFTON (5479grt), and VILLE D'ANVERS (7462grt). Heavy cruiser NORFOLK escorted the convoy from 3 to 11 November and then proceeded to Scapa Flow. Destroyers ECLIPSE and ICARUS escorted the convoy from 3 to 16 November, when they were detached to Kirkwall and then Scapa Flow. Minesweepers BRAMBLE, LEDA, and SEAGULL provided local escort from Archangel and escorted the convoy from 3 to 5 November. Trawlers CELIA and WINDERMERE joined the convoy on the 11th to relieve destroyers ECLIPSE and ICARUS. The trawlers escorted the convoy to 13 November. The destroyers proceeded to Seidisfjord to refuel and rejoined the convoy on the 13th. The convoy arrived at Kirkwall on the 17th and the destroyers arrived at Scapa Flow.

12 NOVEMBER 1941

	U.752 and U.578 began patrolling the mouth of the White Sea until 28 November.

15 NOVEMBER 1941

	U.752 (ObltzS Schroeter) sank Russian minesweeper **T-889/No.34** (ex **RT-3**) (581grt) and missed mine carrier JUSHAR while attacking a small convoy off Cape Gorodetski in 67, 41N, 41, 03E.

18 NOVEMBER 1941

	Submarine TRIDENT was directed to patrol off the Norwegian coast in the area of 62N, 04, 20E, while on passage from Murmansk to Britain.
	Submarine TUNA was directed to patrol in the area of 61, 02N, 03, 50E, while on passage from Scapa Flow to the Northern Patrol area.

25 NOVEMBER 1941

	Submarine TRIDENT departed her patrol area off Norway for Blyth.

27 NOVEMBER 1941

	U.578 lightly damaged Russian patrol boat SKR-25/BRIZ by ramming off Kanin.
	Convoy QP.3 departed Archangel with steamers Russian ANDRE MARTI (2352grt), EMPIRE BAFFIN (6978grt), HARTLEBURY (5082grt), ORIENT CITY (5095grt), Russian REVOLUTSIONER (2900grt), Russian ARCOS (2343grt), HARPALION (5486grt), Russian KUZBASS (3109grt), QUEEN CITY (4814grt), and TEMPLE ARCH (5138grt). Minesweeper HUSSAR escorted the convoy from 27 November to 9 December and minesweeper GOSSAMER escorted the convoy from 27 November to 10 December. These minesweepers took Russian ships to Kirkwall after the dispersal of the convoy. Russian steamers ARCOS and KUZBASS returned to Archangel with defects. Destroyers BEDOUIN and INTREPID, carrying officers and other ranks of RAF 151 Wing from Operation STRENGTH, departed Murmansk to join the convoy and provide escort from the 28th to 2 December. Light cruiser KENYA, carrying 200 personnel from RAF 151 Wing, which had arrived in Operation STRENGTH, departed Murmansk on the 28th. The cruiser joined the convoy at daylight on the 29th and escorted

the convoy to 3 December.
    The convoy was dispersed on 3 December in 73, 45N, 19, 00E.
    The British ships proceeded to Seidisfjord. Trawlers MACBETH and HAMLET escorted them from Seidisfjord to Kirkwall from 9 to 12 December.
    Destroyers BEDOUIN and INTREPID arrived at Scapa Flow on 5 December.
    Light cruiser KENYA arrived at Rosyth on 6 December for repairs and to disembark the RAF personnel. Minesweeper HUSSAR arrived at Scapa Flow on 9 December.
    Minesweeper GOSSAMER arrived at Scapa Flow on 11 December, carrying Russian Commodore Egipko, who was to be the liaison officer with the Home Fleet, to be accommodated in battle cruiser RENOWN.

NORTH ATLANTIC OCEAN

Iceland and North of Britain
Long. W30, 00 – E03, 00   Lat. N68, 00 – N58, 30

1 NOVEMBER 1941

	American PBY aircraft of VP-73 Squadron provided air cover for convoy ON.30 until American Task Unit TU.4.2.1 took over the escort in the North Atlantic and led the convoy far to the south to avoid the German Wolfpack identified off Newfoundland.
	Light cruisers EDINBURGH and SHEFFIELD departed Scapa Flow for Hvalfjord, Iceland.
	The British Admiralty directed that destroyers ARROW, ANTELOPE, ACTIVE, ANTHONY, and ACHATES should join Western Approaches Command from Scapa Flow, when former Force H destroyers FAULKNOR, FORESTER, FORESIGHT, and FURY become available to the Home Fleet.
0430	Heavy cruiser BERWICK departed Scapa Flow for Rosyth with destroyers PUNJABI and ESCAPADE.

2 NOVEMBER 1941

	In response to the report that the German heavy cruiser ADMIRAL SCHEER was preparing to sortie into the North Atlantic, the Home Fleet took up a position south of Iceland with battleship KING GEORGE V, aircraft carrier VICTORIOUS plus cruisers and destroyers.
American Task Group TG.3.1 departed Hvalfjord to cover the Denmark Strait with battleships IDAHO (BB-42) and MISSISSIPPI (BB-41), heavy cruisers TUSCALOOSA (CA-37) and WICHITA (CA-45), plus destroyers GWIN (DD-433), MEREDITH (DD-434), and MONSSEN (DD-436).
	Heavy cruiser BERWICK arrived at Scapa Flow from Rosyth.
	Submarine P.35 departed Scapa Flow to patrol off Norway.
1200	Destroyer SOUTHWOLD departed Scapa Flow for the Clyde after a reduced time to work up to combat efficiency. The destroyer was to carry out boiler cleaning at Greenock before proceeding with convoy WS.12Z for service in the Mediterranean.

3 NOVEMBER 1941

	Light cruisers EDINBURGH and SHEFFIELD arrived at Hvalfjord from Scapa Flow.
	American PBY aircraft of VP-73 Squadron provided air cover for convoy ON.31.
0700	Destroyer IMPULSIVE departed Scapa Flow to relieve destroyer PUNJABI on the escort screen for battleship DUKE OF YORK, which was carrying out sea trials to the west of the Orkneys.
1010	Destroyer PUNJABI arrived at Scapa Flow from her escort duties. The battleship DUKE OF YORK and her remaining destroyers arrived at Scapa Flow later in the day.
1700	Destroyer ESCAPADE departed Scapa Flow to boiler clean at Rosyth.
1730	Destroyer MAORI arrived at Scapa Flow from Sheerness to begin working up to combat efficiency.
1730	Battleship KING GEORGE V, aircraft carrier VICTORIOUS, heavy cruisers KENT, BERWICK, and SUFFOLK departed Scapa Flow for Iceland with destroyers SOMALI, ASHANTI, MATABELE, PUNJABI, OFFA, and ORIBI.

4 NOVEMBER 1941

	U.431, U.402, U.332 and U.105 arrived in the Denmark Strait to support the planned breakout of German heavy cruiser ADMIRAL SCHEER into the North Atlantic. However, the cruiser developed mechanical defects, which cancelled her sortie.
	Battleship KING GEORGE V and aircraft carrier VICTORIOUS arrived at their patrol position south of Iceland with a destroyer escort. They maintained their station in case German heavy cruiser ADMIRAL SCHEER tried to sortie into the North Atlantic.
	American Task Group TG.3.1 patrolled the Denmark Strait with battleships IDAHO (BB-42) and MISSISSIPPI (BB-41), heavy cruisers TUSCALOOSA (CA-37) and WICHITA (CA-45) plus destroyers GWIN (DD-433), MEREDITH (DD-434) and MONSSEN (DD-436). They maintained their station in case German heavy cruiser ADMIRAL SCHEER tried to sortie into the North Atlantic.

1730	Destroyers TARTAR and ESKIMO departed Scapa Flow for Hvalfjord to join the Commander in Chief.
2030	Destroyer MONTROSE departed Scapa Flow for Rosyth.
2055	Light cruiser KENYA departed Seidisfjord with destroyers BEDOUIN and INTREPID to cover the trawler patrol line west of the Iceland-Faeroes minefield. Convoy PQ.3, which these ships were to have escorted, was ordered to remain at Hvalfjord until further notice.

5 NOVEMBER 1941

	American heavy cruisers WICHITA (CA-45) and TUSCALOOSA (CA-37) departed Hvalfjord on patrol in response to a rumour that German heavy cruiser ADMIRAL SCHEER was breaking out of Norwegian waters.
	American battleships IDAHO (BB-42) and MISSISSIPPI (BB-41) departed Hvalfjord on a patrol with destroyers GWIN (DD-433), MEREDITH (DD-434), and MONSSEN (DD-436) of Destroyer Division 22.
	Light cruiser ARETHUSA arrived at Scapa Flow from Rosyth.
0730	Battleship KING GEORGE V, heavy cruisers BERWICK, KENT, and SUFFOLK, arrived at Hvalfjord from Scapa Flow with destroyers SOMALI, MATABELE, and PUNJABI.
>0731	Aircraft carrier VICTORIOUS arrived independently at Hvalfjord with destroyers ASHANTI, OFFA, and ORIBI after exercises.
0800	Minelaying cruisers MANXMAN and WELSHMAN arrived at Scapa Flow from Loch Alsh.
0815	Destroyer WHEATLAND arrived at Scapa Flow from the Clyde to work up to combat efficiency.
1000	Destroyer CHIDDINGFOLD departed Scapa Flow with Vice Admiral Sir Bruce Fraser, Third Sea Lord, and Sir Stanley Goodall, Direction of Naval Construction, for passage to Scrabster.
1330	Destroyer CHIDDINGFOLD arrived back at Scapa Flow from Scrabster.
1730	Destroyers ONSLOW, IMPULSIVE, and ANTELOPE departed Scapa Flow for Londonderry.
1800	Battleship KING GEORGE V, aircraft carrier VICTORIOUS plus heavy cruisers KENT and BERWICK departed Hvalfjord with destroyers SOMALI, PUNJABI, ASHANTI, MATABELE, ORIBI, and OFFA.
1800	Light cruiser EDINBURGH (CS.18), heavy cruiser SUFFOLK, and light cruiser SHEFFIELD departed Hvalfjord on a patrol.
2359	British intelligence indicated that the German heavy cruiser ADMIRAL SCHEER had returned to harbour, the allied warships on patrol were ordered to return to Hvalfjord just before midnight.

6 NOVEMBER 1941

	American heavy cruisers WICHITA (CA-45) and TUSCALOOSA (CA-37) arrived at Hvalfjord from the Denmark Strait.
	Light cruiser EDINBURGH, heavy cruiser SUFFOLK, and light cruiser SHEFFIELD arrived at Hvalfjord.
	The Commander in Chief, Home Fleet, arrived back at Hvalfjord.
	Light cruiser KENYA with destroyers BEDOUIN and INTREPID were ordered to return to Seidisfjord from the Iceland-Faeroes passage patrol. After refuelling, the ships would proceed to cover the laying of Minefield SN.83B, sailing on the 8th. However, the destroyers were forced to return to Seidisfjord in heavy weather.
0800	Destroyer MONTROSE arrived at Scapa Flow and disembarked Vice Admiral, Second in Command Home Fleet and his staff alongside battleship DUKE OF YORK.
0900	Vice Admiral, Second in Command Home Fleet, hoisted his flag in battleship DUKE OF YORK.
>0901	Destroyer MONTROSE departed Scapa Flow with Rear Admiral Destroyers Home Fleet for passage to Scrabster.
1000	Destroyers TARTAR and ESKIMO arrived at Hvalfjord from Scapa Flow.
1330	Destroyer MONTROSE arrived back at Scapa Flow from Scrabster.

7 NOVEMBER 1941

	American battleships IDAHO (BB-42) and MISSISSIPPI (BB-41) arrived at Hvalfjord from the Denmark Strait with destroyers MEREDITH (DD-434), GRAYSON (DD-435), and MONSSEN (DD-436).
	Light cruiser TRINIDAD arrived at Scapa Flow from the Clyde.
	Heavy cruiser BERWICK departed Hvalfjord on a Denmark Strait patrol.
	Destroyer MONTROSE departed Scapa Flow for Loch Alsh to support Rear Admiral Minelaying.
1345	Destroyer NORMAN departed Scapa Flow for Wick to embark Crown Prince Olaf of Norway and his staff for passage to Scapa Flow.
1500	Sloop LOWESTOFT departed Scapa Flow to join convoy WN.2 for onward passage to Rosyth. She had completed working up to combat efficiency and was assigned to Commander in Chief, Rosyth.
1700	Destroyer NORMAN returned to Scapa Flow from Wick.
2100	Destroyer BEAUFORT arrived at Scapa Flow from the Clyde to work up to combat efficiency.

8 NOVEMBER 1941

	American destroyer NIBLACK (DD-424) damaged Norwegian steamer ASTRA (2164grt) in a collision at Reyk-

	javik, Iceland.
	German bombing damaged steamer GASLIGHT (1696grt) two cables southeast of S.1 Buoy off Sutherland. The steamer was towed to Sutherland arriving on the 9th.
0230	Destroyer HURWORTH departed Scapa Flow for Loch Ewe carrying sixty bags of mail for battleship RODNEY and her destroyer screen.

9 NOVEMBER 1941

	Convoy PQ.3 departed Hvalfjord with steamers BRIARWOOD (4019grt), CAPE RACE (3807grt), Panamanian EL CAPITAN (5255grt), TREK IEVE (5244grt), CAPE CORSO (3807grt), Panamanian COCLE (5630grt), SAN AMBROSIO (7410grt), and WANSTEAD (5486grt) escorted by trawlers HAMLET and MACBETH. Trawler HAMLET was detached from the convoy on the 14th and returned with steamer BRIARWOOD, which had been damaged by ice. Trawler MACBETH was detached from the convoy on the 15th. Destroyers BEDOUIN and INTREPID and light cruiser KENYA joined the convoy on the 14th in 70, 30N, 05, 00W. On the 19th, Russian General Gromov and the Russian Mission was transferred from light cruiser KENYA to destroyer BEDOUIN for onward passage to Archangel. Minesweepers BRAMBLE, SEAGULL, and SPEEDY joined the convoy on the 20th. The convoy arrived at Murmansk on the 21st with light cruiser KENYA. The convoy continued to Archangel with local escort only arriving at Archangel on the 22nd. Destroyers BEDOUIN and INTREPID arrived at Murmansk on the 22nd with minesweeper BRAMBLE. Minesweepers SEAGULL and SPEEDY arrived at Murmansk from Archangel on the 24th.
	Minelayers MENETHEUS and PORT QUEBEC laid Minefield SN.83B escorted by destroyers BRIGHTON, NEWARK, CHARLESTOWN, and MONTROSE. Light cruiser KENYA covered the mining group. After the mining, light cruiser KENYA was ordered to return to Seidisfjord to refuel and then join convoy PQ.3 north of Iceland.
2315	Trawlers CELIA and WINDERMERE departed Hvalfjord and joined convoy QP.2 on the 11th to relieve destroyers ECLIPSE and ICARUS.

10 NOVEMBER 1941

0830	Destroyer ECHO arrived at Scapa Flow from Sheerness. En route, she assisted damaged tug BUCCANEER.
1600	Heavy cruiser CUMBERLAND departed Scapa Flow to join the Commander in Chief's force at Hvalfjord.
1600	Destroyer MAORI departed Scapa Flow for the Clyde after she completed a shortened program for working up to combat efficiency.

11 NOVEMBER 1941

	Heavy cruiser KENT departed Hvalfjord for exercises and then a patrol in the Iceland-Faeroes passage.
0030	Destroyer ESCAPADE arrived at Scapa Flow from Rosyth with weather damage sustained en route.
0144	Battleship RODNEY was ordered to Hvalfjord with destroyers ONSLOW, IMPULSIVE, and ANTELOPE from her patrol off the Iceland-Faeroes passage.

12 NOVEMBER 1941

	Heavy cruiser CUMBERLAND arrived at Hvalfjord from Scapa Flow.
	Battleship RODNEY arrived at Hvalfjord with destroyers ONSLOW, IMPULSIVE, and ANTELOPE from their Iceland-Faeroes passage patrol.
	Heavy cruiser KENT arrived at Hvalfjord from a Denmark Strait patrol.
0800	Destroyer MONTROSE arrived at Scapa Flow after being detached at the Minches.
0930	Destroyer HURWORTH departed Scapa Flow for Scrabster with His Royal Highness Crown Prince Olaf of Norway.
1200	Light cruiser KENYA returned to Seidisfjord to refuel and then join convoy PQ.3 north of Iceland.
1200	Destroyer HURWORTH arrived back at Scapa Flow from Scrabster to embark her motorboat and to prepare for boiler cleaning.
>1201	Destroyer HURWORTH departed Scapa Flow for the Clyde to boiler clean prior to proceeding to the Mediterranean.

13 NOVEMBER 1941

	Destroyers BEDOUIN and INTREPID and later light cruiser KENYA departed Seidisfjord to join convoy PQ.3 in 70, 30N, 05, 00W.
	U.431, U.402, U.332 and U.105 were moved from their position in the Denmark Strait to the area off Cape Race. They had been originally sent to the straits when the Germans had planned to move the heavy cruiser ADMIRAL SCHEER into the North Atlantic. Now that her breakout was delayed, the U-boats were released for

	convoy hunting.
	Light cruiser SHEFFIELD departed Hvalfjord for a Faeroes to Iceland patrol.
0730	Minesweeper SHARPSHOOTER arrived at Scapa Flow from Cardiff.
0830	Destroyer ECHO departed Scapa Flow for Hvalfjord to join the Commander in Chief, Home Fleet. She also carried mail for the fleet.
0900	Destroyer PYTCHLEY arrived at Scapa Flow from Leith to begin working up to combat efficiency.

14 NOVEMBER 1941

	Light cruiser EDINBURGH and heavy cruiser SUFFOLK departed Hvalfjord for a Denmark Strait patrol.
	Minesweeper FITZROY departed the Faeroes to boiler clean at Aberdeen.
0830	Destroyer BRIGHTON arrived at Scapa Flow from Loch Alsh to carry out docking and repairs.
1215	An American destroyer attacked a submarine contact in 62, 50N, 24, 40W.
2015	Destroyer ESCAPADE departed Scapa Flow for Hvalfjord to join the force under the Commander in Chief, Home Fleet. The destroyer embarked mail for the fleet before sailing.

15 NOVEMBER 1941

	Destroyers ASHANTI, MATABELE, and PUNJABI departed Hvalfjord for an anti-submarine search for a submarine contact attacked by an American destroyer in 62, 50N, 24, 30W the previous day.
0940	Destroyer ECHO arrived at Hvalfjord from Scapa Flow to join the Home Fleet.

16 NOVEMBER 1941

	German bombing sank fishing trawler **FERNBANK** (211grt) twelve miles northwest of Myggenaes. Five crewmen were lost.
1000	Destroyer ESCAPADE arrived at Hvalfjord from Scapa Flow.
1100	Destroyer ANTELOPE departed Hvalfjord for Scapa Flow.

17 NOVEMBER 1941

	Convoy PQ.4 departed Reykjavik with steamers the Russian ALMA ATA (3611grt), DAN Y BRYN (5117grt), EULIMA (6027grt), the Russian RODINA (4441grt), the Russian BUDENNI (2482grt), EMPIRE METEOR (7457grt), the Russian MOSSOVET (2981grt), and the Russian SUKHONA (3124grt). Trawlers BUTE and STELLA CAPELLA escorted the convoy from 17 to 27 November. Heavy cruiser BERWICK with destroyers OFFA and ONSLOW escorted the convoy from 25 to 27 November. The convoy was to have joined with additional escorts on the 20th, but the warships were unable to locate the convoy. On the 27th, minesweepers GOSSAMER, SEAGULL, and SPEEDY joined the convoy relieving the heavy cruiser, destroyers, and trawlers, which proceeded to Murmansk. The convoy arrived at Archangel on the 28th.
	Heavy cruiser KENT departed the Faeroes-Iceland patrol for Hvalfjord. Light cruiser SHEFFIELD took over the patrol of this area and her own area.
	Light cruiser EDINBURGH departed Denmark Strait patrol for Hvalfjord.
0800	Destroyers ECLIPSE and ICARUS arrived at Kirkwall after being detached from convoy QP.2. They then continued on to Scapa Flow.
0900	Minesweepers HAZARD and HEBE arrived at Scapa Flow from Greenock.
0900	Heavy cruiser BERWICK departed Hvalfjord for Seidisfjord with destroyers ONSLOW and OFFA.
1130	Destroyers ECLIPSE and ICARUS arrived at Scapa Flow from Kirkwall.

18 NOVEMBER 1941

	Heavy cruiser KENT arrived at Hvalfjord from a Faeroes-Iceland patrol.
	Light cruiser EDINBURGH arrived at Hvalfjord from a Denmark Strait patrol.
0730	Destroyer ANTELOPE arrived at Scapa Flow from Hvalfjord.
0900	Heavy cruiser BERWICK arrived at Seidisfjord from Hvalfjord with destroyers ONSLOW and OFFA to refuel.

19 NOVEMBER 1941

	Heavy cruiser NORFOLK departed Scapa Flow for the Faeroes - Iceland patrol and then on to Hvalfjord.
	Minelayer MENETHEUS laid Minefield SN.25A escorted by destroyer NEWARK.
0900	Destroyer ANTELOPE departed Scapa Flow for Hull to carry out a long refit.
0915	Minesweeper HAZARD departed Scapa Flow for Scrabster to embark stores and then joined the Kirkwall section of convoy PQ.5 for passage to Hvalfjord.
0930	The Kirkwall section of convoy PQ.5 departed for Hvalfjord escorted by minesweepers SHARPSHOOTER and HEBE.
1300	Heavy cruiser BERWICK departed Seidisfjord with destroyers ONSLOW and OFFA to rendezvous with con-

	voy PQ.4 and escort it to Archangel.

20 NOVEMBER 1941

	Heavy cruiser SUFFOLK arrived at Hvalfjord from a Denmark Strait patrol.
	Light cruiser SHEFFIELD departed her Faeroes - Iceland patrol for Scapa Flow after being relieved by heavy cruiser NORFOLK.
1500	Destroyers NORMAN and ICARUS departed Scapa Flow to rendezvous with destroyer FAULKNOR and battleship NELSON.

21 NOVEMBER 1941

	Light cruiser SHEFFIELD arrived at Scapa Flow from her Faeroes - Iceland patrol.
0900	Destroyer PUNJABI departed Hvalfjord for Scapa Flow.
1700	Minelaying cruiser MANXMAN departed Scapa Flow for Loch Alsh to boiler clean.

22 NOVEMBER 1941

	Destroyer SARDONYX sank anti-submarine trawler **ST APOLLO** (580grt) (T/Lt R. H. Marchington RNVR) in a collision with off the Hebrides in 59, 13N, 07, 41W. Destroyer PUNJABI, en route from Hvalfjord to Scapa Flow, was ordered to proceed to assist. On arrival, the trawler had already sunk. Destroyer PUNJABI escorted destroyer SARDONYX to Loch Ewe. At the Minches, destroyer SARDONYX continued unescorted to Loch Ewe and destroyer PUNJABI continued to Scapa Flow.
0300	Destroyers ECLIPSE and CHIDDINGFOLD departed Scapa Flow to relieve the escort for monitor EREBUS off Kinnaird Head.
0900	Battle cruiser RENOWN arrived at Scapa Flow from Rosyth. Destroyers ARROW, VIMIERA, and WALLACE were detached outside the anchorage and returned to Rosyth.
1024	Battleship RAMILLIES arrived at Scapa Flow from Liverpool escorted by destroyers VANQUISHER and WITCH.
1030	Battleship NELSON arrived off Scapa Flow with destroyers FAULKNOR, NORMAN, and ICARUS. Destroyer NORMAN was detached before entering the harbour for the Clyde, where she was to boiler clean prior to transfer to the Mediterranean.
1830	Battleship NELSON departed Scapa Flow for Rosyth escorted by destroyers FAULKNOR and ICARUS. Destroyer ECLIPSE was ordered to detach from her monitor EREBUS escort off Duncansby Head and join the battleship escort, but the destroyer was unable to proceed due to bad weather and returned to Scapa Flow.
2000	Monitor EREBUS arrived at Scapa Flow with destroyer CHIDDINGFOLD. Destroyer ECLIPSE was detached from the monitor en route to join the screen for battleship NELSON, but was unable to do so because of bad weather.
2230	Destroyer ECLIPSE returned to Scapa Flow.

23 NOVEMBER 1941

	Heavy cruiser KENT departed Hvalfjord to replace heavy cruiser NORFOLK on the Faeroes - Iceland patrol. Heavy cruiser NORFOLK then proceeded to Hvalfjord, arriving on the 24th.
1230	The Kirkwall section of convoy PQ.5 arrived at Hvalfjord escorted by three minesweepers.
1230	Monitor EREBUS departed Scapa Flow with destroyers WITCH and VANQUISHER to carry out exercises west of the Orkneys, and then she proceeded to Londonderry.
1640	Destroyers FAULKNOR and ICARUS returned to Scapa Flow from Rosyth.
1700	Destroyer PUNJABI arrived at Scapa Flow from Hvalfjord after escorting damaged destroyer SARDONYX to the Minches.

24 NOVEMBER 1941

	Free French submarine MINERVE arrived at Scapa Flow from Dundee for repairs.
	Heavy cruiser CUMBERLAND departed Hvalfjord for a Denmark Strait patrol.
1200	Destroyer PUNJABI departed Scapa Flow for the Tyne to carry out a refit.
2330	Destroyer ICARUS departed Scapa Flow for Hvalfjord to join the Commander in Chief Home Fleet.

25 NOVEMBER 1941

	Free French submarine MINERVE departed Scapa Flow for a patrol off Norway.
	Light cruiser SHEFFIELD departed Scapa Flow for Seidisfjord for escort duty with convoy PQ.5. However, she was forced to heave to in the heavy weather on the 26th and did not arrive until the 27th.
	Minesweeper FITZROY departed Scapa Flow for the Faeroes to resume minesweeping duties.

27 NOVEMBER 1941

	Battleship RESOLUTION arrived at Scapa Flow with destroyers BERKELEY and KUJAWIAK from Plymouth to begin working up to combat efficiency after her refit.
	Armed merchant cruiser CAPE SABLE arrived at Scapa Flow from Oban to work up to combat efficiency.
	Heavy cruiser SUFFOLK departed Hvalfjord for the west Denmark Strait patrol.
	Light cruiser EDINBURGH departed Hvalfjord for the north Faeroes-Iceland patrol area.
	Heavy cruiser KENT changed her position to the south Faeroes-Iceland area patrol area after the light cruiser EDINBURGH arrived.
0800	Destroyer BEAUFORT departed Scapa Flow for the Clyde to boiler clean prior to her transfer to the Mediterranean.
0830	Destroyer ICARUS arrived at Hvalfjord from Scapa Flow to join the Commander in Chief Home Fleet.
1030	Convoy PQ.5 departed Hvalfjord with steamers BRIARWOOD (4019grt), EMPIRE STEVENSON (6209grt), Russian PETROVSKI (3771grt), TREHATA (4817grt), CHUMLEIGH (5445grt), Russian KOMILES (3962grt), and ST CLEARS (4312grt) escorted by minesweepers SHARPSHOOTER, HAZARD, and HEBE. Light cruiser SHEFFIELD departed Seidisfjord early on the 30th and joined the convoy in 70, 20N, 05, 00W. The light cruiser continued with the convoy to 7 December, when she was detached from the convoy to Murmansk. Minesweepers HAZARD and HEBE were detached from the convoy on 7 December with light cruiser SHEFFIELD and proceeded to Murmansk, arriving on 8 December. Minesweepers BRAMBLE and SEAGULL departed Murmansk on 5 December and joined the convoy on 7 December. They escorted the convoy with minesweeper SHARPSHOOTER to its arrival at Archangel on 13 December.
1800	Destroyer BRIGHTON departed Scapa Flow upon the completion of docking and repairs to rendezvous with convoy DS.17 in position 16½ miles 192° from Skerryvore.
2100	Destroyer MONTROSE departed Scapa Flow to rejoin the NORE Command after she worked up to combat efficiency. The destroyer was to provide additional escort for convoy FS.659 en route.
2200	Destroyer MONTROSE was ordered to investigate an RDF contact to the east of the Orkneys. She found fishing trawler PORT ARTHUR at that location.

28 NOVEMBER 1941

	Light cruiser EDINBURGH departed the Faeroes - Iceland patrol for Scapa Flow, where she arrived on the 29th.
	Heavy cruiser CUMBERLAND departed her Denmark Strait patrol for Hvalfjord after being relieved by heavy cruiser SUFFOLK. She arrived later that day.
	Minelayer MENETHEUS laid Minefield SN.25B escorted by destroyer LANCASTER.
0530	Destroyer INGLEFIELD arrived at Scapa Flow from the Humber following her refit.
1400	Battleship KING GEORGE V, aircraft carrier VICTORIOUS, plus heavy cruiser NORFOLK departed Hvalfjord for Scapa Flow with destroyers ASHANTI, TARTAR, ESKIMO, SOMALI, MATABELE, ECHO, and ESCAPADE.

29 NOVEMBER 1941

	Heavy cruiser KENT departed the Faeroes - Iceland patrol for Scapa Flow, where she arrived on the 30th.
0930	Destroyers FURY and FORESIGHT arrived at Scapa Flow from Londonderry to join the Home Fleet.
1000	Destroyer CHIDDINGFOLD departed Scapa Flow to join Floating Dock XIV on passage up the east coast in tow of tug EMPIRE LARCH (487grt) and escorted by trawlers SCALBY WYKE and PRESTON NORTH END. Destroyer CHIDDINGFOLD arrived back at Scapa Flow on the 30th.
1400	Destroyer INGLEFIELD departed Scapa Flow for Scrabster to embark Rear Admiral Destroyers Home Fleet and his staff for passage to Scapa Flow.
1730	Destroyer INGLEFIELD returned to Scapa Flow from Scrabster with Rear Admiral Destroyers Home Fleet and his staff.

30 NOVEMBER 1941

	Light cruiser SHEFFIELD departed Seidisfjord early in the morning and joined convoy PQ.5 in 70, 20N, 05, 00W.
	Armed merchant cruiser CITY OF DURBAN arrived at Scapa Flow from the NORE Command to work up to combat efficiency.
1130	Destroyer FORESTER arrived at Scapa Flow from Londonderry to join the Home Fleet.
1200	Battleship KING GEORGE V, aircraft carrier VICTORIOUS, plus heavy cruiser NORFOLK arrived at Scapa Flow from Hvalfjord with destroyers ASHANTI, TARTAR, ESKIMO, SOMALI, MATABELE, ECHO, and ESCAPADE.

Norwegian Sea

Long. E03, 00 – E20, 00   Lat. N68, 00 – N58, 30

4 NOVEMBER 1941

	Submarine UMBRA began an unsuccessful patrol off Utvaer, Norway until 4 December.
	Submarine TUNA began an unsuccessful patrol off Vestfjord, Norway until 4 December.
	Free French submarine RUBIS began an unsuccessful patrol off Norway until 4 December.

14 NOVEMBER 1941

	Submarine P.35 departed her patrol zone off Norway to return to Dundee, Scotland.

East of Canada

Long. W70, 00 – W30, 00   Lat. N68, 00 – N43, 30

1 NOVEMBER 1941

	American destroyers DALLAS (DD-199), ELLIS (DD-154) and EBERLE (DD-430) dropped depth charges on submarine contacts while escorting convoy HX.157 east of Newfoundland.
	U.569, U.123, U.38, U.82, U.202, U.84, U.203, U.93 and U.85 plus U.74 and U.106 formed Wolfpack RAUBRITTER east of Belle Isle Strait to attack convoy SC.52.
	U.374 (ObltzS v. Fischel) spotted convoy SC.52 east of Newfoundland and radioed her position to the waiting Wolfpack.
	Convoy ON.28 picked up its local Canadian escort at the WESTOMP, where American Task Unit TU.4.1.1 was detached from the convoy.

2 NOVEMBER 1941

0526 0717	U.208 (ObltzS Schlieper) heavily damaged steamer **LARPOOL** (3872grt) (Master Charles Patton) as she was straggling behind convoy ON.27 about 250 miles east, southeast of Cape Race. U.208 sank the steamer with two additional torpedoes. Twenty-two crewmen and four gunners were lost plus four crewmen died of wounds. The master and five crewmen landed their lifeboat at Burin, Newfoundland on 10 November. Canadian corvette BITTERSWEET (Lt Cdr J. A. Woods) rescued eleven survivors and landed them at Halifax.

3 NOVEMBER 1941

	American destroyer UPSHUR (DD-144) dropped depth charges on a submarine contact near convoy HX.157.
	Early in the day, U.123 (Kptlt Hardegen) spotted convoy SC.52 east of Newfoundland and radioed its position to U.38, U.569, U.82 and U.202.
	Convoy HX.158 departed Halifax escorted by destroyer ANNAPOLIS plus corvettes ALGOMA, CHAMBLY, ORILLIA, and PICTOU. American Task Unit TU.4.1.8 with destroyers BUCK (DD-420), COLE (DD-155), LUDLOW (DD-438), MCCORMICK (DD-223), and SWANSON (DD-443) relieved the escorts on the 5th. Destroyer COLE (DD-155) was detached from the convoy the next day. Destroyers BEAGLE and ROXBOROUGH, sloop COMMANDANT DETROYAT, corvettes HEATHER, LOBELIA, and NARCISSUS, plus anti-submarine trawlers ARAB, KIRKELLA, LADY MADELEINE, NORWICH CITY, and STELLA CARINA relieved the American destroyers on the 13th. The trawlers, less KIRKELLA, were detached from the convoy later that day. The escorts, less KIRKELLA, were detached from the convoy on the 17th. The convoy arrived at Liverpool on the 18th.
0454 0458 0505	U.202 (Hans-Heinz Linder) sank steamer **FLYNDERBORG** (2022grt) (ex Danish) (Master P. Petersen) while attacking convoy SC.52 northeast of Notre Dame Bay, Newfoundland in 51, 21N, 51, 45W. Three crewmen were lost and Canadian corvette WINDFLOWER (Lt John Price) rescued the master, eighteen crewmen and two gunners and landed them at St. John's.
0454 0458 0505	U.202 (Hans-Heinz Linder) sank steamer **GRETAVALE** (4586grt) (Master Frank S. Passmore) while attacking convoy SC.52 northeast of Notre Dame Bay, Newfoundland in 51, 21N, 51, 45W. The master, thirty-one crewmen and six gunners were lost. Canadian corvette WINDFLOWER rescued six crewmen and landed them at St. John's.
1828	U.203 (Kptlt Mützelburg) sank steamer **EMPIRE GEMSBUCK** (5626grt) (ex American **SAN FILIPE** (5626grt)) (Master William Stewart Anderson) while attacking convoy SC.52 northeast of Cape Charles in 52, 18N, 53, 05W. Canadian corvette BUCTOUCHE (Lt G. N. Downey) rescued the master, thirty-six crewmen and six gunners and landed them at St. John's, Newfoundland on 6 November.
1828	U.203 sank steamer **EVEROJA** (4830grt) (ex Latvian) (Master Alfred Kirschfeloths) while attacking convoy SC.52 about eighty miles 77° from Belle Isle. Corvette NASTURTIUM (Lt Cdr R. C. Freaker DSO) rescued the master, forty crewmen and five gunners and landed them at St. John's, Newfoundland.

4 NOVEMBER 1941

Steamer **EMPIRE ENERGY** (6584grt) (ex Italian **GABBIANO** (6584grt)) became stranded and lost off Nova Scotia.

Convoy SC.53 departed Sydney, Cape Breton, escorted by corvettes BATTLEFORD, DUNVEGAN, and SOREL.
Corvettes DUNVEGAN and SOREL were detached from the convoy on the 6th when relieved by destroyer BURNHAM with corvettes ALGOMA, ARVIDA, CHAMBLY, DAUPHIN, and MATAPEDIA.
American destroyer DALE (DD-353) was with the convoy on 10 to 12 November.
Corvettes ALGOMA and BATTLEFORD were detached from the convoy on the 11th.
Destroyer BURNHAM and the remaining corvettes were detached from the convoy on the 20th when relieved by destroyers CALDWELL, VANOC, and VOLUNTEER with corvettes HIBISCUS, PERIWINKLE, and SWEETBRIAR.
The convoy arrived at Liverpool on the 24th.

5 NOVEMBER 1941

Panamanian steamer MONTROSE damaged American Naval tanker LARAMIE (AO-16) in a collision in Tunugdliark Fjord, Narsarssuak, Greenland.

Escort Group EG.14 with destroyer OTTAWA plus corvettes ALGOMA, ARVIDA, DAUPHIN and ORILLIA joined convoy SC.53 at the WESTOMP.
Destroyer BURNHAM with corvettes CHAMBLY, MATAPEDIA and NEPANCE later reinforced the convoy escort after ULTRA message intercepts indicated that a German patrol line was near the convoy.

6 NOVEMBER 1941

American destroyer MADISON (DD-425), part of Task Unit TU.4.1.2 escorting convoy ON.39, dropped depth charges on a submarine contact east of Newfoundland.

7 NOVEMBER 1941

While escorting convoy ON.39, American destroyers LANSDALE (DD-426), CHARLES F. HUGHES (DD-428) and GLEAVES (DD-423) dropped depth charges on submarine contacts east of Newfoundland.

2234	While returning to France, U.74 (Kptlt Kentrat) missed steamer **NOTTINGHAM** (8532grt) (Master Francis Cecil Pretty OBE DSC) with two torpedoes while she was sailing alone on her maiden voyage about 550 miles southeast of Cape Farewell in 53, 24N, 31, 51W.
2250	U.74 hit the steamer and the crew abandoned ship.
2259	U.74 sank the steamer with one last torpedo. The master, fifty-five crewmen and six gunners were never found.

8 NOVEMBER 1941

U.123, U.38, U.577, U.106, U.571, U.133, U.82 and U.85 formed Wolfpack RAUBRITTER southeast of Greenland.

Convoy HX.159 departed Halifax with thirty-one ships escorted by destroyer ANNAPOLIS plus corvettes KAMLOOPS and SASKATOON.
On the 10th, American Task Unit TU.4.1.4 from Argentia, Newfoundland with destroyers BADGER (DD-126), COLE (DD-155), DECATUR (DD-341), LIVERMORE (DD-429), and PLUNKETT (DD-431) relieved the Halifax escort group.
On the 18th, destroyer SABRE, corvettes ALISMA and SUNFLOWER, and American Coast Guard cutter CAMPBELL (WPG-32) joined the convoy. CAMPBELL (WPG-32) was the first coast guard cutter to join a convoy escort.
On the 19th, destroyer ROCKINGHAM and corvette KINGCUP joined the convoy and relieved the American destroyers.
The American Coast Guard cutter CAMPBELL (WPG-32) and corvette SUNFLOWER were detached from the convoy on the 22nd.
Anti-submarine trawlers LADY ELSA, LE TIGRE, and WELLARD escorted the convoy in Home Waters.
The convoy arrived at Liverpool on the 23rd.

10 NOVEMBER 1941

Allied convoy WS.12X departed Halifax with the British troops delivered in convoy CT.5/7 in American transports MOUNT VERNON (AP-22), LEONARD WOOD (AP-25), JOSEPH T. DICKMAN (AP-26), ORIZABA (AP-24), WEST POINT (AP-23), and WAKEFIELD (AP-21) escorted by American aircraft carrier RANGER (CV-4) (Flag Rear Admiral Arthur Cook; Harrill), heavy cruisers QUINCY (CA-39) (Battle) and VINCENNES (CA-44) (Riefkohl), and Destroyer Squadron 8 with destroyers WAINWRIGHT (DD-419) and MOFFETT (DD-362), Destroyer Division 17 with destroyers MCDOUGAL (DD-358) and WINSLOW (DD-359), and Destroyer Division 16 with destroyers MAYRANT (DD-402), RHIND (DD-404), ROWAN (DD-405), and TRIPPE (DD-403).
Oiler CIMARRON (AO-22) joined the convoy on the 19th at Trinidad.
Aircraft carrier RANGER (CV-4) was detached from the convoy in 17S, 20W and returned to Trinidad escorted

by destroyers TRIPPE (DD-403) and RHIND (DD-404).

Heavy cruiser QUINCY (CA-39) (Battle) relieved Rear Admiral Cook on aircraft carrier RANGER (CV-4) as force commander.

The convoy arrived at Cape Town on 9 December. The original destination was Basra, but the convoy was ordered to Singapore, via Bombay.

The American escorts were detached from the convoy at Cape Town.

The convoy sailed on 13 December escorted by heavy cruiser DORSETSHIRE.

The American destroyers were employed for a local anti-submarine screen to 14 December and arrived back at Cape Town on 15 December.

On 16 December, heavy cruisers QUINCY (CA-39) and VINCENNES (CA-44) and destroyers MACDOUGAL (DD-358), MAYRANT (DD-402), WINSLOW (DD-359), ROWAN (DD-405), WAINWRIGHT (DD-419), and MOFFET (DD-362) departed Cape Town for the Caribbean.

On 21 December, light cruiser CERES joined the convoy and took troopship ORIZABA (AP-24) to Mombasa.

The convoy arrived at Bombay on 27 December.

American troopship MOUNT VERNON (AP-22) was detached from the convoy to join light cruiser COLOMBO on 23 December, but the rendezvous was not kept so she proceeded to Mombasa alone to join convoy DM.1.

American destroyer ERICSSON (DD-440) dropped depth charges on a submarine contact while escorting convoy HX.157 east of Newfoundland.

Convoy SC.54 departed Sydney, CB, escorted by corvettes BATTLEFORD, DRUMHELLER, DUNVEGAN, SOREL, and SUMMERSIDE, plus minesweeper NIPIGON.

Destroyers COLUMBIA and SKEENA plus corvettes ACONIT, BRANDON, CAMROSE, MIMOSA, SHEDIAC, and WETASKIWIN relieved the Sydney corvettes on the 12th.

Destroyers BROKE and WOLVERINE with corvettes BEGONIA, EGLANTINE, LARKSPUR, and MONTBRETIA relieved destroyers COLUMBIA and SKEENA plus corvettes ACONIT, MIMOSA, SHEDIAC, and WETASKIWIN on the 22nd.

Corvette BRANDON was detached from the convoy on the 25th and the convoy arrived at Liverpool on the 26th.

11 NOVEMBER 1941

American destroyer DECATUR (DD-341) dropped depth charges on a submarine contact while escorting convoy HX.159.

2335 — U.561 (Robert Bartels) sank Panamanian steamer **MERIDIAN** (5592grt) (ex Italian **DINO** (5592grt)) while she was straggling behind convoy SC.53 in the North Atlantic in 52, 50N, 33, 20W. The entire crew of twenty-six were lost. Canadian corvette CHAMBLY was the last ship to see the **MERIDIAN** before she disappeared from the convoy at 1730 on 11 November.

12 NOVEMBER 1941

While escorting convoy HX.159, American destroyers DECATUR (DD-341) and BADGER (DD-126) dropped depth charges on submarine contacts. American destroyer LIVERMORE (DD-429) and Coast Guard cutter CAMPBELL (WPG-32) investigated a sound contact near the convoy.

13 NOVEMBER 1941

American destroyer DECATUR (DD-341) dropped depth charges on submarine contacts while escorting convoy HX.159.

Convoy SC.54 departed St John's escorted by destroyer BURNHAM plus corvettes ALGOMA, CHAMBLY, MATAPEDIA, and NAPANEE.

Canadian troop convoy TC 15 departed Halifax with troopships ANDES (25,689grt), CHRISTIAAN HUYGENS (16,287grt), DUCHESS OF ATHOLL (20,119grt), DURBAN CASTLE (17,388grt), ORCADES (23,456grt), ORONSAY (20,043grt), REINA DEL PACIFICO (17,702grt), SOBIESKI (11,030grt), and WARWICK CASTLE (20,107grt).

The convoy escort joined on the 13th and included American battleship NEW MEXICO (BB-40), light cruisers PHILADELPHIA (CL-41) and SAVANNAH (CL-42), plus and destroyers MORRIS (DD-417), SIMS (DD-409), HUGHES (DD-410), MUSTIN (DD-413), RUSSELL (DD-414), WALKE (DD-416), and O'BRIEN (DD-415).

On the 18th, destroyers HIGHLANDER (SO), HARVESTER, HAVELOCK, HESPERUS, WESTCOTT, and BLANKNEY, which had been escorting convoy CT.6, joined the convoy and provided escort until it arrived on the 21st.

14 NOVEMBER 1941

U.561 (Robert Bartels) sank Panamanian steamer **CRUSADER** (2939grt) (ex Danish **BROSUND** (2939grt)) as she was straggling behind convoy SC.53 in the North Atlantic in 49, 30N, 37, 15W. She failed to join the convoy off Newfoundland and was reported missing. There were no survivors.

15 NOVEMBER 1941

Convoy HX.160 departed Halifax escorted by destroyers ANNAPOLIS and HAMILTON.

On the 17th, American destroyers BABBITT (DD-128), LEARY (DD-158), MAYO (DD-422), NICHOLSON (DD-442), and SCHENCK (DD-159) relieved the Halifax destroyers.

In heavy seas, the American destroyers all sustain storm damage.

On the 25th, destroyers SARDONYX, SCIMITAR, and WATCHMAN plus corvettes DAHLIA and MONKSHOOD relieved the American destroyers at the MOMP.

Corvette MONTBRETIA joined the convoy on the 26th.

Anti-submarine trawlers HUGH WALPOLE, NORTHERN PRIDE, and NORTHERN SPRAY escorted the convoy in Home Waters.

Corvette MONTBRETIA was detached from the convoy on the 28th and the destroyers plus corvettes DAHLIA and MONKSHOOD were detached from the convoy on the 29th.

Anti-submarine trawler KIRKELLA escorted the convoy into Liverpool on the 30th.

16 NOVEMBER 1941

American Task Unit TU.4.1.5 with destroyers BABBITT (DD-128), LEARY (DD-158), MAYO (DD-422), NICHOLSON (DD-442), and SCHENCK (DD-159) departed Argentia, Newfoundland to join convoy HX.160.

American tugboat **TURECAMO BOYS** was lost in the North Atlantic to an unknown cause.

Convoy SC.55 departed Sydney, CB, escorted by corvettes BATTLEFORD, DRUMHELLER, and SUMMERSIDE plus minesweeper NIPIGON.

Corvettes DUNVEGAN, KENOGAMI, LETHBRIDGE, and PRESCOTT joined the convoy on the 18th.

On the 19th, destroyer ST FRANCIS with corvettes MAYFLOWER, NANAIMO, and SOREL replaced the Sydney corvettes.

Destroyer ST FRANCIS was detached from the convoy on the 25th, corvettes DUNVEGAN, PRESCOTT, and SOREL were detached from the convoy on the 28th, and corvettes KENOGAMI and LETHBRIDGE were detached from the convoy on the 29th.

On the 28th, destroyer AMAZON joined the convoy; on the 29th, destroyer FOXHOUND joined the convoy, and on the 30th, corvettes HEARTSEASE and ROSELYS, plus anti-submarine trawlers AYRSHIRE and NOTTS COUNTY joined the convoy.

Corvettes MAYFLOWER and NANAIMO were detached from the convoy on 1 December, destroyer AMAZON was detached from the convoy on 3 December, and corvette HEARTSEASE with trawlers AYRSHIRE and NOTTS COUNTY were detached from the convoy on 4 December.

Anti-submarine trawler ST CATHAN joined the escort on 4 December and arrived with the convoy at Liverpool on 5 December.

17 NOVEMBER 1941

American destroyers EDISON (DD-439) and BENSON (DD-421) dropped depth charges on submarine contacts while escorting convoy ON.34.

19 NOVEMBER 1941

Wolfpack STEUGEN formed west of Newfoundland with U.105, U.434, U.574, U.372, U.43 and U.575.

21 NOVEMBER 1941

Convoy HX.161 departed Halifax escorted by destroyers ANNAPOLIS and HAMILTON.

The destroyers were relieved on the 23rd by American destroyers BERNADOU (DD-153), DUPONT (DD-152), LEA (DD-118), MACLEISH (DD-220), ROE (DD-418), and WOOLSEY (DD-437).

Corvettes ANEMONE, THYME, and VERONICA joined the convoy on 2 December.

On the 24th, destroyer DUPONT (DD-152) was damaged in a collision with Norwegian tanker THORSHOVDI (9944grt).

On 3 December, destroyers DOUGLAS, LEAMINGTON, and VETERAN relieved the American destroyers.

Destroyer LEAMINGTON with corvettes ANEMONE and THYME were detached from the convoy on 5 December.

Anti-submarine trawler KIRKELLA joined the convoy on 6 December and escorted the convoy into Liverpool.

22 NOVEMBER 1941

Convoy SC.56 departed Sydney, CB, escorted by corvettes DRUMHELLER, and SUMMERSIDE plus minesweepers GEORGIAN and THUNDER.

On the 24th destroyer RESTIGOUCHE with corvettes AGASSIZ, ALYSSE, AMHERST, BITTERSWEET, CHICOUTIMI, MORDEN, and ORILLIA joined the convoy and relieved corvettes DRUMHELLER and SUMMERSIDE from the escort.

Corvette ALYSSE was detached from the convoy on 4 December, destroyer RESTIGOUCHE while corvettes AGASSIZ, AMHERST, CHICOUTIMI, MORDEN, and ORILLIA were detached from the convoy on 5 December.

Sloop COMMANDANT DETROYAT joined the convoy on 5 December while destroyers BEAGLE and MONTGOMERY, corvettes HEATHER, LOBELIA, and NARCISSUS, plus anti-submarine trawler LADY MADELEINE joined the convoy on 6 December.

Destroyer MONTGOMERY was detached from the convoy on 8 December and the rest of the escorts were detached from the convoy on 9 December before the convoy arrived at Liverpool on 10 December.

23 NOVEMBER 1941

American Task Unit TU.4.1.6 joined convoy HX.161 as escort to the MOMP.

24 NOVEMBER 1941

Norwegian tanker THORSHOVDI (9944grt) damaged American destroyer DUPONT (DD-152) in a collision while at sea with convoy HX.161.

27 NOVEMBER 1941

American destroyer BABBITT (DD-128) dropped depth charges on a submarine contact while escorting convoy HX.160.

Convoy HX.162 departed Halifax escorted by destroyers ANNAPOLIS and HAMILTON plus corvette COBALT. The escorts were detached from the convoy on the 29th when relieved by American destroyers CHARLES F. HUGHES (DD-428), LANSDALE (DD-426), MADISON (DD-425), STURTEVANT (DD-240), and WICKES (DD-441).

Destroyers CALDWELL and VANOC plus corvettes CALENDULA, GENTIAN, and HONEYSUCKLE relieved the American group on 7 December.

These escorts, except for destroyer CALDWELL, were detached from the convoy on 10 December. Destroyer CALDWELL arrived at Liverpool with the convoy on 11 December.

28 NOVEMBER 1941

Convoy SC.57 departed Sydney, CB, escorted by corvettes BATTLEFORD, KAMSACK, and SHAWNIGAN, plus minesweeper NIPIGON.

Corvettes KAMSACK, and SHAWNIGAN plus minesweeper NIPIGON were detached from the convoy on the 30th when relieved by corvettes ARVIDA, FENNEL, POLYANTHUS, PRIMROSE, SHERBROOKE, and TRAIL.

Corvette FENNEL was detached from the convoy on 1 December when destroyer OTTAWA joined the escort.

Corvettes ALISMA, KINGCUP, and SUNFLOWER with anti-submarine trawlers LADY ELSA and LE TIGRE joined the convoy on 9 December.

Destroyer OTTAWA plus corvettes ARVIDA, BATTLEFORD, POLYANTHUS, PRIMROSE, SHERBROOKE, and TRAIL were detached from the convoy on 9 December.

Destroyers SABRE and SKATE joined the convoy on 10 December.

Destroyers SABRE and SKATE, corvettes ALISMA, KINGCUP, and SUNFLOWER, and the trawlers were detached from the convoy on 13 December. The convoy arrived at Liverpool on 15 December.

29 NOVEMBER 1941

American Task Unit TU.4.1.2 joined convoy HX.162 with its thirty-five ships east of Newfoundland.

American Naval salvage vessel REDWING (ARS-4) supported Task Unit TU.4.1.2 escorting convoy HX.162.

American fleet tanker SAPELO (AO-11) supported Task Unit TU.4.1.3.

American destroyer WOOLSEY (DD-437) dropped depth charges on a submarine contact while escorting convoy HX.161 south of Greenland.

East of United States   Long. W85, 00 – W60,00   Lat. N43, 30 – N25, 00

1 NOVEMBER 1941

Lt A. C. Wilkinson with Leading Airman A. G. Gilbert and Leading Airman N. C. Moulden of light cruiser NEWCASTLE were killed when their Walrus aircraft of 700 Squadron crashed three and a half miles west of Bermuda while they were on a dive bombing exercise.

21 NOVEMBER 1941

American battleship INDIANA (BB-58) was launched.

Caribbean and Gulf of Mexico   Long. W100, 00 – W60, 00   Lat. N31, 00 – N05, 00

3 NOVEMBER 1941

Aircraft carrier INDOMITABLE ran aground off Kingston, Jamaica. Corvette CLARKIA, escorting the aircraft carrier, also ran aground. The damaged aircraft carrier arrived at Norfolk, Virginia on the 12th and departed fully repaired on 12 December.

4 NOVEMBER 1941

Naval oiler OLWEN (6394grt) sent out a Raider Warning after sighting German AMC SCHIFF.45/KOMET on its way to France.

American Task Group TG.3.6 with light cruiser MILWAUKEE (CL-5) and destroyer WARRINGTON (DD-383)

were en route to Yorktown, Virginia from San Juan, Puerto Rica and were too far from the contact area to intercept the raider.
American Task Group TG.3.7 with cruiser MEMPHIS (CL-13) plus destroyers DAVIS (DD-395) and JOUETT (DD-396) were returning from an escort mission to Lagos, Nigeria, and coordinated with Task Group TG.3.5 with light cruiser OMAHA (CL-4) and destroyer SOMERS (DD-381) to intercept.

17 NOVEMBER 1941

American Task Group TG.3.5 with light cruiser OMAHA (CL-4) and destroyer SOMERS (DD-381) arrived at San Juan, Puerto Rico with captured German steamer **ODENWALD** (5098grt).

25 NOVEMBER 1941

Canadian tanker **PROTEUS** (10,653grt) foundered in the Caribbean.

Western Approaches
Long. W30, 00 – W03, 00   Lat. N58, 30 – N49, 00

1 NOVEMBER 1941

	Convoy HX.156 reached the MOMP, where Escort Group EG.6 took over its escort into Britain.
	U.552 and U.567 made unsuccessful attacks on convoy HX.156, both claiming damage to steamers.
	Aircraft carrier ARGUS and aircraft transport ATHENE departed the Clyde ferrying aircraft to Gibraltar, escorted by destroyers LAFOREY, HIGHLANDER, HAVELOCK, and HARVESTER.
	Convoy ON.32 departed Liverpool escorted by New Zealand trawler MOA. The MOA was en route to the Pacific. Destroyers DOUGLAS, LEAMINGTON, and SKATE plus corvettes ABELIA and ANEMONE joined the convoy on the 2nd. On the 6th, the 2 November escorts were detached from the convoy when destroyers RESTIGOUCHE and ST CROIX plus corvettes AGASSIZ, ALBERNI, ALYSSE, AMHERST, and BITTERSWEET joined the convoy. Destroyer RESTIGOUCHE was detached from the convoy on the 13th and the rest of the escort, less trawler MOA, was detached from the convoy on the 14th. The convoy arrived at Halifax on the 16th.
	Trawler CANNING (148grt) damaged destroyer CHELSEA in a collision at Liverpool. The destroyer sustained only minor damage and spent no time out of service.
1100	Destroyer BEAUFORT departed Liverpool for the Clyde, carrying out speed trials en route.
2240	Destroyer BEAUFORT arrived at the Clyde from Liverpool.

2 NOVEMBER 1941

	A Swordfish aircraft of 818 Squadron from aircraft carrier ARGUS ditched at sea and destroyer LAFOREY rescued the pilot, Lt A. S. Campbell, and crew.
	German bombing sank fishing trawler **CALIPH** (226grt) eleven miles south of Old Head of Kinsale. One crewman died of wounds.
	A German aerial mine sank hopper barge **FOREMOST 45** (824grt) in 51, 21, 10N, 06W. One crewman was lost.

3 NOVEMBER 1941

	Convoy ON.33 departed Liverpool. Destroyers BEAGLE and ROXBOROUGH, sloop COMMANDANT DETROYAT, corvettes HEATHER, LOBELIA, and NARCISSUS, plus anti-submarine trawlers ARAB, LADY MADELEINE, NORWICH CITY, and STELLA CARINA joined the convoy on the 4th. Destroyer ROXBOROUGH was detached from the convoy on the 8th and destroyer BEAGLE and the trawlers, less LADY MADELEINE, were detached from the convoy on the 9th. Destroyer ST LAURENT with corvettes SNOWBERRY and TRAIL joined the convoy on the 10th. On the 11th, the sloop, the corvettes, and trawler LADY MADELEINE were detached from the convoy when corvettes CHILLIWACK, COLLINGWOOD, and PRIMROSE joined the convoy. Destroyer ST LAURENT was detached from the convoy on the 13th. Corvette POLYANTHUS joined the convoy on the 16th and was detached from the convoy the next day. Corvette COLLINGWOOD was detached from the convoy on the 17th, TRAIL was detached from the convoy on the 18th, CHILLIWACK was detached from the convoy on the 19th, and SNOWBERRY was detached from the convoy on the 21st. Corvette PRIMROSE was detached from the convoy on the 22nd when the convoy was dispersed.
0730	Destroyer SOUTHWOLD arrived at the Clyde from Scapa Flow for boiler cleaning.

4 NOVEMBER 1941

	Escort Group EG.8 joined convoy SC.51 at the MOMP.
	A German aerial mine sank Dutch motor vessel **MADJOE** (249grt) in 51, 34, 38N, 03, 50, 30W. The crew of

	four, two gunners, and the pilot were all lost.
1245	Destroyer WHEATLAND departed the Clyde for Scapa Flow to work up to combat efficiency.
2300	Minelaying cruisers MANXMAN and WELSHMAN departed Loch Alsh for Scapa Flow.

6 NOVEMBER 1941

	Light cruiser TRINIDAD departed the Clyde for Scapa Flow.
1630	Destroyer BEAUFORT departed the Clyde for Scapa Flow.
<1659	Destroyers ONSLOW, IMPULSIVE, and ANTELOPE arrived at Londonderry from Scapa Flow.
1700	Destroyers ONSLOW, IMPULSIVE, and ANTELOPE departed Londonderry to join battleship RODNEY in 55, 40N, 17, 45W and relieve her escorting destroyers HIGHLANDER, HAVELOCK, and HARVESTER.

7 NOVEMBER 1941

	Convoy ON.34 departed Liverpool escorted by destroyers CALDWELL, VANOC, and VOLUNTEER plus corvettes ACANTHUS, GENTIAN, HIBISCUS, HONEYSUCKLE, MYOSOTIS, and SWEETBRIAR. Corvettes CHICOUTIMI and SHERBROOKE joined the convoy on the 8th and SHERBROOKE was detached from the convoy later that day. Corvettes HIBISCUS, PERIWINKLE, and SWEETBRIAR were detached from the convoy on the 10th. The remainder of the escort was detached from the convoy on the 12th when American destroyers BENSON (DD-421), EDISON (DD-439), HILARY P. JONES (DD-427), NIBLACK (DD-424), and TARBELL (DD-142) joined the convoy. The convoy was dispersed on the 21st and the American escort was detached.
	Convoy OS.11 departed Liverpool. Destroyer CLARE with sloops ABERDEEN, ENCHANTRESS, IBIS, and STORK joined the convoy on the 8th. The destroyer was detached from the convoy on the 25th, sloops ABERDEEN, ENCHANTRESS, and IBIS were detached from the convoy on the 26th, and STORK was detached from the convoy on the 16th. Corvettes COLTSFOOT and ORCHIS plus escort vessel WALNEY also joined the convoy on the 8th. Corvette COLTSFOOT was detached from the convoy on the 12th, escort vessel WALNEY was detached from the convoy on the 25th, and corvette ORCHIS arrived with the convoy on the 28th. On the 10th, escort vessel HARTLAND joined the convoy and was detached from the convoy on the 25th. On the 24th, destroyer BRILLIANT, corvettes BERGAMOT, CROCUS, and NIGELLA, and anti-submarine whaler SOUTHERN PRIDE joined the convoy and arrived with it at Freetown on the 28th.
1200	Destroyers ONSLOW, IMPULSIVE, and ANTELOPE joined battleship RODNEY in 55N, 12W and relieved escorting destroyers HIGHLANDER, HAVELOCK, and HARVESTER. The RODNEY then continued to Loch Ewe to refuel.
1700	Destroyer MONTROSE arrived at Loch Alsh from Scapa Flow to support mining missions under Rear Admiral Minelaying.

8 NOVEMBER 1941

0800	Rear Admiral Minelaying departed Loch Alsh to lay Minefield SN.83B.
0815	Destroyers ONSLOW, IMPULSIVE, and ANTELOPE arrived at Loch Ewe with battleship RODNEY.
0850	Destroyer HURWORTH arrived at Loch Ewe from Scapa Flow carrying sixty bags of mail for battleship RODNEY and her destroyer screen.
1050	Destroyer HURWORTH departed Loch Ewe for Scapa Flow. She carried out gunnery practice off the Orkneys on the return passage.
1600	After refuelling, battleship RODNEY departed Loch Ewe with destroyers ONSLOW, IMPULSIVE, and ANTELOPE to patrol the Iceland/Faeroes passage.

9 NOVEMBER 1941

	Convoy ON.35 departed Liverpool. The convoy was joined on the 10th by destroyers KEPPEL, ROCKINGHAM, and VENOMOUS, corvettes ALISMA, SHERBROOKE, and SUNFLOWER, with anti-submarine trawlers BUTTERMERE, LADY ELSA, THIRLMERE and WELLARD. Destroyers KEPPEL and VENOMOUS were detached from the convoy on the 12th. American destroyers DALLAS (DD-199), EBERLE (DD-430), ELLIS (DD-154), ERICSSON (DD-440), and UPSHUR (DD-144) relieved the rest of the escort on the 15th. The convoy dispersed on the 27th and the American destroyers were detached.
0700	Minelayers MENETHEUS and PORT QUEBEC returned to Loch Alsh after laying Minefield SN.83B escorted by destroyers BRIGHTON, NEWARK, and CHARLESTOWN.

11 NOVEMBER 1941

	German bombing damaged Minesweeper BLYTH off Dartmouth. The damage required sixteen days to repair.
	A/Leading Airman S. H. Tyson of 1 SFTS Netheravon was killed when his Battle aircraft crashed at Shrewton

	LG.
0012	Minesweeper SHARPSHOOTER departed Cardiff for Scapa Flow.
1215	Destroyer MAORI arrived at the Clyde from Scapa Flow.

12 NOVEMBER 1941

	American Task Unit TU.4.1.3 joined convoy ON.34 at the MOMP.
	American destroyer EDISON (DD-439) dropped depth charges on a submarine contact while escorting convoy ON.34.
	Convoy WS.12Z departed Liverpool and the Clyde to rendezvous off Oversay on the 13th with steamers ADRASTUS (7905grt), EMPIRE STAR (11,093grt), SUSSEX (13,647grt), MATAROA (12,390grt), DUCHESS OF BEDFORD (20,123grt), EMPRESS OF ASIA (16,909grt), NARKUNDA (16,632grt), EMPRESS OF JAPAN (26,032grt), AORANGI (17,491grt), ARUNDEL CASTLE (19,118grt), ORDUNA (15,507grt), MONARCH OF BERMUDA (22,424grt), CAPETOWN CASTLE (27,000grt), DEUCALION (7516grt), ABBEKERK (7906grt), and RIMUTAKA (16,576grt). Destroyers WHITEHALL, WITCH, BADSWORTH, VANQUISHER, and EXMOOR escorted the convoy from 13 to 16 November. Destroyer MAORI was with the convoy from 13 to 17 November. She arrived at Gibraltar on the 20th for duty in the 19th Destroyer Flotilla. Battleship ROYAL SOVEREIGN departed the Clyde with destroyers FURY, FORESTER, and FORESIGHT on the 12th to join the convoy. They were routed via Milford Haven and south of Ireland. On the 13th, the warships arrived at Milford Haven and departed later that day to join the convoy. Destroyers FURY, FORESIGHT, and FORESTER escorted the convoy from 16 to 19 November. On the 19th, destroyers FORESIGHT, FORESTER, and FURY parted company with the convoy in 34, 05N, 25, 50W to refuel from oiler DINGLEDALE (8145grt). The destroyers then proceeded to search for an enemy merchant ship reported to be in the area. DINGLEDALE arrived back at Gibraltar on the 25th, escorted by corvettes JONQUIL and COREOPSIS. Destroyer FORESTER later proceeded to Ponta Delgada to complete refuelling. She departed on the 22nd and rejoined destroyers FORESIGHT and FURY. Battleship ROYAL SOVEREIGN with destroyers DULVERTON and SOUTHWOLD escorted the convoy from 16 to 24 November. Destroyers VIMY and VELOX escorted the convoy from 21 to 24 November. Corvette CLOVER escorted the convoy from 22 to 24 November when the convoy arrived at Freetown. On the 24th, the convoy departed Freetown with SUSSEX, ADRASTUS, EMPIRE STAR, DUCHESS OF BEDFORD, EMPRESS OF ASIA, MATAROA, NARKUNDA, EMPRESS OF JAPAN, ARUNDEL CASTLE, MONARCH OF BERMUDA, AORANGI, CAPETOWN CASTLE, ORDUNA, DEUCALION, RIMUTAKA, and ABBEKERK. Destroyers SOUTHWOLD and DULVERTON escorted the convoy from 28 November to 14 December. Battleship ROYAL SOVEREIGN escorted the convoy from 28 November to 18 December. Sloop MILFORD plus corvettes VERBENA and HOLLYHOCK escorted the convoy from 28 November to 15 December.
	A mine sank steamer **MAURITA** (199grt) at Hilbre Swash, in the Dee Estuary.

13 NOVEMBER 1941

	American destroyer EDISON (DD-439) dropped depth charges on a submarine contact while escorting convoy ON.34.
	Convoy ON.36 departed Liverpool escorted by destroyers BROKE, CHELSEA, and WOLVERINE, plus corvettes BEGONIA, EGLANTINE, and LARKSPUR. Destroyer CHELSEA was detached from the convoy on the 16th when destroyer BROADWAY joined the escort. Destroyer BROADWAY was detached from the convoy later that day. On the 18th, destroyer ROCKINGHAM with corvettes ARROWHEAD, BUCTOUCHE, COBALT, MOOSE JAW, NASTURTIUM, PICTOU, and WINDFLOWER relieved the Liverpool escorts. Destroyer ROCKINGHAM was detached from the convoy on the 20th. The remaining escorts were detached from the convoy on the 25th when the convoy was dispersed.
1900	Destroyer BRIGHTON departed Loch Alsh to carry out docking and repairs at Scapa Flow.

14 NOVEMBER 1941

	While escorting convoy ON.34, American destroyers BENSON (DD-421) and NIBLACK (DD-424) dropped depth charges on submarine contacts.
	American destroyer EDISON (DD-439) picked up a SONAR contact while escorting convoy ON.34.
	American Task Unit TU.4.1.1 joined convoy ON.35 at the MOMP and relieved the British escort group.

15 NOVEMBER 1941

	Naval drifter **HARMONY** (24grt) was sunk in a collision off Invergordon.

	Convoy ON.37 departed Liverpool escorted by anti-submarine trawlers HUGH WALPOLE and NORTHERN SPRAY. On the 16th, destroyers BEVERLEY and SARDONYX joined the convoy. On the 18th, destroyers SCIMITAR and WATCHMAN with corvettes DAHLIA and MONKSHOOD, plus anti-submarine trawler NORTHERN PRIDE joined the convoy. Destroyer BEVERLEY was detached from the convoy on the 20th and trawler NORTHERN PRIDE was detached from the convoy on the 21st. American destroyers BUCK (DD-420), GREER (DD-145), LUDLOW (DD-438), MCCORMICK (DD-223), and SWANSON (DD-443) relieved the remaining escorts on the 22nd. The American destroyers were detached from the convoy on the 30th when the convoy was dispersed.

16 NOVEMBER 1941

	Destroyer CHELSEA was damaged in a collision with an unknown merchant ship while escorting convoy ON.36. The destroyer lost six feet of her stern, but was able to reach Liverpool under her own power. The damage was repaired at Liverpool and completed on 14 December.
0300	Minesweepers HAZARD and HEBE departed Greenock for Scapa Flow.
1100	Destroyer FAULKNOR arrived at the Clyde from Portsmouth.

17 NOVEMBER 1941

	T/Sub Lt M. S. H. Christopher RNVR was lost overboard from submarine P.38 while the ship was returning from her patrol southwest of Ireland and west of Land's End. The submarine arrived at Portsmouth on the 22nd.

18 NOVEMBER 1941

	Convoy OS.12 departed Liverpool. Sloops FOLKESTONE, LONDONDERRY, WELLINGTON, and WESTON plus escort vessels SENNEN and TOTLAND joined the convoy on the 19th. Sloop LONDONDERRY was detached from the convoy on 2 December, sloop WESTON was detached from the convoy on 7 December, sloops FOLKESTONE and WELLINGTON and the escort vessels were detached from the convoy on 8 December. Escort vessel GORLESTON joined the convoy on 4 December and was detached from the convoy on 6 December when destroyers VANSITTART and VELOX plus corvettes BERGAMOT, LAVENDER, and STARWORT joined the convoy and escorted it into Freetown, arriving on 11 December.

19 NOVEMBER 1941

	American destroyer LEARY (DD-158) made a RADAR contact with a U-boat while escorting convoy HX.160. This event was the first confirmed instance of making contact with an enemy vessel with surface RADAR for the United States Navy.
	Convoy ON.38 departed Liverpool escorted by corvettes HEARTSEASE, RENONCULE, and ROSELYS plus anti-submarine trawlers KING SOL and ST APOLLO. On the 20th, anti-submarine trawler CAPE WARWICK joined the convoy. Destroyers AMAZON and FOXHOUND joined the convoy on the 21st. Trawler ST APOLLO was detached from the convoy on the 22nd. Corvette GALT joined the convoy on the 24th and was detached from the convoy on the 25th. On the 26th, destroyer BURNHAM with corvettes ALGOMA, CHAMBLY, DAUPHIN, MATAPEDIA, and NAPANEE joined the convoy and the earlier escorts were all detached from the convoy. The convoy was dispersed on the 30th and the escorts were detached to other duties.
	The accidental explosion of a scuttling charge damaged destroyer CASTLETON while at sea on escort duty. She was under repairs at Newport until 20 April 1942.

20 NOVEMBER 1941

	American destroyer NICHOLSON (DD-442) dropped depth charges on a submarine contact while escorting convoy HX.160.
1330	Battleship RAMILLIES departed Liverpool escorted by destroyers VANQUISHER and WITCH for Scapa Flow.
1400	Destroyer FAULKNOR departed the Clyde for Londonderry.
2100	Destroyer FAULKNOR arrived at Londonderry from the Clyde and refuel.

21 NOVEMBER 1941

	Destroyer GURKHA arrived at Londonderry after her escort duty.
	ML.219 was grounded off Stornoway and was declared a constructive total loss.
	Convoy ON.39 departed Liverpool. On the 22nd destroyers DOUGLAS, LEAMINGTON, SHERWOOD, SKATE, and VETERAN, corvettes ANEMONE, THYME, and VERONICA, plus anti-submarine trawlers ST ELSTAN, ST KENAN, and ST ZENO, and VIZALMA joined as escort.

	The destroyers were detached from the convoy on the 27th and rest of the escorts detached from the convoy on the 29th when relieved by American destroyers BADGER (DD-126), COLE (DD-155), DECATUR (DD-341), LIVERMORE (DD-429), and PLUNKETT (DD-431) and Coast Guard cutter CAMPBELL (WPG-32).
	The American ships were detached from the convoy when the convoy was dispersed on 4 December.
	T/A/Sub Lt (A) C. Don RNVR was killed when his Hurricane aircraft of 760 Squadron crashed after an engine failure near Shepton Mallet.

22 NOVEMBER 1941

	Destroyer FAULKNOR departed Londonderry for a position in 55N, 10W with destroyers NORMAN and ICARUS to take over screening duties of battleship NELSON from destroyers ZULU, SIKH, and GURKHA.
	Destroyer ZULU and SIKH arrived at Londonderry after their escort duty.
0900	Minelaying cruiser MANXMAN arrived at Loch Alsh from Scapa Flow to boiler clean.

23 NOVEMBER 1941

| 0930 | Destroyer NORMAN arrived at the Clyde for her boiler cleaning prior to her transfer to the Mediterranean. |

25 NOVEMBER 1941

	Convoy ON.40 departed Liverpool escorted by anti-submarine trawlers COVENTRY CITY and LADY MADELEINE. On the 26th, sloop COMMANDANT DETROYAT, corvettes HEATHER and NARCISSUS, and anti-submarine trawler ARAB joined the convoy. Destroyers BEAGLE and BOADICEA joined the convoy on the 27th. Destroyers COLUMBIA and SKEENA with corvettes ACONIT, GALT, SHEDIAC, and WETASKIWIN relieved the escorts from the convoy on the 30th. The convoy was dispersed on 4 December.
	Convoy OG.77 departed Liverpool escorted by sloops BLACK SWAN and FOWEY plus corvettes CAMPION, HELIOTROPE, LA MALOUINE, and MALLOW. On the 26th, destroyer HARVESTER escorted the convoy through the day and then detached from the convoy and continued on to Gibraltar, arriving on 2 December. Corvette MALLOW was detached from the convoy on the 28th when corvettes BLUEBELL, CARNATION, MYOSOTIS, and STONECROP joined the escort. Destroyers HESPERUS and HARVESTER departed Gibraltar on 7 December and joined the convoy on 9 December. Destroyer HIGHLANDER proceeded to join the convoy after completing current duties. Destroyer HARVESTER was recalled on 10 December. Escorts were detached from the convoy to accompany ships proceeding to Portuguese or Spanish ports on 9 December. The detached escorts rejoined the convoy. Sloop DEPTFORD with corvettes VETCH, SAMPHIRE, PENSTEMON, and CONVOLVULUS departed Gibraltar on an anti-submarine sweep on 9 December and joined the convoy on 13 December for additional escort. The convoy arrived at Gibraltar on 13 December.
0900	Monitor EREBUS arrived at Londonderry with destroyers WITCH and VANQUISHER from Scapa Flow.

26 NOVEMBER 1941

| | Armed merchant cruiser CAPE SABLE departed Oban for Scapa Flow to work up to combat efficiency. |

27 NOVEMBER 1941

| | Destroyers FURY and FORESIGHT arrived at Londonderry after escort duty. |
| | Convoy ON.41 departed Liverpool escorted by corvettes CALENDULA, CELANDINE, GENTIAN, HONEYSUCKLE, PERIWINKLE, and ROSE.
Corvette PERIWINKLE was detached from the convoy on the 28th.
Destroyer VANOC joined the convoy on the 29th and destroyer CALDWELL joined the convoy on the 30th.
Destroyers CALDWELL and VANOC with corvettes CALENDULA and ROSE were detached from the convoy on 4 December when relieved by American destroyers BABBITT (DD-128), LEARY (DD-158), MAYO (DD-422), NICHOLSON (DD-442), and SCHENCK (DD-159).
Corvette HONEYSUCKLE was detached from the convoy on 5 December followed by corvettes CELANDINE and GENTIAN on 6 December.
The American destroyers were detached from the convoy on 10 December.
Corvette LETHBRIDGE was the only escort still with the convoy on 11 December when it was dispersed. |

28 NOVEMBER 1941

| 0700 | Destroyer BEAUFORT arrived at the Clyde from Scapa Flow to boiler clean prior to her transfer to the Mediterranean. |
| 1100 | Destroyer BRIGHTON joined convoy DS.17 in position 16½ miles 192° from Skerryvore. |

1300	Destroyers FURY and FORESIGHT departed Londonderry for Scapa Flow to join the Home Fleet.

29 NOVEMBER 1941

	American Task Unit TU.4.1.4 joined convoy ONS.39 at the MOMP west of Ireland. American destroyers PLUNKETT (DD-431), LIVERMORE (DD-429), DECATUR (DD-341), and COLE (DD-155) suffered storm damage during their escort of convoy ONS.39.
1718	Destroyer FORESTER departed Londonderry for Scapa Flow to join the Home Fleet.

30 NOVEMBER 1941

	American destroyer DECATUR (DD-341) dropped depth charges on a submarine contact while escorting convoy ONS.39 west of Ireland.
	Convoy OS.13 departed Liverpool. On 1 December, destroyer ROCKINGHAM plus sloops LEITH, ROCHESTER, SANDWICH, and SCARBOROUGH joined the convoy. The destroyer was detached from the convoy on 11 December, sloop SCARBOROUGH was detached from the convoy on 3 December, and the other sloops were detached from the convoy on 18 December. On 17 December, the convoy was joined by destroyer VIMY, corvettes BERGAMOT and CLOVER, and anti-submarine trawler SOUTHERN GEM, which arrived at Freetown with the convoy on 20 December.

Central Atlantic Crossing Zone

Long. W60, 00 – W15, 00   Lat. 49, 00 – N05, 00

2 NOVEMBER 1941

	U.98 spotted convoy OS.10 in the North Atlantic, but lost contact in the heavy seas.

4 NOVEMBER 1941

	German Fw200 aircraft briefly spotted convoy OS.10 heading south in the North Atlantic.
	Fleet oiler OLWEN (6394grt) reported sighing a German AMC in the southern North Atlantic. Heavy cruiser DORSETSHIRE and AMC CANTON were ordered to investigate the sighting.

5 NOVEMBER 1941

	Wolfpack STORTEBECKER with U.96, U.98, U.69, U.201, U.103, U.107, U.373 and U.572 set up a patrol line to intercept convoy HG.76 west of Spain. However, four Fw200 aircraft of I/KG.40 failed to find the convoy at sea.

6 NOVEMBER 1941

	Six Fw200 aircraft of I/KG.40 as well as Wolfpack STORTEBECKER failed to find convoy HG.76 west of Spain.

7 NOVEMBER 1941

	In flight operations from escort aircraft carrier AUDACITY, supporting convoy OG.76, the Martlet aircraft piloted by Sub Lt (A) N. H. Patterson went over the side of the ship while landing in heavy seas. An escort ship safely rescued Patterson from the sea.

8 NOVEMBER 1941

	Lt Cdr J. M. Wintour Rtd of 802 Squadron from aircraft carrier AUDACITY was lost when his Martlet aircraft was shot down while engaging German aircraft, which were attacking convoy OG.76. Convoy escort destroyer WANDERER recovered Wintour's body. Sub Lt D. A. Hutchison downed the German Fw200 Condor aircraft that shot down Wintour.

15 NOVEMBER 1941

	Wolfpack STORTEBECKER formed with U.552, U.567, U.98, U.96, U.572, U.69, U.373, U.201 and U.77 to attack convoy OS.11.

16 NOVEMBER 1941

	German aerial reconnaissance failed to find convoy OS.11 at sea.

17 NOVEMBER 1941

	U.332 joined Wolfpack STORTEBECKER.

18 NOVEMBER 1941

	U.402 joined Wolfpack STORTEBECKER.

19 NOVEMBER 1941

	Wolfpack GODECKE with U.98, U.69, U.201, and U.572 formed to intercept convoy OG.77.
	Wolfpack BENECKE with U.332, U.402, U.96, and U.552 formed to intercept convoy OG.77.
	Wolfpack STORTEBECKER with U.85, U.133, U.571 and U.577 formed to intercept convoy OG.77.

20 NOVEMBER 1941

	While returning from a patrol, Dutch submarine K-XIV (Lt Cdr Van Well Groeneveld) unsuccessfully attacked U.552 off the Cape Verde Islands.

21 NOVEMBER 1941

	A Shark aircraft of 750 Squadron was lost in the sea while on a reconnaissance exercise from Ponta Delgada. T/Lt (A) H. V. Hicks RNVR was lost.

24 NOVEMBER 1941

	Destroyers FORESIGHT, FURY, and FORESTER joined convoy SL.92 and provided escort to Londonderry.

25 NOVEMBER 1941

	Destroyers FURY and FORESIGHT were detached from convoy SL.92 for Londonderry, arriving on the 27th.

26 NOVEMBER 1941

	U.69, U.201 and U.402 formed Wolfpack LETZTE RITTER and set up a patrol line to intercept convoy OG.77.

28 NOVEMBER 1941

	U.43 (Kptlt Lüth) sighted convoy OS.12 with Escort Group EG.42 with the Sloops WESTON, SENNEN, TOTLAND, LONDONDERRY, and WELLINGTON west of Portugal.

29 NOVEMBER 1941

	U.43 (Kptlt Lüth) sank steamer **THORNLIEBANK** (5569grt) while attacking convoy OS.12 west of Portugal in 41, 50N, 29, 48W. The entire crew was lost.

30 NOVEMBER 1941

1926	U.43 (Kptlt Lüth) sank steamer **ASHBY** (4868grt) (Master Tom Valentine Frank OBE) as she was straggling behind convoy OS.12 about 170 miles south-southeast of Flores, Azores in 36, 54N, 29, 51W. The master, eleven crewmen and five gunners were lost. The survivors landed their lifeboats at Fayal. Portuguese destroyer LIMA transferred the thirty-three survivors to Portuguese steamer CARVALHO ARAUJO (4560grt) for transfer to Lisbon.

UK East Coast

Long. W04, 00 – E03, 00   Lat. N58, 30 – N51, 30

1 NOVEMBER 1941

	Light cruiser ARETHUSA departed the Tyne to complete her refit at Rosyth escorted by destroyer VALOROUS and torpedo school ship LAIRDS ISLE, where they arrived later that day.
0755	Destroyer TARTAR departed Sheerness for Scapa Flow.
0800	Destroyer MAORI departed London for Sheerness to embark ammunition and fuel after her long refit.
1300	Destroyer MAORI arrived at Sheerness from London to embark ammunition and fuel.
1600	Heavy cruiser BERWICK arrived at Rosyth from Scapa Flow with destroyers PUNJABI and ESCAPADE.

2 NOVEMBER 1941

	German bombing damaged steamer **MARIE DAWN** (2157grt) twenty miles from Spurn Point. The steamer sank the next day at four miles 210° from 59A Buoy, Humber. The entire crew was rescued.
	German bombing sank steamer **BRYNMILL** (743grt) four miles 210° from 59A Buoy, East Dudgeon. The entire crew was rescued.
	German bombing damaged tanker AGILITY (522grt) in Great Yarmouth Roads. She arrived at Great Yarmouth on the 3rd.
	German bombing damaged steamer THYRA III (828grt) in Great Yarmouth Roads. She was towed to Great Yarmouth arriving on the 3rd.
0800	Battleship DUKE OF YORK departed Rosyth with heavy cruiser BERWICK plus destroyers PUNJABI and ESCAPADE for Scapa Flow, and to carry out exercises en route. Destroyer TARTAR joined this force off May Island while she was en route from Sheerness to Scapa Flow.
0845	Destroyer MAORI arrived at Sheerness for Scapa Flow to work up to combat efficiency.

3 NOVEMBER 1941

	A German aerial mine sank patrol vessel **OUZEL** (76grt) (T/Lt G. W. Wilkinson RNR) one half mile east of Mablethorpe. Wilkinson and the entire crew were lost.

4 NOVEMBER 1941

	Free French submarine **MINERVE** arrived at Dundee after a patrol off Norway.
	A German aerial mine sank sailing vessel **BRITISHER** (95grt) just north of West Mouse Buoy, off Maplin. Both crewmen were lost.

5 NOVEMBER 1941

	Light cruiser **ARETHUSA** departed Rosyth after completing her refit and arrived at Scapa Flow later that day.
0700	Destroyer **MONTROSE** arrived at Rosyth from Scapa Flow.
1600	Destroyer **MONTROSE** embarked Vice Admiral, Second in Command Home Fleet and his staff and departed Rosyth for Scapa Flow.

6 NOVEMBER 1941

	Naval trawler **FLOTTA** (530grt) grounded off Buchan Ness on 29 October and foundered on this day.

7 NOVEMBER 1941

	German bombing damaged minesweeper **ALBURY** with a bomb near miss off the east coast of Scotland. The damage required five weeks to repair.
0800	Destroyer **ECHO** departed London for Sheerness after she completed a long refit.
1400	Destroyer **ECHO** arrived at Sheerness from London.

8 NOVEMBER 1941

	Naval drifter **MONARDA** (109grt) foundered in the Thames Estuary.
	German bombing sank Norwegian steamer **VICTO** (3655grt) 1.8 miles 330° from 18B Buoy, Scarborough in 54, 20N, 00, 17W. Two crewmen were killed.
	German bombing sank fishing trawler **CRADOCK** (204grt) fourteen miles north, northeast of St Abb's Head. The entire crew was rescued.
1330	Destroyer **ECHO** departed Sheerness for Scapa Flow.

9 NOVEMBER 1941

	A collision sank Naval drifter **BOY ANDREW** (97grt) (Skipper G. F. Ball RNR) in the Firth of Forth. Ball was lost in the drifter.
	An unknown cause sank tug **LETTIE** (89grt) off St Abb's Head.
	German bombing heavily damaged tug **BUCCANEER** and a battle practice target in tow off Montrose. Destroyer **ECHO** was ordered to proceed to assist the tug while she was en route from Sheerness to Scapa Flow. When the tug drifted ashore the destroyer was ordered to continue to Scapa Flow. The tug was later salvaged.

10 NOVEMBER 1941

	German bombing damaged Examination vessel **LONGSCAR** with bomb near misses off Middlesbrough in 54, 41, 30N, 01, 09, 45W.
0800	Destroyer **ESCAPADE** departed Rosyth for Scapa Flow after she completed her boiler cleaning.
0900	Destroyer **PYTCHLEY** departed the Tyne for Methil to land trial parties before proceeding to Scapa Flow. Due to bad weather, the destroyer was ordered to Leith.
1500	Destroyer **PYTCHLEY** arrived at Leith from the Tyne after encountering bad weather on her way to Scapa Flow.

11 NOVEMBER 1941

	T/Sub Lt (A) G. Black, RNZVR died of injuries after his Swordfish aircraft flew into high ground at Durham.

12 NOVEMBER 1941

	German bombing sank cable ship **FRANCOLIN** (ex-**FARADAY** (322grt) T/A/Skipper Lt J. Dinwoodie RNR) two miles N 25° E from Haisborough Light House.
	German bombing damaged steamer trawler **BEN SCREEL** (195grt) fourteen miles northeast by north of St Abb's Head.
1645	Destroyer **PYTCHLEY** departed Leith for Scapa Flow to work up to combat efficiency.

15 NOVEMBER 1941

	German bombing badly damaged steamer **CORHAMPTON** (2495grt) twenty-six miles northeast of Spurn Point. She sank on the 16th in tow two miles 142° from 62D Buoy in the Humber area. The entire crew was rescued.

16 NOVEMBER 1941

	German bombing damaged Examination vessel **MINNA** (290grt) in 56, 04, 36N, 02, 51, 12W. She arrived at Leith on the 17th.

17 NOVEMBER 1941

	Minesweeper **ROSS** departed the Humber for Aberdeen and the Faeroes.
	German bombing sank steamer **BOVEY TRACEY** (1212grt) in 52, 58N, 02, 05E. The entire crew was rescued.

18 NOVEMBER 1941

	Free French submarine **RUBIS** departed Dundee to patrol off the Norwegian coast.
	T/Sub Lt (A) D. Worth RNVR was killed when his Fulmar aircraft of 884 Squadron crashed near Donibristle.

19 NOVEMBER 1941

	The German 2nd S-Boat Flotilla attacked convoy FS.650 of fifty-nine ships escorted by destroyers WOLSEY, VERDUN, WIDGEON, and KITTIWAKE, plus trawler KINGSTON OLIVINE off Great Yarmouth. Destroyers VESPER, GARTH, and CAMPBELL were nearby as a support force and MGB.87 followed the convoy. Destroyers HAMBLEDON and QUORN were also at sea. MGB.63, MGB.64, and MGB.67 departed to operate near the German activity, but MGB.63 was forced to return at the start with engine room problems. S.104 (ObltzS Rebensburg) sank tanker **WAR MEHTAR** (5502grt) in 52, 50n, 02, 08E. The entire crew was rescued. S.105 sank steamer **ARUBA** (1159grt) in 52, 51N, 02, 07, 30E. One gunner was missing. S.41 (Oblt. Popp) badly damaged steamer **WALDINGE** (2462grt) near 55 A Buoy, Smith's Knoll. One gunner was lost and she sank on the 20th. S.41 was damaged in a collision with a convoy escort and was in tow returning to port, when intercepted by MGB.64 and MGB.67. The British were able to board the S-boat, but could not prevent her sinking. Destroyer GARTH was seriously damaged when she was accidentally struck by 40-mm gunfire from another destroyer in the escort. GARTH was towed to Harwich and the convoy arrived at Southend on the 20th.

20 NOVEMBER 1941

0835	Monitor **EREBUS** departed Sheerness for Londonderry escorted by destroyers MEYNELL and WALPOLE, as far as Kinnaird Head.
0900	Destroyer **ANTELOPE** arrived at Hull from Scapa Flow to begin a long refit.

21 NOVEMBER 1941

	Naval drifter **ROWAN TREE** (91grt) ran aground and capsized at the entrance to Lowestoft Harbour.
1600	Battle cruiser **RENOWN** departed Rosyth escorted by destroyers ARROW, VIMIERA, and WALLACE for Scapa Flow.

22 NOVEMBER 1941

	Free French submarine **MINERVE** departed Dundee for a patrol off the Norwegian coast. On the 23rd, the submarine experienced mechanical problems and was diverted to Scapa Flow for repairs, arriving on the 24th. MINERVE departed Scapa Flow on the 25th for her patrol.
	German bombing damaged Norwegian steamer **BESTUM** (2215grt) off Platters near Harwich.

23 NOVEMBER 1941

1100	Battleship **NELSON** arrived at Rosyth and the escorting destroyers returned to Scapa Flow.

24 NOVEMBER 1941

	The German 4th S-Boat Flotilla (KptLt Bätge) with S.50, S.51, S.52, S.109 and S.110 attacked convoy FS.654 off Orfordness.
	S.109 (LtzS. Bosse) sank tanker **VIRGILIA** (5732grt) while attacking convoy FS.654 during the night three miles north east of Hearty Knoll Buoy in 52, 20N, 01, 59E. Twenty-three crewmen, including seven gunners, were missing and ML.150 and ML.152 rescued seventeen survivors.
	S.52 (ObltzS Karl Müller) sank Dutch steamer **GROENLO** (1984grt) while attacking convoy FS.654 during the

	night one and a half miles 28° from 52E Buoy in 52, 20N, 01, 59E. One crewman was killed and nine crewmen were missing.
	S.51 torpedoed steamer **BLAIRNEVIS** (4155grt) while attacking convoy FS.654 during the night off Hearty Knoll in 52, 28N, 02, 05E. She was beached at Great Yarmouth Roads and was re-floated and towed to London on 16-17 December for repairs. ML.150 rescued the crew after they had abandoned the damaged ship. Destroyers WESTMINSTER and SOUTHDOWN both reported sinking German S-boats, but all returned to base.
	T/Sub Lt (A) L. A. C. Michell RNVR was killed when his Albacore aircraft of 767/769 Squadrons crashed near Arbroath during exercises.
	German bombing damaged steamer **ARDENZA** (933grt) at buoy 54B, ten miles southeast of Orfordness. She arrived at Great Yarmouth the next day.

25 NOVEMBER 1941

	MTBs sank German auxiliary patrol vessel **Vp.412/BREMERHAVEN** (416grt) near St Pol. She was later salvaged and returned to service as patrol boat Vp.805. The entire crew was rescued.
	MTBs sank Vichy French fishing boat **PROSPER BIHEN** (24grt) off Dunkirk, France.
0730	Destroyer PUNJABI arrived at the Tyne from Scapa Flow for a refit.

27 NOVEMBER 1941

0900	Destroyer INGLEFIELD departed the Humber for Scapa Flow following her refit.

29 NOVEMBER 1941

	The German 4th S-Boat Flotilla (Kptlt Bätge) attacked convoy FN.564 northwest of Cromer after laying eighteen TMB mines in 53, 16N, 01, 05E. MGB.86 and MGB.89 engaged the German ships and MGB.89 was damaged during the ensuing combat.
	S.64 (ObltzS Wilcke) sank tanker **ASPERITY** (699grt) in 53, 11N, 01, 07E. Ten crewmen were missing.
	S.52 (ObltzS Karl Müller) sank steamer **EMPIRE NEWCOMEN** (2840grt) five miles south of Dudgeon Light. Ten crewmen were lost.
	S.51 (ObltzS Hans-Jürgen Meyer) sank steamer **CORMARSH** (2848grt) a half mile north of 58 A Buoy, in 53, 16N, 01, 04E. The entire crew was rescued.

30 NOVEMBER 1941

	Submarine TRIDENT arrived at Blyth from Polyarnoe, Russia. She then went on to the Tyne for repairs and docking.

North Sea

Long. E03, 00 – E09, 00   Lat. N58, 30 – N51, 00

1 NOVEMBER 1941

	German bombing damaged steamer **KINGSLAND** (3669grt) in the North Sea.
	RAF bombing damaged Swedish steamer **BRAHEHOLM** (5676grt) off the Dutch coast. One crewman was killed.

2 NOVEMBER 1941

	RAF bombing damaged Swedish steamer **INGEREN** (6123grt) west of Borkum. She arrived at Emden, Germany for repairs.

5 NOVEMBER 1941

	RAF bombing sank German Flak lighter **LAT.5/KURT SANDKAMP** (250grt) in the Ems river mouth.

10 NOVEMBER 1941

	An RAF aerial mine sank Swedish steamer **VOLLRATH THAM** (5787grt) one and half miles from Hubert Gat. The crew was rescued and taken to a German port.

23 NOVEMBER 1941

	A mine sank Swedish steamer **HEDDA** (1498grt) north of Borkum. The entire crew was rescued.

30 NOVEMBER 1941

	German AMC SCHIFF.45/KOMET (KAdm. Eyssen) arrived at Hamburg, Germany after a voyage of 516 days. She sank six ships of 31,005 tons and shared the sinking of two more with German AMC SCHIFF.36/ORION for another 21,125 tons.

English Channel
Long. W07, 00 – E01, 30   Lat. N51, 00 – N49, 00

3 NOVEMBER 1941

	In an attack on a German convoy in the Channel, MGB's claimed torpedoing and badly damaging a MOEWE class torpedo boat (note says MOEWE or GREIF) and sank a 5000-ton ship. The torpedoes sank German **Transport RO.19** (1573grt) (ex Dutch **BATAVIER V** (1573grt)) off Cap Griz Nez, France. She had been converted for the planned invasion of Britain, but was now used to move cargo.

5 NOVEMBER 1941

	German bombing and strafing damaged steamer GLENCREE (481grt) fifteen miles southwest of Bishops Light.

10 NOVEMBER 1941

	Lt E. A. Holloway was killed when his Martlet aircraft of 888 Squadron crashed on approach three miles north of Bishops Waltham, Hants.

13 NOVEMBER 1941

	A mine sank Dutch steamer **JOMA** (372grt) in Falmouth Harbour. Three gunners were lost.

14 NOVEMBER 1941

	T/A/Sub Lt (A) P. R. Cassels RNVR was killed when his Hurricane aircraft of 759/760 Squadron crashed in Dawlish Bay.

15 NOVEMBER 1941

0900	Destroyer FAULKNOR departed Portsmouth for the Clyde to carry out direction finding calibration before proceeding to Scapa Flow.

19 NOVEMBER 1941

	Lt Cdr L. C. D. Ashburner was killed when his ROC aircraft of 834 Squadron crashed at Eastleigh.
>1200	Anti-aircraft cruiser CAIRO arrived at Devonport after she suffered a failure of her steering engine while escorting convoy BB.101 from Belfast to Milford Haven. Her repairs were not completed until early February.

23 NOVEMBER 1941

	Heavy cruiser HAWKINS arrived at Portsmouth from the East Indies escorted by destroyer BLENCATHRA. She began an extensive refit at Portsmouth from 7 December to 7 May.

24 NOVEMBER 1941

	Battleship RESOLUTION departed Plymouth for Scapa Flow escorted by destroyers BERKELEY and KUJAWIAK to work up to combat efficiency.
	Landing ship PRINCE LEOPOLD landed troops on the coast of Normandy, France escorted by MGB.316, MGB.312, MGB.314, and MGB.317 in Operation SUNSTAR. The ships returned to Portsmouth after the desired information was collected.

25 NOVEMBER 1941

	German bombing sank Naval drifter **FISHER GIRL** (85grt) (T/Electrician J. W. Parsons RNVR) at Falmouth Harbour.
	German bombing sank armed patrol trawler **JACQUES MORGAND** (155grt) at Falmouth.

27 NOVEMBER 1941

	German AMC SCHIFF.45/KOMET departed Cherbourg, France early in the morning escorted by torpedo boats T.7, T.4, and T.11 plus minesweepers M.10 and M.153. The SCHIFF.45/KOMET spent the day in Le Havre, France and departed that night with the three torpedo boats, five minesweepers, and six motor minesweepers. Early on the 28th, the Dover Command sent a force to attack the SCHIFF.45/KOMET off Boulogne, France and Dunkirk, France as she returned to Germany. MTB.218, MTB.219, MTB.221, and MTB.56 had departed Dover and proceeded to the number 8 buoy. MTB.45, MTB.44, MTB.47, and MTB.48 had departed Dover and proceeded to the S buoy. MGB.14 and MGB.41 had departed Ramsgate and proceeded to the V buoy. En route MTB.221, MTB.56, and MTB.48 developed engine troubles and returned to Dover. The SCHIFF.45/KOMET was undamaged during the engagement, but MTB.219 damaged one of the escorts, which was last seen with three motor minesweepers standing by. The Coxswain of MTB.219 was wounded and later died.

| | German torpedo boat T.4 was damaged by gunfire from T.12, and a dud shell fired by one of the minesweepers.
One of the MTBs caused personnel casualties on the torpedo boat with machine gun fire, wounding four, including the commanding officer.
German torpedo boat T.7 was also hit by machine gun fire, causing three dead and three wounded.
The SCHIFF.45/KOMET arrived in Hamburg, Germany on the 30th after a lengthy cruise in which she sank 6 1/2 ships (seven of her kills were shared with SCHIFF.36/ORION) for a total of 42,959grt. |
|---|---|

Bay of Biscay

Long. W15, 00 – E03, 00   Lat. N49, 00 – N40, 00

4 NOVEMBER 1941

	New submarines UNA and P.38 began an unsuccessful patrol in the Bay of Biscay until 6 December.

5 NOVEMBER 1941

	U.81, U.205, U.433 and U.565 began departing France to run through the Gibraltar Strait into the Mediterranean from 11 to 16 November. After they assembled east of Gibraltar, they formed Wolfpack ARNAULD.

6 NOVEMBER 1941

	German steamer RIO GRANDE (6062grt) (Kpt v. Allwörden) departed Bordeaux, France for Osaka, Japan.

13 NOVEMBER 1941

	The German 8th Minesweeper Flotilla (KKpt. v. Kamptz) with auxiliary minesweepers M.28, M.24, M.26, M.27 and M.32 sortied into the Bay of Biscay to lead the captured prise ship **SILVAPLANA** (4793grt), taken by German AMC SCHIFF.16/ATLANTIS, to France. When they reached the rendezvous point, they found instead, the captured prise ship **KOTA NOPAN** (7322grt), taken by German AMC SCHIFF.10/THOR. The prise ship thought she had sailed into a trap and rammed M.27, causing heavy damage on the minesweeper before the situation was resolved. The minesweepers then escorted **KOTA NOPAN** and her valuable cargo into Gironde, France.

17 NOVEMBER 1941

	Captured steamers **SILVAPLANA** (4793grt) and **KOTA NOPAN** (7322grt) arrived at Bordeaux with their rich cargo of war material.
	U.652 and U.561 guided German AMC SCHIFF.45/KOMET from the South Atlantic to German controlled waters in the Bay of Biscay. Both U-boats were detached on the 24th.
0001	A probable German supply ship was reported by a submarine in 44, 00N, 02, 00W. Battleship NELSON and light cruiser HERMIONE tried to intercept, but no contact was made.
1845	Battleship NELSON escorted by destroyers ZULU, SIKH, and GURKHA separated from light cruiser HERMIONE, aircraft carrier ARGUS, and destroyers LAFOREY, LIGHTNING, LEGION, and ISAAC SWEERS.
The NELSON group continued north, while the ARGUS group, less HERMIONE returned to Gibraltar.

19 NOVEMBER 1941

| | Submarine RORQUAL (Cdr Dewhurst) laid Minefield FD.34 off La Rochelle, France during the night.
One of the mines sank Vichy French fishing steamer **COLIGNY** (600grt) off La Rochelle. |
|---|---|

23 NOVEMBER 1941

	Destroyers FORESIGHT, FURY, and FORESTER departed the Biscay patrol to join convoy SL.92 and then proceed to Londonderry.

24 NOVEMBER 1941

	German AMC SCHIFF.45/KOMET arrived at Bordeaux, France after a lengthy patrol across the Atlantic, Indian and Pacific Oceans.

26 NOVEMBER 1941

	Submarine P.36 unsuccessfully attacked a German U-boat off St. Nazaire, France in 47, 16N, 03, 20W.

30 NOVEMBER 1941

	An RAF Whitley bomber of 502 Squadron sank **U.206** west of Nantes in 46, 55N, 07, 16W. The entire crew of forty-six were lost. Other sources place the sinking site in 47, 05N, 02, 40W.

West of Gibraltar
Long. W15, 00 – W05, 30   Lat. N40, 00 – N30, 00

1 NOVEMBER 1941

Destroyer WILD SWAN joined convoy OS.9G, escorted by Dutch destroyer ISAAC SWEERS, sloops FOWEY and LEITH, and corvette STONECROP, and led the ships into Gibraltar.

Convoy SL.91G departed Gibraltar to join convoy SL.91 at sea, escorted by corvette CARNATION with destroyers SIKH and VIDETTE, corvette AZALEA, plus anti-submarine trawlers STELLA CARINA and LADY HOGARTH.

Destroyer VIDETTE and the trawlers were detached from the convoy on the 6th and the rest of the escort group detached from the convoy on the 8th.

On the 2nd, sloop FOWEY and corvette STONECROP departed Gibraltar to overtake the convoy and proceed to England.

Sloop LEITH with corvettes HELIOTROPE and CAMPION departed Gibraltar on the 3rd escorting Dutch steamer TYSA (5327grt) to join convoy SL.91G at sea.

Destroyer WILD SWAN was the local escort for this group.

Destroyer DUNCAN and Free French sloop COMMANDANT DUBOC departed Gibraltar on the 4th to join the convoy at sea. The destroyer was en route to Chatham for her refit.

When German raiders were reported moving into the Atlantic, destroyers DUNCAN and SIKH returned to Gibraltar to escort Force H.

Battleship RODNEY, at sea with destroyers ZULU, GURKHA, LIGHTNING, and ISAAC SWEERS to join aircraft carrier ARGUS, was ordered to join destroyers HIGHLANDER, HAVELOCK, and HARVESTER in 55, 40N, 17, 45W.

Oiler DINGLEDALE (8145grt), escorted by corvettes JONQUIL and COREOPSIS with submarine CLYDE, departed Gibraltar on the 7th to patrol in position 34N, 30W.

Sloop COMMANDANT DUBOC had been detached from the convoy with defects and arrived at Gibraltar on the 7th.

On the 8th, destroyer DUNCAN departed Gibraltar to begin a refit at Chatham.

On the 8th, the joined convoys SL.91 and SL.91G split into convoy SL.91GF and convoy SL.91GS.

Convoy SL.91GF arrived at Liverpool on the 18th and convoy SL.91GS arrived on the 19th.

2 NOVEMBER 1941

Battleship RODNEY departed Gibraltar escorted by destroyers GURKHA, ZULU, LIGHTNING, and ISAAC SWEERS to join aircraft carrier ARGUS and aircraft transport ATHENE escorted by destroyers LAFOREY, HIGHLANDER, HAVELOCK, and HARVESTER at sea.

The two groups joined at a position in 42N, 20W.

Battleship RODNEY proceeded to Scapa Flow with destroyers HIGHLANDER, HAVELOCK, and HARVESTER to return to the Home Fleet.

Aircraft carrier ARGUS and transport ATHENE proceeded to Gibraltar with destroyers LAFOREY, ZULU, GURKHA, LIGHTNING, and ISAAC SWEERS, arriving on the 8th.

5 NOVEMBER 1941

Steamers CITY OF LINCOLN (8039grt) and DUNEDIN STAR (11,168grt) departed Gibraltar for Cape Town, South Africa and Panama, respectively.

8 NOVEMBER 1941

Corvette SPIREA departed Gibraltar to join Norwegian tanker THORSHAVET (11,015grt) and escort her into Gibraltar.

On the 15th, corvette AZALEA departed Gibraltar to join the arriving ships.

All three ships arrived at Gibraltar on the 17th.

10 NOVEMBER 1941

Ocean boarding vessel MARSDALE arrived at Gibraltar after a Western Patrol.

12 NOVEMBER 1941

Convoy SL.91GF departed Gibraltar escorted by sloops FOWEY and BLACK SWAN to 18 November, ocean boarding vessel MARON to 15 November, and corvettes CAMPION and HELIOTROPE to 16 November plus corvettes CARNATION and STONECROP to 18 November.

Convoy SL.91 GS departed Gibraltar escorted by destroyer WRESTLER to 16 November, sloops FLEETWOOD, LEITH, SANDWICH, and SCARBOROUGH to 19 November, plus corvettes ANCHUSA, CALENDULA, MIGNONETTE to 19 November.

Corvettes ACANTHUS, GENTIAN, and HONEYSUCKLE provided escort to 19 November, and corvette MYOSOTIS joined on the 13th and provided escort to 15 November.

Anti-submarine whaler SOUTHERN STAR joined the convoy on the 17th and provided escort to 18 November.

13 NOVEMBER 1941

Anti-submarine trawlers ST NECTAN and LADY SHIRLEY departed Gibraltar escorting tanker COWRIE (8197grt) westwards and then joined tanker WINAMAC (8621grt) at sea and escorted her into Gibraltar, arriving on the 21st.

14 NOVEMBER 1941

Ocean boarding vessel MARSDALE departed Gibraltar on a Western Patrol.

16 NOVEMBER 1941

Battleship NELSON departed Gibraltar to return to Britain escorted by destroyers ZULU, SIKH, and GURKHA. Light cruiser HERMIONE, aircraft carrier ARGUS, plus destroyers LAFOREY, LIGHTNING, LEGION, and the Dutch ISAAC SWEERS sailed with the battleship to create a diversion further to the east.

17 NOVEMBER 1941

Anti-submarine trawlers STELLA CARINA and LADY HOGARTH departed Gibraltar to join with arriving Norwegian tanker PRESIDENT DE VOGUE (9320grt) and escort her into Gibraltar.

The trawlers were reassigned to join the escort of outward-bound tanker THORSHAVET (11,015grt) on the 23rd.

Corvette VETCH departed Gibraltar to join inbound tanker PRESIDENT DE VOGUE and returned with her on the 25th.

18 NOVEMBER 1941

Anti-submarine trawler SCOTTISH intercepted Vichy French fishing ketch **BELLE BRETAGNE** twenty-two miles 280° from Cape Espichel. She was sent into Gibraltar.

19 NOVEMBER 1941

Aircraft carrier ARGUS returned to Gibraltar with destroyers LAFOREY, LIGHTNING, LEGION, and the Dutch ISAAC SWEERS.

Submarine UNA arrived at Gibraltar from Holy Loch.

20 NOVEMBER 1941

Sloop STORK arrived at Gibraltar from Britain escorting steamer EMPIRE BARRACUDA (4926grt).

Destroyer MAORI and corvette COLTSFOOT arrived at Gibraltar from Britain. MAORI had recently completed her refit at London.

21 NOVEMBER 1941

Light cruiser HERMIONE returned to Gibraltar.

Destroyer WILD SWAN departed Gibraltar for Freetown to rejoin the South Atlantic Command.

Anti-submarine trawler SCOTTISH intercepted Vichy French fishing ketch **PETITE ANNICK** twenty miles 280° from Cape Espichel and sent her to Gibraltar, arriving on the 23rd.

22 NOVEMBER 1941

Destroyers LAFOREY, LIGHTNING, LEGION, and GURKHA of the 19th Destroyer Flotilla departed Gibraltar for exercises and to carry out an anti-submarine sweep.

Corvette SPIREA departed Gibraltar escorting Norwegian tanker THORSHAVET (11,015grt) out to sea and then to join arriving Dutch tanker VELMA (9720grt) and escort her into Gibraltar.

On the 23rd, anti-submarine trawlers LADY HOGARTH and STELLA CARINA were ordered to join the outward escort.

Corvette GERANIUM departed Gibraltar on the 29th to provide additional escort for the tanker. On 1 December, VELMA and corvette SPIREA arrived at Gibraltar.

23 NOVEMBER 1941

Corvette GERANIUM arrived at Gibraltar escorting steamer EMPIRE PANTHER (5711grt) (ex American **WEST QUECHEE** (5711grt)) after refitting in the UK.

24 NOVEMBER 1941

U.431 successfully navigated through the Gibraltar Strait from the North Atlantic into the Mediterranean.

Submarine CLYDE arrived at Gibraltar after escort duty with RFA oiler DINGLEDALE (8145grt).

25 NOVEMBER 1941

Corvettes JONQUIL and COREOPSIS arrived at Gibraltar with RFA oiler DINGLEDALE (8145grt).

	Destroyers WISHART and VIDETTE arrived at Gibraltar with troopships ROYAL SCOTSMAN, ROYAL ULSTERMAN, and ULSTER MONARCH from Freetown. Destroyer VELOX and corvette CLOVER escorted the troopships out of Freetown, and the corvette was later relieved by destroyer VIMY.
0400	Destroyers LAFOREY, LEGION, LIGHTNING, GURKHA, and ISAAC SWEERS departed Gibraltar to carry out an anti-submarine sweep.
1630	Destroyers WISHART and BRADFORD departed Gibraltar and joined destroyers LAFOREY, LEGION, LIGHTNING, GURKHA, and ISAAC SWEERS to carry out an anti-submarine sweep.

26 NOVEMBER 1941

	U.95 successfully navigated through the Gibraltar Strait from the North Atlantic into the Mediterranean.

27 NOVEMBER 1941

	Destroyer LEGION attacked a submarine contact in 35, 40N, 07, 26W.
	After receiving fuel and provisions in a Spanish harbour, U.557 crossed into the Mediterranean from the North Atlantic through the Gibraltar Strait.

28 NOVEMBER 1941

	After refuelling and provisioning from a German tanker in Cadiz, Spain, U.652 sailed into the Mediterranean through the Gibraltar Strait and patrolled east of Gibraltar.

29 NOVEMBER 1941

	After receiving fuel and provisions in a Spanish harbour, U.562 crossed into the Mediterranean from the North Atlantic through the Gibraltar Strait.
	Free French sloop COMMANDANT DUBOC departed Gibraltar to return to Britain.

West of North Africa   Long. W15, 00 – E11, 00   Lat. N30, 00 – N00, 00

4 NOVEMBER 1941

	Light cruiser DUNEDIN departed Freetown, Sierra Leone with AMCs QUEEN EMMA and PRINCESS BEATRIX to investigate the report of a German AMC sighted west of North Africa.

5 NOVEMBER 1941

	Force G (Adm. Phillips) with battleship PRINCE OF WALES with destroyers ELECTRA and EXPRESS arrived at Freetown from the Clyde on their voyage to the Far East Command.

6 NOVEMBER 1941

	Convoy SL.92 departed Freetown escorted by destroyers VANSITTART and VELOX to 11 November and corvettes BURDOCK and MARGUERITE to 11 November plus corvette STARWORT to 12 November. On the 11th, sloop EGRET joined the convoy and escorted the convoy to 29 November while escort vessels BANFF and FISHGUARD joined the convoy and provided escort to 1 December. On the 12th, heavy cruiser DORSETSHIRE and light cruiser DUNEDIN escorted the convoy to 13 November. Destroyers BADSWORTH, CROOME, FORESIGHT, and FURY escorted the convoy on the 24th and 25 November with destroyer FORESTER escorting the convoy on the 25th for that day only. Corvette MONTBRETIA and anti-submarine trawler MAN O' WAR escorted the convoy on the 30th only. Anti-submarine trawler ARAB provided escort on 1 December until the convoy arrived at Liverpool.

11 NOVEMBER 1941

	Convoy ST.8 departed Freetown, escorted by sloop BRIDGEWATER, corvettes CLOVER, HOLLYHOCK, and WALLFLOWER, plus anti-submarine trawlers KELT and SARABANDE. The convoy arrived at Takoradi on the 16th.

13 NOVEMBER 1941

0042	U.126 (Ernst Bauer) sank unescorted steamer **PERU** (6961grt) (ex Danish) (Master C. V. Frederiksen) southwest of Cape Palmas in 01, 30N, 13, 20W. The whaling tanker UNIWALECO (9755grt) rescued the master, forty-two crewmen and seven gunners and landed them at Freetown on the 16th.

17 NOVEMBER 1941

	Destroyer VELOX and corvette CLOVER departed Freetown with troopships ROYAL SCOTSMAN (3244grt), ROYAL ULSTERMAN (3244grt), and ULSTER MONARCH (3791grt) for Gibraltar. Destroyer VIMY later replaced the corvette at sea.

18 NOVEMBER 1941

Convoy SL.93 departed Freetown escorted by destroyers BRILLIANT to 23 November and STANLEY to 24 November, sloop BIDEFORD to 10 December, corvettes BERGAMOT and CROCUS to 23 November, CYCLAMEN to 10 December, NIGELLA and ORCHIS to 23 November, escort vessels CULVER, LANDGUARD, and LULWORTH to 10 December and GORLESTON to 1 December, and anti-submarine whaler SOUTHERN PRIDE to 23 November.
On the 27th, ocean boarding vessel CORINTHIAN joined the convoy to 10 December.
Sloop LONDONDERRY joined the convoy on 2 December to 10 December.
Anti-submarine trawler ARAB escorted the convoy until it arrived at Liverpool on 10 December.

22 NOVEMBER 1941

Convoy ST.9 departed Freetown escorted by corvettes ARMERIA, BURDOCK, and WALLFLOWER. The convoy arrived at Takoradi on the 27th.

30 NOVEMBER 1941

Convoy SL.94 departed Freetown escorted by destroyers VANSITTART and VELOX to 2 December and STANLEY to 5 December plus corvettes LAVENDER and STARWORT to 2 December.
On 2 December, destroyer CLARE, sloops ABERDEEN, ENCHANTRESS, and IBIS, plus escort vessels HARTLAND and WALNEY joined the convoy to 20 December.
Corvette STARWORT joined the convoy on 7 December to 12 December.
Destroyer ROCKINGHAM joined the convoy on 13 December for that day only.
On 20 December, anti-submarine trawlers COVENTRY CITY and MAN O' WAR joined the convoy for the day.
The convoy arrived at Liverpool on 20 December.

SOUTH ATLANTIC OCEAN

East of South America
Long. W70, 00 – W30, 00   Lat. N05, 00 - S60, 00

6 NOVEMBER 1941

American Task Group TG.3.5 (Capt Chandler) with cruiser OMAHA (CL-4) and destroyer SOMERS (DD-381) intercepted German steamer **ODENWALD** (5098grt) (Kpt. Löhr) off the Brazilian coast. She was disguised as American steamer WILLMOTO (4999grt) and carried a cargo of Japanese rubber.

West of South Africa
Long. W30, 00 – E25, 00   Lat. S00, 00 – S60, 00

1 NOVEMBER 1941

0654 — U.68 (KKpt. Merten) sank unescorted steamer **BRADFORD CITY** (4953grt) (Master Henry Paul) about 300 miles west of Walvis Bay, South West Africa in 22, 59S, 09, 49E. The master, thirty-six crewmen and eight gunners rowed their lifeboats ashore near Walvis Bay. South African anti-submarine trawlers BLOMVLEI and MOOIVLEI stood by the steamer until she sank. (Authors note: please join me in a moment of silence for the loss of 9000 tons of sugar and rum lost with the ship.)

13 NOVEMBER 1941

U.68 (KKpt. Merten) encountered German AMC SCHIFF.16/ATLANTIS south of St. Helena. The AMC provided fuel and provisions to the U-boat.

16 NOVEMBER 1941

Force G (Adm. Phillips) with battleship PRINCE OF WALES plus destroyers ELECTRA and EXPRESS arrived at Simon's Town, South Africa on their way to the Far East Command.

22 NOVEMBER 1941

Heavy cruiser DEVONSHIRE (Capt Oliver) surprised and sank German AMC **SCHIFF.16/ATLANTIS** while she was transferring supplies and fuel to U.126 (KptIt Farmer) off Ascension Island. The crew managed to abandon ship, but due to the U-boat threat, DEVONSHIRE departed the area without stopping to rescue the crew.
U.126 tended to the wounded and took the lifeboats in tow and radioed their position to headquarters.
On the 24th, German supply ship PYTHON arrived and took the survivors aboard.
ATLANTIS had sunk twenty-two allied ships for 145,697 tons in the Atlantic, Pacific, and Indian Oceans.

24 NOVEMBER 1941

>1200 — U.124 (KptIt Mohr) spotted light cruiser DUNEDIN while on her way to rescue survivors of sunken German

	AMC **SCHIFF.16/ATLANTIS.**
1450	DUNEDIN spotted the periscope and changed course to avoid an attack.
1521	U.124 sank light cruiser **DUNEDIN** (4850grt) (Captain R. S. Lovatt, OBE) with a long-range attack with two torpedoes north of Pernambuco in 03S, 26W. She sank in seventeen minutes.
	Lovatt, Cdr (E) C. R. W. Bolt, T/A/Surgeon Lt Cdr H. T. L. Broadway RNVR, Paymaster Lt T. B. N. Caws, Sub Lt E. M. French, T/Lt E. E. Gibson RNVR, T/Sub Lt (E) D. Hanson, Sub Lt J. G. Hollinshead RNR, Lt J. M. Jervelund, Commissioned Gunner (T) H. Lowey, Lt E. B. Mackay RNVR, Lt (A/Captain) R. H. L. Maul, RM, T/Surgeon Lt C. J. Milligan RNVR, T/A/Sub Lt R. A. S. Pratt RNR, Paymaster Lt Cdr R. M. P. Skinner, Lt Cdr R. M. H. Sowdon, Midshipman C. H. S. Wilson, T/Paymaster Lt C. J. G. Wright RNVR, Midshipman K. R. Dutta, RIN, 330 ratings, and fifty-five Marines were missing.
	About 250 men managed to abandon the ship and made it to seven Carley floats and debris.
	Gunner E. M. Goldfinch, T/Instructor Lt G. D. L. Harcombe, A/Warrant Engineer E. W. J. Hickey, Schoolmaster A. R. Hughes, T/A/Lt Cdr A. W. Hughes DSC, Cdr E. O. Unwin, T/Sub Lt W. L. Walters RNR, and six ratings died in the water from exposure and injuries before rescue. One rating was killed.
	American steamer NISHMAHA (6076grt) rescued Lt Cdr A. O. Watson, who was wounded, Lt G. E. Milner RNR Rtd, Gunner C. B. Titheridge, T/Sub Lt E. F. Jolliffe RNVR, and sixty-eight ratings after three days and four nights in the water. Five of the ratings died on the 28th before arriving at Trinidad.
	In all, only sixty-seven men survived from a crew of 486.

27 NOVEMBER 1941

	American steamer NISHMAHA (6076grt) rescued seventy-two survivors from sunken light cruiser **DUNEDIN** north of Pernambuco, Brazil.

30 NOVEMBER 1941

	U.68, U.A, U.129 and U.124 began operations 780 sea miles south of St Helena Island.

BALTIC SEA

Kattegat and Skagerrak
Long. E09, 00 – E12, 00   Lat. N60, 00 – N53, 00

1 NOVEMBER 1941

	An RAF aerial mine sank Swedish steamer **SIGRID** (1093grt) near Kiel, Germany. Ten crewmen were lost.

2 NOVEMBER 1941

	German plans to sortie the heavy cruiser ADMIRAL SCHEER into the North Atlantic were put on hold when she developed mechanical defects.

23 NOVEMBER 1941

	A mine sank German steamer **POLLUX** (518grt) in the western Baltic.

27 NOVEMBER 1941

	RAF bombers sank German steamer **CLARA L. M. RUSS** (1600grt) at Lübeck.

Southern Baltic Area
Long. E12, 00 – E22, 00   Lat. N60, 00 – N53, 00

3 NOVEMBER 1941

	A mine sank German steamer **ANNELIESE** (726grt) off Dievenow.
	German auxiliary minesweepers **M.511** and **M.529** were sunk when they entered a German minefield off Kolberg, Germany.
	Russian submarine SHCH-323 (Lt Cdr Ivantsov) unsuccessfully attacked a German steamer off Karlskrona, Sweden.

5 NOVEMBER 1941

	Russian submarine SHCH-323 (Lt Cdr Ivantsov) unsuccessfully attacked a German tanker off Kalmarsund, Sweden.
	Swedish steamer ELIN (grt) sank Finnish coastal sailing ship **HERTTA** (343grt) in a collision in Kalmarsund, Sweden. She was later salvaged.
	Russian submarine LEMBIT (Lt Cdr Matiyasevich) laid mines in Bjorko Sound, Sweden.

7 NOVEMBER 1941

A mine sank German steamer **FRAUENBURG** (2111grt) (ex Estonian **PEET** (2111grt)) off Windau.

11 NOVEMBER 1941

German target vessel ANGELBURG (3053grt) sank **U.580** (ObltzS Kuhlmann) in a collision during night training exercises off Memel in 55, 45N, 20, 40E. Twelve crewmen were lost, while thirty-two crewmen were rescued.

15 NOVEMBER 1941

U.583 (Kptlt Ratsch) was sunk in a collision during night training with U.153 off Danzig in 55, 23N, 17, 05E. Forty-five crewmen were lost.

17 NOVEMBER 1941

A mine sank German steamer **SCHWANECK** (2194grt) near Stettin, Germany.

19 NOVEMBER 1941

A Russian submarine mine sank German steamer **HENNY** (764grt) off Memel, East Prussia. Some sources have her being sunk on 28 November.

22 NOVEMBER 1941

A Russian mine sank Swedish tanker **UNO** (408grt) three miles off the entrance to Memel. One crewman was lost.

A Russian mine sank German fishing vessel **GERTRUD KAMPF** (471grt) near Libau.

26 NOVEMBER 1941

A Russian mine sank German steamer **EGERAN** (1143grt) off Memel.

Swedish steamer **CAJE** (grt) went missing off Karlshamn, Sweden.

28 NOVEMBER 1941

German steamer **GERDA FERDINAND** (3727grt) foundered north of Stockholm, Sweden.

A Russian submarine mine sank German steamer **HENNY** (764grt) near Memel. Some sources have her being sunk on 19 November.

Gulf of Finland

Long. E22, 00 – E30, 00   Lat. N61, 00 – N57, 00

1 NOVEMBER 1941

The Russian Baltic Fleet (Vice Adm. V. P. Drozd) departed Suursaari with destroyers STOIKI and SLAVNY, Minelayer MARTI (Kpt. 1st Class N. I. Mescherski), minesweepers T-207/SHPIL, T-210/GAK, T-215 and T-217 plus five MO-IV class submarine hunters to begin evacuating Russian troops from Hangö. On the return voyage, the group detonated sixteen mines, which damaged the MARTI and T-210. That night they evacuated 4230 men.

To support the evacuation effort, Russian submarines S-9 and SHCH-324 patrolled the entrance to the gulf of Finland, while S-7 patrolled off Reval, Estonia.

A mine sank Russian submarine **KALEV** (Lt Cdr Nyrov) somewhere between Hangö and Suursaari.

2 NOVEMBER 1941

A second Hangö evacuation convoy (Capt 2nd Class Narykov) departed Kronstadt with destroyer SUROVY and SMETLIVY, minesweepers T-205/GAFEL, T-206/VERP, T-207/SHPIL and T-211/RYM plus four MO-IV class submarine chasers and four TKA boats.

Russian submarine **SHCH-324** (Lt Cdr Tarkhnishvili) departed Kronstadt on a patrol and was lost to a mine between 5 and 7 November.

3 NOVEMBER 1941

Finnish artillery damaged Russian destroyer SMETLIVY with a shell hit off Hangö.

German minelayer KAISER (KKpt. Bohm) laid 150 EMC mines west of Minefield JUMINDA in the Gulf of Finland.

A German mine damaged Finnish minesweeper KUHA 3 (18grt) off Bjerkesund.

Russian submarine S-4 unsuccessfully patrolled off the Finnish coast until 18 November.

Russian submarine S-9 unsuccessfully patrolled in the Aaland Sea until 18 November.

Russian submarine S-7 unsuccessfully patrolled in Narva Bay until 18 November.

4 NOVEMBER 1941

After departing Hangö with the evacuation convoy, Russian destroyer **SMETLIVY** (Capt 2nd Class Maslov †) ran into two mines of the Minefield CORBETHA and sank. Russian minesweeper T-205/GAFEL rescued 350 survivors and took them back to Hangö. The remainder of the convoy arrived at Suursaari with 1200 men.

8 NOVEMBER 1941

German artillery sank Russian Minelaying submarine **L-1** off Leningrad. She was later raised, but not repaired.

9 NOVEMBER 1941

Russian submarine SHCH-309 patrolled German shipping lanes until 21 November.

Russian submarine SHCH-311 patrolled German shipping lanes until 26 November.

The third Russian evacuation convoy (Rear Adm. M. S. Moskalenko) departed Kronstadt with destroyer STOIKI, destroyer leader LENINGRAD, Minelayer URAL (Capt 2nd Class Karpov), troopship ANDREI ZHDANOV (3870grt) (Capt 1st Class Meshchersky), minesweepers T-201/ZARYAD, T-211/RYM, T-215, T-217, and T-218 plus four MO-IV class submarine chasers for Hangö.

10 NOVEMBER 1941

Russian submarine L-2 (Lt Cdr Chebanov) departed Kronstadt to lay mines off Danzig.

Russian submarine M-98 (Lt Cdr Bezzubikov) departed Kronstadt for a patrol off Tallinn, Estonia.

Russian minesweepers T-217 and T-218 were heavily damaged when they collided in heavy fog off the south coast of Finland. Both returned to Kronstadt.

11 NOVEMBER 1941

Due to the heavy fog, the third Russian evacuation convoy temporarily heads back towards Suursaari, but then changed course back to Hangö when darkness fell.

During the night, Russian destroyer leader LENINGRAD (Capt 3rd Class Gorbachev) hit two mines. She heads back to Suursaari escorted by two minesweepers and the troopship ANDREI ZHDANOV (3870grt).

12 NOVEMBER 1941

The remainder of the Russian third evacuation convoy change course in the morning to return to Suursaari.

Finnish minelayers RIILAHTI and RUOTSINSALMI laid one hundred and forty-one EMC mines northwest of Minefield JUMINDA.

13 NOVEMBER 1941

The fourth Russian evacuation convoy (Capt 2nd Class V. N. Narykov) departed Suursaari for Hangö with destroyers SUROVY and GORDY, Minelayer URAL, minesweepers T-206/VERP, T-207/SHPIL, T-211/RYM and T-215 plus four MO-IV-class submarine chasers.

During the late evening, the Russian evacuation convoy entered the newly laid Finnish minefield with Russian destroyer **SUROVY** (Capt 3rd Class Ustinov), minesweeper **T-206/VERP** and submarine chaser **MO-301** being sunk by mines.

14 NOVEMBER 1941

A mine in the newly extended German Minefield JUMINDA sank Russian submarine **M-98** (Lt Cdr Bezzubikov) west of Suursaari.

In the early morning, Russian destroyer **GORDY** (Capt 3rd Class Efet) entered the German Minefield CORBETHA and was sunk by a mine.
Only Russian minesweeper T-215, Minelayer URAL and three submarine chasers reached Hangö.
After the heavy loss of the larger destroyers, the remaining evacuation convoys would use smaller ships.

A mine sank Russian submarine **L-2** between Suursaari and Hangö.

15 NOVEMBER 1941

Russian submarine SHCH-311 (Lt Cdr Sidorenko) unsuccessfully attacked a German steamer with five torpedoes and 45-mm gunfire.

The Russian evacuation convoy departed Hangö for Suursaari with minesweepers T-205/GAFEL, T-217 and T-218 plus three MO-IV-class submarine hunters.

19 NOVEMBER 1941

The next Russian evacuation convoy (Capt 3rd Class D. M. Belkov) departed Suursaari with Netlayer AZIMUT, patrol boat T-297/VIRSAITIS, minesweepers T-58, T-35/MENZHINSKI, T-42 and T-54/KLYUZ to Hangö.

20 NOVEMBER 1941

Another Russian evacuation convoy departed Suursaari with minesweepers T-205/GAFEL, T-217, T-218, Transport No.548/MINNA plus two submarine hunters for Hangö. The transport and the submarine hunters were forced to return to Suursaari.

21 NOVEMBER 1941

The Russian evacuation convoy departed Hangö for Suursaari.
Mines sank Netlayer **AZIMUT** and minesweeper **T-35/MENZHINSKI** during the night.

A mine sank German trawler **FOHN** (303grt) off Hangö.

During the night, Russian Transport No.10 departed Suursaari with five motor minesweepers for Hangö, Finland.

22 NOVEMBER 1941

A German evacuation convoy (KptIt Dus) departed Suursaari with Transport No.568/MINNA, patrol boat T-76/KORALL, minesweeper T-53/UDARNIK and two submarine chasers for Hangö.

23 NOVEMBER 1941

A Russian evacuation convoy (Capt 3rd Class Belkov) departed Suursaari with minesweepers T-42, KLJUZ, and T-297/VISAITIS plus two submarine chasers for Hangö.

During the night, Russian gunboat LAYNE (Capt Verzbitski) evacuated 165 men from Odensholm Island to Hangö.

24 NOVEMBER 1941

A Russian evacuation convoy departed Hangö with Transport No.548/MINNA, minesweepers T-53/UDARNIK, T-54/KLYUZ, and VERSAYTIS for Suursaari.
Mines sank Transport No.548/MINNA, T-54/KLYUZ and VERSAYTIS.
A mine lightly damaged T-53/UDARNIK.
In spite of these heavy losses, by the end of November, the Russians evacuated 4424 men, eighteen tanks, 720-tons of provisions and 250-tons of munitions from Hangö.

25 NOVEMBER 1941

The fourth Russian evacuation convoy arrived at Kronstadt with minesweepers T-205/GAFEL, T-217 and T-218 plus three MO-IV-class submarine chasers carrying 4588 troops from Hangö.

During the night, Russian gunboat LAYNE (Capt Verzbitski) evacuated seventy men from Odensholm Island to Hangö.

26 NOVEMBER 1941

A mine damaged Russian destroyer LENINGRAD off Hangö, Finland. She was later repaired.

28 NOVEMBER 1941

During the night, Russian gunboat LAYNE (Capt Verzbitski) evacuated 206 men from Odensholm Island to Hangö. In all, she evacuated 441 men in three trips to Hangö.

29 NOVEMBER 1941

Another evacuation group (Capt 2nd Class N. A. Mamontov) departed Kronstadt with destroyers STOIKI and SLAVNY, transport JOSIF STALIN, minesweepers T-205/GAFEL, T-207/SHPIL, T-211/RYM, T-215, T-217, T-218, seven submarine hunters and four MTBs for Hangö, Finland.

German aircraft sank Russian Icebreaker **OKTYABR** off Finland near Suursaari.

30 NOVEMBER 1941

The Russian evacuation group (Capt 2nd Class N. A. Mamontov) with destroyers STOIKI and SLAVNY, transport JOSIF STALIN, minesweepers T-205/GAFEL, T-207/SHPIL, T-211/RYM, T-215, T-217, T-218, seven submarine hunters and four MTBs arrived at Hangö, Finland from Kronstadt.

During the night of 30 November/1 December, another Russian evacuation group (Lt Cdr Shevtsov) departed Kronstadt for Hangö with Transport No.539/MAYA, minesweeper T-210/GAK, gunboat VOLGA, minesweepers UDARNIK and T-297/VIRSAITIS, plus submarine chasers MO-405 and MO-406.

A Finnish attack group with gunboats KUUSIMAA and MAMEENMAA, to boats of the 3rd Patrol Boat Flotilla, plus four motor patrol boats unsuccessfully searched for the Russian evacuation convoys.

MEDITERRANEAN SEA & MIDDLE EAST

East of Gibraltar
Long. W05, 30 – E11, 00   Lat. N44, 30 – N35, 00

1 NOVEMBER 1941

	Submarine UTMOST (Lt Cdr Cayley) finally sank damaged Italian steamer **MARIGOLA** (5996grt) 2.3 miles 165° from Kuriat Island.
	Submarine UTMOST and Polish submarine SOKOL (Lt Cdr Karnicki) jointly sank Italian steamer **BALILLA** (2469grt) with gunfire off the northern Tunisian coast.

2 NOVEMBER 1941

	Submarine **TETRARCH** (1095grt) was lost in the western Mediterranean while on passage from Malta to Gibraltar.

4 NOVEMBER 1941

	Italian submarine DANDOLO (Lt Cdr Auconi) damaged French tanker **TARN** (4220grt) with a torpedo off Algiers in 36N, 2E.
	Italian sailing ship **AMBROGIO G.** (81grt) went missing in the Ligurian Sea.

8 NOVEMBER 1941

	Italian submarine DANDOLO (Lt Cdr Auconi) sank Spanish steamer **CASTILLO OROPESA** (6600grt) near Melilla. The entire crew was rescued.

9 NOVEMBER 1941

	Submarine OLYMPUS unsuccessfully attacked Italian store ship MAURO CROCE (1049grt) with torpedoes and gunfire in the Gulf of Genoa.
	Dutch submarine O.21 departed Gibraltar for a patrol in the Mediterranean.

10 NOVEMBER 1941

	Italian submarines ARADAM, SQUALO, TURCHESE, BANDIERA, ONICE and NARVALO patrolled east of Gibraltar.
	In Operation PERPETUAL, Force H (Vice Adm. Somerville) with battleship MALAYA, aircraft carriers ARK ROYAL (Capt Maund) and ARGUS, light cruiser HERMIONE, plus destroyers LAFOREY, LEGION, LIGHTNING, GURKHA, SIKH, ZULU, and the Dutch ISAAC SWEERS departed Gibraltar to launch aircraft to Malta.

12 NOVEMBER 1941

	Submarine OLYMPUS arrived at Gibraltar from a patrol in the Mediterranean.
<1159	An Italian reconnaissance aircraft spotted Force H and alerted U.205 (Kptlt Reschke) and U.81 (Kptlt Guggenberger) of its position south of Sardinia.
>1200	In Operation PERPETUAL, aircraft carriers ARK ROYAL and ARGUS launched seven Blenheim bombers and thirty-four of thirty-seven Hurricane fighter aircraft to Malta. Force H then headed back to Gibraltar.

13 NOVEMBER 1941

	Battleship MALAYA, aircraft carrier ARGUS, and light cruiser HERMIONE arrived at Gibraltar, completing Operation PERPETUAL.
<1159	U.205 (Kptlt Reschke) unsuccessfully attacked destroyer LEGION and the aircraft carrier ARK ROYAL east of Gibraltar. One torpedo detonated when it hit the propeller wash from LEGION. The ARK ROYAL launched six Swordfish aircraft, but they did not spot and U-boats in the area.
1437	U.81 (Kptlt Guggenberger) torpedoed aircraft carrier ARK ROYAL (Capt Maund) with a torpedo amidships out of four launched from long distance east of Gibraltar in 36, 03N, 04, 45W.
>1438	Destroyer WILD SWAN, tugboats ST DAY and THAMES, plus motor-launches ML.121, ML.130, ML.132, ML.135, ML.170, ML.172, and ML.176 departed Gibraltar to assist the ARK ROYAL. Tugs THAMES and ST DAY arrived and took the damaged ARK ROYAL in tow.

14 NOVEMBER 1941

	Italian torpedo bombing sank steamer **EMPIRE PELICAN** (6463grt) while she was en route to Malta from Gibraltar, sailing alone as part of Operation ASTROLOGER, ten miles southwest of Galita Island. One crewman was lost. Thirty-five crewmen and nine gunners were made prisoners of war.
	The German 3rd S-Boat Flotilla (KKpt. Kemnade) arrived at Marseilles, France after a trip up the Rhine river, through the French canals, and then down the Rhone river to reach the Mediterranean. They were placed under the command of the German Naval Command Italy.

0613	Aircraft carrier **ARK ROYAL** (22,600grt) (Capt Maund) sank twenty-five sea miles from Gibraltar. Only one rating, Able Seaman E. Mitchell, was lost.

15 NOVEMBER 1941

	Italian torpedo bombing sank steamer **EMPIRE DEFENDER** (5649grt) while she was en route to Malta from Gibraltar, sailing alone as part of Operation ASTROLOGER, eighteen sea miles south of Galita Island. Four crewmen were lost and the rest of the crew were made prisoners of war.

16 NOVEMBER 1941

	A convoy of steamers BLAIRATHOLL (3319grt), BARON NEWLANDS (3386grt), SHUNA (1575grt), CISNEROS (1886grt), and OTTINGE (2870grt), and oiler BROWN RANGER (3417grt) departed Gibraltar escorted by destroyer WILD SWAN, sloop DEPTFORD, plus corvettes CONVOLVULUS, RHODODENDRON, and MARIGOLD. The convoy, Operation CHIEFTAIN, was a diversion for Operation CRUSADER in the eastern Mediterranean. Destroyer WILD SWAN made a U-boat contact and she was joined by corvette SAMPHIRE. Corvette MARIGOLD sank the **U.433** south of Malaga in 36, 13N, 04, 42W. Six officers and thirty-two ratings were rescued, while six ratings were lost. The convoy proceeded towards Malta, but after nightfall on the 18th, the steamers returned to Gibraltar.

17 NOVEMBER 1941

	Vichy French forces seized Dutch steamers **PLUTO** (1156grt) and **RHEA** (1388grt) at Algiers.

19 NOVEMBER 1941

	Dutch submarine O.21 sank two sailing ships in the Tyrrhenian Sea.

22 NOVEMBER 1941

	Dutch submarine O.21 sank Italian sailing ship **SAN SALVATORE** (92grt) off Sardinia in 41, 25N, 10, 42E.

24 NOVEMBER 1941

	Submarine OLYMPUS departed Gibraltar with aviation petrol and other stores for Malta.

28 NOVEMBER 1941

	Dutch submarine O.21 (Lt Cdr van Dulm) sank **U.95** (Kptlt Schreiber) east of Gibraltar southwest of Almeria in 36, 21N, 03, 27W. The O.21 rescued the German commanding officer, three other officers, and eight ratings. Thirty-three crewmen were lost. The submarine arrived back at Gibraltar later in the day.

29 NOVEMBER 1941

	Submarine CLYDE departed Gibraltar to patrol the area in 35, 50N, 03, 20W.

30 NOVEMBER 1941

	Dutch submarine O.24 departed Gibraltar to patrol off Oran, Algeria.

Middle Mediterranean Sea

Long. E11, 00 – E20, 00   Lat. N46, 00 – N30, 00

1 NOVEMBER 1941

	RAF Wellington bombers attacked Italian steamer CAPO ARMA (3195grt), escorted by torpedo boat PROCIONE, while they were en route to Benghazi, Libya from Brindisi, Italy. The bombing damaged the steamer, but she reached Benghazi later that day.
	Force K with light cruisers AURORA and PENELOPE plus destroyers LANCE and LIVELY departed Malta for a patrol during the night of 1/2 November. No contact was made and the ships returned to Malta on the 2nd.
	A Swordfish aircraft of 830 Squadron failed to return from a mission in which six Swordfish unsuccessfully searched for an Italian convoy. An Italian ship rescued Sub Lt W. E. Cotton, Sub Lt D. H. Stokes RNVR, and Leading Airman E. A. Robson after they spent seven days adrift.

2 NOVEMBER 1941

	Polish submarine SOKOL damaged Italian steamer **BALILLA** (2469grt) (ex **GOTHIC** (2469grt)) northwest of Trapani, Sicily with torpedoes and gunfire in 38, 22N, 12, 20E. Submarine UTMOST sank the damaged steamer with gunfire later in the day.
	Submarine THRASHER unsuccessfully attacked a minelayer off Benghazi.

3 NOVEMBER 1941

	Submarines OTUS and REGENT ended unsuccessful patrols off Libya, while UNIQUE, ULTIMATUM, URSULA and URGE took up patrol positions in the approaches to Tripoli.
	Submarine URGE unsuccessfully attacked a steamer north of Kuriat.
	Submarine UTMOST arrived at Malta after a special mission in the Gulf of Hammamet and a patrol off Kuriat.
	Polish submarine SOKOL arrived at Malta after a patrol off Naples, Italy.

4 NOVEMBER 1941

	An Italian convoy departed Brindisi with steamer BOSFORO (3567grt) and German steamer SAVONA (2120grt) escorted by torpedo boat PEGASO for Benghazi. British aircraft sighted the Benghazi convoy on the 8th as it left the Adriatic. Malta based aircraft heavily attacked the convoy. German steamer SAVONA was damaged in the attack and returned to Brindisi. Italian steamer BOSFORO and torpedo boat PEGASO put into Navarino, Greece. Both ships later departed Navarino and arrived at Benghazi on the 12th.
	Submarine TRUSTY arrived at Malta after off patrol off Cephalonia, Greece.

5 NOVEMBER 1941

	RAF bombing sank Italian steamer **ANNA ZIPPITELLI** (1019grt) west of Benghazi in 31, 49N, 18, 25W. She was in a small convoy with another steamer escorted by Italian torpedo boat CALLIOPE. The other steamer arrived safely at Benghazi the next day.

7 NOVEMBER 1941

	Italian convoy BETA departed Naples for Tripoli with German troopship DUISBERG (7389grt), Italian troopships SAN MARCO (3113grt), MARIA (6339grt), and SAGITTA (5153grt) plus Italian tanker MINATITLAN (7599grt) from Naples with Italian troopship RINA CORRADO (5180grt) and Italian tanker CONTE DI MISURATA (5014grt) from Messina, escorted by destroyers MAESTRALE (KptzS. Bisciani), EURO, FULMINE, GRECALE, ORIANI, and LIBECCIO. Italian heavy cruisers TRENTO and TRIESTE plus destroyers GRANATIERE, FUCILIERE, BERSAGLIERE, and ALPINO provided cover for the convoy on 8 November.
	Submarine UPHOLDER departed Malta for patrol off Cephalonia.

8 NOVEMBER 1941

	Force K with light cruisers AURORA (Capt Agnew) and PENELOPE (Capt Nicholl) plus destroyers LANCE and LIVELY departed Malta to attack the Italian Supply convoy based upon ULTRA messages. An RAF Maryland aircraft of 69 Squadron, out of Malta, located the convoy and provided its exact position to Force K.
	Italian heavy cruisers TRENTO (Capt Parmigiano with Division Adm. Brivonesi on board) and TRIESTE (Capt Rouselle) plus the 13th Destroyer Flottilla (Capt Capponi) with destroyers GRANATIERE, FUCILIERE, BERSAGLIERE, and ALPINO departed Messina, Sicily to cover the troop convoy BETA to Tripoli.
	RAF bombers sank Italian steamer **SANT ANTONIO** (249grt) off Brindisi.
	RAF bombers attacked a small Italian convoy running from Brindisi to Benghazi. The aircraft heavily damaged Italian steamer BOSFORO (3567grt) and lightly damaged German steamer SAVONA (2120grt) during their repeated attacks. The convoy put into Navarino, Greece for protection. The SAVONA returned to Brindisi, while BOSFORO escorted by Italian torpedo boat PEGASO continued on and reached Benghazi on 12 November.
	Submarine UPHOLDER (Lt Cdr Wanklyn) unsuccessfully attacked a submarine south of Italy in 36, 19N, 16, 22E.

9 NOVEMBER 1941

	Italian submarines BEILUL, CORALLO, DELFINO and SETTEMBRINI on patrol to cover Italian convoy BETA were unable to fire their torpedoes due to the chaotic night battle.
	A small Italian convoy with two steamers escorted by torpedo boat CENTAURO successfully ran from Tripoli, Libya to Benghazi, Libya.
	A small return convoy ran from Benghazi with three steamers escorted by Italian torpedo boats CALLIOPE and CASCINO to Tripoli without any British contact.
	Submarine PORPOISE arrived at Malta from Gibraltar with naval stores and kerosene.
0100	Force K gunfire sank convoy BETA troopships **DUISBERG** (7389grt) (German), **SAN MARCO** (3113grt), **MARIA** (6339grt), and **SAGITTA** (5153grt), and **RINA CORRADO** (5180grt), tankers **MINATITLAN** (7599grt) and **CONTE DI MISURATA** (5014grt) plus destroyer **FULMINE**. Force K gunfire also damaged Italian destroyers EURO and GRECALE. Italian destroyer ORIANI towed damaged Italian destroyer GRECALE from the area. Italian destroyers MAESTRALE, EURO, ORIANI, ALPINO, FUCILIERE, and BERSAGLIERE with hospital ship VIRGILIO from Augusta, Sicily and hospital ship ARNO from Benghazi, plus Italian destroyers DA RECCO

	and USODIMARE from Benghazi and destroyer GIOBERTI from Trapani helped rescue 704 Italian and German survivors.
0100	Italian heavy cruisers TRENTO and TRIESTE moved closer to Malta in case any British ships were to attack the convoy with Italian destroyers GRANATIERE, FUCILIERE, BERSAGLIERE, and ALPINO. Unfortunately, they did not have RADAR and sailed right past Force K in the dark. When they saw the gunfire, they thought that the convoy escort had mistaken them as an enemy force, so they did not close in to the area for fear of hitting their own ships. After this fiasco, Italian Division Adm. Brivonesi and Capt Bisciani were both dismissed.
>0101	Force K returned to Malta while avoiding Italian torpedo bombers sent to attack them. The ULTRA messages alerted the ships as to where the Italian aircraft were heading to attack the force. The position information enabled the Force K ships to alter their course sufficiently to miss most of the Italian aircraft.
0640	Submarine UPHOLDER (Lt Cdr Wanklyn) torpedoed Italian destroyer **LIBECCIO** while she rescued survivors in 36, 50N, 18, 10E. Italian destroyer EURO tried to tow the damaged destroyer, but she sank after she experienced an internal collapse.
1107	Submarine UPHOLDER unsuccessfully attacked the Italian heavy cruisers TRENTO and TRIESTE with torpedoes in 37, 12N, 18, 33E.

10 NOVEMBER 1941

	Submarine UPHOLDER arrived at Malta after her patrol.

11 NOVEMBER 1941

	A small Italian supply convoy departed Trapani for Tripoli with two steamers escorted by torpedo boat PRESTINARI. Due to the heavy British air and sea efforts in the area, the convoy was rerouted first to Pantellaria and then towards the coast of Tunisia. The two steamers put in to Zuara for safety. They later reached Tripoli on 17 and 30 November.

12 NOVEMBER 1941

	Submarine PORPOISE departed Malta for Alexandria.
	During a shipping sweep during the night of 11/12 November, seven Swordfish aircraft of 830 Swordfish took off from Malta to attack a convoy of two merchant ships and escorts reported west of Pantellaria. The Swordfish aircraft piloted by Lt P. E. O'Brien, Sub Lt (A) M. Thorpe, and T/A/Sub Lt (A) R. S. Vercoe RNVR were forced to return to Malta with engine problems. Four other Swordfish aircraft were lost when they ran out of fuel while returning to Malta. Lt Cdr J.G. Hunt, Lt G. M. T. Osborn DSC, and Sergeant M. Parke; T/A/Sub Lt (A) S. W. L. Campbell RNVR, and Leading Airman J. R. Fallon; T/Sub Lt (A) R. W. Taylor RNVR and P/T/A/Sub Lt (A) F. L. Robinson RNVR were rescued and made prisoners of war. Lt (A) A. F. Wigram RNVR and Leading Airman K. D. Griffiths were not found.

13 NOVEMBER 1941

	Italian submarines ATROPO, SAINT BON, CAGNI and MILLO began regular supply runs between Taranto, Italy and Bardia, Libya until 26 November. The submarines were used because of the heavy losses in surface ships from the British forces at Malta.
	Submarine REGENT arrived at Malta from Alexandria with passengers, stores, and kerosene. On the 12th, her starboard engine broke down completely and she limped into Malta with only her port engine operating.

14 NOVEMBER 1941

	A small Italian supply convoy departed Taranto, Italy for Benghazi with steamers CITTA DI GENOVA (5413grt) and CITTA DI NAPOLI (5418grt) escorted by Italian destroyers PIGAFETTA and VERAZZANO. They arrived safely on the 16th.
	Submarines TORBAY and TALISMAN landed commandoes on the North African coast to strike at Rommel's Headquarters near Apollonia. The mission failed to get Rommel and submarines arrived back at Alexandria on the 23rd.

15 NOVEMBER 1941

	Dutch submarine O.21 unsuccessfully attacked Italian steamer NINETTO G. (5335grt) while attacking a small convoy in the Tyrrhenian Sea.
	Submarines UPRIGHT and URGE unsuccessfully patrolled the Ionian sea until 28 November. Each unsuccessfully attacked small Italian convoys in the area.

16 NOVEMBER 1941

	Dutch submarine O.21 unsuccessfully attacked Italian steamer ITU (1578grt) while attacking a convoy in the

17 NOVEMBER 1941

	Tyrrhenian Sea.
	A small Italian return convoy departed Benghazi for Taranto with two steamers escorted by Italian destroyers PIGAFETTA and VERAZZANO. They arrived safely on the 20th.
	Submarines UPRIGHT and URGE unsuccessfully attacked a convoy in the Ionian Sea.

18 NOVEMBER 1941

	A small Italian supply convoy departed Taranto for Tripoli with three steamers escorted by Italian torpedo boat CENTAURO. RAF aircraft attacked the convoy on the 19th, but all ships arrived safely on the 20th.
	An Italian convoy of steamers AMBA ARADAM (405grt) and BROOK (1225grt) arrived at Benghazi from Brindisi escorted by torpedo boat PARTENOPE.
	Force K departed Malta with light cruisers AURORA and PENELOPE plus destroyers LANCE and LIVELY to participate in the Operation CHIEFTAIN. The ships arrived back at Malta during the night of 18/19 November.
	Submarine PERSEUS, which had been under repair at Malta, departed Malta on sea trials, but was forced to return with a defective hydroplane.

19 NOVEMBER 1941

	A small Italian supply convoy departed Tripoli for Benghazi with two steamers escorted by Italian torpedo boat PRESTINARI. They arrived safely on the 22nd.
	Submarine THRASHER claimed sinking a small Italian ship near Brindisi.
	Italian convoy A departed Tripoli for Naples with steamers ANKARA (4768grt) and SEBASTINO VENIER (6311grt) escorted by destroyers MAESTRALE, ORIANI, and GIOBERTI. Due to British naval activity, the convoy was diverted from the Messina Strait to Taranto where they arrived on the 22nd.
	An Italian supply convoy departed Taranto with two steamers escorted by destroyers ZENO and MALOCELLO plus torpedo boat PARTENOPE for Benghazi. Due to mechanical defects, one of the steamers was taken to Suda Bay, Crete. The other steamer arrived at Benghazi on 21 November escorted by ZENO and PARTENOPE. The second steamer arrived at Benghazi on 24 November escorted by destroyer MALOCELLO.
	Submarine OSIRIS arrived at Malta after a patrol off Candia, Crete.

20 NOVEMBER 1941

	Italian supply convoy C departed Naples with steamers NAPOLI (6142grt) and VETTOR PISANI (6339grt) escorted by destroyer TURBINE and torpedo boat PERSEO for Tripoli. Italian heavy cruisers GORIZIA (Division Adm. Parona), TRENTO and TRIESTE departed Naples and covered the convoy.
	Submarine URSULA arrived at Malta after a patrol off Misurata.
	Lt W. J. Pangbourne was killed when his Hurricane aircraft of 806 Squadron was shot down south of El Adem.

21 NOVEMBER 1941

	Dutch submarine O.21 unsuccessfully attacked an Italian steamer in the Tyrrhenian Sea.
	Destroyer ZENO departed Benghazi with a steamer that arrived safely at Taranto.
	Cruiser CADORNA departed Brindisi with gasoline for Benghazi. She claimed she was unsuccessfully attacked by a submarine during the night of 22 November, but arrived safely. There are no corresponding submarine reports for an allied submarine attack on this date.
	An Italian convoy departed Taranto with steamers CITTA DI TUNISI (5419grt) and CITTA DI PALERMO (5413grt) escorted by destroyers ZENO and MALOCELLO for Benghazi. This convoy was joined by torpedo boat PARTENOPE from Benghazi.
	An Italian convoy departed Brindisi with tanker BERBERA (2093grt) escorted by torpedo boat PEGASO.
	Submarine URGE arrived at Malta after a patrol off Cephalonia, Greece.
0023	Italian heavy cruisers GORIZIA (Division Adm. Parona), TRENTO and TRIESTE were detached from convoy C.
0530	A second Italian convoy departed Naples with steamers IRIDIO MANTOVANI (10,540grt) and MONGINEVRO (5324grt) escorted by destroyer DA RECCO and torpedo boat COSENZ.
0810	Italian light cruisers GARIBALDI and ABRUZZI, plus destroyers AVIERE, CAMICIA NERA, GENIERE, CORAZZIERE, and CARABINIERE departed Naples to cover the second convoy.
1300	Force K had departed Malta with supply ship BRECONSHIRE (9776grt) plus steamers SYDNEY STAR (11,095grt), AJAX (7540grt), and CLAN FERGUSON (7347grt), escorted by corvette GLOXINIA to draw out Italian forces in Operation LANDMARK. The British ships arrived back at Malta early on the 22nd.
1930	Italian heavy cruisers GORIZIA, TRIESTE, and TRENTO departed Naples to cover the Italian convoys. British bombing damaged heavy cruiser GORIZIA with bomb splinters during a raid on Naples shortly before the Italian ships departed.

2130		British Malta based aircraft attacked the Naples convoys shortly before they cleared the Messina Strait.
2312		Submarine UTMOST (Lt Cdr Cayley) torpedoed Italian heavy cruiser TRIESTE (Capt Rouselle) in 37, 48N, 15, 32E. Light cruiser GARIBALDI and destroyer BERSAGLIERE escorted the TRIESTE to Messina, arriving on the 22nd.

22 NOVEMBER 1941

	The German B-Service reported that Force K had departed Malta to attack the Italian convoys at sea. Italian submarines DELTINO, SQUALO, TRICHECO, SETTEMBRINI and CORALLO patrolled east of Malta, but did not sight any targets.
	A small fast Italian convoy departed Trapani with a steamer escorted by destroyers USODIMARE, SAETTA, and SEBENICO plus torpedo boat CENTAURO for Tripoli. They arrived safely the next day.
0038	Swordfish aircraft of 830 Squadron torpedoed Italian light cruiser DUCA DEGLI ABRUZZI (KptzS. Zannoni). LT P. E. O'Brien and T/Sub Lt (A) A. J. Griffith RNVR of 830 Squadron were shot down. O'Brien was killed and Griffith was rescued by Italian destroyer PESSAGNO and made a prisoner of war. ABRUZZI, her stern blown off, proceeded to Messina for repairs under her own power and was escorted by Italian light cruiser GARIBALDI plus destroyers VIVALDI, DA NOLI, GRANATIERE, FUCILIERE, ALPINO, CORAZZIERE, CARABINIERE, and TURBINE and torpedo boat PERSEO. Despite further air attacks on the ABRUZZI force, particularly on light cruiser GARIBALDI, no further damage was done.
0100	Covered by Italian heavy cruiser GORIZIA and destroyer AVIERE, the Italian convoys were ordered to Taranto in view of continuing air attacks. Italian destroyer GENIERE escorted steamers VETTOR PISANI (6339grt) and NAPOLI (6142grt) to Taranto. Italian destroyer CAMICIA NERA escorted steamer IRIDIO MANTOVANI (10,540grt) to Taranto. Italian destroyer PESSAGNO escorted steamer MONGINEVRO (5324grt) to Taranto.

23 NOVEMBER 1941

	Dutch submarine O.21 unsuccessfully attacked an Italian steamer in the Tyrrhenian Sea.
	Force K departed Malta with light cruisers AURORA (Capt Agnew) and PENELOPE plus destroyers LANCE and LIVELY.
	While Italian light cruiser CARDONA was returning from Benghazi, Italian steamer ADRIATICO (1976grt) departed Reggio, Italy unescorted for Benghazi. Italian steamer VINICOLO (grt) departed Trapani, Sicily unescorted for Tripoli. Italian steamer BOSFORO (3567grt) departed Benghazi escorted by destroyer STRALE to return to Brindisi. Italian steamer FABIO FILZI (6835grt) departed Trapani with destroyers USODIMARE and SAETTA for Tripoli. Italian destroyer SEBENICO and torpedo boat CENTAURO joined a steamer from Tripoli.
	Italian sailing ship **ELENA** (grt) went missing off Palermo, Sicily.
	Italian fishing ship **NUOVO SANT'ANTONIO** (grt) went missing off Terrene.
	T/Sub Lt (A) A. J. C. Willis RNVR was killed when his Hurricane aircraft of 806 Squadron from GREBE crashed at Bir el Gu.

24 NOVEMBER 1941

	Dutch submarine O.21 sank Italian coastal steamer **UNIONE** (216grt) northeast of Troca in 41, 06N, 10, 02E.

25 NOVEMBER 1941

	An Italian mine damaged German steamer **ZIRONA** (grt) (ex Yugoslavian **JASTREB** (grt)) during an air attack on Benghazi. She was beached to prevent her sinking.
	An RAF air attack sank German steamer **TINOS** (2826grt) at Benghazi.
	Submarine THRASHER (Lt Mackenzie) sank Italian AMC **ATTILO DEFFENU** (3510grt) near Brindisi in 40, 37N, 18, 27E from a Patrasso to Brindisi convoy including steamers CATERINA MADRE (4019grt) and RESURRECTIO (979grt).
0730	Force K returned to Malta after a successful convoy hunt.

27 NOVEMBER 1941

	Submarine UPHOLDER unsuccessfully attacked a northbound tanker off eastern Tunisia.
	Italian submarines SQUALO and DELFINO patrolled southeast of Sicily.
	Italian submarines ALAGI and ARADAM patrolled of the Cyrenaica coast.
	Submarine TRUSTY unsuccessfully attacked an unescorted tanker off Argostoli.
	Submarine UTMOST arrived at Malta after a patrol off Del Armi.
	Polish submarine SOKOL arrived at Malta after a patrol off Navarino, Greece.

28 NOVEMBER 1941

	Dutch submarine O.21 sank Italian fishing ship **SAN SALVATORE** (92grt) with gunfire in the Tyrrhenian Sea.

	Dutch submarine O.21 sank Italian coastal sailing ship **UNION** (216grt) off Melilla.
	British bombing sank Italian steamer **PRIARUGGIA** (1196grt) at Benghazi.
	Force K of light cruisers AURORA and PENELOPE plus destroyers LANCE and LIVELY departed Malta to intercept enemy destroyers thought to be departing Benghazi. No contact was made and Force K returned to Malta on the 29th.
	T/Sub Lt (A) E. H. Walshe RNVR, and T/Sub Lt (E) J. H. Lewis of 828 Squadron from ST ANGELO, were taken prisoner after their Albacore aircraft was lost after a night attack on Castel Benito.

29 NOVEMBER 1941

	During the night, Italian submarine TRICHECO unsuccessfully attacked the Force K reinforcements south of Malta.
	Italian steamers ISEO (2366grt) and CAPO FARO (3476grt) departed Brindisi for Benghazi escorted by torpedo boat PROCIONE.
	Steamer IRIDIO MANTOVANI (10,540grt) departed Trapani for Tripoli with destroyer DA MOSTO. This group joined the Italian steamer SEBASTINO VENIER (6311grt) convoy on the 30th.
	Italian tanker VOLTURNO (3363grt) departed Navarino for Benghazi with torpedo boats ARETUSA and PEGASO. Malta based aircraft damaged tanker VOLTURNO and she was forced to return to port.
	Italian steamer ADRIATICO (1976grt) departed Argostoli unescorted for Benghazi.
	Italian steamer SEBASTINO VENIER (6311grt) departed Taranto with destroyer DA VERAZZANO.
	The Italian 7th Cruiser Division (Division Adm de Courten) with light cruisers DUCA D'AOSTA, MONTECUCOLI, and ATTENDOLO departed Taranto with destroyers AVIERE, CAMICIA NERA to provide cover for the Italian convoys.
	Italian battleship CAIO DUILIO (Division Adm. Giovanola) departed Taranto with heavy cruiser GARIBALDI plus destroyers GRANATIERE, ALPINO, BERSAGLIERE, FUCILIERE, CORAZZIERE and CARABINIERE to provide cover for the Italian convoys.
	Submarine UPROAR (Lt Kershaw) unsuccessfully attacked Italian light cruiser MONTECUCOLI south of Italy.

30 NOVEMBER 1941

	Malta based aircraft sank Italian steamer **CAPO FARO** (3476grt) and damaged ISEO (2366grt) between Brindisi for Benghazi in 37, 28N, 19, 20E. Torpedo boat PROCIONE escorted damaged steamer ISEO to Argostoli.
	Italian submarine TRICHECO unsuccessfully attacked a destroyer in 34, 23N, 15, 46E.
	British bombing badly damaged Italian tanker **SPERANZA** (445grt) at Benghazi. She was later scuttled on 23 December.
	Submarine REGENT departed Malta to return to Britain.
	Submarine URSULA departed Malta for Gibraltar.
	Submarine OLYMPUS arrived at Malta from Gibraltar with petrol and stores.
0500	Force B of light cruisers AJAX and NEPTUNE with destroyers KIMBERLEY and KINGSTON and Force K of light cruisers AURORA and PENELOPE with destroyer LIVELY departed Malta to intercept Italian forces in the Ionian Sea.
2330	Force B detached Force K to intercept Italian steamer **ADRIATICO** (1976grt), which was sunk early on 1 December. Destroyer LIVELY picked up two officers and nineteen ratings from the steamer. Italian destroyer VERAZZANO later arrived from Tripoli and rescued further survivors. Force B arrived back at Malta on 1 December. Force K returned to Malta on 2 December.

Eastern Mediterranean Sea
Long. E20, 00 – E38, 00   Lat. N43, 00 – N30, 00

1 NOVEMBER 1941

	British aircraft unsuccessfully attacked U.75 in 33, 44N, 24, 48E.
	Rear Admiral Philip Vian assumed command of Cruiser Squadron 15 with his flag raised on light cruiser NAIAD. The Mediterranean Fleet cruisers at that time included Cruiser Squadron 7 (Rawlings) with AJAX, NEPTUNE, and Australian light cruiser HOBART; Cruiser Squadron 15 (Vian) with NAIAD, GALATEA, EURYALUS, and later by DIDO on 31 December. The cruisers AJAX and NEPTUNE of Cruiser Squadron 7 were later transferred to Malta as Force B and arrived there on the 29th.

2 NOVEMBER 1941

	Minelaying cruiser ABDIEL carried troops to Famagusta, Cyprus escorted by destroyers to relieve the troops garrisoned there in Operation GLENCOE.

	About 250 troops were embarked in each destroyer and three hundred troops and seventy tons of stores were embarked in ABDIEL. The operation called for 11,000 Indian and 3400 British troops to be transport from Alexandria to Famagusta and 15,000 British troops to be transported from Famagusta to Palestine. The Forces were divided into three groups. Minesweeper BAGSHOT sighted a submarine periscope 22 miles 282° from Ras el Tin. Destroyer DECOY and a motor anti-submarine boat were sent from Alexandria to assist in the submarine hunt. Anti-submarine whalers THORGRIM and KOS XIX were sent from patrol to assist in the submarine hunt.
1500	Operation GLENCOE Group A: included Minelaying cruiser ABDIEL (Rear Admiral Destroyers embarked) with destroyers JAGUAR and HASTY departed Alexandria for Famagusta.
1700	Operation GLENCOE Group B: included destroyers JERVIS, KANDAHAR, KIMBERLEY, and KINGSTON departed Alexandria.
1900	Operation GLENCOE Group C: included destroyers NAPIER, NIZAM, KIPLING, and JACKAL departed Alexandria.
2300	En route to Famagusta, destroyer KIPLING broke down in 31, 46N, 30, 22E. Her troops were transferred to destroyer JACKAL, which took the destroyer in tow for Alexandria. Destroyer DECOY departed from Alexandria and took over the tow at daylight on the 3rd. Destroyer JUPITER departed Alexandria and replaced destroyer KIPLING in Group C.

3 NOVEMBER 1941

	Submarine PROTEUS (Lt Francis) damaged Italian tanker TAMPICO (4958grt) in the Gulf of Athens three miles south of Mandili Island in 37, 53N, 24, 30E. Italian torpedo boats MONZAMBANO and CASTELFIDARDO heavily attacked the submarine with depth charges, but she managed to escape.
0730	Operation GLENCOE Group A arrived at Famagusta from Alexandria. Rear Admiral Destroyers disembarked at Famagusta. The destroyers disembarked the new troops and embarked equivalent contingents of troops and departed for Haifa. The ships of Group A arrived at Haifa during the night of 3/4 November.
1230	Operation GLENCOE Group B arrived at Famagusta from Alexandria. The destroyers disembarked the new troops and embarked equivalent contingents of troops and departed for Haifa. The ships of Group B arrived at Haifa during the night of 3/4 November.
1630	Operation GLENCOE Group C arrived at Famagusta from Alexandria. The destroyers disembarked the new troops and embarked equivalent contingents of troops and departed for Haifa.

4 NOVEMBER 1941

	Greek destroyer KONDOURIOTIS departed Alexandria for docking at Suez.
1400	Operation GLENCOE Group C arrived at Haifa, Palestine from Famagusta. All ships disembarked their Famagusta troops, embarked Indian troops, and sailed for Cyprus. The groups arrived at Famagusta during the night of 4/5 November and sailed again at four-hour intervals.

5 NOVEMBER 1941

0400	Operation GLENCOE Group A arrived at Haifa from Famagusta.
0730	Operation GLENCOE Group A departed Haifa for Famagusta. The Group arrived at Famagusta and sailed again with further Indian troop contingents for Haifa.
0830	Operation GLENCOE Group B arrived at Haifa from Famagusta.
1200	Operation GLENCOE Group C arrived at Haifa from Famagusta.
1230	Operation GLENCOE Group B departed Haifa for Famagusta. The Group arrived at Famagusta and sailed again with further Indian troop contingents for Haifa.
1630	Operation GLENCOE Group C departed Haifa for Famagusta. The Group arrived at Famagusta and sailed again with further Indian troop contingents for Haifa.
2220	Anti-submarine whaler KOS XIX reported sighting a periscope thirty-two miles west of Alexandria. Anti-submarine whaler FALK, corvette SNAPDRAGON, and anti-submarine boat MA/SB.2 joined the whaler to search for the submarine. Destroyer ENCOUNTER was also sent from Alexandria to assist.

6 NOVEMBER 1941

	The 15th Cruiser Squadron departed Alexandria for gunnery exercises at sea.
0300	Operation GLENCOE Group A arrived at Haifa from Famagusta. The Group departed for Famagusta after embarking more troops and refuelling.
<0600	Destroyers DECOY and HOTSPUR joined the submarine hunt west of Alexandria at daylight.
0800	Operation GLENCOE Group B arrived at Haifa from Famagusta. The Group departed for Famagusta after embarking more troops and refuelling.

1200	Operation GLENCOE Group C arrived at Haifa from Famagusta. The Group departed for Famagusta after embarking more troops and refuelling.
1800	Destroyers DECOY and HOTSPUR were recalled from the submarine hunt west of Alexandria.

7 NOVEMBER 1941

	The Operation GLENCOE destroyers departed Famagusta during the night of 6/7 November and arrived at Haifa on the 7th. They sailed again during the day with the final troop contingent for Famagusta. Rear Admiral Destroyers re-embarked on cruiser minelayer ABDIEL. Destroyer KINGSTON remained at Haifa with defects and her troops were spread among the other ships of Group B.
	Patches of oil were spotted west of Alexandria where the submarine search had been conducted the day before so destroyers KIPLING and HOTSPUR were sent from Alexandria to search the area again. The search continued during the night of 7/8 November. Destroyer ENCOUNTER joined the destroyers at daylight on 8 November and the three destroyers were then involved in screening light cruiser NEPTUNE during a practice bombardment at Abukir. The destroyers returned to Alexandria on the 9th.

8 NOVEMBER 1941

0300	Operation GLENCOE Group A arrived at Haifa from Famagusta.
0500	Operation GLENCOE Group B arrived at Haifa from Famagusta.
1200	Operation GLENCOE Group C arrived at Haifa from Famagusta.
1400	The entire Operation GLENCOE force departed for Haifa with Minelaying cruiser ABDIEL plus destroyers JERVIS, KANDAHAR, KIMBERLEY, KINGSTON, JAGUAR, HASTY, NAPIER, NIZAM, JACKAL, and JUPITER. The ships carried out an anti-submarine sweep as they returned to Alexandria, where they all arrived on the 9th.

10 NOVEMBER 1941

	Submarine PROTEUS (Lt Francis) sank German steamer **ITHAKA** (1773grt) two sea miles southwest of Milos, Greece. She was carrying 469 Germans from Crete.
	Greek submarine GLAVKOS (KKpt. Arslanoglu) damaged German steamer NORBURG (2392grt) off Candia, Crete.
	Battleship BARHAM and light cruiser GALATEA departed Alexandria with destroyers KANDAHAR, KINGSTON, KIMBERLEY, and JUPITER to conduct exercises.
	Submarines TORBAY and TALISMAN departed Alexandria to land commandoes on the North African coast to strike at Rommel's Headquarters near Apollonia, Libya.

11 NOVEMBER 1941

	Light cruiser EURYALUS arrived at Alexandria to join the Mediterranean Fleet.
	Battleship VALIANT and light cruiser HOBART departed Alexandria with four destroyers to conduct exercises at sea.
	The 7th Destroyer Flotilla departed Alexandria to conduct exercises at sea.

12 NOVEMBER 1941

	Greek submarine GLAVKOS (KKpt. Arslanoglu) sank a coastal sailing ship off Crete with gunfire.
	Greek destroyer AETOS departed Alexandria to transit the Suez Canal, en route to a refit in India.

13 NOVEMBER 1941

	Destroyers KIPLING, JACKAL, and ENCOUNTER departed Alexandria carrying stores to Tobruk on the first Operation APPROACH convoy serial. Polish General Sikorski took passage in destroyer KIPLING to inspect the Polish troops at Tobruk. The ships returned to Alexandria on the 14th.
	Destroyer ERIDGE and sloop FLAMINGO passed through the Suez Canal northbound. Sloop FLAMINGO departed Port Said for Alexandria, arriving on the 14th. Destroyer ERIDGE was held at Port Said to take part in an anti-submarine sweep the next day.
	A mine sank Greek auxiliary ship **AGHIOS NICOLAOS** between Dikili and Mitylene, Greece. The Master and crew of three were all lost.

14 NOVEMBER 1941

	Greek submarine GLAVKOS (KKpt. Arslanoglu) sank a coastal sailing ship off Crete with gunfire.
	Minelaying cruiser ABDIEL departed Alexandria with destroyers HERO, HOTSPUR, and NIZAM for Tobruk in the second convoy series of Operation APPROACH. The ships arrived back at Alexandria on the 15th with General Sikorski aboard ABDIEL.
	Destroyer ERIDGE departed Port Said and joined destroyers NAPIER, KANDAHAR, and HASTY in an anti-

submarine sweep. After an unsuccessful search, the destroyers returned to Alexandria on the 16th.

Anti-aircraft ship CARLISLE, destroyer AVON VALE, plus Australian sloops PARRAMATTA and YARRA passed through the Suez Canal and sailed for Alexandria.
Destroyer AVON VALE was recalled to escort landing ship GLENGYLE the following day.
Destroyer HEYTHROP passed through the Suez Canal on the 15th and on arrival at Port Said departed with destroyer AVON VALE escorting landing ship GLENGYLE to Alexandria.
Destroyer HEYTHROP arrived at Alexandria from Gibraltar, via the Cape.
The anti-aircraft ship and the sloops arrived at Alexandria on the 15th.
The landing ship and destroyers AVON VALE and HEYTHROP arrived at Alexandria on the 16th.
Destroyer HEYTHROP joined the 2nd Destroyer Flotilla for duty in the Mediterranean Fleet.

15 NOVEMBER 1941

Italian submarine ASCIANGHI began an unsuccessful patrol off the Palestinian coast until 24 November.

Destroyers ENCOUNTER and JUPITER departed Alexandria for the Far East Command, via Bombay, India.

Light cruisers NAIAD and EURYALUS were at sea from Alexandria for gunfire practice.

16 NOVEMBER 1941

Destroyers KIPLING, JACKAL, and DECOY departed Alexandria on the 3rd Operation APPROACH serial. The destroyers returned to Alexandria on the 17th.

MTB.68 and MTB.215 patrolled off Bardia, Libya to intercept a submarine reported to be in the area.

17 NOVEMBER 1941

U.331 landed two German officers and seven enlisted men of a Commando group near Daba, Egypt sixty miles west of Alexandria, to mine the railway. All nine German Commandos were captured later the same day before any sabotage was done.

Light cruisers AJAX, NEPTUNE, and the Australian HOBART departed Alexandria with destroyers KANDAHAR, HASTY, and HOTSPUR to bombard the Sollum area during the night of 17/18 November. The bombardment was cancelled due to poor weather and the ships returned to Alexandria.

18 NOVEMBER 1941

Submarine THORN unsuccessfully attacked a steamer in the Aegean. The steamer was later found to be a Turkish Red Crescent relief ship.

To support Operation CRUSADER, Australian sloops PARRAMATTA and YARRA escorted ammunition ship HANNE (1360grt) from Alexandria to Tobruk.

Operation APPROACH was cancelled with the exception of tankers TONELINE (811grt) and LESBOS (1009grt), which departed Alexandria, escorted by Australian sloops YARRA and PARRAMATTA, minesweeping whaler SOTRA, and two anti-submarine trawlers.
When tanker TONELINE broke down, PARRAMATTA assisted the tanker returning to Mersa Matruh. The tanker sailed after dark on the 19th for Tobruk.
Tanker LESBOS arrived late at Tobruk escorted by anti-submarine whaler KLO.
Whaler KLO and motor launch ML.1048 were damaged by shellfire on the 20th.
After temporary repairs to a direct shell hit, whaler KLO was able to depart for Alexandria.

Battleships QUEEN ELIZABETH, BARHAM, and VALIANT, light cruisers NAIAD, GALATEA, and EURYALUS departed Alexandria with destroyers JERVIS, KIMBERLEY, KINGSTON, NAPIER, NIZAM, KIPLING, JACKAL, DECOY, AVON VALE, and ERIDGE to support Operation CHIEFTAIN, the dummy convoy intended to divert attention from Operation CRUSADER in the eastern Mediterranean.
The Mediterranean Fleet turned back after dark and arrived at Alexandria during the morning of 19 November. Light cruisers NAIAD and EURYALUS with destroyers KIPLING and JACKAL, which had been detached late on the 18th, bombarded the axis controlled Halfaya fortifications around Tobruk.
The light cruisers and destroyers arrived at Alexandria later the next day.

British aircraft accidentally attacked anti-submarine whaler SOUTHERN MAID in 31, 15N, 28, 02E, reporting her as a submarine. Destroyers FARNDALE and ERIDGE departed Alexandria to search for the reported submarine.

| 1200 | Light cruisers AJAX, NEPTUNE, and HOBART with destroyers KANDAHAR, HASTY, and HOTSPUR joined the Mediterranean Fleet departing Alexandria. |

19 NOVEMBER 1941

Polish submarine SOKOL (Cdr Karnicki) damaged Italian destroyer AVIERE by firing torpedoes into the Navarino harbour. The destroyer was beached to prevent her sinking.

Submarine TRIUMPH sank a small steamer in the Aegean.

20 NOVEMBER 1941

Light cruisers AJAX and NEPTUNE and Australian light cruiser HOBART departed Alexandria with destroyers

	HEYTHROP and AVON VALE. Destroyers FARNDALE and ERIDGE joined the group at sea. The cruisers bombarded the Bardia area during the night of 20/21 November.
	Submarine THORN unsuccessfully attacked a steamer in the Aegean.

21 NOVEMBER 1941

	Polish submarine SOKOL (Cdr Karnicki) damaged Italian tanker BERBERA (2093grt) off Navarino in 36, 53N, 21, 28E.
	Australian PARRAMATTA and destroyer AVON VALE escorted ammunition ship HANNE (1360grt) from Alexandria to Tobruk
<1200	Battleships QUEEN ELIZABETH, BARHAM, and VALIANT, light cruisers NAIAD, EURYALUS, and GALATEA departed Alexandria with destroyers JERVIS, KANDAHAR, KIMBERLEY, KINGSTON, NAPIER, NIZAM, KIPLING, JACKAL, HASTY, HOTSPUR, and DECOY to operate in coordination with Operation LANDMARK to simulate an attack on Tripoli to draw German and Italian air strength away from Halfaya and Bardia.
1200	Light cruisers AJAX, NEPTUNE, and the Australian HOBART joined the Mediterranean Fleet at sea. The four HUNT destroyers escorting the cruisers had been sent to Alexandria. At dark, the cruisers of the 15th Cruiser Squadron were detached to make W/T reports further to the west to aid in the deception of an attack on Tripoli. The Mediterranean Fleet returned to Alexandria at daylight on the 22nd.

22 NOVEMBER 1941

	Schooner **MARIA DI GIOVANNI** (255grt) (T/Lt A. B. Palmer RNR) was lost when she grounded west of Tobruk. Palmer, T/Lt J. Lucas RNR and the crew were taken prisoner.
>1200	Light cruisers AJAX, NEPTUNE, and the Australian HOBART returned to Alexandria.

23 NOVEMBER 1941

	Damaged Italian tanker BERBERA (2093grt) and torpedo boat PEGASO arrived at Navarino, Greece.
	German steamers MARITZA (2910grt) and PROCIDA (1843grt) departed Piraeus for Benghazi carrying fuel for the Luftwaffe and escorted by Italian torpedo boats LUPO and CASSIOPEA.
	Italian submarines DAGABUR, BEILUL and ZAFFIRO patrolled along the Cyrenaica coast against British night convoys to Tobruk with U.79, U.331 and U.559.
	Pressured by Prime Minister Churchill to support Operation CRUSADER, Admiral Cunningham took the Mediterranean Fleet to sea in two groups. Force A, included battleships QUEEN ELIZABETH, BARHAM and VALIANT with destroyers DECOY, GRIFFIN, HASTY, JACKAL, JERVIS, KIPLING NAPIER and NIZAM. Force B, (KAdm. Rawlings) included light cruisers AJAX, NEPTUNE, NAIAD, EURYALUS and GALATEA with destroyers KANDAHAR, KINGSTON, KIMBERLEY, and HOTSPUR.
	An Axis aerial torpedo damaged landing ship GLENROY (9809grt) while she carried supplies for Tobruk, in 31, 40N, 26, 28E. She was taken in tow by anti-aircraft cruiser CARLISLE, escorted by destroyers AVON VALE and ERIDGE and beached at Mersa Matruh. The troops on the landing ship were transferred to destroyer FARNDALE, which carried them to Tobruk. Destroyers NAPIER, NIZAM, KIPLING, JACKAL, and HASTY were ordered to assist the landing ship. Sloop FLAMINGO and tug ST ISSEY departed Alexandria. GLENROY was re-floated on the 27th and taken in tow by tugs ST ISSEY and ST MONACE. Escorted by destroyers two anti-submarine trawlers, later reinforced by destroyer AVON VALE, and later by destroyers FARNDALE and ERIDGE. She arrived at Alexandria on the 29th.
	Tanker TONELINE (811grt) and steamer GEBIL KEBIR (grt) departed Tobruk escorted by destroyer HEYTHROP, Australian sloop YARRA, and three anti-submarine trawlers.

24 NOVEMBER 1941

	Force K destroyers LANCE and LIVELY sank German steamer **MARITZA** (2910grt) between Crete and Libya. She was carrying fuel for the German air force in North Africa.
	Greek submarine GLAVKOS damaged German steamer NORBURG (2392grt) off Candia, Crete.
	Force K light cruiser PENELOPE sank German steamer **PROCIDA** (1843grt) off Libya. She was carrying fuel for the German air force in North Africa.
	Force K gunfire damaged Italian torpedo boat CASSIOPEA while she was escorting the two German steamers.
	Submarine TRIUMPH (Lt Cdr Woods) sank Italian tug **HERCULES** (632grt) and further damaged German steamer NORBURG (2392grt) off Heraklion, Crete. In spite of the heavy damage, NORBURG was repaired and made sea worthy in 1942.
<2244	Destroyers FARNDALE, AVON VALE, and ERIDGE joined the Mediterranean Fleet at sea.
2245	After completing fuelling, destroyers NAPIER, NIZAM, KIPLING, JACKAL, and HASTY joined with the Mediterranean Fleet and relieved destroyers FARNDALE, AVON VALE, and ERIDGE as escort.

25 NOVEMBER 1941

	Submarine THUNDERBOLT (Lt Cdr Crouch) sank German motor sailing ship **LVII** (300grt) with gunfire off Cape Malea, Greece.
	Steamer HANNE (1360grt) departed Alexandria carrying ammunition for Tobruk escorted by destroyer AVON VALE, Australian sloop PARRAMATTA, plus South African anti-submarine whalers SOUTHERN MAID, SOUTHERN SEA, and SOUTHERN ISLE.
0503	Italian submarine SETTEMBRINI sighted Force K at sea and sent an alert for all convoys to make for the nearest port.
1629	U.331 (ObltzS v. Tiesenhausen) sank battleship **BARHAM** (31,100grt) (Captain G. C. Cooke) with three torpedo hits off Sollum in 32, 34N, 26, 24E. Her magazines exploded as the ship rolled over and she quickly sank. Cooke, T/Paymaster Sub Lt A. J. Allsebrook RNVR, Lt Cdr (E) G. A. O. Andrews, Lt Cdr F. Barchard, T/A/Warrant Electrician T. R. Barnacott, T/Lt (E) A. Bisset, T/Sub Lt K. M. H. Bond RNVR, P/T/Midshipman R. G. Bower RNR, Midshipman T. P. Boyd, Warrant Engineer N. E. Boyes, Cdr G. F. N. Bradford, Lt Cdr W. L. Brodrick, T/Chaplain the Reverend F. Burnett RNVR, Paymaster Lt J. Charles, Midshipman R. E. Cloete, Lt J. M. Corrie, RM, Cdr R. H. Craske DSC, Lt H. Creasy, Commissioned Boatswain E. T. Ford, Commissioned Gunner C. H. George, Warrant Mechanic W. J. O. Goodlad, Lt Cdr D. Grove-White, Midshipman W. T. Hickling, Lt C. St. G. S. Hill, RM, Senior Master C. B. Hockaday, Midshipman A. E. Hutton RNR, T/Midshipman W. J. Jennings RNR, Midshipman the Honourable J. C. Jocelyn, A/Paymaster Sub Lt D. M. Lawder, T/Paymaster Sub Lt H. F. Lacheur RNVR, T/Lt (E) N. C. Lewis, Lt J. W. Lochore, Warrant Supply Officer S. W. Lowes, T/Midshipman W. G. W. Maplesden RNR, A/Lt (E) R. C. V. Molesworth, Cdr G. P. U. Morris DSC, Warrant Telegraphist G. M. Pennington, T/Lt (E) F. V. Percival, Lt W. G. L. Peters, Paymaster Lt D. A. Phillips RNVR, Captain G. S. Pitts, RM, T/Midshipman J. H. Reid RNR, Lt Cdr J. R. Roberts-West DSC, T/Paymaster Lt J. C. Robertson RNVR, Lt J. K. Rodwell, Midshipman H. T. B. Salmon, T/Surgeon Lt A. E. Sherwell RNVR, Surgeon Cdr E. R. Sorley, Commissioned Gunner A. E. Stanley, Lt (E) H. B. Stringer, Paymaster Midshipman F. H. Twycross, Signal Boatswain J. G. Warren, T/Lt R. S. Watson RNVR, Engineering Cdr H. R. Whitehouse, Paymaster Cdr H. G. Williams, Lt S. Woodcock, six hundred and seventy-four ratings, and one hundred and thirty-two Marines were missing from the battleship. Two ratings and one Marine died of wounds after being rescued. About four hundred and fifty survivors, including Vice Admiral Pridham Wippell were rescued by destroyers JERVIS, JACKAL, NIZAM, which rescued 168 men, and HOTSPUR. Only 449 men survived from the 1311 men aboard. After the loss of **BARHAM**, submarine OTUS was withdrawn from operational duties for use as an anti-submarine warfare training ship. (Authors note: The horrible sight of BARHAM exploding continues to be shown in nearly every documentary made of the second World War. It is both fascinating and terrible to watch.)

26 NOVEMBER 1941

	Transport ships carrying tanks departed Port Said for Alexandria escorted by sloop FLAMINGO, corvettes SALIVA, HYACINTH, and ERICA, plus Greek destroyers KONDOURIOTIS and ASPIS from Alexandria. Anti-aircraft ship CARLISLE departed Alexandria and joined the convoy off Port Said. The convoy arrived at Alexandria on the 27th.
1000	Battleships QUEEN ELIZABETH and VALIANT arrived at Alexandria with destroyers NAPIER, GRIFFIN, HASTY, DECOY, HOTSPUR, and KIPLING.
1400	Destroyers JERVIS, NIZAM, and JACKAL arrived at Alexandria.
1800	Force B, light cruisers AJAX, NEPTUNE, NAIAD, EURYALUS and GALATEA returned to Alexandria with destroyers KANDAHAR, KINGSTON, KIMBERLEY, and HOTSPUR.

27 NOVEMBER 1941

	Steamer HANNE (1360grt) safely arrived at Tobruk with her much needed cargo of ammunition.
	Admiral Rawlings transferred light cruisers AJAX (Capt McCarthy) and NEPTUNE from Alexandria to Malta with destroyers KIMBERLEY and KINGSTON to strengthen Force K. Light cruisers NAIAD (Rear Adm. Vian) and EURYALUS escorted the group with destroyers HOTSPUR and GRIFFIN as Force C part of the way and then to sweep off Cyrenaica before returning to Alexandria on the 28th.
	Submarine PROTEUS sighted a submarine sixty miles northwest of Alexandria late in the day. However, the reported was delayed and not received at headquarters until the next morning.
0012 0046 0305	U.559 (Kptlt Heidtmann) fired thee torpedoes from 2000 metres at the sloop and the steamer, but they missed. U.559 sank Australian sloop **PARRAMATTA** (1060grt) (A/Cdr J. H. Walker, MVO RAN) with one torpedo from 1500 metres off Bardia in 32, 20N, 24, 35E. She broke in two and quickly sank. Walker, Lt Cdr P. W. Forwood RANR, Lt G. W. A. Langford, T/Lt V. V. Johnston RANR (S), T/Lt K. R. Hunter RANR (S), Lt A. Moore RANVR, Surgeon Lt C. F. Harrington RANR, Commissioned Engineer R. P. Oram, A/Gunner (T) A. J. Brown, and 151 ratings were lost. Forwood and Johnston perished in the ship's boat. Destroyer AVON VALE rescued twenty-one ratings and three ratings successfully swam ashore. Passengers, Lt R. H. S. Litchfield and seven ratings, formerly of gunboat **GNAT**, were also lost. In all only twenty-four men survived from the crew of 138.

28 NOVEMBER 1941

	During the night, RAF aircraft destroyed damaged Italian tanker **BERBERA** (2093grt) at Navarino, Greece.
	U.205, U.565 and U.81 patrolled the area between Alexandria and Tobruk until 31 November.
	U.79, U.331 and U.559 patrolled Bardia, Derna, Benghazi and Tripoli to protect Axis North African supply convoys.
0800	After receiving the report from submarine PROTEUS, destroyers GRIFFIN and HERO were sent to hunt for a submarine in the area, despite the lateness of the report. Later destroyers HASTY and NIZAM joined the hunt while returning from a supply run to Tobruk.

29 NOVEMBER 1941

	Naval whaler **EGELAND** (153grt) ran aground on the Palestine coast and became a total loss.

30 NOVEMBER 1941

	Destroyers JERVIS, JAGUAR, KIPLING, and JACKAL departed Alexandria to intercept convoys sailing from Navarino, Greece to Derna, Libya. Light cruisers NAIAD and EURYALUS departed Alexandria with destroyers HERO and HASTY to support the destroyers from the east.
1600	Convoy AT.1 departed Alexandria for Tobruk. The slow section, consisting of Greek steamer ELPIS (3651grt), tug ST ISSEY towing two lighters, three landing ship tank A lighters, departed Alexandria escorted by Australian sloop YARRA, sloop FLAMINGO, and two anti-submarine trawlers. Greek destroyers KONDOURIOTIS accompanied the convoy as far as Mersa Matruh.
2130	The fast section of convoy AT.1 departed Alexandria with armed boarding vessel CHAKDINA and tanker KIRKLAND (1361grt) escorted by destroyers HEYTHROP and AVON VALE plus one anti-submarine trawler. Both convoys safely arrived on 2 December.

Black Sea

Long. E27, 00 – E43, 00   Lat. N48, 00 – N41, 00

1 NOVEMBER 1941

	The Russian Black Sea Fleet with cruisers KRASNY KRYM, KRASNY KAVKAZ, and CHERVONA UKRAINA, destroyer leader KHARKOV, with destroyers BODRY, BOIKI, BDITELNY, BEZUPRECHNY, NEZAMOZHNIK, SHAUMYAN and ZHELEZNYAKOV began evacuating Russian troops cut off on the Tendra peninsula, plus those at Tschernomorsk, Yalta, Evpatoria and Feodosia and took them to Sevastopol. By 9 November, they were able to move over 15,000 troops from various isolated Crimean ports to Sevastopol.
	A mine badly damaged Russian cruiser VOROSHILOV off Fidonisi Island in the Black Sea. The cruiser was repaired at Poti, Georgia, completing in February 1942.
	A mine sank Russian submarine **M-59** (Lt Cdr Matveev) east of Constanza, Romania.

2 NOVEMBER 1941

	Three German Ju88 aircraft of KG.51 damaged Russian cruiser VOROSHILOV (Capt 1st Class F. S. Markov) with two bomb hits in the Black Sea. She was towed to Poti, Georgia.
	Russian submarine SHCH-214 (Lt Cdr Vlasov) sank Turkish sailing ship **KAYNAKDERE** (85grt) (also identified as **KARALTEPE** (145grt)) along the Bulgarian/Turkish Border off Cape Midia. The crew of eight were all rescued.
	Russian submarines M-34, M-59, M-60, L-6, D-4, D-5, S-31, SHCH-213 and SHCH-214 patrol the western Black Sea until 18 November.

4 NOVEMBER 1941

	Russian submarines S-33, SHCH-208, A-5, S-34, M-31, A-2, SHCH-211, L-6, SHCH-215, M-35 begin patrols in the western Black Sea.
	Romanian destroyer MARIA sank Russian submarine **M-58** with depth charges off southern Ukraine.

5 NOVEMBER 1941

	Russian submarine SHCH-214 (Lt Cdr Vlasov) sank Italian tanker **TORCELLO** (3336grt) off the Bulgarian coast near Cape Kuruburnu.
	Romanian submarine DELFINUL damaged Russian tanker KREML (7661grt) four miles south of Yalta.

6 NOVEMBER 1941

	Russian submarine S-33 (Lt Cdr Alekseev) unsuccessfully attacked the Romanian destroyer MARASESTI off Mangalia, Romania.

9 NOVEMBER 1941

	Mines laid by Russian destroyers SMYSHLENY and BODRY in Minefield ILYITSCHEWKA sank Romanian steamer **UNGVAR** (1031grt) along with Romanian MTBs **VIFORUL** and **VIJELIA** off Odessa, Ukraine.
	A Russian supply convoy departed the Caucasus for Sevastopol escorted by destroyer leader TASHKENT, destroyers SPOSOBNY, SMYSHLENY and SOOBRAZITELNY, plus patrol boats SHTORM and SHKVAL.
	Russian cruiser MOLOTOV (Capt 1st Class Zinovev) bombarded German and Romanian positions attacking the Russian 51st Army off Feodosia at Cape Chauda.

10 NOVEMBER 1941

	German aircraft unsuccessfully attacked Russian cruiser MOLOTOV (Capt 1st Class Zinovev) off Tuapse.
	Russian cruisers CHERVONA UKRAINA (Capt 2nd Class Basisty) and KRASNY KRYM (Capt 2nd Class Zubkov) with destroyers NEZAMOZHNIK and SHAUMYAN provided gunfire support to the troops defending Sevastopol. The ships shelled German positions north and east of the city.

11 NOVEMBER 1941

	Russian cruisers CHERVONA UKRAINA (Capt 2nd Class Basisty) and KRASNY KRYM (Capt 2nd Class Zubkov) with destroyers NEZAMOZHNIK and SHAUMYAN provided gunfire support to the troops defending Sevastopol.

12 NOVEMBER 1941

	During the night of 12/13 November, a mine sank Russian submarine **S-34** (Capt 3rd Class Chemlnitski) off Cape Emine.
	Russian cruisers CHERVONA UKRAINA (Capt 2nd Class Basisty) and KRASNY KRYM (Capt 2nd Class Zubkov) with destroyers NEZAMOZHNIK and SHAUMYAN provided gunfire support to the troops defending Sevastopol.
1200	German Ju87 aircraft of II/STG.77 (Hptm. Orthofer) from the IV Air Corps made three bomb hits on Russian cruiser **CHERVONA UKRAINA**, which sank off Sevastopol despite efforts to save her. Her guns were later removed and installed ashore.
1200	German aircraft also heavily damaged Russian destroyers SOVERSHENNY, waiting to be fitted for combat and BESPOSHCHADNY, just recently completing repairs from damage sustained on 22 September. On the 17th, destroyer SHAUMYAN towed BESPOSHCHADNY to Poti, Russia for repairs.
1200	German aircraft also damaged Russian steamer KRASNY PROFINTERN (4648grt) in the Black Sea.

15 NOVEMBER 1941

	Russian battleship PARIZHSKAYA KOMMUNA, cruisers KRASNY KAVKAZ and KRASNY KRYM with destroyers BESPOSHCHADNY, BOIKI, SMYSHLENY, SOOBRAZITELNY and ZHELEZNYAKOV supported the Sevastopol defence with gunfire.

16 NOVEMBER 1941

	A mine sank Russian submarine **SHCH-211** off Varna, Bulgaria. Some sources have her being sunk on the 18th.

17 NOVEMBER 1941

	Russian submarine L-6 (Capt 3rd Class Bul) laid mines off Ak-Mechet.
	Russian destroyer SHAUMYAN towed damaged destroyer BESPOSHCHADNY from Sevastopol to Poti.

18 NOVEMBER 1941

	Russian submarine SHCH-215 (Lt Cdr Apostolov) sank Turkish steamer **YENICE** (520grt) off Vasiliko. Twelve crewmen were lost and two survivors were rescued.
	After reporting in for the day, a mine sank Russian submarine **SHCH-211** (Lt Cdr Devyatko) off Varna, Bulgaria. Some sources have her being sunk on the 16th.

20 NOVEMBER 1941

	A mine laid by Russian submarine L-6 sank Romanian lighter **DANUBIUS** (550grt) off Ak-Mechet.

23 NOVEMBER 1941

	Russian battleship PARIZHSKAYA KOMMUNA, cruisers KRASNY KAVKAZ and KRASNY KRYM with destroyers BESPOSHCHADNY, BOIKI, SMYSHLENY, SOOBRAZITELNY and ZHELEZNYAKOV supported the Sevastopol defence with gunfire.

25 NOVEMBER 1941

	Russian battleship PARIZHSKAYA KOMMUNA, cruisers KRASNY KAVKAZ and KRASNY KRYM with destroyers BESPOSHCHADNY, BOIKI, SMYSHLENY, SOOBRAZITELNY and ZHELEZNYAKOV supported the Sevastopol defence with gunfire.
	Russian tankers VARLAAM AVANESOV (6557grt), SAKHALIN (6085grt) and TAUPSE (6320grt) departed Batumi for the Bosporus with Icebreaker MIKOYAN. Russian destroyer leader TASHKENT (Rear Adm. L. A. Vladimirski) with destroyers SOOBRAZITELNY and SPOSOBNY escorted the tankers until 28 November.

28 NOVEMBER 1941

	Russian battleship PARIZHSKAYA KOMMUNA, cruisers KRASNY KAVKAZ and KRASNY KRYM with destroyers BESPOSHCHADNY, BOIKI, SMYSHLENY, SOOBRAZITELNY and ZHELEZNYAKOV supported the Sevastopol defence with gunfire.
	During the night of 28/29 November Russian battleship PARIZHSKAYA KOMMUNA (Capt 1st Class Kravchenko) with destroyer SMYSHLENY bombarded German and Romanian positions around Cape Feolent, south of Sevastopol with 146 rounds of 305-mm shells, 120 rounds of 130-mm shells and 299 rounds of 120-mm shells.

29 NOVEMBER 1941

	Russian battleship PARIZHSKAYA KOMMUNA, cruisers KRASNY KAVKAZ and KRASNY KRYM with destroyers BESPOSHCHADNY, BOIKI, SMYSHLENY, SOOBRAZITELNY and ZHELEZNYAKOV supported the Sevastopol defence with gunfire.
	Russian cruiser KRASNY KAVKAZ (Capt 2nd Class Gushchin) and destroyer ZHELEZNYAKOV bombarded German positions at Kutschuk.

Red Sea
Long. E32, 00 – E43, 00   Lat. N30, 00 – N15, 00

5 NOVEMBER 1941

	Australian sloop YARRA joined the Suez Escort Force, relieving sloop FALMOUTH, which returned to the East Indies Station.

6 NOVEMBER 1941

	Armed boarding vessel ARPHA fractured her propeller shaft while laying beacons at Anchorage G (Ginah) in the Suez Gulf. She was beached at Towila and Indian sloop SUTLEJ was sent to assist her. On the 9th, the ARPHA was re-floated and towed by tug CONFEDERATE, screened by Indian sloop SUTLEJ, to Ginah, Egypt. Damaged ABV ARPHA arrived at Suez in tow of tug CONFEDERATE and escorted by SUTLEJ on the 14th.

10 NOVEMBER 1941

	Light cruiser EURYALUS arrived at Suez from Britain to join the Mediterranean Fleet. She arrived at Alexandria on the 11th.

16 NOVEMBER 1941

	Destroyer FARNDALE arrived at Suez to join the Mediterranean Fleet and passed through the Suez Canal.

29 NOVEMBER 1941

	Light cruiser GALATEA departed Suez.

Arabian Sea
Long. E43, 00 – E77, 00   Lat. N31, 00 – N00, 00

12 NOVEMBER 1941

	Destroyers FARNDALE and HEYTHROP arrived at Aden to join the Mediterranean Fleet. They later departed Aden for the Suez. The destroyers had accompanied light cruiser EURYALUS for most of the passage.

17 NOVEMBER 1941

	Convoy WS.12 steamers DOMINION MONARCH (27,155grt), EMPRESS OF CANADA (21,517grt), DUCHESS OF RICHMOND (20,022grt), and PERSEUS (10,286grt) were detached as convoy WS.12J in 06, 05N, 52, 30E, escorted by light cruiser GLASGOW for Colombo, Ceylon arriving on 23 November.

20 NOVEMBER 1941

	Destroyers ENCOUNTER and JUPITER departed Aden for Colombo.

30 NOVEMBER 1941

	Convoy BA.8 departed Bombay, India escorted by light cruiser GLASGOW. The convoy arrived at Aden on 4 December. There was no convoy BA.9.
	Heavy cruiser CORNWALL captured Vichy French steamer **SURCOUF** (1129grt) south of Cape Guardafui at the end of November and sent her into Aden.

INDIAN OCEAN

East of South Africa
Long. E25, 00 – E60, 00   Lat. S00, 00 – S60, 00

2 NOVEMBER 1941

Heavy cruiser DEVONSHIRE, light cruiser COLOMBO with AMCs CARTHAGE and CARNARVON CASTLE intercepted Vichy French convoy south of the Cape of Good Hope in Operation BELLRINGER.

The Vichy French convoy carried 900 tons of graphite and 30,000 tons of rice and the British force captured steamers **BANKOK** (8056grt) and **COMMANDANT DORISE** (5529grt) plus liners **COMPIEGNE** (9986grt), **CAP TOURANE** (8009grt) and **CAP PADARAN** (8009grt).

The crew immobilised steamer **CAP PADARAN** and she was taken in tow by AMC CARTHAGE, escorted by minesweeping whaler STELLENBERG and taken to Port Elizabeth.

The crew set steamer **BANGKOK** on fire and abandoned the ship, with light cruiser COLOMBO and whaler NIGEL taking off the crew.

The other three steamers were taken to South African ports.

Heavy cruiser DEVONSHIRE and minesweeping whaler STEENBERG escorted the **CAP TOURANE** to Port Elizabeth.

AMC CARNARVON CASTLE and minesweeping whaler GUN 9 escorted **COMMANDANT DORISE** to East London.

Light cruiser COLOMBO and minesweeping whaler NIGEL escorted **COMPIEGNE** to East London.

South African minesweeping whalers SOUTHERN BARRIER and TERJE supported the operation.

Vichy French sloop D'IBERVILLE managed to escape unharmed.

In response to the convoy's capture, the Vichy French Admiralty sent submarines LE GLORIEUX and LE HÉROS to Madagascar.

3 NOVEMBER 1941

Convoy WS.12 arrived at Durban, South Africa with steamers FRANCONIA (20,175grt), DUCHESS OF RICHMOND (20,022grt), EMPRESS OF RUSSIA (16,810grt), HIGHLAND BRIGADE (14,134grt), PERSEUS (10,286grt), ORMONDE (14,982grt), and SAMARIA (19,597grt) escorted by AMC DERBYSHIRE.

5 NOVEMBER 1941

Convoy WS.12 departed Cape Town, South Africa with steamers STRATHAIRD (22,284grt), LEOPOLDVILLE (11,439grt), MENDOZA (5193grt), EMPIRE PRIDE (9248grt), EMPIRE TRUST (8143grt), PERTHSHIRE (10,496grt), EMPRESS OF CANADA (21,517grt), and DOMINION MONARCH (27,155grt) escorted by AMC DUNNOTTAR CASTLE.

8 NOVEMBER 1941

Convoy WS.12 with steamers SAMARIA (19,597grt), CITY OF PARIS (10,902grt), NIEUW AMSTERDAM (36,287grt) from Durban, steamers FRANCONIA (20,175grt), CLAN LAMONT (7268grt), CLAN CAMPBELL (7255grt), EMPRESS OF RUSSIA (16,810grt), ALMANZORA (15,551grt), ASCANIUS (10,048grt) from Mombasa, steamers MENDOZA (5193grt), PERSEUS (10,286grt), NOVA SCOTIA (6796grt) from Durban, and troopship DUCHESS OF RICHMOND (20,022grt) departed Durban and rendezvoused at sea with the Cape Town section.

Battle cruiser REPULSE relieved AMC DUNNOTTAR CASTLE and remained with the convoy until 14 November, when she was detached from the convoy in 05, 10S, 34, 00E when battleship REVENGE joined the convoy.

The convoy arrived at Aden on 20 November.

17 NOVEMBER 1941

Vichy French submarine LE HÉROS sank Norwegian steamer **THODE FAGELUND** (5757grt) thirty-five miles east of East London in 33, 00S, 29, 00E. The entire crew was rescued. The attack was in retaliation for the British capture of a Vichy French convoy on the 2nd.

30 NOVEMBER 1941

Free French destroyer LEOPARD (Lt Cdr Evenou) arrived at Reunion Island and after a short skirmish with the Vichy French forces at the Point de Galets, occupied the Island.

Bay of Bengal
Long. E77, 00 – E95, 00   Lat. N22, 00 – N00, 00

24 NOVEMBER 1941

Convoy WS.12J departed Colombo with steamers DOMINION MONARCH (27,155grt) and EMPRESS OF CANADA (21,517grt) escorted by light cruiser GLASGOW.
In 06, 14N, 92, 00E, steamer AWATEA (13,482grt) joined the convoy escorted by light cruiser DRAGON and light cruiser GLASGOW was detached from the convoy with steamer AWATEA to Colombo. Convoy WS.12J arrived at Singapore on 28 November.

26 NOVEMBER 1941

Destroyers ENCOUNTER and JUPITER arrived at Colombo from Aden.

28 NOVEMBER 1941

Force G (Adm. Phillips) arrived at Colombo, Ceylon with battleship PRINCE OF WALES with destroyers ELECTRA and EXPRESS.

30 NOVEMBER 1941

Battleship PRINCE OF WALES departed Colombo, Ceylon with destroyers EXPRESS and ELECTRA and joined battle cruiser REPULSE with destroyers ENCOUNTER and JUPITER, which departed from Trincomalee, Ceylon. The group arrived at Singapore on 2 December.

Malaya
Long. E95, 00 – E105, 00   Lat. N17, 00 – N00, 00

6 NOVEMBER 1941

Light cruiser MAURITIUS arrived at Singapore with convoy WS.11X from Colombo, Ceylon.

16 NOVEMBER 1941

Minelayer TEVIOTBANK arrived at Singapore.

24 NOVEMBER 1941

Troopship AWATEA (13,482grt) departed Singapore with 420 crewmembers for troopship EMPRESS OF RUSSIA (16,810grt).
Light cruiser DRAGON escorted the troopship to a position in 06, 14N, 98E where light cruiser GLASGOW relieved light cruiser DRAGON.
Light cruiser GLASGOW escorted troopship AWATEA until 27 November and she arrived at Colombo, Ceylon on the 28th.

28 NOVEMBER 1941

Convoy WS.12J arrived at Singapore with steamers DOMINION MONARCH (27,155grt) and EMPRESS OF CANADA (21,517grt) from Colombo, Ceylon escorted by light cruiser DRAGON.

29 NOVEMBER 1941

Troopship KAROA (7009grt) departed Rangoon, Burma with 115 military personnel for Calcutta, India. Heavy cruiser EXETER escorted the troopship until it arrived on 2 December.

West of Australia
Long. E95, 00 – E125, 00   Lat. S15, 00 – S60, 00

11 NOVEMBER 1941

Australian light cruiser SYDNEY departed Fremantle, Australia to escort troopship ZEALANDIA (6683grt), which had departed Sydney, Australia escorted by light cruiser ADELAIDE for Singapore.
Light cruiser DURBAN relieved light cruiser SYDNEY on the 17th.
The SYDNEY was detached to return to Fremantle, arriving on the 20th.

13 NOVEMBER 1941

Australian troop convoy US.13 departed Fremantle, Australia with troopships QUEEN ELIZABETH (83,673grt) and QUEEN MARY (81,235grt). The convoy was dispersed on the 20th and the liners travelled independently to their destination ports.

19 NOVEMBER 1941

Australian light cruiser **SYDNEY** (Capt Burnett) encountered German AMC **SCHIFF.41/KORMORAN** (FKpt.

Detmers) about 170 sea miles west of Sharks bay, Australia.

The AMC managed to lure the SYDNEY into close range with confusing recognition signals and then opened up at 900 meters with every gun she had, plus fired a torpedo. The SYDNEY replied in kind.

In the end, the Germans abandoned their sinking ship and the light cruiser steamed away, but never reached port. The German survivors managed to make it to Australia, but no survivors from the SYDNEY were ever found.

For more information, go to the official Australian Navy report on the incident. They analysed the wreck and did a comprehensive study to determine why the ship sank with all hands and assessed how the battle must have progressed.

PACIFIC OCEAN

South China Sea
Long. E105, 00 – E120, 00   Lat. N27, 00 – N10, 00

1 NOVEMBER 1941

IJN minesweepers W-1, W-2, W-3, W-5 and W-6 were assigned to the Japanese Southern Expeditionary Fleet and the 9th Base Force, both based at Camranh Bay, Indochina.

American gunboat WAKE (PR-3) (Lt Cdr Andrew E. Harris) arrived at Hankow, China.

IJN submarine chaser CH-8 arrived at Camranh Bay, French Indochina. She was assigned to Submarine Chaser Division 11 with CH-7 and CH-9 in the Ninth Base Force of the Japanese Southern Expeditionary Fleet.

2 NOVEMBER 1941

Vichy French liner D'ARTAGNAN (15,105grt) arrived at Saigon, French Indochina. She was immobilized due to the heavy fire damage that remained after her fire at Shanghai, China.

8 NOVEMBER 1941

IJN destroyer HAKAZE was at Cape St. Jacques (Saigon-area) of French Indo-China supporting the Japanese 22nd Air Flotilla.

13 NOVEMBER 1941

IJA AA transport ZENYO MARU (6442grt) arrived at Humen, China from Nanking, China.

14 NOVEMBER 1941

IJA auxiliary transport CALCUTTA MARU (5339grt) departed Sakaide, Shikoku Island, for Haiphong, French Indochina (now Vietnam).

IJN ammunition ship KOTOKU MARU (6702grt) arrived at her support position south of China.

15 NOVEMBER 1941

Troopship AWATEA (13,482grt) arrived at Hong Kong with 2,000 Canadian troops under Brigadier J Lawson.

The Canadians increased the garrison in Hong Kong, but, as Churchill himself has pointed out, two semi-trained battalions were unlikely to deter Japan from war, but would merely increase the numbers of prisoners the Japanese could take.

(Authors note, I remember a story told about two Canadian privates when they arrived at Hong Kong, one said "I don't know mate, but it looks like another Dunkirk to me." Upon which the other replied "No, at Dunkirk we had someplace to retreat to.")

16 NOVEMBER 1941

IJN cargo ship TOYO MARU (2470grt) departed her support position south of China for Sasebo, Kyushu.

17 NOVEMBER 1941

IJN minesweeper W-5 arrived at Sana, Hainan Island with minesweepers W-1, W-2, W-3, W-4 and W-6. The minesweepers began patrols around the area.

20 NOVEMBER 1941

IJA antiaircraft vessel SAKURA MARU (9246grt) departed Canton, China for Haikou, Hainan Island.

IJN transport HOKKAI MARU (5105grt) completed her conversion and was assigned to the Japanese Southern Force (Vice Admiral Kondo Nobutake) in the Japanese Borneo Invasion Group (Rear Admiral Kurita Takeo), as part of the Miri and Seria Invasion unit (Rear Admiral Hashimoto Shintaro). HOKKAI MARU carried the No.2 Yokosuka Naval Landing Force (SNLF) (Captain Tomonari Kiyoshi). She departed Canton, China.

23 NOVEMBER 1941

	IJA AA transport ZENYO MARU (6442grt) departed Humen, China for Saint Jacques, French Indochina.
	IJA antiaircraft vessel SAKURA MARU (9246grt) arrived at Haikou. Hainan, China.
	IJA auxiliary transport CALCUTTA MARU (5339grt) arrived at Haiphong, French Indochina.

24 NOVEMBER 1941

	American gunboat WAKE (PR-3) (Lt Cdr Andrew E. Harris) departed Hankow, China, ignoring Japanese demands to stay, and began a 600-mile voyage down the Yangtze river to Shanghai, China.
	IJA antiaircraft vessel SAKURA MARU (9246grt) departed Haikou, Hainan and returns back that same day. She later departed for Samah, Hainan and arrived there at an unknown date

25 NOVEMBER 1941

	IJA AA transport ZENYO MARU (6442grt) departed Humen, China for Saint Jacques, French Indochina.

26 NOVEMBER 1941

	American Gunboat LUZON (PR-7) (Lt Cdr George M. Brooke) departed Hankow, China with Admiral Glassford aboard, to sail down the Yangtze river to Shanghai, China.
	IJN seaplane tender SAGARA MARU departed Samah, Hainan Island.
	IJN oiler ERIMO arrived at Sana (now Ya Xian), Hainan Island, and joined the anchored warships for fuel transfer operations.

27 NOVEMBER 1941

	IJN seaplane tender KAMIKAWA MARU arrived at Samah, Hainan Island.
	IJN cargo ship TATSUWA MARU (6335grt) arrived at her support position south of China.

28 NOVEMBER 1941

	IJN seaplane tender KAMIKAWA MARU was assigned to the Japanese 12th Naval Air Group, Japanese Third Fleet and moved to Camranh Bay, French Indo-China from Samah.
	While en route to Manila, American submarine rescue ship PIGEON (ASR-6) lost steering in a storm. American auxiliary minesweeper FINCH (AM-9) managed to take the helpless PIGEON under tow to keep her from foundering.

29 NOVEMBER 1941

	IJN minesweeper W-17 arrived at Mako, Pescadores.

30 NOVEMBER 1941

	IJN minesweepers W-12 and W-18 arrived at Mako, Pescadores.
	American river patrol boats LUZON (PR-7) and OAHU (PR-6) joined up with submarine rescue ship PIGEON (ASR-6) and auxiliary minesweeper FINCH (AM-9) on their way to Manila, PI.
	IJN ammunition ship KOTOKU MARU (6702grt) arrived at Mako, Pescadores. She unloaded mines and torpedoes plus 278-tons of other materiel.

Dutch East Indies
Long. E105, 00 – E120, 00   Lat. N10, 00 – S15, 00

17 NOVEMBER 1941

	Dutch patrol boats BANCKERT and PIET HEIN plus submarines K-XI, K-XII and K-XIII were all undergoing their half-yearly maintenance at the Navy maintenance facility at Surabaya, Java when an order was issued to accelerate the work so that the ships would be on a 48-hour notice from 28 November onward.

East China Sea
Long. E120, 00 – E130, 00   Lat. N42, 00 – N20, 00

1 NOVEMBER 1941

	IJN second-class destroyer TSUGA was assigned to the Japanese Shanghai Area Base Force with old destroyers HASU and KURI.
	IJN salvage and repair tug KASASHIMA was assigned to the Japanese Third Fleet, 2nd Base Force at Takao, Formosa.
	IJN cargo ship TATSUWA MARU (6335grt) departed Takao, Formosa.

2 NOVEMBER 1941

IJN patrol boat SHURI MARU arrived at Ryojun from a north China coastal patrol.

IJN river gunboat SAGA (785grt) was attached to the Japanese China Area Fleet in the Second China Expeditionary Fleet (Vice Admiral Hara Kiyoshi) 15th Escort Squadron with gunboat HASHIDATE plus torpedo boats HIYODORI and KASASAGI.

4 NOVEMBER 1941

IJN river gunboat SAGA (785grt) arrived at Hangkow, China, and was attached to the Yangtze Upper River Division. She conducted patrols along the river from Hangkow.

6 NOVEMBER 1941

IJN ammunition ship SOYA arrived at Kojima, Japan.

7 NOVEMBER 1941

IJN aircraft carrier TAIYO departed Takao, Formosa for Sasebo, Kyushu.

IJA AA transport ZENYO MARU (6442grt) arrived at Nanking, China from Ujina, Japan.

IJN oiler HOKUAN MARU (3712grt) arrived at Dairen Kisen K.K. shipyard for maintenance and refit.

8 NOVEMBER 1941

IJN patrol boat SHURI MARU departed Ryojun on a north China coastal patrol.

11 NOVEMBER 1941

IJN aircraft ferry FUJIKAWA MARU departed Takao, Formosa.

IJA AA transport ZENYO MARU (6442grt) departed Nanking, China for Humen, South China.

15 NOVEMBER 1941

Italian steamer CORTELLAZZO (5292grt) departed Dairen, China for Bordeaux, France.

16 NOVEMBER 1941

IJN auxiliary aircraft transport KEIYO MARU departed Takao, Formosa for the south China area and French Indo-China.

17 NOVEMBER 1941

IJN river gunboat ATAKA (725grt) arrived at Shanghai, China.

20 NOVEMBER 1941

IJN river gunboat ATAKA (725grt) entered the dry dock at Shanghai, China.

IJN auxiliary gunboat SEIKYO MARU (2606grt) was attached to Chinkai District in the Rashin Base Force (Vice Admiral Sukigara Tamazo) with auxiliary gunboat HAKKAI MARU (2921grt).

21 NOVEMBER 1941

IJN transport KOMAKI MARU (8525grt) arrived at Takao, Formosa. She was attached to the Japanese 23rd Naval Air Flotilla in the Japanese 11th Air Fleet.

IJN patrol boat SHURI MARU arrived at Ryojun from a north China coastal patrol.

24 NOVEMBER 1941

IJA auxiliary transport CALCUTTA MARU (5339grt) arrived at Nanking, China.

25 NOVEMBER 1941

IJN transport KOMAKI MARU (8525grt) departed Takao, Formosa for exercises with the Japanese 23rd Sentai.

27 NOVEMBER 1941

The 2nd Battalion, 4th United States Marine Corps regiment was evacuated from Shanghai, China aboard liners PRESIDENT MADISON (14,187grt) and PRESIDENT HARRISON (10,509grt). Six men fail to board and were left behind.

American river patrol boat WAKE (PR-3) (Lt Cdr Andrew E. Harris) arrived at Shanghai from Hangkow, China. She was not seaworthy enough to undertake a crossing of the Formosa Straits to Manila, PI, so Harris and most of his crew were transferred to river patrol boats OAHU (PR-6) and LUZON (PR-7).

28 NOVEMBER 1941

	American river patrol boat WAKE (PR-3) (Lt Cdr Columbus D. Smith, USNR) remained at Shanghai, China with a skeleton crew of fourteen reservists, under a Shanghai commercial harbour pilot.

29 NOVEMBER 1941

	IJN minesweepers W-13 and W-14 arrived at Takao, Formosa.
0027	American river gunboats LUZON (PR-7) (Admiral Glassford) and OAHU (PR-6), departed Shanghai, China for Manila, PI.

30 NOVEMBER 1941

2359	American auxiliary minelayer FINCH (AM-9) with submarine rescue vessel PIGEON (ASR-6), joined with river gunboats LUZON (PR-7) and OAHU (PR-6) at sea, for the trip to Manila, PI.

West of Philippine Islands
Long. E120, 00 – E125, 00   Lat. N20, 00 – N00, 00

10 NOVEMBER 1941

	IJN liner/transport ASAMA MARU arrived at Manila, PI.

19 NOVEMBER 1941

	A mine sank American sailing vessel **DEL PIDIO** when she sailed into a prohibited area at the entrance to Manila Bay. Six crewmen were rescued.
	A mine sank Philippine sailing ship **EDRIDIO MINDORO** (67grt) when she sailed into a prohibited area at the entrance to Manila Bay.

20 NOVEMBER 1941

	American destroyer tender BLACK HAWK (AD-9) departed Manila, PI for Balikpapan, Borneo escorted by four American destroyers.

27 NOVEMBER 1941

	American submarine SALMON (SS-182) departed Manila on a defensive patrol along the west coast of Luzon Island. On 8 December, it became her first war patrol.

30 NOVEMBER 1941

	American liner PRESIDENT MADISON (14,187grt) arrived at Olongapo, PI from Shanghai, China.

Sea of Japan
Long. E128, 00 – E143, 00   Lat. N55, 00 – N33, 00

1 NOVEMBER 1941

	IJN cargo ship TOYO MARU (2470grt) departed Sasebo, Kyushu for Shanghai, China.

2 NOVEMBER 1941

	Japanese tanker GENYO MARU (10,018grt) was requisitioned by the IJN and registered in the Sasebo Naval District.

4 NOVEMBER 1941

	IJN oiler HOKUAN MARU (3712grt) arrived at Sasebo, Kyushu.

5 NOVEMBER 1941

	A mine sank Japanese steamer KEHI MARU (4523grt) in the Sea of Japan in 40, 40N, 131E. Of eighty crewmen and four hundred and thirty passengers, twenty were lost and one hundred and eleven were missing.

9 NOVEMBER 1941

	IJN oiler KORYU MARU (880grt) arrived at Sasebo, Kyushu.

10 NOVEMBER 1941

	Japanese passenger/cargo ship KAGU MARU (6806grt) arrived at Nagasaki, Japan and began conversion into a specially installed transport ship at Mitsubishi Heavy Industries' shipyard. She was re-rated as a converted transport (misc) in the Sasebo Naval District.
	IJN aircraft carrier TAIYO arrived at Sasebo, Kyushu.

	IJN oiler TOEI MARU arrived at Sasebo, Kyushu.
	The IJN registered transport NANKAI MARU (5114grt) and she was attached to the Sasebo Naval District as an auxiliary transport, (Ko) category, with her homeport as Sasebo.

11 NOVEMBER 1941

	IJN aircraft carrier KAGA was dry-docked at Sasebo navy yard.
	IJN battleship KIRISHIMA arrived at Sasebo, Kyushu and prepared for war.
	IJN super battleship MUSASHI was launched.

12 NOVEMBER 1941

	IJN oiler KORYU MARU (880grt) departed Sasebo, Kyushu, for the central China coast area.

13 NOVEMBER 1941

	IJN oiler TOEN MARU arrived at Sasebo, Kyushu.

14 NOVEMBER 1941

	IJN aircraft carrier KAGA moved out of dry dock at Sasebo, Kyushu.
	IJN battleship KONGO arrived at Sasebo, Kyushu to make her final war preparations.

17 NOVEMBER 1941

	IJN battleship KIRISHIMA departed Sasebo, Kyushu.

18 NOVEMBER 1941

	IJN transport HOKUROKU MARU (5046grt) departed Sasebo, Kyushu.

19 NOVEMBER 1941

	IJN submarine tender NAGOYA MARU departed Sasebo, Kyushu for the southern Chinese coast.

20 NOVEMBER 1941

	IJN oiler IRO departed Sasebo, Kyushu.
	IJN ammunition ship KOTOKU MARU (6702grt) arrived at Sasebo, Kyushu from Takao, Formosa.
	The IJN registered transport RAKUTO MARU (2962grt) and attached her to the Sasebo Naval District as an auxiliary transport, (Otsu) category, with her homeport as Sasebo.

21 NOVEMBER 1941

	IJN battleship KONGO departed Sasebo, Kyushu.
	IJN ammunition ship KOTOKU MARU (6702grt) received Secret Sasebo Naval District order No.795 to transport staff, materiel and conduct replenishment sorties.

22 NOVEMBER 1941

	IJN seaplane tender SANYO MARU arrived at Sasebo, Kyushu.
	IJN seaplane tender KAMIKAWA MARU departed Sasebo, Kyushu, for Samah, Hainan Island. She now carried fourteen Aichi Type 0 E13A1 "Jake" reconnaissance floatplanes and Mitsubishi F1M2 "Pete" scout float biplanes.

23 NOVEMBER 1941

	Japanese tanker GENYO MARU (10,018grt) began her conversion into an IJN auxiliary oiler at the Sasebo Naval Yard.
	IJN frigates HATSUKARI and TOMOZURU departed Sasebo, Kyushu for Takao, Formosa, via Terashima.
	IJN torpedo boat CHIDORI departed Sasebo, Kyushu for Takao, Formosa.

24 NOVEMBER 1941

	IJN transport ship KAGU MARU completed her conversion at Nagasaki, Kyushu.

26 NOVEMBER 1941

	IJN minesweepers W-13, W-17 and W-18 departed Sasebo, Kyushu.
	I-65 departed Sasebo, Kyushu for Palau with light cruiser YURA along with the 29th Submarine Division and 30th Submarine Division. En route, the 5th Submarine Squadron was diverted to Samah, Hainan Island, China.
	I-66 departed Sasebo, Kyushu for Palau with the light cruiser YURA (Rear Admiral, the Marquis, Daigo Tadashige) plus the 30th Submarine Division and 29th Submarine Division. En route, the 5th Submarine Squadron was

	diverted to Samah, Hainan Island, China.
	IJN submarines I-62 and I-64 departed Sasebo, Kyushu for Palau.
	IJN oiler KORYU MARU (880grt) arrived at Sasebo, Kyushu.

27 NOVEMBER 1941

	IJN minesweepers W-7, W-8 and W-12 departed Sasebo, Kyushu.
	IJN ammunition ship KOTOKU MARU (6702grt) departed Sasebo, Kyushu.
	IJN transport NANKAI MARU (5114grt) completed her conversion at Sasebo, Kyushu.

28 NOVEMBER 1941

	IJN coastal minelayer ITSUKUSHIMA arrived at Sasebo, Kyushu and later departed through the Terajima Straits.
	IJN aircraft carrier TAIYO departed Sasebo, Kyushu carrying Type-96 shipboard fighters to Palau for the Japanese 11th Air Fleet escorted by IJN destroyer HOKAZE.
	IJN hydrographic survey ship HAKUSA (3810grt) departed Sasebo, Kyushu for the central China coast area. She was assigned to the Japanese China Area Fleet.
	IJN oiler KORYU MARU (880grt) departed Sasebo, Kyushu for the central China coast area.
	IJN submarine I-66 and Submarine Division 30 were reassigned to the Japanese Southern Force.
	IJN transport KINAI MARU (5047grt) departed Sasebo, Kyushu.
	IJN transport NANKAI MARU (5114grt) departed Sasebo, Kyushu.

29 NOVEMBER 1941

	IJN destroyers HAGIKAZE, ARASHI, NOWAKI, MAIKAZE, HAYASHIO, ARASHIO, MICHISHIO, OSHIO, ASASHIO, INAZUMA, IKAZUCHI, HIBIKI, and AKATSUKI departed Sasebo, Kyushu through Terashima Straits for Mako, Pescadores.
	IJN destroyer SHIOKAZE escorted light aircraft carrier RYUJO from Sasebo, Kyushu to Palau.

30 NOVEMBER 1941

	IJN oiler KUROSHIO MARU (10,383grt) departed Sasebo, Kyushu.

East of Philippine Islands
Long. E125, 00 – E140, 00   Lat. N20, 00 – N00, 00

28 NOVEMBER 1941

	IJN Submarine Division 30 was reassigned to the Japanese Southern Expeditionary Fleet at Samah, Hainan Island, China.

New Guinea and Solomon Islands
Long. E140, 00 – E180, 00   Lat. N00, 00 – S25, 00

30 NOVEMBER 1941

	Off Fiji, IJN submarine I-10 launched a Watanabe E9W1 "Slim" floatplane piloted by Lt Ando Yasuo to reconnoitre Suva Bay. Lt Ando reported that there are no warships at Suva, but failed to return to the submarine. After a three-day fruitless search under radio silence I-10 departed the area, and reported the loss of its aircraft to the Japanese Sixth Fleet HQ. A recent book dealing with the crypto analytic background of the Japanese attack on Pearl Harbor, suggests that I-10's floatplane was lost at Pago-Pago four days later. Wartime records did not confirm these findings.
	New Zealand light cruiser ACHILLES joined with New Zealand light cruiser LEANDER at Suva, Fiji Islands. Both light cruisers then returned to New Zealand.

East of Australia
Long. E140, 00 – E155, 00   Lat. S12, 00 – S40, 00

7 NOVEMBER 1941

	A German AMC laid mine sank steamer **CAMBRIDGE** (10,855grt) off Wilsons Promontory, Australia.

8 NOVEMBER 1941

	A German AMC laid mine sank American steamer **CITY OF RAYVILLE** (5883grt) off Cape Otway, Australia.

East of Japan

Long. E130, 00 – E180, 00   Lat. N55, 00 – N30, 00

1 NOVEMBER 1941

	Japanese cargo ship KIYOSUMI MARU (8613grt) was requisitioned by the IJN to become a converted light cruiser.
	The aircraft tail code for IJN seaplane tender NOTORO was changed to "N2-xx."
	The CINC Japanese 1st Air Fleet (VAdm Nagumo Chuichi) signalled oiler TOEI MARU that after completing battle preparations, she was to obtain about 750 drums of fuel oil (for use by aircraft carrier AKAGI) and 12,000 kerosene tins of fuel oil (for use by aircraft carrier HIRYU) from Yokosuka and rendezvous with the fleet at Sasebo on 10 November.
	IJN coastal minesweeper TSUGARU departed Yokosuka, Japan.
	IJN battleships MUTSU and NAGATO anchored at Saiki, Japan at full combat readiness.
	IJN submarine tender NAGOYA MARU was assigned to Submarine Squadron 4 of the Japanese Sixth Fleet based at Kure, Japan. NAGOYA MARU was the tender for Submarine Division 18 (I-53, I-54, I-55), Submarine Division 19 (I-56, I-57, I-58) and Submarine Division 21 (RO-33 and RO-34).
	Japanese tanker SAN PEDRO MARU (7268grt) was requisitioned by the IJN.
	IJN oiler HISHI MARU No.2 was assigned to the Japanese Combined Fleet Supply Force.
	Japanese tanker TONAN MARU NO. 2 (19,262grt) began conversion into a fleet oiler. Rated by the IJN as a special transport ship and oil tanker.
	IJN minelayer NARYU (720grt) was assigned to the Maizuru Guard Unit and began working up to combat efficiency.
	IJN minelayer SHIRAKAMI (720grt) was assigned to the Ominato Defence Corps at the Ominato Guard Station.
	Japanese oiler HOKKI MARU (5601grt) was requisitioned by the IJA and served as Army No.751.
	IJN cargo ship MITAKESAN MARU (4441grt) departed Yokosuka, Japan.
	IJN cargo ship NANIWA MARU (4857grt) was attached to the Yokosuka Naval District as an auxiliary transport.
	IJN cargo ship TEISEN MARU (5019grt) arrived at Kushiro, Hokkaido from Yokohama, Japan.
	The IJN requisitioned transport TAITO MARU (4466grt).

2 NOVEMBER 1941

	IJN battleship KIRISHIMA departed Saiki, Japan and arrived at Ariake Bay, Japan later the same day.
	IJN aircraft carrier SHOKAKU departed Oita, Japan with aircraft carrier ZUIKAKU for a training cruise.

3 NOVEMBER 1941

	IJN aircraft carrier SHOKAKU arrived at Ariake Bay, Japan with aircraft carrier ZUIKAKU from a short training cruise.
	IJN auxiliary transport YAMAGIRI MARU (6438grt) departed Tokyo, Japan for Mili Atoll in the Marshall Islands.

4 NOVEMBER 1941

	IJN battleship KIRISHIMA departed Ariake Bay, Japan for Kagoshima, Japan.
	The IJA requisitioned cargo ship ZENYO MARU (6442grt). She was to be converted into a Boku Kikansen (anti-aircraft) vessel, fitted with six Type-88 75-mm AA guns and six Type-98 20-mm AA machine-cannons.

5 NOVEMBER 1941

	Japanese passenger/cargo ship KINUGASA MARU (8407grt) arrived at the Nippon Kokan, K. K. Tsurumi shipyard.
	Before loading additional fuel on oiler TOEI MARU, the Chief, Bureau Military Affairs Section signalled the Chief of Staff, Japanese 1st Air Fleet that loading drums of fuel oil on the tankers would affect the strength of the hull and the ship's performance. He advised that aircraft carrier AKAGI should be loaded under 600 tons; aircraft carrier SORYU and aircraft carrier HIRYU should be loaded under 400 tons, and that an equivalent weight should be removed. The AKAGI and HIRYU should be loaded amidships and the bow and stern areas avoided. The SORYU should be loaded evenly over length of ship.
	IJN submarine chaser CH-27 was launched.
	IJN aircraft carrier SHOKAKU departed Ariake Bay, Japan with aircraft carrier ZUIKAKU.
	IJN oiler HISHI MARU (856grt) completed her conversion into a fleet oiler at Yokosuka, Japan.
	IJN transport CHOKO MARU No.2 GO (3515grt) arrived at Yokosuka, Japan.

6 NOVEMBER 1941

	IJN battleship KIRISHIMA arrived at Kagoshima, Japan from Ariake Bay, Japan.

	IJN liner/transport ASAMA MARU departed Yokohama, Japan for Singapore, Malaya to evacuate approximately 450 Japanese civilians.
	IJN transport CHOKO MARU No.2 GO (3515grt) departed Yokosuka, Japan for Pagan Island, in the northern Marianas Islands.

7 NOVEMBER 1941

	IJN AMC KIYOSUMI MARU was assigned directly to the Japanese Combined Fleet in the 24th Cruiser Squadron (Raider) with AIKOKU MARU and HOKOKU MARU.
	IJN battleship KIRISHIMA departed Kagoshima, Japan for Saiki Bay, Japan.
	IJN aircraft carrier SHOKAKU arrived at Oita Bay, Japan with aircraft carrier ZUIKAKU after their training cruise.
	IJN ammunition ship KOGYO MARU (6353grt) was assigned to the Japanese Southern Force.
	Japanese oiler MANJU MARU (6515grt) was requisitioned by the IJN at Kure, Japan.

8 NOVEMBER 1941

	IJN minesweepers W-1, W-2, W-3, W-4, W-5 and W-6 departed Kure, Japan for Camranh Bay, French Indo-China.
	IJN oiler SHIRETOKO arrived at Yokosuka, Japan.
	Japanese tanker SAN LUIS MARU (7268grt) was requisitioned by the IJN and began conversion in to an auxiliary oil tanker.
	IJN oiler MANJU MARU (6515grt) departed Kure, Japan and made stops at Kanogawa, Hakodate, Otaru, Yokkaichi, Shimotsu, Mako, Takao, Dairen, Tokuyama, Kudamatsu and Mako.
	IJN transport HEITO MARU (4468grt) departed Futami-ko, Hyogo Prefecture to operate in the South Seas area (Japan mandated islands).
	IJN transport TOKAI MARU (5038grt) departed Shibaura, Japan for Truk, in the Caroline Islands.

9 NOVEMBER 1941

	IJN battleship KIRISHIMA arrived at Saiki Bay, Japan from Kagoshima, Japan.
	IJN aircraft carrier SHOKAKU departed Oita Bay, Japan with aircraft carrier ZUIKAKU and arrived at Kure, Japan later the same day.

10 NOVEMBER 1941

	The Chief of Staff of the Kure Naval District advised the Chief of Staff Japanese 1st Air Fleet, that arrangements had been made to re-equip oilers KENYO MARU, KYOKUTO MARU, SHINKOKU MARU and KOKUYO MARU for simultaneous port and starboard re-fuelling by 13 November.
	Japanese passenger/cargo ship KINUGASA MARU (8407grt) began equipment installation.
	IJN tanker TOA MARU arrived at Saiki Bay, Japan as part of the Japanese Sixth Fleet re-fuelling Unit with fleet oiler ONDO.
	IJN battleship KIRISHIMA departed Saiki Bay, Japan.
	IJN battleship NAGATO arrived at Iwakuni, Japan.
	Japanese cargo ship KUNIKAWA MARU (6863grt) began conversion into a seaplane tender at the Innoshima Yard of the Osaka Tekkosho K.K.
	IJN submarine I-1 was in Submarine Division 7 with I-2 and I-3. Admiral Shimizu convened a meeting of all his commanders aboard his flagship, light cruiser KATORI. Cdr Ankyu and the other commanders were briefed on the planned attack on Pearl Harbor, Oahu.
	IJN submarine I-10 and I-26 were assigned to the Japanese Sixth Fleet Reconnaissance Unit. I-10 was assigned to reconnoitre areas in the Fiji, Samoa and Tutuila Islands in the South Pacific and I-26 was assigned to the Aleutians area.
	IJN submarine I-4 was in the Japanese Sixth Fleet Submarine Squadron 2 in Submarine Division 8 with I-5, I-6 and the squadron's flagship, I-7.
	Japanese tanker NICHIEI MARU (10,020grt) began her conversion into a naval auxiliary at Kawasaki Dockyard in Kobe, Japan.
	IJN submarine I-70 departed Saeki, Japan with submarine I-68 for Kwajalein.
	The IJN registered transport EIKO MARU (3535grt) and she was attached to the Kure Naval District as an auxiliary transport, (Otsu) category.
	The IJN registered transport HOKKAI MARU (5105grt) and she was attached to the Yokosuka Naval District as an auxiliary transport, (Ko) category, with her homeport as Yokosuka, Japan.
	The IJN registered transport TAITO MARU (4466grt) and she was attached to the Kure Naval District as an auxiliary transport, (Otsu) category, with her homeport as Kure, Japan.
	The IJN registered transport RAKUTO MARU (2962grt) as a transport (Ippan Choyosen).

11 NOVEMBER 1941

	IJN seaplane tender KIMIKAWA MARU arrived at Yokosuka, Japan and was dry-docked.
	IJN submarines I-69, , I-71, I-72 and I-73 departed Saeki, Japan for Kwajalein.
	IJN submarines I-74 and I-75 departed Saeki, Japan.
	IJN submarine I-8 departed Saeki, Japan.
	The IJN registered auxiliary gunboat NIKKAI MARU (2562grt) as PG-51.

12 NOVEMBER 1941

	IJN battleship HIEI arrived at Yokosuka, Japan for final preparations for the Operation Z.
	IJN hospital ship TAKASAGO MARU was requisitioned by the IJN.
	Japanese tanker KAIJO MARU No.2 (8636grt) was requisitioned by the IJN.
	Japanese cargo ship URAKAMI MARU (4317grt) was requisitioned by the IJN and became a repair ship.
	IJN submarine I-26 departed Yokosuka, Japan on her first war patrol.

13 NOVEMBER 1941

	IJN AMCs AIKOKU MARU and HOKOKU MARU departed Kure, Japan for Iwakuni, Japan.
	IJN oilers KENYO MARU, KYOKUTO MARU, SHINKOKU MARU and KOKUYO MARU conducted fuelling at sea exercises with Japanese Carrier Division 1 aircraft carrier AKAGI, Destroyer Squadron 1, Cruiser Division 8, Japanese Carrier Division 2 aircraft carriers SORYU and HIRYU and Japanese Carrier Division 5 aircraft carriers SHOKAKU and ZUIKAKU, while all were en route to Kagoshima Bay.
	IJN aircraft carrier ZUIKAKU was reassigned to Carrier Division 5 at Kure, Japan.

14 NOVEMBER 1941

	The Flag of Commander Japanese Carrier Division 5 shifted from IJN aircraft carrier SHOKAKU to aircraft carrier ZUIKAKU at Kure, Japan.
	IJN oiler SHIRIYA was assigned to the Japanese 1st Air Fleet Support Force.
	IJN liner TATSUTA MARU arrived at Yokohama, Japan.
	IJN oiler KYOEI MARU No.2 (1192grt) arrived at Saeki Bay, Japan.

15 NOVEMBER 1941

	IJN oiler AKEBONO MARU was assigned to the Japanese 1st Air Fleet.
	IJN battleship KIRISHIMA was assigned to the Japanese First Fleet of the Japanese Combined Fleet anchorage at Hashirajima in Hiroshima Bay in Battleship Division 3 with her sister ships HIEI, HARUNA and KONGO.
	IJN submarine I-9 was assigned to the Japanese Advance Expeditionary Force (Japanese Sixth Fleet) as flagship of Submarine Squadron 1 with submarines I-15 through I-26.
	IJN auxiliary minelayer TENYO MARU (6843grt) departed Kure, Japan.
1735	IJN AMCs AIKOKU MARU and HOKOKU MARU departed Iwakuni, Japan.
	IJN submarines RO-33 and RO-34 were assigned to Submarine Squadron 4 (Rear Admiral Yoshitomi Setsuzo) in Submarine Division 21 (Captain Iwagami Hidetoshi).
	IJN transport SHOHEI MARU (7255grt) departed Yokosuka, Japan.

16 NOVEMBER 1941

	IJN oiler SAN DIEGO MARU was requisitioned by the IJN.
	The boats of Japanese Submarine Squadron 2 departed Yokosuka, Japan for the Hawaiian Islands. I-1, undergoing engine repairs, was unable to sortie with the rest of her unit. Prior to her departure, she was fitted with a long-range very low frequency (VLF) receiver.
	IJN submarine I-10 departed Yokosuka, Japan for the South Pacific on her first war patrol.
	IJN submarine I-4 departed Yokosuka, Japan for the Hawaiian Islands.
	IJN submarine I-5 departed Yokosuka, Japan for the Hawaiian Islands.
	IJN aircraft carrier ZUIKAKU departed Kure, Japan for Saeki Bay, Japan.
	Japanese cargo ship NICHII MARU (6543grt) was requisitioned by the IJN to become an ammunition ship.
1200	IJN submarine I-2 departed Yokosuka, Japan for the Hawaiian Islands with Commander Submarine Division 7 (Capt Shimamoto Hisagoro) aboard.
1200	IJN submarine I-3 departed Yokosuka, Japan for the Hawaiian Islands in the company of submarine I-2.
1300	IJN submarine I-6 departed Yokosuka, Japan for the Hawaiian Islands with Commander Submarine Division 8 (Capt Takezaki Kaoru) aboard.
1300	Japanese Commander Submarine Squadron 2 (Rear Admiral Yamazaki) transferred his flag to I-7. The submarine also embarked a Watanabe E9W1 "Slim" Type 96 floatplane. IJN submarine I-7 departed Yokosuka, Japan for the Hawaiian Islands.

17 NOVEMBER 1941

	IJN aircraft carrier KAGA arrived at Saeki Bay, Japan to load 100 special torpedoes for the impending Operation Z.
	IJN battleship NAGATO departed Hashirajima, Japan for Saeki Bay, Japan.
	IJN oiler KIRISHIMA MARU began conversion into a fleet oiler at Kure Naval Yard.
	IJN oiler KYOKUYO MARU was requisitioned by the IJN and registered in the Yokosuka Naval District as a chartered transport ship (oil supply).
	IJN aircraft carrier SHOKAKU departed Kure, Japan and arrived at Saeki Bay, Japan later the same day.
	IJN aircraft carrier ZUIKAKU departed Saeki, Japan for Oita Bay, Japan.
	Japanese oiler AKATSUKI MARU (10,216grt) was requisitioned by the IJN.
	IJN cargo ship MANKO MARU (4471grt) arrived at Yokohama, Japan.
	The officers of the Japanese Special Attack Unit (Captain Sasaki Hankyu) were briefed on the Hawaii Operation. For Operation Z, IJN submarine I-22 was assigned as the flagship with I-16, I-18, I-20, and I-24.
	Japanese passenger/cargo ship TAIYO MARU (14,503grt) arrived at Yokohama just in time for the IJN officers aboard to brief the midget submarine crews about the latest details at Pearl Harbor.

18 NOVEMBER 1941

	Japanese liner HIKAWA MARU (11,622grt) arrived at Yokohama, Japan and concluded her 74th and last peacetime voyage.
	Seven oilers including KENYO MARU, KOKUYO MARU, KYOKUTO MARU, TOEI MARU, TOHO MARU, NIPPON MARU and SHINKOKU MARU were assigned to Operation Z, but the merchant tanker crews had very little practical experience in refuelling at sea. Earlier in the month, three refuelling exercises were held in Sukumo Bay and the Ariake Sea. Now, while en route to the Kuriles, all units in the carrier formation were refuelled ten times.
	IJN battleship HIEI departed the Kisarazu Naval Base in Tokyo Bay.
	IJN battleship NAGATO arrived at Saeki Bay, Japan. Admiral Yamamoto departed battleship NAGATO by motor launch for aircraft carrier AKAGI anchored nearby, where he hosted a farewell party for the Commander of the Japanese Carrier Striking Force *(Kido Butai)*, Vice Admiral Nagumo Chuichi.
	IJN Destroyer Squadron 1 departed Saeki Bay, Japan, with destroyers AKIGUMO, TANIKAZE, HAMAKAZE, URAKAZE, SHIRANUHI, ISOKAZE, KAGERO, KASUMI, and ARARE to escort the Japanese Carrier Striking Force to Etorofu, in the Kuril Islands.
	Although initially assigned to the No.2 Supply Group for Operation Z, the attack on Pearl Harbor, the hose flanges aboard IJN oiler AKEBONO MARU did not match up with the refuelling hoses used by the fleet ships. She was the last oiler to be so fitted and work had not been completed before the Japanese Carrier Striking Force *(Kido Butai)* sailed from Japan. Due to the deficiency, the AKEBONO MARU did not participate in the operation.
	IJN oiler TOEN MARU began her conversion into a fleet oiler.
	The Japanese Special Attack Unit departed Kure, Japan, with IJN submarines I-16, I-18, I-20, I-22, and I-24. At the Kamegakubi Naval Proving Ground each submarine embarked a top-secret 46-ton two-man Type "A" midget submarine, code-named "Mato".
	IJN submarines of the 1st (RAdm Sato) and 2nd (RAdm Yamazaki) Submarine Flotillas departed Yokosuka, Japan, and Kure, Japan, for operations in the Central Pacific.
	IJN aircraft carrier SHOKAKU departed Saeki, Japan, for Oita Bay, Japan, arriving later the same day.
	IJN aircraft carrier ZUIKAKU departed Oita Bay, Japan, for Hittokappu Bay, Japan.
	Japanese cargo ship NICHII MARU (6543grt) began her conversion to an auxiliary ammunition ship at the Kawasaki shipyard.
	Japanese oiler AKATSUKI MARU (10,216grt) arrived at Kure, Japan, and began her conversion into an auxiliary fleet oiler.
	IJN oiler KYOEI MARU No.2 (1192grt) departed Saeki Bay, Japan.
	IJN cargo ship KUNISHIMA MARU (4083grt) arrived at Yokosuka, Japan.

19 NOVEMBER 1941

	IJN repair ship ASAHI departed Kure, Japan, carrying the Japanese 11th Special Base Unit.
	IJN aircraft carrier SHOKAKU departed the Inland Sea with aircraft carrier ZUIKAKU for Hittokappu Bay in the Kuril Islands to join the ships massing for the Operation Z. For this operation, the assigned complement aircraft squadron aircraft of the SHOKAKU and ZUIKAKU had been increased beyond the standard eighteen by adding aircraft with aircrew temporarily assigned aboard from shore based training squadrons. ZUIKAKU carried eighteen A6M, twenty-seven D3A, and twenty-seven B5N aircraft. Finally, an additional twelve spare aircraft of each type were embarked in a disassembled condition.
	IJN aircraft carrier KAGA departed Saeki Bay, Japan for Hittokappu Bay, the secret assembling point for Operation Z.
	IJN battleship MUTSU arrived at Hashirajima, Japan.

	IJN Admiral Yamamoto returned to Hashirajima, Japan aboard battleship NAGATO.
	IJN seaplane tender KUNIKAWA MARU completed her conversion and was attached directly to the Japanese Combined Fleet as a "converted transport (misc)".
	IJN battleship HYUGA departed for Hashirajima, Japan.
	IJN oiler ITSUKUSHIMA MARU (10,006grt) arrived at Yokohama, Japan.
0215	The Japanese Special Attack Unit departed Kamegakubi, Japan with IJN submarines I-16, I-18, I-20, I-22 (Captain Sasaki), and I-24 each carrying a midget submarine to attack Pearl Harbor. They would take the direct route passing south of Midway Island.
	Japanese transport RAKUTO MARU (2962grt) arrived at the Osaka Iron Works shipyard to start her conversion into an auxiliary transport.

20 NOVEMBER 1941

	Japanese passenger/cargo ship KINUGASA MARU (8407grt) completed her equipment installation.
	IJN patrol boat PB-1/SHIMAKAZE was assigned to Patrol Boat Squadron 1 with PB-2, PB-32, PB-33, PB-34, PB-35, PB-36, PB-37, PB-38 and PB-39.
	IJN oiler ERIMO was assigned to the Japanese Second Fleet.
	IJN Destroyer Squadron 3 departed Kure, Japan, for Samah, Hainan, with destroyers SAGIRI, AMAGIRI, YUGIRI, ASAGIRI, SHIKINAMI, AYANAMI, URANAMI, ISONAMI, SHIRAKUMO, SHINONOME, MURAKUMO, HATSUYUKI, SHIRAYUKI and FUBUTI.
	Japanese tanker GOYO MARU began conversion into a navy transport at Fujinagata Zosen's shipyard, Osaka, Japan.
	Captain Togo advised the chiefs of staff of Japanese Carrier Divisions 1, 2 and 5 and the Japanese Combined Fleet that fleet oiler SHIRIYA was undergoing overhaul and would complete loading fuel oil (aviation gasoline) and other miscellaneous equipment by the next day at Yokosuka, Japan. He further advised that the main generator and other minor repairs would be completed by 23 November. Togo noted that he expected to get underway on the 24th and join up with Japanese 1st Air Fleet units during the morning of 27 November.
	IJN AMC KONGO MARU arrived at Yokosuka, Japan.
	IJN oiler SAN RAMON MARU was completed at Yokosuka, Japan.
	Japanese passenger/cargo ship KINRYU MARU (9310grt) arrived at Yokosuka, Japan.
	IJN destroyer YUZUKI was assigned to Destroyer Division 23 with destroyers KIKUZUKI and UZUKI, Carrier division 2, Japanese 1st Air Fleet.
	IJN submarines I-19 and I-23 departed Yokosuka, Japan, for the Hawaiian Islands.
	IJN cargo ship TATSUWA MARU (6335grt) departed Yawata, Japan, after her refit for Takao, Formosa.
	IJN transport EIKO MARU No.2 GO (3535grt) was renamed EIKO MARU (3026grt) and used by the IJN as a minesweeper tender.
	IJN transport NANKAI MARU (5114grt) was assigned to Japanese Combined Fleet, Japanese Third Fleet, to transport troops to the Southern Area.

21 NOVEMBER 1941

	Japanese passenger/cargo ship HIE MARU (4943grt) arrived at Kobe, Japan.
	Japanese liner HIKAWA MARU (11,622grt) was requisitioned by the IJN and began conversion into a hospital ship at Yokosuka, Japan. She was assigned to the Yokosuka Naval District.
	IJN submarine I-25 departed Yokosuka, Japan, on her first "war" patrol.
	IJN oiler HOYO MARU departed Yokosuka, Japan, for Truk.
	Captain Togo advised Commander Destroyer Division 7 that oiler SHIRIYA expected to depart November 24 and arrive at sea on November 27. Togo requested that he be advised of the rendezvous point with Destroyer Division 7.
	IJN submarine I-9 departed Yokosuka, Japan, with Commander Submarine Squadron 1, RAdm Sato Tsutomu aboard in the company of submarines I-15, I-17 and I-25, carrying a Watanabe E9W1 "Slim" floatplane.
	IJN cargo ship KENYO MARU (6486grt) departed Kobe, Japan.

22 NOVEMBER 1941

	IJN aircraft carrier SHOKAKU and aircraft carrier ZUIKAKU of Japanese Carrier Division 5 arrived at Hittokappu Bay as part of a last-minute addition to the Japanese Carrier Striking Force for Operation Z.
	IJN aircraft carriers AKAGI and KAGA arrived at Hittokappu Bay at Etorofu Island, in the Kuriles, as part of the Japanese Carrier Striking Force.
	IJN battleships KIRISHIMA, HIEI, and KONGO arrived at Hittokappu Bay.
	Japanese oiler FUJISAN MARU (9524grt) was requisitioned by the IJN and registered as a converted merchant transport (oil supply) in the Kure Naval District.
	IJN oiler ERIMO departed Kure, Japan.

	Japanese tanker TEIYO MARU (9849grt) was requisitioned by the IJN and was converted into a fleet oiler at Mitsubishi, Yokohama, Japan.
	IJN oiler SAN CLEMENTE MARU arrived at Kure, Japan.
	Japanese passenger/cargo ship KINRYU MARU (9310grt) departed Yokosuka, Japan.
	IJN battleship HYUGA departed Kure, Japan.
	Japanese tanker OGURA MARU No.2 (7250grt) was requisitioned by the IJN.
	IJN submarine I-21 arrived at Hittokappu Bay, Etorofu Island, Kuriles.
	Japanese oiler ITSUKUSHIMA MARU (10,006grt) was requisitioned by the IJN and registered in the Kure Naval District.
1130	IJN patrol boat PB-35 anchored in Kaneda Bay, Japan.
	IJN transport EIKO MARU No.2 GO (3535grt) completed her conversion and departed Kure, Japan, for Yokosuka, Japan.

23 NOVEMBER 1941

	Japanese passenger/cargo ship AKAGI MARU (7389grt) was requisitioned by the IJN and converted into an AMC.
	IJN Destroyer Division 23 with destroyers YUZUKI, UZUKI and KIKUZUKI escorted a troop convoy from Sakaide, Japan, to Haha-jima, Bonin Islands.
	IJN AMC KONGO MARU departed Yokosuka, Japan, for Truk.
	IJN submarines I-19 and I-23 arrived at Hittokappu Bay, Etorofu Island, Kuriles.
0630	IJN patrol boat PB-35 departed Kaneda Bay, Japan.
>1200	IJN submarine I-1 departed Yokosuka, Japan. After an overnight stop at Tateyama Bight she departed for the Hawaiian area at flank speed, conducting her first dive once she was within six hundred miles of Oahu.
	The IJN requisitioned Japanese transport ANSHU MARU (1469grt).

24 NOVEMBER 1941

	Japanese passenger/cargo ship TATSUTAKE MARU (7068grt) was requisitioned by the IJN and converted into an ammunition ship.
	IJN oiler KIRISHIMA MARU completed her conversion at Kure, Japan.
	IJN oiler MANJU MARU (6515grt) arrived at Kure, Japan.

25 NOVEMBER 1941

	Japanese passenger/cargo ship AKAGI MARU (7389grt) began her conversion into an auxiliary cruiser at Hitachi Zosen's Sakurajima yard at Osaka, Japan. Five 41-Year Type 152-mm (6-inch) single mounts guns, one 76-mm (3-inch)/40 cal. AA gun and two 7.7-mm MGs were installed. Later, she was equipped with two observation floatplanes. The ship was provided a full IJN complement including a relief air crew.
	IJN battleship MUTSU departed Kure, Japan.
	Japanese passenger/cargo ship TATSUTAKE MARU (7068grt) began her conversion into an ammunition ship.
	IJN tanker NICHIEI MARU completed her conversion into a fleet tanker.
	IJN submarine I-26 (Lt Cdr M. Yokota) conducted a reconnaissance of Kiska Island, Alaska.
	IJN oiler ITSUKUSHIMA MARU (10,006grt) arrived at Kure, Japan, from Yokohama, Japan.
	The IJN 2nd Destroyer Squadron with destroyers AMATSUKAZE and OBORO passed through the Terashima Strait to Palau.
0850	IJN patrol boat PB-35 arrived at Kure, Japan.

26 NOVEMBER 1941

	Japanese passenger/cargo ship HIE MARU (4943grt) was requisitioned by the IJN.
	KENYO MARU departed Tenzan Bay (Hittokappu) with Japanese Supply Group No.1 oilers KOKUYO MARU, KYOKUTO MARU and SHINKOKU MARU and Supply Group No.2 oilers TOHO MARU, NIPPON MARU and TOEI MARU. The oilers provided fuel for the Japanese Carrier Striking Force *(Kido Butai)* including Carrier Division 1 with aircraft carriers AKAGI, KAGA, Carrier Division 2 with aircraft carriers HIRYU and SORYU, and Carrier Division 5 with aircraft carriers SHOKAKU and ZUIKAKU. The Support Force consisted of: the 3rd Battleship Division (VAdm Mikawa) with battleships HIEI and KIRISHIMA, the 8th Cruiser Division with heavy cruisers TONE and CHIKUMA, the 1st Destroyer Division with light cruiser ABUKUMA (RAdm Omori) and destroyer AKIGUMO, the 17th Destroyer Division with destroyers ISOKAZE, URAKAZE, TANIKAZE and HAMAKAZE, the 18th Destroyer Division with destroyers ARARE, KASUMI, KAGERO and SHIRANUHI and the Japanese Midway Bombardment Unit, and the 7th Destroyer Division with destroyers SAZANAMI and USHIO.

	IJN submarines I-19, I-21 and I-23 also sailed with the force. Admiral Nagumo's orders from Admiral Yamamoto, CINC, Japanese Combined Fleet, were that, if refuelling proved impossible in the stormy winter waters of the Northern Pacific, Nagumo was to detach aircraft carriers AGAKI, SORYU and HIRYU plus his destroyers and make the attack on Pearl Harbor with only aircraft carriers KAGA, SHOKAKU and ZUIKAKU.
	IJN light cruiser NAGARA, flagship of the Japanese Fourth Surprise Attack Unit, departed the Terashima Strait, Japan.
	IJN torpedo boats HATO and SAGI departed Yokosuka, Japan, for Akkeshi, Japan.
	IJN torpedo boat MANAZURU departed from Terashima, Japan, for Takao, Formosa.
	IJN Destroyer Squadron 2 departed Terashima Strait for Palau with destroyers TOKITSUKAZE, YUKIKAZE, NATSUSHIO, HATSUKAZE, OYASHIO, SUZUKAZE, UMIKAZE, KAWAKAZE, YAMAKAZE and KUROSHIO.
	IJN Destroyer Squadron 4 departed Terashima Strait for Mako, Pescadores Islands, with destroyers ASAGUMO, MINEGUMO, YAMAGUMO, HARUSAME, YADUCHI, SAMIDARE, MURASAME and NATSUGUMO.
	IJN Destroyer Squadron 5 departed Terashima Strait for Mako, Pescadores Islands, with destroyers SATSUKI, NAGATSUKI, MINAZUKI, FUMIZUKI, HATAKAZE, MATSUKAZE, ASAKAZE, and HARUKAZE.
	IJN oiler TSURUMI departed Hashirajima, Japan.
	Japanese cargo ship HITACHI MARU (6540grt) was requisitioned by the IJN and converted into an ammunition ship.
	IJN liner/transport ASAMA MARU arrived at Kobe, Japan.
	IJN battleship HYUGA departed Hashirajima, Japan.
	IJN ammunition ship KOGYO MARU (6353grt) loaded 150 tons of boiler oil, 300 tons of water and weapons. She was assigned directly to HQ, Japanese Combined Fleet, to support the Japanese Malaya Seizure Force.
	IJN cargo ship MITAKESAN MARU (4441grt) arrived at Yokosuka, Japan.
	IJN transport EIKO MARU No.2 GO (3535grt) arrived at Yokosuka, Japan.

27 NOVEMBER 1941

	IJN seaplane tender KIYOKAWA MARU departed Yokosuka, Japan, for Saipan.
	IJN submarines I-19, I-21 and I-23 refuelled from a fleet oiler at sea.
	IJN oiler SAN CLEMENTE MARU departed Kure, Japan.
0615	IJN patrol boat PB-35 departed Kure, Japan.

28 NOVEMBER 1941

	IJN oiler KENYO MARU refuelled IJN aircraft carrier AKAGI at sea.
	IJN minesweeper W-11 departed Yokosuka, Japan.
	IJN seaplane tender KUNIKAWA MARU departed Kure, Japan, for Palau carrying the Kure No.2 Special Naval Landing Force (SNLF) (Cdr Siga Masanari).
	IJN destroyers USHIO and SAZANAMI departed Tateyama, Japan, with tanker SHIRIYA.
	IJN Destroyer Division 7 with destroyers USHIO, SAZANAMI, and AKEBONO was assigned to Carrier Division 1, Japanese 1st Air Fleet.

29 NOVEMBER 1941

	IJN Battleship Division 3 with battleships HARUNA and KONGO was attached to the Japanese Second Fleet, Japanese Southern (Malay) Force that included Battleship Division 3/2, Cruiser Division 4 (VAdm Kondo Nobutake) with heavy cruisers ATAGO, TAKAO and MAYA and eight destroyers. The Southern (Malay) Force departed Hashirajima, Japan, for Mako, Pescadores. Battleship Division 3 with HARUNA and KONGO plus destroyers ARASHI, HAGIKAZE, AKATSUKI, HATAKAZE, NOWAKI, MAIKAZE, MICHISHIO and HIBIKI were referred to as the Malayan Invasion Force Main Body.
	IJN battleship MUTSU returned to Hashirajima, Japan.
	IJN transport MOGAMIGAWA MARU was requisitioned by the IJN. She was armed with a 4.7-inch (120-mm) gun and fitted with mine laying equipment.
	IJN oiler SAN CLEMENTE MARU departed Saiki, Japan.
	IJN transport TAITO MARU (4466grt) departed Kure, Japan, for Palau.

30 NOVEMBER 1941

	IJN seaplane tender KIMIKAWA MARU was undocked and departed Yokosuka, Japan, for Ominato, Honshu.
	Japanese tanker AKEBONO MARU (10,182grt) entered the Naniwa Dockyard to convert her into a naval auxiliary and equip her to replenish ships at sea.
	All three ASAMA MARU class passenger ships were chartered by the IJN.
	IJN oiler KIRISHIMA MARU departed Ujina, Japan, for Palau carrying a unit of Special Naval Landing Force

(SNLF) troops escorted by two unidentified warships.

IJN oiler ITSUKUSHIMA MARU (10,006grt) departed Kure, Japan.

Bonin – Mariana Islands
Long. E130, 00 – E150, 00   Lat. N30, 00 – N00, 00

5 NOVEMBER 1941
IJN coastal minesweeper TSUGARU arrived at Saipan, Mariana Islands.

6 NOVEMBER 1941
IJN coastal minesweeper TSUGARU departed Saipan for Truk.

12 NOVEMBER 1941
IJN transport CHOKO MARU No.2 GO (3515grt) arrived at Pagan, Mariana Islands.

14 NOVEMBER 1941
IJN transport HEITO MARU (4468grt) arrived at Iwo Jima, *Ogasawara Gunto* (Bonin Islands).

15 NOVEMBER 1941
IJN transport CHOKO MARU No.2 GO (3515grt) departed Pagan for Saipan.

16 NOVEMBER 1941
IJN transport CHOKO MARU No.2 GO (3515grt) arrived at Saipan from Pagan.

22 NOVEMBER 1941
IJN transport CHOKO MARU No.2 GO (3515grt) departed Saipan for Otaru, Hokkaido.

24 NOVEMBER 1941
IJN coastal minesweeper TSUGARU arrived at Saipan, Mariana Islands.

28 NOVEMBER 1941
IJN coastal minesweeper TSUGARU departed Saipan.

30 NOVEMBER 1941
IJN oiler TSURUMI arrived at Haha-jima, Bonin Islands, on a water replenishment mission.

Gilbert – Marshall Islands
Long. E150, 00 – E180, 00   Lat. N30, 00 – N00, 00

1 NOVEMBER 1941
The submarine tender JINGEI was in the Japanese Fourth Fleet (VAdm Inoue Shigeyoshi) as flagship of the Japanese 7th Submarine Squadron (RAdm Onishi Shinzo) consisting of the 26th, 27th and 33rd Submarine Divisions. She was equipped with an E7K2 "Alf" floatplane.

IJN cargo ship KENYO MARU (6486grt) arrived at Truk.

8 NOVEMBER 1941
IJN coastal minesweeper TSUGARU arrived at Truk from Saipan.

10 NOVEMBER 1941
IJN seaplane tender KIYOKAWA MARU was assigned to Headquarters, Japanese Fourth Fleet.

11 NOVEMBER 1941
IJN cargo ship TATSUWA MARU (6335grt) departed Truk for Yawata, Japan.

14 NOVEMBER 1941
IJN transport TOKAI MARU (5038grt) arrived at Truk.

20 NOVEMBER 1941
IJN submarines I-71, I-72, I-74 and I-75 arrived at Kwajalein, Marshall Islands.

IJN submarines I-70 and I-73 arrived at Kwajalein. All arriving submarines took on fuel and provisions for Operation Z.

21 NOVEMBER 1941

	Japanese tanker SHIRETOKO MARU (6500grt) arrived at Kwajalein, Marshall Islands.

22 NOVEMBER 1941

	IJN coastal minesweeper TSUGARU departed Truk.

23 NOVEMBER 1941

	IJN submarine I-10 arrived at Kwajalein, Marshall Islands, to refuel and then proceeded to the Fiji Island area.
	IJN submarines I-68, I-69, I-71, and I-72 departed Kwajalein on their first war patrol.
	IJN submarines I-70, I-73, I-74 and I-75 departed Kwajalein for the Hawaiian Islands.

24 NOVEMBER 1941

	IJN submarine I-8 departed Kwajalein for the Hawaiian Islands.

25 NOVEMBER 1941

	IJN AMCs AIKOKU MARU and HOKOKU MARU arrived at the standby position at Jaluit Atoll, Marshall Islands. They refuelled and replenished from the naval supply base on Emidj Island.
	American submarines TRITON (SS-201) and TAMBOR (SS-198) arrived at Wake Island on their training patrol from Pearl Harbor, Oahu, Hawaii.

26 NOVEMBER 1941

	IJN AMCs AIKOKU MARU and HOKOKU MARU departed Jaluit Atoll, Marshall Islands, for their war positions.
	American transport SONOMA (AT-12) departed Wake Island with her barges.

28 NOVEMBER 1941

	The IJN 29th Destroyer Division with destroyers OITE, HAYATE, ASANAGI, and YUNAGI were assigned to the 6th Destroyer Squadron, Japanese Fourth Fleet.
	The IJN 30th Destroyer Division with destroyers MUTSUKI, KISARAGI, YAYOI, and MOCHIZUKI were assigned to the 6th Destroyer Squadron, Japanese Fourth Fleet.
	American seaplane tender WRIGHT (AV-1) arrived at Wake Island.

29 NOVEMBER 1941

	IJN light cruiser YUBARI, flagship of the 6th Destroyer Squadron, departed Truk for Kwajalein, Marshall Islands, with the 29th Destroyer Division of destroyers ASANAGI, OITE, YUNAGI and HAYATE, and the 30th Destroyer Division of destroyers KISARAGI, MUTSUKI, YAYOI and MOCHIZUKI.
	IJN patrol boats PB-32 and PB-33 departed Truk for Kwajalein.
1300	In Operation GI, IJN coastal minelayer TOKIWA departed Truk with the Japanese Gilbert Islands Invasion Force that included minelayers OKINOSHIMA (F), TSUGARU and TENYO MARU carrying the 51st Guards Unit escorted by Section 1 of the 29th Destroyer Division with destroyers ASANAGI and YUNAGI. The light aircraft carrier CHITOSE Naval Air Group was assigned to provide air cover.

30 NOVEMBER 1941

	IJN AMC KONGO MARU and passenger/cargo ship KINRYU MARU (9310grt) departed Truk.

New Zealand

Long. E150, 00 – E180, 00 Lat. S25, 00 – S60, 00

4 NOVEMBER 1941

	New Zealand light cruiser ACHILLES arrived at Auckland, New Zealand.

10 NOVEMBER 1941

	New Zealand light cruiser ACHILLES departed Auckland, New Zealand, with an American liner for Sydney, Australia.

22 NOVEMBER 1941

	New Zealand light cruiser ACHILLES joined with Australian light cruiser ADELAIDE in Cook Strait and took over the escort of convoy VK.21. Light cruiser ACHILLES was detached from the convoy on the 24th 250 miles east of Chatham Island and proceeded to Navulu Passage.

Alaska
Long. W180, 00 – W130, 00   Lat. N70, 00 – N50, 00

27 NOVEMBER 1941

	IJN submarine I-26 (Cdr M. Yokota) made periscope observations of the harbours at Attu, Kiska and Adak Islands in the Aleutians.
	IJN submarine I-26 flew her aircraft over Dutch Harbour, Alaska, during the night.

30 NOVEMBER 1941

	IJN submarine I-26 (Cdr M. Yokota) conducted a reconnaissance of Kodiak Island, Alaska.

Hawaii Area
Long. W180, 00 – W140, 00   Lat. N30, 00 – N00, 00

1 NOVEMBER 1941

0830	IJN passenger/cargo ship TAIYO MARU (14,503grt) arrived at Honolulu, Oahu. Lt Matsuo disembarked to reconnoitre the entrance to Pearl Harbor.

2 NOVEMBER 1941

	IJN liner TATSUTA MARU arrived at Honolulu, Hawaii, to embark Japanese nationals for return to Japan.

1 NOVEMBER 1941

	IJN passenger/cargo ship TAIYO MARU (14,503grt) departed Honolulu, Oahu, for Japan. All three IJN officers returned with her after their reconnaissance of the Pearl Harbor defences.

18 NOVEMBER 1941

	American light cruiser BOISE (CL-47) departed Pearl Harbor escorting convoy 4001 with USA transport PRESIDENT GRANT (14,119grt) and steamers AMERICAN LEADER (6750grt), CAPE FAIRWEATHER (6797grt), JOHN LYKES (6829grt), and DONA NATI (5011grt) to Manila, Philippines. The convoy arrived at Manila on 4 December and the BOISE (CL-47) was ordered to join the American Asiatic Fleet.

19 NOVEMBER 1941

	American submarine TRITON (SS-201) departed Pearl Harbor for a training patrol off Wake Island.

21 NOVEMBER 1941

	American destroyer SHAW (DD-373) and tanker SABINE (AO-25) were damaged in a collision during sea refuelling exercises near Pearl Harbor.

28 NOVEMBER 1941

	American aircraft carrier ENTERPRISE (CV-6) departed Pearl Harbor, Oahu, accompanied by battleships ARIZONA (BB-39), NEVADA (BB-36), and OKLAHOMA (BB-37) of Battleship Division 1, heavy cruisers CHESTER (CA-27), NORTHAMPTON (CA-26), and SALT LAKE CITY (CA-25) of Cruiser Division 5, Commander Destroyer Flotilla 2 in light cruiser DETROIT (CL-8), plus destroyers HENLEY (DD-391), HELM (DD-388), BLUE (DD-387), BAGLEY (DD-386), MUGFORD (DD-389), RALPH TALBOT (DD-390), JARVIS (DD-393), and PATTERSON (DD-392) of Destroyer Squadron 4 and destroyers BALCH (DD-363), GRIDLEY (DD-380), CRAVEN (DD-382), MCCALL (DD-400), MAURY (DD-401), DUNLAP (DD-384), FANNING (DD-385), BENHAM (DD-397), and ELLET (DD-398) of Destroyer Squadron 6. The battleships, light cruiser DETROIT (CL-8), and Destroyer Squadron 4 were detached out of sight of land for exercises, and the aircraft carrier with Cruiser Division 5 and Destroyer Squadron 6 continued on to Wake Island. On 4 December, twelve aircraft of United States Marine Corps VMF-211 Squadron were launched from the ENTERPRISE (CV-6) to the airfield on Wake Island.
	American submarine ARGONAUT (SM-1) departed Pearl Harbor for a practice patrol near Midway Island.

West of United States
Long. W130, 00 – W110, 00   Lat. N50, 00 – N30, 00

2 NOVEMBER 1941

	Japanese oiler ITSUKUSHIMA MARU (10,006grt) departed San Francisco, California, on her last peacetime oil voyage.

Volume 4 Index

Ships in **BOLDFACE** were either sunk or captured and renamed during the period from June 1941 through November 1941. Where possible, the tonnage of merchant ships is listed in the index. Military vessels are listed without tonnage unless the ship was sunk, even when it is known and cited in the text.

There are often two or more ships with the same name. Where this occurs, they have been differentiated in several ways:

1. The merchant vessel will be listed with her tonnage, and the military vessel without, e.g. New Zealand light cruiser ACHILLES and British merchant ACHILLES (11,404grt).

2. Multiple merchants with the same name almost always have different tonnages, and are differentiated by weight.

3. Nationality of a ship is occasionally part of the index reference when it is necessary to differentiate between two ships of identical name belonging to two different nations. For example, CASTOR (Fr) and CASTOR (Neth) were both military vessels belonging to France and the Netherlands, respectively. (There was also a Swedish tanker by that name, which has been indexed as CASTOR (8714grt).)

4. Some ship names are differentiated by the punctuation of their names, e.g. British ACHERON and French ACHÉRON, or British CERES and French CÉRÈS

A.11 .... 258, 259
A.18 .... 319, 320
A.2 .... 258, 259, 319, 320
A.7 .... 259, **319**, 320
A.9 .... 258, 259, **318**
A-2 389
A-3 .... 134, 195, 325
A-4 73
A-5 389
A5/V63/CARLA 250
AAGTEKERK (6811grt) 37
ABBAS COMBE (489grt) 229
ABBEKERK (7906grt) 359
ABDIEL 69, 71, 131, 132, 133, 190, 191, 192, 193, 194, 256, 257, 258, 259, 320, 321, 322, 383, 384, 384, 385
ABEILLE IV 172
ABELIA 32, 34, 97, 102, 157, 164, 222, 226, 229, 232, 288, 294, 295, 357
ABERDARE 69, 318
ABERDEEN 33, 38, 301, 307, 358, 372
ABKHAZIYA (4727grt) 323, 324
ABOSSO (11,030grt) 167, 244, 245
ABRUZZI 188, 381, 382
ABUKUMA 405
ACANTHUS 358, 369
ACHATES 25, 26, 27, 29, 33, 42, 44, 48, 91, 93, 94, 95, 100, 150, 151, 153, 171, 346
ACHILLE (2415grt) 317
ACHILLE PAPA 128
ACHILLES 77, 79, 204, 271, 330, 336, 399, 408
ACONIT 158, 220, 224, 228, 231, 290, 291, 293, 294, 297, 354, 361
ACTÉON 107

ACTIVE 26, 27, 29, 33, 42, 91, 93, 94, 95, 99, 100, 110, 148, 150, 152, **153**, 170, 171, 212, 214, 215, 215, 279, 280, 283, **302**, 346
ADA O (5234grt) 161
ADAMANT (80grt) 110
ADAMELLO (5785grt) 245
ADAMS BECK (2816grt) 110
ADDA (7816grt) 56
ADELAIDE 265, 271, 330, 393, 408
ADJUTANT 79, 102, 140
ADMIRAL MURGESCU 22
ADMIRAL SCHEER 217, 246, 247, 346, 347, 348, 373
ADOUR (1105grt) 69
ADRASTUS (7905grt) 359
ADRIATICO (1976grt) 382, 383
ADUA 250, 251, 252
ADUA (400grt) 186
ADVENTURE 30, 88, 89, 92, 93, 94, 102, 148, 149, 154, 163, 213
AETOS 72, 385
AFRICANA (5869grt) 174
AFRICANDER (5441grt) 160
AGAKI 406
AGAMEMNON 25, 27, 29, 91, 154, 216, 292
AGASSIZ 31, 35, 40, 96, 102, 156, 164, 221, 224, 226, 228, 289, 355, 357
AGATE 170
AGHIA PARASKEVA (120grt) 322
AGHIOS NICOLAOS 385
AGILITY (522grt) 363
AGUILA (3255grt) 165
AHAMO (8621grt) 48
AIDA 326
AIKOKU MARU 202, 266, 267, 332, 335, 401, 402, 408
AIKOKU MARU (10,437grt) 204

AINDERBY (4860grt) 39
AINGERU GUARDAKOA (300grt) 306
AIR FRANCE IV 56
AJAX 67, 68, 69, 71, 129, 130, 131, 132, 193, 194, 231, 256, 257, 258, 259, 319, 320, 321, 322, 323, 383, 386, 387, 388
AJAX (7540grt) 231, 251, 381
AKAGI 334, 400, 402, 403, 404, 405, 406
AKAGI MARU 268
AKAGI MARU (7389grt) 405
AKASHI 136
AKATSUKI 399, 406
AKATSUKI MARU (10,216grt) 403
AKEBONO 406
AKEBONO MARU 402, 403, 406
AKEBONO MARU (10,182grt) 267
AKIGUMO 403, 405
AKITSU MARU (9186grt) 77
AKRANES 108
ALA (933grt) 52
ALABAMA (7004grt) 44
ALAGI 122, 123, 185, 250, 313, 314, 382
ALAR (160grt) 182
ALAUNIA 31, 222
ALBATROS **255**
ALBATROSS 57, 70
ALBERNI 31, 42, 98, 159, 162, 163, 218, 223, 228, 232, 287, 289, 357
ALBERTA (3357grt) 67
ALBERTA (6131grt) 68, 160
ALBERTO FASSIO (2289grt) 187
ALBURY 47, 49, 364
ALCHIBA (4427grt) 148, 153, 214, 280
ALCINOUS (6189grt) 24
ALCIONE (493grt) 187
ALDEBARAN 318, 321
ALDER 303
ALDERGROVE (1974grt) 174
ALDERSDALE (8402grt) 148, 153, 212, 218
ALEXANDER HAMILTON (WPG-34) 155, 160
ALEXANDER VON HUMBOLDE 147
ALEXANDRE ANDRE (5322grt) 190
ALEXANDRU LA ROVARI 22
ALFERRAREDE (1452grt) 168
ALFRED JONES (5013grt) 56
ALFREDO ORIANI (3059grt) 194, 253
ALGOMA 225, 227, 232, 294, 352, 353, 354, 360
ALHAMA (1352grt) 308
ALISMA 32, 37, 40, 102, 103, 115, 156, 158, 163, 166, 230, 289, 297, 353, 356, 358
ALMA ATA (3611grt) 214, 280, 349
ALMAACK (AK-27) 99, 149
ALMANZORA (15,551grt) 292, 392
ALMIRANTE BROWN 310
ALPHARD (5483grt) 43, 44, 130
ALPINO 64, 125, 126, 127, 128, 315, 379, 380, 382, 383
ALRESFORD (2472grt) 45
ALSSUND (3222grt) 295
ALSTERTOR (3039grt) 52, 55
ALTAIR (341grt) 115
ALTAIR (It) 321
ALTKIRCH (4713grt) 343
ALVA (1584grt) 165
ALYNBANK... 25, 26, 27, 28, 29, 30, 48, 49, 50, 51, 90, 91, 92, 93, 94, 95, 108, 149, 150, 151, 152, 170, 171

ALYSSE............... 103, 157, 158, 166, 224, 226, 226, 228, 232, 289, 355, 357
AMABILITAS (5245grt) 178
AMAGIRI 404
AMARANTHUS 102, 116, 117, 162, 177, 229, 244, 292, 309
AMARAPOORA (8173grt) 219
AMATSUKAZE 405
AMAZON 96, 97, 98, 104, 157, 158, 164, 220, 224, 228, 231, 288, 290, 293, 295, 298, 355, 360
AMBA ARADAM (405grt) 316, 381
AMBROGIO G. (81grt) 377
AMBUSCADE 228
American Asiatic Fleet 409
AMERICAN LEADER (6750grt) 409
AMERICAN LEGION (AP-35) 149
AMERIKA (10,218grt) 46, 123, 126, 175
AMETIST 182
AMETISTA 128
AMGUN 182
AMHERST 288, 289, 355, 357
AMIRAL LACAZE (332grt) 190
AMIRAL MURGESCU 72, 323
AMSTERDAM (4220grt) 25, 26, 28, 48, 49, 50
AMSTERDAM (8673grt) 64, 65, 127, 186, 254
AMUR 182
ANCHUSA 103, 177, 232, 292, 309, 369
ANDERS (190grt) 229
ANDERSON (DD-411) 36, 215, 222, 288, 290
ANDES (25,689grt) 33, 161, 263, 288, 290, 354
ANDRE MARTI (2352grt) 345
ANDREA GRITTI (6338grt) 64, 66, 125, 128, 186, 252
ANDREI ZHDANOV (3870grt) 375
ANDROMEDA (658grt) 279
ANEMONE..... 32, 34, 38, 97, 102, 157, 164, 222, 226, 229, 232, 355, 357, 360
ANGELBURG (3053grt) 374
ANGLE 38, 42, 157, 164, 224, 228, 231, 288, 290, 295, 298
ANIMATE (88grt) 39
ANKARA (4768grt) 64, 66, 125, 128, 192, 314, 315, 381
ANNA BULGARIS (4603grt) 34
ANNA ZIPPITELLI (1019grt) 379
ANNAPOLIS 32, 33, 97, 156, 157, 158, 223, 225, 226, 227, 287, 288, 289, 290, 352, 353, 354, 355, 356
ANNELIESE (726grt) 373
ANNELIESE ESSBERGER (5173grt) 77, 140, 241
ANNISTON CITY (5687grt) 198
ANSELM (5954grt) 42, 105
ANSHU MARU (1469grt) 405
ANTAR (389grt) 258
ANTARES 194
ANTELOPE... 25, 27, 28, 29, 33, 38, 40, 42, 91, 94, 95, 99, 147, 150, 151, 152, 153, 163, 165, 212, 216, 217, 219, 220, 221, 237, 238, 279, 281, 282, 283, 284, 285, 296, 298, 302, 303, 303, 346, 347, 348, 349, 358, 365
ANTENOR 57, 74, 197
ANTHONY 25, 26, 27, 28, 39, 40, 41, 48, 50, 88, 89, 93, 94, 95, 147, 149, 151, 152, 153, 165, 212, 215, 216, 217, 218, 219, 220, 221, 237, 280, 281, 283, 284, 284, 295, 296, 302, 303, 303, 346
ANTIKLIA (951grt) 70, 71, 72, 129
ANTIOPE (4545grt) 303
AORANGI (17,491grt) 288, 359
AOSTO (494grt) 64
APHIS 68, 193
AQUITANIA (44,786grt) 79, 264, 266, 271
AQUITANIA (4971grt) 64, 127, 128, 186, 188
ARAB............... 97, 102, 156, 157, 162, 229, 284, 294, 352, 357, **361**, 371, 372

ARABIS 30, 33, 41, 96, 156, 158, 163, 167, 224, 230, 287, 290, 293, 298
ARADAM 185, 250, 251, 313, 377, 382
ARAKAKA 46
ARARE 403, 405
ARASHI 399, 406
ARASHIO 399
ARATAMA MARU 333
ARATAMA MARU (6784grt) 203, 267
ARAWA 56
ARBOREA 317
ARBUTUS 39, 41, 56, 100, 101, 230, 234, 252, 305
ARCHIMEDE (It) 300
ARCOS (2343grt) 345
Arctic Ocean U-boat Command 146
ARCTIC RANGER 100, 242, 307
ARCTURUS (AK-18) 91
ARDEAL 22
ARDENZA (933grt) 366
ARDEOLA (2069grt) 116
ARDOR (8960grt) 254
ARETHUSA (UK) 24, 26, 27, 28, 29, 30, 92, 101, 115, 122, 124, 127, 152, 154, 163, 164, 174, 185, 347, 363, 364
ARETUSA 383
ARGONAUT (SM-1) 409
ARGUN (3487grt) 279
ARGUS 40, 53, 100, 152, **153**, 155, 165, 213, 217, 218, 219, 232, 292, 298, 300, 306, 307, 357, 368, 369, 370, 377
ARICA (5390grt) 37
ARIGUANI 31, 38, 100, 103, 115, 233, 301, 307, 308
ARIOSTO (2176grt) 308
ARIZONA (BB-39) 336, 409
ARK ROYAL ... 53, 54, 55, 62, 63, 122, 123, 124, 165, 183, 184, 185, 233, 242, **250**, 251, 252, **305**, 313, 339, 377, 378
ARKADIA (grt) 318
ARKANSAN (6997grt) 262
ARKANSAS (BB-33) 91, 96, 156, 159, 160, 215, 227
ARMENIYA (4727grt) 323, 324
ARMERIA 46, 56, 117, 162, 177, 243, 244, 245, 292, 293, 309, 372
ARNO 379
ARONDA (4062grt) 57, 263
ARPHA 391
ARRAN 100, 116, 176
ARROW 50, 101, 346, 350, 365
ARROWHEAD 35, 37, 38, 101, 156, 164, 224, 224, 225, 226, 228, 290, 293, 359
ARSIA (736grt) 64
ARTEM 22, 61, 180, 181, 182
ARTHUR CAVANAGH 197, 198
ARTIFEX 297
ARUBA (1159grt) 365
ARUNDEL CASTLE (19,118grt) 42, 359
ARVIDA 157, 158, 159, 222, 353, 356
ASAGIRI 404
ASAGUMO 406
ASAHI 403
ASAKA MARU 267, 268, 333
ASAKAZE 406
ASAMA MARU 330, 397, 401, 406
ASAMA MARU (16,975grt) 76, 78, 139, 202, 204, 205
ASANAGI 408
ASASHIO 399
ASCANIA 33, 35, 36, 97, 104, 169, 223
ASCANIUS (10,048grt) 392

ASCARI 66, 125, 251, 252, 254
ASCIANGHI 258, 386
ASH 48
ASHANTI 110, 172, 217, 219, 220, 221, 236, 237, 281, 282, 282, 286, 287, 346, 347, 349, 351
ASHBY (4868grt) 235, 363
ASHIGARA 136, 268
ASHIZURI (7951grt) 137
ASIA (7014grt) 111
ASPE 240
ASPEN (1305grt) 110
ASPERITY (699grt) 366
ASPHODEL 42, 46, 56, 103, 177, 229, 244, 297, 309
ASPIS 388
ASPROMONTE 186, 187, 188
ASSINIBOINE .. 33, 37, 38, 42, 97, 100, 149, 152, 156, 157, 158, 167, 228, 292
ASSURANCE 94, 150, 151, 153, 171
ASSURANCE (675grt) 296
ASTER 37, 53, 56, 117, 164, 177, 243, 244, 245, 293, 309
ASTRA (2164grt) 347
ASTRID (1195grt) 64
ASTRONOM 182
ASUNCION (4626grt) 344
ATAGO 406
ATAKA 200, 396
ATHENE 357, 369
ATHERSTONE 173
ATHLONE CASTLE (25,564grt) 42
ATLANTIC (167grt) 40
ATLANTIC (5414grt) 221, 279, 281, 345
Atlantic Charter 144, 156
ATLANTIC CITY (5133grt) 103
ATLANTIC COAST (890grt) 176
ATLANTIC COCK (182grt) 231
ATROPO 124, 190, 315, 380
ATTENDOLO 64, 66, 124, 188, 251, 383
ATTILO DEFFENU 382
AUBRIETIA 31, 33, 38, 42, 96, 97, 98, 101, 104, 157, 158, 164, 228
AUCKLAND 66, 67, 68, 69, 70, 71
AUDACIOUS (7grt) 49
AUDACITY 90, 230, 234, 298, 305, 362
AUDITOR (5444grt) 105
AUGUST BOLTEN (3665grt) 148
AUGUSTA (CA-31) 156, 157, 159
AURANIA 25, 39, 97, 297
AURICULA 40, 42, 102, 104, 176, 232, 309
AURIS (8030grt) 55
AURORA 24, 25, 26, 27, 28, 29, 31, 90, 92, 94, 95, 101, 146, 147, 148, 150, 152, 153, 212, 213, 216, 217, 220, 282, 283, 307, 313, 317, 378, 379, 381, 382, 383
AUSEKLIS (1309grt) 59
AUSMA (1791grt) 182
AUSONIA 33, 37, 100, 156, 163, 222
AUSSA (5441grt) 160
AUSTRALIA 77, 79, 167, 198, 326, 327
AUSTRALIND (5020grt) 205
AVEROFF 197
AVIERE 64, 66, 127, 186, 188, 189, 254, 315, 381, 382, 383, 386
AVILA STAR (14,443grt) 101
AVOCETA (3442grt) 236
AVOCETTE 129
AVON VALE ... 38, 39, 55, 56, 63, 106, 114, 115, 122, 123, 124, 175, 176, 241, 262, 319, 320, 322, 322, 323, 326, 386, 387, 387, 388, 389

AWATA MARU	267, 268, 333
AWATA MARU (7397grt)	202, 203
AWATEA (13,482grt)	393, 394
AXEL CARL (2170grt)	181
AXUM	250, 251, 314
AYANAMI	404
AYRSHIRE	32, 39, 102, 156, 162, 165, 229, **355**
AZALEA	55, 101, 103, 175, 176, 177, 241, 242, 243, 306, 309, 369
AZIMUT	**375, 376**
B.1	170
B.247/MARIA IMMANCOLATA	127
BABBITT (DD-128)	221, 227, 284, 291, 294, 297, 355, 355, 356, 361
BABITONGA (4422grt)	57
BABR	197
BACHAQUERO	152, 163
BADDECK	288, 289, 296
BADGER (DD-126)	294, 353, 354, 361
BADSWORTH	153, 155, 165, 167, 217, 219, 220, 225, 230, 237, 238, 290, 292, 359, 371
BAGLEY (DD-386)	409
BAGNOLINI	106, 107
BAGSHOT	318, 384
BAHIA LAURA (8561grt)	148
BAINBRIDGE (DD-246)	99, 223, 223, 226, 289, 298
BAINSIZZA (7933grt)	65, 127, 186, 253, 315, 316
BALCH (DD-363)	409
BALCIC (3495grt)	256, 317
BALEEKA	198
BALFRON (362grt)	108
BALI (1428grt)	343
BALIK	23
BALILLA (2469grt)	377, 378
BALKAN (3838grt)	317
BALKHASH (2191grt)	182
BALLOT (6131grt)	160
BALTA	103, 179
BALTALLINN (1303grt)	234
BALTENLAND (3724grt)	311
BALZAC (5372grt)	57
BANCKERT	76, 395
BANDE NERE	64, 124
BANDIERA	62, 185, 251, 313, 377
BANFF	31, 34, 164, 170, 244, 294, 371
BANGALORE (6067grt)	117
BANGKOK MARU (5350grt)	202, 204, 332
BANKOK (8056grt)	392
BANYAN	182
BARACCA	105, 114, 241
BARBARA (3065grt)	198
BARBARIGO	46, 106, 107, 299
BARBARIGO (5293grt)	66, 125
BARBRO (6325grt)	226
BARCELONA (3101grt)	213, 287
BARFONN (9739grt)	296
BARHAM	196, 255, 256, 259, 319, 339, 385, 386, 387, 388
BARI (120grt)	314
BARLETTA	321
BAROEY (424grt)	221
BARON CARNEGIE (3178grt)	39
BARON KELVIN (3081grt)	307
BARON LOVAT (3395grt)	53
BARON NAIRN (3164grt)	44
BARON NEWLANDS (3386grt)	378
BARON PENTLAND (3410grt)	224, 226
BARON RAMSAY (3650grt)	224
BARRHILL (4972grt)	51
BARRIE	34, 96, 97, 98, 156, 157, 158, 159, 222
BARRISTER (6200grt)	167, 244, 326, 327
BASARABIA	22
BATAVIER V (1573grt)	367
BATH	27, 41, 56, 101, 103, 104, 115, 163, 164, 169
BATHURST	189, 192, 193
BATORY (14,287grt)	152, 163
Battle for the Atlantic	275
Battle of Britain	210
BATTLEFORD	290, 291, 353, 354, 355, 356
Bay of Biscay patrol	152, 168
BDITELNY	22, 134, 325, 389
BEAGLE	32, 39, 97, 102, 156, 157, 162, 165, 222, 226, 227, 229, 232, 284, 289, 294, 352, 355, 357, **361**
BEAR (AG-29)	96
BEATRICE COSTA (6132grt)	64
BEAUCE (4869grt)	315
BEAUFORT	347, 351, 357, 358, 361
BEAUMANOIR (2477grt)	47
Beaverbrook, Lord	212, 214
BEDOUIN	23, 24, 26, 27, 29, 30, 91, 93, 96, 110, 172, 215, 216, 217, 219, 220, 237, 282, 283, 284, 286, 295, 344, 345, 346, 347, 348
BEECH	28
BEGONIA	41, 54, 56, 100, 102, 107, 167, 175, 236, 242, 290, 297, 354, 359
BEILUL	379, 387
BELCHEN (6367grt)	31, 43
BELGRAVIAN (3136grt)	162
BELKNAP (AVD-8)	156
BELLE BRETAGNE	370
BELLONA (1297grt)	191
BELMONT	157, 158, 159, 224, 228, 231, 288, 290, 295
BELOMORETS	23
BELOSTOK (grt)	323
BEN GLAMAIR (198grt)	109
BEN MY CHREE (2586grt)	24
BEN SCREEL (195grt)	47, 364
BEN STROME (198grt)	95
BENBOW	40
BENCRUACHEN (5920grt)	129
BENEDICK (6978grt)	175, 176, 242, 299, **305**
BENHAM (DD-397)	409
BENNEKOM (5998grt)	299
BENNO (8306grt)	113, 174, 331, 332
BENSON (DD-421)	91, 96, 99, 222, 232, 289, 299, 355, 358, 359
BEPPE (4859grt)	316
BERBERA (2093grt)	381, 387, 389
BERGAMOT	102, 116, 161, 358, 360, 362, 372
BERGENSFJORD (11,015grt)	57
BERKELEY	173, 351, 367
BERNADOU (DD-153)	91, 96, 99, 285, 287, 291, 297, 355
BERNHARD (1890grt)	111
BERSAGLIERE	64, 127, 251, 315, **379**, 380, 382, 383
BERURY (4924grt)	225
BERWICK	92, 93, 149, 170, 215, 218, 238, 284, 302, 344, 345, 346, 347, 349, 363
BESPOSHCHADNY	22, 72, 73, 134, 195, 196, 260, 261, 390, 391
BESSHEIM (1774grt)	213, 344
BESTUM (2215grt)	225, 365
BEVERLEY	115, 116, 122, 290, 292, 297, 309, 360

BEZUPRECHNY..................................... 22, 72, 134, 195, 196, 261, 389
BHUTAN (6104grt).. 167, 244, 246
BIANCHI **175**
BIDEFORD........................53, 100, 106, 116, 235, 244, 298, 299, 372
BIRGITTA (1363grt)...108
BIRKA (1000grt)..214
BIRMINGHAM 24, 37, 57
BIRTLEY (2873grt)..238
BISTRITSA 22
BITTERSWEET ... 33, 41, 97, 162, 222, 223, 226, 228, 233, 289, 352, 355, 357
BJORNUNGEN...279
BKA-111 134
BKA-114 134
BKA-134 134
BLACK HAWK (AD-9) 397
BLACK RANGER (3417grt) 88, 93, 94, 214, 221, 279, 280, 281, 283
BLACK SWAN 26, 27, 29, 104, 166, 175, 293, 309, **361**, 369
BLACKHEATH (4637grt) 101
BLAIRATHOLL (3319grt) 378
BLAIRNEVIS (4155grt)........................... 221, 279, 281, 345, 366
BLANKNEY 225, 231, 292, 305, 354
BLENCATHRA 367
BLOMVLEI..372
BLOOMFIELD (1417grt)...218
BLUE (DD-387)..409
BLUE MERMAID (97grt)...109
BLUEBELL ... 101, 104, 116, 117, 162, 163, 164, 177, 178, 233, 241, 301, 307, **361**
BLYTH..358
BOADICEA............................. 32, 97, 102, 156, 157, 162, 165, 222, 229, 361
BODNY..73
BODRY................................22, 134, 195, 196, 261, 323, 324, 325, 389, 390
BOIKI..................................22, 72, 134, 195, 196, 260, 261, 323, 325, 389, 390, 391
BOISE (CL-47)..409
BOKN (698grt)..39
BOLD VENTURE (3222grt)..295
BOLLWERK (4173grt)..245
BOLSHEVIK (1412grt)... 323, 324
BOLZANO 66, 122, 125, 188, 253
BOMBARDIERE (613grt)..184
BOREAS 37, 42, 57, 107, 163, 165, 166, 169, 174, 175, 176, 177, 178, 231, 241
BOREAS (grt) 40
BORGNY (3015grt)..286
BOSEMULLER 228, 233
BOSFORO (3567grt) 186, 379, 382
BOTWEY (5106grt)..104
BOUGAINVILLE (7110grt)...74
BOVEY TRACEY (1212grt)...365
BOWDOIN (IX-50)...31
BOY ANDREW 364
BP-21..181
BRADFORD.. 292, 298, 371
BRADFORD CITY (4953grt)...372
BRADGLEN (4741grt)...238
BRAHEHOLM (5676grt)..366
BRAMBLE 282, 284, 293, 344, 345, 348, 351
BRANDON... 225, 227, 293, 295, 354
BRARENA (6996grt)...126
BRECONSHIRE (9776grt)........................116, 123, 126, 231, 251, 381
BREMSE 88, 213
BRIARWOOD (4019grt) 348, 351
BRIDGEWATER 56, 102, 243, 245, 309, 371

BRIGHTON..... 25, 27, 29, 30, 37, **230**, 286, 292, 299, 348, 349, 351, 358, 359, 361
BRILLIANT 37, 42, 43, 44, 162, 164, 177, 229, 230, 232, 244, 309, 358, 372
BRIN.. 44, 45
BRIONI...259
BRISBANE STAR (11,076grt).. 164, 244
BRITANNIC (26,943grt).. 33, 161, 245, 263
BRITISH COLONEL (6999grt)...322
BRITISH FORTUNE (4696grt)...303
BRITISH FREEDOM (6985grt) 242, 308
BRITISH HONOUR (6991grt) 115, 116
BRITISH MARINER (6996grt)...309
BRITISH PRINCE (4979grt)..239
BRITISHER (95grt)...364
BRITOMART........31, 33, 38, 42, 104, 157, 164, 221, 232, 279, 280, 281, 285, 286, 303
BROADWATER 41, 97, 103, 157, 226, 226, 228, 288, 295, 296
BROADWAY 158, 161, 227, 228, 290, 293, 297, 359
BROCKLESBY...231
BROCKLEY HILL (5297grt)...34
BROKE..................... 32, 34, 103, 116, 227, 244, 289, 293, 297, 354, 359
BRONTE (4769grt)...198
BROOK (1225grt)..381
BROOKLYN (CL-40) 91, 96, 98, 99, 159, 160, 169, 227
BROOME (DD-210) 221, 227, 282, 284, 294
BRORA (530grt)...229
BROSUND (2939grt)..354
BROWN RANGER (3417grt) 122, 124, 251, 378
BRUMMER 58, 60, 61, 118, 181, 248
BRUNO HEINEMANN 113, 240
BRUSTEROT..261
BRUSTEROT (101grt)...325
BRYNJE (3916grt) 118
BRYNMILL (743grt)...363
B-Service..382
BUCCANEER 348, 364
BUCCARI (4543grt)..65
BUCK (DD-420) 91, 291, 297, 352, 360
BUCOVINA..22
BUCTOUCHE 32, 97, 156, 158, 227, 228, 290, 293, 352, 359
BUDENNI (2482grt)... 214, 280, 349
BULLDOG 31, 33, 38, 42, 96, 101, 157, 158, 163, 164, 220, 224, 228, 231, 288, 293, 295
BULLFINCH..322
BULOLO.. 39, 40
BULYSSES (7519grt)...224
BUNTE KUH (262grt)...246
BURDOCK.............46, 56, 117, 164, 177, 244, 245, 294, 298, 309, 371, 372
BURGENLAND (7320grt) 269
BURKE..233
BURNHAM...................31, 35, 39, 102, 156, 157, 164, 223, 228, 353, 354, 360
BURRA..293
BURWELL 41, 97, 103, 104, 155, 157, 167, 227, 228, 291, 293
BURYA..182
BURZA... 93, 96, 98, 104, 164, 229
BUSKOE..218
BUTE... 297, 344, 349
BUTTERMERE 159, 225, 358
BUXTON 33, 97, 288, 290, 297
BYSTRY 22, 72, 134
C. JON (744grt)...305
C.307..320
CABOTO (5225grt)...198

CACHALOT	65, 69, 125, 128, 130
CADAMOSTO (1010grt)	64, 187
CADORNA	381
CAFFARO (6476grt)	64, 126, 186, 189, 253
CAGNI	315, 380
CAIMAN	68, 129, 130
CAIO DUILIO	383
CAIRNDALE (8447grt)	53
CAIRO	37, 42, 43, 97, 161, 167, 288, 290, 292, 367
CAITHNESS (4970grt)	44
CAJE (grt)	374
CALABRIA (1277grt)	41
CALATAFIMI	130, 318
CALCUTTA	66
CALCUTTA MARU (5339grt)	394, 395, 396
CALDEA (2703grt)	125
CALDWELL	166, 176, 178, 227, 232, 241, 290, 353, 356, 358, 361
CALEDON	196
CALENDULA	103, 177, 245, 292, 309, 356, 361, 369
CALIFORNIA	35, 39, 40, 101, 157, 167
CALIFORNIA (13,060grt)	186
CALIPH (226grt)	357
CALLIOPE (It)	186, 187, 189, 314, 315, 316, 379
CALMAR (3946grt)	59
CALVI (It)	106, 107, 169, 241
CALYPSO (AG-35)	159
CAMBRIDGE (10,855grt)	399
CAMELLIA	35, 38, 101, 164, 224, 225, 226, 289, 290, 297
CAMERONIA (16,287grt)	113
CAMERONIA (16,297grt)	56, 161, 263
CAMICIA NERA	64, 127, 186, 188, 189, 254, 315, 381, 382, 383
CAMILLIA	156
CAMPANULA	101, 116, 117, 163, 164, 165, 174, 176, 177, 178, 241, 289, 295
CAMPBELL	365
CAMPBELL (WPG-32)	287, 291, 297, 353, 354, 361
CAMPBELTOWN	104, 114, 117, 164, 167, 177, 222, 230
CAMPECHE (6382grt)	106, 107, 108
CAMPERO (6382grt)	108
CAMPION	163, 164, 164, 174, 174, 176, 178, 233, 241, 300, 301, 307, 309, **361**, 369
CAMPUS (3667grt)	219
CAMROSE	288, 295, 354
CAMROUX II (324grt)	50
CANADA (9684grt)	70
Canadian Newfoundland Escort Force	211
CANADIAN STAR (8293grt)	103
CANBERRA	135
CANDYTUFT	32, 35, 97, 99, 162, 222, 223, 228
CANNA	38, 55, 116
CANNING (148grt)	357
CANSO	79
CANTON	74, 116, 117, 362
CANTORE	253
CAP CANTIN (3317grt)	114
CAP PADARAN (8009grt)	392
CAP TOURANE (8009grt)	392
CAP VARELLA (7677grt)	137
CAPACITAS (5371grt)	64
CAPE CORSO (3807grt)	348
CAPE FAIRWEATHER (6797grt)	409
CAPE NYEMETSKI	284
CAPE PALLISER	215
CAPE PORTLAND	25
CAPE RACE (3807grt)	348
CAPE RODNEY (4512grt)	162
CAPE SABLE	117, 351, 361
CAPE WARWICK	157, 164, 224, 228, 231, 288, 290, 295, 298, 360
CAPETOWN CASTLE (27,000grt)	37, 57, 288, 359
CAPIRA (5565grt)	221, 279, 281, 345
CAPITAN DUMITRESCU	22
CAPITAN ROMANO MIHAIL	22
CAPO ARMA (3195grt)	318, 378
CAPO D'ORSO (5293grt)	125
CAPO FARO (3476grt)	383
CAPO ORSO (3149grt)	317
CAPO ROSA (4699grt)	178
CAPODOGLIO (184grt)	255
CAPPELLINI	169, 241
CAPSA (8229grt)	175, 176
Captain of the Fleet	220
CARABINIERE	66, 125, 251, 254, 381, 382, 383
CARADOC	291
CARDIUM (8236grt)	176
CARDONA	382
CARIBIA (12,049grt)	111
CARLISLE	71, 129, 130, 131, 132, 190, 194, 196, 197, 262, 322, 326, 386, 387, 388
CARLTON (5162grt)	44
CARMELLA	228
CARMELO NOLI (109grt)	251
CARNARVON CASTLE	245, 263, 392
CARNATION	31, 33, 38, 42, 103, 115, 117, 165, 177, 178, 233, 241, 300, 301, 307, 308, 309, **361**, 369
CAROLINA (227grt)	65
CARSBRECK (3670grt)	308
CARTHAGE	319, 392
CARVALHO ARAUJO (4560grt)	363
CASAREGIS (6485grt)	315
CASCINO	315, 316, 379
CASH HALL (4972grt)	51
CASSIOPEA	387
CASTELBIANCO (4895grt)	178
CASTELFIDARDO	319, 384
CASTELLON (2086grt)	314
CASTELVERDE (6666grt)	127, 128, 186, 254
CASTILLO MONTJUICH (6581grt)	246
CASTILLO OROPESA (6600grt)	377
CASTLETON	27, 29, 42, 91, 93, 94, 95, 110, 149, 152, 154, 163, 166, 176, 216, 217, 218, 219, 230, 231, 360
CASTORE	64
CATERINA (4786grt)	254, 316
CATERINA MADRE (4019grt)	382
CATHAY	42, 105, 177, 292
CATHRINE (2727grt)	40
CATTISTOCK	111
CAVA	284
CAVE (grt)	39
CAVINA	56, 101, 105, 168, 176, 178
CEDARWOOD (899grt)	239
CELANDINE	29, 33, 40, 102, 157, 166, 224, 225, 226, 228, 293, 298, **361**
CELANO	109
CELIA	26, 27, 148, 151, 153, 297, 345, 348
CENTAURO	125, 252, 253, 379, 381, 382
Central Atlantic patrol	98
CERAMIC (18,713grt)	42

CERES 135, 197, 244, 327, 354
CERVANTES (1810grt) 236
CERVINO (4363grt) 178
CH-17 .... 138, 330, 334
CH-18 138
CH-19 269
CH-20 203
CH-21 203
CH-22 332
CH-23 202
CH-25 331
CH-26 203
CH-27 400
CH-39 77
CH-7 394
CH-8 394
CH-9 394
CHAKDINA 73, 192, 389
CHALLENGER 105
CHAMBLY 33, 42, 44, 97, 104, 159, 218, 223, 224, 227, 228, 294, 352, 353, 354, 360
CHAMBRUM 129
CHANTALA 192, 321, 322, 323
CHAPAEV 182
CHAPAEV (2638grt) 324
CHARLES F. HUGHES (DD-428) 34, 91, 96, 99, 154, 155, 159, 159, 160, 215, 218, 220, 223, 232, 287, 288, 289, 295, 298, 353, 356
CHARLESTON 283, 284, 290, 294
CHARLESTOWN 27, 42, 94, 95, 110, 149, 150, 152, 154, 163, 348, 358
CHARLOTTE (200grt) 172
CHARLOTTE SCHLIEMANN (7747grt) 46
CHAROGH **198**
CHATEAU THIERRY (AP-31) 96
CHATEAU YQUEM (2536grt) 129
CHAUCER (5792grt) 107
CHAZBAAZ 197
CHEKHOV (grt) 323
CHELSEA 41, 54, 56, 100, 103, 116, 162, 165, 177, 244, 357, 359, 360
CHERNOMORETS 23, 324
CHEROKEE (ATF-66) 91, 291
CHERVONA UKRAINA 22, 72, 196, 260, 261, 323, 324, 325, 389, 390
CHESHIRE 32, 40, 96, 98
CHESTER (CA-27) 409
CHESTERFIELD 35, 38, 39, 96, 101, 156, 163, 223, 224, 226, 228
CHEVALIER PAUL 69
CHEVINGTON (1537grt) 302
CHEVREUIL 166
CHEYNYSHEVSKI (3588grt) 345
CHICOUTIMI 97, 98, 156, 157, 158, 226, 227, 355, 358
CHIDDINGFOLD 284, 296, 347, 350, 351
CHIDORI 398
CHIKUMA 405
CHILLIWACK 157, 167, 226, 228, 233, 290, 357
CHINA MAIL (7842grt) 290
CHINESE PRINCE (8593grt) 39
CHIPKA (2304grt) 260
CHITOSE 408
CHITRAL 42, 98, 157
CHIYODA 77, 200, 266, 270
CHOGEI 139, 332
CHOKO MARU No.2 GO (3515grt) 332, 334, 400, 401, 407
CHRISTIAAN HUYGENS (16,287grt) 57, 354
CHRISTIAN KROHG (1992grt) 45

CHRISTINE MARIE (3895grt) 45
CHRISTINE ROSE 230
CHRISTUS REGNAT (28grt) 112
Chuichi, VAdm Nagumo 400, 403
CHUMLEIGH (5445grt) 154, 351
CHURCHILL .. 31, 35, 39, 96, 101, 152, 156, 157, 164, 223, 224, 225, 226, 228
Churchill, Prime Minister Winston 144, 152, 157, 387
CHURRUCA 318
CICLOPE 126, 316
CIGNO 187, 316
CILICIA 56
CILICIA (2747grt) 194
CIMARRON (AO-22) 223, 353
CINCINNATI (CL-6) 228, 291, 292
CINGALESE PRINCE (8474grt) 246
CIRCASSIA 96, 103, 168, 169, 177
CIRCE (It) 126, 253
CISCAR (1809grt) 165, 236
CISIL (1847grt) 179
CISNEROS (1886grt) 378
CITO (124grt) 155
CITTA DI AGRIGENTO (2480grt) 321
CITTA DI BASTIA (2499grt) 259
CITTA DI GENOVA (5413grt) 380
CITTA DI MARSALA (2480grt) 259, 321
CITTA DI NAPOLI (5418grt) 380
CITTA DI PALERMO (5413grt) 317, 381
CITTA DI SIMI (25grt) 319
CITTA DI TRIPOLI (2933grt) 128
CITTA DI TUNISI (5419grt) 381
CITY OF AUCKLAND (8336grt) 262
CITY OF CALCUTTA (8063grt) 231, 251, **255**
CITY OF CANTERBURY (8331grt) 327
CITY OF DURBAN (5850grt) 177, 306, 351
CITY OF EDINBURGH (8036grt) 167, 244, 246, 327
CITY OF EMDEN (grt) 173
CITY OF HONG KONG (9606grt) 300
CITY OF KIMBERLEY (6169grt) 134
CITY OF LINCOLN (8039grt) 231, 251, 313, 317, 369
CITY OF MANCHESTER (8917grt) 167, 244, 246
CITY OF PARIS (10,902grt) 292, 392
CITY OF PRETORIA (8046grt) 101, 122, 252, 254, **255**
CITY OF RAYVILLE (5883grt) 399
CITY OF WATERFORD (1071grt) 234
CLAM (7404grt) 32
CLAN CAMPBELL (7255grt) 292, 392
CLAN FERGUSON (7347grt) 231, 251, 317, 381
CLAN FORBES (7529grt) 42, 262
CLAN LAMONT (7268grt) 292, 392
CLAN MACDONALD (9653grt) 152, 163, 231, 251, 308, 316
CLAN MACNAUGHTON (6088grt) 116
CLARA (6131grt) 36
CLARA L. M. RUSS (1600grt) 373
CLARE 358, 372
CLARKIA 38, 100, 356
CLEARPOOL (5404grt) 48
CLEMATIS 117, 164, 297, 309
CLEVELLA 172
CLIMENE 130
CLIO 64, 65, 188, **254**
CLIVE 73
CLONLARA (1203grt) 165, 174

CLOVER	102, 115, 168, 230, 232, 294, 309, 359, 362, 371
CLYDE	55, 62, 63, 64, 65, 101, 105, 114, 115, 116, 174, 175, 176, 236, 241, 243, 369, 370, 378
COBALT	32, 41, 97, 103, 158, 227, 228, 291, 293, 297, 356, 359
COBRA	58, 180, 248, 249
COCKCHAFER	197, 198
COCLE (5630grt)	348
COL DI LANA (5891grt)	64, 65, 127, 186, 188, 253, 254
COLE (DD-155)	99, 352, 353, **361**, 362
COLIGNY (600grt)	368
COLLINGDOC (1780grt)	109
COLLINGWOOD	33, 35, 42, 156, 157, 158, 166, 226, 228, 233, 289, 357
COLLIOPE	189
COLOMBO	135, 354, 392
COLONNA	62
COLORADO (5039grt)	161
COLTSFOOT	358, 370
COLUMBIA	32, 97, 98, 104, 157, 158, 159, 216, 218, 228, 230, 295, 354, 361
COLUMBINE	57, 309
COMANCHE (CGC-57)	31
COMANDOR EUGEN STIHI	22
Combined Operations Training Centre	258
COMMANDANT BAFILE (1790grt)	249
COMMANDANT DETROYAT	352, 355, 357, 361
COMMANDANT DOMINE	162, 177, 241, 294
COMMANDANT DORISE (5529grt)	392
COMMANDANT DUBOC	235, 243, 244, 300, 301, 306, 307, 308, 369, 371
COMPIEGNE (9986grt)	392
CONDOURIOTIS	190
CONFEDERATE	391
CONSBRO	103
CONSTANZA (582grt)	188
CONSUL HINTZ (1847grt)	51
CONTE DI MISURATA (5014grt)	379
CONTE GRANDE (23,861grt)	178
CONVOLVULUS	56, 100, 104, 175, 176, 243, 298, 305, 361, 378
COPELAND	104
COPINSAY	100, 116, 245
COR JESU	48
CORALLO	63, 122, 379, 382
CORAZZIERE	66, 125, 251, 254, 381, 382, 383
CORBRAE	38, 55
CORDELIA	41, 114
CORDELIA (1357grt)	260
CORDELIA (8190grt)	176, 177, 241, 297
CORDENE (2345grt)	170
COREOPSIS	38, 41, 53, 100, 104, 113, 114, 116, 176, 299, 305, 306, 307, 308, 359, 369, 370
CORFIELD	**237**
CORHAMPTON (2495grt)	365
CORINTHIAN	43, 107, 116, 177, 230, 234, 305, 372
CORMARSH (2848grt)	366
CORMEAD (2848grt)	237
CORMORANT	165
CORMOUNT (2841grt)	49
CORNOUAILLE (3290grt)	148
CORNWALL	73, 135, 262, 392
CORNWALLIS	197
CORRIDONI	124, 190
CORRIENTES	310
CORRIENTES (4565grt)	105
CORRISPONDENTE BETA	314
CORTE REAL (2044grt)	306
CORTELLAZZO (5292grt)	396
CORTELSBURG (1309grt)	59
CORTES (1374grt)	236
COSENZ	65, 381
COSSACK	24, 33, 37, 40, 42, 101, 115, 122, 124, 127, 167, 175, 183, 231, 242, 243, 251, 300, 305, 306, 307, 308, 313
COTSWOLD	49, 302
COVENTRY	66, 67, 68, 69, 71, 125, 131, 191, 192, 193, 196, 197, 262, 319, 325
COVENTRY CITY	293, 361, 372
COWRIE (8197grt)	308, 370
COWSLIP	230, 298, 305
CRADOCK (204grt)	364
CRAVEN (DD-382)	409
CRICKET	72, 130, 322
CRITON (4564grt)	56
CROCUS	57, 164, 309, 358, 372
CROOME	42, 90, 94, 95, 97, 110, 149, 150, 163, 165, 234, 241, 243, 290, 306, 309, 371
CRUSADER (2939grt)	354
CUBA MARU (5950grt)	331
CULVER	31, 34, 102, 177, 298, 299, 372
CUMBERLAND	27, 29, 51, 284, 302, 348, 350, 351
CURAÇOA	90, 91, 92, 93, 94, 95, 96, 109, 110, 149, 150, 152, 153, 170, 171, 172
CUSHENDALL (626grt)	51
CYCLAMEN	56, 57, 117, 161, 230, 232, 293, 309, 372
CYCLOPS	258, 259
CYRUS (405grt)	129
CZESTOCHOWA (1971grt)	171
D'ARTAGNAN (15,105grt)	328, 394
D'IBERVILLE	392
D-3	23, 87, 147, 212, 214, 344
D-4	325, 389
D-5	134, 260, 261, 324, 389
DA BARBIANO	122
DA MOSTO	64, 66, 124, 125, 128, 186, 187, 188, 383
DA NOLI	188, 189, 254, 254, 314, 315, 316, 317, 382
DA RECCO	64, 66, 124, 187, 251, 252, 253, 254, 254, 315, 316, 379, 381
DA VERAZZANO	64, 66, 124, 186, 187, 188
DA VINCI	46, 55, 105, 114, 234, 235, 241, 242
DACIA	72, 323
DAGABUR	128, 256, 320, 387
DAGMAR (844grt)	52
DAGNY I (1392grt)	90, 150
DAHLIA	287, 290, 293, 298, 355, 360
DAIF	197
DAINTY	70
DALE (DD-353)	353
DALEMOOR (5796grt)	49
DALEWOOD (2774grt)	171
DALLAS (DD-199)	99, 225, 282, 290, 293, 352, 358
DALNY (6672grt)	198
DALTONHALL (7253grt)	232
DAN Y BRYN (5117grt)	349
DANAE	75, 135, 199, 264
DANDOLO	251, 377
DANDOLO (4964grt)	127
DANEMAN	31, 38, 96, 98, 104, 157, 158, 164, 224, 228, 231
DANTE (4901grt)	178
DANUBIUS (550grt)	390
DARDO	64, 66, 127, 186, 252, 254
DARKDALE (8145grt)	310

DARU (3854grt) 231
DASHWOOD (2154grt) 50
DAUGAVA (1430grt) 181
DAUNTLESS 75, 197, 263, 264
DAUPHIN 33, 96, 97, 98, 156, 157, 222, 353, 360
DAVIS (DD-395) 161, 228, 291, 357
DAXHOUND (1128grt) 93, 94
DE LUTTI 124
DE RUYTER 76
DE VERAZZANO 315
DECATUR (DD-341) 226, 288, 294, 295, 296, 353, 354, 361, 362
DECOY 70, 71, 72, 128, 130, 131, 189, 190, 191, 192, 193, 194, 256, 257, 259, 319, 320, 321, 322, 384, 385, 386, 387, 388
DEFENDER 68, 69, 70, 71, 72, 129, 130
DEL PIDIO 397
DELAVAR 197, 198
DELAWARE (2441grt) 110
DELFINO 133, 189, 190, 251, 313, 379, 382
DELFINUL 22, 72, 195, 196, 389
DELNORTE (4982grt) 246
DELPHIN (109grt) 182
DELPHINIUM 133, 259, 319, 320
DELTA (AR-9) 223
DELTINO 382
DENBYDALE (8145grt) 250
Denmark Strait 24, 25, 26, 225, 346, 347, 348
Denmark Strait patrol 24, 27, 28, 30, 90, 91, 94, 95, 148, 155, 215, 217, 220, 346, 347, 348, 349, 350, 351
DENNIS ROSE (1600grt) 52
DEPTFORD 40, 104, 114, 175, 176, 230, 234, 235, 241, 298, 305, 361, 378
DERBYSHIRE 31, 40, 107, 117, 167, 244, 245, 246, 292, 310, 327, 392
DERZKY 323
DESIGNER (5945grt) 105
DESIRADE (9645grt) 37
DESMOULEA (8120grt) 189
DESPATCH 178
DETROIT (CL-8) 409
DEUCALION (7516grt) 101, 122, 185, 188, 241, 359
DEUTSCHLAND 19
DEVON (9036grt) 205
DEVON COUNTY 108
DEVONSHIRE 26, 91, 94, 95, 148, 149, 150, **153**, 154, 213, 215, 217, 218, 220, 221, 292, 372, 392
DEWDALE 152, 163
DEZZA 187, 254
DI GUISSANO 64, 122, 124
DIANA 182
DIANA (942grt) 25
DIANA (It) 127
DIANELLA 35, 96, 100, 102, 103, 115, 156, 158, 163, 166, 227, **230**, 233
DIANTHUS 38, 39, 96, 102, 157, 166, 226, 228, 293, 294
DIASPRO 62, 122, 123, 185, 251, 252, 313, 314
DIDO 73, 383
DILWARA (11,080grt) 327
DINGLEDALE (8145grt) 309, 359, 369, 370
DINO (5592grt) 159, 354
DIOMED (10,374grt) 161, 263
DIOMEDE 169
DIPAVATI 197, 198
DIRPHYS (4240grt) 44
DITMAR KOEL (4479grt) 59
DIVANA (1530grt) 313
DIXCOVE (3790grt) 235

DJEBEL SAMIN 129
DJURDJURA (3460grt) 45
DNEPR 72
DNEPR (3071grt) 261, 323
DNESTR (3580grt) 59
DOBROTITS 23
DOLPHIN (SS-169) 335
DOLPHIN cipher 144
DOMINION MONARCH (27,155grt) 158, 292, 391, 392, 393
DONA NATI (5011grt) 409
DONAU 309
DONAU II (2931grt) 148
Dönitz, Adm Karl 20, 208, 210
DONOVANIA (8149grt) 167
DORINE (3176grt) 50
DORIS II (6grt) 49
DOROSTOR 23
DORSETSHIRE 95, 110, 151, 164, 178, 246, 292, 354, 362, 371
DOUGLAS .. 34, 97, 98, 102, 104, 152, 157, 159, 163, 164, 225, 229, 288, 290, 294, 355, 357, 360
DRAGON 393
DRAUG 220, 238, 281, 282, 286
DRIN (426grt) 68
DROSSEL (175grt) 261, 325
DRUMHELLER 289, 354, **355**
DUANE (WPG-33) 45
DUCA D'AOSTA 64, 66, 124, 315, 383
DUCA DEGLI ABRUZZI 64, 251, 382
DUCHESS OF ATHOLL (20,119grt) 290, 354
DUCHESS OF BEDFORD (20,123grt) 37, 359
DUCHESS OF RICHMOND (20,022grt) 292, 391, 392
DUCHESS OF YORK (20,021grt) 97, 167, 244, 246, 327
DUILO 122
DUISBERG (7389grt) 379
DUKE OF YORK 173, 216, 217, 229, 230, 237, 346, 347, 363
DULVERTON 233, 281, 285, 298, 359
DUMITRESCU 72, 260, 323
DUNCAN ...54, 55, 116, 122, 165, 167, 175, 176, 177, 242, 251, 252, 300, 301, 305, 307, 308, 369
DUNCARRON (478grt) 237
DUNEDIN 46, 74, 118, 177, 243, 371, 373, 373
DUNEDIN STAR (11,168grt) 152, 163, 231, 251, 313, 317, 369
DUNERA (11,162grt) 193, 319
DUNLAP (DD-384) 409
DUNLUCE CASTLE 91, 92
DUNNOTTAR CASTLE 37, 57, 164, 392
DUNVEGAN 290, 291, 353, 354, **355**
DUPONT (DD-152) 285, 287, 291, 297, 299, 355, 356
DURAZZO (1153grt) 99
DURBAN 37, 57, 75, 135, 354, 393
DURBAN CASTLE (17,388grt) 37, 57, 178, 290, 354
DURENDA (7241grt) 68
DURHAM (10,893grt) 101, 122, 187, 250
DURMITOR 128, 132, 192, 194
DUROSTOR 72
DZERZHINSKI 22, 72, 195, 196, 260, 261, 323, 325
EAGLE 44, 46, 177, 178, 243, 246, 298, 300, 306, 307
EAGLESCLIFFE HALL (1900grt) 170
East Indies Fleet 192
East Indies Station 391
Eastern Atlantic patrol 114, 116
Eastern Fleet 298
EASTERN PRINCE (10,926grt) 37, 57, 327

EBERLE (DD-430) ... 35, 99, 159, 160, 169, 220, 225, 290, 293, 352, 358
ECHO ... 27, 28, 29, 49, 92, 94, 95, 149, 151, 163, **170**, 348, 349, 351, 364
ECHODALE ... 178
ECLIPSE ... 27, 28, 29, 30, 40, 42, 52, 91, 92, 93, 94, 95, 96, 148, 149, 150, 151, 152, 153, 154, 163, 171, 213, 215, 217, 218, 219, 221, 239, 283, 284, 345, 348, 349, 350
EDENVALE (444grt) ... 295
EDINBURGH ... 24, 25, 26, 27, 28, 42, 101, 113, 114, 115, 122, 127, 161, 243, 244, 246, 251, 284, 295, 305, 306, 346, 347, 349, 351
EDISON (DD-439) ... 355, 358, 359
EDITH GERMAINE ... 56, 107, 117
EDRIDIO MINDORO (67grt) ... 397
EDWARD BLYDEN (5003grt) ... 235
EESTIRAND (4444grt) ... 311
EG.1 ... 286, 297
EG.14 ... 228, 353
EG.15 ... 228
EG.16 ... 228
EG.17 ... 228
EG.18 ... 228
EG.19 ... 228
EG.2 ... 218, 225, 295
EG.20 ... 216, 228
EG.21 ... 228
EG.22 ... 228
EG.23 ... 228
EG.24 ... 223, 228
EG.25 ... 228
EG.3 ... 220, 295
EG.36 ... 234
EG.37 ... 300
EG.4 ... 284, 289
EG.42 ... 363
EG.5 ... 285, 289
EG.6 ... 357
EG.8 ... 357
EGADI (861grt) ... 189
EGELAND ... 389
EGERAN (1143grt) ... 374
EGERLAND (9789grt) ... 43, 44, 56
EGLANTINE ... 227, 290, 293, 297, 354, 359
EGLINTON ... 50
EGRA (5108grt) ... 197
EGRET ... 164, 244, 294, 371
EIBERGEN (4801grt) ... 43
EIKHAUG (1436grt) ... 237
EIKO MARU (3026grt) ... 404
EIKO MARU (3535grt) ... 335, 401
EIKO MARU No.2 GO (3535grt) ... 404, 405, 406
EILEEN DUNCAN ... 239
EINVIK (2000grt) ... 216
EIRINI KYRIAKIDES (3781grt) ... 45
EKMA (5101grt) ... 197
EL CAPITAN (5255grt) ... 348
EL FATH (311grt) ... 193
EL MADINA (3962grt) ... 197
ÉLAN (VFr) ... 129
ELBE (9179grt) ... 44
ELBING III (315grt) ... 119
ELECTRA ... 24, 25, 26, 27, 28, 38, 39, 40, 41, 50, 148, 150, 152, 153, 170, 212, 214, 215, 215, 280, 283, 285, 298, 301, 302, 303, 307, 371, 372, 393
ELENA (grt) ... 382
ELGIN ... 47, 49, 284
ELIN (grt) ... 310, **373**
ELISA (216grt) ... 185
ELISABETH BAKKE (5450grt) ... 42
ELIZABETE (2039grt) ... 109
ELLENGA (5196grt) ... 75, 135, 264, 327
ELLET (DD-398) ... 409
ELLINICO (3059grt) ... 34
ELLIS (DD-154) ... 91, 96, 99, 225, 290, 293, 352, 358
ELM ... 147, 153, 212
ELMDENE (4853grt) ... 44
ELNA II (3221grt) ... 221, 279, 281
ELPIS (3651grt) ... 389
ELSA ESSBERGER (6103grt) ... 329
ELTON (1799grt) ... 59
ELWOOD (5932grt) ... 160
EMBASSAGE (4954grt) ... 44, 166
EMDEN ... 58, 246, 247, 249
EMERALD ... 74, 75, 199, 263, 264
EMERALD QUEEN (481grt) ... 109
EMILION ... 303
EMPIRE ABILITY (7603grt) ... 46
EMPIRE AUDACITY (5537grt) ... 90
EMPIRE BAFFIN (6978grt) ... 284, 345
EMPIRE BARON (5890grt) ... 74
EMPIRE BARRACUDA (4926grt) ... 370
EMPIRE BURTON (6966grt) ... 226
EMPIRE CONDOR (7773grt) ... 37
EMPIRE CREEK (332grt) ... 49
EMPIRE CROSSBILL (5463grt) ... 225
EMPIRE CURLEW (7101grt) ... 37
EMPIRE DEFENDER (5649grt) ... 378
EMPIRE DEW (7005grt) ... 33
EMPIRE EGRET (7248grt) ... 37, 290
EMPIRE ELAND (5613grt) ... 231
EMPIRE ENERGY (6584grt) ... 353
EMPIRE FULMAR (7775grt) ... 290
EMPIRE GARDEN (8923grt) ... 43
EMPIRE GEMSBUCK (5626grt) ... 352
EMPIRE GHYLL (2011grt) ... 302
EMPIRE GUILLEMOT (5641grt) ... 250, 314, 316, 317
EMPIRE GUNNER (4492grt) ... 229
EMPIRE HERON (6023grt) ... 295
EMPIRE HUDSON (7465grt) ... 224
EMPIRE HURST (2852grt) ... 176
EMPIRE KANGAROO (6219grt) ... 191
EMPIRE KUMARI (6288grt) ... 197
EMPIRE LARCH (487grt) ... 51, 351
EMPIRE METEOR (7457grt) ... 51, 349
EMPIRE MOAT (2922grt) ... 234
EMPIRE NEWCOMEN (2840grt) ... 366
EMPIRE OAK (484grt) ... 165, 174
EMPIRE ORIOLE (6551grt) ... 290
EMPIRE PANTHER (5711grt) ... 370
EMPIRE PELICAN (6463grt) ... 377
EMPIRE PEREGRINE (7842grt) ... 290
EMPIRE PERI (4769grt) ... 198
EMPIRE PINTAIL (7773grt) ... 290
EMPIRE PLANET (4272grt) ... 168
EMPIRE PRIDE (9248grt) ... 292, 392
EMPIRE RAJA (6224grt) ... 197
EMPIRE RANI (7575grt) ... 197
EMPIRE SALVAGE (10,746grt) ... 46

EMPIRE SPRINGBUCK (5591grt) ... 223
EMPIRE STAR (11,093grt) ... 359
EMPIRE STEVENSON (6209grt) ... 351
EMPIRE STREAM (2922grt) ... 236
EMPIRE TAJ (3065grt) ... 198
EMPIRE TRUST (8143grt) ... 292, 392
EMPIRE WARRIOR (1306grt) ... 54
EMPIRE WAVE (7463grt) ... 102, 287
EMPIRE WIDGEON (6736grt) ... 37, 57, 290
EMPRESS OF ASIA (16,909grt) ... 359
EMPRESS OF AUSTRALIA (21,833grt) ... 167, 244, 326, 327
EMPRESS OF CANADA (21,517grt) ... 97, 147, 148, 152, 153, 165, 212, 216, 229, 292, 391, 392, 393
EMPRESS OF JAPAN (26,032grt) ... 37, 57, 359
EMPRESS OF RUSSIA (16,810grt) ... 158, 292, 392, 393
EMULATOR (168grt) ... 48
ENCHANTRESS ... 229, 245, 305, 358, 372
ENCOUNTER ... 104, 123, 124, 126, 175, 184, 241, 244, 298, 321, 322, 326, 384, 385, 386, 391, 393
ENGELS ... 120, 181
ENGGANO (5412grt) ... 47
ENGLES ... 22
ENIGMA ... 23, 54, 82, 83, 144, 274, 277
ENNERDALE ... 152, 163
ENOTRIA (852grt) ... 187
ENRICO COSTA (4080grt) ... 66
ENSIS (6207grt) ... 44
ENTERPRISE ... 74
ENTERPRISE (CV-6) ... 409
EQUIPOISE (6140grt) ... 160
EQURTSA (grt) ... 323
ERATO (1335grt) ... 107
EREBUS ... 148, 216, 218, 220, 238, 239, 350, 361, 365
EREVAN ... 195
ERICA ... 70, 128, 258, 259, 320, 322, 388
ERICH STEINBRINCK ... 113, 240
ERICSSON (DD-440) ... 225, 290, 293, 354, 358
ERIDGE ... 38, 39, 41, 55, 114, 115, 122, 123, 124, 175, 176, 262, 319, 320, 322, 322, 323, 326, 385, 386, 387, 387
ERIMO ... 395, 404
ERIN ... 243, 244
ERINPURA (5143grt) ... 135
ERITREA ... 189
ERITREA (2517grt) ... 124
ERLANGEN (6101grt) ... 117
ERNA (1590grt) ... 227
ERNA III (1590grt) ... 227
ERNA OLDENDORFF (2095grt) ... 240
ERNANI (6619grt) ... 46, 47
ERNESTO (7272grt) ... 64, 65, 127, 128, 186, 188, 253
ERVIKEN (6595grt) ... 296
ESCAPADE ... 93, 94, 95, 148, 149, 150, 151, 152, 153, 154, 212, 213, 215, 218, 219, 221, 279, 280, 281, 285, 286, 346, 348, 349, 351, 363, 364
ESCAUT (1087grt) ... 189
ESKIMO ... 24, 25, 26, 27, 29, 30, 37, 38, 90, 109, 216, 217, 218, 219, 220, 231, 237, 282, 286, 287, 347, 351
ESNEH (1931grt) ... 148, 153, 214, 280
ESPERANCE BAY ... 37, 43, 47, 56, 95, 110, 116
ESPERIA (11,398grt) ... 66, 187
ESPERIA (384grt) ... 317
ESSO HAMBURG (9849grt) ... 43, 56
ESTONIA (1181grt) ... 60
ESTONIAN PEETER (2727grt) ... 40

ETHIOPIA (5574grt) ... 197
EUGENIO DI SAVOIA ... 64, 315
EULIMA (6027grt) ... 349
EURO ... 65, 126, 186, 188, 189, 254, 314, 315, 379, 380
EURYALUS ... 50, 94, 110, 155, 215, 218, 231, 237, 238, 243, 251, 305, 383, 385, 386, 387, 388, 389, 391
EVANGELISTRA (28grt) ... 187
EVERITA (3251grt) ... 182
EVEROJA (4830grt) ... 352
EVEROLANDA (3379grt) ... 120
EVROS (5283grt) ... 296
Examination vessel No.10 ... 38
EXCALIBUR (9359grt) ... 45
EXCELLENT ... 91
EXEMPLAR (6736grt) ... 290
Exercise LEAPFROG ... 152, 163
EXETER ... 74, 135, 197, 198, 263, 326, 393
EXMOOR ... 359
EXPORTADOR I (318grt) ... 52
EXPRESS ... 170, 285, 298, 301, 307, 371, 372, 393
EXTANTIA (6551grt) ... 290
EYEBRIGHT ... 35, 38, 101, 156, 164, 221, 224, 224, 226, 228, 288, 289, 297
FABIO FILZI (6835grt) ... 314, 315, 382
FABRIZI ... 253
FALK (UK) ... 259, 384
FALMOUTH ... 198, 326, 391
FANA (1345grt) ... 235
FANDANGO ... 41, 114, 245
FANNING (DD-385) ... 409
Far East Command ... 371, 372, 386
FARADAY (322grt) ... 364
FARFIELD (468grt) ... 102
FARNDALE ... 38, 39, 41, 55, 114, 115, 122, 126, 127, 167, 185, 188, 231, 241, 242, 243, 251, 305, 386, 387, 387, 391
FAULKNOR ... 41, 52, 53, 54, 55, 62, 63, 102, 113, 122, 124, 175, 184, 241, 346, 350, 360, 361, 367
FAUSTO (5285grt) ... 245
FEARLESS ... 41, 53, 54, 55, 62, 63, 101, 113, 114, 115, 122, 123, 185
FEDERICO C. (1466grt) ... 127
FELLOWSHIP ... 131
FELVISHI ... 23
FENIX (1894grt) ... 25
FENNEL ... 41, 97, 162, 222, 223, 228, 231, 356
FERNBANK (211grt) ... 349
FERNBANK (4333grt) ... 47
FERNCOURT (9918grt) ... 100
FERNIE ... 240
FERRARIS ... 300, 301
FERTILE VALE (91grt) ... 109
FIAMMETTA (393grt) ... 189
FIANONA (6660grt) ... 65
FIDELITY ... 166
FILEY BAY ... 172
FILUCCIO (248grt) ... 254
FINCH (AM-9) ... 395, 397
Finnish Navy ... 82, 142, 208
FINZI ... 168, 169
FIONA SHELL (2444grt) ... 250
FIREDRAKE ... 50, 101, 115, 122, 123, 242
First Lord of the Admiralty ... 154, 155, 166
FISALIA ... 259
FISHER GIRL ... 367
FISHGUARD ... 31, 34, 164, 244, 294, 371

FITZROY 284, 349, 350
FLAMINGO ... 68, 70, 71, 72, 130, 131, 132, 133, 189, 190, 191, 192, 193, 194, 256, 321, 322, 326, 385, 387, 388, 389
Fleet Tender C 47
FLEETWOOD 33, 40, 42, 97, 293, 309, 369
FLEUR DE LYS ... 38, 53, 56, 102, 115, 175, 176, 177, 233, 241, 242, 251, 252, 299, **305**, 306
Floating Crane 72, 310
Floating Crane (500grt) 306
Floating Dock G022 127
Floating Dock XIV 351
FLOTTA 303, 364
FLOTTBEK (1930grt) 343
FLUVIOR (389grt) 255
FLYING KITE (260grt) 231
FLYNDERBORG (2022grt) 352
FOHN (303grt) 376
FOLGORE 65, 126, 127, 128, 186, 251, 252, 253, 254, 316
FOLKESTONE 38, 55, 103, 177, 232, 309, 360
FORCE 50
Force A 63, 90, 94, 95, 146, 147, 152, 212, 251, 387
Force B 63, 67, 68, 70, 383, 387, 388
Force C 67, 388
Force F 46, 95, 178
Force G 298, 371, 372, 393
Force H 50, 53, 54, 55, 62, 63, 122, 123, 124, 127, 142, 145, 151, 183, 184, 185, 188, 250, 252, 259, 283, 296, 297, 305, 313, 346, 369, 377
Force K 89, 146, 147, 152, 153, 215, 313, 317, 378, 379, 380, 381, 382, 383, 387, 388
Force L 155, 212, 213, 215, 217, 218
Force M 154, 212, 213, 215, 217, 221
Force S 124, 251
Force X 124, 251, 252
FOREMOST 45 (824grt) 357
FORERUNNER 302
FORESIGHT . 52, 53, 54, 62, 101, 104, 114, 115, 122, 124, 165, 175, 177, 184, 231, 233, 242, 243, 250, 251, 252, 298, 305, 307, 313, 346, 351, 359, 361, 362, 363, 368, 371
FORESTER 41, 52, 53, 54, 55, 62, 63, 101, 102, 113, 114, 115, 122, 123, 124, 175, 176, 177, 184, 231, 233, 242, 243, 250, 251, 252, 298, 305, 307, 313, 346, 351, 359, 362, 363, 368, 371
FORMIDABLE 132
FORT RICHEPANSE (3485grt) 229
FORTH 284, 296, 302, 303
FORTUNE 54
FORTUNSTELLA (4864grt) 178
FOUADIEH (1853grt) 258
FOWEY 167, 242, 294, 300, 309, 361, 369
FOWEY ROSE (470grt) 100
FOXHOUND 52, 53, 54, 55, 62, 63, 101, 114, 115, 122, 123, 124, 151, 175, 184, **355**, 360
FRAM (92grt) 221
FRANCESCO BARBARO (6343grt) 66, 128, 186, 252
FRANCESCO GARRE (395grt) 188
FRANCOLIN 364
FRANCONIA (20,175grt) 37, 292, 392
FRANDALE 305
FRANKENSTEIN (3703grt) 31
FRANKFURT (5522grt) 105, 168
FRANKLIN 51, 109
FRATELLI BERTOLLI (429grt) 125
FRATELLI GARRE (413grt) 188
FRAUENBURG (2111grt) 374
FRECCIA 66, 127, 186, 253, 254

FREESIA 40, 42, 55, 103, 298, 299
FRIEDA (245grt) 64
FRIEDRICH BREME (10,396grt) 39
FRIEDRICH ECKHOLDT 30, 31, 58, 87, 88, 146, 279
FRIEDRICH IHN 112, 113
FRIESLAND (2662grt) 303
FRODE (1535grt) 111
FRUNZE 22, 195, 196, 261, 324
FUBUTI 404
FUCILIERE 64, 125, 126, 127, 128, 251, 315, 379, 380, 382, 383
FUGLOYGJIN (81grt) 283
FUJIKAWA MARU 77, 78, 138, 199, 266, 396
FUJISAN MARU (9524grt) 404
FULLER (AP-14) 91
FULMINE 65, 126, 127, 128, 186, 253, 254, 316, 379
FUMIZUKI 406
FURIOUS 28, 40, 41, 52, 53, 55, 62, 63, 89, 90, 94, 95, 113, 145, 149, **153**, 166, 167, 231, 242, 250, 291
FURY 52, 53, 54, 55, 62, 63, 101, 102, 113, 114, 115, 122, 124, 167, 175, 176, 177, 184, 231, 233, 242, 251, 252, 298, 307, 313, 346, 351, 359, 361, 362, 363, 368, 371
FUSHIMI 78, 138, 200, 328
FUSO 267, 268, 270
GABBIANO (6584grt) 353
GADA (grt) 126
GAISMA (3077grt) 59
GALATEA 24, 42, 193, 194, 196, 257, 259, 320, 321, 326, 383, 385, 386, 387, 388, 391
GALT 156, 158, 227, 228, 290, 293, 297, 360, **361**
GAMMA (696grt) 182
GANDA (4333grt) 55
GARDENIA 56, 117, 235, 244
GARIBALDI 64, 122, 127, 128, 381, 382, 383
GARLAND 42, 55, 90, 94, 95, 101, 146, 150, 167, 229, 231, 243, 251, 252, 306
GARM (1231grt) 225
GARTH 111, 365
GASFIRE (2972grt) 50
GASLIGHT (1696grt) 348
GEBIL KEBIR (grt) 321, 387
GEDANIA (8923grt) 43
GEMSTONE (4986grt) 221, 279, 281, 345
GENIERE 64, 66, 125, 127, 186, 381, 382
GENTIAN 39, 116, 162, 167, 242, 250, 289, 295, 356, 358, 361, 369
GENYO MARU (10,018grt) 397, 398
GEORGE J. GOULANDRIS (4345grt) 47
GEORGES LEYGUES 107
GEORGETOWN 96, 98, 101, 104, 152, 157, 163, 164, 220, 224, 231, 288, 290, 293, 295, 298
GEORGIAN 355
GEORGIC (27,759grt) 134
GEORGIOS AVEROFF 72, 263
GERANIUM 40, 53, 54, 114, 115, 370
GERDA FERDINAND (3727grt) 374
German Naval Command Italy 377
GERTRUD III (210grt) 179
GERTRUD KAMPF (471grt) 374
GESUE E MARIA (239grt) 69
GHIGULESCU 72, 323
GIANFRANCO (8081grt) 178
GIBEL DRIS (744grt) 305
GILLHAUSEN (4339grt) 222

GIOBERTI........ 64, 66, 125, 127, 186, 187, 188, 189, 251, 254, 254, 314, 315, 316, 380, 381
GIORGINA (253grt)....65
GIOVANNI BOTTIGLIERE (331grt)....63
GIULIA (5921grt).... 64, 65, 186, 189, 253, 315
GIUSEPPINA GHIRARDI (3319grt)....68
GIUSEPPINA V. (367grt)....189
GLADIOLUS....... 29, 32, 33, 39, 97, 98, 99, 104, 158, 159, 216, 225, 228, 231, 287, 288, 289, 295, 296
GLADYS MOLLER (5285grt)....193
GLASGOW.... 263, 327, 391, 392, 393
GLAUCO....55
GLAUCUS (7586grt).... 167, 244, 246, 310, 327
GLAVKOS.... 65, 130, 132, 385, 387
GLEAVES (DD-423)........... 91, 96, 99, 218, 220, 223, 232, 284, 288, 298, 353
GLEN ALVA (6grt)....238
GLEN HEAD (2011grt)....53
GLENCREE (481grt)....367
GLENDALOUGH (868grt)....170
GLENEARN (8986grt)....68, 134
GLENGYLE (9919grt)....67, 196, 258, 386
GLENORCHY (10,000grt)....167, 244, 246, 327
GLENROY (9809grt)....70, 191, 258, 262, 321, 387
GLOIRE....107
GLORIA (5896grt)....107
GLORIA IN EXCELSIO DEO....173
GLOXINIA.... 126, 381
GLYNN (1134grt)....302
GNAT.... 130, 193, 256, 320, 321, 322, 388
GNEISENAU.... 113, 174
GNEVNY....22, 59
GOLD SHELL (8208grt)....170
GOLDEN GRAIN (101grt)....171
GOLDFINCH (454grt)....100
GOLDSBOROUGH (AVD-5)....90
GONZENHEIM (4104grt)....43, 53
GORDY.... 22, 59, 120, 181, 182, 183, 249, 375
GORIZIA....66, 122, 188, 251, 381, 382
GORLESTON.... 105, 166, 235, 236, 244, 298, 299, 360, 372
GOS II....40, 113
GOS III....40, 114
GOS VII....55
GOSHAWK....40
GOSHU MARU.... 203, 331
GOSSAMER.... 32, 40, 157, 221, 232, 281, 284, 344, 345, 346, 349
GOTEBORG....247
GOTHIC (2469grt)....378
GOYO MARU.... 333, 404
GRANATIERE.... 64, 127, 251, 315, 379, 380, 382, 383
GRANBY....79
GRAYBURN (6342grt)....30
GRAYSON (DD-435)....99, 159, 160, 169, 215, 227, 347
GRAZIELLA (2137grt)....344
GRAZIOLI LANTE....64, 188
GREBE.... 133, 257, 382
GRECALE.... 65, 124, 187, 251, 379
GREENWICH....100
GREER (DD-145)....99, 209, 210, 216, 288, 294, 295, 296, 360
GREIF....367
GREMYAHCHI....344
GREMYASHCHI....22, 88, 213, 214
GRETAVALE (4586grt)....352
GRIBB....197
GRIDLEY (DD-380)....409
GRIFFIN..... 68, 69, 71, 128, 129, 130, 131, 132, 193, 194, 256, 257, 258, 259, 318, 319, 320, 321, 322, 322, 387, 388, 389
GRILLE....58
GROENLO (1984grt)....365
GROMKI.... 22, 88, 213, 214, 344
GROUIN DU COU....115
Group 1....62
Group 2....62
Group A.... 384, 385
Group B.... 384, 385
Group C.... 384, 385
GROZA....87, 88
GROZJASHCHI....120
GROZNY.... 22, 23, 90, 147, 148, 213
GROZYASHCHI....22, 60, 62, 120, 183, 249, 249
GRUZIYA (4857grt)....261, 324
GUARDIAN.... 167, 244, 245
GUELMA (4402grt)....46
GUÉPARD....68, 69, 70, 128, 129
GUGLIELMO (331grt)....65
GUIDONIA (5060grt)....160
GUILLEMOT....47, 49
GUJARAT (4148grt)....132, 133, 190, 192
GUN 9....392
GUNDA (1770grt)....54
GUNLOG (1424grt)....304
GUNTHER (252grt)....310
GURKHA........ 97, 101, 161, 163, 164, 164, 169, 231, 243, 250, 251, 252, 292, 300, 305, 307, 308, 309, 360, 361, 368, 369, 370, 371, 377
GURNA....322
GUSTAV EUGENE (120grt)....112
GUSTAV JEANNE (39grt)....112
GWIN (DD-433)....35, 99, 160, 215, 227, 346, 347
GYLFE (6129grt)....197
GYPSUM QUEEN (3915grt)....225
H.32....39
H-27....247
HAAKON ADALSTEIN (710grt)....286
HAAKON JARL (1482grt)....147
HAARLEM....307
HAGIKAZE.... 399, 406
HAKAZE....394
HAKKAI MARU....396
HAKUSA....399
HALCYON.... 94, 95, 148, 151, 153, 214, 280, 285, 286, 303
HAMAKAZE.... 403, 405
HAMBLEDON.... 24, 26, 27, 28, 29, 48, 49, 50, 108, 365
HAMILTON....223, 354, 355, 356
HAMLET.... 148, 151, 153, 215, 280, 297, 346, 348
HAMMANN (DD-412).... 36, 98, 215, 223, 288, 290
HAMMARLAND (3875grt)....32
HAMUL (AK-30)....91
HANAU (5892grt)....88
HANNE (1360grt).... 386, 387, 388
HANNOVER....234
HANS CHRISTOPHERSON (1599grt)....111
HANS LODY....30, 31, 58, 87, 88, 146, 148
HANSA (21,131grt)....146
HANSA (7603grt)....46
HANSEAT (224grt)....247
HANSESTADT DANZIG.... 58, 61, 118
HARLINGEN (5415grt)....162

HARMONIC (4558grt) 221, 279, 281, 345
HARMONY 359
HARPALION (5486grt) 284, 345
HARPALYCUS (5629grt) 262
HARRIER 148, 149, 150, 151, 153, 214, 279, 280, 285, 286, 303
Harriman, Averell 214
HARROW 70, 131
HARTLAND 31, 34, 51, 229, 245, 305, 358, 372
HARTLEBURY (5082grt) 284, 345
HARUKAZE 406
HARUNA 203, 268, 402, 406
HARUSAME 406
HARVESTER 38, 97, 100, 149, 158, 231, 288, 297, 354, 357, 358, 361, 369
HASHIDATE 396
HASTY 69, 70, 71, 128, 129, 130, 131, 132, 191, 192, 193, 194, 256, 257, 258, 259, 319, 320, 321, 322, 323, 384, 385, 386, 387, 388, 389
HASU 395
HATAKAZE 406
HATASU (3198grt) 287, 295
HATO 406
HATSUKARI 398
HATSUKAZE 406
HATSUTAKA 328
HATSUYUKI 404
HAVBRIS (1315grt) 279
HAVELOCK ... 33, 38, 42, 97, 149, 158, 228, 231, 288, 297, 354, 357, 358, 369
HAVOCK 69, 70, 71, 128, 129, 131, 132, 189, 190, 191, 192, 194, 256, 257, 258, 320, 321
HAVPRINS (8066grt) 35
HAVTOR (1524grt) 26
HAWAIIAN SHIPPER (7775grt) 290
HAWKINGE (2475grt) 107
HAWKINS 57, 179, 198, 245, 263, 367
HAYASHIO 399
HAYATE 408
HAYTIAN 304
HAZARD 32, 40, 156, 157, 163, 349, 351, 360
HAZEL 147, 153, 212, 218
HAZELSIDE (5297grt) 310
HEARTSEASE .. 97, 98, 104, 157, 158, 164, 220, 224, 228, 231, 288, 290, 293, 295, 298, 355, 360
HEATHER .97, 99, 102, 156, 157, 158, 162, 165, 226, 227, 229, 232, 284, 289, 294, 352, 355, 357, 361
HEBE 32, 35, 40, 97, 156, 157, 158, 163, 349, 351, 360
HECLA 152, 155
HECTOR 57, 197, 198, 327
HEDDA (1498grt) 366
HEEMSKERK 33, 42, 101, 164
HEIAN MARU (11,614grt) 202, 331, 332
HEINA (4028grt) 43
HEITO MARU (4468grt) 332, 401, 407
HEKLA (1215grt) 35
HELEN BARBARA 284
HELIOTROPE ... 31, 96, 103, 115, 117, 165, 177, 178, 233, 241, 300, 301, 307, 309, **361**, 369
HELM (DD-388) 409
HENLEY (DD-391) 409
HENNY (764grt) 374
HEPATICA 33, 38, 100, 156, 163, 222, 228, 231
HERCULES (632grt) 387
HERMANN FRITZEN (3845grt) 111
HERMANN SCHOEMANN 31, 87, 88, 147
HERMES (7209grt) 117

HERMIONE 24, 25, 27, 28, 41, 55, 63, 113, 114, 122, 124, 127, 173, 175, 184, 185, 250, 251, 255, 305, 307, 308, 313, 368, 370, 377
HERMIS (5234grt) 161
HERO 67, 68, 70, 71, 130, 131, 132, 189, 190, 191, 256, 257, 258, 259, 319, 320, 322, 323, 385, 389
HERTA ENGELINE FRITZEN (5100grt) 304
HERTTA (343grt) 310, 373
HESPERUS 54, 62, 97, 100, 149, 298, 301, 307, 308, 354, 361
HEYTHROP 28, 91, 92, 93, 94, 95, 97, 100, 101, 149, 162, 165, 231, 242, 243, 251, 305, 386, 387, 387, 389, 391
HEYWOOD (AP-12) 91
HIBIKI 399, 406
HIBISCUS 40, 42, 102, 116, 162, 167, 233, 242, 295, 353, 358
HIDE MARU 267, 333
HIDE MARU (5181grt) 202, 203
HIE MARU (4943grt) 140, 269, 404, 405
HIEI 77, 78, 79, 138, 139, 201, 203, 267, 268, 329, 330, 331, 334, 402, 403, 404, 405
HIGHLAND BRIGADE (14,134grt) 37, 292, 392
HIGHLAND MONARCH (14,139grt) 161
HIGHLAND PATRIOT (14,172grt) 263
HIGHLAND PRINCESS (14,133grt) 292
HIGHLANDER 37, 107, 108, 116, 167, 175, 242, 288, 295, 354, 357, 358, 361, 369
HIGHWOOD (1177grt) 99
HIIUSAAR 182
HIKAWA MARU (11,622grt) 77, 333, 403, 404
HILARY 38, 44, 56, 101, 116, 167, 244
HILARY P. JONES (DD-427) 91, 96, 99, 223, 223, 232, 285, 289, 290, 299, 358
HILDA (1237grt) 304
HILDA (4901grt) 198
HILDUR (1856grt) 59
HILMI 258
HIMALAYA (3540grt) 52
HIMALAYA (6240grt) 174
HIPHAISTOS 72
HIRYU 400, 402, 405, 406
HISHI MARU 333, 400
HISHI MARU No.2 .... 334, 400
HISHI MARU No.2 (856grt) 268
HITACHI MARU (6540grt) 406
Hitler, Adolph .. 6, 7, 10, 19, 20, 85, 86, 142, 144, 145, 211, 274, 277, 278, 338, 339, 342
HIYODORI 396
HM King George VI 150, 151
HOBART 131, 132, 133, 134, 190, 191, 192, 194, 255, 256, 257, 258, 259, 319, 320, 321, 322, 323, 383, 385, 386, 387
HOEGH HOOD (9351grt) 123, 126, 308
HOGLAND (4360grt) 172
HOHENFELS (7862grt) 197
HOHENHORN (grt) 312
HOKAZE 399
HOKKAI MARU (5105grt) 331, 394, 401
HOKKI MARU (5601grt) 400
HOKOKU MARU 202, 269, 332, 401, 402, 408
HOKOKU MARU (10,439grt) 204
HOKUAN MARU (3712grt) 327, 329, 330, 396, 397
HOKUROKU MARU (5046grt) 332, 398
HOLDERNESS 47, 110, 237, 238
HOLLAND (1991grt) 246
HOLLY 40, 113
HOLLYHOCK 33, 38, 42, 294, 359, 371
HOLMSIDE (3433grt) 106

HOLMSTEINN (16grt) 24
Home Fleet... 19, 24, 25, 26, 28, 50, 91, 94, 122, 142, 150, 151, 153, 164, 208, 217, 221, 275, 282, 346, 346, 347, 349, 350, 351, 362, 364, 369
HOMEFIRE (1262grt) 108
HONDO (229grt) 25
HONDURAS (4524grt) 262
HONEYSUCKLE.......32, 96, 102, 157, 166, 224, 225, 226, 226, 228, 289, 295, 356, 358, 361, 369
HOPEWELL (DD-181) 169
HOPTON (202grt) 25
HORN SHELL (8272grt) 46, 106, 114, 115, 116
HOSHO 202, 269, 270
HOTSPUR...... 67, 68, 69, 70, 71, 129, 131, 133, 190, 192, 193, 194, 256, 257, 258, 259, 318, 319, 320, 321, 322, 384, 385, 386, 387, 388
HOWELL LYKES (7773grt) 290
HOYO MARU 78, 136, 201, 204, 332, 333, 404
HRABRI 23
HUDSON 309
HUGH WALPOLE 355, **360**
HUGHES (DD-410) 99, 288, 290, 354
HULL TRADER (717grt) 50
HURWORTH 282, 301, 348, 358
HUSSAR 32, 34, 221, 232, 281, 284, 344, 345, 346
HYACINTH 69, 70, 128, 129, 131, 133, 189, 258, 259, 318, 319, 388
HYDRANGEA......41, 53, 56, 101, 104, 116, 117, 161, 162, 163, 164, 169, 176, 177, 178, 232, 241
HYUGA....... 77, 78, 79, 138, 139, 201, 203, 267, 268, 269, 270, 331, 332, 334, 404, 405, 406
I. C. WHITE (7052grt) 246
I-1 ....401, 402, 405
I-10 ....330, 399, 401, 402, 408
I-121 332
I-122 332
I-123 332
I-124 332
I-15 ....402, 404
I-16 ....403, 404
I-17 404
I-18 ....403, 404
I-19 ....404, 405, 406, 406
I-2 ....401, 402
I-20 ....403, 404
I-21 ....405, 406, 406
I-22 ....334, 335, 403, 404
I-23 ....404, 405, 406, 406
I-24 ....403, 404
I-25 ....333, 404
I-26 ....401, 402, 405, 409
I-3 ....401, 402
I-4 ....401, 402
I-5 ....201, 401, 402
I-53 400
I-54 400
I-55 400
I-56 400
I-57 400
I-58 400
I-6 ....401, 402
I-61 ....**332**
I-62 399
I-64 399
I-65 398
I-66 ....334, 398, 399

I-68 ....401, 408
I-69 ....402, 408
I-7 ....334, 401, 402
I-70 ....401, 407, 408
I-71 ....402, 407, 408
I-72 ....402, 407, 408
I-73 ....402, 407, 408
I-74 ....402, 407, 408
I-75 ....402, 407, 408
I-8 ....**182**, 402, 408
I-9 ....402, 404
IBERVILLE (5685grt) 196
IBIS 220, 239, 284, 285, 297, 358, 372
ICARUS...... 24, 26, 29, 33, 37, 38, 88, 92, 93, 94, 95, 100, 101, 110, 147, 149, 150, 151, 152, 153, 212, 216, 217, 229, 230, 237, 283, 284, 302, 345, 348, 349, 350, 351, 361
Iceland Command 221
Iceland-Faeroes passage 24-30, 347, 348
ICEMAID (1964grt) 302
IDA KNUDSEN (8913grt) 55, 115
IDAHO (BB-42) 215, 220, 222, 223, 346, 347
IERAX 72
IGEA (160grt) 128
IHSAN 198
IJORA (2815grt) 345
IKAZUCHI 399
IKI KARDESHLER 67
IKU-TURSO 61, 120
ILA (1583grt) 295
ÎLE DE FRANCE (43,450grt) 197
ILEX 67, 68, 69, 71, 132, 135
ILMARINEN 247, 248
ILSE (2844grt) 49
ILVANIA (487grt) 252
IMHOFF 197
IMPERIA (222grt) 252
IMPERIAL STAR (10,733grt) 231, 251
IMPERIALIST 54, 106
IMPULSIVE 25, 26, 27, 38, 49, 148, 150, 151, 152, 153, 163, 170, 171, 215, 217, 218, 219, 220, 221, 280, 281, 285, 346, 347, 348, 358
INAZUMA 399
INCHKEITH 298
INDIAN PRINCE (6376grt) 161, 263
INDIANA (BB-58) 356
INDOMITABLE 47, 285, 293, 356
INDRA (2032grt) 307
INDRAPOERA (10,825grt) 33, 161, 245, 263, 319
INDUS 73
INDUS (733grt) 240
INES CORRADO (5159grt) 178
INGA ESSBERGER (grt) 111
INGA I (1304grt) 107
INGER (1418grt) 154
INGEREN (6123grt) 304, 366
INGERTO (3089grt) 147, 153
INGLEFIELD... 26, 27, 29, 33, 42, 88, 91, 94, 95, 100, 148, 149, 150, 151, 152, **153**, 154, 163, 171, 213, 215, 217, 218, 219, 238, 351, 366
INGRIA (4391grt) 166
INSTERBURG (1799grt) 59
INTREPID... 25, 27, 28, 29, 33, 42, 48, 91, 94, 95, 99, 149, 152, 153, 154, 162, 163, 165, 172, 285, 286, 303, 344, 345, 346, 347, 348
INVERARDER (5578grt) 52
INVERLANE (9141grt) 283

INVERLEE (9158grt)	241, 242, 306, 307
INVERNESS (4897grt)	105
INVERSUIR (9456grt)	43
ION C. BRATIANU	22
IRENE VERNICOS (250grt)	66
IRIDIO MANTOVANI (10,540grt)	381, 382, 383
IRIS (1974grt)	109
IRO	335, 398
ISAAC SWEERS	91, 95, 97, 161, 164, 167, 231, 243, 251, 292, 300, 305, 307, 308, 309, 368, 369, 370, 371, 377
ISABELLA FOWLIE (196grt)	109
ISAC (2385grt)	112, 115
ISARCO (5738grt)	249
ISE	79, 138, 139, 267, 268, 270
ISEO	186
ISEO (2366grt)	383
ISIS	67, 68, 69, 133
ISLE OF WIGHT (176grt)	50
ISOKAZE	403, 405
ISONAMI	404
ISORA (316grt)	322
Italian Commando Supremo	123
Italian Fleet	17, 82, 86, 122, 123, 142, 185, 208, 251, 255, 338, 342
Italian Navy	274
ITALO BALBO (5114grt)	250
ITHAKA (1773grt)	385
ITSUKUSHIMA	77, 267, 268, 269, 329, 331, 399
ITSUKUSHIMA MARU	404, 405
ITSUKUSHIMA MARU (10,006grt)	205, 405, 407, 409
ITU (1578grt)	380
IVY	**198**
JAAKARHU	248
JACKAL	67, 68, 69, 70, 72, 128, 129, 130, 131, 132, 189, 190, 191, 192, 193, 194, 196, 257, 258, 259, 320, 326, 384, 385, 386, 387, 388, 389
JACQUES MORGAND	**367**
JADE	65
JAGUAR	68, 69, 70, 71, 131, 132, 133, 190, 191, 192, 256, 257, 258, 259, 318, 319, 320, 321, 322, 323, 384, 385, 389
JAMAICA PLANTER (4098grt)	99
JAMES AND STANLEY (grt)	168
JAN HUBERT (460grt)	96
JANA (2917grt)	182
JANSSENS	76
JANTINA	71, 129
JANUS	67, 68
Japanese 11th Air Fleet	328, 396, 399
Japanese 11th Naval Air Fleet	334
Japanese 1st Air Fleet	334, 335, 400, 401, 402, 404, 406
Japanese Advance Expeditionary Force	402
Japanese Borneo Invasion Group	394
Japanese Carrier Striking Force	403, 404, 405
Japanese China Area Fleet	200, 265, 396, 399
Japanese Combined Fleet	202, 210, 268, 331, 332, 333, 334, 335, 400, 401, 402, 404, 406, 406
Japanese Fifth Fleet	139, 267, 268, 333
Japanese First Air Fleet	203, 266, 267, 268, 270
Japanese First China Expeditionary Fleet	200
Japanese First China Fleet	328
Japanese First Fleet	203, 267, 268, 270, 402
Japanese Fourth Fleet	204, 267, 270, 332, 335, 336, 407, 408
Japanese Fourth Surprise Attack Unit	406
Japanese Gilbert Islands Invasion Force	343, 408
Japanese Malaya Seizure Force	406
Japanese Midway Bombardment Unit	405
Japanese Second Fleet	270, 404, 406
Japanese Shanghai Area Base Force	395
Japanese Sixth Fleet	139, 333, 399, 400, 401, 402
Japanese Southern (Malay) Force	406
Japanese Southern Expeditionary Fleet	139, 199, 330, 394, 399
Japanese Southern Force	394, 399, 401
Japanese Southwest Area Fleet	328
Japanese Special Attack Unit	403, 404
Japanese Third Fleet	76, 77, 139, 265, 267, 268, 333, 395, 404
JARLINN (190grt)	216
JARVIS (DD-393)	409
JASMINE	41, 54, 56, 100, 102, 167, 175, 233, 242, 250
JASTREB (grt)	382
JEAN MIC	129
JEDMOOR (4392grt)	219, 223
JERVIS	69, 70, 71, 72, 131, 132, 133, 189, 190, 191, 192, 193, 194, 257, 258, 259, 319, 320, 321, 322, 323, 384, 385, 386, 387, 388, 389
JESUS ANTONIO (988grt)	66
JIM (833grt)	49
JINGEI	407
JOHAN DE WITT (10,474grt)	327
JOHAN VAN OLDENBARNEVELDT (19,429grt)	137, 264
JOHANN WESSELS (4659grt)	239
JOHN (197grt)	37
JOHN HOLT (4975grt)	235
JOHN LYKES (6829grt)	409
JOMA (372grt)	367
JON (744grt)	305
JONQUIL	40, 53, 54, 100, 104, 114, 116, 176, 242, 243, 252, 301, 307, 308, 359, 369, 370
JOSEPH T. DICKMAN (AP-26)	353
JOSIF STALIN	376
JOUETT (DD-396)	161, 228, 291, 292, 357
JULIET (173grt)	165
JULIUS HUGH STINNES 27 (2530grt)	246
JUMNA	29, 30, 90, 100, 230
JUNO (grt)	182
JUPITER	23, 27, 29, 30, 91, 101, 161, 182, 259, 262, 298, 318, 319, 320, 321, 322, 323, 384, 385, 386, 391, 393
JUSHAR	345
K-1	212, 280, **287**, 343
K-2	146, 212, 213
K-21	61, 148, 214, 343, 344
K-22	61, 148, 214, 343
K-23	61, 148, 214, 280, 343, 344
K-3	61, 119, 214, 344
KAAPAREN (3393grt)	293
KAGA	77, 138, 334, 398, 403, 404, 405, 406
KAGANOVITCH (3663grt)	59
KAGERO	403, 405
KAGU MARU	398
KAGU MARU (6806grt)	397
KAIHEI MARU (4575grt)	204, 270, 333, 334, 335
KAIJA (1876grt)	310
KAIJA (244grt)	247
KAIJO MARU No.2 (8636grt)	402
KAISER	58, 180, 247, 248, 374
KAISHO MARU (4164grt)	138, 269, 270, 331
KAISSAAR (1893grt)	311
KAJE (1547grt)	51
KAJMAKALAN	128, 132, 192, 194
KAKO	269

KALEV..59, 179, 182, 247, 312, 374
KALININ...22, 182
KALININ (4156grt)...323, 324
KALOSERKA...23
KALYPSO VERGOTTI (5686grt)..47
KAMAKURA MARU (17,526grt)...........................202, 203, 267, 270, 335
KAMCHIYA...23
KAMIKAWA MARU....................................77, 139, 265, 395, 398
KAMIKAZE MARU...202, 270, 327
KAMIKAZE MARU (4916grt)...77, 139
KAMLOOPS...353
KAMOGAWA MARU..267
KAMSACK..356
KANDAHAR..67, 68, 69, 71, 128, 131, 132, 133, 190, 191, 192, 193, 194, 256, 258, 259, 318, 319, 320, 321, 322, 384, 385, 386, 387, 388
KANIMBLA..197
KANIN..90
KANTARA...**233**
KANTO MARU (8606grt)...201
KAPITAN MINKOV...23
KARALTEPE (145grt)..389
KARANJA (9891grt)..152, 163
KARKAZ...**197**
KARL GALSTER..30, 31, 58, 87, 88, 148, 279
KARL LIBKNECHT...22
KARL MARKS...22, 61, 180
KARNAK (7209grt)...117
KAROA (7009grt)..393
KASASAGI...396
KASASHIMA...395
KASATKA...182
KASHINO...331
KASTEHOLM (5417grt)..24
KASUGA MARU..267
KASUMI...403, 405
KATERINA GRUBO...23
KATOOMBA (9424grt)...137
KATORI...401
KATSONIS..65, 72
KATSURIKI...335, 336
KAWAKAZE...406
KAYNAKDERE (85grt)..389
KAZAK POYAKOV (1035grt)..138
KEARNY (DD-432)..........................160, 226, 284, 288, 294, 295, 296
KEDGREREE..144, 198
KEHI MARU (4523grt)...397
KEIJO MARU...335
KEIYO MARU...334, 396
KEIYO MARU (6442grt)...202
KELLETT...284
KELLWYN (1459grt)..107
KELT..371
KELVIN...68
KENNETH HAWKSFIELD (1546grt)..50
KENOGAMI..........158, 159, 218, 223, 224, 225, 228, 232, 288, 289, 297, 355
KENRYU MARU (4575grt)...75, 136, 199
KENT..240, 281, 284, 346, 347, 348, 349, 350, 351
KENYA........24, 25, 27, 28, 29, 31, 51, 110, 154, 172, 215, 216, 217, 230, 231, 236, 243, 251, 252, 283, 286, 293, 294, 299, 305, 344, 345, 346, 347, 348
KENYO MARU...401, 402, 403, 405, 406
KENYO MARU (6486grt)...........................202, 267, 270, 331, 404, 407
KEPHALLINIA..191
KEPPEL......35, 97, 103, 156, 158, 163, 166, 222, 227, 230, 233, 289, 358

KEVINBANK..132, 133, 189, 191, 192
KHABRI...323
KHARKOV..............................22, 72, 73, 134, 196, 260, 389
KHASAN (3979grt)..59
KHEDIVE ISMAIL (7290grt)...197
KHEYR EL DINE..258
KIEV...195
KIHELKONNA (120grt)...182
KIKU MARU...202, 268, 333
KIKUZUKI..404, 405
KIMBERLEY...67, 68, 69, 70, 71, 129, 130, 131, 132, 133, 190, 191, 192, 193, 194, 256, 257, 258, 259, 323, 383, 384, 385, 386, 387, 388
KIMIKAWA MARU..................................201, 266, 267, 335, 402, 406
KIMIKAWA MARU (6863grt)...138
KIMISHIMA MARU (5193grt)......................................75, 136, 199, 264
KINA II (9823grt)...167, 244, 246, 327
KINAI MARU (5047grt)..329, 399
KINDERSLEY (1999grt)..171
KINDIA (1972grt)...270, 334
KING EDGAR (4536grt)...262
KING ERIK (228grt)...216
KING GEORGE V.24, 26, 27, 94, 153, 171, 216, 217, 220, 221, 237, 281, 282, 286, 346, 347, 351
KING HENRY...49
KING MALCOLM (5120grt)...290
KING SOL...38, 42, 227, 290, 293, 297, 360
KINGCUP...................35, 37, 96, 100, 102, 115, 289, 297, 353, 356
KINGSLAND (3669grt)..366
KINGSTON..........69, 70, 71, 128, 129, 130, 132, 189, 190, 191, 193, 194, 196, 256, 257, 258, 259, 321, 322, 383, 384, 385, 386, 387, 388
KINGSTON AGATE..155
KINGSTON HILL (7628grt)..44
KINGSTON OLIVINE...365
KINGSTOWN (628grt)..39
KINROSS (4956grt)..34
KINRYU MARU (9310grt).........................267, 333, 334, 404, 405, 408
KINUGASA..269
KINUGASA MARU (8407grt)....................................400, 401, 404
KIPLING........131, 132, 134, 190, 192, 193, 194, 196, 256, 257, 259, 318, 319, 320, 384, 385, 386, 387, 388, 389
KIRISHIMA.77, 78, 79, 138, 139, 200, 201, 202, 203, 268, 329, 331, 333, 398, 400, 401, 402, 404, 405
KIRISHIMA MARU.....................................330, 403, 405, 406
KIRKELLA..352, 355, 355
KIRKLAND (1361grt)..389
KIROV........................22, 58, 60, 62, 181, 182, 183, 247, 248, 249
KISARAGI..408
KISO...267
KISO MARU..332
KITTIWAKE...365
KIYOKAWA MARU..331, 406, 407
KIYOKAWA MARU (6862grt)...270
KIYOSUMI MARU..202, 332, 401
KIYOSUMI MARU (8613grt)..400
KLARA (7277grt)..299
KLAS HORN..247
KLAS UGGLA...247
KLJUZ..376
KLO...67, 318, 322, 386
KNOLL (1151grt)...219
KNUD VILLEMOES (1582grt)..111
KODU (grt)..182
KOFUKU MARU (3209grt)..................................202, 268, 270

KOGYO MARU	267, 401, 406
KOGYO MARU (6353grt)	204, 268
KOKUYO MARU	78, 139, 401, 402, 403, 405
KOKUYO MARU (10,026grt)	269, 333, 334
KÖLN	246, 247, 311
KOLYVAN	182
KOMAHASHI	336
KOMAKI MARU	76, 78, 137, 139, 200, 268, 396
KOMAKI MARU (8525grt)	330, 396
KOMILES (3962grt)	351
KOMINTERN	22, 72, 134, 195, 260, 261, 324, 324
KOMZIL	23
KONDOURIOTIS	384, 388, 389
KONGO	203, 266, 268, 329, 398, 402, 404, 406
KONGO MARU	267, 270, 332, 334, 404, 405, 408
KONGO MARU (8624grt)	201
KONGSGAARD (9467grt)	35
KÖNIGIN LUISE	58, 170, 180, 249
KOOLGA (1110grt)	170
KORYU MARU	137, 138, 266, 329, 330, 399
KORYU MARU (880grt)	77, 397, 398, 399
KOS IX	103, 157
KOS VII	38
KOS VIII	157
KOS X	38, 55
KOS XI	38, 55
KOS XII	38, 113
KOS XIX	320, 321, 322, 384
KOS XVI	**166**
KOS XX	35
KOS XXI	**318**
KOS XXII	67
KOSHU	336
KOTA NOPAN (7322grt)	205, 368
KOTA PINANG (7277grt)	236, 299
KOTOKU MARU (6702grt)	328, 394, 395, 398, 399
KOTOVSKI (grt)	323, 324
KRAKOWIAK	26, 29, 30, 52, 92, 101, 309
KRASNAYA ABCHAZIYA	195
KRASNAYA ABCHAZIYA (grt)	261
KRASNAYA ARMENIYA	134, 195, 196, 261
KRASNAYA GRUZIYA	134, 195, 196
KRASNOE ZNAMYA	247
KRASNY ADZHARISTAN	195, 323
KRASNY KAVKAZ	22, 72, 196, 260, 261, 323, 324, 325, 389, 390, 391
KRASNY KRYM	22, 196, 261, 323, 325, 389, 390, 391
KRASNY KUBAN (3113grt)	134
KRASNY PROFINTERN (4648grt)	390
KREML (7661grt)	389
KRISYJANIS VALDEMARS (2250grt)	182, 182
KRONOBORG (6537grt)	26
KTS-1101	182
KTS-1104	182
KTS-1105	182
KTS-1107	182
KTS-1201	182
KTS-1204	182
KTS-1205	182
KTS-1206	182
KTS-1510	182
KTS-1511	182
KTS-1512	182
KTS-1524	182
KUHA 3	374
KUIBYSHEV	23, 88
KUJAWIAK	92, 94, 101, 305, 309, 351, 367
KUJBYSHEV	146, 148, 195
KUJIWIAK	28, 49
KUMA	268
KUMAGAWA MARU	334
KUMAGAWA MARU (6641grt)	269
KUMASIAN (4922grt)	162
KUNIKAWA MARU	404, 406
KUNIKAWA MARU (6863grt)	335, 401
KUNISHIMA MARU (4083grt)	78, 139, 267, 333, 403
KURFURST	228, 234
KURI	395
KUROSHIO	406
KUROSHIO MARU	266, 333
KUROSHIO MARU (10,383grt)	202, 203, 399
KURSK (5801grt)	324
KUUSIMAA	376
KUYBYSHEV	22
KUZBASS (3109grt)	345
K-XI	395
K-XII	395
K-XIII	395
K-XIV	363
K-XVII	76
K-XVIII	76
KYMA (3959grt)	302
KYOEI MARU 3	79
KYOEI MARU No.2	269, 332
KYOEI MARU No.2 (1192grt)	204, 402, 403
KYOKUTO MARU	78, 138, 401, 402, 403, 405
KYOKUTO MARU (10,051grt)	335
KYOKUYO MARU	403
L.26	42
L.27	304
L-1	375
L-2	247, 312, 375
L-20	61, 214, 280
L-22	61, 214, 280
L-23	195
L-24	195
L-25	195
L-3	59, 60, 118, 119, 249, 310, 311
L-4	195, 196, 260, 261, 323, 324, 325
L-5	195, 196, 260, 261
L-6	325, 389, 390
LA CARRIERE (5685grt)	243, 306
LA CORDELIERE	229
LA DIEPPOISE	306
LA MALOUINE	103, 115, 117, 162, 165, 177, 178, 233, 241, 300, 301, 307, 361
LA VAILLANTE	129
LACONIA	33, 36, 158
LACONIA (5932grt)	160
L'ADOUR (4500grt)	129
LADY DENISON-PENDER (1984grt)	177
LADY ELSA	35, 37, 40, 100, 158, 166, 227, 230, 233, 289, 293, 353, 356, 358
LADY HOGARTH	41, 54, 102, 113, 115, 174, 175, 176, 241, 242, 306, 307, 369, 370
LADY MADELEINE	32, 39, 97, 102, 162, 165, 229, 284, 294, 352, 355, 357, **361**

LADY OF MANN (3104grt) 25, 26, 28, 48, 49, 50
LADY SHIRLEY 38, 41, 102, 113, 115, 175, 235, 241, 242, 243, 244, 299, 308, 370
LADY SOMERS 53, 100, 106
LADY SOMERS (8194grt) 45
LADYLOVE 154, 155
LAERTES 38, 55
LAFIAN (4876grt) 235
LAFOREY 155, 216, 217, 218, 231, 237, 243, 251, 252, 282, 283, 284, 296, 297, 305, 357, 368, 369, 370, 371, 377
LAIRDS ISLE 363
LAMERTON .. 152, 154, 171, 217, 219, 220, 230, 232, 233, 237, 238, 300, 301, 307, 308
LAMOTTE-PICQUET 264, 268, 270, 327, 333, 334
LANCASHIRE (9557grt) 197
LANCASTER 219, 220, 232, 238, 283, 292, 351
LANCASTRIAN PRINCE (1914grt) 148, 153, 214, 280
LANCE 27, 41, 55, 63, 97, 113, 114, 161, 163, 164, 164, 165, 231, 243, 250, 251, 252, 299, 305, 313, 317, 378, 379, 381, 382, 383, 387
LANCIERE 125, 251, 252, 254
LANDBY (4150grt) 226
LANDGUARD 102, 177, 298, 299, 372
LANG (DD-399) 36
LANSDALE (DD-426) .. 91, 96, 99, 158, 216, 218, 220, 223, 232, 288, 298, 353, 356
LAPCHEV 23
LAPINO 254
LAPLAND (1330grt) 107
LAPWING (1348grt) 236
LARAMIE (AO-16) 353
LARGS BAY (14,182grt) 167, 244, 246, 327
LARKSPUR 41, 56, 100, 102, 167, 175, 242, 289, 297, 354, 359
LARPOOL (3872grt) 352
LASCAR CATARGIU 22
LASHPLESIS (253grt) 121
LAT.5/KURT SANDKAMP 366
LATONA 70, 71, 131, 132, 133, 191, 193, 194, 256, 257, 258, 259, 320, 321, 322, 323
LAUENBURG 29
LAURA COSULICH (5870grt) 124
LAUREL 230
LAURELWOOD (7347grt) 174
LAURETTA (grt) 318
LAVENDER 105, 177, 179, 360, 372
LAVINIA L. 48
LAWRENCE 197, 198
LAYNE 376
LCA.119 99
LCP(L).59 255
LCP(L).71 255
LCT.102 300
LCT.12 192
LCT.13 321
LCT.14 191
LCT.16 67
LCT.17 321
LCT.18 .... 319, 321
LCT.2 319
LCT.20 66
LCT.6 66
LCT.7 .... **319**
LCT.8 133
LE CID 129
LE GLORIEUX 392
LE HÉROS 392
LE LUTTEUR 151, 153, 171
LE PROGRÈS (grt) 324
LE TIGRE 148, 151, 153, 353, 356
LEA (DD-118) 91, 96, 99, 285, 287, 291, 297, 299, 355
LEAMINGTON .. 97, 98, 102, 104, 152, 157, 159, 163, 164, 225, 226, 229, 232, 355, 357, 360
LEANDER 67, 68, 69, 70, 71, 73, 130, 131, 132, 133, 266, 271, 399
LEARY (DD-158) 221, 227, 284, 291, 294, 297, 355, 355, 360, 361
LECONTE DE LISLE (9877grt) 122
LEDA 157, 164, 221, 232, 281, 284, 345
LEGION ... 37, 41, 55, 63, 97, 113, 114, 116, 161, 167, 169, 231, 233, 242, 250, 251, 252, 298, 300, 301, 305, 307, 308, 313, 368, 370, 371, 377
LEHIGH (4983grt) 309
LEICESTER CITY 150
LEIDUS (grt) 182
LEIESTEN (6118grt) 51
LEINSTER (4302grt) 101, 115, 122, 124, 175, 231, 243, 306
LEIPZIG 58, 246, 247, 249
LEITH 41, 97, 163, 164, 178, 241, 294, 300, 362, 369
LEMBIT 59, 179, 182, 249, 311, 373
LENA REHDER (262grt) 118
LENIN 22, 60
LENINGRAD 22, 61, 181, 182, 183, 375, 376
LENINGRADSOVIET (1270grt) 182, 183
LEONARD WOOD (AP-25) 353
LEONTES (338grt) 120, 247
LEOPARD (FFr) 392
LEOPOLDVILLE (11,439grt) 292, 392
LEPARI 198
LESBOS (1009grt) 193, 386
LETHBRIDGE 222, 224, 227, 288, 289, 297, 355, 361
LETTIE (89grt) 364
LEVANTE (4770grt) 147
LEVENWOOD (803grt) 50
LEVIS 156, 164, 224, 226, 228
LI 129
LIBAU (3663grt) 59
LIBECCIO 379, 380
LIBERTAD (5441grt) 161
LIBRA 259, 318
LIDDESDALE 51
LIDVARD (4785grt) 107
Lighter A.10 131
Lighter A.11 131
Lighter A.14 .... 133, 191
Lighter A.8 133
LIGHTNING .. 29, 30, 91, 92, 101, 115, 122, 124, 151, 153, 154, 155, 164, 167, 171, 172, 175, 185, 216, 217, 219, 229, 230, 231, 237, 243, 251, 252, 282, 283, 284, 296, 297, 300, 302, 305, 308, 368, 369, 370, 371, 377
LIISA (782grt) 61
LILAC 197
LILAVATI 198
LILIYA 23
LIMA 363
LINCOLN 32, 37, 40, 97, 156, 158, 163, 166, 216
LINOIS (7473grt) 198
LISMORE 189, 192
LISSA (1511grt) 235
LITTORIO 122, 188, 251
LIVELY .. 148, 152, 154, 155, 167, 172, 231, 233, 242, 243, 250, 251, 305, 313, 317, 378, 379, 381, 382, 383, 387

LIVERMORE (DD-429)	160, 226, 288, 294, 295, 296, 296, 353, 354, 361, 362
LIVORNO (1829grt)	253
LLANDAFF CASTLE (10,786grt)	327
LLANGIBBY CASTLE (11,951grt)	37, 57
LLANSTEPHAN CASTLE (11,299grt)	280, 283, 294
LLANSTEPHAN CASTLE (11,348grt)	148, **153**, 214
LOBELIA	159, 226, 227, 229, 232, 284, 289, 352, 355, 357
LOCH OSKAIG	106, 306
LOCHGARRY (1627grt)	93
LOCOTENENT DIMITRIE CALINESCU	22
LOCOTENENT LEPRI REMUS	22
LOFOTEN (1517grt)	213
LONDON	43, 44, 57, 94, 95, 114, 115, 152, 154, 161, 165, 166, 168, 172, 173, 214, 215, 215, 217, 218, 219, 220, 221, 278, 279, 280, 282, 284, 285, 303
LONDONDERRY	34, 38, 103, 177, 232, 246, 301, 307, 309, 360, 363, 372
LONG ISLAND (AVG-1)	35, 157, 159, 160
LONGSCAR	364
LONGTAKER (1700grt)	158, 216
L'ORAGE	115
LORCA (4875grt)	221, 279, 281, 345
LORD AUSTIN	94
LORD GAINSFORD	103
LORD IRWIN	38, 55
LORD ST VINCENT	108
LORINDA	103, 179
LOTHRINGEN (10,746grt)	46
LOTTE HALM (1198grt)	172
LOWESTOFT	283, 302, 347
LÜBECK (3703grt)	31, 146
LUCIENNE JEANNE	303
LUDLOW (DD-438)	352, 360
LUGA (2329grt)	61
LUIGI DI SAVOIA	188
LUKOMSKI	195, 324
LULWORTH	166, 235, 244, 298, 299, 372
LUNACHARSKI (3618grt)	181
LUNAN (363grt)	100
LUPO	321, 387
LUSSIN (3958grt)	187
LÜTZOW	19, 26, 30, 31, 58
LUVSEE (2373grt)	254
LUZON (PR-7)	395, 396, 397
LV	130
LVI	130
LVII (300grt)	388
LXII	130
LXIV	129
LYDD	284
LYDIARD	131, 318
LYONS MARU	139, 204
LYONS MARU (7017grt)	328
M.10	367
M.1101/FOCH & HUBERT	286
M.1102/H. A. W. MULLER	155, 239
M.153	367
M.1707/LUNEBURG	181, 248
M.1708/ALDEBARAN	311
M.18	113
M.201	60, 119
M.22	343
M.23	119
M.24	368
M.25	113
M.26	368
M.27	113, 368
M.28	368
M.30	113
M.31	73, 120
M.3131/NORDMARK	119
M.32	368
M.3823	241
M.4030	240
M.509	118
M.511	373
M.529	373
M.6	305
M-101	60
M-102	59, 60, 182, 248
M-111	260, 261
M-112	260, 325
M-171	87, 212, 213, 214, 278, 343
M-172	87, 147, 181, 212, 214, 222, 343
M-173	23, 146, 212, 213, 214, 343
M-174	87, 146, 212, 214
M-175	23, 87, 146, 212, 214, 278, 279, 343
M-176	23, 87, 214, 278, 279, 280
M-31	134, 195, 260, 389
M-32	73, 134, 195, 260, 323
M-33	73, 134, 195, 196, 260, 323, 324
M-34	73, 134, 195, 196, 260, 261, 323, 325, 389
M-35	73, 134, 195, 260, 324, 325, 389
M-36	73, 134, 195, 196, 260, 324
M-49	138
M-51	260
M-52	134, 323
M-58	134, 260, 323, 324, **325**, 389
M-59	260, 323, **325**, 389
M-60	260, 323, **325**, 389
M-62	134, 195, 260, 324
M-63	138, 200
M-71	60
M-72	60
M-74	249
M-77	59, 62, 120, 248
M-78	59
M-79	59, 62, 120
M-80	60
M-81	59, 120
M-83	59, 60
M-89	62
M-90	61, 62
M-94	59, 60, 121
M-95	62, 121, 182, 249, 311
M-96	59, 121
M-97	62, 182, 248, 312
M-98	62, 121, 182, 248, 249, 311, 312, 375
M-99	59, 60
MA/SB.2	384
MAASDAM (8810grt)	35
MACBETH	148, 151, 215, 280, 297, 346, 348
MACBETH (545grt)	153
MACERO (3235grt)	245
MACHARDA (7998grt)	152, 163
MACLEISH (DD-220)	218, 223, 223, 285, 287, 291, 297, 299, 355

MACON (5135grt)	46, 106
MADDALENA ODERO (5479grt)	65, 122, 126, 186, 187
MADISON (DD-425)	35, 99, 156, 218, 220, 223, 232, 288, 298, 353, 356
MADJOE (249grt)	357
MAESTRALE	65, 124, 187, 251, 379, 381
MAGGIORE BARACCA	234
MAGNITOGORSK (3566grt)	59
MAHSEER (7911grt)	302
MAIDSTONE	165
MAIKAZE	399, 406
MAINE	256
MAISTER IVAN	23
MAJA	59
MAKSIM GORKI	22, 59, 247, 248, 249
MALACHITE	128, 129, 258
MALASPINA	45, 46, 106, 114, 234, 242
MALAYA	95, 97, 110, 155, 284, 297, 300, 308, 377
MALAYA II (8651grt)	35
Malayan Invasion Force Main Body	406
MALAYAN PRINCE (8593grt)	310
MALCOLM	30, 33, 41, 97, 103, 156, 158, 163, 167, 224, 230, 287, 290, 293
MALLOW	96, 103, 115, 117, 165, 178, 233, 241, 300, 301, 307, 361
MALOCELLO	64, 65, 125, 128, 186, 315, 381
MALOJA	32, 33, 36, 99, 156, 157, 167, 306
MALSEDO (5285grt)	245
MALVERNIAN	41, 53, 56, 104
MAMARI (7924grt)	47
MAMEENMAA	376
MAMIYA	269
MAN O' WAR	37, 40, 100, 156, 158, 162, 166, 227, 230, 233, 297, 371, 372
MANARA	62, 185
MANAZURU	406
MANCHESTER	24, 25, 26, 27, 28, 30, 90, 92, 101, 115, 122, 123, 124, 175, 185, 242
MANCHESTER PORT (5469grt)	161, 321
MANCHESTER PROGRESS (5620grt)	167, 326, 327
MANJU MARU	268, 269
MANJU MARU (6515grt)	201, 202, 204, 401, 405
MANKO MARU (4471grt)	75, 136, 199, 265, 329
Mannerheim, Field Marshal Carl Gustaf	210
MANSFIELD	41, 54, 56, 227, 229, 244, 293
MANXMAN	28, 92, 101, 115, 122, 124, 127, 174, 176, 185, 216, 217, 240, 294, 304, 305, 347, 350, 358, 361
MAORI	24, 37, 40, 42, 55, 101, 115, 122, 124, 127, 175, 183, 303, 346, 348, 359, 363, 370
MAPLIN	30, 32, 33, 38, 39, 41, 102, 104, 114, 117, 161, 165, 241
MARASESTI	22, 72, 389
MARASTI	22, 72, 73
MARAT	22, 183, 247, 248, 249
MARAUDER	29
MARCO POLO (12,272grt)	66, 125, 127, 187
MARCONI (322grt)	238
MARCONI (It)	44, 52, 53, 168, 169, 176, 300, 301
MARCREST (4224grt)	237
MAREEBA (3472grt)	74
MARGARETA (3103grt)	233
MARGHERITA MADRE (296grt)	186
MARGUERITE	56, 117, 245, 298, 309, 371
MARIA	389
MARIA (6339grt)	379
MARIA DI GIOVANNI (255grt)	387
MARIA IMMACOLATA (23grt)	125
MARIA LEONOR (280grt)	106
MARIA POMPEI (1407grt)	317
MARIANN (1991grt)	246
MARIE DAWN (2157grt)	363
MARIENFELS (7575grt)	197
MARIGOLA (5996grt)	250, 313, 314, 377
MARIGOLD	40, 42, 102, 104, 176, 230, 234, 298, 305, 378
MARIJA ULJANOVA (3870grt)	147
MARIN SANUDO (5081grt)	186, 189, 254, 316
MARISTELLA (4862grt)	178
MARITZA (2910grt)	387
MARIUS	129
MARKEN (5719grt)	234
MARKGRAF	180, 210, 215, 216, 223
MARMARI (7924grt)	48
MARNIX VAN ST ALDEGONDE (19,355grt)	137, 264
MARON	164, 242, 243, 299, 306, 369
MARSDALE	43, 52, 54, 55, 56, 57, 114, 369, 370
MARSEILLAISE	129
MARTA (1414grt)	62
MARTI	60, 61, 183, 249, 310, 345, 374
MARTYNOV	73, 134
MAS.451	127
MAS.452	127
MAS.532	127
MAS.533	127
MASON (DD-191)	296
MASSACHUSETTS (BB-59)	228
MASSALIA	129
MATABELE	38, 152, 153, 155, 171, 213, 215, 217, 218, 219, 220, 221, 281, 282, 282, 286, 287, 346, 347, 349, 351
MATAPEDIA	34, 96, 97, 98, 156, 157, 158, 226, 227, 294, 353, 354, 360
MATAROA (12,390grt)	42, 359
MATSUKAZE	406
MAURADER	30
MAURETANIA (35,677grt)	198
MAURITA (199grt)	359
MAURITIUS	57, 74, 135, 327, 393
MAURO CROCE (1049grt)	377
MAURY (DD-401)	409
MAX BERENDT	126, 315, 316
MAXIM GORKI	183
MAYA	406
MAYA (3867grt)	256
MAYFLOWER	35, 38, 102, 156, 164, 224, 226, 228, 232, 287, 288, 289, 297, **355**
MAYO (DD-422)	91, 96, 99, 221, 227, 284, 293, 294, 355, 355, 361
MAYRANT (DD-402)	28, 106, 156, 157, 159, 160, 215, 288, 290, 353, 354
MCCALL (DD-400)	409
MCCORMICK (DD-223)	99, 224, 352, 360
MCDOUGAL (DD-358)	35, 156, 157, 220, 224, 290, 353
MDS.11	118
MDS.6	118
Mediterranean Fleet	18, 19, 67, 70, 71, 83, 131, 132, 133, 134, 142, 176, 189, 192, 193, 194, 196, 241, 255, 259, 262, 275, 315, 318, 319, 320, 326, 339, 383, 385, 386, 387, 391
MEDWAY	128
MEERO (1866grt)	247
MEITEN MARU (4474grt)	138, 202, 270, 331, 334
MELBOURNE STAR (12,806grt)	101, 122, 252, 254, 255, 305
MEMELLAND (542grt)	181
MEMPHIS (CL-13)	161, 228, 291, 357
MENDIP	49, 51, 111, 238, 301
MENDOZA (5193grt)	40, 392

MENDOZA (8199grt)	292
MENES (5609grt)	126
MENESTHEUS	25, 27, 29
MENETHEUS	91, 286, 299, 348, 349, 351, 358
MERCIER (7886grt)	45
MEREDITH (DD-434)	99, 160, 215, 227, 287, 346, 347
MERIDIAN	88
MERIDIAN (5592grt)	159, 354
METEOR	183
METEOR (1685grt)	318
METZ (733grt)	240
MEYNELL	237, 238, 365
MGB.14	367
MGB.312	240, 367
MGB.314	240, 367
MGB.316	240, 367
MGB.317	367
MGB.41	367
MGB.62	172
MGB.63	365
MGB.64	365
MGB.67	240, 365
MGB.86	366
MGB.87	365
MGB.89	366
MGB.90	111
MGB.92	111
MGLA	279
MICHAEL E (7628grt)	24
MICHELE BIANCHI	112
MICHISHIO	399, 406
Middle Atlantic patrol	98, 99, 228
MIDNATSOL (978grt)	213
MIGNONETTE	117, 177, 232, 243, 244, 292, 309, 369
MIHAIL KOGALRICEANU	22
MIKAGE MARU No.3 (3111grt)	327
MIKOYAN	195, 196, 391
MILFORD	177, 309, 359
MILLO	380
MILWAUKEE (CL-5)	161, 228, 291, 356
MIMOSA	97, 98, 99, 104, 158, 159, 216, 225, 228, 231, 288, 289, 295, 354
MINATITLAN (7599grt)	186, 189, 254, 379
MINAZUKI	406
MINDANAO (PR-8)	327
Minefield ALLIRAHU	180
Minefield APOLDA	59, 60, 61, 118
Minefield B	315
Minefield BS.57	47
Minefield BS.58	49
Minefield BS.59	49
Minefield BS.60	50
Minefield BS.63	47
Minefield BS.64	51
Minefield BS.65	50
Minefield BS.66	108
Minefield BS.67	108
Minefield COBURG	61, 180
Minefield CORBETHA	58, 60, 118, 312, 375
Minefield D.10	180
Minefield D.30	180
Minefield D2	60
Minefield EH	216
Minefield EISENACH	58
Minefield ERFURT	58
Minefield F.15	120
Minefield F.16	121
Minefield F.17	180
Minefield F.18	180
Minefield F.19	180
Minefield F.20	180
Minefield F.21	180
Minefield F.22	180
Minefield F.5	120
Minefield F3	61
Minefield F4	61
Minefield F5	61
Minefield F6	62
Minefield FD.33	171, 172
Minefield FD.34	368
Minefield GOTHA	61, 120
Minefield HF	240
Minefield HG	304
Minefield ILYITSCHEWKA	390
Minefield JT	240
Minefield JU	240
Minefield Juminda	180
Minefield JUMINDA	181, 182, 183, 247, 248, 374, 375
Minefield JXA	305
Minefield JXB	305
Minefield KIPINOLA	61
Minefield KULEMAJARVI	62
Minefield M.6	254
Minefield M.6A	254
Minefield MONA I	180
Minefield PINNASS I	180
Minefield PINNASS II	180
Minefield PINNASS III	180
Minefield PINNASS IV	180
Minefield PINNASS V	180
Minefield PINNASS VI	180
Minefield QZX.385	94
Minefield RUSTO	181
Minefield S.2	66
Minefield S.31	124
Minefield S.32	124
Minefield SN.21A	93
Minefield SN.21B	94
Minefield SN.21C	95
Minefield SN.22A	151
Minefield SN.22B	154
Minefield SN.23A	216
Minefield SN.23B	219
Minefield SN.23C	220
Minefield SN.24A	282
Minefield SN.24B	283
Minefield SN.24C	285
Minefield SN.25A	349
Minefield SN.25B	351
Minefield SN.41	186
Minefield SN.42	186
Minefield SN.43	187
Minefield SN.44	188
Minefield SN.61	216
Minefield SN.64	25, 26

Minefield SN.66	27
Minefield SN.67A	91, 92, 101
Minefield SN.69	94
Minefield SN.70A	154
Minefield SN.70B	28, 29
Minefield SN.83A	286, 299
Minefield SN.83B	347, 348, 358
Minefield VALKJARVI	62, 121, 183
Minefield WARTBURG I	58
Minefield WARTBURG II	58
Minefield WARTBURG III	58
Minefield WEIMAR	58
MINEGUMO	406
MINEKAZE	329
Minelaying Command	153
MINERVE (sub)	91, 149, 156, 221, 222, 284, 287, 350, 364, 365
Minesweeper 27/T-413	73
MINNA	365, 376
MINNALAID (grt)	182
MINONA (grt)	279
MINSK	22, 61, 181, 182, 183, 249
MIRANDA (279grt)	72
MISOA	152, 163
MISSISSIPPI (BB-41)	98, 99, 149, 160, 215, 227, 346, 347
MITAKESAN MARU (4141grt)	331
MITAKESAN MARU (4441grt)	267, 269, 270, 331, 400, 406
MITTNATSOL	148
MIZAR (AF-12)	99
MIZAR (AF-120)	149
ML.1023	321
ML.1032	128, 131
ML.1043	152
ML.1045	152
ML.1048	386
ML.1061	321
ML.121	123, 377
ML.122	92, 93
ML.124	92, 93
ML.125	92, 93
ML.126	115, 123
ML.128	92, 93
ML.129	123, 184
ML.130	123, 184, 377
ML.132	377
ML.135	377
ML.144	**240**
ML.150	365, 366
ML.152	365
ML.168	123, 184
ML.169	115, 123
ML.170	115, 176, 377
ML.172	115, 176, 377
ML.173	115, 123
ML.174	115
ML.175	115
ML.176	115, 377
ML.188	216, 218
ML.208	92, 93
ML.209	243
ML.210	92, 93
ML.213	92, 93
ML.218	26
ML.219	360
ML.233	92, 93
ML.242	175, 176
ML.244	243, 306
ML.251	243
ML.256	175, 176
ML.261	175, 176
ML.263	175, 176
ML.265	175, 176
ML.266	175, 176
ML.271	243
ML.272	175, 176
ML.274	175, 176
ML.277	243
ML.279	243
ML.281	243
ML.288	302
ML.289	243
MLR-33/OLONKA	182
MLR-35/SHUYA	182
MLR-58/OSETR	182
MLR-93	182
MMS.39	170
MO-112	182
MO-121	23
MO-123	23
MO-131	87, 182
MO-132	87
MO-133	87, 182
MO-142	182
MO-200	182
MO-202	**182**
MO-204	182
MO-207	182, 182
MO-212	182
MO-213	182
MO-218	59
MO-238	61
MO-301	375
MO-310	311
MO-405	376
MO-406	376
MO-501	182
MO-502	182
MO-510	182
MOA	357
MOCENIGO	44
MOCHIZUKI	408
MODOC (CGC-39)	31
MOEWE	367
MOFFETT (DD-362)	156, 220, 224, 290, 353
MOGAMIGAWA MARU	406
MOGAMIGAWA MARU (7497grt)	204
MOJI MARU	329
MOKAMBO (4996grt)	37
MOLOTOV	22, 325, 390
MOMP	284, 285, 286, 289, 290, 293, 294, 297, 298, 355, 356, 357, 359, 362
MONARCH OF BERMUDA (22,424grt)	42, 288, 359
MONARDA	364
MONDOC (1926grt)	291
MONGINEVRO (5324grt)	381, 382
MONKSHOOD	158, 167, 224, 287, 288, 290, 293, 298, 355, **360**

MONOWAI	330
MONROSA (6703grt)	323
MONSELET (3372grt)	250
MONSSEN (DD-436)	160, 215, 227, 346, 347
MONSUN (6590grt)	181
MONTANA (1549grt)	225
MONTANARI	125
MONTBRETIA	289, 297, 354, 355, 371
MONTCLARE	98, 163
MONTE PIANA (5890grt)	74
MONTE SANTO (5850grt)	178
MONTECUCOLI	122, 127, 188, 315, 383
MONTELLO (6117grt)	64
MONTENOL (2646grt)	101
MONTEPONI (747grt)	127
MONTEVIDEO (5785grt)	245
MONTFERLAND (6790grt)	50
MONTGOMERY	222, 226, 227, 232, 355
MONTICELLO (AP-61)	178
MONTROSE	285, 303, 347, 348, 351, 353, 358, 364
MONZAMBANO	318, 321, 384
MOOIVLEI	372
MOOLTAN (20,952grt)	37, 167, 244, 326, 327
MOORWOOD (2056grt)	48
MOOSE JAW	158, 159, 223, 224, 225, 297, 359
MORDEN	355
MORETON BAY	42, 47, 117
MOROSINI	45, 105, 106, 114, 234, 242
MORRIS (DD-417)	215, 223, 223, 290, 354
MORRIS DANCE	41, 114, 245
MORSE	130
MOSCARDIN (4492grt)	229
MOSEL	247, 310
MOSEL (8428grt)	137
MOSEL (9492grt)	268
MOSELLA (6023grt)	295
MOSKVA	22, 73, 182
MOSKVA (6086grt)	323
MOSSOVET (2981grt)	214, 280, 349
MOSSOVET (grt)	23
MOTIA (2473grt)	65
MOUNT VERNON (AP-22)	353, 354
MOY	131
MRS.3	343
MS-52/BUYOK	182
MS-56/BAROMETR	182
MS-57/IMANTA	182
MS-71/KRAB	182
MS-72/DHZERZHINSKI	182
MS-91/LYAPIDEVSKI	182
MTB.104	133
MTB.215	66, 67, 128, 255, 320, 323, 386
MTB.218	367
MTB.219	367
MTB.221	367
MTB.44	367
MTB.45	367
MTB.47	367
MTB.48	367
MTB.54	240
MTB.56	220, 239, 281, 282, 286, 367
MTB.68	66, 128, 129, 255, 320, 323, 386

MUGFORD (DD-389)	409
MUNARGO (AP-20)	96
MUNCHEN	19, 24
MUNERIC (5229grt)	224
MUNIN (1285grt)	147, 153
MUNSTERLAND (6408grt)	271
MURAKUMO	404
MURASAME	406
MUREFTE (691grt)	257
MURENA (8252grt)	156
MURIELLE (96grt)	233
MUSASHI	331, 398
MUSTIN (DD-413)	36, 98, 215, 222, 223, 290, 354
MUTSU	202, 204, 269, 270, 400, 403, 405, 406
MUTSUKI	408
MYOKO MARU (5086grt)	75, 136, 137, 264
MYOSOTIS	42, 55, 116, 162, 167, 242, 289, 295, 358, 361, 369
MYRMIDON (6278grt)	38
NACHISAN MARU (4433grt)	77, 136, 137, 199, 265, 268
NACHISAN MARU (4441grt)	327
NADIA (247grt)	65
NAGARA	268, 406
NAGATO	202, 332, 400, 401, 403, 404
NAGATSUKI	406
NAGOYA MARU	398, 400
NAGOYA MARU (6072grt)	138
NAIAD	69, 70, 71, 72, 128, 129, 131, 132, 190, 193, 194, 256, 257, 258, 326, 383, 386, 387, 388, 389
NAILSEA MANOR (4926grt)	300
NAIRANA (225grt)	216
NALUCA	22, 72, 134, 323
NANAIMO	98, 288, 289, 297, 355
NANDI (1999grt)	147, 153
NANIWA MARU (4857grt)	333, 400
NANKAI MARU (5114grt)	398, 399, 404
NAPANEE	33, 96, 97, 98, 156, 157, 159, 224, 227, 294, 354, 360
NAPIER	130, 191, 193, 194, 256, 257, 258, 259, 321, 322, 323, 326, 384, 385, 386, 387, 388
NAPIR	259
NAPOLI (6142grt)	381, 382
NARCISSUS	157, 158, 159, 165, 227, 229, 232, 284, 289, 294, 352, 355, 357, 361
NARKUNDA (16,632grt)	152, 163, 292, 359
NARUTO MARU (7149grt)	331
NARVALO	251, 313, 377
NARVIK (4281grt)	239
NARWHAL (SS-168)	335
NARYU	400
NASHVILLE (CL-43)	36, 91, 96, 98, 160
NASTURTIUM	29, 33, 38, 40, 97, 98, 99, 104, 352, 359
NATAL (3172grt)	113
NATORI	268
NATSUGUMO	406
NATSUSHIO	406
NEA HELLAS (16,991grt)	40, 53, 161, 263, 319
NELSON	24, 25, 26, 27, 38, 43, 92, 101, 122, 124, 184, 185, 236, 250, 251, 252, 305, 350, 361, 365, 368, 370
NEPANCE	353
NEPTUN	182
NEPTUNE	24, 37, 43, 53, 54, 57, 132, 133, 135, 190, 191, 193, 194, 256, 257, 258, 259, 322, 323, 383, 385, 386, 387, 388
NEPTUNIA (19,475grt)	125, 127, 187, 188, 189, 254, 254
NEPTUNIA (798grt)	66

NEPTUNUS (395grt) 189
NEREIDE 131
NEREO (214grt) 316
NEREUS (Gk) 65, 130, 189
NESS POINT **171**
NESTOR 26, 27, 29, 30, 91, 101, 104, 115, 122, 123, 124, 127, 175, 176, 184, 241, 243, 244
NETTUNO 125
NEUENFELDE (193grt) 118
neutrality patrol 159, 160
NEVADA (BB-36) 409
NEVASA (9213grt) 197
NEW MEXICO (BB-40) ... 99, 152, 155, 159, 160, 215, 220, 223, 288, 290, 291, 354
NEW WESTMINSTER CITY (4747grt) 148, 153, 214, 280
NEW YORK (BB-34) 91, 96, 227
NEWARK................152, 153, 154, 216, 219, 285, 290, 292, 348, 349, 358
NEWBURY (5102grt) 231
NEWCASTLE 117, 178, 356
NEYROU 198
NEZAMOZHNIK 22, 195, 260, 261, 323, 324, 325, 389, 390
NIAGARA 32, 41, 155, 156, 157, 158, 166, 228
NIBLACK (DD-424) 91, 96, 99, 223, 223, 232, 289, 299, 347, 358, 359
NICETO DE LARRINAGA (5591grt) 235
NICHIEI MARU 405
NICHIEI MARU (10,020grt) 335, 401
NICHII MARU (6543grt) 402, 403
NICHOLSON (DD-442) 355, 355, 360, 361
NICITA 133
NICOLAOS PIANGOS (4499grt) 303
NICOLAS PATERAS (4362grt) 34
NICOLO ODERO (6003grt) 65, 126, 186, 189, 253
NIEUW AMSTERDAM (36,287grt) 73, 197, 392
NIEUW HOLLAND (11,066grt) 327
NIEUW ZEELAND (11,069grt) 245, 246, 327
NIGARISTAN (5993grt) 220, 225
NIGEL 392
NIGELLA 32, 33, 39, 42, 96, 97, 98, 101, 104, 157, 158, 164, 228, 294, 309, 358, 372
NIGER 30, 33, 41, 94, 96, 148, 149, 170
NIGERIA....23, 24, 25, 26, 27, 28, 29, 47, 90, 91, 92, 94, 95, 96, 146, 147, 150, 152, 153, 212, 213, 216, 217, 237, 238
NIGERSTROOM (4639grt) 161, 245, 263
NIGHTINGALE (7248grt) 290
NIKKAI MARU 335, 402
NIKOLKIS (3575grt) 45
NIKOLKIS (3576grt) 106
NILE 194
NINETTO G. (5335grt) 380
NINFEA (607grt) 124
NINGPO (6079grt) 75
NIPIGON 354, **355**, 356
NIPPON MARU 269, 403, 405
NIPPON MARU (9975grt) 201, 268
NIRVA (5164grt) 127, 128
NIRVO (5164grt) 64, 186, 253, 315
NISHMAHA (6076grt) 373, 373
NITA (6813grt) 127, 128, 186
NITTA MARU 332
NIZAM 70, 71, 129, 130, 131, 132, 189, 190, 191, 192, 193, 196, 256, 257, 258, 319, 320, 321, 322, 323, 384, 385, 386, 387, 388, 389
NK.08/CANONIER 96
No.80 ....**181**

NOGI 50
NOJIMA MARU (7190grt) 139, 269
NOLI 64, 66
NORBURG (2392grt) 385, 387
NORDERNEY (3667grt) 178
NORE Command 27, 50, 351
NOREG (7605grt) 241, 242
NORFOLD (6370grt) 326
NORFOLK 30, 37, 51, 56, 218, 220, 238, 283, 284, 345, 349, 350, 351
NORFOLK (10,948grt) 40
NORITA (1516grt) 107
NORLINDO (2686grt) 161
NORMAN 240, 279, 280, 281, 281, 282, 286, 347, 350, **361**
NORSE 41, 114
NORTELOIDE (4173grt) 245
North Channel 163, 166, 167
NORTH DEVON (3658grt) 108
North East Greenland Patrol 96
NORTH KING (4934grt) 221, 279, 281, 345
NORTH STAR (WPG-59) 96, 218
NORTHAMPTON (CA-26) 201, 409
Northern Barrage 91, 93, 94, 95, 151, 154
NORTHERN CHIEF 155
NORTHERN DAWN 37, 40, 100, 103, 156, 162, 227, **230**, 233
NORTHERN DUKE 29, 30
NORTHERN FOAM 29, 91
NORTHERN GEM........31, 33, 41, 96, 156, 158, 167, 224, 230, 290, 293, 298
Northern Patrol 25, 27, 215
NORTHERN PRIDE....31, 33, 41, 103, 156, 158, 163, 167, 224, 230, 287, 293, 355, 360
NORTHERN PRINCESS 91
NORTHERN REWARD 28
NORTHERN SKY 28, 91, 93
NORTHERN SPRAY....41, 96, 97, 103, 163, 167, 224, 230, 290, 298, 355, 360
NORTHERN WAVE 30, 33, 41, 97, 103, 156, 158, 163, 167, 287, 293
NORTHLAND (WPG-49) 96, 218
NORTHUMBERLAND (11,558grt) 167, 244, 245
NORVINN (6322grt) 55, 116, 174
NORWICH CITY 102, 156, 157, 162, 227, 232, 284, 352, 357
NOTORO 330, 400
NOTTINGHAM (8532grt) 353
NOTTS COUNTY 42, 98, 104, 157, 164, 224, 231, 289, 293, **355**
NOVA SCOTIA (6796grt) 392
NOWAKI 399, 406
NT.05/TOGO 213, 214
NUBIA **302**
NUBIAN 68, 69
NUOVO SANT'ANTONIO (grt) 382
NÜRNBERG 247
O.10 (SS-171) 36
O.14 ....37, 150, 156, 221, 284
O.21 ....38, 53, 55, 65, 113, 114, 122, 127, 184, 185, 249, 251, 252, 253, 255, **312**, 377, 378, 380, 381, 382, 383
O.23 ....63, 64, 65, 122, 130, 184, 187, 239, 241
O.24 .....62, 63, 65, 100, 114, 124, 130, 184, 185, 186, 250, **312**, 313, 315, 378
O.6 (SS-167) 36
O.9 (SS-170) 36
O'BRIEN (DD-415) 98, 99, 160, 290
OAHU (PR-6) 395, 396, 397
OBERON (1996grt) 46
OBORO 405
O'BRIEN (DD-415) 215, 222, 223, 354
OBSHITELNY **195**

OBUCHENNY	195
OCEAN VICTOR (202grt)	150
OCEANIA (19,507grt)	66, 125, 126, 127, 187, 188, 189, 254, 254
ODENWALD (5098grt)	203, 357, 372
OERSEO	253
OFFA	221, 233, 282, 283, 286, 299, 344, 345, 346, 347, 349
OGADEN (2703grt)	125
OGNEVOI	195
OGURA MARU No.2 (7250grt)	405
OITE	408
OKA	183
OKINOSHIMA	204, 335, 408
OKITSU MARU (6666grt)	334
OKLAHOMA (BB-37)	336, 409
OKTYABR	181, 376
OKTYABRSKAYA REVOLUTSIYA	22, 183, 247, 249, 249
OLE JACOB (8306grt)	113, 174, 331, 332
OLEN (4924grt)	225
OLIGARCH (6897grt)	90, 94, 95, 146, 147, 150, 152, 153, 212, 216, 218
OLWEN (6394grt)	356, 362
OLYMPUS	40, 54, 122, 124, 126, 314, 377, 378, 383
OMAHA (CL-4)	161, 228, 291, 292, 357, 357, 372
OMFLEET (130grt)	110
ONDINA	70
ONDO	401
ONEGA	182
ONICE	377
ONOE MARU (6667grt)	201, 202, 203, 267, 331, 333
ONSLOW	282, 286, 294, 344, 345, 347, 348, 349, 358
ONWARD (209grt)	95
OP-8	261
Operation APPROACH	341, 385, 386
Operation AR	342, 344
Operation ASTROLOGER	341, 377, 378
Operation BARBAROSSA	20
Operation BAREFOOT	277, 281, 286
Operation BATTLEAXE	19, 20
Operation BELLRINGER	341, 392
Operation BENEDICT	145, 153
Operation BEOWULF I	210, 211, 246, 248
Operation BISHOP	145, 197
Operation CALLBOY	278, 313, 316, 317
Operation CHESS	87, 112
Operation CHIEFTAIN	341, 378, 381, 386
Operation CHOPPER	211, 240
Operation CHRONOMETER	19, 73
Operation COUNTENANCE	145, 197
Operation CRACKLER	145, 198
Operation CRUSADER	339, 341, 378, **386**, 387
Operation CULTIVATE	277, 320, 321, 321, 322
Operation CUTTING	145, 177
Operation DEMON	145, 198
Operation DN	85, 91, 96
Operation EAST PRUSSIA	277, 311
Operation EC	21, 23, 29, 30
Operation EF	86, 87, 88, 89, 94, 95, 144, 149, 150, 162
Operation EGV.1	145, 154, 210, 212, 218, 221
Operation EGV.2	145, 154, 217, 218, 221
Operation EJ	211, 220, 277, 282, 283, 286, 287
Operation EVG.2	210, 212
Operation EXPORTER	19, 67
Operation FB	87, 90, 95, 150
Operation GAUNTLET	145, **147**, 148, 153
Operation GI	343, 408
Operation GIDEON	86, 111
Operation GLENCOE	341, 383, 384, 385
Operation GOEBEN	211, 243
Operation GUILLOTINE	86, 131, 132, 133, 144, 189, 190, 191, 192, **193**, **194**
Operation HALBERD	211, 231, 243, 250, 251, 252, 255, 259, 314
Operation HERCULES	20
Operation ILIAD	145, 173
Operation INDIGO III	210, 222
Operation LANDMARK	342, 381, 387
Operation MARMALADE	145, 198
Operation MERCURY	19
Operation MINCEMEAT	145, 184, 185
Operation MOPUP	145, 198
Operation PERPETUAL	341, 377
Operation PROPELLER	211, 250
Operation RAILWAY	21, 63
Operation RAILWAY 2	21, 63
Operation RAPIER	145, 197
Operation RATION	144, 198
Operation RHEINBUNG	19, 24
Operation ROCKET	19, 62
Operation ROMULUS	211, 271
Operation SALVAGE	20, 46
Operation SEELOWE	247
Operation SIEGFRIED	277, 278
Operation SILVER FOX	21
Operation STATUS	210, 211, 250
Operation STRENGTH	145, 155, 210, 212, 213, 342, 344, 345
Operation STYLE	87, 102, 124, 144, 183, 184, 185
Operation SUBSTANCE	85, 86, 101, 115, 122, 123, 124, 126, 127, 132, 208, 242
Operation SUNSTAR	342, 367
Operation SUPERCHARGE	211, 257, 258, 259
Operation TAIFUN	277
Operation TRACER	20, 62
Operation TREACLE	144, 192, 193, 194
Operation VIGOROUS	21, 55, 114
Operation WESTFALEN	277, 311
Operation Z	341, 402, 403, 404, 407
OPHELIA	26, 27, 148, 153, 215, 279, 280, 283, 284
OPHIR II (213grt)	237
OPYTNY	183
ORBITA (15,495grt)	37
ORCADES (23,456grt)	161, 263, 290, 354
ORCHIS	32, 39, 97, 102, 156, 162, 358, 372
ORDUNA (15,507grt)	359
ORDZHONIKIDZE	195
ORIANI	125, 127, 186, 187, 188, 189, 253, 254, 379, 381
ORIBI	93, 149, 152, **153**, 166, 231, 243, 251, 252, 282, 283, 286, 294, 299, 305, 346, 347
ORIENT CITY (5095grt)	284, 345
ORILLIA	33, 34, 42, 98, 159, 162, 163, 223, 224, 227, 228, 230, 294, 352, 353, 355
ORIOLE (489grt)	233
ORION	69, 70
ORION (23,371grt)	97, 164, 197, 244, 327
ORIONE	128
ORIZABA (AP-24)	91, 353, 354
ORMONDALE (4645grt)	36
ORMONDE (14,982grt)	152, 163, 292, 392
ORONSAY (20,043grt)	42, 290, 354

ORONTES (20,097grt) 167, 244, 246, 327
ORSA 64, 65, 125, 186, 188, 189, 253
ORSOLINA (344grt) 313
OSHIO 399
OSIRIS 55, 63, 65, 66, 124, 125, 186, 253, 257, 258, 381
OSLEBSHAUSEN (4989grt) 221
OSORIO 44
OSTPREUSSEN (3030grt) 147
OSTROVSKI 72
OTAIO (10,298grt) 167
OTCHAYANNY 195
OTMENNY 195
OTOWASAN MARU 140
OTRA 213, 214
OTRANTO (20,032grt) 167, 244, 326, 327
OTTAR JARL (1459grt) 213
OTTAWA 33, 37, 99, 100, 227, 288, 294, 353, 356
OTTINGE (2870grt) 378
OTTUL 22
OTUS 65, 122, 126, 187, 190, 191, 252, 257, 379, 388
OUED GROU (792grt) 108
OUED YQUEM (1369grt) 312
OUZEL 364
OVERTON (DD-239) 223, 223, 226, 289, 298
OYASHIO 406
OZORNOI 195
P.31 .... 91, 306, 313, 316
P.32 .... 52, 53, 65, 122, 133, 187
P.33 .... 40, 52, 55, 63, 65, 124, 125, 126, 186, 187, 188
P.34 .... 231, 241, 243, 312, 315, 316
P.35 .... 286, 287, 303, 346, 352
P.36 .... 305, 368
P.38 .... 360, 368
P.L.M. 22 (5646grt) 46
P-1 248
P-2 249
PACIFIC (6034grt) 308
PADENNA (1589grt) 317
PAGAO (6101grt) 54
PALANG 198
PALATIA (3979grt) 59
PALLADE 64, 126, 252
PALMA (2715grt) 164, 244
PALMA (5419grt) 103
PALMAIOLO 127
PALOMARES 93, 152, 166, 176
PAMPAS (5415grt) 42
PAMPERO (1153grt) 99
PANAJOTIS KRAMOTTOS (120grt) 259
PANDIAS (4981grt) 45
PANDORA 45, 65
PANGIOTIS (120grt) 322
PANORAMA 103
PANTHER (Gk) 72, 256
PANUCO (6212grt) 125
PAOLINA (4994grt) 316
PAOLO Z. PODESTA (863grt) 315
PAPANICOLIS 65, 130, 256
PARA (3986grt) 43
PARIZHSKAYA KOMMUNA 22, 325, 390, 391
PARRAMATTA 67, 69, 70, 71, 131, 132, 133, 189, 190, 191, 192, 194, 256, 326, **386**, 387, 388

PARTENOPE 128, 186, 188, 315, 381
PARTHIAN 65, 67, 68, 70, 71, 130, 132, 173, 176, 184
PASS OF BALMAHA (758grt) 66, 67, 70, 71, 259, 320
PASTEUR (29,253grt) 33, 101, 115, 175
PATRAI (1977grt) 130
PATRICIA McQUEEN 32
PATRICK HENRY (7191grt) 228
PATTERSON (DD-392) 409
PAULA (1549grt) 225
PAULA FAULBAUM (1922grt) 311
PAULINE FRIEDRICH (4645grt) 36
PB-1/SHIMAKAZE 404
PB-2 .... 203, 404
PB-32 .... 404, 408
PB-33 .... 404, 408
PB-34 .... 138, 404
PB-35 .... 404, 405, 406
PB-36 404
PB-37 404
PB-38 404
PB-39 404
PC-457 161
PEARY (DD-225) 329
PEET (2111grt) 374
PEGASO 64, 65, 125, 128, 186, 187, 187, 188, 189, 253, 314, 318, 379, 381, 383, 387
PEGASUS 32, 40, 56, 100, 109
PEGASUS (3597grt) 130
PEGASUS (5762grt) 231
PELES (5708grt) 196
PELORUM (5314grt) 178
PENDRECHT (10,746grt) 45
PENELOPE .. 171, 216, 218, 219, 220, 229, 230, 282, 282, 283, 286, 307, 313, 317, 378, 379, 381, 382, 383, 387
PENSTEMON 103, 230, 361
PENTSTEMON 230, 234, 298, 305
PEONY 70, 129, 132, 133, 192, 257, 258, 318, 319, 320, 322
PERIWINKLE 37, 40, 42, 102, 116, 167, 233, 234, 236, 242, 289, 295, 353, 358, 361
PERLA (5741grt) 254
PERNAU (3580grt) 59
PERSEO 187, 253, 381, 382
PERSEUS 65, 130, 132, 256, 314, 315, 381
PERSEUS (10,286grt) 292, 391, 392
PERTH 71, 128, 129, 130, 131, 132, 135, 166
PERTHSHIRE (10,496grt) 292, 392
PERU (6961grt) 371
PESSAGNO 66, 124, 186, 187, 188, 189, 251, 254, 254, 316, 317, 382
PETER (252grt) 304
PETER (643grt) 310
PETER HENDRIKS 109
PETER WESSELS (135grt) 239
PETEREL 54
PETEREL (1354grt) 165, 236
PETITE ANNICK 370
PETROPAVLOVSK 183, 248
PETROVSKI (3771grt) 351
PETUNIA 31, 105, 114, 158, 167, 224, 230, 293
PG-51 402
PHEMIUS (7406grt) 161, 245, 263
PHIDIAS (5623grt) 44
PHILADELPHIA (CL-41) 36, 98, 99, 290, 291, 354
PHILANTE 35, 38, 96, 162, 178, 241

PHOEBE	67, 68, 69, 71, 129, 130, 131, 132, 193, 194
PHYLLISIA	103
PICKHUBEN (238grt)	111
PICOTEE	33, 97, 102, 151, 162
PICTOU	31, 32, 41, 97, 104, 158, 226, 228, 288, 294, 295, 352, 359
PIET HEIN	76, 395
PIETA	247
PIETRO CAMPANELLA (6140grt)	160
PIETRO QUERINI (1004grt)	65
PIGAFETTA	64, 66, 124, 186, 187, 188, 315, 380, 381
PIGEON (ASR-6)	395, 397
PILAR DE LARRINAGA (7046grt)	102
PILLSBURY (DD-227)	329
PILOT (grt)	26
PIMPERNEL	39, 41, 56, 100, 101, 102, 175
PINK STAR (4150grt)	226
PINTAIL	48
PINZON (1365grt)	114
PIORUN	37, 42, 97, 113, 116, 161, 164, 167, 229, 231, 243, 251, 252, 306
PK-233 (grt)	182
PLAUDIT (5060grt)	160
PLEIADI	316
PLOVER	47, 49, 50, 108
PLUNKETT (DD-431)	91, 96, 99, 226, 288, 294, 295, 296, 353, 361, 362
PLUTO (1156grt)	378
PLUTO (3496grt)	30
POL IX	140
POLINNIA (1292grt)	66
POLLUCE	64, 253, 316
POLLUX (518grt)	373
POLYANTHUS	32, 33, 39, 41, 97, 103, 158, 228, 290, 356, 357
PONTFIELD (8290grt)	238
PORPOISE	293, 306, 313, 316, 379, 380
PORT ARTHUR	351
PORT CHALMERS (8535grt)	101, 122, 252, 254, 255, 305
PORT JACKSON (9687grt)	164, 244
PORT QUEBEC	91, 95, 151, 154, 216, 219, 282, 283, 285, 286, 299, 348, 358
PORT WYNDHAM (8580grt)	37
PORTLAND	136
PORTLAND (7132grt)	305
PORTSDOWN (342grt)	232
POSEIDONE (6613grt)	255
POTARO (5410grt)	163
POTOMAC (AG-25)	157, 159
POZARICA	92, 93, 148, 151, 152, 153, 163
POZARICA (7599grt)	64, 186, 188, 189, 253
PRESCOTT	158, 221, 222, 228, 288, 289, 297, 355
PRESIDENT DE VOGUE (9320grt)	370
PRESIDENT GRANT (14,119grt)	409
PRESIDENT HARRISON (10,509grt)	396
PRESIDENT III	287
PRESIDENT MADISON (14,187grt)	396, 397
PRESTATYN ROSE (1151grt)	238
PRESTINARI	380, 381
PRESTON NORTH END	351
PRETORIA CASTLE	37, 178
PREUSSEN	58, 118
PREUSSEN (8230grt)	65, 126
PRIARUGGIA (1196grt)	383
PRILIV	88
PRIMROSE	33, 38, 98, 100, 162, 163, 290, 356, 357
PRIMULA	262
PRINCE BAUDOUIN (3050grt)	292
PRINCE CHARLES	152, 163
PRINCE DAVID	34, 36, 158, 160, 169
PRINCE LEOPOLD	240, 367
PRINCE OF WALES	28, 93, 110, 149, 151, 152, 153, 154, 156, 157, 217, 218, 231, 243, 251, 252, 282, 285, 298, 301, 305, 307, 371, 372, 393
PRINCE PHILIPPE	102
PRINCE RUPERT CITY (4749grt)	24
PRINCESS BEATRIX (4135grt)	231, 371
PRINCIPESSA MARIA (8918grt)	178
PRINZ EUGEN	52, 112, 113, 174
PROBITAS (5084grt)	316
PROCIDA	62
PROCIDA (1843grt)	387
PROCIONE	64, 65, 125, 128, 187, 188, 253, 378, 383
PROCRIS (1033grt)	106
PROSERPINA (4869grt)	315
PROSPER BIHEN (24grt)	366
PROSPERO (971grt)	255
PROTEA	262, 320
PROTECTOR	68, 70, 190, 191
PROTEUS	229, 242, 250, 318, 384, 385, 388, 389
PROTEUS (10,653grt)	357
PS-70 (558grt)	146
PUCKERIDGE	150, 153, 155, 217, 218, 240
PUERTO RICO (6076grt)	198
PULASKI (6345grt)	42, 327
PUNJABI	24, 25, 26, 27, 37, 38, 90, 91, 94, 95, 96, 146, 150, 151, 152, 153, 155, 171, 213, 215, 217, 218, 219, 220, 221, 282, 282, 283, 284, 286, 346, 347, 349, 350, 363, 366
PYTCHLEY	50, 349, 364
PYTHON	372
QUANTOCK	48
QUEEN CITY (4814grt)	284, 345
QUEEN ELIZABETH	71, 131, 132, 190, 255, 257, 259, 319, 320, 386, 387, 388
QUEEN ELIZABETH (83,673grt)	79, 264, 393
QUEEN EMMA	152, 163, 231, 371
QUEEN MARY (81,235grt)	79, 264, 393
QUEEN OF BERMUDA	42, 178
QUEENSBURY (3911grt)	48
QUENTIN ROOSEVELT (grt)	30
QUINCY (CA-39)	36, 98, 99, 149, 152, 155, 220, 288, 353, 354
QUORN	111, 148, 149, 171, 302, 365
R.11	120
R.153	148
R.158	214
R.165	304
R.166	304
R.169	119
R.202	60
R.203	60
R.205	60, **311**
R.33	304
R.35	304
R.36	304
R.38	304
R.53	60, 119
R.55	249
R.57	249
R.58	247
R.60	248

R.61 248
R.62 248
R.63 ....60, 119
R-101/RYBINCI 180
RABAUL (6809grt) 52
RABY CASTLE (4996grt) 68
RACCOON 31, 32, 33
RAF Launch.20 197
RAJULA (8478grt) 197
RAKUTO MARU (2962grt) 398, 401, 404
RALPH TALBOT (DD-390) 409
RAMILLIES 30, 31, 33, 152, 350, 360
RAMSEY 32, 37, 41, 97, 158, 227, 228
RANDA (1558grt) 225
RANELLA (5590grt) 45
RANGER (CV-4) 35, 353, 354
RANGITATA (16,737grt) 42
RANGITIKI (16,698grt) 161, 263, 327
RANOY (286grt) 213
RANPURA 32, 41, 97, 104, 158, 226, 306
RAPIDOL (2648grt) 244
RARITAN (CGC-72) 31
RASK (632grt) 296
RASMA (3204grt) 119, 120
RAU IV (354grt) 343
RAYON D'OR 31, 33
RAZVECHIK 182
READING 42, 96, 102, 156, 157, 222, 228
RECCA (5441grt) 161
RECEPTIVE 108
Red Sea Escort Force 257
REDWING (ARS-4) 356
REFAH (3805grt) 70
REGELE CAROL I 72, 323, 324
REGELE FERDINAND 22, 72
REGENSBURG (8068grt) 52
REGENT 62, 65, 128, 130, 132, 192, 314, 318, 379, 380, 383
REGGIO 186, 187, 188
REGIN (1386grt) 224
REGINA MARIA 22, 72, 73, 323
REGULUS (AK-14) 204
REICHENFELS (7744grt) 314, 315
REINA DEL PACIFICO (17,702grt) 161, 245, 288, 290, 354
REINDEER 32, 33, 34
REMAGIO (174grt) 45
RENONCULE 229, 290, 298, 360
RENOWN 53, 54, 55, 62, 63, 122, 124, 151, 163, 171, 175, 184, 298, 346, 350, **365**
REPULSE 32, 33, 42, 91, 93, 100, 110, 152, 155, 167, 171, 241, 244, 245, 298, 327, 392, 393
RESMILO 49
RESOLUTION 351, 367
RESTIGOUCHE 32, 37, 97, 149, 156, 157, 288, 289, 355, 357
RESURRECTIO (979grt) 382
REUBEN JAMES (DD-245) 99, 223, 223, 226, 232, 275, 278, 289, 299
REVENGE 32, 33, 39, 40, 169, 244, 392
REVOLUTSIONER (2900grt) 345
RHEA (1388grt) 378
RHIND (DD-404) 28, 106, 156, 157, 159, 160, 215, 288, 290, 353, 354
RHINELAND (1381grt) 235
RHODODENDRON 41, 56, 100, 102, 107, 175, 230, 298, 305, 378
RIALTO (6099grt) 64, 66, 125, 128, 186, 252, 314, 315
RICHARD BEITZEN 31, 87, 88, 146, 147

RICHARD WITH (905grt) 212, 213
RICHMOND 32, 37, 41, 97, 103, 158, 220, 222, 223, 227, 231, 288, 295
RICHMOND CASTLE (7798grt) 117
RIILAHTI 61, 62, 180, 247, 375
RILA 23
RIMAGE (1856grt) 59
RIMOUSKI 31, 32, 41, 97, 103, 157, 228, 230
RIMUTAKA (16,576grt) 204, 359
RINA CORRADO (5180grt) 379
RIO ATUELE (4862grt) 178
RIO AZUL (4088grt) 47
RIO BERMEJO (5245grt) 178
RIO CHICO (5314grt) 178
RIO CHUBUT (4900grt) 178
RIO COLORADO (5850grt) 178
RIO CORRIENTES (4966grt) 178
RIO DE LA PLATA (8918grt) 179
RIO DIAMANTE (5159grt) 178
RIO DULCE (4699grt) 178
RIO GRANDE (6062grt) 241, 293, 305, 368
RIO GUALEGUAY (4595grt) 178
RIO NEUQUEN (5696grt) 178
RIO PRIMERO (4363grt) 178
RIO SALADO (8081grt) 178
RIO SEGUNDO (4901grt) 178
RIO TERCERO (4864grt) 178
RIO TEUCO (5597grt) 178
RIPLEY 33, 40, 97, 99, 149, 156, 157, 158, 163, 237
RIV (6630grt) 189
RIVER AFTON (5479grt) 221, 279, 281, 345
RIVER LUGAR (5423grt) 46
RIVER TRENT (246grt) 109
RO-33 ....400, 402
RO-34 ....400, 402
ROBERT HUGHES (2879grt) 56
ROBERT L. HOLT (2918grt) 105
ROBERT MAX (172grt) 168
ROBIN MOOR (4999grt) 20, 44
ROCHESTER 165, 233, 241, 300, 307, 308, 362
ROCKINGHAM 230, 252, 289, 305, 306, 353, 358, 359, 362, 372
RODI (3220grt) 194
RODINA (4159grt) 261
RODINA (4441grt) 214, 280, 349
RODNEY 24, 25, 36, 38, 160, 228, 243, 251, 305, 313, 348, 358, 369
ROE (DD-418) 99, 159, 160, 169, 289, 298, 355
ROHNA (8602grt) 197
ROLAND 181
ROLFSBORG (1831grt) 26
ROLLICKER 123, 308
Romanian Danube Flotilla 324, 325
Romanian Navy 72, 82, 83, 142
RONALDSAY 284
RONIS 60
Roosevelt, President Franklin D 20, 86, 144, 156, 157, 159, 210, 277, 278, 338, 341, 342
RORQUAL..65, 67, 71, 125, 130, 131, 186, 193, 194, 308, 313, 314, 315, 316, 318, 319, 321, 368
ROSA (246grt) 315
ROSALIE MOLLER (3963grt) 326
ROSE 361
ROSELYS 290, 298, 355, 360
ROSEMARY 229
ROSLEA (642grt) 304

Index

ROSME ... 108
ROSS ... 284, 365
ROSS (4978grt) ... 262
ROSTHERN ... 156, 288
ROSTOVTSEV ... 72, 73, 134
ROTTVER (grt) ... 88
ROVER ... 65
ROWALLAN CASTLE (7798grt) ... 231, 251, 255
ROWAN (DD-405) ... 36, 98, 160, 215, 288, 290, 353, 354
ROWAN TREE ... 365
ROXBOROUGH ... 33, 38, 97, 102, 162, 226, 227, 232, 284, 289, 352, 357
ROY (1768grt) ... 302
ROYAL FUSILIER (2187grt) ... 48
ROYAL SCOT (1444grt) ... 48
ROYAL SCOTSMAN (3244grt) ... 152, 163, 231, 371
ROYAL SOVEREIGN ... 113, 283, 285, 295, 298, 359
ROYAL ULSTERMAN (3244grt) ... 167, 292, 371
ROZENBURG (2068grt) ... 156
RT-3 ... 345
RT-32/KUMZHA ... 87
RT-66 ... 87
RT-67/MOLOTOV ... 87
RT-70/KAPITAN VORONIN ... 146
RT-8/SELD ... 279, 281
RUBIS ... 154, 155, 156, 171, 172, 240, 352, 365
RUDAU (2833grt) ... 59
RUHNO (499grt) ... 61
RUHR (5954grt) ... 255
RUMBA ... 40
RUNA (1575grt) ... 235
RUNSWICK BAY ... 54
RUOTSINSALMI ... 61, 62, 180, 375
RUPERT DE LARRINAGA (5358grt) ... 45, 106
RUSSELL (DD-414) ... 99, 155, 159, 159, 160, 215, 218, 220, 290, 354
Russian Arctic Fleet ... 17, 18, 87
Russian Baltic Fleet ... 17, 18, 22, 83, 143, 181, 183, 208, 209, 247, 248, 274, 275, 338, 339, 374
Russian Black Sea Fleet ... 17, 21, 22, 82, 83, 134, 142, 143, 195, 196, 208, 209, 261, 274, 275, 324, 339, 389
Russian Danube Flotilla ... 73, 195
Russian Danube Reni Group ... 134
Russian Fleet ... 20
Russian Northern Fleet ... 22, 23, 83, 143, 144, 209, 213, 214, 275, 280, 339, 343
Russian Pacific Fleet ... 22, 143
Russian Reserve Fleet ... 22
RYM (1369grt) ... 296
RYUJO ... 399
S.1 (Ro) ... 22
S.101 ... 119, 120, 182
S.104 ... 60, 302, 365
S.105 ... 60, 302, 365
S.106 ... 60
S.107 ... 237, 304
S.109 ... 365
S.110 ... 365
S.19 ... 51
S.2 (Ro) ... 22
S.20 ... 51, 173
S.22 ... 48, 51
S.24 ... 48, 51
S.25 ... 51
S.26 ... 119, 120, 182
S.27 ... 59, 120, 182
S.28 ... 60, 119, 120
S.29 ... 121
S.31 ... 59, 60
S.34 ... 60
S.35 ... 59, 60
S.39 ... 119, 182
S.40 ... 119, 120, 182
S.41 ... 302, 365
S.42 ... 60
S.43 ... 60
S.44 ... 60, 61
S.46 ... 60
S.47 ... 60, 120, 302
S.48 ... 171, 237
S.49 ... 173, 237
S.50 ... 237, 238, 365
S.51 ... 238, 304, 365, 366
S.52 ... 237, 238, 304, 365, 366
S.53 ... 302
S.54 ... 60, 120, 121
S.55 ... 121, 180
S.57 ... 120, 121
S.58 ... 120, 121, 180, 181
S.59 ... 59, 60
S.60 ... 59, 60
S.61 ... 60
S.62 ... 302
S-1 ... 59, 60, 311
S-10 ... 59, 60, 61
S-101 ... 59, 61, 62, 214
S-102 ... 61, 62, 119, 214
S-11 ... 119, 180
S-3 ... 59
S-31 ... 134, 260, 325, 389
S-32 ... 134, 196, 260
S-33 ... 134, 196, 260, 323, 389
S-34 ... 134, 260, 324, 389, 390
S-35 ... 195
S-36 ... 195
S-37 ... 195
S-38 ... 195
S-39 ... 196
S-4 ... 59, 60, 179, 182, 249, 312, 374
S-5 ... 59, 62, 179, 182
S-6 ... 59, 61, 179, 182
S-7 ... 59, 60, 61, 118, 248, 312, 374
S-8 ... 59, 62, 119, 310, 311
S-9 ... 59, 118, 121, 312, 374
SABINA (2421grt) ... 62
SABINE ... 48
SABINE (AO-25) ... 409
SABRE ... 32, 35, 37, 40, 96, 100, 156, 158, 166, 222, 227, 230, 233, 289, 297, 353, 356
SACRAMENTO VALLEY (4573grt) ... 44
SAETTA ... 65, 126, 127, 128, 382
SAGA ... 76, 328, 396
SAGARA MARU ... 330, 335, 395
SAGARA MARU (7189grt) ... 268, 269
SAGI ... 406
SAGIRI ... 404
SAGITTA (5153grt) ... 379

SAGITTAIRE (7706grt)..198
SAGUENAY..............................32, 37, 41, 102, 157, 158, 228, 292
SAIGON MARU................................78, 269, 270, 332, 333
SAIGON MARU (5350grt)..203
SAINT ANSELM (5614grt)..47
SAINT BON..315, 380
SAINT CLAIR (3753grt)..235
SAINT DIDIER (2778grt)..129
SAKHALIN (6085grt)..391
SAKURA MARU (9246grt)..........................328, 331, 333, 394, 395
SALADIN..............32, 34, 97, 152, 159, 163, 164, 225, 229, 232, 288, 294
SALAMANDER .. 31, 33, 38, 42, 94, 95, 148, 151, 153, 214, 280, 285, 286, 303
SALAMAUA (6676grt)..................131, 133, 189, 190, 192, 194, 256, 257, 326
SALAMONIE (AO-16)..91
SALINAS (AO-19)..156, 282, 285, 291
SALISBURY.....32, 33, 38, 96, 97, 102, 156, 157, 158, 159, 162, 165, 226, 227, 229, 232, 284, 289, 294
SALIVA..388
SALLY MAERSK (3252grt)..224
SALMI (185grt)..182
SALMON (SS-182)..397
SALPA..71
SALPI (2710grt)..313
SALT LAKE CITY (CA-25)..201, 409
SALVIA..131, 189, 191, 257, 319, 320
SALVONIA..155
SALZBURG (1756grt)..319, 321
SAMARIA (19,597grt)..37, 292, 392
SAMIDARE..406
SAMOS (1208grt)..259, 320
SAMPHIRE..104, 176, 243, 252, 298, 361, 378
SAMPSON (DD-394)..........35, 99, 156, 218, 222, 223, 285, 287, 291, 297, 299
SAN AMBROSIO (7410grt)..348
SAN ANGELO (5591grt)..223
SAN CLEMENTE MARU..334, 405, 406
SAN CLEMENTE MARU (7335grt)..268
SAN DIEGO MARU..199, 265, 270, 402
SAN FILIPE (5626grt)..352
SAN FLORENTINO (12,842grt)..287
SAN FRANCISCO DI PAOLA (50grt)..254
SAN LUIS MARU (7268grt)..401
SAN MARCO (3076grt)..62
SAN MARCO (3113grt)..379
SAN MICHELE..189
SAN NICOLA (21grt)..132
SAN PEDRO MARU..136, 137, 200, 201
SAN PEDRO MARU (7268grt)..400
SAN RAMON MARU..404
SAN SALVATORE (92grt)..378, 382
SAN STEFANO..193
SANDAR (7624grt)..306, 307
SANDWICH..........................33, 38, 96, 162, 177, 241, 293, 309, 362, 369
SANGARA (5445grt)..177
SANT ANTONIO (249grt)..379
SANT ANTONIO (736grt)..64
SANTAGANTA (4299grt)..259, 323
SANTAROSA..63, 314
SANTHIA (7754grt)..197
SANTOS MARU..201, 203
SANUKI MARU..265, 267
SANUKI MARU (7158grt)..202
SANYO MARU..200, 265, 398
SANYO MARU (8360grt)..200
SAPELO (AO-11)..356
SARABANDE..41, 114, 177, 229, 244, 371
SARASTONE (2473grt)..308
SARDELLA (329grt)..113
SARDONYX.........31, 55, 97, 100, 103, 104, 156, 158, 163, 167, 230, 287, 290, 293, 298, 350, 355, 360
SARPEDON (11,321grt)..292
Sasebo Raiding Force..211
SASKATOON..32, 353
SATA (6500grt)..332
SATSUKI..406
SATURN..182, 182
SATURN (403grt)..182
SAUGOR (6303grt)..34, 166
SAVANNAH (CL-42)..................36, 98, 99, 160, 227, 288, 290, 291, 354
SAVNY..182
SAVONA (2120grt)..379
SAVONA (2210grt)..314
SAWAKAZE..267
SAZANAMI..405, 406
SBORUL..22, 72, 323
SC-206..134
SC-307..180
SC-402..148
SCALARIA (5683grt)..326
SCALBY WYKE..351
SCANIA (1980grt)..225
SCARBOROUGH..........................41, 104, 114, 115, 293, 309, 362, 369
SCHARNHORST..94, 113, 174
SCHENCK (DD-159)..........................221, 227, 284, 294, 297, 355, 355, 361
SCHIE (1967grt)..34
SCHIELAND (2249grt)..49
SCHIFF.10/THOR..368
SCHIFF.11/OSNABRUCK..119, 120, 121
SCHIFF.16/ATLANTIS..........................57, 74, 135, 271, 368, 372, 373
SCHIFF.33/PINGUIN..74
SCHIFF.36/ORION..........................74, 107, 117, 174, 366, 368
SCHIFF.41/KORMORAN..74, 305, 393
SCHIFF.45/KOMET.........74, 85, 140, 174, 205, 356, 366, 367, 368, 368
SCHLETTSTADT (8028grt)..111
SCHWANECK (2194grt)..374
SCIMITAR..........................30, 33, 41, 96, 97, 103, 104, 156, 163, 355, 360
SCIRE..250
SCIROCCO..64, 124, 187, 251
SCORTON (4813grt)..109
SCOTT..93, 94, 95, 151, 282
SCOTTISH..370
SCOTTISH MONARCH (4719grt)..43, 44, 45
SCYTHIA (19,761grt)..54, 55, 113, 167, 244, 326, 327
SEABELLE..198
SEAFORD..136
SEAGULL... 32, 33, 39, 156, 157, 162, 165, 283, 284, 294, 344, 345, 348, 349, 351
SEAL..118
SEALION..112, 241, 285, 286, 343, 344
SEALYHAM..90, 95, 146, 147, 150, 153
SEAWOLF..113, 241, 286, 343, 344
SEBASTINO VENIER (6311grt).........64, 66, 125, 186, 252, 314, 315, 381, 383
SEBENICO..315, 316, 382
SECURITY..52
SEEWULF..217
SEGUNDO (4414grt)..166

SEIKAI MARU	335
SEIKYO MARU	330, 333, 396
SEINE (1358grt)	39
SEKSERN	197
SELKIRK	150, 284
SELLA	259, 319, 323
SEMMES (AG-24)	99
SENKO MARU (2618grt)	203, 266
SENNEN	39, 97, 100, 166, 167, 244, 306, 309, 360, 363
SERBINO (4099grt)	297
SERDITY	22, 60, 120, 121
SERENITAS (5171grt)	258
SERENITY (557grt)	292
SERGO (7956grt)	323, 324
SERP I MOLOT	182, 183
SERPENTE	185, 250, 251, 252, 313
SESSA (1700grt)	158
SESTRORETSK	183
SETA	200
SETE CIDADES (grt)	106
SETTEMBRINI	128, 250, 313, 379, 382, 388
SETTIMO	185
SETTLER (6000grt)	116, 123, 126
SEVASTOPOL	195
SEVERN	53, 63, 65, 66, 114, 116, 122, 174, 175, 176, 241, 307
SEVZAPLES (3947grt)	214, 280
SF.16	325
SF.25	325
SF.36	325
SHAHRISTAN (6935grt)	107
SHARPSHOOTER	32, 33, 39, 102, 349, 351, 359
SHAUMYAN	22, 73, 134, 195, 260, 323, 324, 324, 325, 389, 390
SHAW (DD-373)	409
SHAWNIGAN	356
SHCH-201	134, 195, 323
SHCH-202	73, 195, 323
SHCH-203	323
SHCH-204	73
SHCH-205	72
SHCH-206	72, 73, 261
SHCH-207	324, 325
SHCH-208	195, 260, 389
SHCH-209	72, 195, 260
SHCH-210	134, 323, 324
SHCH-211	134, 195, 196, 260, 261, 389, 390
SHCH-212	195, 196, 260, 324
SHCH-213	260, 325, 389
SHCH-214	260, 325, 389
SHCH-215	195, 323, 389, 390
SHCH-216	196, 260, 324
SHCH-301	179, 182, 195
SHCH-302	249
SHCH-303	249
SHCH-304	312
SHCH-305	59, 60
SHCH-306	59, 60, 249
SHCH-307	121, 182
SHCH-308	182
SHCH-309	59, 61, 62, 249, 311, 375
SHCH-310	59, 61, 62
SHCH-311	59, 61, 62, 249, 311, 375
SHCH-317	248, 249, 311
SHCH-318	179, 249
SHCH-319	179, 248, 249
SHCH-320	179, 247, 248, 311
SHCH-322	59, 119, 182, 183, 249, 311
SHCH-323	59, 119, 311, 373
SHCH-324	59, 312, 374
SHCH-401	23, 87, 88, 146, 212, 214, 280, 343
SHCH-402	87, 88, 146, 212, 278, 279
SHCH-403	23, 87
SHCH-404	23, 280
SHCH-406	119
SHCH-421	23, 88, 146, 280, 343
SHCH-422	87, 212, 213, 278
SHEARWATER	239
SHEBA	262
SHEDIAC	222, 224, 227, 288, 295, 354, 361
SHEFFIELD	24, 27, 28, 39, 53, 62, 151, 155, 167, 170, 215, 217, 230, 231, 236, 242, 243, 251, 252, 283, 286, 293, 294, 305, 345, 346, 347, 349, 350, 351
SHERBROOKE	32, 222, 226, 227, 356, 358
SHERWOOD	29, 33, 37, 40, 284, 288, 289, 295, 360
SHIKARI	32, 35, 40, 96, 97, 100, 103, 156, 158, 163, 166, 222, 227, 230
SHIKINAMI	404
SHIMUSHU	199
SHINKOKU MARU	270, 401, 402, 403, 405
SHINKOKU MARU (10,020grt)	203, 334, 335
SHINKYO MARU	329
SHINONOME	404
SHINYO MARU (4163grt)	139
SHIOKAZE	399
SHIP.19/LOLA	325
SHIRAKAMI	400
SHIRAKUMO	404
SHIRANUHI	403, 405
SHIRAYUKI	404
SHIRETOKO	401
SHIRETOKO MARU (6500grt)	332, 408
SHIRIYA	402, 404, 406
SHKVAL	390
SHOAN MARU (5624grt)	332
SHOHEI MARU (7255grt)	331, 402
SHOKA MARU (4467grt)	335
SHOKAKU	201, 203, 267, 268, 330, 331, 332, 334, 335, 400, 401, 402, 403, 404, 405, 406
SHOREHAM	198, 326
SHROPSHIRE	56, 74, 91, 94, 95, 148, 149, 150, 152, 153, 154, 155, 213, 215, 215, 217, 218, 219, 221, 278, 280, 283, 302
SHTORM	390
SHUKA (316grt)	59
SHUNA (1575grt)	378
SHURI MARU	76, 137, 200, 265, 328, 396
SIBAJAK (12,226grt)	135, 137, 264
SIBIR (3767grt)	181
SIDAMO (2384grt)	255
SIGRID (1093grt)	373
SIGULDA	183
SIKH	24, 33, 37, 40, 42, 101, 115, 122, 123, 124, 127, 175, 185, 292, 300, 306, 308, 313, 361, 368, 369, 370, 377
SILACH (541grt)	60
SILDRA (7313grt)	55, 177
SILNY	22, 60, 120, 183, 249
SILVA (127grt)	283
SILVAPLANA (4793grt)	271, 368

SILVERBELLE (5302grt) 235, 243
SILVERCEDAR (4354grt) 295
SILVERLAUREL (6142grt) 51
SILVERPALM (6373grt) 39
SILVERTEAK (6770grt) 152, 163
SILVIO SCARONI (1367grt) 64
SIMEON 23
SIMORGH 198
SIMPSON (DD-221) 220, 223, 232, 288, 298
SIMS (DD-409) 155, 159, 215, 218, 223, 288, 290, 354
SIR RUSSELL (1548grt) 173
SIREMALM (2468grt) 233
SIRENA (974grt) 252, 253
SIRETUL 22
SIRIO 192, 256, 323
SIRLY 120
SIRTORI 127, 128, 187
SISAPON 48
SITOEBONDO (7049grt) 108
SITORI 187
SJOBORG (158grt) 151
SKAGERAK (1283grt) 171
SKAGERRAK 58
SKATE 34, 38, 40, 53, 97, 98, 102, 104, 156, 157, 158, 159, 225, 226, 229, 232, 288, 294, 356, 357, 360
SKEENA 33, 98, 159, 163, 218, 223, 228, 230, 288, 295, 354, 361
SKORY 182
SKR-102/PETRAS 324
SKR-107/KUBAN 324
SKR-11/Patrol Boat 70 87
SKR-11/RT-66/URAL 281
SKR-113/BUG 323, 324
SKR-114/DNESTR 323, 324
SKR-12/TUMAN 146
SKR-20/SHTIL 88
SKR-22/PASSAT 87
SKR-23/MUSSON 87, 88
SKR-25/BRIZ 345
SKR-27/ZHEMCHUG 146
SKR-29/BRILLIANT 87
SKUDD III 194
SKUM (1304grt) 50
SLAVNY 22, 182, 183, 374, 376
SMELI 323
SMELY 22, 61
SMERALDO 254
SMERCH 88
SMERI 87
SMETLIVY 22, 60, 62, 120, 182, 183, 374, 375
SMEUL 22, 323
SMIELY 121
SMOLNY 249
SMYSHLENY 22, 73, 196, 324, 325, 390, 391
SNAEFELL 108
SNAPDRAGON 197, 198, 326, 384
SNEG 120, 182
SNOWBERRY 38, 96, 102, 157, 166, 226, 228, 233, 290, 357
SNOWDROP 104, 156, 162
SOAVITA (80grt) 110
SOBIESKI (11,030grt) 290, 306, 354
SOIKA 189, 259, 318, 320, 322
SOKOL ..105, 113, 242, 250, 255, 314, 315, 317, 320, 377, 378, 379, 382, 386, 387

SOKRUSHITELNY 22, 23, 88, 90, 147, 148, 213, 214, 279
SOLARRIS 153
SOLOY (4402grt) 34
SOLSKIN (372grt) 304
SOMALI 150, 153, 154, 155, 163, 166, 173, 213, 215, 217, 218, 220, 221, 281, 282, 286, 287, 346, 347, 351
SOMERS (DD-381) 161, 228, 291, 292, 357, 357, 372
SONAVATI 198
SONOMA (AT-12) 408
SOOBRAZITELNY 22, 73, 196, 260, 261, 325, 390, 391
SOREL 289, 290, 291, 353, 354, 355
SORYU 400, 402, 405, 406
SOTRA 189, 190, 318, 386
SOUFFLEUR 71
SOURIYA 198
SOUTA PRINCESCA (grt) 105
South Atlantic Command 54, 232, 370
SOUTHDOWN 366
SOUTHERN BARRIER 392
SOUTHERN GEM 175, 176, 362
SOUTHERN ISLE 72, 258, 388
SOUTHERN MAID 66, 67, 71, 322, 386, 388
SOUTHERN PRIDE 175, 176, 358, 372
SOUTHERN PRINCE 154
SOUTHERN SEA 69, 259, 388
SOUTHERN STAR 369
SOUTHPORT (572grt) 301
SOUTHWOLD 239, 283, 284, 304, 346, 357, 359
SOVERSHENNY 262, 390
SOVETSKAYA UKRANIA 195
SOYA 396
SP-12 72
SP-14 .... 261, 323
SPARTA (1724grt) 124, 125
SPARVIERO (498grt) 252
SPEEDWELL 30, 33, 41, 96, 97, 158, 173
SPEEDY 98, 157, 164, 283, 284, 294, 344, 348, 349
SPERANZA (445grt) 383
SPEZIA (1825grt) 127, 253
SPHENDONI 72
SPIDOLA 60
SPIDOLA (2833grt) 59
SPIKENARD 38, 39, 96, 103, 157, 167, 226, 228
SPIND (2129grt) 174
SPIREA 40, 54, 100, 104, 106, 114, 116, 164, 242, 243, 306, 309, 369, 370
SPOSOBNY 196, 260, 261, 390, 391
SPREEWALD (5083grt) 328
SPRINGBANK (5155grt) 37, 41, 54, 167, 177, 233, 235, 236, 242
SPRINGDALE 38, 55
SPRINGTIDE 38, 55
SQUALO 106, 131, 185, 251, 313, 377, 382
SREMITELNY 22
ST ALBANS 33, 42, 55, 102, 104, 114, 117, 161, 164, 167, 177, 222, 230, 293
ST ANGELO 128, 383
ST APOLLO .. 31, 33, 42, 96, 101, 104, 158, 224, 228, 231, 288, 295, 298, 350, 360
ST ATHAN 197
ST CATHAN 148, 151, 153, 355
ST CLAIR II (3753grt) 235
ST CLEARS (4312grt) 351
ST CROIX 31, 33, 34, 97, 158, 159, 218, 221, 228, 231, 289
ST DAY 123, 305, 377

ST ELSTAN	32, 34, 97, 98, 102, 104, 164, 232, 288, 360
ST FRANCIS	42, 288, 289, 355
ST ISSEY	69, 72, 129, 130, 387, 389
ST JULIEN (1952grt)	173
ST KENAN	32, 34, 164, 229, 232, 360
ST LAURENT	33, 97, 103, 158, 226, 228, 233, 357
ST LINDSAY (5370grt)	40
ST LOMAN	32, 39, 97, 157, 162, 227
ST MARYS	25, 27, 37, 42, 167
ST MELANTE	54
ST MONACE	322, 387
ST NECTAN	102, 107, 175, 176, 307, 308, 370
ST OMAR	123
ST PATRICK (1922grt)	39
ST PIERRE (10,086grt)	137
ST PIERRE D'ALCANTARA (329grt)	112
ST WISTAN	177
ST ZENO	32, 34, 97, 98, 102, 104, 164, 222, 229, 288, 294, 360
STACK (DD-406)	36, 98, 160, 215, 220
Stalin, Josef	6, 7, 21, 83, 85, 86, 144, 211, 214, 277, 339, 341
STAMATIOS G. EMBIRICOS (3941grt)	264
STANLEY	298, 299, 372
STANMOUNT (4468grt)	237
STANVAC CAPE TOWN (grt)	44
STAR OF DEVERON	239
STARGARD (1113grt)	224
STARLING	236
START (grt)	344
STARWORT	105, 164, 177, 244, 293, 298, 360, 371, 372
STARY BOLSHEVIK (2974grt)	214, 280
STATNY	180, 181
ST-CERGUE (4260grt)	91
STEEL SEAFARER (5718grt)	262
STEENBERG	392
STELLA (4272grt)	168
STELLA CAPELLA	344, 349
STELLA CARINA	53, 55, 104, 116, 176, 306, 352, 357, 369, 370
STELLENBERG	392
STEREGUSHCHI	22, 59, 120, 121, 180, 183, 249
STERETT (DD-407)	98, 160, 215
STIG GORTHON (2241grt)	110
STIHI EUGEN	72, 134
STIRLING CASTLE (25,550grt)	33, 161, 245, 263
STOIKI	22, 60, 62, 120, 183, 374, 375, 376
STONE STREET (6131grt)	36
STONECROP	167, 242, 294, 300, 361, 369
STONEPOOL (4815grt)	225
STORK	24, 26, 27, 28, 90, 101, 103, 175, 230, 309, 358, 370
STORK (787grt)	174
STOROZHEVOI	22, 60, 183
STRALE	66, 127, 186, 252, 253, 254, 317, 382
STRASHNY	60, 120, 183
STRATHAIRD (22,281grt)	292
STRATHAIRD (22,284grt)	392
STRATHALLAN (23,722grt)	161, 245
STRATHBORVE	237
STRATHEDEN (23,722grt)	158, 231
STRATHGAIRN (211grt)	99
STRATHGELDIE (192grt)	237
STRATHLOCHY (212grt)	95
STRATHMORE (23,428grt)	97, 164, 244
STRATHNAVER (22,283grt)	97, 164, 244

STREMITELNY	88
STROGI	23, 183
STROMBO (5232grt)	67, 130, 193
STRONGHOLD	321
STROYNI	183
STUART	68, 69, 70, 71, 129, 130, 132, 193
STURLA (1195grt)	63, 64
STURMFELS (6288grt)	197
STURTEVANT (DD-240)	99, 289, 298, 356
SUBLOCOTENENT CHICULESCU	22
SUD (2689grt)	168
Suez Escort Force	258, 259, 322, 323, 325, 326, 391
SUFFOLK	24, 25, 26, 27, 28, 30, 91, 94, 95, 148, 149, 153, 154, 213, 215, 217, 218, 219, 220, 221, 231, 232, 280, 281, 285, 346, 347, 349, 350, 351
SUFFOLK (11,063grt)	163
SUKHONA (3124grt)	214, 280, 283, 349
SULEV	182
SULOIDE (3235grt)	245
SUMIDA	76, 77, 200
SUMMERSIDE	289, 354, 355
SUNFISH	239
SUNFLOWER	32, 37, 40, 102, 103, 107, 115, 156, 158, 163, 227, 230, 233, 282, 287, 298, 353, 356, 358
SUPERGA (6154grt)	261
SURCOUF (1129grt)	392
SUROVY	22, 180, 181, 182, 183, 374, 375
SURPRISE	56, 116, 287
SUSAN MAERSK (2355grt)	45
SUSSEX (13, 647grt)	359
SUTLEJ	24, 27, 167, 391
SUTTON	47, 49
SUUR TOLL	182
SUZUKAZE	406
SVAM I (388grt)	253
SVANA	318
SVEND FOYN (14,795grt)	282
SVENOR (7616grt)	124, 126
SVERDLOV	195
SVINT (1174grt)	101
SVIREPY	181, 183
SVOBODNY	195
SWANSON (DD-443)	352, 360
SWEETBRIAR	289, 295, 353, 358
SWIFTPOOL (5205grt)	162
SYDHAV (7587grt)	54
SYDNEY	271, 393, 394
SYDNEY STAR (11,095grt)	381
SYDNEY STAR (11,219grt)	101, 122, 127
SYDNEY THUBRON	198
SYOKSY	247, 249
SYRINGA	40, 114
SYZRAN	323, 324
SZEGED (grt)	260, 324
T. J. WILLIAMS (8212grt)	226
T.11	247, 248, 249, 367
T.12	368
T.2	247, 248, 311
T.3	119
T.4	367, 368
T.5	247, 248, 311
T.7	247, 249, 311, 367, 368
T.8	247, 248, 249, 311
T-201/ZARYAD	180, 375

T-202/BUI ... 120
T-202/BUJ ... 181
T-203/PATRON ... 312
T-204/FUGAS ... 59, 60, 61, 118, 119, 182, 311
T-205 ... 182
T-205/GAFEL ... 182, 374, 375, 376
T-206/VERP ... 182, 374, 375
T-207/SHPIL ... 182, 374, 375, 376
T-208/SHKIV ... 60
T-209/KNECHT ... 181
T-210/GAK ... 182, 374, 376
T-211/RYM ... 374, 375, 376
T-212/SHTAG ... 181
T-213/KRAMBOL ... 181
T-214 ... 182
T-215 ... 182, 374, 375, 376
T-216 ... 182
T-217 ... 182, 374, 375, 376
T-218 ... 182, 375, 376
T-297/VIRSAITIS ... 375, 376
T-297/VISAITIS ... 376
T-32/ZEMLJAK ... 323
T-35/MENZHINSKI ... 375, 376
T-38/RAIKOMVOD ... 323
T-39/DOROTEYA ... 323, 324
T-405/VZRYVATEL ... 324
T-406/ISKATEL ... 324
T-408/YAKOR ... 324
T-41/KHENKIN ... 323
T-41/SERGEY KIROV ... 249
T-42 ... 375, 376
T-4O4/SHCHIT ... 324
T-51/PIRMUNAS ... 181
T-53/UDARNIK ... 376
T-54/KLYUZ ... 375, 376
T-58 ... 375
T-76/KORALL ... 376
T-889/No.34 ... 345
T-890 ... 87
T-891 ... 87
T-898/DVINA ... 147
TABERG (1392grt) ... 53
TAGLIAMENTO (5448grt) ... 321
TAHCHEE (6508grt) ... 224
TAI KOO (688grt) ... 262
TAIFUN ... 249
TAITO MARU (4466grt) ... 400, 401, 406
TAIYO ... 266, 267, 328, 330, 396, 397, 399
TAIYO MARU (14,457grt) ... 332
TAIYO MARU (14,503grt) ... 334, 403, 409
TAKAO ... 406
TAKASAGO MARU ... 402
TAKU ... 64, 65, 68, 125, 132, 187, 188
TALABOT (6798grt) ... 123, 126, 175
TALISMAN ... 96, 115, 124, 189, 191, 193, 258, 259, 314, **316**, 318, 319, 380, 385
TALLINN (4479grt) ... 59
TALMA (10,000grt) ... 197
TALODI (1585grt) ... 257
TAMA ... 267
TAMAROA (12,405grt) ... 42
TAMBOR (SS-198) ... 408

TAMPICO (4958grt) ... 196, 261, 384
TAN 8 ... 76
TANIKAZE ... 403, 405
Tanker TN-12 (1700grt) ... 182
TANNENBERG ... 58, 61, 118
TARBELL (DD-142) ... 99, 224, 289, 299, 358
TARMO ... 248
TARN (4220grt) ... 377
TARTAR ... 23, 25, 29, 30, 37, 38, 90, 91, 92, 93, 94, 95, 96, 146, 150, 151, 152, **153**, 171, 172, **303**, 347, 351, 363
TASHKENT ... 22, 134, 196, 325, 390, 391
Task Force TF.2.6 ... 36
Task Force TF.2.8 ... 36
Task Group TG.2.5 ... 35
Task Group TG.3 ... 35
TATEKAWA MARU ... 139
TATSUGAMI MARU ... 269, 334
TATSUGAMI MARU (7064grt) ... 268
TATSUHO MARU (6334grt) ... 331
TATSUMIYA MARU ... 266
TATSUTA ... 204
TATSUTA MARU ... 402, 409
TATSUTA MARU (16,975grt) ... 138, 139, 202, 203, 204, 205, 265, 332, 333, 336
TATSUTAKE MARU (7068grt) ... 405
TATSUWA MARU (6335grt) ... 75, 76, 136, 137, 199, 265, 327, 328, 395, 404, 407
TAUPSE (6320grt) ... 391
TAURI (2517grt) ... 221
TAURUS (4767grt) ... 48
TAXIARCHIS ... 67
TAZZOLI ... 177
TEDDINGTON (4762grt) ... 238
TEDWORTH ... 109
TEIKAI MARU (9492grt) ... 268, 270
TEISEN MARU (5019grt) ... 203, 400
TEIYO MARU (6081grt) ... 268
TEIYO MARU (9849grt) ... 405
TEIZUI MARU (8428grt) ... 137
TEMBIEN ... 185
TEMBIEN (5584grt) ... 64, 65, 253
TEMPLE ARCH (5138grt) ... 284, 345
TENACEMENTE ... 189
TENRYU ... 204
TENYO MARU ... 204, 269, 335, 402, 408
TENYO MARU (6843grt) ... 268, 269
TERJE ... 392
TERUKAWA MARU (6433grt) ... 267
TESEO (4966grt) ... 178
TETELA (5389grt) ... 238
TETRARCH ... 65, 70, 127, 132, 133, 187, 188, 259, 314, 317, 377
TEVIOTBANK ... 47, 50, 51, 93, 94, 393
TEXAS (BB-35) ... 28, 106
TF.1 ... 99
TF.14 ... 290, 291
TF.15 ... 210, 218, 220, 222, 223
TF.16 ... 99
TF.19 ... 91, 92, 96
TF.3 ... 161, 228, 291
TF.4 ... 211
TG.1.1.2 ... 155
TG.17.4 ... 288
TG.2.5 ... 99, 159, 160, 169

TG.2.6	160
TG.2.7	99, 160
TG.2.8	98
TG.3.1	346
TG.3.5	228, 291, 292, 357, 357, 372
TG.3.6	228, 291, 356
TG.3.7	228, 291, 357
TG.3.8	228, 291, 292
THALIA (5875grt)	306, 307
THAMES	29, 30, 234, 301, 308, 377
THEODOR RIEDEL	155, 172
THEOPHILE GAUTIER (8194grt)	318
THERESE WALLNER	324, 325
THERESIA WALLNER	261
THERMOPYLAE (6655grt)	123, 126, 175
THIRLMERE	358
THISTLEGLEN (4748grt)	223
THISTLEGORM (4898grt)	326
THODE FAGELUND (5757grt)	392
THORBRYN	192
THORGRIM	194, 384
THORN	232, 243, 312, 315, 316, 386, 387
THORNLIEBANK (5569grt)	363
THORPEBAY (2183grt)	47
THORSHAVET (11,015grt)	369, 370
THORSHOVDI (9944grt)	355, 356
THRASHER	40, 55, 63, 66, 112, 133, 192, 193, 253, 254, 255, 314, 317, 378, 381, 382
THUNDER	355
THUNDERBOLT	46, 96, 116, 184, 186, 192, 253, 317, 319, 320, 321, 388
THYME	355, 360
THYRA III (828grt)	363
THYSVILLE (8351grt)	57
TIBERIO	259
TIBIA (10,356grt)	35
TIGRIS	86, 95, 112, 146, 147, 175, 212, 213, 214, 221, 222, 278, 279, 280
TIIR	182
TILA	23
TILLY L. M. RUSS (1600grt)	65
TINOS (2826grt)	382
TINOS (2827grt)	253, 317
TIRPITZ	220, 227, 247
TIRPITZ (7970grt)	126
TKA-103	182
TKA-11	213
TKA-113	182
TKA-12	213, 249, 279
TKA-122	180
TKA-13	213
TKA-14	213, 279
TKA-15	213, 279
TKA-17	60
TKA-27	60
TKA-37	60
TKA-47	60
TKA-57	60
TKA-67	60, 248
TKA-71	121
TKA-73	182
TKA-74	182
TKA-94	182
TOA MARU	401
TOA MARU (10,052grt)	266, 269
TOBA	265, 328
TOEI MARU	78, 138, 140, 201, 267, 398, 400, 403, 405
TOEI MARU (10,023grt)	331, 332, 333
TOEN MARU	75, 76, 199, 200, 328, 329, 398, 403
TOHO MARU	403, 405
TOHO MARU (9997grt)	203, 270, 334
TOKAI MARU (5038grt)	332, 334, 401, 407
TOKITSUKAZE	406
TOKIWA	204, 335, 408
TOLWORTH (1351grt)	50
TOM (3056grt)	47
TOMOZURU	398
TON S. (466grt)	229
TONAN MARU NO. 2 (19,262grt)	332, 400
TONBRIDGE	173
TONE	405
TONELINE (811grt)	321, 322, 386, 387
TOPAZIO	185, 257, 320
TORBAY	65, 66, 67, 68, 69, 72, 128, 129, 130, 186, 187, 192, 256, 258, 259, **316**, 380, 385
TORCELLO (3336grt)	318, 389
TORELLI	55, 105, 106, 114, 115, 234, 242
TORNATOR (4964grt)	77, 78
TORNATOR GO (4964grt)	78
TORONTO CITY (2486grt)	104
TOTLAND	97, 100, 166, 167, 244, 306, 309, 360, 363
TOTTENHAM (4762grt)	57
TOYO MARU (2470grt)	76, 138, 199, 200, 265, 327, 328, 329, 394, 397
TOYO MARU No.2 (2480grt)	333
TRAFALGAR (5542grt)	52
TRAIL	98, 158, 167, 226, 228, 233, 290, 356, 357
TRAJANUS (1712grt)	132
TRANIO	50
Transport No.10	376
Transport No.539/MAYA	376
Transport No.548/MINNA	376
Transport RO.19	367
TRAPANI (1855grt)	259, 319
TRAUTENFELS (6418grt)	213
TRAVELLER	100
TRAVELLER (3963grt)	34
TRECARRELL (5271grt)	43
TREERN	197
TREGARTHEN (5201grt)	44
TREHATA (4817grt)	148, 153, 214, 280, 351
TREK IEVE (5244grt)	348
TRELISSICK (5265grt)	50
TREMODA (4736grt)	166
TRENTO	188, 251, 379, 380, 381
TRESILLIAN (4743grt)	45
TREVARRACK (5270grt)	45
TREVERBYN (5218grt)	297
TRICHECO	185, 258, 382, 383
TRIDENT	86, 146, 147, 148, 212, 214, 222, 280, 343, 345, 366
TRIDENT (4317grt)	170
TRIESTE	66, 122, 125, 188, 251, 379, 380, 381, 382
TRIFELS (6189grt)	240
TRILLIUM	33, 38, 100, 156, 163
TRINIDAD	304, 305, 347, 358
TRINIDAD (434grt)	234
TRIO FRASSINETTI (244grt)	64

TRIOMPHANT	112, 330, 336
TRIPPE (DD-403)	28, 288, 290, 353, 354
TRITON (Gk/sub)	65, 131, 133, 258, 259
TRITON (SS-201)	36, 408, 409
TRIUMPH	64, 65, 71, 124, 125, 188, 252, 254, 255, 322, 323, 386, 387
TROOPER	100
TROSTBURG (3566grt)	59
TROYBURG (2288grt)	179
TRSAT (1369grt)	237
TRUANT	65, 226, 243, 312, 316, 317, 318
TRUSTY	229, 242, 250, 255, 314, 316, 317, 379, 382
TRUXTUN (DD-229)	218, 223, 223, 226, 289, 298
TSAR ASSEN	23
TSENIT	324
TSIKLON	182
TSUGA	395
TSUGARU	334, 400, 407, 408
TSURUMI	406, 407
TTS-121	182
TTS-42/IZHORETS-17	182
TTS-43	182
TTS-44	182
TTS-47	182
TTS-56/BAROMETR	182
TTS-71/KRAB	182
TU.1.1.5	216
TU.1.1.7	216
TU.4.1.1	225, 293, 352, 359
TU.4.1.2	353, 356
TU.4.1.3	221, 285, 292, 297, 356, 359
TU.4.1.4	294, 295, 353, 362
TU.4.1.5	221, 284, 285, 288, 355
TU.4.1.6	285, 286, 293, 297, 356
TU.4.1.7	289
TU.4.1.8	352
TU.4.2.1	346
TUCHA	120
Tug No.307	321
TUGELA (5559grt)	279
TULIP	100
TUMAN	87
TUNA	112, 113, 263, 345, 352
TUNGUS (2607grt)	200
TUNGUSKA	60
TUNISIA (4337grt)	162
TURBINE	66, 127, 186, 381, 382
TURBO (4782grt)	193
TURCHESE	251, 313, 377
TURECAMO BOYS	355
TURQUOISE (430grt)	49
TUSCALOOSA (CA-37)	35, 36, 156, 157, 159, 215, 220, 222, 346, 347
TUTUILA (PR-4)	20, 75, 137
TUVA (4652grt)	292
TYNE	150
TYNEFIELD (5856grt)	326
TYPHOON (5039grt)	161
TYSA (5327grt)	369
U.101	34, 39, 43, 46, 162, 166, 230, 289, 294, 296, 297
U.103	44, 46, 47, 105, 235, 236, 299, 300, 362
U.105	43, 155, 162, 215, 225, 346, 348, 355
U.106	44, 163, 169, 230, 286, 290, 291, 352, 353
U.107	44, 45, 56, 235, 236, 299, 300, 362
U.108	24, 30, 34, 44, 45, 46, 47, 104, 169, 233, 236
U.109	116, 168, 288, 289, 295
U.110	19, 24
U.111	30, 34, 43, 46, 104, 169, 233, 234, 236, 246, 299
U.123	46, 47, 55, 105, 106, 168, 297, 352, 353
U.124	106, 112, 168, 234, 235, 236, 372, 373
U.125	169, 233, 236, 300
U.126	103, 106, 107, 168, 300, 309, 310, 371, 372
U.129	162, 168, 236, 299, 373
U.132	279, 281
U.133	291, 353, 363
U.138	54
U.140	58, 61, 121
U.141	41, 103, 104, 166, 216, 229
U.142	58
U.143	154, 166, 167
U.144	58, 59, 121, 180
U.145	58
U.146	30
U.147	37
U.149	58, 60
U.153	374
U.201	29, 30, 45, 46, 104, 163, 165, 169, 173, 174, 233, 234, 235, 362, 363
U.202	30, 46, 104, 155, 162, 215, 225, 286, 297, 352
U.203	28, 34, 46, 103, 106, 107, 112, 233, 236, 286, 297, 352
U.204	24, 45, 46, 162, 163, 165, 167, 168, 169, 241, 293, 299, 300, 305, 306, 307
U.205	161, 168, 174, 233, 236, 368, 377, 389
U.206	150, 162, 168, 228, 293, 300, 306, 307, 368
U.207	155, 215, 225
U.208	288, 289, 295, 352
U.331	106, 107, 168, 243, 318, 319, 386, 387, 388, 389
U.332	346, 348, 362, 363
U.371	34, 39, 45, 46, 107, 108, 116, 168, 242, 243, 255, 300, 318, 321
U.372	106, 161, 162, 168, 224, 226, 287, 355
U.373	218, 226, 362
U.374	288, 289, 291, 295, 352
U.38	44, 155, 158, 162, 215, 286, 297, 352, 353
U.401	106, 161
U.402	346, 348, 362, 363
U.43	32, 40, 43, 45, 46, 155, 162, 168, 215, 355, 363
U.431	106, 161, 162, 168, 226, 287, 346, 348, 370
U.432	155, 215, 218, 224, 225, 289, 294, 295, 296, 297, 301
U.433	155, 215, 218, 225, 368, 378
U.434	355
U.451	145, 146, 147, 213, 222
U.452	154
U.46	32, 43, 44, 45, 168
U.48	33, 43, 44, 45, 46, 58
U.501	155, 162, 163, 215, 216, 223
U.502	282, 288, 289, 291, 294, 295, 297, 299
U.552	39, 40, 163, 169, 174, 218, 226, 278, 291, 299, 357, 362, 363
U.553	30, 34, 45, 46, 104, 155, 162, 228, 230, 288, 289, 295, 296
U.556	29, 46
U.557	30, 43, 46, 104, 166, 167, 217, 228, 234, 371
U.558	34, 46, 102, 161, 162, 167, 228, 289, 294, 295, 296
U.559	30, 46, 104, 161, 162, 163, 165, 168, 169, 243, 318, 319, 321, 387, 388, 389
U.561	30, 104, 106, 107, 166, 217, 218, 228, 230, 354, 368
U.562	30, 46, 104, 106, 113, 168, 226, 227, 228, 287, 371
U.563	162, 168, 228, 230, 293, 294, 300, 301, 308
U.564	29, 30, 35, 46, 104, 106, 163, 164, 165, 169, 173, 174, 226, 293, 300, 301, 306, 308

U.565 .... 106, 161, 162, 168, 217, 218, 368, 389
U.566 .... 145, 146, 147, 212
U.567 .... 155, 162, 168, 228, 229, 291, 299, 357, 362
U.568 .... 162, 228, 286, 288, 289, 291, 294, 295, 296, 297, 299
U.569 .... 155, 162, 215, 223, 224, 230, 286, 297, 352
U.570 155
U.571 .... 146, 147, 291, 353, 363
U.572 .... 218, 226, 287, 299, 362, 363
U.573 .... 288, 289, 295
U.574 355
U.575 .... 218, 226, 292, 355
U.576 .... 281, 345
U.577 .... 291, 353, 363
U.578 345
U.580 374
U.583 374
U.586 151
U.588 168
U.651 .... 30, 34, 46
U.652 .... 87, 88, 145, 146, 147, 154, 155, 162, 215, 216, 224, 368, 371
U.66 .... 43, 47, 105, 106, 107, 236, 246, 299, 300
U.67 .... 235, 236, 299
U.68 .... 106, 107, 235, 236, 310, 372, 373
U.69 .... 20, 46, 56, 105, 217, 226, 362, 363
U.71 .... 34, 46, 162, 167, 168, 228, 230, 293, 300, 308
U.73 .... 45, 46, 162, 230, 233, 286, 289, 294, 296, 297
U.74 .... 106, 162, 226, 285, 286, 352, 353
U.75 .... 34, 43, 46, 161, 162, 163, 168, 174, 243, 318, 319, 322, 323, 383
U.751 .... 40, 46, 162, 166, 168, 228, 230, 286, 289, 291, 294, 296, 297, 299
U.752 .... 146, 147, 345
U.77 .... 30, 34, 45, 46, 104, 162, 228, 230, 286, 289, 291, 294, 296, 297, 299, 362
U.79 .... 26, 34, 35, 46, 104, 106, 107, 168, 236, 243, 250, 299, 318, 321, 387, 389
U.81 .... 87, 88, 146, 155, 215, 223, 224, 368, 377, 389
U.82 .... 155, 162, 215, 224, 225, 286, 297, 352, 353
U.83 .... 162, 163, 166, 168, 228, 230, 293, 300, 301, 306, 307
U.84 .... 155, 162, 215, 218, 286, 297, 300, 301, 352
U.85 .... 155, 215, **223**, 286, 297, 352, 353, 363
U.93 .... 31, 43, 106, 168, 175, 176, 286, 297, 352
U.94 .... 106, 168, 176, 217, 226, 231, 287
U.95 .... 46, 103, 106, 166, 168, 217, 218, 228, 234, 371, 378
U.96 .... 30, 46, 104, 105, 162, 168, 228, 230, 291, 299, 362, 363
U.97 .... 46, 106, 168, 243, 318, 320, 322
U.98 .... 30, 46, 104, 105, 106, 217, 219, 234, 362, 363
U.A 46, 168, 373
U.B 118
UARSCIEK 131, 320
UDARNIK 376
UDARNY 73, 261
UGO BASSI (2900grt) 63
UJ.113/NORTHLAND 119
UJ.117/GUSTAV KRONER 310
UJ.1201 214
UJ.1213 343
UJ.1709/CARL KAMPF 287
UJ.176 148
UJ.177 .... 88, 148
UJ.178 .... 88, 148
UKRAINA (4727grt) 324
ULEA (1574grt) 301
ULSTER MONARCH (3791grt) 152, 163, 231, 292, 371
ULSTER QUEEN 154, 220, 232

ULTIMATUM 243, 379
ULTRA ... 102, 106, 112, 227, 277, 283, 284, 285, 288, 289, 315, 316, 317, 339, 342, 353, 379, 380
ULYSSES (14,652grt) 40
UMBRA 352
UMIKAZE 406
UMPIRE 109
UMVUMA (4419grt) 110
UNA 368, 370
UNBEATEN 65, 66, 125, 126, 133, 185, 187, 188, 189, 252, 254, 255, 316, 317
UNGVAR (1031grt) 390
UNION 65, 125, 126
UNION (216grt) 383
UNIONE (216grt) 382
UNIQUE 64, 65, 66, 122, 126, 128, 133, 186, 187, 252, 314, 315, 316, 317, 379
United States Asiatic Fleet 341
United States Atlantic Fleet 83, 144, 211, 275, 339
United States Navy 215, 220, 225
United States Pacific Fleet 86, 274, 275
UNIWALECO (9755grt) 371
UNO (408grt) 374
UPHOLDER 65, 66, 122, 124, 125, 126, 127, 187, 188, 189, 252, 254, 255, 314, 315, 316, 379, 380, 382
UPRIGHT ... 65, 66, 122, 126, 127, 130, 252, 254, 255, 314, 316, 317, 380, 381
UPROAR 383
UPSHUR (DD-144) 91, 96, 99, 225, 288, 290, 293, 352, 358
URAKAMI MARU (4317grt) 402
URAKAZE 403, 405
URAL 61, 182, 375
URALETS (grt) 323
URANAMI 404
URGE .. 64, 65, 66, 122, 124, 126, 127, 185, 187, 188, 252, 255, 313, 316, 317, 379, 380, 381
URITSKI 22, 23, 146, 148
UROLA (grt) 307
URSULA .. 65, 125, 133, 185, 189, 252, 254, 255, 315, 316, 317, 379, 381, 383
URSULA RICKMERS (5019grt) 203
USHIO 405, 406
USODIMARE 64, 65, 188, 189, 254, 254, 314, 315, 316, 380, 382
UTENA (542grt) 180
UTILITAS (5342grt) 68
UTMOST ... 65, 66, 122, 124, 126, 127, 186, 188, 189, 252, 253, 254, 255, 314, 377, 378, 379, 382
UXUM 131
UZUKI 404, 405
V.1106 304
V.1107 304
V.1109 304
V.121/CARLOFORTE 65
V.125/GIOVANNI BOTTIGLIERE 65
V.1506 170
V.1512 240
V.202 240
V.208 240
V.308/OSCAR NEYNABER 249
V.309/MARTIN DONANDT 119
V.51/ALFA 189
V.5505/SEETEUFEL 286
V.6109 343
VAAGEN (687grt) 279
VAINAMOINEN 247, 248
VAINDLO 182
VALDARNO (5696grt) 178

VALIANT 71, 130, 131, 132, 255, 259, 319, 320, 385, 386, 387, 388
VALK 265
VALKYRIE 54
VALMY 68, 69, 128, 129
VALOROSO 64
VALOROUS 363
VAMPIRE 70
VAN KINSBERGEN 37
VAN MEERLANT 48
VAN OOST 212, 218
VANCOUVER (5729grt) 238
VANCOUVER ISLAND (9472grt) 102, 294
VANESSA 49
VANITY 240
VANJA (6198grt) 306
VANOC 41, 56, 101, 103, 104, 107, 115, 117, 166, 167, 178, 227, 232, 241, 295, 353, 356, 358, 361
VANQUISHER 37, 42, 97, 309, 350, 359, 360, 361
VANSITTART 37, 42, 53, 57, 108, 117, 166, 177, 244, 245, 292, 298, 309, 360, 371, 372
VARANBERG (2842grt) 236
VARD (681grt) 222
VARELA (4651grt) 197
VARLAAM AVANESOV (6557grt) 391
VARNA 23
VARSOVA (4701grt) 197
VASCAMA 283
VASILISSA OLGA 191, 319
VAUQUELIN 69, 70, 128, 129
VECHTSTROOM (845grt) 238
VELEBIT (4153grt) 74
VELELLA 44, 45, 53
VELMA (9720grt) 307, 308, 370
VELOX 37, 42, 57, 108, 161, 164, 165, 174, 177, 244, 245, 292, 309, 359, 360, 371, 372
VENDETTA 67, 70, 71, 129, 130, 133, 189, 190, 191, 193, 256, 257, 258, 259, 260, 318, 319, 321
VENERSBORG (1065grt) 179
VENETO 122, 178, 188
VENIERO 45, 53, 168
VENOMOUS 32, 37, 40, 97, 100, 103, 158, 166, 222, 227, 230, 233, 289, 297, 358
VENUS (2546grt) 172
VERAZZANO 380, 381, 383
VERBENA 31, 96, 97, 103, 156, 163, 298, 299, 359
VERDUN 216, 237, 365
VERITY 41, 54, 56, 100, 103, 116, 289, 292, 297
VERONICA... 32, 34, 38, 98, 104, 157, 164, 222, 226, 229, 232, 288, 294, 295, 296, 355, 360
VERSAILLES 58
VERSAYTIS 376
VERVAIN 102, 115, 168, 177, 245, 305
VESCO (331grt) 344
VESIHIISI 61, 120, 180
VESIKKO 120
VESPER 49, 365
VESTERAALEN (682grt) 279
VESTKYST I (370grt) 96
VESTLAND (1934grt) 225
VETCH 230, 298, 305, 361, 370
VETEHINEN 61, 62, 120
VETERAN 39, 41, 54, 157, 159, 164, 225, 226, 229, 232, 288, 294, 355, 360
VETTOR PISANI (6339grt) 128, 186, 252, 314, 315, 381, 382

VIBORG (4100grt) 120
VICEROY 117, 162
VICEROY OF INDIA (19,627grt) 244, 246, 327
Vichy French Fleet 17
Vichy French Navy 82
VICTO (3655grt) 364
VICTORIA (13,098grt) 188, 189
VICTORIOUS ... 29, 30, 37, 41, 42, 43, 53, 54, 62, 88, 90, 92, 94, 95, 145, 146, 148, 149, 150, 153, 154, 212, 213, 215, 217, 218, 219, 220, 221, 282, 282, 283, 284, 285, 286, 296, 297, 346, 347, 351
VIDETTE 115, 116, 123, 164, 167, 169, 175, 176, 233, 241, 250, 298, 300, 301, 307, 369, 371
VIFORUL 72, 195, 390
VIGRID (4765grt) 34
VIJELIA 72, 195, 390
VILLE D'ANVERS (7462grt) 345
VILLE D'ANVERS (7462grt) 221, 279, 281
VILLE DE ROUEN (5383grt) 118
VILLE DE TAMATAVE (4993grt) 74
VILLE DE VERDUN (7007grt) 122
VILLE D'ORAN (10,172grt) 198
VIMIERA 350, 365
VIMY 115, 116, 123, 176, 184, 234, 241, 242, 243, 245, 292, 309, 359, 362, 371
VINCENNES (CA-44) 35, 36, 98, 99, 220, 222, 223, 353, 354
VINCENZO PADRE 125
VINGA (7321grt) 231
VINHA 249
VINICOLO (grt) 382
VIOLET 30, 31, 33, 41, 96, 97, 103, 156, 163, 232, 300
VIRGILIA (5732grt) 365
VIRGILIO 379
VIRGINIA S. (3885grt) 317
VIRGO FIDELIS (129grt) 112
VIRONIA (2026grt) 182
VIRRE (80grt) 182
VISCOLUL 72, 195
VISENDA 28, 154
VITA 240
VITTORIO VENETO 251
VITTORIO VENETO (4595grt) 178
VIVACIOUS .. 154, 155, 167, 171, 216, 217, 219, 220, 230, 237, 238, 239, 302, 304
VIVALDI 64, 186, 187, 315, 382
VIZALMA 164, 229, 232, 294, 360
VMV.1 248
VMV.14 248
VMV.15 248
VMV.16 248
VODNIK (125grt) 180
VOLENDAM (15,434grt) 161, 245, 263, 319
VOLGA 183, 376
VOLGA (3113grt) 323
VOLGOLES (3946grt) 59
VOLLRATH THAM (5787grt) 366
VOLODARSKI 22, 61, 182
VOLTURNO (3363grt) 383
VOLTURNO (3424grt) 162
VOLUNTAS (5597grt) 178
VOLUNTEER 104, 166, 178, 227, 232, 241, 289, 295, 353, 358
VOROSHILOV 22, 73, 261, 389
VORTIGERN 50
VOSTOK 182

VOSTOK (grt) 324
VOYAGER 67, 70, 130, 133
Vp.1508/RAU III 111
VP.308/OSCAR NEYNABER 248
Vp.309/MARTIN DONANDT 311
Vp.412/BREMERHAVEN 366
Vp.6111 148
Vp.6113 148
Vp.805 366
VT-501/BALHASH 183
VT-505/IVAN PAPANIN (3974grt) 182, 183
VT-511/ALEV (1446grt) 182, 182
VT-512/KUMARI (237grt) 182
VT-512/TOBOL (2758grt) 182
VT-518/LUGA (2329grt) 182
VT-520/EVALD 183
VT-523/KAZAKHSTAN 182, 183
VT-524/KALPAKS (2190grt) 182, 183
VT-529/SKRUNDA (2414grt) 182, 183
VT-530/ELLA (1522grt) 182, 182
VT-537/ERGONAUTIS (206grt) 182, 183
VT-543/VTORAYA PYATILETKA (3974grt) 182, 183
VT-546/AUSMA (1791grt) 183
VT-547/JARVAMAA (1363grt) 182, 182
VT-550/SIAULIA (1207grt) 182, 183
VT-563/ATIS KRONVALDIS (1423grt) 182, 182, 183
VT-574/KUMARI 182
VT-581/LAKE LUCERNE (2317grt) 182, 183
VT-584/NAISSAAR (1839grt) 182
VULCAN 128, 227, 255
VULCAN (AR-5) 227, 284, 296
VULCANIA (24,469grt) 253, 254
VULKAN (395grt) 240
VYACHESLAV MOLOTOV (7484grt) 180
VYATKA 182
VZRIV 23
W. C. TEAGLE (9552grt) 296
W-1 .... 394, 401
W-10 77
W-11 .... 77, 269, 406
W-12 .... 77, 269, 395, 399
W-13 .... 76, 397, 398
W-14 .... 76, 397
W-15 76
W-16 76
W-17 .... 76, 395, 398
W-18 .... 76, 395, 398
W-19 76
W-2 .... 394, 401
W-2 (Ru) 261
W-20 269
W-3 .... 394, 401
W-5 .... 394, 401
W-6 .... 394, 401
W-7 .... 77, 269, 399
W-8 .... 77, 269, 399
W-9 77
WACHTFELS (8467grt) 64, 65
WAINWRIGHT (DD-419) 36, 353, 354
WAINWRIGHT (DD-420) 98, 290
WAIWERA (10,800grt) 37
WAKE (DD-416) 160, 290

WAKE (PR-3) 394, 395, 396, 397
WAKEFIELD (AP-21) 353
WALDINGE (2462grt) 365
WALKE (DD-416) 98, 99, 215, 223, 354
WALKER 39, 41, 53, 56, 101, 103, 104, 115, 117, 166, 178, 227, 232, 241
WALLACE 350, 365
WALLFLOWER ... 39, 53, 56, 101, 116, 117, 163, 164, 165, 174, 176, 177, 178, 241, 371, 372
WALMER CASTLE (906grt) 234
WALNEY 97, 100, 229, 245, 358, 372
WALPOLE 50, 365
WANDERER 37, 43, 101, 104, 114, 117, 161, 164, 167, 169, 177, 362
WANDSBEK (2388grt) 88
WANSTEAD (5486grt) 348
WAR BHARATA (5604grt) 29
WAR DIWAN (5551grt) 30
WAR GREY (246grt) 237
WAR MEHTAR (5502grt) 365
WAR PINDARI (5559grt) 94
WAR SUDRA (5627grt) 93
WARRINGTON (DD-383) 161, 228, 291, 356
WARSPITE 70, 71
WARWICK CASTLE (20,107grt) 161, 288, 290, 354
WASP (CV-7) 36, 99, 149, 160, 227
WASTWATER 90, 95, 150, 152, 155
WATCHMAN 31, 33, 41, 97, 100, 103, 156, 158, 163, 167, 216, 224, 230, 287, 290, 293, 298, 355, 360
WATERHEN 70, 71, 72
WBS.3/LAUENBURG 23
WEISSENFELS (7861grt) 197
WELLARD 35, 100, 103, 297, 353, 358
WELLFIELD (6054grt) 43
WELLINGTON (NZ) 54, 102, 177, 230, 297, 309, 360, 363
WELLS 27, 29, 42, 91, 93, 102
WELSH COAST (646grt) 51
WELSHMAN 154, 172, 217, 218, 220, 286, 294, 299, 304, 305, 347, 358
WENDINGEN (grt) 344
WESER (9179grt) 214
WESER (9472grt) 294
WEST ARMAGOSA (5463grt) 225
WEST GROUP 46
WEST KEDRON (5613grt) 231
WEST NILUS (5565grt) 246
WEST POINT (AP-23) 98, 116, 159, 353
WEST QUECHEE (5711grt) 370
WESTBURN (2842grt) 48
WESTCOTT 40, 42, 55, 102, 157, 167, 177, 222, 230, 297, 354
Western Approaches Command 27, 28, 29, 90, 91, 93, 150, 151, 152, 164, 220, 221, 232, 346
Western Hemisphere Defence Plan 4 (WPL-51) 86
WESTERNLAND (16,231grt) 263, 264
WESTERWALD (10,845grt) 58
WESTFIELD (140grt) 100
WESTMINSTER 280, 302, 366
WESTOMP 352, 353
WESTON 103, 177, 232, 246, 309, 360, 363
WETASKIWIN 31, 35, 40, 96, 102, 158, 159, 216, 225, 228, 230, 288, 289, 295, 296, 354, 361
WHEATLAND 347, 358
WHIPPET 318
WHITE PATROL 220
White Sea Fleet 280
WHITEHALL 157, 161, 163, 164, 222, 231, 292, 359

WICHITA (CA-45) 98, 99, 149, 215, 227, 346, 347
WICKES (DD-441) 297, 356
WIDGEON 365
WILD SWAN 37, 42, 53, 57, 164, 167, 175, 176, 177, 241, 242, 243, 245, 300, 306, 369, 370, 377, 378
WILDENFELS (6224grt) 197
WILLIAM P. BIDDLE (AP-15) 91
WILLMOTO (4999grt) 372
WILSON (DD-408) 36
WINAMAC (8621grt) 370
WINCHELSEA 37, 42, 97, 101, 161, 163, 165, 167, 222
WINCHESTER 27, 29, 30, 42, 92, 93, 238
WINCHESTER CASTLE (20,109grt) 152, 163
WINDERMERE 155, 159, 345, 348
WINDFLOWER 33, 38, 100, 156, 163, 289, 290, 297, 352, 359
WINDSOR 27, 29, 49, 95, 110, 238
WINDSOR CASTLE (19,141grt) 33, 38, 161, 245
WINSLOW (DD-359) 156, 222, 226, 232, 290, 292, 353, 354
WINTERSWIJK (3205grt) 224
WISA (3845grt) 173
WISHART 54, 55, 56, 62, 63, 101, 113, 115, 123, 173, 174, 175, 298, 308, 371
WISLA (3106grt) 224
WISTARIA 167
WITCH ... 157, 158, 161, 163, 164, 222, 225, 231, 292, 309, 350, 359, 360, 361
WIVERN 37, 42, 53, 164, 166, 169, 175, 177, 242
WOLBOROUGH 259, 321
WOLFE 32, 33, 35, 41, 156, 164, 224, 306
WOLFHOUND 171, 172, 239
Wolfpack ARNAULD 368
Wolfpack BENECKE 363
Wolfpack BRANDENBURG 226, 227, 231, **287**
Wolfpack BRESLAU 293
Wolfpack GODECKE 363
Wolfpack LETZTE RITTER 363
Wolfpack MARKGRAF 155
Wolfpack MORDBRENNER 289, 295
Wolfpack RAUBRITTER 352, 353
Wolfpack REISSEWOLF 284, 297
Wolfpack SCHLAGETOT 286, 297
Wolfpack STEUGEN 355
Wolfpack STORTEBECKER 362, 363
Wolfpack STOSSTRUPP 291
WOLSEY 166, 302, 365
WOLVERINE ... 42, 116, 162, 165, 177, 227, 229, 242, 289, 293, 297, 354, 359
WOODRUFF 53, 117, 162, 177, 232, 243, 244, 309
WOOLSEY (DD-437) 355, 356
WOOLSTON 117, 162
WOOLWICH 256
WORCESTER 95, 110
WORCESTERSHIRE 158, 161, 228, 290
WRESTLER 38, 53, 54, 102, 117, 161, 164, 244, 245, 292, 309, 369
WRIGHT (AV-1) 408

WROTHAM (1884grt) 107
WYREEMA (31grt) 129
YADUCHI 406
YAKOV SVERDLOV 22, **182**
YALOVA (3750grt) 259, **318**
YAMABIKO MARU (6795grt) 201, 202, 333
YAMAGIRI MARU (6438grt) 329, 331, 400
YAMAGUMO 406
YAMAKAZE 406
Yamamoto, Adm Isoroku 210, 274, 403, 404, 406
YAMASHIMO MARU 267
YAMASHIMO MARU (6776grt) 203
YAMASHIRO 267, 268, 270
YAMATO 202, 269
YARRA 197, 198, 386, 387, 389, 391
YARRAWONGA (4900grt) 239
YAYOI 408
YENICE (520grt) 390
YORKTOWN (CV-5) 35, 36, 98, 99, 159, 160, 169, 227, 288, 290, 291
YSELHAVEN (4802grt) 32
YUBARI 335, 408
YUGIRI 404
YUKIKAZE 406
YUNAGI 408
YURA 398
YUZUKI 404, 405
Z.23 .... 30, 31, 58, 113, **305**
Z.24 .... 30, 31, 58, 113, **305**
Z.25 .... 31, 247
Z.26 247
Z.27 247
ZAAFARAN 30, 295
ZAFFIRO 185, 320, 387
ZARAGOZA (6101grt) 54
ZARTE ZEE 162
ZEALANDIA (6683grt) 393
ZENA (5219grt) 315
ZENO 186, 187, 188, **316**, 317, 381
ZENOBIA 198
ZENYO MARU (6442grt) 394, 395, 396, 400
ZEYA 183
ZHAN ZHORES (grt) 323, 324
ZHELEZNODOROZHNIK (2029grt) 59, 181
ZHELEZNYAKOV 22, 72, 73, 325, 389, 390, 391
ZHEMCHUZHIN 72, 73, 134
ZINNIA 39, 101, 116, 117, 162, 163, 164, 174, 177
ZIRONA 253
ZIRONA (grt) 382
ZOEA 124, 190
ZUIKAKU 270, 331, 332, 333, 334, 400, 401, 402, 403, 404, 405, 406
ZULU 24, 37, 167, 231, 242, 250, 251, 300, 305, 306, 308, 313, **361**, 368, 369, 370, 377
ZYPERN 320

WORLD WAR II SEA WAR

VOLUME 4
GERMANY SENDS RUSSIA TO THE ALLIES

Errata Form

E-mail below information to: **bertkepubs@email.com**

or complete form and mail to:
**Bertke Publications
1740 E. Stroop Rd.
P.O. Box 291974
Dayton, OH 45429-9998**

SECTION #	PAGE #	DESCRIPTION OF ERROR OR CHANGE AND YOUR PROPOSED SOLUTION